G.A. Henty, 1832–1902
A Bibliographical Study

G.A. HENTY

G. A. HENTY
1832–1902

**A Bibliographical Study of his British editions
with short accounts of his publishers, illustrators and designers,
and notes on production methods used for his books**

PETER NEWBOLT

SCOLAR
PRESS

Published by
SCOLAR PRESS
Gower House
Croft Road
Aldershot
Hants GU11 3HR
England

Ashgate Publishing Company
Old Post Road
Brookfield
Vermont 05036–9704
USA

British Library Cataloguing-in-Publication data

G.A. Henty, 1832–1902: A Bibliographical Study of his British editions with Short Accounts of his Publishers, Illustrators and Designers and Notes on Production Methods Used for his Books
    I. Newbolt, Peter
    016.8238

Library of Congress Cataloging-in-Publication Data

Newbolt, Peter
    G.A. Henty, 1832–1902: a Bibliographical Study of his British editions, with short accounts of his publishers, illustrators and designers, and notes on production methods used for his books / by Peter Newbolt.
        p.   cm.
    Includes bibliographical references and index.
    ISBN 1–85928–208–3
    1. Henty, G.A. (George Alfred), 1832–1902—Bibliography. 2. Book industries and trade—Great Britain—History—19th century. 3. Children's stories—Publishing—Great Britain—History—19th century. 4. Authors and publishers—Great Britain—History—19th century. 5. Children's stories, English—Bibliography. I. Title.
    Z8397.47.N49 1996
    [PR4785.H55]
    016.823'8—dc20   95–14702
                          CIP

ISBN 1 85928 208 3

Typeset in Times by Bournemouth Colour Press and printed in Great Britain at the University Press, Cambridge

CONTENTS

ILLUSTRATIONS

THE PLATES

ILLUSTRATIONS ON TEXT PAGES

PREFACE

I started making bibliographical notes on Henty's writings about twenty years ago, and for a time some of them appeared in Supplements to the quarterly Bulletins of the Henty Society. Other matters intervened, and I was unable to return to the work until five years ago. The original material had been issued only to members of the Society, and amounted to a mere fraction of the present work.

When I began I had not intended to compile a comprehensive catalogue of the later editions and issues of Henty's books. But as the work progressed it became clear that the editions produced from 1910 by what was at the time known as the 'Joint Venture', between Hodder & Stoughton and the Oxford University Press, could not be omitted. They are now valued by collectors, and some of the volumes are physically more attractive than many earlier editions. The story of this unusual publishing enterprise, and how it revived interest in Henty's earliest boys' books published by Griffith & Farran, is briefly told in Appendix II.

To include the Joint Venture, and the eventual take-over of its children's books by the O.U.P., meant bibliographical entries had to follow Henty's work into the 1920s. That happened to fit well with the activities of Henty's main publisher, Blackie & Son. In 1903 they started re-issuing their boys' novels in a cheap edition with bindings largely decorated by John Hassall, and they were still adding to the series up to the autumn of 1917. In August 1917 the Blackie archive, as far as Henty is concerned, for some reason comes to an end. But after the first war they re-issued Henty's novels again, in a second cheap edition, giving each book a coloured frontispiece. That series was launched while the Oxford University Press was doing much the same thing for titles originally published by Griffith & Farran.

By the end of the 1920s the production of Henty's books had gone into decline. Blackie seems to have lost enthusiasm for decorative productions of Henty for which they had been famous. They dropped the colour frontispieces, and they dropped pictorial blocking from the binding cases, front board first, then spine as well. They even edited and cut the texts. The results are not, for the enthusiast, whether reader or collector, truly recognisable Henty. For the bibliographer a line had to be drawn somewhere, and this compilation was in danger of growing too cumbersome to be useful. The end of the 1920s, without putting too precise a date on it, seemed the right place to stop.

Of the 122 books written by Henty, descriptive entries are given in §1 for over 550 separate editions or issues published before 1930. In §2 there are listed 72 books and annuals to which Henty contributed, with separate entries for well over a hundred editions or issues. §3 lists 34 periodicals and newspapers to which he contributed, although at present much diligent searching by Stuart Wilson, a Henty Society member, and myself has failed to reveal the names of some other weekly newspapers in which the adult novels were serialised before publication in book form.

For anyone who wishes to take the matter further than the period covered here, it should perhaps be added that among the rather drab later versions of the books, Blackie published some of the stories 'Retold by Douglas V. Duff' in the language of the 1930s and 1940s. At the beginning of the 1950s, Tambimuttu, famous as the founder of Editions Poetry London, but also operating under other imprints, was one of several publishers with an eye to the future who were perusing Henty. The copyright expired at the end of 1952, and in 1953 a number of abridged or re-written versions of the novels appeared for sale at low prices.

Henty, in one form or another, was being kept alive by a small group of hopeful publishers with varying degrees of skill in book-design. They included Latimer House, Dean, Foulsham, and Collins. Dragon Books issued a series of abridged but good-looking paperbacks in the 1960s, and before that there had even been English editions of a New York publisher's 'comic strip' books, cheaply printed in colour in Poland with very little text at all.

A short but comparatively well produced series of hardback titles, with brightly illustrated dust-wrappers, was produced by Foulsham as late as 1977, 'carefully edited and slightly abridged to meet the tastes of the Modern Boy'. Just over a hundred years after his first book for boys was published, I am sure Henty would have been delighted, possibly even with the careful editing.

A few booksellers have been aware for some time that this book was in preparation. Several have quite independently urged me strongly to provide a background to Henty's dealings with his publishers. I had always intended to do so in brief notes, but I found, once I had started, that the publishers' personalities, and their businesses, affected Henty's career as a writer perhaps more than I had realised. They have ended up with an Appendix to themselves.

The eccentric William Tinsley, who in ten years turned himself from farm lad to wealthy publisher, lived and worked in a Bohemian world experienced but not written about by Henty. The section dealing with his activities is longer than the others for two reasons. Partly because little has previously been written of his Dickensian way of life and business, and partly because it was through him that Henty was brought in touch with the world of Charles Edward Mudie and his Library, the most important single influence in Victorian fiction.

Edward Marston, of Sampson Low, probably understood Henty as well as any of his publishers. It was to Marston that he admitted his suffering 'for some years from gouty diabetes', the gout perhaps a cause, beyond lingering melancholy after his first wife's early death, of his recurring outbursts of irritability.

Andrew Chatto, whose romantic feeling for the 'luxurious form' of the three-decker was almost irrational in its persistence, recognised and encouraged Henty's ability as a writer for adults. Chatto's belief in Henty was justified by his sales figures: they demonstrate conclusively the success he achieved, whatever may have been written in later times by uninformed commentators. A study of their disparagements shows they have not simply and blindly repeated each other, but tended in turn to exaggerate what their predecessors wrote. Only Guy Arnold, the most recent critic, who actually read some of the novels, including the successful *Rujub, the Juggler*, has dared to question the myth.

And finally the workaholic Alexander Blackie, a publisher with a touch of genius, who took on Henty wholeheartedly as his leading author in Blackie's first-ever list of reward books, learned to manage the economics, as well as the aesthetics, of book production with a skill that set him a generation ahead of his contemporaries.

These men, and their fellows, moved in and out of Henty's life, as friends gained, and friends lost and gained again, and provided his daily bread. Many of them knew him after his days as a newspaper correspondent were over, although there were years when Henty was simultaneously writing books and sending dispatches from distant places. I have not attempted to identify the many dispatches that were published 'by Our Special Correspondent' in the *Standard*. But I have unearthed some reports, and even some of Henty's own illustrations, that were published in periodicals and have not been previously recorded. Details of those will be found here, together with a note about one report previously ascribed to Henty which I believe he did not write.

Other parts of this book attempt to explain in not-too-technical terms the processes involved in the production and the illustration of Henty's books. Members of the Henty Society have over the years asked numerous questions on these subjects, and I have tried to include answers to those and to others as well. I hope that the result will prove useful not only to those interested in Henty, but to those who read or collect other authors of the same period. It happens to be a period of great advances in printing and illustration techniques, and also in the writing of stories for children.

Cley-next-the-Sea   Peter Newbolt
Norfolk   February 1996

INTRODUCTION

The following notes are intended to explain briefly the lines on which this book has been compiled, and I hope they will make it easier to use.

The cataloguing of Henty's work is divided into four sections, which form the main part of this book. Because of Henty's very large output it has been necessary to make these divisions, but for anyone unsure in which section a particular title is to be found, the comprehensive index shows the main entry for it in **bold** type.

The first section, dealing with books written solely by Henty, is arranged chronologically, with its own alphabetical index. That method proved far more useful to an understanding of Henty's career as a writer, than earlier attempts, including my own, to arrange the works alphabetically. All the other sections, however, are alphabetical, as that proved a more convenient system for reference.

The descriptions of the books all follow a pattern which was to some extent suggested by Dartt's earlier bibliography. But it gives much greater detail: for example, of illustration, which Dartt barely mentioned. I have not described the collation of each item in the standard shorthand formula (see Gaskell, *A New Introduction to Bibliography*, p.328) which is necessary for books of an earlier time or whose make-up is less straightforward. Any irregularities or unusual features of make-up are, nevertheless, recorded, and from the entries it should be possible to analyse without difficulty the details of construction of each book.

It order to make such an analysis there are a few points that should be understood by the reader: they are constant to all entries in §1 and §2.

1. All Henty's books, unless otherwise specified, are bound in 16-page sections.

2. In the title-page descriptions the use of *italic* type is not distinguished; the use of gothic type is always mentioned.

3. In describing preliminary pages, I have used 'list of Illustrations' (with only one capital) to denote a page-heading which appears simply as 'Illustrations'. Where the publisher has headed the page 'List of Illustrations', I have shown it in the same way, with a capital 'L'.

4. In the descriptions of bindings, the colours given are in most cases those used in one of a number of alternative colour schemes. It was for many years exceptional for children's books to be bound in only one cloth-colour, and the alternative states of many of Henty's early editions incorporate changes of pigments for blocking as well as of cloth. The variants are, consequently, rarely significant, and too numerous for all to be described in detail. The subject is discussed more fully in Appendix III, Part 2.

5. Many of the first editions from Blackie were reprinted a number of times, and show small alterations to advertisements, up-dated bound-in catalogues, and changes to publisher's imprint and addresses as overseas offices were opened or closed. Similarly, numerous variants are found among their later reprints in the 1920s. The variations, and sometimes those among reprints from other publishers,

may be numerous, but appear to have no special significance. I have therefore devised a system of describing such reprints of a single edition under the heading of a 'generic' code-number. These codes are distinguished by having an asterisk before them, for example: *10.5. The descriptions under such headings indicate the nature of variations that may be found.

6. The 'References' in each entry are to selected Libraries and private collections holding copies examined or described, and then, after a vertical stroke, to entries in earlier bibliographies. Between them, separated by another vertical stroke, will occasionally be found references to a publisher's archive. The abbreviations of references given are listed at the end of this Introduction.

Dartt listed both British and American editions, but, by not giving separate entries for each, managed to confuse himself. That, sadly, was the cause of numerous errors. I hope that this volume will be followed by another dealing separately with the authorised and the 'pirated' editions of Henty published in the United States, as well as those published in Canada.

Arrangements made by Scribners in New York, in conjunction with Blackie in Glasgow, resulted in many of Henty's first American editions carrying dates earlier than those of the first British editions. It was Blackie's policy to print on title pages the date of the year following publication, even, when a book was published as early as February 1888, dating it 1889. There has been some consequent confusion as to whether certain titles appeared in the States before they were published in Britain. Such confusion continues to the present day in catalogues from international booksellers and auction houses. In 1948 it was unfortunately worse confounded by a distinguished American librarian, who published in an authoritative journal incorrect information about Blackie's publication dates (see Appendix VI, Note 14). In fact, the only title not published first in Britain was *In the Hands of the Cave-Dwellers*, a 'long short-story', produced by Harper & Brothers, New York, in 1900, and by Blackie, undated, in 1902. Wherever known, precise publication dates are given in relevant entries: also, for Blackie titles, in Appendix VII, Part 1.

I have barely mentioned dust-wrappers, nor the 'summaries' on thin paper and other ephemeral leaflets often loosely inserted in early issues by Blackie, and occasionally by other publishers. Many of these items are scarce, especially early dust-wrappers: perhaps one day someone will make a separate study of them.

The European editions and translations of Henty's work have proved too extensive to be included in this volume, as was originally intended. I have collected, with generous help from a number of sources, considerable information about them. Many listings have been compiled, and I hope that in due course it will be possible to cover the editions from nine European countries in a separate volume.

P.N.

Abbreviations used in the text under 'References'

BG   Bethnal Green Museum of Childhood
BL   British Library
Bod Bodleian Library, Oxford
B-R Bodleian Library, Rhodes House, Oxford
NS   National Library of Scotland
WL   Wandsworth Public Library

AG   Anthony Gadd collection
AK   Ann King collection
AP   Alex Pyne collection
BB   Revd Basil Brown collection
BU   Brian Burgess collection
CH   Christopher Holtom
CT   Cargill Thompson collection
DS   David Sandler collection
GD   Gerald Duin collection
HE   Harland Eastman collection
IM   Ivan McClymont collection
JJ   Kate and Tom Jackson
MH   Mildred Hoad collection
OD   Clive Orbell-Durrant collection
PN   Peter Newbolt collection
RC   Roger Childs collection
RH   Roy Henty collection
RS   Revd David Shacklock collection
SH   Norman Shaw
SW   Stuart Wilson collection
TC   Terry Corrigan collection

Farmer   Kennedy & Farmer, *Bibliography of G.A. Henty & Hentyana*
Dartt   Robert L. Dartt, *G.A. Henty, A Bibliography*
Companion R.L. Dartt, *A Companion to G.A. Henty, A Bibliography*
Sadleir   Michael Sadleir, *XIX Century Fiction, A Bibliographical Record*
Hannabuss C.S. Hannabuss, *Works by G.A. Henty included in the Wandsworth Collection*

§1

BOOKS WRITTEN BY HENTY

This section is arranged in chronological order:
references in the index below are to entry numbers, not to pages

1. A SEARCH FOR A SECRET

1.1

A SEARCH FOR A SECRET. | A Novel. | BY | G.A. HENTY. | IN THREE VOLUMES | VOL.I. (VOL.II., VOL.III.) | LONDON: | TINSLEY BROTHERS, 18, CATHERINE ST., STRAND. | 1867.
(Note: A Novel. *is in gothic type).*

Contents, Volume I
191 x 125 mm. (i)–iv | 1–(300) | no catalogue. No illustrations.

(i) Title p. | (ii) printer's imprint (LONDON: | WYMAN AND SONS, PRINTERS, GREAT QUEEN STREET, | LINCOLN'S-INN FIELDS, W.C.) | (iii)–iv. Contents of Vol.I | 1–298. text | (299) printer's imprint, exactly as on p.(ii) | (300) blank.

Volume II
191 x 125 mm. (i)–iv | 1–(272) | no catalogue. No illustrations.

(i) Title p. | (ii) printer's imprint, as on p.(ii) of Vol.I | (iii)–iv. Contents of Vol.II | 1–269. text, with printer's imprint at foot of p.269, below 6cm. rule (WYMAN AND SONS, PRINTERS, GREAT QUEEN STREET, LONDON, W.C.) | (270)–(272) blank.

Volume III
191 x 125 mm. (i)–iv | 1–(264) | no catalogue. No illustrations.

(i) Title p. | (ii) printer's imprint, as on p.(ii) of previous volumes | (iii)–iv. Contents of Vol.III | 1–263. text, with printer's imprint at foot of p.263, below 6cm. rule, on one line, as on p.269 of Vol.II | (264) blank.

Binding (see Plate 1)
Blue, stipple-grained cloth boards, blocked blind and gilt; edges uncut; plain off-white wove endpapers.

Front board: Blind decorative rules at edges, forming panel. **Spine:** Three rules (thin, thick, thin) full width of spine: A | SEARCH | FOR A | SECRET | (1cm. rule) | G.A.HENTY. | (decorative rule, full width of spine) | VOL I. (VOL II., VOL III.) | TINSLEY BROs | three rules, as at head of spine, (all blocking gilt). **Back board:** as front board.

References: Bod | *Farmer*, p.60; *Dartt*, p.118, *Companion*, p.26; *Sadleir*, I, 1190.

Notes
1. This was Henty's first published fiction: he was aged 35.
2. *Farmer* reports an alternative binding in green cloth boards. *Dartt* appears to take his information from *Farmer*, omitting some details and misquoting the page size. Neither *Farmer* nor *Dartt* gives any sources. There is no copy in the British Library, and neither of the earlier bibliographers saw the more comprehensive Henty collection in the Bodleian Library at Oxford.
3. A brief history of Tinsley Brothers is at Appendix II, Part 1. No records of the firm survive, and the size of the edition is unknown. It is likely to have been in the region of 300–400 copies, possibly smaller, and was sold at £1.11s.6d., the standard price for three-volume novels.

1.2

A SEARCH I FOR A SECRET I BY I G.A. HENTY I (ornamental rule) I London: I GALL AND INGLIS, 31 HENRIETTA STREET, STRAND, W.C.: I AND EDINBURGH.

(Note: London: *is in gothic type).*

Contents

200 x 138 mm. (i)–(ii) I 1–286 I no catalogue. Frontispiece from watercolour-drawing, signed (? R.T. Davidson), printed from three-colour halftone blocks on coated paper.

(Frontispiece, tipped in) I (i) title p. I (ii) printer's imprint (PRINTED AND BOUND BY I GALL AND INGLIS, I NEWINGTON PRINTING AND BOOKBINDING WORKS, I EDINBURGH.) I (1)–286. text.

Binding (see Plate 16)

Red cloth boards, blocked black, red, white, pale blue, and gilt; top edge machine-gilded, other edges stained matt-green (see Note 2); off-white calendered endpapers. Run-on copies of frontispiece trimmed and laid down on front board.

Front board: A SEARCH I FOR A SECRET (gilt) above laid-down illustration within black-ruled border. Six decorative flowers (black) at each side of illustration; G.A.HENTY (black) below. All within black ruled panel. **Spine:** A I SEARCH I FOR A I SECRET I by I G.A. Henty (gilt) on solid black panel forming upper part of illustration (black, merging to white and to pale blue). GALL & INGLIS (black) at foot, above black rule at foot of illustration panel. **Back board:** plain.

References: BL; Bod; PN I *Farmer*, p.61; *Dartt*, p.118, *Companion*, p.26.

Notes

1. A cheaply-produced edition on featherweight paper, received by the Copyright Libraries in 1911. *Farmer* in a moment of madness dated it (1869), and *Dartt* followed, compounding the error by giving it both dates, (1869) and (1911).
2. Copies are known with all edges machine-gilded, perhaps from early issues.

2. THE MARCH TO MAGDALA

2.1

THE I MARCH TO MAGDALA. I BY G.A. HENTY, I SPECIAL CORRESPONDENT OF THE "STANDARD;" AUTHOR OF I "A SEARCH FOR A SECRET," ETC. I (6-em rule) I LONDON: I TINSLEY BROTHERS, I CATHERINE STREET, STRAND. I 1868.

Contents

224 x 142 mm. (i)–(viii) I (1)–(432) I no catalogue. No illustrations.

(i) Half-title p. I (ii) printer's imprint (LONDON: I ROBSON AND SON, GREAT NORTHERN PRINTING WORKS, I PANCRAS ROAD, N.W.) I (iii) title p. I (iv) blank I (v)–vii. Preface I (viii) blank I (1)–24. Introductory Chapter I 25–431. text, with printer's imprint on p.431, exactly as on p.(ii) I (432) blank.

Binding (see Plate 8)
Royal-blue cloth boards, blocked blind and gilt; edges uncut; plain off-white endpapers.

Front board: Blind decorative panelling. **Spine:** THE MARCH | TO | MAGDALA | (short rule) | G.A. HENTY. (all gilt) with decorative rules above and below (all gilt) above small decorative emblem (gilt). At foot: TINSLEY BROTHERS (gilt) between plain and decorative rules (gilt). **Back board:** blind decorative panelling.

References: BL; Bod; BB | *Farmer*, p.50; *Dartt*, p.96; *Sadleir*, I, 1188.

Note: *Sadleir* writes that the binding is 'in the style adopted by the publishers for several non-fiction 8vos at this period . . . Although not fiction, it is recorded as a specimen of a characteristic Tinsley style'. He lists three other Tinsley titles 'generally uniform with this work'.

3. ALL BUT LOST

3.1

ALL BUT LOST. | A Novel. | BY | G.A. HENTY, | AUTHOR OF "THE MARCH TO MAGDALA," ETC., ETC. | IN THREE VOLUMES. | VOL.I. (VOL.II., VOL.III.) | LONDON: | TINSLEY BROTHERS, 18, CATHERINE ST., STRAND. | 1869. | [The Right of Translation is reserved.]
(Notes: A Novel. is in gothic type; the E *in the first* ETC., *under author's name, is missing in Volume III only).*

Contents, Volume I
190 x 126 mm. (i)–(vi) unfolioed | (1)–290 | no catalogue. No illustrations.

(i) Half-title p. | (ii) blank | (iii) title p. | (iv) printer's imprint (LONDON: | BRADBURY, EVANS, AND CO., PRINTERS, WHITEFRIARS.) | (v) Contents | (vi) blank | (1)–290, text, with printer's imprint at foot of p.290 (BRADBURY, EVANS, AND CO., PRINTERS, WHITEFRIARS.)

Volume II
190 x 127 mm. (i)–(vi) unfolioed | (1)–278 | no catalogue. No illustrations.

(i) Half-title p. | (ii) blank | (iii) title p. | (iv) printer's imprint, as in Vol.I | (v) Contents | (vi) blank | (1)–278. text, with printer's imprint at foot of p.278 (as on p.290 of Vol.I).

Volume III
190 x 127 mm. (i)–(vi) unfolioed | (1)–(294) | no catalogue. No illustrations.

(i) Half-title p. | (ii) blank | (iii) title p. | (iv) printer's imprint, as in previous volumes | (v) Contents | (vi) blank | 1–293. text, with printer's imprint at foot of p.293 (as on p.290 of Vol.I) | (294) blank.

Binding (see Plate 2)
Royal blue, stipple-grained cloth boards, blocked blind and gilt; edges uncut; yellow surface-paper endpapers.

Front board: Treble rules at edges of boards (thin, thick, thin); rules and decorative flowers, etc., forming central panel (all blind). **Spine:** Decorative rules at head; ALL BUT | LOST | (11mm. rule) | G.A. HENTY | (decorated rule) | VOL.I. (VOL.II., VOL.III.) | (plain rule) | TINSLEY BROTHERS | (decorative rules, as at head) (all gilt). **Back board:** as front board.

References: BL; Bod | *Farmer*, p.4; *Dartt*, p.2, *Companion*, p.1.

Notes
1. No publisher's records exist of this one-and-only edition.
2. The imposition is clumsy. In Vol.I the prelims consist of two conjugate leaves plus a single leaf tipped on, making 6 pages; and the final 16-page section also has a single leaf tipped on, forming pages 289–290. In Vol.II the prelims and the first six pages of text are made up as a pair of conjugate leaves (pp.(i)–(iv)) pasted to an 8-page gathering (pp.(v)–6). In Vol.III the six pages of prelims are made up as in Vol.I; the last 16-page gathering (sig.T) has a pair of conjugate leaves tipped on (as sig.V) and a final single leaf tipped on after that.

4. OUT ON THE PAMPAS

4.1
OUT ON THE PAMPAS; | OR, | THE YOUNG SETTLERS. | A Tale for Boys. | BY | G.A. HENTY, | AUTHOR OF 'ALL BUT LOST,' 'THE MARCH TO MAGDALA,' ETC. ETC. | WITH ILLUSTRATIONS BY J.B. ZWECKER. | (publisher's device) | LONDON: | GRIFFITH AND FARRAN, | SUCCESSORS TO NEWBERY AD HARRIS, | CORNER OF ST. PAUL'S CHURCHYARD. | MDCCCLXXI.
(Notes: (a) A Tale for Boys. *is in gothic type. (b) The* L *in* SETTLERS *is slightly raised in the forme and prints bolder than the rest of the line. (c) Misprint* AD *for* AND *in* SUCCESSORS TO NEWBERY AD HARRIS,*).*

Contents
175 x 117 mm. (i)–viii | (1)–(376) | catalogue (1)–32. Four full-page black-and-white engravings after J.B. Zwecker by Pearson, unbacked, unfolioed, tipped in.

(i) Half-title p. | (ii) printer's imprint (MURRAY AND GIBB, EDINBURGH, | PRINTERS TO HER MAJESTY'S STATIONERY OFFICE.) | (frontispiece, tipped in) | (iii) title p. | (iv) blank | (v)–vii. Contents | (viii) blank | (1)–374. text | (375) printer's imprint, as on p.(ii) | (376) blank | (1)–32. catalogue, undated.

Binding (see Plate 32)
Brown cloth boards, blocked black, blind, and gilt; edges plain; pinkish-yellow surface-paper endpapers. (See Note 2).
Front board: OUT | ON THE PAMPAS (gilt), the first initial O being incorporated in a design of palm trees with a rifle, and birds (all gilt); OR | THE YOUNG | SETTLERS (black); decorative panelling in black, including small panel enclosing . BY . G.A. HENTY . (black). **Spine:** decorative panelling and palm-tree design in black: OUT | ON THE | PAMPAS (cloth-colour out of gilt decorative scrollwork with bows and arrows, birds, etc.); publisher's device (gilt) at foot. **Back board:** decorative blind panelling; publisher's monogram (blind) as central medallion.

References: BL; Bod; PN | *Farmer*, p.54; *Dartt*, p.104, *Companion*, p.22.

Notes
1. Henty's first book for children, written in 1868 for his own offspring, Charles, Hubert, Maud and Ethel, whose names were given to the main characters. In an interview reported in *The Captain*, Vol.1, No.1, April 1899, p.3, Henty said the book was published in 1868, and the error has been often repeated, in *The Dictionary of National Biography* and elsewhere.
2. Published in November 1870 (title-page date 1871), at 5s. with plain edges, and at 5s.6d. with all edges gilt. Also bound in blue and green cloth.
3. The caption to the plate facing p.242 shows a misprint: 'Hulbert' for 'Hubert'. This continued until the Zwecker illustrations were replaced (see 4.7 below). *Dartt* has several errors of detail.

4.2

OUT ON THE PAMPAS: | OR, | THE YOUNG SETTLERS. | A Tale for Boys. | BY | G.A. HENTY, | AUTHOR OF 'THE YOUNG FRANC-TIREURS,' 'THE MARCH TO MAGDALA,' ETC. | WITH ILLUSTRATIONS BY J.B. ZWECKER. | SECOND EDITION. | (publisher's device) | LONDON: | GRIFFITH AND FARRAN, | SUCCESSORS TO NEWBERY AND HARRIS, | WEST CORNER OF ST. PAUL'S CHURCHYARD. | MDCCCLXXVI.
(Note: A Tale for Boys. *is in gothic type).*

Contents: As for 4.1, but no catalogue in copies examined (see Note 1).

Binding: Details not known as no copy has been found in original state. It seems probable that it would have followed the style of 4.1.

References: GD; WL | *Hannabuss*, p.53.

Notes
1. Only two copies of this impression are known to me, neither of them in the publisher's binding. Some details in the above description are therefore lacking.
2. The Wandsworth collection copy is from a set of his works that Henty had specially bound, and is inscribed by him on the title page to his second wife: 'Bessie Keylock | from her's always | the author'. This is one of the examples of Henty's uncertain grammar alluded to in Appendix I.

4.3

OUT ON THE PAMPAS; | OR, | THE YOUNG SETTLERS. | BY | G.A. HENTY, | AUTHOR OF 'THE YOUNG FRANC-TIREURS,' 'THE YOUNG BUGLERS,' | 'THE MARCH TO MAGDALA,' ETC. ETC. | WITH ILLUSTRATIONS BY J.B. ZWECKER. | (publisher's device) | GRIFFITH AND FARRAN, | SUCCESSORS TO NEWBERY AND HARRIS, | WEST CORNER OF ST. PAUL'S CHURCHYARD, LONDON. | E.P. DUTTON & CO. NEW YORK.

Contents
181 x 122 mm. (i)–(iv) | (1)–374 | catalogue (1)–(32) (See Note 2 below). Four full-page black-and-white engravings after J.B. Zwecker by Pearson, printed on unbacked text pages, unfolioed, but still keyed to the facing text page.

(i) Blank I (ii) frontispiece I (iii) title p. I (iv) The Rights of Translation and of Reproduction are reserved. I (1)–374. text I (1)–(32) catalogue, dated 10.81.

Binding (see Plate 33)
Green, diagonally-grained cloth boards, blocked black, yellow, blind and gilt; edges plain; grey floral-patterned endpapers.

Front board: Illustration of boy sitting in tree, reading a book, enclosed in decorative rules at head, foot, and foredge (black and yellow), with lettering superimposed: THE BOYS' OWN I FAVOURITE I LIBRARY (yellow, cased black). In lower part of design: Out on the Pampas I G.A. Henty . (black, and cloth-colour out of solid-gilt rectangular panel). **Spine:** Illustration continues from front board, with the same decorative rules at head and foot. OUT I ON THE I PAMPAS (black, and cloth-colour out of three solid-gilt panels), branch of tree obscuring part of lettering. Beneath this: . G . A . I HENTY (gilt) above small black panel with: GRIFFITH & FARRAN reversed out (cloth-colour). **Back board:** three rules at head and foot (blind), with publisher's device at centre (blind).

Reference: PN.

Notes
1. This impression of 2000 copies, now issued in a cheaper format, was printed from plates made from the original typesetting. The preliminary pages were reduced from eight to four, and the four full-page illustrations were printed with the text instead of being run off separately, on heavier paper, and tipped in.
2. This arrangement, involving the re-imposition of the entire book, makes the figures given under *Contents* above appear misleading: the frontispiece is now included in the pagination shown for the prelims (as pp.(i)–(ii)), and the other three plates, being unbacked and unfolioed, although printed on text pages, do not show up in the figures given for the text (pp.(1)–374). The last page of text carries the folio 374, but in fact there are 380 pages in this part of the book – 374 pages of text, plus 6 unfolioed pages for the three plates. So, whereas 4.1 and 4.2 each had a total of 392 pages of text and illustrations, 4.3 has a total of only 384 pages. In practical terms this means a saving of paper and machining costs (12 sheets of paper per book instead of 12$\frac{1}{2}$ sheets) and a saving in the bindery by removing the need for hand-work in tipping-in plates.
3. *Out on the Pampas* was one of six titles with which Griffith & Farran launched 'The Boys' Own Favourite Library' in 1881. They announced their intention 'to publish One Volume a fortnight', but although there were 27 titles in 1885 the series had grown to only 38 titles some ten years later. During that period four binding styles were introduced: that used in 1881, and described above, was replaced in 1884, and the others followed successively, although erratically, c.1886 and c.1895.
4. W.D. Griffith had died in 1877, and it was Robert Farran who devised the new series (see Appendix II, Part 2). Management changes resulted in a degree of confusion, and much variation is found in books in 'The Boys' Own Favourite Library', and no doubt in the publisher's other titles, during the 1880s and 1890s.
5. It is unlikely that during those decades the books were ever out of print. An examination of many books has shown that most titles in the series were reprinted several times, in regular impressions of 2000 copies, and title-page imprints were adjusted when appropriate, or at least when someone remembered to tell the printer

to change them. The styles of binding were changed at apparently arbitrary moments (see Note 3), presumably to boost sales. So printed sheets from any one impression were often bound up in more than one binding style, and, by the same token, each style of binding case is found with title pages bearing varying imprints. I have consequently tried, in listing books in 'The Boys' Own Favourite Library', which include 4.3, 4.4, 4.5, and 4.6, mainly to distinguish between the binding styles rather than to cover all the variants of title pages, etc., contained within them.

4.4

Title page: As for 4.3, except publishers' imprint (GRIFFITH, FARRAN, OKEDEN & WELSH, | SUCCESSORS TO NEWBERY AND HARRIS, | WEST CORNER OF ST. PAUL'S CHURCHYARD, LONDON. | E.P. DUTTON & CO., NEW YORK.).

Contents: 184 x 122 mm. As for 4.3, except (a) p.(iv) (The rights of Translation and of Reproduction are reserved.); (b) printer's imprint on p.374 (MORRISON AND GIBB, EDINBURGH, | PRINTERS TO HER MAJESTY'S STATIONERY OFFICE.); (c) catalogue, dated 12.85.

Binding (see Plate 33)
Green, diagonally-grained cloth boards, blocked black, light-green, silver, and gilt; edges plain; yellow-green floral-patterned endpapers.
   Front board: OUT ON THE | PAMPAS (black, and cloth-colour out of solid gilt rectangular panel) superimposed over a confused multiple illustration, including palm trees, sunset, gun on carriage, anchor, sailing ship in moonlight, etc. (black, light-green and silver), with: BY | G.A. | HENTY (black) beneath title, and: ILLUSTRATED (black over light-green shading) at foot. **Spine:** OUT | ON THE | PAMPAS (cloth-colour out of solid-gilt rectangle) with rules (black and light green) above and below. By G.A. | HENTY (cloth-colour out of smaller solid-gilt rectangle) with similar rules above and below. GRIFFITH FARRAN & Co (cloth-colour out of even smaller solid-gilt rectangle) at foot, with similar rules above and below. Illustrations of weapons and satchel, as a trophy, above cricket bat, ball and stumps (black and light green) between top and bottom rectangles and running behind the central one. **Back board:** publisher's monogram (black) in roughly rectangular panel in design of palm tree (black) at centre.

Reference: PN.

Notes
1. From an impression of 2000 copies, dated by printer's code 25 September 1884.
2. The binding style is the second used for books in 'The Boys' Own Favourite Library', and came into use in 1884.
3. See 4.3, Notes 3–5, above.

4.5

Title page: As for 4.4.

Contents
181 x 120 mm. (i)–(iv) | (1)–374 | catalogue (1)–16. Illustrations as in 4.3.
   (i) Blank | (ii) frontispiece | (iii) title p. | (iv) printer's imprint (MORRISON AND

GIBB, EDINBURGH | PRINTERS TO HER MAJESTY'S STATIONERY OFFICE.) | (1)–374. text | (1)–16. catalogue, dated by printer's code 15 November 1888.

Binding (see Plate 33)
Brown, diagonally-grained cloth boards, bevelled, and blocked black, light brown, and gilt; all edges gilt; yellow-green floral-patterned endpapers.

Front board: OUT ON THE PAMPAS (black, and cloth-colour out of solid-gilt rectangular panel) with rules (black and light brown) above and below, superimposed across a trophy (black, light brown, and gilt) of rifles, oars, and an anchor. Beneath this: By | G.A. HENTY (black) above crossed swords (black and light brown). **Spine:** Six bands across width of spine (light brown, with black above and below); between the second and third bands: OUT | ON THE | PAMPAS (black, and cloth-colour out of solid-gilt panel). Between fourth and fifth bands: HENTY (black, and cloth-colour out of smaller solid-gilt panel). Above sixth band: GRIFFITH, FARRAN & Co (gilt). **Back board:** plain.

Reference: PN.

Notes
1. In either 1887 or 1888 Griffith & Farran improved the appearance of all books in 'The Boys' Own Favourite Library' with gilt edges and bevelled boards: they still sold at 3s.6d. a copy.
2. This binding style is the third used for the series, from about 1886.
3. See 4.3, Notes 3 to 5, above.

4.6

OUT ON THE PAMPAS | OR | THE YOUNG SETTLERS | BY | G.A. HENTY | AUTHOR OF 'THE YOUNG FRANC-TIREURS,' 'THE YOUNG BUGLERS | 'THE MARCH TO MAGDALA,' ETC. ETC. | WITH ILLUSTRATIONS BY J.B.ZWECKER. | GRIFFITH FARRAN BROWNE & CO. LTD. | 35 BOW STREET, | COVENT GARDEN | LONDON
(*Note: The comma and quotation mark following* THE YOUNG BUGLERS *are missing*).

Contents: 181 x 123 mm. As for 4.3, except (a) no catalogue; (b) p.(iv) blank; (c) printer's imprint at foot of p.374 (PRINTED BY MORRISON AND GIBB LIMITED, EDINBURGH).

Binding (see Plate 33)
Blue, vertically-ribbed, cloth boards, bevelled, and blocked black, white, red, and gilt; all edges gilt; dark-blue surface-paper endpapers.

Front board: Elaborate decorative framework at edges, illustrating military and naval equipment, etc. (black and, at foot, red) and sailing ship against setting sun (gilt) at top left corner. Right of this, in scrolls (outlined black): BoYS' [*sic*] OWN | FAVOURITE | LIBRARY. (red). At centre: OUT ON | THE PAMPAS (gilt) | BY (black) | G.A. HENTY (gilt). **Spine:** OUT ON | THE PAMPAS (gilt) above trophy of flags, anchor, rifles, etc. (black, white, red). Beneath: BY (black) | G.A. | HENTY (gilt). Emblem of bugle and palm leaves (red) above: GRIFFITH FARRAN | BROWNE & CO. (black). **Back board:** plain.

Reference: PN.

Notes
1. From an impression of 2000 copies, dated by printer's code November 1897.
2. This binding style is the fourth, and last, used for books in 'The Boys' Own Favourite Library', from about 1895.
3. See 4.3, Notes 3–5, above.

4.7
OUT ON THE PAMPAS I OR I THE YOUNG SETTLERS I BY I G.A. HENTY I AUTHOR OF I "THE YOUNG FRANC-TIREURS" "THE YOUNG BUGLERS" I ETC. ETC. I WITH ILLUSTRATIONS BY FRANK FELLER I GRIFFITH FARRAN BROWNE & CO. LIMITED I 35 BOW STREET, COVENT GARDEN I LONDON

Contents
190 x 134 mm. (1)–320 I no catalogue. Eight full-page wash-drawings by Frank Feller, reproduced by black-and-white halftone blocks printed on unbacked text pages, folioed.
(1) Blank I (2) frontispiece I (3) title p. I (4) [The Rights of Translation and of Reproduction are Reserved] I (5) Contents I (6) blank I (7) List of Illustrations I (8) blank I 9–315. text I (316) printer's imprint (PRINTED BY I MORRISON AND GIBB LIMITED, EDINBURGH.) I (317)–(320) blank.

Binding (see Plate 34)
Blue, vertically-ribbed cloth boards, blocked gilt; top edge gilt; plain off-white wove endpapers.
Front board: OUT (decoration of formal roses and leaves) I ON THE I PAMPAS (all gilt) above illustration, with arms and trophy, etc.: G.A. HENTY (all gilt), all placed high and to the left. **Spine:** OUT I ON THE I PAMPAS (gilt) within shield forming part of gilt decoration. G.A. HENTY (gilt) towards the foot of it, and, below: GRIFFITH, FARRAN I BROWNE & CO. (gilt). **Back board:** plain.

Reference: PN.

Notes
1. One of a set in similar format of Griffith & Farran's five Henty novels. Copies examined show that all were printed at least twice, in impressions of 2000 copies, between 1895 and 1899. The printer's code on p.(316) of my copy records an edition of 2000, June 1899. The other titles are: *The Young Franc-Tireurs*, 5.10; *The Young Buglers*, 7.6; *In Times of Peril*, 9.5; and *Friends, though Divided*, 12.5.
2. The type was newly set for each title except *Friends, though Divided*, for which the first-edition typesetting was still used. The other four, including *Out on the Pampas*, are therefore truly new editions.
3. The four new editions (only) were newly illustrated with wash-drawings, but the paper used was unsuitable for fine-screen halftones, and the reproductions do not do justice to the pictures.

4.8
Title page: As for 4.7, but add *(Note: The quotation marks after* BUGLERS *are battered).*

Contents

188 x 132 mm. (1)–(320) | no catalogue. Frontispiece from hand-coloured impression of black-and-white illustration (see Note 1), reproduced by four-colour blocks printed on coated paper, unbacked, tipped in; seven black-and-white illustrations printed on unbacked text pages as in 4.7.

(1)–(2) blank | (frontispiece, tipped in) | (3) title p. | (4) [The Rights of Translation and Reproduction are Reserved.] | (5) Contents | (6) blank | (7) List of Illustrations | (8) blank | 9–315. text | (316) printer's imprint (Printed by | MORRISON & GIBB LIMITED | Edinburgh) | (317)–(320) blank.

Binding (see Note 3)

Streaked pink cloth boards, blocked blind and gilt; top edge gilt, others plain; plain off-white endpapers.

Front board: OUT | ON THE | PAMPAS | G.A. HENTY (gilt) enclosed on three sides by art-nouveau decoration of plant (gilt), all framed by several decorative borders (blind). **Spine:** OUT | ON THE | PAMPAS | HENTY (gilt) with art-nouveau decorations of plants (gilt) above and below. Blind rules at head and foot, with: GRIFFITH FARRAN, BROWNE & CO. (gilt) between rules at foot. **Back board:** plain.

Reference: BB.

Notes

1. A reprint from the typesetting for 4.7. The frontispiece block has been taken out of the forme, and p.(2) is now blank. A light impression made from the block was hand-coloured; the result became a new original, from which a set of four-colour blocks was made, printed on coated paper, and tipped in as a colour-frontispiece. The other seven black-and-white illustrations appear exactly as in 4.7.

2. The printer's imprint has been reset, and there is no printer's code.

3. The case is blocked from a 'binder's blank' (see Glossary). I have not seen this design used for other titles by Henty.

4.9

OUT ON THE PAMPAS | OR | THE YOUNG SETTLERS | BY | G.A. HENTY | AUTHOR OF | "THE YOUNG FRANC-TIREURS" "THE YOUNG BUGLERS" | ETC. ETC. | GRIFFITH FARRAN BROWNE & CO. LIMITED | 35 BOW STREET, COVENT GARDEN | LONDON

Contents

188 x 130 mm. (1)–(304) | no catalogue. Frontispiece from wash-drawing by Frank Feller reproduced by halftone block printed in dark blue ink on coated paper, unbacked, tipped in.

(1)–(4) all blank | (frontispiece, tipped in) | (5) title p. | (6) [The Rights of Translation and of Reproduction are Reserved] | (7) Contents | (8) blank | 9–301. text | (302) printer's imprint (Printed by | MORRISON & GIBB LIMITED | Edinburgh) | (303)–(304) blanks.

Binding (see Note 3)

Red, vertically-ribbed cloth boards, blocked gilt; top edge gilt; plain off-white wove endpapers.

Front board: OUT ON THE | PAMPAS (gilt), with formal leaf-decoration (gilt) above and below. Beneath this: G.A. HENTY (gilt). **Spine:** OUT ON | THE | PAMPAS | G.A. | HENTY (gilt) above formal leaf-decoration (gilt). At foot: GRIFFITH, FARRAN | BROWNE & CO. (gilt). **Back board:** plain.

Reference: CT.

Notes
1. A further reprint from the type set for 4.7. The colour-frontispiece has now been abandoned, and only one of the black-and-white illustrations by Frank Feller retained. This is now printed on coated paper, to great advantage. As it is tipped in, as in 4.8, and other illustrations removed, the book is re-imposed, and shorter by 16 pages.
2. The printer's imprint is now on p.(302); there is again no printer's code. The copy described has a school-prize label inscribed 1911.
3. The binding style is similar to, although not exactly the same as, that used for *In Times of Peril*, 9.7 (Plate 45).

4.10
OUT ON THE PAMPAS | OR | THE YOUNG SETTLERS | BY | G.A. HENTY | AUTHOR OF | "THE YOUNG FRANC-TIREURS" "THE YOUNG BUGLERS" | ETC. ETC. | NEW EDITION | ILLUSTRATED IN COLOUR BY A.J.GOUGH | LONDON | HENRY FROWDE | HODDER AND STOUGHTON | 1910

Contents
190 x 131 mm. (1)–(302) (see Note 4 below) | catalogue (1)–16. Six full-page watercolour drawings by A.J. Gough (signed and dated 1909), reproduced by three-colour halftone blocks printed on coated paper, unbacked, unfolioed, tipped in.
   (1)–(2) Blank | (3) half-title p. | (4) blank | (frontispiece, tipped in) | (5) title p. | (6) [The Rights of Translation and of Reproduction are Reserved.] | (7) Contents | (8) List of Illustrations | 9–301. text | (302) printer's imprint (Printed by | MORRISON & GIBB LIMITED | Edinburgh) | (1)–16. catalogue.

Binding (see Plate 35)
Dark-green cloth boards, blocked black, white, red, brown and gilt; edges stained dark brown; plain off-white wove endpapers.
   Front board: OUT | on the | PAMPAS | G.A. HENTY (gilt) at top right of illustration of cowboy on white horse (black, white, red, brown), the whole design within double-ruled panel (black). **Spine:** OUT | on the | PAMPAS | (14mm. rule) | G.A. HENTY (all gilt) above illustration of mounted cowboy with lasso (black, white, red, brown) above: HENRY FROWDE | HODDER & STOUGHTON (gilt). **Back board:** plain.

References: BL; Bod.

Notes
1. The stock and goodwill of Griffith & Farran, including *Out on the Pampas* and four other novels by Henty, were bought by Hodder & Stoughton in 1906. The books were re-issued by Hodders in conjunction with the Oxford University Press, of which Henry Frowde was then the Publisher, in what was known as the 'Joint Venture' (see Appendix II, Part 2).

2. The new editions (except *In Times of Peril*, 1911) appeared in 1910, with dated title pages. In true Blackie style, later impressions omitted the date, and various cloth-colours were used for each title, all blocked in numerous colours and gilt.

3. The prelims are re-organised and partly re-set; the text is from stereos of the type used by the same printer for the last Griffith & Farran edition, 4.8.

4. The final gathering consists of 14 pages, the odd leaf, forming pages 289–290, being tipped on. What would have been its conjugate leaf, as pages (303)–(304), appears to have been deliberately removed from all copies I have examined.

4.11

Title page: As for 4.10, except (a) NEW EDITION deleted; (b) no date.

Contents

185 x 123 mm. (1)–(304) | no catalogue. Illustrations as in 4.10.

(1) Half-title p. | (2) publisher's advertisement (STORIES FOR BOYS) listing 14 titles | (frontispiece, tipped in) | (3) title p. | (4) printer's imprint (PRINTED IN GREAT BRITAIN BY R. CLAY AND SONS, LTD., | BRUNSWICK STREET, STAMFORD STREET, S.E., AND BUNGAY, SUFFOLK.) | (5) Contents | (6) blank | (7) List of Illustrations | (8) blank | 9–301. text | (302)–(304) blank.

Binding (see Plate 37)

Green, grained cloth boards, blocked black and white; with two onlays printed on coated paper from three-colour halftones, rectangular on front board, oval on spine; edges plain; plain off-white endpapers.

Front board: OUT ON THE | PAMPAS | G.A. HENTY (white) within rectangular frame forming upper panel in art-nouveau decoration (black), above larger rectangle (black), framing onlay printed in colour on coated paper and cut down from illustration facing p.224. **Spine:** OUT | ON THE | PAMPAS | G.A. HENTY (white) in square panel, framed black, forming upper part of art-nouveau decoration. At centre, within oval panel, framed black, oval onlay of illustration of standing figure printed in colour on coated paper. (This picture does not appear in the illustrations.) At foot: HENRY FROWDE | HODDER & STOUGHTON (black) with small rectangle, framed black. **Back board:** plain.

Reference: PN.

Notes

1. A cheaper reprint of 4.10, from the same or duplicate plates, but by a new printer, Richard Clay, who were ultimately to print all, except 4.14, of the Henty novels acquired by the Joint Venture (see Appendix II, Part 2).

2. In re-imposing, the printer has moved the blank leaf from the front to the back of the book.

3. The publisher's advertisement on p.(2) includes this book and *The Young Franc-Tireurs*, but no other Henty titles yet. They are the only ones here advertised as being available in two cloth bindings, at 3s.6d. and 2s.6d. Cheaper versions were later to be published concurrently with these (see 4.12 and 4.13, below).

4.12

OUT I on . the I PAMPAS I G . A I HENTY I LONDON I HENRY . FROWDE I HODDER & I STOUGHTON
(Note: All lettering is hand-drawn within elaborate decorated framework).

Contents

164 x 110 mm. (1)–(304) I no catalogue. Frontispiece from watercolour drawing by A.J. Gough (signed and dated 1909) reproduced by three-colour halftone blocks printed on coated paper, unbacked, keyed to p.152, tipped in.

(1)–(2) Blank I (3) half-title p. I (4) publisher's advertisement (THE BOYS' NEW 7d. NET LIBRARY I With frontispiece in colour) listing 11 titles including this one I (frontispiece, tipped in) I (5) title p. I (6) printer's imprint (RICHARD CLAY & SONS, LIMITED, I BRUNSWICK STREET, STAMFORD STREET, S.E., I AND BUNGAY, SUFFOLK.) I (7) Contents I (8) blank I 9–301. text I (302)–(304) blank.

Binding (see Note 3)

Red cloth boards, blind embossed, blocked gilt; edges plain; light-blue endpapers printed in dark-blue with line illustration of arabs riding camels near palm-trees in desert (signed, W.Herbert Holloway, and with caption, Sudan).

Front board: Over-all pattern of vertical rules with medallion over horizontal band at centre, with head and shoulders of knight in armour, holding a lance (all blind-embossed). **Spine:** Art-nouveau floral decoration (blind) at centre with, above: OUT I ON THE I PAM- I PAS I (triangle of three dots) I G . A I HENTY (all gilt) and, below: HENRY I FROWDE I HODDER . & I STOUGHTON (blind). **Back board:** over-all pattern of vertical rules with horizontal band as on front board, but without medallion (blind-embossed).

Reference: BB.

Notes

1. This impression is on smaller paper of a very light weight; consequently it has narrow margins and is much less bulky. It is sewn in 32-page sections. The only illustration is the frontispiece, so the preliminary pages have been re-arranged, omitting the list of illustrations.

2. The illustrations used as frontispiece vary from one copy to another. It seems that at first they were all taken from printed sheets of the pictures for 4.11. But later, probably, a set of electrotypes was made from one of the three-colour sets, chosen to become the permanent frontispiece, and to be printed on a small machine.

3. This edition, in 'The Boys' New 7d. Net Library', is the first of two Henty titles published by the Joint Venture in a 'pocket' size, and the only one listed on p.(4). Later, *The Young Buglers* was added (see 7.11, Plate 42), but the name of the series was changed to 'The Boys' Pocket Library' (see 4.13 below).

4. The text is still printed from stereos of the typesetting used for the last Griffith & Farran edition, 4.9.

5. The gilt blocking is done with real gold, but books that followed in 'The Boys' Pocket Library' were blocked with imitation gold foil (see 4.13, Note 3, below).

4.13

Title page, Contents: As for 4.12, but on p.(4) publisher's advertisement (THE BOY'S POCKET LIBRARY).

Binding: As for 4.12, except (a) Pale-green endpapers printed olive-green; and (b) Spine blocked with over-all pattern of vertical rules with superimposed decorations (blind), and three sunken panels for title; author; and publisher: OUT I ON THE I PAM- I PAS ; G . A I HENTY ; HENRY I FROWDE I HODDER . & I STOUGHTON (all lettering imitation gold).

Reference: PN.

Notes

1. One of two Henty novels (see 4.12, Note 3, above) now listed on p.(4) in 'The Boy's Pocket Library' issued by the 'Joint Venture'. The series was continued by the Oxford University Press when the 'Joint Venture' ended (see Appendix II, Part 2).
2. My copy has a dust-wrapper with the O.U.P. imprint, which dates it after March 1916, when the Oxford University Press was using up sheets with the joint imprint.
3. The use of real gold for blocking went generally out of use during the first war, and this issue shows a change from 4.12. The imitation gold foil that took its place continued in use by some publishers for many years after the war, but was never satisfactory, invariably going almost black within a short time.

4.14

Title page: As for 4.11, but with changed imprint (HUMPHREY MILFORD I OXFORD UNIVERSITY PRESS I LONDON EDINBURGH GLASGOW I TORONTO MELBOURNE CAPE TOWN BOMBAY).

Contents

186 x 120 mm. (1)–(304) I no catalogue. Illustrations as in 4.10.
   (1) Half-title p. I (2) publisher's announcement of 16 books, headed STORIES FOR BOYS I (frontispiece, tipped in) I (3) title p. I (4) printer's imprint (Printed in Great Britain I by Turnbull & Spears, Edinburgh) I (5) Contents I (6) blank I (7) List of Illustrations I (8) blank I 9–301. text I (302)–(304) blank.

Binding (see Plate 37)

Grey-green paper boards (grained to imitate cloth), blocked black, with colour-printed oval onlay; edges plain; plain off-white endpapers.
   Front board: OUT ON THE PAMPAS I G.A. HENTY (paper-colour out of black) in rectangular solid-black decorative panel above oval, outlined with heavy black line and decorative art-nouveau scroll design. Within the oval is laid down a cut-out section of the colour plate facing p.118. **Spine:** OUT ON I THE I PAMPAS I HENTY (paper-colour out of black) in solid rectangular panel, above decorative art-nouveau scrolls. At foot: OXFORD (paper-colour out of black) in solid rectangular panel. **Back board:** plain.

Reference: PN.

Notes

1. Apart from the preliminary pages this is a reprint of 4.11 by yet another new printer, now under the O.U.P. imprint and still in a cheaper binding style.

2. Reprints continued in this format, simultaneously with the pocket edition, 4.13 (see 4.11, Note 3).

4.15

OUT | on . the | PAMPAS | G . A | HENTY | . HUMPHREY . | MILFORD | OXFORD | UNIVERSITY | PRESS . LONDON
(Note: All lettering is hand-drawn within elaborate decorated framework).

Contents: As for 4.13, except: (a) Changed imprint on title p. and p.(4) etc.; (b) Printer's imprint on p.(6): (REPRINTED 1926 IN GREAT BRITAIN BY R. CLAY AND SONS LTD., | BUNGAY, SUFFOLK.).

Binding: As for 4.13, but (a) yellow-buff endpapers printed in black; (b) case blocked in black instead of imitation gold, with imprint changed to 'OXFORD'.

Reference: PN.

Notes
1. An issue from the Oxford University Press after they had taken over the children's books from the Joint Venture (see Appendix II, Part 2).
2. It became customary for Richard Clay, who eventually took over the printing of all O.U.P. books by Henty, to include in their imprint the date of each reprint. There may have been earlier issues from the O.U.P. than the copy described here.
3. Following the disappointing appearance of imitation-gold foil the publisher for a time used black ink, which was even cheaper (see 4.12, Note 5, and 4.13, Note 3).

4.16

OUT | ON THE PAMPAS | OR | THE YOUNG SETTLERS | A TALE FOR BOYS | BY | G.A. HENTY | AUTHOR OF 'ALL BUT LOST' 'THE MARCH TO MAGDALA,' ETC. ETC. | LONDON | HOLDEN & HARDINGHAM | ADELPHI
(Note: There is no comma after 'ALL BUT LOST').

Contents
191 x 135 mm. (i)–(iv) unfolioed, plus i–(iv) | 1–(312). Frontispiece from water-colour by unknown hand (see Note 3) reproduced by three-colour halftone blocks printed on coated paper, unbacked, unfolioed, tipped in.
(i) Half-title p. | (ii) blank | (frontispiece, tipped in) | (iii) title p. | (iv) blank | i–iii. Contents | (iv) blank | 1–(310) text | (311) publisher's advertisement | (312) printer's imprint (Printed by Ebenezer Baylis & Son, Trinity Works, Worcester.)

Binding (see Plate 38)
Brown cloth boards, blocked black, brown, gilt, and blue merging through light olive-green to darker green; edges plain; plain off-white wove endpapers.
Front board: OUT ON THE | PAMPAS (black) above illustration of horseman with spear chasing another (black, brown, blue merging to green) partly enclosed by thick black rule. At foot: G.A. HENTY (black). **Spine:** OUT | ON THE | PAMPAS | G.A. HENTY | HOLDEN & | HARDINGHAM (all gilt). **Back board:** plain.

References: PN | *Farmer*, p.54

Notes
1. Little is known of this publisher, but see 4.17, Note 1, below. They issued the book about 1913, in October of which year they also published *With Hunter, Trapper and Scout in Camp and Field*, a collection of boys' stories (see §2, 191), edited by Alfred H. Miles, who also edited all the 'Fifty-Two' series of books (see §2, 143 to 154). It includes 'Seth Harpur's Story', an edited extract from *Out on the Pampas*.
2. In the two publications mentioned above, Holden and Hardingham announce a total of only four 'Gift Books'. This edition of *Out on the Pampas* is advertised at 2s.6d.; I have seen copies bound in red cloth instead of brown.
3. The frontispiece is from an unsigned watercolour based on the original engraving by J.B. Zwecker illustrating 'The Fight with the Puma' (keyed to p.59 in 4.1).

4.17
OUT ON THE PAMPAS | OR | THE YOUNG SETTLERS | BY | G.A. HENTY | AUTHOR OF | "THE YOUNG FRANC-TIREURS," "THE YOUNG BUGLERS," ETC. | NEW EDITION | ILLUSTRATED IN COLOUR | LONDON | HUMPHREY MILFORD | OXFORD UNIVERSITY PRESS

Contents
188 x 124 mm. (i)–(iv) unfolioed, plus i–(iv) | (1)–(312), of which p.(331) advertises books published by Holden & Hardingham. Three full-page watercolour drawings by A.J.Gough reproduced by three-colour halftone blocks on coated paper, unbacked, unfolioed, tipped in.
(i) Half-title p. | (ii) blank | (frontispiece, tipped in) | (iii) title p. | (iv) blank | i–iii. Contents | (iv) blank | 1–(310) text | (311) advertisement for Holden & Hardingham publications | (312) printer's imprint (Printed by Ebenezer Baylis & Son, Trinity Works, Worcester.)

Binding
Red cloth boards, blocked buff and gilt, with oval overlays printed on coated paper from three-colour blocks (illustrations in the book) on front board and spine; edges plain; plain off-white endpapers.
Front board: OUT ON THE PAMPAS | G.A. HENTY (cloth colour) out of solid gilt rectangular panel with ornamental lower corners, all outlined (buff) as part of decorative art-nouveau framework (buff) to printed onlay. **Spine:** OUT ON | THE | PAMPAS | HENTY (cloth colour) out of solid gilt rectangular panel. That, and printed onlay below, outlined and with decorative art-nouveau framework (buff). At foot: MILFORD (buff) above buff rule. **Back board:** plain.

Reference: PN.

Notes
1. It is clear from the above that the Holden & Hardingham list was taken over by the Oxford University Press. This edition is basically a reissue of 4.16, but the old frontispiece has been discarded and a new title page tipped in as a cancel. The illustrations are some of those used first by the Joint Venture in 1910 (see 4.10).
2. My copy has a presentation inscription dated 10 April 1922.

5. THE YOUNG FRANC-TIREURS

5.1

THE YOUNG FRANC- | TIREURS | And their Adventures in the Franco- | Prussian War. | BY | G.A. HENTY, | SPECIAL CORRESPONDENT OF THE "STANDARD," AND AUTHOR OF "A MARCH | TO MAGDALA," "OUT ON THE PAMPAS," &c. | WITH ILLUSTRATIONS BY R.T. LANDELLS, | ARTIST TO THE "ILLUSTRATED LONDON NEWS," | (publisher's device) | LONDON: | GRIFFITH AND FARRAN, | SUCCESSORS TO NEWBERY AND HARRIS, | CORNER OF ST. PAUL'S CHURCHYARD. | MDCCCLXXII.
(Note: The subtitle is in gothic type).

Contents
175 x 118 mm. (i)–(viii) | (1)–376 | catalogue (1)–32. Eight full-page wood-engravings after R.T. Landells by Swain, unbacked, unfolioed, tipped in.

(Frontispiece, tipped in) | (i) title p. | (ii) printer's imprint (LONDON; | GILBERT AND RIVINGTON, PRINTERS, | ST. JOHN'S SQUARE.) | (iii)–iv. Foreword | (v)–vii. Contents | (viii) blank | (1)–376. text, with printer's imprint on p.376 (GILBERT AND RIVINGTON, PRINTERS, ST. JOHN'S SQUARE, LONDON.) | (1)–32. catalogue, undated, with printer's imprint at foot of p.32 (WERTHEIMER, LEA AND CO., CIRCUS PLACE, FINSBURY CIRCUS.)

Binding (see Plate 32)
Green, stipple-grained cloth boards, blocked black, blind, and gilt; edges plain; plain pinkish-yellow surface-paper endpapers. (See Note 1).
Front board: THE YOUNG | FRANC-TIREURS (gilt) above figure of franc-tireur with rifle and bayonet (gilt) in simple line representation of landscape (black), all within elaborate decorative panelling with battle-trophies at head and foot (all black). **Spine:** THE | YOUNG | FRANC- | TIREURS (gilt) | G.A. HENTY (black) above trophy of military equipment (gilt). At foot: GRIFFITH & FARRAN (green cloth-colour out of gilt panel). Other decorations (black). **Back board:** decorative panelling with publisher's monogram at centre (all blind).

References: BL; Bod; PN | *Farmer*, p.88; *Dartt*, p.172, *Companion*, p.37; *Sadleir*, I, 1192.

Notes
1. The book was sold as described above at 5s.; also, with bevelled boards and all edges gilt, at 5s.6d. It was almost certainly published in the autumn of 1871.
2. In the line under the author's name on the title page, *The March to Magdala* is incorrectly shown as *A March to Magdala*.
3. The story later appeared as a serial in the *Union Jack* (see §3, 225).
4. The illustration facing p.302, captioned 'The Sea! The Sea!', was not used for the serialisation, being replaced by a similar picture from a French translation. It was used in the *Union Jack*, however, by its economical Editor, to illustrate 'A Ballooning Adventure' by E.G. Salmon (Vol.III, No.141, 7 September 1882, p.781).
5. Other illustrations from the French edition were also used in later English editions: see 5.3, Note 1.
6. At The National Book League, London, in 1947, John Carter and Michael Sadleir

arranged an Exhibition of 'Original Editions' of Victorian Fiction. It included this first edition, as one of a collection of eleven 'Adventure Stories' by leading British writers, published between 1841 and 1898. In the exhibition catalogue the authors declare 'Many of these books are rarities in fine state: one or two – notably *The Young Franc-Tireurs* – are rare in any condition'. (Carter and Sadleir, *Victorian Fiction*, p.29).

5.2

Title page: As for 5.1, but with 'Second Edition' in gothic type above the publisher's device.

Contents: As for 5.1, but catalogues bound-in with this edition vary: the earliest I have seen has 32 pages, is headed '1877–1878' on p.3 , and dated '11.77' on p.1.

Binding: As for 5.1, but brown, ungrained-cloth boards.

References: BL; PN | *Dartt*, p.173, Note (1).

Notes

1. This is really a second impression of 5.1, not a new edition, in spite of the wording on the title page. Neither 5.1 nor 5.2 contains printer's codes.

2. For notes on the early reprints of Henty's books from Griffith & Farran, see Appendix II, Part 2.

3. As in 5.1 (and numerous subsequent impressions) the title of *The March to Magdala* is incorrectly shown under the author's name on the title page.

5.3

THE YOUNG FRANC- | TIREURS | AND THEIR ADVENTURES IN THE | FRANCO-PRUSSIAN WAR. | BY | G.A. HENTY, | SPECIAL CORRESPONDENT OF THE "STANDARD," AND AUTHOR OF "A MARCH | TO MAGDALA," "OUT ON THE PAMPAS," &c. | ILLUSTRATED | (publisher's device) | GRIFFITH AND FARRAN, | SUCCESSORS TO NEWBERY AND HARRIS, | WEST CORNER OF ST. PAUL'S CHURCHYARD, LONDON. | E.P. DUTTON & CO., NEW YORK.

Contents

181 x 122 mm. (i)–(ii) unfolioed | (i)–(viii) | (1)–376 plus seven unfolioed leaves | catalogue (1)–(32). Eight full-page black-and-white engravings after R.T. Landells by Swain, printed on text pages, unbacked, unfolioed, the leaves not counted in pagination. Seven smaller black-and-white engravings after Janet-Lange by various engravers, printed on text pages with typematter (see Note 1).

(i) Blank | (ii) (frontispiece) | (i) title p. | (ii) [The rights of Translation and of Reproduction are reserved.] | (iii)–iv. Preface to the Present Edition | (v)–vii. Contents | (viii) blank | (1)–376. text; printer's imprint on p.376 (GILBERT AND RIVINGTON, LIMITED, ST. JOHN'S SQUARE, LONDON.) | (1)–(32) catalogue, dated 1882.

Binding: In the first style of 'The Boys' Own Favourite Library' (see Plate 33); red cloth boards; edges plain; yellow-green floral endpapers. (See Notes 3 and 4).

References: PN | *Dartt*, p.173, Note (2).

Notes

1. The first-edition typesetting is used again for this impression of 2000 copies, now issued in cheaper format. New plates have been made to include seven engravings with the typematter. The illustrations are by Janet-Lange, and appeared first in a French translation of the book published by Librairie Hachette & Cie, Paris, 1873 (see also 5.1, Note 4).

2. The full-page illustrations are on unfolioed leaves, as frontispiece, and following pp.48, 94, 144, 190, 276, 302, and 338. The book is imposed in twenty-five 16-page sections, the first consisting of a blank leaf (frontispiece), pp.(i)–(viii), and pp.1–6.

3. In 1881 Griffith & Farran had announced the first six titles in 'The Boys' Own Favourite Library', which included Henty's *Out on the Pampas*. The dated, bound-in catalogue shows that *The Young Franc-Tireurs* was now added to the list.

4. For notes on 'The Boys' Own Favourite Library' editions, which include 5.3, 5.4, 5.5, and 5.6, see *Out on the Pampas*, 4.3, Notes 3–5.

5. Henty's Preface has been re-written, and now begins: 'My dear Lads,'.

6. On the title page the error in the name of *The March to Magdala* is continued from earlier impressions.

5.4

Title-page: As for 5.3 but with changed imprint (GRIFFITH, FARRAN, OKEDEN & WELSH, | SUCCESSORS TO NEWBERY AND HARRIS, | WEST CORNER OF ST. PAUL'S CHURCHYARD, LONDON. | E.P. DUTTON & CO., NEW YORK.).

Contents: 185 x 122 mm. As for 5.3, but final page of catalogue is folioed 32.

Binding: In the second style of the Boys' Own Favourite Library (see Plate 33); blue cloth boards; edges plain; yellow-green floral endpapers. (See Note 2).

References: PN | *Dartt*, p.173, Note (2)

Notes

1. An impression of 2000 copies, using the text plates made for 5.3.

2. See 5.3, Notes 4 and 6.

5.5

Title-page: As for 5.3.

Contents: As for 5.3, but publisher's catalogue is (1)–16, dated 12 November 1888.

Binding: In the third style of 'The Boys' Own Favourite Library' (see Plate 33); red cloth boards, bevelled; all edges gilt; yellow-green floral endpapers.

Reference: PN.

Notes

1. The plates made for 5.3 are used again. Below the imprint on p.376 the printer's code identifies an impression of 2000 copies, dated 4 January 1886.

2. For details of 'The Boys' Own Favourite Library', which includes 5.3, 5.4, 5.5, and 5.6, see *Out on the Pampas*, 4.3, Notes 3–5, and, with especial relevance to 5.5 and 5.6, *Out on the Pampas,* 4.5, Note 1.

5.6

THE YOUNG | FRANC-TIREURS | AND THEIR ADVENTURES IN THE | FRANCO-PRUSSIAN WAR | BY | G.A. HENTY | SPECIAL CORRESPONDENT OF THE "STANDARD," AND AUTHOR OF "A MARCH | TO MAGDALA," "OUT ON THE PAMPAS," &c. | ILLUSTRATED | (publisher's device) | NEW EDITION. | LONDON | GRIFFITH FARRAN & CO., | NEWBURY HOUSE, 39, CHARING CROSS ROAD

Contents: 182 x 120 mm. As for 5.3, except (a) no catalogue; (b) printer's imprint reset on p.376 (Gilbert and Rivington, Ld., St. John's House, Clerkenwell Road, London).

Binding: In the fourth style of 'The Boys' Own Favourite Library' (see Plate 33); crimson, vertically-ribbed, cloth boards, bevelled, blocked black, scarlet, and gilt; all edges gilt; brown surface-paper endpapers.

Reference: PN.

Note: A further reprint from the original typesetting: I can find no reason for the words 'NEW EDITION' on the title page. No printer's code. See 5.5, Note 2.

5.7

THE | YOUNG FRANC-TIREURS | AND THEIR ADVENTURES IN THE | FRANCO-PRUSSIAN WAR | BY | G.A. HENTY | SPECIAL CORRESPONDENT OF THE 'STANDARD,' | AND AUTHOR OF 'THE YOUNG BUGLERS,' 'FRIENDS THOUGH DIVIDED,' | 'IN TIMES OF PERIL,' 'OUT ON THE PAMPAS,' ETC. | (publishers device) | LONDON | GRIFFITH FARRAN OKEDEN & WELSH | NEWBERY HOUSE, CHARING CROSS ROAD | AND SYDNEY

Contents

230 x 150 mm. (1)–160 | catalogue (1)–8. No illustrations.

(1) Title p. | (2) printer's imprint (MORRISON AND GIBB, PRINTERS, EDINBURGH.); at foot: [The Rights of Translation and Reproduction are Reserved.] | 3. Preface to the Present Edition | (4) blank | 5. Contents | (6) blank | 7–160. text, set in two columns, with rule between. On p.160 an engraved vignette, 'The End', decorated with daffodils; printer's imprint as on p.(2) | (1)–8. general catalogue (see Note 2).

Cover

Red paper, printed black; edges cut flush.
(1) The Young | Franc-Tireurs | And their Adventures in the | Franco-Prussian War | By G.A. HENTY | SPECIAL CORRESPONDENT OF THE 'STANDARD,' AND | AUTHOR OF 'A MARCH TO MAGDALA,' 'OUT ON THE PAMPAS,' ETC. | (cut-out vignette halftone portrait from photograph of G.A. Henty, 82 x 65 mm.) | London: Griffith Farran Okden & Welsh | Newbery House, Charing Cross Road | And Sydney
(All above is in double-ruled panel, 206 x 125 mm.) Below it: PRICE SIXPENCE
(2) Full-page advertisement for Oetzmann & Co., furniture manufacturers.

(3) Full-page advertisement for Bovril.

(4) Full-page advertisement for Liebig's Extract of Beef.

(Spine) THE YOUNG FRANC-TIREURS (at centre, running from foot to head), see Note 1.

References: BL; Bod; PN | *Dartt*, p.173, Note (2).

Notes

1. I cannot be certain of the details of the spine: in 1991 that of the only known copy with cover, at the Bodleian Library, was damaged: and now the front (pp.1–2) cover of that copy is missing. But I did then record details, and on p.(1) of cover the title of *The March to Magdala* is given incorrectly with the indefinite article.

2. The bound-in catalogue, in addition to the publisher's announcements of Books for Boys and Girls, contains announcements of books from other publishers and stamp dealers. Other advertisements include one for tea and coffee, showing price-reductions following the 1890 budget.

3. Probably the earliest issue of an edition in two-columns, cheaply printed on poor quality paper, and possibly for sale mainly from railway-station bookstalls (see 5.8, 5.11, 5.12). It was received by the Copyright Libraries in February 1891.

5.8

Title-page: As for 5.7.

Contents: 222 x 126 mm. Otherwise as for 5.7.

Binding (see Plate 41)

Red cloth boards, blocked black; edges plain; plain off-white endpapers.

   Front board: The | Young Franc-Tireurs | (short rule) | G.A. Henty (black) above a head-and-shoulders portrait of Henty (black) from a line engraving. **Spine:** THE YOUNG FRANC-TIREURS (black) running from head to foot. **Back board:** plain.

References: BB; PN.

Note: Only two copies are known to me. Sheets of 5.7, including the catalogue, are trimmed and cased in red cloth boards, uniquely blocked with Henty's portrait. The publishers's name is not on the binding case. In spite of the inclusion of a catalogue this may be a private issue, perhaps made as a reward book for a school or institution. Neither copy, however, has any prize label or inscription.

5.9

Title-page: As for 5.6.

Contents

182 x 133 mm. (i)–(viii) | (1)–376 | no catalogue. Illustrations as in 5.3.

   (Frontispiece, tipped in) | (i) title p. | (ii) [The rights of Translation and of Reproduction are reserved.] | (iii)–iv. Preface to the Present Edition | (v)–vii. Contents | (viii) blank | (1)–376. text, with printer's imprint at foot of p.376 (Gilbert and Rivington, Ld., St. John's House, Clerkenwell Road, London.)

Binding (see Note 3)

Light-blue, diagonally-ribbed cloth boards, blocked black and gilt; all edges gilt; light brownish-yellow floral-patterned endpapers.

Front board: THE YOUNG | FRANC-TIREURS (gilt) between two thick black rules forming open panel towards top of illustration of five sailors in a boat, rowing away from natives firing arrows from a pursuing canoe, near an island of palm trees, etc. (all black except the five sailors, gilt). G.A. Henty (black) within small ruled panel set at centre of illustration. **Spine:** THE | YOUNG | FRANC- | TIREURS (gilt) between two black rules forming open panel towards top of illustration of two monkeys throwing down coconuts from palm tree to white man in boat (all black except man, gilt). At foot: GRIFFITH, FARRAN & Co. (gilt). **Back board:** plain.

Reference: BB.

Notes
1. A straightforward reprint of 5.6, on slightly larger paper and in a different binding. The printer's code on p.376 indicates 2000 copies, 28 December 1892.
2. Although the use of gilt edges is continued from 5.6, the boards are not now bevelled. This is a slightly cheaper binding, using a 'binder's blank'.
3. I have a copy of *In Times of Peril* (9.3, Plate 43), bound in the same style, but with a different cloth: in it the printer's code indicates 2000 copies, January 1893. I have not found other Henty novels in this binding style.

5.10

The | Young Franc-Tireurs | And their Adventures in the | Franco-Prussian War | BY | G.A. HENTY | AUTHOR OF "THE YOUNG BUGLERS" "FRIENDS THOUGH DIVIDED" | "IN TIMES OF PERIL" "OUT ON THE PAMPAS" ETC. | ILLUS-TRATED BY FRANK FELLER | GRIFFITH FARRAN BROWNE & CO. LIMITED | 35 BOW STREET, COVENT GARDEN | LONDON

Contents
190 x 133 mm. (1)–352 | no catalogue. Eight full-page black-and-white wash-drawings by Frank Feller, reproduced by halftone blocks printed on MF text paper, unbacked, some of them unfolioed but all counted in pagination.
   (1) Blank | (2) frontispiece | (3) title p. | (4) [The Rights of Translation and of Reproduction are Reserved] | 5–6. Preface to the Present Edition | 7. Contents | 8. List of Illustrations | 9–352. text and illustrations, with printer's imprint at foot of p.352 (PRINTED BY MORRISON AND GIBB LIMITED, EDINBURGH).

Binding (see Plate 34)
Blue, vertically-grained cloth boards, blocked gilt; top edge gilt; plain off-white laid endpapers.
   Front board: THE YOUNG (engraved eagle) | FRANC | TIREURS (all gilt) above decorative illustration, with arms and trophy, etc.: G.A. HENTY (all gilt) placed high and at left. **Spine:** THE | YOUNG | FRANC | TIREURS (gilt) within shield forming part of gilt decoration. G.A. HENTY (gilt) towards the foot of it, and, below: GRIFFITH, FARRAN | BROWNE & CO. (gilt). **Back board:** plain.

Reference: PN.

Notes
1. One of a set in similar format of Griffith & Farran's five Henty novels. Copies examined show that all were printed at least twice in this style, in impressions of

2000 copies, between 1895 and 1899. The other titles are: *Out on the Pampas*, 4.7; *The Young Buglers*, 7.6; *In Times of Peril*, 9.5; and *Friends, though Divided*, 12.5.

2. The type is newly set for all titles except *Friends, though Divided*, for which the first-edition typesetting was still used. The other four, including *The Young Franc-Tireurs*, are therefore truly new editions.

3. The four new editions (only) were newly illustrated with wash-drawings reproduced by halftone blocks, but the paper used was unsuitable for the fine-screen halftones and the reproductions do not do justice to the pictures.

5.11

THE | YOUNG FRANC-TIREURS | AND THEIR ADVENTURES IN THE | FRANCO-PRUSSIAN WAR | BY | G.A. HENTY | SPECIAL CORRESPONDENT OF THE "STANDARD," | AND AUTHOR OF "THE YOUNG BUGLERS," "FRIENDS THOUGH DIVIDED," | "IN TIMES OF PERIL," "OUT ON THE PAMPAS," ETC. | LONDON | GRIFFITH FARRAN BROWNE & CO., LTD. | 35, BOW STREET, COVENT GARDEN

Contents

214 x 139 mm. (1)–(2) | 7–160 (see Note 2). No illustrations.

(1) Title p. | (2) blank) | 7–160. text, in two columns, with rule between. On p.160 an engaved vignette, 'The End', decorated with daffodils; printer's imprint (Printed by GILBERT and RIVINGTON, Limited, St. John's House, Clerkenwell, E.C.) | (161)–(164) general advertisements, mainly for household goods, but including one quarter-page publisher's advertisement listing 5 Henty titles (see Note 4).

Cover (see Plate 39)

White paper, printed black-and-white (inners), and full colour (outers), wrapped round, and cut flush.

(1) PRICE SIXPENCE. (black) | THE (black) | YOUNG | FRANC-TIREURS (red, cased black) over area of sky in illustration (full colour) of man in hedge, with gun, accosting mounted officer in woodland scene. At foot: G.A. HENTY. | GRIFFITH, FARRAN, BROWNE & CO., LONDON. (all black).

(2) Full-page advertisement for furniture: Oetzmann & Co. (black line).

(3) Full-page advertisement for Keating's Powder (black line).

(4) Full-page advertisement for STEEDMAN'S SOOTHING POWDERS (full-colour), with printer's imprint at foot (ENGRAVED AND PRINTED BY EDMUND EVANS, THE RACQUET COURT PRESS SWAN STREET, LONDON, S.E.) (black).

(Spine) (partly missing in copy examined) THE YOUNG FRANC-TIREURS. G.A. HENTY. (black on coloured background) reading from foot to head.

Reference: SW.

Notes

1. I have seen only one copy of this attractively-presented booklet, its cover typical of Edmund Evans's work. It was probably the last issue of the double-column setting in paper covers (see 5.7, Note 3). The text is printed from plates made from the type used, and probably set, by Morrison and Gibb of Edinburgh, for 5.7.

2. The title page is reset by the new printer, with double-quotes for the titles after the author's name, with the publisher's current imprint, and without their device. The original preliminary pages (3) to (6) of 5.7 have been omitted; consequently what should now be page 3 is still folioed 7. The imposition makes it clear that this was planned intentionally, the first 32-page gathering ending at p.36, with the central threads visible between pages 20 and 21. The last 32-page gathering ends with four pages of general advertisements to complete the even working.

3. The printing is not good, and the paper is of poor quality, now brittle and brown at the edges. The book was sold at 6d., probably mainly from railway bookstalls.

4. The publisher's advertisement lists all five Henty titles as 'Large Crown 8vo, Cloth gilt, Gilt Top, with New Illustrations. Price 3s.6d.'. These include *The Young Franc-Tireurs* as described at 5.10 above. The others are listed in 5.10, Note 1.

5. On p. (4) of the cover, the comma is missing after 'RACQUET COURT PRESS'.

5.12

Title page: As for 5.11.

Contents

216 x 140 mm. (1)–(2) I 7–160 (see 5.11, Note 2) I (1)–(160) bound-in edition of *The Young Buglers* (see Note 3) I no catalogue. No illustrations.

(1) Title p. I (2) blank I 7–160. text, set in two columns, with rule between. On p.160 an engraved vignette, 'The End', decorated with daffodils. At foot, below rule, printer's imprint (Printed by GILBERT and RIVINGTON, Limited, St. John's House, Clerkenwell, E.C.) I (1)–(160) bound-in edition of *The Young Buglers*.

Binding (see plate 43)

Red, vertically ribbed cloth boards, blocked gilt; edges plain; plain off-white endpapers.

Front board: Young Franc-Tireurs I Young Buglers (all gilt). **Spine:** YOUNG I FRANC- I TIREURS I (2-em rule) I YOUNG I BUGLERS I (2-em rule) I G.A. I HENTY (all gilt). At foot: GRIFFITH FARRAN, I BROWNE & CO. (gilt). **Back board:** plain.

Reference: PN.

Notes

1. The text is printed from the plates used for 5.11. The advertisement leaves (pages 161–164) have been cut away, and the stubs held and concealed by glue and the lower endpaper. The book was no doubt sold at a cheap price in an attempt to dispose of the remaining sheets of the two-column editions of both titles.

2. My copy is inscribed with the date, April '05.

3. The bound-in edition of *The Young Buglers* is described below as 7.8.

5.13

The I Young Franc-Tireurs I And their Adventures in the I Franco-Prussian War I BY I G.A. HENTY I AUTHOR OF I "THE YOUNG BUGLERS" "FRIENDS THOUGH DIVIDED I "OUT ON THE PAMPAS" ETC. ETC. I NEW EDITION I ILLUSTRATED IN COLOUR BY T.C. DUGDALE I LONDON I HENRY FROWDE I HODDER AND STOUGHTON I 1910

(*Note: The quotation marks after FRIENDS THOUGH DIVIDED are missing*).

Contents

187 x 129 mm. (1)–352 | catalogue (1)–16. Six full-page plates from watercolour drawings by T.C. Dugdale, reproduced by three-colour halftone blocks printed on coated paper, unbacked, unfolioed, tipped in. Two full-page black-and-white illustrations from wash-drawings by Frank Feller, reproduced by halftone blocks printed on unbacked MF text paper.

(1) Half-title p. | (2) blank | (frontispiece, tipped in) | (3) title p. | (4) [The Rights of Translation and Reproduction are Reserved.] | 5–6. Preface | 7. Contents | (8) List of Illustrations | 9-352. text and illustrations; printer's imprint on p.352 (PRINTED BY MORRISON AND GIBB LIMITED, EDINBURGH) | (1)–16. catalogue.

Binding (see Plate 36)

Red cloth boards, blocked black, brown, white, blue, yellow merging to orange, gilt; all edges stained blue-grey; plain off-white endpapers.

Front board: THE YOUNG | FRANC-TIREURS | G.A. HENTY (gilt with black shadow) on sky (yellow merging to orange) of illustration of franc-tireurs in twilight landscape (black, brown, white, blue, yellow merging to orange). **Spine:** THE YOUNG | FRANC- | TIREURS | (3-em rule) | G.A. HENTY (all gilt) above illustration of franc-tireur against starlit sky (black, brown, white, blue). At foot: HENRY FROWDE | HODDER & STOUGHTON (gilt). **Back board:** plain.

References: BL; Bod; PN | *Dartt*, p.173, Note (2).

Notes

1. The stock and goodwill of Griffith & Farran, including *The Young Franc-Tireurs* and four other novels by Henty, were bought by Hodder & Stoughton in 1906. The books were re-issued by Hodders, with the Oxford University Press, of which Henry Frowde was then the Publisher, in their 'Joint Venture' (see Appendix II, Part 2).

2. The new editions (except *In Times of Peril*, 1911) appeared in 1910, with dated title pages. In true Blackie style, later impressions omitted the date, and various cloth-colours were used for each title, blocked in numerous pigments and gold.

3. The prelims are at least partly reset, but the typesetting of the text is that used by the same printer for the last Griffith & Farran edition, 5.10.

4. Two of the Frank Feller black-and-white illustrations (see 5.10) remain in their positions on text pages 77 and 200. The text has not been re-imposed but the other six Feller plates were cut away after the books were folded, leaving only stubs, to which the new colour plates have been pasted. This hand-operation in the bindery indicates that the new publisher was using up sheets printed for Griffith & Farran, and found this to be the cheapest way of introducing the six colour plates. For any impression made to the order of the Joint Venture the type (or stereos) would have had to be newly imposed before machining, as the pages would have been carefully packed away after the last impression.

5. The List of Illustrations on p.(8) shows only the six new colour plates, and neither this nor the title page makes any reference to the two black-and-white plates retained from the earlier printing (see 5.14, Note 1, below).

5.14

Title page, Contents: As for 5.13, but see Notes 1–5.

Binding: As for 5.13, but my copy has changed colour-scheme: Blue cloth boards, blocked black, brown, white, red, yellow merging to orange, gilt; all edges stained green-grey; plain off-white endpapers.

Reference: PN.

Notes

1. A second issue of 5.13, following the publisher's realisation that errors had been made (see 5.13, Note 5) in the List of Illustrations on p.(8). The leaf forming pp.7–(8) was reprinted and inserted as a cancel, being tipped on to the stub of the now excised original leaf.

2. A different illustration is used as frontispiece. In 5.13 it was the illustration captioned 'The boys made a rush through the crowd': in 5.14 it is the one captioned 'Set off to a point where they could see the entrance to the tunnel'.

3. The List of Illustrations now includes the two retained Frank Feller pictures, entered in their correct positions. The order of the first two illustrations has now been reversed (showing them as 'Frontispiece' and 'Facing p.50', instead of 'Frontispiece' and 'Facing p.94' as in 5.13). The previously incorrect reference, 'Facing p.174', has been amended to 'Facing p.172'.

4. The cancel may have been added both to bound stock and to unbound sheet-stock. It is not possible to tell how soon it was done after publication of the edition, and I have no evidence on the relative scarcity of 5.13 and 5.14.

5. No attempt was made to credit Frank Feller with the two black-and-white illustrations, the title page mentioning only T.C. Dugdale. In subsequent comparable editions the text was re-imposed (see 5.13, Note 4) and the last two Frank Feller illustrations were omitted (see 5.16).

5.15

The | YOUNG | FRANC- | TIREURS | G . A | HENTY | LONDON | HENRY . FROWDE | HODDER & | STOUGHTON
(Note: All lettering is hand-drawn within an art-nouveau frame).

Contents

190 x 120 mm. (1)–336 | no catalogue. Frontispiece from watercolour drawing by T.C. Dugdale, reproduced by three-colour halftone blocks printed on coated paper, unbacked, tipped in.

(Frontispiece, tipped in) | (1) title p. | (2) publisher's advertisement for 'The Boy's New Library', with printer's imprint at foot (Richard Clay & Sons, Limited, London and Bungay.) | 3–4. Preface | (5) Contents | (6) blank | 7–336. text.

Binding (see Note 3)
Red cloth boards, blind embossed, blocked gilt, edges plain, light-green endpapers, printed in dark-green with bled-off illustration of nautical scene. ·
    Front board: Step-and-repeat pattern of lions passants within ruled border; over this a ribboned seal showing representation of St George slaying the dragon (all blind-embossed). **Spine:** Blind-embossed art-nouveau design of flower, and rules, with three sunken panels, showing title; author; and publisher: THE | YOUNG |

FRANC- I TIREURS (gilt); G . A . I HENTY (gilt); and: HENRY FROWDE I HODDER & I STOUGHTON (blind). (See Note 1). **Back board:** All-over step-and-repeat design of lions passants within ruled border (all blind-embossed).

References: PN; TC.

Notes
1. This binding design was used both by the 'Joint Venture', and by the Oxford University Press (see 5.17 below) after they took full control of the old Griffith & Farran children's books. Apart from the prelims, the type is not reset.
2. The illustrations used as frontispiece vary from one copy to another. It seems that at first they were all taken from printed sheets of the pictures for 5.13. But later, probably, a set of electros was made from one of the three-colour sets, chosen to become the permanent frontispiece, and to be printed on a small machine.
3. This format was devised for a series, 'The Boy's New Library' (or 'The Boys' New Library'), in which three of Henty's books appeared (see Appendix V and, for binding style, Plate 42).
4. Terry Corrigan has shown me a freak copy bound in green cloth which otherwise follows the above description but has in error 'HARRY COLLINGWOOD' in gilt lettering on the spine in place of 'G.A. HENTY'.

5.16

The I Young Franc-Tireurs I And their Adventures in the I Franco-Prussian War I BY I G.A.HENTY I AUTHOR OF I "THE YOUNG BUGLERS" "FRIENDS THOUGH DIVIDED I "OUT ON THE PAMPAS" ETC. ETC. I ILLUSTRATED IN COLOUR BY T.C. DUGDALE I HUMPHREY MILFORD I OXFORD UNIVERSITY PRESS I LONDON, EDINBURGH, GLASGOW I TORONTO, MELBOURNE, CAPE TOWN, BOMBAY
(Note: The quotation marks after FRIENDS THOUGH DIVIDED *are missing).*

Contents
188 x 125 mm. (1)–336 I no catalogue. Six full-colour plates from watercolour drawings by T.C. Dugdale, reproduced by three-colour halftone blocks printed on coated paper, unbacked, unfolioed, tipped in.
 (Frontispiece, tipped in) I (1) title p. I (2) printer's imprint (REPRINTED 1917 IN GREAT BRITAIN BY R. CLAY AND SONS, LTD., I BRUNSWICK STREET, STAMFORD STREET, S.E., AND BUNGAY, SUFFOLK.) I 3–4. Preface I 5. Contents I 6. List of Illustrations I 7–336. text.

Binding (see Note 3)
Light-blue cloth boards, blocked red, black, brown and white; all edges stained blue-grey; plain off-white endpapers.
 Front board: THE YOUNG I FRANC-TIREURS I G.A. HENTY (red with black shadow) at upper left corner of illustration of franc-tireurs in wooded landscape (black, red, brown and white). **Spine:** THE YOUNG I FRANC- I TIREURS I (3-em rule) I G.A. HENTY (all black) above illustration of franc-tireur standing on patch of ground (black, red, brown and white). At foot: MILFORD (black). **Back board:** plain.

Reference: CH.

Notes

1. During 1916–1917 new arrangements were made between the members of the 'Joint Venture' (see 5.13, Note 1). On 31 March 1916 the children's books came under sole authority of the Oxford University Press, whose Publisher at that date was Henry Frowde's successor, Humphrey Milford. From then on the 5 Henty novels were issued under this new imprint. For further details see Appendix II, Part 2.

2. In this edition of *The Young Franc-Tireurs*, the last two Frank Feller drawings have been finally abandoned. The text is re-imposed, with re-organised prelims, making a saving of 16 pages. The six colour-plates remain, tipped in conventionally.

3. This binding design is as for 5.13, but cheaper cloth and lighter boards were used; and two runs of blocking dispensed with, including gilt, the most expensive.

4. This impression is dated 1917 in the printer's imprint on p.(2).

5.17

The I YOUNG I FRANC- I TIREURS I G . A I HENTY I HUMPHREY . MILFORD I OXFORD . UNIVERSITY I . PRESS . I LONDON
(Note: All lettering is hand-drawn within an art-nouveau frame).

Contents: 185 x 121 mm. As for 5.15, but on p.(2) publisher's advertisement is for 'The Boys' New Library' (not Boy's), and printer's imprint re-set (REPRINTED 1918 IN GREAT BRITAIN BY R. CLAY AND SONS, LTD., I BRUNSWICK STREET, STAMFORD STREET, S.E.1, AND BUNGAY, SUFFOLK.)

Binding: As for 5.15, except publisher's imprint at foot of spine, which now reads simply: MILFORD (blind, sometimes gilt).

Reference: PN.

Note: See 5.15, Notes 1–3, above. Dates of reprints were generally given in the printer's imprint (p.(2)). The first I have found for this title is 1918, but there may have been an earlier O.U.P. impression. I have another copy dated 1922.

5.18

THE I YOUNG FRANC-TIREURS I AND THEIR ADVENTURES IN THE I FRANCO-PRUSSIAN WAR I BY I G.A. HENTY I SPECIAL CORRESPONDENT OF THE "STANDARD," I AND AUTHOR OF "THE YOUNG BUGLERS," "FRIENDS THOUGH DIVIDED," I "IN TIMES OF PERIL," "OUT ON THE PAMPAS," ETC. I LONDON I GRIFFITH FARRAN BROWNE & CO., LTD. I 35, BOW STREET, COVENT GARDEN

Contents: 213 x 140 mm. Otherwise as for 5.12. These details relate to the edition of *The Young Franc-Tireurs* bound-in with, and following, an edition of *The Young Buglers* (see 7.9).

Binding (see Note 3 and Plate 43)
Red cloth boards, blocked black, white and gilt; edges plain; plain off-white endpapers.
Front board: The YOUNG I BUGLERS (gilt, with two black casings) above illustration of two buglers wearing pill-box caps (black and white). **Spine:** THE I YOUNG I BUGLERS I (1cm. rule) I G.A. HENTY (all gilt) beneath four rules

(black). At foot: ASKEW & SON I PRESTON (gilt) above four rules (black). **Back board:** plain.

References: PN I *Dartt*, p.173, Note (4).

Notes
1. This volume has almost exactly the same contents as 5.11, but the two titles are bound in reverse order. The issue of *The Young Buglers* is described as 7.9.
2. In 5.18, the title page for *The Young Buglers* is cancelled by a joint title page: THE YOUNG BUGLERS. I A Tale of the Peninsular War. I AND I THE YOUNG FRANC-TIREURS, I Their Adventures in the Franco-Prussian War. I BY I G.A.HENTY, I (printer's ornament) I PRESTON: I JAMES ASKEW & SON, I CORPORATION STREET.
3. The binding case makes no mention of *The Young Franc-Tireurs*.
4. James Askew & Son were booksellers and publishers in Preston, Lancashire. In the early years of this century they were one of a number of firms who bound books for presentation purposes. For more details of them and of this publication see *The Young Buglers*, 7.9, Notes 2–5.

6. THE MARCH TO COOMASSIE

6.1
THE I MARCH TO COOMASSIE. I BY I G.A. HENTY, I SPECIAL CORRESPONDENT OF THE "STANDARD," I AUTHOR OF "THE MARCH TO MAGDALA," "A SEARCH FOR A SECRET," ETC. I (34mm. rule) I LONDON: I TINSLEY BROTHERS, CATHERINE STREET, STRAND. I (5mm. rule) I 1874.

Contents
220 x 142 mm. (i)–(iv) unfolioed I (1)–(472) I no catalogue. No illustrations.

(i) Half-title p. I (ii) blank I (iii) title p. I (iv) printer's imprint (LONDON: I SWEETING AND CO., PRINTERS I 80, GRAY'S INN ROAD.) I (1)–453. text I 453–470. Appendix, with printer's imprint at foot of p.470 (LONDON: SWEETING AND CO., PRINTERS, 80 GRAY'S INN ROAD.) I (471)–(472) blank.

Binding (see Plate 9)
Blue cloth boards, blocked black, blind, and gilt; edges rough-trimmed, top uncut; pale-yellow surface-paper endpapers.

Front board: Double rules near edges of board; panel at centre, of triple rules with ornaments on all sides (all black). **Spine:** three thick rules (gilt, blind, gilt) above: THE MARCH I TO I COOMASSIE I BY I G.A. HENTY. (all gilt) I (decorative rule) (black) I AUTHOR OF I "THE MARCH TO MAGDALA" (gilt). At foot, above three thick rules, as at head: TINSLEY BROTHERS (gilt). **Back board:** as front board.

References: BU I *Farmer*, p.50; *Dartt*, p.96.

Notes
1. *Farmer* and *Dartt* describe copies as above; *Farmer* gives (as normal practice) the page-size, while *Dartt* (as always) gives the approximate size of the binding case.

2. Copies of 6.1 are very scarce. It is possible there may have been some accident, such as a warehouse fire, soon after they were printed, especially as the publisher failed to send copies to the Copyright Libraries. They received copies of 6.2.

6.2

Title page: As for 6.1, but: SECOND EDITION. replaces 34mm. rule (see Note 1).

Contents: 221 x 143 mm. Otherwise as for 6.1.

Binding
Brown cloth boards, blocked blind and gilt; top edge stained brown; pale-yellow surface-paper endpapers.

Front board: Five variegated rules forming panel, with central decoration (all blind). **Spine:** THE | MARCH TO | COOMASSIE | (short rule) | G.A. HENTY. | (decorative flower) (All gilt), with gilt decorative rules head and foot. **Back board:** as front board.

References: BL; B-R; TC | *Dartt Companion:* p.21.

Notes
1. See 6.1, Note 2. This is really a reprint of 6.1, not a second edition.
2. A copy examined has a variant binding, as follows:
Blue cloth boards, blocked black and gilt; edges uncut; plain off-white endpapers.

Front board: Rules near edges of board; decoration at centre (all black). **Spine:** Two black rules between two thicker rules in gilt, above: THE MARCH | TO | COOMASSIE | BY | G.A. HENTY | (gilt rule) | AUTHOR OF | "THE MARCH TO MAGDALA" | (rule) | SECOND EDITION (all gilt); at foot: TINSLEY BROTHERS (gilt) above two black rules between two thicker rules in gilt. **Back board:** as front board.

7. THE YOUNG BUGLERS

7.1
THE YOUNG BUGLERS. | A TALE OF THE PENINSULAR WAR. | BY G.A. HENTY, | AUTHOR OF "THE MARCH TO MAGDALA," "THE MARCH TO COOMASSIE," "THE YOUNG | FRANC-TIREURS," "OUT ON THE PAMPAS,": ETC., ETC. | WITH EIGHT ILLUSTRATIONS BY JOHN PROCTOR | AND ELEVEN PLANS OF BATTLES. | (publisher's device) | GRIFFITH AND FARRAN, | SUCCESSORS TO NEWBERY AND HARRIS, | WEST CORNER OF ST. PAUL'S CHURCHYARD, LONDON. | E.P. DUTTON AND CO., NEW YORK. | MDCCCLXXX.

Contents
192 x 129 mm. (i)–(viii) | (1)–336 | catalogue (1)–(24). Eight full-page black-and-white engravings after John Proctor by W.H. (?), unbacked, unfolioed, tipped in. Eleven fold-out black-and-white engraved battle-plans.

(Frontispiece, tipped in) | (i) title p. | (ii) [The Rights of Translation and of Reproduction are reserved.] | (iii) Preface | (iv) blank | (v)–vi. Contents | (vii) List of Illustrations | (viii) List of Plans of Battles | (1)–336. text, with printer's imprint at foot of p.336 (GILBERT AND RIVINGTON, PRINTERS, ST. JOHN'S SQUARE, E.C.) | (1)–(24) catalogue, dated 11/79.

Binding (see Plate 32)
Red cloth boards, bevelled, and blocked black, blind, and gilt; edges plain; pinkish-yellow surface-paper endpapers; all gatherings wire-stitched.
   Front board: THE | YOUNG | BUGLERS (gilt) diagonally; G.A. | HENTY (black) diagonally; illustration of man sitting in drum, buglers, etc. (gilt); all enclosed in panels and with other decorations and rules (black). **Spine:** THE | YOUNG | BUGLERS (gilt); G.A. HENTY (black); trophy of drum and bugles, etc. (gilt); ILLUSTRATED (black); GRIFFITH & FARRAN (gilt); with additional decorations and rules (black). **Back board:** Two diagonal blind rules within blind panelling; publisher's monogram (blind) at centre.

References: BL; Bod; PN | *Farmer,* p.86 and Addenda; *Dartt,* p.167.

Notes
1. Griffith & Farran's records were almost certainly destroyed in the bombing of London in the second war, and there is no printer's code in this, Henty's third book for boys. The first impression is unlikely to have exceeded 2000 copies. It was published in 1879, although dated 1880 on the title page.
2. The published price of 7s.6d. was higher than that of any other boys' book by Henty; the page size is slightly larger than the others (small post 8vo instead of the usual crown 8vo). There are eleven fold-out battle-plans and eight full-page illustrations. It is not clear why the larger page-size was chosen, nor why the plans had to be so lavishly presented. In the sizes they were reproduced they would have fitted on the usual smaller pages, and the total number of pages would not have been greater than in either *Out on the Pampas* or *The Young Franc-Tireurs.* By saving on the paper size, and consequently on the size of binding case, it would have been possible to more-than-cover the cost of thread-sewing instead of wire-stitching. This undesirable alternative is probably one reason for the present scarcity of the book: wire-stitching rusted quickly and that caused books to disintegrate. But it was an innovation in bookwork at this date, and no doubt its weaknesses were not foreseen by Griffith & Farran. They never used it again for Henty's books.
3. I have found no evidence of a second impression in this format, but *Farmer* reports a second issue of this impression with catalogue dated 1/80.
4. In my copy the catalogue is incorrectly folded, so the pages appear in the wrong order.

7.2

Title page: As for 7.1, but with changed imprint, and no date, below publisher's device (LONDON: | GRIFFITH, FARRAN, OKEDEN & WELSH, | WEST CORNER OF ST. PAUL'S CHURCHYARD, | E.P. DUTTON AND CO., NEW YORK.). Also add: *(Note: After* COOMASSIE *the comma is damaged, the two quotation marks are missing, and the following word* THE *and the quotation marks before it are damaged).*

Contents: 183 x 135 mm. As for 7.1, except (a) no catalogue; (b) printer's imprint on p.336 re-set (GILBERT AND RIVINGTON, LIMITED, ST. JOHN'S SQUARE, E.C.)

Binding (see Plate 40)

Turquoise cloth boards, bevelled, and blocked dark-blue, white, red, blind, and gilt; all edges gilt; yellow surface-paper endpapers.

Front board: The Young | Buglers | . G . A . Henty . (all dark-blue) on stippled solid-gilt panels with dark-blue shadow, superimposed on crossed flags (red, white and dark-blue) which in turn are superimposed over a series of illustrations of naval and military activities in separate panels (red, white and dark-blue). **Spine:** THE (gilt) above stippled solid-gilt scroll with: YOUNG | BUGLERS (reversed out cloth-colour). Below is illustration of soldier and sailor (red, white and dark-blue) above solid-gilt strip with: G.A. HENTY (reversed out cloth-colour); another solid-gilt scroll with: ILLUSTRATED (reversed out cloth-colour). At foot: GRIFFITH FARRAN & Co (gilt). **Back board:** publisher's monogram in circle (blind) at centre.

References: Bod; TC.

Notes

1. This edition was received by the Bodleian Library on 4 March 1887. The printer's code on p.336 shows that 2000 copies were printed, 25 April 1886. There seems to have been no urgency to get this issue into circulation. The present scarcity of these early editions, and the fact that six years elapsed between the first two, indicate the book was not selling fast.

2. Contemporary Griffith & Farran catalogues show a price reduction: with works by other authors the book is listed in the 'Kingston Series of Six-Shilling Books'.

3. The book is now thread-sewn, and the binding is more lavish: perhaps this is an attempt to keep up with the bindings from the rival firm, Blackie & Son.

7.3

Title page: As for 7.2, but with changed imprint below publisher's device (GRIFFITH FARRAN OKEDEN & WELSH, | NEWBERY HOUSE, CHARING CROSS ROAD, | LONDON, AND SYDNEY.).

(Note: The quotation marks after COOMASSIE *are missing).*

Contents: 182 x 131 mm. As for 7.2, but printer's imprint on p.336 re-set (GILBERT AND RIVINGTON, LD., ST. JOHN'S HOUSE, CLERKENWELL ROAD, LONDON.).

Binding (see Plate 44)

Olive-green cloth boards, blocked black, red, and gilt; all edges gilt; light-brown patterned endpapers with publisher's device in a decorative step-and-repeat design.

Front board: The Young | Buglers | . G . A . Henty . (black) on stippled-gilt rectangular solid panel at upper left corner. At lower right corner is a drawing of a crown (red and black). **Spine:** THE (gilt) above YOUNG | BUGLERS (black) on stippled-gilt decorative solid scroll. At centre: drawing of crown (red and black). At foot: G . A . HENTY (cloth-colour out of solid-gilt strip); ILLUSTRATED (cloth-colour out of solid-gilt scroll); GRIFFITH FARRAN & Co (gilt). **Back board:** Publisher's monogram in double circle (black) at centre.

Reference: PN.

Notes

1. The printer's code on p.336 shows 1000 copies, dated 3 January 1891. Five years have passed since 7.2 was printed, and eleven years since first publication, and there is no evidence of more than three impressions in this time (7.1, 7.2 and 7.3), which would account for a maximum of 5000 copies. This third impression was to be given yet another binding design (see 7.4), presumably in an attempt to boost sales.

2. A contemporary Griffith & Farran catalogue lists *The Young Buglers* in 'The Crown Library for Boys'. The books are described as 'Illustrated. Large crown 8vo, gilt edges. Price 5s.': that represents a second price-reduction (see 7.2, Note 2). The crowns in the binding design may relate to the name of the series, but although *Friends, though Divided* appears in the same list I have not found it so bound. There were no books by Henty listed in 'The Crown Library' by 1897 (see 7.5, Note 5).

7.4

Title page: As for 7.3.

Contents: 185 x 131 mm. Otherwise as for 7.3.

Binding
Olive-green cloth boards, blocked black, red, bright-green, and gilt; all edges gilt; light-green patterned endpapers showing publisher's device in a decorative step-and-repeat design.

Front board: The Young | Buglers (gilt) beneath thick and thin black rules across head of board, with: . G . A . Henty . (black) above illustration of uniformed but hatless bugler (red and black) blowing his bugle on a bushy hillside overlooking a distant valley (black, bright-green and red), with cavalry soldiers at right (black).
Spine: THE | YOUNG | BUGLERS | (15mm. rule) | G.A. HENTY (all gilt) beneath thick and thin black rules across head, continued from front board. Illustration of soldiers in tented camp (red and black); at foot: GRIFFITH FARRAN & Co (gilt).
Back board: Publisher's device (black) at centre.

Reference: CT.

Notes

1. This varies from 7.3 only in the binding design. This second design seems to confirm that the impression of 1000 copies, dated 3 January 1891, was not selling fast (see 7.2, Note 1; 7.3, Note 1).

2. It is not clear whether this was an alternative binding style for books in 'The Crown Library' (see 7.3, Note 2) or whether the title had already been removed from that series, as it certainly was within a few years (see 7.5, Note 5).

7.5

THE YOUNG BUGLERS. | A TALE OF THE PENINSULAR WAR. | BY G.A. HENTY, | AUTHOR OF "FRIENDS THOUGH DIVIDED," "THE CURSE OF CARNE'S HOLD,' | "THE YOUNG FRANC-TIREURS," "OUT ON THE PAMPAS,' ETC., ETC. | WITH EIGHT ILLUSTRATIONS BY JOHN PROCTOR | AND ELEVEN PLANS OF BATTLES | GRIFFITH FARRAN BROWNE & CO. LIMITED, | 35 BOW STREET, COVENT GARDEN, | LONDON.
(Note: One of the two quotation marks has broken away both after HOLD and after PAMPAS in the book titles following the author's name).

Contents

187 x 130 mm. (i)–(viii) plus one unfolioed leaf | (1)–336 plus seven unfolioed leaves | catalogue (1)–(8) unfolioed. Eight full-page black-and-white engravings after John Proctor by W.H. (?), printed by line blocks on unbacked text pages, unfolioed. Eleven fold-out black-and-white battle-plans.

(Frontispiece, on verso of unfolioed leaf) | (i) title p. | (ii) [The Rights of Translation and of Reproduction are Reserved.] | (iii) Preface | (iv) blank | (v)–vi. Contents | (vii) List of Illustrations | (viii) List of Plans of Battles | (1)–336. text, and seven unfolioed leaves with illustrations on recto pages; printer's imprint at foot of p.336 (PRINTED BY MORRISON AND GIBB LIMITED, EDINBURGH) | (1)–(8) catalogue.

Binding (see Plate 44)

Blue cloth boards, bevelled, and blocked black, gilt, and white merging through yellow, and brown, to blue-grey; all edges gilt; dark-brown surface-paper endpapers.

Front board: THE | YOUNG | BUGLERS (gilt) | (leaf-decoration, black) | G.A. | HENTY. (gilt), all within panel outlined in shape of a shield (gilt) over decorative illustration of flag and sporting equipment (black, and white merging through yellow and brown to blue-grey). Three rules (black) frame this decoration. **Spine:** Three rules at head (gilt); THE | YOUNG | BUGLERS (gilt) between ornamental rules (gilt) forming panel above trophy of bow and arrow, sword and bugle (white merging through yellow to brown). G.A. | HENTY (gilt) between ornamental rules and decorations (gilt). At foot: GRIFFITH FARRAN | BROWNE & CO. (gilt) between ornamental rules (gilt). **Back board:** plain.

Reference: PN.

Notes

1. A handsome and elegant book. The boards are heavier than before, and bevelled; and the pictorial blocking more complicated. The firm's new imprint shows the change of management from 1897, which resulted in a more active sales policy (see *Out on the Pampas*, 4.3, Note 5; and Appendix II, Part 2).

2. The eight illustrations are now printed on text pages, instead of as a separate working. They appear in the same positions as before, and the leaves are unbacked, unfolioed, and not counted in the pagination, so no alteration was required to the List of Illustrations on p. (vii).

3. Gilbert and Rivington have lost the printing contract to Morrison and Gibb of Edinburgh. The printing is still from stereos made from the original typesetting.

4. The printer's code on p.336 shows 2000 copies, June, 1897. That the publisher decided this time on a longer print-run, following the rather desultory sales-history of *The Young Buglers* so far, could simply reflect confidence in their new sales policy, or possibly be the result of an increasing demand for Henty's work as his books from Blackie widened his popularity.

5. The publisher's bound-in catalogue shows that this title is no longer in 'The Crown Library'. It is now part of another series, 'Tales of Adventure', described as 'Large crown 8vo, cloth elegant, bevelled boards, gilt edges. Fully illustrated. Price 5s. per volume'. There are nine other titles in the list, including Henty's *Friends, though Divided*, 12.4.

6. This new series, 'Tales of Adventure', should not be confused with the earlier Griffith & Farran series, 'Tales of Travel and Adventure' (see Appendix V).

7.6

THE YOUNG BUGLERS. | A TALE OF THE PENINSULAR WAR. | BY | G.A. HENTY, | AUTHOR OF | "FRIENDS THOUGH DIVIDED," "THE YOUNG FRANC-TIREURS," | "OUT ON THE PAMPAS," "IN TIMES OF PERIL," | ETC. ETC. | WITH EIGHT ILLUSTRATIONS BY J. SCHÖNBERG | AND TEN PLANS OF BATTLES. | GRIFFITH FARRAN BROWNE & CO. LIMITED, | 35 BOW STREET, COVENT GARDEN, | LONDON.

Contents

189 x 134 mm. (i)–(viii) unfolioed | (1)–346 | no catalogue. Eight full-page wash-drawings by J. Schönberg reproduced by black-and-white halftone blocks (signed by engraver A R C°) printed on unbacked text pages, unfolioed and not counted in pagination. Ten black-and-white battle-plans printed by line blocks on text pages, backed by text, unfolioed but counted in pagination.

(i) Blank | (ii) frontispiece | (iii) title p. | (iv) [The Rights of Translation and Reproduction are Reserved.] | (v) Preface | (vi) blank | (vii) List of Illustrations | (viii) List of Plans of Battles | (1)–346. text and plans, with unfolioed illustrations; printer's imprint on p.346 (PRINTED BY MORRISON AND GIBB LIMITED, EDINBURGH).

Binding (see Plate 34)

Blue, vertically-grained cloth boards, blocked gilt; top edge gilt; plain off-white laid endpapers.

Front board: THE (decoration of formal roses and leaves) | YOUNG | BUGLERS (all gilt) above illustration, with arms and trophy, etc.; G.A. HENTY (all gilt) placed high at left. **Spine:** THE | YOUNG | BUGLERS (gilt) within shield forming part of gilt decoration. Towards the foot of this: G.A. HENTY (gilt), and, below: GRIFFITH FARRAN | BROWNE & CO. (gilt). **Back board:** plain.

Reference: PN.

Notes

1. One of a set in similar format of the five Griffith & Farran novels. Copies examined show that at least two impressions of 2000 copies were printed of each between 1895 and 1899. The other titles are: *Out on the Pampas*, 4.7; *The Young Franc-Tireurs*, 5.10; *In Times of Peril*, 9.5; and *Friends, though Divided*, 12.5.

2. The type was reset for all except *Friends, though Divided*, which also kept its original illustrations. The rest are therefore truly new editions, and were newly illustrated with wash-drawings printed from halftone blocks. *The Young Buglers* was late to join the group (some plates dated 1899). The paper used for the set was not suitable for a fine screen, and the reproductions do not do justice to the pictures.

3. Economies in binding were made with lighter boards and no bevels, blocking in gilt only, and gilding only the top edges of the leaves. The plans no longer fold out: they and the illustrations were printed on text pages, causing re-imposition of the whole book. But that, with the omission of one battle-plan and the list of Contents, resulted in an even working of 356 pages. It is surprising that these economies, considerably reducing the cost per copy, were not made years earlier.

4. The printer's code on p.346 indicates an impression of 2000 copies, dated July, 1899. The larger print-orders for 7.5 and 7.6 must indicate a distinct improvement in sales of this title, some fifteen years after first publication.

7.7

Title page: As for 7.6, except that the title itself (only) is set in a different typeface, with the first word (THE) on a separate line at the head of the page.

Contents

188 x 134 mm. (i)–(viii) unfolioed | (1)–346 | no catalogue. Full-page black-and-white wash-drawing by J. Schönberg converted to full colour and reproduced by four-colour halftone blocks printed on coated paper, tipped in as frontispiece; the remaining seven wash-drawings by J. Schönberg, and the ten battle-plans, appear exactly as in 7.6.

(i)–(ii) Blank | (frontispiece, tipped in) | (iii) title p. | (iv) [The Rights of Translation and of Reproduction are Reserved] | (v)–(viii) and (1)–346. as for 7.6.

Binding: As for 7.6.

Reference: PN.

Notes

1. There is no printer's code, so size and date of the impression are unknown, but the omission shows it is from a later printing than 7.6. Apart from the changed frontispiece, and the part-resetting of the title page, the copyright line on p. (iv), which in Griffith & Farran titles frequently varies from one impression to another, shows small changes both in punctuation and wording.

2. The transformation of the frontispiece was probably undertaken by the blockmaker rather than by the artist. The drawing was not re-made: every detail, including the signature on the black plate of the new four-colour set, can be seen to repeat identically the original black halftone. Process engravers devised their own methods of achieving colour plates from monochrome originals, and they differed in detail. The simplest involved the making of a series of four negatives, identical except for the angling of the screen, to produce plates to print in yellow, red, blue, and black. Each plate was then etched, the etcher having to use his judgement as to the relative densities of tone required in each colour at every point. Great skill was required, and experience was an important factor in the production of successful four-colour sets of halftones. This is an extremely simplified description of one process devised by blockmakers, at this period and later. It was used even after the full development of commercial colour photography, when a coloured illustration or postcard was required and only a black-and-white photograph was available. For further notes on blockmaking, etc., see Appendix IV, Part 1.

3. The new frontispiece is a reversal of the publisher's policy of economy (see 7.6, Note 3), for apart from their initial cost the blocks had to be printed on expensive art-paper. It may, perhaps, have been a concession to booksellers by then accustomed to colour in children's books. Frontispieces printed in colour by Kronheim had been common since the 1870s, even in sixpenny Sunday-School reward books, and although Blackie were not yet printing in colour in Henty's books they were making up for that with multi-coloured pictorial bindings. By comparison, Griffith & Farran's five new bindings seemed distinctly plain.

7.8

THE | YOUNG BUGLERS | A TALE OF THE PENINSULAR WAR | BY | G.A. HENTY | AUTHOR OF "THE YOUNG FRANC-TIREURS," " IN TIMES OF PERIL," | "OUT ON THE PAMPAS," "FRIENDS THOUGH DIVIDED," ETC. | LONDON | GRIFFITH FARRAN BROWNE & CO. LTD. | 35, BOW STREET, COVENT GARDEN

Contents

216 x 140 mm. Bound-in edition of *The Young Franc-Tireurs* (see 5.12), followed by (1)–158 (see Note 4) | no catalogue. Frontispiece from black-and-white engraving after John Proctor by W.H. (?), reproduced by line block printed on text paper.

(1) Blank | (2) frontispiece | (3) title p. | (4) blank | (5)–158. text, set in two columns with rule between; printer's imprint at foot of p.158 (GILBERT AND RIVINGTON, LD., ST. JOHN'S HOUSE, CLERKENWELL, LONDON.) (See Note 4.).

Binding (see Plate 43, under 5.12)

Red, vertically-ribbed cloth boards, blocked gilt; edges plain; plain off-white endpapers.

Front board: Young Franc-Tireurs | Young Buglers (all gilt). **Spine:** YOUNG | FRANC- | TIREURS | (2-em rule) | YOUNG | BUGLERS | (2-em rule) | G.A. | HENTY (all gilt). At foot: GRIFFITH FARRAN, | BROWNE & CO. (gilt). **Back board:** plain.

Reference: PN.

Notes

1. This is the earliest issue I have seen of *The Young Buglers* set in two columns. My copy is inscribed 'April '05', but was probably printed earlier. The printing-quality is not good, and the cheap paper is now brittle and browning at the edges. The edition probably appeared first by itself in paper covers, as did the bound-in edition of *The Young Franc-Tireurs* (see 5.7 and 5.11), but I have not seen it thus.

2. The frontispiece illustration appears in the earlier 8vo editions (7.1 to 7.5), facing p. 102. This edition has no other illustrations and no battle-plans.

3. The printer was Gilbert and Rivington, who lost the contract for the standard 8vo editions to Morrison and Gibb after the issue of 7.4. *The Young Franc-Tireurs* similarly changed printer about then, but the cheap, two-column edition of that book (5.7, 5.11) was printed by Morrison and Gibb. Both cheap editions were probably issued simultaneouly, but not before 1897, when the publisher's imprint changed.

4. The final leaf in my copy of *The Young Buglers*, here referred to as blank pages (159)–(160), has been neatly removed, and the conjugate leaf, forming pages 129–130, is held in position by the glue in the back of the binding, or is possibly tipped in. The leaf may have been removed after the book was sold, but the neatness of the work, and the fact that identical treatment was given to 7.9, below, suggest it may have carried some matter no longer considered appropriate (see 7.9, Note 4).

7.9

THE YOUNG BUGLERS. | A Tale of the Peninsular War. | AND | THE YOUNG FRANC-TIREURS, | Their Adventures in the Franco-Prussian War. | BY | G.A. HENTY. | (printer's ornament) | PRESTON: | JAMES ASKEW & SON, | CORPORATION STREET.

Contents

213 x 140 mm. (1)–158 (see Note 4) | no catalogue. Frontispiece as in 7.8. Followed by a bound-in edition of *The Young Franc-Tireurs* (see 5.18).

(1) Blank | (2) frontispiece | (3) cancel title-page, tipped in | (4) blank | (5)–158, text, set in two columns with rule between; printer's imprint at foot of p.158 (GILBERT AND RIVINGTON, LD., ST. JOHN'S HOUSE, CLERKENWELL, LONDON.) (See Note 4) | bound-in edition of *The Young Franc-Tireurs* (see 5.18).

Binding (see Plate 43)

Red cloth boards, blocked black, white and gilt; edges plain; plain off-white endpapers.

Front board: The YOUNG | BUGLERS (gilt, with two black casings) above illustration of two buglers wearing pill-box caps (black and white). **Spine:** THE | YOUNG | BUGLERS | (1 cm. rule) | G.A. HENTY (all gilt) beneath four rules (black). At foot: ASKEW & SON | PRESTON (gilt) above four rules (black). **Back board:** plain.

References: PN | *Dartt*, p.173, Note (4).

Notes

1. Contents almost exactly the same as 7.8 with the order of the titles reversed.
2. James Askew & Son were booksellers and publishers in Preston, Lancashire. They moved from Corporation Street in 1964, and are now James Askew & Son Limited, in North Road, Preston. In August 1991 their Managing Director told me how, as a junior member of the firm, he was instructed at the time of the move to dispose of boxes of Company records and other papers, a task he found very distressing. He consequently regretted being unable to throw light on the history of this publication.
3. At the time the firm produced books for school prizes, using sheets bought from publishers at special rates. They were bound inexpensively for the special market, with cancel title pages. An example of such treatment by Messrs Combridge of Birmingham, another 'Publisher of Prize Literature', is a variant and re-titled edition of one volume from a set of *Battles of the Nineteenth Century* (see §2, *The World's Battles*, 192.1, Notes 2–3).
4. The final leaf in my copy has been neatly removed, and the conjugate leaf, forming pages 129–130, is pasted in position at the back of the binding. Another copy of the same impression appears in 7.8, similarly treated (see 7.8, Note 4).

7.10

THE | YOUNG BUGLERS | A TALE OF THE PENINSULAR WAR | BY | G.A. HENTY | AUTHOR OF | "FRIENDS THOUGH DIVIDED" "THE YOUNG FRANC-TIREURS" | "OUT ON THE PAMPAS" ETC. ETC. | NEW EDITION | ILLUSTRATED IN COLOUR BY CONRAD H. LEIGH | LONDON | HENRY FROWDE | HODDER AND STOUGHTON | 1910

Contents
186 x 123 mm. (i)–(iv) | (1)–336 | (i)–(x) | catalogue (1)–16. Four watercolour drawings by Conrad H. Leigh reproduced by three-colour halftones printed on coated paper, unbacked, tipped in. Ten engraved battle-plans printed in black line on ten pages of coated paper at end of text.

(i) Half-title p. | (ii) blank | (frontispiece, tipped in) | (iii) title p. | (iv) printer's imprint (RICHARD CLAY & SONS, LIMITED, | BREAD STREET HILL, E.C., AND | BUNGAY, SUFFOLK.) | (v) Preface | (vi) blank | (vii) List of Illustrations | (viii) List of Plans of Battles at end of Book | (1)–336. text, with printer's imprint at foot of p.336 (Richard Clay & Sons, Limited, London and Bungay.) | (i)–(x) battle plans | (1)–16. catalogue.

Binding (see Plate 36)
Blue cloth boards, blocked grey and gilt; illustrations, printed in three-colour halftone on coated paper, laid down on front board and spine; edges plain; plain off-white endpapers.

Front board: YOUNG BUGLERS | G.A. HENTY (cloth-colour) out of decorative solid-gilt panel above rectangular illustration of cavalry battle-scene (printed in three-colour halftone on coated paper) laid down in decorative art-nouveau panel (grey). **Spine:** YOUNG | BUGLERS | HENTY (cloth-colour) out of rectangular gilt panel above oval illustration of sailor and redcoat in dinghy (printed in three-colour halftone on coated paper) laid down in decorative art-nouveau panel (grey). At foot, in irregular grey panel: HENRY FROWDE | HODDER & | STOUGHTON (grey). **Back board:** plain.

References: BB.

Notes
1. The stock and goodwill of Griffith & Farran, including *The Young Buglers* and four other novels by Henty, were bought by Hodder & Stoughton in 1906. The books were re-issued by them with the Oxford University Press, of which Henry Frowde was then the Publisher, in their 'Joint Venture' (see Appendix II, Part 2).
2. The books (except *In Times of Peril*, 1911) appeared in 1910, with dated title pages. Later impressions, in the old Blackie manner, omitted the date.
3. This book was given four new colour-plates by Conrad Leigh, Standards of production were higher than ever for the five titles. This is the only one of the five, however, to have colour plates laid on the front board and spine instead of having the case decorated with multi-coloured blocking (see Plates 35–36).

7.11
YOUNG | BUGLERS | G . A | HENTY | LONDON | HENRY . FROWDE | HODDER & | STOUGHTON
(Note: All lettering is hand-drawn within elaborate decorated framework).

Contents
163 x 110 mm. (i)–(viii) | (1)–336 | catalogue 1–8. Frontispiece from watercolour drawing by Conrad H. Leigh, reproduced by three-colour halftone blocks printed on coated paper, unbacked, keyed to p.218, tipped in.

(i)–(ii) Blank | (iii) half-title p. | (iv) publisher's advertisement (THE BOY'S

POCKET LIBRARY) listing 14 titles | (frontispiece, tipped in) | (v) title p. | (vi) printer's imprint (PRINTED IN GREAT BRITAIN BY R. CLAY AND SONS, LTD., | BRUNSWICK STREET, STAMFORD STREET, S.E. AND BUNGAY, SUFFOLK.) | (vii) Preface | (viii) blank | (1)–336. text | 1–8. catalogue.

Binding (see Plate 42)
Red cloth boards, blind embossed, blocked imitation gold; edges plain; pale-green endpapers printed in olive-green with line-illustration of arabs riding camels near palm-trees in desert (signed, W. Herbert Holloway, and with caption, Sudan).
 Front board: Over-all pattern of vertical rules with medallion over horizontal band at centre, with head and shoulders of knight in armour, holding a lance (all blind-embossed). **Spine:** over-all pattern of vertical rules with superimposed decorations, and three sunken panels for title; author; and publisher: YOUNG | BUGLERS (imitation gold); G . A | HENTY (imitation gold); HENRY | FROWDE | HODDER . & | STOUGHTON (imitation gold). **Back board:** over-all pattern of vertical rules with horizonal band, as on front board, but without medallion (blind embossed).

Reference: PN.

Notes
1. Printed on a smaller sheet of very light weight; this issue has narrow margins and is much less bulky. It is sewn in eleven 32-page sections. Frontispieces vary from copy to copy, being taken from sheets of colour-plates printed for earlier editions. No list of illustrations was needed and the prelims were re-arranged.
2. The publisher's catalogue is printed on the last eight leaves of the final gathering, folioed 1–8 instead of 337–344.
3. This was one of two Henty novels in 'The Boy's Pocket Library', issued by the 'Joint Venture'. The other was *Out on the Pampas* (4.10), the only title by Henty in the list on p. (iv). The series continued under the O.U.P. imprint (see 7.12, below) when they took over from the 'Joint Venture' (see Appendix II, Part 2).
4. Stereos of the typesetting from the last Griffith & Farran edition, 7.7, are used by the new printer, who also printed *Out on the Pampas* in the same series.
5. Imitation gold foil was used for blocking, an unsatisfactory substance at that date, which usually went almost black within a short time.

7.12
YOUNG | BUGLERS | G . A | HENTY | . HUMPHREY . | MILFORD | OXFORD | UNIVERSITY | PRESS . LONDON
(Note: All lettering is hand-drawn within elaborate decorated framework).

Contents
162 x 110 mm. (i)–(viii) | (1)–336 | catalogue (1)–8. Frontispiece as in 7.11.
 (i)–(ii) Blank | (iii) half-title p. | (iv) publisher's advertisement (THE BOY'S POCKET LIBRARY) listing 28 titles | (frontispiece, tipped in) | (v) title p. | (vi) printer's imprint (REPRINTED 1919 IN GREAT BRITAIN BY R. CLAY AND SONS, LTD., | BRUNSWICK STREET, STAMFORD STREET, S.E.I, AND BUNGAY, SUFFOLK.) | (vii) Preface | (viii) blank | (1)–336. text | (1) half-title to catalogue (A Select List of Books | for Boys: Published by | Humphrey Milford, Oxford | University Press) | 2–8. publisher's catalogue.

Binding: As for 7.11 (see Plate 42), but in pink cloth and with pale-blue endpapers printed dark blue. Publisher's imprint on spine changed to: OXFORD (imitation gold).

Reference: PN.

Notes
1. The Oxford University Press issued several impressions in the 'Boy's Pocket Library' after they took over from the 'Joint Venture' (see 7.11, Note 3, above, and Appendix II, Part 2). They were usually dated in the printer's imprint on p.(vi).
2. The publisher's advertisement on p.(iv) includes this title and *Out on the Pampas*, the only titles by Henty to be included in the series.

7.13
THE | YOUNG BUGLERS | A TALE OF THE PENINSULAR WAR | BY | G.A. HENTY | NEW EDITION | ILLUSTRATED IN COLOUR BY CONRAD H. LEIGH | (publisher's device) | HUMPHREY MILFORD | OXFORD UNIVERSITY PRESS | LONDON, EDINBURGH, GLASGOW | TORONTO, MELBOURNE, CAPE TOWN, BOMBAY

Contents
186 x 122 mm. (i)–(viii) | (1)–336 | battle-plans (i)–(x) | catalogue (1)–8. Four full-page watercolour drawings by Conrad H. Leigh reproduced by three-colour halftone blocks on coated paper, unbacked, unfolioed, tipped in. Fourteen plans of twelve battles reproduced by line blocks, printed in black on calendered MF paper.
(i) Half-title p. | (ii) publisher's advertisement (STORIES BY G.A. HENTY) listing 4 titles | (frontispiece, tipped in) | (iii) title p. | (iv) printer's imprint (REPRINTED 1929 IN GREAT BRITAIN BY R. CLAY AND SONS, LTD., | BUNGAY, SUFFOLK.) | (v) Preface | (vi) blank | (vii) List of Illustrations | (viii) List of Plans of Battles at end of Book | (1)–336. text | (i)–(x) Battle-plans | (1)–8. catalogue.

Binding (see Plate 46)
Pale-blue paper boards, grained to imitate cloth, blocked black; edges plain; plain off-white endpapers.
Front board: THE | YOUNG | BUGLERS | BY . G . A . HENTY (black) above small decorative drawing of bugler blowing bugle, and with decorative borders running from head to foot about 4mm. from edges of board (all black).
Spine: THE | YOUNG | BUGLERS | (small vertical rule) | G.A | HENTY (all black) above small decorative drawing of heads and shoulders of three redcoat soldiers advancing with bayonets fixed (black). At foot: OXFORD (black). With decorative border running from head to foot near edges of spine (black). **Back board:** plain.

Reference: PN.

Notes
1. A reprint of the text of 7.10, now taken over by the Oxford University Press (see Appendix II, Part 2) and given new preliminary pages and imprint.
2. The book was sold in this 8vo format both during and after the period of the 'Joint Venture', concurrently with the issues in the 'Boy's Pocket Library' (see 7.11 and

7.12). My copy is dated 1929 in the printer's imprint on p. (iv).

3. The battle-plans form a separate gathering on smooth MF paper, between the end of the text and the publisher's catalogue, both of which are printed on antique wove.

8. THE CORNET OF HORSE

8.1

THE | CORNET OF HORSE. | A Tale of Marlborough's Wars. | BY G.A. HENTY, | WAR CORRESPONDENT OF THE "STANDARD," | AUTHOR OF "THE YOUNG BUGLERS," "THE YOUNG FRANC-TIREURS," ETC., ETC. | WITH TWENTY FULL-PAGE ILLUSTRATIONS BY H. PETHERICK, | AND FIVE PLANS OF BATTLE-FIELDS. | LONDON: | SAMPSON LOW, MARSTON, SEARLE, & RIVINGTON, | CROWN BUILDINGS, 188, FLEET STREET. | 1881. | [All rights reserved.]
(Note: The subtitle is in gothic type).

Contents
183 x 123 mm. (i)–(viii) | (1)–278 | catalogue (1)–32 (see Note 8) | (279)–(280). Full-page engraved portrait of John, Duke of Marlborough, after H. Petherick, as frontispiece on text page (ii); and twenty full-page black-and-white engraved illustrations after the same artist by an unknown engraver, unbacked, unfolioed, tipped in. Five fold-out black-and-white battle-plans.

(i) Blank | (ii) frontispiece | (iii) title p. | (iv) printer's imprint (LONDON: | GILBERT AND RIVINGTON, LIMITED, | ST. JOHN'S SQUARE.) | (v)–vi. Preface | (vii) Contents | (viii) List of Illustrations | (tipped-in illustration) | (1)–278. text | (1)–32. catalogue, dated January 1881 | (279) printer's imprint (LONDON: | PRINTED BY GILBERT AND RIVINGTON, LIMITED, | ST. JOHN'S SQUARE.) | (280) blank.

Binding (see Plate 47)
Red, diagonally-grained cloth boards, blocked black, blind, and gilt; all edges gilt; blue-flowered off-white endpapers.
Front board: THE | CORNET OF HORSE (gilt, with black shadow) in gilt decorative frame; BY | G.A. HENTY. (gilt); all superimposed on elaborate design of panels, trophies and emblems, with illustration in largest panel of man in ship throwing barrel overboard, centre right (all black). **Spine:** THE | CORNET | OF | HORSE (black) above illustration of standing figure (black). G.A. HENTY (gilt) between black and gilt rules. ILLUSTRATED (cloth-colour out of solid-black strip) over decorative panel (black); SAMPSON LOW & Co. (black) between series of rules (black). **Back board:** publisher's device in decorative circle (blind) at centre.

References: BL; Bod; PN | *Farmer*, p.22; *Dartt*, p.41, *Companion*, p.10.

Notes
1. The story was serialised in the *Union Jack* (see §3, 225) in 26 weekly parts, from 7 October 1880. In book form it was published, with all edges gilt, at 5s.
2. In July 1881 Sampson Low took over publication of the *Union Jack*, which Henty had edited for over a year following the death of its first Editor, W.H.G. Kingston.

Griffith & Farran had given up the magazine in February 1881 as it failed to pay its way. After an interim arrangement, costly for Henty (see Appendix II, Part 2), it was a great relief to him to be again in the hands of a regular publisher, and Sampson Low inevitably took over the publication of his books from Griffith & Farran. The latter did, however, continue with books already planned or in production: *In Times of Peril* was published by them in the same year, 1881, and *Friends, though Divided* a year later (title-page date 1883).

3. On 31 May 1881 Henty signed a contract with Sampson Low for *The Cornet of Horse* (see Appendix VI, Part I). There it is clear that production of the book had already begun, and that stereos were made at Henty's expense or at least his to assign.

4. *The Cornet of Horse* was the first of only two books by Henty to be printed from the actual type set for the *Union Jack*. The magazine was set in two columns, and each was a suitable width for the page of a book. After printing, the type was taken out of the formes and made up into book-pages with running headlines and folio numbers; stereos were made of each page. The type itself could have been kept for making further stereos for later impressions should the first set get worn out. But judging from later impressions the type for this book had already been distributed and was not available by the time it was badly needed.

5. It is clear that Griffith & Farran had not been in any way involved in producing *The Cornet of Horse* as a book. If they had started the work they would surely have completed it, as they were about to do for two other Henty stories (see Note 2). In any case they would not have used the *Union Jack* type, something they never did for any other books. I am drawn to the conclusion, therefore, that Henty had made his own arrangements with Gilbert and Rivington, the printers of the *Union Jack*, and of his earlier books. Before Sampson Low took on the magazine Henty was in direct touch with them, and probably expressed concern about the future publication of his books. Gilbert & Rivington very likely suggested the use of standing type from the magazine as the cheapest way of getting *The Cornet of Horse* into production as a book.

6. One other book, *Winning his Spurs*, was begun in the same way during the short period when Henty had no contract with a book publisher (see 11.1, Note 2).

7. *The Cornet of Horse* was the most lavishly illustrated of Henty's books for boys. The drawings in the *Union Jack* were by several hands, including Horace Petherick, who was a regular illustrator for the magazine and regarded by Henty as their star turn (see Appendix IV, Part 2, Note 33). The pictures in the book were all his: some were new drawings, and smaller blocks were needed for those from the magazine. For editions after 1886 (see 8.1A below) more than half of the twenty plates were dropped, although the battle-plans, also from the *Union Jack*, were all retained.

8. The catalogue is inserted in a technically cumbersome way. Normally it would be treated as a final gathering following the text. In this case the last section of the text makes only eight pages. (Probably printed on one sheet of paper with the 8-page section of prelims). This catalogue is a 32-page section, folded and sewn through the centre in the usual way (the threads can be seen between pages 16 and 17). But, instead of following the final 8-page text gathering as usual, it has been inserted just before the final leaf of that gathering.

9. To achieve this, without pages becoming loose and falling out, the binder had to take his thread-sewing through the final text section twice. First, in the normal way,

at the centre of the 8-page section (between pages 276 and 277), and then again, through the middle of the catalogue and on through the 8-page section between pages 278 and (279). (For a similar arrangement see *Our Sailors*, §2, 167.2, Note 3).
10. Perhaps Sampson Low wished to make the catalogue immediately obvious to readers when they reached the end of the text, and not have it obscured by a blank leaf.

8.1A

Title page: As for 8.1, but date changed to 1886.

Contents: As for 8.1, but (a) p.(iv) publisher's advertisement (UNIFORM WITH THIS VOLUME) including *Jack Archer* and *Winning his Spurs*, all cloth, gilt edges, 5s.; printer's imprint omitted; (b) p.278. printer's imprint at foot (GILBERT AND RIVINGTON, LIMITED, ST. JOHN'S SQUARE, LONDON.); (c) publisher's advertisements: p.(279) (BOOKS BY JULES VERNE.); p.(280) (BOOKS BY MAUD JEANNE FRANC.) (d) publisher's catalogue, dated October 1886, pp.(1)–32 (see Note 3).

Binding: As for 8.1, but grey-flowered off-white endpapers.

Reference: AK.

Notes
1. I know only one copy of this early reprint. As I first saw it at a late stage in the production of this bibliography, I have had to give it the code 8.1A.
2. It contains the full quota of illustrations that appear in 8.1. All subsequent reprints contain only eight, including the frontispiece (see 8.2, Note 2).
3. The earlier cumbersome placing and sewing of the catalogue (see 8.1, Notes 8–10) has been avoided by printing advertisements on pp. (279)–(280).

*8.2

THE | CORNET OF HORSE | A Tale of Marlborough's Wars | BY G.A. HENTY | WAR CORRESPONDENT OF THE "STANDARD," | AUTHOR OF "THE YOUNG BUGLERS," "THE YOUNG FRANC-TIREURS," ETC., ETC. | WITH EIGHT FULL-PAGE ILLUSTRATIONS BY H. PETHERICK, | AND FIVE PLANS OF BATTLE-FIELDS. | NEW EDITION. | LONDON | SAMPSON LOW, MARSTON & COMPANY | Limited | St. Dunstan's House | FETTER LANE, FLEET STREET, E.C.
(Note: The sub-title and the line St. Dunstan's House *are in gothic type).*

Contents
182 x 122 mm. (i)–(viii) | 1–(280) | no catalogue. Full-page engraved portrait of John, Duke of Marlborough, after H. Petherick, and seven full-page illustrations after the same artist by an unknown engraver, all printed on unbacked text-pages, unfolioed and not counted in pagination. Five fold-out black-and-white battle-plans.
(i) Half-title p. | (ii) printer's imprint (LONDON: | PRINTED BY GILBERT AND RIVINGTON, LD., | ST. JOHN'S HOUSE, CLERKENWELL ROAD, E.C.) | frontispiece, printed on text leaf, unbacked, unfolioed, not counted in pagination | (iii) title p. | (iv) blank | (v)–vi. Preface | (vii) Contents | (viii) List of Illustrations | (1)–278. text, with seven leaves unfolioed and not counted in pagination |

(279)–(280) blank.

Binding: As for 8.1, except (a) grey-blue diagonally ribbed cloth boards; (b) edges plain; (c) plain off-white endpapers; (d) spine brass for blocking 'ILLUSTRATED' has been opened up to give the effect of bolder lettering, and publisher's name at foot is blocked with a line of ranging caps, instead of caps and small caps as before; (e) back board has treble rule (blind) at edges of board, and publisher's device is omitted.

References: PN I *Farmer*, p.22; *Dartt*, p.41, *Companion*, p.10.

Notes

1. Reprints after 1886 were sometimes dated on the title page, sometimes not.

2. The number of illustrations was reduced to eight, including frontispiece, all printed on text pages, unbacked, and not counted in the pagination. An added half-title page made an even working of 304 pages. The battle-plans remained as in 8.1.

3. There were numerous minor variations: details of imprint; advertisements (on pp.(279)–(280) or verso of the half-title page); type of text paper; design of endpapers, etc. All are grouped together under this 'generic' heading, *8.2.

4. With the two other books by Henty, *Winning his Spurs*, 1882, and *Jack Archer*, 1883, *The Cornet of Horse* was included towards the end of the 1880s in the series of 'Low's Standard Books for Boys'. That did not affect the format, but the books became available at 2s.6d. with edges plain, and at 3s.6d. with all edges gilt.

5. By the end of the 1890s the original stereos had still not been replaced, and were in a very poor state: the quality of both printing and paper was far from what should have been acceptable from a reputable publisher. Griffith & Farran had hard times in the 1890s (see Appendix II, Part 2), but the quality of their publications never sank to the depths endured by Sampson Low's readers at this period.

8.3

THE I CORNET OF HORSE I A Tale of Marlborough's Wars I BY G.A. HENTY I AUTHOR OF "WINNING HIS SPURS," "JACK ARCHER,' I "HIDDEN FOE," ETC. I WITH EIGHT FULL-PAGE ILLUSTRATIONS BY H. PETHERICK I AND FIVE PLANS OF BATTLE-FIELDS I NEW EDITION I LONDON I SAMPSON LOW, MARSTON & COMPANY I Limited I St. Dunstan's House I FETTER LANE, FLEET STREET, E.C. I 1903

(Note: The sub-title; and the line St. Dunstan's House, *are in gothic type. The second quotation mark after* ARCHER *has broken away).*

Contents: 181 x 121 mm. Otherwise as for 8.2.

Binding (see Plate 48)

Grey-blue cloth boards, blocked black, blue, orange merging through yellow back to orange, buff, and gilt; edges plain; plain off-white endpapers.

    Front board: Thick black rules dividing the design into three panels, with, in top panel: THE . CORNET I . OF . HORSE . (gilt) in strong 'egyptian' lettering; in central panel: illustration, based on the one facing p.212, of gaolers with keys and lantern standing over figure on a stretcher (black, blue, orange merging through yellow to orange, and buff); in bottom panel: G.A. HENTY (black). **Spine:** Black rules as on front board, forming panels, with, in top panel: THE I CORNET I OF I

HORSE | (centre-dot) | G.A. HENTY (all gilt); illustration in central panel of uniformed figure with sword (black, blue, orange merging to yellow, and buff); in bottom panel: SAMPSON | LOW & Co. (gilt). **Back board:** plain.

Reference: PN.

Notes

1. In about 1900 Sampson Low changed the appearance of all three of their Henty novels with a stronger, simpler, and more colourful binding design of some quality (see *Winning his Spurs*, 11.3 and 11.4; and *Jack Archer*, 14.5 and 14.6).

2. The quality of paper and printing of the text still left much to be desired.

3. Sampson Low seem to have dated or not dated title pages quite arbitrarily. For later impressions this title page was reset in a more up-to-date style.

8.4

THE | CORNET OF HORSE | A Tale of Marlborough's Wars | BY G.A. HENTY | AUTHOR OF "WINNING HIS SPURS," "JACK ARCHER,' | "HIDDEN FOE," ETC. | THIRTY-FIFTH THOUSAND. | LONDON | SAMPSON LOW, MARSTON & COMPANY | Limited
(Note: The second quotation mark after ARCHER has broken away).

Contents

195 x 128 mm. (i)–(viii) | (1)–(280) | no catalogue. Full-page black-and-white illustration by H. Petherick converted to colour and reproduced by three-colour halftone blocks printed on coated paper, tipped in as frontispiece; the seven remaining illustrations by H. Petherick, including the portrait of John, Duke of Marlborough, printed in black line on coated paper, unbacked, unfolioed, tipped in. Five fold-out black-and-white battle-plans.

(i) Half-title p. | (ii) printer's imprint (Printed by | REA & INCHBOULD, 224, Blackfriars Road, | London, S.E.) | (frontispiece, tipped in) | (iii) title p. | (iv) blank | (v)–vi. Preface | (vii) Contents | (viii) List of Illustrations | (portrait of John, Duke of Marlborough, tipped in) | (1)–278. text, with printer's imprint at foot of p.278 (LONDON: PRINTED BY REA AND INCHBOULD, 224, BLACKFRIARS ROAD, S.E.) | (279)–(280) blank.

Binding (see Plate 49)

Red cloth boards, blocked black and gilt, with colour plate laid down on front board; edges plain; plain off-white endpapers.

Front board: THE CORNET | OF HORSE | G.A. HENTY (black), the upper two lines of lettering drawn on a double curve, the third line straight, all above printed colour-plate, cut down from run-on copies of the frontispiece and laid down within ruled frame (black). At foot: AUTHORISED COPYRIGHT | EDITION (black). **Spine:** THE CORNET | OF | HORSE (gilt) above semi-abstract decoration with moon, stars, earth, birds flying (all gilt). At centre of this: . G . A . | HENTY (gilt). At foot: LOW MARSTON & CO. LTD. (gilt). **Back board:** plain.

Reference: PN.

Notes

1. The same worn-out stereos of the original typesetting were used on bulky featherweight paper in a larger page-size. However smart the publisher believed this edition appeared outwardly, he failed to lift the text out of its wretched state.

2. But it has been re-imposed, and the illustrations are now on coated paper, tipped in. That was not necessary for the line drawings, but it was for the frontispiece, a coloured version of the picture previously facing p.12 in 8.2 and 8.3. This transformation was no doubt undertaken by the blockmaker, similarly to that in *The Young Buglers* (see 7.7, Note 2). The result here is a three-colour set of halftones, the black plate being omitted (see Appendix IV, Part 1).

3. No relevant Sampson Low records survive, and the edition cannot be dated from internal evidence. My copy contains an inscription dated Christmas 1911. The size of this impression remains unknown, but the title page claims the completion of thirty-five thousand copies of the book since first publication.

4. The words AUTHORISED COPYRIGHT EDITION on the front board may have been an attempt, even at this late stage, to boost sales where the numerous pirate editions of United States publishers were sold. As far as I know Low produced no American nor colonial editions, and UK editions would have been exported without alteration.

5. I have a second copy of this impression. It varies only in details of blocking on the binding case. On the front board Henty's name is in a larger size, impressed with the blocking piece used on the front board of 8.3 (an 'egyptian' face). Below the colour plate, AUTHORISED COPYRIGHT EDITION is very crudely and heavily impressed, each word appearing to have been applied separately by hand, out of alignment with the others, and independently of the rest of the blocking. On the spine the publisher's imprint at the foot is given as: SAMPSON LOW & Co. (gilt).

*8.5

Title page: As for 8.4, except (a) publisher's device replaces THIRTY-FIFTH THOUSAND; (b) imprint reads: LONDON: | SAMPSON LOW, MARSTON & CO., LTD.

Contents

182 x 120 mm. (i)–(iv) | (1)–(280) | catalogue (1)–(4). No illustrations.

(i) Title p. | (ii) printer's imprint (Printed in Great Britain by | The Union Press 66-68 Union Street London S.E.1) | (iii) Contents | (iv) blank | (1)–278. text | (1)–(4) catalogue (see Note 1).

Binding (see Note 3)

Red cloth boards, blocked black; edges plain; plain off-white endpapers.

Front board: THE CORNET OF | HORSE | G.A. HENTY (black) within ruled rectangular panel beneath illustration of sailing ships in sea battle, with boats, all contained in larger ruled rectangle (black). **Spine:** THE | CORNET | OF HORSE (black) between two black rules, above illustration of ships, in upper half of tall narrow panel, with: G.A. | HENTY (black) and four small black ornaments in lower half. At foot: SAMPSON LOW (black) between two black rules. **Back board:** plain.

Reference: PN.

Notes

1. In the 1920s 'Sampson Low's New Series' included their three Henty novels for boys, and *A Hidden Foe*, first published as an adult novel, all at 2s.6d. *The Cornet of Horse* (only) had no illustrations, but their catalogues announced 'If you look in the booksellers' windows you will know these books by the pictures on the coloured wrappers'. Sampson Low's address was then 100 Southwark Street, London, S.E.1.

2. The text is printed on featherweight paper by a new printer, but still from the old worn plates. The Union Press may be a new name for Walter H. Jackson Limited of the same address, who printed an impression of *Winning his Spurs*, see 11.6.

3. There were substantial variants of this edition, with alternative advertisements, and the series was given other names over a number of years: the constant factor is the colour and style of binding. The design is shown at Plate 50, used for *Winning his Spurs*, 11.8. My copy of this title is inscribed and dated 1923. All the variants are included here under this 'generic' heading *8.5.

4. The final leaf of text paper in my copy, described here as blank pages (279)–(280), has been neatly removed, possibly by the binder before publication, so that a reader finishing the book would not miss the tipped in (unsewn) 4-page catalogue.

5. Later editions, some in variant bindings of the one described here, were issued under the Sampson Low imprint in the 1930s (see Appendix II, Part 3), but are beyond the period covered by this bibliography.

9. IN TIMES OF PERIL

9.1

IN TIMES OF PERIL. | A TALE OF INDIA. | BY | G.A.HENTY, | Special War Correspondent of the "Standard"; Author of "The Young Buglers," | "The Young Franc Tireurs," "Out on the Pampas," etc. | With Nineteen Illustrations. | GRIFFITH AND FARRAN, | (SUCCESSORS TO NEWBERY AND HARRIS,) | WEST CORNER OF ST. PAUL'S CHURCHYARD, LONDON, | E.P. DUTTON & CO., NEW YORK. | 1881.
(Note: With Nineteen Illustrations. *is in gothic type).*

Contents
181 x 120 mm. (i)–(viii) | (1)–(344) | catalogue (1)–(32). Eighteen full-page and one half-page black-and-white engravings after several artists, the majority by J.H. (? Joseph Henderson, 1832–1908), engraved by W.J. Welch. (See Notes 3–10).

(i) Half-title p. | (ii) publisher's advertisement for *The Young Buglers* and *Out on the Pampas* | (frontispiece, tipped in) | (iii) title p. | (iv) [The rights of translation and of reproduction are reserved.] | (v)–vii. Contents | (viii) List of Illustrations | (1)–343. text, with printer's imprint at foot of p.343 (Butler & Tanner, The Selwood Printing Works, Frome, and London.) | (344) blank | (1)–(32) catalogue.

Binding (see Plate 32)
Red, lightly diagonally-grained, cloth boards, blocked black, blind and gilt; edges plain; grey-flowered endpapers.

Front board: IN TIMES OF PERIL (gilt) beneath decorative rules (black) and above illustration of soldiers with guns, between two pairs of plain rules (all black). Under this, at right: G.A. HENTY (gilt) with decorative rules below (black). **Spine:** IN | TIMES | OF | PERIL | G.A. HENTY (all gilt) above illustration (black and gilt); decorative rules (black); GRIFFITH & FARRAN (gilt). **Back board:** publisher's monogram in central decorative panel (all blind).

References: BL; Bod; PN | *Farmer*, p.43; *Dartt*, p.85, *Companion*, p.20.

Notes

1. The story was serialised in the *Union Jack*, starting in Vol. 1, No 1, dated 1 January 1880, under the title 'Times of Peril'. After six weekly parts it was 'concluded' without explanation, the final sentence of Chapter VI reading: 'Some day or other, the story of their further adventures in these "Times of Peril" may be told'. Fifteen weeks later the serialisation began again, with Chapter VII, under the revised title 'In Times of Peril', and continued thus for twenty weeks. The resumption was soon after Henty had taken over the Editorship of the *Union Jack* from W.H.G. Kingston. In that issue (Vol. I, No.21, 20 May 1880, p.336) he wrote that his readers 'will see that I have . . . continued the publication of "In Times of Peril". I fear that here and there the story will be found almost too historical for a magazine appearing weekly. However, if occasionally they get a number in which the story seems a little dull, they willl get so much adventure at other times that they will, I hope, be pleased with it in the long run'.

2. There is no printer's code, and no publisher's records survive. The earliest catalogues I have seen are dated July 1881 and October 1881. The book was sold at 5s. with plain edges and 5s.6d. with all edges gilt.

3. There is strange confusion about the number of illustrations. The title page correctly announces nineteen, but only sixteen are shown in the List of Illustrations, and the catalogue confirms the latter number. All nineteen appeared in the *Union Jack* serialisation, which had a total of thirty illustrations, but it is clear that the publisher originally intended to include only sixteen in the book.

4. The plates shown in the List of Illustrations are all full-page pictures, printed as a separate working, unbacked, unfolioed and tipped in. But the first three illustrations to appear, excluding the frontispiece, are not listed: they are uncaptioned and printed on text pages. Of these, one fits in half an ordinary page of text, but the two full-page pictures are unbacked, and both sides of the leaves are unfolioed, although they are counted in the pagination.

5. The sixteen initially chosen for the book are all by the same artist, although only one of them, facing p.225, bears his signature, 'J.H.'. He may be Joseph Henderson, RWS (1832–1908), who normally signed his work with exactly this style of interleaved monogram (see Appendix IV, Part 2).

6. In the magazine, most illustrations of the early chapters were by Stanley Berkeley, and his initials, or even his name, are on seven of them. Another drawing, on p.85, also appears by coincidence on p.85 of the book: the original, as printed in the *Union Jack* is signed 'H.F.' (?), but the initials were cut away when the electro from the wood block was trimmed to fit the page-size of the book.

7. The later drawings, by J.H., and the work of his engraver, W.J. Welch, had a more robust quality than the others. Welch's signature appears on thirteen of the sixteen original engravings, but was lost when the plates were trimmed for the book.

8. At first sight the publisher's choice of the sixteen illustrations for the book was sound. Unfortunately, Henderson, if indeed he is 'J.H.', illustrated the story only after serialisation was resumed on 20 May 1880 (see Note 1). So, when the book was made up, the first six chapters, two-fifths of the total, were unillustrated.

9. At a late stage it was decided to choose two more full-page pictures from the early part of the serialisation. They could not, of course, be printed with the other illustrations, which already filled a complete sheet of paper, so the only possibility was to print them on text pages, including p.85 (see Note 6 above). To make them appear to the reader like the other pictures, those text pages were not backed up: few would then have distinguished them from the sixteen tipped-in plates.

10. Thus the book became four pages longer. Without causing any further increase in extent it was found possible to fit a small illustration from the *Union Jack* within Chapter V of the book. All the three new pictures were printed without captions, possibly to justify their omission from the List of Illustrations.

11. A common arrangement in book-printing is to make up an even working by imposing the first and last gatherings of a book together, to print on a single sheet. That may be what had been planned here. The gaining of four extra text pages was perhaps made possible by two chances. First, that there was in any case going to be a blank leaf at the end of the book and, second, that another leaf could be saved by re-arranging the prelims (see Note 12). By re-imposing the text the two leaves could be used in appropriate positions for the added illustrations.

12. The typograpical treatment of the List of Illustrations as it was finally printed looks very cramped compared with the Contents. The latter is spread lavishly over three pages, while the List of Illustrations, in the same type-size, is squeezed on to the verso of p.vii. Two pages may have been saved by closing it up.

13. This is one of few books by Henty to be given no Preface.

9.2

Title page: As for 9.1, but with changed imprint (GRIFFITH, FARRAN, OKEDEN AND WELSH, | (SUCCESSORS TO NEWBERY & HARRIS,) | WEST CORNER OF ST. PAUL'S CHURCHYARD, LONDON; | AND SYDNEY, N.S.W.

Contents: 179 x 120 mm. Otherwise as for 9.1, except (a) printer's code, p.343 (see Note 3); (b) catalogue is (1)–16.

Binding: As for 9.1, except (a) brown, lightly diagonally-grained cloth boards, bevelled; all edges gilt; yellow surface-paper endpapers; (b) publisher's name at foot of spine is now given as GRIFFITH FARRAN & Co. (gilt).

Reference: PN.

Notes

1. Reprints of the first impression show small alterations to the prelims. By 1886 the book was issued in a series, 'Tales of Travel and Adventure', 'Crown 8vo, cloth elegant, bevelled boards, gilt edges, price 5s.'. That involved no change of format, but all copies had the bevels and gilt edges. It was in effect a price-reduction, as an additional 6d. had been charged for those 'extras' (see 9.1, Note 2).

2. *Friends, though Divided*, 12.2, was also in the 'Tales of Travel and Adventure' series, not to be confused with the later 'Tales of Adventure' (see Appendix V).

3. The printer's code on p.343 records 1000 copies, dated November 1888.

9.3

Title page: As for 9.1, but with changed imprint (LONDON: | GRIFFITH, FARRAN AND CO., | NEWBERY HOUSE, 39, CHARING CROSS ROAD.)

Contents

181 x 120 mm. (i)–(viii) | (1)–(344) | no catalogue. Illustrations as in 9.1, the eighteen full-page pictures now printed on unbacked text pages, those on pp.67 and 85 still uncaptioned and unfolioed, but counted in the pagination. The remainder are captioned and keyed to the text, but unfolioed and not counted in the pagination.

(i) Half-title p. | (ii) publisher's advertisement for *The Young Buglers, The Young Franc-Tireurs*, and *Out on the Pampas* | (frontispiece, leaf not counted in pagination) | (iii) title p. | (iv) [The rights of translation and of reproduction are reserved.] | (v)–vii. Contents | (viii) List of Illustrations | (1)–343. text, with printer's imprint at foot of p.343 (Butler & Tanner, The Selwood Printing Works, Frome, and London.) | (344) blank.

Binding (see Plate 43)

Olive-green cloth boards, blocked black and gilt; all edges gilt; light-brown flowered endpapers.

Front board: IN TIMES | OF PERIL (gilt) between two thick black rules forming clear panel towards top of illustration of five sailors in a boat, rowing away from natives firing arrows from a pursuing canoe, near an island of palm trees, etc. (all black except the five sailors, gilt). G.A. Henty (black) within small ruled panel set at centre of illustration. **Spine:** IN | TIMES | OF | PERIL | (6mm. rule) | G.A. HENTY (all gilt) between two black rules forming clear panel towards the top of illustration of two monkeys throwing down coconuts from palm tree to white man in boat (all black except man, gilt). At foot, below illustration: GRIFFITH & FARRAN (gilt). **Back board:** plain.

Reference: PN.

Notes

1. Apart from small alterations to the prelims the content is unchanged from 9.2. The make-up, however, has changed. All illustrations are now printed on text pages, and the book is therefore re-imposed. Some earlier eccentricities remain (see under *Contents* above). But, although some full-page pictures are counted in the pagination and some are not, the book is now an even working of twenty-four 16-page sections.
2. The printer's code on p.343 records 2000 copies, dated January 1893.
3. The case is a 'binder's blank' (see Glossary). A copy of *The Young Franc-Tireurs*, 5.9, the only other Henty title I have found in this binding style, is dated by printer's code 28 December 1892, by which time it was being advertised in 'The Boys' Own Favourite Library'. *In Times of Peril*, printed scarcely a month later, was advertised in 'The Boys' Own Favourite Library' shortly afterwards, when both it and *The Curse of Carne's Hold*, 40.4, were taken into the series.

9.4

Title page: As for 9.3.

Contents: 184 x 120 mm. Otherwise as for 9.3.

Binding (see Note 2)

Red cloth with light diagonal grain, blocked black, brown, and gilt; all edges gilt; yellow-brown floral-patterned endpapers.

Front board: IN TIMES OF PERIL (black, and cloth-colour out of solid-gilt rectangular panel) with rules (black and brown) above and below, superimposed across a trophy (black, brown, gilt) of rifles, oars, and an anchor. Beneath this: By | G.A. HENTY (black) above crossed swords (black and brown). **Spine:** Six bands across width of spine (brown, with black above and below); between the second and third bands: IN TIMES | OF | PERIL (black, and cloth-colour out of solid-gilt panel). Between third and fourth bands: HENTY (black, and cloth-colour out of smaller solid-gilt panel). Above sixth band: GRIFFITH, FARRAN & Co (gilt). **Back board:** plain.

Reference: PN.

Notes

1. The printer's code on p.34 shows this issue is from the impression of 2000 copies, dated January 1893, that was used for 9.3.

2. In the third binding style for 'The Boys' Own Favourite Library', used mainly in 1886–1895. From 1887 or 1888 virtually all books in the series were given gilt edges and bevelled boards, my copy of this book being the only exception I have found. It has gilt edges, but the boards are not bevelled. For more details of 'The Boys' Own Favourite Library' see *Out on the Pampas*, 4.3, Notes 3–5; Plate 33.

9.5

Title page: As for 9.3.

Contents: 182 x 122 mm. Otherwise as for 9.3.

Binding (see Note 2)

Light-maroon, vertically-ribbed cloth boards, bevelled, and blocked black, orange, brown and gilt; all edges gilt; dark-brown surface-paper endpapers.

  Front board: Elaborate decorative framework around edges, illustrating military and naval equipment, etc. (black, with part of background at foot orange) and sailing ship against setting sun (gilt) at top left corner. At right of this, in scrolls (outlined black): BoYS' OWN FAVOURITE | LIBRARY. (orange). At centre: IN TIMES | OF PERIL (all gilt) | BY (black) | G.A. HENTY (gilt). **Spine:** IN TIMES | OF PERIL (gilt) above trophy of anchor, rifles and flags (black, orange and brown): BY (black) | G.A. | HENTY (gilt); emblem of bugle and palm leaves (black and orange) above: GRIFFITH FARRAN | BROWNE & CO. (black). **Back board:** plain.

Reference: PN.

Notes

1. The printer's code on p.343 records 2000 copies, dated March 1895.

2. This binding style is the fourth and last used for books in 'The Boys' Own Favourite Library': in the year of this printing it replaced the earlier design used for 9.4. For details of the series see *Out on the Pampas*, 4.3, Notes 3–5; Plate 33.

9.6

IN TIMES OF PERIL | A TALE OF INDIA | BY | G.A. HENTY | AUTHOR OF "THE YOUNG BUGLERS" "THE YOUNG FRANC-TIREURS" | "OUT ON THE PAMPAS" ETC. | WITH ILLUSTRATIONS BY FRANK FELLER | GRIFFITH FARRAN BROWNE & CO. LIMITED | 35 BOW STREET, COVENT GARDEN | LONDON

Contents
189 x 134 mm. (1)–384 | no catalogue. Eight full-page wash-drawings by Frank Feller reproduced by black-and-white halftone blocks printed on unbacked text pages, unfolioed.

(1) Blank | (2) frontispiece | (3) title p. | (4) [The Rights of Translation and of Reproduction are Reserved] | 5–6. Contents | 7. List of Illustrations | (8) blank | 9–384. text, with printer's imprint at foot of p.384 (PRINTED BY MORRISON AND GIBB LIMITED, EDINBURGH).

Binding (see Plate 34)
Blue, vertically-ribbed cloth boards, blocked gilt; top edge gilt; plain off-white laid endpapers.

Front board: IN TIMES (decoration of formal roses and leaves) | OF | PERIL (all gilt) above illustration, with arms and trophy, etc.: G.A. HENTY (all gilt), all placed high and at left. **Spine:** IN TIMES | OF PERIL (gilt) within shield forming part of gilt decoration. G.A. Henty (gilt) towards the foot of it, and, below: GRIFFITH FARRAN | BROWNE & CO. (gilt). **Back board:** plain.

Reference: PN.

Notes
1. One of a set in similar format of Griffith & Farran's five Henty novels. Copies examined show that all were printed at least twice, in impressions of 2000 copies, between 1895 and 1899. The other titles are: *Out on the Pampas*, 4.7; *The Young Franc-Tireurs*, 5.10; *The Young Buglers*, 7.6; and *Friends, though Divided*, 12.5.
2. The type was re-set for them all except *Friends, though Divided*, which also kept its original illustrations. The rest were newly illustrated with wash-drawings.

9.7
Title page: As for 9.6.

Contents
187 x 132 mm. (1)–368 | no catalogue. Frontispiece from wash-drawing by Frank Feller reproduced by halftone block printed in dark blue-green ink on coated paper, keyed to text, unbacked, tipped in.

(1) Half-title p. | (2) blank | (frontispiece, tipped in) | (3) title p. | (4) [The Rights of Translation and of Reproduction are Reserved] | 5–6. Contents | 7–368. text, with printer's imprint at foot of p.368 (PRINTED BY MORRISON AND GIBB LIMITED, EDINBURGH).

Binding (see Plate 45)
Green, vertically-ribbed cloth boards, blocked gilt; top edge gilt; plain off-white endpapers.

Front board: IN TIMES | OF PERIL (gilt) with formal leaf-decoration (gilt) above and below. Beneath this: G.A. HENTY (gilt). **Spine:** IN TIMES | OF | PERIL | G.A. | HENTY (gilt) with formal leaf-decoration (gilt) above and below. At foot: GRIFFITH, FARRAN | BROWNE & CO. (gilt). **Back board:** plain.

Reference: PN.

Notes
1. A reprint from the type set for 9.5. Only one of the eight drawings is kept, as frontispiece, on coated paper, tipped in. Although not in black it is a far better reproduction. The book is re-imposed, and shorter by sixteen pages.
2. There is no printer's code to give size or date of the impression.
3. The binding design is similar to, although not exactly the same as, that used for *Out on the Pampas*, 4.9, of which a copy examined was inscribed 1911.

9.8

IN TIMES OF PERIL I A STORY OF INDIA I BY I G.A. HENTY I ILLUSTRATED IN COLOUR BY T.C. DUGDALE I LONDON I HENRY FROWDE I HODDER AND STOUGHTON I 1911

Contents
191 x 137 mm. (1)–368 I catalogue (1)–16. Six watercolour drawings by T.C. Dugdale reproduced by three-colour halftone blocks printed on coated paper, unbacked, unfolioed, tipped in.
(1) Half-title p. I (2) blank I (frontispiece, tipped in) I (3) title p. I (4) printer's imprint (RICHARD CLAY & SONS, LIMITED, I BREAD STREET HILL, E.C., AND I BUNGAY, SUFFOLK.) I (5) Contents I 6. List of Illustrations I 7–368. text, with printer's imprint at foot of p.368 (Richard Clay & Sons, Limited, London and Bungay.) I 1–16. catalogue, undated.

Binding (see Plate 35)
Green cloth boards, blocked black, cream, red, brown, and gilt; all edges stained dark green; grey lined endpapers.
Front board: IN TIMES OF PERIL (gilt) over illustration of three uniformed figures in undergrowth (black, cream, red, brown). **Spine:** IN TIMES I OF PERIL I G.A. HENTY (all gilt) above illustration of soldiers in battle (black, cream, red, brown). At foot: HENRY FROWDE I HODDER & STOUGHTON (gilt). **Back board:** plain.

References: BL; Bod.

Note: The stock and goodwill of Griffith & Farran were bought by Hodder & Stoughton in 1906. Henty's books were re-issued by them with the Oxford University Press in what was known as the 'Joint Venture' (see Appendix II, Part 2). The four other books were dated 1910. This one, dated 1911, was issued in 1910.

9.9

IN I TIMES OF I PERIL I G . A I HENTY I LONDON I HENRY . FROWDE I HODDER & I STOUGHTON
(Note: All lettering is hand-drawn within an art-nouveau frame).

Contents
187 x 121 mm. (1)–368 I catalogue (1)–(16) unfolioed. Frontispiece from watercolour drawing by T.C. Dugdale, reproduced by three-colour halftone blocks printed on coated paper, unbacked, unfolioed, tipped in.
(1) Half-title p. I (2) blank I (frontispiece, tipped in) I (3) title p. I (4) blank I (5) Contents I (6) blank I 7–368. text, with printer's imprint on p.368 (Richard Clay & Sons, Limited, London and Bungay.) I (1)–(16) catalogue.

Binding (see Note 1)

Yellow-green cloth boards, blind embossed, and blocked gilt; edges plain; light-green endpapers printed in dark green with bled-off illustration of nautical scene.

Front board: Step-and-repeat design of lions passants within ruled border; over this a ribboned seal showing St George slaying the dragon (all blind embossed). **Spine:** Blind-embossed art-nouveau design of flower, and rules, with three sunken panels, showing title, author, and publisher: IN | TIMES | of | PERIL (gilt); G . A | Henty (gilt); and: HENRY FROWDE | HODDER & | STOUGHTON (blind). **Back board:** All-over step-and-repeat design of lions passants within ruled border (blind embossed).

References: Bod; PN.

Notes

1. 'The Boys' New Library' (also advertised as 'The Boy's New Library') was issued by the 'Joint Venture' and later by the Oxford University Press (see 9.11, below). For changes in imprint during the period from 1906 to 1917 see Appendix II, Part 2. The series included *The Young Franc-Tireurs*, 5.15, and *Friends, though Divided*, 12.10, Plate 42.

2. My copy of this 'Joint Venture' edition has a prize-inscription dated 1913.

9.10

IN TIMES OF PERIL | A STORY OF INDIA | BY | G.A. HENTY | ILLUSTRATED IN COLOUR BY T.C. DUGDALE | LONDON | HENRY FROWDE | HODDER & STOUGHTON

Contents

190 x 124 mm. (1)–368 | no catalogue. Illustrations as in 9.8.

(1) Half-title p. | (2) publisher's advertisment (STORIES FOR BOYS) (see Note 3 below) | (frontispiece, tipped in) | (3) title p. | (4) printer's imprint (PRINTED IN GREAT BRITAIN BY R. CLAY AND SONS, LTD., | BRUNSWICK STREET, STAMFORD STREET, S.E., AND BUNGAY, SUFFOLK.) | (5) Contents | 6. List of Illustrations | 7–368. text.

Binding (see Plate 45)

Light-brown cloth boards, blocked dark-blue, red, white, and khaki; edges plain; plain off-white endpapers.

Front board: IN TIMES | OF PERIL (red) out of khaki panel, framed white, at top of illustration of British soldier with bugle, in khaki uniform of first war period, with Union flag behind (dark-blue, red, white, khaki). **Spine:** IN TIMES | OF PERIL | G.A. HENTY (dark-blue) above illustration of British soldier, running with Union flag (dark-blue, red, white, khaki). At foot: MILFORD (dark-blue). **Back board:** plain.

Reference: PN.

Notes

1. The binding design must have had strong patriotic appeal during the first war. It is quite out of period for this book, and was a kind of binder's blank used for Herbert Strang titles (with both 'Joint Venture' and O.U.P. imprints).

2. The imprint on the binding case does not correspond with that on the title page and advertisement on p.(2). Remnants of existing Joint Venture sheets were bound up for the O.U.P. shortly after they had taken control, and this issue can therefore be dated shortly after 1917.

3. The publisher's advertisement on p.(2) lists 14 titles, of which two are by Henty: *Out on the Pampas* and *The Young Franc-Tireurs* are both shown as available in cloth at 3s.6d. and 2s.6d. This is a reprint of 9.8, sold at 3s.6d., and the edition sold at 2s.6d. was in 'The Boys' New Library', see 9.9 and 9.11.

9.11

IN I TIMES OF I PERIL I G . A I HENTY I HUMPHREY . MILFORD I OXFORD . UNIVERSITY I . PRESS . I LONDON
(Note: All lettering is hand-drawn within an art-nouveau frame).

Contents
187 x 123 mm. (1)–368 I no catalogue. Frontispiece as in 9.9.

(1) Half-title p. I (2) publisher's advertisement (THE BOYS' NEW LIBRARY) listing 36 titles including this and two others by Henty I (frontispiece, tipped in) I (3) title p. I (4) printer's imprint (REPRINTED 1921 IN GREAT BRITAIN BY R. CLAY AND SONS, LTD., I BUNGAY, SUFFOLK.) I (5) Contents I (6) blank I 7–368. text.

Binding: As for 9.9, except (a) smooth red cloth; (b) author's name on spine now in caps: G.A I HENTY (gilt); (c) publisher's imprint on spine changed to: MILFORD (gilt, see Note 2).

Reference: PN.

Notes
1. See 9.9, Note 1. During and after the period of the 'Joint Venture' the book was sold both in this format and in the more standard, illustrated, 8vo editions (see 9.8 and 9.10). This impression is dated 1921 on p.(4).
2. During the first war the blocking of books in this 'Boys' New Library' series was done with imitation gold foil, a poor substitute for real gold, that soon tarnished and turned black. From 1922 there was a partial return to real gold.
3. The position of the apostrophe in 'Boys' varies in lists throughout the series.

9.12

Title page: As for 9.11.

Contents: As for 9.11, except (a) publisher's advertisement lists 46 titles; (b) printer's imprint includes date, 1924.

Binding (see Plate 46)
White paper boards, printed by offset lithography, yellow, red, blue, grey and black; edges plain; buff endpapers, printed in brown ink with bled-off illustration of nautical scene.

Front board: IN TIMES OF I PERIL (white, with grey shadow, out of solid black) above decorative illustration showing large tiger and smaller figures below (yellow, red, blue and grey, with solid-black background). **Spine:** IN . TIMES I OF

. PERIL (white out of solid black) | (small red vertical rule) | G.A. HENTY (yellow lettering with red dots, all out of solid black) above illustration of figure being grasped from behind by tiger from front board (yellow, red, grey and blue, all out of solid black). At foot: OXFORD (black on small grey panel). **Back board:** publisher's advertisement for 'The New Ensign Series' (black on white panel in blue background).

Reference: PN.

Notes
1. An eye-catching binding design from the O.U.P. in 1924, to replace the rather drab blind-embossed cloth boards of 9.9 and 9.11, although these paper-boards do not have the strength of the earlier bindings.
2. The advertisement on the back of the binding case lists six titles for boys and five for girls, all under the title of 'The New Ensign Series'. *In Times of Peril* is the only title by Henty to be included, and it may be that it was the first of a series in this binding design.

10. FACING DEATH

10.1
FACING DEATH: | OR, | THE HERO OF THE VAUGHAN PIT. | A TALE OF THE COAL MINES. | BY | G.A. HENTY, | AUTHOR OF "IN TIMES OF PERIL;" "THE YOUNG BUGLERS;" | "CORNET OF HORSE;" ETC. ETC. | (publisher's device) | LONDON: | BLACKIE & SON, 49 OLD BAILEY, E.C.; | GLASGOW, EDINBURGH, AND DUBLIN. | 1882.

Contents
184 x 124 mm. (1)–304 | catalogue (1)–16. Six line-and-tint drawings by Gordon Browne, reproduced by black line and sepia tint-plates, unbacked, unfolioed, tipped in.
  (1) Half-title p. | (2) blank | (frontispiece, tipped in) | (3) title p. | (4) blank | (5) Contents | (6) blank | (7) list of Illustrations | (8) blank | (9)–304. text | (1)–16. catalogue.

Binding (see Plate 64)
Light-brown, grained cloth boards, blocked black, red, blind, and gilt; edges plain; dark-brown surface-paper endpapers.
  Front board: Frame in black and red enclosing illustration (gilt, red and black) of miner with lamp, and fuse. FACING . DEATH (gilt) at top; A TALE | OF THE | COAL MINES (red, cased with gilt); BY G.A. HENTY (gilt) at foot. **Spine:** series of five panels contained in a simple black-rule framework, with gilt rules at upper and lower extremities of spine, and also between each panel. Top panel shows double wheels operating the cable of the lift 'cage' above the mineshaft (cloth-colour reversed out of red); bottom panel shows the cage itself (cloth-colour reversed out of red). Second panel from top is delicately ornamented gilt, with decorations and FACING | DEATH (cloth-colour reversed out of gilt). Beneath it, the largest panel is solid red with a small circular dot (cloth-colour, reversed out) at

each corner, and a circle, to full width of spine panel (cloth-colour, reversed out), with trophy of miner's lamp and pickaxes (all gilt). Below this, in the smallest panel: . BY . | G.A. HENTY (gilt). **Back board:** Triple rules at edges of board (blind).

Reference: BB.

Notes
1. The story was serialised in the *Union Jack* in five instalments, 15 April to 13 May 1880 (Vol.1, No.16–20): there are considerable differences between that version and this shorter one published by Blackie.
2. This was the first of Henty's stories to be published by Blackie (see Appendix II, Part 5), the beginning of a famous series of 67 full-length novels for boys, of which 24 were to be published at 5s. each, and 43 at 6s. The fixed formats used for the two price-ranges, which were used for children's books by many authors, were planned by Blackie during the early years of this new publishing venture. They came into use gradually, but were fully operational by 1885.
3. *Facing Death* became the first of the 5s. novels, but only after a number of vicissitudes in its early stages. The story is considerably shorter than most of Henty's novels, and was originally planned by Blackie to sell at 3s.6d., with six full-page illustrations printed in two colours. The type was set, to make 304 pages, which is 48 pages less than any of the subsequent 5s. titles; and six illustrations were commissioned from Gordon Browne, the about-to-be-famous son of a famous father (Hablôt Browne, perhaps better known as 'Phiz'), though not yet, apparently, considered a name worth mentioning on the title page.
4. The book was printed and bound, and ready to put on sale, with a bound-in catalogue in which it was advertised 'With 6 full-page Illustrations in black and tint. Crown 8vo, cloth elegant, 3s.6d.'. In comparison with the content and prices of Blackie's other books, this seems a straightforward and reasonable pricing. But Blackie had sudden and serious second thoughts, and the book was withdrawn almost as soon as it had been issued. Indeed, there is only one known copy of the book in this original state, as described above. The others were altered before distribution to booksellers. The alterations, and others that followed, are discussed in the Notes under 10.2, 10.3 and 10.4. The catalogue includes no other book by Henty.
5. Blackie lists publication date as 31 May 1882, but does not indicate whether that date is for 10.1, or for the book in its revised state as 10.2.

10.2
Title page: As for 10.1 (see Plate 65).

Contents: As for 10.1, except (a) eight full-page line-and-tint drawings by Gordon Browne; (b) cancel leaf A4 (pp.(7)–(8)); (c) catalogue pp.(1)–32.

Binding: As for 10.1, except (a) green cloth; (b) part of the spine brasses were recut so that in the central panel, showing a miner's lamp and crossed pickaxes, the small circular dots at each corner were replaced with small stars (see Plate 67).

References: NS; PN | *Farmer*, p.28; *Dartt*, p.52, *Companion*, p.14.

Notes

1. The second state of the first edition of *Facing Death* varies from 10.1 in having two additional illustrations by Gordon Browne: they face pages 58 and 237.

2. It was consequently necessary to revise the list of Illustrations on p.(7), and to print a cancel. The original leaf, forming pp.(7)–(8), was removed from each bound book, and the replacement, showing details of all eight plates, was tipped on to the stub.

3. The Blackie catalogue that appeared in 10.1 was destroyed, to remove all trace of the 3s.6d. price. Copies may have appeared in titles by other authors, but none have been reported. Catalogues in 10.2 also announce *Under Drake's Flag*, 13.1.

4. There seems to have been no economic reason for changing the price of the book. Indeed, the inclusion of two extra illustrations may be seen merely as an excuse for so doing. The real reason was probably not economic, but a result of negotiation with the author. Possibly Henty was upset to find Blackie about to charge 30% less for one of his novels than the price of any of those already published. At that time four were selling at 5s. each, and *The Young Buglers*, in a larger format, was priced by Griffith & Farran at 7s.6d. His thoughts may have been on the possibility of future royalties (at this stage they did not come into his agreement with Blackie) on something like the terms promised by Sampson Low in his contract for *The Cornet of Horse* (see Appendix VI). Or he may simply have been suffering from injured pride. *Facing Death* had been heavily reduced in length since its appearance in the *Union Jack*. Henty had no doubt agreed in principle to Blackie's editing, but its extent may have been an unpleasant surprise.

5. By the end of 1881 Henty had had four full-length stories serialised in the *Union Jack*, and of them only the earliest, *Facing Death*, had not been published in book form. The story seems to have lacked appeal for both Griffith & Farran and Sampson Low, so he should have been pleased that Blackie was prepared to publish it, even if they insisted on substantial editing. In later life he always maintained in spite of everything that *Facing Death* was his own favourite among his books for boys.

6. However the arguments went, Blackie decided to re-issue the book at five shillings and commissioned two more pictures from Gordon Browne. That they agreed to make such changes at so late a stage implies they already valued Henty highly as an author. Perhaps they would have acted differently had they foreseen the trouble that was to follow. The story is told in the Notes under 10.3 and 10.4 below.

7. Meanwhile remark must be made of the entries in *Farmer* and *Dartt*. Neither knew of the existence of 10.1, believing 10.2 to be the first issue. Nevertheless, it must be said that entries and notes in *Dartt* and his *Companion* are confused and inaccurate. His readers should note, in particular, that in *all* Blackie editions the subtitle on the title page is 'The Hero of the Vaughan Pit', and that on the first page of text is 'How Stokebridge was Civilized'.

8. In the list of Illustrations on p.(7) one of the new pictures is given as 'In the Old Shaft – Can he be Saved?', whereas the caption to the plate, facing p.58, is 'In the Old Shaft – Will he be Saved?'. At p.107 the figure 7 in the folio number is battered. Both these faults continued in subsequent reprints.

10.3

Title page: As for 10.2, with date changed to 1883.
(Note: The last digit of the date, and the full-point following it, have been erased and re-entered by hand, see Plate 68 and Notes 1–6 below).

Contents: 182 x 124 mm Otherwise as for 10.2, but with eight full-page illustrations; cancel leaf A4 (pp.(7)–(8)); and title page altered (see above).

Binding: Orange-brown diagonally-grained cloth boards, otherwise as for 10.2, but see 10.4, Note 10.

References: BL; Bod; PN | *Dartt*, p.52.

Notes

1. Blackie must have acted very fast in making the changes from 10.1 to 10.2, and may have asked booksellers to return any copies they held of 10.1 to be exchanged for the later issue. But even if, as seems extremely likely, only a very small number of copies of 10.1 had left the bindery, the fact remained that the book had been published, both technically and in the eyes of the law, in two different states and at two different prices, both bearing the same title-page date. Blackie were advertising a new book by their leading children's author at five shillings; that would seem at least a bit fishy to the few booksellers and others who knew that it had already appeared at a cheaper price.

2. To this conscientous publisher the situation no doubt seemed, on reflection, rather reprehensible, and Blackie decided to do something about it. It seemed that the only solution was to make a distinction between the two issues, so that the book being offered at 5s. was seen to be a later edition of the one previously priced at 3s.6d. To do that it was only necessary to change the title-page date from 1882 to 1883 in the remaining copies. Those included the ones already bound, as well as the flat sheets awaiting binding.

3. The book described here as 10.3 was the result of Blackie's treatment of the books already bound. From the evident scarcity of 10.2 (I know of less than a dozen copies) it is clear that only a small number had been sent out to booksellers. Copies of 10.3 are scarce, but they are not as scarce as 10.2. It is significant that the copies sent to the Copyright Libraries were 10.3, and even more so that copies specially bound for Henty himself were also 10.3. (The copy in the National Library of Scotland is 10.2, but was acquired secondhand at a later date). From all the above it may reasonably be supposed that 10.1, 10.2, and 10.3 were all issued within a few days of each other.

4. A decision was taken to alter the bound copies by changing the title-page date. The method was one rarely used by letterpress printers (I have only once seen it being done), being limited to occasions where both the area to be altered, and the number of copies to be altered, were very small. Unless those conditions applied it would be cheaper, and quicker, to reprint the faulty leaf and insert a cancel, as had already been done for the list of Illustrations. The operation was done by scraping the paper surface with a very sharp knife, or a razor blade, until the offending character was erased, and then 'printing in' the replacement character by holding a small piece of type in the fingers and using it like a rubber stamp.

5. It was always difficult, and risked wasting a number of sheets. In this case the operation was carried out on title pages in bound books, rather than on unbound sheets, so a mistake would be the more costly. It was not easy to scrape away a printed impression without making a mess of the surface, or even making a hole in the paper, especially as the process was not one in which the operator was ever likely to become very experienced. Nor was it easy to get an even film of ink, of the right thickness, on the end of a single, very small, piece of metal. Perhaps it was even more difficult to impress this fiddly piece of type in exactly the right place, at the right angle, and with appropriate pressure.

6. Plate 68 shows, in considerable enlargement of the detail, that this method of making corrections was very crude, and of course the results varied from copy to copy. All those I have examined show a blind impression of the hand-held type, for the figure 3, and the full-point, clearly visible on two or three leaves following the title page, proving that the work was done in bound copies.

7. From the foregoing it will be clear that all copies of 10.1, 10.2, and 10.3 formed part of a single printing, and all are equally first editions in spite of their variations caused by subsequent treatment.

8. The final stage for Blackie was to deal with the still-unbound flat sheets of this first printing. Their solution to this part of the problem was not difficult – nor was it cheap – and is discussed in the Notes under 10.4 below.

10.4

FACING DEATH | OR, | THE HERO OF THE VAUGHAN PIT. | A TALE OF THE COAL MINES. | BY | G.A. HENTY, | Author of "Under Drake's Flag;" "In Times of Peril;" "The Young Buglers;" | "Cornet of Horse;" &c. &c. | ILLUSTRATED BY GORDON BROWNE. | SECOND EDITION. | (publisher's device) | LONDON: BLACKIE & SON, 49 OLD BAILEY, E.C.; | GLASGOW, EDINBURGH, AND DUBLIN. | 1883.

Contents: 185 x 122 mm. Otherwise as for 10.2, except (a) revised title page (see Plate 66); (b) A4 (pp.(7)–(8)) now an integral leaf.

Binding: (see Plates 64, 67). As for 10.2, except (a) orange-brown, stipple-grained cloth boards (see Note 10); (b) Spine as for 10.1, the brasses for the central panel, with miner's lamp and crossed pickaxes, being cut to a smaller size, and the other brasses for the spine being re-spaced. The stars in the corners of the central panel were replaced by circular dots again.

References: PN | *Dartt*, p.53.

Notes
1. Blackie's final solution to the problems arising from the first printing of *Facing Death* was to reprint the eight preliminary pages, including the revised list of Illustrations. The title page was amended to show the date as 1883, and the words SECOND EDITION were added. While they were at it Blackie added Gordon Browne's name as illustrator, and changed the titles given under the author's name to include *Under Drake's Flag* which at that time was either just published, or just about to be. They removed the colon after the title, and re-centred the line, but made no other changes in punctuation. The remaining sheets of the first printing of text could now be bound with the new preliminary pages. The whole was presented as a completely new edition, implicitly unconnected with what had originally been produced as 10.1 or 10.2. It was not, in fact, a new edition at all, indeed the text was not even a new impression, but that was unlikely to cause anyone much concern. It was in this state that the majority of sheets from the first printing of *Facing Death* reached readers' hands.
2. At about this time Blackie made some general decisions about the dating of title

pages. It will have been noticed by collectors that they were among the most reticent of publishers in the matter of bibliographical information. In their books no details are given of impressions printed: the words SECOND EDITION on the title page of 10.4 are a unique occurrence, used on this occasion just as part of a scheme to get out of difficulties. The only information they routinely gave was the date, shown on title pages of the first printings of the 5s. and 6s. series. And even that was misleading, as the date given was always that of the year *following* first publication. Blackie was by no means the only publisher to adopt that practice: indeed Griffith & Farran did the same thing for *Out on the Pampas* (see 4.1, Note 2) and other titles. Hence, *Under Drake's Flag*, published in August 1882, was dated 1883 on the title page, and the rule applied however early in the year a book was published, so when *The Lion of St. Mark* was published on 29 February 1888 it was given the title-page date 1889 (see Appendix VII, Part 1). Thus the alterations made by hand to the date in 10.3, and the subsequent dating of 10.4, both conformed quite fortuitously to the new rules.

3. In 1884 the rules were modified. When a book sold well enough for a reprint to be ordered during the calendar year of first printing, as happened with *With Clive in India* (see 15.3, Note 1), that reprint would also carry on its title page the date shown in the first printing. Any later reprints were issued, as before, with no date. Blackie modified the rules again during the first decade of the twentieth century (see 10.6, Note 3 below).

4. In Note 1 under 10.3 I suggested that 10.1, 10.2, and 10.3 were all issued in quick succession. It is probable that 10.4 was issued no more than a few weeks later. In the absence of most of Blackie's records, the evidence can only be circumstantial. But it may be found convincing. First, the comparative scarcity of 10.3 today, reinforced by the fact that the essential hand-work could have been done in only a very small number of copies, suggests that the issue in that state could have done little to stave off the need for supplies to booksellers. Second, the catalogues in early issues of 10.4 contain announcements of *Facing Death* and *Under Drake's Flag* without quotations from press reviews. Catalogues with such simple announcements appear in only the early issues of each title. Blackie revised and reprinted catalogues frequently, and included quotations from press notices as soon as possible. The implication is that no new catalogues had been printed, and therefore little time had passed, between the distribution of 10.2 and of 10.4.

5. At this period it was normal practice for publishers to bind a sufficiently large number of copies of a book to meet initial demand, and thereafter to bind small batches as and when more copies were needed. This is explained in more detail in Appendix III, Part 2. Thus an edition of 3000 books could produce a number of different 'issues' with variations in catalogues, and sometimes variations also in the colours of cloth and blocking of binding cases.

6. There were, in fact, several issues of 10.4. From an examination of some of them, and from Blackie's sales figures, it is possible to guess (no more than that) at a little more of the publishing-history of *Facing Death*. The figures show that at the end of February 1883 a total of 2162 copies had been sold. The totals at the end of the three subsequent Februaries were: (1884) 648 copies; (1885) 1343 copies; (1886) 1244 copies. Considering those in the context of figures for other books over the years, I suggest that the initial print order was for 3000 copies, and that at some time near the end of 1883, or early in 1884, the stock ran very low or possibly ran out altogether. Blackie were feeling their way at the start of a new venture. They could not possibly foresee the great success that was to come, but had to decide whether or not to risk reprinting this first 5s. title. Naturally they hesitated: if the book should fail to go on selling, much of the profit already made from it would be wastefully spent in piling up copies of an unsaleable product. Indeed it is doubtful, in view of its past history, whether there actually was any profit so far from this particular title. Swayed perhaps by pre-publication orders for *By Sheer Pluck* and *With Clive in India*; Blackie took the plunge and ordered a reprint, probably (judging from the figures) of another 3000 copies.

7. From then on there were no fears about the success of the book. Reprints in this format (see *10.5 below) averaged sales of 1041 copies a year for the next fifteen years, achieving a grand total of 20,501 copies by the end of August 1907 when the book was re-issued in Blackie's cheaper 'New and Popular Edition' (see 10.6). At that time there was a balance of 114 copies in stock, and they were sold over the next five years, concurrently with the cheap edition.

8. The earliest issue of 10.4 in my collection has an undated catalogue, identical with that in my copy of 10.2 (see Note 4): it is headed 'New Series for the Young', and the announcements of *Facing Death* and *Under Drake's Flag* do not include quotations from reviews. A second copy has a catalogue dated '11.83' on page 1. Under 'New Series for Season 1884' the first titles beneath Henty's name are *By Sheer Pluck* and *With Clive in India*, both of which were published in September 1883 and have title pages dated 1884. The announcements of *Facing Death* and *Under Drake's Flag* both include quotations from press reviews. A third copy has an undated catalogue which also proclaims the 'New Series for 1884', includes excerpts from press notices of *By Sheer Pluck* and *With Clive in India*, and also displays, at the head of page (1), a quotation from '*The Academy*, Dec.1, 1883' (see Note 9 below). This may have been the last issue, early in 1884, before supplies of 10.4 were exhausted, as suggested in Note 6. It certainly appears, from the drop in sales of *Facing Death* in the year ending February 1884, that there was a period when the book was out of print: sales picked up well again thereafter, probably when supplies of a reprint (*10.5) became available. The delay in providing them may have been caused partly by the hesitation postulated in Note 6, but also perhaps partly because the printing machines were busy at the critical time printing *In Freedom's Cause, True to the Old Flag*, and *St. George for England*, all to be published that year, in addition to books by other authors.

9. The quotation from *The Academy*, mentioned in Note 8 above, reads as follows: 'It is due to Messrs. Blackie to say that no firm of publishers turns out this class of literature with more finish. We refer not only to the novel tinting of the illustrations and the richness of the cover, but more particularly to the solidity of the binding, a matter of great importance in boys' books'.

10. 10.1, 10.2, and some copies of 10.3 are bound in cloth with a very fine, almost imperceptible, diagonal straight-line grain. The cloth used for other copies of 10.3, and for the first issue of 10.4, is fairly heavily stipple-grained, and is similar to that used for the first edition of *Under Drake's Flag*, for at least two issues. An examination of the latter book, in particular, shows that this heavy grain did not accept pictorial blocking satisfactorily. An extra-heavy impression of the brasses was clearly necessary, which tended to spoil the general effect of the design, and even then the gilt and pigments did not sit well on the material. For the second and third issues of 10.4 referred to in Note 8 above, pale-brown and red cloths were used, both with the very light, diagonal, straight-line (or ribbed) grain, as for 10.1, 10.2 and 10.3. Cloths with the same grain were used for some later issues of the first edition of *Under Drake's Flag*, 1883 (see 13.3, under the heading *Binding*), for the first editions of *By Sheer Pluck* and *With Clive in India*, both dated 1884, and for some copies of titles with 1885 title-page dates. Thereafter, apart from a few copies of *Yarns on the Beach*, 1886 (published in September 1885), Blackie abandoned the use of grained cloth for Henty's books.

*10.5

Reprints of the five-shilling edition followed the style of 10.4, but the date and the words NEW EDITION were removed from the title page. Alterations were made to title-page imprint and address as necessary: Blackie became a Limited Company in 1890; the Edinburgh address was not used after 1894; and the Indian office was opened in 1901, although Bombay did not appear regularly in the imprint until 1906. The list of books after Henty's name on the title page was changed to include more recent titles, and only those published by Blackie. The printing of illustrations was in due course modified, the second-colour tint being either transferred to the black plate or omitted (see Appendix IV, Part I).

Bindings showed variations in colour of cloth, blocking, and endpapers. From 1883 some books were given 'olivine edges' (see Appendix II, Part 5, Note 73), and within a few years this became standard for all the novels.

The slightly-varying issues of this title in its first-edition format are all grouped together under this 'generic' heading, *10.5.

10.6

Facing Death | OR | THE HERO OF THE VAUGHAN PIT | A TALE OF THE COAL MINES | BY | G.A. HENTY | Author of "With Clive in India" "In Freedom's Cause" "By Sheer Pluck" | "Under Drake's Flag" &c. | ILLUSTRATED | NEW EDITION | BLACKIE AND SON LIMITED | LONDON GLASGOW DUBLIN BOMBAY | 1908

Contents
185 x 128 mm. (1)–304 | catalogue 1–16. Eight unsigned wash-drawings based on the line-illustrations in 10.2, reproduced by black-and-white halftone blocks printed on coated paper, unbacked, unfolioed, tipped in.

(1) Half-title p. | (2) publisher's advertisement (HISTORICAL STORIES BY G.A. HENTY) listing 30 titles | (frontispiece, tipped in) | (3) title p. | (4) blank | 5. Contents | (6) blank | (7) list of Illustrations | (8) blank | 9–304. text | 1–16. catalogue.

Binding (see Plate 173)
Red cloth boards, blocked dark grey, warm buff, black, and gilt; all edges stained green; grey endpapers, lined off-white.
Front board: FACING DEATH | A TALE OF THE COAL MINES (gilt) above illustration of young miner with pick and lamp (dark grey, warm buff, black). At foot: G.A. HENTY. (warm buff). **Spine:** FACING | DEATH | G.A. HENTY. (gilt) above illustration of miner on chain-held seat with lamp (dark grey, warm buff, black). At foot: BLACKIE & SON, LTD. (black). **Back board:** plain.

References: BL; Bod.

Notes

1. In 1907 (title-page date 1908) *Facing Death* was re-issued in the cheaper 'New and Popular Edition'.

2. The price of all books in the series was 3s.6d., and they were bound in a more contemporary style, many binding designs being by John Hassall. A number of them are signed, and probably almost all those unsigned are also by Hassall.

3. Later issues were printed with no date on the title page, and, when necessary, with alterations to imprint and addresses, this treatment repeating Blackie's custom with first editions (see 10.4, Notes 2 and 3). The Dublin office was removed from the imprint after 1910. On later binding cases gilt blocking was replaced with pigment, first on the front board, and then on the spine as well.

4. In this edition Blackie sold 2438 copies during 1908, and a further 6126 copies up to the end of August 1917. No figures are available after that date.

5. The caption to the illustration facing page 58 has now been amended to correspond with the entry in the list of Illustrations (see 10.2, Note 8).

*10.7

Facing Death | OR | THE HERO OF THE VAUGHAN PIT | A TALE OF THE COAL MINES | BY | G.A. HENTY | Author of "With Clive in India" "In Freedom's Cause" "By Sheer Pluck" | "Under Drake's Flag" &c. | ILLUSTRATED | BLACKIE AND SON LIMITED | LONDON GLASGOW AND BOMBAY

Contents

186 x 125 mm. (1)–304 | no catalogue. Frontispiece from watercolour drawing by unknown artist, reproduced by three-colour halftone blocks; four full-page wash-drawings reproduced by halftone blocks printed in black; all on coated paper, unbacked, tipped in.

(1) Half-title p. | (2) publisher's advertisement (G.A. HENTY'S BOOKS) listing 12 titles | (frontispiece, tipped in) | (3) title p. | (4) blank (see Note 3, below) | (5) Contents | (6) blank | (7) list of Illustrations | (8) blank | 9–304. text, with printer's imprint at foot of p.304 (PRINTED AND BOUND IN GREAT BRITAIN | By Blackie & Son, Limited, Glasgow).

Binding

Red cloth boards, blocked black, dark-grey, buff; edges plain; plain off-white endpapers.

Front board: FACING DEATH | A TALE OF THE COAL MINES (buff) above illustration of miner with pick and lamp (black, dark-grey, buff). At foot: G.A. HENTY. (buff). **Spine:** FACING | DEATH | G.A. HENTY. (buff) above illustration of miner with lamp, on chain-held seat (black, dark-grey, buff). At foot: BLACKIE & SON. LTD. (black). **Back board:** plain.

Reference: PN.

Notes

1. During the 1920s Blackie re-issued Henty's novels in a series called 'The New Popular Henty', a title very close to that of the series begun in 1903 (The 'New and Popular Edition'). Although details of presentation varied from title to title, according to the date of issue, all the books had a standard set of illustrations, consisting of a colour-frontispiece and four black-and-white plates.

2. Variations are also found between issues of individual titles, even to re-setting of title pages, and re-arrangement of preliminary pages and advertisements.

3. Most of the bindings were blocked from brasses cut for the 'New and Popular Edition', but for this series no gold was used. Examples from the series are at Plates 174–175. The watercolour frontispiece was also used on the dust-wrapper.

4. In my copy p.(4) is impressed, near the foot, with a rubber stamp: 'PRINTED AND BOUND IN GREAT BRITAIN'.

5. All the minor variants of *Facing Death* in this series are grouped together under the 'generic' heading, *10.7.

6. After a few years Blackie produced the novels even more cheaply. In later series the colour-frontispieces were abandoned, and in each book one of the four black-and-white plates took its place.

7. Binding cases were also simplified. Pictorial blocking was removed from the front board, and later from the spine as well, leaving only lettering and rules. (I have found only a single exception: see *By Pike and Dyke*, 43.5). The dust-wrappers, with coloured illustrations, continued in use.

8. These later formats fall outside the scope of this bibliography.

11. WINNING HIS SPURS

11.1

WINNING HIS SPURS: | A Tale of the Crusades. | BY G.A. HENTY, | AUTHOR OF "THE YOUNG BUGLERS," "THE CORNET OF HORSE," | "IN TIMES OF PERIL," ETC. | WITH NUMEROUS ILLUSTRATIONS. | London; | SAMPSON LOW, MARSTON, SEARLE, & RIVINGTON, | CROWN BUILDINGS, 188, FLEET STREET. | 1882. | [All rights reserved.]
(Note: the subtitle, and London;, *are in gothic type).*

Contents
182 x 120 mm. (i)–(viii) | (1)–324 | catalogue (1)–32. Seventy-four small black-and-white engravings after Horace Petherick by Lefman on text pages.

(i) Half-title p. | (ii) printer's imprint (LONDON: | GILBERT AND RIVINGTON, LIMITED, | ST. JOHN'S SQUARE.) | (iii) title p. | (iv) blank | (v)–vii. Contents | (viii) blank | (1)–324. text; printer's imprint on p.324 (GILBERT AND RIVINGTON, LIMITED, ST. JOHN'S SQUARE, LONDON.) | (1)–32. catalogue, dated December 1881.

Binding (see Plate 47)
Red cloth boards, blocked black, blind, and gilt; all edges gilt; grey-and-white flowered endpapers.

Front board: WINNING | HIS SPURS (gilt); A TALE OF THE CRUSADES (black) with two long-stemmed flowers (gilt), all on black decorative banner forming part of illustration (black). By | G.A. HENTY (gilt) superimposed on illustration. **Spine:** WINNING | HIS | SPURS (gilt) with gilt scallop below, on elaborate decorative black panel; BY G.A. HENTY (gilt) between black rules; black illustration; ILLUSTRATED (black) between black rules; SAMPSON LOW & Co. (black) between black rules and below truncated trophy (black). **Back board:** double rules at edges of board, with publisher's monogram forming central medallion (all blind).

References: BL; Bod; PN I *Farmer*, p.78; *Dartt*, p.157.

Notes
1. The story was serialised in the *Union Jack* in 26 weekly instalments, beginning in Vol.III, No.119, 6 April 1882, p.425.
2. This was the second of two books by Henty for which standing type from the *Union Jack* was used (see *The Cornet of Horse*, 8.1, Notes 4–6).
3. There are no full-page plates. The many small illustrations all appear exactly as in the *Union Jack*, with no trimming or cutting as was required for those in *The Cornet of Horse*. Thus the composition and make-up of text and illustrations were cheaper than for any book by Henty so far.
4. The final section of text, signature Y, consists of four pages, tipped on to the end of the previous gathering. This section, and the 8-page section of prelims, are extra to the twenty 16-page text gatherings: a rather costly make-up.
5. No publisher's records survive, and there is no printer's code to show the size of the edition.

*11.2
WINNING HIS SPURS: I A Tale of the Crusades. I BY G.A. HENTY, I AUTHOR OF "THE YOUNG BUGLERS," "THE CORNET OF HORSE," I "IN TIMES OF PERIL," ETC. I WITH NUMEROUS ILLUSTRATIONS. I LONDON: I SAMPSON LOW, MARSTON, SEARLE, & RIVINGTON, I Limited, I St. Dunstan's House, I FETTER LANE, FLEET STREET, E.C. I 1890. I [All rights reserved.]
(Note: The subtitle, and St. Dunstan's House, *are in gothic type).*

Contents
181 x 118 mm. (i)–(viii) I (1)–324 I (325)–(327) publisher's lists I (328) blank I catalogue (1)–32. Illustrations as in 11.1.
    (i) Half-title p. I (ii) printer's imprint (LONDON: I GILBERT AND RIVINGTON, LIMITED, I ST. JOHN'S HOUSE, CLERKENWELL ROAD, E.C.) I (iii) title p. I (iv) publisher's advertisement I (v)–vii. Contents I (viii) blank I (1)–324. text, with printer's imprint on p.324 (Gilbert & Rivington, Limited, St. John's House, Clerkenwell Road, London, E.C.) I (325)–(327) publisher's advertisements I (328) blank I (1)–32. catalogue, dated October 1890.

Binding: As for 11.1, except (a) brown cloth; (b) edges plain; (c) brown-and-white flowered endpapers.

References: PN I *Farmer*, p.78.

Notes
1. In numerous reprints, some title pages were dated and some were not, apparently quite arbitrarily. The copy described is no more than representative of them: all follow the basic style of 11.1, with minor variations. Those consist, externally, in the

colour of cloth and endpapers, and blind blocking on the back board; internally, in the publisher's imprint and address, and alteration or omission of advertisements and catalogues. The majority appeared in the 1890s.

2. For most copies of *11.2, including this one, machining and binding costs have been reduced by making the final gathering one of eight pages. This was probably printed with the eight pages of prelims as one full sheet (see 11.1, Note 4).

3. Together with *The Cornet of Horse* and *Jack Archer, Winning his Spurs* was included towards the end of the 1880s in the series, 'Low's Standard Books for Boys'. That involved no changes of style beyond those outlined in Note 1, but the books were then sold at 2s.6d. with all edges plain, or alternatively at 3s.6d. with all edges gilt. All minor variants are included under this 'generic' heading, *11.2.

11.3

WINNING HIS SPURS I A Tale of the Crusades I BY G.A. HENTY I AUTHOR OF "THE YOUNG BUGLERS," "THE CORNET OF HORSE," I "IN TIMES OF PERIL," ETC. I WITH NUMEROUS ILLUSTRATIONS I LONDON I SAMPSON LOW, MARSTON & COMPANY I Limited I St. Dunstan's House I FETTER LANE, FLEET STREET, E.C.

(Note: The subtitle and St. Dunstan's House *are in gothic type).*

Contents

182 x 121 mm. (i)–(viii) I (1)–324 I no catalogue. Illustrations as in 11.1.

(i) Half-title p. I (ii) printer's imprint (LONDON I PRINTED BY GILBERT AND RIVINGTON, LD. I ST. JOHN'S HOUSE, CLERKENWELL, E.C.) I (iii) title p. I (iv) blank I (v)–vii. Contents I (viii) blank I (1)–324. text, with printer's imprint on p.324 (Gilbert & Rivington, Limited, St. John's House, Clerkenwell London, E.C.).

Binding (see Plate 48)

Green cloth boards, blocked black, blue, yellow-green merging to orange-brown, buff, and gilt; edges plain; plain off-white endpapers.

Front board: Thick black rules dividing the design into three panels, with, in top panel: WINNING I HIS . SPURS (gilt) in strong 'egyptian' lettering; in central panel: illustration, based on the one on p.86, showing man on horseback escaping from a group of attackers (black, blue, yellow-green merging to orange-brown, buff); in bottom panel: G.A. HENTY (black). **Spine:** Black rules as on front board, forming panels with, in top panel: WINNING I HIS . SPURS I (centre dot) I G.A. HENTY (all gilt); in central panel: illustration of figure standing over dead man and holding flag (black, blue, yellow-green merging to orange-brown, buff); in bottom panel: SAMPSON I LOW & Co. (gilt). **Back board:** plain.

Reference: PN.

Notes

1. From about 1900 Sampson Low used this bolder and brighter binding design, with variations, for all three of their Henty novels (see *The Cornet of Horse*, 8.3, and *Jack Archer*, 14.5 and 14.6). This copy is inscribed and dated Christmas 1903.

2. Unusually for Sampson Low, this impression is on a cream laid paper, bulkier than the usual wove, and the book is nearly a quarter of an inch thicker. The plates from the original *Union Jack* typesetting are by now very worn, and the presswork is poor: in particular the make-ready of the line blocks is inadequate.

3. The imposition of the book has reverted to that used for 11.1, once again leaving the uneconomical 4-page section at the end.

4. The comma is missing after 'Clerkenwell' in the printer's imprint on p.324.

11.4

WINNING HIS SPURS | A Tale of the Crusades | BY | G.A. HENTY | AUTHOR OF "THE YOUNG BUGLERS," "THE CORNET OF HORSE," | "IN TIMES OF PERIL," ETC. | THIRTY-THIRD THOUSAND | LONDON | SAMPSON LOW, MARSTON & COMPANY | Limited | 1905
(Note: The subtitle is in gothic type).

Contents
181 x 125 mm. (i)–(viii) | (1)–324 | no catalogue. Illustrations as in 11.1.

(i) Half-title p. | (ii) printer's imprint (LONDON | PRINTED BY GILBERT AND RIVINGTON, LD. | ST. JOHN'S HOUSE, CLERKENWELL, E.C.) | (iii) title p. | (iv) blank | (v)–vii. Contents | (viii) blank | (1)–324. text, with printer's imprint at foot of p.324 (Gilbert & Rivington, Limited, St. John's House, Clerkenwell London, E.C.).

Binding: As for 11.3, except colour scheme (Dark olive-green cloth boards, blocked black, light-green merging to warm buff, yellow, blue, and gilt).

Reference: PN.

Notes
1. For some of the numerous reprints in this style, including this one, Sampson Low reverted to a poor quality wove paper, now yellowing at the edges.
2. The old *Union Jack* stereos continue to be used for the text, but the quality of the printing, especially of the line blocks, is much better than for 11.3.

11.5

WINNING HIS SPURS | A Tale of the Crusades. | BY G.A. HENTY | AUTHOR OF "THE YOUNG BUGLERS," "THE CORNET OF HORSE," | "IN TIMES OF PERIL," ETC. | THIRTY-EIGHTH THOUSAND. | LONDON | SAMPSON LOW, MARSTON & COMPANY | Limited
(Note: The subtitle is in gothic type).

Contents: 191 x 128 mm. As for 11.4, except (a) catalogue (1)–32; (b) printer's imprint on p.(ii) (PRINTED BY | REA & INCHBOULD, 224, BLACKFRIARS ROAD, | LONDON, S.E.); (c) printer's imprint at foot of p.324 (LONDON: PRINTED BY REA & INCHBOULD, 224, BLACKFRIARS ROAD, S.E.).

Binding (see Plate 51)
Brown cloth boards, blocked black, red merging to yellow, grey-blue merging to violet, and gilt; edges plain; plain off-white endpapers.

Front board: As for 11.3, except (a) changed colour-scheme; (b) additonal heavy black rules at head and foot because of larger board. **Spine:** WINNING | HIS | SPURS (gilt) above semi-abstract decoration with moon, stars, earth, flying birds (all gilt). At centre of this: . G . A . | HENTY (gilt). At foot: SAMPSON LOW & Co. (gilt). **Back board:** plain.

Reference: PN.

Notes

1. The design of the front board is that of 11.3, but in yet another colour-scheme, and that of the spine is a new style, later used more appropriately for 11.7. Both designs were used independently for other titles, but I have not seen them in this combination on other Henty titles.

2. The text is on a bulkier paper; the presswork is even worse than before. The new printer, Rea and Inchbould, took over *The Cornet of Horse* at about the same date.

3. There are no publisher's records for this title, the catalogue is undated, and there is no printer's code in this issue, so the date and size of the impression are unknown. My copy has a school-prize label dated March 1913. I have seen a similar copy, with the binding blocked in a different colour-scheme, which has THIRTY-SEVENTH THOUSAND on the title page, and a prize-label inscribed March 1912.

4. The bound-in catalogue shows two new addresses for Sampson Low, no mention being made of their earlier offices at Fetter Lane, Fleet Street. They are: Overy House, 100 Southwark Street, S.E., and Tudor House, 32 Warwick Lane, E.C.

11.6

WINNING HIS SPURS | A Tale of the Crusades | BY G.A. HENTY | Author of The Young Buglers, The Cornet of Horse, | In Times of Peril, etc. | (publisher's monogram, SLM&Co, with date MDCCCXLIV) | LONDON & EDINBURGH | SAMPSON LOW, MARSTON & COMPANY | LIMITED.
(Note: The subtitle is in gothic type).

Contents

196 x 127 mm. (1)–320 | no catalogue. Frontispiece from watercolour drawing by E.S. Farmer, reproduced by three-colour halftone blocks, printed on coated paper, unbacked, keyed to p.264, tipped in. Forty black-and-white drawings re-drawn from some originals in earlier editions, printed on text pages (see Note 1).

(1) Half-title p. | (2) blank | (frontispiece, tipped in) | (3) title p. | (4) blank | (5)–(6) Contents | (7) blank | (8) printer's imprint (PRINTED BY WALTER H. JACKSON, LTD., | 66-68, UNION STREET, LONDON, S.E.1.) | 9–320. text, with printer's imprint on p.320 (Walter H. Jackson, Ltd., Printers, 66-68 Union Street, Southwark, S.E.1.).

Binding: As for 11.5, except (a) brown cloth boards, blocked black, blue merging to grey, red merging to pink, and gilt; (b) spine blocked in grey only.

Reference: BB.

Notes

1. For this new edition the printer has been changed again, and at last the worn-out stereos have been discarded and the type reset in a more up-to-date style. The line blocks originally made by Lefman from Horace Petherick's drawings for the *Union Jack* are now also acknowledged to be worn out. An unknown artist made copies of just over half of them, which are reproduced here.

2. This is the first appearance of Edinburgh in the Sampson Low imprint.

3. There is no printer's code. This copy has an inscription dated March 1921.

11.7

WINNING HIS SPURS | A Tale of the Crusades | BY G.A. HENTY | Author of The Young Buglers, The Cornet of Horse, | In Times of Peril, etc. | NEW EDITION | LONDON | SAMPSON LOW, MARSTON & COMPANY | LIMITED
(Note: The subtitle is in gothic type).

Contents
194 x 138 mm. (1)–320 | no catalogue. Illustrations as in 11.6.
　　(1) Half-title p. | (2) blank | (frontispiece, tipped in) | (3) title p. | (4) blank | (5)–(6) Contents | (7) repeat half-title p. | (8) blank | 9–320. text, with printer's imprint at foot of p.320 (EDINBURGH　J.C. THOMPSON | AT THE MERCAT PRESS).

Binding (see Plate 50)
Royal-blue cloth boards, blocked black, light-blue, and gilt; with three-colour plate, consisting of trimmed run-on copy of frontispiece, laid down; edges plain; plain off-white endpapers.
　　Front board: WINNING | HIS | SPURS (black) at top left of semi-abstract decoration of stars, whorls, etc., all within ruled border (light-blue), also including, at foot: G.A. HENTY (black). At centre, colour plate laid down within ruled border (light-blue). **Spine:** WINNING | HIS SPURS (gilt) above semi-abstract decoration with moon, stars, earth, and flying birds (light-blue). At centre of this: G.A. HENTY (gilt). At foot: SAMPSON LOW & Co. LTD. (gilt). **Back board:** plain.

Reference: PN.

Notes
1. Once again Sampson Low placed the book with a new printer, possibly one recommended by their Edinburgh staff, but the imprint now omits the Scottish office. The text is printed from plates of the setting used for 11.6.
2. I have seen copies with prize labels dated from July 1915 to March 1929.
3. Once again there is no clue to the size of the impression.

*11.8

WINNING HIS SPURS | A TALE OF THE CRUSADES | BY | G.A. HENTY | AUTHOR OF | The Young Buglers, The Cornet of Horse, | In Times of Peril, etc. | (publisher's device) | LONDON | SAMPSON LOW, MARSTON & Co. LTD.

Contents
181 x 121 mm. (i)–(viii) | 9–320 | no catalogue. Two full-page wash-drawings by unknown artist (frontispiece signed 'M.L.P.') reproduced by halftone blocks printed black on coated paper, unbacked, tipped in, keyed to text. Line drawings in text as in 11.6.
　　(i) Half-title p. | (ii) blank | (frontispiece, tipped in) | (iii) title p. | (iv) printer's imprint (PRINTED IN GREAT BRITAIN BY PURNELL AND SONS | PAULTON, SOMERSET, ENGLAND) | v–vi. Contents | (vii) half-title p. | (viii) blank | 9–320. text.

Binding (see Plate 50)
Red cloth boards, blocked black; edges plain; plain off-white endpapers.

Front board: WINNING HIS SPURS | G.A. HENTY (black) within ruled rectangular panel beneath illustration of sailing ships in sea battle, with boats, all contained in larger ruled rectangle (black). **Spine:** WINNING | HIS SPURS (black) between two black rules, above illustration of ships in upper half of tall narrow panel, with: G.A. | HENTY (black) and four small black ornaments in lower half. At foot: SAMPSON LOW (black) between two black rules. **Back board:** plain.

Reference: PN.

Notes
1. In the 1920s 'Sampson Low's New Series' included their three Henty novels for boys, and *A Hidden Foe*, originally issued as an adult novel, all at 2s.6d. The publisher's address was 100 Southwark Street, London, S.E.1.
2. A third printer has taken over plates for the text and line illustrations used for 11.6 and 11.7.
3. The colour plate is now omitted. Two wash-drawings, reproduced by halftones on coated paper, tipped in, are by an unknown artist, 'M.L.P.', who also made two wash-drawings for *Jack Archer*, *14.9, in this series.
4. There were substantial variants of this edition, and the series was given other names over a period of years. The colour and style of binding were constant factors. All the varying issues are grouped together under this 'generic' heading, *11.8.
5. Later versions of the book, some in variant bindings of the one described here, were issued under the Sampson Low imprint in the 1930s (see Appendix II, Part 3), but are beyond the period covered by this bibliography.

12. FRIENDS, THOUGH DIVIDED

12.1
FRIENDS, THOUGH DIVIDED | A TALE OF THE CIVIL WAR | BY G.A. HENTY | AUTHOR OF 'IN TIMES OF PERIL,' 'THE YOUNG FRANC-TIREURS,' | 'CORNET OF HORSE,' 'THE YOUNG BUGLERS,' ETC. | ILLUSTRATED. | GRIFFITH & FARRAN | SUCCESSORS TO NEWBERY AND HARRIS | WEST CORNER ST. PAUL'S CHURCHYARD, LONDON | E.P. DUTTON & CO., NEW YORK | 1883

Contents
182 x 123 mm. (i)–viii | (1)–384 | catalogue (1)–(32). Eight full-page black-and-white engravings signed with monogram of R and T, unbacked, unfolioed, tipped in.
   (i) Half-title p. | (ii) blank | (frontispiece, tipped in) | (iii) title p. | (iv) printer's imprint (COLSTON AND SON, PRINTERS, EDINBURGH.): [All rights of Translation and Reproduction are reserved.] | (v)–vi. Preface | (vii)–viii. Contents | (1)–384. text; printer's imprint on p.384, as on p.(iv) | (1)–(32) catalogue, dated 5.82 (see Notes 2–4).

Binding (see Note 1)
Blue cloth boards with light diagonal grain, blocked black, blind, and gilt; edges plain; green flowered endpapers (but see Note 3).
   Front board: FRIENDS | THOUGH DIVIDED (gilt) | A TALE OF THE CIVIL

WAR | G.A. HENTY (black); illustration with panelled trophy at right and decorative border at foot (all black). **Spine:** FRIENDS | THOUGH | DIVIDED | G.A. HENTY (gilt); illustration (black and gilt); ILLUSTRATED (gilt); decorative border (black); GRIFFITH & FARRAN (gilt); decorative border (black). **Back board:** publisher's monogram as central medallion (blind).

References: BL; Bod; PN | *Farmer*, p.31; *Dartt*, p.61, *Companion*, p.15.

Notes
1. The earliest issues of the first edition have plain edges to the leaves, and boards without bevels. Later issues (see 12.2, Plate 32, and 12.3) have all edges gilt and bevelled boards. The price remained at 5s. for all issues.
2. The earliest bound-in catalogue is dated May 1882 (Catalogue B). That is three months earlier than the date in the printer's code on p.(iv), which indicates an edition of 3000 copies, 22 August. As with many Griffith & Farran books the title-page date is that of the year following actual publication, 1882.
3. Catalogues dated '9.83' (Catalogue A) are also found in copies of 12.1, so the change of binding style (to 12.2) cannot have happened very quickly. Copies of 12.1 that I have seen with Catalogue A have yellow surface-paper endpapers. The September 1883 catalogue is also found in later issues (see 12.2, Note 1).
4. Catalogue A was headed 'Books for the Young', while Catalogue B, not really intended for boys' books, was of 'General Literature, Devotional and Religious Books, and Educational Books and Appliances'. (The 'appliances' were items of equipment for needlework).
5. Griffith & Farran presumably contracted to publish the book while they still owned the *Union Jack*. Sampson Low took over the magazine in July 1881, but had no claim on this story as it had never been serialised.
6. The comma is omitted after FRIENDS on both front board and spine of the binding case. This variation was common in the publisher's literature, and more frequent in later years.
7. The illustration facing p.118 is keyed to that page, although the reference should be to p.106 (see 12.2, Note 3).

12.2
Title page: As for 12.1.

Contents: As for 12.1, except bound-in catalogue (see Note 1).

Binding: (See Plate 32). As for 12.1, except: Red cloth boards with light diagonal grain, bevelled, blocked black, blind, and gilt; all edges gilt; yellow surface-paper endpapers.

References: PN | *Farmer*, p.32; *Dartt*, p.62.

Notes
1. This issue, from the same impression as 12.1, is found with publisher's catalogues dated 1883 (Catalogue A) or 1884 (Catalogue B). See 12.1, Notes 3–4.
2. The imprint on the spine of the binding case is the same as on 12.1.
3. The illustration keyed incorrectly to p.118 is now tipped in to face its proper reference on p.106 (see 12.1, Note 7).

12.3

Title page: As for 12.1.

Contents: As for 12.1, except bound-in catalogue (see Note 1).

Binding: As for 12.1, except (a) bevelled boards; (b) all edges gilt; (c) yellow surface-paper endpapers; (c) imprint at foot of spine (GRIFFITH FARRAN & Co.).

Reference: PN.

Notes

1. The catalogues found in this binding style are dated 1885, 1886 or 1888.

2. 12.1, 12.2, and 12.3 are all from the first printing of 3000 copies in August 1882. The book was clearly not a fast seller. It is now generally agreed that *Friends, though Divided* does not represent Henty's writing at its best.

3. Certainly by 1888, possibly earlier, the book was included in the series 'Tales of Travel and Adventure', not to be confused with 'Tales of Adventure', which appeared in the 1890s (see Appendix V). No change in format was involved: books in the series had bevelled boards and all edges gilt. The price was still 5s.

4. A contemporary catalogue lists *Friends, though Divided* in another series, c.1891, 'The Crown Library'. *The Young Buglers* was in the same list, and is identified as 7.3, but I have found no copy of *Friends, though Divided* bound in similar format.

5. See 12.2, Note 3: the correction is also made in this issue.

12.4

Title page: As for 12.1, except (a) full point deleted after ILLUSTRATED; (b) changed imprint (LONDON I GRIFFITH FARRAN & CO I NEWBERY HOUSE, CHARING CROSS ROAD).

Contents

189 x 130 mm. (i)–viii I (1)–(386) (see Note 3) I no catalogue. Illustrations as in 12.1.

(i) Blank I (ii) frontispiece I (iii) title p. I (iv) [The Rights of Translation and of Reproduction are reserved.] I (v)–vi. Preface I (vii)–viii. Contents I (1)–384. text I (385)–(386) blank.

Binding (see Note 1)

Maroon cloth boards, blocked black, white, yellow merging through orange to grey-blue, and gilt; all edges gilt; dark-blue surface-paper endpapers.

Front board: FRIENDS I THOUGH I DIVIDED I G.A I HENTY. (all gilt) within panel outlined as a shield (gilt) over decorative illustration of flag and sporting equipment (black, white, and yellow merging through orange to grey-blue). Three rules (black) frame this decoration. **Spine:** Three rules at head (gilt); FRIENDS I THOUGH I DIVIDED (gilt) between ornamental rules (gilt) forming panel above trophy of bow and arrow, sword and bugle (black, white, yellow merging to orange). G.A. HENTY (gilt) between ornamental rules and decorations (gilt). At foot: GRIFFITH FARRAN I BROWNE & CO. (gilt) between ornamental rules (gilt). **Back board:** plain.

Reference: PN.

Notes

1. A handsome and elegant book, on heavy-quality, smooth paper, in heavy boards, bevelled, and blocked in an elaborate and colourful style. It is part of a series, 'Tales of Adventure', which also included *The Young Buglers*, 7.5, Plate 44.

2. 'Tales of Adventure', should not be confused with the earlier series, 'Tales of Travel and Adventure', issued in the 1880s (see Appendix V).

3. As in *The Young Buglers*, the illustrations are now more economically printed on text pages. They are closer to their text references, and no longer incorrectly keyed. In particular, the plate now properly keyed to face p.106 (see 12.1, Note 7 and 12.2, Note 3) is now used as frontispiece. The illustration-leaves are unbacked, unfolioed, and not counted in the pagination, except for the frontispiece – which accounts for the apparently strange make-up of the book. In fact, the text pages, following the eight pages of prelims, number 400. Taken all together they thus make an even working, although 14 pages are unfolioed (accounting for the seven illustrations other than the frontispiece) and the last two are blank.

4. The original printer has lost the contract for this book, as happened with *The Young Buglers* when it became part of the series. In this case there is no proper imprint for the new printer: his name is given only in the printer's code on p.(iv) as 'D. & Co.'. The text is printed from stereos of the original typesetting.

5. The printer's code records 1000 copies, dated March 1894. The selling price was 5s. The short print-run confirms that the book was still selling slowly.

12.5

FRIENDS | THOUGH DIVIDED | A TALE OF THE CIVIL WAR | BY | G.A. HENTY | AUTHOR OF | 'IN TIMES OF PERIL' 'THE YOUNG FRANC-TIREURS' | 'THE YOUNG BUGLERS' | ETC. ETC. | ILLUSTRATED | GRIFFITH FARRAN BROWNE & CO. LTD | 35 BOW STREET, COVENT GARDEN | LONDON

Contents

188 x 133 mm. (i)–viii | (1)–(386) | no catalogue. Illustrations as in 12.4 (see Note 3 below).

(i) Blank | (ii) frontispiece | (iii) title p. | (iv) [The Rights of Translation and Reproduction are Reserved.] | (v)–vi. Preface | (vii)–viii. Contents | (1)–384. text, with printer's imprint at foot of p.384 (PRINTED BY MORRISON AND GIBB LIMITED, EDINBURGH) | (385)–(386) blank.

Binding (see Plate 34)

Blue, vertically-ribbed cloth boards, blocked gilt; top edge gilt; plain off-white laid endpapers.

Front board: FRIENDS (decoration of formal roses and leaves) | THOUGH (single rose) | DIVIDED (all gilt) above illustration, with arms and trophy, etc.; G.A. HENTY (all gilt), all placed high and to the left. **Spine:** FRIENDS | THOUGH | DIVIDED (gilt) within shield forming part of gilt decoration. G.A. HENTY (gilt) towards the foot of it, and, below: GRIFFITH, FARRAN | BROWNE & CO. (gilt). **Back board:** plain.

Reference: PN.

Notes

1. One of a set in similar format of Griffith & Farran's five Henty novels. Copies examined show that all were printed at least twice, in impressions of 2000, between 1895 and 1899. The other titles are: *Out on the Pampas*, 4.7; *The Young Franc-Tireurs*, 5.10; *The Young Buglers*, 7.6; and *In Times of Peril*, 9.5.

2. The type was newly set for the other four titles, which were also given new illustrations from wash-drawings. They were, therefore, truly new editions, whereas *Friends, though Divided* had been reprinted less frequently, and the type was still in good condition. The pictures, also, are of better quality than some from this publisher: there probably seemed little point in commissioning new ones.

3. Although the illustration leaves are not folioed, and not counted in the pagination, folio numbers are now added beneath the captions. These duplicate folios are confusing, and in any case incorrect if intended as keys to text references.

12.6

Title page: As for 12.5, but with the word ILLUSTRATED omitted.

Contents

192 x 138 mm. (i)–viii | (1)–384 | no catalogue. Frontispiece from line-and-wash drawing by an unknown hand, based on the frontispiece in previous impressions, reproduced by halftone block printed in dark-green ink on coated paper, unbacked, keyed to book, tipped in.

(i) Half-title p. | (ii) blank | (frontispiece, tipped in) | (iii) title p. | (iv) [The Rights of Translation and of Reproduction are Reserved] | (v)–vi. Preface | (vii)–viii. Contents | (1)-384. text, with printer's imprint at foot of p.384 (PRINTED BY MORRISON AND GIBB LIMITED, EDINBURGH).

Binding (see Plate 27)

Red, vertically-ribbed cloth boards, blocked black and gilt; all edges gilt; plain off-white endpapers.

Front board: Two panels of art-nouveau designs of leaves and flowers, enclosed in a series of rules (all black). Between these panels: FRIENDS | THOUGH DIVIDED (black). **Spine:** Three rules across head (black) above: Friends | Though | Divided (gilt) within decorative art-nouveau border (gilt), and all above: Henty (black) and panel of art-nouveau design of leaves and flowers (black). At foot: GRIFFITH, FARRAN | BROWNE & CO. (gilt) above three rules (black). **Back board:** plain.

Reference: PN.

Notes

1. The binding case is a 'binder's blank' (see Glossary). A very similar design was used for *The Curse of Carne's Hold* (see 40.10, also at Plate 27). Its size, heavily-ribbed cloth, and (crude) gilt edges were meant to give the volume a 'de-luxe' appearance when new, but it is in fact a cheaply produced book in every way.

2. For the frontispiece a heavy-handed wash-drawing has been made over a print of the original line illustration, much of the original drawing, including the signature, remaining visible. The conversion was probably undertaken for the publisher by a blockmaker. All other illustrations are omitted, and the text has been re-imposed, with a blank leaf at the end as in 12.1.

12.7

FRIENDS | THOUGH DIVIDED | A TALE OF THE CIVIL WAR | BY | G.A. HENTY | AUTHOR OF | 'THE YOUNG FRANC-TIREURS' 'THE YOUNG BUGLERS' | ETC. ETC. | NEW EDITION | ILLUSTRATED IN COLOUR BY A.P.COLE | LONDON | HENRY FROWDE | HODDER AND STOUGHTON | 1910

Contents

188 x 129 mm. (i)–viii | (1)–384 | catalogue (1)–16. Six full-page watercolour drawings by A.P. Cole, reproduced by three-colour halftone blocks printed on coated paper, unbacked, unfolioed, tipped in.

(i) Half-title p. | (ii) blank | (frontispiece, tipped in) | (iii) title p. | (iv) blank | (v)–vi. Preface | (vii)–viii. Contents | (1)–384. text; printer's imprint on p.384 (Richard Clay & Sons, Limited, London and Bungay.) | (1)–16. catalogue.

Binding (see Plate 36)

Green cloth boards, blocked black, white, red, brown, buff, light-blue, and gilt; all edges stained grey-green; plain off-white endpapers.

Front board: FRIENDS THOUGH | DIVIDED | G.A. | HENTY (all gilt, shaded black) on sky (light-blue and white) of illustration of cavalier on horseback (black, white, red, brown, buff); the whole within black ruled border. **Spine:** FRIENDS | THOUGH | DIVIDED | G.A. HENTY (gilt) above illustration of figures in boat on river (black, white, red, brown, light-blue) in black ruled frame, above: HENRY FROWDE | HODDER & STOUGHTON (gilt). **Back board:** plain.

References: BL; Bod; PN.

Notes

1. The stock and goodwill of Griffith & Farran, including *Friends, though Divided* and their other novels by Henty, were bought by Hodder & Stoughton in 1906. They re-issued the books, in conjunction with the Oxford University Press, in what was known as the 'Joint Venture' (see Appendix II, Part 2).

2. These new editions (except *In Times of Peril*, 1911) appeared in 1910 with dated title pages. In the old Blackie style, later impressions omitted the date; various cloth-colours were used for each title, blocked in numerous pigments and gilt.

3. Apart from the preliminary pages this title is still printed from stereos of the type set for the first 1883 edition.

12.8

FRIENDS | THOUGH | DIVIDED | G . A | HENTY | LONDON | HENRY . FROWDE | HODDER & | STOUGHTON

(Note: All lettering is hand-drawn within elaborate decorative framework).

Contents

188 x 121 mm. (i)–viii | (1)–384 | catalogue (1)–(4). Frontispiece from watercolour drawing by A.P.Cole, reproduced by three-colour halftone blocks printed on coated paper, unbacked, tipped in.

(i) Half-title p. | (ii) advertisement for 'The Boy's New Library' | (frontispiece, tipped in) | (iii) title p. | (iv) printer's imprint (PRINTED IN GREAT BRITAIN BY R. CLAY AND SONS, LTD., | BRUNSWICK STREET, STAMFORD STREET,

S.E., AND BUNGAY, SUFFOLK.) I (v)–vi. Preface I (vii)–viii. Contents I (1)–384. text I (1)-(4) catalogue.

Binding (see Note 1)
Red cloth boards, blind embossed, and blocked gilt; edges plain; olive-green endpapers printed in darker green with bled-off illustration of nautical scene.
    Front board: Step-and-repeat design of lions passants within ruled border; over this a ribboned seal showing representation of St George slaying the dragon (all blind-embossed). **Spine:** Blind-embossed art-nouveau design of flower, and rules, with three sunken panels, showing title, author, and publisher: FRIENDS I THOUGH I DIVIDED (gilt); G . A I HENTY (gilt); and: HENRY FROWDE I HODDER & I STOUGHTON (blind). **Back board:** All-over step-and-repeat design of lions passants within ruled border (all blind-embossed).

Reference: PN.

Notes
1. This design, for 'The Boy's New Library', was used by the Joint Venture, as above, and later by the Oxford University Press (see 12.10, Plate 42). My copy has a school-prize label inscribed and dated 'Advent 1915'.
2. The frontispiece is from a three-colour set used in 12.7.
3. The advertisement on p.(ii) lists 15 titles in 'The Boy's New Library', including three by Henty: *Friends, though Divided, The Young Franc-Tireurs,* and *In Times of Peril.* (The position of the apostrophe in the series title varies, throughout the publisher's literature).

12.9
FRIENDS I THOUGH DIVIDED I A TALE OF THE CIVIL WAR I BY I G.A. HENTY I NEW EDITION I ILLUSTRATED IN COLOUR BY A.P. COLE I HUMPHREY MILFORD I OXFORD UNIVERSITY PRESS I LONDON, EDINBURGH, GLASGOW I TORONTO, MELBOURNE, CAPE TOWN, BOMBAY

Contents
185 x 122 mm. (i)–viii I (1)–384 I catalogue (1)–32, not always present. Six full-page watercolour drawings by A.P. Cole, reproduced by three-colour halftone blocks printed on coated paper, unbacked, unfolioed, tipped in.
    (i) Half-title p. I (ii) publisher's advertisement (STORIES OF ADVENTURE I BY G.A. HENTY) I (frontispiece, tipped in) I (iii) title p. I (iv) printer's imprint (REPRINTED 1923 IN GREAT BRITAIN BY R. CLAY AND SONS, LTD., I BUNGAY, SUFFOLK.) I (v)-vi. Preface I (vii)-viii. Contents I (1)-384. text.

Binding (see Note 2)
Blue grained-cloth boards, blocked black, with oval illustration, printed by three-colour halftone blocks on coated paper, laid down; edges plain; plain off-white endpapers.
    Front board: FRIENDS THOUGH I DIVIDED I G.A. HENTY (all cloth-colour out of black) in rectangular solid-black decorative panel above oval, outlined with heavy black line and decorative art-nouveau scroll design. Within the oval is laid down a cut-out colour plate. **Spine:** FRIENDS I THOUGH I DIVIDED I

G.A. HENTY (cloth-colour out of black) in solid rectangular panel, above decorative art-nouveau scrolls. At foot: OXFORD (cloth-colour out of black) in solid rectangular panel. **Back board:** plain.

Reference: PN.

Notes

1. Apart from the preliminary pages this is a reprint of 12.7, now issued under the O.U.P. imprint. Later issues were bound in paper boards, grained to imitate cloth.

2. Reprints in this style, which was also used for *Out on the Pampas*, 4.14, Plate 37, were usually dated in the printer's imprint, and issued simultaneously with the cheaper edition in 'The Boy's New Library', 12.8.

3. The publisher's advertisement on p.(ii) lists *Out on the Pampas, Friends though Divided, In Times of Peril, The Young Franc-Tireurs*, and *The Young Buglers*.

12.10

FRIENDS | THOUGH | DIVIDED | G . A | HENTY | HUMPHREY . MILFORD | OXFORD . UNIVERSITY | . PRESS . | LONDON
(Note: All lettering is hand-drawn within elaborate decorative framework).

Contents: 186 x 123 mm. Text and illustrations as for 12.8, except (a) no catalogue; (b) printer's imprint on p.(iv) (REPRINTED 1917 IN GREAT BRITAIN BY R. CLAY AND SONS, LTD., | BRUNSWICK STREET, STAMFORD STREET, S.E., AND BUNGAY, SUFFOLK.).

Binding: (see Plate 42). As for 12.8, except (a) green cloth boards; (b) plain off-white endpapers; (c) publisher's imprint on spine (MILFORD (gilt)).

Reference: PN.

Notes

1. The stereos are still from the type set for 12.1, apart from the prelims. This impression is dated 1917 in the printer's imprint on p.(iv).

2. Some copies have the word OXFORD in gilt at the foot of the spine, instead of MILFORD. Reprints show variations in the printer's imprint on p.(iv), for example: (REPRINTED 1921 IN GREAT BRITAIN BY R. CLAY AND SONS, LTD., | BUNGAY SUFFOLK.) Other dates in the 1920s are found; text paper varies considerably, and endpapers were often printed in brown or green ink (see 12.8 above).

3. The binding case for the 1921 reprint is made of smoother cloth, and is blocked with real gold in place of the poor-quality imitation used for earlier issues.

4. The frontispiece in all copies I have seen, with both the Joint Venture imprint and the Oxford University Press imprint, is the illustration from 12.7 captioned 'In a moment a dozen sturdy hands seized him by the collar'.

5. The apostrophe in the series title varies, both 'Boy's' and 'Boys'' being used.

13. UNDER DRAKE'S FLAG

13.1

UNDER DRAKE'S FLAG: | A | TALE OF THE SPANISH MAIN. | BY | G.A. HENTY, | SPECIAL CORRESPONDENT OF THE "STANDARD;" | AUTHOR OF "THE MARCH TO MAGDALA;" "THE YOUNG BUGLERS;" "THE CORNET | OF HORSE;" "IN TIMES OF PERIL;" "FACING DEATH," ETC. | ILLUSTRATED | (publisher's device) | LONDON: | BLACKIE & SON, 49 & 50 OLD BAILEY, E.C.; | GLASGOW, EDINBURGH, AND DUBLIN. | 1883. *(Note: Comma in place of semi-colon after* FACING DEATH*).*

Contents

183 x 130 mm. (1)–368 | catalogue (1)–32. Twelve full-page line-and-wash drawings by Gordon Browne, reproduced in two-colour line by the French engraver Lefman, printed in black and sepia on uncoated paper, unbacked, unfolioed, keyed to text, tipped in.

(1) Half-title p. | (2) blank | (frontispiece, tipped in) | (3) title p. | (4) blank | (5) Contents | (6) blank | (7) List of Illustrations | (8) blank | (9)–368. text | (1)–32. catalogue.

Binding (see Plate 86)

Red, stipple-grained cloth boards, bevelled, blocked black, dark green, blind, and gilt; edges plain; dark-brown surface-paper endpapers. (See Notes 2 and 3 below).
   Front board: UNDER (gilt, shaded black) | (black and gilt ornaments formed of groups of 5 dots) | DRAKE'S FLAG (gilt, shaded black) | . BY . | G.A. HENTY (gilt) above illustration (black, dark green, and gilt). The whole design within double rules (black). **Spine:** UNDER | DRAKE'S | FLAG (red cloth-colour out of gilt decorative scrolled panel) | BY G.A. HENTY (gilt on continuation of scroll), all superimposed on illustration (black and gilt) between black and gilt rules. **Back board:** Three rules at edges of board (blind).

References: BL; Bod; PN | *Farmer*, p.75; *Dartt*, p.144, *Companion*, p.33.

Notes

1. Published on 31 August 1882: Henty's first novel in Blackie's six-shilling series.
2. Early issues were bound in cloth with a pronounced stipple-grain, my copies being red, and brown. An extra-heavy impression of the brasses seems to have been needed on its surface, especially for the black pigment. The effect was not pleasing, and Blackie soon changed to a much less pronounced, diagonal, straight-line grain. This was used in other colours, my copy being grass-green. On this subject see also *Facing Death*, 10.4, Note 10.
3. *Farmer* mistakenly calls for burnished olivine edges. They were not introduced by Blackie until the autumn of 1883. *Dartt* follows the error, and in his *Companion* even reports gilt edges, confusing, as often, Blackie editions with Scribner's.
4. Catalogues slightly later than those in the first issue may be distinguished as follows: (a) On p.2, the full-point after the last word on the page has dropped out of the forme. (b) On p.3, there is a signature mark (A²), not present in the earliest catalogues. (c) On p.14, the early catalogues announce a book, '*Patriot Martyr. Being the Life and Times of Jeanne d'Arc, commonly called the Maid of Orleans*',

which was emended in later catalogues to the title under which it was ultimately published: '*Jeanne d'Arc, the Patriot Martyr:* And other Narratives of Female Heroism in Peace and War'.

5. From August 1882 to the end of February 1883 Blackie sold 2094 copies; over the next sixteen years sales remained fairly steady, at an average of 798 copies each year. When the cheap edition was issued at the end of 1909 (see 13.4 below) Blackie had sold a total of 19,437 copies at 6s., and the remaining 140 copies were sold off over the next four years.

*13.2

UNDER DRAKE'S FLAG: I A I TALE OF THE SPANISH MAIN. I BY I G.A. HENTY I Author of "True to the Old Flag," "St. George for England," "In Freedom's Cause,' I "With Clive in India," "By Sheer Pluck," "Facing Death," &c. &c. I WITH TWELVE FULL-PAGE ILLUSTRATIONS I BY GORDON BROWNE. I (publisher's device) I LONDON: I BLACKIE & SON, 49 & 50 OLD BAILEY, E.C.; I GLASGOW, EDINBURGH, AND DUBLIN.
(Note: One of the two quotation marks has fallen out after In Freedom's Cause*).*

Contents
185 x 130 mm. (1)–368 I catalogue (1)–48. Illustrations as in 13.1, except that the plates are no longer keyed to text pages.

(1) Half-title p. (2) advertisement (BOOKS BY G.A. HENTY) listing seven titles I (frontispiece, tipped in) I (3) title p. I (4) blank I (5) Contents I (6) blank I (7) List of Illustrations I (8) blank I (9)–368. text I (1)–48. catalogue.

Binding: (See Plate 86). As for 13.1, except (a) colour scheme (blue, ungrained cloth boards, bevelled, blocked black, maroon, blind, and gilt); (b) all edges burnished yellowish olive-green; (c) a totally different effect from much smoother cloth-texture.

Reference: PN.

Notes
1. Reprints of the first edition followed Blackie's usual pattern. The date was dropped from the title page; alterations were made to title-page imprint and address as necessary. Blackie became a Limited Company in 1890; the Edinburgh address was not used after 1894; and the Indian office was opened in 1901 although Bombay did not appear regularly in the imprint until 1906. The list of books after Henty's name on the title page was changed to include more recent titles, and, before long, only those published by Blackie. The illustrations were modified, the second-colour tint either transferred to the black plate or omitted (see Appendix IV, Part 1).
2. Bindings showed variations in colour of cloth, blocking, and endpapers. From 1883 some issues were given 'olivine edges' (see Appendix II, Part 5, Note 73).
3. The catalogue is undated, as usual with Blackie, but is headed 'The New Season's Books' and lists Henty titles issued with 1887 title-page dates. These titles are described without quotations from press notices, and it is therefore reasonable to assume that the catalogue was printed in 1886.
4. The slightly-varying issues of this title in its first-edition format are all grouped together under this 'generic' heading, *13.2.

13.3

UNDER DRAKE'S FLAG | A | TALE OF THE SPANISH MAIN | BY | G.A. HENTY | Author of "True to the Old Flag" "St. George for England" "In Freedom's Cause" | "With Clive in India" "By Sheer Pluck" "Facing Death" &c. | WITH TWELVE FULL-PAGE ILLUSTRATIONS BY GORDON BROWNE | LONDON | BLACKIE & SON, LIMITED, 50 OLD BAILEY, E.C. | GLASGOW AND DUBLIN

Contents

184 x 130 mm. (1)–368 | catalogue 1–16. Twelve full-page illustrations from line drawings by Gordon Browne, reproduced by line blocks in black only, omitting the wash reproduced in earlier impressions by second-colour (sepia) plates, unbacked, unfolioed, tipped in.

(1) Half-title p. | (2) advertisement (MR. HENTY'S HISTORICAL TALES.) listing 35 titles | (frontispiece, tipped in) | (3) title p. | (4) blank | 5. Contents | (6) blank | 7. List of Illustrations | (8) blank | 9–368. text | 1–16. catalogue.

Binding (see Plate 86)

Designed by Ralph Peacock (see Note 2). Dark-green cloth boards, bevelled, blocked black, red, yellow, and gilt; all edges burnished olive-green; plain grey endpapers, lined off-white.

Front board: UNDER | DRAKE'S | FLAG (gilt, shaded black) at lower right corner of illustration (black, red, yellow, and gilt) and with: BY G.A. HENTY (gilt) centred beneath. Art-nouveau design of leaves and flowers (black and red) at head and foot of board. Illustration signed at lower right corner with initials: R.P. (black). **Spine:** UNDER | DRAKE'S | FLAG (gilt) superimposed on art-nouveau design (black) above illustration (black, red, yellow, and gilt). At foot: G.A. HENTY (gilt) above art-nouveau design (black and red).

References: PN | *Dartt*, p.144 (Note); Blackie, Agnes A.C.: *Blackie & Son, 1809–1959*, p.38.

Notes

1. This binding design is illustrated in Agnes Blackie's short history of the firm, with the caption: 'A First Edition Henty'. This is strictly true, in bibliographical terms, as the type has not been reset. But for many Henty collectors, who tend to regard only first impressions as first editions, and for *Dartt* (p.144), it has been confusing.

2. The design is by Ralph Peacock, and is signed with his initials. He was later commissioned by Talwin Morris, head of Blackie's art department, to design cases for several more novels by Henty. This design first appeared in 1895, or possibly late 1894, and may have been a trial of Peacock's aptitude for such work, before he embarked on a new title. If so, it clearly succeeded, as the later designs show. The cloth-colour chosen for each of Peacock's case designs was rarely changed, but for this book he seems to have agreed to two alternatives, dark blue and dark green. Notes on Peacock and Morris are in Appendix IV, Part 2.

3. Contrary to my opinion given in *A.B.M.R.* (March 1977, p.91) about the co-existence of two binding designs, I now believe that the old design for 13.1, 13.2 and 13.3, was abandoned when this one was introduced. As in all Blackie reprints, variations occur from one to another in details of prelims and advertisements, etc.

13.4

Under Drake's Flag | A Tale of the Spanish Main | BY | G.A. HENTY | Author of "True to the Old Flag" "St. George for England" "In Freedom's Cause" | "With Clive in India" "With Buller in Natal" &c. | ILLUSTRATED BY GORDON BROWNE | NEW EDITION | BLACKIE AND SON LIMITED | LONDON GLASGOW DUBLIN BOMBAY | 1910

Contents

186 x 126 mm. (1)–368 | catalogue 1–32. Eight wash-drawings attributed to Gordon Browne (see Note 3), reproduced by halftone blocks printed in sepia on coated paper, unbacked, unfolioed, tipped in.

(1) Half-title p. | (2) advertisement (NEW AND POPULAR EDITION OF | G.A. HENTY'S WORKS) listing 27 titles | (frontispiece, tipped in) | (3) title p. | (4) blank | 5. Contents | (6) blank | 7. List of Illustrations | (8) blank | 9–368. text | 1–32. catalogue.

Binding (see Plate 173)

Red cloth boards, blocked black, orange, buff, and gilt; all edges stained olive-green; plain grey endpapers, lined off-white.

Front board: UNDER DRAKE'S | FLAG | G.A. HENTY (gilt) above illustration, framed by black line, of soldier standing over bodies of two others (black, orange and buff). **Spine:** UNDER | DRAKE'S | FLAG | G.A. HENTY (gilt) over illustration of young soldier with sword (black, orange, and buff). At foot: BLACKIE AND SON LTD (black). **Back board:** plain.

References: BL; Bod; PN.

Notes

1. Late in 1909 (title-page date 1910) Blackie re-issued *Under Drake's Flag* in their cheaper 'New and Popular Edition'. For notes on the series see *Facing Death*, 10.6, Notes 2 and 3.

2. In this edition Blackie sold 3825 copies in 1910, over 1000 copies in each of the following five years, and a total of 10,216 copies by the end of August 1917. No figures are available after that date.

3. The eight wash-drawings are copies of original line illustrations in 13.1, and are attributed on the title page to Gordon Browne. I believe the copies were not made by him. Four of them re-appear in *13.7, with a new frontispiece, and are no longer attributed. Similar copying of Browne's line drawings was done for late editions of other titles, and none of those is credited to him.

13.5

THE TALISMAN LIBRARY (underlined) | UNDER | DRAKE'S FLAG | BY | G.A. HENTY | (publisher's device) | BLACKIE AND SON LIMITED | 50 OLD BAILEY LONDON | GLASGOW AND BOMBAY | 1920

Contents

171 x 113 mm. (i)–xii | 1–164 | no catalogue. Frontispiece from wash-drawing by unknown artist, based on an original line-drawing by Gordon Browne, reproduced by halftone block printed in black on coated paper, unbacked, tipped in.

(i) Half-title p. | (ii) unheaded introduction to the Talisman Library | (frontispiece, tipped in) | (iii) title p. | (iv) list of titles in series, and printer's imprint (Printed in Great Britain by | Blackie & Son, Limited, Glasgow) | v–xii. Introduction | 1–155. text | (156) blank | 157–164. Notes.

Binding (see Note 3)
Grey cloth boards, blocked blue (see Note 3); edges plain; plain off-white endpapers.
  Front board: UNDER | DRAKE'S . FLAG | G.A. Henty | (publisher's trade mark for the series, including the wording: The | TALISMAN | Library of | ENGLISH | AUTHORS) | Blackie.&.Son.Limited (all blue) within frame of decorative rules (blue). **Spine:** UNDER . DRAKE'S . FLAG : HENTY (blue) running from foot to head. **Back board:** plain.

References: BL; Bod; BB.

Notes
1. In 1920 four of Henty's novels for boys were abridged for use in schools and included in Blackie's 'The Talisman Library of English Authors'. (That full title ignores the fact that the first two books were by Sir Walter Scott!) Thereafter two by Charles Kingsley were followed by the four by Henty. The other titles by Henty are: *With Clive in India; With Wolfe in Canada;* and *Redskin and Cowboy.* Two more were added, in 1921 and 1922 (see 13.6, Note 2).
2. The frontispiece is a wash-drawing copied from a line illustration used in 13.1.
3. Books in the series (example at Plate 145) were also issued in limp cloth covers, cut flush, in the same design, and with no alteration to the contents.
4. Later impressions in both styles of binding were issued with undated title pages.

13.6
THE TALISMAN LIBRARY (underlined) | UNDER | DRAKE'S FLAG | BY | G.A. HENTY | (publisher's device) | BLACKIE & SON LIMITED | LONDON AND GLASGOW

Contents
173 x 114 mm. (i)–xii | 1–164 | no catalogue. Frontispiece as in 13.5.
  (i)–(ii) Introduction to the series with bold heading on p.(i): 'The Talisman Library of English Authors', and the titles in the series listed on p.(ii) | (frontispiece, tipped in) | (iii) title p. | (iv) Blackie addresses, and printer's imprint at foot (Printed in Great Britain by Blackie & Son, Ltd., Glasgow) | v–xii. Introduction | 1–155. text | (156) blank | 157–164. Notes.

Binding: As for 13.5.

Reference: BB.

Notes
1. Following the dated and undated issues of 13.5 (see 13.5, Note 4), the prelims were reset. Apart from the title-page imprint, changes were made to the introductory notes and list of titles in the series. Otherwise the text appears to be unaltered.
2. Two more of Henty's books were added to the series: *The Dragon and the Raven* in 1921, and *Beric the Briton* in 1922. There seems to have been only one later title: *Gulliver's Travels* by Dean Swift.
3. The series continued in production, both in limp cloth and in cloth boards, at least

for two decades. Copies of some titles are found with the Book Production War Economy symbol on p.(iv), a measure required of British publishers during the second war (see *With Wolfe in Canada*, 27.4, Note 3).

*13.7

Under Drake's Flag I A Tale of the Spanish Main I BY I G.A. HENTY I Author of "True to the Old Flag" "St. George for England" "In Freedom's I Cause" "With Clive in India" "With Buller in Natal" &c. I ILLUSTRATED I BLACKIE & SON LIMITED I LONDON AND GLASGOW

Contents
186 x 125 mm. (1)–368 I advertisement (1)–(2). Frontispiece from watercolour drawing by Arch. Webb, printed by three-colour halftone blocks; four full-page wash-drawings based on pen-drawings by Gordon Browne (see Note 2), printed by halftone blocks in black; all on coated paper, unbacked, unfolioed, tipped in.

(1) Half-title p. I (2) Blackie addresses I (frontispiece, tipped in) I (3) title p. I (4) publisher's imprint (Printed in Great Britain by I Blackie & Son, Limited, Glasgow) I (5) Contents I (6) blank I (7) list of Illustrations I (8) blank I 9-368. text I (1)-(2) advertisement (THE NEW POPULAR HENTY) listing 64 titles.

Binding
Blue cloth boards, blocked black, red, buff; edges plain; plain off-white endpapers.
    Front board: UNDER DRAKE'S I FLAG I G.A. HENTY (buff), above illustration, framed by black line, of soldier standing over bodies of two others (black, red, and buff). **Spine:** UNDER I DRAKE'S I FLAG I G.A. HENTY (buff), above illustration of young soldier with sword (black, red, and buff). At foot: BLACKIE & SON LTD (black). **Back board:** plain.

Reference: PN.

Notes
1. For notes on Blackie's second cheaper series, 'The New Popular Henty', see *Facing Death*, 10.7, Notes 1–3; and examples of binding style at Plates 174–175.
2. The black-and-white plates are four of the eight wash-drawings credited to Gordon Browne in *13.4, although they are not credited to him in *13.7 (see 13.4, Note 4).
3. All the minor variants of *Under Drake's Flag* in the series are grouped together under this 'generic' heading, *13.7.

14. JACK ARCHER

14.1
JACK ARCHER I A Tale of the Crimea I BY G.A. HENTY I AUTHOR OF "WINNING HIS SPURS," "CORNET OF HORSE," "FACING DEATH," I ETC., ETC. I WITH ILLUSTRATIONS I London I SAMPSON LOW, MARSTON, SEARLE, & RIVINGTON I CROWN BUILDINGS, 188, FLEET STREET I 1883 I [All rights reserved]
(Note: The subtitle and London *are in gothic type).*

Contents

181 x 123 mm. (i)–(viii) | (1)–(304) | catalogue (1)–32. Sixteen full-page black-and-white illustrations, including wood-engravings and pen-drawings after several artists: two of them are signed J.J. (? John Jellicoe), and that facing p.3 unsigned but credited in the *Union Jack* to Gordon Browne (see Note 4); all are printed in black line on MF wove paper, unbacked, unfolioed, and tipped in. Five black-and-white fold-out engravings of battle-plans.

(Frontispiece, tipped in) | (i) title p. | (ii) printer's imprint (LONDON: | GILBERT AND RIVINGTON, LIMITED | ST. JOHN'S SQUARE.) | (iii)-vi. Contents | (vii)–viii. List of Illustrations | (1)–302. text | (303) printer's imprint (LONDON: GILBERT AND RIVINGTON, LIMITED, | ST. JOHN'S SQUARE.) | (304) blank | (1)–32. catalogue, dated September 1883.

Binding (see Plate 47)

Red cloth boards with light diagonal graining, blocked black, white, blind, and gilt; all edges gilt; grey flowered endpapers.

Front board: JACK | ARCHER (gilt, cased in black) on decorative scrollwork; A TALE | OF THE CRIMEA | BY | G.A. HENTY. (black), all above illustration (black and white). **Spine:** Emblem, with flags, medal, and wreath (black and gilt) above: JACK | ARCHER | (rule) | G.A. HENTY (gilt); band across spine (black); ILLUSTRATED (black) lettered on curve; illustration of two young soldiers (black). At foot: SAMPSON LOW & Co (gilt) between two black bands. **Back board:** double rules at edges of board, with publisher's monogram as central medallion (all blind).

References: BL; Bod; PN | *Farmer*, p.45; *Dartt*, p.87.

Notes

1. The story was serialised in the *Union Jack* in 25 weekly instalments, beginning in Vol.IV (New Series, Vol.I), No.27, 3 April 1883, p.426. To Henty's bitter disappointment the magazine was forced to cease publication almost immediately afterwards, at the end of September 1883 (see §3, 225). The serialisation of 'Jack Archer' was only completed in the penultimate issue, dated 18 September.

2. No publisher's records for this title have survived, and there is no printer's code. The bound-in catalogue advertises this book, together with *Winning his Spurs* and *Cornet of Horse* [*sic*], each at 5s.

3. On p.(iii) the page references given as 56 and 66 should be 46 and 56. These errors were repeated in later impressions for well over a decade.

4. The first three instalments of the story in the *Union Jack* carried in their headings a credit to Gordon Browne for the illustrations. Of these, the first (see Note 1) was actually illustrated with one engraving by Gordon Browne; the others had no illustrations at all. Subsequently Browne's name was dropped from the headings and other instalments were illustrated with a hotch-potch of old and new engravings and pen-drawings. Browne's engraving appears in the book facing p.3.

*14.2

JACK ARCHER | A Tale of the Crimea | BY G.A. HENTY | AUTHOR OF "WINNING HIS SPURS," "CORNET OF HORSE," "FACING DEATH," | ETC., ETC. | NEW AND CHEAPER EDITION. | LONDON | SAMPSON LOW, MARSTON, SEARLE, & RIVINGTON | Limited | St. Dunstan's House | FETTER LANE, FLEET STREET, E.C. | 1888 | [All rights reserved]
(Note: The subtitle and St. Dunstan's House *are in gothic type).*

Contents
184 x 121 mm. (i)–(viii) | (1)–(304) | catalogue (1)–32. Eight full-page black-and-white engravings after several artists, unbacked, unfolioed, tipped in. Five black-and-white fold-out engravings of battle plans.

(Frontispiece, tipped in) | (i) title p. | (ii) publisher's advertisement listing 26 titles 'Uniform with this Volume' | (iii)–vi. Contents | (vii) List of Illustrations | (viii) blank | (1)–302. text | (303) printer's imprint (LONDON. | PRINTED BY GILBERT AND RIVINGTON, LD., | ST. JOHN'S HOUSE, CLERKENWELL ROAD, E.C.) | (304) blank | (1)–32. catalogue, dated September 1888.

Binding: As for 14.1, except (a) blue-grey cloth; (b) edges of leaves plain.

References: PN | *Farmer*, p.45.

Notes
1. With their two other books by Henty, Sampson Low included *Jack Archer* in 1887 or 1888 in the series 'Low's Standard Books for Boys'. There was no significant change from the first-edition format apart from a reduction in the number of illustrations from twelve to eight, but the books were reduced in price and now sold at 2s.6d. with plain edges, or 3s.6d. with all edges gilt. One of the omitted illustrations was the engraving by Gordon Browne.
2. There were numerous reprints, many with dated title pages, of which this is an example. Many small variations appear in title-page imprint, advertisements and catalogues, binding cloth, etc. Such issues are all grouped together under the 'generic' headings, *14.2 and *14.3.

*14.3

JACK ARCHER | A Tale of the Crimea | BY G.A. HENTY | AUTHOR OF "WINNING HIS SPURS," "CORNET OF HORSE," "FACING DEATH," | ETC., ETC. | NEW AND CHEAPER EDITION. | LONDON | SAMPSON LOW, MARSTON & COMPANY | LIMITED | St. Dunstan's House | FETTER LANE, FLEET STREET, E.C. | 1895 | [All rights reserved]
(Note: The subtitle and St. Dunstan's House *are in gothic type).*

Contents
182 x 123 mm. (i)–(viii) | (1)–(304) | no catalogue. Illustrations and battle-plans as in *14.2.

(Frontispiece, tipped in) | (i) title p. | (ii) publisher's advertisement listing 60 titles 'Uniform with this Volume' | (iii)–vi. Contents | (vii) List of Illustrations | (viii) blank | (1)–302. text, with printer's imprint at foot of p.302 (Woodfall & Kinder, Printers, 70 to 76, Long Acre, London, W.C.) | (303)–(304) blank.

Binding: As for *14.2, except (a) greenish-grey cloth boards; (b) endpapers printed in blue with repeat-pattern including publisher's monogram and part of tall building; (c) back board has blind triple-rules near edges, and publisher's monogram is omitted.

References: PN | *Farmer*, p.45.

Notes
1. A new printer has been used for this impression. The plates are still from the original type-setting used for 14.1.
2. This is a later example than *14.2 of the reprints that followed the first edition. Apart from the date they had only minor variations: those apparent here are: (a) amended publisher's imprint on title page; (b) changed advertisements on p.(ii); (c) no catalogue bound in; (d) new style of endpapers; (e) smoother cloth used for binding, and alteration to blocking on back board.
3. See *14.2, Note 2.

14.4
JACK ARCHER | A TALE OF THE CRIMEA | BY | G.A. HENTY | AUTHOR OF | "WINNING HIS SPURS," "CORNET OF HORSE," "FACING DEATH," ETC. | POPULAR EDITION | LONDON | SAMPSON LOW, MARSTON AND COMPANY | LIMITED | St. Dunstan's House | FETTER LANE, FLEET STREET, E.C. | 1898
(Note: St. Dunstan's House *is in gothic type).*

Contents
214 x 146 mm. (1)–128 including catalogue. One illustration printed from line block on front cover. Five full-page battle plans printed from line blocks on text pages.
    (1)–(2) See Note 1 | (3) title p. | (4) blank | (5) Contents | (6) blank | (7)–119. text, set in two columns, with rule between, and with printer's imprint at foot of p.119 (Richard Clay & Sons, Limited, London & Bungay.) | 120–128. catalogue.

Cover (see Plate 52)
Orange paper, printed in black ink; edges cut flush.
(1) Price Sixpence | JACK ARCHER | A TALE OF THE CRIMEA | BY | G.A. HENTY | (line illustration with caption 'DRAWING HIS LONG KNIFE, HE RUSHED AT THEM', also appearing as plate facing p.30) | COPYRIGHT | LONDON | SAMPSON LOW, MARSTON AND COMPANY | LIMITED | St. Dunstan's House, Fetter Lane, E.C.
    (Note: the last line is in gothic type).
(2) Full-page advertisement for Brooke's Monkey Brand Soap.
(3) Full-page advertisement for Oetzmann & Co., furniture manufacturers.
(4) Full-page advertisement for Pears Soap, with printer's imprint at foot (RICHARD CLAY AND SONS, LIMITED, LONDON AND BUNGAY.).
(Spine) JACK ARCHER (at centre running from foot to head).

Reference: PN.

Notes
1. Only a single copy of this paperback edition is known to me, and unfortunately

the first leaf of text-paper is missing. It may, perhaps, have been a half-title page, a frontispiece, or possibly have carried more advertisements.

2. Set in two columns, and reminiscent of Griffith & Farran's paper-back edition of *The Young Franc-Tireurs*, 14.7, it was probably designed to be sold from railway-station bookstalls; the price, sixpence, is printed on the front cover.

3. The text is folded in four 32-page sections, and side-stabbed with two wire stitches. The paper is cheap, brittle, and now browning at the edges.

4. Pages 121–123 give a list of Low's 'Standard Books for Boys'. On p.123 is included 'BEVIS. By the late RICHARD JEFFERIES. Edited by G.A. HENTY'. Books in the series are described as 'In very handsome cloth binding. Crown 8vo. Price 2s.6d.'. This 1898 edition of *Jack Archer* is the last known publication from Sampson Low to carry an advertisement for *Bevis* giving Henty's name as editor (see *Bevis*, §2, 128; and Miller and Matthews, *Richard Jefferies, a bibliographical study*, p.279).

14.5

Title page: As for *14.3, except (a) no full point after 'E.C' at end of imprint; (b) no date; (c) '[All rights reserved]' omitted.

Contents: 181 x 123 mm. As for *14.3, except (a) advertisement (STANDARD BOOKS FOR BOYS) (see Note 2); (b) printer's imprint at foot of p.302 (WOODFALL AND KINDER, PRINTERS, LONG ACRE, LONDON.).

Binding (see Plate 48)
Blue cloth boards, blocked black, blue merging through green and yellow to orange-brown, buff, and gilt; edges plain; plain off-white endpapers.

Front board: Thick black rules dividing the design into three panels, with, in top panel: . JACK . | ARCHER (gilt) in strong 'egyptian' lettering; in centre panel: illustration, based on the one facing p.30, showing Spanish soldier attacking two young men with dagger (black, blue merging through green and yellow to orange-brown, buff); in bottom panel: G.A. HENTY (black). **Spine:** Black rules as on front board, forming panels, with, in top panel: JACK | ARCHER | (centre dot) | G.A. HENTY (all gilt); illustration in centre panel of cloaked figure with rifle (black, blue merging through green and yellow to orange-brown, buff); in bottom panel: SAMPSON LOW | & Co. (gilt). **Back board:** plain.

Reference: PN.

Notes
1. About 1900 Sampson Low re-issued all three of their Henty novels in a simpler and more colourful binding design of some quality (see *The Cornet of Horse*, 8.3, and *Winning his Spurs*, 11.3 and 11.4). My copy is inscribed, and dated February 1902.

2. On p.(ii) are listed 83 titles, headed with the name of the series (see *14.2, Note 1). The three by Henty are numbered 7, 16, and 25. The books are described as 'Fully illustrated. In very handsome cloth binding. Crown 8vo. Price 2s.6d.'.

14.6

JACK ARCHER | A Tale of the Crimea | BY | G.A. HENTY | AUTHOR OF "WINNING HIS SPURS," "CORNET OF HORSE," "FACING DEATH," | ETC., ETC. | THIRTY-THIRD THOUSAND | LONDON | SAMPSON LOW, MARSTON & COMPANY | LIMITED | 1906

Contents: As for 14.5, except (a) p.(ii) blank; (b) printer's imprint at foot of p.302 (GILBERT AND RIVINGTON, LTD., ST. JOHN'S HOUSE, CLERKENWELL, E.C.).

Binding: As for 14.5, but red cloth boards.

Reference: PN.

Notes
1. The stereo plates are still from the original typesetting, but printed again by Gilbert and Rivington. The title page has been reset without the use of gothic type, is dated, and carries the line 'Thirty-third thousand'.
2. The full-page plates are now printed on coated paper, quite unnecessary for line illustrations, but perhaps helping to brighten up the book.

14.7

JACK ARCHER | A TALE OF THE CRIMEA | BY | G.A. HENTY | (device) | Authorised Copyright Edition | LONDON | BENNETT & CO. | (The Century Press) | 8, Henrietta Street, WC. | All rights reserved
(Note: the full point after W *is missing in* W C.*).*

Contents
179 x 121 mm. (i)–x | (11)–192 | no catalogue. No illustrations.
  (i)-(ii) General advertisements | (iii) half-title p. (B-P's Books for Boys | JACK ARCHER | Edited by | Lt.-Gen. Sir R. Baden-Powell, K.C.B., K.C.V.O.) | (iv) advertisements | (v) title p. | (vi) blank | (vii) Contents (see Note 3) | (viii) advertisement | (ix)–(x) Foreword (to Parents and Scoutmasters) (see Note 1) | 11–192. text, with printer's imprint at foot of p.192 (BENNETT, PRINTER, PORTSMOUTH.).

Cover (see Plate 53)
White coated paper, lined off-white uncoated paper; exterior printed red and dark-blue; interior printed black; edges cut flush.
(1) B-P's BOOKS | FOR BOYS | JACK ARCHER | BY | G.A. Henty (all white out of solid red background, cased dark blue), above illustration of soldiers in uniform with rifle, pistol, etc. (dark-blue on white out of solid red). At foot: 4ᴅ Net (red and dark blue in white circle, outlined dark blue, all out of solid red).
(2) advertisements (black)
(3) advertisements (black)
(4) advertisement for Fry's Cocoa (dark blue and red)
(Spine, from foot) B-P's Books for Boys. JACK ARCHER, by G.A. HENTY (dark-blue).

References: BL; Bod.

Notes

1. This is the only Henty title among six books produced by Sir Robert Baden-Powell, the Chief Scout (and founder of the Scouting movement), at the phenomenally low price of 4d. His own Foreword on pp.(ix)–(x) explains his aims, achieved no doubt by persuading publishers, printers, and advertisers of the rightness of his cause:

Just a line to Parents and Scoutmasters. You know – or perhaps you do not know – what awful stuff is put before boys in the form of cheap literature nowadays. It is stuff that is made to sell without regard to how it affects the mind and character of the boy.

Personally, I believe this trash to be responsible for half the crime and brutality among young offenders.

I am not squeamish, but when I took up the other day one out of three of the cheap biographies of a celebrated criminal, and read the morbid, dirty detail thus pushed into the minds of our little lads, I marvelled what kind of a beast the writer could be who could prostitute his abilities to such an end.

And this book was only typical of hundreds of the same kind.

Boys read a great deal more nowadays than they used to, and they naturally like something that will interest and grip them. Their appetite is for literature of an exciting kind, and there is no reason why the food they are supplied with to this end should not be clean and wholesome.

As a rule, however, the books of good writers have been too high in price to be within the reach of the ordinary boy, and the cheap "dreadfuls" and "shockers" have been his only resource.

By means of the Edition which we are now bringing out we hope to meet this want, in reproducing at a cheap rate a selected series of good books by known authors – and by "good" we mean books not only good from the parents' point of view, but from that of the boy as well.

May, 1910.   R.J.Baden-Powell.

2. Needless to say, the book is very cheaply produced both as regards printing and paper, the latter brittle and browning at the edges.

3. There is a note on p.(vii), at the end of the list of Contents:

'B-P's BOOKS FOR BOYS.

Readers desirous of having 'JACK ARCHER' by G.A. Henty . . . in more permanent form, can be supplied with copies handsomely bound in cloth gilt and profusely illustrated, 2s.9d. each, post free, upon application to BENNETT & Co., 8, Henrietta Street, London, W.C.'.

This implies that a cloth-bound edition printed by Bennett & Co was produced at the same time, but I have not found a copy of such an edition.

14.8

Title page: As for 14.6, except (a) THIRTY-FIFTH THOUSAND; (b) no date.

Contents

193 x 130 mm. (i)–(viii) | (1)–(304) | no catalogue. Full-page black-and-white illustration converted to colour and reproduced by three-colour halftone blocks printed on coated paper, tipped in as frontispiece; the seven remaining illustrations from 14.2 printed in black line on coated paper, unbacked, keyed to facing pages, tipped in. Five fold-out black-and-white battle-plans.

(Frontispiece, tipped in) | (i) title p. | (ii) blank | (iii)–vi. Contents | (vii) List of Illustrations | (viii) printer's imprint (Printed by | REA & INCHBOULD, 224, Blackfriars Road, | London, S.E.) | (1)–302. text, with printer's imprint at foot of p.302 (LONDON: PRINTED BY REA AND INCHBOULD, 224, BLACKFRIARS ROAD, S.E.) | (303)–(304) blank.

Binding (see Plate 49)
Blue cloth boards, blocked black and gilt, with colour plate laid down on front board; edges plain; plain off-white endpapers.
　　Front board: JACK | ARCHER (black), the two lines of lettering drawn on a double curve; . G . A . | HENTY (black) at right of laid down colour-plate enclosed in black rules. At lower right corner: AUTHORISED | COPYRIGHT | EDITION (black). **Spine:** JACK | ARCHER (gilt) above semi-abstract decoration with moon, stars, earth, birds flying (all gilt). At centre: . G . A . | HENTY (gilt). **Back board:** plain.

Reference: PN.

Notes
1. This binding, blocked with the words AUTHORISED COPYRIGHT EDITION, is similar to one used at about the same date for *The Cornet of Horse*, 8.4. For the use of these words, see 8.4, Note 4. Both editions appeared towards the end of the first war.
2. The book is now with yet another printer, the fourth used for this title. Rea and Inchbould also printed the edition of *The Cornet of Horse* mentioned above. Of the two sets of stereos supplied the one for this title is slightly less worn.
3. The new frontispiece is a coloured version of what had previously been the illustration facing p.226. For the process of transformation see *The Cornet of Horse*, 8.4, Note 2, and especially *The Young Buglers*, 7.7, Note 2.

14.8A
JACK ARCHER | A TALE OF THE CRIMEA | BY | G.A. HENTY | AUTHOR OF "WINNING HIS SPURS," "CORNET OF HORSE," "FACING DEATH," | ETC., ETC. | ILLUSTRATED | LONDON | SAMPSON LOW, MARSTON & COMPANY, LIMITED

Contents
194 x 127 mm. (i)–(viii) | (9)–352 | catalogue (1)–(16) unfolioed. Eight full-page watercolour drawings reproduced by three-colour halftones on coated paper, unbacked, keyed to text pages, tipped in. Four fold-out black-and-white battle-plans.
　　(i) Half-title p. | (ii) blank | (frontispiece, tipped in) | (iii) title p. | (iv) blank | (v) Contents | (vi) blank | (vii) List of Illustrations | (viii) printer's imprint (Printed by | W. Mate & Sons, Ltd., | Bournemouth.) | (9)–352. text, with printer's imprint below rule at foot of p.352 (Printed by W. Mate & Sons, Ltd., Bournemouth.) | (1)–(16) unfolioed, publisher's catalogue.

Binding
Light-blue cloth boards, blocked black, dark blue, and gilt; edges plain; light-green endpapers, printed dark green: romantic landscape garden scene at edge of water with large sailing ship and setting sun behind, and in rectangular panel: SAMPSON

LOW MARSTON & C^O., L^{TD} | MDCCXCIV (all within thick dark-green border).

Front board: JACK | ARCHER (black) at left of, and above, design of flourishes, moon, and stars (dark blue). At centre, within dark-blue rectangular frame, is laid down illustration printed in three-colour halftone on coated paper. At foot: G.A. HENTY (black). The whole within dark-blue ruled border. **Spine:** JACK | ARCHER (gilt) above semi-abstract decoration with moon, stars, earth, birds flying (all dark blue). At centre: G.A. | HENTY (gilt); at foot: SAMPSON LOW & C^O, L^{TD} **Back board:** plain.

Reference: PN.

Notes

1. A new edition, entirely re-set by a printer whose imprint apparently has not previously appeared in a book by Henty. The much improved quality was long overdue.

2. The significance of the endpaper design is something of a mystery. The date, 1794, in roman numerals, is positioned close to the name of Sampson Low Marston & Co., Ltd on the line above. I have not seen the design used in other books by Henty, and certainly the illustration seems to have little relevance to any of Sampson Low's Henty titles. It seems likely that the design was planned for more than one book, possibly for a Sampson Low series, but I am unable to explain the date. Sampson Low, Senior, did not start his business until 1819, setting up as a general publisher in 1848; Edward Marston became a partner in 1856, and on the death of Low in 1886 he became the owner of the business (see Appendix II, Part 3). There was no centenary, nor even apparently an anniversary, to celebrate in 1894.

3. The anonymous watercolour illustrations are all closely based on the earlier black-and-white drawings. There are only four battle-plans in this edition, that for the Battle of the Tchernaya being omitted. The plans are from the same originals as before, but the type for the captions has been re-set.

*14.9

JACK ARCHER | A TALE OF THE CRIMEA | BY | G.A. HENTY | AUTHOR OF | "WINNING HIS SPURS," "CORNET OF HORSE," | "FACING DEATH," ETC. | LONDON | SAMPSON LOW, MARSTON AND CO., LTD.

Contents

183 x 120 mm. (i)–(ii) | (1)–302 | biographies (1)–(16) | catalogue (1)–32. Two full-page wash-drawings signed 'M.L.P.', reproduced by halftone blocks printed in black on coated paper, unbacked, keyed to text pages, tipped in.

(i) (Frontispiece, tipped in) | (i) title p. | (ii) printer's imprint (PRINTED IN GREAT BRITAIN BY PURNELL AND SONS | PAULTON (SOMERSET) AND LONDON) | (1)–302. text | (1)-(16) biographies, see Note 3 | (1)–32. catalogue.

Binding (see Note 1)

Red cloth boards, blocked black; edges plain; plain off-white endpapers.

Front board: JACK ARCHER | G.A. HENTY (black) within ruled rectangular panel beneath illustration of sailing ships in sea battle, with boats, all contained in larger ruled rectangle (black). **Spine:** JACK | ARCHER (black) between two black rules, above illustration of ships in upper half of tall narrow panel, with: G.A. |

HENTY (black) and four small black ornaments in lower half. At foot: SAMPSON LOW (black) between two black rules. **Back board:** plain.

Reference: AK.

Notes

1. In the 1920s 'Sampson Low's New Series' included their other Henty novels for boys, *The Cornet of Horse*, 8.5, and *Winning his Spurs*, 11.8 (see Plate 50); as well as *A Hidden Foe*, 46.6, originally published as an adult novel, all at 2s.6d. The publisher's address was then 100 Southwark Street, London, S.E.1.

2. The text is printed from stereos of the old typesetting, but since 14.8 was printed the engraved headpieces and tailpieces to chapters have been cut away. All that remains of the prelims is a title page, set by the new printer.

3. Following the text, an unfolioed 16-page section with title page 'Favourite Books for Girls and Boys', gives short biographies, with lists of principal works, of three Sampson Low authors: Louisa M. Alcott, Jules Verne, and Clark Russell.

4. The unknown artist, 'M.L.P.', also illustrated *Winning his Spurs*, *11.8.

5. There were substantial variants of this edition, with alternative advertising material, and the series was given other names over a period of years. The constant factor was the colour and style of binding. All the varying issues are grouped together under this 'generic' heading, *14.9.

6. Later versions of this title, some in variant bindings of the one described here, were issued under the Sampson Low imprint in the 1930s (see Appendix II, Part 3), but are beyond the period covered by this bibliography.

15. WITH CLIVE IN INDIA

15.1

WITH CLIVE IN INDIA: | OR THE | BEGINNINGS OF AN EMPIRE. | BY | G.A. HENTY, | Author of "Under Drake's Flag;" "Facing Death;" "Winning | his Spurs;" "The Cornet of Horse;" &c. &c. | WITH TWELVE FULL-PAGE ILLUSTRATIONS BY GORDON BROWNE. | (publisher's device) | LONDON: | BLACKIE & SON, 49 & 50 OLD BAILEY, E.C.; | GLASGOW, EDINBURGH, AND DUBLIN. | 1884.
(Note: There is a black mark made by a raised space following &c. &c.; *the second line of the publisher's imprint, starting* BLACKIE & SON, *is letterspaced).*

Contents

186 x 129 mm. (i)–(viii) | (9)–(384) | catalogue (1)–32. Twelve full-page line-and-wash drawings by Gordon Browne, reproduced by two-colour line blocks with mechanical tints for second-colour wash (yellowish sepia). Five battle-plans printed in black from line blocks on text pages.

(i) Half-title p. | (ii) advertisement for *Under Drake's Flag* and *Facing Death* | (frontispiece, tipped in) | (iii) title p. | (iv) blank | (v) Preface (see Note 3 below) | (vi) blank | (vii) Contents | (viii) list of Illustrations | (9)–382. text | (383)–(384) blank | (1)–32. catalogue.

Binding (see Plate 88)

Light-brown lightly diagonally-grained cloth boards, bevelled, and blocked black, red, blind,and gilt; all edges burnished yellowish olive-green; maroon surface-paper endpapers.

Front board: WITH I CLIVE I IN I INDIA (gilt, cased black) superimposed over illustration (black, red, and gilt). At foot: . BY . G . A . HENTY . (light-brown cloth-colour out of solid gilt panel within thick black-ruled frame). The whole within two black rules (thick and thin) forming panel. **Spine:** WITH I CLIVE I IN INDIA (light-brown cloth-colour out of decorated gilt panel) above illustration (black, red, and gilt); BY I G.A. HENTY (gilt) separated by two black rules from: BLACKIE & SON (gilt). The whole within black rule forming panel, with double gilt rules at extremities of spine. **Back board:** Triple blind rule (thin, thick, thin) near edges of board.

Reference: PN.

Notes

1. First published at 6s. on 24 September 1883, the book was well received: by the end of February 1884 Blackie had sold 2773 copies. Annual sales over the next fifteen years averaged 1008 copies, and when the cheap edition was issued at the end of August 1906, a grand total of 22,168 copies had been sold in the 6s. format. A balance of 259 copies was sold over five years, concurrently with the cheap edition.

2. This first issue contains no map. The bound-in catalogue has a heading 'New Series for Season 1884': *With Clive in India* and *By Sheer Pluck* are both advertised without quotations from press reviews.

3. Early issues, including this one and 15.2 (below), have the Preface on a single page in small type. This changed when the book was reprinted (see 15.3, Note 2).

4. The five battle-plans, printed from line blocks on text pages, are not included in the list of Illustrations on p.(viii).

15.2

Title page: As for 15.1.

Contents: As for 15.1, except for Map of India, printed by lithography in black line, unbacked, unfolioed, now guarded in as double-page spread following p.(viii).

Binding: As for 15.1, but (a) cloth is smooth, ungrained; (b) edges burnished more of a yellow ochre than olive-green; (c) dark-brown surface-paper endpapers.

Reference: PN.

Notes

1. The main difference between this issue and 15.1 is the inclusion, soon after publication, of a double-spread map of India, guarded in after p.(viii).

2. The text and preliminary pages are from the original printing, with the Preface set in small type on p.(v).

3. Among the catalogues bound in 15.2, announcements of this book and *By Sheer Pluck* may be found both with and without quotations from press reviews, .

15.3

Title page: As for 15.1.

Contents: 184 x 130 mm. As for 15.2, but see Notes 2–5 below.

Binding: As for 15.2, except that blind rules on back board are wider than previously.

Reference: PN.

Notes

1. Early sales were very good (see 15.1, Note 1), and a reprint was needed during the first year. At this time Blackie considered the dating of title pages. It had been agreed that first impressions of books should have dated title pages, but was now decided that any reprint in the first calendar year of publication would be treated in the same way (see *Facing Death*, 10.4, Notes 2 and 3). Therefore the first two printings of *With Clive in India* both have title pages with the date 1884.

2. Blackie took the opportunity to re-set the Preface: the type is still smaller than that for the text, but the division into paragraphs, and changed punctuation, are distinct improvements. On the half-title page there is slightly more space than in the first impression between book-title and ornament. The list of Illustrations on p.(viii) still omits the map of India, and the battle-plans.

3. When reprinting the illustrations Blackie used a greenish-grey ink for the second-colour tint plates, instead of sepia.

4. In my copy the endpapers are of an even darker shade of brown than in 15.2.

5. Later issues of 15.3 include catalogues headed 'New Series for Season 1885'. In them the announcements of this book and of *By Sheer Pluck* include press reviews, but those of the books for the next year, *True to the Old Flag, In Freedom's Cause*, and *St. George for England*, do not.

*15.4

WITH CLIVE IN INDIA I OR THE I BEGINNINGS OF AN EMPIRE. I BY I G.A. HENTY, I Author of "The Lion of the North," "Through the Fray," "In Freedom's Cause," I "True to the Old Flag," "For Name and Fame," "Facing Death," &c. I WITH TWELVE FULL-PAGE ILLUSTRATIONS BY GORDON BROWNE. I (publisher's device) I LONDON: I BLACKIE & SON, 49 & 50 OLD BAILEY, E.C. I GLASGOW, EDINBURGH, AND DUBLIN.

Contents: 185 x 132 mm. As for 15.3, except (a) page (ii) advertisement (BOOKS BY G.A. HENTY.) listing six titles at 6s. and five at 5s.; (b) catalogue (1)-40.

Binding: As for 15.3, but red cloth boards, blocked black, red, blind, and gilt; edges burnished olive-green; dark-brown surface-paper endpapers.

Reference: PN.

Notes

1. Reprints of the six-shilling edition were in the style of 15.3, following Blackie's usual pattern. The date was removed from the title page, and alterations were made to title-page imprint and address as necessary. Blackie became a Limited Company in 1890; the Edinburgh address went after 1894; the Indian office opened in 1901, although Bombay did not appear regularly in the imprint before 1906. The books listed after Henty's name on the title page included more recent titles, and soon only those published by Blackie.

2. The illustrations were modified in late issues, the second-colour tint either transferred to the black plate or omitted (see Appendix IV, Part 1).

3. Bindings continued to show variations in colour of cloth, blocking, and end-papers, often also having the publisher's name removed from the spine.

4. Blackie did not regularly date their catalogues, but it is possible from them to date the issue of the book. This catalogue is headed 'The New Season's Books' and at the head of the list are four by Henty: *The Lion of the North, Through the Fray, For Name and Fame*, and *The Dragon and the Raven*. The last to be issued was *Through the Fray*, on 5 September 1885. Announcements of all include quotations from press reviews, so the catalogue would not have been printed until early in 1886. There are no announcements of books for the following year, of which the first due to be published was *With Wolfe in Canada*, on 18 May 1886. Blackie would have announced the next season's books as soon as possible, certainly by March or April: therefore this catalogue was almost certainly printed in the first quarter of 1886.

5. The advertisement on p.(ii) lists all the novels published up to 1885, each with a brief excerpt from a press review. This reprint can therefore be dated to approximately the same date as the catalogue bound in it. It is an early reprint of this often reprinted book, still having the illustrations printed in two colours.

6. In late issues the Preface was slightly amended, the main changes being the omission of 'My dear Lads,' and of the last sentence of the second paragraph.

7. The impression described here is one of numerous slightly-varying issues in the first-edition format: all are included under this 'generic' heading, *15.4.

15.5

Blackie's Colonial Library | (15-em rule) | WITH CLIVE IN INDIA | OR THE | BEGINNINGS OF AN EMPIRE | BY | G.A. HENTY | Author of "The Lion of the North", "Through the Fray", "In Freedom's Cause", | "True to the Old Flag", "For Name and Fame", "Facing Death", &c. | (publisher's device) | LONDON | BLACKIE & SON, LIMITED, 50 OLD BAILEY, E.C. | GLASGOW AND DUBLIN | 1896 | (7-em rule) | This Edition is for circulation only in India | and the British Colonies

(Note: Blackie's Colonial Library *is in gothic type; the last two lines in bold).*

Contents

185 x 125 mm. (1)–(2) | (i)–(viii) | (9)–(384) | no catalogue. Frontispiece from line drawing by Gordon Browne, reproduced by line block printed in black on coated paper, unbacked, tipped in.

(1) Advertisement (Blackie's Colonial Library) listing 12 titles | (2) blank | (i) half-title p. | (ii) blank | (iii) title p. | (iv) blank | (v)–vi. Preface | (vii) Contents | (viii) blank | (1)–382. text | (383)–(384) blank.

Binding (see Note 1)

Designed by Talwin Morris (see Appendix IV, Part 2). Green cloth boards, blocked pale-green and gilt; edges plain; plain off-white endpapers.

Front board: BLACKIE'S COLONIAL LIBRARY | WITH CLIVE | IN INDIA | G.A. HENTY (all pale-green) within decorative panel formed by over-all art-nouveau design (pale-green). **Spine:** Over-all design similar to that on front board (pale-green), leaving two panels with lettering. Upper panel: WITH CLIVE | IN INDIA | (three small ornaments, placed asymmetrically) | G.A. HENTY (all gilt) in gilt ruled frame. Lower panel: BLACKIE'S | COLONIAL | LIBRARY (gilt) in gilt ruled frame. **Back board:** plain.

References: BB | Cargill Thompson: *The Boys' Dumas*, pp.3–4.

Notes

1. Only four of Henty's novels for boys are known to have been included in Blackie's Colonial Library (see Appendix V). The first twelve titles are advertised on p.(1): 'In crown 8vo, with Frontispiece, in Paper Covers, also in Cloth boards'. An example of the latter is at Plate 54.

2. I have examined only three titles: two of them have title pages dated 1896, but *The Dash for Khartoum*, in my collection, is undated, probably indicating a reprint. The colonial edition of *When London Burned* has proved extremely elusive. Equally elusive are all issues in paper covers, of which I have found no trace at all.

3. The text paper, and especially the paper used for the endpapers, are poor in quality by comparison with those used for Blackie's UK editions, both containing some wood pulp and consequently yellowing with age.

4. In 15.5 the advertisement for the series is on a single unfolioed leaf, tipped on to the first 16-page gathering.

5. The frontispiece by Gordon Browne is captioned 'The Fate of the Assassins', a caption used for a different drawing by the same artist in earlier editions of the book. The drawing used here does not appear in the UK editions.

15.6

With Clive in India | Or, The Beginnings of an Empire | BY | G.A. HENTY | Author of "The Lion of the North," "Through the Fray," "True to the | Old Flag," "In Freedom's Cause," "For Name and Fame," | "Facing Death," &c. | ILLUSTRATED | BLACKIE AND SON LIMITED | LONDON GLASGOW DUBLIN BOMBAY | 1907

Contents

186 x 125 mm. (1)–(380) | catalogue 1–16. Six full-page illustrations from wash-drawings by an unknown hand, based on the earlier illustrations by Gordon Browne, reproduced by halftone blocks printed in sepia on coated paper, unbacked, unfolioed, tipped in. Map of India and five battle-plans as in earlier editions.

(1) Half-title p. | (2) advertisement (HENTY'S TALES OF BRITISH HISTORY.) listing 38 titles | (frontispiece, tipped in) | (3) title p. | (4) blank | 5–6. Preface | 7. Contents | (8) blank | 9. list of Illustrations | (10) blank | (map of India, guarded in) | 11–378. text | (379)–(380) blank | 1–16. catalogue.

Binding (see Plate 172)

Blue cloth boards, blocked black, red, buff, and gilt; edges burnished olive-green; grey endpapers, lined off-white.

Front board: WITH CLIVE | IN INDIA | G.A. HENTY (gilt) above illustration of turbaned boy with ladder, standing near wall of building (black, red, buff) framed with black rule, and with signature, J Hassall (black) at bottom right corner. **Spine:** WITH | CLIVE | IN | INDIA | G.A. HENTY (all gilt) above illustration of turbaned boy standing with cutlass and lamp (black, red, buff). At foot: BLACKIE & SON LTD. **Back board:** plain.

Reference: PN.

Notes
1. In 1906 (title-page date 1907) *With Clive in India* was issued in the 'New and Popular Edition'. For details of the series see *Facing Death*, 10.6, Notes 2–3.
2. This is a true new edition, the type completely reset. For the first time, both the map of India and the battle-plans appear in the list of Illustrations (p.9).
3. Blackie sold 3936 copies of this 3s.6d. edition in 1907, and a further 15,811 copies by the end of August 1917. During the period 1908–1917 the average number of copies sold each year other than 1911 was 1416. In 1911 the number sold was 3050. No explanation is apparent; it may be that a special order was placed by, say, the London County Council, for use as school prizes. Blackie's sales records show that the London County Council did in fact order 1108 copies of *Both Sides the Border* 'as a 2s.6d. book' in that very year, but no further explanation is given.

15.7
THE TALISMAN LIBRARY (underlined) | WITH CLIVE IN INDIA | BY | G.A. HENTY | (publisher's device) | BLACKIE AND SON LIMITED | 50 OLD BAILEY LONDON | GLASGOW AND BOMBAY | 1920

Contents
171 x 115 mm. (i)–xvi | 1–168 | catalogue (169)–(176). Frontispiece from wash-drawing by unknown artist, based on an original line-illustration by Gordon Browne, reproduced by halftone block printed in black on coated paper, unbacked, tipped in.
(i) Half-title p. | (ii) unheaded introduction to the Talisman Library | (frontispiece, tipped in) | (iii) title p. | (iv) list of titles in series, and printer's imprint (Printed in Great Britain by | Blackie & Son, Limited, Glasgow) | v–xvi. Introduction | 1–158. text | (159)–168. Notes | (169)–(174) catalogue of school textbooks | (175)–(176) blank.

Binding (see Plate 145)
Grey cloth boards, blocked blue (see Note 3); edges plain; plain off-white endpapers.
Front board: WITH . CLIVE | IN . INDIA | G.A. Henty | (publisher's trade mark for the series, including the wording: The | TALISMAN | Library of | ENGLISH | AUTHORS) | Blackie.&.Son.Limited (all blue) within frame of decorative rules (blue). **Spine:** WITH . CLIVE . IN . INDIA : HENTY (blue) running from foot to head. **Back board:** plain.

References: BL; Bod; BB.

Notes
1. In 1920 four of Henty's novels for boys were abridged for use in schools and included in Blackie's 'The Talisman Library of English Authors' (see Appendix V). (That title ignores the fact that the first two titles were by Walter Scott!) Two more by Henty were added in 1921 and 1922 (see 15.8, Note 2).
2. The frontispiece is from one of the illustrations used in 15.6.

3. The series was also issued in limp cloth, without change of design or content.

4. Later impressions in both styles of binding were issued with undated title pages.

15.8

THE TALISMAN LIBRARY (underlined) | WITH | CLIVE IN INDIA | BY | G.A. HENTY | (publisher's device) | BLACKIE & SON LIMITED | LONDON AND GLASGOW

Contents

175 x 120 mm. (i)–xvi | 1–168 | catalogue (169)–(176). Frontispiece as in 15.7.

(i)-(ii) Introduction to the series with bold heading on p.(i): 'The Talisman Library of English Authors', and the titles in the series listed on p.(ii) | (frontispiece, tipped in) | (iii) title p. | (iv) Blackie addresses, and printer's imprint at foot (Printed in Great Britain by Blackie & Son, Ltd., Glasgow) | v–xvi. Introduction | 1–158. text | (159)–168. Notes | (169)–(174) catalogue of school text-books | (175)–(176) blank.

Binding: As for 15.7.

References: PN; BB.

Notes

1. Following the issues both dated and undated of 15.7 (see 15.7, Note 4), the preliminary pages were reset. The main changes, apart from the title-page imprint, were the re-arrangement of the introductory notes, and the list of titles within the series. Otherwise the text appears to be unaltered.

2. Two more of Henty's books were added to the series: *The Dragon and the Raven* in 1921, and *Beric the Briton* in 1922.

3. The series continued in production, both in limp cloth and in cloth boards, at least for two decades. Copies of some titles are found with the Book Production War Economy symbol on p.(iv), a measure required of British publishers during the second war (see *With Wolfe in Canada*, 27.4, Note 3).

*15.9

With Clive in India | Or, The Beginnings of an Empire | BY | G.A. HENTY | Author of "The Lion of the North" "Through the Fray" | "True to the Old Flag" "In Freedom's Cause" | "For Name and Fame" | "Facing Death" | &c. | ILLUSTRATED | BLACKIE AND SON LIMITED | LONDON GLASGOW AND BOMBAY

Contents

184 x 123 mm. (1)–(380) | no catalogue. Frontispiece from watercolour drawing by John de Walton, reproduced by three-colour halftone blocks; four full-page wash-drawings by an unknown hand, based on the original line illustrations by Gordon Browne, reproduced by halftone blocks printed in black; all on coated paper, unbacked, tipped in. Map of India and five battle-plans printed from line blocks on text pages.

(1) Half-title p. | (2) Blackie addresses | (frontispiece, tipped in) | (3) title p. | (4) printer's imprint (Printed in Great Britain by | Blackie & Son, Limited, Glasgow) | 5–6. Preface | (7) Contents | (8) blank | (9) list of Illustrations | (10) map | 11–378. text | (379)–(380) blank.

Binding
Red cloth boards, blocked black, pink, and buff; edges plain; plain off-white endpapers.
Front board: WITH CLIVE | IN INDIA | G.A. HENTY (buff) above illustration, framed by black line, of turbaned boy standing by ladder (black, pink, buff), with signature at lower right corner: J Hassall (black). **Spine:** WITH | CLIVE | IN | INDIA | G.A. HENTY (buff) above illustration of turbaned boy standing with cutlass and lamp (black, pink, buff). At foot: BLACKIE & SON LTD (black). **Back board:** plain.

Reference: PN.

Notes
1. For notes on Blackie's second cheaper series, 'The New Popular Henty', see *Facing Death*, 10.7, Notes 1–3; and examples of binding style at Plates 174–175.
2. All the minor variants of With *Clive in India* in this series are grouped together under this 'generic' heading, *15.9.

16. BY SHEER PLUCK

16.1
BY SHEER PLUCK: | A TALE OF THE ASHANTI WAR: | BY | G.A. HENTY, | Author of "The Young Buglers;" "Under Drake's Flag;" "The Cornet | of Horse;" "Facing Death;" &c. &c. | WITH EIGHT FULL-PAGE ILLUSTRATIONS BY GORDON BROWNE. | (publisher's device) | LONDON: | BLACKIE & SON, 49 & 50 OLD BAILEY, E.C.; | GLASGOW, EDINBURGH, AND DUBLIN. | 1884.

Contents
185 x 122 mm. (1)–352 | catalogue (1)–32. Eight full-page line-and-wash drawings by Gordon Browne, reproduced by two-colour line blocks with mechanical tints laid for second colour (sepia), unbacked, unfolioed, tipped in.
(1) Half-title p. | (2) advertisement for *Under Drake's Flag* and *Facing Death* | (frontispiece, tipped in) | (3) title p. | (4) blank | (5) Contents | (6) blank | (7) list of Illustrations | (8) blank | (9)–352. text | (1)–32. catalogue.

Binding (see Plate 60)
Grey-green, diagonally-grained cloth boards, blocked dark green, brown, blind, and gilt; edges plain; greenish-brown surface-paper endpapers.
Front board: BY | SHEER PLUCK – | G.A. HENTY. (gilt, cased brown, out of dark-green L-shaped panel with illustration of figure of hunter with gun, knife and bag (brown and gilt). A second illustration, of jungle scene with alligator (brown and gilt), at right in lower panel, inverted L-shaped. The whole enclosed by brown rule. **Spine:** BY | SHEER | PLUCK (cloth-colour out of decorative gilt panel); G.A. HENTY (cloth-colour out of rectangular gilt panel); all-over illustration of jungle scene with alligator (brown). At foot: BLACKIE & SON (gilt) with rectangular brown ruled surround. The whole enclosed by brown rule. **Back board:** Triple blind rule (thin, thick, thin) near edges of board.

References: BL; Bod; PN | *Farmer*, p.17; *Dartt*, p.31, *Companion*, p.7.

Notes

1. The second book by Henty in Blackie's five-shilling series, published 28 September 1883.

2. Earliest bound-in catalogues are headed 'New Series for Season 1884', with announcements of *With Clive in India* and *By Sheer Pluck* without quotations from press notices. Catalogues in later issues included extracts from press reviews. As the book was published late in the year, copies of 16.1 are also found with catalogues headed 'New Series for Season 1885'.

3. By the end of February 1884 Blackie had sold 2177 copies, and over the next fifteen years a further 15,600 copies: a yearly average of 1040 in that period. In the following eighteen years a further 6422 copies were sold, making a grand total from publication date to the end of August 1917 of 24,199 copies. They were all at 5s.: the book was not re-issued in Blackie's 'New and Popular Edition'.

4. For notes on grained cloth see *Facing Death*, 10.4, Note 10. At some time in 1884 Blackie abandoned the use of grained cloth for all Henty's books.

*16.2

BY SHEER PLUCK | A TALE OF THE ASHANTI WAR. | BY | G.A. HENTY, | Author of "With Clive in India;" "Under Drake's Flag;" "In Freedom's Cause;" | "The Young Carthaginian;" "Facing Death;" &c. | WITH EIGHT FULL-PAGE ILLUSTRATIONS BY GORDON BROWNE. | (publisher's device) | LONDON | BLACKIE & SON, LIMITED, 50 OLD BAILEY, E.C. | GLASGOW AND DUBLIN

Contents: 186 x 124 mm. As for 16.1, but (a) illustrations usually printed in black instead of sepia (see Note 2); (b) advertisement (MR. HENTY'S HISTORICAL TALES.) listing 35 titles.

Binding: As for 16.1, except (a) blue cloth boards, blocked brown, green, and gilt; (b) edges burnished olive-green; (c) grey endpapers, lined off-white; (d) spine: publisher's imprint omitted; (e) back board: plain.

Reference: PN.

Notes

1. Reprints of the 5s. edition were issued for about 33 years, with small variations, following Blackie's usual pattern. The date was dropped from the title page, and alterations made to imprint and address as necessary. Blackie became a Limited Company in 1890; the Edinburgh address was not used after 1894; an Indian office opened in 1901, although Bombay did not appear regularly in the imprint until 1906; Dublin did not appear after 1910. Books listed after Henty's name on the title page soon included more recent titles and excluded any not published by Blackie.

2. Illustrations were modified, the second-colour tint either transferred to the black plate or omitted (see Appendix IV, Part 1).

3. Bindings showed variations in colour of cloth, blocking, and endpapers, often also having the publisher's name removed from the foot of the spine.

4. This copy has a bound-in catalogue listing first *The Tiger of Mysore* and *A Knight of the White Cross*, both without quotations from press reviews. The two books were published in June and August of 1895, so this reprint probably appeared that summer.

5. *By Sheer Pluck* was not re-issued in the cheaper 'New and Popular Edition'. There were, however, several variant issues of the book in its first-edition format, especially as it ran for so many years. This copy is no more than representative of them, and all are grouped together under this 'generic' heading, *16.2.

*16.3
By Sheer Pluck I A Tale of the Ashanti War I BY I G.A. HENTY I Author of "With Clive in India" "Under Drake's Flag" I "In Freedom's Cause" "The Young Carthaginian" I "Facing Death" &c. I Illustrated by Gordon Browne I BLACKIE & SON LIMITED I LONDON AND GLASGOW

Contents
181 x 125 mm. (1)–352 I no catalogue. Frontispiece from watercolour drawing, reproduced by three-colour halftone blocks; four full-page pen-drawings reproduced by line blocks printed in black-and-white; all by Gordon Browne; all on coated paper, unbacked, tipped in.

(1) Half-title p. I (2) Blackie addresses (in London, Glasgow, Bombay and Toronto) I (frontispiece, tipped in) I (3) title p. I (4) printer's imprint (Printed in Great Britain by I Blackie & Son, Limited, Glasgow) I 5. Contents I (6) blank I (7) list of Illustrations I (8) blank I 9–352. text.

Binding (see Note 1)
Light olive-green cloth boards, blocked black, brown, buff; edges plain; plain off-white endpapers.

Front board: BY SHEER I PLUCK (buff) I A TALE OF THE ASHANTI WAR (black) above illustration of British soldier in wide-brimmed hat, with rifle (black, brown, buff). At foot: G.A. HENTY. (buff). **Spine:** BY I SHEER I PLUCK I G.A. HENTY (black) above illustration of Ashanti warrior with spear (black, brown, buff). At foot: BLACKIE & SON LTD. (black). **Back board:** plain.

Reference: PN.

Notes
1. For notes on Blackie's second cheaper series, 'The New Popular Henty', see *Facing Death*, 10.7, Notes 1–3; and examples of binding style at Plates 174–175.
2. The black-and-white plates are from Gordon Browne's line drawings made for the first edition.
3. All the minor variants of *By Sheer Pluck* in the series are grouped together under this 'generic' heading, *16.3.

17. THE YOUNG COLONISTS

GENERAL NOTES

1. The publishing history of this book is very unusual. Work on its production was done in turn by three different publishers, of which the second, George Routledge and Sons, was the first to issue it. Routledge worked simultaneously from London and New York offices, and that resulted in the then rare occurrence of an English edition of an English book being printed and bound in the United States. It is therefore convenient, as a special case for this title only, to list both the British and authorised American editions in this bibliography.

2. On 24 October 1883 Henty sold to Sampson Low 'at the price or sum of Seventy Five Pounds [of] all my Copyright and interest, present and future, vested and contingent or otherwise, of and in "THE YOUNG COLONIST" [*sic*] a tale of the Zulu and Boer Wars, composed by me'. For this contract, and others mentioned below, see Appendix VI.

3. It may be wondered why Henty should have sold this book outright, and for only £75, when two years earlier he had contracted with Sampson Low for the publication of *The Cornet of Horse* for a down payment plus royalties (see 8.1, Note 3). It could be argued that considering the sums that must have been made from the book by three publishers over the years, the author came off very poorly. But there are two important considerations. First, at that period many authors preferred a down payment to royalties. Trollope held this view, believing a publisher would work harder to sell works that were his own property. Second, the contract for *The Cornet of Horse* was negotiated in exceptional circumstances, when Henty had already begun his own arrangements with a printer to produce the book (see 8.1, Notes 3–5). Further, had Henty negotiated a royalty for *The Young Colonists* on the terms offered by Sampson Low for *The Cornet of Horse*, beginning at ten per cent of the trade price, it would have amounted to only about £32.10s. on the first edition.

4. The first publisher made his profit (probably amounting to about £50) extremely quickly and unexpectedly, without ever having put the book on sale. After five months, on 27 March 1884, Sampson Low signed a contract with George Routledge & Sons to sell 'at the price or sum of two hundred and fifty pounds all our Copyright and interest, present and future, vested and contingent or otherwise, of and in the book, illustrations, and stereotype plates of the Young Colonists composed by G.A. Henty'.

5. Apart from the fact that the book had changed its title slightly between the two contracts, it will be seen that Sampson Low had already been working on its production. They had clearly intended to publish it themselves, and when they sold the rights they had more than just the manuscript to dispose of. The two contracts are in the archives of Sampson Low, together with a receipt, signed by Sampson Low, for the sum mentioned. The Routledge account book shows, however, that the sum they paid for the package was only £225, so there must have been some late bargaining after the original deal was done.

6. The obvious question – why did Sampson Low sell the book? – has not been explicitly answered. But new evidence is considered in Appendix II, Part 3, relating both to Henty's health, and to his work for Sampson Low about seven years later, and I have suggested some explanations for the sequence of events.

7. Routledge's account book shows that for the sum of £225 they acquired from Sampson Low 'Young Colonists, G.A. Henty: copyright, stereos, and 2000 sets of illustrations, with electros of do.'. They thus owned the stereos made from the type set for Sampson Low (by Gilbert and Rivington, who were asked to continue with the production of the book), but no printed sheets of the text. They received electros made from the engravings of the illustrations, but not the engravings themselves, because those, or at least some of them, were not exclusive to this book (see 17.1, Note 3). And they received 2000 sets of printed sheets of the eight illustrations. So, to produce the first issue, Routledge just had to print the text, with their own imprint on the title page, and to bind the book.

8. The two book-titles recorded under the author's name on the title page are Blackie publications, nothing from Sampson Low being allowed a mention. Blackie had started publishing Henty's 'books for young people' two years earlier, but he had not yet signed a contract with them (see Appendix VI).

17.1

THE | YOUNG COLONISTS | BY | G.A. HENTY | AUTHOR OF "CLIVE IN INDIA," "UNDER DRAKE'S FLAG," ETC. | LONDON | GEORGE ROUTLEDGE AND SONS | BROADWAY, LUDGATE HILL | NEW YORK: 9 LAFAYETTE PLACE | 1885

Contents

182 x 120 mm. (i)–(viii) | (1)–(304) catalogue (1)–8. Eight full-page engravings after various artists, including Godefroy Durand, John Schönberg, Horace Petherick, and R.C. Woodville, on uncoated paper, unbacked, unfolioed, tipped in.

(i) Half-title p. | (ii) printer's imprint (LONDON: | PRINTED BY GILBERT AND RIVINGTON, LIMITED, | ST. JOHN'S SQUARE.) (frontispiece, tipped in) | (iii) title p. | (iv) advertisement | (v)–vi. Contents | (vii) List of Illustrations | (viii) (printer's ornament) | (1)–303. text | (304) printer's imprint (LONDON: | GILBERT AND RIVINGTON, LIMITED | ST. JOHN'S SQUARE.) | (1)–8. catalogue.

Binding (see Plate 97)

Red cloth boards, bevelled, blocked black, blue, brown, blind, and gilt; or, blue cloth boards, bevelled, blocked black, red, brown, blind, and gilt; all edges gilt; blue flowered endpapers.

Front board: Decorative rules (three colours) above THE | YOUNG COLONISTS (gilt, shaded black) at top of illustration of armed African (gilt and three colours). Superimposed at lower left corner: BY | G.A. | HENTY (gilt, shaded black). **Spine:** Decorative rules (three colours); THE | YOUNG | COLONISTS (gilt) on black panel with gilt rules and grass; G.A. HENTY (gilt) on coloured panel with gilt rules over top of illustration of men shooting tiger (gilt and two colours). At foot: ROUTLEDGE (black out of gilt panel with black rules). **Back board:** Three rules near edges of bevel; publisher's monogram as central medallion (all blind).

References: BL; Bod; BB | *Farmer*, p.87; *Dartt*, p.169, *Companion*, p.36.

Notes

1. Routledge's account book (see General Note 5 above) records an edition of 2000 copies published in 1884 at 5s. Their costs are detailed thus: Payment to Sampson Low (see Notes 4 and 5 above) £225; binder's brasses £12.12s.; 20 reams of quad-crown paper £38.15s.; machining text £11.8s.; binding (at 6d. a copy) £50.3s.: Total £337.18s. The figures show an actual edition of 2006 copies and, allowing for booksellers' discounts and review copies, it was unlikely to have shewn a return of more than about £375: a profit of perhaps ten to twelve per cent on outlay.

2. Had the whole edition not been sold, the publisher would probably have made a loss. However, a profitable reprint was to follow (see 17.2, Notes 2–3).

3. The illustrations are a mixed bag, with almost as many artists as pictures. Most had been engraved to illustrate other works. That facing p.168 illustrated a story by Captain Mayne Reid on p.225 of the *Union Jack*, Vol. IV, No.15, dated 9 January 1883. The electro from the original engraving has been trimmed to fit the book page.
4. The title *With Clive in India* is incorrectly given on this and later title pages.
5. The title page has a joint London and New York imprint, and copies of this edition were at this stage possibly also on sale in the United States.
6. The book is imposed to make nineteen 16-page gatherings of text, following an 8-page section of prelims. The 8-page catalogue was also printed on text paper. We know quad-crown paper was used (see Note 1), and therefore that each sheet would consist of 32 pages. These were cut in half before folding, to make the 16-page sections, and one of the resulting half-sheets, consisting of the prelims and the catalogue, cut in half again. When a later edition was printed in the U.S., the imposition scheme was changed (see 17.3, Note 3).

17.2
Title page: As for 17.1, but date omitted.

Contents: 184 x 123 mm. As for 17.1, but printer's imprint on p.304 (LONDON: | GILBERT AND RIVINGTON, LIMITED, | ST. JOHN'S SQUARE.).

Binding (see Plate 97)
Dark-green cloth boards, bevelled, blocked black, red, bright green, blind, and gilt; edges plain; grey flowered endpapers.
  Front board: Decorative rules (black, red, bright green) above: THE | YOUNG COLONISTS (red, shaded black) at top of illustration of armed African (black, red, bright green, and gilt). Superimposed at lower left corner: BY | G.A. | HENTY (red, shaded black). **Spine, and Back board:** as for 17.1.

Reference: PN.

Notes
1. Economies in binding were made by the omission of some gilt blocking, and by leaving the edges of the leaves plain. Publisher's advertising is up-dated.
2. Routledge's account book shows the date for this impression (described by them as the second edition) as 28 October 1886. The print order was for 1000 copies.
3. Routledge's costs for the 1000 copies, including binding, amount to £56.1s.2d., which works out at 1s.1½d. per copy. If all copies were sold this should show a profit, allowing for booksellers' discounts, of about £140.
4. As for 17.1, the title page has a joint London and New York imprint.

17.3
THE | YOUNG COLONISTS | BY | G.A. HENTY | AUTHOR OF "CLIVE IN INDIA," "UNDER DRAKE'S FLAG," ETC. | LONDON | GEORGE ROUTLEDGE AND SONS, LIMITED | BROADWAY, LUDGATE HILL | MANCHESTER AND NEW YORK | 1892

Contents: 185 x 123mm. As for 17.1, except (a) p.(ii) blank; (b) frontispiece is now illustration listed to face p.71, not p.84; (c) changed imprint, etc., on title p.; (d) p.(iv) printer's imprint (LONDON: | BRADBURY, AGNEW, & CO. LIMD.

PRINTERS, WHITEFRIARS); (e) p.304, printer's imprint as on p.(iv) but has comma after 'LIMD.'; (f) catalogue up-dated.

Binding (see Plate 98)
Green cloth boards, blocked black, red, and gilt; edges plain; off-white endpapers printed in sepia with a step-and-repeat pattern of publisher's monogram.
   Front board: Series of superimposed panels, with leaves, geometrical pattern, and enlarged snowflake (red and black) with, also in superimposed panels: THE YOUNG | COLONISTS (black out of two decorative gilt rectangles), with geometrical shapes also reversed out (cloth-colour), and: ILLUSTRATED (black with black rule surround). Black rules across board at head and foot. **Spine:** similar decoration (red and black); THE YOUNG | COLONISTS (black out of gilt panel) with rules also reversed out (cloth-colour); G.A. HENTY (cloth-colour reversed out of solid gilt rectangle) with rules also reversed out (cloth colour) and black rule surround; ROUTLEDGE (black) with black rule surround. **Back board:** central vignette of leaves (black).

References: PN | *Farmer*, p.88; *Dartt*, p.169, *Companion*, p.36.

Notes
1. Routledge records a further 1000 copies to sell at the reduced price of 3s.6d., 9 March 1892. Cost of paper, and machining text and illustrations, was £23.12s.2d.; no price is shown for binding. At the old price it would have been £25 for 1000 copies.
2. The new, cheaper binding design has thinner boards, without bevels, and is blocked in fewer colours. The old stereos and electros are sent to a new printer.
3. The title, [*With*] *Clive in India*, is still incorrectly given on the title page.
4. The title-page imprint shows that Routledge became a limited liability company at some time between 1886 and 1892.
5. The entry in the Routledge account book has an added note: 'Plates sent to New York, June 1892'. The reason for this may be seen in 17.4 below.

17.4
THE | YOUNG COLONISTS | BY | G.A. HENTY | AUTHOR OF "THE CAT OF BUBASTES," "WITH CLIVE IN INDIA," "IN THE | REIGN OF TERROR," "IN FREEDOM'S CAUSE," "BY ENGLAND'S AID," | "BY PIKE AND DYKE," "HELD FAST FOR ENGLAND," ETC., ETC. | GEORGE ROUTLEDGE AND SONS, LIMITED | NEW YORK: 9 LAFAYETTE PLACE | LONDON AND MANCHESTER

Contents
183 x 132 mm. One blank leaf plus (i)–(viii) | (1)–(304) | catalogue (1)–(16) un-folioed, plus one blank leaf. Illustrations as in 17.1, printed on coated paper.
   (One blank leaf of text paper, tipped on) | (i) half-title p. | (ii) blank | (frontispiece, tipped in) | (iii) title p. | (iv) printer's imprint (The Caxton Press | 171, 173 Macdougal Street, New York) | (v)–vi. Contents | (vii) List of Illustrations | (viii) printer's ornament | (1)–303. text | (304) blank | (1)–(16) catalogue | (one blank leaf of text paper, tipped on).

Binding (see Plate 99)
Light olive-green cloth boards, blocked black, brown, white, and gilt; all edges stained green; blue surface-paper endpapers.

Front board: THE | YOUNG | COLONISTS (ornamental lettering in gilt outline, partly filled with white) above illustration of helmeted cavalryman attacking African, with sword through his shield (black, brown, and white). Beneath this: BY | G.A. HENTY (black). The whole enclosed in black ruled frame. **Spine:** THE | YOUNG | COLONISTS (gilt ornamental lettering) above illustration of African soldier with shield and spear (black, brown, and white). At foot: G.A. HENTY (gilt). **Back board:** plain.

Reference: PN.

Notes
1. The first true US edition was printed from plates sent from London in June 1892: the title page was reset (note the change of typeface) giving the New York address precedence. The edition was no doubt on sale that autumn. The catalogue is of American Routledge editions. Unfortunately no records are available.
2. The quality of production is better, the design more controlled than Routledge's UK editions. It was perhaps influenced by Scribner versions of Blackie's bindings.
3. The US printer changed the imposition of the stereos of the text sent from England. Here they make twenty 16-page gatherings: the first consisting of pp.(i)–(viii) plus (1)–8; the last of pp.297–(304) plus the 8-page catalogue. That saved the need to cut one of the half-sheets (see 17.1, Note 6), and to sew it as two 8-page gatherings. On the other hand, once the sheets were folded, all signature marks were hidden from the binder, in the centre of each section, and so lost all purpose. Also, the catalogue could not be revised until the book was reprinted.
4. The extra cost of pasting a blank leaf of text paper to the first and last gatherings can only have been justified on cosmetic grounds. Certainly the papers used for text, illustrations, and perhaps especially endpapers, although made with wood and therefore brittle, are of quality at least as good as in any other edition.
5. In the printer's imprint on p. (iv), 'The Caxton Press' is in gothic type.

17.5
Title page: As for 17.4.

Contents: 187 x 126 mm. As for 17.4, but without blank leaves tipped on first and last gatherings.

Binding (see Plate 99)
Red, rough-weave cloth boards, blocked black and white; edges plain; plain off-white laid endpapers.

Front board: plain. **Spine:** THE | YOUNG | COLONISTS (white ornamental lettering) above binder's ornament (black). At foot: G.A. HENTY (white). **Back board:** plain.

Reference: PN.

Notes
1. An American reprint of 17.4, on paper with a fractionally rougher surface. The imposition scheme remains the same (see 17.4, Note 3).

2. 17.5 followed fairly closely on 17.4: the bound-in catalogues are identical.

3. The savings made include the omission of the two blank leaves; cheaper cloth; minimal blocking; plain edges to the leaves; and cheaper endpapers.

17.6

Title page: As for 17.4, but publisher's imprint revised (LONDON | GEORGE ROUTLEDGE & SONS, LIMITED | BROADWAY, LUDGATE HILL | MANCHESTER AND NEW YORK).

Contents: 183 x 125 mm. As for 17.5, except (a) p. (iv) printer's imprint (PRINTED BY | BURR PRINTING HOUSE, | NEW YORK, U.S.A.); (b) no catalogue; (c) illustrations printed on uncoated paper. The imposition scheme is unchanged.

Binding: As for 17.3 (Plate 98), except (a) smaller boards, bevelled; (b) 'French' joints; (c) cloth colour is bluer green; (c) endpapers a warmer shade of brown; (d) single, heavy black rules, at head and foot of front board and spine, omitted.

Reference: PN.

Notes

1. Printed in New York, not by the printer of 17.4 and 17.5, but still with stereos of the original Sampson Low typesetting. The half-title and title had been reset in New York by The Caxton Press, and they remain the same here except for one important change: the title page now shows the Routledge imprint for UK editions.

2. The binding cloth, and especially the style of binding, with 'French' joints, are signs of American workmanship. It was extremely unusual for the UK edition of a book from a British publisher to be printed and also bound in the USA for sale in the UK. The late Percy Muir told me he thought this might be the very first case.

3. The binding case was blocked from electros made from the 1892 UK-edition brasses. As the boards were smaller, and made effectively smaller still by the bevels, black rules at the head and foot of the front board and spine had to be cut away.

4. The Routledge decision to print and bind a new UK edition in New York was doubtless based on some financial saving. Perhaps it was convenient to print US and UK editions in one impression, with alternative prelims. Points to be noted about this issue are: (a) The title page imprint might easily have been a joint one for London and New York, but is clearly not so; (b) There is no bound-in catalogue: for the UK market the American catalogue would have been useless, even an embarrassment, and UK catalogues would not have been worth transporting to the US binder. (c) Electros of the UK-edition brasses were sent to New York. The American binding design had not been seen in UK, and would appear strange both to booksellers and public. By the same token there would have been no advantage in using the UK design for books to be sold in the USA following the appearance of 17.4 and 17.5.

5. A final entry in the Routledge account book relating to *The Young Colonists* is dated 3 August 1894. It reads: '3s.6d. Edn. 1650 copies. £51.13s.4d. New York'. And beneath that is written: 'Ret'd to G.R. & Sons, & sold to Blackie & Son. November 1895'. The implications will be seen in 17.7, 17.8, and 17.9 below.

The Henty Society was founded in 1977 by a small group of enthusiasts, led by Roy Henty, a distant relation of G. A. Henty.

George Alfred Henty
1832-1902

was best known as a writer of boys' books which combine adventure with history. He wrote novels, including three-deckers, of which one in particular was extremely successful, and many short stories and articles. Educated at Westminster School, London, and at Gonville & Caius College, Cambridge, Henty had a wide range of interests. He was a keen yachtsman, and later owned an ocean-going yacht. He spent some years in mining operations in Italy and the UK. In the Crimea he rose to the rank of Captain in the Purveyors Department of the British army.

For short periods Henty edited boys' magazines and other periodicals including the *United Service Gazette*. From 1865 he was for many years Special Correspondent to the London daily newspaper, the *Standard,* covering many minor 19th century wars, and other events, including the Royal Tour of India by the Prince of Wales, later Edward VII.

The Henty Society has a world-wide membership; it encourages research into Henty's life and work and operates for the benefit of readers and collectors. Members receive a quarterly *Bulletin* with articles on Henty-related topics. Occasional literary and bibliographical Supplements are also issued.

UK meetings are regularly attended by members from overseas, and a strong Canadian membership organises its own functions. The Society has always encouraged the compilation of bibliographical records, and strongly supported Peter Newbolt's work on his *G. A. Henty 1832 - 1902: A Bibliographical Study*, published by Scolar Press. This book includes accounts of Henty's publishers, illustrators and designers, with essays on printing and binding methods. The Society continues to generate research into American and 'pirate' editions as well as those from European and Commonwealth countries.

The Society is also supporting the writing of a new biography, and intends to publish a collection of Henty's lesser-known short stories. David Sandler's *Ready Reference* guide to Henty titles has been highly acclaimed by collectors. and dealers alike.

Details of membership can be obtained from;
Hon. Secretary: Mrs Ann J. King, Fox Hall, Kelshall, Royston, Hertfordshire, SG8 9SE, England. Telephone: 01763 287208.

17.7

THE YOUNG COLONISTS | A STORY OF | THE ZULU AND BOER WARS | BY | G.A. HENTY | Author of "With Clive in India", "The Cat of Bubastes", "In the Reign of Terror" | "In Freedom's Cause", "By England's Aid", "By Pike and Dyke", "Held Fast for England" | &c. &c. | (5½–em rule) | WITH SIX ILLUSTRATIONS BY SIMON H. VEDDER | (5½–em rule) | NEW EDITION | (publisher's device) | LONDON | BLACKIE & SON, LIMITED, 50 OLD BAILEY, E.C. | GLASGOW AND DUBLIN | 1897

Contents

185 x 124 mm. (i)–(viii) unfolioed | (1)–(304) | catalogue (1)–32. Six full-page black-and-white wash-drawings by Simon Harmon Vedder, reproduced by halftone blocks printed on coated paper, unbacked, unfolioed, tipped in.

(Frontispiece, tipped in) | (i) title p. | (ii) blank | (iii) Preface | (iv) blank | (v) Contents | (vi) blank | (vii) list of Illustrations | (viii) blank | (1)–303. text | (304) blank | (1)–32. catalogue.

Binding (see Plate 100)

Olive-green cloth boards, blocked black, orange, red-brown, and gilt; edges plain; grey endpapers, lined off-white.

Front board: THE | YOUNG | COLONISTS (cloth-colour out of orange panel) with orange rule surround, overlapped by illustration of horseman wih rifle (black, orange, and red-brown). At right: A TALE | OF THE | ZULU | AND | BOER | WARS | G.A. HENTY (all black). **Spine:** THE | YOUNG | COLONISTS (gilt) between pairs of gilt rules; pictorial emblem (black and orange); at foot: G.A. HENTY (gilt). **Back board:** plain.

References: BL; Bod; PN | *Farmer*, p.88; *Dartt*, p.169.

Notes

1. Apart from the note in the Routledge account book (see 17.6, Note 5, above) there is no surviving record of the transaction with Blackie, nor of what led up to it. But in November 1895 Blackie bought from Routledge, for an unknown sum, their rights in the book, stereos of the text and electros of the illustrations, together with a substantial number of sets of printed sheets of the complete book. The sheets were part of the impression from the Burr Printing House, New York, which first appeared as 17.6 above. The way Blackie disposed of them may be seen under 17.8 and 17.9.
2. Although the rights were acquired in 1895, the book was not re-published by Blackie until 4 August 1896. Then, according to their usual practice, Blackie printed on the title page the date (of the year following publication), and also the words NEW EDITION. One similar use of those words was to follow later, after Blackie bought *John Hawke's Fortune* from Chapman & Hall (see 93.4).
3. The preliminary pages were reset in Blackie's familiar style, and for the first time Henty provided a Preface.
4. The book was not part of the five-shilling series of novels, but priced at 3s.6d. It has, in fact, the same number of pages as *Facing Death*, of which the price had caused so many problems at the start of Henty's association with Blackie (see *Facing Death*, 10.1 to 10.4, Notes). Since then, however, Blackie had published *A Chapter of Adventures* (1891), a book of comparable length, at 3s.6d.

5. The second general contract between Blackie and Henty, in 1891, related exclusively to 5s. and 6s. novels (see Appendix VI). It is possible an agreement existed for the cheaper books, including this one, but none has come to light.

6. Blackie commissioned a new set of six illustrations in a very different style from the originals. The text was printed by them, on their regular book paper, from stereos from the type first set for Sampson Low by Gilbert & Rivington. The result demonstrates admirably the difference between Blackie's standards and those of the earlier publishers.

17.8

Title page: As for 17.6.

Contents: 185 x 124 mm. As for 17.6.

Binding: As for 17.7, except (a) new lettering pieces in smaller size to fit narrower spine; (b) pictorial emblem trimmed at sides for the same reason.

Reference: PN.

Notes

1. This book consists of sheets of text and illustrations printed for Routledge at the Burr Printing House, New York (see 17.6, above), which were bought by Blackie with the rights (see 17.7, Note 1).

2. The binding design is that commissioned by Blackie for 17.7, now modified to fit a book with a narrower spine. Blackie's name does not appear on the binding case, nor anywhere else in the book; there is no bound-in catalogue. Indeed, there is no indication that this is not a book published by Routledge.

3. The copy described has a school prize-label dated 1899, but I suspect the book was issued considerably earlier.

17.9

Title page: As for 17.6.

Contents: 184 x 123 mm. As for 17.6, except Blackie's bound-in catalogue (1)–32.

Binding (see Plate 100)

Blue, lightly diagonally-grained cloth, blocked black and gilt; edges plain; plain off-white endpapers.

    Front board: Overall 'binder's blank' geometric and decorative design, with, at centre: THE I YOUNG I COLONISTS (cloth-colour reversed out of solid black) in rhomboid panel. **Spine:** Similar overall 'binder's blank' design, with: THE I YOUNG I COLONISTS (gilt) in upper panel, and: G.A. HENTY (gilt) in lower panel. **Back board:** plain.

Reference: PN.

Notes

1. This is a further stage in Blackie's disposal of the Routledge sheets bought in November 1895. They had already issued the book in their own style, with new illustrations and new prelims, and with only the stereos of the text remaining from earlier editions (17.7). They had also issued the old Routledge edition in a modified version of their new binding style (17.8). Now they preferred to get rid of the remaining sheets of that edition in a really cheap binding, using 'binder's blanks', and probably at a cut price. The blocking pieces for the lettering cost little enough: the spine repeated the narrow spine brasses of 17.8; and for the front board an electro was made of the brass used for the title on 17.7 and 17.8. This explains the rhomboid shape of the panel: a comparison of the lettering of the front boards of 17.9 with 17.7 or 17.8 will show that the electro could be cut only in that way in order to exclude the illustration.

2. Unexpectedly, perhaps, in a book which otherwise appeared, like 17.8, to be a Routledge production, Blackie bound in their own catalogue. Observant readers were no doubt puzzled to find it in a book with a Routledge title page, particularly if they noticed on page 9 of the catalogue an announcement of *The Young Colonists* at 3s.6d. with illustrations by Simon Vedder.

3. The latest Henty title advertised in the bound-in catalogue is *With Frederick the Great*, published 26 August 1897. The announcement includes a quotation from a press notice, so the catalogue was probably printed in the Spring or Summer of 1898.

17.10

The Young Colonists | A Story of the Zulu and | Boer Wars | BY | G.A. HENTY | Author of "With Clive in India" "In the Reign of Terror" | "Held Fast for England" &c. | ILLUSTRATED | BLACKIE AND SON LIMITED | LONDON GLASGOW AND BOMBAY

Contents: 184 × 126 mm. As for 17.7, except (a) catalogue 1–16; (b) p.(ii) advertisement (NEW AND POPULAR EDITION OF | G.A. HENTY'S WORKS) listing 36 titles including this one; (c) printer's imprint at foot of p.303 (PRINTED IN GREAT BRITAIN | At the Villafield Press, Glasgow, Scotland).

Binding: As for 17.7, but all edges stained olive-green.

Reference: PN.

Notes

1. The title page is again re-set, and the book is now included in Blackie's 'New and Popular Edition'. It is on bulky featherweight paper, but still from stereos of the original typesetting for the publisher who never published it, Sampson Low.

2. *The Young Colonists* has at last caught up with books in the Blackie 5s. and 6s. series of novels, being sold on equal terms with titles from both price ranges, for all Henty's works in the 'New and Popular Edition' were priced at 3s.6d. In this case, however, Blackie had never sold the book at any other price.

3. As it did not start as one of Blackie's regular novels *The Young Colonists* is not listed in their surviving sales records, and no date is known for its inclusion in this series. My copy was issued after 1910, being without the Dublin address in the title-page imprint, and is inscribed with the date 1914. Copies may possibly be found with alternative imprints.

4. The book was not included in the second cheaper series, the 'New Popular Henty', issued during the 1920s (see Appendix V). Possibly it appeared in even later formats: for them the bindings were modified by dropping the pictorial blocking from the front board, and eventually from the spine, until only rules and simple lettering remained. Those later issues fall outside the scope of this bibliography.

18. IN FREEDOM'S CAUSE

18.1

IN FREEDOM'S CAUSE: | A STORY OF | WALLACE AND BRUCE. | BY | G.A HENTY, | Author of "With Clive in India," "By Sheer Pluck," "Facing Death," | "Under Drake's Flag," &c. | WITH TWELVE FULL-PAGE ILLUSTRATIONS BY GORDON BROWNE. | (publisher's device) | LONDON: | BLACKIE & SON, 49 & 50 OLD BAILEY, E.C.; | GLASGOW, EDINBURGH, AND DUBLIN | 1885. *(Note: The full point after* A *in* G.A HENTY *is missing).*

Contents

186 x 131 mm. (i)–(viii) | (9)–392 | catalogue (1)–32. Twelve full-page line-and-tint drawings by Gordon Browne, reproduced as two-colour line blocks by the Parisian engravers Guillaume Frères, printed in black and sepia on uncoated paper, unbacked, unfolioed, tipped in.

(Frontispiece, tipped in) | (i) title p. | (ii) blank | (iii)–iv. Preface | (v)–vi. Contents | (vii) list of Illustrations | (viii) blank | (9)–392. text | (1)–32. catalogue.

Binding (see Plate 71)

Turquoise cloth boards, bevelled, blocked black, maroon, blind, and gilt; all edges burnished yellow-green; maroon surface-paper endpapers.

Front board: IN FREEDOM'S | (ornament) CAUSE. (ornament) (all gilt, cased black) on maroon rectangular panel within black and gilt rules. A | STORY | . OF . | WALLACE (between rules) | . & . | BRUCE (between decorative rules) (all black) within black-ruled frame, inset in upper right corner of illustration of armed knight on charger (black, maroon, and gilt). At foot: BY . G . A . HENTY (gilt) on maroon panel with gilt decorations, all within double gilt-ruled frame. The whole enclosed in black and maroon ruled frame. **Spine:** IN | FREEDOM'S | CAUSE (black, and cloth-colour) reversed out of solid gilt panel with other rules, formal thistle-decorations, etc. reversed out (cloth-colour). Illustration of armed figure with shield and lance (black, maroon, gilt) above: G.A HENTY [*sic*] | (ornament) (gilt). At foot: BLACKIE & SON. (gilt) within gilt-ruled frame. The whole enclosed by black rules. **Back board:** triple rules near edges of board (blind).

References: BL; Bod; PN | *Farmer*, p.44; *Dartt*, p.79, *Companion*, p.18.

Notes

1. Publication date was 16 July 1884. By the end of February 1885 Blackie had sold 2698 copies at six shillings. Over the following fifteen years the book had a regular sale, though not quite as strong as Blackie's previous books by Henty. The total over this period was 9379 copies; average annual sales over the first sixteen years were 755 copies. A further 1619 copies were sold in the next five years, up to August 1905, when the book was re-issued in the cheaper edition (see 18.3 below). Eight copies remained, and they were sold sold concurrently with the 'New and Popular Edition'. A total of 11,006 copies was sold at six shillings.

2. As usual with Blackie novels, the earliest issues contain the catalogue advertising books for the current year (in this case 'New Series for Season 1885') without quotations from press reviews.

*18.2

Reprints of the six-shilling edition were in the style of 18.1, following Blackie's usual pattern. The date was removed from the title page. Alterations were made to title-page imprint and address as necessary: Blackie became a Limited Company in 1890; the Edinburgh address was not used after 1904; and the Indian office was opened in 1901, although Bombay did not appear regularly in the imprint before 1906. The illustrations were in due course modified, the second-colour tint either transferred to the black plate or omitted (see Appendix IV, Part 1).

Binding continued to show variations in colour of cloth, blocking, and endpapers, often also having the publisher's name removed from the spine. From 1883 some books were given 'olivine edges', see Appendix II, Part 5, Note 73), and in a few years they became standard for all the novels.

The slightly-varying issues of this title in its first-edition format are all grouped together under this 'generic' heading, *18.2.

18.3

In Freedom's Cause I A Story of Wallace and Bruce I BY I G.A.HENTY I Author of "The Lion of the North" "With Clive in India" "By Sheer Pluck" I "True to the Old Flag" "Facing Death" "Under Drake's Flag" &c. I ILLUSTRATED I NEW EDITION I BLACKIE AND SON LIMITED I LONDON GLASGOW DUBLIN BOMBAY I 1906

Contents

186 x 124 mm. (1)–392 I catalogue 1–32. Eight wash-drawings by an unknown hand reproduced by halftone blocks printed in sepia on coated paper, unbacked, unfolioed, tipped in.

(Frontispiece, tipped in) I (1) title p. I (2) blank I 3. Preface I iv. [roman numerals in error] Preface, continued I 5. Contents I vi. [roman numerals in error] Contents, continued I 7. list of Illustrations I (8) blank I 9–392. text I 1–32. catalogue.

Binding (see Note 2)

Red cloth boards, blocked black, orange, buff, and gilt; all edges stained olive-green; grey endpapers, lined off-white.

Front board: IN I FREEDOM'S I CAUSE I G.A. HENTY (buff) above illustration of horseman waving his hat (black, orange, buff), signed at foot: J Hassall (black). **Spine:** IN I FREEDOM'S I CAUSE I G.A. HENTY (gilt) above illustration of standing figure with shield and sword, wearing feathered Tam o'Shanter (black, orange, buff). At foot: BLACKIE & SON LTD (gilt). **Back board:** plain.

References: BL; Bod.

Notes

1. The illustrations are based on Gordon Browne's original line-and-tint drawings.

2. This impression in the 'New and Popular Edition', was isued in 1905 (title-page date 1906). For details of the series see *Facing Death*, 10.6, Notes 2–3; and examples of binding style, Plates 172–173.

3. At the end of 1906 Blackie had sold 3084 copies, and over the years from 1906 to 1917, when records cease, the total sold at 3s.6d. was 12,771. The grand total of copies of this title sold by Blackie from 1884 to 1917 was 23,777.

*18.4

Title page: As for 18.3, except (a) NEW EDITION deleted; (b) changed imprint (BLACKIE AND SON LIMITED | LONDON GLASGOW AND BOMBAY); (c) no date.

Contents

184 x 123 mm. (1)–392 | no catalogue. Frontispiece from watercolour drawing by Gordon Browne, reproduced by three-colour halftone blocks; four full-page wash-drawings by an unknown hand based on the original two-colour line-drawings by Gordon Browne, reproduced by halftone blocks printed in black; all on coated paper, unbacked, keyed to text pages, tipped in.

(1) Half-title p. | (2) advertisement (G.A. HENTY'S BOOKS) listing 56 titles | (frontispiece, tipped in) | (3) title p. | (4) printer's imprint (Printed in Great Britain by | Blackie & Son, Limited, Glasgow) | 5–6. Preface | 7–8. Contents | (9) list of Illustrations | (10) blank | 11–392. text.

Binding: (see Plate 175). As for 18.3, except (a) no gilt: front-board lettering now buff, spine lettering now black; (b) edges plain; (c) plain off-white endpapers.

Reference: PN.

Notes

1. For notes on Blackie's second cheaper series, 'The New Popular Henty', and subsequent editions of this book, see *Facing Death*, 10.7, Notes 1–3 and 6–8.
2. All the minor variants of *In Freedom's Cause* in the series are grouped together under this 'generic' heading, *18.4.

19. TRUE TO THE OLD FLAG

19.1

TRUE TO THE OLD FLAG: | A TALE OF THE | AMERICAN WAR OF INDEPENDENCE. | BY | G.A. HENTY, | Author of "With Clive in India," "By Sheer Pluck," "Facing Death," | "Under Drake's Flag," &c. | WITH TWELVE FULL-PAGE ILLUSTRATIONS BY GORDON BROWNE. | (publisher's device) | LONDON: | BLACKIE & SON, 49 & 50 OLD BAILEY, E.C.; | GLASGOW, EDINBURGH, AND DUBLIN. | 1885.

Contents

186 x 130 mm. (i)–(viii) | (9)–390 | catalogue (1)–32. Twelve full-page engravings in two colours by Gillaume Frères after line-and-wash drawings by Gordon Browne (see Appendix IV, Part 2), printed in black and sepia. Six battle-plans in black line printed on text pages.

(i) Half-title p. | (ii) blank | (frontispiece, tipped in) | (iii) title p. | (iv) blank | (v)–vi. Preface | (vii) Contents | (viii) list of Illustrations and Maps | (9)–390. text | (1)–32. catalogue.

Binding (see Plate 85)

Blue, diagonally-grained cloth boards, bevelled, blocked black, maroon, blind, and gilt; all edges burnished yellowish olive-green; maroon surface-paper endpapers.

Front board: TRUE | TO | THE OLD | FLag. [*sic*] (gilt, cased in black) above illustration of British soldier with sword and banner standing over two fallen. At right, between two decorative flourishes: A | TALE | . OF . THE . | . AMERICAN . | WAR | OF | INDEPENDENCE (black, with maroon ornament each side of WAR). At foot: (ornament) BY (ornament) G . A . HENTY (ornament) (all gilt, within double-ruled gilt frame). **Spine:** (ornament) TRUE (ornament) | TO . THE | OLD . FLAG | (3-cm. rule) (all gilt, within gilt ruled border) above illustration of standing British soldier, wounded, with pistol and lowered flag (black and gilt) and: BY | G.A. HENTY. (black) within black ruled border; the whole within gilt ruled frame. At foot: + BLACKIE & SON + (gilt) within double gilt ruled frame. Black and gilt rules at head and foot of spine. **Back board:** Three rules (thin, thick, thin) at edges of board (blind).

References: BL; Bod; PN | *Farmer*, p.72; *Dartt*, p.141, *Companion*, p.31.

Notes

1. The book was published on 2 August 1884 at six shillings. By the end of February 1885 Blackie had sold 2528 copies. Over the next fifteen years a further 8406 copies were sold, the average yearly sales for the first sixteen years being 683. Between August 1900 and August 1912, when the cheaper edition was issued, Blackie sold 2897 more copies, and the last 28 copies at six shillings were sold concurrently with the 'New and Popular Edition' at 3s.6d. (see 19.3).

2. *Farmer* remarks: 'This is one of the most important of Henty's contributions to historical fiction as it gives, alone of all contemporary writers, the British side of the War of American Independence, and is taken from the best authentic accounts'.

3. *Dartt* mistakenly reports 'first page of catalogue a full-page sketch of Henty' being once again confused between Blackie and Scribner editions. In his *Companion* he appears surprised to find 'full-page Henty foto not in' three copies in well-known English collections. As far as I know Blackie never used a full-page sketch or photograph of Henty on the *first* page of any catalogue bound in Henty titles. A small photograph of Henty did appear on the first page of a catalogue printed in 1900 which was bound in copies of books with title-page date 1901.

4. For a note on Blackie's use of grained cloth see *Facing Death* (10.4, Note 10).

5. As usual with Blackie novels, the earliest issues contain the catalogue advertising books for the current year (in this case 'New Series for Season 1885') without quotations from press reviews.

*19.2

Reprints of the six-shilling edition, in the style of 19.1, followed Blackie's usual pattern. The date was removed from the title page. Alterations were made to title-page imprint and address as necessary: Blackie became a Limited Company in 1890; the Edinburgh address was not used after 1904; and the Indian office was opened in 1901, although Bombay did not appear regularly in the imprint until 1906; Dublin was removed after 1910.

Illustrations were in due course modified, the second-colour tint either transferred to the black plate or omitted (see Appendix IV, Part 1).

Bindings continued to show variation in colour of cloth, blocking, and endpapers, often also having the publisher's name removed from the foot of the spine.

The slightly-varying issues in the first-edition format are all grouped together under this 'generic' heading, *19.2.

19.3

True to the Old Flag | A Tale of the American War of Independence | BY | G.A. HENTY | Author of "The Lion of the North" "With Clive in India" "Through the Fray" | "In Freedom's Cause" "The Dragon and the Raven" "Facing Death" &c. | ILLUSTRATED BY CHARLES M. SHELDON | NEW EDITION | BLACKIE AND SON LIMITED | LONDON GLASGOW AND BOMBAY

Contents

183 x 126 mm. (1)–390 | catalogue 1–16. Six full-page wash-drawings by Charles M. Sheldon, reproduced by halftone blocks printed in sepia on coated paper, unbacked, unfolioed, tipped in. Six battle-plans printed from line blocks on text pages.

(1) Half-title p. | (2) advertisement (NEW AND POPULAR EDITION OF | G.A. HENTY'S WORKS) listing 36 titles | (frontispiece, tipped in) | (3) title p. | (4) blank | 5. Preface | vi. [roman numerals in error] Preface, continued | (7) Contents | (8) list of Illustrations | 9–390. text, with printer's imprint at foot of p.390 (PRINTED IN GREAT BRITAIN | At the Villafield Press, Glasgow, Scotland) | 1–16. catalogue.

Binding (see Note 1)

Green cloth boards, blocked black, brown, vermilion, and gilt; all edges stained olive-green; grey endpapers lined off-white.

Front board: TRUE TO THE | OLD FLAG (three square dots) | A TALE OF THE AMERICAN WAR | OF INDEPENDENCE (two square dots) | BY | G.A. HENTY (all gilt) above illustration framed by black rules, of soldier sitting on rocks among trees (black, brown, vermilion). **Spine:** TRUE TO | THE OLD | . FLAG . | G.A. HENTY (all gilt) above illustration framed by black rules, of standing figure of young Indian (black, brown, vermilion); signature: J Hassall (black). At foot: BLACKIE & SON LTD (black). **Back board:** plain.

Reference: BL.

Notes

1. In 1912 Blackie re-issued this title in their 'New and Popular Edition'. 1911 had been the last year in which dated title pages (dated 1912) were used in the series, so the first re-issues of *True to the Old Flag* were printed with no date. Further details of the series are given under *Facing Death*, 10.6, Notes 2–3, and examples of binding style at Plates 172–173.

2. By the end of August 1913 Blackie had sold 1861 copies in this edition, and in the four years to 1917, when Blackie's records cease, they sold 1772 more. Average annual sales for the five years were 727 copies. The grand total of copies sold at both prices from 1884 to 1917 is 17,492.

*19.4

True to the Old Flag | A Tale of the American War | of Independence | BY | G.A. HENTY | Author of "The Lion of the North" "With Clive in India" | "Through the Fray" "In Freedom's Cause" | "The Dragon and the Raven" | "Facing Death" &c. | ILLUSTRATED | BLACKIE AND SON LIMITED | LONDON GLASGOW AND BOMBAY

Contents
185 x 125 mm. (i)–(viii) | 9–(392) | no catalogue. Frontispiece from watercolour drawing by John de Walton, reproduced by three-colour halftone blocks; four full-page wash-drawings by Charles M. Sheldon, reproduced by halftone blocks printed in black; all on coated paper unbacked, unfolioed, tipped in.

(i) Half-title p. | (ii) publisher's advertisement (G.A. HENTY'S BOOKS) listing 46 titles | (frontispiece, tipped in) | (iii) title p. | (iv) blank | v–vi. Preface | vii. Contents | (viii) list of Illustrations | 9–390. text, with printer's imprint at foot of p.390 (PRINTED IN GREAT BRITAIN | By Blackie & Son, Limited, Glasgow) | (391)–(392) blank.

Binding: As for 19.3, except (a) Grey-blue cloth boards, blocked black, dark-grey, and orange; (b) edges plain; (c) plain off-white endpapers; (d) no gilt blocking: all lettering on case is black.

Reference: PN.

Notes
1. For notes on Blackie's second cheaper series, 'The New Popular Henty', and subsequent editions of this book, see *Facing Death*, 10.7, Notes 1–3 and 6–8. Examples of binding style are at Plates 174–175.
2. All the minor variants of *True to the Old Flag* in the series are grouped together under this 'generic' heading, *19.4.

20. ST. GEORGE FOR ENGLAND

20.1
ST. GEORGE FOR ENGLAND: | A TALE OF | CRESSY AND POITIERS. | BY | G.A. HENTY, | Author of "With Clive in India," "By Sheer Pluck," Facing Death," | "Under Drake's Flag," &c. | WITH EIGHT FULL-PAGE ILLUSTRATIONS BY GORDON BROWNE. | (publisher's device) | LONDON: | BLACKIE & SON, 49 & 50 OLD BAILEY, E.C.; | GLASGOW, EDINBURGH, AND DUBLIN. | 1885.

Contents
186 x 123 mm. (i)–(viii) | (9)–352 | catalogue (1)–32. Eight full-page line-and-wash drawings by Gordon Browne, printed in black and grey, with some mechanical tints, on uncoated paper, unbacked, unfolioed, tipped in.

(Frontispiece, tipped in) | (i) title p. | (ii) blank | (iii)–iv. Preface | (v) Contents | (vi) blank | (vii) list of Illustrations | (viii) blank | (9)–352. text | (1)–32. catalogue.

Binding (see Plate 81)
Olive-green cloth boards, blocked black, maroon, blind, and gilt; edges plain; dark-brown surface-paper endpapers.
Front board: ST. GEORGE . FOR . ENGLAND. (gilt, cased black) above illustration of mounted knight in armour (black, maroon, and gilt). Beneath this: + A + TALE + OF + CRESSY + | AND POITIERS. (maroon). At foot: G.A.HENTY. (gilt, cased black) with two ornaments at each side (maroon). Thick and thin rules (black) at head and foot of board. **Spine:** ST. GEORGE . | . . . FOR . . . | ENGLAND (cloth-colour out of solid gilt panel) with other dots and rules reversed out, and with

black decorative rules above and below. Illustration of mounted knight in armour, with lance (black, maroon, gilt) above: . G . A . HENTY . I (rule) I (three ornaments) (all maroon). At foot: BLACKIE & SON (cloth-colour reversed out of gilt panel) with black rules above and below. **Back board:** three rules near edges of board (blind).

References: BL; Bod; PN I *Farmer*, p.62; *Dartt*, p.116, *Companion*, p.25.

Notes

1. Publication date was 27 August 1884. By the end of February 1885 Blackie had sold 2650 copies at five shillings. Over the next fifteen years they sold a further 10,882 copies, the average annual sale for the sixteen years being 846. The book continued to have a steady sale, and in August 1916, at the end of another sixteen-year period, 7063 more copies had been sold, still at the original price of five shillings. Thus, over the first 32 years, the average annual sale was 644 copies. Early in 1917 the book was re-issued in the cheaper 'New and Popular Edition' (see 20.4 below). Of the 5s. edition 34 remaining copies were sold in 1917.

2. *Dartt* shows confusion between the Blackie and first Scribner editions in the matter of 'burnished olivine edges'. (See also Appendix II, Part 5, Note 73).

3. As usual with Blackie novels, the earliest issues contain the catalogue advertising books for the current year (in this case 'New Series for Season 1885') without quotations from press reviews.

*20.2

Reprints of the five-shilling edition, in the style of 20.1, followed Blackie's usual pattern. The date was removed from the title page. Alterations were made to title-page imprint and addresses as necessary: Blackie became a Limited Company in 1890; the Edinburgh address was not used after 1904, and the Indian office was opened in 1901, although Bombay did not appear regularly in the imprint until 1906. A half-title page was later introduced, and the preliminary pages re-arranged. In later issues the title page was reset. Illustrations were modified, the second colour, and mechanical tints, being omitted (see Appendix IV, Part 1).

Bindings continued to show variations in colour of cloth, blocking, and endpapers, often having the publisher's name removed from the spine.

The slightly varying issues of this title in its first-edition format are all grouped together under this 'generic' heading, *20.2.

20.3

St. George for England I A Tale of Cressy and Poitiers I BY I G.A. HENTY I Author of "With Clive in India" "By Sheer Pluck" "Facing Death" I "Under Drake's Flag" "Redskin and Cowboy" "The Dash for Khartoum" &c. I WITH EIGHT FULL-PAGE ILLUSTRATIONS I BY GORDON BROWNE (see Note 4 below) I BLACKIE AND SON LIMITED I LONDON GLASGOW AND BOMBAY

Contents

185 x 124 mm. (1)–352 I no catalogue. Six full-page wash and pencil drawings by Frank Gillett, reproduced by halftone blocks printed on coated paper, unbacked, tipped in (see Note 4 below).

(1) Half-title p. I (2) publisher's advertisement (NEW AND POPULAR

EDITION OF I G.A. HENTY'S WORKS) listing 45 titles I (frontispiece, tipped in)
I (3) title p. I (4) blank I 5. Preface I vi. [roman numerals in error] Preface, continued
I (7) Contents I (8) blank I (9) list of Illustrations I (10) blank I 11–352. text, with
printer's imprint at foot of p.352 (PRINTED IN GREAT BRITAIN I At the
Villafield Press, Glasgow, Scotland).

Binding
Red cloth boards, blocked black, orange, buff, and gilt; edges plain; grey endpapers,
lined off-white.
Front board: ST GEORGE I FOR I ENGLAND. I G.A. HENTY. (buff) above
and at left of illustration of standard-bearer with sword and shield, St George and
dragon shown on standard (black, orange, buff). **Spine:** ST GEORGE I FOR I
ENGLAND. I G.A. HENTY (gilt) above illustration of soldier with long sword,
drawn (black, orange, buff). At foot: BLACKIE & SON LTD (black). **Back board:**
plain.

Reference: PN.

Notes
1. Issued in 1916 in the 'New and Popular Edition' of Henty's novels, and sold at
3s.6d. Blackie record this and *With Kitchener in the Soudan* as the last to appear in
the series, although *In the Reign of Terror* was added the following year. For details
of the series see *Facing Death*, 10.6, Notes 2–3, and for examples of binding style,
Plates 172–173. Blackie's custom of dating title pages of first impressions in the
'New and Popular Edition' ceased after those issued in 1911 and dated 1912.
2. Wartime economies caused less gold to be used for blocking, and gilt lettering
tended to disappear from all titles. By 1916 gilt was omitted from the front board,
even of the first issue. For later issues it was removed from the spine as well.
3. Blackie's records for these books cease at the end of August 1917, so all that is
known about this impression is that 1498 copies were sold in that year.
4. The type was completely reset for this edition, and six new illustrations were
commissioned from Frank Gillett. The title-page credit to the illustrator has not been
changed from that in the earlier edition, so both the name of the artist and the number
of illustrations are given incorrectly. The new pictures are correctly listed on p.(9).
The Preface has been slightly re-worded.

*20.4
St. George for England I A Tale of Cressy and Poitiers I BY I G.A. HENTY I Author
of "With Clive in India" "By Sheer Pluck" "Facing Death" I "Under Drake's Flag"
"Redskin and Cowboy" "The Dash for Khartoum" &c. I ILLUSTRATED BY
FRANK GILLETT, R.I. I BLACKIE AND SON LIMITED I LONDON
GLASGOW BOMBAY

Contents
185 x 125 mm. (1)–352 I no catalogue. Frontispiece from watercolour drawing
reproduced by three-colour halftone blocks; four full-page wash and pencil drawings
reproduced by halftone blocks; all by Frank Gillett, R.I., printed on coated paper,
unbacked, tipped in.
(1) Half-title p. I (2) publisher's advertisement (G.A. HENTY'S BOOKS) listing

45 titles I (frontispiece, tipped in) I (3) title p. I (4) blank I 5. Preface I vi. [roman numerals in error] Preface, continued I (7) Contents I (8) blank I (9) list of Illustrations I (10) blank I 11–352. text, with printer's imprint at foot of p.352 (PRINTED IN GREAT BRITAIN I By Blackie & Son, Limited, Glasgow).

Binding: As for 20.3, except (a) dark-blue cloth boards, blocked black, red, and buff; (b) plain off-white endpapers; (c) title and author on spine are now buff.

References: Bod; PN.

Notes
1. Issued in 1923 in Blackie's second cheaper series, 'The New Popular Henty'. For details of that, and subsequent editions, see under *Facing Death*, 10.7, Notes 1–3 and 6–8. Examples of the series binding style are at Plates 174–175.
2. All the minor variants of *St. George for England* in the series are grouped together under this 'generic' heading *20.5.

21. THE DRAGON AND THE RAVEN

21.1
THE I DRAGON AND THE RAVEN: I OR; I THE DAYS OF KING ALFRED. I BY I G.A. HENTY, I Author of "True to the Old Flag," "St. George for England," "In Freedom's Cause," I "With Clive in India," "By Sheer Pluck," "Facing Death," &c. &c. I WITH EIGHT FULL-PAGE ILLUSTRATIONS I BY C.J. STANILAND, R.I. I (publisher's device) I LONDON: I BLACKIE & SON, 49 & 50 OLD BAILEY, E.C.; I GLASGOW, EDINBURGH, AND DUBLIN. I 1886.

Contents
187 x 125 mm. (i)–(viii) I (9)–352 I catalogue (1)–40. Eight full-page line-and-wash drawings by C.J. Staniland, R.I., reproduced by two-colour line blocks, with sepia tint plates including mechanical tints, unbacked, unfolioed, tipped in.
(i) Half-title p. I (ii) advertisement (BOOKS BY G.A. HENTY.) I (frontispiece, tipped in) I (iii) title p. I (iv) blank I (v)–vi. Preface I (vii) Contents I (viii) list of Illustrations I (9)–352. text I (1)–40. catalogue.

Binding (see Plate 63)
Brown cloth boards, blocked black, orange, blind, and gilt; edges plain; brown surface-paper endpapers.
Front board: Overall elaborately decorated panels, with three gilt rules at head and foot. In upper triangular panel: THE I DRAGON . AND I . THE I RAVEN (gilt, cased black, with gilt embellishment). In lower horizontal rectangular panels: OR THE DAYS OF KING ALFRED. (gilt, cased orange) I G.A. HENTY (between two pairs of decorative 'flowers') (all cloth-colour reversed out of orange, with black casing). **Spine:** THE I DRAGON I AND THE I RAVEN. (cloth-colour reversed out of solid gilt panel) with small decorations also reversed out. Beneath this: trophy including helmet and weapons, etc. (black, orange, gilt); G.A. HENTY (cloth-colour reversed out of solid gilt rectangle) with ruled frame also reversed out; Blackie & Son (gilt) between two decorative rules (black). All these panels enclosed in a series of gilt and black rules. **Back board:** three rules (thin, thick, thin) near edges of board (blind).

References: BL; Bod; PN | *Farmer*, p.27; *Dartt*, p.51, *Companion*, p.14.

Notes
1. Publication was on 2 May 1885 at five shillings. By the end of February 1886 Blackie had sold 2628 copies. During the following fifteen years they sold 6912 more, a smaller total in such a time than for any of Henty's novels from Blackie so far. That gave an average annual sale, over the first sixteen years, of 596 copies. Blackie sold 1650 more copies by the end of August 1907; then the book was re-issued in the cheaper 'New and Popular Series' (see 21.3, below). The last 92 copies were sold over three years, concurrently with the 3s.6d. edition.
2. As usual in Blackie novels, catalogues in the earliest issues show books for the current year (in this case dated 1886) without quotations from press reviews.
3. This is the first of Henty's novels from Blackie that was not illustrated by Gordon Browne.

*21.2
Reprints of the five-shilling edition were issued in the style of 21.1, but with no date on the title-page. Alterations were made to title-page imprint and addresses as necessary: Blackie became a Limited Company in 1890; the Edinburgh address was not used after 1894; the Indian office was opened in 1901 although Bombay did not appear regularly in the imprint until 1906.
Illustrations were in due course modified, the second-colour tint either transferred to the black plate or omitted (see Appendix IV, Part 1). Bindings continued to show variations in colour of cloth, blocking and endpapers, sometimes also having the publisher's name removed from the foot of the spine.
The slightly-varying issues of this title in its first-edition format are all grouped together under this 'generic' heading, *21.2.

21.3
The Dragon and the Raven | Or, The Days of King Alfred | BY | G.A. HENTY | Author of "With Clive in India" "The Lion of the North" "In Freedom's Cause" | "Through the Fray" "By Sheer Pluck" "Facing Death" &c. | ILLUSTRATED | NEW EDITION | BLACKIE AND SON LIMITED | LONDON GLASGOW DUBLIN BOMBAY | 1908

Contents
184 x 127 mm. (1)–352 | catalogue 1–16. Eight full-page wash-drawings by an unknown hand, reproduced by halftone blocks printed in sepia, unbacked, unfolioed, tipped in.
  (1) Half-title p. | (2) advertisement (HENTY'S TALES OF BRITISH HISTORY) listing 38 titles | (frontispiece, tipped in) | (3) title p. | (4) blank | 5. Preface | vi. [roman numerals in error] Preface, continued | 7. Contents | 8. list of Illustrations | 9–352. text | 1–16. catalogue.

Binding (see Note 3)
Red cloth boards, blocked black, buff, orange, and gilt; edges stained olive-green; grey endpapers lined off-white.
  Front board: THE DRAGON & | THE RAVEN (gilt) | OR THE DAYS OF KING ALFRED (black) above illustration of soldier with winged helmet, sword and

shield, under fire from arrows (black, buff, orange). At foot: G.A. HENTY. (buff). **Spine:** THE I DRAGON I & THE I RAVEN. I G.A. HENTY (gilt) above illustration of similar soldier standing, with bow, shield and sword, etc. (black, buff, orange). At foot: BLACKIE & SON. LTD (black). **Back board:** plain.

References: BL; Bod.

Notes

1. This impression, in Blackie's 'New and Popular Edition' of Henty's novels, all of which were sold at 3s.6d., was issued in 1907. By the following year 2086 copies had been sold, and over the next nine years up to 1917, when records cease, 4328 more, making a total of 6414 at this price. The grand total from 1885 to 1917 was 17,696.

2. The anonymous illustrations are closely based on the original line-and-wash drawings by C.J. Staniland.

3. Details of the series are given under *Facing Death*, 10.6, Notes 2–3; examples of binding style at Plates 172–173.

21.4

THE TALISMAN LIBRARY (underlined) I THE DRAGON AND I THE RAVEN I BY I G.A. HENTY I (publisher's device) I BLACKIE AND SON LIMITED I 50 OLD BAILEY LONDON I GLASGOW AND BOMBAY I 1921

Contents

174 x 113 mm. (i)–(xx) I 1–72 I no catalogue. Frontispiece from pen-drawing by C.J. Staniland, R.I., reproduced by line block printed in black on coated paper, unbacked, tipped in.

   (i) Half-title p. I (ii) unheaded introduction to the Talisman Library I (frontispiece, tipped in) I (iii) title p. I (iv) list of titles in series I v–xix. Introduction I (xx) blank I 1–157. text I 158–172. Notes, with printer's imprint on p.172 (PRINTED AND BOUND IN GREAT BRITAIN I By Blackie & Son, Limited, Glasgow).

Binding (see Note 3)

Grey cloth boards, blocked blue (see Note 3); edges plain; plain off-white endpapers.

   Front board: THE . DRAGON I & . THE . RAVEN I G.A. Henty I (publisher's trade mark for the series, including: The I TALISMAN I Library of I ENGLISH I AUTHORS) I Blackie.&.Son.Limited (all blue) within framework of decorative rules (blue). **Spine:** DRAGON . AND . RAVEN (blue) runnng from foot to head. **Back board:** plain.

References: BL; Bod; BB.

Notes

1. In 1921 Blackie issued this as the fifth Henty title in 'The Talisman Library of English Authors'. (The full title takes no account of the fact that the first two books, issued in 1920, were by Sir Walter Scott!). In the same year two by Charles Kinglsey were followed by the first four Henty titles: *With Clive in India, Under Drake's Flag, With Wolfe in Canada* and *Redskin and Cowboy*. One more, *Beric the Briton*, followed in 1922.

2. The frontispiece is from the black plate only of one of the two-colour illustrations in 21.1.

3. Books in the series (example at Plate 145) were also issued in limp cloth covers, cut flush, in the same design, and with no alteration to the contents.
4. Later impressions in both styles of binding were issued with undated title pages.

21.5

THE TALISMAN LIBRARY (underlined) | THE DRAGON AND | THE RAVEN | BY | G.A. HENTY | (publisher's device) | BLACKIE & SON LIMITED | LONDON AND GLASGOW

Contents

171 x 115 mm. (i)–(xx) | 1–172 | no catalogue. Frontispiece as in 21.4.
  (i)–(ii) Introduction to the series with bold heading on p.(i): 'The Talisman Library of English Authors', and the titles in the series listed on p.(ii) | (frontispiece, tipped in) | (iii) title p. | (iv) Blackie addresses, and printer's imprint (Printed in Great Britain by Blackie & Son, Ltd., Glasgow) | v–xix. Introduction | (xx) blank | 1–157. text | 158–172. Notes, with imprint at foot of p.172 (PRINTED AND BOUND IN GREAT BRITAIN | By Blackie & Son, Limited, Glasgow).

Binding: As for 21.4.

Reference: BU.

Notes

1. Following the issues both dated and undated of 21.4 (see also 21.4, Note 4), the preliminary pages were reset. The main changes, apart from the title-page imprint, were the re-arrangement of the introductory notes and the list of titles in the series. Otherwise the text appears to be unaltered.
2. The series continued in production, both in limp cloth and in cloth boards, at least for two decades. Copies of some titles are found with the Book Production War Economy symbol on p. (iv), a measure required of British publishers during the second war (see *With Wolfe in Canada*, 27.4, Note 3).

*21.6

The Dragon and | the Raven | Or, The Days of King Alfred | BY | G.A. HENTY | Author of "With Clive in India" "The Lion of the North" "In Freedom's Cause" | "By Sheer Pluck" "Facing Death" &c. | ILLUSTRATED | BLACKIE & SON LIMITED | LONDON AND GLASGOW

Contents

186 x 125 mm. (1)–352 | advertisements (1)–(2). Frontispiece from watercolour drawing by Frank Gillett, R.I., reproduced by three-colour halftone blocks; four full-page wash-drawings by unknown artist, reproduced by halftone blocks printed in black; all on coated paper, unbacked, tipped in.
  (1) Half-title p. | (2) Blackie addresses | (frontispiece, tipped in) | (3) title p. | (4) printer's imprint (Printed in Great Britain by | Blackie & Son, Limited, Glasgow) | 5. Preface to the Original Edition | vi. [roman numerals in error] Preface, continued | (7) Contents | (8) list of Illustrations | 9–352. text | (1)–(2) advertisement (THE NEW POPULAR HENTY) listing 64 titles.

Binding (see Plate 174)

Green cloth boards, blocked black, orange, and buff; edges plain; plain off-white endpapers.

Front board: THE DRAGON & | THE RAVEN (buff) | OR THE DAYS OF KING ALFRED (black) above illustration of soldier with winged helmet, sword and shield, under fire from arrows (black, orange, buff). At foot: BY G.A. HENTY. (buff). **Spine:** THE | DRAGON | AND THE | RAVEN | G.A. HENTY (black) above illustration of similar soldier, with bow, shield and sword, etc. (black, orange, buff). At foot: BLACKIE & SON LTD (black). **Back board:** plain.

References: Bod; PN.

Notes

1. Issued in 1922 in Blackie's second cheaper series, 'The New Popular Henty'. For that, and subsequent editions, see *Facing Death*, 10.7, Notes 1–3 and 6–8.

2. All the minor variants of *The Dragon and the Raven* in the series are grouped together under this 'generic' heading, *21.6.

22. FOR NAME AND FAME

22.1

FOR NAME AND FAME: | OR, | THROUGH AFGHAN PASSES. | BY | G.A. HENTY, | Author of "True to the Old Flag," "St. George for England," "In Freedom's Cause," | "With Clive in India," "By Sheer Pluck," "Facing Death," &c. &c. | WITH EIGHT FULL-PAGE ILLUSTRATIONS | BY GORDON BROWNE. | (publisher's device) | LONDON: | BLACKIE & SON, 49 & 50 OLD BAILEY, E.C.; | GLASGOW, EDINBURGH, AND DUBLIN | 1886.

Contents

186 x 125 mm. (i)–(viii) | (9)–352 | catalogue (1)–40. Eight full-page line-and-wash drawings by Gordon Browne, reproduced by two-colour line blocks, the second-colour plates (sepia) including mechanical tints, printed on coated paper, unbacked, unfolioed, tipped in.

(Frontispiece, tipped in) | (i) title p. | (ii) blank | (iii)–iv. Preface | (v) Contents | (vi) blank | (vii) list of Illustrations | (viii) blank | (9)–352. text | (1)–40. catalogue.

Binding (see Plate 69)

Sage-green cloth boards, blocked dark-green, red, blind, and gilt; edges plain; brown surface-paper endpapers.

Front board: Series of decorative panels (red and dark green) with illustration of soldier with rifle and grenade in vertical panel at left (red, dark green, and gilt). At head: For Name and | Fame | or, Through | Afghan Passes. (gilt); at foot: BY G.A. HENTY. (gilt). **Spine:** FOR (gilt decoration) | . NAME | & FAME. (gilt) above illustration of soldier with drawn sword (dark green and gilt) and decorative panel (red, dark green, and gilt). G.A. HENTY. (cloth-colour reversed out of red panel) above: BLACKIE & SON (gilt) within gilt frame. The whole enclosed in red ruled borders, and with additional gilt rules at extreme head and foot of spine. **Back board:** Three rules (thin, thick, thin) near edges of board (blind).

References: BL; Bod; PN | *Farmer* p.30; *Dartt*, p.60, *Companion*, p.15.

Notes

1. The story appeared in twelve monthly instalments in Routledge's *Every Boy's Magazine*, starting on 1 October 1884. Magazine-parts were bound up to form the cloth-bound *Every Boy's Annual* for 1886, sold at six shillings for Christmas 1885.

2. Blackie published on 2 May 1885, when only eight instalments had appeared.

3. The subtitle on p.(9), at the head of Chapter I, differs from that on the title page, being shown as 'A Tale of the Afghan War'.

4. In the index to the Routledge *Annual* the story is said to be Illustrated. In fact there is not a single illustration to any of the twelve parts. In the headings to the parts Henty's name is followed by the names of a number of his books. These include 'Out with Clive'. That was perhaps the originally intended title of *With Clive in India*, but it seems strange that the mistake was not spotted in the Routledge proofs as the book had been published in August 1883 (title-page date 1884), over a year before the first instalment appeared.

5. By the end of February 1886 Blackie had sold 2798 copies of the book at five shillings. During the next fourteen years they sold 8776 more, giving an average annual sale during the first fifteen years of 772 copies. In the following year, 1901, the figures were affected by current events in an unusual way (see 22.3).

6. As usual with Blackie novels, catalogues in the earliest issues advertise books for the current year (in this case dated 1886) without quotations from press reviews.

*22.2

Reprints of the five-shilling edition were issued in the style of 22.1, but with the date removed from the title page. Alterations were made as necessary to title-page imprint and addresses: Blackie became a Limited Company in 1890; the Edinburgh address was not used after 1894; and the Indian office was opened in 1901, although Bombay did not appear regularly in the imprint until 1906.

Illustrations were in due course modified, the second-colour tint either transferred to the black plate or omitted (see Appendix IV, Part 1).

Bindings continued to show variations in colour of cloth, blocking and endpapers, often also having the publisher's name removed from the spine.

The slightly-varying issues of this title in its first-edition format are all grouped together under this 'generic' heading, *22.2.

22.3

FOR NAME AND FAME | OR | TO CABUL WITH ROBERTS | BY | G.A. HENTY | Author of "True to the Old Flag" "St. George for England" "With Clive in India" | "In Freedom's Cause" "By Sheer Pluck" "Facing Death" &c. &c. | WITH EIGHT FULL-PAGE ILLUSTRATIONS | LONDON | BLACKIE & SON, LIMITED, 50 OLD BAILEY, E.C. | GLASGOW AND DUBLIN

Contents

185 x 124 mm. (i)–(viii) | (9)–352 | catalogue 1–32. Eight full-page wash-drawings by an unknown hand, reproduced by halftone blocks on coated paper, unbacked, unfolioed, tipped in.

(Frontispiece, tipped in) | (i) title p. | (ii) blank | (iii)–iv. Preface | (v) Contents | (vi) blank | (vii) list of Illustrations | (viii) blank | (9)–352. text | 1–32. catalogue.

Binding (see Plate 69)

Blue cloth boards, blocked red, brown, pale yellow, and gilt; all edges burnished olive-green; grey endpapers, lined off-white.

Front board: For Name | and Fame (gilt) | or | With Roberts | to Cabul | By G.A. Henty (all pale yellow) above, at right of, and below illustration of soldier with sword and pistol (red, brown, and pale yellow), the whole within a ruled framework (pale yellow, and red). **Spine:** For | Name | and | Fame (gilt) above illustration of turbaned Indian with rifle, etc. (red, brown, and pale yellow). At foot: By | G.A. Henty. (gilt). The whole within a ruled framework (pale yellow, and red). **Back board:** plain. *(Note: all lettering is in gothic style).*

References: BL; Bod; PN.

Notes

1. This impression was issued in 1900 wth a re-written Preface by Henty, a new subtitle and a reset title page. The Gordon Browne illustrations have been replaced with wash-drawings based closely on them by an unknown hand.

2. The subtitle on the title page reads 'To Cabul with Roberts' while that on the binding case reads 'With Roberts to Cabul'. The text is unchanged, with the original subtitle, 'A Tale of the Afghan War', at the head of Chapter I.

3. The binding must be easily the least effective of Blackie's usually very good designs, the arrangement of the lettering being decidedly amateurish. It was abandoned before long, and a revised version of the earlier design brought back. The binding orders for 22.3 are not recorded: the total was probably about 2000.

4. Sales figures for the first fifteen years are given at 22.1, Note 4. In 1901, in this new dress, 1947 copies were sold, still at the 5s. price: over four times as many as in the previous year.

5. When Roberts returned from South Africa in 1901, Blackie was ready with this impression of *For Name and Fame*, his name now on the cover. It was done hurriedly, accounting for a poor binding design and a muddle over the subtitle. But it was Blackie's celebration of Roberts's triumphal return to England, to succeed Wolsley as Commander-in-Chief and to receive the Garter and an Earldom from Queen Victoria.

6. *For Name and Fame* and *Under Drake's Flag* were Henty's only novels from Blackie that were given new binding designs without a simultaneous price reduction.

*22.4

FOR NAME AND FAME | OR | TO CABUL WITH ROBERTS | BY | G.A. HENTY | Author of "True to the Old Flag" "St George for England" "With Clive in India" | "In Freedom's Cause" "By Sheer Pluck" "Facing Death" &c. &c. | WITH EIGHT FULL-PAGE ILLUSTRATIONS | LONDON | BLACKIE & SON, LIMITED, 50 OLD BAILEY, E.C. | GLASGOW AND DUBLIN

Contents

185 x 124 mm. (i)–(viii) | (9)–352 | catalogue 1–16. Illustrations as in 22.3.

(Frontispiece, tipped in) | (i) title p. | (ii) blank | (iii)–iv. Preface | (v) Contents | (vi) blank | (vii) list of Illustrations | (viii) blank | (9)–352. text | 1–16. catalogue.

Binding (see Note 1)

Sage-green cloth boards, blocked dark-green, red, and gilt; all edges burnished olive-green; grey endpapers, lined off-white.

Front board: Exactly as for 22.1. **Spine:** As for 22.1, except: (a) gilt omitted from centres of six decorative flowers in panel beneath illustration; (b) BLACKIE & SON (gilt) and surrounding gilt frame all omitted; (c) gilt rules at extreme head and foot of spine omitted.

Reference: MH.

Notes

1. Following the special issue of 22.3 in 1900, Blackie reverted to a slightly modified version of the original binding design. From the title-page imprint and the bound-in catalogue this copy can be dated between 1905 and 1910.

2. There had been a substantial increase in sales in 1901 (see 22.3, Note 4), and then, in the sixteen years up to 1917, when records cease, Blackie sold 4280 more copies at five shillings. A cheaper edition was not issued until after the first war. Total sales, from 1885 to 1917, were 17,801 copies.

*22.5

For Name and Fame | Or | To Cabul with Roberts | BY | G.A. HENTY | Author of "True to the Old Flag" "St. George for England" "With Clive in India" | "In Freedom's Cause" "By Sheer Pluck" "Facing Death" &c. | ILLUSTRATED | BLACKIE AND SON LIMITED | LONDON GLASGOW AND BOMBAY

Contents

186 x 125 mm. (1)–352 | no catalogue. Frontispiece from watercolour drawing signed 'ARCH: WEBB', reproduced by three-colour halftone blocks; four anonymous full-page wash-drawings printed in black; all on coated paper, unbacked, tipped in.

(Frontispiece, tipped in) | (1) title p. | (2) advertisement (G.A. HENTY'S BOOKS) listing 45 titles | 3. Preface | iv. [roman numerals in error] Preface, continued | (5) Contents | (6) blank | (7) list of Illustrations | (8) blank | 9–352. text, with printers's imprint on p.352 (PRINTED IN GREAT BRITAIN | By Blackie & Son, Limited, Glasgow).

Binding

Blue cloth boards, blocked black, brown, and orange; edges plain; plain off-white endpapers.

Front board: FOR NAME & FAME | WITH ROBERTS TO CABUL | G.A. HENTY (black) above illustration of turbaned warrior, with shield, sword, etc. (black, brown, orange). **Spine:** FOR | NAME | & | FAME | G.A. HENTY (black) above illustration of British soldier, hatless, with pistol in hand and sword in scabbard (black, brown, orange). At foot: BLACKIE & SON LTD (black). **Back board:** plain.

Reference: PN.

Notes

1. For notes on Blackie's second cheaper series, 'The New Popular Henty', issued in

the 1920s, and subsequent editions, see *Facing Death*, 10.7, Notes 1–3 and 6–8.
Examples of the series binding style are at Plates 174–175.

2. As with 22.3 and 22.4, three varieties of subtitle are given: on the case, on the title page, and on p.(9).

3. All the minor variants of *For Name and Fame* in the series are grouped together under this 'generic' heading, *22.5.

23. THE LION OF THE NORTH

23.1

THE LION OF THE NORTH: I A TALE OF THE TIMES OF I GUSTAVUS
ADOLPHUS AND THE WARS OF RELIGION. I BY I G.A. HENTY, I Author of
"True to the Old Flag," "St. George for England," "In Freedom's Cause," I "With
Clive in India," "By Sheer Pluck," "Facing Death," &c. &c. I WITH TWELVE
FULL-PAGE ILLUSTRATIONS I BY JOHN SCHÖNBERG. I (publisher's device)
I LONDON: I BLACKIE & SON, 49 & 50 OLD BAILEY, E.C.; I GLASGOW,
EDINBURGH, AND DUBLIN. I 1886.

Contents
186 x 130 mm. (i)–(viii) I (9)–(384) I catalogue (1)–40. Twelve line-and-wash
drawings by John Schönberg, reproduced by black line and sepia tint plates,
unbacked, unfolioed, tipped in.

(i) Half-title p. I (ii) advertisement (BOOKS BY G.A. HENTY.) listing 7 titles I
(frontispiece, tipped in) I (iii) title p. I (iv) blank I (v)–vi. Preface I (vii) Contents I
(viii) list of Illustrations I (9)–382. text I (383)–(384) blank I (1)–40. catalogue.

Binding (see Plate 76)
Brown cloth boards, bevelled, blocked dark-brown, green, blind, and gilt; all edges
burnished olive-green; maroon surface-paper endpapers.

Front board: THE LION OF THE NORTH. (dark-brown, cased gilt) I A TALE
OF THE TIMES OF I GUSTAVUS ADOLPHUS (dark-brown out of solid green
rectangle) with two brown ornaments, all above illustration of half-kneeling figure
(dark-brown) against screen showing scene, very dimly, of figures with pikes, guns
and banners (all gilt) with decorative trefoil border above and below (dark-brown
and gilt). Beneath this: decorative green and dark-brown panel, with: . BY . G . A .
HENTY . (cloth-colour, reversed out of green). Rules at head and foot of boards
(dark-brown and gilt). **Spine:** THE LION I (ornament) OF THE I NORTH. (cloth-
colour reversed out of solid gilt rectangle) with dark-brown rule surround; trefoil
border (dark-brown and gilt); illustration of standing figure with gun against
decorative screen panel (dark-brown and gilt); trefoil border (dark-brown and gilt);
G.A. HENTY. (cloth-colour reversed out of solid gilt) with reversed out rule
surround; decorative border (cloth-colour out of dark-brown); BLACKIE & SON
(gilt). Dark brown and gilt rules at head and foot. **Back board:** three rules (thin, thin,
thick) near edges of board (blind).

References: BL; Bod; PN I *Farmer*, p.48; *Dartt*, p.92, *Companion*, p.21.

Notes
1. The book was published on 19 August 1885. Blackie sold 2770 copies by the end of February 1886, and a further 7451 over the next fifteen years. The average annual sale during the first sixteen years was 639 copies, all at six shillings. Four years later, by August 1905, 778 more copies had been sold; the book was then re-issued in cheaper form, see 23.3 below. The remaining 20 copies at six shillings were sold over three years, concurrently with the cheap edition.
2. As usual with Blackie novels, catalogues in the earliest issues show books for the current year (in this case dated 1886) without quotations from press reviews. Dartt, *Companion*, reports catalogues with 32 pages.

*23.2
Title page: As for 23.1, but with no date.

Contents: 187 × 133 mm. As for 23.1, except (a) catalogue (1)–32; (b) illustrations as in 23.1, but brighter sepia ink; (c) page (ii) advertisement lists 15 titles.

Binding (see Plate 76)
Blue cloth boards, blocked maroon, bright grass-green, blind, and gilt; all edges burnished olive-green; maroon surface-paper endpapers.
   Details as for 23.1, except for blocking of front board. The brass blocking piece for the gilt panelled screen behind the main figure in the illustration has been modified. The engraved lines in the brass plate have been made wider and deeper with a graving tool, so that the details of the 'reversed out' picture appear clearer and bolder. The rest of the design remains unaltered.

Reference: PN.

Notes
1. The changes to the blocking piece used for gilt on the front board were made fairly soon after the book was published. My copy contains advertisements for books published in 1886 (with 1887 title-page dates) and none later than that. I wrote about the alterations and illustrated them in *A.B.M.R.*, March 1977, p.90.
2. This impression is representative of the many slightly-varying reprints of the first edition. They followed the usual Blackie pattern: the date was removed from the title page, and alterations were made as necessary to title-page imprint and addresses (Blackie became a Limited Company in 1890; the Edinburgh address was not used after 1894; and the Indian office was opened in 1901, although Bombay did not appear regularly in the imprint until 1906).
Illustrations were in due course modified, the second-colour tints either transferred to the black plates or omitted (see Appendix IV, Part 1). Bindings continued to vary in colours of cloth, blocking, and endpapers, often, also, having the publisher's name removed from the spine.
3. All the slightly-varying issues of this title in its first-edition format are grouped together under the 'generic' heading, *23.2.

23.3
The Lion of the North | A Tale of the Times of | Gustavus Adolphus and the Wars of Religion | BY | G.A. HENTY | Author of "True to the Old Flag" "St. George for

England" "Facing Death" | "In Freedom's Cause" "With Clive in India" "By Sheer Pluck" &c. | ILLUSTRATED | NEW EDITION | BLACKIE AND SON LIMITED | LONDON GLASGOW DUBLIN BOMBAY | 1906

Contents

184 x 122 mm. (1)–382 | catalogue 1–32. Eight full-page wash-drawings by an unknown hand based on some of the original illustrations by John Schönberg, reproduced by halftone blocks printed in sepia on coated paper, unbacked, unfolioed, tipped in.

(1) Half-title p. | (2) advertisement (HISTORICAL TALES OF G.A. HENTY) listing 30 titles | (frontispiece, tipped in) | (3) title p. | (4) blank | v–vi. [roman numerals in error] Preface | 7. Contents | 8. list of Illustrations | 9–382. text | 1–32. catalogue.

Binding

Royal-blue cloth boards, blocked black, buff, red, and gilt; all edges stained olive-green; grey endpapers, lined off-white.

Front-board: THE | LION OF THE NORTH | G.A. HENTY. (all buff) above illustration of soldier with drawn sword and pistol (black, buff, red), with signature: J Hassall (black) at bottom left corner. **Spine:** THE | LION | OF THE | NORTH | G.A. HENTY (all gilt) above illustration of standing soldier firing pistol at ground in front of his feet (black, buff, red); at foot: BLACKIE & SON, LTD (gilt). **Back board:** plain.

References: BL; Bod; PN.

Notes

1. Issued in 1905 in Blackie's 'New and Popular Edition' of Henty's novels, at 3s.6d. For details of the series see *Facing Death*, 10.6, Notes 2–3, and examples of the series binding style, Plates 172–173.

2. By 1906 Blackie had sold 2694 copies, and over the following eleven years to 1917, when records cease, they sold 6093 more, thus averaging a sale of 732 copies a year for the twelve years. The grand total sold between 1885 and 1917 was 19,806.

3. I have two copies, varying only in the catalogues. In the earlier one a portrait photograph, captioned THE LATE G.A. HENTY, is tipped in to face p.2. The verso shows the frontispiece to *By Conduct and Courage*: it is attributed to that book, with the price given as 6s., but the catalogue contains no announcement of it. The later catalogue announces *By Conduct and Courage* as the first item on p.1, with a quotation from one review. The portrait of Henty is omitted.

*23.4

The | Lion of the North | A Tale of the Times of Gustavus | Adolphus and the Wars of Religion | BY | G.A. HENTY | Author of "With Kitchener in the Soudan" | "With Roberts to Pretoria" "With Clive in India" | "True to the Old Flag" "Beric the Briton" | &c. &c. | Illustrated by Frank Gillett, R.I. | BLACKIE & SON LIMITED | LONDON GLASGOW BOMBAY

Contents

184 x 123 mm. (1)–368 | no catalogue. Frontispiece from watercolour drawing, reproduced by three-colour halftone blocks; four pencil drawings reproduced by

halftone blocks printed in black; all by Frank Gillett; all on coated paper, unbacked, tipped in.

(1) Half-title p. | (2) advertisement (G.A. HENTY'S BOOKS) listing 45 titles | (frontispiece, tipped in) | (3) title p. | (4) blank | 5–6. Preface | 7. Contents | (8) list of Illustrations | 9–368. text, with printer's imprint on p.368 (PRINTED IN GREAT BRITAIN | By Blackie & Son, Limited, Glasgow).

Binding: As for 23.3, except (a) lighter boards and cheaper cloth, and with changed colour-scheme, without gilt (blue cloth boards, blocked black, red, and buff): spine lettering, at head, buff, and at foot, black; (b) edges plain; (c) plain off-white endpapers.

Reference: AK.

Notes
1. For notes on Blackie's second cheaper series, 'The New Popular Henty', and subsequent editions of this book, see *Facing Death*, 10.7, Notes 1–3 and 6–8.
2. In most books in this series the black-and-white plates were printed from the blocks used in the previous edition. Here, however, Frank Gillett was commissioned to make four new illustrations to replace those used in 23.3.
3. All the minor variants of *The Lion of the North* in the series are grouped together under this 'generic' heading, *23.4.

24. THROUGH THE FRAY

24.1
THROUGH THE FRAY: | A TALE | OF THE LUDDITE RIOTS. BY | G.A. HENTY, | Author of "True to the Old Flag," "St. George for England," "In Freedom's Cause," | "With Clive in India," "By Sheer Pluck," "Facing Death," &c. &c. | WITH TWELVE FULL-PAGE ILLUSTRATIONS | BY H.M. PAGET. | (publisher's device) | LONDON: | BLACKIE & SON, 49 & 50 OLD BAILEY, E.C.; | GLASGOW, EDINBURGH , AND DUBLIN. | 1886.

Contents
185 x 130 mm. (i)–(viii) | (9)–384 | catalogue (1)–40. Twelve full-page line-and-wash drawings by H.M. Paget, reproduced by two-colour line blocks with mechanical tints laid for second colour, printed in black and sepia, unbacked, unfolioed, tipped in.

(Frontispiece, tipped in) | (i) title p. | (ii) blank | (iii)–iv. Preface | (v) Contents | (vi) blank | (vii) list of Illustrations | (viii) blank | (9)-384. text | (1)–40. catalogue.

Binding (see Plate 82)
Red cloth boards, bevelled, blocked black, brown, blind, and gilt; all edges burnished olive-green; dark-brown surface-paper endpapers.
Front board: THROUGH . THE . FRAY (gilt, cased brown) | . (brown) A . TALE . OF . THE (gilt) . (brown) | . – (gilt) LUDDITE RIOTS (gilt, cased brown) – . (gilt), all in upper panel enclosed by brown rule, above illustration of boy in tail coat aiming pistol at rows of powder kegs (black, brown, and gilt), enclosed by brown rule. In lowest panel: . BY . G.A. HENTY . (cloth-colour of solid brown

rectangle, cased gilt. The whole enclosed by thick black rules, with similar rules between the three panels. **Spine:** Four panels composed of variations of black, brown, and gilt rules. At top: THROUGH I THE I FRAY (cloth-colour out of decorated gilt solid); in second panel: illustration (black, brown, and gilt). In third panel: A . TALE . OF . THE I LUDDITE I RIOTS . I G.A. HENTY (all gilt, with some gilt underlines and brown ornaments); at foot: BLACKIE & SON (cloth-colour out of gilt solid) in brown rectangle. Black rules surrounding and between panels. **Back board:** Three rules (thin, thin, thick) near edges of board (blind).

References: BL; Bod; PN I *Farmer*, p.69; *Dartt*, p.137, *Companion*, p.30.

Notes

1. Published on 5 September 1885 at six shillings: by February 1886 Blackie had sold 2631 copies. In the year to February 1887 only 65 copies were sold: this is a very low figure for any of Henty's books, and it is possible that the book went out of print by some mistake or accident. The following year sales were still low at 252 copies, and during the following fourteen years only 4836 more copies were sold. That makes a total of 7784 copies in seventeen years – an average of 458 copies a year before the book was re-issued in a cheaper edition (see 24.3). 158 more copies were sold at six shillings concurrently with the cheap edition.

2. As usual with Blackie novels, the earliest issues contain catalogues advertising books for the current year (in this case those with 1886 title-page dates) without quotations from press reviews.

*24.2

Reprints of the six-shilling edition were issued in the same style as 24.1, but with the date removed from the title page. Alterations were made from time to time to the title-page imprint and addresses: Blackie became a Limited Company in 1890; the Edinburgh address was not used after 1894; and the Indian office was opened in 1901, though Bombay did not appear regularly in the imprint until 1906. The illustrations were later modified, the second-colour tints either transferred to the black plates or omitted (see Appendix IV, Part 1).

Bindings continued to show variations in colour of cloth, blocking, and endpapers, often also having the publisher's name removed from the spine.

The slightly-varying issues of this title in its first-edition format are all grouped together under this 'generic' heading, *24.2.

24.3

Through the Fray I A Tale of the Luddite Riots I BY I G.A. HENTY I Author of "True to the Old Flag" "St. George for England" "By Sheer Pluck" I "In Freedom's Cause" "With Clive in India" "Facing Death" &c. I WITH SIX FULL-PAGE ILLUSTRATIONS I NEW EDITION I BLACKIE AND SON LIMITED I LONDON GLASGOW AND DUBLIN I 1903

Contents

185 x 120 mm. (1)–384 I catalogue 1–16. Six full-page wash drawings by an unknown hand, based on some of the original illustrations by H.M. Paget, reproduced by halftone blocks, printed in black on coated paper, unbacked, unfolioed, tipped in.

(Frontispiece, tipped in) | (1) title p. | (2) blank | (3) Preface | iv. [roman numeral in error] Preface, continued | 5. Contents | (6) blank | 7. list of Illustrations | (8) blank | 9–384. text | 1–16. catalogue.

Binding (see Plate 173)
Red cloth boards, blocked black, buff, green, and gilt; all edges stained olive-green; grey endpapers, lined off-white.
Front board: THROUGH | THE FRAY | G.A. HENTY (all gilt) above illustration of man with musket (black, buff, green). **Spine:** THROUGH | THE | FRAY | G.A. HENTY (all gilt) above illustration of young man, pointing, with pistol and two powder kegs (black, buff, and green). **Back board:** plain.

Reference: PN.

Notes
1. This and *The Lion of St. Mark* were the first two titles issued in the cheaper 'New and Popular Edition'. That was in 1902: by the end of August 1903 Blackie had sold 2663 copies of *Through the Fray*, almost exactly a third of the total number sold at six shillings in the seventeen years since the book was published in 1885. By 1917, when Blackie records cease, they had sold 11,174 copies at the reduced price of 3s.6d. This gives a grand total of 19,116 copies between 1885 and 1917.
2. The catalogue in my copy contains a full-page photograph of 'THE LATE G.A. HENTY', who died on 16 November 1902. The series began either just before or just after Henty's death: there may be an earlier issue without the catalogue portrait.
3. Details of the series are given under *Facing Death*, 10.6, Notes 2 and 3.

*24.4
THROUGH THE FRAY | A Tale of the Luddite Riots | BY | G.A. HENTY | Author of "True to the Old Flag" "St. George for England" | "By Sheer Pluck" "Facing Death" &c. | Illustrated | BLACKIE AND SON LIMITED | LONDON GLASGOW AND BOMBAY

Contents
185 x 123 mm. (1)–384 | no catalogue. Frontispiece from watercolour drawing, signed John de Walton, reproduced by three-colour halftone blocks; four full-page wash-drawings reproduced by halftone blocks printed in black; all on coated paper, unbacked, tipped in.
(Frontispiece, tipped in) | (1) title p. | (2) advertisement (G.A. HENTY'S BOOKS) listing 50 titles | 3. Preface | iv. [roman numerals in error] Preface, continued | 5. Contents | (6) blank | (7) list of Illustrations | (8) blank | 9–384. text, with printer's imprint on p.384 (PRINTED IN GREAT BRITAIN | At the Villafield Press, Glasgow, Scotland).

Binding: As for 24.3, except (a) lighter boards, cheaper cloth, and changed colour scheme (green cloth boards, blocked black, blue, and buff): no gilt, front-board lettering buff, spine lettering black; (b) edges plain; (c) plain off-white endpapers.

Reference: AK.

Notes
1. For notes on Blackie second cheaper series, 'The New Popular Henty', and subsequent editons of this book, see *Facing Death*, 10.7, Notes 1–3 and 6–8.
2. All the minor variants of *Through the Fray* in the series are grouped together under this 'generic' heading, *24.4.

25. YARNS ON THE BEACH

25.1
YARNS ON THE BEACH | A BUNDLE OF TALES. | BY | G.A. HENTY, | Author of "By Sheer Pluck;" "Facing Death;" "True to the Old Flag;" | "With Clive in India;" "Under Drake's Flag;" &c. | WITH TWO FULL-PAGE ILLUSTRATIONS | BY J.J. PROCTOR. | (publisher's device) | LONDON: | BLACKIE & SON, 49 & 50 OLD BAILEY, E.C. | GLASGOW, EDINBURGH, AND DUBLIN. | 1886.

Contents
179 x 120 mm. (1)–160 | catalogue (1)–40. Two full-page line-and-wash drawings by J.J. Proctor reproduced as two-colour line blocks, with mechanical tints laid on second-colour plate (sepia), unbacked, unfolioed, tipped in as frontispiece and to face p.82.
(Frontispiece, tipped in) | (1) title p. | (2) blank | (3) Contents | (4) blank | (5)–96. text of 'Do Your Duty' | (97) half-title p. to 'Surly Joe' | (98) blank | (99)–133. text of 'Surly Joe' | (134) blank | (135) half-title p. to 'A Fish-wife's Dream' | (136) blank | (137)–160. text of 'A Fish-wife's Dream' | (1)–40. catalogue.

Binding (see Plate 115)
Blue cloth boards, blocked black, blind, and gilt; edges plain; dark-blue surface-paper endpapers.
Front board: YARNS on the BEACH. (gilt) below decorative border and above drawing of boys with football within decorative borders (all black). Beneath this: By | G.A. Henty | (three small ornaments) (all black). Decorative border (black) at foot.
Spine: Yarns | on the | Beach (cloth-colour out of solid gilt rectangle) beneath decorative border continued from front board, and above illustration of boy with cricket bat, and borders (all black) also continued from front board. Beneath this: . by . | . G . A . | . Henty . (all gilt) and, within two pairs of black rules: BLACKIE & SON (gilt). **Back board:** two rules near edges of board (blind).

References: BL; Bod; PN | *Farmer*, p.85; *Dartt*, p.166, *Companion*, p.35

Notes
1. All three stories were printed elsewhere: for details see §4.
2. Publication was on 15 September 1885, at 1s.6d. By February 1886 Blackie had sold 2515 copies. By 31 August 1917, when Blackie's sales records cease, they had sold 37,142 copies, at an average of 1161 copies a year for all those 32 years – and the book still sold only just under 1000 copies for each of the last three years.
3. In all copies of the first impression examined the title page is a cancel, hard to see because it is so neatly inserted and has the frontispiece tipped in afterwards. The insertion must have been done after the book was folded and before it was cased.

4. Catalogues in the earliest issues announce this title, among others with title pages dated 1886, without quotations from press reviews.

5. *Farmer* has the illustration on the spine of the binding case as 'a boy with an oar on his shoulder'. This is surely a misreading of the picture, not a variant.

6. The copy in the Bodleian Library is bound in blue, diagonally-grained cloth. For Blackie's use of grained cloth for Henty's books, see *Facing Death*, 10.4, Note 10.

*25.2

Reprints of the first edition were issued in the same style as 25.1, with the date removed from the title page. Alterations were made to the title-page imprint and addresses as necessary: Blackie became a Limited Company in 1890; the Edinburgh address was not used after 1894; and the Indian office was opened in 1901, although Bombay did not regularly appear in the imprint before 1906. The illustrations were later modified, with the second colour tint either transferred to the black plate or omitted (see Appendix IV, Part 1).

Binding continued to show variation in colours of cloth, blocking, and endpapers, often also having the publisher's name removed from the foot of the spine.

All the slightly-differing reprints of this title in its first-edition format are grouped together under this 'generic' heading, *25.2.

25.3

YARNS ON THE BEACH I A BUNDLE OF TALES I BY I G.A. HENTY I Author of "By Sheer Pluck" "Facing Death" "True to the Old Flag" I "With Clive in India" "Under Drake's Flag" &c. I WITH TWO FULL-PAGE ILLUSTRATIONS BY J.J. PROCTOR I LONDON I BLACKIE & SON, LIMITED, 50 OLD BAILEY, E.C. I GLASGOW AND DUBLIN

Contents: 182 x 122 mm. Otherwise as for 25.1, except (a) catalogue 1–32 (see Note 1); (b) illustrations printed in black only, the tint being omitted.

Binding (see Note 2)
Red cloth boards, blocked grey, yellow, and gilt; edges plain; grey-brown endpapers, lined off-white.

 Front-board: . YARNS . ON . THE . BEACH . I (rule) BY (rule) I . G.A. HENTY . (all cloth-colour out of solid gilt rectangle, decorated at upper and lower edges). The rectangle is superimposed on an overall pattern of twining tendrils and flowers (grey and yellow) with grey rules at edges of board. **Spine:** YARNS I ON THE I BEACH I (ornament) BY (ornament) I G.A. HENTY (all cloth-colour out of solid gilt rectangle, decorated at upper and lower edges), and all superimposed on repeat of pattern on front board (grey and yellow) all enclosed by grey rules. **Back board:** plain.

Reference: PN.

Notes
1. My copy can be dated 1902 by the catalogue entries, and by a school-prize inscription. It is printed on a bulkier featherweight paper, and in this version the illustrations are printed in black line only, with no mechanical tints.
2. This binding style was also used for *Tales of Daring and Danger*, 42.4, Plate 114.

3. As with the earlier reprints of 25.1, the usual variations of title-page imprint and address, colour schemes in binding, etc. will be found in issues of 25.3.

25.4

Yarns on the Beach I A Bundle of Tales I BY I G.A. HENTY I Author of "By Sheer Pluck" "Facing Death" "True to the Old Flag" I "With Clive in India" "Under Drake's Flag" I ILLUSTRATED BY J.J. PROCTOR I BLACKIE AND SON, LIMITED I LONDON GLASGOW AND BOMBAY

Contents: 179 x 121 mm. As for 25.1, except (a) no catalogue; (b) illustrations printed in black line only, as in 25.3.

Binding (see Note 1)
Dark-green cloth boards, blocked black, orange, yellow, gilt; edges plain; grey endpapers, lined off-white.
    Front board: YARNS ON THE I BEACH (gilt) within decorative panel (black and orange) at head of art-nouveau design of orange tree with leaves, fruit, and shoots, in several panels (black, orange, yellow). **Spine:** YARNS I ON THE I BEACH I G.A. HENTY (all gilt) within decorative panel (black and orange) at head of smaller design similar to that on front board. At foot, in black ruled panel: BLACKIE & SON LD. (black). **Back board:** plain.

Reference: PN.

Notes
1. This binding design seems to have appeared first in 1911: it was also used for *Tales of Daring and Danger*, 42.5, Plate 114, and is advertised as the 'Excelsior Series' although this name does not appear in the actual copies of either title.
2. The title page has been reset in the general style used by Blackie for their 'New and Popular Edition' of Henty's novels. In catalogues of 1915, listing books in that series, both this book and the other collection of short stories, *Tales of Daring and Danger*, are still advertised at their old price, 1s.6d.
3. For later issues the lettering on the front boards, and eventually that on the spine also, was blocked in yellow instead of gilt.

25.5

Yarns on the Beach I A Bundle of Tales I BY I G.A. HENTY I Author of "By Sheer Pluck" "Facing Death" I "True to the Old Flag" "With Clive in India" I "Under Drake's Flag" &c. I BLACKIE & SON LIMITED I LONDON AND GLASGOW

Contents
180 x 120 mm. (1)–160 I no catalogue. Frontispiece from wash-drawing by 'Nick' reproduced by halftone block printed in black on coated paper, unbacked, tipped in.
    (Frontispiece, tipped in) I (1) title p. I (2) (At head) Names and addresses of Blackie Companies in London, Glasgow, Bombay, and Toronto. (At centre) publisher's advertisement (The I Boys' and Girls' Bookshelf) listing 17 titles including only this one by Henty. (At foot) Printer's imprint (Printed in Great Britain by Blackie & Son, Ltd., Glasgow) I (3) Contents I (4) blank I 5–160. text (for details see under 25.1).

Binding (see Plate 115)
Designed by Charles Rennie Mackintosh (see Appendix IV, Part 2). Grey cloth boards, blocked brown and blue; edges plain; plain off-white endpapers.
 Front board: YARNS ON | THE BEACH | G.A. HENTY(all cloth-colour out of solid blue rectangle) enclosed in series of rules, etc., in geometric design (brown and blue). **Spine:** YARNS | ON THE | BEACH | G.A. HENTY (brown) beneath brown rule, and above geometrical pattern (brown and blue). At foot: BLACKIE | AND . SON . LD . (brown) above brown rule. **Back board:** plain.

Reference: PN.

Notes
1. The title page, and the half-title pages to the second and third stories, have been reset. So have the first paragraphs of all three stories, in order to modernise the typographical appearance by removing decorative three-line initials.
2. There is no catalogue, and the only way of dating this impression from internal evidence is from the new frontispiece, which is signed (? 'Nick'), and dated 1927.
3. The advertisement on p.(2) shows this is Henty's only title in 'The Boys' and Girls' Bookshelf', a series bound in a striking design by the architect and painter, Charles Rennie Mackintosh (see Appendix IV, Part 2).
4. Walter W. Blackie, younger brother of Alexander Blackie, was supervising the design of Blackie's books, some years after the deaths of his brother and of Talwin Morris. Walter was a keen admirer of Mackintosh's work, and had an idea for a cheap edition of Henty's novels in uniform bindings. In 1921 he asked Mackintosh to make a suitable design (see Appendix II, Part 5). The project was abandoned but the design produced by Mackintosh was used instead for 'The Boys' and Girls' Bookshelf'.
5. The series, 'The Boys' and Girls' Bookshelf' should not be confused with 'Blackie's Library for Boys and Girls' which existed simultaneously and contained five other books by Henty (see Appendix V). Books in 'The Boys' and Girls' Bookshelf' were priced at 1s.6d., the price at which *Yarns on the Beach* had been sold since it was first published.

26. THE SOVEREIGN READER

26.1
THE SOVEREIGN READER: | SCENES FROM THE | LIFE AND REIGN OF QUEEN VICTORIA. | BY | G.A.HENTY, | Author of "By Sheer Pluck;" "Facing Death;" "With Clive in India;" &c. | FOR UPPER CLASSES IN SCHOOLS. | (publisher's device) | LONDON: | BLACKIE & SON, 49 & 50 OLD BAILEY, E.C. | GLASGOW, EDINBURGH, AND DUBLIN.

Contents
164 x 108 mm. (i)–viii | (9)–256 | no catalogue. Numerous engravings by various hands, printed in black from line blocks on text pages.
 (i) Title p. | (ii) blank | (iii) Preface | (iv) blank | (v)–vi. Contents | (vii)–viii. List of Illustrations | (9)–239. text | (240)–245. List of the more Difficult Words | (246)–256. Meanings of the more Difficult Words and Phrases.

Binding (see Plate 142)
Red cloth boards, blocked black; edges plain; yellow-green endpapers, printed black.
    Front board: . THE . SOVEREIGN . I . READER . (in upper panel). Pattern of acorns, leaves and flowers (at centre). In lower panel: . Scenes from . I . the Life and Reign of . I . Queen Victoria . (all black). All panels framed by black rules. **Spine:** . THE . I SOVEREIGN I READER (in upper panel). Pattern of acorns, leaves and flowers (in central panel); publisher's monogram in oval (lower panel) (all black). All panels framed by black rules. **Back board:** plain.

References: BL; Bod; PN I *Farmer*, p.65; *Dartt*, p.122.

Notes
1. The Reader was published on 26 August 1887. *Farmer* erroneously reports a first edition with the date 1887 printed on the title page. *Dartt* repeats this information, although ambiguously, giving both 1887 and (1887). The earliest copies I have seen are rubber-stamped 'PRESENTED BY THE PUBLISHERS', and used as sales-promotion items. See 26.3, Note.
2. The endpapers are folioed 1, 2, and 3, 4, each folio number being in parentheses. Pages 2 and 3 are printed with a catalogue of 'BLACKIE & SON'S EDUCATIONAL WORKS.'

26.2
THE I SOVEREIGN READER I SCENES FROM THE I LIFE AND REIGN OF QUEEN VICTORIA I BY I G.A. HENTY I Author of "By Sheer Pluck", "Facing Death", "With Clive in India", &c. I NEW EDITION I LONDON I BLACKIE & SON, LIMITED, 50 OLD BAILEY, E.C. I GLASGOW AND DUBLIN I 1896

Contents
170 x 115 mm. (i)–viii I (9)–266 I catalogue (267)–(268). Illustrations as in 26.1, with additions in the extra pages (see Note 2).
    (i) Title p. I (ii) blank I (iii) Preface I (iv) blank I (v)–vi. Contents I (vii)–viii. List of Illustrations I (9)–254. text I (255)–266. Meanings of the more Difficult Words and Phrases I (267)–(268) catalogue.

Binding (see Plate 142)
Purple cloth boards, blocked black; edges plain; plain off-white endpapers.
    Front board: (three ornaments) THE (three ornaments) I SOVEREIGN READER (black) above device from parts of royal coat of arms, and: SCENES FROM THE LIFE AND I REIGN OF QUEEN VICTORIA I (five ornaments) (all black). Below dividing rule: (ornament) BLACKIE AND SON: LIMITED (ornament) (all black). The whole framed by double black rules. **Spine:** THE SOVEREIGN READER (black, running from foot to head) between two ornaments in double-ruled panel. **Back board:** device from parts of royal coat of arms at centre (black).

References: BL; Bod; PN.

Notes
1. On p. (iii) is a Note: 'In the new edition the story of the Queen's reign has been

brought down to the year 1896. G.A.H.'. The extent was increased by twelve pages, and more room made for text by omitting the six-page List of the more Difficult Words. Some re-writing was also necessary, from p.236 onwards. The book is no longer an even working, having a 12-page section printed as 8-pages and 4-pages.
2. The page-size is slightly larger than for 26.1. There is a new illustration on the old p.238; two more full-page pictures and a map of South Africa are also added.

26.3
Title page: As for 26.2, but date changed to 1897.

Contents, Binding: As for 26.2.

References: PN | *Dartt*, p. 122.

Note: Blackie's customs for the dating of title pages of educational books clearly differ from those for fiction. 26.2 and 26.3 are identical in content, and each form part of a second edition of 26.1. Had the book been fiction, 26.1 would have been dated on the title page, and the two later impressions would have been undated. As it is, it appears that the originally undated title page of a school reader was dated every time the book was reprinted. But the ways of Blackie were mysterious, as may be seen from 26.4, Henty's next revision of the text.

26.4
TWENTIETH CENTURY EDITION | (52mm. rule) | THE | SOVEREIGN READER | SCENES FROM THE | LIFE AND REIGN OF QUEEN VICTORIA | TO END OF NINETEENTH CENTURY | BY | G.A. HENTY | Author of "By Sheer Pluck" "Facing Death" "With Clive in India" &c. | LONDON | BLACKIE & SON, LIMITED, 50 OLD BAILEY, E.C. | GLASGOW AND DUBLIN

Contents
172 × 115 mm. (i)–viii | (9)–272 | no catalogue. Illustrations as in 26.2, with alterations and additions in the extra pages, including photographs reproduced by halftone blocks printed on text pages.
(i) Title p. | (ii) blank | (iii) Preface | (iv) blank | (v)–vi. Contents | (vii)–viii. List of Illustrations | (9)–260. text | (261)–272. Meanings of the more Difficult Words and Phrases.

Binding (see Plate 142)
Red cloth boards, blocked black; edges plain; plain off-white endpapers.
Front board: As for 26.2, but with title and device from parts of royal coat of arms lowered within panel, and new line inserted above title: TWENTIETH CENTURY EDITION (black). **Spine:** as for 26.2. **Back board:** as for 26.2.

References: BL; Bod; PN | *Dartt*, p.122.

Notes
1. On p. (iii) is a Note: 'In the new edition the story of the Queen's reign has been brought down to the end of the nineteenth century, thus covering the reconquest of the Soudan, the war in Africa, and the Chinese troubles. G.A.H.'.
2. Henty's revisions start at p.229. The text is six pages longer, but the removal of the 2-page catalogue (at the end of 26.2 and 26.3) resulted in the total extent being increased by only four pages. It is again an even working, now of 272 pages.

3. The engraving of Mr Gladstone has had to go, as has that of the German Emperor, Frederick; also two full-page pictures, showing The Loss of *H.M.S. Victoria*, and a cunning delineation of the Manchester Ship Canal. There are nine new pictures, all from photographs, reproduced by the first halftone blocks to appear in this work. Portraits include Kitchener, Buller, Joseph Chamberlain, and Roberts, and there is a photograph of the Gordon Memorial Service at Khartoum.

26.5 [94.2]

Queen Victoria I Scenes from her Life and Reign I BY I G.A.HENTY I BLACKIE & SON LIMITED I LONDON GLASGOW AND DUBLIN I 1901

Contents

172 x 115 mm. (i)–viii I (9)–272 I no catalogue. Frontispiece photograph of Queen Victoria, reproduced by halftone block printed in black on coated paper, unbacked, tipped in. Numerous engravings reproduced by line blocks, and photographs reproduced by halftone blocks, all printed on text pages.

(i) Half-title p. (Queen Victoria) I (ii) blank I (frontispiece, tipped in) I (iii) title p. I (iv) blank I (v) Preface I (vi) Note (see Note 4) I (vii)–viii. Contents I (9)–260. text I (261)–272. Meanings of the more Difficult Words and Phrases.

Binding (see Plate 142)

Red cloth boards, blocked black; edges plain; plain off-white endpapers.
Front board: TWENTIETH CENTURY EDITION I (row of five ornaments) I QUEEN VICTORIA (all black) above device from parts of royal coat of arms. Beneath this: SCENES FROM HER LIFE AND REIGN I [THE SOVEREIGN READER] I (row of five ornaments) (all black). Beneath a dividing rule: BLACKIE AND SON: LIMITED (black, between two ornaments). The whole framed by black double-rules. **Spine, Back board:** as for 26.2.

Reference: PN.

Notes

1. This is a strange book, the binding bearing two titles simultaneously. In the bookshelf, with only the spine visible, the title is clearly *The Sovereign Reader*, in the style of 26.2, 26.3, and 26.4. On the front board, however, that title is now in brackets, with a new main title, *Queen Victoria*, in its original position.
2. Henty revised the book for the last time on the Queen's death, and Blackie then issued it in a new binding design as *Queen Victoria*, 1901 (see 94.1). That edition was intended for general reading or as a reward book; the only reference to the original title is a Note in small type on p.(iv). The notes at the end of the book on the meanings of difficult words are, in 94.1, omitted.
3. Simultaneously Blackie issued the same sheets, with the twelve pages of notes on difficult words added, in the binding described above (26.5) as a final edition of *The Sovereign Reader* for school use. As the sheets carried the title *Queen Victoria* on the title-page and half-title page it was necessary to make some compromise on the binding case, with the rather confusing result described in Note 1 above.
4. The note on p. (iv) appears of course, in both the two versions of the book, and reads as follows: 'The earlier editions of this book have been known and appreciated by a wide circle under the title of *The Sovereign Reader*. The present edition completes the story of the great reign.'

5. Henty had finished his work by re-writing the last pages of the book, without increasing the overall extent. The book ended up, therefore, after its various changes, as an even working.

6. Strictly (and in spite of a transcription-practice by some modern librarians of avoiding the use of most capital letters), the title of a book is that given on its title page. Accordingly I have listed this edition, with binding described above, and with the school notes, under *Queen Victoria* as 94.2, cross-referenced to this entry. The edition thus has two code numbers, 26.5 and 94.2. I hope this will not increase the confusion begun by its publisher!

27. WITH WOLFE IN CANADA

27.1

WITH WOLFE IN CANADA: I OR I THE WINNING OF A CONTINENT. I BY I G.A.HENTY, I Author of "With Clive in India;" "The Lion of the North;" "In Freedom's Cause;" I "The Dragon and the Raven;" "By Sheer Pluck;" "Facing Death;" &c. I WITH TWELVE FULL-PAGE ILLUSTRATIONS I BY GORDON BROWNE. I (publisher's device) I LONDON: I BLACKIE & SON, 49 & 50 OLD BAILEY, E.C. I GLASGOW, EDINBURGH, AND DUBLIN. I 1887.

Contents
188 x 133 mm. (i)–(viii) I (9)–384 I catalogue (1)–48. Twelve full-page illustrations from pen-drawings by Gordon Browne, reproduced by line blocks printed on coated paper, unbacked, unfolioed, tipped in.
    (Frontispiece, tipped in) I (i) title p. I (ii) blank I (iii)–iv. Preface I (v) Contents I (vi) blank I (vii) list of Illustrations I (9)–384. text I (1)–48. catalogue.

Binding (see Plate 96)
Brown cloth boards, bevelled, blocked black, cream, blind, and gilt; all edges burnished olive-green; maroon surface-paper endpapers.
    Front board: WITH . WOLFE I IN . CANADA . I . G . A . HENTY . (all gilt) at upper left corner, above illustration of mounted cavalry officer with sword drawn (black, cream, and gilt). All enclosed in frame of two black rules. **Spine:** WITH I WOLFE IN I CANADA (gilt) above illustration of Indian with axe and dagger (black and cream); . BY . I G.A.HENTY . I . BLACKIE . & . I . SON . (all gilt). The whole within frame of black rules, single at sides, double at head and foot. **Back board:** single rule at edges of board (blind).

References: BL; Bod; PN I *Farmer*, p.83; *Dartt*, p.163, *Companion*, p.35.

Notes
1. The book was published on 18 May 1886 at six shillings. By the end of February 1887 Blackie had sold 2719 copies. Over the first fifteen years the average annual sale was 779 copies. Over the next sixteen years to 1917, when Blackie's records cease, the average annual sale was 374 copies. The total sold in the 31 years from 1886 to 1917 was 17,662 copies, all at the published price, for the book was not put into a cheaper edition during the period covered by the surviving records.
2. The illustrations mark a departure from Blackie's first-edition style: they are in black line only, with no tints, and no second colour. (See Appendix IV, Part 1).

3. As usual with Blackie novels, the earliest issues contain catalogues advertising books for the current year (in this case those with 1887 title-page dates) without quotations from press reviews.

4. *Dartt* is muddled, as unfortunately he so often is, between various editions which he attempts to describe simultaneously. Here he wrongly calls for 'Leaves all edges gilt'. He also follows *Farmer*, mistakenly calling for a half-title page, but corrects himself, not very carefully, in his *Companion*.

*27.2

Title page: As for 27.1, but with no date.

Contents: 186 x 129 mm. As for 27.1, except (a) catalogue (1)–32; (b) additional sketch map and plan, both printed in line on text pages, see Note 1.

Binding: As for 27.1, but changed colours (grey-blue cloth boards, bevelled, blocked black, cream, blind, and gilt).

Reference: PN.

Notes
1. Shortly after the publication of the book it was decided to add a sketch map, and a plan of Quebec. The easiest way of doing this was to include them in the text, as there was no way of fitting them economically into a sheet with the illustrations. They had to appear at appropriate places in the narrative, and that had to be arranged with minimal alteration to the book. In fact it was necessary to edit, and partly re-write, the text, to make room for each of the new line blocks.
2. In 27.1, Chapter X ends with only five lines on p.186. It might have been possible to slip in the sketch map beneath those lines, without making any change to the text. Unfortunately the block of the sketch map would have had to be made very narrow, because of its shape, and it needed the depth of a full page. So two paragraphs on p.185 were re-written to form only one, and the result was a saving of seven lines. Chapter X therefore ends two lines from the foot of p.185, and the whole of p.186 is devoted to the sketch plan.
3. It was rather more difficult to get the plan of Quebec in the desired place. That was in Chapter XVIII, which is headed 'Quebec', and which ends two-thirds of the way down p.325. Even if there had been room for it on that page it would have appeared too late in the narrative: the right place for it was near the beginning of the chapter. Luckily the previous chapter ended on p.301, with only six lines on that page; unluckily it was a right-hand page, and the Quebec chapter started on its verso, so if put on p.301 the plan would appear to be part of the wrong chapter. The solution was to cut seven lines on p.300, again by re-writing two paragraphs, so that the chapter finished on that page. The first two pages of Chapter XVIII were then moved back from pages 302 and 303 to become pages 301 and 302, and the plan was put on page 303.
4. The list of Illustrations on p.(vii) was amended to include entries for the two new blocks. The editor forgot, however, to amend the list of Contents on p.(v), so that Chapter XVIII, Quebec, is still shown as beginning on p.302.
5. No correspondence survives to show whether Henty did the re-writing within Chapter X and Chapter XVIII. It is more likely that it would have been done by his editor at Blackie, who should have submitted his suggestions for approval.

6. As usual, reprints of the first edition were issued in the same style, but with the date removed from the title page. The impression described here is an early one, issued almost exactly a year after first publication of 27.1, judging from the books listed in the catalogue. I have not found a copy of a reprint without the addition of the map and plan.

7. As mentioned above (27.1, Note 1) this book was not re-issued in a cheaper edition until after the first war. Later reprints of the six-shilling edition followed the usual pattern of Blackie's novels: alterations were made to title-page imprint and addresses as necessary. Blackie became a Limited Company in 1890; the Edinburgh address was not used after 1894; the Indian office was opened in 1901, although Bombay did not appear regularly in the imprint until 1906; and Dublin was removed from it after 1910.

8. Bindings continued to show variation in colours of cloth and endpapers, and the publisher's name was sometimes removed from the spine.

9. The impression described here is no more than representative of the reprints, of which there were more than was usual for Henty's novels, as *With Wolfe in Canada* was not re-issued in the cheaper 'New and Popular Edition'. The slightly-differing issues in the first-edition format are all grouped together under this 'generic' heading, *27.2.

27.3

THE TALISMAN LIBRARY (underlined) | WITH | WOLFE IN CANADA | BY | G.A.HENTY | (publisher's device) | BLACKIE AND SON LIMITED | 50 OLD BAILEY LONDON | GLASGOW AND BOMBAY | 1920

Contents

171 x 114 mm. (i)–(xvi) | 1–(188) | no catalogue. Frontispiece from wash-drawing by Charles Sheldon, reproduced by halftone block printed in black on coated paper, unbacked, tipped in.

(i) Half-title p. | (ii) unheaded introduction to the Talisman Library | (frontispiece, tipped in) | (iii) title p. | (iv) list of titles in series, and printer's imprint (Printed and bound in Great Britain) | v–xv. Introduction | (xvi) blank | 1–175. text | (176) blank | 177–187. Notes | (188) printer's imprint (PRINTED AND BOUND IN GREAT BRITAIN | By Blackie & Son, Limited, Glasgow).

Binding (see Note 3)

Grey cloth boards, blocked blue (see Note 3); edges plain; plain off-white endpapers.
Front board: WITH . WOLFE | IN . CANADA | G.A.Henty | (publisher's trade mark for the series, including the wording: The | TALISMAN | Library of | ENGLISH | AUTHORS) | Blackie.&.Son.Limited (all blue) within frame of decorative rules (blue). **Spine:** WITH . WOLFE . IN . CANADA : HENTY (blue) running from foot to head. **Back board:** plain.

References: BL; Bod.

Notes

1. In 1920 four of Henty's novels for boys were abridged for use in schools and included in Blackie's 'The Talisman Library of English Authors'. (The Scottish publisher ignores the fact that the first two books were by Sir Walter Scott!).

Thereafter two by Charles Kingsley were followed by the four by Henty. His other titles were: *Under Drake's Flag; With Clive in India; and Redskin and Cowboy. Two* more were added, in 1921 and 1922 (see 27.4, Note 2).

2. The frontispiece also appeared as an illustration in 27.5.

3. Books in the series (example at Plate 145) were also issued in limp cloth covers, cut flush, in the same design, and with no alteration to the contents.

4. Later impressions in both styles of binding were issued with undated title pages.

27.4

THE TALISMAN LIBRARY (underlined) | WITH | WOLFE IN CANADA | BY | G.A.HENTY | (publisher's device) | BLACKIE & SON LIMITED | LONDON AND GLASGOW

Contents

170 x 113 mm. (i)–(xvi) | 1–(188) | catalogue (189)–(192). Frontispiece as in 27.3.

(i)–(ii) Introduction to the series with bold heading on p.(i): 'The Talisman Library of English Authors', and the titles in the series listed on p.(ii) | (frontispiece, tipped in) | (iii) title p. | (iv) Blackie addresses, and printer's imprint at foot (Printed in Great Britain by Blackie & Son, Ltd., Glasgow) | v–xv. Introduction | (xvi) blank | 1–175. text | (176) blank | 177–187. Notes | (188) blank | (189)–(192) catalogue of school textbooks.

Binding: As for 27.3.

References: BB; OD.

Notes

1. Following the issues both dated and undated of 27.3 (see 27.3, Note 4), the preliminary pages were reset. The main changes, apart from the title-page imprint, were the re-arrangement of the introductory notes, and the list of titles in the series. Otherwise the text appears to be unaltered.

2. *The Dragon and the Raven* and *Beric the Briton* joined the series in 1921 and 1922, and it continued, both in limp cloth and cloth boards, at least for two decades. I have seen *With Wolfe in Canada* in limp cloth, with the Book Production War Economy symbol on p.(iv), a measure required of British publishers in the second war.

*27.5

With | Wolfe in Canada | Or, The Winning of a Continent | BY | G.A.HENTY | Author of "With Clive in India" "The Lion of the North" | "In Freedom's Cause" "The Dragon and the Raven" | "By Sheer Pluck" "Facing Death" &c. | Illustrated | BLACKIE & SON LIMITED | LONDON AND GLASGOW

Contents

184 x 125 mm. (1)–384 | advertisement (1)–(2). Frontispiece from watercolour drawing by John de Walton, reproduced by three-colour halftone blocks; four wash-drawings by Charles Sheldon, reproduced by halftone blocks printed in black; all on coated paper, unbacked, unfolioed, tipped in. One map and one plan printed from line blocks on text pages.

(1) Half-title p. | (2) Blackie addresses | (frontispiece, tipped in) | (3) title p. | (4)

printer's imprint (Printed in Great Britain by | Blackie & Son, Limited, Glasgow) | 5–6. Preface | 7. Contents | (8) blank | 9. list of Illustrations | (10) blank | 11–384. text | (1)–(2) advertisement (THE NEW POPULAR HENTY) listing 62 titles.

Binding
Dark-green cloth boards, blocked black, red, and buff; edges plain; plain off-white endpapers.
   Front board: WITH WOLFE | IN CANADA | G.A.HENTY. (buff), above illustration of redcoat soldier with sword, waving (black, red, buff). **Spine:** WITH | WOLFE | IN | CANADA | G.A.HENTY (buff), above illustration of young Indian (black, red, buff). At foot: BLACKIE & SON LTD (black). **Back board:** plain.

References: Bod; PN.

Notes
1. For notes on Blackie's second cheaper series, 'The New Popular Henty', see *Facing Death*, 10.7, Notes 1–3. Examples of the series binding style are at Plates 174–175. This title was issued in 1922.
2. All the minor variants of *With Wolfe in Canada* in the series are grouped together under this 'generic' heading, *27.5.

28. THE BRAVEST OF THE BRAVE

28.1
THE | BRAVEST OF THE BRAVE: | OR | WITH PETERBOROUGH IN SPAIN. | BY | G.A.HENTY, | Author of "With Clive in India;" "The Lion of the North;" "In Freedom's Cause;" | "The Dragon and the Raven;" "By Sheer Pluck;" "Facing Death;" &c. | WITH EIGHT FULL-PAGE ILLUSTRATIONS | BY H.M.PAGET. | (publisher's device) | LONDON: | BLACKIE & SON, 49 & 50 OLD BAILEY, E.C. | GLASGOW, EDINBURGH, AND DUBLIN. | 1887.

Contents
187 x 125 mm. (i)–(viii) | (9)–352 | catalogue (1)–48. Eight full-page line-and-wash drawings by H.M.Paget, reproduced by two-colour line blocks, with mechanical tints laid on the second-colour plates (sepia), printed on coated paper, unbacked, unfolioed, tipped in.
   (i) Half-title p. | (ii) advertisement (BOOKS BY G.A.HENTY.) listing 11 titles | (frontispiece, tipped in) | (iii) title p. | (iv) blank | (v)–vi. Preface | (vii) Contents | (viii) list of Illustrations | (9)–352. text | (1)–48. catalogue.

Binding (see Plate 58)
Green cloth boards, blocked black, light-brown, blind, and gilt; edges plain; maroon surface-paper endpapers.
   Front board: Two panels formed by black rules, within frame of heavy black rule. In upper panel: THE | BRAVEST | OF THE | BRAVE | OR | WITH | PETERBOROUGH | IN SPAIN. (all black) at left of illustration of mounted soldier (black, light-brown and gilt). In lower panel: BY | G.A.HENTY (black) at right of illustration of boy (black and light-brown). **Spine:** THE | BRAVEST | OF THE | BRAVE (reversed out and gilt) on solid black rectangle with black rule frame. In

central panel: illustration of Spaniard (black and light-brown), with black rule frame. In lower panel: BY | G.A.HENTY (reversed out and gilt) on solid black rectangle with black rule frame. At foot: BLACKIE & SON (gilt). Black and gilt rules at head and foot. **Back board:** Three rules (thin, thick, thin) near edges of board (blind).

References: BL; Bod; PN | *Farmer*, p.14; *Dartt*, p.27, *Companion*, p.5.

Notes

1. Publication day was 1 June 1886. By the end of February 1887 Blackie had sold 2392 copies at five shillings. Over the next fifteen years they sold 7700 more, giving an annual average of 631 copies for the sixteen years to August 1902. In the next twelve years Blackie sold 3521 copies: the book was then issued in the 'New and Popular Edition' (see 28.3). In that year, 1915, Blackie sold the last 11 copies. Altogether, 13,624 copies were sold in the first-edition format at five shillings.

2. As usual with Blackie novels, the earliest issues contain catalogues advertising books for the current year (in this case those with 1887 title-page dates) without quotations from press reviews.

3. *Dartt* did not have a copy of the first impression and describes a reprint instead. This omits the title-page punctuation, and has a much later version of the Blackie imprint and addresses. Consequently he wrongly calls for 'burnished olivine edges' to the leaves, and for 'grey endpapers'. In his *Companion* he corrects the error about the edges of the leaves, but overlooks the others.

*28.2

Reprints of the first edition were issued in the same style as 28.1, but with the date removed from the title page. Alterations were made when necessary to the title-page imprint and addresses: Blackie became a Limited Company in 1890; the Edinburgh address was not used after 1894; and the Indian office was opened in 1901, although Bombay did not appear regularly in the imprint until 1906.

The printing of illustrations was changed later: for all but the earliest reprints the mechanical tints were laid on the black plates and the second colour omitted (see Appendix IV, Part 1).

Bindings continued to show variations in colour of cloth, blocking, and endpapers, often also having the publisher's name removed from the spine.

The slightly-differing issues of this title in its first-edition format are all grouped together under this 'generic' heading, *28.2.

28.3

The | Bravest of the Brave | Or, With Peterborough in Spain | BY | G.A.HENTY | Author of "In the Irish Brigade" "A Knight of the White Cross" | "At the Point of the Bayonet" "The Tiger of Mysore" &c. | ILLUSTRATED BY WILLIAM RAINEY, R.I. | NEW EDITION | BLACKIE AND SON, LIMITED | LONDON GLASGOW AND BOMBAY

Contents

183 x 126 mm. (1)–352 | catalogue 1–16. Six full-page illustrations from wash-drawings by William Rainey, R.I., reproduced by black-and-white halftone blocks printed on coated paper, unbacked, unfolioed, tipped in.

(1) Half-title p. | (2) advertisement (NEW AND POPULAR EDITION OF

G.A.HENTY'S WORKS) listing 39 titles | (frontispiece, tipped in) | (3) title p. | (4) blank | 5–6. Preface | (7) Contents | (8) list of Illustrations | 9–352. text, with printer's imprint on p.352 (PRINTED IN GREAT BRITAIN | At the Villafield Press, Glasgow, Scotland) | 1–16. catalogue.

Binding (see Note 1)
Blue cloth boards, blocked black, dark-blue, pink, and gilt; all edges stained olive-green; grey endpapers, lined off-white.
   Front board: THE BRAVEST | OF THE BRAVE (gilt) | WITH PETERBOROUGH IN SPAIN (black) above illustration of figure with sword and hat, standing astride gun barrel (black, dark-blue, pink). At foot: G.A.HENTY. (pink). **Spine:** THE | BRAVEST | OF THE | BRAVE (gilt) | G.A.HENTY. (black) above illustration of man loading musket (black, dark-blue, pink). At foot: BLACKIE & SON LTD (black). **Back board:** plain.

References: BL; Bod.

Notes
1. Late in 1914 the book was issued in the 'New and Popular Edition'. For details see *Facing Death*, 10.6, Notes 2–3, and for examples of the binding style, Plates 172–173. After 1912 Blackie gave up the practice of dating title pages of first issues.
2. By the end of August 1915 Blackie had sold 1426 copies at 3s.6d. And up to the end of August 1917, when records cease, a further 586 copies in this edition. The grand total of copies sold, at both prices, between 1886 and 1917 was 15,636.

*28.4
The | Bravest of the Brave | Or, With Peterborough in Spain | BY | G.A.HENTY | Author of "In the Irish Brigade" "A Knight of the White Cross" | "At the Point of the Bayonet" "The Tiger of Mysore" &c. | Illustrated | BLACKIE & SON LIMITED | LONDON AND GLASGOW

Contents
186 x 125 mm. (1)–352 | no catalogue. Frontispiece from watercolour drawing by Frank Gillett, R.I., reproduced by three-colour halftone blocks; four full-page wash-drawings by William Rainey, reproduced by halftone blocks printed in black; all on coated paper, unbacked, unfolioed, tipped in.
   (1) Half-title p. | (2) Blackie addresses | (frontispiece, tipped in) | (3) title p. | (4) printer's imprint (Printed in Great Britain by | Blackie & Son, Limited, Glasgow) | 5–6. Preface | (7) Contents | (8) list of Illustrations | 9–352. text.

Binding: (See Plate 174). As for 28.3, except (a) linen-textured silver-grey cloth; lighter boards, blocked black, blue, orange; no gilt: front-board title and author in orange, other lettering black; (b) edges plain; (c) plain off-white endpapers.

Reference: PN.

Notes
1. For notes on Blackie's second cheaper Henty series, 'The New Popular Henty', and subsequent editions of this book, see *Facing Death*, 10.7, Notes 1–3 and 6–8.
2. All the minor variants of *The Bravest of the Brave* in the series are grouped together under this 'generic' heading, *28.4.

29. A FINAL RECKONING

29.1

A FINAL RECKONING | A TALE OF BUSH LIFE IN AUSTRALIA. | BY | G.A.HENTY, | Author of "With Clive in India;" "The Lion of the North;" "In Freedom's Cause;" | "The Dragon and the Raven;" "By Sheer Pluck;" "Facing Death;" &c. | WITH EIGHT FULL-PAGE ILLUSTRATIONS | BY W.B.WOLLEN. | (publisher's device) | LONDON: BLACKIE & SON, 49 & 50 OLD BAILEY, E.C. | GLASGOW, EDINBURGH, AND DUBLIN. | 1887.

Contents
187 x 125 mm. (i)–(viii) | (9)–352 | catalogue (1)–48. Eight full-page line-and-wash drawings by W.B.Wollen, reproduced by two-colour line blocks, with mechanical tints laid on second-colour plates (sepia), printed on coated paper, unbacked, unfolioed, tipped in.

(i) Half-title p. | (ii) advertisement (BOOKS BY G.A.HENTY.) listing 11 titles | (frontispiece, tipped in) | (iii) title p. | (iv) blank | (v)–vi. Preface | (vii) Contents | (viii) list of Illustrations | (9)–352. text | (1)–48. catalogue.

Binding: (see Plate 63)
Green cloth boards, blocked black, pink, blind, and gilt; edges plain; dark olive-green surface-paper endpapers.
Front board: . A . FINAL . RECKONING . | A TALE OF BUSH LIFE IN AUSTRALIA | BY G.A.HENTY. (all gilt) above illustration of white man firing rifle over rock, with black man; spear landed in foreground (black, pink), all enclosed in frame of three black rules. **Spine:** A FINAL | RECKONING | (15mm. rule) | G.A.HENTY | (15mm. rule) (all gilt) above illustration of black man crouching with spear (black, pink). At foot: BLACKIE & SON. (gilt). All within black rules, three at head and foot, one at sides. **Back board:** Three rules (thin, thick, thin) near edges of board (blind).

References: BL; Bod; PN | *Farmer*, p.30; *Dartt*, p.59, *Companion*, p.15.

Notes
1. This book was published on 8 June 1886 at five shillings. By the end of February 1887 Blackie had sold 2445 copies. During the next fifteen years to the end of February 1902 they sold 8491 more, the average annual sales throughout the sixteen years being 684 copies. In the next seven years 1786 more copies were sold, and then the book was re-issued in the 'New and Popular Edition' (see 29.3 below).
2. *Dartt* reports a copy in his own collection without a half-title page, but as he declares ownership of both Blackie and Blackie/Scribner editions, I must assume that it was either the latter or a damaged, rather than a variant, issue of the former.
3. As usual with Blackie novels, the earliest issues contain catalogues advertising the books for the current year (in this case those with title pages dated 1887) without quotations from press reviews.
4. On 21 February 1928 Charles Scribner's Sons, who were Henty's authorised publishers in the USA of the Blackie titles, wrote to Blackie: 'The Universal Pictures Corporation desire to purchase the picture rights to *The Final Reckoning* [*sic*] by G.A.Henty'. There followed a correspondence between Blackie, Scribners,

Universal Pictures Corporation of Fifth Avenue, New York, and their various legal representatives, largely concerned with problems of copyright. This continued for a number of months: by June they were quoting the title of the book correctly, and in July an assignment of rights was finally legalised between Scribners and Universal Pictures. Blackie's film rights were shortly due to revert by contract to Henty's Estate, but in waiving those rights early they managed to get all parties to agree that Scribners should act for them. The total fee quoted for the film rights was one thousand dollars. The terms set out by Blackie were that Scribners should take 20% and the Henty Estate 80%. Copies of the correspondence are in the Lilly Library of Indiana University, but there is no evidence that the film was ever made.

*29.2
Reprints of the first edition were issued in the style of 29.1, with no date on the title page, and with alterations as necessary to Blackie's imprint and addresses. Blackie became a Limited Company in 1890; the Edinburgh address was not used after 1894; and the Indian office was opened in 1901, although Bombay did not regularly appear in the imprint until 1906.

Other changes followed Blackie's usual pattern: the illustrations were modified in due course, with the second-colour tints either transferred to the black plates or omitted altogether (see Appendix IV, Part 1). Bindings continued to show variation in colours of cloth, blocking, and endpapers, often also having the publisher's name removed from the spine.

All the slightly-differing issues of this title in its first-edition format are grouped together under this 'generic' heading, *29.2.

29.3
Blackie's Colonial Library | (15–em rule) | A FINAL RECKONING | A TALE OF BUSH LIFE IN AUSTRALIA | BY | G.A.HENTY | Author of "With Clive in India", "In Greek Waters", "The Tiger of Mysore", | "The Dragon and the Raven", "By Sheer Pluck", "Maori and Settler", &c. | (publisher's device) | LONDON | BLACKIE & SON, LIMITED, 50 OLD BAILEY, E.C. | GLASGOW AND DUBLIN | 1896 | (7–em rule) | This Edition is for circulation only in India | and the British Colonies
(*Note:* Blackie's Colonial Library *is in gothic type, the last two lines in bold*).

Contents
186 x 124 mm. (1)–352 | no catalogue. Frontispiece from line-and-wash drawing by W.B.Wollen, reproduced by two-colour line blocks, with mechanical tint laid on second-colour plate (sepia), printed on coated paper, unbacked, tipped in.

(1) Half-title p. | (2) blank | (frontispiece, tipped in) | (3) title p. | (4) blank | (5) Preface | (6) blank | (7) Contents | (8) blank | (9)–352. text.

Binding (see Note 1)
Designed by Talwin Morris (see Appendix IV, Part 2). Green cloth boards, blocked pale-green and gilt; edges plain; grey surface-paper endpapers.
Front board: BLACKIE'S COLONIAL LIBRARY | A FINAL RECKONING | G.A.HENTY (all pale-green) within decorative panel formed by art-nouveau design (pale-green). **Spine:** Over-all design similar to that on front board (pale-green), leaving two panels with lettering. Upper panel: A . FINAL | RECKONING | (three

small decorations, placed asymmetrically) | G.A.HENTY (all gilt) within a gilt ruled frame. Lower panel: BLACKIE'S | COLONIAL | LIBRARY (all gilt) within a gilt ruled frame. **Back board:** plain.

References: CT | Cargill Thompson, *The Boys' Dumas*, pp.3–4.

Notes
1. Only four of Henty's novels for boys are known to have been included in Blackie's Colonial Library. The others: 1.*With Clive in India* (15.5); 7.*When London Burned* (68.3); 8. *The Dash for Khartoum* (53.3). A list of the first twelve titles in the series is given on the first pages of both *With Clive in India* and *The Dash for Khartoum*. The books are advertised as 'In crown 8vo, with Frontispiece, in Paper Covers, also in Cloth boards'. An example of the latter binding is at Plate 54.
2. Further details are given under *With Clive in India*, 15.5, Notes 2–3.

29.4

A Final Reckoning | A Tale of Bush Life in Australia | BY | G.A.HENTY | Author of "With Clive in India" "The Lion of the North" "In Freedom's Cause" | "By Conduct and Courage" "With Kitchener in the Soudan" "Facing Death" &c. | ILLUSTRATED BY W.B.WOLLEN | NEW EDITION | BLACKIE AND SON LIMITED | LONDON GLASGOW DUBLIN BOMBAY | 1910

Contents
185 x 124 mm. (1)–352 | catalogue 1–16. Eight full-page wash drawings by an unknown hand based on the original illustrations by W.B.Wollen, reproduced by halftone blocks printed in black on coated paper, unbacked, unfolioed, tipped in.

(1) Half-title p. | (2) advertisement (NEW AND POPULAR EDITION OF G.A.HENTY'S WORKS) listing 27 titles | (frontispiece, tipped in) | (3) title p. | (4) blank | (5) Preface | (6) blank | 7. Contents | 8. list of Illustrations | (9)–352. text | 1–16. catalogue.

Binding (see Note 1)
Dark-green cloth boards, blocked black, dark-grey, light-grey, and gilt; all edges stained olive-green; grey endpapers, lined off-white.
Front board: A | FINAL RECKONING (gilt) | A TALE OF | BUSH LIFE | IN AUSTRALIA (black) above illustration of rider with rifle on grey horse (black, dark-grey, light-grey); beneath this: G.A.HENTY (black). **Spine:** A | FINAL | RECKONING (gilt) | G.A.HENTY (black) above illustration of native standing, with spear (black, dark-grey, light grey). At foot: BLACKIE & SON, LTD (black). **Back board:** plain.

References: BL; Bod.

Notes
1. In 1909 (title-page date 1910) *A Final Reckoning* was re-issued in the 'New and Popular Edition'. For details of the series see *Facing Death*, 10.6, Notes 2–3, and for examples of the binding style see Plates 172–173.
2. In this edition Blackie had sold 1977 copies by the end of August 1910. Another 2962 copies were sold in the following seven years, up to the end of August 1917, when records cease. That makes a total of 4939 copies sold at 3s.6d. over the eight

years: average annual sales being 617 copies. The grand total of copies sold, at both prices, between 1886 and 1917, was 17,661.

*29.5

A Final Reckoning | A Tale of Bush Life in Australia | BY | G.A.HENTY | Author of "With Clive in India" "The Lion of the North" | "In Freedom's Cause" "By Conduct and Courage" | "With Kitchener in the Soudan" | "Facing Death" &c. | ILLUSTRATED | BLACKIE AND SON LIMITED | LONDON GLASGOW AND BOMBAY

Contents

183 x 124 mm. (1)–352 | no catalogue. Frontispiece from watercolour drawing by William Rainey reproduced by three-colour halftone blocks; four full-page wash-drawings by an unknown hand, based on some of the original illustrations by W.B.Wollen, reproduced by halftone blocks printed in black; all on coated paper, unbacked, unfolioed, tipped in.

(1) Half-title p. | (2) publisher's advertisement (G.A.HENTY'S BOOKS) listing 56 titles | (frontispiece, tipped in) | (3) title p. | (4) printer's imprint (Printed in Great Britain by | Blackie & Son, Limited, Glasgow) | 5–6. Preface | 7. Contents | (8) list of Illustrations | 9–352. text.

Binding: As for 29.5, except (a) red cloth boards, blocked black, grey, and buff, with no gilt: all lettering black; (b) edges plain; (c) plain off-white endpapers.

Reference: PN.

Notes

1. For notes on Blackie's second cheaper series, 'The New Popular Henty', and later editions of *A Final Reckoning*, see *Facing Death*, 10.7, Notes 1–3 and 6–8. Examples of the series binding style are at Plates 174–175.

2. All the minor variants of *A Final Reckoning* in the series are grouped together under this 'generic' heading, *29.5.

29.6

Title page: As for *29.5, except (a) Illustrated (not ILLUSTRATED); (b) publisher's device included above revised imprint (BLACKIE & SON LIMITED | LONDON AND GLASGOW).

Contents

180 x 120 mm. (1)–352 | no catalogue. Four watercolour drawings by William Rainey reproduced by three-colour halftone blocks printed on coated paper, keyed to text pages, unbacked, tipped in.

(1) Half-title p. | Blackie addresses | (frontispiece, tipped in) | (3) title p. | (4) printer's imprint (Printed in Great Britain by | Blackie & Son, Limited, Glasgow) | 5–6. Preface | 7. Contents | (8) list of Illustrations | 9–352. text.

Binding (see Note 1)
Blue cloth boards, blocked blind and gilt; edges plain; plain off-white endpapers.

Front board: Over-all design (blind) of decorative rules and panels including roses and, at head: A FINAL | RECKONING | HENTY (gilt). **Spine:** Similar over-all blind decorations and, in panel at head: A | FINAL | RECKONING | HENTY (gilt). At foot: BLACKIE | & SON LTD (blind). **Back board:** plain.

Reference: TC.

Notes

1. This binding design was also used for *A Chapter of Adventures*, 48.10, Plate 104, and *Tales from Henty*, 57.5, as well as titles by other authors in Blackie's 'Library of Famous Books' (see Appendix V). *A Final Reckoning* appears to have been added to the series late in the 1920s.

2. William Rainey was commissioned to make three more watercolour drawings for this edition, the resulting four colour-plates bringing it into line with the corresponding issue of *A Chapter of Adventures* (48.10). *Tales from Henty* (57.5) in the same series has a colour frontispiece only.

3. The dust-wrapper for this issue carries the two illustrations used on the dust-wrapper for *29.5. One of these is the frontispiece; the other is a part of the plate facing p.296. A set of electros was made from the three-colour halftones for the latter plate, and cut to an oval shape for the spines of both dust-wrappers. The two editions, *29.5 and 29.6, were probably both on sale at the same time.

30. THE YOUNG CARTHAGINIAN

30.1

THE YOUNG CARTHAGINIAN: | OR | A STRUGGLE FOR EMPIRE. | BY | G.A.HENTY, | Author of "With Clive in India;" "The Lion of the North;" "In Freedom's Cause;" | "By Sheer Pluck;" "Facing Death;" &c. | WITH TWELVE FULL-PAGE ILLUSTRATIONS | BY C.J.STANILAND, R.I. | (publisher's device) | LONDON: | BLACKIE & SON, 49 & 50 OLD BAILEY, E.C. | GLASGOW, EDINBURGH, AND DUBLIN. | 1887.

Contents

185 x 130 mm. (i)–(viii) | (9)–384 | catalogue (1)–48. Twelve full-page pen-drawings by C.J.Staniland, R.I., reproduced by line blocks printed in black on coated paper, unbacked, unfolioed, tipped in.

(i) Half-title p. | (ii) advertisement (BOOKS BY G.A.HENTY.) listing 11 titles | (frontispiece, tipped in) | (iii) title p. | (iv) blank | (v)–vi. Preface | (vii) Contents | (viii) list of Illustrations | (9)–384. text | (1)–48. catalogue.

Binding (see Plate 70)

Grey-green cloth boards, bevelled, blocked maroon, yellow, blind, and gilt; all edges burnished olive-green; maroon surface-paper endpapers.

Front board: THE . YOUNG . CARTHAGINIAN . | A . STORY . OF . THE . TIMES . OF . HANNIBAL | (decorative rule) | G . A . HENTY | (decorative rule) (all gilt) at right of medallion (gilt) and all within frame of gilt and maroon rules. Below: illustration of battle scene (maroon and yellow) within frame of maroon rules. **Spine:** THE YOUNG (set as the upper arc of a circle) | ... | CARTHAGINIAN | (decorative rule) | G.A.HENTY (all cloth-colour reversed out of solid-gilt circle) with surrounding rules and decoration to form rectangle (gilt) in upper part of plain panel with frame of maroon and gilt rules. Beneath this: illustration as on front board (maroon and yellow) in frame of maroon rules. Gilt rules at head and foot. **Back board:** single rule at edges of bevel (blind).

References: BL; Bod; PN | *Farmer*, p.87; *Dartt*, p.168, *Companion*, p.36.

Notes

1. The book was published on 8 June 1886. By the end of the following February Blackie had sold 2561 copies. During the following ten years they sold 4725 more, making an average annual sale for the eleven years of 729 copies. Over the next eight years only 1741 copies were sold, and the average annual figure dropped to 218 copies. The book was then re-issued in the cheaper 'New and Popular Edition', see 30.3 below. The remaining stock of the six-shilling edition, amounting to 132 copies, was sold between 1906 and 1914, concurrently with the cheaper series.

2. In an interview with Raymond Blathwayt published in *Great Thoughts from Master Minds* on 4 October 1902 (p.9), shortly before he died, Henty said 'The ancient history doesn't sell well. Quite ancient, I mean. There was one on the Punic wars in which I told of the killing of Hannibal. I should have loved that book as a boy, but no, it failed.' The total sales of the six-shilling edition were only just over 9000 copies, which was low for Henty, though by 1917 Blackie sold about 6700 more in the first cheap edition. There was a second cheap edition in the 1920s so the book was not a failure: certainly some of Henty's books came off much worse.

3. As usual with Blackie novels, the earliest issues contain catalogues advertising the books for the current year (in this case those with 1887 title-page dates) without quotations from press reviews.

4. The subtitle on the title page is not the same as that on the binding case. The advertisement in the bound-in catalogue gives the subtitle as on the case. The title page was soon corrected, see 30.2.

30.2

THE YOUNG CARTHAGINIAN: | A STORY OF | THE TIMES OF HANNIBAL. | BY | G.A.HENTY, | Author of "With Clive in India;" "The Lion of the North;" "In Freedom's Cause;" | "By Sheer Pluck;" "Facing Death;" &c. | WITH TWELVE FULL-PAGE ILLUSTRATIONS | BY C.J.STANILAND, R.I. | (publisher's device) | LONDON: | BLACKIE & SON, 49 & 50 OLD BAILEY, E.C. | GLASGOW, EDINBURGH, AND DUBLIN. | 1887.

Contents: 187 x 130 mm. As for 30.1, but see Note 1 below.

Binding: As for 30.1.

Reference: PN.

Notes

1. At some point very shortly after publication of *The Young Carthaginian* cancel title pages were inserted in copies of the first impression. The purpose was to change the subtitle to correspond with the binding case and the bound-in catalogues. The new subtitle was clearly agreed after the type was set, but some time before publication, since there had been time to cut the brasses for the first copies.

2. The catalogue bound in 30.2 still has advertisements for the current year's books, including this one, without quotations from press reviews. It is, however, a slightly later edition, with noticeable differences, especially on p.39.

3. Neither *Farmer* nor *Dartt* was aware of 30.2. The Copyright Libraries have 30.1, and it is likely that it was also used for review copies and to meet booksellers' pre-publication subscription orders (which would have amounted to at least 2000 copies: see 30.1, Note 1). So the cancel title-page would have been inserted in the comparatively few remaining copies of the first printing.

*30.3

Reprints of the first edition were issued in the same style as 30.2, but with the date removed from the title page. Alterations were later made, as necessary, to the publisher's imprint and addresses: Blackie became a Limited Company in 1890; the Edinburgh address was not used after 1894; and the Indian office was opened in 1901, although Bombay did not appear regularly in the imprint until 1906.

Bindings continued to show variations in colours of cloth, blocking and endpapers.

The minor variants among the reprints of this title in its first-edition format are all grouped together under this 'generic' heading, *30.3.

30.4

The Young Carthaginian I A Story of the Times of Hannibal I BY I G.A.HENTY I Author of I "With Clive in India" "The Lion of the North" "The Tiger of Mysore" I "In Freedom's Cause" "Won by the Sword" "Facing Death" &c. I ILLUSTRATED I NEW EDITION I BLACKIE AND SON LIMITED I LONDON GLASGOW DUBLIN BOMBAY I 1906

Contents

187 x 123 mm. (1)–384 I catalogue 1–32. Eight full-page wash-drawings by an unknown hand, based on some of the original illustrations by C.J.Staniland, reproduced by halftone blocks printed in sepia on coated paper, unbacked, unfolioed, tipped in.

(1) Half-title p. I (2) advertisement (HISTORICAL TALES BY G.A.HENTY) listing 30 titles I (frontispiece, tipped in) I (3) title p. I (4) blank I 5. Preface I vi. [roman numerals in error] Preface, continued I 7. Contents I 8. list of Illustrations I 9–384. text I 1–32. catalogue.

Binding (see Note 1)

Blue cloth boards, blocked black, green, pink, and gilt; all edges stained olive-green; grey endpapers, lined off-white.

Front board: THE YOUNG I CARTHAGINIAN I G.A.HENTY (all pink) above illustration of soldier with sword and shield, under fire from arrows (black, pink, green). Signature: J Hassall (black) at foot. **Spine:** THE I YOUNG I CARTHAGINIAN I G.A.HENTY. (gilt) above illustration of soldier firing arrow from bow (black, pink, green). At foot: BLACKIE & SON, LTD (gilt). **Back board:** plain.

References: BL; Bod.

Notes

1. In 1905 (title-page date 1906) Blackie re-issued *The Young Carthaginian* in their 'New and Popular Edition' of Henty's novels. Details of the series are given under *Facing Death*, 10.6, Notes 2–3, and examples of the binding style at Plates 172–173.
2. In this edition Blackie sold 2200 copies by the end of August 1906, and 4532 more over the following eleven years up to the end of August 1917, when records cease. The average annual sale over those twelve years was 561 copies. The grand total of copies sold at both prices from 1886 to 1917 was 15,891.

*30.5

The | YOUNG CARTHAGINIAN | A Story of the Times of Hannibal | BY | G.A.HENTY | Author of | "With Clive in India" "The Lion of the North" "The Tiger of Mysore" | "Beric the Briton" "Maori and Settler" "Facing Death" &c. | Illustrated | BLACKIE & SON LIMITED | LONDON AND GLASGOW

Contents

187 x 125 mm. (1)–384 | advertisement (1)–(2). Frontispiece from watercolour drawing by Frank Gillett, R.I., reproduced by three-colour halftone blocks; four full-page black-and-white wash-drawings by an unknown artist, based on some of the original illustrations by C.J.Staniland, reproduced by halftone blocks printed in black; all on coated paper, unbacked, keyed to text pages, tipped in.

(1) Half-title p. | (2) Blackie addresses | (frontispiece, tipped in) | (3) title p. | (4) printer's imprint (Printed in Great Britain by | Blackie & Son, Limited, Glasgow) | 5. Preface | vi.[roman numerals in error] Preface, continued | (vii) [roman numerals in error] Contents | (viii) [roman numerals in error] list of Illustrations | 9–384. text | (1)–(2) advertisement (THE NEW POPULAR HENTY) listing 64 titles.

Binding

Red cloth boards, blocked black, blue, and buff; edges plain; plain off-white endpapers.
Front board: THE YOUNG | CARTHAGINIAN | G.A.HENTY (buff), above illustration of soldier with sword and shield, under fire from arrows (black, blue, buff), with signature at foot: J Hassall (black). **Spine:** THE | YOUNG | CARTHAG- | INIAN (black) above illustration of soldier firing arrow from longbow (black, blue, buff). At foot: BLACKIE & SON LTD (black). **Back board:** plain.

Reference: PN.

Notes

1. For notes on Blackie's second cheaper series, 'The New Popular Henty', and subsequent editions of this book, see *Facing Death*, 10.7, Notes 1–3 and 6–8. Examples of the series binding style are at Plates 174–175.
2. All the minor variants of *The Young Carthaginian* in the series are grouped together under this 'generic' heading, *30.5.

31. BONNIE PRINCE CHARLIE

31.1

BONNIE PRINCE CHARLIE: I A TALE OF FONTENOY AND CULLODEN. I BY I G.A.HENTY, I Author of "The Young Carthaginian;" "With Clive in India;" "In Freedom's Cause;" I "The Lion of the North;" "With Wolfe in Canada;" "Facing Death;" &c. I WITH TWELVE FULL-PAGE ILLUSTRATIONS I BY GORDON BROWNE. I (publisher's device) I LONDON: I BLACKIE & SON, 49 & 50 OLD BAILEY, E.C. I GLASGOW, EDINBURGH, AND DUBLIN. I 1888.

Contents

187 x 131 mm. (i)–(viii) I (9)–384 I catalogue (1)–32. Twelve full-page pen-drawings by Gordon Browne, reproduced by line blocks printed in black on coated paper, unbacked, unfolioed, tipped in.

(Frontispiece, tipped in) I (i) title p. I (ii) blank I (iii)–iv. Preface I (v) Contents I (vi) blank I (vii) list of Illustrations I (viii) blank I (9)–384. text I (1)–32. catalogue.

Binding (see Plate 57)

Blue cloth boards, bevelled, blocked black, blind, and gilt; all edges burnished olive-green; maroon surface-paper endpapers.

Front board: Bonnie Prince Charlie I by I G.A.Henty. (gilt) below illustration of Scottish soldier with shield and sword (black and gilt), and above decoration of sword, pistol and powder horn (black), all within frame of black rules. **Spine:** Bonnie I (decoration) Prince (decoration) I Charlie. (gilt) above trophy including portrait in frame with ribbons, and military equipment (black and gilt) with lettering enclosed: G.A.HENTY. (gilt). Beneath this: BLACKIE & SON. (gilt). Black and gilt rules at head and foot. **Back board:** Single rule at edges of bevel (blind).

References: BL; Bod; PN I *Farmer*, p.11; *Dartt*, p.19.

Notes

1. The book was published on 6 June 1887 at six shillings. From the first it was a popular title, and Blackie sold 3298 copies by the end of February 1888. Over the following fifteen years, to the end of August 1903, they sold 9982 more – an average annual sale over the first sixteen years of 830 copies. In the next fourteen years another 3479 copies were sold, and it was the end of August 1917 when those figures were recorded, with the information that the book was to be re-issued in the 'New and Popular Edition'. At that point Blackie's surviving records come to an end. The grand total of copies sold, from 1887 up to the end of August 1917, all at six shillings, was 16,759.

2. As usual with Blackie novels, the earliest issues contain catalogues advertising books for the current year (in this case those with 1888 title-page dates) without quotations from press reviews.

*31.2

Reprints of the first edition were issued in the same style as 31.1, but with the date removed from the title page. Alterations were made when necessary to the title-page imprint and addresses: Blackie became a Limited Company in 1890; the Edinburgh address was not used after 1894; the Indian office was opened in 1901, although

Bombay did not appear regularly in the imprint until 1906; and Dublin was removed from it after 1910.

Bindings continued to show variations in colours of cloth, blocking, and endpapers, and often also had the publisher's name removed from the spine.

The slightly differing issues in the first-edition format, produced over a period of thirty years, are all grouped together under this 'generic' heading, *31.2.

31.3

Bonnie Prince Charlie | A Tale of Fontenoy and Culloden | BY | G.A.HENTY | Author of "The Young Carthaginian" "With Clive in India | "In Freedom's Cause" "The Lion of the North' | "With Wolfe in Canada" "Facing Death" &c. | ILLUSTRATED BY GORDON BROWNE, R.I. | BLACKIE AND SON LIMITED | LONDON GLASGOW AND BOMBAY

(Note: In the titles following the author's name, both quotation marks after India are missing, and one of the pair is missing after North).

Contents

186 x 125 mm. (1)–384 | no catalogue. Six full-page pen drawings by Gordon Browne, R.I., reproduced by line blocks printed in black on coated paper, unbacked, unfolioed, tipped in.

(Frontispiece, tipped in) | (1) title p. | (2) blank | 3–4. Preface | (5) Contents | (6) blank | (7) list of Iluustrations | (8) blank | (9)–384. text.

Binding (see Note 2)

Pink cloth boards, blocked black, cream, and grey; edges plain; plain light-grey endpapers.

Front board: BONNIE PRINCE | CHARLIE | A TALE | OF FONTENOY | AND | CULLODEN | G.A.HENTY (all cream) above illustration of Scottish soldier defending himself with sword and shield (black, cream, and grey). **Spine:** BONNIE | PRINCE | CHARLIE | G.A.HENTY (all cream) above illustration of Scottish soldier standing with shield and sword (black, cream and grey). At foot: BLACKIE AND SON LTD (black). **Back board:** plain.

References: BL; Bod; NS.

Notes

1. At the end of 1917 this title and *In the Reign of Terror*, 33.3, were the last to be re-issued in the 'New and Popular Edition'. That is not recorded in Blackie's records, which finish at the end of August 1917, but both were received by the Copyright Libraries in February 1918.

2. Details of the series are given under *Facing Death*, 10.6, Notes 2–3; examples of binding style at Plates 172–173. In common with many other titles re-issued during the first war, this one was produced in a more economical way than earlier books in the series. *With Kitchener in the Soudan*, the final title to be recorded as part of the series, was first issued with gold blocking on the spine but no gold on the front board. The first issue of this later book has no gold blocking at all. Nor does it have the customary new wash-drawings to replace the original line illustrations. For all the later additions to the series, from 1913 onwards, Blackie had also abandoned their custom of dating the title pages of first issues.

*31.4

Title page: As for 31.3.

Contents

184 x 125 mm. (1)–384 I no catalogue. Frontispiece from watercolour drawing, reproduced by three-colour halftone blocks; four full-page drawings reproduced by line blocks printed in black; all by Gordon Browne; all on coated paper, unbacked, keyed to text pages, tipped in.

(Frontispiece, tipped in) I (1) title p. I (2) publisher's advertisement (G.A.HENTY'S BOOKS) listing 45 titles I 3–4. Preface I (5) Contents I (6) blank I (7) list of Illustrations I (8) blank I 9–384. text, with printer's imprint at foot of p.384 (PRINTED AND BOUND IN GREAT BRITAIN I By Blackie & Son, Limited, Glasgow).

Binding: As for 31.3, except (a) red cloth boards, blocked black, brown, and buff: no gilt, all front-board lettering is buff, all spine lettering black; (b) edges plain; (c) plain off-white endpapers.

References: Bod; PN.

Notes

1. Issued (1922) in Blackie's second cheaper series, 'The New Popular Henty'. For details of that, and of subsequent editions, see *Facing Death*, 10.7, Notes 1–3 and 6–8. Examples of the series binding style are at Plates 174–175.

2. All the variants of *Bonnie Prince Charlie* in the series are grouped together under this 'generic' heading, *31.4.

32. ORANGE AND GREEN

32.1

ORANGE AND GREEN: I A TALE OF THE BOYNE AND LIMERICK. I BY I G.A.HENTY, I Author of "The Young Carthaginian;" "With Clive in India;" "In Freedom's Cause;" I "The Lion of the North;" "With Wolfe in Canada;" "Facing Death;" &c. I WITH EIGHT FULL-PAGE ILLUSTRATIONS I BY GORDON BROWNE. I (publisher's device) I LONDON: I BLACKIE & SON, 49 & 50 OLD BAILEY, E.C. I GLASGOW, EDINBURGH, AND DUBLIN. I 1888.

Contents

184 x 123 mm. (i)–(viii) I (9)–352 I catalogue (1)–32. Eight full-page pen-drawings by Gordon Browne, reproduced by line blocks printed in black on coated paper, unbacked, unfolioed, tipped in.

(Frontispiece, tipped in) I (i) title p. I (ii) blank I (iii)–iv. Preface I (v) Contents I (vi) blank I (vii) list of Illustrations I (viii) blank I (9)–352. text I (1)–32. catalogue.

Binding (see Plate 79)

Turquoise cloth boards, blocked black, blind, and gilt; all edges burnished olive-green; maroon surface-paper endpapers.

Front board: ORANGE AND GREEN. I A TALE OF THE BOYNE I AND LIMERICK. (gilt) above illustration of two young soldiers (black and gilt). At foot:

G.A.HENTY. (gilt). All framed by single black rule. **Spine:** ORANGE I . AND . I GREEN. (gilt) above illustration of young soldier (black and gilt). Beneath this: G.A.HENTY. (gilt) above shamrock-leaf decoration (black). At foot: BLACKIE & SON (gilt). Black and gilt rules at head and foot. **Back board:** three rules (thin, thick, thin) near edges of board (blind).

References: BL; Bod; PN I *Farmer*, p.53; *Dartt*, p.102.

Notes

1. The book was published on 2 July 1887 at five shillings. By the end of February 1888 Blackie had sold 2417 copies, and in the following twelve years they sold 4903 more, the average annual sale for the first thirteen years being 563 copies. During the next nine years a further 1677 copies were sold, with the lower yearly average of 186, and at the end of 1909 the book was re-issued in the 'New and Popular Edition' (see 32.3, below). A balance of 79 copies of the five-shilling edition was sold over the next four years, concurrently with the cheaper edition.

2. As usual with Blackie novels, the earliest issues contain catalogues advertising the books for the current year (in this case with 1888 title-page dates) without quotations from press reviews.

*32.2

Reprints of the first edition were issued in the same style as 32.1, but with the date removed from the title page. Alterations were made when necessary to the title- page imprint and addresses; Blackie became a Limited Company in 1890; the Edinburgh address was not used after 1894; and the Indian office was opened in 1901, although Bombay did not appear regularly in the imprint until 1906.

Bindings continued to show variation in colours of cloth, blocking, and endpapers, often also having the publisher's name removed from the spine.

The slightly-differing issues of this title in its first-edition format are all grouped together under this 'generic' heading, *32.2.

32.3

Orange and Green I A Tale of the Boyne and Limerick I BY I G.A.HENTY I Author of "The Young Carthaginian" "With Clive in India" "In Freedom's Cause" I "The Lion of the North" "By Conduct and Courage" "The Dash for Khartoum" &c. I ILLUSTRATED BY GORDON BROWNE I NEW EDITION I BLACKIE AND SON LIMITED I LONDON GLASGOW DUBLIN BOMBAY I 1910

Contents

184 x 128 mm. (1)–352 I catalogue 1–16. Eight full-page wash-drawings credited to Gordon Browne (see Note 3), reproduced by halftone blocks printed in sepia on coated paper, unbacked, unfolioed, tipped in.

(Frontispiece, tipped in) I (1) title p. I (2) advertisement (NEW AND POPULAR EDITION OF I G.A.HENTY'S WORKS) listing 27 titles I 3. Preface I iv.[roman numerals in error] Preface, continued I 5. Contents I (6) blank I 7. list of Illustrations I (8) blank I 9–352. text I 1–16. catalogue.

Binding (see Note 1)

Sage-green cloth boards, blocked black, orange, buff, gilt; all edges stained olive-green; grey endpapers, lined off-white.

Front board: ORANGE AND | GREEN (gilt) | A TALE OF BOYNE AND LIMERICK (black) | G.A.HENTY. (gilt) above illustration, in frame of black rules, of King James standing by stairway, about to draw sword (black, orange, buff). **Spine:** ORANGE | AND | GREEN. | G.A.HENTY. (gilt) over illustration of officer with sword (black, orange, buff). At foot: BLACKIE & SON. LTD (black). **Back board:** plain.

References: BL; Bod.

Notes
1. In 1909 (title-page date 1910) Blackie re-issued *Orange and Green* in the 'New and Popular Edition'. For details of the series see *Facing Death*, 10.6, Notes 2–3, and for examples of the binding style see Plates 172–173.
2. In this edition Blackie sold 1773 copies by the end of August 1910, and a further 1869 copies over the next seven years to the end of 1917, when records cease. That represents a total sale of 3642 in this edition, and an average annual sale over eight years of 455 copies. It was not one of the most popular titles in the series: in its eighth year it sold only 68 copies. The total number of copies sold at both prices from 1887 to 1917 is 12,718, which is not a high figure by Henty's standards.
3. For many books originally illustrated in line, Blackie commissioned anonymous wash-drawings based on some of the original pictures. On the title page of this book Gordon Browne is himself credited with the new illustrations. They are not signed, however, and I think the copies from the pen-drawings were made by another hand: they do not have the vigour usually found in Gordon Browne's work.

*32.4

Title page: As for 32.3, except (a) Illustrated by Gordon Browne (not in capitals); (b) no date; (c) publisher's imprint (BLACKIE & SON LIMITED | LONDON AND GLASGOW).

Contents
184 x 123 mm. (1)–(352) | catalogue (i)–(ii). Frontispiece from watercolour drawing by Gordon Browne reproduced by three-colour halftone blocks; four wash-drawings credited to Gordon Browne (see 32.3, Note 3 above), reproduced by halftone blocks printed in black; all on coated paper, unbacked, keyed to text pages, tipped in.
(Frontispiece, tipped in) | (1) title p. | (2) Blackie addresses; printer's imprint at foot (Printed in Great Britain by Blackie & Son, Limited, Glasgow) | 3. Preface | iv.[roman numerals in error] Preface, continued | (5) Contents | (6) blank | (7) list of Illustrations | (8) blank | 9–352. text | (i)–(ii) advertisement, tipped in (THE NEW POPULAR HENTY) listing 62 titles.

Binding: As for 32.3, except (a) grey-green cloth boards, blocked black, orange, buff, but no gilt: front-board has subtitle black, and spine has publisher's imprint black. All other lettering buff; (b) edges plain; (c) plain off-white endpapers.

Notes
1. For notes on Blackie's second cheaper series, 'The New Popular Henty', and subsequent editions of this book, see *Facing Death*, 10.7, Notes 1–3 and 6–8. Examples of the series binding style are at Plates 174–175.
2. All the minor variants of *Orange and Green* in the series are grouped together under this 'generic' heading, *32.4.

33. IN THE REIGN OF TERROR

33.1

IN THE REIGN OF TERROR: I THE I ADVENTURES OF A WESTMINSTER BOY. I by I G.A.HENTY. I Author of "The Young Carthaginian;" "With Wolfe in Canada" "In Freedom's Cause," I "The Lion of the North;" "With Clive in India;" "Facing Death;" &c. I WITH EIGHT FULL-PAGE ILLUSTRSATIONS I BY J.SCHÖNBERG. I (publisher's device) I LONDON: I BLACKIE & SON, 49 & 50 OLD BAILEY, E.C. I GLASGOW, EDINBURGH, AND DUBLIN. I 1888.
(Note: (a) Semi-colon dropped out after With Wolfe in Canada; *(b) Semi-colon broken and appears as a comma after* In Freedom's Cause*).*

Contents
185 x 125 mm. (i)–(viii) I (9)–352 I catalogue (1)–32. Eight full-page wash-drawings by J.Schönberg, reproduced by halftone blocks printed in black on coated paper, unbacked, unfolioed, tipped in. (See Note 2).
  (Frontispiece, tipped in) I (i) title p. I (ii) blank I (iii) Preface I (iv) blank I (v) Contents I (vi) blank I (vii) list of Illustrations I (viii) blank I (9)–351. text I (352) blank I (1)–32. catalogue.

Binding (see Plate 73)
Green cloth boards, blocked black, blind, and gilt; all edges burnished olive-green; brown surface-paper endpapers.
  Front board: IN THE I REIGN OF TERROR. I . G.A.HENTY . (all gilt) at upper right corner and at right of illustration of man reading proclamation (black and gilt) with gilt rules at top and upper parts of sides, all enclosed in black rules, double at head and foot. **Spine:** IN . THE . REIGN I OF I TERROR. (all cloth-colour reversed out of solid gilt background) of illustration of drummer girl (black and gilt) headed by row of sixteen gilt dots. Beneath this: G.A.HENTY. (gilt). All enclosed in black rules, double at head and foot, with additional pair of gilt rules at both head and foot. **Back board:** double rules near edges of board (blind).

References: BL; Bod; PN I *Farmer*, p.42; *Dartt*, p.85, *Companion*, p.19.

Notes
1. Published on 8 July 1887 at five shillings. By the end of February 1888 Blackie had sold 2690 copies, and in the next twelve years 9456 more, the average annual sale for the first thirteen years being 934 copies. (*Orange and Green*, published the previous week, averaged annual sales of only 563 copies over exactly the same period). During the next nine years *In the Reign of Terror* sold 3439 more copies (cf. *Orange and Green*, 1677), and remained on sale at five shillings until the end of August 1917, when Blackie's records cease: 17,246 copies had then been sold.
2. The illustrations are printed from fine-screen halftone blocks, the first in a book by Henty, and among the earliest to be used in book-printing in this country. Much hand-work and 'deep-etching' was done on the blocks, to accentuate highlights and give life to what might otherwise have been a rather flat result. That treatment was not, however, required for the plate facing p.196, a very effective night scene. Examination with a glass shows that Blackie had printing problems with these very fine screens, which tended to get clogged by dust and ink (see Appendix IV, Part 1).

3. As usual with Blackie novels, the earliest issues contain catalogues advertising the books for the current year (in this case those with title pages dated 1888) without quotations from press reviews.

*33.2

Reprints of the first edition were issued in the same style as 33.1, but with no date on the title page. Alterations were made when necessary to the title-page imprint and addresses: Blackie became a Limited Company in 1890; the Edinburgh address was not used after 1894; the Indian office was opened in 1901, although Bombay did not appear regularly in the imprint until 1906; and Dublin was omitted after 1910.

Bindings continued to show variation in colours of cloth, blocking, and endpapers, and sometimes had the publisher's name removed from the spine. All the minor variants of the book in its first-edition format are grouped together under this 'generic' heading, *33.2.

33.3

In the | Reign of Terror | The Adventures of a | Westminster Boy | BY | G.A.HENTY | Author of "The Young Carthaginian" "With Wolfe in Canada" | "In Freedom's Cause" "The Lion of the North" "With Clive in India" | "Facing Death" &c. | ILLUSTRATED BY FRANK GILLETT, R.I. | BLACKIE AND SON LIMITED | LONDON GLASGOW AND BOMBAY

Contents

185 x 124 mm. (1)–352 | no catalogue. Six full-page pencil drawings by Frank Gillett, reproduced by halftone blocks printed in black on coated paper, unbacked, unfolioed, tipped in.

(1) Half-title p. | (2) publisher's advertisement (NEW AND POPULAR EDITION OF | G.A.HENTY'S WORKS) listing 45 titles (excluding this one) | (frontispiece, tipped in) | (3) title p. | (4) blank | (5) Preface | (6) blank | (7) Contents | (8) blank | (9) list of Illustrations | (10) blank | 11–352. text, with printer's imprint at foot of p.352 (PRINTED IN GREAT BRITAIN | At the Villafield Press, Glasgow, Scotland).

Binding

Pink cloth boards, blocked black, orange, and buff; edges plain; plain off-white endpapers.

Front board: IN THE REIGN OF | TERROR (buff) | THE ADVENTURES OF A WESTMINSTER BOY (black) above illustration of boy waving cap (black, orange, buff). At foot: G.A.HENTY. (buff). **Spine:** IN THE | REIGN | OF | TERROR (buff) | G.A.HENTY. (black) above illustration of uniformed figure (black, orange, buff). At foot: BLACKIE & SON LTD (black). **Back board:** plain.

References: BL; Bod; NS.

Notes

1. At the very end of 1917, this title and *Bonnie Prince Charlie* were the last to be re-issued in the cheaper 'New and Popular Edition'. For details of the series see *Facing Death*, 10.6, Notes 2–3, and for examples of binding style, Plates 172–173.

2. Blackie's surviving records end in August 1917, and do not record this issue, so no sales figures are available. But it was received by the Copyright Libraries in February 1918, in varying cloth-colours (pink and dark-green), and was probably in the shops in time for Christmas 1917.

3. Five years earlier Blackie had ceased dating title-pages in this series, and their use of gold for blocking cases had gradually come to an end for Henty's books.

4. *In the Reign of Terror* in this style is not very common, and it is likely that it was not reprinted. The title was re-issued a few years later in Blackie's second cheap edition with virtually no alteration apart from the addition of a colour-frontispiece and the omission of two black-and-white plates (see *33.4 below).

*33.4

Title page: As for 33.3.

Contents

183 x 125 mm. (1)–352 | no catalogue. Frontispiece from watercolour drawing, reproduced by three-colour halftone blocks; four full-page pencil drawings, reproduced by halftone blocks printed in black, all by Frank Gillett, all on coated paper, unbacked, unfolioed, tipped in.

(1) Half-title p. | (2) publisher's advertisement (G.A.HENTY'S BOOKS) listing 12 titles | (frontispiece, tipped in) | (3) title p. | (4) blank | (5) Preface | (6) blank | (7) Contents | (8) blank | (9) list of Illustrations | (10) blank | 11–352. text, with printer's imprint at foot of p.352 (PRINTED AND BOUND IN GREAT BRITAIN | By Blackie & Son, Limited, Glasgow).

Binding: (See Plate 175). As for 33.3, but blue cloth boards.

Reference: PN.

Notes

1. For notes on Blackie's second cheaper series 'The New Popular Henty', and subsequent editions of this book, see *Facing Death*, 10.7, Notes 1–3 and 6–8.

2. All the minor variants of *In the Reign of Terror* in the series are grouped together under this 'generic' heading, *33.4.

34. STURDY AND STRONG

34.1

STURDY AND STRONG: | OR, | HOW GEORGE ANDREWS MADE HIS WAY. | BY | G.A.HENTY, | Author of "The Young Carthaginian;" "With Clive in India;" "In Freedom's Cause;" | "The Lion of the North;" "With Wolfe in Canada;" "Facing Death;" &c. | WITH FOUR FULL-PAGE ILLUSTRATIONS | BY ROBERT FOWLER. | (publisher's device) | LONDON: | BLACKIE & SON, 49 & 50 OLD BAILEY, E.C. | GLASGOW, EDINBURGH, AND DUBLIN. | 1888.

Contents

178 x 118 mm. (i)–(vi) | (7)–224 | catalogue (1)–32. Four full-page line-and-wash drawings by Robert Fowler reproduced by two-colour line blocks, with mechanical tints laid on the second-colour plates (sepia), printed on coated paper, unbacked, unfolioed, tipped in.

(Frontispiece, tipped in) | (i) title p. | (ii) blank | (iii)–iv. Preface | (v) Contents | (vi) list of Illustrations | (7)–224. text | (1)–32. catalogue.

Binding (see Plate 116)
Blue cloth boards, blocked black, orange, dark-green merging to indian red, blind, and gilt; edges plain; maroon surface-paper endpapers.
Front board: STURDY . & . STRONG | . BY . | G.A.HENTY. (orange, cased black) in upper left corner and above illustration of schoolboy (black, orange, dark-green merging to indian-red, and gilt), all framed with black rule, rounded corners at top. **Spine:** STURDY | AND | STRONG (cloth-colour reversed out of solid gilt rectangle) with decorative rules above and below (gilt). Illustration of lily (black, dark-green merging to indian-red) bisected by: . G . A . HENTY . (gilt). At foot: . BLACKIE . & . SON . (gilt). Black and gilt rules at head and foot. **Back board:** single rule near edges of board (blind).

References: BL; Bod; PN | *Farmer*, p.64; *Dartt*, p.130, *Companion*, p.28.

Notes
1. This long short-story was published on 27 July 1887 at 2s.6d. As will be seen below, it appeared in various bindings, but kept selling extremely well from publication day until Blackie's records cease at the end of August 1917, and seems to have gone on doing so for some time after that.
2. By the end of February 1888 Blackie had sold 2555 copies. In the following fifteen years they sold 16,461 more, the average annual sale over the first sixteen years being 1189 copies. In the next fourteen years up to 1917 Blackie sold another 12,042 copies, making a grand total, from 1887 to 1917, of 31,058 copies. Not many writers of books for boys can claim to have produced a book that sold for thirty consecutive years in the UK alone at not less than 1000 copies every year.
3. At its first appearance Blackie's catalogue briefly summed up the book: 'The aim of the story is to show how steadfastness, truth, and watchfulness may aid a lad to win his way through the greatest difficulties and be of assistance to others in the endeavour'. Henty would have relished the sales figures of such a work!

*34.2

Reprints of the first edition were produced in the style of 34.1, but with no date on the title page. They followed Blackie's usual pattern: alterations were made when necessary to title-page imprint and addresses (Blackie had become a Limited Company in 1890; the Indian office was to be opened in 1901, although Bombay did not appear regularly in the imprint until 1906).
Illustrations were modified, the second-colour tint being first transferred to the black plate (see Appendix IV, Part 1). Bindings continued to show variations in colours of cloth, blocking, and endpapers.
In later issues the opening words of the Preface, 'My dear Lads', were omitted. Some are found with the text on a bulkier cream-laid paper: laid papers were not often used by Blackie. The increased bulk resulted in the brasses being too narrow for the spine, and margins were left down both sides (see 34.3, Notes 1–2 below).
All the minor variants of the book in its first-edition format are grouped together uinder this 'generic' heading, *34.2.

34.3

Title page: As for 34.1, but revised imprint (LONDON | BLACKIE & SON, LIMITED, 50 OLD BAILEY, E.C. | GLASGOW AND DUBLIN).

Contents: 182 x 123 mm. As for 34.1, except (a) text on laid paper; (b) illustrations printed in black only, the tints being omitted.

Binding (see Plate 116)
Green cloth boards, blocked black, white, orange, and gilt; edges plain; plain off-white endpapers.
    Front board: STURDY AND | STRONG (orange, cased black) above illustration of two young men operating fire-fighting hose (black, white, orange, and gilt). **Spine:** STURDY | AND | STRONG (gilt) above illustration of boy running (black, white, orange, and gilt). At foot: G.A.HENTY (black). **Back board:** plain.

References: PN | *Dartt Companion*, p.28.

Notes
1. The binding seems planned for the wider spine caused, in the late 1890s, by impressions of *34.2 on cream laid paper. At first 34.3 was also on that paper.
2. But later impressions of 34.3 were on a featherweight wove that was bulkier still. Again margins appeared at the sides of the blocking, on an even wider spine.
3. The only constant internal difference between *34.2 and 34.3 is that in the latter the illustration tints were dropped. They had already been transferred to the black plates, the second colour having been abandoned, so it may seem surprising that at this stage Blackie should have gone to the expense of remaking the blocks at all. But the old ones had had a lot of wear over the years. Line blocks were made of zinc, which was not as strong as the copper used for halftones, and blocks were worn out not so much by long print-runs as by being repeatedly put to press for reprints, with all the 'make-ready' necessary each time: see Appendix IV, Part 1, Note 6.
4. Blackie changed very few binding designs of Henty's books before their issue of cheap editions early in the twentieth century. Apart from this one, Talwin Morris, head of their art department from 1892 (see Appendix IV, Part 2) commissioned replacements for *Under Drake's Flag*, 13.3, and *Tales of Daring and Danger*, 42.3.

34.4

The book was advertised by Blackie in the series of 'English Authors for School Reading', but I have been unable to find such a copy. The other books in the series are *A Chapter of Adventures*, 48.6, Plate 103; Tales from Henty, 57.3; and *In the Hands of the Malays*, 113.4. A copy of the last-named has also eluded me. This series does not appear in Blackie's surviving records, but the title-page imprints of 48.6 and 57.3 both indicate publication after 1910. The descriptions of those two titles should give a fair clue to the appearance of 34.4.

34.5

Sturdy and Strong | or | How George Andrews made His Way | BY | G.A.HENTY | Author of "Under Drake's Flag" "With Clive in India" | "In Freedom's Cause" "The Lion of the North" | "With Wolfe in Canada" "Facing Death" &c. | ILLUSTRATED BY GORDON BROWNE, R.I. | BLACKIE & SON LIMITED | LONDON AND GLASGOW

Contents

182 × 123 mm. (1)–224 | no catalogue. Four wash-drawings by Gordon Browne, printed from halftone blocks in black on coated paper, unbacked, keyed to text pages, tipped in.

(1) Half-title p. | (2) Blackie addresses | (frontispiece, tipped in) | (3) title p. | (4) printer's imprint (Printed in Great Britain by | Blackie & Son, Linited, Glasgow) | 5–6. Preface | (7) Contents | (8) list of Illustrations | 9–224. text.

Binding

Grey cloth boards, blocked dark-blue and green; edges plain; plain off-white endpapers.

Front board: STURDY AND | STRONG | G.A.HENTY (cloth-colour) out of dark part of illustration, framed by dark-blue line, of two boys in rowing boat, one standing and waving to large ship shewn in silhouette behind (dark-blue and green). **Spine:** STURDY | AND | STRONG | G.A.HENTY (dark-blue) above illustration of boy with fire-fighting hose (dark-blue and green). At foot: BLACKIE & SON LTD (dark-blue). **Back board:** plain.

Reference: PN.

Notes

1. The text of this cheap impression is on featherweight antique paper, and new wash-drawings by Gordon Browne replace Robert Fowler's line drawings.

2. Inscriptions show a date around 1925.

3. Another copy seen has variations. On p.(2): Blackie addresses replaced by publisher's advertisement (BOOKS OF THIS SERIES) listing 10 titles under heading 'BOYS'; 10 titles under heading 'GIRLS'; and 10 titles under heading 'BOYS AND GIRLS'. On p.(3): below publisher's imprint 'Printed and bound in Great Britain'. At foot of p.224: printer's imprint (PRINTED AND BOUND IN GREAT BRITAIN | By Blackie & Son, Limited, Glasgow).

34.6

Sturdy and Strong | BY | G.A.HENTY | Author of "Under Drake's Flag" "With Clive in India" | "In Freedom's Cause" "The Lion of the North" | "With Wolfe in Canada" "Facing Death" &c. | (publisher's device) | BLACKIE & SON LIMITED | LONDON AND GLASGOW

Contents

182 × 126 mm. (1)–224 | catalogue (1)–(2). Frontispiece from watercolour drawing by unknown hand, reproduced by three-colour halftone blocks printed on coated paper, unbacked, tipped in.

(1) Half-title p. | (2) Blackie addresses | (frontispiece, tipped in) | (3) title p. | (4) printer's imprint (Printed in Great Britain by | Blackie & Son, Limited, Glasgow) | 5–6. Preface | (7) Contents | (8) blank | 9–224. text | (1)–(2) catalogue.

Binding (see Note 3)

Possibly designed by Charles Rennie Mackintosh. Buff grained-paper boards (imitating cloth), blocked blue; edges plain; plain off-white endpapers.

Front board: STURDY | AND STRONG | G.A.HENTY (blue) in rectangular panel within over-all geometric pattern of (?) abstract swallows (blue). **Spine:**

STURDY | AND | STRONG (blue) in panel cutting across pattern as on front board (blue). In small rectangle at foot: BLACKIE | & SON . LTD (blue). **Back board:** plain.

Reference: PN.

Notes
1. The type was completely re-set for this new edition.
2. It forms part of a 1s.6d. series that appeared in the 1920s: 'Blackie's Library for Boys and Girls', which should not be confused with 'The Boys' and Girls' Bookshelf'. The two-page catalogue, tipped on to the last leaf of the final gathering, gives lists of books in both these series, as well as 'The Young Folk's Library' and 'The Happy Home library', all with Henty titles (see Appendix V).
3. It has been suggested that the binding for the series was designed by Charles Rennie Mackintosh: see *Tales from Henty*, 57.6, Note 5, and Plate 111.

35. FOR THE TEMPLE

35.1
FOR THE TEMPLE: | A TALE OF THE FALL OF JERUSALEM. | BY | G.A.HENTY, | Author of "The Young Carthaginian;" "With Wolfe in Canada;" "The Lion of the North;" | "A Final Reckoning;" "With Clive in India;" "Facing Death;" &c. | (6–em rule) | ILLUSTRATED BY SOLOMON J.SOLOMON | (6–em rule) (publisher's device) | LONDON: | BLACKIE & SON, 49 & 50 OLD BAILEY, E.C. | GLASGOW, EDINBURGH, AND DUBLIN. | 1888.

Contents
187 x 131 mm. (i)–(viii) | (9)–384 | catalogue (1)–32. Ten full-page wood-engravings by Edmund Evans and R.Taylor after wash-drawings by Solomon J.Solomon, unbacked, unfolioed, tipped in, each with loose tissue overlay. Plan of Jerusalem, printed in four colours as double-page spread, unbacked, guarded in between pages 274 and 275.

(Frontispiece, tipped in) | (i) title p. | (ii) blank | (iii)–iv. Preface | (v) Contents | (vi) blank | (vii) list of Illustrations | (viii) blank | (9)–384. text | (1)–32. catalogue.

Binding (see Plate 70)
Red cloth boards, bevelled, blocked black, blind, and gilt; all edges burnished olive-green; maroon surface-paper endpapers. (See Note 3, below).
   Front board: Three black rules near edges of board, enclosing, in upper left corner: landscape including the Temple (black and gilt); in lower right corner: illustration of two soldiers (black and gilt). At left, below landscape: FOR THE TEMPLE | (rule) A TALE OF THE (rule) | FALL OF JERUSALEM. | (small decoration) | G.A.HENTY (all gilt). **Spine:** Two gilt rules at head and two at foot. Between them, two panels enclosed by black rule, and with black rule dividing them; in upper panel: (ornament) FOR (ornament) | THE TEMPLE. | (short rule between two dots) | . G. A. HENTY . (all cloth-colour reversed out of gilt rectangle with thick gilt rule surround). In lower panel: illustration of the Temple at head and a seated rabbi in foreground (at foot) (all black and gilt). **Back board:** single rule near edges of board (blind).

References: BL; Bod; PN I *Farmer*, p.31; *Dartt*, p.61, *Companion*, p.15.

Notes
1. This book was first published on 19 August 1887. By the end of February the following year Blackie had sold 2694 copies at six shillings. In the next fifteen years they sold 5910 more, before it was re-issued in Blackie's cheaper 'New and Popular Edition' (see 35.3). During the first sixteen years the average annual sale had been 538 copies. The remaining stock of the six-shilling edition was 158 copies, sold by 1908, concurrently with the cheaper edition.
2. There are two interesting technical features, both relating in a sense to illustration. The first is the method of reproduction of the wash-drawings by Solomon J.Solomon. Up to this date Blackie had been moving very much with the times and exploiting the latest developments in photo-engraving, led on, probably, by the enthusiasm and skill of Gordon Browne (see Appendix IV, Part 2). His work for Henty had so far been entirely in line, but he made the most of the process and explored the latest techniques. The next stage forward was the halftone block, only 'perfected' in this country in the 1880s and first used to illustrate Henty in *In the Reign of Terror* (see 33.1, Note 2). Three weeks after its appearance, however, Blackie appeared to have changed direction by publishing this book with wood-engravings. These are, without doubt, of a very high standard, not unexpected from the engravers employed, one of whom was Edmund Evans (see 35.3, Note 3, below).
3. The second feature is a novel technique used for making the brasses for gold-blocking on the binding case. The brass pieces used for blocking are made of that metal because it is hard enough to stand up to repeated impressions made with some force on a fairly hard surface, and because it is soft enough to be engraved by hand without great difficulty. (In more recent times methods have been developed of starting the process of brass-cutting by photographing the image on to the surface and starting with a light etch, similar to the beginning of the making of a printer's line block on zinc, before the heavy hand-work begins). For this book additional work has been done by hand on the surface of the brass plate, after the usual 'cutting'. Fine incisions have been engraved, which produce a 'two-tone' effect when the gold is impressed on the cloth. This is a rare technique, and I have not seen it used elsewhere at this date.
4. As usual with Blackie novels, the earliest issues contain catalogues advertising the books for the current year (in this case those with 1888 title-page dates) without quotations from press reviews.

*35.2
Reprints of the first edition were issued in the same style as 35.1, but with the date removed from the title page. Alterations were made as necessary to title-page imprint and addresses: Blackie became a Limited Company in 1890; the Edinburgh address was not used after 1894; and the Indian office was opened in 1901, although Bombay did not appear regularly in the imprint until 1906.
Bindings continued to show variation in colours of cloth, blocking, and endpapers.
The slightly-differing issues among the reprints of the book in its first-edition format are all grouped together under this 'generic' heading, *35.2.

35.3

For the Temple | A Tale of the Fall of Jerusalem | BY | G.A.HENTY | Author of "The Young Carthaginian" "With Wolfe in Canada" "Facing Death" | "The Lion of the North" "A Final Reckoning" "With Clive in India" &c. | WITH SIX FULL-PAGE ILLUSTRATIONS BY SOLOMON J.SOLOMON | NEW EDITION | BLACKIE AND SON LIMITED | LONDON GLASGOW AND DUBLIN | 1904

Contents

186 x 126 mm. (1)–384 | catalogue 1–32. Six full-page wash-drawings by Solomon J.Solomon, reproduced by halftone blocks printed in black on coated paper, unbacked, unfolioed, tipped in. Plan of Jerusalem printed in black-and-white as double-page spread, on coated paper, guarded in between pages 274 and 275.

(Frontispiece, tipped in) | (1) title p. | (2) blank | (3) Preface | iv.[roman numerals used in error] Preface, continued | (5) Contents | (6) blank | 7. list of Illustrations | (8) blank | 9–384. text | 1–32. catalogue.

Binding (see Plate 173)

Red cloth boards, blocked black, brown, and gilt; edges plain; grey endpapers, lined off-white.

Front board: FOR THE | TEMPLE . | BY | G.A.HENTY. (all gilt) above illustration of figure holding spear and blowing horn (black, brown, and gilt). **Spine:** FOR THE | TEMPLE | BY | G.A.HENTY (all gilt) above illustration of standing figure with hands on sheathed dagger (black, brown, and gilt). **Back board:** plain.

Reference: PN.

Notes

1. In 1903 (title-page date 1904) Blackie re-issued the book in the 'New and Popular Edition'. Details of the series are given under *Facing Death*, 10.6, Notes 2–3.
2. In this edition Blackie sold 2804 copies by the end of August 1904. After exactly thirteen years they had sold 6770 more, and at that point Blackie's records cease. The average annual sale for those fourteen years was 684 copies. The grand total of copies sold at both prices from 1887 to 1917 was 18,336.
3. The illustrations are of especial interest in view of what has gone before (see 35.1, Note 2). By 1903 Blackie were skilled printers of halftone blocks, and decided to illustrate the 3s.6d. edition by that process. They had many of the first-edition line drawings copies in wash, mostly anonymously. In this case Solomon's original drawings had actually been made in wash, but reproduced as wood engravings.
4. Now the electros made from the wood blocks could be abandoned. the old wash-drawings could be reproduced photographically as halftone blocks. Solomon's originals had been well preserved, and even mounted, perhaps for exhibition, as may be seen from marks near the edges of some of the plates in 35.3. This circumstance gives a rare and interesting opportunity to compare the work of the wood-engravers with photographic reproductions of the drawings from which they had worked.
5. The plan of Jerusalem is printed from the black plate only of the colour-set made for 35.1.

*35.4

FOR THE TEMPLE | A Tale of the Fall of Jerusalem | BY | G.A.HENTY | Author of "The Young Carthaginian" "With Wolfe in Canada" | "Facing Death" "The Lion of the North" &c. | Illustrated | BLACKIE AND SON LIMITED | LONDON GLASGOW AND BOMBAY

Contents

184 x 123 mm. (i)–(viii) | 9–384 | no catalogue. Frontispiece from watercolour drawing by Frank Gillett reproduced by three-colour halftone blocks; four wash-drawings by Solomon J.Solomon reproduced by halftone blocks printed in black; all on coated paper, unbacked, keyed to text pages, tipped in.

(Frontispiece, tipped in) | (1) title p. | (2) advertisement (G.A.HENTY'S BOOKS) listing 56 titles; at foot, printer's imprint (Printed in Great Britain by | Blackie & Son, Limited, Glasgow) | iii-iv. Preface | (v) Contents | (vi) blank | (vii) list of Illustrations | (viii) blank | 9–384. text.

Binding

Grey-blue cloth boards, blocked black, red, and brown; edges plain; plain off-white endpapers.

Front board: FOR THE | TEMPLE . | BY | G.A.HENTY. (all black) above and at right of illustration of figure holding spear and blowing horn (black, red, brown). **Spine:** FOR THE | TEMPLE | BY | G.A.HENTY (black) above illustration of standing figure with hands on sheathed dagger (black, red, brown). **Back board:** plain.

Reference: IM.

Notes

1. For notes on Blackie's second cheaper series, 'The New Popular Henty', and subsequent editions of this book, see *Facing Death*, 10.7, Notes 1–3 and 6–8. Examples of the series binding style are at Plates 174–175.

2. All the minor variants of *For the Temple* in the series are grouped together under the 'generic' heading, *35.4.

36. THE LION OF ST. MARK

36.1

THE LION OF ST. MARK: | A TALE OF VENICE. | BY | G.A.HENTY, | Author of "Bonnie Prince Charlie;" "For the Temple;" "By Sheer Pluck;" | "With Clive in India;" &c. | WITH TEN FULL-PAGE ILLUSTRATIONS | BY GORDON BROWNE. | (publisher's device) | LONDON: | BLACKIE & SON, 49 & 50 OLD BAILEY, E.C. | GLASGOW, EDINBURGH, AND DUBLIN. | 1889.

Contents

187 x 130 mm. (i)–(x) | (11)–384 | catalogue (1)–32. Ten full-page line-and-wash drawings by Gordon Browne, reproduced by two-colour line blocks (see Note 6) printed in black and grey on coated paper, unbacked, unfolioed, tipped in.

(i) Half-title p. | (ii) advertisement (CONCERNING MR. HENTY | THE PRESS

SAYS:) giving 7 quotations from press notices | (frontispiece, tipped in) | (iii) cancel title p. (see Note 3) | (iv) blank | (v) Preface | (vi) blank | (vii) Contents | (viii) blank | (ix) list of Illustrations | (x) blank | (11)–384. text | (1)–32. catalogue.

Binding (see Plate 75)
Grey-blue cloth boards, bevelled, blocked black, blind, and gilt; all edges burnished olive-green; maroon surface-paper endpapers.
    Front board: (ornament) The Lion of ST. MARK, (ornament) | G.A.HENTY, (all gilt) above illustration of Venetian sculpture of the Lion of St Mark at top of column (black and gilt), all enclosed in a frame of three black rules. **Spine:** The Lion | (ornament) of (ornament) | ST. MARK. (gilt) within three-sided ruled frame (gilt); above illustration of the Doge of Venice (black and gilt). Beneath this: – BY – | . G . A . HENTY . (gilt) above small gilt ornament. All within frame of rules: three black and one gilt at head and foot, and single black at sides. **Back board:** single rule near edges of board (blind).

References: PN | *Farmer*, p.47; *Dartt*, p.91, *Companion*, p.20.

Notes
1. The book was published on 29 February 1888 at six shillings: by the end of February 1889 Blackie had sold 3831 copies. That is a high figure at this date for the first year's sales of a Henty novel, but it was published extremely early in the year and had in fact been on sale for exactly twelve months at the time this total was calculated. Over the next thirteen years 6994 more copies were sold, and then the book was re-issued in the cheaper series, Blackie's 'New and Popular Edition' of Henty's novels (see 36.4, below). The average annual figure for the fourteen years the book was on sale at six shillings is 773 copies. The remaining stock of 269 copies was sold over six years, concurrently with the cheaper edition.
2. For a book published as early as February it may seem odd that Blackie should stick to their policy of dating the title page for the following year. It is an unusual publication date: Blackie published only one other of Henty's novels earlier in the year than May (*At the Point of the Bayonet* was published on 6 April 1901). The Easter market seems not to have been a very good one: Blackie most commonly published in June and August; July or May came next in choice, but some way behind.
3. All copies of this first impression (36.1) have cancel title pages. A number of reasons are possible, including errors by printer or publisher, but I believe the most likely explanation is a decision by Blackie to change the publication date. No copy with an original title page has come to light, but probably it was first printed with the date 1888. Four other full-length titles by Henty were published that year, and it may have been thought a good plan to postpone this one.
4. A result of the early date was that a reprint was needed before the end of 1888. Blackie's policy for title pages (see *Facing Death*, 10.4, Notes 2–3) was that a reprint ordered before the end of the calendar year in which the book was published would carry the same date as the first printing – in this case, 1889. The dated reprint for this book was printed rather hurriedly (see 36.2, Note 2).
5. Meanwhile a difficulty arises from variations between copies of 36.1. It is clear that two different batches of paper were used for printing the text: I have two copies which are identical in all respects except for their bulk. One of them is 2mm. thicker

than the other, and although that may not seem a matter of great import it does nevertheless show that the paper used for the two copies was not all from the same making. Both copies are considerably bulkier than other novels from Blackie with the same number of pages: the latter, and, indeed, subsequent printings of *The Lion of St. Mark*, bulk 5mm. less than the thicker of the two copies mentioned. That indicates that for the first printing Blackie set out stock from their paper warehouse that was thicker than normal for Henty's books, and then, before printing began, decided to increase the print order (say, from 2000 to 3000 copies). When the paper warehouse was called on for further supplies, the quantity needed was made up with some of their normal paper. The formes of type were consequently allocated to machine-minders, with stacks of paper in two different weights (or thicknesses). When printed sheets were later sent to the bindery it would be a matter of chance whether thick or thin sheets for each gathering were brought together for sewing; thus the books would inevitably vary in bulk. If this is a proper reading of the facts, then variations in bulk will be found throughout all the books from the first printing, and no precedence can be established between thicker and thinner copies.

6. Gordon Browne has used a new technique (for him) in the preparation of his two-colour line blocks. The second-colour tint blocks are, like many others of his, hand-drawn and printed from 'solid' line plates, i.e. without mechanical tints, the 'broken-up' effect being achieved partly with the brush in making the drawing, and partly with a graver on the block itself. For one of these pictures, however, he appears to have used some kind of mechanical tint, or perhaps a graver's wheel, on the *black* plate, something not apparent in earlier illustrations for Henty. It can be seen in the darkest parts of the drawing, at the foot of the frontispiece.

7. As usual with Blackie novels, the earliest issues contain catalogues advertising the books for the current year (in this case those with title pages dated 1889) without quotations from press reviews. There was certainly more than one such issue of the Blackie catalogue printed in time for inclusion in copies of this title. The other Henty titles of that year (with 1889 title pages) were not published until August and September, and Blackie probably waited for them all to be reviewed before adding quotations to the catalogue. Copies of the second printing of *The Lion of St. Mark*, with integral, dated, title pages, also have catalogues without press notices. But they are later editions of the catalogue than those in copies of 36.1 (see 36.2, Note 3).

8. *Dartt* is confused between editions from UK and USA, in this case over the subtitle. In the Blackie editions it was changed in later reprints, see 36.3, below.

36.2

Title page: As for 36.1, but now integral (see Note 1 below).

Contents: 184 x 130 mm. As for 36.1, except (a) p.(ii) blank; (b) p.(iii) now integral.

Binding: As for 36.1.

References: BL; Bod; PN.

Notes

1. This is the first reprint of the book, with the date kept on the title page (see 36.1, Note 4, above). Properly, it is the first edition, second impression. The date, or whatever had been amiss with the original title page, had been corrected by a cancel in 36.1, and now the page is integral, without further alteration. This reprint was deposited with the Copyright Libraries, which do not have 36.1.

2. All copies examined show that the impression was made, and bound, hurriedly. The plates have overlays, or guards, loosely inserted in the bindery to prevent the still-not-dry ink from off-setting on to text pages. In some copies set-off is clearly visible on the overlays.

3. The whole book is now printed on Blackie's standard paper, used normally for Henty's novels and similar works by other authors (see 36.1, Note 5).

4. Apart from the difference between the paper used for 36.1 and that used for 36.2, the bound-in catalogues show variations. If confirmation is required of the chronological order of the two issues, the catalogues give it. Those in 36.2 list, at p.12, a book by Harry Collingwood entitled *The Missing Merchantman*, a title that was actually published by Blackie, whereas the catalogues in 36.1 list the same book under the title *Missing: A Tale of the Merchant Marine*, which seems to have been a provisional title given to the book before publication. Similar examples of the use of provisional titles in Blackie's catalogues can be found elsewhere. (*The Missing Merchantman* appears in the catalogue bound in 36.3, below, under that title and with press reviews). Catalogues in later copies of 36.2 advertise books dated 1889 with quotations from press reviews, whereas no similar catalogues have been found in copies of 36.1. Furthermore these catalogues announce *The Lion of St. Mark* with the subtitle 'A Tale of Venice in the Fourteenth Century'; that was clearly a provisional version of a new subtitle that was about to appear in 36.3.

5. There is one small variation that is found between copies of 36.2. Some have the illustrations printed with the second colour in much the same shade of grey as that used for 36.1. Others have it in a warmer sepia, easily distinguishable. The most likely explanation is that the grey ink in the duct of the machine ran low and was replenished by a machine minder, perhaps carelessly, from a tin of sepia ink. It was almost certainly an error, over which no one at the time was likely to be unduly concerned. Later reprints reverted to the original grey ink.

*36.3

THE LION OF ST. MARK: | A STORY OF VENICE | IN THE FOURTEENTH CENTURY. | BY | G.A.HENTY, | Author of "Bonnie Prince Charlie;" "For the Temple;" "By Sheer Pluck;" | "With Clive in India;" &c. | WITH TEN FULL-PAGE ILLUSTRATIONS | BY GORDON BROWNE. | (publisher's device) | LONDON: | BLACKIE & SON, LIMITED, 49 OLD BAILEY, E.C. | GLASGOW, EDINBURGH, AND DUBLIN.

Contents: 185 x 131 mm. As for 36.2, except p.(ii) advertisement (MR. HENTY'S HISTORICAL TALES.) listing 22 titles.

Binding: As for 36.1, except (a) red cloth boards; (b) dark-blue surface-paper endpapers.

Reference: PN.

Notes

1. The book has been given a new subtitle, not quite the same as that provisionally announced in Blackie's earlier catalogues (see 36.2, Note 4).

2. Reprints of the six-shilling edition continued to be issued in the same style as before, but with the date removed from the title page. Alterations were made to title-page imprint and addresses when necessary: Blackie became a Limited Company in 1890; from May 1894 the Edinburgh address ceased to be used, and the Indian office was opened in 1901 although Bombay did not appear regularly in the imprint before 1906.

3. Bindings continued to show variation in colours of cloth, blocking, and endpapers.

4. The slightly differing issues of this title in its first-edition format are all grouped together under this 'generic' heading, *36.3.

36.4

The Lion of St. Mark | A Story of Venice | in the Fourteenth Century | BY | G.A.HENTY | Author of "Bonnie Prince Charlie" "For the Temple" "By Sheer Pluck" | "With Clive in India" &c. | WITH SIX FULL-PAGE ILLUSTRATIONS | NEW EDITION | BLACKIE AND SON LIMITED | LONDON GLASGOW AND DUBLIN | 1903

Contents

191 x 125 mm. (1)–384 | catalogue 1–32. Eight full-page line-and-wash drawings, unsigned, based on some of the original illustrations by Gordon Browne, reproduced by halftone blocks printed in black on coated paper, unbacked, unfolioed, tipped in.

(1) Half-title p. | (2) advertisement (HISTORICAL TALES BY G.A.HENTY) listing 28 titles | (frontispiece, tipped in) | (3) title p. | (4) blank | 5. Preface | (6) blank | 7. Contents | (8) blank | 9. list of Illustrations | (10) blank | 11–384. text | 1–32. catalogue.

Binding

Red cloth boards, blocked black, light-brown, red, and gilt; edges plain; grey endpapers, lined off-white.

Front board: THE LION | OF ST. MARK | G.A.HENTY (gilt) above illustration of soldier with drawn sword and dagger (black, light-brown, red). **Spine:** THE | LION | OF | ST. MARK | G.A.HENTY (gilt) above illustration of soldier replacing sword in scabbard (black, light-brown, red). **Back board:** plain.

Reference: PN.

Notes

1. In 1902 (title-page date 1903) Blackie re-issued *The Lion of St. Mark* in their cheaper 'New and Popular Edition'. Details of the series are given under *Facing Death*, 10.6, Notes 2–3; examples of binding style are at Plates 172–173.

2. This book, and *Through the Fray*, were the first two books to be re-issued in this way, in 1902. By the end of August 1903 Blackie had sold 3301 copies of *The Lion of St. Mark* at the cheaper price, and over the following fourteen years they sold 11,686 more, the average annual sale for those fifteen years being 999 copies. The grand total of copies sold at both prices between 1888 and 1917 is 26,081.

*36.5

The Lion of | St. Mark | A Story of Venice in the Fourteenth Century | BY | G.A.HENTY | Author of "In Freedom's Cause" "For the Temple" "By Sheer Pluck"

| "With Clive in India" &c. | ILLUSTRATED | BLACKIE AND SON LIMITED | LONDON GLASGOW AND BOMBAY

Contents

186 x 122 mm. (1)–384 | no catalogue. Frontispiece from watercolour drawing by Gordon Browne, reproduced by three-colour halftone blocks; four full-page wash-drawings based on some of the original illustrations by Gordon Browne, reproduced by halftone blocks printed in black on coated paper, unbacked, keyed to text pages, tipped in.

(1) Half-title p. | (2) publisher's advertisement (G.A.HENTY'S BOOKS) listing 40 titles | (frontispiece, tipped in) | (3) title p. | (4) imprint (Printed and bound in Great Britain) | (5) Preface | (6) blank | (7) Contents | (8) blank | (9) list of Illustrations | (10) blank | 11–384. text, with printer's imprint at foot of p.384 (PRINTED AND BOUND IN GREAT BRITAIN | By Blackie & Son, Limited, Glasgow).

Binding: As for 36.4, except (a) dark-green cloth boards, blocked black, red, and buff, and no gilt: all lettering buff; (b) plain off-white endpapers.

Reference: PN.

Notes

1. For notes on Blackie's second cheaper series, 'The New Popular Henty', and subsequent editions of this book, see *Facing Death*, 10.7, Notes 1–3 and 6–8.
2. All the minor variants of *The Lion of St. Mark* in the series are grouped together under this 'generic' heading, *36.5.

37. CAPTAIN BAYLEY'S HEIR

37.1

CAPTAIN BAYLEY'S HEIR: | A TALE | OF THE GOLD FIELDS OF CALIFORNIA. | BY | G.A.HENTY, | Author of "With Clive in India;" "Facing Death;" "For Name and Fame;" | "True to the Old Flag;" "A Final Reckoning;" &c. | WITH TWELVE FULL-PAGE ILLUSTRATIONS | BY H.M.PAGET. | (publisher's device) | LONDON: | BLACKIE & SON, 49 & 50 OLD BAILEY, E.C. | GLASGOW, EDINBURGH, AND DUBLIN. | 1889.

Contents

185 x 130 mm. (i)–(viii) | (9)–386 | catalogue (1)–32. Twelve full-page line-and-wash drawings by H.M.Paget, reproduced by deep-etched halftone blocks printed in black on coated paper, unbacked, unfolioed, tipped in (see Note 5).

(i) Half-title p. | (ii) blank | (frontispiece, tipped in) | (iii) title p. | (iv) blank | (v) Contents | (vi) blank | (vii) list of Illustrations | (viii) blank | (9)–386. text | (1)–32. catalogue.

Binding (see Plate 61)

Blue cloth boards, bevelled, blocked black, blind, and gilt; all edges burnished olive-green; maroon surface-paper endpapers.

Front board: CAPTAIN BAYLEY'S HEIR (gilt, cloth-colour 'shadow') | A

TALE OF THE | GOLD FIELDS OF CALIFORNIA. (cloth-colour) all out of gilt sky of illustration of two gold-diggers with donkey (black and gilt), above: BY | G.A.HENTY. (black). All within frame of single black rule. **Spine:** CAPTAIN | BAYLEY'S | HEIR. (cloth-colour) out of gilt sky of illustration of prospector on horse (black and gilt). Beneath this: – BY – | . G . A . HENTY . (gilt). All within frame of single black rule. **Back board:** single rule near edges of board (blind).

References: Bod; PN | *Farmer*, p.18; *Dartt*, p.33, *Companion*, p.7.

Notes
1. Publication day was 15 August 1888. By the end of the following February Blackie had sold 3214 copies, and in the next fifteen years they sold 5443 more. That gives an average annual sale over the sixteen years of 541 copies: not a high figure by Henty's standards. At the end of that time, in 1904 (title-page date 1905), the book was re-issued in the 'New and Popular Edition' (see 37.3 below). The remaining stock of 158 copies at six shillings was sold over the next seven years.
2. This book suffered from some error in planning. It has 386 pages, not the usual 384 in Blackie's six-shilling series. There must have been an incorrect cast-off, or perhaps some heavy proof-correcting (see Appendix III, Part 1). That resulted in the additional cost of printing one text leaf on a small machine, and pasting it on to the end of the last gathering. Such a situation is something publishers go to great lengths to avoid, and is quite unexpected in a Blackie book at this period.
3. This is one of only a few novels by Henty to have no Preface. Had one been included, causing the text to start on p.11, the book would have made two more pages over the even working, i.e. 388 pages instead of 384. The omission of a Preface was probably not connected with the over-run, but it is surprising that Blackie was still prepared to countenance the single extra leaf, which could have been avoided by two minor cuts of only five lines each to save pages in Chapters XII and XIII.
4. *Dartt* incorrectly reports no catalogue. As usual with Blackie novels, the earliest issues contain catalogues advertising the books for the current year (in this case those with title pages dated 1889) without quotations from press reviews. The early catalogues contain another error by Blackie: at p.3 they announce this book as 'Captain Bailey's Heir'. The mis-spelling was corrected in later catalogues.
5. The illustrations are from early examples of deep-etched halftone blocks, made for H.M.Paget by Angerer & Göschl, a well-known firm of process engravers in Vienna (see Appendix IV, Part 2, under the artist's name).

*37.2
Reprints of the first edition were issued in the same style as 37.1, but with the date removed from the title page. Alterations were made to the title-page imprint and addresses when necessary: Blackie became a Limited Company in 1890; the Edinburgh address was not used after May 1894; and the Indian office was opened in 1901, although Bombay did not appear regularly in the imprint until 1906.
Bindings continued to show variation in colours of cloth, blocking, and endpapers. The slightly-differing reprints of this title in its first-edition format are all grouped together under this 'generic' heading, *37.2.

37.3

Captain Bayley's Heir | A Tale of the Gold Fields of California | BY | G.A.HENTY | Author of "With Clive in India" "For Name and Fame" "True to the Old Flag" | "Facing Death" "A Final Reckoning" &c. | WITH TWELVE FULL-PAGE ILLUSTRATIONS BY H.M.PAGET | NEW EDITION | BLACKIE AND SON LIMITED | LONDON GLASGOW AND DUBLIN | 1905

Contents

188 x 124 mm. (1)–386 | catalogue 1–16. Illustrations as in 37.1.

(1) Half-title p. | (2) advertisement (MR. HENTY'S HISTORICAL TALES.) listing 53 titles | (frontispiece, tipped in) | (3) title p. | (4) blank | 5. Contents | (6) blank | 7. list of Illustrations | (8) blank | 9–386. text | 1–16. catalogue with two leaves of coated paper tipped in, printed with black-and-white halftone plates, including full-page portrait of Henty, captioned 'THE LATE G.A.HENTY'.

Binding (see Note 1)

Red cloth boards, blocked black, dark-grey, light-grey, and gilt; all edges stained olive-green; grey endpapers, lined off-white.

Front board: CAPTAIN BAYLEY'S | HEIR | G.A.HENTY. (all gilt) above illustration of horse-rider with pistol (black, dark-grey, light-grey). **Spine:** CAPTAIN | BAYLEY'S | HEIR | G.A.HENTY. (all gilt) above illustration of figure with rifle (black, dark-grey, light-grey). At foot: BLACKIE & SON. LIMITED. (gilt). **Back board:** plain.

References: BL; Bod.

Notes

1. In 1904 (title-page date 1905) Blackie re-issued *Captain Bayley's Heir* in their cheaper 'New and Popular Edition'. Details of the series are given under *Facing Death*, 10.6, Notes 2–3, and examples of binding style at Plates 172–173.

2. In this edition Blackie sold 2395 copies by the end of August 1905, and 6220 more by the same date in 1917, twelve years later, when their records cease. The average annual sale over those thirteen years was 663 copies. The grand total of copies sold at the two prices from 1888 to 1917 is 17,430.

3. The book is unusual in having twelve illustrations in this edition. Most titles had fewer than in the earlier full-price editions, and the reason for the exception is probably an economic one. The majority of the books had been first illustrated in line, which looked rather old-fashioned by the time of the 'New and Popular Edition'. Blackie therefore commissioned other artists, usually anonymous, to re-draw the original pictures in wash, to be reproduced by halftone blocks. *Captain Bayley's Heir* was only the second of Henty's novels to have been already illustrated with halftone blocks in its first edition, and so there would have been no additional costs for artist's work in re-drawing, nor any extra blockmaking costs. Those savings perhaps made it possible to include all twelve of the existing plates.

4. Unbelievably, the text still makes 386 pages, with a single leaf tipped on the end of the final gathering (see 37.1, Notes 2–3). It would have been a simple matter to save a leaf in the prelims by printing the list of Illustrations on the verso of the Contents, i.e. on p.(6), and the text could then have started on p.7.

*37.4

Captain Bayley's Heir | A Tale of | the Gold Fields of California | BY | G.A.HENTY | Author of "With Clive in India" "For Name and Fame" "A Final Reckoning" | "True to the Old Flag" "Facing Death" &c. | ILLUSTRATED | BLACKIE AND SON LIMITED | LONDON GLASGOW AND BOMBAY | Printed in Great Britain

Contents

185 x 123 mm. (1)–388 | no catalogue. Frontispiece from watercolour drawing by Frank Gillett reproduced by three-colour halftone blocks; four full-page line-and-wash drawings by H.M.Paget reproduced by halftone blocks printed in black; all on coated paper, unbacked, unfolioed, tipped in.

(1) Half-title p. | (2) advertisement (G.A.HENTY'S BOOKS) listing 18 titles | (frontispiece, tipped in) | (3) title p. | (4) blank | (5) Contents | (6) blank | (7) list of Illustrations | (8) blank | 9–386. text, with printer's imprint on p.386 (PRINTED AND BOUND IN GREAT BRITAIN | By Blackie & Son, Limited, Glasgow) | (387)–(388) blank.

Binding: As for 37.3, except (a) red cloth boards, blocked black, grey, and buff, with no gilt; all front-board lettering buff, all spine lettering black; (b) edges plain; (c) plain off-white endpapers.

Reference: PN.

Notes

1. For notes on Blackie's second cheaper series, 'The New Popular Henty', and subsequent editions of this book, see *Facing Death*, 10.7, Notes 1–3 and 6–8. Examples of the binding style are at Plates 174–175.

2. All the minor variants of *Captain Bayley's Heir* in the series are grouped together under this 'generic' heading, *37.4.

3. The miscalculation, or other error, that caused all earlier editions to be made up with a single leaf over the even working of 384 pages, was still causing trouble (see 37.1, Notes 2–3; and 37.3, Note 4). For this edition the binding was made theoretically stronger by replacing the single tipped-in leaf with a 4–page section wrapped round the final signature. That, of course resulted in a book of 388 pages, of which the last two are blank. The fibres of antique wove are not strong, and without this modification the binding itself would have been distinctly weak. It is astonishing that after all this time it had not occurred to Blackie that by saving a leaf in the prelims they could have made the book an even working.

38. THE CAT OF BUBASTES

38.1

THE CAT OF BUBASTES: | A TALE OF ANCIENT EGYPT. | BY | G.A. HENTY, | Author of "By Sheer Pluck;" "The Young Carthaginian;" "For the Temple;" | "In the Reign of Terror;" "A Final Reckoning;" &c. | WITH EIGHT FULL-PAGE ILLUSTRATIONS | BY J.R. WEGUELIN. | (publisher's device) | LONDON: | BLACKIE & SON, 49 & 50 OLD BAILEY, E.C. | GLASGOW, EDINBURGH, AND DUBLIN. | 1889.

Contents
186 x 122 mm. (i)–(viii) | (9)–352 | catalogue (1)–32. Eight full-page wash-drawings by J.R. Weguelin, reproduced by halftone blocks printed in sepia on coated paper, unbacked, unfolioed, tipped in.

(Frontispiece, tipped in) | (i) title p. | (ii) blank | (iii)–iv. Preface | (v) Contents | (vi) blank | (vii) list of Illustrations | (viii) blank | (9)–352. text | (1)–32. catalogue.

Binding (see Plate 61)
Brown cloth boards, blocked black, red, blind, and gilt; all edges burnished olive-green; maroon surface-paper endpapers.

Front board: A series of rectangular panels formed by rules in black, red, and gilt, surrounding illustration of Egyptian figure (black) and cat (gilt). In panel of multiple rules at head: THE CAT OF BUBASTES (gilt, open lettering); in similar panel at foot: . A . TALE . OF . ANCIENT . EGYPT . | . BY . G . A . HENTY . (gilt). **Spine:** Similar but simpler arrangement of rules forming panels (black, red, and gilt); at head: THE CAT | . OF . | BUBASTES (gilt, open lettering), above illustration of seated Egyptian figure (black); at foot: . G . A . HENTY . (gilt). **Back board:** three rules (thin, thick, thin) near edges of board (blind).

References: BL; Bod; PN | *Farmer*, p.19; *Dartt*, p.35, *Companion*, p.8.

Notes
1. The book was published on 3 September 1888 at five shillings. By the end of the following February Blackie had sold 3529 copies, and in the next thirteen years they sold 5891 more. The average annual sale for the first fourteen years was 673 copies. Another 1077 copies were sold over five years, and in 1907 (title-page date 1908) the book was re-issued in Blackie's 'New and Popular Edition' of Henty's novels (see 38.3 below). The remaining stock of 83 copies at six shillings was sold over six years, concurrently with the cheaper edition.
2. As already noted in connection with *The Young Carthaginian* (see 30.1, Note 2) Henty told Raymond Blathwayt in October 1902 that 'The ancient history doesn't sell well. Quite ancient, I mean', and continued: 'I wrote a story dealing with ancient Egypt that I expected would have done very well. It fell extremely flat.' The total sales of the five-shilling edition were 10,582 copies, and the first cheap edition sold nearly 5000 copies by 1917. There was a second cheap edition in the 1920s (*38.4), so altogether it did not do as badly as some of Henty's other books, including some of those dealing with later periods. Perhaps for this particular one Henty had especially high hopes that were at the time disappointed, although in more recent times it has been one of the titles most closely associated with his name.
3. This is the third of Henty's novels that Blackie illustrated with halftone blocks in a first edition. These blocks are printed in sepia instead of black. Some early letterpress printers thought sepia was kinder to what they saw as a rather harsh and 'contrasty' reproduction process, and believed it would help to give the appearance of tone where in fact there was really none (see Appendix IV, Part 1). Sixty years later, when the quality of blockmaking had risen to much greater heights, a leaning towards sepia ink still survived among some members of the printing trade. Blackie used it only once again in the first edition of a full-length Henty novel, and that was the last one, *By Conduct and Courage*, 109.1. They also used it occasionally in some of the 'New and Popular Editions'.

4. As usual with Blackie novels, the earliest issues contain catalogues advertising the books for the current year (in this case those with 1889 title-page dates) without quotations from press reviews.

*38.2

Reprints of the five-shilling edition were issued in the same style as 38.1, but with the date removed from the title page. Alterations were made when necessary to title-page imprint and addresses: Blackie became a Limited Company in 1890; the Edinburgh address was not used after 1894; and the Indian office was opened in 1901, although Bombay did not appear regularly in the imprint until 1906.

Bindings continued to show variation in colours of cloth, blocking, and endpapers. The slightly-varying issues of this title in its first-edition format are all grouped together under this 'generic' heading, *38.2.

38.3

The Cat of Bubastes I A Tale of Ancient Egypt I BY I G.A. HENTY I Author of "By Sheer Pluck" "The Young Carthaginian" "For the Temple" I "In the Reign of Terror" "A Final Reckoning" &c. I ILLUSTRATED BY J.R. WEGUELIN I NEW EDITION I BLACKIE AND SON LIMITED I LONDON GLASGOW DUBLIN BOMBAY I 1908

Contents

185 x 128 mm. (1)–352 I catalogue 1–16. Eight full-page wash-drawings by J.R. Weguelin, reproduced by halftone blocks printed in sepia on coated paper, unbacked, unfolioed, tipped in.

(Frontispiece, tipped in) I (1) title p. I (2) blank I 3. Preface I iv. [roman numerals in error] Preface, continued I 5. Contents I (6) blank I 7. list of Illustrations I (8) blank I 9–352. text I 1–16. catalogue.

Binding (see Note 1)

Dark-green cloth boards, blocked black, red, buff, and gilt; all edges stained olive-green; grey endpapers, lined off-white.

Front board: THE CAT OF I BUBASTES I A TALE OF I ANCIENT EGYPT (gilt) above illustration of soldier firing arrow from bow (black, red, buff); BY I G.A. HENTY (buff). Signature at foot: J Hassall (black). **Spine:** THE CAT I OF I BUBASTES I G.A. HENTY (gilt) above illustration of cat (black and buff). At foot: BLACKIE & SON LTD (black). **Back board:** plain.

References: BL; Bod.

Notes

1. In 1907 (title-page date 1908) Blackie re-issued *The Cat of Bubastes* in the 'New and Popular Edition'. For details of the series see *Facing Death*, 10.6, Notes 2–3, and examples of the binding style, Plates 172–173.

2. In this edition Blackie sold 1809 copies by the end of August 1908, and 2929 more in the following nine years, up to the time Blackie's records cease. The average annual sale over the ten years was 474 copies. The total number of copies sold, at both prices, from 1888 to 1917, was 15,318.

3. The first edition had been one of the early novels to be illustrated with halftone blocks. Consequently Blackie felt able to use all the illustrations in the cheaper edition, something they had not done when re-issuing Henty's early novels. For an explanation of this see *Captain Bayley's Heir*, 37.3, Note 3.

*38.4

The Cat of Bubastes | A Tale of Ancient Egypt | BY | G.A. HENTY | Author of "By Sheer Pluck" "In the Reign of Terror" | "A Final Reckoning" &c. | ILLUSTRATED | BLACKIE AND SON LIMITED | LONDON GLASGOW AND BOMBAY

Contents

186 x 126 mm. (1)–352 | no catalogue. Frontispiece from watercolour drawing by Frank Gillett reproduced by three-colour halftone blocks; four wash-drawings by J.R. Weguelin reproduced by halftone blocks printed in black; all on coated paper, unbacked, tipped in.

(1) Half-title p. | (2) publisher's advertisement (G.A. HENTY'S BOOKS) listing 45 titles | (frontispiece, tipped in) | (3) title p. | (4) blank | (5)–(6) Preface to the Original Edition | (7) Contents | (8) list of Illustrations | 9–352. text, with printer's imprint at foot of p.352 (PRINTED AND BOUND IN GREAT BRITAIN | By Blackie & Son, Limited, Glasgow).

Binding: As for 38.3, except (a) blue cloth boards, blocked black, orange, and buff, with no gilt: lettering of title and sub-title on front board, orange, and of author, buff. All spine lettering, black; (b) edges plain; (c) plain off-white endpapers.

References: Bod; TC.

Notes

1. Issued, 1922, in Blackie's second cheaper series, 'The New Popular Henty'. For that, and subsequent editions, see *Facing Death*, 10.7, Notes 1–3 and 6–8. Examples of the series binding style are at Plates 174–175.
2. All the minor variants of *The Cat of the Bubastes* in the series are grouped together under this 'generic' heading, *38.4.

39. GABRIEL ALLEN, M.P.

39.1

GABRIEL ALLEN, M.P. | BY | G.A. HENTY, | AUTHOR OF "ALL BUT LOST," "A SEARCH FOR A SECRET," "THE MARCH TO MAGDALA," ETC., ETC. | LONDON | SPENCER BLACKETT | (Successor to J.& R. Maxwell) | MILTON HOUSE, 35, ST BRIDE STREET, LUDGATE CIRCUS, E.C. | (short rule) | [All rights reserved]
(Note: Successor to J.& R.Maxwell *is in gothic type).*

Contents

178 x 117 mm. (1)–190 | catalogue 191–192. No illustrations.

(1) Half-title p. | (2) advertisement (BLACKETT'S | SELECT SHILLING NOVELS.) listing 4 titles of which this book is the last | (3) title p. | (4) blank | (5)–190. text, with printer's imprint on p.190 (LONDON: SPENCER BLACKETT, ST. BRIDE STREET, E.C.) | 191–192. catalogue.

Binding (see Plate 28)
Maroon cloth boards, blocked blind and gilt; edges plain; plain off-white endpapers.
Front board: Two rules (thick and thin) near edges of board (blind). **Spine:**
GABRIEL ALLEN, M.P. – G.A. Henty. (gilt italic) running from foot to head. **Back
board:** as front board.

References: BB | *Farmer*, p.33; *Dartt*, p.62, *Companion*, pp.15, 40; *Hannabuss*,
p.30.

Notes
1. Notes on this publisher are in Appendix II, Part 6, but I have been unable to find
any records, and there is no way of dating this book from internal sources. *Farmer*
writes 'we have reason to think that the first edition should be dated 1888'.
Unfortunately he gives no source for this belief, and the book is not mentioned in
Henty's entry in the *Dictionary of National Biography*, nor in his entry in the
Cambridge Bibliography of English Literature. It seems certain that *Dartt*, who
dates the book '(1888)' simply took the date from *Farmer*. I have seen a copy of a
letter dated 28 July 1947 from Chapman & Hall, London, in reply to a query from
an American Public Library, giving The National Book League, London, as
authority for the publication date of 1888. But that probably also derived from
Farmer.
2. Blackett's 'Select Shilling Novels', advertised on p.(2), and not to be confused
with their other 'Shilling Novels', were sold 'in paper covers, and at 1s.6d. in cloth,
postage 2d'. (The 'Select' list is catalogued by Blackett, with a Note: 'This series
will be exclusively reserved to the works of well-known Authors').
3. No copy of *Gabriel Allen, M.P.* is known to have survived in original paper
covers, but the one described above, in the collection of the Revd Basil Brown, is
possibly in the publisher's cloth binding, although it is not blocked with the
publisher's name. It is, nevertheless, certainly in its original contemporary binding
as it bears on the inside front board the label of Smith's circulating library:
'W.H. SMITH & SON | SUBSCRIPTION LIBRARY | 186, STRAND, LONDON |
AND AT RAILWAY BOOKSTALLS.' The label then gives terms for library
subscribers.
4. At this period it was customary for books to be sometimes supplied to Mudie's,
Smith's, or other circulating libraries in flat sheets so that the library could arrange
the binding. This copy of *Gabriel Allen, M.P.*, bearing the W.H. Smith label,
evidently reached their Library shelves in this binding, which therefore must have
been made either by the publisher's binder or by the librarian's binder. In either case
it is a unique and valuable book, being the only copy known in its original cloth case.
(Further details of the great Victorian circulating, or subscription, libraries are given
in Appendix II, Parts 1 and 4).
5. Several other copies of this title are known, but all were bound up (at least
originally) with other titles. Among them is one bound with another Blackett novel,
The Queen's Token, by Mrs Cashel Hoey, in half-roan, marbled boards: in the
publisher's advertisement on p.(2) of that book the list of Select Novels has grown
to six. (By October 1890, the date of the catalogue in *The Curse of Carne's Hold*,
40.2, the list had further increased to twenty-five). *Dartt* mentions copies of *Gabriel
Allen, M.P.* in two American University Libraries, neither of them in their original
bindings. One of Henty's own copies is listed by *Hannabuss* in his catalogue of the

Wandsworth Library, but this had been taken from its original binding and rebound in Henty's personal dark-blue cloth, together with *Yarns on the Beach* and *Tales of Daring and Danger.*

40. THE CURSE OF CARNE'S HOLD

40.1
THE I CURSE OF CARNE'S HOLD I A Tale of Adventure I BY I G.A. HENTY I AUTHOR OF "ALL BUT LOST," "GABRIEL ALLEN, M.P.," ETC., ETC. I IN TWO VOLUMES I VOL.I. (VOL.II.) I LONDON I SPENCER BLACKETT & HALLAM I 35, ST. BRIDE STREET, LUDGATE CIRCUS, E.C. I 1889 I (14mm. rule) I [All rights reserved]
(Note: the subtitle is in gothic type).

Contents, Volume I
184 x 121 mm. (i)–(viii) I (1)–288 I no catalogue. No illustrations.
(i) Half-title p. I (ii) blank I (iii) title p. I (iv) blank I (v)–vi. Contents I (vii) repeat half-title p. I (viii) blank I (1)–286. text, with 'END OF VOL.I' on p.286, above printer's imprint (LONDON: SPENCER BLACKETT AND HALLAM, ST. BRIDE STREET, E.C.) I (287)–(288) blank.

Volume II
184 x 121 mm. (i)–(viii) I (1)–276 I catalogue (1)–(32). No illustrations.
(i) Half-title p. I (ii) blank I (iii) title p. I (iv) blank I (v)–vi. Contents I (vii) repeat half-title p. I (viii) blank I (1)–276. text, with 'THE END'. on p.276, above printer's imprint as on p.286 of Vol.I I (1)–(32) publisher's catalogue (see Note 3).

Binding (see Plate 3)
Blue cloth boards, blocked black, bronze, and gilt; edges plain; dark-brown surface-paper endpapers.
Front board: THE CURSE OF I CARNE'S HOLD (bronze) above ornamental decoration (black and bronze). At foot: BY I G.A. HENTY. (bronze). **Spine:** THE CURSE I OF I CARNE'S I HOLD I (7mm. rule) I VOL.I. (VOL II.) (see Note 5) I G.A. I HENTY I BLACKETT & HALLAM (all gilt). **Back board:** plain.

References: BL; Bod I *Farmer*, p.23; *Dartt*, p.44.

Notes
1. Details of edition and sales remain unknown as no publisher's records survive, but for notes on Spencer Blackett see Appendix II, Part 6.
2. The story first appeared in the Glasgow weekly paper, *Scottish Nights*, published at 1d. It was announced as 'A New and Brilliant Story of Love and War, Romance and Adventure', and serialisation began on 6 July 1889 (see §3, 220). *Dartt* (p.45) incorrectly states that it was serialised in the *Union Jack*, Vol.II.
3. The catalogue in the second volume is dated September 1889. On p.6, under the heading 'NEW TWO AND THREE VOLUME NOVELS.' is a list of eight titles, including: '*The Curse of Carne's Hold.* By G.A. HENTY. 2 vols. In November.'
4. The imprint on the spine of the binding case is abbreviated to 'BLACKETT & HALLAM'. The single-volume edition, 40.2, shows the imprint on both title page

and binding case as 'SPENCER BLACKETT'. As no publisher's archive is available it is impossible to know the significance of these variations.

5. The brass blocking piece for the volume number on the spine of the second volume differs from that for the first volume in having no full point after 'VOL'.

6. The Lilly Library of Indiana University has a copy of a letter from Tillotsons' Newspaper Literature, New York branch of the British syndication agency in Bolton that operated for Henty, dated 3 April 1889 and addressed to Messrs Scribner & Welford, the New York publisher. It includes the following: 'in reply to your favor of the 2nd current, we will be most happy to wait until this day week for your verdict upon the sheets (all we yet have) of Mr. Henty's "Curse of Carne's Hold" sent by this mail. It is quite a young man's story, as you will see'. No doubt Tillotsons in Bolton had contracted with Spencer Blackett & Hallam for the British book rights, but their New York letter to Scribner & Welford is pencilled across the head 'Declined 4/4/89'.

40.2

The | CURSE OF CARNE'S HOLD | A Tale of Adventure | BY | G.A. HENTY | AUTHOR OF "ALL BUT LOST," "GABRIEL ALLEN, M.P.," ETC., ETC. | LONDON | SPENCER BLACKETT | 35, ST. BRIDE STREET, E.C.
(Note: the subtitle is in gothic type).

Contents
182 x 121 mm. (1)–356 | catalogue (1)–(32). Eight full-page pen-drawings by Charles Kerr reproduced by line blocks printed in black on coated paper, unbacked, unfolioed but keyed to text pages, tipped in.

(Frontispiece, tipped in) | (1) title p. | (2) blank | (3)–4. Contents | (5)–356. text, with printer's imprint at foot of p.356 (LONDON: SPENCER BLACKETT ST. BRIDE STREET, E.C.) | (1)–(32) catalogue.

Binding (see Plate 23)
Red-brown cloth boards, blocked black, grey, yellow, and gilt; edges plain; maroon surface-paper endpapers.

Front board: The . Curse . of (gilt) | CARNE'S HOLD (gilt, shaded black) beneath gilt decorative 'frieze' and rules, and above illustration based on frontispiece drawing (black, grey, yellow, and gilt). At foot: ILLUSTRATED (black) | G.A. HENTY. (gilt). **Spine:** The | . CURSE . | of | CARNE'S | HOLD | G.A. HENTY (all gilt) beneath gilt decorative 'frieze' and rules continued from front board. Beneath this: illustration of two standing uniformed figures (black and gilt); at foot: SPENCER . BLACKETT (gilt). **Back board:** plain.

References: PN | *Dartt*, p.44.

Notes
1. This, the first single-volume edition, can be dated only by its bound-in catalogue, October 1890. It shows the selling price as 3s.6d.

2. The book has not been well planned. The text is not set as an even working, the last gathering, signature Z, consisting of only 4 pages.

3. The archives of this publisher are lost, as are those of the publisher who was shortly to take on this book, Griffith & Farran. I do not know, therefore, the circumstances in which the book changed hands, or whether it was issued by Griffith & Farran under licence only (see Appendix II, Part 2).

40.3

THE | CURSE OF CARNE'S HOLD | A Tale of Adventure | BY | G.A. HENTY | AUTHOR OF "ALL BUT LOST," "GABRIEL ALLEN, M.P.," ETC., ETC. | LONDON | GRIFFITH FARRAN & CO. | NEWBERY HOUSE, 39, CHARING CROSS ROAD
(Note: the subtitle is in gothic type).

Contents
175 x 115 mm. (1)–356 | no catalogue. No illustrations.
    (1) Title p. | (2) The Right of Translation and Reproduction is reserved. | (3)–4. Contents | (5)–356. text.

Binding (see Plate 24)
In the style of a Victorian 'yellowback' (see Note 2 below). Pictorial paper boards, printed red and black on yellow, with coloured illustration and decorative panels; edges plain; all endpapers carry advertisements, printed black on white wove paper, for household and medical products.
    Front board: BY G.A. HENTY. (black) in narrow upper part of double solid panel (red) enclosed by black rules and with black rule dividing the two parts; THE (black) CURSE (reversed yellow out of red, with black casing) OF (black) | CARNE'S HOLD (reversed yellow out of red, with black casing). Illustration from engraving of man and woman struggling in clearing of a wood (black and red). In another narrow solid panel (red): GRIFFITH, FARRAN & Co. LONDON (black); this and the illustration enclosed by black rules. **Spine:** All-over decoration of oak leaves and acorns on vertical stem, with: THE | CURSE | OF | CARNE'S | HOLD. (black) in plain yellow ruled panel at head; G.A. HENTY. (black) in plain yellow diagonal scroll across decoration. At foot: TWO SHILLINGS. (black) in yellow rectangle, with red and black rules beneath. **Back board:** Advertisement for Cleaver's Juvenia Toilet Soap (black).

Reference: DS.

Notes
1. I am unable to date this issue accurately but it appears to have come from the new publisher, Griffith & Farran, about 1893, possibly before their first edition in cloth boards (see 40.3A). As stated in 40.2, Note 3, no information is available about the change of publisher.
2. 'Yellowback' editions were mainly fiction, cheaply produced by a number of publishers, and frequently sold from railway-station bookstalls, nearly always at two shillings each. See also *Rujub, the Juggler*, 56.6.

40.3A
Title page: As for 40.3.

Contents
176 x 115 mm. (1)–356 | no catalogue. No illustrations.
    (1) Title p. | (2) The Right of Translation and Reproduction is reserved. | (3)–4.

Contents | (5)–356, text, with printer's imprint below rule at foot of p.356 (CHARLES DICKENS AND EVANS, CRYSTAL PALACE PRESS.)

Binding
Red cloth boards, blocked black and gilt; edges plain; plain off-white endpapers.
Front board: THE CURSE OF | CARNE'S HOLD | BY | G.A. HENTY (black).
Spine: THE CURSE | OF | CARNE'S | HOLD | BY | G.A. | HENTY | GRIFFITH
FARRAN & Co. (all gilt). **Back board:** plain.

Reference: PN.

Notes
1. I have found no other copy of this issue, the first single-volume edition in cloth boards from Griffith & Farran. It was probably issued simultaneously with 40.3.
2. The text is printed by a new printer, whose senior partner was the son of a famous father: this imprint has not previously appeared in one of Henty's books. The plates used are from the Spencer Blackett typesetting for 40.2.
3. The economical (and unillustrated) nature of this issue and the apparently extreme scarcity of both it and 40.3, suggest that both were issued in very small numbers while Griffith & Farran prepared to market the book to a different public in 'The Boys' Own Favourite Library' (see 40.4, Note 1).

*40.4
Title page: As for 40.3, but with an additional line (NEW EDITION) above the imprint.

Contents
182 x 121 mm. (1)–356 | catalogue (1)–(48). Illustrations as in 40.2.
(Frontispiece, tipped in) | (1) title p. | (2) The Right of Translation and Reproduction is reserved. | (3)–4. Contents | (5)–356. text | (1)–47. catalogue | (48) printer's imprint (LONDON: | PRINTED BY GILBERT AND RIVINGTON, LD., | ST. JOHN'S HOUSE, CLERKENWELL, E.C.)

Binding (see Note 3)
Brown, diagonally-ribbed cloth boards, blocked black, yellow, and gilt; all edges gilt; yellow-buff flowered endpapers with 'step-and-repeat' publisher's monogram.
Front board: THE CURSE OF CARNE'S HOLD (black, and cloth-colour) reversed out of solid-gilt rectangle, lettering cased with line (cloth-colour); with black and yellow rules above and below. The whole over trophy of guns, oars, and anchor (black, yellow, and gilt). Beneath this: By | G.A. HENTY (black) above crossed swords (black and yellow). **Spine:** Six black-edged yellow bands, forming five spine-panels. In second panel from top: THE CURSE OF | CARNE'S | HOLD (black, and cloth-colour out of gilt rectangle). In fourth panel: HENTY (black, and cloth-colour out of solid gilt). At foot of fifth panel: GRIFFITH, FARRAN & CO (gilt). **Back board:** plain.

Reference: PN.

Notes
1. The first single-volume edition, 40.2, was presented by the original publisher as

though it were a boys' book, in contrast with the first edition in two volumes.

2. Now, in turn, Griffith & Farran present *The Curse of Carne's Hold* explicitly in 'The Boy's Own Favourite Library', also providing a contrast with *their* earlier, unillustrated issue, 40.3A.

3. The illustrations are from 40.2, and the text printed by Gilbert and Rivington, using plates of the Spencer Blackett typesetting for 40.2.

4. The binding style is the third of four designs used for 'The Boys' Own Favourite Library' (see Plate 33), and was in use for books in the series from c.1886 to c.1895. For more detailed notes about the styles and variations within this series see *Out on the Pampas*, 4.3, Notes 3–5. The variants of title page and of catalogues that may be found in this binding style are several, and they are here grouped together under this 'generic' heading, *40.4.

*40.5

Title page, Contents: As for *40.4.

Binding

Blue, vertically-ribbed cloth boards, bevelled, blocked black, red, white, and gilt; all edges gilt; dark-blue surface-paper endpapers.
In the fourth binding style of 'The Boys' Own Favourite Library' (see Plate 33).

References: SW; BB.

Note: See 40.4, Notes 1–3. Later issues of the book, published by Griffith & Farran in 'The Boys' Own Favourite Library', appeared in this fourth and final binding design for the series from c.1895. All minor variants in the fourth binding style are grouped together under this 'generic' heading, *40.5.

40.6

THE I CURSE OF CARNE'S HOLD I A Tale of Adventure I BY I G.A. HENTY, I Author of "All but Lost," etc., etc. I NEW EDITION I LONDON: I THE STANDARD LIBRARY COMPANY, I 15, CLERKENWELL ROAD, E.C.
(Note: the subtitle is in gothic type).

Contents

178 x 116 mm. (1)–356 I no catalogue. No illustrations.
  (1) Title p. I (2) blank I (3)–4. Contents I (5)–356. text.

Binding (see Plate 25)

Red, diagonally-ribbed cloth, blocked blind and gilt; edges plain; plain off-white endpapers.
  Front board: THE CURSE I OF CARNE'S HOLD (gilt) in upper panel of all-over elaborate art-nouveau design (blind). The decoration extends over the whole board, leaving a second, unused, panel below. **Spine:** THE CURSE I OF I CARNE'S HOLD (gilt) in upper panel of similar art-nouveau design (blind); beneath this: G.A. HENTY. (gilt). At foot, in a small panel: ENTERPRISE LIBRARY (gilt, the first word set as the upper arc of a circle). **Back board:** plain.

Reference: SW.

Notes

1. This is probably a one-off issue arranged between Griffith & Farran and an undertaking variously known as the Standard Library Company and the Enterprise Library. The title page is a cancel; as in 40.3, there is no printer's imprint but the text is from rather battered stereos of the original typesetting by Spencer Blackett for 40.2. The plates were re-imposed for this page size which, like that for 40.3, is smaller than that of usual Griffith & Farran editions.

2. The production has been carried out as cheaply as possible: a small page-size for the text; omission of all illustration; and the binding case made from 'binder's blanks' (see Glossary).

40.7

THE CURSE OF | CARNE'S HOLD | A TALE OF ADVENTURE | BY | G.A. HENTY | NEW EDITION | GRIFFITH FARRAN BROWNE & CO. LIMITED | 35 BOW STREET, COVENT GARDEN | LONDON

Contents

191 x 128 mm. (i)–(iv) | (1)–356 | no catalogue. Frontispiece from wash-drawing, after original pen-drawing by Charles Kerr, reproduced by halftone block printed in black on coated paper, tipped in (see Note 1, below).

(i)–(ii) blank | (iii) half-title p. | (iv) blank | (1) title p. | (2) [The Rights of Translation and of Reproduction are reserved.] | (3)–4. Contents | (5)–356. text, with printer's imprint on p.356 (PRINTED BY MORRISON AND GIBB LIMITED, EDINBURGH).

Binding (see Plate 26)

Grey cloth boards, blocked green, orange, and gilt; edges plain; plain off-white endpapers. (See Note 2, below.)

Front board: CARNE'S | HOLD (gilt) within floral wreath with ribbons (green and orange), the whole enclosed by art-nouveau line-panelling (green). **Spine:** CARNE'S | HOLD | HENTY (gilt) in space between wreath and panelling similar to that on front board (green and orange). At foot: GRIFFITH FARRAN | BROWNE & Co. (orange). **Back board:** plain.

References BB; SW.

Notes

1. The frontispiece appears to be reproduced from a wash-drawing that has been made over the top of a printed impression of Charles Kerr's original line drawing. It bears his signature, but the work was probably done for Griffith & Farran by an anonymous artist. The signature is clearly identical with the one on the line drawing: had Kerr redrawn the picture himself, and signed it, there would surely have been some slight difference between the two signatures.

2. Another copy has the case blocked in black, white, and gilt.

3. The abbreviation of the title, on the case only, is of interest. Two other binding designs show the title abbreviated in the same way (see 40.8 and 40.9).

4. This binding design was also used for *Our Sailors*, see §2, 167.7.

40.8

Title page: As for 40.7.

Contents: 183 x 122 mm. Otherwise as for 40.7.

Binding (see Plate 26)
Blue cloth boards, blocked black, red, buff, and gilt; edges plain; plain off-white endpapers.
Front board: CARNE'S | HOLD (black, shadowed red) in decorative black-framed panel above illustration (black, red, buff). **Spine:** CARNE'S | HOLD (gilt) | HENTY (red) in black-framed decorative panel over illustration (black and buff). At foot: GRIFFITH FARRAN | BROWNE & CO. (black). **Back board:** plain.

Reference: BB.

Note: A second binding design with abbreviated title (see 40.7, Note 3).

40.9

Title page: As for 40.7.

Contents: As for 40.8.

Binding
Grey cloth boards, blocked black, red, green, white, and gilt; edges plain; plain off-white endpapers.
Front board: Series of ruled panels with art-nouveau decorations of flowers, etc. (black, red, green); in upper panel: Carne's Hold (gilt); in centre panel: illustration of boy with book, in cap and blazer, sitting on wall overlooking seaside scene (black, red, green, white). **Spine:** Panels of similar design to those on front board, with blank spaces for lettering (black, red, green). At head: Carne's | Hold (gilt); at centre: Henty (black); at foot: GRIFFITH FARRAN | . BROWNE & CO. . (black). **Back board:** plain.

References: BB; TC.

Note: A third binding design with abbreviated title (see 40.7, Note 3).

40.10

Title page: As for 40.7.

Contents
196 x 137 mm. (1)–356 | no catalogue. Frontispiece from line drawing by Charles Kerr, reproduced by line block printed in black on coated paper, unbacked, tipped in.
(Frontispiece, tipped in) | (1) title p. | (2) The Right of Translation and Reproduction is reserved. | (3)–4. Contents | (5)–356. text, with printer's imprint at foot of p.356 (PRINTED BY MORRISON AND GIBB LIMITED, EDINBURGH).

Binding (see Plate 27)
Red, vertically-ribbed cloth boards, blocked black and gilt; all edges gilt; plain off-white endpapers.
Front board: Two panels of art-nouveau designs of leaves and flowers, enclosed in a series of rules (all black). Between these panels: THE CURSE | OF | CARNE'S

HOLD (black). **Spine:** Three rules across head (black) above: THE CURSE | OF | CARNE'S HOLD (cloth-colour out of gilt decorative art-nouveau panel). Beneath this: G.A. | HENTY (black) and panel of art-nouveau design of leaves and flowers (black). At foot: GRIFFITH FARRAN | BROWNE & CO. (gilt) above three rules (black). **Back board:** plain.

Reference: PN.

Notes

1. The case is a binder's blank: a very similar design was used by Griffith & Farran for *Friends, though Divided* (see 12.6 above, also shown at Plate 27). Its size, heavily-ribbed cloth, and (crude) gilt edges were meant to give the volume a 'de luxe' feeling when new, but it is in fact a cheaply produced book.

2. The frontispiece is from the original line drawing used in this position in 40.2, now printed on very poor quality art-paper.

3. The text is still printed from the old Spencer Blackett typesetting, but this impression is by Morrison and Gibb of Edinburgh. It appears to have been issued at the same time as *Friends, though Divided*, 12.6 (see Note 1 above), also printed by Morrison and Gibb, and these two were probably the last impressions of the titles before the sale of the stock and goodwill of this publisher (see Appendix II, Part 2). However, sheets from this impression were still to be issued by Griffith Farran in one more new binding design (see 40.11).

40.11

Title page, Contents: As for 40.10.

Binding

Blue, vertically-ribbed cloth, blocked black, grey, and gilt; all edges gilt; plain off-white endpapers.

Front board: Over-all 'wallpaper pattern' of formal leaves and flowers (black and grey) with: THE CURSE | OF | CARNE'S HOLD (black) superimposed. **Spine:** similar over-all pattern, with panels at head and foot. Upper panel: THE CURSE | OF | CARNE'S HOLD (cloth-colour out of gilt solid rectangle with surrounding border of flower petals (gilt) and black rules above and below. Panel at foot: GRIFFITH FARRAN | BROWNE & COMP. (black) with black rules above and below. **Back board:** plain.

Reference: TC.

Notes

1. See 40.10, Notes 1–3.

2. I have found no trace of any edition of *The Curse of Carne's Hold* having been published, or even advertised, by the 'Joint Venture' of Henry Frowde, the Publisher at the Oxford University Press, and Hodder & Stoughton, nor later by Humphrey Milford at the O.U.P. after the 'Joint Venture' came to an end. It seems certain that for some reason this title was not included in the 1906 sale to Hodder & Stoughton. Sadly the relevant records of all the publishers concerned are lost, mostly destroyed in the bombing of London in the second war. Furthermore I have found no trace of the title having been taken over by any other British publisher following the demise of Griffith & Farran, and it is hard to understand why it was allowed to disappear from the bookshops while all the rest of Henty's books from their list continued to be reprinted at least into the 1920s. (For details of the 'Joint Venture' see Appendix II, Part 2).

41. THE PLAGUE SHIP

41.1

THE PLAGUE SHIP. | BY | G.A. HENTY, | AUTHOR OF "UNDER DRAKE'S FLAG," "IN TIMES OF PERIL," ETC. | (S.P.C.K. device) | LONDON: | NORTHUMBERLAND AVENUE, CHARING CROSS, W.C. | BRIGHTON: 135, NORTH STREET. | NEW YORK: E.& J.B. YOUNG & CO. | [The Right of Translation is reserved.]

Contents
214 x 136 mm. (1)–32 | no catalogue. Five small black-and-white line drawings by unknown hands, printed on text pages.
    (1) Title p. | (2) blank | (3)–32. text, set in two columns with rule between, and illustrations, with printer's imprint at foot of p.32 (PRINTED BY J.S. VIRTUE AND CO., LIMITED, CITY ROAD, LONDON.)

Cover (see Plate 139)
Off-white paper, printed in dark-brown, red, greenish-blue, yellow-ochre; wrapped around the single gathering of text, saddle-stitched, edges cut flush.
(1) The PENNY LIBRARY of | FICTION (dark-brown) in decorative panel with stipple texture of red and yellow, out of solid background (dark-brown and blue, making black): THE PLAGUE | SHIP (blue) out of same dark solid; S.P.C.K. device (brown on red circle ringed white and brown), all over illustration of three men on deck of ship, one waving (dark-brown, red, greenish-blue, yellow-ochre). Superimposed at lower left corner: By | G.A. | Henty (dark-brown). The whole enclosed by dark-brown and red ruled border.
(2) advertisements for James Nisbet & Co.; for Epps's Cocoa; and for S.P.C.K. 'FICTION FOR THE MILLION'. (All in black-and-white).
(3) full-page advertisement for Aspinall's Enamel; with note at foot: 'All communications respecting Advertisements for these Novels should be addressed to Hart's | Advertising Offices, 33, Southampton Street, Strand, W.C.' (all in black-and-white).
(4) Full-page advertisement in colour for Pears' Soap.

References: Bod; NS | *Dartt*, p.107.

Notes
1. The format of the booklet, in the 'S.P.C.K. Penny Library of Fiction', was used for stories by many authors, including Henty's *The Ranche in the Valley*, 52.1.
2. *Dartt* believed this to be 'the rarest of all Henty publications'. The copy he describes, and illustrates at p.(7) of his illustration section, is in the Indiana University Library. It has been trimmed at the edges.
3. The Bodleian Library copy is described above; it arrived there in 1889. The copy in the National Library of Scotland is bound up among a set of the booklets, with edges trimmed. There is no copy in the British Library.

4. Copies of 41.1, either left-over sheets or reprints, were later bound up with other titles in the 'S.P.C.K. Penny Library of Fiction', forming a book entitled *S.P.C.K. Library of Fiction (Third Series)* (see §2, 177).

41.2

THE PLAGUE SHIP | BY | G.A. HENTY | LONDON | THE SHELDON PRESS | NORTHUMBERLAND AVENUE, W.C. | NEW YORK AND TORONTO: THE MACMILLAN COMPANY

Contents

183 x 120 mm. (1)–(64) | catalogue (1)–8 (see Note 1). No illustrations.

(1) Half-title p. | (2) blank | (3) title p. | (4) printer's imprint at foot (Made and Printed in Great Britain. C. TINLING & CO., LTD., | 53, Victoria Street, Liverpool, and at London and Prescot.) | 5–62. text | (63)–(64) blank | (1)–8. catalogue.

Binding (see Plate 141)

Brown paper boards (grained to imitate cloth), blocked black and off-white; edges plain; plain ivory-wove endpapers.

Front board: THE PLAGUE | SHIP | . G . A . HENTY . (all black in frame of black double rules) above illustration of sailing ship at sea (black and off-white); the whole framed by black double rules. **Spine:** THE PLAGUE SHIP – G.A. HENTY. (black) running from foot to head. **Back board:** plain.

References: BL; PN; RC | *Farmer*, p.56; *Dartt*, p.107, *Companion*, p.23.

Notes

1. The Sheldon Press edition was received by the British Library in 1923. The earliest issues of this impression, including some inscribed in 1924, have no catalogue, but 8-page catalogues were bound in most copies: my own copy is dated 20 June 1925; other dates reported are: 10 October 1925, 1 June 1927 and 1 July 1928.

2. The style and format is similar to that of *The Ranche in the Valley*, 52.2. The Sheldon Press was another imprint of the S.P.C.K.

3. Later issues sometimes had the binding case blocked in black only. Some also have a line added at the foot of the title page (Printed in Great Britain.).

42. TALES OF DARING AND DANGER

42.1

TALES OF | DARING AND DANGER. | BY | G.A. HENTY, | Author of "Yarns on the Beach;" "Sturdy and Strong;" "Facing Death;" | "By Sheer Pluck;" "With Clive in India;" &c. | ILLUSTRATED. | (publisher's device) | LONDON: | BLACKIE & SON, 49 & 50 OLD BAILEY, E.C. | GLASGOW, EDINBURGH, AND DUBLIN. | 1890.

Contents

178 x 120 mm. (1)–160 | catalogue (1)–32. Two full-page drawings by J.A. Christie, reproduced by line blocks printed in black on coated paper, unbacked, tipped in.

(1) Half-title p. | (2) advertisement (MR. HENTY'S HISTORICAL TALES.)

listing 19 titles | (frontispiece, tipped in) | (3) title p. | (4) blank | (5) Contents | (6) blank | (7)–36. text of 'Bears and Dacoits' | (37)–69. text of 'The Paternosters' | (70) blank | (71)–98. text of 'A Pipe of Mystery' | (99)–117. text of 'White-Faced Dick' | (118) blank | (119)–160. text of 'A Brush with the Chinese' | (1)–32. catalogue.

Binding (see Plate 112)
Brown cloth boards, blocked black, red, blue, blind, and gilt; edges plain; dark-blue surface-paper endpapers.
    Front board: TALES . OF . DARING . & . DANGER | . BY . G . A . HENTY . (all gilt, underlined gilt) in plain panel enclosed in over-all decorative design of rules, circles, dots and ornaments (black and red) with, as if superimposed, illustration of gentians (black and blue) on and overlapping from a black circle.
Spine: TALES | – OF – | DARING | AND | DANGER (gilt) in plain panel, as on front board enclosed in design of rules, etc. (black and red). Illustration of gentian (black and blue), as if superimposed on this design, but without black circle behind.
Back board: three rules close to edges of board (blind).

References: PN | *Farmer*, p.67; *Dartt*, p.134, *Companion*, p.30.

Notes
1. This collection of short stories was published on 20 July 1889, in 'Blackie's Eighteenpenny Series'. By the end of February 1890 Blackie had sold 3268 copies, and over the following 27 years a further 38,418 copies were sold at the same price. At that point (end of August 1917) Blackie's records cease. The average annual sale over the long period of 28 years was 1489 copies, the yearly total only twice falling below 1000.
2. *Farmer* is uncharacteristically inaccurate. He gives the title of the book as 'Tales of Danger and Daring' (i.e. with the two main words transposed). He gives the title-page date as 1889 instead of 1890, and a Blackie imprint that did not appear on title pages before 1891. He seems to have relied on hearsay for this entry.
3. *Dartt*, no doubt confused by *Farmer*, on whom he relied heavily, also shows an incorrect title-page date of 1889, but reports that both copies he inspected were dated 1890. His version of the title-page imprint, apart from the date, is correct.
4. Copies of 42.1 are not held by the Copyright Libraries. The Bodleian Library has a copy of *42.2 in greyish-green cloth boards.
5. Other appearances of the individual stories are listed in §4.
6. As usual with Blackie titles, the earliest issues contain catalogues advertising books for the current year (in this case those with title pages dated 1890) without quotations from press reviews.

*42.2
Reprints of the first edition were issued in the same style as 42.1, but with the date removed from the title page. They followed Blackie's usual pattern: alterations were made when necessary to title-page imprint and addresses, and although Blackie became a Limited Company in 1890, the books with that date on the title page did not show the change as they had been published the previous year. The Edinburgh address was not used after 1894, and the Indian office was opened in Bombay in 1901 although that address did not appear regularly in the imprint until 1906. Bindings continued to show variation in colours of cloth, blocking and endpapers.

The slightly-differing issues of this title in its first-edition format are all grouped together under this 'generic' heading, *42.2.

42.3

Title page: As for 42.1, except (a) no date; (b) imprint (LONDON I BLACKIE & SON, LIMITED, 50 OLD BAILEY, E.C. I GLASGOW AND DUBLIN).

Contents: 182 x 123 mm. As for 42.1, but p.(2) blank.

Binding (see Plate 113)
Probably designed by Talwin Morris (see Note 2). Purple cloth boards, blocked green and gilt; edges plain; plain off-white endpapers.
  Front board: TALES OF I DARING & I DANGER I BY I G.A. (small ornament) I (small ornament) Henty (all gilt) in irregular-shaped panel outlined in green at head of art-nouveau floral design (green). **Spine:** TALES OF I DARING I AND I DANGER I (three small ornaments) I G.A. I Henty (all gilt), with green floral art-nouveau decoration above and below. **Back board:** plain.

Reference: PN.

Notes
1. Printed on a larger, laid paper of good quality, also used for some later impressions of *Sturdy and Strong*. It is bulkier than the usual Blackie MF paper, but not as bulky as some of the featherweight antique woves that were to follow it.
2. The binding design is striking, probably designed by Talwin Morris, (see Appendix IV, Part 2). But as Gerald Cinamon points out, 'he had at least one assistant, A.A.Campbell, a fine designer in his own right, who worked very much in the Talwin Morris style and therefore correct attributions . . . may be difficult'. 'Talwin Morris, Blackie and The Glasgow Style', in *The Private Library*, Vol.10, No.1, p.45.
3. The bound-in catalogue places this issue chronologically as the successor to the first-edition binding design. My copy is inscribed 1899.

42.4

Title page: As for 42.3.

Contents: 181 x 122 mm. Otherwise as for 42.3.

Binding (see Plate 114)
Green cloth boards, blocked yellow, pale-green, and gilt; edges plain; cream wove endpapers.
  Front board: . TALES . OF . I . DARING . AND . DANGER . I (rule) BY (rule) I . G.A. HENTY . (all cloth-colour out of solid gilt rectangle, decorated at upper and lower edges). Above and below is over-all design of twining tendrils and flowers (yellow and pale-green) with pale-green rules at edges of board. **Spine:** TALES I . OF . I DARING I . AND . I DANGER I (ornament) BY (ornament) I G.A. HENTY (all cloth-colour out of solid gilt panel, decorated at upper and lower edges). Above and below is over-all design as on front board (yellow and pale-green). **Back board:** plain.

References: PN I *Dartt Companion*, p.30.

Notes
1. The earliest impression was on the cream laid used for 42.3, but later ones were on featherweight antique wove. Inscription dates seen are between 1900 and 1902.
2. Following the binding design used for 42.3 this is a rather humdrum affair, but perhaps more characteristic of Blackie's designs for cheaper children's books of the period. The same design was used for *Yarns on the Beach*, 25.3.

42.5

Tales of I Daring and Danger I BY I G.A. HENTY I Author of "Yarns on the Beach" "Sturdy and Strong" "Facing Death" I "By Sheer Pluck" "With Clive in India" &c. I ILLUSTRATED I BLACKIE & SON LIMITED I LONDON GLASGOW BOMBAY

Contents
179 x 120 mm. (1)–160 I catalogue 1–32. Illustrations as in 42.1.
   (1) Half-title p. I (2) blank I (frontispiece, tipped in) I (3) title p. I (4) blank I (5) Contents I (6) blank I 7–160. text, see 42.1 I 1–32. catalogue.

Binding (see Plate 114)
Green cloth boards, blocked black, orange, pale-yellow, and gilt; edges plain; grey endpapers lined off-white.
   Front board: TALES OF DARING I AND DANGER (gilt) within decorative panel outlined black and orange, at head of art-nouveau design of orange tree with leaves, fruit, and shoots in several panels (black, orange, and yellow). **Spine:** TALES OF I DARING I AND I DANGER I G.A. HENTY (all gilt) within decorative panel outlined black and orange) at head of a similar design to that on front board. At foot, in black ruled panel: BLACKIE & SON LD. (black). **Back board:** plain.

Reference: PN.

Notes
1. The binding case was designed for Blackie's 1s.6d. 'Excelsior Series' (see Appendix V).
2. The text and catalogue are both printed on a bulky featherweight antique wove.
3. Later issues were blocked with no gilt on the front board, and later none on the spine, yellow being used for the lettering.

42.6

Tales of I Daring and Danger I BY I G.A. HENTY I Author of "Facing Death" "By Sheer Pluck I "With Clive in India" &c. I ILLUSTRATED I BLACKIE AND SON LIMITED I LONDON GLASGOW AND BOMBAY
(Note: The quotation marks after By Sheer Pluck *are missing).*

Contents
180 x 120 mm. (1)–160 I no catalogue. Three wash-drawings signed 'A.P.' (Alfred Pearse), reproduced by halftone blocks printed in black on coated paper, unbacked, unfolioed, tipped in.
   (1) Half-title p. I (2) advertisement (BOOKS OF THIS SERIES) (see Note 2) I (frontispiece, tipped in) I (3) title p. I (4) Printed and bound in Great Britain I (5)

Contents | (6) list of Illustrations | 7–160. text, with printer's imprint on p.160 (PRINTED AND BOUND IN GREAT BRITAIN | By Blackie & Son, Limited, Glasgow).

Binding (see Plate 113)
Purplish-blue cloth boards, blocked orange and green; edges plain; grey-white endpapers.
    Front board: TALES OF DARING | AND DANGER (cloth-colour out of solid orange rectangle) framed by orange rules, above semi-abstract over-all design of orange trees (orange and green) in green border. **Spine:** TALES OF | DARING & | DANGER | G.A. Henty (all orange) between two green rules, and above semi-abstract design as on front board (orange and green). At foot: BLACKIE & SON LTD (orange). **Back board:** plain.

Reference: PN.

Notes
1. I am unable to date this edition more precisely than the early 1920s.
2. The advertisement on p.(2) is frustrating: the heading, 'Books of this Series', gives no name to the series. Perhaps this is a later binding design for the 'Excelsior Library' (see 42.5) as, although the treatment is quite different, the subject of the decorations on both cases is the same. On the other hand, this book is included on p.(2), but not *Yarns on the Beach*.
3. The new illustrator is given no credit in the book. But his initials are quite distinctive, as is his work. Alfred Pearse illustrated many children's books and stories in magazines. His first work for Henty was in *By England's Aid*, 47.1, published by Blackie in 1890, with title page dated 1891 (see Appendix IV, Part 2).

43. BY PIKE AND DYKE

43.1
BY PIKE AND DYKE: | A TALE OF THE RISE OF THE DUTCH REPUBLIC. | BY | G.A. HENTY, | Author of "The Lion of St. Mark;" "Bonnie Prince Charlie;" "With Clive in India;" | "With Lee in Virginia;" "The Cat of Bubastes;" &c. | WITH FULL-PAGE ILLUSTRATIONS BY MAYNARD BROWN, | AND FOUR MAPS. | (publisher's device) | LONDON: | BLACKIE & SON, 49 & 50 OLD BAILEY, E.C. | GLASGOW, EDINBURGH, AND DUBLIN. | 1890.

Contents
185 x 130 mm. (i)–(viii) | (9)–384 | catalogue (1)–32. Ten full-page pen-drawings by Maynard Brown, reproduced by line blocks printed in black on coated paper, unbacked, unfolioed, tipped in. Map of the Netherlands as double-page spread, guarded in; two plans on one leaf tipped in; one full-page map tipped in; all printed in black line on coated paper, unbacked.
    (i) Half-title p. | (ii) advertisement (MR. HENTY'S HISTORICAL TALES.) listing 19 titles | (frontispiece, tipped in) | (iii) title p. | (iv) blank | (v)–vi. Preface | (vii) Contents | (viii) list of Illustrations | (9)–384. text | (1)–32. catalogue.

Binding (see Plate 59)

Brown cloth boards, bevelled, blocked black, dark-blue merging to light-blue, blind, and gilt; all edges burnished olive-green; maroon surface-paper endpapers.

Front board: BY PIKE AND DYKE. | A TALE OF THE RISE OF THE DUTCH REPUBLIC. (cloth-colour out of decorated solid gilt panel), the second line set as the upper arc of a circle, above illustration of soldier with pike (black, and dark-blue merging to light-blue). At foot: (ornament and rules) BY G.A. HENTY. (rules and ornament) (all gilt). The whole surrounded by black rules. **Spine:** BY PIKE – | AND DYKE. (cloth-colour out of decorated gilt panel) above illustration of soldier standing with pike (black, and dark-blue merging to light-blue). At foot: BY | G.A. HENTY. (gilt). The whole surrounded by black rule, with additional gilt rule at head and foot. **Back board:** single rule at edges of bevel (blind).

References: BL; Bod; PN | *Farmer*, p.16; *Dartt*, p.29.

Notes

1. The book was published on 7 August 1889 at six shillings. By the end of February 1890 Blackie had sold 3952 copies, and over the next fourteen years they sold 5151 more, the average annual sale over the fifteen year period being 607 copies. The book was then re-issued in Blackie's 'New and Popular Edition' (see 43.3). The remaining stock of 91 copies was sold by the end of August 1908.

2. As usual with Blackie novels, the earliest issues contain catalogues advertising books for the current year (in this case those with title pages dated 1890) without quotations from press reviews.

3. *Dartt*, p.30, Note (1), is ambiguous. The four maps were always present in the first edition, but they were not listed on p.(viii) in the early issues.

*43.2

Reprints of the first edition were issued in the same style as 43.1, but with the date removed from the title page. Changes were made when necessary to the title-page imprint and addresses, and although Blackie became a Limited Company in 1890, the books with that date on the title page had not shown the change as they were published the previous year. The Edinburgh address was not used after 1894, and the Indian office was opened in Bombay in 1901, although that address did not appear regularly in the Blackie imprint until 1906. Bindings continued to show variation in colours of cloth, blocking, and endpapers. The variants of the book in its first-edition format are all grouped together under this 'generic' heading, *43.2.

43.3

By Pike and Dyke | A Tale of the Rise of the Dutch Republic | BY | G.A. HENTY | Author of "The Lion of St. Mark" "Bonnie Prince Charlie" "With Clive in | India" "With Lee in Virginia" "The Cat of Bubastes" &c | WITH TEN FULL-PAGE ILLUSTRATIONS AND FOUR MAPS | NEW EDITION | BLACKIE AND SON LIMITED | LONDON GLASGOW AND DUBLIN | 1905

(Note: the full point is missing after &c at the end of the list of titles).

Contents

187 x 125 mm. (1)–384 | catalogue 1–16. Illustrations, maps and plans as in 43.1.

(1) Half-title p. | (2) advertisement (BY ENGLAND'S AID) | (frontispiece,

tipped in) | (3) title p. | (4) blank | 5. Preface | vi. [roman numerals in error] Preface, continued | 7. Contents | 8. list of Illustrations | 9–384. text | 1–16. catalogue.

Binding (see Note 1)
Green cloth boards, blocked black, light-grey merging to dark-grey, and gilt; all edges stained olive-green; grey endpapers lined off-white.
   Front board: By Pike | and Dyke | G.A. Henty (all gilt) above illustration of soldier with pike against sky-background outlined by circle (black, light-grey merging to dark-grey). **Spine:** By Pike | and Dyke | by | G.A. Henty (gilt) above illustration of soldier with pike (black), and background (light-grey merging to dark-grey) framed (black) in panel with curved top. At foot: Blackie & Son Ltd (gilt). **Back board:** plain.

References: BL; Bod.

Notes
1. Re-issued 1904 (title-page date 1905) in the cheaper 'New and Popular Edition'. For details of the series see *Facing Death*, 10.6, Notes 2–3, and, for examples of the binding style, Plates 172–173.
2. Of this edition Blackie sold 2495 copies by the end of August 1905. Another 9371 copies were sold over the next twelve years, up to the end of August 1917, when Blackie's records cease.

*43.4

By Pike and Dyke | A Tale of the Rise of the Dutch Republic | BY | G.A. HENTY | Author of "The Lion of St. Mark" "Bonnie Prince Charlie" "With Clive in | India" "With Lee in Virginia" "The Cat of Bubastes" &c. | ILLUSTRATED | BLACKIE AND SON LIMITED | LONDON GLASGOW AND BOMBAY

Contents
185 x 126 mm. (1)–384 | no catalogue. Frontispiece from watercolour drawing by Frank Gillett, R.I., printed from three-colour halftone blocks; four full-page pen drawings by Maynard Brown printed in black from line blocks, on coated paper, unbacked, unfolioed, tipped in. Maps and plans as in 43.1.
   (1) Half-title p. | (2) advertisement (G.A. HENTY'S BOOKS) listing 45 titles | (frontispiece, tipped in) | (3) title p. | (4) blank | 5. Preface | vi. [roman numeral in error] Preface, continued | (7) Contents | (8) list of Illustrations | 9–384. text, with printer's imprint on p.384 (PRINTED IN GREAT BRITAIN | By Blackie & Son, Limited, Glasgow).

Binding: As for 43.3, except (a) blue cloth boards, blocked black, light-grey merging to dark-grey, with no gilt: imprint on spine black, all other lettering light-grey; (b) edges plain; (c) plain off-white endpapers.

References: Bod; PN.

Notes
1. For notes on Blackie's second cheaper series, 'The New Popular Henty', and subsequent editions of this book, see *Facing Death*, 10.7, Notes 1–3 and 6–8. This title was issued in 1922.
2. All the minor variants of *By Pike and Dyke* in the series are grouped together under this 'generic' heading, *43.4.

43.5

By Pike and Dyke | A Tale of the Rise of the Dutch Republic | BY | G.A. HENTY | Author of "The Lion of St. Mark" "Bonnie Prince Charlie" "With Clive | in India" "With Lee in Virginia" "The Cat of Bubastes" &c. | Illustrated | BLACKIE & SON LIMITED | LONDON AND GLASGOW

Contents

180 x 121 mm. (1)–384 | no catalogue. Four full-page pen-drawings by Maynard Brown, as in *43.4. Two plans and one map printed in black line on text pages.

(Frontispiece, tipped in) | (1) title p. | (2) Blackie addresses, and printer's imprint (Printed in Great Britain by Blackie & Son, Ltd., Glasgow) | 3–4. Preface | (5) Contents | (6) list of Illustrations | (7) two plans | (8) map | 9–384. text.

Binding: As for 43.3, except (a) grey-blue linen-grained cloth boards, blocked black and orange; edges plain; plain off-white endpapers; (b) all blocking black except framed panels behind figures, solid orange; (c) spine lettering now: BY PIKE | AND | DYKE | G.A. HENTY (at head), BLACKIE & SON LD (at foot); (c) spine illustration trimmed and re-drawn; framed panel behind figure now rectangular.

Reference: PN.

Notes

1. This is the only title I have found in this format, later than 'The New Popular Henty' series, with pictorial blocking on front board and spine, but with four plates in black-and-white only. The colour plate in *43.4 is omitted: the black-and-white plate previously facing p.216 is listed on p.(6) in its place as frontispiece.
2. The prelims are re-set in a different typeface, with no half-title p., but include the plans and smaller map. The earlier, double-page, map is omitted.
3. Bombay is dropped from the title-page imprint, but both Bombay and Toronto are included in the addresses on p.(2).
4. The spine brasses have been completely remade since *43.4.

44. ONE OF THE 28TH

44.1

ONE OF THE 28TH | A TALE OF WATERLOO. | BY | G.A. HENTY, | Author of "The Lion of St. Mark;" "The Cat of Bubastes;" "For Name and Fame;" | "A Final Reckoning;" "Orange and Green;" &c. | WITH EIGHT FULL-PAGE ILLUSTRATIONS BY W.H.OVEREND, | AND TWO MAPS. | (publisher's device) | LONDON: | BLACKIE & SON, 49 & 50 OLD BAILEY, E.C. | GLASGOW, EDINBURGH, AND DUBLIN. | 1890.

Contents

187 x 124 mm. (i)–(viii) | (9)–352 | catalogue (1)–32. Eight full-page wood-engravings by W.H. Overend, printed in black on coated paper; one map and one plan, both printed in black from line blocks on uncoated paper; all unbacked, unfolioed, tipped in.

(i) Half-title p. | (2) advertisement (MR. HENTY'S HISTORICAL TALES.)

listing 19 titles | (frontispiece, tipped in) | (iii) title p. | (iv) blank | (v)–vi. Preface | (vii) Contents | (viii) list of Illustrations | (9)–352. text | (1)–32. catalogue.

Binding (see Plate 78)
Blue cloth boards, blocked black, pink merging to bistre, blind, and gilt; all edges burnished olive-green; maroon surface-paper endpapers.
  Front board: ONE OF THE 28TH. | A TALE OF WATERLOO. (gilt) above illustration of soldier kneeling on one knee and aiming rifle (black, pink merging to bistre). At foot: BY | . G . A . HENTY . (gilt). The whole enclosed in double black rules. **Spine:** ONE | OF . THE | 28TH | (25mm. rule) | A TALE OF | WATERLOO. | (15mm. rule) (all gilt) above illustration of soldier (black, pink merging to bistre). Beneath this: G.A. HENTY. (gilt). Two black rules and one gilt at head and foot.
Back board: Three rules (thin, thick, thin) near edges of board (blind).

References: BL; Bod; PN | *Farmer*, p.52; *Dartt*, p.100, *Companion*, p.22.

Notes
1. This book was published on 8 August 1889 at five shillings. By the end of February 1890 Blackie had sold 4581 copies, and over the next eleven years they sold 10,112 more, the average annual sale for the twelve-year period being 1224 copies, a high figure even by Henty's standards. In the six following years, up to the end of August 1907, a further 2351 copies were sold (average annual sale of 392 copies) and Blackie re-issued the book in their 'New and Popular Edition' (see 44.3 below). The remaining stock of 266 copies in the six-shilling edition was sold over six years.
2. *Dartt* misquotes the wording of the advertisement on p.(2).
3. This is another reversion by Blackie to illustration by wood engravings (see *For the Temple*, 35.1). Overend almost certainly engraved his own blocks.
4. As usual with Blackie novels, the earliest issues contain catalogues advertising the books for the current year, in this case those with title pages dated 1890, without quotations from press reviews.

*44.2

Reprints of the first edition were issued in the same style as 44.1, but with the date removed from the title page. The map and plan, facing pages 266 and 322, were added to the list of Illustrations on p.(viii) in all but the earliest reprints. The title-page imprint and addresses were revised when necessary, and although Blackie became a Limited Company in 1890 no change was made in the impression with that date on the title page because the book had been published the previous year. The Edinburgh address was not used after 1894; the Indian office was opened in 1901 but Bombay did not appear regularly in the Blackie imprint until 1906.
The slightly-differing issues of the book in its first-edition format are all grouped together under this 'generic' heading, *44.2.

44.3

One of the 28th | A Tale of Waterloo | BY | G.A. HENTY | Author of "The Lion of St. Mark" "The Cat of Bubastes" "For Name and Fame" | "A Final Reckoning" "Orange and Green" &c. | ILLUSTRATED BY F.A. STEWART | BLACKIE AND SON LIMITED | LONDON GLASGOW DUBLIN | BOMBAY | 1908

Contents
186 x 128 mm. (1)–352 | catalogue 1–16. Six full-page wash-drawings by F.A. Stewart reproduced by halftone blocks; one map and one plan as line blocks; all printed in black on coated paper, unbacked, unfolioed, tipped in.
    (1) Half-title p. | (2) advertisement (HENTY'S TALES OF BRITISH HISTORY) listing 38 titles | (frontispiece, tipped in) | (3) title p. | (4) blank | 5. Preface | vi. [roman numerals in error] Preface, continued | 7. Contents | 8. list of Illustrations (including map and plan) | 9–352. text | 1–16. catalogue.

Binding (see Note 1)
Red cloth boards, blocked black, brown, warm buff, and gilt; all edges stained olive-green; grey endpapers, lined off-white.
    Front board: ONE OF THE 28th | A TALE OF WATERLOO. | G.A. HENTY (all gilt) above illustration of British soldier with exploding grenade behind (black, brown, warm buff). **Spine:** ONE | OF THE | 28th | G.A. HENTY (all gilt) above illustration of figure with lantern (black, brown, warm buff). At foot: BLACKIE & SON LTD (black). **Back board:** plain.

References: BL; Bod.

Notes
1. Reissued 1907 (title-page date 1908) in the 'New and Popular Edition', see *Facing Death*, 10.6, Notes 2–3. Examples of the series binding style are at Plates 172–173..
2. In this edition Blackie sold 2721 copies by the end of August 1808, and 5708 more over the following nine years up to 1917, when their records cease. The average annual sale over the ten-year period was 843 copies. The grand total of copies sold, at 6s. and at 3s.6d., from 1889 to 1917, is 25,739.

*44.4
One of the 28th | A Tale of Waterloo | BY | G.A. HENTY | Author of "The Lion of St. Mark" "The Cat of Bubastes" "For Name and Fame" | "A Final Reckoning" "Orange and Green" &c. | ILLUSTRATED | BLACKIE AND SON LIMITED | LONDON GLASGOW AND BOMBAY

Contents
184 x 122 mm. (1)–352 | no catalogue. Frontispiece from watercolour drawing reproduced by three-colour halftone blocks; four full-page wash drawings reproduced by halftone blocks printed in black; all by F.A. Stewart; one map and one plan, printed from line blocks; all on coated paper, unbacked, tipped in.
    (1) Half-title p. | (2) advertisement (G.A. HENTY'S BOOKS) listing 45 titles | (frontispiece, tipped in) | (3) title p. | (4) blank | 5. Preface | vi. [roman numerals in error] Preface, continued | (7) Contents | (8) list of Illustrations | 9–352. text, with printer's imprint at foot of p.352 (PRINTED IN GREAT BRITAIN | By Blackie & Son, Limited, Glasgow).

Binding: As for 44.3, except (a) red cloth boards, blocked black, brown, and buff, with no gilt: imprint on spine black, all other lettering buff; (b) edges plain; (c) plain off-white endpapers.

Reference: PN.

Notes

1. For notes on Blackie's second cheaper series, 'The New Popular Henty', and subsequent editions of this book, see *Facing Death*, 10.7, Notes 1–3 and 6–8. Examples of the series binding style are at Plates 174–175.

2. All the minor variants of *One of the 28th* in the series are grouped together under this 'generic' heading, *44.4.

45. WITH LEE IN VIRGINIA

45.1

WITH LEE IN VIRGINIA: | A STORY OF THE AMERICAN CIVIL WAR. | BY | G.A. HENTY, | Author of "With Clive in India;" "With Wolfe in Canada;" "The Lion of St. Mark;" | "Bonnie Prince Charlie;" "The Cat of Bubastes;" &c. | (3-em rule) | ILLUSTRATED BY GORDON BROWNE. | (3-em rule) | (publisher's device) | LONDON: | BLACKIE & SON; 49 & 50 OLD BAILEY, E.C. | GLASGOW, EDINBURGH, AND DUBLIN. | 1890.

Contents

186 x 131 mm. (i)–(viii) | (9)–384 | catalogue (1)–32. Ten full-page line-and-wash drawings by Gordon Browne, reproduced by two-colour line blocks with mechanical and hand-worked tints for second colour (sepia), printed on coated paper; map of Virginia as double-page spread printed in black on uncoated paper and guarded in after p.92; one full-page map and two pairs of battle-plans printed in black on uncoated paper; all unbacked and tipped in.

(i) Half-title p. | (2) advertisement (MR. HENTY'S HISTORICAL TALES.) listing 19 titles | (frontispiece, tipped in) | (iii) title p. | (iv) blank | (v)–vi. Preface | (vii) Contents | (viii) list of Illustrations | (9)–384. text | (1)–32. catalogue.

Binding (see Plate 94)

Light-brown cloth boards, bevelled, blocked in black, dark-brown, blind, and gilt; all edges burnished olive-green; maroon surface-paper endpapers.

Front board: With | (dot and rules) LEE (rules and dot) | in | VIRGINIA. | G.A. Henty. (all gilt), beneath illustration of Confederate soldiers (black, dark-brown, and gilt); the whole framed by black rules. **Spine:** With | Lee | in | Virginia. (cloth-colour) out of decorated solid gilt panel forming background to picture of U.S. flags (black, dark-brown, and gilt). Beneath this: G.A. Henty. (gilt script, with tail of y forming a flourish). The whole framed by black rules. **Back board:** single rule at edges of bevel (blind).

References: BL; Bod; PN | *Farmer*, p.81; *Dartt*, p.161, *Companion*, p.34.

Notes

1. The book was published on 8 August 1889 at six shillings. By the end of February 1890 Blackie had sold 4057 copies: the highest figure so far for any of Henty's books in the first year of publication. Over the next fourteen years, to the end of August 1904, they sold 5880 more, the average annual sale over the fifteen-year period being 663 copies, so the initial impetus was not maintained. It is perhaps surprising that Blackie did not put the book into their cheap edition in the 1900s: they persevered at the six-shilling price, and had sold another 1715 copies by the end of August 1917 when their records cease. The total number of books sold between publication date and 1917 is 11,652: disappointing after such a good start.

2. *Dartt* is confused about the inclusion of the maps and battle-plans in the list of Illustrations on p.(viii), and appears still to be so in his *Companion*. In 45.1 only the ten Gordon Browne illustrations are listed. The maps and plans were added to the list when the book was reprinted.

3. Gordon Browne continued to experiment with tints for his illustrations, here appearing to use a combination of mechanical and hand-drawn effects, with some hand engraving on the blocks themselves (see Appendix IV, Part 2).

4. As usual with Blackie novels, the earliest issues contain catalogues advertising the books for the current year (in this case those with title pages dated 1890) without quotations from press reviews.

5. In an interview with James Barr in 1898 Henty was asked whether he had written of American history. He replied: 'Twice only, and both times I took the unpopular side, for I write only as I believe; and . . . my sympathies are entirely with the Loyalists and confederates in their struggles . . . *With Lee in Virginia* sold very largely in the South, and I received many flattering letters from Dixie land in reference to the tale' (James Barr, *The Golden Penny*).

6. Gerald Duin of California reports an alternative Preface by Henty, which is in the 1890 Scribner & Welford edition, but not in any other US editions he has examined. Although it does not properly belong in this bibliography I believe it will be of interest to British readers:

Preface: To my Readers beyond the Atlantic:

My Dear Lads,

The Great Civil War which your fathers fought to the bitter end has, happily, left but few traces in the life of your generation. The generous treatment of the vanquished by the victors, the entire absence of any persecuting spirit, enabled the wounds to heal rapidly, and the divided parts have again grown strongly together. No doubt you have all fixed convictions as to which side was in the right, but this is only natural, for in England we are still almost as divided as we were in the days of Cromwell, as to the rights and wrongs of our own Civil War a couple of hundred years ago.

I have written this story from the Confederate point of view, but I have drawn the facts most carefully from the official dispatches and writings on both sides, and when these differed have relied upon the reports of the English officers who were attached to the headquarters of both armies, and who viewed events from a military point of view only, and without any bias towards one party or the other. I have also been assisted personally by an American friend, who has given me material aid as to facts, places, and positions.

All the brave deeds, whether done on one side or the other, are, now that you are one people again, your common inheritance, and you have as much right to be proud of such great commanders and noble men as Grant, Sherman, Lee, and Jackson, and of the brave men who fought under them, as you have to share in the glory won by your ancestors and ours in the marvellous victories of Cressy, Poitiers and Agincourt.

Yours sincerely, G.A.Henty.

*45.2

Reprints of the first edition were issued in the style of 45.1, with the date removed from the title page. Alterations were made when necessary to the title-page imprint and addresses. The fact that Blackie became a Limited Company in 1890 is now shown (it was not shown on the 45.1 title page, although dated 1890, because publication was in fact in 1889). The address is now shortened to '49 Old Bailey', perhaps in order to give an aesthetically more pleasing shorter line. In other books the address was shortened to '50 Old Bailey', but I have been unable to find any reason for these variations. Edinburgh was not included in the imprint after 1894; an Indian office was opened in 1901 but Bombay did not appear regularly in the imprint until 1906. Dublin was removed from the addresses after 1910.

The illustrations were later printed in a single colour only, the detail of the second-colour tints being transferred to the black plates (see Appendix IV, Part 1). Bindings still showed variation in colours of cloth, blocking, and endpapers.

There are more variants than of some titles as the book continued in the six-shilling edition for 29 years and was not re-issued in the 'New and Popular Edition'. All the variant issues in the first-edition format are grouped together under this 'generic' heading, *45.2.

*45.3

With Lee in Virginia | A Story of the American Civil War | BY | G.A. HENTY | Author of "With Clive in India" "With Wolfe in Canada" | "The Lion of St. Mark" "Bonnie Prince Charlie" | "The Cat of Bubastes" &c. | Illustrated by Gordon Browne | BLACKIE & SON LIMITED | LONDON AND GLASGOW

Contents
184 x 125 mm. (1)–384 | no catalogue. Frontispiece from watercolour drawing by Gordon Browne, reproduced by three-colour halftone blocks; four full-page pen-drawings by Gordon Browne; one double-spread map, one full-page map, and four half-page plans, all reproduced by line blocks printed in black; all on coated paper, unbacked, keyed to text pages, tipped in.

(1) Half-title p. | (2) Blackie addresses | (frontispiece, tipped in) | (3) title p. | (iv) printer's imprint (Printed in Great Britain by | Blackie & Son, Limited, Glasgow) | 5–6. Preface | 7. Contents | (8) list of Illustrations | 9–384. text.

Binding
Blue cloth boards, blocked black, dark-brown, light-orange; edges plain; plain off-white endpapers.

Front board: WITH LEE IN | VIRGINIA | G.A. HENTY. (light-orange), above illustration of Confederate soldier in wide-brimmed hat, with pistol (black, dark-brown, light-orange). **Spine:** WITH | LEE IN | VIRGINIA | G.A. HENTY (black) above illustration of soldier with sword and rifle (black, dark-brown, light-orange). At foot: BLACKIE & SON LTD. (black). **Back board:** plain.

Reference: PN.

Notes

1. For notes on Blackie's second cheaper series, 'The New Popular Henty', and subsequent editions of this book, see *Facing Death*, 10.7, Notes 1–3 and 6–8. Examples of the series binding style are at Plates 174–175.

2. All the minor variants of *With Lee in Virginia* in the series are grouped together under this 'generic' heading, *45.3.

46. A HIDDEN FOE

46.1

A HIDDEN FOE I BY I G.A. HENTY I AUTHOR OF "THE CURSE OF CARNE'S HOLD," "GABRIEL ALLEN," I "ALL BUT LOST," ETC. I IN TWO VOLUMES. I VOL.I. (VOL.II.) I LONDON: I SAMPSON LOW, MARSTON, AND COMPANY, I LIMITED, I St. Dunstan's House, I FETTER LANE, FLEET STREET, E.C. I 1891. I [All rights reserved.]
(Note: St. Dunstan's House *is in gothic type).*

Contents, Volume I

190 x 125 mm. (i)–(iv) I (1)–296 I no catalogue. No illustrations.

(i) Half-title p. I (ii) blank I (iii) title p. I (iv) printer's imprint (LONDON: PRINTED BY WILLIAM CLOWES AND SONS, LIMITED, I STAMFORD STREET AND CHARING CROSS.) I (1)–293. text, with 'END OF VOL.I.' on p.293, above printer's imprint (LONDON: PRINTED BY WILLIAM CLOWES AND SONS, LIMITED I STAMFORD STREET AND CHARING CROSS.) I (294)–(296) blank.

Volume II

190 x 125 mm. (i)–(iv) I (1)–304 I no catalogue. No illustrations.

(i) Half-title p. I (ii) blank I (iii) title p. I (iv) printer's imprint, as in Vol.I. I (1)–301. text, with 'THE END.' on p.301, above printer's imprint, as on p.293 of Vol.I. I (302)–(304) blank.

Binding (see Plate 4)

Dark-blue cloth boards, blocked gilt; edges uncut; yellow surface-paper endpapers.

Front board: A HIDDEN FOE I (decorative rule) I G.A. HENTY. (gilt). **Spine:** A I HIDDEN I FOE I (17mm. rule) I G.A. Henty I VOL.I. (VOL.II.) I LONDON I SAMPSON LOW & Co. (all gilt). **Back board:** plain.

References: BL; Bod.

Notes

1. Henty signed a contract on 21 January 1891 with Edward Marston 'as agent for and on behalf of Sampson Low, Marston, Searle and Rivington, Limited', for the publication, distribution, translation, and other rights. Sampson Low were to pay Henty 'sixty pounds on account of the two-volume edition: a royalty of ten per cent on the published price of the six-shilling edition; and a royalty of ten per cent on the net proceeds of popular editions' (see Appendix VI).

2. Unfortunately Sampson Low's archive survives only in fragments, and there are few records relating to Henty's work. But see Appendix II, Part 3, in connection with the unusual circumstances of the publication of this book, by a firm that had not dealt with Henty for eight years. It is unlikely that more than a few hundreds of copies of *A Hidden Foe* appeared in this two-volume edition, a format in any case not popular with the circulating libraries. There is no evidence of a reprint, and there was a long interval before the appearance of a single-volume edition (see 46.2).

46.2

A HIDDEN FOE I A NOVEL I BY I G.A. HENTY I AUTHOR OF "THE CURSE OF CARNE'S HOLD," "GABRIEL ALLEN," I "ALL BUT LOST," ETC. I WITH SIX ILLUSTRATIONS BY PERCY F.S. SPENCE I LONDON I SAMPSON LOW, MARSTON & COMPANY I LIMITED I St. Dunstan's House I 1901
(Note: St. Dunstan's House *is in gothic type).*

Contents
186 x 124 mm. (i)–(iv) I (1)–316 I no catalogue. Six full-page wash drawings by Percy F.S. Spence, reproduced by halftone blocks printed in black on coated paper, unbacked, unfolioed but keyed to text pages, tipped in.

(i) Half-title p. I (ii) blank I (frontispiece, tipped in) I (iii) title p. I (iv) List of Illustrations I (1)–316. text, with printer's imprint on p.316 (LONDON: PRINTED BY WILLIAM CLOWES AND SONS, LIMITED, I STAMFORD STREET AND CHARING CROSS.)

Binding (see Plate 17)
Light-turquoise cloth boards, blocked black, grey, white, and gilt; top edge gilt; plain off-white endpapers.

Front board: A HIDDEN I FOE I G.A. HENTY (all white, cased black) above illustration of two sailing ships colliding in heavy seas (black, grey, white), the whole framed by black rules. **Spine:** A I HIDDEN I FOE I G.A. I HENTY I SAMPSON LOW & Co. (all gilt). **Back board:** plain.

References: BL; Bod; PN I *Farmer*, p.38; *Dartt*, p.73, Note 2.

Notes
1. This is the first single-volume edition, referred to in Henty's contract (see 46.1, Note 1) as the 'six-shilling edition' on which he was to be paid royalties at ten per cent of the published price. Henty had to wait ten years for it to follow the two-volume edition, and it also followed a prevalent pattern in his adult novels in being re-issued with illustrations and apparently aimed at a juvenile market, although the words 'A NOVEL' remain on the title page. Certainly Henty would have asked Sampson Low to include them as he had for a time been worried about contravening the terms of his contract for boys' books with Blackie (see Appendix II, Part 3, Note 43). He had made similar requests to Chatto & Windus (see *Rujub, the Juggler*, 56.3, Note 3, and *Colonel Thorndyke's Secret*, 79.1, Note 6).
2. The white ink used on the front board is unusually tenacious and solid. White blocking on cloth rarely stays in place for long, tending to crack and flake.
3. The gilt top, on the other hand, is not of the best quality. The fault results from the publisher's over-optimism in having it applied to the edges of a bulky, featherweight antique wove.

46.3

Title page: As for 46.2, but last two lines (St. Dunstan's House I 1901) omitted.

Contents: 192 x 128 mm. Otherwise as for 46.2, except (a) p.(ii) printer's imprint (Printed by I REA & INCHBOULD, 224, Blackfriars Road, I London, S.E.); (b) printer's imprint at foot of p.316 (LONDON: REA & INCHBOULD, 224, BLACKFRIARS ROAD, S.E.).

Binding (see Plate 17)
Red, horizontally-grained cloth boards, blocked blind, and gilt; edges plain; plain off-white endpapers.
    Front board: A HIDDEN I FOE (blind) to right of art-nouveau scroll, with, in rectangular panel: G.A. HENTY (all blind). The whole framed by single rules. (blind). **Spine:** Elaborate art-nouveau blind and gilt design, with: A I HIDDEN I FOE (gilt) in gilt ruled panel within gilt decoration. Beneath this: G.A. HENTY (gilt) in blind rectangle within blind decoration. In gilt decorated panel at foot: SAMPSON LOW I MARSTON & CO. (gilt). **Back board:** plain.

Reference: PN.

Notes
1. The binding case is a 'binder's blank': this is the earliest issue I have found of the cheap 'popular editions' referred to in Henty's contract (see 46.1, Note 1).
2. Sampson Low had stereos of the type sent to Rea & Inchbould, who were cheaper than William Clowes and some other printers, just as they did between 1910 and 1920 for *The Cornet of Horse*, 8.4; *Winning his Spurs*, 11.4; and *Jack Archer*, 14.7.
3. The paper is lighter in weight but gives a larger page size than that for 46.2.

46.4

Title page: As for 46.3, but the second line (A NOVEL) omitted.

Contents: As for 46.3.

Binding (see Plate 17)
Green cloth boards, blocked black, grey, bluish-white merging to deep-green, and gilt; edges plain; plain off-white endpapers.
    Front board: A HIDDEN I FOE I . G . A . HENTY (all black) above illustration, framed by black rule, of two sailing ships colliding in heavy seas (black, grey, bluish-white merging to deep-green). Beneath this: AUTHORISED COPYRIGHT I EDITION (black). **Spine:** A I HIDDEN I FOE (gilt) above semi-abstract decoration with moon, stars, earth, birds flying (all gilt). At centre of this: . G . A . I HENTY (gilt). At foot: SAMPSON LOW & Co. (gilt). **Back board:** plain.

Reference: PN.

Notes
1. A second cheap issue, of sheets from the first Rea & Inchbould impression, but with the prelims, pp.(i)–(iv), reprinted.
2. The words 'A NOVEL' have been removed from the title page, and the book seems now to be marketed quite explicitly for boys rather than adults (see 46.2, Note 1). The reversion to a pictorial binding, following 46.3, tends to confirm that view.

3. Such a policy was followed by several publishers of Henty's adult novels. Here, combined with the use of various cheap binding styles, it may well indicate that Sampson Low had a struggle to dispose of the second single-volume impression.

4. The words 'AUTHORISED COPYRIGHT EDITION' are blocked on the front board of the binding case, crudely and not well aligned, just as they were for the other titles (see *The Cornet of Horse*, 8.4, Notes 4 and 5).

5. The front-board lettering is blocked with a hotch-potch of brasses from other books and from 46.2. The title is blocked in black from the brass used for the white working on 46.2, with that for the original black casing omitted. The illustration is from a cut-down electro of brasses used for 46.2, now blocked in alternative colours. The spine, too, is from brasses used for Henty's other books, with lettering-pieces borrowed from 46.2 and elsewhere.

46.5

Title page, Contents: As for 46.4.

Binding
Blue cloth boards, blocked black, grey, bluish-white merging to deep blue-green; edges plain; plain off-white endpapers.

Front board: A HIDDEN | FOE (black) above illustration, framed by black rule, of two sailing ships colliding in heavy seas (black, grey, bluish-white merging to deep blue-green). Beneath this: . G . A . HENTY (black). **Spine:** A | HIDDEN | FOE (black) above semi-abstract decoration with moon, stars, earth, birds flying ((bluish-white merging to deep blue-green). At foot: SAMPSON LOW & Co. (black). **Back board:** plain.

References: TC; PN.

Notes
1. A further issue of the Rea & Inchbould sheets, with the binding case produced more economically by the use of a cheaper cloth and the omission of gold.

2. The words 'AUTHORISED COPYRIGHT EDITION' are also omitted, and the author's name now blocked below the illustration on the front board. My copy has the word 'LTD.' in the imprint blocked on the spine, the first time it has appeared thus on any binding of this title, in spite of the word being used on the title pages of all editions. This copy also has a school-prize inscription dated 1920.

46.6

Title page: As for 46.4, except (a) type has been reset; (b) publisher's imprint now reads: LONDON | SAMPSON LOW, MARSTON & CO., LTD.

Contents: 183 x 123 mm. As 46.4, but the type is reset for the preliminary pages.

Binding (see Note 1)
Red cloth boards, blocked black; edges plain; plain off-white endpapers.

Front board: A HIDDEN | FOE | G.A. HENTY (black) within ruled rectangular panel beneath illustration of sailing ships in sea battle, with boats, all contained in larger ruled rectangle (black). **Spine:** A | HIDDEN | FOE (black) between two black rules, above illustration of ships, in upper half of tall narrow panel, with: G.A. | HENTY (black) and four small black ornaments in lower half. At foot: SAMPSON LOW (black) between two black rules. **Back board:** plain.

Reference: AK.

Notes

1. By the mid-1920s 'Sampson Low's New Series' included their three Henty novels for boys (*The Cornet of Horse*, 8.5, *Winning his Spurs*, 11.8, see Plate 50, and *Jack Archer*, 14.9), as well as this title, all at 2s.6d. The publisher's address was then 100 Southwark Street, London, S.E., although it is not given in this book.

2. The text paper is a featherweight very similar to that used for 46.3, 46.4, and 46.5, but the plates have had to be reimposed for the smaller page-size, and the quality of machining is crisper.

3. The preliminary pages (only) have been reset, in a slightly different typeface.

47. BY ENGLAND'S AID

47.1

BY ENGLAND'S AID: | OR, | THE FREEING OF THE NETHERLANDS. | (1585–1604). | BY | G.A. HENTY, | Author of "By Pike and Dyke;" "The Lion of St. Mark;" "Maori and Settler;" | "Bonnie Prince Charlie;" "For the Temple;" &c. | WITH TEN PAGE ILLUSTRATIONS   BY ALFRED PEARSE, | AND FOUR MAPS. | (publisher's device) | BLACKIE & SON, LIMITED, | LONDON, GLASGOW, EDINBURGH, AND DUBLIN. | 1891.

Contents

185 x 130 mm. (i)–(x) | (11)–384 | catalogue (1)–32. Ten full-page wash drawings by Alfred Pearse, reproduced by halftone blocks printed in black on coated paper, unbacked, unfolioed, tipped in. Three plans and one map printed from line blocks on text pages.

   (i) Half-title p. | (ii) advertisement (MR. HENTY'S HISTORICAL TALES.) listing 19 titles | (frontispiece, tipped in) | (iii) title p. | (iv) blank | (v)–vi. Preface | (vii) Contents | (viii) blank | (ix) list of Illustrations | (x) blank | (11)–384. text | (1)–32. catalogue.

Binding (see Plate 59)

Brown cloth boards, bevelled, blocked black, light-brown merging to dark-brown, blind, and gilt; all edges burnished olive-green; maroon surface-paper endpapers.

   Front board: BY ENGLAND'S | AID | OR | THE FREEING | OF THE | NETHERLANDS | (double rule) | G.A. HENTY (all gilt), with numerous flourishes, dots, and decorative symbols (gilt) within double black rules enclosing upper part only of design, and above illustration of horseman in armour flourishing sword (black, light-brown merging to dark-brown). **Spine:** BY | ENGLAND'S | AID | (ornamental rule) | . G . A . HENTY . (all gilt) in style of lettering on front board, within double black rules enclosing upper part only of design, and above illustration of helmeted man with keys and pistol standing over body of another (black, and darker tones of brown). **Back board:** single rule near edges of bevel (blind).

References: BL; Bod; PN | *Farmer*, p.16; *Dartt*, p.28.

Notes

1. This book was published on 14 June 1890 at six shillings. By the end of February

1891 Blackie had sold 4270 copies, and over the next ten years they sold 5370 more. The average annual sale over the eleven years was 876 copies. At the end of 1903 it was re-issued in the 'New and Popular Edition' (see 47.3 below). The remaining stock of 117 copies at six shillings was sold over six years.

2. This was the first of Henty's books published by Blackie as a Limited Company. In this year they used a simple style of imprint on title pages, but it was elaborated again for books dated 1892 and later. *Dartt* was probably working from a reprint in place of a first edition, and gives the details of the imprint wrongly.

3. As usual with Blackie novels, the earliest issues contain catalogues advertising the books for the current year (in this case with title pages dated 1891) without quotations from press reviews.

*47.2

Reprints of the six-shilling edition were issued in the style of 47.1, but with no date on the title page. Alterations were made when necessary to title-page imprint and addresses: the Edinburgh address was not used after 1894; the Indian office was opened in 1901 but Bombay did not appear regularly in the imprint until 1906.

Bindings continued to show variation in colours of cloth, blocking, and endpapers. The slightly-differing issues among the reprints of the book in its first-edition format are all grouped together under this 'generic' heading, *47.2.

47.3

By England's Aid | Or, The Freeing of the Netherlands, 1585–1604 | BY | G.A. HENTY | Author of "By Pike and Dyke" "The Lion of St. Mark" "Maori and Settler" | "Bonnie Prince Charlie" "For the Temple" &c. | WITH SIX PAGE ILLUSTRATIONS BY ALFRED PEARSE | AND FOUR MAPS | NEW EDITION | BLACKIE AND SON LIMITED | LONDON GLASGOW AND DUBLIN | 1904

Contents
187 x 125 mm. (1)–384 | catalogue 1–32. Six full-page wash-drawings by Alfred Pearse, reproduced by halftone blocks printed in black on coated paper, unbacked, unfolioed, tipped in. Three plans and one map printed from line blocks on text pages.

(1) Half-title p. | (2) advertisement (HISTORICAL TALES BY G.A.HENTY) listing 28 titles | (frontispiece, tipped in) | (3) title p. | (4) blank | 5. Preface | vi. [roman numerals in error] Preface, continued | 7. Contents | (8) blank | 9. list of Illustrations | (10) blank | 11–384. text | 1–32. catalogue.

Binding (see Plate 172)
Red cloth boards, blocked black, brown, buff, and gilt; edges plain; grey endpapers, lined off-white.

Front board: BY ENGLAND'S | AID | BY | G.A. HENTY. (all gilt) above illustration of two soldiers with flaming torch and two powder kegs (black, brown, buff). **Spine:** BY | ENGLAND'S AID | G.A. HENTY (gilt) above illustration of soldier with sword, descending a rope (black, brown, buff). **Back board:** plain.

Reference: MH.

Notes
1. Towards the end of 1903 Blackie re-issued the book in their cheaper 'New and Popular Edition'. For details of the series see *Facing Death*, 10.6, Notes 2–3.

2. In this edition Blackie sold 2849 copies the first year, and 7446 more in the following six years, giving an average annual sale for the seven years of 1471 copies. For the next seven years the annual average was 520 copies, and at that point, at the end of August 1917, Blackie's records come to an end. The total number of copies sold in this edition was 14,445, and the grand total of copies of the book sold in both prices, between 1890 and 1917, is 24,212.

3. Undated reprints of this title show greater variation than I have found in others. Title pages give varying numbers of illustrations by Alfred Pearse: sometimes 'WITH EIGHT PAGE ILLUSTRATIONS . . ', sometimes 'WITH TEN PAGE ILLUSTRATIONS . . '. In each case the list of Illustrations is amended accordingly, showing the page numbers and captions for the illustrations specified, and the illustrations themselves appear, tipped in at their correct positions, the largest number representing the full complement of pictures printed in 47.1.

*47.4

By England's Aid | Or, The Freeing of the Netherlands, 1585–1604 | BY | G.A. HENTY | Author of "By Pike and Dyke" "The Lion of St. Mark" "Maori and Settler" | "Bonnie Prince Charlie" "For the Temple" &c. | WITH FIVE ILLUSTRATIONS BY ALFRED PEARSE | AND FOUR MAPS | BLACKIE AND SON LIMITED | LONDON GLASGOW AND BOMBAY

Contents

184 x 124 mm. (1)–384 | no catalogue. Frontispiece from watercolour drawing reproduced by three-colour halftone blocks; four full-page wash-drawings reproduced by halftone blocks printed in black; all by Alfred Pearse; all printed on coated paper, unbacked, tipped in. Three plans and one map printed from line blocks on text pages.

(1) Half-title p. | (2) advertisement (G.A. HENTY'S BOOKS) listing 56 titles | (frontispiece, tipped in) | (3) title p. | (4) printer's imprint (Printed in Great Britain by | Blackie & Son, Limited, Glasgow) | 5. Preface | vi. [roman numerals in error] Preface, continued | 7. Contents | (8) blank | 9. list of Illustrations | (10) blank | 11–384. text.

Binding

Dark-green cloth boards, blocked black, brown, and yellow, edges plain; plain off-white endpapers.

Front board: BY ENGLAND'S | AID | BY | G.A. HENTY. (yellow) above illustration of two soldiers with flaming torch and two powder kegs (black, brown, yellow). **Spine:** BY | ENGLAND'S | AID | G.A. HENTY (yellow) above illustration of soldier with sword, descending a rope (black, brown, yellow). At foot: BLACKIE & SON LTD (black). **Back board:** plain.

References: Bod; PN.

Notes

1. For details of Blackie's second cheaper series, 'The New Popular Henty', and subsequent editions of this book, see *Facing Death*, 10.7, Notes 1–3 and 6–8. Examples of the series binding style are at Plates 174–175. This title was issued in the series in 1923.

2. Variations in presentation (see Note 1), are also found between issues of individual titles. To demonstrate this, I show below, as *47.5, a slightly later issue of this edition, where the setting of the title page, and many details of the setting and arrangement of the preliminary pages vary from the corresponding pages in *47.4. Other variations occur, and all such minor variants are grouped together under these 'generic' headings, *47.4 and *47.5.

3. See also *47.5, Note 2.

*47.5

BY ENGLAND'S AID | Or, The Freeing of the Netherlands | 1585–1604 | BY | G.A. HENTY | Author of "By Pike and Dyke" "The Lion of St. Mark" | "Maori and Settler" "Bonnie Prince Charlie" | "For the Temple" &c. | With Five Illustrations by Alfred Pearse | And Four Maps | BLACKIE & SON LIMITED | LONDON AND GLASGOW

Contents

187 x 125 mm. (1)–368 | catalogue (1)–(2). Illustrations as in *47,4.

(1) Half-title p. | (2) Blackie addresses (in London, Glasgow, Bombay and Toronto) | (frontispiece, tipped in) | (3) title p. | (4) printer's imprint (Printed in Great Britain by Blackie & Son, Ltd., Glasgow) | 5–6. Preface | (7) Contents | (8) blank | (9) list of Illustrations | (10) blank | 11–367. text | (368) blank | (1)–(2) catalogue (THE NEW POPULAR HENTY) listing 64 titles.

Binding: As for *47.4, but blue cloth boards.

Reference: AK.

Notes

1. See *47.4, Notes 1 and 2; the several variants occurring within this edition are grouped together under *47.4 and *47.5.

2. The considerable differences between the two versions of this book within 'The New Popular Henty' series include the complete re-setting of the text, and this copy makes sixteen less pages than *47.4. The two-page advertisement at the end is a single tipped-on leaf.

48. A CHAPTER OF ADVENTURES

48.1

A CHAPTER OF ADVENTURES: | OR, | THROUGH THE BOMBARDMENT OF ALEXANDRIA. | BY | G.A. HENTY, | Author of "By Pike and Dyke;" "The Lion of St. Mark;" "The Cat of Bubastes;" | "Bonnie Prince Charlie;" "By England's Aid;" &c. | WITH SIX FULL-PAGE ILLUSTRATIONS BY | W.H. OVEREND. | (publisher's device) | BLACKIE & SON, LIMITED, | LONDON, GLASGOW, EDINBURGH, AND DUBLIN. | 1891.

Contents

186 x 124 mm. (i)–(viii) | (9)–288 | catalogue (1)–32. Six full-page wood engravings by W.H. Overend, printed in black on coated paper, unbacked, unfolioed, tipped in.

(i) Half-title p. | (ii) advertisement (MR. HENTY'S HISTORICAL TALES.)

listing 19 titles I (frontispiece, tipped in) I (iii) title p. I (iv) blank I (v) Contents I (vi) blank I (vii) list of Illustrations I (viii) blank I (9)–288. text I (1)–32. catalogue.

Binding (see Plate 102)
Blue cloth boards, blocked black, buff, metallic bronze, and blind; edges plain; maroon surface-paper endpapers.
   Front board: A I CHAPTER OF ADVENTURES. (buff, cased black) out of solid bronze sky in illustration of small boat, with two figures, tossed in the air in a cyclone (black, buff, bronze). Beneath this: – BY – I G.A. HENTY. (bronze, cased black). Two black rules at head and foot. **Spine:** – A – I CHAPTER I – OF – I ADVENTURES. (buff, cased black) out of solid bronze sky in illustration (continued from front board) of wrecked ship (black, buff, bronze). Beneath this: BY I G.A. HENTY. (bronze, cased black). Two black rules at head and foot. **Back board:** three rules (thin, thick, thin) near edges of bevel (blind).

References: BL; Bod; PN I *Farmer*, p.21; *Dartt*, p.36, *Companion*, p.9.

Notes
1. The book was published on 14 June 1890 at three shillings and sixpence. By the end of February 1891 Blackie had sold 3770 copies, and over the next 26 years they sold 16,152 more. At that point, the end of August 1917, Blackie's records cease. During the period of 27 years, the average annual sale was 738 copies, but towards the end of this time the demand had lessened: during the first sixteen years the annual sale had averaged 1022 copies.
2. As usual with books from Blackie, the earliest issues contain catalogues advertising titles for the current year (in this case those with title pages dated 1891) without quotations from press reviews.
3. It was still a period of transition in processes of illustration. By now Blackie had used the new halftone process for several books, and Gordon Browne was still experimenting with line-and-tone-tints as second colours for his pen drawings. This is the third use of wood engravings, almost the oldest of all the processes, and the second time in two years they have been by W.H. Overend (see *One of the 28th*, 44.1).

*48.2

Title page: As for 48.1, except (a) no date; (b) changed imprint (LONDON: I BLACKIE & SON, LIMITED, 49 OLD BAILEY, E.C. I GLASGOW, EDINBURGH, AND DUBLIN.).

Contents: As for 48.1, but advertisement on p.(ii) lists 22 titles.

Binding (see Plate 102)
Brown cloth boards, blocked black, yellow merging to blue, dark-brown, mauve merging to yellow; edges plain; maroon surface-paper endpapers.
   Front board: As 48.1, except that sky is yellow at top, merging to blue lower; title lettering is mauve, which turns to yellow at lowest part and for the boat; lettering at foot is dark-brown. **Spine:** As 48.1, except that colours are as on new front board. **Back board:** plain.

Reference: PN.

Notes
1. Reprints of the first edition were issued in the style of 48.1, with the date removed from the title page. The simplified form of imprint used in the books issued in 1890 (title-page date 1891) when Blackie became a Limited Company, was abandoned the following year, and a new form is shown here. Later changes included the removal of Edinburgh from the imprint after 1894; Blackie opened an Indian office in 1901 but Bombay did not regularly appear until 1906. Dublin was removed after 1910. Other variations appeared in the prelims and advertisement page.
2. Bindings showed variation in colours of cloth, blocking, and endpapers.
3. The impression described is representative of the reprints in the first-edition format: the slightly-differing issues are all grouped together under this 'generic' heading, *48.2.

48.3
BLACKIE'S CONTINUOUS READERS | (rule) | A CHAPTER | OF ADVENTURES | BY | G.A. HENTY | WITH FRONTISPIECE | LONDON | BLACKIE & SON, LIMITED, 50 OLD BAILEY, E.C. | GLASGOW AND DUBLIN | 1899

Contents
181 x 120 mm. (1)–216 | no catalogue. Frontispiece from wood engraving after W.H. Overend, printed in black on coated paper, tipped in. Three engravings of ships (two small, one full-page) reproduced by line blocks, printed on text paper.
(Frontispiece, tipped in) | (1) title p. | (2) blank | 3. Note | 4. Contents | 5–212. text | 213–216. Notes.

Binding (see Plate 103)
Red cloth boards, blocked black; edges plain; plain off-white endpapers.
Front board: BLACKIES | CONTINUOUS READERS | A CHAPTER | OF ADVENTURES | (publisher's device) | G.A. HENTY | 1/- (all black). **Spine:** BLACKIE'S | CONTINUOUS | READERS | A | CHAPTER | OF | ADVENTURES | BLACKIE & SON | LIMITED (all black). **Back board:** plain.

References: BB | *Farmer*, p.21.

Notes
1. *Farmer* reports the date, 1899, on the title page. The copies in the Copyright Libraries are reprints (see 48.4) and are undated. The only dated copy I have seen is in the collection of the Revd Basil Brown.
2. The Note on p.3 is really a salesman's blurb directed at schoolteachers, to recommend Blackie's new Continuous Readers.
3. The Notes on pp.213–216 are mainly a glossary of nautical terms and expressions, with the three pictures of ships keyed to show the names of the constituent parts of a cutter and a full-rigged ship.
4. For details of the books by Henty published as School Readers see Appendix V.

48.4
BLACKIE'S CONTINUOUS READERS | (rule) | A CHAPTER | OF | ADVENTURES | BY | G.A. HENTY | LONDON | BLACKIE & SON, LIMITED, 50 OLD BAILEY, E.C. | GLASGOW AND DUBLIN

Contents: As for 48.3, except p.(2) has advertisement (BLACKIE'S CONTINUOUS READERS.) listing 4 titles (this one being the first).

Binding: As for 48.3.

References: BL; Bod; PN.

Note: For this reprint of 48.3, the title page has been reset, with no date. A panel advertising the series of Readers has been added on p.(2).

48.5
Title page: As for 48.4.

Contents
182 x 122 mm. (1)–216 | no catalogue. Illustrations as in 48.3.
(Frontispiece, tipped in) | (1) title p. | (2) blank | (3) Contents | (4) blank | (5)–212. text | (213)–216. Notes.

Binding: As for 48.3.

Reference: PN.

Notes
1. This second reprint of 48.3 omits the advertisement on p.(2), and the list of Contents has been brought back from p.4 to replace the introductory Note that has now been removed from p.3.
2. The folio numbers have been omitted from pages 3, 4, 5, and 213.

48.6
Title page: As for 48.4.

Contents
181 x 120 mm. (1)–216 | no catalogue. Illustrations as in 48.3.
(Frontispiece, tipped in) | (1) title p. | (2) blank | 3. Note | 4. Contents | 5–212. text | 213–216. Notes.

Binding (see Plate 103)
Designed by Talwin Morris (see Appendix IV, Part 2). Mauve cloth boards, blocked black; edges plain; plain off-white endpapers.
Front board: ENGLISH AUTHORS FOR SCHOOL READING (black) | A CHAPTER OF | . ADVENTURES . | HENTY (cloth-colour reversed out of solid black rectangle) above art-nouveau floral design (black). At foot: BLACKIE . AND . SON . LIMITED . LONDON (black). The whole enclosed in double framework of ornamental black rules. **Spine:** In upper panel of black rules: A | CHAPTER | OF | ADVEN- | TURES | HENTY (black). In central panel, between thick rules: art-nouveau floral decoration (all black). In lower panel: 8d. NET (black). **Back board:** plain.

Reference: TC.

Notes

1. This issue, with features of both 48.5 and 48.7, is somewhat confusing, being described on the title page as one of 'BLACKIE'S CONTINUOUS READERS', and on the binding case as from a series called 'ENGLISH AUTHORS FOR SCHOOL READING'.

2. The title-page imprint, including DUBLIN, is not later than 1910.

48.7

A Chapter I of I Adventures I BY I G.A. HENTY I BLACKIE AND SON LIMITED I LONDON GLASGOW AND BOMBAY

Contents

181 x 121 mm. (1)–216 I no catalogue. Frontispiece from watercolour drawing (unsigned) reproduced by three-colour halftone blocks printed on coated paper, unbacked, tipped in.

(Frontispiece, tipped in) I (1) title p. I (2) blank I (3) Contents I (4) blank I (5)–212. text I 213–216. Notes.

Binding: As for 48.6.

Reference: PN.

Notes

1. That this issue is in the series 'ENGLISH AUTHORS FOR SCHOOL READING' is confirmed on the binding case (see 48.6, Note 1). I cannot date it precisely, but the omisssion of Dublin from the imprint shows it was issued after 1910.

2. A colour frontispiece has been added: the watercolour is based very closely on the Overend wood-engraving appearing as the frontispiece in 48.1.

3. In spite of the changes the price has been reduced from 1s. to 8d.

4. My copy has a small leaflet loosely inserted, which may perhaps have been added by a collector at a later date. It is headed 'ENGLISH AUTHORS AND I SCHOOLROOM FAVOURITES I FOR SCHOOL READING', and lists some 48 titles which are described as 'A collection of established favourites issued as Continuous Readers'. Among them, this title only is shown under Henty's name. Blackie's imprint on the leaflet omits Dublin from the addresses, and it is therefore post-1910. The books are advertised as 'With Frontispiece. Price 1s.2d. each'. The confusion of 'Continuous Readers' and 'English Authors for School Reading' appears, therefore, to have persisted into a later period when the price had risen from 8d. to 1s.2d.

48.8

Title page: As for 48.7.

Contents

180 x 121 mm. Catalogue (1)–2 I (1)–212. Frontispiece as in 48.7.

(1)–2. Catalogue (Blackie's Library of Famous Books) (see Note 2) I (frontispiece, tipped in) I (1) title p. I (2) blank I (3) Contents I (4) blank I (5)–212. text.

Binding (see Plate 103)
Designed by Talwin Morris (see Appendix IV, Part 2). Bright-blue cloth boards, blocked white, orange, and gilt; edges plain; plain off-white endpapers.

Front board: A CHAPTER OF ADVENTURES (gilt) above art-nouveau abstract decoration (orange and white). **Spine:** Over-all art-nouveau abstract decoration (orange and white) with, near head: A CHAPTER | OF ADVEN- | (small vertical rule) TURES (small vertical rule) (all gilt). Near foot: . BLACKIE'S . | LIBRARY OF | FAMOUS BOOKS (gilt). **Back board:** plain.

References: BL; Bod; PN.

Notes
1. The Copyright Libraries received this undated impression in 1911. My copy comes from a Library, with acquisition stamp on the title page, dated 9 November 1911.
2. At this date Blackie's 'Library of Famous Books' included this title but no other book by Henty. *Tales from Henty* was added later (see 48.10).
3. In this edition the Notes at the end of the book, being mainly a glossary of nautical terms, with illustrations of ships, added for the schoolbook editions, have been omitted.
4. The two-page catalogue at the beginning of the book is tipped on to the frontispiece, which, in turn, is tipped on to the first leaf of the first text gathering. This is a cumbersome arrangement which inevitably weakened the binding.
5. The book had an odd 8-page working when the type was reset for the Continuous Reader editions. As the Notes are now omitted it finishes with an odd 4-page section at the end: this is tipped on to the last gathering, causing another weakness where the endpapers are tipped on to the final, unsewn, text leaf.

48.9
Title page: As for 48.7.

Contents
180 x 122 mm. (1)–212 | catalogue (1)–(2) | catalogue 1–16. Four full-page unsigned watercolour drawings reproduced by three-colour halftone blocks printed on coated paper, unbacked, unfolioed, three tipped in and one guarded in.

(Frontispiece, tipped in) | (1) title p. | (2) Biographical Note | (3) Contents | (4) blank | (5)–212. text | (1)–(2) catalogue (Blackie's Crown Library) | 1–16. Blackie's general catalogue.

Binding (see Plate 104)
Blue cloth boards, blocked yellow, orange, and gilt; edges plain; plain off-white endpapers.

Front board: Over-all elaborate design of art-nouveau panels (yellow and orange) with: A CHAPTER OF | ADVENTURES (cloth-colour reversed out of solid yellow rectangle) at head. **Spine:** Similar elaborate decorative panels (yellow and orange) with: A | CHAPTER | OF ADVEN= | TURES (cloth-colour reversed out of solid gilt rectangle) at head, and: BLACKIE | AND SON | LIMITED (yellow out of orange rectangle) at foot. **Back board:** plain.

Reference: PN.

Notes

1. Three more colour plates have been added. One of them is loosely based on the illustration in 48.1 which was adapted for use on the front board of the first edition. The others are entirely original. The artist's name is not given.

2. The book still has an odd 4-page working, tipped on to the end of the last gathering. However, one of the new colour plates is guarded round the penultimate gathering (appearing between pp.192 and 193), leaving a stub following p.208, on to which the last four-page section is pasted. This odd arrangement gave the book slightly more strength.

3. The two-page catalogue following the text is a list of books in Blackie's 'Crown Library'. The books are said to be 'Selected from the World's best literature for boys and girls. Handsomely bound in cloth, 1s. each'. This book is the only one by Henty to be included although *Tales from Henty* is found in this binding style (see 57.4). Nearly all the titles appear also in the lists of Blackie's 'Library of Famous Books'. Although it might appear that one list was mainly intended for adult readers and the other for 'boys and girls', that was not so (see 48.11, Note 2).

4. This edition contains a Biographical Note about Henty on p.(2). It is very brief, but contains the erroneous information that Henty's first book for boys was published in 1868. The mistake originated in an interview given by Henty and printed in *The Captain*, April 1899, p.7. It has been repeated many times, notably in *The Dictionary of National Biography* (see *Out on the Pampas*, 4.1, Note 1).

5. A later impression is bound in dark-blue cloth: it is slightly less bulky but otherwise the same externally as described above. There are small differences internally: (a) The Biographical Note on p.(2) is omitted; (b) An additional (non-Henty) title is given at the end of the list on p.(2) of the publisher's catalogue of 'Blackie's Crown Library' immediately following the text. That list still does not include include *Tales from Henty* (see Note 2). (c) There are small alterations and additions to the bound-in 16-page catalogue.

48.10

A Chapter | of | Adventures | BY | G.A. HENTY | (publisher's device) | BLACKIE AND SON LIMITED | LONDON GLASGOW AND BOMBAY

Contents

178 x 119 mm. (1)–212 | no catalogue. Illustrations as in 48.9.

(Frontispiece, tipped in) | (1) title p. | (2) Printed and bound in Great Britain | (3) Contents | (4) List of Colour Plates | (5)–212. text, with printer's imprint at foot of p.212 (PRINTED AND BOUND IN GREAT BRITAIN | By Blackie & Son, Limited, Glasgow).

Binding (see Plate 104)

Red, linen-grained cloth boards, blocked blind and gilt; edges plain; plain off-white endpapers.

Front board: Over-all design of decorative rules and panels including roses and, at head: A CHAPTER | OF ADVEN- | TURES (all blind). **Spine:** Similar over-all blind decorations, and in panel at head: A CHAPTER | OF ADVEN- | TURES | G.A. HENTY (all gilt). At foot: BLACKIE | & SON LTD. (blind). **Back board:** plain.

Reference: PN.

Notes

1. This impression is bound in a case designed for later issues of Blackie's 'Library of Famous Books'. It appeared about 1915, and by then *Tales from Henty* was also issued in this series (see Appendix V).

2. The book was published for many years in this style, and there are variations in details of imprint, etc., such as are evident in 48.11 below.

48.11

Title page: As for 48.10.

Contents

180 x 121 mm. (1)–212 | catalogue (1)–(2). Illustrations as in 48.9.

(Frontispiece, tipped in) | (1) title p. | (2) Blackie's addresses in London, Glasgow, Bombay, and Toronto, with, at foot, printer's imprint (Printed in Great Britain by Blackie & Son, Ltd., Glasgow) | (3) Contents | (4) List of Colour Plates | (5)–212. text | (1)–(2) catalogue (Blackie's | Library of Famous Books | for Boys and Girls).

Binding: As for 48.10, but bright-red, bead-grained cloth boards.

Reference: PN.

Notes

1. This reprint of 48.10 was printed a year or two after the first world war, and the paper for text, illustrations, and endpapers, is all of much improved quality.

2. The catalogue at the end of the book is a single leaf, tipped on to the end of the final gathering. The 'Library of Famous Books' is here explicitly stated to be 'for Boys and Girls', and the books listed are from both the older catalogue and from the list of Blackie's 'Crown Library'. I do not pretend to understand the distinction between these two series (see 48.9, Note 3). This list now includes both *A Chapter of Adventures* and *Tales from Henty*.

3. The copy described here is inscribed January 1929, but could perhaps have been issued a little earlier.

49. MAORI AND SETTLER

49.1

MAORI AND SETTLER: | A STORY OF THE NEW ZEALAND WAR. | BY | G.A. HENTY, | Author of "By Pike and Dyke;" "One of the 28th;" "The Lion of St. Mark;" | "Bonnie Prince Charlie;' "By England's Aid;" &c. | WITH EIGHT FULL-PAGE ILLUSTRATIONS BY ALFRED PEARSE, | AND A MAP. | (publisher's device) | BLACKIE & SON, LIMITED, | LONDON, GLASGOW, EDINBURGH, AND DUBLIN. | 1891.

(Note: the first of the two quotation marks after Bonnie Prince Charlie *has broken off).*

Contents

186 x 123 mm. (i)–(x) | (11)–352 | catalogue (1)–32. Eight full-page wash-drawings by Alfred Pearse, reproduced by halftone blocks printed in black on coated paper; full-page map printed from line block in black on coated paper; all unbacked, unfolioed, tipped in.

(i) Half-title p. | (ii) advertisement (MR. HENTY'S HISTORICAL TALES.) listing 22 titles | (frontispiece, tipped in) | (iii) title p. | (iv) blank | (v)–vi. Preface | (vii) Contents | (viii) blank | (ix) list of Illustrations | (x) blank | (11)–352. text | (1)–32. catalogue.

Binding (see Plate 75)

Brown cloth boards, blocked black, cream merging through yellow to dark-green, blind, and gilt; all edges burnished olive-green; maroon surface-paper endpapers.
Front board: MAORI & SETTLER | A TALE OF THE | NEW ZEALAND | WAR (gilt) above illustration of boy aiming pistol over edge of a cliff (black, cream merging to yellow-green). At foot: BY | . G . A . HENTY . (gilt). All enclosed in black rules. **Spine:** MAORI | – AND – | SETTLER | (decorative rule) (gilt) above illustration of Maori advancing with club and rifle (black, and cream merging through yellow to dark-green). At foot: G.A.HENTY (gilt). All enclosed in black rules. **Back board:** double rule at edges of board (blind).

References: Bod; PN | *Farmer*, p.49; *Dartt*, p.95.

Notes

1. Publication date was 15 July 1890, the price five shillings. By the end of February 1891 Blackie had sold 3910 copies, and nineteen years later, by the end of August 1910, they had sold 7809 more. That gives an average annual sale for the twenty years of 586 copies. The book was then re-issued in Blackie's 'New and Popular Edition' (see 49.3). The stock balance of 67 copies in the six-shilling edition was sold between 1911 and 1913.
2. As usual with Blackie novels, the earliest issues contain catalogues advertising the books for the current year (in this case with title pages dated 1891) without quotations from press reviews.
3. See notes on plagiarism, Appendix I.

*49.2

Reprints of the five-shilling edition were issued in the same style as 49.1, but with the date removed from the title page. Alterations were made when necessary to the title-page imprint and addresses: the Edinburgh address was not used after 1894; the Indian office was opened in 1901, although Bombay did not appear regularly in the imprint until 1906; and Dublin was omitted after 1910.

Bindings continued to show variation in colours of cloth, blocking and endpapers.

The publisher's advertisement page, and catalogues, were constantly updated.

The slightly-differing issues among the reprints of the book in its first-edition format are all grouped together under this 'generic' heading, *49.2.

49.3

Maori and Settler | A STORY OF | THE NEW ZEALAND WAR | BY | G.A. HENTY | Author of "By Pike and Dyke" "One of the 28th" "The Lion of St. Mark" | "Bonnie Prince Charlie" "By England's Aid" &c. | ILLUSTRATED BY ALFRED PEARSE | AND A MAP | NEW EDITION | BLACKIE AND SON LIMITED | LONDON GLASGOW DUBLIN BOMBAY | 1911

Contents

187 x 127 mm. (1)–352 | catalogue 1–16. Illustrations as in 49.1, but halftones printed in sepia.

(1) Half-title p. | (2) advertisement (NEW & POPULAR EDITION OF | G.A. HENTY'S WORKS) listing 27 titles | (frontispiece, tipped in) | (3) title p. | (4) blank | 5. Preface | vi. [roman numerals in error] Preface, continued | (7) Contents | (8) blank | (9) list of Illustrations | (10) blank | 11–352. text | 1–16. catalogue.

Binding (see Note 1)

Blue cloth boards, blocked black, brown, red, and gilt; all edges stained olive-green; grey endpapers, lined off-white.

Front board: MAORI AND | SETTLER (gilt) | A TALE OF THE NEW ZEALAND WAR (black) above illustration of Maori with spears (black, brown, red). Beneath this: G.A. HENTY (red). **Spine:** MAORI | AND | SETTLER (gilt) | G.A. HENTY (black) above illustration of settler standing with axe (black, brown, red). At foot: BLACKIE & SON LTD (black). **Back board:** plain.

References: BL; Bod; PN.

Notes

1. Re-issued 1910 (title-page date 1911) in the 'New and Popular Edition'. For details see *Facing Death*, 10.6, Notes 2–3, and for examples of the series binding style see Plates 172–173.

2. In this edition Blackie sold 1898 copies by the end of August 1911, and 2044 more by the end of August 1917 when their records cease. The average annual sale over the seven years was 563 copies. The grand total of copies sold at both prices from 1890 to 1917 was 15,728.

3. Dublin was omitted from the imprint *after* 1910. It appears on the first issue of this edition because it was published during 1910, although dated 1911.

*49.4

Maori and Settler | A STORY OF | THE NEW ZEALAND WAR | BY | G.A. HENTY | Author of "Redskin and Cowboy" "In Freedom's Cause" | "Bonnie Prince Charlie" &c. | ILLUSTRATED | BLACKIE AND SON LIMITED | LONDON GLASGOW AND BOMBAY | Printed in Great Britain

Contents

186 x 124 mm. (1)–352 | no catalogue. Frontispiece from watercolour drawing reproduced by three-colour halftone blocks; four wash-drawings reproduced by halftone blocks printed in black; all by Alfred Pearse; full-page map printed in black from line block; all on coated paper, keyed to text pages, unbacked, tipped in.

(1) Half-title p. | (2) advertisement (G.A. HENTY'S BOOKS) listing 18 titles | (frontispiece, tipped in) | (3) title p. | (4) blank | 5. Preface to the Original Edition |

vi. [roman numerals in error] Preface, continued I (7) Contents I (8) blank I (9) list of Illustrations I (10) blank I 11–352. text, with printer's imprint at foot of p.352 (PRINTED AND BOUND IN GREAT BRITAIN I By Blackie & Son, Limited, Glasgow).

Binding: As for 49.3, except (a) red cloth boards, blocked black, grey, and orange, with no gilt: title and author's name on front board orange, all other lettering black; (b) edges plain; (c) plain off-white endpapers.

References: Bod; OD.

Notes
1. For notes on Blackie's second cheaper series, 'The New Popular Henty', and subsequent editions of this book, see *Facing Death*, 10.7, Notes 1–3 and 6–8. This title was issued in 1922.
2. All the minor variants of *Maori and Settler* in the series are grouped together under this 'generic' heading, *49.4.

50. BY RIGHT OF CONQUEST

50.1
BY RIGHT OF CONQUEST: I OR, WITH CORTEZ IN MEXICO. I BY I G.A. HENTY, I Author of "With Clive in India;" "The Lion of the North;" "With Lee in Virginia;" I "In Freedom's Cause;" &c. I WITH TEN PAGE ILLUSTRATIONS BY W.S. STACEY, I AND TWO MAPS. I (publisher's device) I BLACKIE & SON, LIMITED, I LONDON, GLASGOW, EDINBURGH, AND DUBLIN. I 1891.

Contents
185 x 130 mm. (i)–(x) I (11)–384 I catalogue (1)–32. Ten full-page wash-drawings by W.S. Stacey, reproduced by halftone blocks printed in black on coated paper, unbacked, unfolioed, tipped in. Two maps printed from line blocks on text pages.
    (i) Half-title p. I (ii) advertisement (MR. HENTY'S HISTORICAL TALES.) listing 22 titles I (frontispiece, tipped in) I (iii) title p. I (iv) blank I (v)–vi. Preface I (vii) Contents I (viii) blank I (ix) list of Illustrations I (x) Map I (11)–384. text I (1)–32. catalogue.

Binding (see Plate 60)
Grey-green cloth boards, bevelled, blocked black, cream, brown, blind, and gilt; all edges burnished olive-green; dark-blue surface-paper endpapers.
    Front board: BY RIGHT OF CONQUEST I OR I WITH CORTEZ I IN I MEXICO. (black) above illustration of Montezuma under fire from arrows (black, cream, brown, and gilt). At foot: By I G.A. HENTY. (black). **Spine:** BY RIGHT I – . OF . – I CONQUEST. (gilt) above illustration of Spanish soldier in armour (black, cream, brown). At foot: G.A. HENTY (gilt). Gilt rule at head and foot. **Back board:** single rule near edges of bevel (blind).

References: BL; Bod; PN I *Farmer*, p.17; *Dartt*, p.30, *Companion*, p.6.

Notes

1. The book was published on 3 October 1890 at six shillings. By the end of February 1891 Blackie had sold 3780 copies, and eleven years later, at the end of August 1902, they had sold 4732 more. That gives an average annual sale for the twelve years of 709 copies. The annual rate of sales fell during the next seven years to an average of 198 copies, the total sales up to the end of August 1909 being 9901. The book was then re-issued in Blackie's 'New and Popular Edition' (see 50.3 below). The remaining stock of 65 copies of the six-shilling edition was sold over five years.

2. As usual with Blackie novels, the earliest issues contain catalogues advertising the books for the current year (in this case with title pages dated 1891) without quotations from press reviews.

*50. 2

Reprints of the six-shilling edition were issued in the same style as 50.1, but with the date removed from the title page. Changes were made when necessary to the title-page imprint and addresses: the Edinburgh office was not used after 1894; the Indian office was opened in 1901 although Bombay did not appear regularly in the imprint until 1906; and Dublin was omitted after 1910.

Bindings continued to show variation in colours of cloth, blocking, and endpapers. The slightly-varying issues of this title in its first-edition format are all grouped together under this 'generic' heading, *50.2.

50.3

By Right of Conquest | OR | With Cortez in Mexico | BY | G.A. HENTY | Author of "With Clive in India" "The Lion of the North" "With Lee in Virginia" | "With Roberts to Pretoria" "The Dash for Khartoum" &c. | ILLUSTRATED BY W.S. STACEY | NEW EDITION | BLACKIE AND SON LIMITED | LONDON GLASGOW DUBLIN BOMBAY | 1910

Contents

186 x 126 mm. (1)–384 | catalogue 1–16. Illustrations as in 50.1, but halftones printed in sepia.

(1) Half-title p. | (2) advertisement (NEW AND POPULAR EDITION OF | G.A. HENTY'S WORKS) listing 27 titles | (frontispiece, tipped in) | (3) title p. | (4) blank | 5. Preface | vi. [roman numerals in error] Preface, continued | 7. Contents | (8) blank | 9–384. text | 1–16. catalogue.

Binding (see Plate 172)

Green cloth boards, blocked black, pink, buff, and gilt; all edges stained olive-green; grey endpapers, lined off-white.

Front board: BY RIGHT OF | CONQUEST (gilt) | WITH CORTEZ | IN MEXICO | G.A. HENTY (buff) above illustration of armed Indian carrying headdress (black, pink, buff). **Spine:** BY RIGHT | OF | CONQUEST | G.A. HENTY (gilt) above illustration of man with dagger in his belt (black, pink, buff). At foot: BLACKIE AND SON LTD (black). **Back board:** plain.

References: BL; Bod.

Notes

1. In 1909 (title-page date 1910) Blackie re-issued *By Right of Conquest* in the 'New and Popular Edition'. For details of the series see *Facing Death*, 10.6, Notes 2–3.

2. In this edition Blackie sold 1865 copies by the end of August 1910. In the seven years before their records cease, at the end of August 1917, they sold 2539 more, the average annual sale over the eight years being 551 copies. The grand total, sold at both prices from 1890 to 1917, was 14,370 copies.

*50.4

By Right of Conquest I OR I With Cortez in Mexico I BY I G.A. HENTY I Author of "With Clive in India" "The Lion of the North" I "With Lee in Virginia" I "With Roberts to Pretoria" "The Dash for Khartoum" &c. I ILLUSTRATED BY W.S. STACEY I BLACKIE AND SON LIMITED I LONDON GLASGOW AND BOMBAY

Contents

184 x 124 mm. (1)–384 I advertisement (1)–(2). Frontispiece from watercolour drawing, reproduced by three-colour halftone blocks; four full-page wash-drawings reproduced by halftone blocks printed in black; all by W.S. Stacey; all on coated paper, unbacked, tipped in. Two maps printed from line blocks on text pages.

(1) Half-title p. I (2) advertisement (G.A. HENTY'S BOOKS) listing 56 titles I (frontispiece, tipped in) I (3) title p. I (4) printer's imprint (Printed in Great Britain by I Blackie & Son, Limited, Glasgow) I 5. Preface I vi. [roman numerals in error] Preface, continued I (7) Contents I (8) blank I (9) list of Illustrations I 10. map I 11–384. text.

Binding: As for 50.3, except (a) green cloth boards, blocked black, orange, and buff, with no gilt: imprint on spine black, all other lettering buff; (b) spine imprint reads 'BLACKIE & SON LD.'; (c) edges plain; (d) plain off-white endpapers.

Reference: PN.

Notes

1. For notes on Blackie's second cheaper series. 'The New Popular Henty', and subsequent editions of this book, see *Facing Death*, 10.7, Notes 1–3 and 6–8. Examples of the series binding style are at Plates 174–175.

2. All the minor variants of *By Right of Conquest* in the series are grouped together under this 'generic' heading, *50.4.

51. THOSE OTHER ANIMALS

51.1

THOSE OTHER ANIMALS. I BY I G.A. HENTY. I WITH PORTRAIT OF THE AUTHOR I (line drawing by Harrison Weir) I AND TWENTY-TWO ILLUSTRATIONS BY HARRISON WEIR. I LONDON: I HENRY AND CO., BOUVERIE STREET, E.C.

Contents

184 x 123 mm. (i)–viii I 1–217 I catalogue (218)–(224). Portrait photograph of

G.A.Henty reproduced by halftone block printed in black on coated paper, unbacked, tipped in as frontispiece. Twenty-two drawings by Harrison Weir reproduced by line blocks printed on text pages.

(i) Half-title p., headed: (SECOND SERIES. | THE WHITEFRIARS LIBRARY | OF WIT AND HUMOUR. | EDITED BY W.H. DAVENPORT ADAMS.) | (ii) blank | (frontispiece, tipped in) | (iii) title p. | (iv) advertisement (The Whitefriars Library of Wit | and Humour.) | (v)–vi. TO THE READER. (Preface by G.A. Henty) | (vii)–viii. Contents | 1–217. text, with printer's imprint at foot of p.217 (Printed by Hazell, Watson, and Viney, Ld., London and Aylesbury.) | (218)–(224) catalogue.

Binding (see Plate 18)
Green cloth boards, blocked white and gilt; edges plain; dark-blue surface-paper endpapers.
Front board: THE | Whitefriars Library | of Wit and Humour. (gilt) above illustration of two monks (white). Beneath this: THOSE OTHER ANIMALS | by G.A. Henty (gilt). **Spine:** THOSE | OTHER | ANIMALS | HENRY & Co. (gilt). **Back board:** plain.

References: BL; Bod; PN | *Farmer*, p.68; *Dartt*, p.135.

Notes
1. The book was published in 1891, and advertised at 3s.6d. I have been unable to find any archive or records of the publisher.
2. The Series Editor of the 'Whitefriars Library of Wit and Humour', William Henry Davenport Adams (1828–1891), also devised the project. A writer and journalist who had contributed to the *Union Jack* in 1882–83, he worked as a reader for various leading publishers including Blackie & Son. Henty had been contracted exclusively to Blackie for boys' books since 14 May 1887, but not for other work, and in a letter of 3 December (?1890), now in the collection of Terry Corrigan, he wrote 'My dear Mr Adams, I *am* tied to Blackie for boy's [*sic*] books, and to Tillotson for novels, so that practically I am not open to engagements of any kind'. This book falls into neither category: Adams may have suggested to Henty a collection of essays, to be written in the style of a few he had already published. In his introduction, 'To the Reader' on p.v, Henty wrote 'some of these essays were first presented to the world in the columns of the *Evening Standard*'.
3. The book is imposed as fourteen 16-page sections with a separate 8-page section for the prelims. The publisher's catalogue is set on the last seven pages of the final text gathering.

51.2

Those Other | Animals | By | G.A. Henty | With Illustrations by Harrison Weir | Second (publisher's device) Thousand | London H. Henry & Co. Ltd. | 93 Saint Martin's Lane W.C. | MDCCCXCVII
(Note: the above is set in a framework of double rules, forming three panels: for the title, the author and illustrator, and the publisher and his device).

Contents
182 x 123 mm. (i)–viii | 1–(218) | no catalogue. No frontispiece; other illustrations as in 51.1.

(i) Half-title p. (THE RANDOM SERIES) I (ii) advertisement (UNIFORM WITH THIS VOLUME) listing 25 titles I (iii) title p. I (iv) blank I (v)–vi. TO THE READER. (Preface by G.A. Henty) I (vii)–viii. Contents I 1–217. text, with printer's imprint at foot of p.217 (Printed by Hazell, Watson, & Viney, Ld., London and Aylesbury.) I (218) blank

Binding (see Plate 18)
Grey cloth boards, blocked brown and blue; edges plain; pale olive-grey flowered endpapers.

Front board: THE I RANDOM SERIES (brown) in panel in upper part of over-all art-nouveau design (brown and blue). **Spine:** THOSE I OTHER I ANIMALS (blue) above design similar to that on front board (brown and blue). At centre: G.A. HENTY (blue). At foot: HENRY & Co. (blue). **Back board:** plain.

References: PN I *Dartt*, p.179, *Companion*, p.39.

Notes
1. This reprint of 51.1 is printed on paper with a less-smooth texture but of a much better quality. Of the eight titles advertised in the original 'Whitefriars Library', five are now listed in this new 'Random Series'. The publisher's catalogue has been omitted, as have some of the preliminary pages (including the portrait of Henty), and the make-up of the book is now in a real muddle. It starts with a simple-fold 4-page cancel (half-title, title, etc.); then two single leaves, which are not conjugate, are both (separately) tipped on to the first 16-page gathering of text (sig.1), which begins at p.(1). There are then straightforward 16-page gatherings, up to and including sig.13, which consists of pp.193–208. The book ends in an 8-page gathering (sig.14) with a single leaf tipped on to it. All copies examined were made up in exactly the same way.
2. This sort of confusion can only be the result of some sort of rescue operation, and it is clear that the book was issued in a form in which it was not originally planned. There may have been an intention to re-issue the book in, or close to, its original form in the Whitefriars Library: it may even have been reprinted and then held back for some reason. William Davenport Adams, the original Series Editor, died in December 1891, very shortly after the publication of 51.1. The publisher moved to new premises. Without access to any records it is impossible to do more than make wild guesses at what happened.

52. THE RANCHE IN THE VALLEY

52.1
THE I RANCHE IN THE VALLEY. I BY I G.A. HENTY, I AUTHOR OF "THE PLAGUE SHIP." I LONDON: I S.P.C.K. I NORTHUMBERLAND AVENUE, W.C.; 43, QUEEN VICTORIA STREET, E.C. I BRIGHTON: 135, NORTH STREET. I NEW YORK: E.& J.B. YOUNG & CO.

Contents
210 x 140 mm. (1)–(32) I no catalogue. No illustrations.
    (1) Title p. I (2) blank I (3)–30. text, set in two columns with rule between I (31)–(32) advertisements.

Cover (see Plate 140)

Off-white paper, printed in black, red, blue and yellow; wrapped around the single gathering of text, saddle-stitched, edges cut flush.

(1) THE | RANCHE IN THE | VALLEY (blue); BY | G.A. HENTY (white) out of coloured illustration of captive watching redskins around camp fire at night. In panel beneath this: THE PENNY | LIBRARY of FICTION (red on blue), with S.P.C.K. device in circle over trophy including tomahawk.

(2) Advertisement for Edwards' 'Harlene', World-Renowned Hair Producer and Restorer, printed in black.

(3) Advertisement for Sunlight Soap, printed in black.

(4) Full-page advertisement in colour for Pears' Soap.

References: BL; Bod; BB | *Farmer*, p.57; *Dartt*, p.110.

Notes

1. The booklet was received by the Copyright Libraries in 1892. Its style and format, in the 'S.P.C.K. Penny Library of Fiction', was repeated for a number of similar stories by other authors. Henty's *The Plague Ship*, 41.1, was also published in the series, and is in a list of titles in the advertisement on p.(32).

2. The story was also printed elsewhere (see §4).

3. The advertisement on p.(32) lists 19 titles, and announces 'Three Volumes (containing Six Stories each), paper boards, 6d. each', see *S.P.C.K. Library of Fiction*, §2, 177.

52.2

THE RANCHE IN | THE VALLEY | BY | G.A. HENTY | LONDON | THE SHELDON PRESS | NORTHUMBERLAND AVENUE, W.C. | NEW YORK AND TORONTO: THE MACMILLAN CO.

Contents

185 x 122 mm. (1)–64 | no catalogue. No illustrations.

(1) Half-title p. | (2) blank | (3) title p. | (4) printer's imprint (Made and Printed in Great Britain. C. TINLING & CO., LTD., | 53, Victoria Street, Liverpool, and at London and Prescot.) | 5–64. text.

Binding (see Plate 141)

Brown paper boards (grained to imitate cloth), blocked black and brown; edges plain; plain ivory wove endpapers.

Front board: THE . RANCHE | IN . THE . VALLEY (brown) within black and brown panel decorated with tomahawks, and above illustration of kneeling red indian with carbine. Beneath this: . G . A . HENTY . (black) over brown and black decoration. **Spine:** THE RANCHE IN THE VALLEY – G.A. HENTY. (black) running from foot to head. **Back board:** plain.

References: BL; RS; PN | *Farmer*, p.58; *Dartt*, p.111.

Notes

1. The earliest issues of this new edition contained no bound-in catalogue. The copy in the Shacklock collection is inscribed and dated 'Christmas 1923'. The copy in the British Library was received in 1923. Later issues, more commonly found, contain publisher's catalogues, folioed (1)–8, and dated on the final page: the earliest date recorded, by *Dartt*, p.111, is 1 May 1924.

2. The catalogue includes, under the heading of books 'For Younger Children', both this title and *The Plague Ship*. Both are priced at one shilling.

3. *Dartt* incorrectly calls for binding in cloth boards.

52.3

THE RANCHE IN | THE VALLEY | BY | G.A. HENTY | LONDON | THE SHELDON PRESS | NORTHUMBERLAND AVENUE, W.C. | NEW YORK AND TORONTO: THE MACMILLAN CO. | Printed in Great Britain

Contents: As for 52.2, with catalogue pp.(1)–8.

Binding

Red cloth boards, blocked black; edges plain; plain ivory laid endpapers.

Details as for 52.2, except that all blocking originally in brown is now omitted, apart from the book title on the front board which now appears in black.

Reference: PN.

Notes

1. This is a late issue, with catalogue dated 1 April 1932. It varies from 52.3 in some small details, but the main difference is in the blocking of the binding case.

2. Note that having saved expense by blocking in only one colour, extra money is spent by using cloth instead of the 'Linson'-type grained paper used for 52.2. The latter was available in a number of grains, to imitate cloth, and seems to have successfully deceived both *Farmer* and *Dartt*.

53. THE DASH FOR KHARTOUM

53.1

THE | DASH FOR KHARTOUM: | A TALE OF | THE NILE EXPEDITION. | BY | G.A. HENTY, | Author of "With Clive in India;" "True to the Old Flag;" "Bonnie Prince Charlie;" | "By Sheer Pluck;" "Facing Death;" "One of the 28th;" &c. | WITH TEN PAGE ILLUSTRATIONS BY JOSEPH NASH, R.I. | AND JOHN SCHÖNBERG. | (publisher's device) | LONDON: | BLACKIE & SON, LIMITED, 49 OLD BAILEY, E.C. | GLASGOW, EDINBURGH, AND DUBLIN. | 1892.

Contents

184 x 130 mm. (i)–(x) | (11)–(384) | catalogue (1)–32. Ten full-page wood engravings after Joseph Nash and John Schönberg, printed in black on coated paper; four plans printed in black from line blocks, two to a page, on coated paper; all unbacked, unfolioed, tipped in.

(i) Half-title p. | (ii) advertisement (MR. HENTY'S HISTORICAL TALES.) listing 22 titles | (frontispiece, tipped in) | (iii) title p. | (iv) blank | (v)–vi. Preface | (vii) Contents | (viii) blank | (ix) list of Illustrations | (x) blank | (11)–382. text | (383)–(384) blank | (1)–32. catalogue.

Binding (see Plate 62)
Brown cloth boards, bevelled, blocked black, yellow, blue, blind, and gilt; all edges burnished olive-green; maroon surface-paper endpapers.

Front board: THE (yellow, cased black) DASH FOR KHARTOUM (gilt, cased black) | A TALE | OF THE NILE | EXPEDITION (black, open lettering), above illustration of soldier running and waving sword (black, yellow, blue). At foot: BY G.A. HENTY. (yellow, cased black). All framed by a single black rule. **Spine:** THE DASH | FOR | KHARTOUM (gilt) above illustration of soldier advancing with fixed bayonet (black and yellow). At foot: G A HENTY. (gilt). Gilt rule at head and foot. **Back board:** single rule near edges of bevel (blind).

References: BL; Bod; PN | *Farmer*, p.25; *Dartt*, p.46, *Companion*, p.12.

Notes
1. The book was published on 14 July 1891 at six shillings. By the end of February 1892 Blackie had sold 6465 copies, by far the greatest number of any novel so far in its first year. The book continued to sell extremely well for many years and was never re-issued in a cheaper edition up to the time Blackie's records cease in 1917. In the first ten years the average annual sale was 1775 copies; in the second ten years the average was 452 copies; and in the next six years the figure fell to 193 copies. The grand total of copies sold from 1891 to 1917, all at six shillings, was 23,432.
2. In all copies examined the plans which, according to the list of Illustrations on p.(ix), should face p.122, are tipped in to face p.118.
3. As usual with Blackie novels, the earliest issues contain catalogues advertising the books for the current year (in this case with title pages dated 1891) without quotations from press reviews. As *Dartt* reports, the British Library copy is not one of the earliest issues. This is no doubt accounted for by the enormous initial demand for the book: it probably took Blackie by surprise, and apart from having to order a quick reprint they would have been concerned more about meeting booksellers' orders than with sending free copies to the Copyright Libraries.

*53.2

Reprints of the six-shilling edition were in the style of 53.1, but with no date on the title page. Alterations were made when necessary to the title-page imprint and addresses: the Edinburgh address was not used after 1894; the Indian office was opened in 1901 although Bombay did not appear regularly in the imprint until 1906; and Dublin was omitted after 1910.
Bindings continued to show variation in colours of cloth, blocking, and endpapers. The slightly-varying issues of the book in its first-edition format are all grouped together under this 'generic' heading, *53.2.

53.3

Blackie's Colonial Library | (15-em rule) | THE | DASH FOR KHARTOUM | A TALE OF | THE NILE EXPEDITION | BY | G.A. HENTY | Author of "With Clive in India", "Wulf the Saxon", "Bonnie Prince Charlie", | "By England's Aid", "St. Bartholomew's Eve", "Condemned as a Nihilist", &c. | (publisher's device) | LONDON | BLACKIE & SON, LIMITED, 50 OLD BAILEY, E.C. | GLASGOW AND DUBLIN | (7-em rule) | This Edition is for circulation only in India | and the British Colonies
(Note: Blackie's Colonial Library *is in gothic type; the last two lines in bold).*

Contents
186 x 124 mm. (1)-384 I no catalogue. Frontispiece from wood engraving after John Schönberg, printed in black on coated paper, unbacked, tipped in.

(1) Advertisement (Blackie's Colonial Library) listing 12 titles I (2) blank I (3) half-title p. I (4) blank I (frontispiece, tipped in) I (5) title p. I (6) blank I (7) Preface I (8) blank I (9) Contents I (10) blank I (11)–382. text I (383)–(384) blank.

Binding (see Plate 54)
Designed by Talwin Morris (see Appendix IV, Part 2). Green cloth boards, blocked pale-green and gilt; edges plain; plain off-white endpapers.
Front board: BLACKIE'S COLONIAL LIBRARY I THE DASH FOR I KHARTOUM I G.A. HENTY (all pale-green) within decorative panel formed by over-all art-nouveau design (pale-green). **Spine:** Over-all design similar to that on front board (pale-green), leaving two panels with lettering. Upper panel: THE DASH FOR I KHARTOUM I (three small ornaments, placed asymmetrically) I G.A. HENTY (all gilt) in gilt ruled frame. Lower panel: BLACKIE'S I COLONIAL I LIBRARY (gilt) in gilt ruled frame. **Back board:** plain.

References: PN I Cargill Thompson: *The Boys' Dumas*, pp.3–4.

Notes
1. Only four of Henty's novels for boys are known to have been included with those by other authors in Blackie's Colonial Library (see Appendix V). A list of the first twelve titles is given on p.(1). The books are advertised as being 'In crown 8vo, with Frontispiece, in Paper Covers, also in Cloth boards'. I have not found copies of any books in the series in paper covers.
2. Further details are given under *With Clive in India*, 15.5, Notes 1–3.

*53.4
The I Dash for Khartoum I A Tale of the Nile Expedition I BY I G.A. HENTY I Author of "With Clive in India" "True to the Old Flag" I "By Sheer Pluck" "Bonnie Prince Charlie" I "Facing Death" &c. I ILLUSTRATED I BLACKIE AND SON LIMITED I LONDON GLASGOW AND BOMBAY

Contents
184 x 123 mm. (1)–(384) I no catalogue. Frontispiece from watercolour drawing by William Rainey, reproduced by three-colour halftone blocks; four full-page wood-engravings by Joseph Nash, R.I., and John Schönberg, reproduced by line plates; one map and four battle-plans from line blocks; all printed on coated paper, unbacked, unfolioed, tipped in.

(1) Half-title p. I (2) advertisement (G.A. HENTY'S BOOKS) listing 18 titles I (frontispiece, tipped in) I (3) title p. I (4) blank I (5) Preface I (6) blank I (7) Contents I (8) blank I (9) list of Illustrations I (10) blank I 11–382. text, with printer's imprint at foot of p.382 (PRINTED AND BOUND IN GREAT BRITAIN I By Blackie & Son, Limited, Glasgow) I (383)–(384) blank.

Binding (see Note 1)
Red cloth boards, blocked black, dark-grey, and yellow; edges plain; plain off-white endpapers.

Front board: THE DASH FOR | KHARTOUM | A TALE OF THE NILE EXPEDITION (black) above illustration of Arab soldier, sitting, with shield and spear, etc., (black, dark-grey, yellow). At right: G.A. HENTY (black). **Spine:** THE DASH | FOR | KHARTOUM | G.A. HENTY (black) above illustration of same Arab soldier, standing (black, dark-grey, yellow). At foot: BLACKIE & SON LTD (black). **Back board:** plain.

Reference: PN.

Notes
1. During the 1920s Blackie re-issued this title in 'The New Popular Henty' series, a title very close to the earlier 'New and Popular Edition', in which this title was not issued (see 53.1, Note 1). For details of the 1920s series and notes on subsequent editions, see *Facing Death*, 10.7, Notes 1–3 and 6–8; examples of the series binding style are at Plates 174–175.
2. All the minor variants of *The Dash for Khartoum* in this series are grouped together under this 'generic' heading, *53.4.

54. REDSKIN AND COW-BOY

54.1
REDSKIN AND COW-BOY | A TALE OF | THE WESTERN PLAINS. | BY | G.A. HENTY, | Author of "With Lee in Virginia;" "By Right of Conquest;" "Through the Fray;" | "Facing Death;" "A Final Reckoning;" &c. | WITH TWELVE PAGE ILLUSTRATIONS BY | ALFRED PEARSE. | (publisher's device) | LONDON: | BLACKIE & SON, LIMITED, 49 OLD BAILEY, E.C. | GLASGOW, EDINBURGH, AND DUBLIN. | 1892.

Contents
186 x 130 mm. (i)–(x) | (11)–384 | catalogue (1)–32. Twelve full-page wash-drawings by Alfred Pearse, reproduced by halftone blocks printed in black on coated paper, unbacked, unfolioed, tipped in.
(i) Half-title p. | (ii) advertisement (MR. HENTY'S HISTORICAL TALES.) | (frontispiece, tipped in) | (iii) title p. | (iv) blank | (v) Preface | (vi) blank | (vii) Contents | (viii) blank | (ix) list of Illustrations | (x) blank | (11)–384. text | (1)–32. catalogue.

Binding (see Plate 80)
Brown cloth boards, bevelled, blocked black, red-brown, yellow-buff, blind, and gilt; all edges burnished olive-green; dark-blue surface-paper endpapers.
Front board: REDSKIN | AND COW-BOY. (gilt) with gilt flourishes; A Tale of the | Western | Plains. (lettering black), the capital A scrolled into the rule framing three sides of the board, and: By | G A Henty. (gilt), at right of illustration of cow-boy on horse, with lasso (black, red-brown, yellow-buff). **Spine:** REDSKIN | AND | COW-BOY. | BY . G. A. HENTY. (gilt), above illustration of redskin with gun (black, red-brown, yellow-buff). Gilt rule at head and foot. **Back board:** single rule near edges of bevel (blind).

References: BL; Bod; PN | *Farmer*, p.58; *Dartt*, p.113.

Notes

1. The book was published on 14 July 1891 at six shillings. By the end of February 1892 Blackie had sold 5880 copies, and at the end of thirteen years they had sold a total of 18,143 copies, giving an average annual sale over that period of 1396 copies. During the next thirteen years, up to the end of August 1917, when Blackie's records cease, they sold 6327 more copies at an annual average of 487 copies. The grand total of copies sold, from 1891 to 1917, was 24,470, all at six shillings, for the book was not re-issued in a cheaper edition during that time.

2. As usual with Blackie novels, the earliest issues contain catalogues advertising the books for the current year (in this case with title pages dated 1892) without quotations from press reviews.

3. The intricate and skilfully organised plot of *Redskin and Cow-boy* departs from Henty's usual formula (see Appendix I). This is not a historical novel but a straightforward adventure story: it has been suggested to me that it may be the first 'Western' novel ever written.

*54.2

Reprints of the six-shilling edition were issued in the style of 54.1, with the date removed from the title page. Alterations were made when necessary to the title-page imprint and addresses: the Edinburgh address was not used after 1894; the Indian office was opened in 1901 although Bombay did not appear regularly in the Blackie imprint until 1906; and Dublin was omitted after 1910.

Bindings continued to show variation in colours of cloth, blocking, and endpapers.

This was one of Henty's most popular novels, and it was not re-issued in Blackie's first cheaper series, the 'New and Popular Edition'. The several variant reprints of the book in its first-edition format are all grouped together under this 'generic' heading, *54.2.

54.3

THE TALISMAN LIBRARY (underlined) | REDSKIN AND | COWBOY | BY | G.A. HENTY | (publisher's device) | BLACKIE AND SON LIMITED | 50 OLD BAILEY LONDON | GLASGOW AND BOMBAY | 1920

Contents

175 x 117 mm. (i)–(xii) | 1–184 | no catalogue. Frontispiece from wash-drawing by Alfred Pearse reproduced by halftone block printed in black on coated paper, unbacked, tipped in.

(i) Half-title p. | (ii) unheaded introduction to the Talisman Library | (frontispiece, tipped in) | (iii) title p. | (iv) list of titles in series, and printer's imprint (Printed in Great Britain by | Blackie & Son, Limited, Glasgow) | v–xii. Introduction | 1–175. text | (176) blank | 177–184. Notes.

Binding (see Note 3)

Brownish-grey cloth boards, blocked blue (see Note 3); edges plain; plain off-white endpapers.

Front board: REDSKIN . & | COWBOY | G.A. Henty | (publisher's trade mark for the series, including the wording: The | TALISMAN | Library of | ENGLISH |

AUTHORS) | Blackie.&.Son.Limited (all blue) within framework of decorative rules (blue). **Spine:** REDSKIN . AND . COWBOY : HENTY (blue) running from foot to head. **Back board:** plain.

References: BL; Bod; BB; BU.

Notes
1. In 1920 four of Henty's novels for boys were abridged for school use in 'The Talisman Library of English Authors'. (The Scottish publisher ignores the fact that the first two books were by Sir Walter Scott!) Two more by Henty were added in 1921 and 1922 (see 54.4, Note 2).
2. The frontispiece is from one of the illustrations in 54.1, with a new caption.
3. Books in the series (example at Plate 145) were also issued in limp cloth covers, cut flush, in the same design, and with no alteration to the contents.
4. Later impressions in both styles of binding were issued with undated title pages.

54.4
THE TALISMAN LIBRARY (underlined) | REDSKIN AND | COWBOY | BY | G.A. HENTY | (publisher's device) | BLACKIE & SON LIMITED | LONDON AND GLASGOW

Contents
172 x 118 mm. (i)–xii | 1–184 | no catalogue. Frontispiece as in 54.3.
   (i)–(ii) Introduction to the series with bold heading on p.(i): 'The Talisman Library of English Authors', and the titles in the series listed on p.(ii) | (frontispiece, tipped in) | (iii) title p. | (iv) Blackie addresses, and printer's imprint at foot (Printed in Great Britain by Blackie & Son, Ltd., Glasgow) | v–xii. Introduction | 1–175. text | (176) blank | 177–184. Notes.

Binding: As for 54.3, but grey cloth boards, and see Note 3.

Reference: BU.

Notes
1. Following the issues both dated and undated of 54.3 (see also 54.3, Note 4), the preliminary pages were reset. The main changes, apart from the title-page imprint, were the re-arrangement of the introductory notes and the list of titles in the series. Otherwise the text appears to be unaltered.
2. Two more of Henty's books were added to the series: *The Dragon and the Raven* in 1921, and *Beric the Briton* in 1922.
3. The series continued in production, both in limp cloth and in cloth boards, at least for two decades. Copies of some titles are found with the Book Production War Economy symbol on p.(iv), a measure required of British publishers during the second war (see *With Wolfe in Canada*, 27.4, Note 3).

*54.5
Redskin and Cowboy | A Tale of the Western Plains | BY | G.A. HENTY | Author of "With Lee in Virginia" "By Right of Conquest" | "Through the Fray" "Facing Death" | "A Final Reckoning" &c. | ILLUSTRATED BY ALFRED PEARSE | BLACKIE AND SON LIMITED | LONDON GLASGOW AND BOMBAY

Contents

183 x 124 mm. (1)–384 | no catalogue. Frontispiece from watercolour drawing reproduced by three-colour halftone blocks; four full-page wash-drawings reproduced by halftone blocks; all by Alfred Pearse; all printed on coated paper, unbacked, unfolioed, tipped in.

(1) Half-title p. | (2) advertisement (G.A. HENTY'S BOOKS) listing 56 titles | (frontispiece, tipped in) | (3) title p. | (4) printer's imprint (Printed in Great Britain by | Blackie & Son, Limited, Glasgow) | (5) Preface | (6) blank | (7) Contents | (8) blank | (9) list of Illustrations | (10) blank | 11–384. text.

Binding (see Note 1)

Grey-blue cloth boards, blocked black, brown, red; edges plain; plain off-white endpapers.

Front board: REDSKIN AND | COWBOY | A Tale of the Western Plains | G.A. HENTY (black) above illustration of mounted cowboy looking back over his shoulder (black. brown, red). At lower right corner, signature: J Hassall (black). **Spine:** REDSKIN | AND | COWBOY | G.A. HENTY (black) above illustration of Indian, standing, with rifle (black, brown, red). At foot: BLACKIE & SON LTD. (black). **Back board:** plain.

Reference: PN.

Notes

1. During the 1920s Blackie re-issued the book in a series called 'The New Popular Henty', a name very close to that of the series begun in 1903 ('The New and Popular Edition'), in which this title was never issued (see 54.1, Note 1). For details of the second cheaper series, and later editions, see *Facing Death*, 10.7, Notes 1–3 and 6–8; examples of the series binding style are at Plates 174–175.

2. John Hassall designed the binding in the style he had made famous for the 'New and Popular Edition'. For this series all blocking was in pigments, with no gilt.

3. All the minor variants of *Redskin and Cowboy* in the series are grouped together under this 'generic' heading, *54.5.

55. HELD FAST FOR ENGLAND

55.1

HELD FAST FOR ENGLAND | A TALE OF THE SIEGE OF GIBRALTAR | (1779–83). | BY | G.A. HENTY, | Author of "With Clive in India;" "By Right of Conquest;" "By England's Aid;" | "The Dash for Khartoum;" "One of the 28th;" "In the Reign of Terror;" &c. | ILLUSTRATED BY GORDON BROWNE. | (publisher's device) | LONDON: | BLACKIE & SON, LIMITED, 49 OLD BAILEY, E.C. | GLASGOW, EDINBURGH, AND DUBLIN. | 1892.

Contents

185 x 124 mm. (i)–(x) | (11)–352 | catalogue (1)–32. Seven full-page wash-drawings by Gordon Browne, reproduced by halftone blocks printed in black on coated paper; two views of Gibraltar engraved on wood and printed in black on one page, coated paper; all unbacked, unfolioed, tipped in. Plan of Gibraltar printed from line block on text page.

(i) Half-title p. | (ii) advertisement (MR. HENTY'S HISTORICAL TALES.) listing 22 titles | (frontispiece, tipped in) | (iii) title p. | (iv) blank | (v)–vi. Preface | (vii) Contents | (viii) blank | (ix) list of Illustrations | (x) blank | (11)–352. text | (1)–32. catalogue.

Binding (see Plate 71)
Grey cloth boards, blocked black, blue merging through green to yellow and back to green and yellow, blind, and gilt; all edges burnished olive-green; dark-blue surface-paper endpapers.
   Front board: HELD FAST | FOR ENGLAND. (gilt, cased black) | A TALE OF | THE SIEGE OF GIBRALTAR | . BY . | G A HENTY. (merging colours, blue at top, down to yellow, all cased black) above illustration of the Rock of Gibraltar (black, gilt, and yellow merging to green and back to yellow). All framed by black rule. **Spine:** HELD FAST | . FOR . | ENGLAND (all gilt, cased black) | BY | G.A. HENTY (gilt) above illustration of man with cannon (black, gilt, green merging to yellow). All framed by black rules. **Back board:** Three rules (thin, thick, thin) near edges of board (blind).

References: BL; Bod; PN | *Farmer*, p.36; *Dartt*, p.71, *Companion*, p.17.

Notes
1. Publication was on 1 August 1891 at five shillings. By the end of February 1892 Blackie had sold 5880 copies, and in the next twenty-five years they sold 14,257 more, making a total of 20,137 up to the time Blackie's records cease, at the end of August 1917. The average annual sales were, for the first eleven years, 1329 copies; for the next ten years, 441 copies, and for the last five years, 223 copies. The book was not re-issued in a cheaper edition until after the first war.
2. As usual with Blackie novels, the earliest issues contain catalogues advertising the books for the current year (in this case with title pages dated 1892) without quotations from press reviews.
3. This is the first of Henty's books to be illustrated by Gordon Browne with wash-drawings reproduced by halftone blocks.

*55.2

Reprints of the first edition were issued in the style of 55.1, with no date on the title page. Alterations were made as necessary to title-page imprint and addresses: the Edinburgh address was not used after 1894; the Indian office was opened in 1901 although Bombay did not appear regularly in the Blackie imprint until 1906; and Dublin was omitted after 1910.
Bindings continued to show variation in colours of cloth, blocking, and endpapers. The book was not re-issued in the cheaper 'New and Popular Edition'.
All the variant reprints of *Held Fast for England* in its first-edition format are grouped together under this 'generic' heading, *55.2.

*55.3

Held Fast for England | A Tale of the Siege of Gibraltar | (1779–83) | BY | G.A. HENTY | Author of "With Clive in India" "By Right of Conquest" "By England's Aid" | "The Dash for Khartoum" "One of the 28th" "In the Reign of Terror" &c. | ILLUSTRATED BY GORDON BROWNE | BLACKIE AND SON LIMITED | LONDON GLASGOW AND BOMBAY

Contents

187 x 125 mm. (i)–(x) | 11–352 | no catalogue. Frontispiece from watercolour drawing, reproduced by three-colour halftone blocks, and four full-page wash-drawings reproduced by halftone blocks printed in black, all by Gordon Browne, all on coated paper, unbacked, tipped in. Plan of Gibraltar printed from line block on text page.

(i) Half-title p. | (ii) advertisement (G.A. HENTY'S BOOKS) listing 56 titles | (frontispiece, tipped in) | (iii) title p. | (iv) publisher's imprint (Printed in Great Britain by | Blackie & Son, Limited, Glasgow) | v–vi. Preface | (vii) Contents | (viii) blank | (ix) list of Illustrations | (x) blank | 11–352. text.

Binding (see Note 1)

Grey-blue cloth boards, blocked black, dark-grey, and yellow; edges plain; plain off-white endpapers.

Front board: HELD FAST | FOR ENGLAND | A TALE OF THE SIEGE | OF GIBRALTAR | G.A. HENTY (all black) above and at left of illustration, framed by black line, of the Rock of Gibraltar (black, dark-grey, yellow). **Spine:** HELD | FAST | FOR | ENGLAND | G.A. HENTY (black) above illustration of sailor with sword (black, dark-grey, yellow). At foot: BLACKIE & SON LD. (black). **Back board:** plain.

Reference: PN.

Notes

1. During the 1920s Blackie re-issued Henty's novels in a series called 'The New Popular Henty', a name very close to that of the series begun in 1903 ('The New and Popular Edition') in which this title was never issued. For details of the second cheaper series, and later editions, see *Facing Death*, 10.7, Notes 1–3 and 6–8. Examples of 'The New Popular Henty' binding style are at Plates 174–175.

2. All the minor variants of *Held Fast for England* in the series are grouped together under this 'generic' heading, *55.3.

56. RUJUB, THE JUGGLER

56.1

RUJUB, THE JUGGLER | BY | G.A. HENTY | AUTHOR OF | "THE CURSE OF CARNE'S HOLD," "A HIDDEN FOE," ETC. | (publisher's device) | IN THREE VOLUMES | VOL.I. (VOL.II., VOL.III.) | London | CHATTO & WINDUS, PICCADILLY | 1893

(Note: London is in gothic type; quotation marks preceding THE CURSE OF . . . are missing in Volume II only).

Contents, Volume I

184 x 122 mm. (i)–(iv) | (1)–(296) | no catalogue. No illustrations.

(i) Half-title p. | (ii) advertisement (NEW NOVELS AT ALL LIBRARIES) | (iii) title p. | (iv) blank | (1)–294. text, with printer's imprint at foot of p.294 (PRINTED BY BALLANTYNE, HANSON AND CO. | EDINBURGH AND LONDON) | (295)–(296) blank.

Volume II
184 x 122 mm. (i)–(iv) | (1)–(280) | no catalogue. No illustrations.

(i) Half-title p. | (ii) advertisement, as in Vol.I. | (iii) title p. | (iv) blank | (1)–277. text, with printer's imprint at foot of p.277, as in Vol.I. but with full point following last word, LONDON. | (278)–(280) all blank.

Volume III
184 x 122 mm. (i)–(iv) | (1)–(268) | catalogue (1)–32. No illustrations.

(i) Half-title p. | (ii) advertisement, as in Vol.I. | (iii) title p. | (iv) blank | (1)–266. text, with printer's imprint at foot of p.266, as in Volume II | (267)–(268) blank | (1)–32. catalogue, dated October 1892, with printer's imprint at foot of p.32 (OGDEN, SMALE AND CO. LIMITED, PRINTERS, GREAT SAFFRON HILL, E.C.).

Binding (see Plate 5)
Blue cloth boards, blocked gilt; edges plain; yellow-sepia flowered endpapers.

Front board: Over-all repeat floral pattern in reddish gilt. **Spine:** RUJUB | THE | JUGGLER | G.A. | HENTY | VOL.I (VOL.II, VOL.III) | CHATTO & WINDUS (all gilt). **Back board:** as front board.

References: BL; Bod; BB | Chatto & Windus Archive: MS 2444/27 | *Farmer*, p.59; *Dartt*, p.114, *Companion*, p.24; *Sadleir*, I, 1189.

Notes
1. In the summer of 1892 Henty had signed an agreement with Tillotson and Sons of Bolton, making them his exclusive agent for all adult fiction. Tillotsons' business was substantial: they were owners of a group of newspapers, printers in several fields, and, by then, agents 'for Supplying the Newspaper Press with Special Articles and the Works of Popular Novelists' (see Appendix II, Part 4).
2. This was the first story Henty sent them. Unfortunately Tillotsons' archives have survived only in very incomplete form, so the terms of his contract with them and the fees he received are not known. Nor have I been able to identify the newspaper or newspapers in which this story was serialised.
3. Towards the end of 1892 Tillotsons sent Chatto & Windus proofs of the type set for newspaper serialisation, under the title 'In the Days of the Mutiny', offering them the book rights for £125. Andrew Chatto expressed interest but, as was his usual and no-doubt expected practice, asked for a reduction in price. He also expressed doubt about the title of the story as serialised.
4. With regard to the price, Tillotsons went through what had become by then a sort of ritual dance carried on with Chatto, and wrote in reply on 6 December 1892, 'We had thought the price quoted for Mr Henty's story "In the Days of the Mutiny" would have struck you as low. We are satisfied that the story is worth the amount we have quoted, but with a wish to meet you – in consequence of other business we are doing with you – we are willing to make the price £115'.
5. In the same letter, Tillotsons wrote, 'Mr Henty originally submitted the title "Isobel" (the heroine's name), and when we asked for something more striking, suggested "Rujub: The Juggler of Cawnpore". For volume publication we know his preference is to avoid a title that would seem to indicate that the story is a boys' book. It is a novel written for adult readers'. Often, in dealing with other publishers,

Henty showed concern that Blackie might think he was straying from the terms of his contract with them (see 56.3, Note 6 below, and Appendix VI).

6. On the following day the final stage of the ritual was carried through: 'Your obliging concession', wrote Andrew Chatto, 'in respect to the price of the English volume rights of publication throughout the world with the exception of America and Canada of Mr Henty's new story "In the Days of the Mutiny" decides us to accept it at the price (£115) you name.' He then turned again to the title: 'We hope you may be able to induce him to allow us to publish it under the title of "Rujub the Juggler", which we are pleased to learn is one that he himself suggested. We think that this title is very suitable for the library form of issue, and does not suggest the idea of its being a boys' book, whilst there are already very many books on the market with titles like In the Days of the Mutiny'.

7. On 19 December 1892 Chatto sent a print order to Ballantynes for a three-volume edition of 500 copies. On the same day he wrote for the first time direct to Henty: 'We have arranged with Messrs Tillotson & Sons of Bolton to publish in library form in 3 volumes the story by you which they have been issuing serially entitled *In the Days of the Mutiny*. We are however strongly of opinion that the title *Rujub the Juggler*, which we understand from Messrs Tillotsons is one that you had originally chosen for the novel would be much more attractive for the library form in which we are intending to issue it and we hope that you may concur in the idea. We enclose proofs of the first sixteen pages, although we do not propose to trouble you with any further proofs unless you specially wish it'.

8. On 31 December Chatto wrote again: 'We sent some proofs of vol.iii yesterday . . . the book is being printed in Edinburgh, so that delay is unavoidable, sometimes. We always make chapters continuous from beginning to end of a novel: to begin each volume with *ch.i* is surely indefensible!' Some years later, in 1896, Henty corresponded with Chatto about the practice of publishing novels in 'library form' in three volumes or two volumes (see *The Queen's Cup*, 78.1, Notes 4–5).

9. *Rujub, the Juggler* was published, at the then standard price for three-volume novels, £1.11.6d., on 23 February 1893.

10. On 19 December 1892 Chatto also ordered 2000 copies of an unillustrated single-volume colonial edition, that being a regular practice at the time. I have, regrettably, been unable to find a copy of the colonial edition (see 56.2, Notes).

11. In September 1893 Chatto ordered an illustrated, single-volume edition for publication the same year (see 56.3, Notes 1–3). This may have risked the wrath of Mudie, who asked that re-issues of novels should not be made until a year after the three-decker appeared. Certainly Chatto rejected the opportunity, which some publishers took, of observing Mudie's second-hand sales of the three-decker before deciding on whether, and how many copies, to reprint.

12. On 27 January 1893 Andrew Chatto wrote to Tillotsons enclosing an application from the US publisher, Worthington, for the American book rights 'which are reserved for you. Will you kindly reply to it direct?' It is interesting that this American publisher, often regarded as a 'pirate' of the work of English writers, should have made this formal application.

56.2

Notes

1. On 19 December 1892, the day that Chatto & Windus instructed Ballantynes to produce an edition of 500 copies of 56.1, described above, they also ordered from the same printer an edition of 2000 copies (and 'overs') of a single-volume Colonial Edition. No copy of this edition has come to light.

2. From the publisher's records it is nevertheless possible to give some information about the edition. It was on paper that would produce a page size of about 170 x 115 mm., rather smaller than their standard octavo size used for 56.3. Three binding orders were issued: the first on 20 February 1893 for 1300 copies, and two subsequently, on 15 June 1893 for 200 copies, and on 3 March 1896 for 514 copies. 13 sets of sheets were otherwise disposed of, making a total of 2027 complete sets.

3. Later, a further 483 copies were produced, by using sheets printed for the 2s. edition (56.7), with cancel title pages, of which 500 were printed in February 1896. 56.7 was printed on paper of exactly the same size as 56.2, although trimmed to give a slightly smaller page (see also *Dorothy's Double*, 61.2 and 61.4).

56.3

RUJUB, THE JUGGLER | BY | G.A. HENTY | AUTHOR OF "THE CURSE OF CARNE'S HOLD," "A HIDDEN FOE," ETC. | (publisher's device) | A NEW EDITION | WITH EIGHT ILLUSTRATIONS BY STANLEY L. WOOD | London | CHATTO & WINDUS, PICCADILLY | 1893
(Note: London *is in gothic type).*

Contents

185 x 122 mm. (i)–(iv) | (1)–332 | catalogue (1)–32. Eight full-page wash-drawings by Stanley L. Wood, reproduced by halftone blocks printed in black on coated paper, unbacked, unfolioed, tipped in.

(Frontispiece, tipped in) | (i) title p. | (ii) blank | (iii) list of Illustrations | (iv) blank | (1)–332. text, with printer's imprint at foot of p.332 (PRINTED BY BALLANTYNE, HANSON AND CO. | EDINBURGH AND LONDON.) | (1)–32. catalogue, with printer's imprint at foot of p.32 (OGDEN, SMALE AND CO. LIMITED, PRINTERS, GREAT SAFFRON HILL, E.C.)

Binding (see Plate 19)

Red cloth boards, bevelled, blocked black, white, yellow, and gilt; all edges gilt; grey flowered endpapers.

Front board: RUJUB | THE | JUGGLER (white, shaded black) above illustration of man standing over body, threatening tiger with whip (black, white, yellow). **Spine:** RUJUB | THE | JUGGLER | G.A. | HENTY (gilt) above illustration of tiger's head (black, white, yellow). At foot: CHATTO & WINDUS (gilt). **Back board:** plain.

References: PN | *Dartt*, p.115, *Companion*, p.24.

Notes

1. On 11 September 1893, only six months after the order for the three-volume and colonial editions, a further 3000 copies were ordered for this first illustrated, single-volume edition. Chatto's confidence in the book was clearly firm, although he wrote to Tillotsons only ten days later, when negotiating a price for *Dorothy's Double*, 'We are sorry to say that our experience with the story we last bought of you, "Rujub the Juggler" has been disappointing'. Such a comment by Chatto was no doubt little more than a mandatory ploy, for he continued rather ambiguously: 'although we shall be glad to venture upon the new story by Mr Henty which you offer us, we feel we are not justified in giving more for it than we paid for "Rujub the Juggler", which we consider a very good and promising story'. But see 61.1, Note 1.

2. The selling price was 5s. Blue and green cloths were also used.

3. Earliest recorded dates of bound-in catalogues are July 1893 (from catalogue stock printed before this edition of the book) and September 1893. An issue with catalogue dated April 1894, later than the earliest found in 56.4, contains a single leaf of advertisement for 'The Piccadilly Novels' tipped in before the frontispiece.

4. Stanley Wood's illustrations all carry the name of George Meisenbach, an early and renowned Munich process-engraver. His system had been patented in England in 1882 (see Appendix IV, Part 1).

5. The entries and Notes that follow, for the various editions of *Rujub, the Juggler*, accounting for over 11,000 copies printed between 1892 and 1902, do not bear out the claim made by the writer of Henty's obituary in the *Dictionary of National Biography*: 'He issued about a dozen orthodox novels, including *Colonel Thorndyke's Secret*, published as late as 1898, but none of them achieved much success'. While that may be true of some of his adult novels, especially the earliest ones, it is evident that *Rujub, the Juggler* was a real success (see Appendix II, Part 4, Note 61). It is also true, I think, that the style of story-telling Henty developed over many years of writing for boys tended to overflow into the stories he wrote for adults. This meant that these novels were not, as Mr Woods describes them, 'orthodox', but tended generally to fall between two stools. Although acceptable to older readers, they were also, in an old-fashioned sense, 'suitable' for the young also, and often had the elements of adventure that appealed to readers of his books expressly written for boys. By adding illustrations to later editions, and giving them pictorial bindings, publishers traded on those tendencies, and often gave Henty's adult novels a second market in the juvenile field.

6. Henty was well aware of what was happening, and showed much concern over the years that single-volume editions of his novels, even without illustrations, might appear to Blackie to be close to, if not actually, breaking the terms of his contract with them. He had undertaken to write books for young people for them only (see Appendix VI, and *Colonel Thorndyke's Secret*, 79.1, Note 4). This 1893 edition of *Rujub, the Juggler* was a good example of the problem, and in 1899 Chatto worried him even more with a Presentation Edition (see 56.8). In that year he confided his fears to a journalist (see Appendix II, Part 3, Note 43).

56.4

RUJUB, THE JUGGLER | BY | G.A. HENTY | AUTHOR OF "A HIDDEN FOE," "DOROTHY'S DOUBLE," ETC. | (publisher's device) | A NEW EDITION | WITH EIGHT ILLUSTRATIONS BY STANLEY L. WOOD | London | CHATTO & WINDUS, PICCADILLY | 1894
(Note: London is in gothic type).

Contents: 190 x 126 mm. As for 56.3, but single unfolioed advertisement leaf tipped in before first signature (The Piccadilly Novels).

Binding (see Plate 22)
Red-brown, pebble-grain cloth boards, blocked black and blind; edges rough-trimmed and uncut at heads; endpapers printed with grey-green leaf-and-dot pattern.
   Front board: Over-all geometric design, with leaves. In upper panel: RUJUB, THE JUGGLER; in lower panel: G.A. HENTY (all black). **Spine:** Similar over-all geometric design, with flowers (black), with three spaces for lettering. In top panel: RUJUB I THE JUGGLER (gilt); at centre: G.A. HENTY (gilt); at foot: CHATTO & WINDUS (cloth-colour) out of solid gilt rectangle over potted palm (gilt). **Back board:** double rule near edges of board (blind).

References: TC; RC.

Notes
1. The text consists of sheets from the original printing for 56.3, with the preliminary pages, including the title-page date, revised and reprinted.
2. Bound-in catalogues are dated February 1894, and September 1894.
3. Blocked with a set of 'binder's blanks'. The price was reduced to 3s.6d.

56.5

A further set of preliminary pages, with title page as for 56.4 but dated 1895, was bound up with sheets from the standard single-volume impression, of which some had already been used for 56.3 and 56.4. The binding was exactly as for 56.4, and apart from the omission of the advertisement leaf before the frontispiece, the contents are unchanged. The 32-page catalogue bound in a copy examined is dated March, 1896. The price remained at 3s.6d.

56.6

Title page: As for 56.4, but dated 1895.

Contents: 192 x 130 mm. As for 56.3 (see Note 1 below).

Binding (see Plate 19)
Red canvas boards, blocked gilt; edges uncut; plain off-white laid endpapers.
   Front board: RUJUB I THE JUGGLER (gilt) above a gilt decorative flower, all within a gilt ornamental heart-shaped frame, in upper right corner. **Spine:** RUJUB I THE JUGGLER I G.A. HENTY I CHATTO & WINDUS (all gilt). **Back board:** plain.

References: PN I *Dartt Companion*, p.24.

Notes
1. Catalogues recorded in this format are dated: February 1897 and January 1898.
2. The publisher's price, in this new binding style, was unchanged at 3s.6d.
3. In October 1894 a further 1000 copies had been printed, making a total to date of 6000 copies of single-volume editions.

56.7

Title page: As for 56.4, but date changed to 1896.

Contents
165 x 108 mm. (i)–(iv) I (1)–332 I catalogue (1)–32. No illustrations.

(i) Half-title p. | (ii) advertisement (OPINIONS OF THE PRESS) | (iii) title p. | (iv) printer's imprint (PRINTED BY BALLANTYNE, HANSON & CO. | EDINBURGH AND LONDON.) | (1)–332. text, with printer's imprint on p.332, as on p.(iv) | (1)–32. catalogue.

Binding (see Plate 21)
In the style of a Victorian 'yellowback' (see Note 1). Pictorial paper boards, printed red and black on yellow-cream, with coloured illustration and decorative panels; edges plain; all endpapers carry advertisements, printed black on white wove, for food and medical products, etc.
    Front board: RUJUB, THE JUGGLER (red) | BY G.A. HENTY (black) above illustration of man standing over body, threatening tiger with whip (full-colour). At foot: Chatto & Windus, Piccadilly (black). All framed by black rule. **Spine:** RUJUB | THE | JUGGLER (black) beneath, and above, flower decorations. At centre: G.A. HENTY (black); at foot: TWO SHILLINGS (black). **Back board:** advertisement (black).

References: BB | *Dartt Companion*, p.25.

Notes
1. This, and *Dorothy's Double*, were Henty's only novels to be published by Chatto and Windus in 'yellowback' paper-boards format. Griffith & Farran also published *The Curse of Carne's Hold* as a yellowback (see 40.3). Such editions were produced by many publishers, were mainly fiction, and frequently sold from railway-station bookstalls, nearly always at two shillings, the price in this case.
2. A further 2500 copies had been ordered on 6 February 1896, making a total so far of 9000 single-volume copies. This impression was printed on paper of the smaller, non-standard size that Chatto used for the early colonial edition, 56.2.
3. Chatto arranged that at the same time as the 2500 copies of the text were printed, Ballantynes should also run off an additional 500 title pages for the colonial edition, 56.2. By using them as cancel title pages, with 500 sets of the newly printed sheets, they were able to sell that number of extra copies of the colonial edition. In fact, with the overs delivered by the printer, they were able to sell a total of 2510 copies to the colonies. As no copies of 56.2 have been found, nor any copies of the later printing with cancel title pages, I have made no attempt to distinguish between the two versions and so give no specific code number for the latter.
4. The catalogue in this impression is dated February 1899.
5. Neither the colonial edition nor the yellow back edition was illustrated, but the 3s.6d., illustrated edition remained on sale simultaneously with them both.

56.8
RUJUB, THE JUGGLER | BY | G.A. HENTY | AUTHOR OF | "THE QUEEN'S CUP," "DOROTHY'S DOUBLE," "COLONEL THORNDYKE'S SECRET," "THE CURSE OF CARNE'S HOLD," ETC. | (publisher's device) | PRESENTATION EDITION | WITH 8 ILLUSTRATIONS BY STANLEY WOOD | LONDON | CHATTO & WINDUS | 1899

Contents
186 x 132 mm. (i)–(viii) | (1)–332 | catalogue (1)–32. Illustrations as in 56.3.

(i) Advertisement (NOVELS BY G.A. HENTY) | (ii) blank | (iii) half-title p. | (iv) blank | (frontispiece, tipped in) | (v) title p. | (vi) printer's imprint (Printed by BALLANTYNE, HANSON & Co. | At the Ballantyne Press) | (vii) list of Illustrations | (viii) blank | (1)–332. text, with printer's imprint at foot of p.332 (Printed by BALLANTYNE, HANSON & CO. | Edinburgh & London) | (1)–32. catalogue.

Binding (see Plate 20)

Dark-blue cloth boards, bevelled, blocked black, white, orange, and gilt; all edges gilt; dark-blue surface-paper endpapers.

Front board: RUJUB THE | JUGGLER (white, shaded cloth-colour) out of solid-gilt irregular panel, above illustration of man standing over body and threatening tiger with whip (black, white, orange). At foot: G.A. HENTY (white). **Spine:** RUJUB | THE | JUGGLER (white, shaded cloth-colour) out of solid-gilt irregular panel, above: G.A. HENTY (white); illustration of tiger's head (black, white, orange). At foot: CHATTO & WINDUS (orange) between white rules. **Back board:** plain.

References: PN | *Farmer*, p.60; *Dartt*, p.115, *Companion*, p.24.

Notes

1. On 12 January 1899 Chatto sent Ballantynes an order to print 1000 copies on paper in a new size, described by the publisher as 'small demy octavo' but in fact a small imperial, as a 'de luxe' Presentation Edition, to sell at 5s.

2. This Presentation Edition may be compared with that issued by Chatto & Windus in the same year for *Colonel Thorndyke's Secret* , 79.2. On the front board of the latter book the illustration fits neatly into the irregular shape of the gilt panel containing the title. Possibly the title-panel on the front board of 56.8 was designed with an irregular base so that it, also, could take, neatly fitted into it, part of the illustration – in this case perhaps the end of the whip held by the man standing over a tiger. If such a drawing was prepared for this edition the publisher must have had second thoughts about it, for it was never used. Instead, Chatto used the illustration from the front board of 56.3, and the whip does not rise above the man's head to fit into the 'slot' in the panel that seems to have been designed for it. The spine illustration is, similarly, a repeat of the one from 56.3.

3. At the turn of the century *Rujub, the Juggler* was available in bookshops in three formats simultaneously: 'Presentation Edition, small demy 8vo, cloth bevelled, gilt edges, with 8 illustrations by Stanley Wood, 5s.; crown 8vo, cloth, with 8 illustrations, 3s.6d.; and post 8vo, illustrated boards, 2s.'. This wording is taken from the publisher's catalogue, and the use of the words 'demy', 'crown', and 'post', which in reality have very precise definitions as descriptions of paper sizes, seem to have been used by publishers then as loosely as they are by many antiquarian booksellers today. A fourth edition, not advertised in this country, was available in the colonies (see 56.2; and 56.7, Note 3).

56.9

Title page: As for 56.8, but date changed to 1903.

Contents

183 x 131 mm. (i)–(iv) | (1)–332 | no catalogue. Illustrations as in 56.3.

(Frontispiece, tipped in) | (i) title p. | (ii) printer's imprint (Printed by BALLANTYNE, HANSON & CO. | At the Ballantyne Press) | (iii) list of Illustrations | (iv) blank | (1)–332. text, with printer's imprint on p.332, exactly as on p.(ii).

Binding: As for 56.8, except (a) all edges stained green; (b) plain cream laid endpapers.

Reference: PN.

Notes

1. This is a cheap reprint of the original 'de luxe' Presentation Edition (56.8): in view of its comparatively shoddy appearance it is perhaps surprising that the words 'Presentation Edition' remained on the title page. The thin featherweight contrasts both in texture and weight with the smoother, heavier, and more expensive paper used for the earlier editions.

2. The other differences between 56.9 and 56.8 are the slightly smaller page-size; the coloured edges of the leaves (the edges of featherweight paper cannot be satisfactorily gilded – nor, as it appears from this example, satisfactorily stained!); the reduction of the prelims from eight to four pages; the paper used for the endpapers; and the omission of all advertising.

3. The print order was for 500 copies only, and was given on 29 December 1902.

56.10

Notes

1. One final reprint is recorded in Chatto's archive. The order for an impression of 500 copies was given to Ballantynes on 14 October 1910, and the ledger entry shows that 487 sets of sheets had been bound by 1920, in six main batches varying from 50 to 100 copies, to be sold in both the 2s. and the 3s.6d. series. All editions of the book are comparatively scarce, and I have been unable to find copies from this printing distinguishable from earlier impressions in the two series.

2. From first publication in 1893 to the end of 1920 Chatto had produced a total of 11,000 copies of *Rujub the Juggler*, of which 10,500 were in single-volume editions following the initial 500 three-volume sets.

57. TALES FROM THE WORKS OF G.A.HENTY

57.1

TALES | FROM THE WORKS OF | G.A. HENTY | AUTHOR OF | "FACING DEATH;" "FOR NAME AND FAME;" &c. | (39mm. rule) | ADAPTED FOR CLASS READING. | (39mm. rule) | (publisher's device) | LONDON: | BLACKIE & SON, LIMITED, 49 OLD BAILEY, E.C. | GLASGOW, EDINBURGH, AND DUBLIN. | 1893.

Contents

172 x 114 mm. (i)–(iv) I (5)–240 I no catalogue. Ten full-page illustrations from line-drawings and wood engravings, reproduced by line blocks printed on text pages, unfolioed but counted in pagination. Numerous small engravings printed in the explanatory notes at end of the book.

(i) Title p. I (ii) blank I (iii) Publisher's Preface I (iv) Contents I (5)–227. text I (228)–240. Explanations of the more Difficult Words and Phrases.

Binding (see Plate 110)

Probably designed by Talwin Morris (see Note 3). Red cloth boards, blocked black; edges plain; plain off-white endpapers.

Front board: TALES I FROM I HENTY I 1/6 (black) within over-all design of black decorative panels, rules, and ornaments. **Spine:** TALES I FROM I HENTY (black) set in design of similar black panels, rules, and ornaments. **Back board:** plain.

References: BL; Bod; PN I *Farmer*, p.67; *Dartt*, p.132.

Notes

1. This School Reader contains thirteen excerpts from eleven of Henty's books published by Blackie, and from *The Plague Ship*, published by the S.P.C.K.
2. The book does not appear in Blackie's surviving records.
3. The binding is almost certainly one of Talwin Morris's earliest designs for Blackie: he was appointed Art Manager in February 1893 (see Appendix IV, Part 2).

57.2

Reprints of the first edition were issued with the date removed from the title page. No other differences are noticeable, except for the use of very-slightly thinner paper for the text, and boards of a slightly lighter weight for the binding case.

57.3

Tales from the Works I of I G.A. Henty I (publisher's device) I BLACKIE & SON LIMITED I LONDON AND GLASGOW

Contents

173 x 117 mm. (1)–(224) including 4pp. catalogue. Frontispiece from unsigned watercolour drawing, reproduced by three-colour halftone blocks printed on coated paper, unbacked, tipped in.

(Frontispiece, tipped in) I (1) title p. I (2) publisher's addresses at head; printer's imprint at foot (Printed in Great Britain by Blackie & Son, Ltd., Glasgow) I 3. Biographical Note I iv. [roman numerals in error] Biographical Note, continued I (5) Contents I (6) blank I 7–219. text I (220) blank I (1)–(4) catalogue.

Binding (see Note 1)

Designed by Talwin Morris. Red cloth boards, blocked black; edges plain; plain off-white endpapers.

Front board: ENGLISH AUTHORS FOR SCHOOL READING (black) I TALES I FROM . HENTY (cloth-colour out of black rectangle) above art-nouveau floral design (black). At foot: BLACKIE . AND . SON . LIMITED . LONDON (black). The whole enclosed in double framework of ornamental black rules. **Spine:**

(ornament) TALES (ornament) FROM (ornament) HENTY (ornament) (all black) in panel of decorative black rules, running from foot to head. The ornaments are shaped like teardrops. **Back board:** plain.

Reference: CH.

Notes
1. The publisher's catalogue, printed on the last four pages of the final gathering, is headed: 'ENGLISH AUTHORS for School Reading. A collection of established favourites issued as Continuous Readers. Strongly bound in cloth boards. With Frontispiece. 1s.4d. each.', and includes, among many English classics: *Sturdy and Strong*, 34.4, *In the Hands of the Malays*, 113.4, and this title. I have not been able to find copies of the first two of these titles, but another book in the series, possibly added later, is *A Chapter of Adventures*, 48.6, Plate 103. That title, although similarly bound, has a variant spine, with the price, 8d., blocked on it.
2. The design for the spine appears to have been made for a book printed on a less bulky paper. No indication of price is blocked on this spine (see Note 1).
3. The Biographical Note, starting on p.3, includes many incorrect dates.
4. The frontispiece, captioned 'Caught in the Cyclone' is from a set of three-colour halftone blocks made to illustrate *A Chapter of Adventures*. It appears first in the 'Crown Library' edition of that book, 48.9 (see 57.4, Note 3), facing p.192.

57.4

Tales from the Works | of | G.A. Henty | (publisher's device) | BLACKIE AND SON LIMITED | 50 OLD BAILEY LONDON | GLASGOW AND BOMBAY

Contents
180 x 122 mm. (1)–(224) including 4pp. catalogue | catalogue (1)–(2). Frontispiece from watercolour drawing by an unknown hand, reproduced by three-colour halftone blocks printed on unbacked coated paper, tipped in.

(Frontispiece, tipped in) | (1) title p. | (2) blank | 3. Biographical Note | iv. [roman numerals in error] Biographical Note, continued | (5) Contents | (6) blank | 7–219, text | (220) blank | (221)–(224) folioed 1–4. catalogue of books by Henty | (1)–(2) catalogue (Blackie's Crown Library).

Binding (see Note 3)
Dark-blue cloth boards, blocked yellow, orange, and gilt; edges plain; plain off-white endpapers.

Front board: Over-all elaborate design of art-nouveau panels (yellow and orange) with: . TALES . | FROM HENTY (cloth-colour reversed out of solid yellow rectangle) at head. **Spine:** Similar elaborate panels (yellow and orange) with: TALES | FROM | HENTY (cloth-colour reversed out of solid gilt rectangle) at head, and: BLACKIE | AND SON | LIMITED (yellow out of orange rectangle) at foot. **Back board:** plain.

References: BL; Bod; PN.

Notes
1. This issue was received by the Copyright Libraries in 1915.
2. As in 57.3, Blackie have made up an even working by including a 4-page

catalogue of Henty's books at the end of the first text gathering. The catalogue lists *St. George for England*, at its full first-published price of 5s.: the price was reduced in 1916, which confirms the date given in Note 1.

3. The second (two-page) catalogue is of Blackie's 'Crown Library' (including *A Chapter of Adventures*, 48.9, Plate 104): 'Selected from the World's best literature for boys and girls. Handsomely bound in cloth, 1s. each'. Most of the books were also in Blackie's 'Library of Famous Books' (see 57.5). See also Appendix V.

4. The Biographical Note on p.3 repeats the errors in 57.3 (see 57.3, Note 4). The explanatory notes at the end of the earlier, school-reader editions are omitted.

*57.5

Title page: As for 57.4.

Contents: As for 57.4, but without second (two-page) catalogue.

Binding (see Note 1)
Dark-green, linen-grained cloth boards, blocked blind and gilt; edges plain; plain off-white endpapers.
   Front board: Over-all design of decorative rules and panels including roses and, at head: TALES | FROM | HENTY (all blind). **Spine:** Similar over-all blind decorations and, in panel at head: TALES | FROM | HENTY (gilt). At foot: BLACKIE | & SON LTD. (blind). **Back board:** plain.

References: PN | *Dartt*, p.133.

Notes
1. This binding design for Blackie's 'Library of Famous Books' (see Appendix V), was for a time in use concurrently with 57.6 (see 57.6, Note 4). It was used for *A Final Reckoning*, 29.6, and *A Chapter of Adventures*, 48.10, Plate 104.
2. Many slightly-varying issues were reprinted in this style in the 1920s and 1930s. Cloth colours were numerous, pink, red, and green being the most common; text papers were of varying bulk; publisher's advertisements were sometimes omitted, often causing the final gathering to be of 12 pages instead of 16; the publisher's addresses and printer's imprint were included in late issues on p.(2) and/or p.212. These minor variants are all grouped together under this 'generic' heading, *57.5.

57.6

Tales from the Works | of | G.A. Henty | (publisher's device) | BLACKIE AND SON LIMITED | LONDON GLASGOW AND BOMBAY

Contents
171 x 115 mm. (1)–(220) | no catalogue. Frontispiece from watercolour drawing by unknown artist, reproduced by three-colour halftone blocks printed on coated paper, unbacked, tipped in.
   (Frontispiece, tipped in) | (1) title p. | (2) printer's imprint (Printed in Great Britain by | Blackie & Son, Limited, Glasgow) | 3. Biographical Note | iv. [roman numerals in error] Biographical Note, continued | (vii) Contents | (viii) blank | (1)–219. text | (220) blank.

Binding (see Plate 111)
Possibly designed by Charles Rennie Mackintosh (see Note 5). Buff grained-paper boards (imitating cloth), blocked blue; edges plain; plain off-white endpapers.
   Front board: TALES FROM | HENTY (blue) in rectangular panel within overall geometric pattern of (?) abstract swallows (blue). **Spine:** TALES | FROM | HENTY (blue) in panel cutting across pattern as on front board (blue). In small rectangle at foot: BLACKIE | & SON . LTD (blue). **Back board:** plain.

References: NS; PN.

Notes
1. Part of a series that appeared in the 1920s, 'Blackie's Library for Boys and Girls', not to be confused with 'The Boys' and Girls' Bookshelf' (see Appendix V).
2. The text is still printed from stereos of the type set for the first edition. The address line on the title page, and the addition of the printer's imprint on p.(2), are the only changes from *57.5.
3. The frontispiece remains unchanged; the colour plate on the dust-wrapper shows three seamen struggling to sail a ship in a gale; on the back is a list of 28 titles in Blackie's 'Library for Boys and Girls'.
4. Many books in the series were issued concurrently in Blackie's 'Library of Famous Books' (see Appendix V), at least for most of the 1920s. The latter series appears to have outlived this one, however, some of its titles being found in bright cloth with inscription dates well into the 1930s. See *57.5, Notes 1 and 2.
5. Robert J. Gibbs wrote in the Charles Rennie Mackintosh Society's Newsletter, No.12, Summer 1976, of Mackintosh's binding designs for Blackie, and of an 'example from the twenties, featuring rows of Vorticist swallows which could conceivably be his: this replaced Talwin Morris's design for the shilling series "Blackie's Library for Boys and Girls"'. (Books in the series were in fact priced at 1s.6d.) Morris had died in 1911: later design work was commissioned – some of it at least – by Walter Blackie who had taken over as Chairman after the death of his elder brother Alexander in 1918. As John Morris of the National Library of Scotland recently remarked to me, 'If not Mackintosh, who else could have made this design?' For further notes on Mackintosh and Walter Blackie see Appendix II, Part 5; Appendix IV, Part 2; and *Yarns on the Beach*, 25.5, Notes 3–4.

58. CONDEMNED AS A NIHILIST

58.1
CONDEMNED AS A NIHILIST: | A STORY OF | ESCAPE FROM SIBERIA. | BY | G.A. HENTY, | Author of "In Freedom's Cause;" "The Lion of the North;" | "The Young Carthaginian;" &c. | (15mm. rule) | ILLUSTRATED BY WALTER PAGET. | (15mm. rule) | (publisher's device) | LONDON: | BLACKIE & SON, LIMITED, 49 OLD BAILEY, E.C. | GLASGOW, EDINBURGH, AND DUBLIN. | 1893.

Contents
185 x 124 mm. (i)–(x) | (11)–352 | catalogue (1)–32. Eight full-page wash-drawings by Walter Paget, reproduced by halftone blocks printed in black on coated paper,

unbacked, unfolioed, tipped in. Map of Russia printed in three colours as double-page spread, unbacked, guarded in between pp.80 and 81.

(i) Half-title p. | (ii) advertisement (MR. HENTY'S HISTORICAL TALES.) listing 22 titles | (frontispiece, tipped in) | (iii) title p. | (iv) blank | (v) Preface | (vi) blank | (vii) Contents | (viii) blank | (ix) list of Illustrations | (x) blank | (11)–352. text | (1)–32. catalogue.

Binding (see Plate 62)
Yellow-grey cloth boards, blocked black, brown, bronze, blind, and gilt; all edges burnished olive-green; maroon surface-paper endpapers.
Front board: CONDEMNED | AS A | NIHILIST. (gilt), the cap C only shaded black and entwined with a whip (black and gilt) forming part of the illustration of man being tied up with rope (black, brown, bronze). At foot: BY | G.A. HENTY. (black). The whole in a border of decorative rules (black). **Spine:** CONDEMNED | . AS . A . | NIHILIST. (gilt, shaded black) above illustration of hands in chains (black and gilt). Below: . G . A . | . HENTY . (black). The whole within a border of black decorative rules, with single gilt rule at head and foot. **Back board:** Three rules (thin, thick, thin) near edges of board (blind).

References: BL; Bod; PN | *Farmer*, p.21; *Dartt*, p.40, *Companion*, p.10.

Notes
1. The book was published on 21 June 1892 at five shillings. By the end of February 1893 Blackie had sold 6370 copies, and during the next thirteen years they sold 7451 more, the average annual sale over the fourteen-year period being 987 copies. At this point, the end of August 1906, the book was re-issued in a cheaper edition (see 58.3 below). The remaining 315 copies at five shillings were sold over seven years.
2. Dartt (*Companion*, p.10) uses cloth-colour as a guide to the chronological order of issues. This is not a valid method of dating (see Appendix III, Part 2).
3. As usual with Blackie novels, the earliest issues contain catalogues advertising the books for the current year (in this case with title pages dated 1893) without quotations from press reviews.

*58.2
Reprints of the five-shilling edition were issued in the style of 58.1, with the date removed from the title page. Alterations were made to the title-page imprint and addresses when necessary: the Edinburgh address was not used after 1894; and the Indian office was opened in 1901 although Bombay did not appear regularly in the Blackie imprint until 1906.
Bindings continued to show variation in colours of cloth, blocking, and endpapers. The slightly varying issues among the reprints of the book in its first-edition format are all grouped together under this 'generic' heading, *58.2.

58.3
Condemned as a Nihilist | A Story of Escape from Siberia | BY | G.A. HENTY | Author of "Beric the Briton" "In Freedom's Cause" "The Lion of the North' | "The Young Carthaginian" "Under Wellington's Command" &c. | ILLUSTRATED BY WAL PAGET | NEW EDITION | BLACKIE AND SON LIMITED | LONDON GLASGOW DUBLIN BOMBAY | 1907
(Note: the final quotation mark after North *has broken off).*

Contents

185 × 128 mm. (1)–352 | catalogue 1–16. Eight full-page wash-drawings by Wal Paget, reproduced by halftone blocks printed in sepia on coated paper, unbacked, unfolioed, tipped in. Map printed in three colours as double-page spread, unbacked, guarded in between pages 80 and 81.

(1) Half-title p. | (2) advertisement (HISTORICAL TALES BY G.A. HENTY) listing 30 titles | (frontispiece, tipped in) | (3) title p. | (4) blank | (5) Preface | (6) blank | 7. Contents | (8) blank | 9. list of Illustrations | (10) blank | 11–352. text | 1–16. catalogue.

Binding (see Note 1)

Green cloth boards, blocked black, brown, buff, and gilt; all edges stained olive-green; grey endpapers, lined off-white.
Front board: CONDEMNED | AS A NIHILIST | G.A. HENTY (gilt) above illustration of young fur-clad figure with paddle and rifle (black, brown, buff). **Spine:** CONDEMNED | AS A | NIHILIST. | G.A. HENTY (all gilt) above illustration of similar figure with gun and game-bird (black, brown, buff). At foot: BLACKIE AND SON LTD. (black). **Back board:** plain.

Reference: IM.

Notes

1. Re-issued 1906 in the 'New and Popular Edition'. For details see *Facing Death*, 10.6, Notes 2–3, and, for examples of the series binding style, Plates 172–173.
2. The copy in Ivan McClymont's collection is inscribed with the date 23 December 1906. I have seen another copy, bound in slate-grey cloth, with the spine imprint 'BLACKIE & SON LTD.', and with plain, off-white endpapers.
3. In this edition Blackie had sold 2427 copies by the end of 1907, and during the following ten years, to the end of August 1917 when Blackie's records cease, they sold 5586 more, at an annual average of 759 copies for the first five years, and of 358 copies for the last five. The grand total of copies sold at both prices from 1892 to 1917 is 22,149.

*58.4

CONDEMNED AS A | NIHILIST | A Story of Siberia | BY | G.A. HENTY | Author of "Beric the Briton" "In Freedom's Cause" | "The Lion of the North" "The Young Carthaginian" | "Under Wellington's Command" &c. | Illustrated | BLACKIE AND SON LIMITED | LONDON GLASGOW AND BOMBAY

Contents

185 × 122 mm. (1)–352 | no catalogue. Frontispiece from watercolour drawing by Frank Gillett, R.I., reproduced by three-colour halftone blocks; four full-page wash-drawings by Wal Paget, reproduced by halftone blocks printed in black; all on coated paper, unbacked, keyed to text, tipped in. Map printed from line block on text page.

(1) Half-title p. | (2) advertisement (G.A. HENTY'S BOOKS) listing 56 titles | (frontispiece, tipped in) | (3) title p. | (4) printer's imprint (Printed in Great Britain by | Blackie & Son, Limited, Glasgow) | (5) Preface | (6) blank | (7) Contents | (8) blank | (9) list of Illustrations | (10) map | 11–352. text.

Binding: (See Plate 174). As for 58.3, except (a) red cloth boards, blocked black, brown, and buff, with no gilt: all lettering black; (b) imprint on spine is now simply BLACKIE; (c) edges plain; (d) plain off-white endpapers.

References: BL; PN.

Notes
1. For notes on Blackie's second cheaper series, 'The New Popular Henty', and subsequent editions of this book, see *Facing Death*, 10.7, Notes 1–3 and 6–8. This title was issued in 1926.
2. All the minor variants of *Condemned as a Nihilist* in the series are grouped together under this 'generic' heading, *58.4.

59. BERIC THE BRITON

59.1
BERIC THE BRITON: | A STORY OF | THE ROMAN INVASION. | BY | G.A. HENTY, | Author of "The Dash for Khartoum;" "In Freedom's Cause;" "With Clive in India;" | "St. George for England;" "Facing Death;" &c. | (41mm. rule) | WITH TWELVE ILLUSTRATIONS BY W. PARKINSON. | (41mm. rule) | (publisher's device) | LONDON: | BLACKIE & SON, LIMITED, 49 OLD BAILEY, E.C. | GLASGOW, EDINBURGH, AND DUBLIN. | 1893.

Contents
185 x 130 mm. (i)–(x) | (11)–384 | catalogue (1)–32. Twelve full-page wash-drawings by W. Parkinson and W.H. Margetson (see Note 3), reproduced by halftone blocks printed in black on coated paper, unbacked, unfolioed, tipped in.
   (i) Half-title p. | (ii) blank | (frontispiece, tipped in) | (iii) title p. | (iv) blank | (v)–vi. Preface | (vii) Contents | (viii) blank | (ix) list of Illustrations | (x) blank | (11)–383. text | (384) blank | (1)–32. catalogue.

Binding (see Plate 56)
Light-brown cloth boards, bevelled, blocked black, white, yellow, blind, and gilt; all edges burnished olive-green; maroon surface-paper endpapers.
   Front board: BERIC | THE | BRITON | . | A STORY | OF THE | . ROMAN . | INVASION | . | BY | G A HENTY | . (all black) at right of illustration of British soldier (black, white, yellow). All framed by black rule. **Spine:** From head: three rules (black, gilt, black); row of six gilt ornaments; BERIC | . | . THE . | . | BRITON (all gilt, shaded black) above two crossed daggers (black and gilt); . BY . | G.A. HENTY | . o . (all black), with black rule at foot. **Back board:** Single rule near edges of bevel (blind).

References: BL; Bod; PN | *Farmer*, p.10: *Dartt*, p.17, *Companion*, p.3.

Notes
1. The book was published on 22 June 1892 at six shillings. By the end of February 1893 Blackie had sold 7260 copies, and during the next twelve years they sold 9088 more, the average annual sale over the thirteen years being 1258 copies. Over the next twelve years they sold a further 3774 copies, making a grand total up to the end

of August 1917, when Blackie's records cease, of 20,122 copies, all at six shillings. The book was not re-issued in the 'New and Popular Edition'.

2. As usual with Blackie novels, the earliest issues contain catalogues advertising the books for the current year (in this case with title pages dated 1893) without quotations from press reviews.

3. Although the title page announces twelve illustrations by W. Parkinson, the plate facing page 314 is in fact drawn and signed by W.H. Margetson.

*59.2

Reprints of the six-shilling edition were in the style of 59.1, with the date removed from the title page. Alterations were made when necessary to the title-page imprint and addresses: the Edinburgh address was not used after 1894; the Indian office was opened in 1901 although Bombay did not appear regularly in the Blackie imprint until 1906; and Dublin was omitted after 1910.

Bindings continued to show variation in colours of cloth, blocking, and endpapers. The book was not re-issued in a cheaper edition until the 1920s (see *59.3).

The many slightly-varying issues among the reprints of the book in its first-edition format, in which it remained for twenty-five years, are all grouped together under this 'generic' heading, *59.2.

*59.3

Beric the Briton | A Story of the Roman Invasion | BY | G.A. HENTY | Author of "The Dash for Khartoum" "In Freedom's Cause" | "With Clive in India" "St. George for England" | "Facing Death" &c. | Illustrated | BLACKIE & SON LIMITED | LONDON AND GLASGOW

Contents

186 x 125 mm. (1)–384 | no catalogue. Frontispiece from watercolour drawing by Frank Gillett, R.I., reproduced by three-colour halftone blocks; four full-page wash-drawings by W. Parkinson and W.H. Margetson (see Note 2), reproduced by halftone blocks printed in black; all on coated paper, unbacked, unfolioed, tipped in.

(1) Half-title p. | (2) Blackie addresses | (frontispiece, tipped in) | (3) title p. | (4) printer's imprint (Printed in Great Britain by | Blackie & Son, Limited, Glasgow) | 5–384. text.

Binding (see Note 1)

Grey-blue cloth boards, blocked black, red, and warm-buff; edges plain; plain off-white endpapers.

Front board: BERIC THE BRITON | A Story of the | ROMAN INVASION (black) above illustration of Roman soldier with shield, pike and sword (black, red, warm-buff). At lower left corner, signature: J Hassall (black); at right: G.A. HENTY (black). **Spine:** BERIC | THE | BRITON | G.A. HENTY (black) above illustration of Briton with shield and sword (black, red, warm-buff). At foot: BLACKIE & SON LD. (black). **Back board:** plain.

Reference: PN.

Notes

1. For notes on Blackie's second cheaper series, 'The New Popular Henty', and later editions, see *Facing Death*, 10.7, Notes 1–3 and 6–8. Examples of the series binding style are at Plates 174–175.

2. The black-and-white plates include, facing p.312, the drawing by W.H. Margetson (see 59.1, Note 3).

3. All the minor variants of *Beric the Briton* in the series are grouped together under this 'generic' heading, *59.3.

59.4

THE TALISMAN LIBRARY (underlined) | BERIC THE BRITON | BY | G.A. HENTY | (publisher's device) | BLACKIE AND SON LIMITED | 50 OLD BAILEY LONDON | GLASGOW AND BOMBAY | 1922

Contents

174 x 113 mm. (i)–x | 1–182 | no catalogue. Frontispiece from wash-drawing by W. Parkinson reproduced by halftone block printed in black on coated paper, unbacked, tipped in.

(i) Half-title p. | (ii) unheaded introduction to the Talisman Library | (frontispiece, tipped in) | (iii) title p. | (iv) list of titles in series | v–x. Introduction | 1–171. text | 172–182. Notes.

Binding (see Note 3)

Grey cloth boards, blocked blue (see Note 3); edges plain; plain off-white endpapers.

Front board: BERIC | THE . BRITON | G.A. Henty | (publisher's trade mark for the series, including the wording: The | TALISMAN | Library of | ENGLISH | AUTHORS) | Blackie.&.Son.Limited (all blue) within framework of decorative rules (blue). **Spine:** BERIC . THE . BRITON : HENTY (blue) running from foot to head. **Back board:** plain.

References: BL; Bod; BB.

Notes

1. In 1922 Blackie issued this as the sixth Henty title in 'The Talisman Library of English Authors'. (The full title takes no account of the fact that the first two books, issued in 1920, were by Sir Walter Scott!). In the same year two by Charles Kingsley were followed by the first four Henty titles. These were: *With Clive in India; Under Drake's Flag; With Wolfe in Canada* and *Redskin and Cowboy*. A fifth book by Henty, *The Dragon and the Raven*, entered the series in 1921.

2. The frontispiece is the same as that in 59.1.

3. Books in the series (example at Plate 145) were also issued in limp cloth covers, cut flush, in the same design, and with no alteration to the contents.

4. Later impressions in both styles of binding were issued with undated title pages.

59.5

THE TALISMAN LIBRARY (underlined) | BERIC THE BRITON | BY | G.A. HENTY | (publisher's device) | BLACKIE & SON LIMITED | LONDON AND GLASGOW

Contents

172 x 115 mm. (i)–x | 1–182 | no catalogue. Frontispiece as in 59.4.

(i)–(ii) Introduction to the series with bold heading on p.(i): 'The Talisman

Library of English Authors', and the titles in the series listed on p.(ii) | (frontispiece, tipped in) | (iii) title p. | (iv) Blackie addresses, and printer's imprint (Printed in Great Britain by Blackie & Son, Limited, Glasgow) | v–x. Introduction | 1–171. text | 172–182. Notes, with imprint at foot of p.182 (PRINTED AND BOUND IN GREAT BRITAIN | By Blackie & Son, Limited, Glasgow).

Binding: As for 59.4, but see Note 3.

Reference: BU.

Notes

1. Following the issues both dated and undated of 59.4 (see also 59.4, Note 4), the preliminary pages were reset. The main changes, apart from the title-page imprint, were the re-arrangement of the introductory notes and the list of titles in the series. Otherwise the text appears to be unaltered.

2. At this date (1922) the Talisman Library consisted of ten titles: two by Scott, two by Kingsley, and six by Henty.

3. The series continued in production, both in limp cloth and in cloth boards, at least for two decades. Copies of some titles are found with the Book Production War Economy symbol on p.(iv), a measure required of British publishers during the second war (see *With Wolfe in Canada*, 27.4, Note 3).

60. IN GREEK WATERS

60.1

IN GREEK WATERS: | A STORY OF | THE GRECIAN WAR OF INDEPENDENCE. | (1821–1827) | BY | G.A. HENTY, | Author of "The Dash for Khartoum;" "In the Reign of Terror;" | "With Clive in India;" &c. | (19mm. rule) | WITH TWELVE ILLUSTRATIONS BY W.S. STACEY, AND | A MAP OF THE GRECIAN ARCHIPELAGO. | (19mm. rule) | (publisher's device) | LONDON: | BLACKIE & SON, LIMITED, 49 OLD BAILEY, E.C. | GLASGOW, EDINBURGH, AND DUBLIN. | 1893.

Contents

185 x 130 mm. (i)–(x) | (11)–384 | catalogue (1)–32. Twelve full-page wash-drawings by W.S. Stacey, reproduced by halftone blocks printed in black on coated paper, unbacked, unfolioed, tipped in. Map printed from line block on text page.

(i) Half-title p. | (ii) blank | (frontispiece, tipped in) | (iii) title p. | (iv) blank | (v) Preface | (vi) blank | (vii) Contents | (viii) blank | (ix) list of Illustrations | (x) map | (11)–384. text | (1)–32. catalogue.

Binding (see Plate 72)

Green cloth boards, bevelled, blocked black, blue, blind, and gilt; all edges burnished olive-green; maroon surface-paper endpapers.

Front board: IN GREEK | WATERS (gilt, black shadow) | A | STORY OF | . THE . | GREEK WAR | . OF . | INDEPENDENCE | 1821–1827 (all black) above and at left of illustration of man loading a musket (black, blue, gilt). All with a black rule border. **Spine:** . IN . | GREEK | WATERS | (rule) | G.A. | HENTY. (all gilt) above illustration of turbaned man with lance (black, blue, gilt). Two gilt rules and one black at head; one black, one gilt at foot. **Back board:** Single rule near edges of bevel (blind).

References: BL; Bod; PN I *Farmer*, p.44; *Dartt*, p.79.

Notes

1. The book was published on 29 June 1892 at six shillings. By the end of February 1893 Blackie had sold 5950 copies, and during the next eleven years they sold 3600 more. This was not one of the best sellers, the average annual sale over those twelve years amounting to 796 copies, and over the following six years to 118 copies. At the end of that time the total number of copies sold was 10,260, and in that year, 1910, Blackie re-issued the book (title-page date 1911) in their cheaper 'New and Popular Edition' (see 60.3, below).

2. As usual with Blackie novels, the earliest issues contain catalogues advertising the books for the current year (in this case with title pages dated 1893) without quotations from press reviews.

*60.2

Reprints of the six-shilling edition were issued in the style of 60.1, with the date removed from the title page. Alterations were made when necessary to the title-page imprint and addresses: the Edinburgh address was not used after 1894; the Indian office was opened in 1901 although Bombay did not appear regularly in the Blackie imprint until 1906; and Dublin was omitted after 1910.

Bindings continued to show variation in colours of cloth, blocking, and endpapers. The slightly-varying issues among the reprints of the book in its first-edition format are all grouped together under this 'generic' heading, *60.2.

60.3

In Greek Waters I A STORY OF I THE GRECIAN WAR OF INDEPENDENCE I (1821–1827) I BY I G.A. HENTY I Author of "The Dash for Khartoum" "In the Reign of Terror" I "With Clive in India" &c. I ILLUSTRATED BY W.S. STACEY I AND A MAP I NEW EDITION I BLACKIE AND SON LIMITED I LONDON GLASGOW DUBLIN BOMBAY I 1911

Contents

187 x 128 mm. (1)–384 I catalogue 1–16. Eight full-page wash-drawings by W.S. Stacey, reproduced by halftone blocks printed in sepia on coated paper, unbacked, unfolioed, tipped in. Map printed from line block on text page.

(1) Half-title p. I (2) advertisement (NEW AND POPULAR EDITION OF I G.A. HENTY'S WORKS) listing 27 titles I (frontispiece, tipped in) I (3) title p. I (4) blank I (5) Preface I (6) blank I (7) Contents I (8) blank I (9) list of Illustrations I 10. Map of the Grecian Archipelago I 11–384. text I 1–16. catalogue.

Binding (see Plate 172)

Royal-blue cloth boards, blocked black, light-blue, warm-buff, and gilt; all edges stained olive-green; grey endpapers, lined off-white.

Front board: IN GREEK I . WATERS . I . BY G.A. HENTY . (all gilt) above illustration, framed by black line, of two sailors fighting (black, light-blue, warm-buff). **Spine:** . IN . I GREEK I WATERS I G.A. HENTY (all gilt) above illustration framed by black line, of young sailor with short sword (black, light-blue, warm-buff). At foot: BLACKIE & SON LTD (black). **Back board:** plain.

References: BL; Bod.

Notes
1. This was never one of Henty's most successful books (see 60.1, Note 1), and when re-issued in Blackie's 'New and Popular Edition' in 1910 it had sold only 1711 copies by the end of August 1911. Over the next six years, up to the end of August 1917, when Blackie's records cease, it had sold another 1193 copies at the cheaper price. The grand total of copies sold at both prices from 1892 to 1917 was 13,164.
2. For details of Blackie's first cheaper edition see *Facing Death*, 10.6, Notes 2–3.

*60.4

IN GREEK WATERS | A Story of the Grecian War of | Independence (1821–1827) | BY | G.A. HENTY | Author of "The Dash for Khartoum" "In the Reign of Terror" | "With Clive in India" &c. | Illustrated | BLACKIE AND SON LIMITED | LONDON GLASGOW AND BOMBAY

Contents
184 x 123 mm. (1)–384 | no catalogue. Frontispiece from watercolour drawing by Frank Gillett reproduced by three-colour halftone blocks; four full-page wash-drawings by W.S. Stacey, reproduced by halftone blocks printed in black; all on coated paper, unbacked, tipped in. Map printed from line block on text page 10.

(1) Half-title p. | (2) advertisement (G.A. HENTY'S BOOKS) listing 50 titles | (frontispiece, tipped in) | (3) title p. | (4) statement of origin (Printed and bound in Great Britain) | (5) Preface | (6) blank | (7) Contents | (8) blank | (9) list of Illustrations | 10. map | 11–384. text.

Binding (see Note 1)
Dark-blue cloth boards, blocked black, light-blue, and buff; edges plain; plain off-white endpapers.
Front board: IN GREEK | . WATERS . | . BY G.A. HENTY . (buff) above illustration, framed by black line, of two sailors fighting (black, light-blue, buff).
Spine: IN | GREEK | WATERS | G.A. HENTY (black) above illustration, framed by black line, of young sailor with short sword (black, light-blue, buff). At foot: BLACKIE & SON LTD (black). **Back board:** plain.

Reference: AK.

Notes
1. For notes on Blackie's second cheaper series, and later editions, see *Facing Death*, 10.7, Notes 1–3 and 6–8. Examples of the series binding style are at Plates 174–175.
2. All the minor variants of *In Greek Waters* in the series are grouped together under this 'generic' heading, *60.4.

61. DOROTHY'S DOUBLE

61.1

DOROTHY'S DOUBLE | BY | G.A.HENTY | AUTHOR OF 'RUJUB THE JUGGLER' 'IN THE DAYS OF THE MUTINY' | 'THE CURSE OF CARNE'S HOLD' ETC. | (publisher's device) | IN THREE VOLUMES – VOL.I. (VOL.II., VOL.III.) | London | CHATTO & WINDUS, PICCADILLY | 1894
(Note: London *is in gothic type; the comma after* WINDUS *is missing in Vol.I).*

Contents, Volume I
186 × 120 mm. (i)–(iv) | (1)–272 | no catalogue. No illustrations.
(i) Half-title p. | (ii) advertisement (NEW LIBRARY NOVELS) including this book | (iii) title p. | (iv) printer's imprint (PRINTED BY | SPOTTISWOODE AND CO., NEW-STREET SQUARE | LONDON) | (1)–6. Prologue | 7–272. text, with 'END OF THE FIRST VOLUME' on p.272, above printer's imprint (Spottiswoode & Co. Printers, New-street Square, London.).

Volume II
186 × 120 mm. (i)–(iv) | (1)–264 | no catalogue. No illustrations.
(i) Half-title p. | (ii) advertisement, as in Vol.I | (iii) title p. | (iv) printer's imprint, as in Vol.I | (1)–261. text, with 'END OF THE SECOND VOLUME' on p.261, above printer's imprint (PRINTED BY | SPOTTISWOODE AND CO., NEW-STREET SQUARE | LONDON) | (262) blank | (263) publisher's device | (264) blank.

Volume III
186 × 120 mm. (i)–(iv) | (1)–(224) | catalogue (1)–32. No illustrations.
(i) Half-title p. | (ii) advertisement, as in Vol.I | (iii) title p. | (iv) printer's imprint, as in Vol.I | (1)–221. text, with 'THE END' on p.261, above printer's imprint (Spottiswoode & Co. Printers, New-street Square, London.) | (222) blank | (223) publisher's device | (224) blank | (1)–32 catalogue, dated February 1894.

Binding (see Plate 6)
Blue, pattern-embossed boards, blocked blind and gilt; edges plain; blue-grey flowered endpapers.
Front board: plain, pattern-embossed (blind, see Note 7). **Spine:** DOROTHY'S | DOUBLE | G.A. | HENTY | VOL.I (VOL.II, VOL.III) | CHATTO & WINDUS (all gilt). **Back board:** publisher's monogram at centre (blind).

References: BL; Bod | Chatto & Windus Archive: MSS 2444/28/29 | *Farmer*, p.26; *Dartt*, p.47, *Companion*, p.12.

Notes
1. On 21 September 1893 Chatto wrote to Tillotsons acknowledging their offer of 'a new 3-volume novel by Mr G.A. Henty, now in course of serial issue, for £150'. The writer, expressing disappointment with their sales of *Rujub, the Juggler* (see 56.3, Note 1), feels 'not justified in giving more' for the new story than they paid before: 'We shall be glad to know that you are disposed to accept the £125'. This overlooks the fact that they were offered *Rujub* for £125, but agreed to pay only £115. The following day Tillotson wrote to acknowledge receipt of the offer of £125 for 'The

Hawtrey Mystery': 'Perhaps you will allow us a few days to consider the matter, and in the meantime we will undertake not to make an offer of the story elsewhere'. They took a fortnight to accept Chatto's 'offer of £125 for the English volume rights outside the United States and Canada of Mr Henty's new story "Dorothy's Double" or "The Hawtrey Mystery". We have a very favourable report upon the story from our Reader, and we trust that its issue in your series will be so satisfactory that you will be able to make us an offer for other stories of similar length by this author'.

2. Tillotsons had sold the first serial rights in the story to the *Western Weekly News*, who published it in weekly parts from 16 September to 30 December 1893 (see §3, 227). Tillotsons offered the story to Chatto & Windus as 'The Hawtrey Mystery', although it had been published in serial form as 'Dorothy's Double'. A third title, 'Hawtrey's Double' also appears in the documents in the Chatto & Windus archive.

3. The publisher's records show that Spottiswoode received an order on 1 January 1894 to print 400 copies of the three-volume edition. Publication date was 5 March, and the books were put on sale at 15s. This anticipated the new price for three-volume novels that was to be agreed by Andrew Chatto, following circulars issued simultaneously by the Mudie and W.H. Smith Libraries on 27 June 1894. The agreement was made without hesitation, by similar letters to both Libraries, dated 29 June: 'We are of opinion that the course you recommend to be adopted by publishers, of reducing the trade price of library novels, may tend to lessen the present overproduction and thus afford opportunities for the larger circulation of fiction of the better class. We shall therefore be willing to accede to the suggestions you have made, and to supply you with any library novels which we may issue after 1st of January next at the uniform rate of 4/= nett per volume, 25 as 24. We would also agree not to issue cheaper editions without your sanction within twelve months, unless at the time of subscription you are informed that we may wish to do so at shorter notice. Trusting that the very slight modifications which we desire in your proposals will meet with your approval and that beneficial results will accrue alike to readers, librarians and publishers'.

4. The books listed after Henty's name on the title page include *In the Days of the Mutiny*. That was the title used in the USA and Canada for the book published in the UK as *Rujub, the Juggler*. However, both names were printed here because the story had first appeared as 'In the Days of the Mutiny' when serialised by Tillotsons (see *Rujub, the Juggler*, 56.1, Notes 3–7).

5. Once again, as with *Rujub, the Juggler*, Chatto ordered, simultaneously with the three-volume edition, a colonial edition of 2000 copies (see 61.2).

6. On 7 November 1893 a correspondence began between Tillotsons and Chatto & Windus about granting rights to Tauchnitz in three novels, including one (unspecified) by Henty. The conclusion was that the rights were owned by Tillotsons, but I have found no record of any of Henty's work having been issued in a Tauchnitz edition. (Christian Bernhard von Tauchnitz owned a Leipzig publishing house which in 1841 started, in the absence of any international copyright agreement, to issue a 'Collection of British and American Authors', printed in English. The series was intended for sale on the Continent but became available also in the United Kingdom).

7. The Bodleian Library copy, received 10 March 1894, is bound in green pattern-embossed boards, blocked blind, bronze and gilt: the front board is blocked with a variant, all-over repeating leaf-pattern in bronze.

8. In 'amending' his original entry (*Dartt*, p.47) Dartt confuses matters in his *Companion*. He deletes his whole reference to a single-volume edition from Chatto & Windus, and inserts under the heading to the three-volume edition: 'U.S. copyright, November 1, 1893, Tillotson & Son.'. That is misplaced, and presumably refers to a purchase from Tillotsons of the US rights by Rand McNally, who published a single-volume edition in the States, described later by Dartt as 'first American'.

9. Such a sale by Tillotsons was allowed for in their agreement with Chatto (see Note 1). 1893 was the Tillotson copyright date, i.e. the date of first publication (see Note 2). But in the same entry Dartt amends his earlier description of the Rand McNally edition, adding on the verso of its title page: 'copyrights by G.A. Henty, 1893 and 1895'. I cannot unravel these convolutions, beyond adding that Dartt's copyright attributions (*Companion*, pp.12–13) do not appear in Chatto & Windus editions.

61.2
Notes
1. On 1 January 1894, the day that Chatto & Windus instructed their printer to produce an edition of 400 copies of 61.1, described above, they also ordered from the same printer an edition of 2000 copies of a single-volume Colonial Edition.

2. No copies of the true Colonial Edition have come to light, but the publisher's records show that after a time some sheets were bound up with revised preliminary pages, and sold in this country, probably after the standard single-volume octavo edition had gone out of print. These copies are described as 61.4.

3. It is nevertheless possible to give some information here about the impression originally made for the colonial edition. It was printed on paper which would produce a page size of approximately 170 x 115 mm., rather smaller than their standard octavo size used for 61.3. The size is the same as that of the paper used for the colonial edition of *Rujub, the Juggler*, 56.2, but the weight is rather less. The 'overs' printed for this order resulted in a total of 2020 sets of sheets.

61.3
DOROTHY'S DOUBLE | BY | G.A.HENTY | AUTHOR OF 'RUJUB THE JUGGLER' 'IN THE DAYS OF THE MUTINY | 'THE CURSE OF CARNE'S HOLD' ETC. | (publisher's device) | A NEW EDITION | London | CHATTO & WINDUS, PICCADILLY | 1895
(Note: The quotation mark after MUTINY *is missing;* London *is in gothic type).*

Contents
193 x 130 mm. (i)–(iv) | (1)–336 | catalogue (1)–32. No illustrations.

(i) Half-title p. | (ii) advertisement (OPINIONS OF THE PRESS | ON | DOROTHY'S DOUBLE.) giving ten quotations from reviews | (iii) title p. | (iv) blank | (1)–336. text, with printer's imprint on p.336 (PRINTED BY | SPOTTISWOODE AND CO., NEW-STREET SQUARE | LONDON) | (1)–32. catalogue (see Note 3).

Binding (see Note 5)
Red canvas boards, blocked gilt; edges uncut; ivory laid endpapers.
   Front board: DOROTHY'S | DOUBLE (gilt) within a gilt ornamental heart-shaped frame, in upper right corner. **Spine:** DOROTHY'S | DOUBLE | G.A.HENTY | CHATTO & WINDUS (all gilt). **Back board:** plain.

References: PN I *Farmer*, p.26; *Dartt*, p.47, *Companion*, p.12.

Notes

1. Spottiswoode received an order from Chatto & Windus on 3 December 1894 to print 2000 copies of a standard single-volume octavo edition for sale at 3s.6d., eleven months after the first publication of the book in three volumes. As with *Rujub, the Juggler*, Chatto did not wait for the Mudie second-hand sale of the three-volume edition (see 56.1, Note 10).

2. The catalogue bound in the first issue of this edition was dated September 1894, and in it, on p.11, this edition is announced, followed by the word 'Shortly'. Dartt (*Companion*, p.13) reports an issue with catalogue dated September 1896.

3. See 61.1, Note 4, regarding the books listed after Henty's name on the title page. In 61.3 the quotation mark following the word MUTINY is missing.

4. This edition was never reprinted, but Chatto supplemented supplies of a single-volume edition for the UK by printing alternative preliminary pages to be bound up with sheets originally intended for the colonial edition, which had been printed in January 1894. Issues of this 'ad hoc' edition are described as *61.4.

5. This binding style was also used for *Rujub, the Juggler*, 56.6, Plate 19, and for *The Queen's Cup*, 78.2.

*61.4

DOROTHY'S DOUBLE I BY I G.A.HENTY I AUTHOR OF I 'RUJUB THE JUGGLER' 'COLONEL THORNDYKE'S SECRET' I ETC. I (publisher's device) I A NEW EDITION [see Notes 2–3 for variants] I LONDON I CHATTO & WINDUS I 1901

Contents

180 × 122 mm. (i)–(iv) I (1)–336 I catalogues (1)–(4) & (1)–32. No illustrations.

(i) Half-title p. I (ii) blank I (iii) title p. I (iv) blank I (1)–336. text, with printer's imprint on p.336 (PRINTED BY I SPOTTISWOODE AND CO., NEW-STREET SQUARE I LONDON I (1)–(4) catalogue (LIST OF CHEAP POPULAR NOVELS) I (1)–32. general catalogue.

Binding: As for 61.3, except (a) smaller, red, smooth linen boards, blocked gilt; (b) heads trimmed, other edges uncut; (c) plain off-white wove endpapers.

References: PN I *Dartt Companion*, p.13.

Notes

1. This edition is made up of sheets originally printed in January 1894 for the Colonial Edition (61.2), bound up with a new set of preliminary pages, specially printed to use as cancels, and thus to produce copies for the UK. That accounts for the lack of illustrations, and the smaller page size. (See 61.3, Note 4).

2. It is possible that other variations will be found in the preliminary pages bound up with the text sheets of the original 'colonial' impression (see Note 3). For this reason this entry is given a 'generic' code number: *61.4.

3. Dartt (*Companion*, p.13, Note) describes a copy with prelims having the title page dated 1894. That would indicate that a further set of prelims was printed in that year for this purpose, although the publisher's records give no indication of such an impression. Dartt's description gives other details: the title page has the words

'SPECIAL EDITION' in place of the publisher's device and 'A NEW EDITION' shown here. It also has the quotation mark intact after 'MUTINY'. (There is no mention of the words 'Colonial Edition', nor of the usual proviso that copies may not be sold in the United Kingdom.) Apart from all that, Dartt's copy has a 32-page bound-in catalogue dated 1906. Although the main catalogue in my copy has no printed date, it is possible to date it post-1904 by the advertisements for novels by other authors.

4. There is first a 4-page list of 'yellowback' novels ('Cheap popular novels, Picture Covers, Two Shillings each'), with no mention of any book by Henty. The main catalogue follows, and at the end there is a section of 'yellowbacks' in which is included, at p.30, *Rujub the Juggler*.

61.5

Chatto & Windus's catalogues in copies of *Rujub the Juggler* advertised *Dorothy's Double* in their two-shilling 'yellowback' series of cheap novels. No copy of this edition has come to light, and I regret I cannot give a detailed description.

62. A JACOBITE EXILE

62.1

A JACOBITE EXILE: | BEING | THE ADVENTURES OF A YOUNG ENGLISHMAN IN | THE SERVICE OF CHARLES XII. OF SWEDEN. | BY | G.A.HENTY, | Author of "Beric the Briton;" "The Dash for Khartoum;" "The Lion of St. Mark;" | "With Clive in India;" &c. | (16mm. rule) | WITH EIGHT ILLUSTRATIONS BY PAUL HARDY, | AND A MAP OF CENTRAL EUROPE. | (16mm. rule) | (publisher's device) | LONDON: | BLACKIE & SON, LIMITED, 49 OLD BAILEY, E.C. | GLASGOW, EDINBURGH, AND DUBLIN. | 1894.

Contents
186 × 123 mm. (i)–(x) | (11)–352 | catalogue (1)–32. Eight full-page wash-drawings by Paul Hardy, reproduced by halftone blocks printed in black on coated paper, unbacked, unfolioed, tipped in. Fold-out map (two folds) printed in three colours with mechanical tints laid, unbacked, unfolioed, tipped in to face p.(x).

(i) Half-title p. | (ii) advertisement (MR. HENTY'S HISTORICAL TALES.) listing 24 titles | (frontispiece, tipped in) | (iii) title p. | (iv) blank | (v) Preface | (vi) blank | (vii) Contents | (viii) blank | (ix) list of Illustrations | (x) blank | (11)–352. text | (1)–32. catalogue.

Binding (see Plate 74)
Dark-green cloth boards, blocked black, yellow, red merging to pink and back to red, blind, and gilt; all edges burnished olive-green; maroon surface-paper endpapers.

Front board: A | Jacobite Exile (gilt) in decorative scroll, with flower (black, red, gilt) above illustration of two cavaliers holding hands (black, yellow, red merging to pink). At foot: By G.A.Henty. (gilt) in scroll (black and red). All framed in double black rule. **Spine:** A | Jacobite | Exile (gilt) in decorative scroll, with flower (black, red, gilt) above trophy of sword and hat (black, yellow, red, gilt). At foot: G.A.Henty. (gilt) in scroll (black and red). **Back board:** three rules (thin, thick, thin) near edges of bevel (blind).

References: BL; Bod; PN | *Farmer*, p.46; *Dartt*, p.88.

Notes
1. Publication date was 13 June 1893, and by the end of February 1894 Blackie had sold 5590 copies at five shillings. This was not a popular book in comparison with others by Henty, and after fourteen years only another 3910 copies had been sold, giving an average annual sale over the fifteen years of 633 copies. At this point, in 1908 (title-page date 1909) Blackie re-issued it in their cheaper edition (see 62.3 below). The remaining 76 copies of the five-shilling edition were sold over the next five years, concurrently with the cheaper books.
2. As usual with Blackie novels, the earliest issues contain catalogues advertising the books for the current year (in this case with title pages dated 1894) without quotations from press reviews.

*62.2

Reprints of the five-shilling edition were issued in the same style as 62.1, but with the date removed from the title page. Alterations were made when necessary to the title-page imprint and addresses. From the year following publication of this book the Edinburgh address was not used; the Indian office was opened in 1901, although Bombay did not appear regularly in the Blackie imprint until 1906; and Dublin was omitted after 1910.
Bindings continued to show variation in colours of cloth, blocking, and endpapers. The slightly-differing issues among the reprints of the book in its first-edition format are all grouped together under this 'generic' heading, *62.2.

62.3

A Jacobite Exile | being | The Adventures of a Young Englishman in | the Service of Charles XII of Sweden | BY | G.A.HENTY | Author of "Beric the Briton" "The Dash for Khartoum" "The Lion of St. Mark" | "With Clive in India" &c. | ILLUSTRATED BY PAUL HARDY | NEW EDITION | BLACKIE AND SON LIMITED | LONDON GLASGOW DUBLIN BOMBAY | 1909

Contents
182 × 126 mm. (1)–352 | catalogue 1–16. Eight full-page wash-drawings by Paul Hardy, reproduced by halftone blocks printed in sepia on coated paper, unbacked, unfolioed, tipped in. Map as in 62.1.
(1) Half-title p. | (2) advertisement (HENTY'S TALES OF BRITISH HISTORY) listing 38 titles | (frontispiece, tipped in) | (3) title p. | (4) blank | (5) Preface | (6) blank | 7. Contents | (8) blank | 9. list of Illustrations | (10) blank | (fold-out map, tipped in) | 11–352. text | 1–16. catalogue.

Binding (see Note 1)
Red cloth boards, blocked black, grey, orange, buff, and gilt; all edges stained olive-green; grey endpapers, lined off-white.
Front board: A JACOBITE | EXILE (gilt) above illustration, and: ADVENTURES | OF A YOUNG | ENGLISHMAN | IN THE | SERVICE OF | CHARLES XII | OF SWEDEN | G.A.HENTY (all gilt) at left of illustration, framed by black rules, of soldier with rifle (black, grey, orange, buff) and signature: J Hassall (black). **Spine:** A | JACOBITE | EXILE | G.A.HENTY (all gilt) above

illustration, framed by black rules, of soldier standing in front of a wood (black, orange, buff). At foot: BLACKIE & SON LTD (black). **Back board:** plain.

References: BL; Bod; PN.

Notes

1. Re-issued 1908 (title-page date 1909) in the 'New and Popular Edition'. For details see *Facing Death*, 10.6, Notes 2–3, and for examples of the series binding style, Plates 172–173.

2. In this edition Blackie sold 2015 copies by the end of August 1909, and during the following eight years, up to the end of August 1917 when Blackie's records cease, they sold 2061 more. The average annual sale for the nine years was 453 copies. The grand total of copies sold at both prices from 1893 to 1917 was 13,652.

*62.4

A JACOBITE EXILE | Being the Adventures of a Young | Englishman in the Service of | Charles XII of Sweden | BY | G.A.HENTY | Author of | "Beric the Briton" "The Dash for Khartoum" | "The Lion of St. Mark" | "The Tiger of Mysore" | &c. | Illustrated | BLACKIE AND SON LIMITED | LONDON GLASGOW AND BOMBAY

Contents

185 × 123 mm. (1)–352 | no catalogue. Frontispiece from watercolour drawing by Frank Gillett, reproduced by three-colour halftone blocks; four full-page wash-drawings by Paul Hardy, reproduced by halftone blocks printed in black; all on coated paper, unbacked, keyed to text pages, tipped in.

(1) Half-title p. | (2) advertisement (G.A.HENTY'S BOOKS) listing 20 titles | (frontispiece, tipped in) | (3) title p. | (4) Imprint (Printed and bound in Great Britain) | (5) Preface | (6) blank | (7) Contents | (8) blank | (9) list of Illustrations | (10) blank | 11–352. text.

Binding: As for 62.3, except (a) green cloth boards, blocked black, brown, and buff, with no gilt: front-board lettering all buff, spine lettering all black; (b) edges plain; (c) plain off-white endpapers.

Reference: IM.

Notes

1. For notes on Blackie's second cheaper series, 'The New Popular Henty', and subsequent editions of this book, see *Facing Death*, 10.7, Notes 1–3 and 6–8. Examples of the binding style for the series are at Plates 174–175.

2. All the minor variants of *A Jacobite Exile* in the series are grouped together under the 'generic' heading, *62.4.

63. ST. BARTHOLOMEW'S EVE

63.1

ST. BARTHOLOMEW'S EVE: | A TALE OF | THE HUGUENOT WARS. | BY | G.A.HENTY, | Author of "Beric the Briton;" "In Freedom's Cause;" "The Dash for

Khartoum;" | "By England's Aid;" "In the Reign of Terror;" &c. | (14mm. rule) | WITH TWELVE ILLUSTRATIONS BY H.J.DRAPER, | AND MAP OF FRANCE. | (14mm. rule) | (publisher's device) | LONDON: | BLACKIE & SON, LIMITED, 49 OLD BAILEY, E.C. | GLASGOW, EDINBURGH, AND DUBLIN. | 1894.

Contents

185 × 130 mm. (i)–(x) | (11)–384 | catalogue (1)–32. Twelve full-page wash-drawings by H.J.Draper, reproduced by halftone blocks printed in black on coated paper, unbacked, unfolioed, tipped in. Map of France, printed in three colours with mechanical tints, as double-page spread, guarded in after p.(x).

(i) Half-title p. | (ii) advertisement (MR. HENTY'S HISTORICAL TALES.) listing 24 titles | (frontispiece, tipped in) | (iii) title p. | (iv) blank | (v)–vi. Preface | (vii) Contents | (viii) blank | (ix) list of Illustrations | (x) blank | (map, guarded in) | (11)–384. text | (1)–32. catalogue.

Binding (see Plate 81)

Plum-red cloth boards, bevelled, blocked black, blind, silver, and gilt; all edges burnished olive-green; maroon surface-paper endpapers.

Front board: ST. | BARTHOLOMEW'S | EVE | BY | G.A.HENTY (silver) at right of trophy of belted sword, cross, etc. (black, silver, gilt). **Spine:** SAINT | BARTHOLOMEW'S | EVE | BY | G.A.HENTY (gilt) between areas of pictorial decoration (black and gilt). **Back board:** single rule near edges of bevel (blind).

References: BL; Bod; PN | *Farmer*, p.61; *Dartt*, p.116.

Notes

1. The book was published on 13 June 1893 at six shillings, and by the end of February 1894 Blackie had sold 7345 copies. After nine more years they had sold a further 5770, the average annual sale being 1312 copies for the first ten years. The book was on sale at 6s. until the end of 1910, by which time 1473 more copies had been sold (average annual sale being 246 copies), and then Blackie re-issued it in the cheaper edition (see 63.3). The remaining 113 copies of the 6s. edition were sold between 1911 and 1914, concurrently with the cheaper books.

2. The book is printed on heavier paper than Blackie normally used for Henty's books. That resulted in it being about 7mm. thicker than the other six-shilling novels, which meant that binding cases had to be made specially, and could not be taken from the stock generally available for all Blackie's children's novels at 6s. (see Appendix II, Part 5). It almost certainly came about by accident, probably because Blackie ran out of the proper paper at a critical moment, and had to find alternative stock in a hurry. But it meant that for reprints more paper of the heavier weight would have to be used, or narrower brasses would have to be made for the spine. They seem to have made the latter choice, but some issues exist which fit their cases rather loosely.

3. As usual with Blackie novels, the earliest issues contain catalogues advertising the books for the current year (in this case with title pages dated 1894) without quotations from press reviews.

*63.2

Reprints of the six-shilling edition were issued in the style of 63.1, with the date removed from the title page. Alterations were made when necessary to the title-page imprint and addresses: the Edinburgh address was not used after 1894; and the Indian office was opened in 1901 although Bombay did not appear regularly in the Blackie imprint until 1906.

Bindings continued to show variation in colours of cloth, blocking, and endpapers. The slightly-varying issues among the reprints of the book in its first-edition format are all grouped together under this 'generic' heading, *63.2.

63.3

St. Bartholomew's Eve | A TALE OF | THE HUGUENOT WARS | BY | G.A.HENTY | Author of "Beric the Briton" "In Freedom's Cause" "The Dash for Khartoum" | "By England's Aid" "In the Reign of Terror" &c. | ILLUSTRATED BY H.J.DRAPER | AND A MAP | NEW EDITION | BLACKIE AND SON LIMITED | LONDON GLASGOW DUBLIN BOMBAY | 1911

Contents
185 × 129 mm. (1)–384 | catalogue 1–16. Eight full-page wash-drawings by H.J.Draper, reproduced by halftone blocks printed in sepia on coated paper, unbacked, unfolioed, tipped in. Map as in 63.1.

(1) Half-title p. | (2) advertisement (NEW AND POPULAR EDITION OF | G.A.HENTY'S WORKS) listing 27 titles | (frontispiece, tipped in) | (3) title p. | (4) blank | 5. Preface | vi. [roman numerals in error] Preface, continued | (7) Contents | (8) blank | (9) list of Illustrations | (10) blank | (map, guarded in) | 11–384. text | 1–16. catalogue.

Binding (see Note 1)
Dark-green cloth boards, blocked black, brown, warm-buff, and gilt; all edges stained olive-green; grey endpapers, lined off-white.

Front board: ST. BARTHOLOMEW'S | . EVE . | . BY G.A.HENTY . | (gilt) above illustration, within black ruled frame, of three men in boat (black, brown, warm-buff). **Spine:** ST. BAR- | THOLOMEW'S | EVE | G.A.HENTY (all gilt) above illustration of standing figure in sixteenth-century costume (black, brown, warm-buff). At foot: BLACKIE & SON LTD (black). **Back board:** plain.

References: BL; Bod.

Notes
1. Re-issued 1910 (title-page date 1911) in the 'New and Popular Edition'. For details see *Facing Death*, 10.6, Notes 2–3, and, for examples of the series binding style, Plates 172–173.

2. In this edition Blackie had sold 1906 copies by the end of August 1911, and during the next six years, up to the end of August 1917 when their records cease, they sold 2242 more. That gives an average annual sale of 593 copies over the seven years. The grand total of copies sold at both prices, from 1893 to 1917 is 18,849.

*63.4

Title page: As for 63.3, except (a) NEW EDITION deleted; (b) date deleted; (c) imprint changed (BLACKIE AND SON LIMITED | LONDON GLASGOW AND BOMBAY).

Contents

186 x 125 mm. (1)–384 | no catalogue. Frontispiece from watercolour drawing by Frank Gillett, R.I., reproduced by three-colour halftone blocks; four full-page wash-drawings by H.J.Draper, reproduced by halftone blocks printed in black; all on coated paper, unbacked, tipped in. Map as in 63.1.

(1) Half-title p. | (2) advertisement (G.A.HENTY'S BOOKS) listing 30 titles | (frontispiece, tipped in) | (3) title p. | (4) blank | 5. Preface | vi. [roman numerals in error] Preface, continued | (7) Contents | (8) blank | (9) list of Illustrations | (10) blank | 11-384. text, with printer's imprint at foot of p.384 (PRINTED AND BOUND IN GREAT BRITAIN | By Blackie & Son, Limited, Glasgow).

Binding: As for 63.3, except (a) olive-green cloth boards, blocked black, indian red, and buff, with no gilt: front-board lettering all buff, spine lettering all black; (b) edges plain; (c) plain off-white endpapers.

Reference: PN.

Notes

1. For notes on Blackie's second cheaper series, 'The New Popular Henty', and subsequent editions of this book, see *Facing Death*, 10.7, Notes 1–3 and 6–8.

2. All the minor variants of *St. Bartholomew's Eve* in the series are grouped together under this 'generic' heading, *63.4.

64. THROUGH THE SIKH WAR

64.1

THROUGH THE SIKH WAR: | A TALE OF | THE CONQUEST OF THE PUNJAUB. | BY | G.A.HENTY, | Author of "Beric the Briton;" "The Dash for Khartoum;" "Held Fast for England;" | "With Clive in India;" &c. | (18mm. rule) | WITH TWELVE ILLUSTRATIONS BY HAL HURST, | AND A MAP OF THE PUNJAUB. | (18mm. rule) | (publisher's device) | LONDON: | BLACKIE & SON, LIMITED, 49 OLD BAILEY, E.C. | GLASGOW, EDINBURGH, AND DUBLIN. | 1894.

Contents

186 x 130 mm. (i)–(x) | (11)–384 | catalogue (1)–32. Twelve full-page wash-drawings by Hal Hurst, reproduced by halftone blocks printed in black on coated paper, unbacked, unfolioed, tipped in. Map printed in three colours with mechanical tints, as double-page spread, unbacked, guarded in after p.(x).

(i) Half-title p. | (ii) advertisement (MR. HENTY'S HISTORICAL TALES.) listing 24 titles. | (frontispiece, tipped in) | (iii) title p. | (iv) blank | (v) Preface | (vi) blank | (vii) Contents | (viii) blank | (ix) list of Illustrations | (x) blank | (map, guarded in) | (11)-384. text | (1)–32. catalogue.

Binding (see Plate 83)

Olive-green cloth boards, bevelled, blocked black, red, white, blind, and gilt; all edges burnished olive-green; dark-blue surface-paper endpapers.

Front board: THROUGH THE | SIKH WAR. | G.A.HENTY. (red, cased black) above and at right of illustration of Sikh warrior with shield and bloody sword, framed in crescent moon and star (black, red, white, gilt). **Spine:** THROUGH | THE | SIKH | WAR (red, cased black) above trophy of military equipment and triptych (black, red, white, gilt). Below this: G.A.HENTY. (red, cased black), over ornamental border (black and red). **Back board:** plain.

References: BL; Bod; PN | *Farmer*, p.70; *Dartt*, p.137, *Companion*, p.30.

Notes

1. The book was published on 13 June 1893 at six shillings. By the end of February 1894 Blackie had sold 6725 copies, and in the next ten years they sold 4818 more, the average annual sale over the eleven years being 1049 copies. In the following seven years 1450 copies were sold, the annual average for this period being 207 copies, and at this point, in 1911, Blackie re-issued the book in their cheaper edition (see 64.3). The remaining 108 copies of the six-shilling edition were sold over three years, concurrently with the cheaper books.

2. As usual with Blackie novels, the earliest issues contain catalogues advertising the books for the current year (in this case with title pages dated 1894) without quotations from press reviews.

*64.2

Reprints of the six-shilling edition were issued in the same style as 64.1, but with the date removed from the title page. Alterations were made when necessary to the title-page imprint and addresses: the Edinburgh address was not used after 1894; the Indian office was opened in 1901 although Bombay did not appear regularly in the Blackie imprint until 1906; and Dublin was omitted after 1910.

Bindings continued to show variation in colours of cloth, blocking, and endpapers. The slightly-varying issues among the reprints of the book in its first-edition format are all grouped together under this 'generic' heading, *64.2.

64.3

Through the Sikh War | A Tale of the Conquest of the Punjaub | BY | G.A.HENTY | Author of "Beric the Briton" "The Dash for Khartoum" "Held Fast for England" | "With Clive in India" &c. | WITH EIGHT ILLUSTRATIONS BY HAL HURST | AND MAP OF THE PUNJAUB | NEW EDITION | BLACKIE AND SON LIMITED | LONDON GLASGOW AND BOMBAY | 1912

Contents

183 x 125 mm. (1)–384 | no catalogue. Eight full-page wash-drawings by Hal Hurst, reproduced by halftone blocks printed in black on coated paper, unbacked, unfolioed, tipped in. Map, as in 64.1.

    (1) Half-title p. | (2) advertisement (NEW AND POPULAR EDITION OF | G.A.HENTY'S WORKS) listing 33 titles | (frontispiece, tipped in) | (3) title p. | (4) blank | (5) Preface | (6) blank | (7) Contents | (8) blank | (9) list of Illustrations | (10) blank | (map, guarded in) | 11–384. text.

Binding (see Note 1)

Red cloth boards, blocked black, orange, buff, and gilt; all edges stained olive-green; grey endpapers, lined off-white.

    Front board: THROUGH THE | SIKH WAR | G.A.HENTY (gilt) above illustration, framed by black line, of look-out and two Sikh riflemen in rocky landscape (black, orange, buff). **Spine:** THROUGH | THE | SIKH WAR | G.A.HENTY (gilt) above illustration, framed by black line, of man holding sword (black, orange, buff). At foot: BLACKIE & SON LTD (black). **Back board:** plain.

Reference: MH.

Notes

1. Re-issued 1911 (title-page date 1912) in the 'New and Popular Edition'. For details see *Facing Death*, 10.6, Notes 2–3, and for examples of the series binding style, Plates 172–173.

2. In this edition Blackie had sold 1816 copies by the end of August 1912, and during the next five years, to the end of August 1917 when their records cease, they sold 1790 more. That gives an average annual sale of 601 copies over the six years. The grand total of copies sold at both prices, from 1893 to 1917 is 16,707.

*64.4

Through the Sikh War | A Tale of the Conquest of the Punjaub | BY | G.A.HENTY | Author of "Beric the Briton" "The Dash for Khartoum" | "Held Fast for England" "With Clive in India" &c. | Illustrated | BLACKIE & SON LIMITED | LONDON AND GLASGOW

Contents

184 x 123 mm. (1)–(384) | catalogue (i)–(ii). Frontispiece from watercolour drawing by Frank Gillett, reproduced by three-colour halftone blocks; four wash-drawings by Hal Hurst reproduced by halftone blocks printed in black; all on coated paper, unbacked, keyed to text pages, tipped in.

(1) Half-title p. | (2) Blackie addresses | (frontispiece, tipped in) | (3) title p. | (4) printer's imprint (Printed in Great Britain by | Blackie & Son, Limited, Glasgow) | (5) Preface | (6) blank | 7. Contents | (8) blank | (9) list of Illustrations | (10) blank | 11–383. text | (384) blank | (i)–(ii) advertisement (The New Popular Henty) tipped in, listing 62 titles.

Binding (see Note 1)

Green cloth boards, blocked black, red, and buff; edges plain; plain off-white endpapers.

Front board: THROUGH THE | SIKH WAR | G.A.HENTY (black) above illustration, framed by black rules, of look-out and two Sikh riflemen in rocky landscape (black, red, buff). **Spine:** THROUGH | THE | SIKH | WAR | G.A.HENTY (black) above illustration, framed by black rules, of Sikh soldier standing in rocky landscape (black, red, buff). At foot: BLACKIE & SON LD. (black). **Back board:** plain.

Reference: PN.

Notes

1. For notes on Blackie's second cheaper series, 'The New Popular Henty', and later editions, see *Facing Death*, 10.7, Notes 1–3 and 6–8. Examples of the series binding style are at Plates 174–175.

2. All the minor variants of *Through the Sikh War* in the series are grouped together under this 'generic' heading, *64.4.

65. A WOMAN OF THE COMMUNE

65.1

A WOMAN | OF THE | COMMUNE | A TALE OF TWO SIEGES OF PARIS | BY | G.A.HENTY | Author of | 'In the Days of the Mutiny,' 'The Curse of Carne's Hold,' | 'Dorothy's Double,' Etc., Etc. | LONDON | F.V.WHITE & CO. | 14 BEDFORD STREET, STRAND, W. | (6mm. rule) | 1895

Contents
190 × 126 mm. approximately (pages unopened). (i)–(viii) | (1)–292 | catalogue (293)–308. No illustrations.
    (i) Half-title p. | (ii) blank | (iii) title p. | (iv) blank | (v)–vi. Contents | (vii) repeat half-title p. | (viii) blank | (1)–292. text, with printer's imprint at foot of p. 292 (Colston & Company Ltd., Printers, Edinburgh) | (293)–308. catalogue (see Note 5).

Binding (see Plate 11)
Mottled pink-red cloth boards, bevelled, blocked black and gilt; edges uncut; brown and cream patterned endpapers.
    Front board: A | WOMAN | OF THE | COMMUNE | G.A.HENTY (all black) above long gilt rule. Double black rules at head and foot. **Spine:** A | WOMAN | OF THE | COMMUNE | (short rule) | G.A.HENTY (all gilt) above gilt rule. F.V.White & Co. (gilt). Double black rules at head and foot. **Back board:** publisher's monogram (black) at centre.

References: BL; Bod | Chatto & Windus Archive: MSS 2444/30/31 | *Farmer*, p.84; *Dartt*, p.164.

Notes
1. Henty sent the story to Tillotsons, under the terms of his contract for adult fiction (see Appendix II, Part 4). They arranged for serialisation in *The Preston Guardian* (see §3, 218), a weekly newspaper that was not part of the Tillotson Group. The story appeared in 25 Saturday instalments, from 4 May to 19 October 1895.
2. On 25 January 1895 Chatto & Windus wrote to Tillotsons, after receiving their new list of available Fiction Serials. They picked five titles from the list, including Henty's *A Woman of the Commune*, and asked to be offered the British Book Rights of them all. Three days later Chatto wrote again to say they would be pleased to see the slips, when ready, of three of the titles, again including *A Woman of the Commune*, and adding: 'We observe that the prices you put on Mr Henty's and Mr [Justin] McCarthy's stories are much higher than those we paid you for these authors' previous works, while we must again remind you that the action of the circulating libraries is making it so difficult to secure a remunerative sale for 2 and 3 volume novels, that the value of them is now much less than when we had the others from you. The prices ought therefore certainly to be less, rather than higher than before'. That letter may possibly have affected Chatto's chances of acquiring the rights in the two novels. After eight months they wrote again, to remind Tillotsons that the slips of neither story had been received.
3. Tillotson's reply is not recorded, but its content is evident from Chatto's next letter to them: 'We are extremely disappointed that you should have disposed of the stories by Mr Justin McCarthy and Mr Henty as we publish nearly all of Mr McCarthy's

previous works, and Mr Henty's two last stories we took from you, and we think it always desirable that an author's work should, as far as possible, be kept together. After our letter to you of January 28th last, asking for a sight of the slips in reply to yours of the 26th January offering these two stories, we certainly relied upon your letting us have the perusal of them before offering them elsewhere, or, at any rate, that you would not have accepted another offer without giving us the first option. That you should have omitted to again refer the matter to us, after our letter of the 5th May last reminding you of our desire to take these two stories into consideration causes us much regret. We need hardly say that we are always ready to give immediate attention to any story that you may favour us with.'

4. Why Tillotsons should have ignored several letters from Chatto is far from clear. It is possible, if unlikely, that it was partly a result of Chatto's rather premature vehemence on 28 January about not being prepared to pay what Tillotsons were asking. The novel by Justin McCarthy did eventually come Chatto's way, and although the price first mentioned was £225, Chatto wrote that they 'would go up to £250 rather than lose it'. The correspondence droned on. Finally, in September, Chatto wrote of 'lamenting the misunderstanding', but ended: 'Thanking you for your desire to serve us, we remain Very faithfully Yours'. Henty's *A Woman of the Commune* was not mentioned again by either party.

5. I have found no records of the publisher, F.V.White, who succeeded in buying the story from Tillotsons. Their bound-in catalogue is undated, but includes an announcement of this book: 'Cloth gilt, bevelled boards, 6s.'.

6. The titles following Henty's name on the title page include *In the Days of the Mutiny*, which was the title under which *Rujub, the Juggler* first appeared in England, serialised by Tillotsons before it was published in book form by Chatto & Windus (see *Rujub, the Juggler*, 56.1, Notes 3–6).

7. The make-up of this book has not been very carefully planned. After an 8-page section of prelims, the text consists of twenty-four 16-page gatherings followed by an odd four pages, 289-292. These two conjugate leaves are folded and tipped in, without sewing, causing a weakness in the binding, between the main part of the text and the catalogue.

8. On p.46, line 21, there is a misprint 'hear' for 'here'. This ran, unchanged, through all printings of the book under this title, but was corrected by the same printer, Colston, when it was taken over by a new publisher, Partridge, and issued with two alternative titles (see 65.5, Note 4).

*65.2

A WOMAN | OF THE | COMMUNE | A TALE OF TWO SIEGES OF PARIS | BY | G.A.HENTY | Author of | 'In the Days of the Mutiny,' 'The Curse of Carne's Hold,' | 'Dorothy's Double,' Etc., Etc. | SECOND EDITION | LONDON | F.V.WHITE & CO. | 14 BEDFORD STREET, STRAND, W. | (6mm. rule) | 1895

Contents, Binding: As for 65.1.

Reference: PN.

Notes

1. The make-up has not changed (see 65.1, Note 7). In my copy the last pair of conjugate leaves, forming pp.289–292, has been folded incorrectly, and is bound in so that the pages appear as 291, 292, 289, 290.

2. Copies of this book have been reported to me with the words 'THIRD EDITION' and 'FOURTH EDITION' on the title page. These copies all carry the date 1895 at the foot of the page. It may be that the book sold well and had to be reprinted three times in quick succession. These variant title pages may, alternatively, be evidence of an old publisher's dodge to make books appear to be selling quicker than they actually were. It was not a great difficulty to stop the press every 500 copies, or every 1000 copies, and change one line of type on the title page before carrying on with the run. I have not found an example of this elsewhere in Henty's works, and if it did happen in this case it was an unnecessary ploy, as the book was re-issued with illustrations the following year. But in view of the revelation in 65.4, Note 1, I cover these variants within this 'generic' heading, *65.2.

3. A small economy was made in binding the third and fourth 'editions': the horizontal rule across the centre of the spine and front board was blocked in black, instead of gilt.

4. The leaves in the third and fourth 'editions' are trimmed at all edges, giving a page size of 183 × 123 mm.

65.3

A WOMAN | OF THE | COMMUNE | A TALE OF THE SIEGES OF PARIS | BY | G.A.HENTY | (publisher's device) | LONDON | GEORGE BELL & SONS | AND BOMBAY | (6mm. rule) | 1895

Contents
190 × 120 mm. (i)–(viii) | (1)–292 | catalogue (1)–(14). No illustrations.
　　(i) Half-title p., headed in gothic type, underlined: 'Bell's Indian and Colonial Library.' | (ii) notice (This Edition is issued for circulation in India and the Colonies only) | (iii) title p. | (iv) blank | (v)–vi. Contents | (vii) repeat half-title p. (without heading) | (viii) blank | (1)–292. text, with printer's imprint at foot of p.292 (Colston & Company Ltd., Printers, Edinburgh) | (1)–(14) catalogue, dated August 1895.

Binding
Pink mottled cloth, blocked brown and gilt; top edge uncut, others plain; plain off-white endpapers.
　　Front board: Bell's Indian & Colonial Library | A WOMAN | OF THE COMMUNE | (large version of publisher's device) (all brown). **Spine:** A WOMAN | OF THE | COMMUNE | (1cm. rule) | G.A. | HENTY (all brown) with intricate gilt decoration above and below. At foot: GEORGE BELL & SONS (brown) below small version of publisher's device (brown). **Back board:** plain.

References: AK | *Dartt*, p.165.

Notes
1. *Dartt* describes a copy of Bell's Indian and Colonial Edition with no date on the title page, in a binding case with the imprint of the Canadian publishers, The Copp, Clark Co. Limited. If the description is accurate it implies that there must have been a reprint with the changed title page, although the date of the catalogue bound in is the same as in the copy described here. It is more likely that the title-page date was omitted in error from *Dartt's* description of 'an unusual 1895 edition'.

2. The catalogue, strangely and uneconomically consisting of 14 pages, starts with a section headed 'BELL'S I INDIAN & COLONIAL LIBRARY.', and this is followed by an 'ALPHABETICAL LIST OF BOOKS I CONTAINED IN I BOHN'S LIBRARIES.'. Messrs Bell and Daldy had acquired the stock and copyrights of the firm of H.G.Bohn in 1864, and took over the Bohn premises in York Street, Covent Garden, London, W.C. After F.R. Daldy's death in 1873 the firm became known as George Bell & Sons.

3. There is a slip, 94 × 120 mm., tipped-in between the upper endpaper and the half-title page, on which is printed in red ink: 'Bell's Indian and Colonial Library. I NOTICE. I MESSRS. GEORGE BELL AND SONS beg to I announce that they will issue before Christmas I a Special Colonial Edition of I The Amazing Marriage I BY I GEORGE MEREDITH.'

4. The text is printed from the type or plates used for the F.V. White editions, and the edition may be made up from sheets already printed, which would help to account for the number of 'editions' ascribed by the publisher to 65.2 (see 65.2, Note 2). The prelims are in the same style as before, modified for the new publisher.

65.4

A WOMAN I OF THE I COMMUNE I A TALE OF TWO SIEGES OF PARIS I BY I G.A.HENTY I Author of I 'In the Days of the Mutiny,' 'The Curse of Carne's Hold,' I 'Dorothy's Double,' Etc., Etc. I WITH ILLUSTRATIONS BY HAL HURST I LONDON I F.V.WHITE & CO. I 14 BEDFORD STREET, STRAND, W. I (6mm. rule) I 1896

Contents

196 × 133 mm. (i)–(viii) I (1)–292 I catalogue (293)–308. Six full-page wash-drawings by Hal Hurst, reproduced by halftone blocks printed in black on coated paper, unbacked, unfolioed, tipped in.

(i) Half-title p. I (ii) blank I (frontispiece, tipped in) I (iii) title p. I (iv) blank I (v)–vi. Contents I (vii) List of Illustrations I (viii) blank I (1)–292. text I (293)–308. catalogue.

Binding (see Plate 11)

Brown cloth boards, bevelled, blocked black, red, pink, blind, and gilt; all edges gilt; plain ivory laid endpapers.

Front board: A WOMAN I OF THE COMMUNE (gilt, shaded black) above illustration of girl in black with red flag, etc. (black, red, pink). At bottom right corner: BY (black) I G.A.HENTY (gilt, shaded black). **Spine:** Four rules at head (red, gilt, red, black) above: A I WOMAN I OF THE I COMMUNE (gilt, shaded black) I G.A.HENTY. (gilt); illustration of girl facing firing squad (black, red, pink). At foot: F.V.WHITE & Co (black on solid gilt panel) with black and red rules. **Back board:** publisher's monogram (blind) at centre.

References: PN I *Dartt*, pp.164–165.

Notes

1. The bound-in catalogue includes this title: 'Bevelled boards, 6s. 2nd edition', which seems strange as there were supposedly third and fourth 'editions' before this one. See 65.2, Note 2.

2. This is yet another example of one of Henty's adult novels being changed in appearance to look like one of his books for boys (see Appendix II, Part 6, and especially Note 43). This was generally achieved, as by this publisher, with the addition of illustrations and a pictorial binding.

3. Two of the halftone blocks are marked with a process engraver's initials, V & C.

65.5

Title page: As for 65.4, but with date changed to 1897, and a slightly wider rule (8mm.) above it.

Contents: 189 x 126 mm. Otherwise as for 65.4.

Binding: (See Plate 11). As for 65.4, except (a) smaller, brown cloth boards, not bevelled, blocked black, red, pink, blind, and gilt; (b) edges plain; (c) plain off-white wove endpapers.

References: PN I *Dartt Companion*, p.35.

Notes

1. This is a cheaper version of 65.4, printed on smaller paper of a slightly poorer quality, but with no alteration to text or prelims apart from the title-page date.

2. The binding is modified by the abandonment of bevelled edges to the boards and gilt edges to the leaves.

3. Dartt reports in his *Companion* a copy bound in blue cloth boards.

4. This story was later published in book form by S.W.Partridge & Co., Ltd: in 1899 under the title *Cuthbert Hartington* (§1, 86), and in 1916 as *Two Sieges* (§1, 112).

66. WULF THE SAXON

66.1

WULF THE SAXON I A STORY OF I THE NORMAN CONQUEST I BY I G.A.HENTY I Author of "Beric the Briton;" "A Jacobite Exile;" "In Freedom's Cause;" I "The Dragon and the Raven;" "Bonnie Prince Charlie;" &c. I (19mm. rule) I WITH TWELVE ILLUSTRATIONS BY RALPH PEACOCK I (19mm. rule) I (publisher's device) I LONDON I BLACKIE & SON, LIMITED, 49 OLD BAILEY, E.C. I GLASGOW, AND DUBLIN I 1895

Contents

184 x 131 mm. (i)–(x) I (11)–384 I catalogue (1)–32. Twelve full-page wash-drawings by Ralph Peacock, reproduced by halftone blocks printed in black on coated paper, unbacked, unfolioed, tipped in.

(i) Half-title p. I (ii) advertisement (MR. HENTY'S HISTORICAL TALES.) listing 30 titles I (frontispiece, tipped in) I (iii) title p. I (iv) blank I (v)–vi. Preface I (vii) Contents I (viii) blank I (ix) list of Illustrations I (x) blank I (11)–384. text I (1)–32. catalogue.

Binding (see Plate 101)

Light-green cloth boards, bevelled, blocked brown, yellow, dark-green; blind; and gilt; all edges burnished olive-green; grey endpapers, lined off-white.

Front board: WULF THE I SAXON (gilt, cased brown) out of two dark-green panels, cased brown, on solid-yellow background of illustration of mounted Norman soldier, attacking with lance a Saxon foot soldier with shield and dagger (brown, yellow, dark-green). In scroll, superimposed at foot: BY G.A.HENTY (cloth-colour out of solid gilt, brown). All framed by brown line. **Spine:** WULF | (ornament) THE (ornament) | SAXON (gilt) on dark-green rectangle with rules above and below (brown and gilt). Beneath this: illustration of Saxon with shield and dagger (brown, yellow, dark-green). At foot: G.A.HENTY (cloth-colour out of solid gilt panel, cased brown) over brown and gilt rules. All framed by brown line. **Back board:** single rule near edges of bevel (blind).

References: BL; Bod; PN | *Farmer*, p.85; *Dartt*, p.166.

Notes
1. The book was published on 8 May 1894 at six shillings. By the end of February 1895 Blackie had sold 8090 copies, and in the following nine years they sold 5525 more, the average annual sale over the ten-year period being 1362 copies. The six-shilling edition was still on sale thirteen years later, at the end of August 1917, when Blackie's records cease: during those years 3347 more copies were sold at an average yearly rate of 258. No cheaper edition was issued until 1922.
2. As usual with Blackie novels, the earliest issues contain catalogues advertising the books for the current year (in this case with title pages dated 1895) without quotations from press reviews.

*66.2

Reprints of the six-shilling edition were issued in the same style as 66.1, but with the date removed from the title page. Changes were made when necessary to the title-page imprint and addresses: the Indian office was opened in 1901 although Bombay did not appear regularly in the Blackie imprint until 1906; after 1910 the Dublin address was removed. Bindings continued to show variation in colours of cloth, blocking, and endpapers.

There were several variant issues among the reprints of the book in its first-edition format, especially as it remained in this form for twenty-three years: they are all grouped together under this 'generic' heading, *66.2.

*66.3

WULF THE SAXON | A STORY OF | THE NORMAN CONQUEST | BY | G.A.HENTY | Author of "Beric the Briton" "A Jacobite Exile" "In Freedom's Cause" | "The Dragon and the Raven" "Bonnie Prince Charlie" &c. | ILLUSTRATED BY RALPH PEACOCK | BLACKIE AND SON LIMITED | LONDON GLASGOW AND BOMBAY

Contents
185 × 125 mm. (1)–384 | no catalogue. Frontispiece from watercolour drawing, reproduced by three-colour halftone blocks; four full-page wash-drawings; all by Ralph Peacock; printed on coated paper, unbacked, keyed to text pages, tipped in.
    (1) Half-title p. | (2) blank | (frontispiece, tipped in) | (3) title p. | (4) blank | 5. Preface | vi. [roman numerals in error] Preface, continued | 7. Contents | (8) blank | (9) list of Illustrations | (10) blank | 11–384. text, with printer's imprint at foot of p.384 (PRINTED AND BOUND IN GREAT BRITAIN | By Blackie & Son, Limited, Glasgow).

Binding (see Note 1)
Red cloth boards, blocked black, and buff; edges plain; plain off-white endpapers.

Front board: WULF (buff, cased black) | THE (black) | SAXON (buff, cased black) above illustration of soldier with shield and long sword, under fire from arrows (black, buff). At lower right corner, signature: J Hassall (black). **Spine:** WULF | THE | SAXON | G.A.HENTY (black) above illustration of same soldier, standing, at rest (black, buff). At foot: BLACKIE & SON LTD (black). **Back board:** plain.

References: Bod; PN.

Notes
1. Re-issued 1922 in 'The New Popular Henty', a name very close to that used for Blackie's first cheaper series ('The New and Popular Edition', begun in 1903) in which this title never appeared (see 66.1, Note 1). For details of the later series see *Facing Death*, 10.7, Notes 1–3 and 6–8, and examples of the binding style, Plates 174–175.
2. All the minor variants of *Wulf the Saxon* in the series are grouped together under this 'generic' heading, *66.3.

67. IN THE HEART OF THE ROCKIES

67.1

IN THE | HEART OF THE ROCKIES | A STORY OF | ADVENTURE IN COLORADO | BY | G.A.HENTY | Author of "Redskin and Cow-boy;" "With Lee in Virginia" | "By Right of Conquest;" &c. | (16mm. rule) | WITH EIGHT FULL-PAGE ILLUSTRATIONS BY G.C.HINDLEY | (16mm. rule) | (publisher's device) | LONDON | BLACKIE & SON, LIMITED, 50 OLD BAILEY, E.C. | GLASGOW, AND DUBLIN. | 1895
(Note: the semicolon after With Lee in Virginia *is missing).*

Contents
185 x 124 mm. (i)–(x) | (11)–352 | catalogue (1)–32. Eight full-page wash-drawings by G.C.Hindley, reproduced by halftone blocks printed in black on coated paper, unbacked, unfolioed, tipped in.

(i) Half-title p. | (ii) blank | (frontispiece, tipped in) | (iii) title p. | (iv) blank | (v)–vi. Preface | (vii) Contents | (viii) blank | (ix) list of Illustrations | (x) blank | (11)–352. text | (1)–32. catalogue.

Binding (see Plate 72)
Grey cloth boards, blocked black, blue, maroon, blind, and gilt; all edges burnished olive-green; grey endpapers, lined off-white.

Front board: . IN . | . THE . | . HEART . | . OF . THE . | . ROCKIES | . BY . | . G.A.HENTY . (all gilt) on blue rocks of illustration (black, blue, maroon). All framed by black and maroon rules. **Spine:** IN | THE | HEART | OF | THE | ROCKIES (all gilt on blue panel) above decoration of feathers and arrowheads (black, blue, maroon, gilt). At foot: . BY . | . G . A . HENTY . (gilt on blue). The whole framed by black rule, and with gilt rules at head and foot. **Back board:** three rules (thin, thick, thin) near edges of board (blind).

References: BL; Bod; PN | *Farmer*, p.41; *Dartt*, p.84.

Notes

1. The book was published on 19 July 1894 at five shillings. By the end of February Blackie had sold 7375 copies, and after eleven more years they had sold an additional 6941. The average annual sale over the twelve-year period was 1193 copies. In another eleven years, by the end of August 1917, when Blackie's records cease, 3288 more copies had been sold, making a grand total of 17,604, all at five shillings, in the period from 1894 to 1917. The book was not re-issued in a cheaper edition until 1922.

2. As usual with Blackie novels, the earliest issues contain catalogues advertising the books for the current year (in this case with title pages dated 1895) without quotations from press reviews.

*67.2

Reprints of the five-shilling edition were issued in the same style as 67.1, but with the date removed from the title page. Changes were made when necessary to the title-page imprint and addresses: the Indian office was opened in 1901 although Bombay did not appear regularly in the Blackie imprint until 1906; after 1910 Dublin was removed.

Bindings continued to show variation in colours of cloth and blocking.

There were several slightly-varying issues among the reprints of the book in its first-edition format, in which it appeared for so many years: these are all grouped together under this 'generic' heading, *67.2.

*67.3

In the | Heart of the Rockies | A Story of Adventure in Colorado | BY | G.A.HENTY | Author of "Redskin and Cowboy" "With Lee in Virginia" | "Beric the Briton" &c. | ILLUSTRATED | BLACKIE AND SON LIMITED | LONDON GLASGOW AND BOMBAY

Contents

184 x 122 mm. (1)–352 | no catalogue. Frontispiece from watercolour drawing by Frank Gillett, R.I., reproduced by three-colour halftone blocks; four full-page wash-drawings by G.C.Hindley, reproduced by halftone blocks printed in black; all on coated paper, unbacked, keyed to text pages, tipped in.

(1) Half-title p. | (2) advertisement (G.A.HENTY'S BOOKS) listing 56 titles | (frontispiece, tipped in) | (3) title p. | (4) printer's imprint (Printed in Great Britain by | Blackie & Son, Limited, Glasgow) | 5. Preface | vi. [roman numerals in error] Preface, continued | (7) Contents | (8) blank | (9) list of Illustrations | (10) blank | 11–352. text.

Binding (see Note 1)

Green cloth boards, blocked black and buff; edges plain; plain off-white endpapers.

Front board: IN THE HEART | OF THE ROCKIES | BY G.A.HENTY (black) above illustration of Indian advancing with rifle (black, buff). At lower right corner, signature: J Hassall (black). **Spine:** IN THE | HEART | OF THE | ROCKIES | G.A.HENTY (black) above illustration of Indian with rifle (black, buff). At foot: BLACKIE & SON LTD (black). **Back board:** plain.

References: Bod; PN.

Notes

1. Re-issued in the 1920s in 'The New Popular Henty', a name very close to that used for the series begun in 1903 ('The New and Popular Edition'), in which this title never appeared (see 67.1, Note 1, above). Details of this second series, and later editions, are under *Facing Death*, 10.7, Notes 1–3 and 6–8, and examples of the series binding style at Plates 174–175.

2. All the minor variants of *In the Heart of the Rockies* in the series are grouped together under this 'generic' heading, *67.3.

68. WHEN LONDON BURNED

68.1

WHEN LONDON BURNED | A STORY OF | RESTORATION TIMES AND THE GREAT FIRE | BY | G.A.HENTY | Author of "Beric the Briton", "By Pike and Dyke", "One of the 28th", "The Lion of St. Mark", | "In the Reign of Terror", "The Dash for Khartoum", &c. | (18mm. rule) | WITH TWELVE PAGE ILLUSTRATIONS BY J.FINNEMORE | (18mm. rule) | (publisher's device) | LONDON | BLACKIE & SON, LIMITED, 50 OLD BAILEY, E.C. | GLASGOW AND DUBLIN | 1895

Contents

185 × 128 mm. (i)–(x) | (11)–388 | catalogue (1)–32. Twelve full-page wash-drawings by J.Finnemore, reproduced by halftone blocks printed in black on coated paper, unbacked, unfolioed, tipped in.

(i) Half-title p. | (ii) advertisement (MR. HENTY'S HISTORICAL TALES.) listing 30 titles | (frontispiece, tipped in) | (iii) title p. | (iv) blank | (v) Preface | (vi) blank | (vii) Contents | (viii) blank | (ix) list of Illustrations | (x) blank | (11)–388. text | (1)–32. catalogue.

Binding (see Plate 87)

Grey-blue cloth boards, bevelled, blocked black, yellow, orange, and gilt; all edges burnished olive-green; grey endpapers, lined off-white.

Front board: When | London | Burned (orange, cased black) above and over decoration of heads and shoulders of two figures in restoration dress (black and yellow) against fiery back-ground (gilt), above: A Story | of Restoration Times | and the | Great | Fire | BY | G.A.HENTY (all orange). **Spine:** When | London | Burned (gilt, cased black) | A Story of | Restoration Times | and the | Great Fire (gilt), all above illustration of full-length figure with stick (black and yellow). At foot: G.A.HENTY (gilt, shaded black). **Back board:** plain.

References: BL; Bod; PN | *Farmer*, p.77; *Dartt*, p.155, *Companion*, p.33.

Notes

1. The book was published on 4 August 1894, at six shillings. By the end of February 1895 Blackie had sold 9075 copies, and during the next eleven years they sold 6401 more: the average annual sale over the twelve years being 1290 copies. Over the following eleven years, up to the end of August 1917 when Blackie records cease, a

further 2595 copies were sold, all at six shillings. The book was not re-issued in a cheaper edition during that period. The grand total from 1894 to 1917 was 18,071.
2. Unusually for Blackie, this book does not make an even working, there being an odd 4-page section at the end, between the final text gathering and the catalogue. Whether this was the result of an error in cast-off, or of some final corrections by Henty, we shall never know (see Appendix III, Part 1).
3. As usual, the earliest issues contain catalogues advertising the books for the current year (title pages dated 1895) without quotations from press reviews.

*68.2

Reprints of the six-shilling edition were issued in the style of 68.1, with the date removed from the title page. Changes were made when necessary to the title-page imprint and addresses: the Indian office was opened in 1901 although Bombay did not appear regularly in the Blackie imprint until 1906; after 1910 Dublin was removed.
Bindings continued to show variation in colours of cloth and blocking.
The slightly-varying issues among the many reprints of this popular title in its first-edition format are all grouped together under this 'generic' heading, *68.2.

68.3
Notes
1. This was one of four Henty titles published in Blackie's Colonial Library in 1896. I have examined copies of the other three, and they are listed under the titles given in Note 2 below. No copy of *When London Burned* has come to light.
2. The series included 12 books for young people, and the other three titles by Henty were: (1).*With Clive in India*, 15.5; (2). *A Final Reckoning*, 29.3; (8).*The Dash for Khartoum*, 53.3. The books were advertised: 'In crown 8vo, with Frontispiece, in Paper Covers, also in Cloth boards'.
3. In cloth boards, the colonial edition of this title has proved extremely elusive, as have all four titles in paper covers. I have found no trace of any of them.
4. The descriptions of the other three titles will give a reasonable notion of the appearance of 68.3: the binding design, by Talwin Morris (see Appendix IV, Part 2), was used in the same colour scheme for the other Henty titles (see *The Dash for Khartoum*, 53.3, Plate 54), and the general style and make-up of them all is the same.
5. More details of the series are given under *With Clive in India*, 15.5, Notes 2–3.

*68.4

When London Burned | A Story of Restoration Times | and the Great Fire | BY | G.A.HENTY | Author of "Beric the Briton" "By Pike and Dyke" "One of the 28th" | "The Lion of St. Mark" "In the Reign of Terror" | "The Dash for Khartoum" &c. | ILLUSTRATED | BLACKIE AND SON LIMITED | LONDON GLASGOW AND BOMBAY

Contents
185 × 123 mm. (1)–392 | no catalogue. Frontispiece from watercolour drawing by Frank Gillett, R.I., reproduced by three-colour halftone blocks; four full-page wash-drawings by J.Finnemore, reproduced by halftone blocks printed in black; all on coated paper, unbacked, keyed to text pages, tipped in.

(1) Half-title p. | (2) advertisement (G.A.HENTY'S BOOKS) listing 40 titles | (frontispiece, tipped in) | (3) title p. | (4) imprint (Printed and bound in Great Britain) | 5. Preface | vi. [roman numerals in error] Preface, continued | (7) Contents | (8) blank | (9) list of Illustrations | (10) blank | 11–392. text, with printer's imprint at foot of p.392 (PRINTED AND BOUND IN GREAT BRITAIN | By Blackie & Son, Limited, Glasgow).

Binding (see Note 1)
Blue cloth boards, blocked black, white, and green; edges plain; plain off-white endpapers.
Front board: When | London | Burned (white, cased black) above and overlapping decoration of heads and shoulders of two figures in restoration dress (black, white, green). At lower left corner: By | G.A.Henty (black). **Spine:** WHEN | LONDON | BURNED | A Story of | Restoration | Times (black) above illustration of full-length figure with stick (black, white). At foot: G.A.Henty | BLACKIE & SON LTD (black). **Back board:** plain.

Reference: PN.

Notes
1. Re-issued in the 1920s in 'The New Popular Henty', a name very close to that of the series begun in 1903 ('The New and Popular Edition'), in which this title never appeared (see 68.1, Note 1). For details of 'The New Popular Henty' series, and later editions, see *Facing Death*, 10.7, Notes 1–3 and 6–8. Examples of the series binding style are at Plates 174–175.
2. Of the binding cases in 'The New Popular Henty' series, this is one that does not have the familiar stamp of John Hassall's design. All the minor variants of *When London Burned* in the series are grouped together under this generic heading, *68.4.

69. BEARS AND DACOITS

69.1
BEARS AND DACOITS | A TALE OF THE GHAUTS | BY | G.A.HENTY | Author of "By England's Aid", "One of the 28th", | "By Right of Conquest", &c. &c. | (publisher's device) | LONDON | BLACKIE & SON, LIMITED, 50 OLD BAILEY, E.C. | GLASGOW AND DUBLIN

Contents
152 × 121 mm. (1)–48 | no catalogue. Frontispiece from pen-drawing, unsigned, reproduced by line block printed in black on text page.
(1) Blank | (2) frontispiece | (3) title p. | (4) blank | (5)–48. text.

Cover (see Plate 120)
Sage-green limp cloth, lined off-white paper, printed dark-brown on cloth, black on paper; saddle-stitched, two wires, cut flush; edges plain.
(1) BEARS AND | DACOITS (dark-brown) in panel at top left corner of illustration of children with flowers (dark-brown).
(2) Blank.
(3) Advert. (NEW SERIES OF | CHILDREN'S BOOKS.) (black) (see Note 3).
(4) Blank.

References: BL; Bod; PN | *Farmer*, p.10; *Dartt*, p.12.

Notes

1. No records of this booklet exist among the surviving Blackie papers. The Copyright Libraries received it in 1896.

2. The story first appeared in the *Union Jack*, June 1881: see also §4.

3. The publisher's advertisement on p.3 of the cover lists three groups of booklets at different prices, 'in prettily-designed Cloth Covers. Illustrated'. The group at 'One Penny each' contains nothing by Henty. The second group, at 'Twopence each,' includes *White-Faced Dick*, and the third group at 'Threepence each' includes *Surly Joe* as well as this booklet, *Bears and Dacoits*.

4. *Farmer* is extremely confused, and so is *Dartt*. Much of the trouble stems from the fact that Blackie later issued a collection of Henty's short stories, including this one, under the title *Bears and Dacoits and Other Stories* (see 69.2, below), of which only the first three words appear on the binding case. Thus, the collection, which is bound in cloth boards, and is an octavo, has been regarded as a later edition of this little limp cloth booklet, which is a sixteenmo. To save even more confusion it seems the best plan to treat it so here. The earlier edition is scarce, and although *Farmer* and *Dartt* both refer to the copy in the British Library it is clear that neither of them had fully examined it. Dartt had seen Henty's presentation copy in the Wandsworth Collection: Farmer had not. Nevertheless both entries are inaccurate and unreliable, containing too many errors to mention in detail.

69. 2

BEARS AND DACOITS | AND OTHER STORIES | BY | G.A.HENTY | Author of "With Buller in Natal" "Out with Garibaldi" "For Name and Fame" | "The Bravest of the Brave" &c. &c. | WITH COLOURED FRONTISPIECE | AND SEVEN FULL-PAGE ILLUSTRATIONS | BLACKIE AND SON LIMITED | LONDON GLASGOW AND DUBLIN

Contents

176 x 120 mm. (1)–(112) | catalogue 1–16. Frontispiece from watercolour by H.M.Brock, dated 1900, reproduced by three-colour halftone blocks printed on coated paper, unbacked, tipped in. Seven full-page pen-drawings by unknown artist, reproduced by line blocks printed on text pages, folioed, unbacked.

(1) Half-title p. | (2) blank | (frontispiece, tipped in) | (3) title p. | (4) blank | 5. Contents | 6. list of Illustrations | 7–42. text and illustrations of 'Bears and Dacoits' | 43–65. text and illustrations of 'White-Faced Dick' | 66–111. text and illustrations of 'A Brush with the Chinese' | (112) blank | 1–16. catalogue.

Binding (see Plate 121)

Red cloth boards, blocked black, green, and gilt; edges plain; plain off-white endpapers.

Front board: Bears and | Dacoits | By G.A.Henty (all gilt) framed in black rules above illustration, also framed in black rules, of girl with a book, and boy, walking near trees (black and green). Illustration is signed with monogram of the letters O and F (black) at lower left corner. **Spine:** BEARS | AND | DACOITS (gilt) above illustration of the same children walking (black and green). At foot: BY | G.A. | HENTY (black). **Back board:** plain.

References: BL; Bod; PN | *Farmer*, p.10; *Dartt*, p.13, *Companion*, p.3.

Notes
1. The book was published by Blackie in this entirely different form on 28 May 1901. It is really a separate publication from *Bears and Dacoits* described as 69.1 above, but is catalogued as 69.2, in line with *Dartt* and to avoid even further confusion (see 69.1, Note 4).
2. For other appearances of the short stories see §4.
3. Later issues have the gilt blocking replaced with pigment on the front board, and eventually on the spine as well.

69.3

Bears and Dacoits | And Other Stories | BY | G.A.HENTY | Author of "With Buller in Natal" "Out with Garibaldi" | "For Name and Fame" "The Bravest of the Brave" &c. &c. | WITH COLOURED FRONTISPIECE | AND SEVEN FULL-PAGE ILLUSTRATIONS | BLACKIE AND SON LIMITED | LONDON GLASGOW AND BOMBAY

Contents: 176 × 118 mm. As for 69.2, but catalogue 1–8.

Binding (see Note 1)
Blue cloth boards, blocked black, bistre, white, and gilt; edges plain; plain off-white endpapers.
   Front board: Bears and | Dacoits | By G.A.Henty (white) on panel across illustration of girl and boy running with dog (black, bistre, white). All framed by black rules. **Spine:** BEARS | AND | DACOITS (gilt in ruled black panel) above illustration of boy, girl, dog, and book (black, bistre, white). At foot: BLACKIE & SON | LIMITED (black). All framed by black rules. **Back board:** plain.

Reference: BB.

Notes
1. This binding design was also used for *Do Your Duty*, 89.5, Plate 118, of which a copy in my possession is inscribed May, 1914, on a school-prize label. Another copy which, unlike 69.3, has Dublin still in the imprint, is inscribed 1910.
2. The bistre blocking on the spine is usually uniformly faded to yellow ochre.

69.4

Title page: As for 69.3.

Contents: 177 × 117 mm. Otherwise as for 69.2.

Binding (see Plate 122)
Brown cloth boards, blocked black; illustration printed on coated paper, laid down; edges plain; plain off-white endpapers.
   Front board: BEARS AND | DACOITS (cloth-colour out of solid-black rectangle) above laid-down illustration, reproduced by three-colour halftone blocks on coated paper, of boy and girl playing with ball, and jumping dog, all framed by black rules. At the top, one hand of the girl, and the ball, project beyond the edge of the rectangular shape, and the plate is cut out irregularly, so that the two small projecting areas of the illustration overlap the word DACOITS blocked above.

Spine: BEARS I AND I DACOITS I G.A.HENTY (all black) framed by black rules, above another ruled panel containing a floral art-nouveau design (black). At foot, a third, small, ruled panel, containing BLACKIE I & SON LTD (all black). **Back board:** plain.

Notes
1. The copy described has an inscription dated 1917.
2. This binding design was also used for *Do Your Duty*, 89.7. Both titles are found in various cloth-colours.

69.5
Title page: As for 69.3.

Contents: As for 69.2, but no catalogue.

Binding
Greenish-grey cloth, blocked dark-green; edges plain; plain off-white endpapers.
    Front board: BEARS AND I DACOITS (cloth-colour out of solid dark-green rectangle) within dark-green rules, above laid-down illustration, reproduced by three-colour halftone blocks printed on coated paper, of girl, and boy with hat, holding large basket of apples; all framed by dark-green rules. **Spine:** BEARS I AND I DACOITS I G.A.HENTY (dark-green) framed by dark-green rules, above illustration of boy in mediaeval dress in a second ruled panel. At foot: BLACKIE I & SON LTD (dark green) framed by dark-green rules. **Back board:** plain.

Note: Designs similar to the bindings of 69.4 and 69.5, using colour plates printed on paper and laid down on the upper boards, were introduced by Blackie at about this time for other titles, notably *Do Your Duty* and *John Hawke's Fortune*, probably as an economy during wartime. Inscriptions in such copies are found with dates between 1915 and 1920.

70. SURLY JOE

70.1
(Double horizontal 2-em rule) SURLY JOE (double horizontal 2-em rule) I THE STORY OF A TRUE HERO I BY I G.A.HENTY I Author of "Wulf the Saxon", "A Knight of the White Cross", &c.&c. I (publisher's device) I LONDON I BLACKIE & SON, LIMITED, 50 OLD BAILEY, E.C. I GLASGOW AND DUBLIN

Contents
150 × 130 mm. (1)–48 I no catalogue. Frontispiece from pen-drawing, signed P.H. (possibly Paul Hardy), reproduced by line block on text page, unbacked, unfolioed but counted in pagination.
    (1) Blank I (2) frontispiece I (3) title p. I (4) blank I (5)–48. text.

Cover (see Note 4)
Sage-green limp cloth, lined off-white paper, printed dark-brown on cloth, black on paper; saddle stitched, two wires, cut flush; edges plain.
    (1) SURLY I JOE (dark-brown) in panel at top left, above illustration of children and flowers (dark-brown).

(2) Blank.
(3) Advert. (NEW SERIES OF | CHILDREN'S BOOKS) (black) (see Note 4).
(4) Blank.

References: BL; Bod; BB | *Farmer*, p.66; *Dartt*, p.131.

Notes
1. *Dartt* reports a copy in 'green-brown paper' instead of cloth.
2. No records of this booklet exist among the surviving Blackie papers. The Copyright Libraries received their copies in 1896.
3. For other appearances of the story see §4. It was also published, in a school reader, as 'The Boatman's Story'.
4. The cover design is the same as for other books in the series: see *Bears and Dacoits*, 69.1, Note 3, Plate 120.

71. WHITE-FACED DICK

71.1
WHITE-FACED DICK | A STORY OF PINE-TREE GULCH | BY | G.A.HENTY | Author of "Wulf the Saxon", "By England's Aid", &c.&c. | (publisher's device) | LONDON | BLACKIE & SON, LIMITED, 50 OLD BAILEY, E.C. | GLASGOW AND DUBLIN

Contents
150 x 130 mm. (1)–(32) | no catalogue. Frontispiece from pen-drawing, signed P.H., reproduced by line block printed black on text page, unbacked, unfolioed but counted in pagination.
    (1) blank | (2) frontispiece | (3) title p. | (4) blank | (5)–31. text | (32) blank.

Cover
Orange limp cloth, lined off-white paper, printed dark-brown on cloth, black on paper; saddle-stitched, two wires, cut flush; edges plain.
(1) WHITE-FACED | DICK (dark-brown), all except the three initial letters under-lined, in panel at top left of illustration of children dancing around tree (dark-brown).
(2) Blank.
(3) Advert. (NEW SERIES OF | CHILDREN'S BOOKS) (black) (see Note 3).
(4) Blank.

References: BL; Bod; BB | *Farmer*, p.77; *Dartt*, p.156.

Notes
1. No records exist for this booklet among the surviving Blackie papers. The Copyright Libraries received their copies in 1896.
2. For other appearances of the story see §4. A short excerpt appears in *Tales from Henty*, Blackie, 1893, entitled 'The Flood in Pine-Tree Gulch'.
3. Details of the advertisement on p.3 of the cover are the same as in other books in the series: see *Bears and Dacoits*, 69.1, and *Surly Joe*, 70.1.

4. As with *Bears and Dacoits* Blackie made confusion for bibliographers by re-issuing the story as part of a collection but with the same volume-title. In this case they did it twice: *White-Faced Dick And Two Other Stories*, and *White-Faced Dick And Another Story*. Although these are really separate publications, it seems less confusing now to follow *Dartt* and deal with them both as later editions of 71.1.

71.2

WHITE-FACED DICK | And Two Other Stories | BY | G.A.HENTY | Author of "Sturdy and Strong" | "In the Hands of the Cave Dwellers" &c. | BLACKIE & SON, LIMITED | LONDON AND GLASGOW

Contents
182 × 121 mm. (1)–(80) | no catalogue. Frontispiece from wash-drawing by D.C.Eyles, reproduced by halftone block printed in black on coated paper, tipped in.

(1)–(2) Blank, pasted down as endpaper | (3) half-title p. | (4) publisher's addresses | (frontispiece, tipped in) | (5) title p. | (6) printer's imprint (Printed in Great Britain by Blackie & Son, Ltd., Glasgow) | (7) Contents | (8) blank | 9–26. text of 'White-Faced Dick' | 27–68. text of 'A Brush with the Chinese' | 69–78. text of 'A Battle with Wolves' | (79)–(80) blank, pasted down as endpaper.

Binding (see Plate 137)
Paper boards, printed in full colour; edges plain; endpapers formed by pasting down first and last leaves of text.

Front board: WHITE-FACED | DICK (black) on yellow panel above full-colour illustration of cowboy with his arm on shoulder of a boy, signed, 'D.C.Eyles'. **Spine:** WHITE- | FACED | DICK | G.A.Henty (black) on yellow panel at head, continued from front board, above illustration of cowboy standing, with drawn gun (full-colour). At foot: BLACKIE (black). **Back board:** THE . PINNACLE . LIBRARY (blue) on yellow strip across head of board, on blue background. At lower left corner: BLACKIE | & SON | LIMITED | (decoration) (blue) on yellow shield out of blue background. A white border at edges of board.

References: BB | *Dartt*, p.156 (Note).

Notes
1. It is not possible to date this edition from internal sources, and it is not mentioned in surviving Blackie records. It is likely that it preceded 71.3, also in 'The Pinnacle Library', but little evidence is available (see 71.3, Note 1).
2. For other appearances of the stories see §4.

71.3

WHITE-FACED DICK | And Another Story | BY | G.A.HENTY | Author of "Sturdy and Strong" | "In the Hands of the Cave Dwellers" &c. | BLACKIE & SON LIMITED | LONDON AND GLASGOW

Contents
180 × 121 mm. (1)–64 | no catalogue. Frontispiece as in 71.2.

(Frontispiece, tipped in) | (1) title p. | (2) publisher's addresses at head; printer's imprint at foot (Printed in Great Britain by Blackie & Son, Ltd., Glasgow) | (3) Contents | (4) blank | 5–22. text of 'White-Faced Dick' | 23–64. text of 'A Brush with the Chinese'.

Binding: (See Plate 137). As for 71.2, except (a) plain off-white endpapers; (b) design of spine cut down to fit this thinner book (from 28mm. to 20mm.).

References: BB | *Dartt*, p.156, Note.

Notes

1. I cannot be certain of the relative chronological order of 71.2 and 71.3: no publisher's record has survived, and there is little else to go on. But both volumes are in 'The Pinnacle Library' and have the same binding design. As the spine widths differ, it seems more likely that the wider spine came first, and was later cut down, than that a completely new set of plates was made with a wider spine for a second book.

2. For other appearances of the stories see §4.

72. A KNIGHT OF THE WHITE CROSS

72.1

A KNIGHT | OF THE WHITE CROSS | A TALE OF THE SIEGE OF RHODES | BY | G.A.HENTY | Author of "When London Burned", "For the Temple", "St. Bartholomew's Eve" | "Under Drake's Flag", "Beric the Briton", &c. | (29mm. rule) | WITH TWELVE ILLUSTRATIONS BY RALPH PEACOCK | AND A PLAN | (29mm. rule) | (publisher's device) | LONDON | BLACKIE & SON, LIMITED, 50 OLD BAILEY, E.C. | GLASGOW AND DUBLIN | 1896

Contents

186 × 130 mm. (i)–(x) | (11)–392 | catalogue (1)–(32). Twelve full-page wash-drawings by Ralph Peacock, reproduced by halftone blocks; full-page photograph of G.A.Henty with signature, reproduced by combined line and halftone block; all printed in black on coated paper, unbacked, unfolioed, tipped in. Plan of the Fortress of Rhodes printed from line block in black on coated paper, guarded in following p.48 (between sig.C and sig.D).

(i) Half-title p. | (ii) advertisement (MR. HENTY'S HISTORICAL TALES.) listing 30 titles | (frontispiece, tipped in) | (iii) title p. | (iv) blank | (v)–vi. Preface | (vii) Contents | (viii) blank | (ix) list of Illustrations | (x) blank | (portrait of G.A.Henty, tipped in) | (11)–392. text | (1)–(32) catalogue.

Binding (see Plate 74)

Designed by Ralph Peacock (see Note 2). Dark-green cloth boards, bevelled, blocked black, brown, cream, and gilt; all edges burnished olive-green; grey endpapers, lined off-white.

Front board: A KNIGHT | OF THE | WHITE | CROSS | G.A.HENTY. (all gilt) at right of illustration (black, brown, cream, gilt), framed by brown rules, of knight in full armour with white cross. At lower left corner, artists initials RP. (Ralph Peacock) (brown) in small brown rectangle. **Spine:** A KNIGHT | OF THE | WHITE | CROSS (gilt) above heraldic decorations and head of knight (black, brown, cream, gilt) with ornamental panelling (brown). At foot: G.A.HENTY (gilt). **Back board:** plain.

References: BL; Bod; PN I *Farmer*, p.47; *Dartt*, p.91, *Companion*, p.20.

Notes

1. The book was published on 13 June 1895 at six shillings. By the end of February 1896 Blackie had sold 9200 copies, and in the next eight years they sold 3734 more, the average annual sale over the nine years being 1437 copies. In the following nine years the annual average sank to 174 copies, and then, at the end of August 1913, Blackie re-issued the book in their cheaper edition. One more copy was sold at six shillings in 1914. The total sales at this price were 14,497 copies.

2. This is one of the few novels by Henty which, in its first format, is not found in more than one cloth-colour. That was probably at the insistence of the artist, Ralph Peacock, who not only illustrated the book but also provided a striking design for the binding case. The work would have been commissioned by Talwin Morris (see entries under both names in Appendix IV, Part 2).

3. The portrait of Henty appeared also, without explanation, in the other novels published the same year as this, see *Through Russian Snows*, 73.1, and *The Tiger of Mysore*, 74.1.

4. As usual with Blackie novels, the earliest issues contain catalogues advertising the books for the current year (in this case with title pages dated 1896) without quotations from press reviews.

5. This book is longer than any of Henty's other novels published by Blackie. The normal length for a six-shilling novel was 384 pages, but this has a final 8-page section added at the end, making it 392 pages.

*72.2

Reprints of the first edition were in the style of 72.1, but without the date on the title page. Alterations were made when necessary to the title-page imprint and addresses: the Indian office was opened in Bombay in 1901 although Bombay did not appear regularly in the imprint until 1906; after 1910 Dublin was deleted.

Other changes found in reprints include: the omission of the ornament from the half-title page, and the addition to the list of Illustrations, on p.(ix), of an entry for the Plan of the Fortress of Rhodes.

Some issues have pages v and vii folioed, but incorrectly, in arabic numerals, as 5 and 7. (Page vi remains in roman numerals).

In late issues the front board has G.A.HENTY blocked in cream instead of gilt.

There were many such small variations among the reprints of the book in its first-edition format: all are grouped together under this 'generic' heading, *72.2.

72.3

A Knight I of the White Cross I A Tale of the Siege of Rhodes I BY I G.A.HENTY I Author of "When London Burned" "For the Temple" "St. Bartholomew's Eve" I "Under Drake's Flag" "Beric the Briton" &c. I ILLUSTRATED BY RALPH PEACOCK I NEW EDITION I BLACKIE AND SON LIMITED I LONDON GLASGOW AND BOMBAY

Contents

185 × 126 mm. (1)–392 I catalogue 1–16. Eight full-page wash-drawings by Ralph Peacock reproduced by halftone blocks printed in sepia on coated paper, unbacked, unfolioed, tipped in. Plan as in 72.1.

(1) Half-title p. | (2) advertisement (NEW AND POPULAR EDITION OF | G.A.HENTY'S WORKS) listing 39 titles | (frontispiece, tipped in) | (3) title p. | (4) blank | 5. Preface | vi. [roman numerals in error] Preface, continued | (7) Contents | (8) blank | (9) list of Illustrations | (10) blank | 11–392. text | 1–16 catalogue.

Binding (see Note 1)
Blue cloth boards, blocked black, light-blue, red, buff, and gilt; all edges stained olive-green; grey endpapers, lined off-white.
    Front board: A KNIGHT OF THE | WHITE CROSS | BY G.A.HENTY (all gilt) above illustration, framed by black line, of knight with shield, under fire from arrows (black, light-blue, red, buff), with signature: J Hassall (black) at lower right corner. **Spine:** A KNIGHT | OF THE | WHITE | CROSS | G.A.HENTY (gilt) above illustration, framed by black line, of knight in armour with sword and shield (black, light-blue, red, buff). At foot: BLACKIE & SON LTD (black). **Back board:** plain.

References: BL; Bod.

Notes
1. Re-issued, late 1913, in the 'New and Popular Edition': for details see *Facing Death*, 10.6, Notes 2–3, and examples of the series binding style, Plates 172–173.
2. In this edition Blackie had sold 1601 copies by the end of August 1914, and they sold 607 more copies by the same date in 1917. At this point Blackie's records cease. The grand total of copies sold at both prices from 1895 to 1917 is 16,706.
3. From 1913 Blackie printed all issues of the 'New and Popular Edition' without dates on title pages: the first issue of this edition of *A Knight of the White Cross* was therefore undated, unlike first issues of titles re-issued in earlier years.

*72.4
A Knight | of the White Cross | A Tale of the Siege of Rhodes | BY | G.A.HENTY | Author of "When London Burned" "For the Temple" | "St. Bartholomew's Eve" &c. | Illustrated | BLACKIE AND SON LIMITED | LONDON GLASGOW AND BOMBAY

Contents
184 × 124 mm. (1)–392 | no catalogue. Frontispiece from watercolour drawing by Frank Gillett, R.I., reproduced by three-colour halftone blocks; four wash-drawings by Ralph Peacock, reproduced by halftone blocks printed in black; all on coated paper, unbacked, tipped in.
    (1) Half-title p. | (2) advertisement (G.A.HENTY'S BOOKS) listing 56 titles | (frontispiece, tipped in) | (3) title p. | (4) printer's imprint (Printed in Great Britain by | Blackie & Son Limited, Glasgow) | 5. Preface | vi. [roman numerals in error] Preface, continued | (7) Contents | (8) blank | (9) list of Illustrations | (10) blank | 11–392. text.

Binding (see Note 1)
Green cloth boards, blocked black, red, blue, and buff; edges plain; plain off-white endpapers.
    Front board: A KNIGHT OF THE | WHITE CROSS | BY G.A.HENTY (black) above illustration, framed by black line, of knight with shield, under fire from arrows (black, red, blue, buff), with signature: J Hassall (black) at lower right corner.

Spine: A | KNIGHT | OF THE | WHITE | CROSS | G.A.HENTY (black) above illustration, framed by black line, of knight in armour with sword and shield (black, red, blue, buff). At foot: BLACKIE & SON LTD (black). **Back board:** plain.

References: BL; Bod; AK.

Notes

1. For details of Blackie's second cheaper series, 'The New Popular Henty', and later editions, see *Facing Death*, 10.7, Notes 1–3 and 6–8. Examples of the series binding style are at Plates 174–175. This title was added to the series in 1925.

2. In this bibliography all the minor variants of a title within the 'New Popular Henty' series are normally grouped together under one 'generic' heading, indicated by an asterisk. In the case of *A Knight of the White Cross*, however, they are grouped under two such 'generic' headings, the first being this one, *72.4. A second heading is needed for this book as one or more impressions were sub-contracted by Blackie to another printer in Glasgow, where the entire setting and imposition of the book was changed, resulting in a new edition with the extent of the book reduced by 8 pages. The out-worked edition is described as *72.5 below.

*72.5

Title page: As for *72.4, but changed imprint (BLACKIE & SON LIMITED | LONDON AND GLASGOW).

Contents

186 × 125 mm. (1)–384 | advertisement (1)–(2). Illustrations as in *72.4.

(1) Half-title p. | (2) Blackie addresses | (frontispiece, tipped in) | (3) title p. | (4) printer's imprint (Printed in Great Britain by Thomson & Cully, Glasgow) | 5–6. Preface | 7. Contents | (8) list of Illustrations | 9–384. text | (1)–(2) advertisement (THE NEW POPULAR HENTY) listing 64 titles.

Binding: As for *72.4, but red cloth boards.

Reference: PN.

Notes

1. See *72.4, Notes 1 and 2, for an explanation of this second edition in 'The New Popular Henty' series, given the 'generic' heading *72.5.

2. A very unusual example of a Blackie edition being out-worked to another printer, presumably for lack of machine-room space. The only other cases I have come across are late reprints of *Through Three Campaigns* (see *107.3, Note 5) and *With Frederick the Great* (see *82.4, Note 4). Here, strangely, the type has been re-set: it would have been more usual for Blackie to have supplied the type, or a set of plates made from it, to the other printer. Presumably the original type was damaged or pied, and no stereos had been made. Thomson and Cully arrived at an extent of six pages less than Blackie, probably being unable to match Blackie's type face, and in order to save the full half-sheet (of eight pages) they re-imposed the prelims. The text proper therefore begins at page 9 instead of page 11.

73. THROUGH RUSSIAN SNOWS

73.1

THROUGH RUSSIAN SNOWS | A STORY OF | NAPOLEON'S RETREAT FROM MOSCOW | BY | G.A.HENTY | Author of "Beric the Briton", "One of the 28th", "Condemned as a Nihilist" | "For Name and Fame", "In the Heart of the Rockies", &c. | (27mm. rule) | WITH EIGHT ILLUSTRATIONS BY W.H.OVEREND | AND A MAP | (27mm. rule) | (publisher's device) | LONDON | BLACKIE & SON, LIMITED, 50 OLD BAILEY, E.C. | GLASGOW AND DUBLIN | 1896

Contents
184 x 123 mm. (i)–(x) | (11)–352 | catalogue (1)–(32). Eight full-page wash-drawings by W.H. Overend, reproduced by halftone blocks; full-page photograph of G.A.Henty, with signature, reproduced by combined line and halftone block; a map and two battle-plans reproduced by line blocks; all printed in black on coated paper, unbacked, unfolioed, tipped in.

(i) Half-title p. | (ii) advertisement (MR. HENTY'S HISTORICAL TALES.) listing 35 titles | (frontispiece, tipped in) | (iii) title p. | (iv) blank | (v) Preface | (vi) blank | (vii) Contents | (viii) blank | (ix) list of Illustrations | (x) blank | (portrait of G.A.Henty, tipped in) | (11)–352. text | (1)–(32) catalogue.

Binding (see Plate 82)
Designed by Ralph Peacock (see Note 2). Blue cloth boards, blocked black, white, and gilt; all edges burnished olive-green; grey endpapers, lined off-white.
Front board: THROUGH | RUSSIAN | SNOWS | A STORY OF | NAPOLEON'S | RETREAT FROM | MOSCOW (all white) | BY | G.A.HENTY (black), all framed in hexagonal decorative panel of black rules at lower right corner of illustration of Napoleonic soldier in snow scene (black, white, gilt); the whole framed by black and white rules. **Spine:** All within decorative white panels: symbol of eagle (gilt) above: THROUGH | RUSSIAN | SNOWS | BY | G.A.HENTY (all gilt) ; N within wreath (all gilt). At foot: BLACKIE & SON | LIMITED (gilt). The whole framed in black rules. **Back board:** plain.

References: BL; Bod; PN | *Farmer*, p.69; *Dartt*, p.136, *Companion*, p.30.

Notes
1. The book was published on 14 August 1895 at five shillings. By the end of February 1896 Blackie had sold 10,090 copies, and during the next nine years they sold 6600 more, giving an average annual sale over the ten years of 1669 copies. The average annual sale over the following ten years was 367 copies, and the total number of copies sold at five shillings was 20,357. At this point, at the end of 1915, Blackie re-issued the book in their cheaper edition (see 73.3 below).
2. This is one the novels which, before the cheaper editions, was virtually always bound in cloth of the same colour, a feature of several case designs by Ralph Peacock (see Appendix IV, Part 2).
3. The portrait of Henty appeared also, without explanation, in the other novels published the same year (see *A Knight of the White Cross*, 72.1, and *The Tiger of Mysore*), 74.1.

4. As usual with Blackie novels, the earliest issues contain catalogues advertising the books for the current year (in this case with title pages dated 1896) without quotations from press reviews.

*73.2

Reprints of the five-shilling edition were in the style of 73.1, with no date on the title page. Changes were made when necessary to the title-page imprint and addresses: the Indian office was opened in 1901 although Bombay did not appear regularly in the Blackie imprint until 1906; after 1910 Dublin was omitted.

The slightly-differing issues among the reprints of this title in its first-edition format are all grouped together under this 'generic' heading, *73.2.

73.3

Through Russian Snows | A Story of | Napoleon's Retreat from Moscow | BY | G.A.HENTY | Author of "Beric the Briton" "One of the 28th" "Condemned as a Nihilist" | "For Name and Fame" "In the Heart of the Rockies" &c. | ILLUSTRATED BY W.H.OVEREND | NEW EDITION | BLACKIE AND SON LIMITED | LONDON GLASGOW AND BOMBAY

Contents
183 x 127 mm. (1)–352 | no catalogue. Five full-page wash-drawings by W.H.Overend reproduced by halftone blocks; a full-page map and two full-page battle-plans reproduced by line blocks; all printed in black on coated paper, unbacked, unfolioed, tipped in.

(1) Half-title p. | (2) advertisement (NEW AND POPULAR EDITION OF G.A.HENTY'S WORKS) listing 41 titles | (frontispiece, tipped in) | (3) title page | (4) blank | (5) Preface | (6) blank | (7) Contents | (8) blank | (9) list of Illustrations | (10) blank | 11–352. text.

Binding (see Note 1)
Blue cloth boards, blocked black, white, orange, buff, and gilt; all edges stained olive-green; grey endpapers, lined off-white.
Front board: THROUGH | RUSSIAN SNOWS (white) | NAPOLEON'S RETREAT FROM MOSCOW | G.A.HENTY (black) above illustration, framed by black lines, of soldier marching in snow (black, white, orange, buff). **Spine:** THROUGH | RUSSIAN | SNOWS | G.A.HENTY (gilt) above illustration, framed by black lines, of Napoleon-like figure (black, white, orange, buff). At foot: BLACKIE & SON LTD (black). **Back board:** plain.

References: BL; Bod.

Notes
1. Re-issued, late 1915, in the 'New and Popular Edition'. For details see *Facing Death*, 10.6, Notes 2–3, and examples of the series binding style, Plates 172–173.
2. In this edition Blackie sold 1517 copies in 1916, and 745 copies in 1917. Their records cease at this date, though the book no doubt continued to sell in this format for some years. The grand total of copies sold at both prices from 1895 to 1917 is 22,619.
3. From 1913 Blackie had printed all issues of the 'New and Popular Edition'

without dates on title pages; the first issue of this edition of *Through Russian Snows* was therefore undated, unlike first issues of titles produced up to 1912.

*73.4

THROUGH I RUSSIAN SNOWS I A Story of Napoleon's Retreat I from Moscow I BY I G.A.HENTY I Author of "Beric the Briton" "One of the 28th" I "In the Reign of Terror" &c. I Illustrated I BLACKIE & SON LIMITED I LONDON AND GLASGOW

Contents
184 x 125 mm. (1)–352 I advertisement (1)–(2). Frontispiece from watercolour drawing by John de Walton, reproduced by three-colour blocks; four full-page wash-drawings by W.H.Overend reproduced by halftone blocks printed in black; all on coated paper, unbacked, keyed to text pages, tipped in.

(1) Half-title p. I (2) Blackie addresses I (frontispiece, tipped in) I (3) title p. I (4) printer's imprint (Printed in Great Britain by I Blackie & Son, Limited, Glasgow) I (5) Preface I (6) blank I (7) Contents I (8) blank I (9) list of Illustrations I (10) blank I 11–352. text I (1)–(2) advertisement (THE NEW POPULAR HENTY) listing 62 titles.

Binding (see Plate 175)
Blue cloth boards, blocked black, cream, red, and buff; edges plain; plain off-white endpapers.

Front board: THROUGH I RUSSIAN SNOWS (cream) I NAPOLEON'S RETREAT FROM MOSCOW I G.A.HENTY (black) above illustration, framed by black lines, of soldier marching in snow (black, cream, red, buff). **Spine:** THROUGH I RUSSIAN I SNOWS I G.A.HENTY (black) above illustration, framed by black rules, of Napoleon-like figure (black, cream, red, buff). At foot: BLACKIE & SON LTD. (black). **Back board:** plain.

Reference: PN.

Notes
1. For details of Blackie's second cheaper series, 'The New Popular Henty', and subsequent editions of this book, see *Facing Death*, 10.7, Notes 1–3 and 6–8.
2. All the minor variants of *Through Russian Snows* in the series are grouped together under this 'generic' heading, *73.4.

74. THE TIGER OF MYSORE

74.1
THE TIGER OF MYSORE I A STORY OF I THE WAR WITH TIPPOO SAIB I BY I G.A.HENTY I Author of "With Clive in India", "Through the Sikh War", "Beric the Briton" I "Held Fast for England", "For Name and Fame", &c. I (29mm. rule) I WITH TWELVE ILLUSTRATIONS BY W.H.MARGETSON I AND A MAP I (29mm. rule) I (publisher's device) I LONDON I BLACKIE & SON, LIMITED, 50 OLD BAILEY, E.C. I GLASGOW AND DUBLIN I 1896

Contents

186 × 130 mm. (i)–(x) | (11)–(380) | catalogue (1)–(32). Twelve full-page wash drawings by W.H. Margetson, reproduced by halftone blocks; full-page photograph of G.A. Henty, with signature, reproduced by combined line and halftone block; all printed in black on coated paper, unbacked, unfolioed, tipped in. Map of Southern India printed by litho in three colours with mechanical tints, unbacked, unfolioed, guarded in as double-page spread (see Note 4). Two battle-plans printed from line blocks on text pages.

(i) Half-title p. | (ii) advertisement (MR. HENTY'S HISTORICAL TALES.) listing 35 titles | (frontispiece, tipped in) | (iii) title p. | (iv) blank | (v) Preface | (vi) blank | (vii) Contents | (viii) blank | (ix) list of Illustrations | (x) blank | (portrait of G.A. Henty, tipped in) | (11)–379. text | (380) blank | (1)–(32) catalogue.

Binding (see Plate 84)

Turquoise-blue cloth boards, bevelled, blocked black, white, ultramarine, brown, and gilt; all edges burnished olive-green; grey endpapers, lined off-white.

Front board: THE TIGER | OF | MYSORE (white, cased brown) out of geometrical pattern forming rectangular background (ultramarine) to illustration of Indian figure with turban and sword (black, white, ultramarine, brown. See Note 7 below). At right: BY | G.A.HENTY. (white). **Spine:** THE | TIGER | OF | MYSORE (gilt) on geometrical pattern similar to that on front board (ultramarine), above: BY | G.A.HENTY (white) and illustration of tiger's head (black, white, brown). At foot: BLACKIE & SON LIMITED (white). **Back board:** plain.

References: BL; Bod; PN | *Farmer*, p.71; *Dartt*, p.138, *Companion*, p.31.

Notes

1. This book was published on 12 September 1895 at six shillings. By the end of February 1896 Blackie had sold 9400 copies, and in the next eight years they sold 4454 more, the average annual sale over the nine-year period being 1539 copies. In the next nine years 2459 copies were sold (at an annual average of 273 copies), and then, at the end of 1913, Blackie re-issued the book in their cheaper series (see 74.3). The last 20 copies of the six-shilling edition were sold in 1914.

2. The portrait of Henty appeared also, without explanation, in the other novels published that year, see *A Knight of the White Cross*, 72.1, and *Through Russian Snows*, 73.1.

3. This is one of very few examples of Blackie's novels not printed as an even working. The normal length for the six-shilling novels was 384 pages, and this was regularly achieved with manuscripts of varying length by careful cast-off (see Appendix III, Part 1). It was only rarely that something went wrong in Blackie productions, and on this occasion the book finished with a twelve-page gathering at the end instead of the normal sixteen pages.

4. The map is guarded-in between pages 72 and 73, and not, as stated in the list of Illustrations, to face page 71, where one of the illustrations is tipped in.

5. I have not seen this book in other cloth-colours, nor blocked with alternative pigments, except for one variant detailed in Note 7. The use of white pigment was not usually satisfactory, as it tended to flake off. That certainly happened with *The Tiger of Mysore*, and it is not easy to find fine copies. (An exception to this tendency seems to be the first single-volume edition of *A Hidden Foe*, see 46.2, Note 2).

6. As usual with Blackie novels at this period, the earliest issues contain catalogues with announcements of the current year's books, including this one, but without quotations from press reviews.

7. I have a second copy of the first printing, an early issue with an inscription dated Christmas 1895, and with the catalogue described in Note 6. My friend Peter Allen, of Messrs Robert Temple, kindly drew my attention to a variation in the blocking of the binding case, of which I would otherwise have doubtless remained ignorant. The variation is in the jewel of the turban illustrated on the front board, which, on this copy, is blocked in gilt. When examined under a glass there is quite clearly a small semi-circle of brown pigment at the right of the gilt. All other copies I have seen have the jewel blocked entirely in brown pigment.

At first I was inclined to believe that this copy had been 'doctored' in some way: it seemed so unlikely that this small solid circle, between 1mm. and 2mm. in diameter, would have been thought worth blocking as the *only* part of the design in gilt on the front board. The copy in question has suffered a little from damp, and the gilt is not in pristine condition. However, the gilt on the turban is exactly the same in colour and condition as that on the spine of the book, and to achieve such a match would be beyond the powers of most amateur 'doctors'.

Certainly, I can see that the idea of one small jewel, brighter than anything else on the front board, would appeal to a designer. I can also see what a troublesome business it would have been for the blocking-machine operator to position accurately this tiny impression. And there would have been extra cost in terms of time, and in an extra (necessarily largely wasted) ribbon of gold leaf to be fed through the machine. That might well have caused Blackie to abandon the idea, if they did actually agree to it in the first instance. I cannot tell, from this single example, what really happened, but I must confess to some scepticism about the genuineness of this 'variant' blocking, largely because of the clear semicircle of brown pigment alongside the gilt. It seems more likely that the jewel would have been blocked *either* in gilt or in brown. But both colours are present, and it is possible that the gilt was blocked over the brown which is clearly there on all other copies.

8. The book has the publisher's name blocked on the spine of the binding case: this is a return to Blackie's early practice, and something they had not done, at any rate for Henty's books, for six years.

*74.2

Reprints of the six-shilling edition were in the style of 74.1, but with the date removed from the title page. Changes were made when necessary to the title-page imprint and addresses: the Indian office was opened in 1901 although Bombay did not appear regularly in the Blackie imprint until 1906; after 1910 Dublin was omitted. The slightly-varying issues among the reprints of the book in its first-edition format are all grouped together under this 'generic' heading, *74.2.

74.3

The Tiger of Mysore | A Story of the War with Tippoo Saib | BY | G.A.HENTY | Author of "With Clive in India" "Through the Sikh War" "Beric the Briton" | "Held Fast for England" "For Name and Fame" &c. | ILLUSTRATED BY W.H.MARGETSON | NEW EDITION | BLACKIE AND SON LIMITED | LONDON GLASGOW AND BOMBAY

Contents

186 × 125 mm. (1)–380 | catalogue 1–16. Eight full-page wash-drawings by W.H.Margetson, reproduced by halftone blocks printed in sepia on coated paper, unbacked, unfolioed, tipped in. Map of Southern India, and two plans, as in 74.1.

(1) Half-title p. | (2) advertisement (NEW AND POPULAR EDITION OF G.A.HENTY'S WORKS) listing 39 titles | (frontispiece, tipped in) | (3) title p. | (4) blank | (5) Preface | (6) blank | (7) Contents | (8) blank | (9) list of Illustrations | (10) blank | 11–379. text, with printer's imprint at foot of p.379 (PRINTED IN GREAT BRITAIN | At the Villafield Press, Glasgow, Scotland) | (380) blank | 1–16. catalogue.

Binding (see Note 1)

Dark-green cloth boards, blocked black, light-blue, buff, and gilt; all edges stained olive-green; grey endpapers, lined off-white.

Front board: THE TIGER OF | MYSORE | BY G.A.HENTY (gilt) above illustration framed by black line, of two turbaned figures in conversation (black, light-blue, buff), with signature at foot: J Hassall (black). **Spine:** THE | TIGER OF | MYSORE | G.A.HENTY | (gilt) above illustration of turbaned boy on rope-ladder (black, light-blue, buff). At foot: BLACKIE & SON LTD (black). **Back board:** plain.

References: BL; Bod.

Notes

1. Re-issued, late 1913, in the 'New and Popular Edition'. For details see *Facing Death*, 10.6, Notes 2–3, and examples of the series binding style, Plates 172–173.
2. In this edition Blackie sold 1804 copies by the end of August 1914, and in the remaining three years before Blackie's records cease, in 1917, they sold 887 more. No doubt the book continued to sell in this format after that. The total number of copies sold at both prices from 1895 to 1917 is 19,024.
3. From 1913 all issues of the 'New and Popular Edition' were printed without dated title pages. Unlike first issues of books in the series issued up to 1912, this first cheap issue of *The Tiger of Mysore* was therefore undated.

*74.4

Title page: As for 74.3, but the line above NEW EDITION now reads simply: ILLUSTRATED.

Contents

185 × 123 mm. (1)–(380) | no catalogue. Frontispiece from watercolour by Frank Gillett, R.I. reproduced by three-colour halftone blocks; four full-page wash-drawings by W.H. Margetson reproduced by halftone blocks printed in sepia; all on coated paper, unbacked, tipped in. Map of Southern India printed in line in black ink on coated paper, tipped in as double-page spread. Two battle-plans printed from line blocks on text pages.

(1) Half-title p. | (2) publisher's advertisement (G.A.HENTY'S BOOKS) listing 16 titles | (frontispiece, tipped in) | (3) title p. | (4) blank | (5) Preface | (6) blank | (7) Contents | (8) blank | (9) list of Illustrations | (10) blank | 11–379. text | (380) printer's imprint (PRINTED AND BOUND IN GREAT BRITAIN | By Blackie & Son, Limited, Glasgow).

Binding: As for 74.3, except (a) blue cloth boards, blocked black, green, and buff, with no gilt: front-board lettering all buff, spine lettering all black; (b) edges plain; (c) plain off-white endpapers.

Reference: TC.

Notes

1. For details of Blackie's second cheaper series, 'The New Popular Henty', and of subsequent editions of this book, see *Facing Death*, 10.7, Notes 1–3 and 6–8.

2. All the minor variants within this series, of the edition of *The Tiger of Mysore* having 380 pages, are grouped together under this 'generic' heading, *74.4. Those of the edition with 368 pages are given below, under *74.5.

*74.5

The Tiger of Mysore | A Story of the War with Tippoo Saib | BY | G.A.HENTY | Author of "With Clive in India" "Through the Sikh War" | "Beric the Briton" "Held Fast for England" | "For Name and Fame" &c. | Illustrated | NEW EDITION | BLACKIE & SON LIMITED | LONDON AND GLASGOW

Contents

184 x 124 mm. (1)–368 | advertisement (i)–(ii). Illustrations, map and battle-plans as in *74.4.

(1) Half-title p. | (2) Blackie addresses | (frontispiece, tipped in) | (3) title p. | (4) printer's imprint (Printed in Great Britain by | Blackie & Son, Limited, Glasgow) | (5) Preface | (6) blank | (7) Contents | (8) blank | (9) list of Illustrations | (10) blank | 11–368. text | (i)–(ii) advertisement (THE NEW POPULAR HENTY) listing 60 titles.

Binding: As for *74.4, but grey-blue cloth boards.

Reference: PN.

Notes

1. This is a later impression than *74.4 in 'The New Popular Henty' series, and a fine example of the degree to which books in the series varied. In this case not only has the title page been reset, and the details of the preliminary pages and advertisements re-arranged, but the entire text has been reset by Blackie's own printers in a smaller typeface, reducing the extent by 16 pages.

2. It is, in fact, a true new edition in the bibliographical definition. This, and the later, outworked, edition of *A Knight of the White Cross*, *72.5, are the only 'New Popular Henty' examples I have seen of complete textual resetting by Blackie, but the series was in print for a long time and it is possible that other examples may be found.

3. The single leaf of publisher's catalogue is tipped on to the final page of the last gathering.

4. All minor variants of this edition, with only 368 pages, are grouped together under this 'generic' heading, *74.5.

5. For subsequent editions see under *Facing Death*, 10.7, Notes 6–8.

75. WITH COCHRANE THE DAUNTLESS

75.1

WITH | COCHRANE THE DAUNTLESS | A TALE OF | THE EXPLOITS OF LORD COCHRANE IN | SOUTH AMERICAN WATERS | BY | G.A.HENTY | Author of "Under Drake's Flag", "The Dash for Khartoum", "In Greek Waters" | "The Lion of St. Mark", "Through Russian Snows", &c. | (5-em rule) | WITH TWELVE ILLUSTRATIONS BY W.H.MARGETSON | (5-em rule) | publisher's device) | LONDON | BLACKIE & SON, LIMITED, 50 OLD BAILEY, E.C. | GLASGOW AND DUBLIN | 1897

Contents

185 × 130 mm. (i)–(x) | (11)–384 | catalogue (1)–32. Twelve full-page wash-drawings by W.H. Margetson, reproduced by halftone blocks printed in black on coated paper, unbacked, unfolioed, tipped in.

(i) Half-title p. | (ii) advertisement (MR. HENTY'S HISTORICAL TALES.) listing 38 titles | (frontispiece, tipped in) | (iii) title p. | (iv) blank | (v)–vi. Preface | (vii) Contents | (viii) blank | (ix) list of Illustrations | (x) blank | (11)–384. text; printer's imprint on p.384 (PRINTED BY BLACKIE AND SON, LIMITED, GLASGOW.) | (1)–32. catalogue.

Binding (see Plate 88)

Blue cloth boards, bevelled, blocked black, white, light-blue, and gilt; all edges burnished olive-green; grey endpapers, lined off-white.

Front board: WITH | COCHRANE | THE | DAUNTLESS (light-blue, cased black) below illustration of two sailing ships firing at each other (white, light-blue, gilt), and above trophy of hat and sword (black and gilt). At foot: BY | G.A.HENTY (light-blue). **Spine:** WITH | COCHRANE | THE | DAUNTLESS (white) out of solid-gilt sky of illustration of officer with ratings rowing dinghy (black, white, light-blue). At centre of illustration: G.A.HENTY (light-blue). Light-blue and white rules at foot. **Back board:** plain.

References: BL; Bod; PN | *Farmer*, p.79; *Dartt*, p.158, *Companion*, p.34.

Notes

1. *With Cochrane the Dauntless* was published on 9 June 1896 at six shillings. By the end of February 1897 Blackie had sold 9180 copies, and over the next eleven years they sold 3351 more. The average annual sale over the twelve years was 1044 copies. At the end of 1908 (title-page date 1909) Blackie re-issued the book in their cheaper edition (see 75.3). The remaining five copies of the six-shilling edition were not all sold until 1912

2. *Dartt*, as so often, confuses Blackie and Scribner editions, and incorrectly reports publisher's name in gilt on the spine of the binding case.

3. The earliest issues of this first edition contain catalogues with no mention of the books with title pages dated 1897. These catalogues include earlier titles up to those dated 1896, with press reviews, but they were printed before the titles for the following year were announced.

4. Margetson's halftone illustrations are marked 'Swantype', a product name of the Swan Engraving Company, earlier known as the Swan Electric Company, pioneer

English process engravers. Their work both in line and halftone was much praised by Joseph Pennell in his *Pen Drawing and Pen Draughtsmen,* 1889, and their small, independent workshop was still making fine blocks in the 1960s.

*75.2

Reprints of the six-shilling edition were issued in the same style as 75.1, but with the date removed from the title page. Alterations were made from time to time to the title-page imprint and addresses; the Indian office was opened in 1901 although Bombay did not appear regularly in the Blackie imprint until 1906.

The slightly-varying issues among the reprints of the book in its first-edition format are all grouped together under this 'generic' heading, *75.2.

75.3

With I Cochrane the Dauntless I A Tale of I the Exploits of Lord Cochrane in I South American Waters I BY I G.A.HENTY I Author of "Under Drake's Flag" I "The Dash for Khartoum" "In Greek Waters" I "The Lion of St. Mark" "Through Russian Snows" &c. I ILLUSTRATED BY W.H.MARGETSON I NEW EDITION I BLACKIE AND SON LIMITED I LONDON GLASGOW DUBLIN BOMBAY I 1909

Contents
186 × 127 mm. (1)–384 I catalogue 1–16. Eight full-page wash-drawings by W.H.Margetson, reproduced by halftone blocks printed in sepia on coated paper, unbacked, unfolioed, tipped in.

(1) Half-title p. I (2) advertisement (HENTY'S TALES OF BRITISH HISTORY) listing 38 titles I (frontispiece, tipped in) I (3) title p. I (4) blank I 5. Preface I vi. [roman numerals in error] Preface, continued I 7. Contents I (8) blank I 9–384. text I 1–16. catalogue.

Binding (see Note 1)
Red cloth boards, blocked black, grey, buff, pink, and gilt; all edges stained olive-green; grey endpapers, lined off-white.
Front board: WITH COCHRANE I THE DAUNTLESS I THE EXPLOITS OF LORD COCHRANE IN I SOUTH AMERICAN WATERS I G.A.HENTY (all gilt) above illustration, framed by black rules, of boy paddling boat (black, grey, buff, pink), with signature at foot: J Hassall (black). **Spine:** WITH I COCHRANE I THE I DAUNTLESS I G.A.HENTY (all gilt) above figure of boy with sword (black, buff, pink). At foot: BLACKIE & SON LTD (black). **Back board:** plain.

References: BL; Bod.

Notes
1. Re-issued 1908 (title-page date 1909) in the 'New and Popular Edition'. For details see *Facing Death,* 10.6, Notes 2–3, and examples of the series binding style, Plates 172–173.
2. In this edition Blackie sold 2251 copies by the end of August 1909, and up to the end of August 1917 when Blackie's records cease they sold 3105 more: that represents an average annual sale over the nine-year period of 595 copies. The grand total of copies sold at both prices from 1896 to 1917 is 17,892.

*75.4

Title page: As for 75.3, but last five lines replaced by: Illustrated | BLACKIE & SON LIMITED | LONDON AND GLASGOW

Contents

185 × 125 mm. (1)–384 | no catalogue. Frontispiece from watercolour drawing by Frank Gillett, reproduced by three-colour halftone blocks, and four full-page wash-drawings by W.H.Margetson reproduced by halftone blocks printed in black; all on coated paper, unbacked, keyed to text pages, tipped in.

    (1) Half-title p. | (2) Blackie addresses | (frontispiece, tipped in) | (3) title p. | (4) printer's imprint (Printed in Great Britain by | Blackie & Son, Limited, Glasgow) | 5. Preface | vi. [roman numerals in error] Preface, continued | (7) Contents | (8) blank | (9) list of Illustrations | (10) blank | 11–384. text.

Binding: As for 75.3, except (a) green cloth boards, blocked black, grey. yellow-ochre, and light buff, with no gilt: front-board lettering all light-buff, spine lettering all black; (b) edges plain; (c) plain off-white endpapers.

Reference: IM.

Notes:
1. For details of Blackie's second cheaper series, 'The New Popular Henty', and subsequent editions of this title, see *Facing Death*, 10.7, Notes 1–3 and 6–8.
2. All the minor variants of *With Cochrane the Dauntless* in the series are included under this 'generic' heading, *75.4.

76. AT AGINCOURT

76.1

AT AGINCOURT | A TALE OF | THE WHITE HOODS OF PARIS | BY | G.A.HENTY | Author of "Beric the Briton", "St. Bartholomew's Eve", "In the Reign of Terror" | "St. George for England", "The Tiger of Mysore", &c. | (28mm. rule) | WITH TWELVE ILLUSTRATIONS BY WAL. PAGET | (28mm. rule) | (publisher's device) | LONDON | BLACKIE & SON, LIMITED, 50 OLD BAILEY, E.C. | GLASGOW AND DUBLIN | 1897

Contents

186 × 130 mm. (i)–(x) | (11)–384 | catalogue (1)–32. Twelve full-page wash-drawings by Wal. Paget, printed in black from halftone blocks, signed 'Swantype' by the Swan Engraving Company, on coated paper, unbacked, unfolioed, tipped in.

    (i) Half-title p. | (ii) advertisement (MR. HENTY'S HISTORICAL TALES.) listing 38 titles | (frontispiece, tipped in) | (iii) title p. | (iv) blank | (v) Preface | (vi) blank | (vii) Contents | (viii) blank | (ix) list of Illustrations | (x) blank | (11)–384. text, with printer's imprint at foot of p.384 (PRINTED BY BLACKIE AND SON, LIMITED, GLASGOW.) | (1)–32. catalogue.

Binding (see Plate 55)

Designed by Ralph Peacock (see Note 2). Grey-green cloth boards, bevelled, blocked black, red, white, and gilt; all edges burnished olive-green; grey endpapers, lined off-white.

Front board: AT | AGINCOURT (gilt) | A TALE | OF THE (red) | WHITE | HOODS | of | PARIS (white) | G.A.HENTY (red), at left of illustration of man with white hood and a flaming torch (black, red, white); all within white line. **Spine:** AT | AGINCOURT | (gilt) above trophy of helmet, lances, English & French shields (black, red, white, and gilt). At foot: G.A.HENTY (gilt). All within white line. **Back board:** plain.

References: BL; Bod; PN | *Farmer*, p.7; *Dartt*, p.8.

Notes

1. *At Agincourt* was published on 27 June 1896 at six shillings. By the end of February 1897 Blackie had sold 9440 copies, and in the next fifteen years they sold 4952 more, the average annual sale over the sixteen years being 900 copies. Then, at the end of August 1912, Blackie re-issued the book in their cheaper edition, see 76.3 below. The remaining 7 copies of the six-shilling edition were sold in 1913.

2. Ralph Peacock was commissioned by Talwin Morris to design binding cases for Henty between 1895 and 1898. He also illustrated some books. (See Appendix IV, Part 2).

3. The earliest issues have the same bound-in catalogues as *With Cochrane the Dauntless* (see 75.1, Note 3). They make no mention of the books with title pages dated 1897: they include earlier titles up to those dated 1896, with quotations from press reviews, but were printed before titles for the following year were announced.

*76.2

Reprints of the six-shilling edition were in the style of 76.1, but with no date on the title page. From time to time changes were made to the title-page imprint and addresses: the Indian office was opened in 1901 although Bombay did not appear regularly in the Blackie imprint until 1906; and after 1910 Dublin was omitted.

The slightly-varying issues among the reprints of the book in its first-edition format are all grouped together under this 'generic' heading, *76.2.

76.3

At Agincourt | A Tale of the White Hoods of Paris | BY | G.A.HENTY | Author of "Beric the Briton" "St. Bartholomew's Eve" "In the Reign of Terror" | "St. George for England" "The Tiger of Mysore" &c. | ILLUSTRATED BY WAL PAGET | NEW EDITION | BLACKIE AND SON LIMITED | LONDON GLASGOW AND BOMBAY

(*Note: The* T *of* PAGET *is broken*).

Contents

185 × 127 mm. (1)–384 | catalogue 1–16. Eight wash-drawings by Wal Paget reproduced by halftone blocks printed in black on coated paper, unbacked, tipped in.

(1) Half-title p. | (2) advertisement (NEW AND POPULAR EDITION OF | G.A.HENTY'S WORKS) listing 36 titles | (frontispiece, tipped in) | (3) title p. | (4) blank | (5) Preface | (6) blank | (7) Contents | (8) blank | (9) list of Illustrations | (10) blank | 11–384. text, with printer's imprint at foot of p.384 (PRINTED IN GREAT BRITAIN | At the Villafield Press, Glasgow, Scotland) | 1–16. catalogue.

Binding (see Note 1)

Red cloth boards blocked black, blue, buff, and gilt; edges stained olive-green; grey endpapers, lined off-white.

Front board: AT AGINCOURT | A TALE OF THE WHITE HOODS | OF PARIS. | BY G.A.HENTY (gilt) above illustration, within black line, of English archers in action (black, blue, buff), with signature at lower right corner: J Hassall (black). **Spine:** AT | AGINCOURT | G.A.HENTY (gilt) above illustration, within black line, of single English archer with long bow and quiver full of arrows, and with flag of St George behind (black, blue, buff). At foot: BLACKIE & SON, LTD (black). **Back board:** plain.

Reference: BB.

Notes

1. Re-issued, late 1912, in the 'New and Popular Edition'. For details see *Facing Death*, 10.6, Notes 2–3, and examples of the series binding style, Plates 172–173.

2. In this edition Blackie sold 2098 copies by the end of August 1913, and up to the end of August 1917 when Blackie's records cease they sold 1696 more; this represents an average annual sale over the five-year period of 759 copies. The grand total of copies sold at both 6s. and 3s.6d. from 1896 to 1917 is 18,193.

3. After 1912 Blackie no longer dated title pages in the 'New and Popular Edition'; this book would otherwise have carried the date 1913 on the title page of its first impression in this series.

*76.4

Title page: As for 76.3, but all three capital Ts in 'ILLUSTRATED BY WAL PAGET' are broken.

Contents

185 × 123 mm. (1)–384 | no catalogue. Frontispiece from watercolour drawing reproduced by three-colour halftone blocks; four wash-drawings reproduced by halftone blocks printed in black; all illustrations by Wal Paget; all on coated paper, unbacked, keyed to text pages, tipped in.

(1) Half-title p. | (2) advertisement (G.A.HENTY'S BOOKS) listing 45 titles | (frontispiece, tipped in) | (3) title p. | (4) blank | (5) Preface | (6) blank | (7) Contents | (8) blank | (9) list of Illustrations | (10) blank | 11–384. text, with printer's imprint on p.384 (PRINTED IN GREAT BRITAIN | By Blackie & Son, Limited, Glasgow).

Binding: As for 76.3, except (a) grey-blue cloth boards, blocked black, blue, and buff, with no gilt: spine imprint blocked black, all other lettering buff; (b) edges plain; (c) plain off-white endpapers.

Reference: PN.

Notes

1. For details of Blackie's second cheaper series, 'The New Popular Henty', and later editions, see *Facing Death*, 10.7, Notes 1–3 and 6–8. Examples of the series binding style are at Plates 174–175.

2. The cloth used for this book has a slightly rougher texture than that used for many books in the series.

3. All the minor variants of *At Agincourt* in the series are grouped together under this 'generic' heading, *76.4.

77. ON THE IRRAWADDY

77.1

ON THE IRRAWADDY | A STORY OF | THE FIRST BURMESE WAR | BY | G.A.HENTY | Author of "With Clive in India", "In the Heart of the Rockies", "Through Russian Snows" | "When London Burned", "The Dash for Khartoum", "Through the Sikh War", &c. | (6-em rule) | WITH EIGHT ILLUSTRATIONS BY W.H.OVEREND | (6-em rule) | (publisher's device) | LONDON | BLACKIE & SON, LIMITED, 50 OLD BAILEY, E.C. | GLASGOW AND DUBLIN | 1897

Contents
185 × 123 mm. (i)–(x) | (11)–352 | catalogue (1)–32. Eight full-page wash-drawings by W.H.Overend, reproduced by halftone blocks printed in black on coated paper, unbacked, unfolioed, tipped in.
  (i) Half-title p. | (ii) advertisement (MR. HENTY'S HISTORICAL TALES.) listing 38 titles | (frontispiece, tipped in) | (iii) title p. | (iv) blank | (v)–vi. Preface | (vii) Contents | (viii) blank | (ix) list of Illustrations | (x) blank | (11)–352. text, with printer's imprint at foot of p.352 (PRINTED BY BLACKIE AND SON, LIMITED, GLASGOW.) | (1)–32. catalogue.

Binding (see Plate 78)
Designed by Ralph Peacock (see Note 2). Grey-blue cloth boards, blocked brown, pink, white, and gilt; all edges burnished olive-green; grey endpapers, lined off-white.
  Front board: ON THE | IRRAWADDY | A STORY | OF THE FIRST | BURMESE WAR | G.A.HENTY (all gilt) superimposed on semi-abstract illustration of parts of sailing ship, Burmese figures, smoke, sword, etc. (brown, pink, white) with initials of artist: RP (pink). **Spine:** ON | THE | IRRAWADDY (gilt) over decoration of sun behind boat (pink and white), above illustration of group of figures with building behind (brown, pink, white, and gilt). At foot: G.A.HENTY (pink). **Back board:** plain.

References: BL; Bod; PN; MH | *Farmer*, p.51; *Dartt*, p.100.

Notes
1. The book was published on 13 August 1896 at five shillings. By the end of February 1897 Blackie had sold 8415 copies, and in the following fourteen years 3125 more, the average annual sale over the fifteen years being 769 copies. Then Blackie re-issued the book in their cheaper series (see 77.3). The last 67 copies at five shillings were sold by 1913, total sales in this edition being 11,607 copies.
2. That this is one of the few binding designs normally found in only one cloth-colour was probably the wish of Ralph Peacock (see Appendix IV, Part 2), whose initials are on the front board. But I have seen one copy only of 77.1 in bright-green cloth, blocked in the usual style.
3. As usual at this period, catalogues in the earliest issues give no announcement of

the books for the current year, but details of those for the previous year (with title pages dated 1896) include quotations from press reviews.

4. The halftone illustrations are marked by the process engraver with the product name 'Swantype': see 76.1, Note 4.

*77.2

Reprints of the five-shilling edition were in the style of 77.1, but with the date removed from the title page. Changes were made when necessary to the title-page imprint and addresses: the Indian office was opened in 1901 although Bombay did not appear regularly in the Blackie imprint until 1906; after 1910 Dublin was omitted.

The slightly differing issues among the reprints of this title in its first-edition format are all grouped together under this 'generic' heading, *77.2.

77.3

On the Irrawaddy | A Story of the First Burmese War | BY | G.A.HENTY | Author of "With Clive in India" "In the Heart of the Rockies" | "Through Russian Snows" "When London Burned" "The Dash for Khartoum" | "Through the Sikh War" &c. | WITH EIGHT ILLUSTRATIONS BY W.H.OVEREND | NEW EDITION | BLACKIE AND SON LIMITED | LONDON GLASGOW AND BOMBAY | 1912

Contents
185 × 125 mm. (1)–352 | catalogue 1–16. Eight wash-drawings by W.H.Overend reproduced by halftone blocks printed in sepia on coated paper, unbacked, tipped in.
(1) Half-title p. | (2) advertisement (NEW AND POPULAR EDITION OF | G.A.HENTY'S WORKS) listing 33 titles | (frontispiece, tipped in) | (3) title p. | (4) blank | 5. Preface | vi. [roman numerals in error] Preface, continued | (7) Contents | (8) blank | (9) list of Illustrations | (10) blank | 11–352. text | 1–16. catalogue.

Binding (see Plate 172)
Dark-green cloth boards, blocked black, blue, buff, and gilt; edges stained olive-green; grey endpapers, lined off-white.
Front board: ON THE | IRRAWADDY | G.A.HENTY. (gilt) above illustration, framed by black line, of two men paddling small boat (black, blue, buff). **Spine:** ON | THE | IRRAWADDY | G.A.HENTY. (gilt) above illustration, framed by black line, of girl with head covered and with sun-hat on her back (black, blue, buff). At foot: BLACKIE & SON . LTD. (black). **Back board:** plain.

Reference: PN.

Notes
1. In 1911 (title-page date 1912) Blackie re-issued *On the Irrawaddy* in their 'New and Popular Edition'. For details of the series see *Facing Death*, 10.6, Notes 2–3.
2. In this edition Blackie sold 1803 copies by the end of August 1912, and up to the end of August 1917 when Blackie's records cease they sold 1203 more; this represents an average annual sale over the six-year period of 501 copies. The grand total of copies sold at 5s. and 3s.6d. from 1896 to 1917 is 14,613.
3. After 1911 Blackie did not date title pages in this series. It had been their custom to date first impressions in the 'New and Popular Edition', as they had with first

editions. But books issued in 1912, that would normally have been dated 1913, were undated, as were all subsequent first-impressions, in this and other series.

*77.4

ON THE IRRAWADDY | A Story of the First Burmese War | BY | G.A.HENTY | Author of "With Clive in India" "In the Heart of the Rockies" | "Through Russian Snows" "When London Burned" &c. | Illustrated | BLACKIE AND SON LIMITED | LONDON GLASGOW AND BOMBAY

Contents
185 x 123 mm. (1)–352 | no catalogue. Frontispiece from watercolour drawing by Frank Gillett, reproduced by three-colour halftone blocks; four wash-drawings by W.H. Overend reproduced by halftone blocks printed in black; all on coated paper, unbacked, keyed to text pages; tipped in.

(1) Half-title p. | (2) advertisement (G.A.HENTY'S BOOKS) listing 50 titles | (frontispiece, tipped in) | (3) title p. | (4) imprint (Printed and bound in Great Britain) | 5. Preface | vi. [roman numerals in error] Preface, continued | (7) Contents | (8) blank | (9) list of Illustrations | (10) blank | 11–352. text, with printer's imprint at foot of p.352 (PRINTED IN GREAT BRITAIN | At the Villafield Press, Glasgow, Scotland).

Binding: As for 77.3, except (a) all gilding omitted from blocking: front-board lettering all buff, spine lettering all black; (b) edges plain; (c) plain off-white endpapers.

Reference: IM.

Notes
1. For details of Blackie's second cheaper series, 'The New Popular Henty', and subsequent editions of this title, see *Facing Death*, 10.7, Notes 1–3 and 6–8.
2. All the minor variants of *On the Irrawaddy* in the series are grouped together under this 'generic' heading, *77.4.

78. THE QUEEN'S CUP

78.1
THE QUEEN'S CUP | A NOVEL | BY | G.A.HENTY | AUTHOR OF | 'RUJUB THE JUGGLER,' 'DOROTHY'S DOUBLE,' 'THE CURSE OF | CARNE'S HOLD,' ETC. | (publisher's device) | IN THREE VOLUMES | VOL.I. (VOL.II., VOL.III.) | LONDON | CHATTO & WINDUS | 1897
(Note: the quotation mark before RUJUB *is missing in Volume I only).*

Contents, Volume I
186 x 122 mm. (i)–(ii) | (1)–(252) | no catalogue. No illustrations.

(i) Half-title p. | (ii) advertisement (NEW BOOKS AT EVERY LIBRARY) | (1)–250. text, with printer's imprint at foot of p.250 (BILLING AND SONS, PRINTERS, GUILDFORD.) | (251) publisher's device | (252) blank.

Volume II

186 × 122 mm. (i)–(ii) | (1)–(256) | no catalogue. No illustrations.

(i) Half-title p. | (ii) advertisement (NEW BOOKS AT EVERY LIBRARY) | (1)–253. text, with printer's imprint at foot of p.253, as in Vol.I, p.250 | (254) blank | (255) publisher's device | (256) blank.

Volume III

186 × 122 mm. (i)–(ii) | (1)–(224) | catalogue (1)–32. No illustrations.

(i) Half-title p. | (ii) advertisement (NEW BOOKS AT EVERY LIBRARY) | (1)–221. text, with printer's imprint at foot of p.221, as in Vol.I, p.250 | (222) blank | (223) publisher's device | (224) blank | (1)–32. catalogue, dated Nov. 1896, with printer's imprint at foot of p.32 (OGDEN, SMALE AND CO. LIMITED, PRINTERS, GREAT SAFFRON HILL, E.C.).

Binding (see Plate 7)

Dark bottle-green, ribbed cloth boards, blocked blind and gilt; edges plain; olive-green, decorative endpapers.

Front board: Elegant art-nouveau decoration of leaves, etc. (blind). **Spine:** The | Queen's | Cup | G.A. | Henty | Vol.I (Vol.II, Vol.III) | Chatto & Windus (all gilt). **Back board:** publisher's monogram at centre (blind).

References: BL; Bod; BB | Chatto & Windus Archive: MSS 2444/32/33 | *Farmer*, p.56; *Dartt*, p.108.

Notes

1. Negotiations between Tillotsons and Chatto & Windus were smooth and fast, following the difficulties over *A Woman of the Commune* (see 65.1, Notes 1–4). Indeed, there was not even any bargaining, as there had been with both the earlier novels (see *Rujub, the Juggler*, 56.1, Notes 3–6; and *Dorothy's Double*, 66.1, Notes 1–2). On 10 August 1896 Tillotson sent a complete set of proofs, reminding Chatto that they had been asked for on 20 April, following the initial offer of book rights in the United Kingdom, the Cape, India, and the Australian Colonies. The price asked was £125, and Chatto accepted within a fortnight. It was the same sum that they had paid for *Dorothy's Double*, and the correspondence shows both parties keen to make sure that nothing went wrong this time, after the fiasco of the previous year.

Tillotsons even asked to 'be allowed to intimate our willingness to tender for the printing of the story, if you are prepared to consider such a proposal'. Chatto did not, however, regard Tillotsons as book printers (see Appendix III, Part 1, Note 1), and preferred Billing of Guildford. Billing's skills were well-known to publishers for many decades, and in the 1950s Bertram Billing was still touchingly proud of their long-standing reputation for fine pioneering work with Bibles on India paper (as well as having a fine personal palate for well-made Indian tea). *The Queen's Cup* was the first of Henty's novels from Chatto & Windus to be printed on laid paper.

2. On 22 August 1896 Henty heard from Chatto: 'We have bought from Messrs Tillotson & Son the volume rights in your novel *The Queen's Cup*: and they have sent us a set of proof-slips of the story as it appeared in their newspapers. We understand that you have corrected these for press – Will you kindly say if you would like to see the slips again, with a view to revision before we get the book into type: or may we print from them without further troubling you. Our printers are, we think, careful'. Wisely, Henty asked to see the galleys, or 'slips', which were sent to him five days later, by a publisher obviously anxious to avoid delay: 'Will you kindly let us have them again when corrected. Our printers are very careful, and we hope we may not have to trouble you with proofs in book form'. And on 9 September Chatto wrote: 'We enclose proofs of the first 32 pp. and title pages of *The Queen's Cup*, but do not propose to trouble you with further proofs unless you really wish it. Our printers shall read carefully. Will you kindly say – and return the enclosed proofs.'

3. If this repeated chivvying by Chatto was aimed at getting the book out in time for Christmas, their hopes were frustrated. Henty, perhaps uncertain of the wisdom of Chatto's publishing politics, embarked on a correspondence about the pros and cons of novels in three volumes. The correspondence developed, making Chatto's views about three-deckers appear almost obsessive. Further details of the events that followed are given in Appendix II, Part 4.

4. On 28 November 1896 Chatto wrote to say that 'we are not publishing *The Queen's Cup* until January – perhaps in the second week of the month', and it duly appeared on 12 January 1897. In that year the total number of three-volume novels published by all British publishers totalled a mere four. It was, therefore, one of the last of the three-deckers ever to appear.

5. Of the three-volume edition, 350 copies were printed in September 1896: less than the three-deckers of *Rujub, the Juggler* (500) and *Dorothy's Double* (400). That is hardly surprising, as there can be no doubt that it was unwelcome to Mudie and W.H.Smith purely on account of its format. In terms of total numbers printed, *The Queen's Cup* was the least successful of Henty's novels published by Chatto & Windus (see 78.3, Note 4), and the cause of that may have largely been the publisher's misjudgement of the state of the market. It is indeed evident that the book was very well received by the critics: substantial quotations from reviews in eleven leading publications are quoted on p.(i) of 61.2. No colonial edition was printed.

78.2

THE QUEEN'S CUP | A NOVEL | BY | G.A.HENTY | AUTHOR OF | 'RUJUB THE JUGGLER,' 'DOROTHY'S DOUBLE,' 'THE CURSE OF | CARNE'S HOLD,' ETC. | (publisher's device) | A NEW EDITION | LONDON | CHATTO & WINDUS | 1897

Contents
193 x 128 mm. (i)–(vi) | (1)–(314) | catalogue (1)–32. No illustrations.

(i) Extracts from reviews (OPINIONS OF THE PRESS) | (ii) blank | (iii) half-title p. | (iv) advertisement (NOVELS BY G.A.HENTY) | (v) title p. | (vi) blank | (1)–311. text, with printer's imprint on p.311 (BILLING AND SONS, PRINTERS, GUILDFORD) | (312) blank | (313) publisher's device | (314) blank | (1)–32. catalogue, dated May 1897 (see Note 1), with printer's imprint at foot of p.32 (OGDEN, SMALE AND CO. LIMITED, PRINTERS, GREAT SAFFRON HILL, E.C.).

Binding (see Note 6)
Red canvas boards, blocked gilt; edges uncut; plain off-white laid endpapers.
  Front board: THE QUEEN'S | CUP (gilt) within heart-shaped decorative frame

in upper right corner. **Spine:** THE QUEEN'S | CUP | G.A.HENTY | CHATTO & WINDUS (all gilt). **Back board:** plain.

References: PN | *Dartt*, p.109, *Companion*, p.23.

Notes
1. 1500 copies of this first single-volume edition were ordered from Billing in July 1897. Chatto had used wove paper for Henty's earlier novels, but they had changed to the more elegant laid for 78.1, and continued with laid paper for 78.2. They were still binding-in catalogues dated May 1897; later issues of 78.2 have been reported with catalogues dated as late as September 1897. This edition sold at 3s.6d.
2. *Farmer* does not notice this impression, but mentions 78.3.
3. *Dartt* (p.109) is more or less accurate as far as it goes, but his *Companion* (p.23) mistakenly substitutes IMPRESSION for EDITION on the title page. That was a confusion with the 1907 impression (see 78.4) which he had just discovered.
4. On 30 August 1897 Chatto informed Tillotsons that they had received an order from a Canadian bookseller for 100 copies of the one-volume edition: 'As the work will bear our imprint, and be supplied from the new edition which we have nearly ready [78.2] we shall feel greatly obliged if you will kindly send us a line to say that you have no objection to our doing so, as we are desirous of not disappointing our client' (Chatto & Windus Archive: MS 2444/34). I have found no evidence of Tillotson's reply, but it seems likely they would have agreed to the request, and, if so, the copies supplied would be indistinguishable from those supplied to UK booksellers, unless containing a Canadian bookseller's ticket.
5. The imposition and collation of this book seems unnecessarily complicated and clumsy. The prelims make six pages, and were printed together with the last signature (sig.20, starting at p.305) which makes ten pages, thus producing an even working of 16 pages. That involved the division of the sheet into (a) two conjugate leaves, forming 4 pages, plus a single leaf, tipped in with paste, to make up the prelims; and (b) half the sheet, folded, to make 8 pages, plus another single leaf tipped in with paste, to produce signature 20. Altogether an expensive arrangement, apparently just to allow for the publisher's device to appear on an otherwise blank leaf at the end of the text.
6. The binding style was also used for *Rujub, the Juggler*, 56.6, Plate 19, and for *Dorothy's Double*, 61.3.

78.3

Title page: As for 78.2, but date changed to 1898.

Contents
191 x 128 mm. (i)–(viii) | (1)–(312) | catalogue (1)–32. No illustrations.

(i)–(ii) blank | (iii) extracts from reviews (OPINIONS OF THE PRESS) | (iv) blank | (v) half-title p. | (vi) advertisement (NOVELS BY G.A.HENTY) | (vii) title p. | (viii) blank | (1)–311. text, with printer's imprint at foot of p.311 (BILLING AND SONS, PRINTERS, GUILDFORD.) | (312) blank | (1)–32. publisher's catalogue, with printer's imprint at foot of p.32 (UNWIN BROTHERS, Printers, 27, Pilgrim Street, London, E.C.).

Binding: As for 78.2, but the boards are about 3mm. shorter, because of the smaller page size.

References: PN | *Farmer*, p.57.

Notes

1. On 15 August 1898 Chatto ordered a further 500 copies, still on an antique laid, but of a slightly lighter weight than before. The imposition and collation are now simplified (see 78.2, Note 4), the prelims, and signature 20, each a folded half-sheet of eight pages. The publisher's device following the text has disappeared.

2. This reprint sold slowly: bound-in catalogues are known with dates including March 1901 and September 1906, so part of the small impression of only 500 copies had lain in stock for eight years. It is therefore very surprising to find Chatto & Windus ordering yet another edition of 500 copies the following year (see 78.4).

78.4

THE QUEEN'S CUP | A NOVEL | G.A.HENTY | AUTHOR OF | 'RUJUB THE JUGGLER,' 'DOROTHY'S DOUBLE,' 'THE CURSE OF | CARNE'S HOLD,' ETC. | (publisher's device) | A NEW IMPRESSION | LONDON | CHATTO & WINDUS | 1907

Contents

188 × 122 mm. (i)–(viii) | (1)–(312) | no catalogue. No illustrations.

(i) Advertisement (NOVELS BY G.A.HENTY) | (ii) blank | (iii) extracts from reviews (OPINIONS OF THE PRESS | ON | THE QUEEN'S CUP) | (iv) blank | (v) half-title p. | (vi) blank | (vii) title p. | (viii) blank | (1)–311. text, with printer's imprint at foot of p.311 (BILLING AND SONS, LIMITED, PRINTERS, GUILDFORD) | (312) blank.

Binding

Dark-blue, horizontally-ribbed cloth boards, blocked blind and gilt, edges plain; plain off-white wove endpapers.

Front board: THE QUEEN'S | CUP | G.A.HENTY (all blind) at left of centre and in upper part of board, all enclosed within blind rule near edges of board. **Spine:** THE QUEEN'S | CUP | G.A.HENTY (all gilt). At foot: CHATTO & WINDUS (gilt). Gilt rules at head and foot. **Back board:** plain.

References: SW | *Dartt Companion*, p.23.

Notes

1. This impression of 500 copies was ordered in August 1907. It is a surprising move since the 500 copies printed eight years earlier were only just exhausted. This new impression is on a cheaper, wove paper, and the imposition scheme follows that of 78.3. The prelims have been reset, but there appears to be no other variation from 78.3 apart from a dropped full-point at the end of the printer's imprint on p.311.

2. Less surprisingly this edition proved very hard to dispose of. The sheets were bound between 26 September 1907 and 19 May 1925, mostly in batches to make 50 copies, some for sale at 3s.6d. and the later batches, dated 12 July 1924 and 19 May 1925, at 5s. On 1 April 1926 the outstanding balance of 176 copies was remaindered.

3. The advertisement on p.(i) shows: *Rujub the Juggler* ('Demy 8vo., cloth, gilt edges, with eight illustrations by S.L.Wood, 5s.; post 8vo., cloth, 3s.6d.; illustrated boards, 2s.'); *Dorothy's Double* ('Crown 8vo., cloth, 3s.6d.'); *The Queen's Cup* ('Crown 8vo., cloth, 3s.6d.'); and *Colonel Thorndyke's Secret* (With Frontispiece by

Stanley L.Wood. Crown 8vo., cloth, 3s.6d.'). Extracts from press reviews are given for each title.

4. No colonial edition was printed. The total number of copies printed in both the three-volume edition and the single-volume editions was 2850.

79. COLONEL THORNDYKE'S SECRET

79.1

COLONEL THORNDYKE'S | SECRET | BY | G.A.HENTY | AUTHOR OF | "THE QUEEN'S CUP," "DOROTHY'S DOUBLE," "RUJUB THE JUGGLER," | "THE CURSE OF CARNE'S HOLD," ETC. | (publisher's device) | LONDON | CHATTO & WINDUS | 1898
(Note: The title, and CHATTO & WINDUS, *are printed in red).*

Contents
189 × 130 mm. approx. (i)–(iv) | (1)–400 | catalogue (1)–32. No illustrations.

(i) Half-title p. | (ii) advertisement (NOVELS BY G.A.HENTY) | (iii) title p. | (iv) blank | (1)–400. text, with printer's imprint at foot of p.400 (PRINTED BY WILLIAM CLOWES AND SONS, LIMITED, LONDON AND BECCLES.) | (1)–32. catalogue, dated January 1898, with printer's imprint at foot of p.32 (OGDEN, SMALE AND CO. LIMITED, PRINTERS, GREAT SAFFRON HILL, E.C.).

Binding (see Plate 10)
Light-red cloth boards, blocked black and gilt; top edge gilt, others uncut; light olive-green flowered endpapers.
Front board: Colonel | Thorndyke's | Secret (gilt) in small panel in art-nouveau design of leaves and flowers (black). **Spine:** Colonel | Thorndyke's | Secret | G.A. | Henty (gilt) above art-nouveau design of leaves, etc. (black). At foot: Chatto & Windus (gilt). **Back board:** device with publisher's monogram at centre (black).

References: BL; Bod; PN | Chatto & Windus Archive: MSS 2444/34/35 | *Farmer*, p.21; *Dartt*, p.39, *Companion*, p.9.

Notes
1. On 9 November 1897 Chatto acknowledged receipt from Tillotsons of slips of two novels: George Manville Fenn's *A Woman worth Winning*, and Henty's *Colonel Thorndyke's Secret*, which were offered for £175 and £125 respectively. Chatto wrote: 'We have given very careful consideration to the two stories, but we find that the utmost that we can give for the two tales would be £225. The excessive output of works of fiction makes it very difficult in the present state of the book market to secure a sale that shall promise a remunerative return on the above offer which we are sure is the largest that the times will allow us to make'.
2. Tillotsons wrote again, not quite splitting the difference, and Chatto took the two books for a joint fee of £250: 'We are desirous of meeting you whenever we can, and we trust you will bear this in mind, when you kindly favour us with the next novel'. It is noticeable, however, from Chatto's letter books, that business between the two firms had been dwindling, and by this date correspondence was infrequent.

3. On 15 December 1897 Chatto wrote to thank Henty for correcting and returning the first batch of the slips supplied by Tillotsons: 'We are intending to publish the story as a 1-volume novel (the library 3-volume form being now unfortunately quite obsolete)'. On 21 December, acknowledging another batch, Chatto wrote: 'The recent refusal of the large circulating libraries to circulate novels in three or even in two volumes, has caused authors to greatly vary the length of their tales, which now are generally ordered in one volume at the nominal publishing price of 5/-; some uniformity being obtained between long and short works by using larger or smaller type and a closer page. We are very pleased to learn that *Colonel Thorndyke* is of the average length of a 3-vol story, as we find that the reading public seem to expect this quantity in one volume'.

4. In the same letter of 21 December Chatto agreed to describe the book on the title page 'as a "novel" in accordance with your instructions'. Henty had several times shown concern about appearing to be breaking the terms of his agreement with Blackie (see Appendix VI). Although not (yet) illustrated it might be thought to be intended 'for young people', and he was evidently anxious to make it clear from the start that, whoever might ultimately enjoy reading the book, it was first published as an adult novel (see *Rujub, the Juggler*, 56.1, Note 5, and 56.3, Note 6). Chatto did not, however, keep his promise: the word 'novel' was omitted from the title page. On the other hand the facing page displayed a small panel with a heading 'NOVELS BY G.A.HENTY', in which were listed all four of the books published by Chatto.

5. This was the last book by Henty they published, and the only one of the four not to appear as a three-decker. The publication date was 10 March 1898, and it was put on sale at six shillings (not five shillings as forecast, see Note 3).

6. For this first edition 2000 sets of sheets had been ordered on 30 December 1897, to be printed on laid paper. The first binding order, for 1000 copies, was dated 24 January 1898, and the catalogues bound in were dated January 1898.

7. To begin with, the book went well, 1800 copies being sold by May, and another 150 by October. In all, 1972 copies were sold by 1904 from the total of 2024 copies (including overs) produced by Clowes. There was a small balance remaindered in 1918. Dartt (*Companion*, p.9) reports a catalogue dated February 1899 in a late issue, probably from the last batch of 50 copies, ordered from the bindery in October 1898.

79.2

COLONEL THORNDYKE'S | SECRET | BY | G.A.HENTY | AUTHOR OF | "THE QUEEN'S CUP," "DOROTHY'S DOUBLE," "RUJUB THE JUGGLER," | "THE CURSE OF CARNE'S HOLD," ETC. | (publisher's device) | PRESENTATION EDITION | WITH A FRONTISPIECE BY STANLEY WOOD | LONDON | CHATTO & WINDUS | 1899

Contents

198 × 135 mm. (i)–(iv) | (1)–400 | catalogue (1)–32. Frontispiece from wash-drawing by Stanley L.Wood, reproduced by halftone block printed in black on coated paper, unbacked, tipped in.

(i) Half-title p. | (ii) advertisement (NOVELS BY G.A.HENTY) | (frontispiece, tipped in) | (iii) title p. | (iv) blank | (1)–400. text, with printer's imprint at foot of p.400 (PRINTED BY WILLIAM CLOWES AND SONS, LIMITED, LONDON

AND BECCLES.) | (1)–32. catalogue, with printer's imprint at foot of p.32 (OGDEN, SMALE AND PETTY, LIMITED, PRINTERS, GREAT SAFFRON HILL, E.C.).

Binding (see Plate 10)
Grey-blue cloth boards, bevelled, blocked black, white, yellow, and gilt; all edges gilt; dark blue-green surface-paper endpapers.
  Front board: COLONEL . THORNDYKE'S | SECRET (yellow, cased black, out of solid-gilt panel) above illustration of 'smoke' rising from open casket (black, white, yellow); at left: G.A.HENTY (white). **Spine:** COLONEL | THORNDYKE'S | SECRET (yellow out of solid-gilt panel) above: G.A.HENTY (white); illustration of Indian figure dressed in yellow (black, white, yellow). White and yellow rules at foot. **Back board:** plain.

References: PN | *Dartt Companion*, p.9.

Notes
1. Ten months after publication of the first edition, on 13 January 1899, Chatto ordered a further 1000 sets of sheets, to be printed this time on good-quality wove paper in place of the equally good-quality laid paper used for 79.1.
2. This Presentation Edition was the kind of book production that worried Henty. The pictorial binding, and the inclusion of an illustration by Stanley Wood, made the book appear just like some of his books for boys. There was, in fact, only one illustration, but it was exactly the sort of picture that appeared in boys' adventure stories, and when pasted in as frontispiece it concealed the advertisement containing the word 'novel' (see 79.1, Note 4). A strong case could be made that Chatto was deliberately aiming at buyers of gift books for boys. From the Chatto ledger it is clear there was an immediate, if not prolonged, revival of demand for the book in its changed format.
3. The first binding order, on 17 April 1899, was for 400 copies, and there followed two more orders, for 250 and 100 respectively, in September and November of that year. After that there were orders in August 1900 and August 1901, for 100 copies and 50 copies respectively, in time for the Christmas trade. By August 1903 there was a balance of 85 copies still unsold.
4. Dartt (*Companion*, p.9) reports a catalogue with all four Henty titles listed under 'Piccadilly Novels', but gives no date for it. Catalogues in the earliest issue I have found are dated February 1899, and show three Henty titles only: indeed I have never found *Colonel Thorndyke's Secret* listed as a Piccadilly novel.
5. On the other hand, the advertisement on p.(ii) gives more details of the current availability of the four novels than I have found elsewhere: *Rujub the Juggler* ('Presentation Edition, small demy 8vo, cloth bevelled, gilt edges, with 8 Illustrations by Stanley Wood, 5s.; or crown 8vo, cloth, with 8 Illustrations, 3s.6d.; post 8vo, illustrated boards, 2s.'); *Dorothy's Double* ('Crown 8vo, cloth, 3s.6d.; post 8vo, illustrated boards, 2s.'); *The Queen's Cup* ('Crown 8vo, cloth, 3s.6d.'); *Colonel Thorndyke's Secret* ('Presentation Edition, small demy 8vo, cloth bevelled, gilt edges, with a Frontispiece by Stanley Wood, 5s.; or crown 8vo, cloth, gilt top, 6s.'). The term 'illustrated boards', which appears under both *Rujub the Juggler* and *Dorothy's Double*, refers to what were generally known as 'yellowbacks'.

79.3

Notes

1. The publisher's records show that 500 sets of sheets, including frontispieces, were printed in December 1905. Chatto's ledger records a wove paper for the text. I have not been able to find a copy of this 1905 issue.

2. But it also records that 150 copies were first bound on 22 January 1906; further batches of 50 and 100 copies were bound in April and September of 1907; and the balance was bound, and probably sold, by 1915. There were no later impressions.

3. In all editions, 3500 copies were printed of *Colonel Thorndyke's Secret.*

80. WITH MOORE AT CORUNNA

80.1

WITH MOORE AT CORUNNA | BY | G.A.HENTY | Author of "With Cochrane the Dauntless", "A Knight of the White Cross" | "In Freedom's Cause", "St. Bartholomew's Eve", "Wulf the Saxon", &c. | (5-em rule) | WITH TWELVE ILLUSTRATIONS BY WAL PAGET | (5-em rule) | (publisher's device) | LONDON | BLACKIE & SON, LIMITED, 50 OLD BAILEY, E.C. | GLASGOW AND DUBLIN | 1898

(Note: Both serifs at the top of the second N *in* CORUNNA *are slightly battered).*

Contents

186 x 130 mm. (i)–(x) | (11)–384 | catalogue (1)–32. Twelve full-page wash-drawings by Wal Paget, reproduced by halftone blocks (see Note 4) printed in black on coated paper, unbacked, unfolioed, tipped in. Three battle-plans printed from line blocks on text pages.

(i) Half-title p. | (ii) advertisement (MR. HENTY'S HISTORICAL TALES.) listing 41 titles | (frontispiece, tipped in) | (iii) title p. | (iv) blank | (v)–vi. Preface | (vii) Contents | (viii) blank | (ix) list of Illustrations | (x) blank | (11)–384. text, with printer's imprint at foot of p.384 (PRINTED BY BLACKIE AND SON, LIMITED, GLASGOW.) | (1)–32. catalogue.

Binding (see Plate 94)

Designed by Ralph Peacock (see Note 3). Green cloth boards, bevelled, blocked black, white, red, pink, and gilt; all edges burnished olive-green; grey endpapers, lined off-white.

Front board: WITH MOORE | AT | CORUNNA (gilt) above and at right of illustration of cloaked soldier with arm in sling (black, white, red, pink, gilt). At lower right corner: G.A.HENTY (gilt). All framed by broken white line. **Spine:** WITH | MOORE | AT | CORUNNA (gilt) above trophy of hat, pouch, and sword (black, white, red, gilt). At foot: G.A.HENTY (gilt). All framed by white line. **Back board:** plain.

References: BL; Bod; PN | *Farmer*, p.82; *Dartt*, p.161, *Companion*, p.34.

Notes

1. This book was published on 22 May 1897 at six shillings. By the end of February 1898 Blackie had sold 9150 copies, and ten years later, at the end of August 1908, they had sold 3177 more, the average annual sale over the eleven-year period being 1121 copies. The book was then re-issued in Blackie's first cheaper edition (see 80.3). The remaining stock of 68 copies was sold over five years.

2. *Dartt* (pp.l61–162) is very confusing, mainly because he once again tries to describe the Blackie and Scribner editions together. As far as I know, the 'light blue' cloth was never used for a Blackie edition; he omits the vital 'red' from the colours used for blocking the case. The 'map of Northern Portugal' does not appear in Blackie editions, nor do 'dark blue' endpapers. The copy in the Battersea Library (one of Henty's own) is in binder's cloth, not in 'publisher's cloth'.

3. This binding design, in common with others by Ralph Peacock (see Appendix IV, Part 2), is virtually always found in the same cloth-colour.

4. The halftone illustrations are marked by the process engraver with the product name 'Swantype': see 76.1, Note 4.

*80.2

Reprints of the six-shilling edition were in the style of 80.1, but with the date removed from the title page. Alterations were made when necessary to the title-page imprint and addresses: the Indian office was opened in 1901 although Bombay did not appear regularly in the Blackie imprint until 1906; after 1910 Dublin was omitted.

The slightly-varying issues among the reprints of the book in its first-edition format are all grouped together under this 'generic' heading, *80.2.

80.3

With | Moore at Corunna | BY | G.A.HENTY | Author of "With Cochrane the Dauntless" "A Knight of the White Cross" | "In Freedom's Cause" "St. Bartholomew's Eve" "Wulf the Saxon" &c. | ILLUSTRATED BY WAL PAGET | NEW EDITION | BLACKIE AND SON LIMITED | LONDON GLASGOW DUBLIN BOMBAY | 1909

Contents

187 × 127 mm. (1)–384 | catalogue 1–16. Eight full-page wash-drawings by Wal Paget, reproduced by halftone blocks printed in black on coated paper, unbacked, unfolioed, tipped in. Battle-plans as in 80.1.

(1) Half-title p. | (2) advertisement (HENTY'S TALES OF BRITISH HISTORY) listing 38 titles | (frontispiece, tipped in) | (3) title p. | (4) blank | (5) Preface | vi. [roman numerals in error] Preface, continued | 7. Contents | (8) blank | 9. list of Illustrations | (10) blank | 11–384. text | 1–16. catalogue.

Binding (see Note 1)

Red cloth boards, blocked black, brown, vermilion, buff, and gilt; all edges stained olive-green; grey endpapers, lined off-white.

Front board: WITH MOORE | AT CORUNNA | G.A.HENTY (gilt) above illustration, framed by black line border, of soldiers (black, brown, vermilion, and buff), with signature: J Hassall (black). **Spine:** WITH | MOORE | AT | CORUNNA | G.A.HENTY (gilt) above illustration of soldier aiming pistol (black, brown, vermilion, buff). At foot: BLACKIE & SON LTD. (black). **Back board:** plain.

References: BL; Bod.

Notes

1. Re-issued late 1908 (title-page date 1909) in the 'New and Popular Edition'. For details see *Facing Death*, 10.6, Notes 2–3, and for examples of the series binding style, Plates 172–173.

2. In this edition Blackie had sold 2375 copies by the end of August 1909, and by the same date eight years later, when Blackie's records cease, they had sold 4160 more. The average annual sale over those nine years was 726 copies. The grand total of copies sold at both prices, from 1897 to 1917, is 18,930.

*80.4

With I Moore at Corunna I A Tale of the Peninsular War I BY I G.A.HENTY I Author of "Beric the Briton" "Redskin and Cowboy" "In Freedom's Cause" I "St. Bartholomew's Eve" "Wulf the Saxon" &c. I ILLUSTRATED BY WAL PAGET I BLACKIE AND SON LIMITED I LONDON GLASGOW AND BOMBAY

Contents

185 × 124 mm. (1)–384 I no catalogue. Frontispiece from watercolour drawing reproduced by three-colour halftone blocks; four full-page wash-drawings reproduced by halftone blocks printed in black; all by Wal Paget; all on coated paper, unbacked, keyed to text pages, tipped in.

(1) Half-title p. I (2) advertisement (G.A.HENTY'S BOOKS) listing 45 titles I (frontispiece, tipped in) I (3) title p. I (4) blank I 5. Preface I vi. [roman numerals in error] Preface, continued I (7) Contents I (8) blank I (9) list of Illustrations I (10) blank I 11–384. text, with printer's imprint at foot of p.384 (PRINTED IN GREAT BRITAIN I By Blackie & Son, Limited, Glasgow).

Binding: As for 80.3, except (a) green cloth boards, blocked black, red, brown, and buff, with no gilt: imprint on spine blocked black, all other lettering buff; (b) edges plain; (c) plain off-white endpapers.

Reference: PN.

Notes

1. For details of Blackie's second cheaper series, 'The New Popular Henty', and subsequent editions of this title, see *Facing Death*, 10.7, Notes 1–3 and 6–8.

2. All the minor variants of *With Moore at Corunna* in the series are grouped together under this 'generic' heading, *80.4.

81. A MARCH ON LONDON

81.1

A MARCH ON LONDON I BEING A STORY OF I WAT TYLER'S INSURRECTION I BY I G.A.HENTY I Author of "Beric the Briton", "When London Burned," "With Clive in India", &c. I (6-em rule) I WITH EIGHT ILLUSTRATIONS BY W.H.MARGETSON I (6-em rule) I (publisher's device) I LONDON I BLACKIE & SON, LIMITED, 50 OLD BAILEY, E.C. I GLASGOW AND DUBLIN I 1898

Contents

185 × 123 mm. (i)–(x) | (11)–352 | catalogue (1)–32. Eight full-page wash-drawings by W.H. Margetson, reproduced by halftone blocks printed in black on coated paper, unbacked, unfolioed, tipped in.

(i) Half-title p. | (ii) advertisement (MR. HENTY'S HISTORICAL TALES.) listing 41 titles | (frontispiece, tipped in) | (iii) title p. | (iv) blank | (v)–vi. Preface | (vii) Contents | (viii) blank | (ix) list of Illustrations | (x) blank | (11)–352. text; printer's imprint on p.352 (PRINTED BY BLACKIE AND SON, LIMITED, GLASGOW.) | (1)–32. catalogue.

Binding (see Plate 77)

Designed by Ralph Peacock (see Note 4). Blue cloth boards, blocked black, blue, green, and gilt; all edges burnished olive-green; grey endpapers, lined off-white (see Note 3).

Front board: A MARCH | ON | LONDON (green, cased black) above illustration of man with weapon on caparisoned horse (black, blue, green, and gilt). At right: A | TALE | OF | WAT TYLER'S | RISING (green). At foot: BY | G.A.HENTY. (black). **Spine:** A | MARCH | ON | LONDON (gilt) over illustration of man holding home-made weapon (black, blue, green). At foot: BY | G.A.HENTY (black) within gilt chain of office (black and gilt). **Back board:** plain.

References: BL; Bod; PN | *Farmer*, p.49; *Dartt*, p.95, *Companion*, p.21.

Notes

1. The book was published on 15 June 1897 at five shillings. By the end of February 1898 Blackie had sold 8870 copies, but thirteen years later, at the end of August 1911, they had sold only 3566 more. The average annual sale over the fourteen years, boosted by pre-publication sales, was 888 copies, but for the thirteen years from 1899 to 1911 it was only 274 copies. In 1911 (title-page date 1912) Blackie re-issued the book in the cheaper series (see 81.3). 120 more copies were sold over the years up to August 1914, concurrently with the cheaper books.

2. The earliest catalogues were printed before the announcement of the books with 1898 title-page dates. The advertisements include books with title pages dated 1897.

3. I have a second copy, an early issue, inscribed December 1897, which has plain off-white endpapers in place of the grey ones normally seen in Blackie novels of this period. These endpapers carry the dated inscription, and there is no doubt that they are original. The catalogue in this copy is as described in Note 2 above. This is the only Henty novel from Blackie with such endpapers, in either the five-shilling or the six-shilling series, that has come to my notice.

4. The binding case, in common with others by Ralph Peacock (see Appendix IV, Part 2), is virtually always found in cloth of the same colour. The subtitle on the front board differs from that on the title page, perhaps because 'insurrection' is a long and awkward word to fit into the design.

5. *Dartt* incorrectly reports the publisher's name blocked on the spine, probably once again confusing the Blackie edition with his own from Scribners. This, and his description of the illustration on the front board, is corrected in his *Companion*.

6. The halftone illustrations are marked by the process engraver with the product name 'Swantype': see 76.1, Note 4.

*81.2
Reprints of the five-shilling edition were in the style of 81.1, but with no date on the title page. Alterations were made when necessary to the title-page imprint and addresses: the Indian office was opened in 1901 although Bombay did not appear regularly in the Blackie imprint until 1906; after 1910 Dublin was omitted.

The slightly-varying issues among the reprints of the book in its first-edition format are all grouped together under this 'generic' heading, *81.2.

81.3
A March on London | Being a Story of | Wat Tyler's Insurrection | BY | G.A.HENTY | Author of "Beric the Briton" "When London Burned" "With Clive in India" | "One of the 28th" "The Dash for Khartoum" &c. | WITH EIGHT ILLUSTRATIONS | BY W.H.MARGETSON | NEW EDITION | BLACKIE AND SON LIMITED | LONDON GLASGOW AND BOMBAY | 1912

Contents
184 x 125 mm. (1)–352 | catalogue 1–16. Eight full-page wash drawings by W.H.Margetson, reproduced by halftone blocks printed in sepia on coated paper, unbacked, unfolioed, tipped in.

(1) Half-title p. | (2) advertisement (NEW AND POPULAR EDITION OF | G.A.HENTY'S WORKS) listing 33 titles | (frontispiece, tipped in) | (3) title p. | (4) blank | 5. Preface | vi. [roman numerals in error] Preface, continued | (7) Contents | (8) blank | (9) list of Illustrations | (10) blank | 11–352. text | 1–16. catalogue.

Binding (see Note 1)
Olive-green cloth boards, blocked black, blue, buff, and gilt; edges stained olive-green; grey endpapers, lined off-white.

Front board: A MARCH | ON LONDON | G.A.HENTY. (all gilt) above illustration, framed by black line, of young man in front of house, with woman in doorway (black, blue, buff). **Spine:** A | MARCH | ON | LONDON | G.A.HENTY (all gilt) above illustration, framed by black line, of helmeted soldier on horseback (black, blue, buff). At foot: BLACKIE & SON LTD (black). **Back board:** plain.

Reference: AK.

Notes
1. Re-issued late 1911 (title-page date 1912) in the 'New and Popular Edition'. For details see *Facing Death*, 10.6, Notes 2–3, and for examples of the series binding style, Plates 172–173.
2. In this edition Blackie had sold 1788 copies by the end of August 1912, and by the same date five years later, when Blackie's records cease, they had sold 1329 more. The grand total of copies sold at both prices, from 1897 to 1917, was 15,673.

*81.4
A March on London | Being a Story of | Wat Tyler's Insurrection | BY | G.A.HENTY | Author of "Beric the Briton" "When London Burned" "With Clive in India" | "One of the 28th" "The Dash for Khartoum" &c. | ILLUSTRATED | BLACKIE AND SON LIMITED | LONDON GLASGOW AND BOMBAY

Contents
184 × 124 mm. (1)–352 | no catalogue. Frontispiece from watercolour drawing by John de Walton, reproduced by three-colour halftone blocks; four full-page wash-drawings by W.H. Margetson, reproduced by halftone blocks printed in black; all on coated paper, unbacked, unfolioed, tipped in.

(1) Half-title p. | (2) advertisement (G.A.HENTY'S BOOKS) listing 45 titles | (frontispiece, tipped in) | (3) title p. | (4) blank | 5. Preface | vi. [roman numerals in error] Preface, continued | (7) Contents | (8) blank | (9) list of Illustrations | (10) blank | 11–352. text, with printer's imprint at foot of p.352 (PRINTED IN GREAT BRITAIN | By Blackie & Son, Limited, Glasgow).

Binding: As for 81.3, except (a) dark-green cloth boards, blocked black, blue, and buff, with no gilt: all lettering buff; (b) publisher's imprint omitted from spine; (c) edges plain; (d) plain off-white endpapers.

Reference: PN.

Notes
1. For details of Blackie's second cheaper series, 'The New Popular Henty', and subsequent editions of this title, see *Facing Death*, 10.7, Notes 1–3 and 6–8.
2. All the minor variants of *A March on London* in the series are grouped together under this 'generic' heading, *81.4.

82. WITH FREDERICK THE GREAT

82.1
WITH FREDERICK THE GREAT | A STORY OF THE SEVEN YEARS' WAR | BY | G.A.HENTY | Author of "At Agincourt", "By England's Aid", "In Greek Waters" | "One of the 28th", &c. | (5-em rule) | WITH TWELVE ILLUSTRATIONS BY WAL. PAGET | (5-em rule) | (publisher's device) | LONDON | BLACKIE & SON, LIMITED, 50 OLD BAILEY, E.C. | GLASGOW AND DUBLIN | 1898

Contents
186 × 130 mm. (i)–(x) | (11)–384 | catalogue (1)–32. Twelve full-page wash-drawings by Wal. Paget, reproduced by halftone blocks printed in black on coated paper, unbacked, unfolioed, tipped in. One map and seven battle-plans printed from line blocks on text pages.

(i) Half-title p. | (ii) advertisement (MR. HENTY'S HISTORICAL TALES.) listing 41 titles | (frontispiece, tipped in) | (iii) title p. | (iv) blank | (v)–vi. Preface | (vii) Contents | (viii) blank | (ix) list of Illustrations | (x) map | (11)–384. text; printer's imprint on p.384 (PRINTED BY BLACKIE AND SON, LIMITED, GLASGOW.) | (1)–32. catalogue.

Binding (see Plate 93)
Designed by Ralph Peacock (see Note 5). Red cloth boards, bevelled, blocked black, white, and gilt; all edges burnished olive-green; grey endpapers, lined off-white.

Front board: With Frederick | the | Great (gilt, gothic lettering) | A | TALE | OF THE | SEVEN YEARS | WAR (all black) | G.A.HENTY (white), all above and at left of illustration of Frederick the Great in uniform, reading a map (black, white).

All framed by broken white line. **Spine:** With | Frederick | the | Great (gilt, gothic lettering) above illustration of officer on horse (black, white). At foot: G.A.HENTY (black). All framed by broken white line. **Back board:** plain.

References: BL; Bod; PN | *Farmer*, p.80; *Dartt*, p.159.

Notes

1. The book was published on 26 August 1897 at six shillings. By the end of February 1898 Blackie had sold 8990 copies, and by the end of August 1908 they had sold 2392 more, the average annual sale over the eleven years being 1034 copies. Then Blackie re-issued the book in their cheaper edition (see 82.3). The remaining stock of 21 copies of the six-shilling edition was sold by August 1912.

2. *Farmer* reports copies in 'light brown paper dust wrapper with cover designs reproduced on front and spine'.

3. *Dartt* is confusing, in his usual attempt to describe the Blackie and Scribner editions together. In particular, 'dark blue' endpapers do not occur in Blackie issues; the pigments used for blocking the binding case are not correctly described.

4. The subtitle on the binding case differs from that on the title page, substituting 'Tale' for 'Story'. It also omits the apostrophe after 'Seven Years'.

5. This binding case is another example of the work of Ralph Peacock: his lettering as well as his general style is quite distinctive (see Appendix IV, Part 2), and once again the cloth-colour is invariably the same.

6. The earliest issues contain catalogues with no mention of books for the current year (with title pages dated 1898). Henty's books up to and including those for the previous year (dated 1897) are listed, with quotations from press notices.

*82.2

Reprints of the six-shilling edition were in the style of 82.1, with the date removed from the title page. Changes were made when necessary to the title-page imprint and addresses: the Indian office was opened in 1901 although Bombay did not appear regularly in the Blackie imprint until 1906; Dublin was omitted after 1910.

The slightly-varying issues among the reprints of the book in its first-edition format are all grouped together under this 'generic' heading, *82.2.

82.3

With | Frederick the Great | A Story of the Seven Years' War | BY | G.A.HENTY | Author of "At Agincourt" "By England's Aid" "In Greek Waters" | "One of the 28th" &c. | ILLUSTRATED BY WAL PAGET | NEW EDITION | BLACKIE AND SON LIMITED | LONDON GLASGOW DUBLIN BOMBAY | 1909

Contents

185 × 125 mm. (1)–384 | catalogue 1–16. Eight full-page wash-drawings by Wal Paget, reproduced by halftone blocks printed in sepia on coated paper, unbacked, unfolioed, tipped in. Map and battle-plans as in 82.1.

(1) Half-title p. | (2) advertisement (HENTY'S TALES OF BRITISH HISTORY) listing 38 titles | (frontispiece, tipped in) | (3) title p. | (4) blank | 5. Preface | vi. [roman numerals in error] Preface, continued | 7. Contents | (8) blank | 9. list of Illustrations | (10) map | 11–384. text | 1–16. catalogue.

Binding (see Note 1)

Green cloth boards, blocked black, orange, buff, brown, and gilt; all edges stained olive-green; grey endpapers, lined off-white.

Front board: WITH FREDERICK | THE GREAT | A STORY OF THE SEVEN YEARS WAR | G.A.HENTY (all gilt) above illustration, framed by black line, of windblown figure on horseback crossing desert landscape (black, orange, buff, brown), with signature: J Hassall (black) at foot. **Spine:** WITH | FREDERICK | THE | GREAT | G.A.HENTY (all gilt) above illustration of figure with sword (black, orange, buff, brown). At foot: BLACKIE & SON LTD (black). **Back board:** plain.

References: BL; Bod.

Notes

1. Re-issued, late 1908, in the 'New and Popular Edition'. For details see *Facing Death*, 10.6, Notes 2–3; for examples of the series binding style, Plates 172–173.

2. In this edition Blackie had sold 2301 copies by the end of August 1909, and by the same date in 1917, when their records cease, they had sold 3257 more, averaging sales of 618 copies each year over the nine-year period. The grand total of sales at both prices from 1897 to 1917 was 16,961 copies.

*82.4

With Frederick the Great | A Story of the Seven Years' War | BY | G.A.HENTY | Author of "At Agincourt" "By England's Aid" | "In Greek Waters" "One of the 28th" &c. | Illustrated | BLACKIE & SON LIMITED | LONDON AND GLASGOW

Contents

184 × 124 mm. (1)–384 | advertisement (i)–(ii). Frontispiece from watercolour drawing, unsigned, reproduced by three-colour halftone blocks; four wash-drawings by Wal Paget reproduced by halftone blocks; all printed on coated paper, unbacked, tipped in. Map and battle-plans as in 82.1.

(1) Half-title p. | (2) Blackie addresses | (frontispiece, tipped in) | (3) title p. | (4) printer's imprint (Printed in Great Britain by Thomson & Cully, Glasgow) (see Note 2) | (5) Preface | vi. [roman numerals in error] Preface, continued | (7) Contents | (8) blank | (9) list of Illustrations | (10) map | 11–384. text | (i)–(ii) advertisement (THE NEW POPULAR HENTY) listing 62 titles.

Binding: As for 82.3, except (a) blue cloth boards, blocked black, grey, and buff, with no gilt: all lettering black; (b) edges plain; (c) plain off-white endpapers.

Reference: TC.

Notes

1. For details of Blackie's second cheaper series, 'The New Popular Henty', and subsequent editions of this book, see *Facing Death*, 10.7, Notes 1–3 and 6–8.

2. This issue is one of very few that Blackie outworked to other printers, no doubt because of a heavy work-load. I have found only two other examples among Henty's novels (*A Knight of the White Cross*, *72.5, and *Through Three Campaigns*, *107.3).

3. All the minor variants of *With Frederick the Great* in the series are grouped together under this 'generic' heading, *82.4.

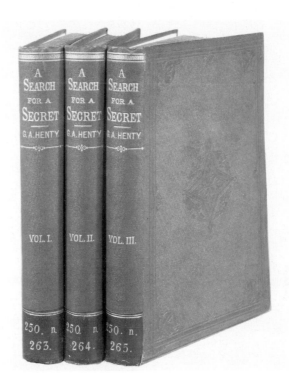

1. *A Search for a Secret*, 1.1

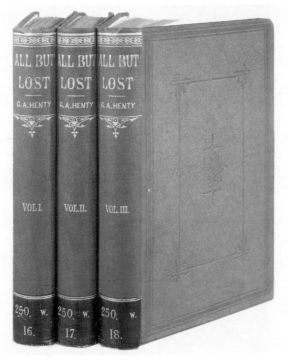

2. *All but Lost*, 3.1

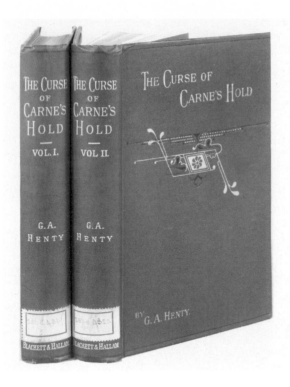

3. *The Curse of Carne's Hold,* 40.1

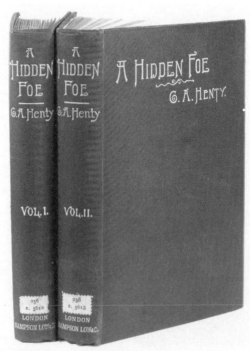

4. *A Hidden Foe,* 46.1

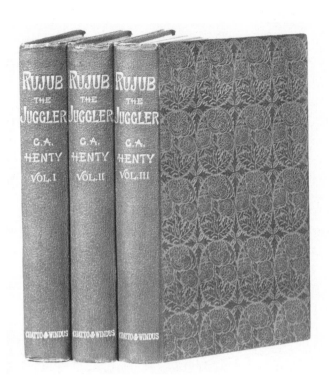

5. *Rujub,*
the Juggler, 56.1

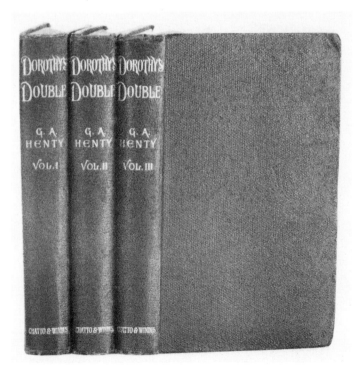

6. *Dorothy's*
Double, 61.1

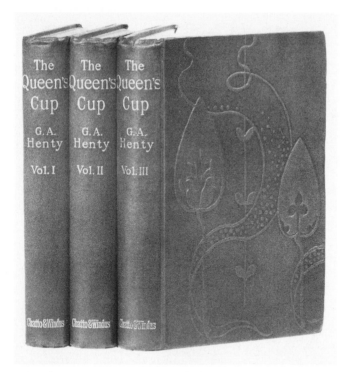

7. *The Queen's Cup,* 78.1

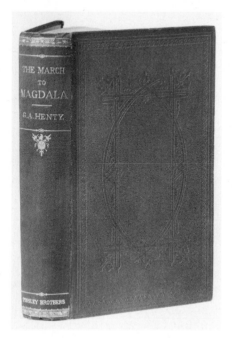

8. *The March to Magdala,* 2.1

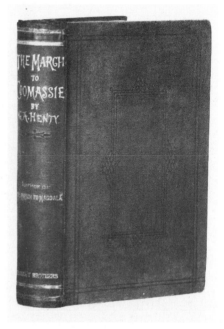

9. *The March to Coomassie,* 6.1

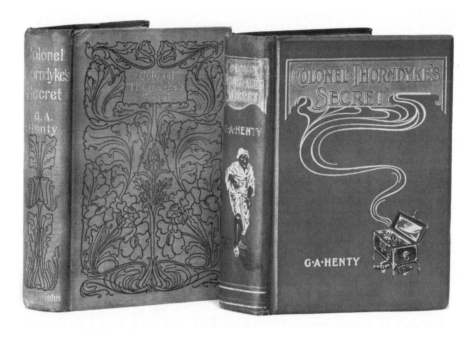

10. *Colonel Thorndyke's Secret*, 79.1, 79.2

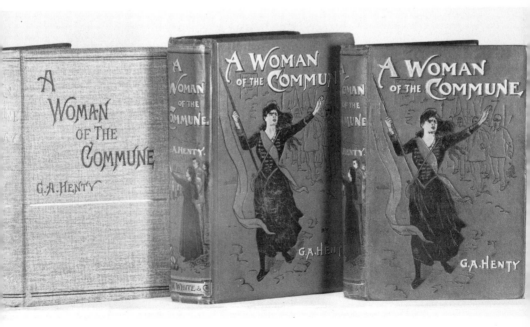

11. *A Woman of the Commune*, 65.1, 65.4, 65.5

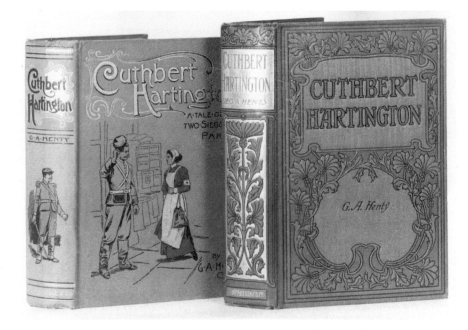

12. *Cuthbert Hartington*, 86.1, 86.2

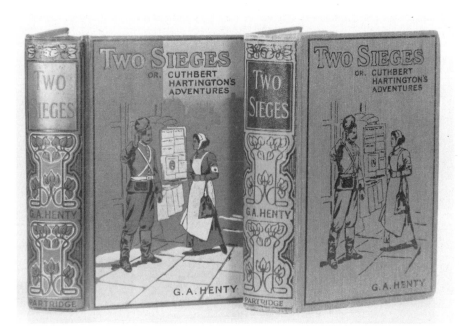

13. *Two Sieges*, 112.1, 112.2

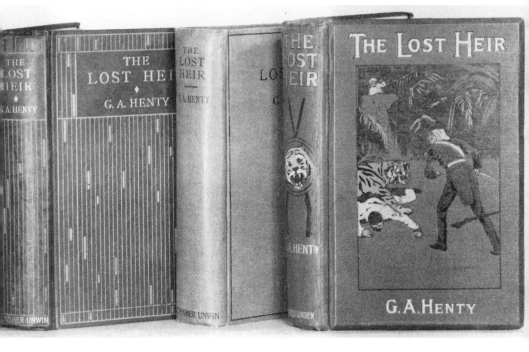

14. *The Lost Heir*, 87.2, 87.3, 87.1

15. *The Lost Heir*, 87.4

16. *A Search for a Secret*, 1.2

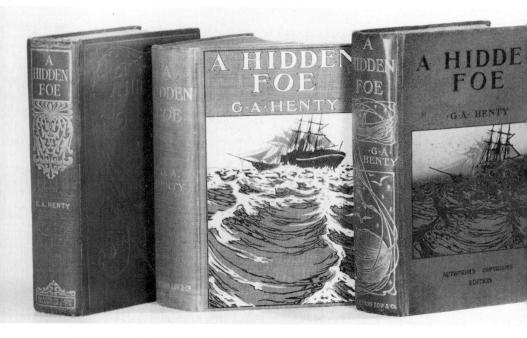

17. *A Hidden Foe*, 46.3, 46.2, 46.4

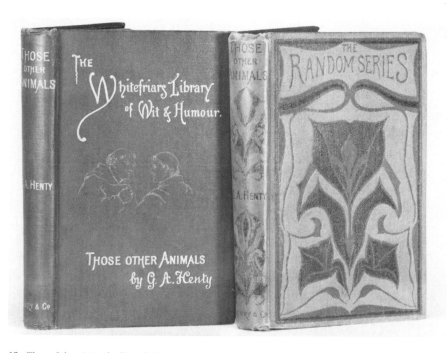

18. *Those Other Animals*, 51.1, 51.2

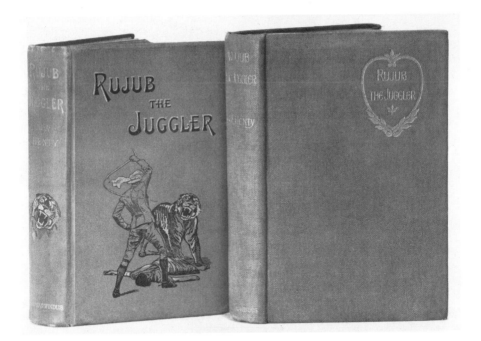

19. *Rujub, the Juggler,* 56.3, 56.6

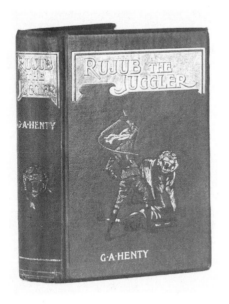

20. *Rujub, the Juggler,* 56.8

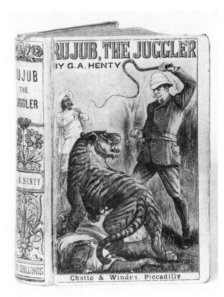

21. *Rujub, the Juggler,* 56.7

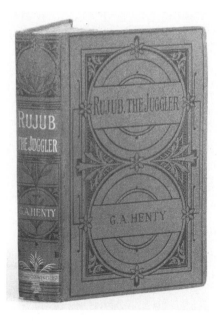

22. *Rujub, the Juggler*, 56.4

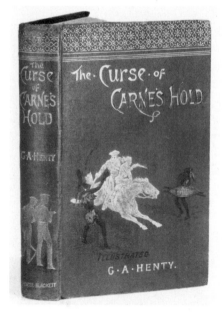

23. *The Curse of Carne's Hold*, 40.2

24. *The Curse of Carne's Hold*, 40.3

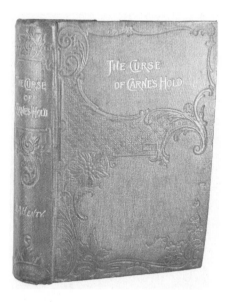

25. *The Curse of Carne's Hold*, 40.6

26. *The Curse of Carne's Hold*, 40.7, 40.8

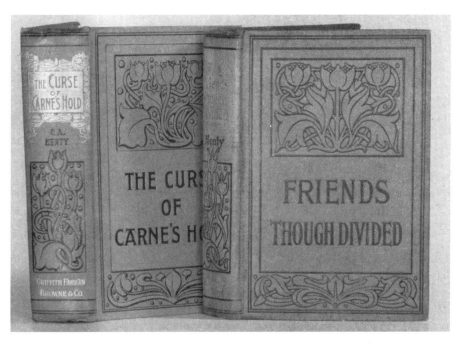

27. *The Curse of Carne's Hold*, 40.10; *Friends, though Divided*, 12.6

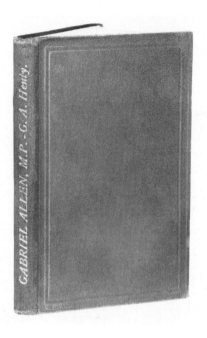

28. *Gabriel Allen, M.P.*, 39.1

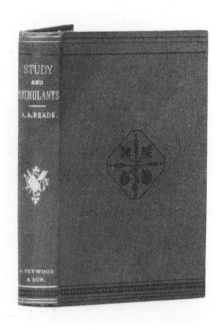

29. *Study and Stimulants*, 188.1

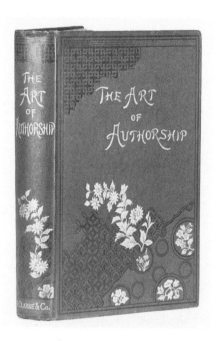

30. *The Art of Authorship*, 124.1

31. *The Ashantees*, 125.1

32. *In Times of Peril,* 9.1; *The Young Franc-Tireurs,* 5.1; *The Young Buglers,* 7.1; *Out on the Pampas,* 4.1; *Friends, though Divided,* 12.2

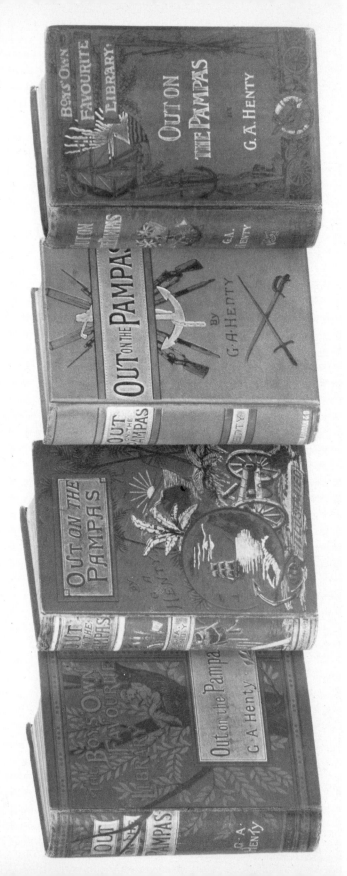

33. The Griffith & Farran binding designs for 'The Boys' Own Favourite Library', here all shown for issues of *Out on the Pampas*: left to right, 4.3, 4.4, 4.5, 4.6

34. *Out on the Pampas*, 4.7; *In Times of Peril*, 9.6; *Friends, though Divided*, 12.5; *The Young Franc-Tireurs*, 5.10; *The Young Buglers*, 7.6

35. *In Times of Peril*, 9.8; *Out on the Pampas*, 4.10

36. *The Young Franc-Tireurs*, 5.13; *The Young Buglers*, 7.10; *Friends, though Divided*, 12.7

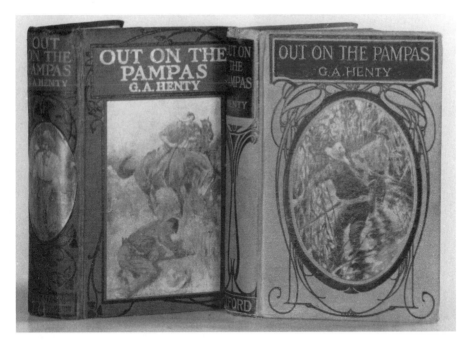

37. *Out on the Pampas*, 4.11, 4.14

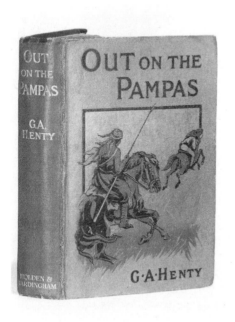

38. *Out on the Pampas*, 4.16

39. *The Young Franc-Tireurs*, 5.11

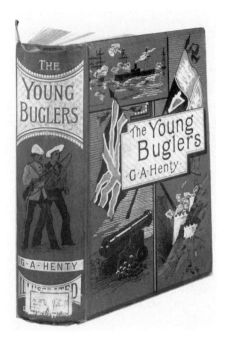
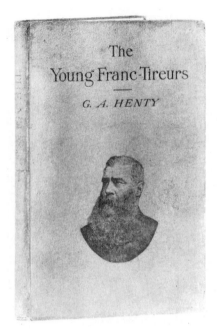

40. *The Young Buglers*, 7.2   **41.** *The Young Franc-Tireurs*, 5.8

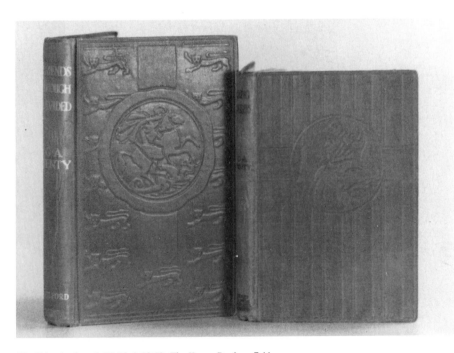

42. *Friends, though Divided*, 12.10; *The Young Buglers*, 7.11

43. *The Young Franc-Tireurs*, 5.12; *The Young Buglers*, 7.9; *In Times of Peril*, 9.3

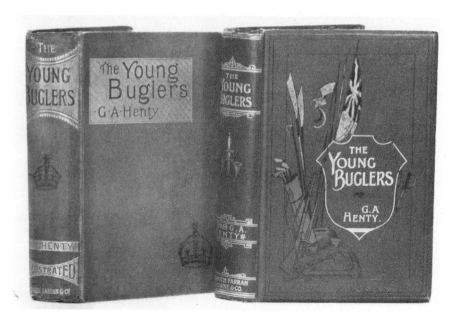

44. *The Young Buglers*, 7.3, 7.5

45. *In Times of Peril*, 9.7, 9.10

46. *The Young Buglers*, 7.13; *In Times of Peril*, 9.12

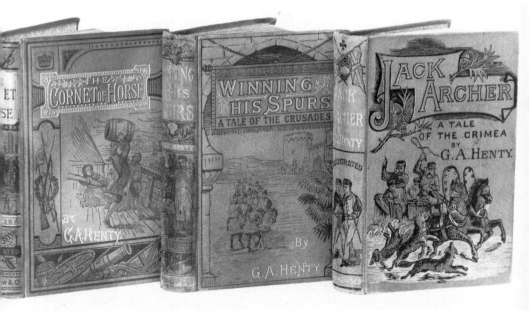

47. *The Cornet of Horse*, 8.1; *Winning his Spurs*, 11.1; *Jack Archer*, 14.1

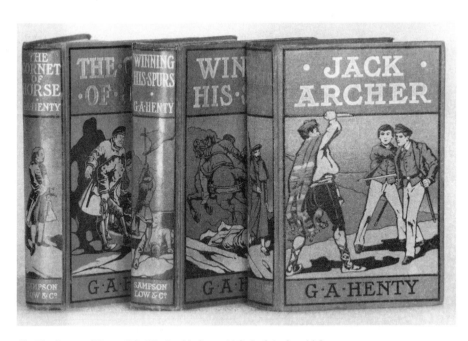

48. *The Cornet of Horse*, 8.3; *Winning his Spurs*, 11.3; *Jack Archer*, 14.5

49. *The Cornet of Horse*, 8.4; *Jack Archer*, 14.8

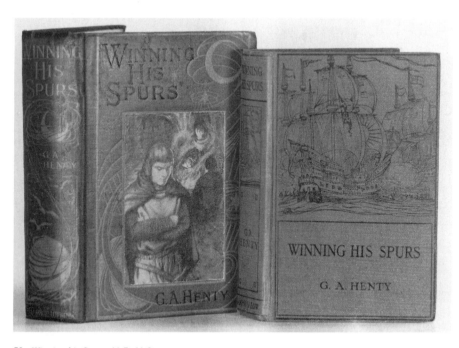

50. *Winning his Spurs*, 11.7; 11.8

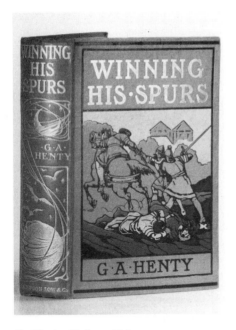

51. *Winning his Spurs*, 11.5

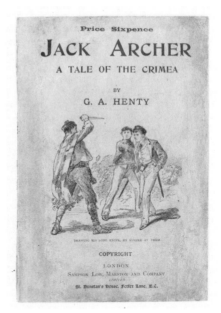

52. *Jack Archer*, 14.4

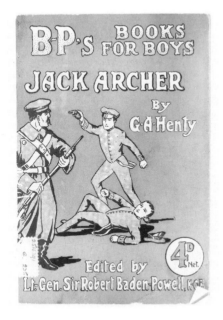

53. *Jack Archer*, 14.7

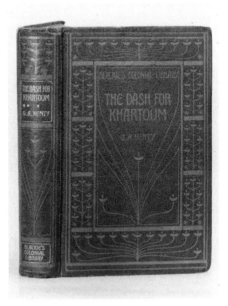

54. *The Dash for Khartoum*, 53.3

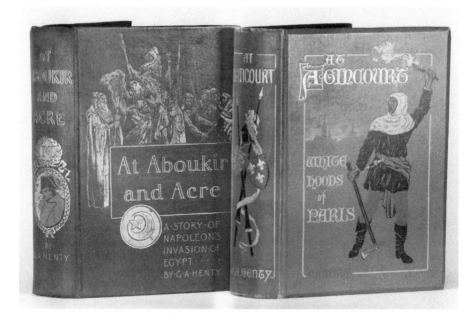

55. *At Aboukir and Acre*, 85.1; *At Agincourt*, 76.1

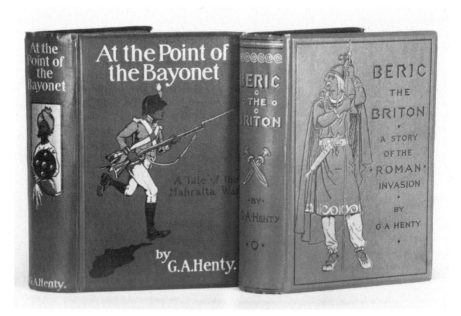

56. *At the Point of the Bayonet*, 99.1; *Beric the Briton*, 59.1

57. *Bonnie Prince Charlie*, 31.1; *Both Sides the Border*, 84.1

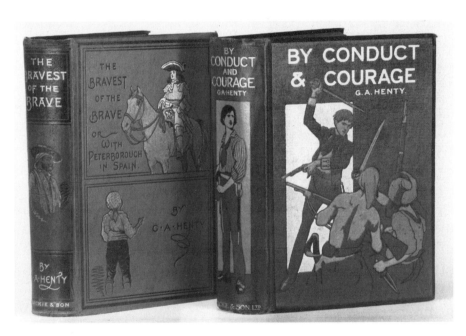

58. *The Bravest of the Brave*, 28.1; *By Conduct and Courage*, 109.1

59. *By England's Aid*, 47.1; *By Pike and Dyke*, 43.1

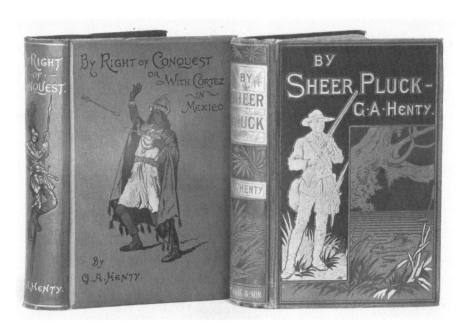

60. *By Right of Conquest*, 50.1; *By Sheer Pluck*, 16.1

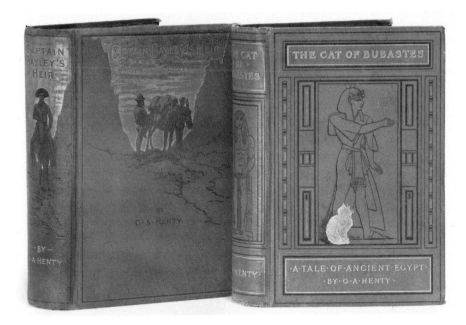

61. *Captain Bayley's Heir*, 37.1; *The Cat of Bubastes*, 38.1

62. *Condemned as a Nihilist*, 58.1; *The Dash for Khartoum*, 53.1

63. *The Dragon and the Raven*, 21.1; *A Final Reckoning*, 29.1

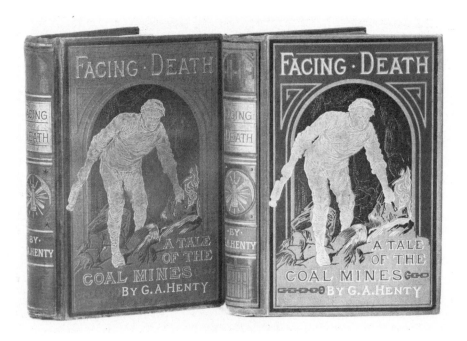

64. *Facing Death*, 10.1, 10.4

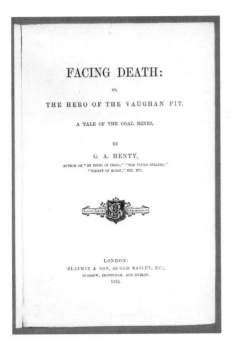

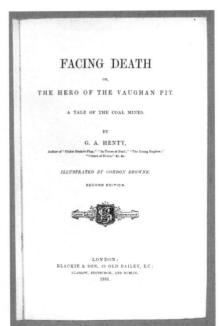

65. *Facing Death*, 10.1

66. *Facing Death*, 10.4

67. *Facing Death*, 10.2, 10.4

68. *Facing Death*, 10.3

69. *For Name and Fame,* 22.1, 22.3

70. *For the Temple,* 35.1; *The Young Carthaginian,* 30.1

71. *Held Fast for England*, 55.1; *In Freedom's Cause*, 18.1

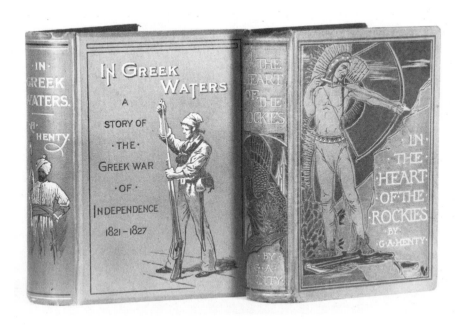

72. *In Greek Waters*, 60.1; *In the Heart of the Rockies*, 67.1

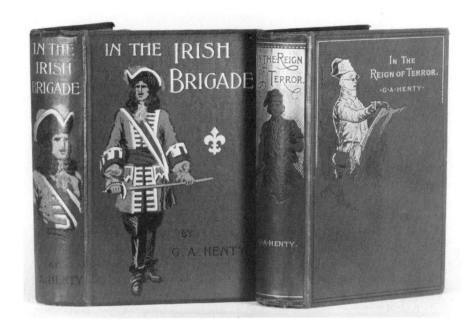

73. *In the Irish Brigade*, 96.1; *In the Reign of Terror*, 33.1

74. *A Jacobite Exile*, 62.1; *A Knight of the White Cross*, 72.1

75. *The Lion of St. Mark*, 36.1; *Maori and Settler*, 49.1

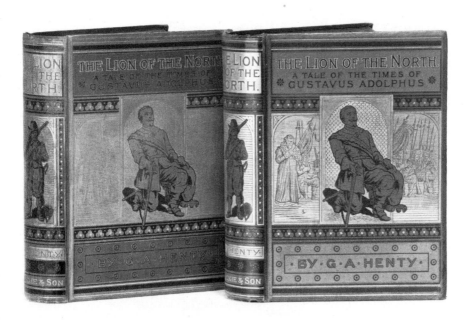

76. *The Lion of the North*, 23.1, 23.2

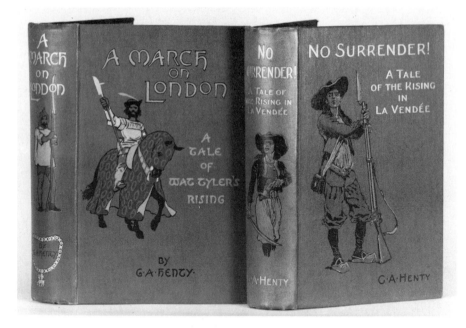

77. *A March on London*, 81.1; *No Surrender!*, 92.1

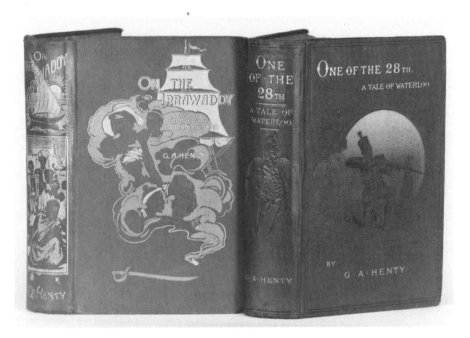

78. *On the Irrawaddy*, 77.1; *One of the 28th*, 44.1

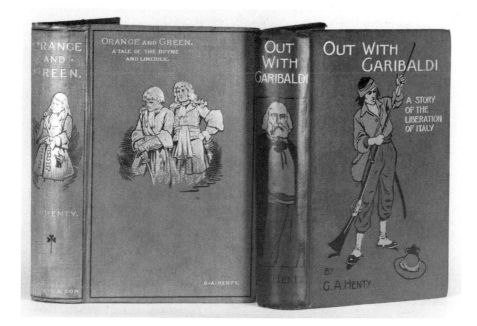

79. *Orange and Green*, 32.1; *Out with Garibaldi*, 98.1

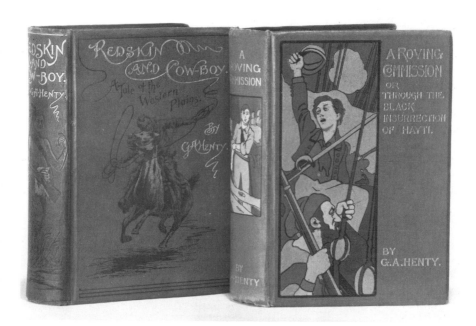

80. *Redskin and Cow-boy*, 54.1; *A Roving Commission*, 91.1

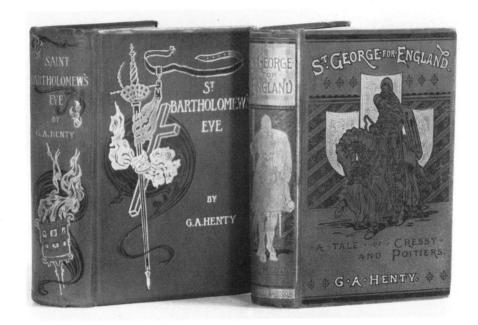

81. *St. Bartholomew's Eve*, 63.1; *St. George for England*, 20.1

82. *Through Russian Snows*, 73.1; *Through the Fray*, 24.1

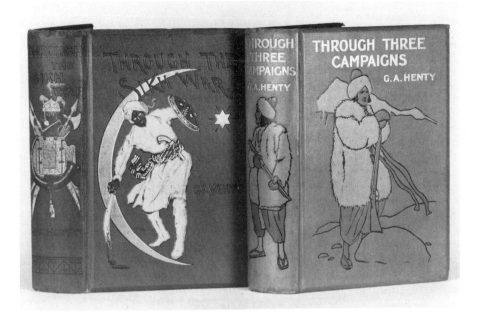

83. *Through the Sikh War*, 64.1; *Through Three Campaigns*, 107.1

84. *The Tiger of Mysore*, 74.1; *The Treasure of the Incas*, 105.1

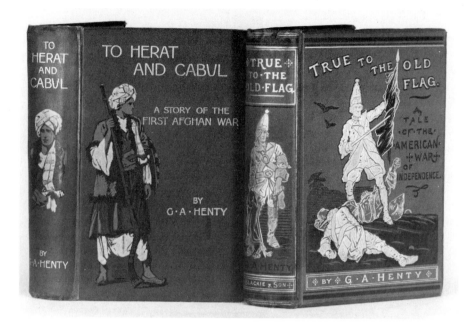

85. *To Herat and Cabul*, 100.1; *True to the Old Flag*, 19.1

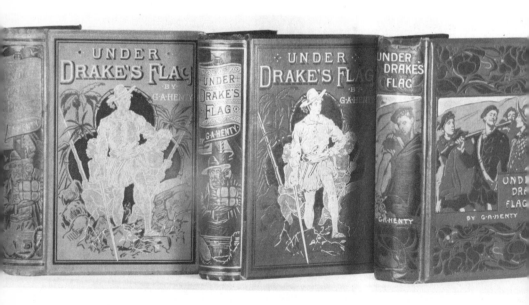

86. *Under Drake's Flag*, 13.1, 13.2, 13.3

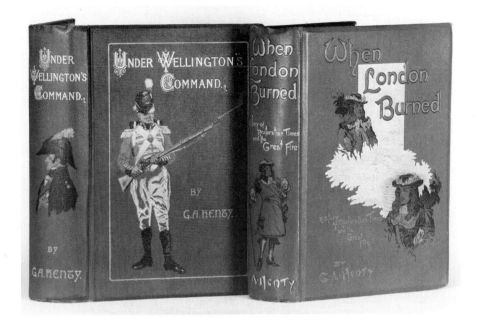

87. *Under Wellington's Command*, 83.1; *When London Burned*, 68.1

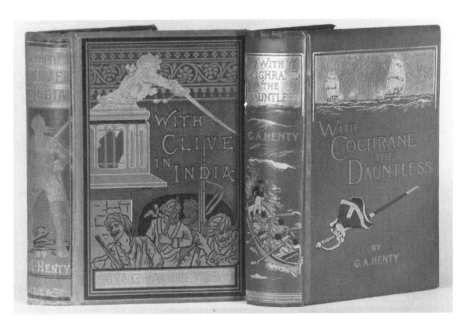

88. *With Clive in India*, 15.1; *With Cochrane the Dauntless*, 75.1

89. (above) *With Buller in Natal*, 97.1, 97.4
90. (below) details, 97.1, 97.2   **91., 92.** (opposite) details, 97.1, 97.2

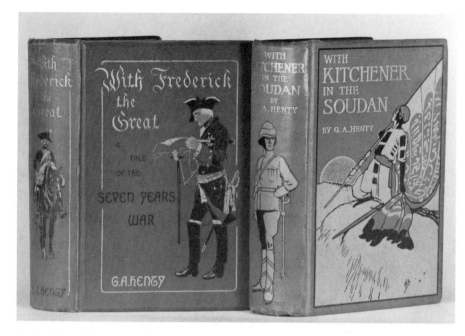

93. *With Frederick the Great*, 82.1; *With Kitchener in the Soudan*, 104.1

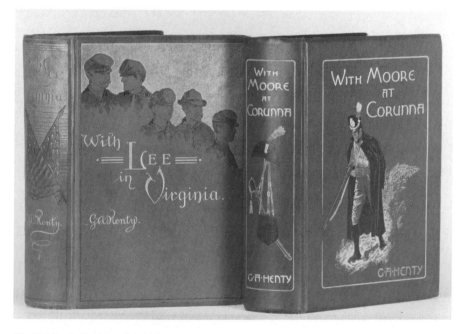

94. *With Lee in Virginia*, 45.1; *With Moore at Corunna*, 80.1

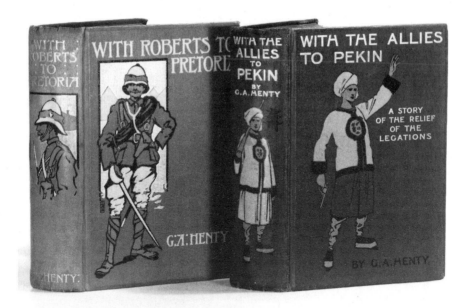

95. *With Roberts to Pretoria*, 101.1; *With the Allies to Pekin*, 108.1

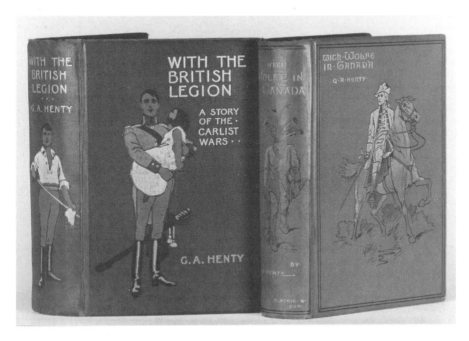

96. *With the British Legion*, 106.1; *With Wolfe in Canada*, 27.1

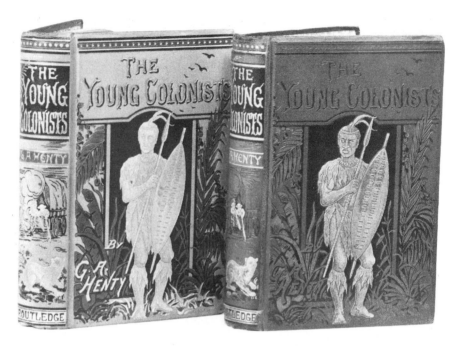

97. *The Young Colonists*, 17.1, 17.2

98. *The Young Colonists*, 17.3, 17.6

99. *The Young Colonists*, 17.5, 17.4

100. *The Young Colonists*, 17.7, 17.9

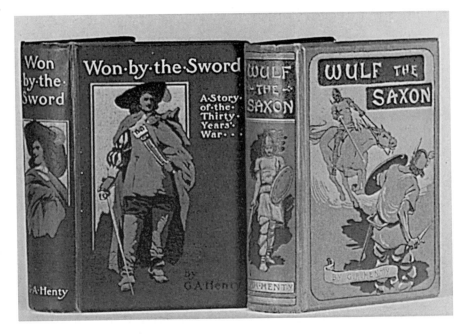

101. *Won by the Sword*, 90.1; *Wulf the Saxon*, 66.1

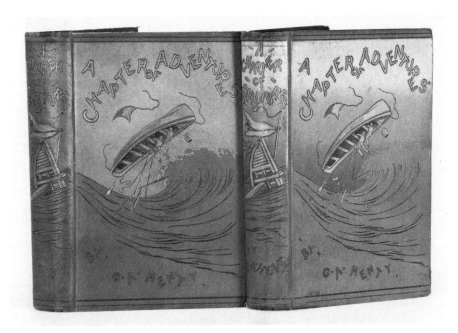

102. *A Chapter of Adventures*, 48.1, 48.2

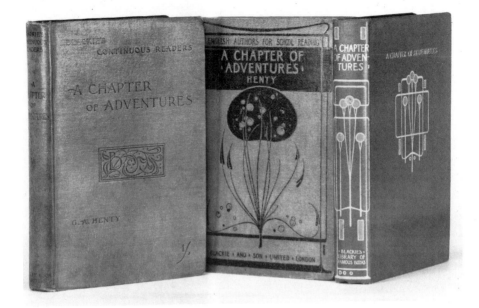

103. *A Chapter of Adventures*, 48.3, 48.6, 48.8

104. *A Chapter of Adventures*, 48.9, 48.10

105. *John Hawke's Fortune*, 93.1

106. *John Hawke's Fortune*, 93.2

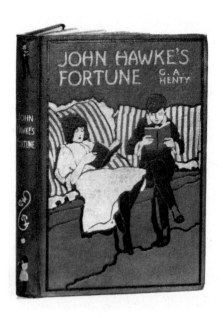

107. *John Hawke's Fortune*, 93.5

108. *John Hawke's Fortune*, 93.7

109. *John Hawke's Fortune*, 93.4, 93.9, 93.10, 93.6

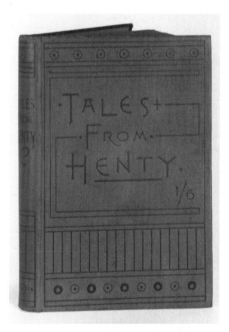

110. *Tales from Henty,* 57.1

111. *Tales from Henty,* 57.6

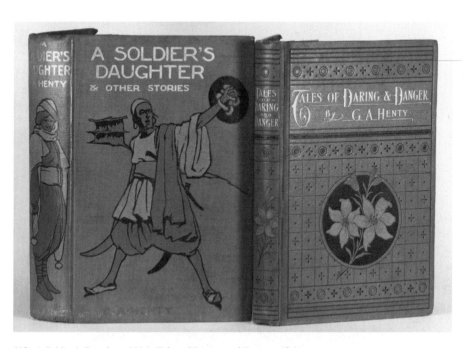

112. *A Soldier's Daughter,* 111.1; *Tales of Daring and Danger,* 42.1

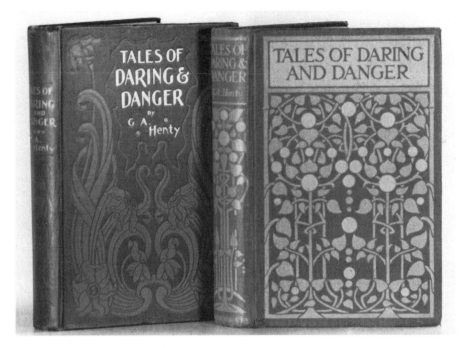

113. *Tales of Daring and Danger,* 42.3, 42.6

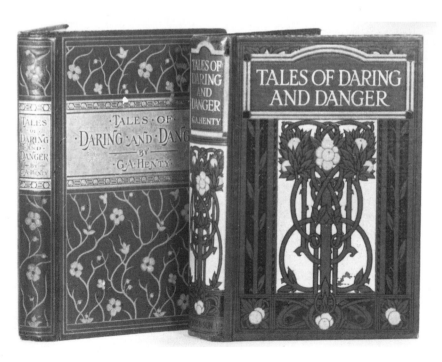

114. *Tales of Daring and Danger,* 42.4, 42.5

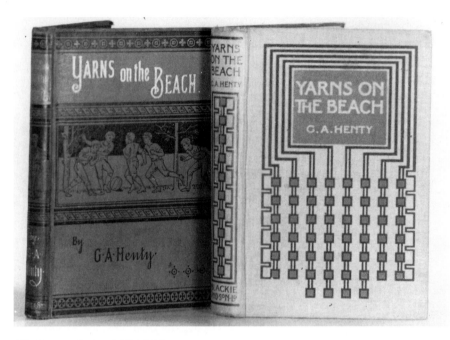

115. *Yarns on the Beach*, 25.1, 25.5

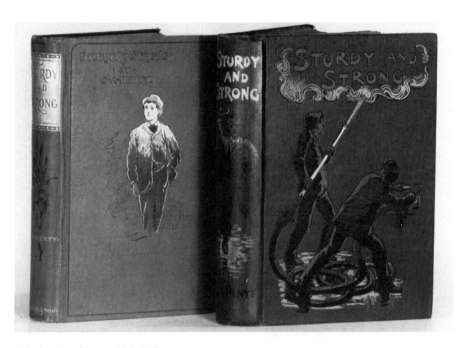

116. *Sturdy and Strong*, 34.1, 34.3

117. *In the Hands of the Cave-Dwellers*, 102.1; *In the Hands of the Malays*, 113.1

118. *Do Your Duty*, 89.1, 89.8, 89.9, 89.5

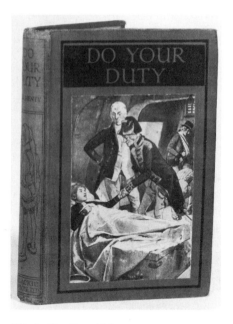

119. *Do Your Duty*, 89.6

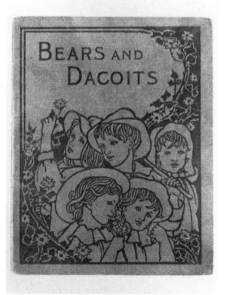

120. *Bears and Dacoits*, 69.1

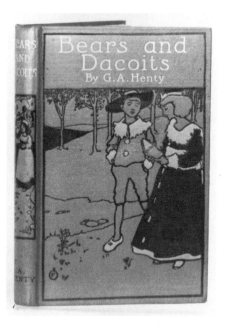

121. *Bears and Dacoits*, 69.2

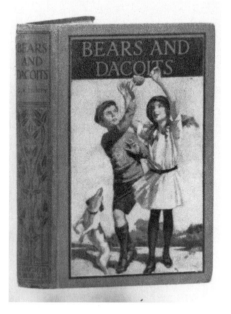

122. *Bears and Dacoits*, 69.4

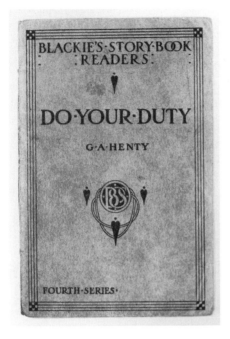

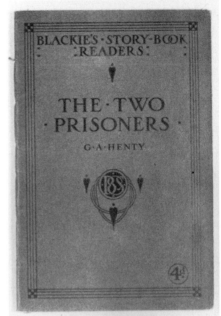

123. *Do Your Duty*, 89.3

124. *The Two Prisoners*, 120.1

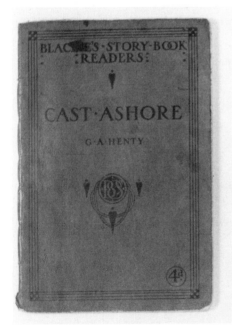

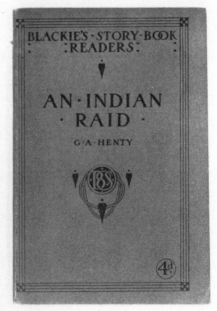

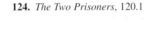

125. *Cast Ashore*, 115.1; *An Indian Raid*, 119.1

126. *Cast Ashore*, 115.2; *Cornet Walter*, 117.2; *Among the Bushrangers*, 114.2; *An Indian Raid*, 119.2

127. *On the Spanish Main*, 88.2, 88.1

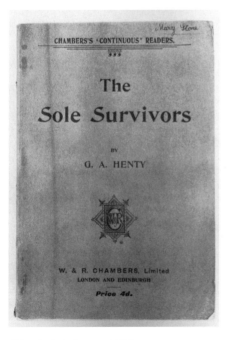

128. *The Sole Survivors*, 95.2

129. *Gallant Deeds*, 110.2

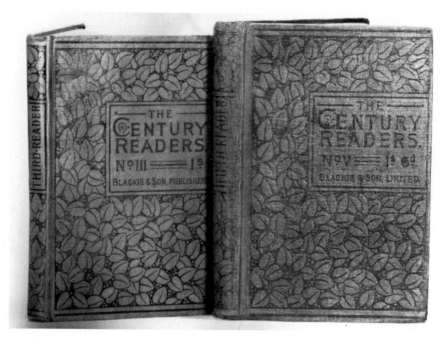

130. *Blackie's Century Readers*, 129.1, 130.1

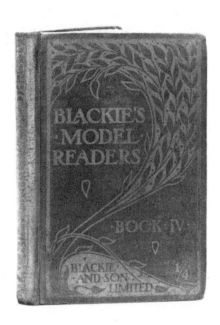

131. *Blackie's Model Readers*, 132.1

132. *A Young Patriot*, 122.1

133. *Charlie Marryat*, 116.3, 116.3s, 116.4

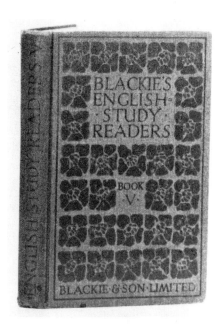

134. *Blackie's English-Study Readers*, 131.1

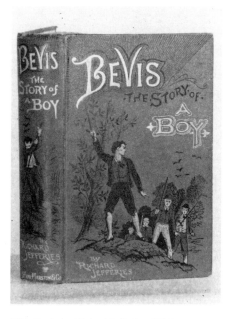

135. *Bevis*, by Richard Jefferies, 128.2

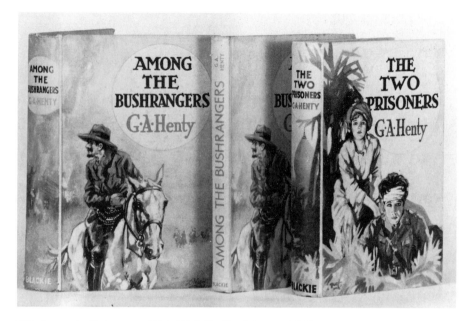

136. Among the *Bushrangers*, 114.4, 114.5; *The Two Prisoners*, 120.4

137. *White-Faced Dick*, 71.2, 71.3

138. *S.P.C.K. Library of Fiction*, 177.1

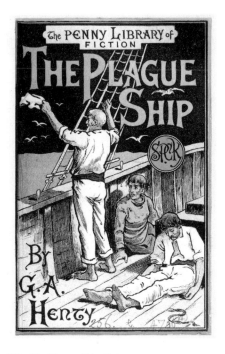

139. *The Plague Ship*, 41.1

140. *The Ranche in the Valley*, 52.1

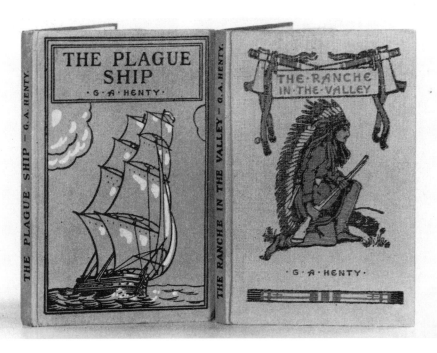

141. *The Plague Ship*, 41.2; *The Ranche in the Valley*, 52.2

142. *The Sovereign Reader*, 26.1, 26.2, 26.4, 26.5

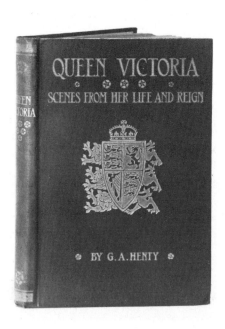

143. *Queen Victoria*, 94.1

144. *Queen Victoria*, 94.3

145. *With Clive in India*, 15.7

146. *A Dozen All Told*, 141.1

147. *The Red Book for Boys*, 174.1; *The Green Book for Boys*, 156.1; *Brave and True*, 135.1; *By Land and Sea*, 137.1

148. *52 Stories for Boyhood and Youth*, 147.1; *52 Other Stories for Boys*, 145.1; *52 Further Stories*, 143.1; *52 Stories of Boy-Life*, 148.1; *52 Stories of Pluck & Peril*, 153.1; *52 Stories of Heroism*, 151.1; *52 Stories of Duty & Daring*, 150.1; *52 Stories of Life & Adventure*, 152.1; *52 Holiday Stories*, 144.1; *52 Stories of the Brave & True*, 154.1; *52 Stirring Stories*, 146.1; *52 Stories of Courage & Adventure*, 149.1

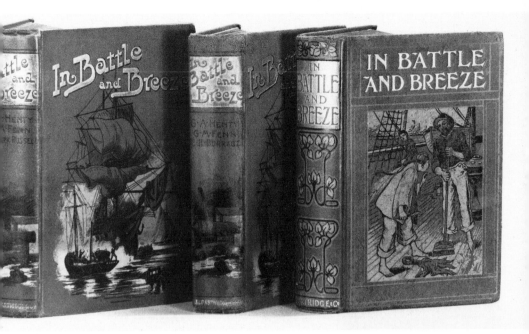

149. *In Battle and Breeze*, 159.1, 159.2, 159.3

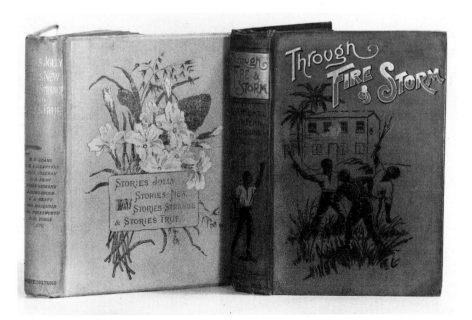

150. *Stories Jolly, Stories New, &c.*, 182.1; *Through Fire & Storm*, 189.1

151. *Brains & Bravery*, 134.1; *Courage and Conflict*, 139.1

152. *Dash and Daring*, 140.1; *Grit and Go*, 157.1

153. *Hazard and Heroism*, 158.1; *Peril and Prowess*, 170.1

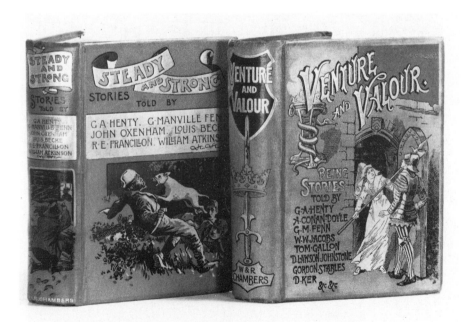

154. *Steady & Strong*, 178.1; *Venture and Valour*, 190.1

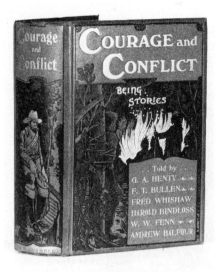

155. *Courage and Conflict*, 139.2

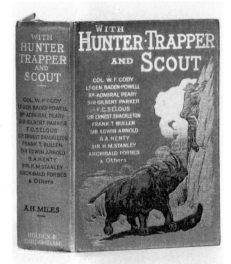

156. *With Hunter, Trapper, &c.*, 191.1

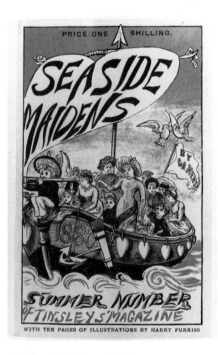

157. *Seaside Maidens*, 176.1

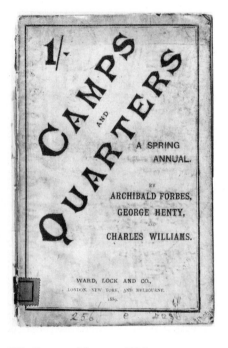

158. *Camps and Quarters*, 138.1

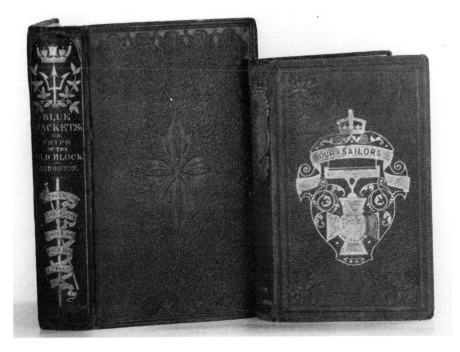

159. *Blue Jackets*, 167.A; *Our Sailors*, 167.1

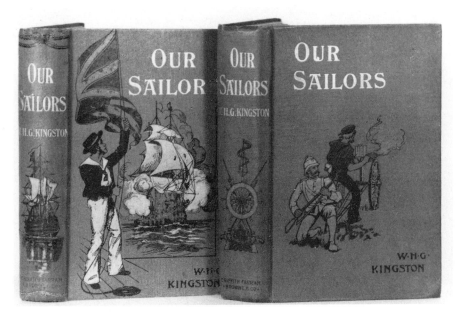

160. *Our Sailors*, 167.5, 167.6

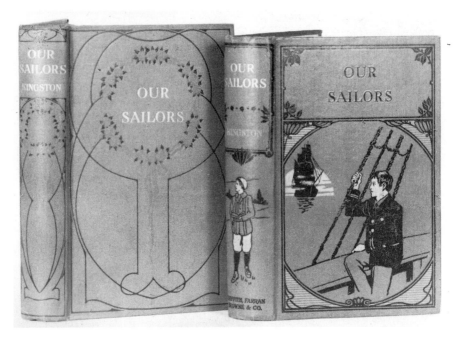

161. *Our Sailors*, 167.7, 167.8

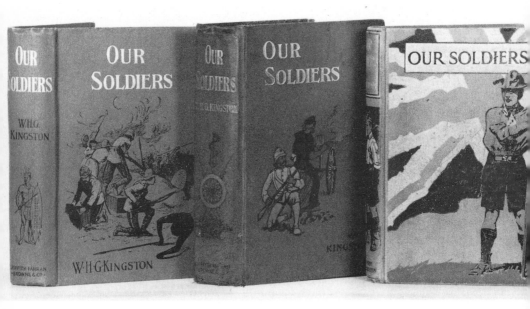

162. *Our Soldiers*, 168.8, 168.9, 168.10

163. *Our Soldiers*, 168.1

164. *Savage Club Papers*, 175.1

165. *Please Tell Me Another Tale*, 172.1; *Now for a Story!*, 165.1

166. *Yule Logs*, 193.4, 193.1, 193.2

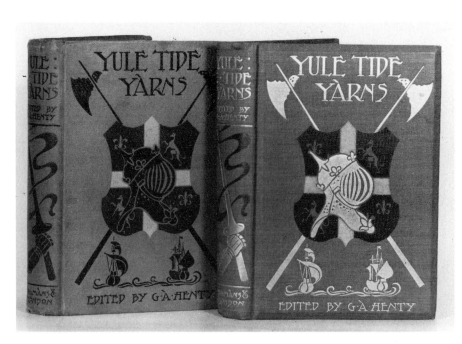

167. *Yule-Tide Yarns*, 194.2, 194.1

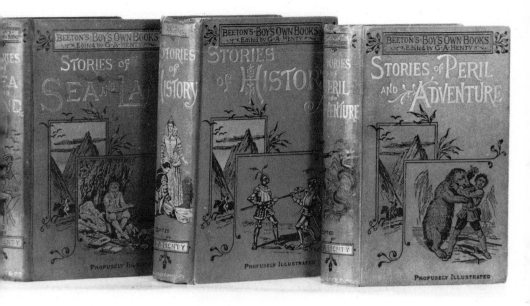

168. *Stories of Sea and Land*, 187.1; *Stories of History*, 185.1; *Stories of Peril and Adventure*, 186.1

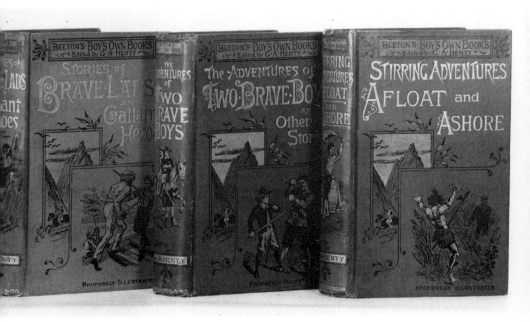

169. *Stories of Brave Boys & Gallant Heroes*, 184.1; *The Adventures of Two Brave Boys*, 123.1; *Stirring Adventures Afloat & Ashore*, 179.1

170. *Nister's Holiday Annual*, 163.1, 162.1, 164.1

171. A random selection of Nister story books: *Pastime Tales*, 169.1; *In Storyland*, 160.1; *The Golden Story Book*, 155.1; *In the Chimney Corner*, 161.1

172. A selection of titles from Blackie's first cheaper re-issue, 'The New & Popular Edition': *By Right of Conquest*, 50.3; *In Greek Waters*, 60.3; *With Clive in India*, 15.6; *On the Irrawaddy*, 77.3; *By England's Aid*, 47.3

173. More titles from 'The New & Popular Edition': *Under Drake's Flag*, 13.4; *In the Irish Brigade*, 96.2; *Through the Fray*, 24.3; *Facing Death*, 10.6; *For the Temple*, 35.3

174. A selection of titles from Blackie's second cheaper re-issue, 'The New Popular Henty': *By Conduct & Courage*, 109.2; *Condemned as a Nihilist*, 58.4; *The Bravest of the Brave*, 28.4; *Both Sides the Border*, 84.4; *The Dragon & The Raven*, 21.6

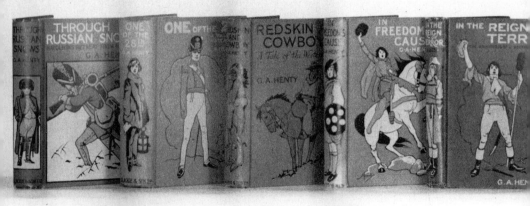

175. More titles from 'The New Popular Henty': *Through Russian Snows*, 73.4; *One of the 28th*, 44.4; *Redskin and Cowboy*, 54.5; *In Freedom's Cause*, 18.4; *In the Reign of Terror*, 33.4

83. UNDER WELLINGTON'S COMMAND

83.1
UNDER | WELLINGTON'S COMMAND | A TALE OF THE PENINSULAR WAR | BY | G.A.HENTY | Author of "With Moore at Corunna" "At Agincourt" "The Dash for Khartoum" | "Through the Sikh War" &c. | (5-em rule) | WITH TWELVE ILLUSTRATIONS BY WAL PAGET | (5-em rule) | LONDON | BLACKIE & SON, LIMITED, 50 OLD BAILEY, E.C. | GLASGOW AND DUBLIN | 1899

Contents
185 x 132 mm. (i)–(x) | (11)–384 | catalogue (1)–32. Twelve full-page wash-drawings by Wal Paget, reproduced by halftone blocks printed in black on coated paper, unbacked, unfolioed, tipped in. Five battle-plans printed from line blocks on text pages.

(Frontispiece, tipped in) | (i) title p. | (ii) blank | (iii)–v. Preface | (vi) blank | (vii) Contents | (viii) blank | (ix) list of Illustrations | (x) blank | (11)–383. text, with printer's imprint at foot of p.383 (PRINTED BY BLACKIE AND SON, LIMITED.) | (384) blank | (1)–32. catalogue.

Binding (see Plate 87)
Designed by Ralph Peacock (see Note 3). Royal-blue cloth boards, bevelled, blocked black, white, red, pink, and gilt; all edges burnished olive-green; grey endpapers, lined off-white.
   Front board: UNDER WELLINGTON'S | COMMAND. (gilt) | BY | G.A.HENTY. (white) above and at right of illustration of soldier with rifle and fixed bayonet (black, white, red, pink). All framed by white line. **Spine:** UNDER | WELLINGTON'S | COMMAND. (gilt) above illustration of Duke of Wellington (black, white, red, pink). Beneath this: BY | G.A.HENTY. (white). **Back board:** plain.

References: BL; Bod; PN | *Farmer*, p.75; *Dartt*, p.145, *Companion*, p.33.

Notes
1. The book was published on 2 June 1898 at six shillings. By the end of February 1899 Blackie had sold 10,566 copies, and in the next seven years, up to the end of August 1906, they sold 3671 more. As a result of the very large initial demand, the average annual sale for the first eight years was 1780 copies. At that point Blackie re-issued the book in their cheaper edition (see 83.3), and sold the remaining stock of 38 copies at six shillings by 1910.
2. This book is a sequel to *With Moore at Corunna*, and has a longer-than-usual Preface: Henty recapitulates 'the story so far' of his young hero.
3. The binding design is a characteristic work of Ralph Peacock (see Appendix IV, Part 2), and in common with others by him is invariably on cloth of the same colour.
4. The earliest catalogues do not mention the books with title pages dated 1899, having been printed before those books were announced. Books up to and including those with 1898 title pages are listed, with extracts from their reviews.

*83.2

Reprints of the six-shilling edition were in the style of 83.1, with the date removed from the title page. Changes were made when necessary to the title-page imprint and addresses: the Indian office was opened in 1901 although Bombay did not appear regularly in the Blackie imprint until 1906.

The slightly-varying issues among the reprints of the book in its first-edition format are all grouped together under this 'generic' heading, *83.2.

83.3

Under Wellington's Command | A Tale of the Peninsular War | BY | G.A.HENTY | Author of "With Moore at Corunna" "At Agincourt" "The Dash for Khartoum" | "Through the Sikh War" &c. | ILLUSTRATED BY WAL PAGET | NEW EDITION | BLACKIE AND SON LIMITED | LONDON GLASGOW DUBLIN BOMBAY | 1907

Contents

184 × 127 mm. (1)–(384) | catalogue 1–16. Eight full-page wash-drawings by Wal Paget, reproduced by halftone blocks printed in black on coated paper, unbacked, unfolioed, tipped in. Five battle-plans printed from line blocks on text pages.

(Frontispiece, tipped in) | (1) title p. | (2) blank | (3) Preface | iv–v. [roman numerals in error] Preface, continued | (6) blank | 7. Contents | (8) blank | 9. list of Illustrations | (10) blank | 11–383. text | (384) blank | 1–16. catalogue.

Binding (see Note 1)

Blue cloth boards, blocked black, green, buff, and gilt; all edges stained olive-green; grey endpapers, lined off-white.

Front board: UNDER WELLINGTON'S COMMAND (gilt) | A TALE OF THE | PENINSULAR WAR | G.A.HENTY (all buff) above illustration of soldier with drawn sword (black, green, buff). **Spine:** UNDER | WELLINGTON'S | COMMAND | G.A.HENTY (all gilt) above illustration of hatless soldier with drawn sword (black, green, buff). At foot: BLACKIE & SON LTD (black). **Back board:** plain.

Reference: CH.

Notes

1. Re-issued, late 1906, in the 'New and Popular Edition'. For details see *Facing Death*, 10.6, Notes 2–3; for examples of the series binding style, Plates 172–173.

2. In this edition Blackie sold 2993 copies in the first year, and during the following ten years, up to the end of August 1917 when Blackie's records end, 9269 more. That gives an average annual sale over the eleven years of 1115 copies. The grand total of copies sold, at both prices, from 1898 to 1917, is 26,537.

*83.4

Under Wellington's | Command | A Tale of the Peninsular War | BY | G.A.HENTY | Author of "With Moore at Corunna" "At Agincourt" "The Dash for Khartoum" | "Through the Sikh War" &c. | ILLUSTRATED BY WAL PAGET | BLACKIE & SON LIMITED | LONDON AND GLASGOW

Contents

186 × 125 mm. (1)–(384) | no catalogue. Frontispiece from watercolour drawing reproduced by three-colour halftone blocks; four full-page wash-drawings reproduced by halftone blocks printed in black; all by Wal Paget, on coated paper, unbacked, keyed to text, tipped in. Five battle-plans from line blocks on text pages.

(Frontispiece, tipped in) | (1) title p. | (2) publisher's addresses; printer's imprint (Printed in Great Britain by Blackie & Son, Ltd., Glasgow) | 3. Preface | iv–v. [roman numerals in error] Preface, continued | (6) blank | (7) Contents | (8) blank | (9) list of Illustrations | (10) blank | 11–383. text | (384) blank.

Binding: As for 83.3, except (a) red cloth boards, blocked black, dark-green, and buff, with no gilt: publisher's imprint on spine blocked black, all other lettering buff; (b) brasses for spine lettering re-cut, and 'WELLINGTON'S' is now shown as 'WELLING- | TON'S'; (c) top edge stained red; (d) plain off-white endpapers.

References: Bod; PN.

Notes

1. For details of Blackie's second cheaper series, 'The New Popular Henty', and subsequent editions of this title, see *Facing Death*, 10.7, Notes 1–3 and 6–8.
2. All the minor variants of *Under Wellington's Command* in the series are grouped together under this 'generic' heading, *83.4.
3. This is the only issue of a Henty title from Blackie I have seen with top edge stained red.

84. BOTH SIDES THE BORDER

84.1

BOTH SIDES THE BORDER | A TALE OF | HOTSPUR AND GLENDOWER | BY | G.A.HENTY | Author of "A March on London" "Beric the Briton" "By England's Aid" | "For Name and Fame" &c, &c. | (8-em rule) | WITH TWELVE ILLUSTRATIONS BY RALPH PEACOCK | (8-em rule) | LONDON | BLACKIE & SON, LIMITED, 50 OLD BAILEY, E.C. | GLASGOW AND DUBLIN | 1899

Contents

188 × 132 mm. (i)–(x) | (11)–384 | catalogue (1)–32. Twelve full-page wash-drawings by Ralph Peacock, reproduced by halftone blocks printed in black on coated paper, unbacked, unfolioed, tipped in.

(i) Half-title p. | (ii) advertisement (MR. HENTY'S HISTORICAL TALES.) listing 44 titles | (frontispiece, tipped in) | (iii) title p. | (iv) blank | (v) Preface | (vi) blank | (vii) Contents | (viii) blank | (ix) list of Illustrations | (x) blank (11)–384. text | (1)–32. catalogue.

Binding (see Plate 57)
Designed by Ralph Peacock (see Note 2). Blue cloth boards, bevelled, blocked brown, ochre, and gilt; all edges burnished olive-green; grey endpapers, lined off-white.

Front board: BOTH SIDES | THE BORDER | A TALE OF HOTSPUR | AND GLENDOWER (cloth-colour out of solid-gilt panel). Three representations of heraldic shield with crest (ochre); spear (brown) and elaborate scroll (brown) with lettering reversed out: FIGHT THE GOOD FIGHT, AND IF | THOU WOUNDED | BE | FIGHT ON: THROUGH DEATH DO | SOME REACH VICTORY (cloth-colour). At foot: SEE! THE ARMS AND | THE CREST OF THE | PERCIES | AND THE SPEAR OF THE | WARRIOR | AND THE LONG SCROLL OF FAME (brown). **Spine:** (two rose ornaments) BOTH | SIDES THE | BORDER (thistle ornament) (all cloth-colour reversed out of solid-gilt panel) over spear and scrolling (brown), with heraldic shield and crest (ochre). At foot: BY | G.A.HENTY (part brown, and part cloth-colour reversed out of brown scroll). **Back board:** plain.

References: BL; Bod; PN | *Farmer*, p.11; *Dartt*, p.20, *Companion*, p.4.

Notes
1. The book was published on 28 June 1898 at six shillings. By the end of February 1899 Blackie had sold 8227 copies, and in the next seven years, to the end of August 1906, they sold 1916 more. The average annual sale over the eight-year period was 1268 copies. The remaining stock of 24 copies at six shillings was sold by 1910.
2. Ralph Peacock (see Appendix IV, Part 2) drew the illustrations and designed the binding case, no doubt making his usual request for only one cloth-colour.
3. The earliest issues contain catalogues with no mention of the books with title pages dated 1899. These catalogues include titles up to and including those dated 1898, but were printed before the titles for the following year were announced.
4. *Dartt* has the line-division of the subtitle given incorrectly.

*84.2
Reprints of the six-shilling edition were in the style of 84.1, with the date omitted from the title page. Changes were made when necessary to the title-page imprint and addresses: the Indian office was opened in 1901 although Bombay did not appear regularly in the Blackie imprint until 1906.
The slightly-varying issues of the reprints of the book in its first-edition format are all grouped together under this 'generic' heading, *84.2.

84.3
Both Sides the Border | A Tale of Hotspur and Glendower | BY | G.A.HENTY | Author of "A March on London" "Beric the Briton" "By England's Aid" | "For Name and Fame" &c.&c. | ILLUSTRATED BY RALPH PEACOCK | NEW EDITION | BLACKIE AND SON LIMITED | LONDON GLASGOW DUBLIN BOMBAY | 1907

Contents
186 × 127 mm. (1)–384 | catalogue 1–16. Eight full-page wash-drawings by Ralph Peacock reproduced by halftone blocks printed in black on coated paper, unbacked, unfolioed, tipped in.
(1) Half-title p. | (2) advertisement (HISTORICAL TALES BY G.A.HENTY) listing 30 titles | (frontispiece, tipped in) | (3) title p. | (4) blank | (5) Preface | (6) blank | 7. Contents | (8) blank | 9. list of Illustrations | (10) blank | 11–384. text | 1–16. catalogue, with full-page photographic portrait tipped in to face p.2, captioned 'THE LATE G.A.HENTY'.

Binding (see Note 1)
Red cloth boards, blocked black, blue, buff, and gilt; all edges stained olive-green; grey endpapers, lined off-white.
  Front board: BOTH SIDES THE | BORDER (gilt) | A TALE OF HOTSPUR | & GLENDOWER | G.A.HENTY (buff) above and at right of illustration of standard-bearer with drawn sword, shield, and standard leant against his right shoulder (black, blue, buff). **Spine:** BOTH SIDES | THE | BORDER | G.A.HENTY (gilt) above illustration of soldier with sword, shield, dagger, and halberd (black, blue, buff). At foot: BLACKIE & SON LTD (black). **Back board:** plain.

Reference: MH.

Notes
1. Re-issued 1906 (title-page date 1907) in the 'New and Popular Edition'. For details see *Facing Death*, 10.6, Notes 2–3; for examples of the series binding style, Plates 172–173.
2. In this edition Blackie sold 2444 copies in the first year, and during the following ten years, up to the end of 1917 when Blackie's records come to an end, 5253 more. In addition, 1108 copies were sold to the London County Council in 1911 at 2s.6d.: no explanation is recorded, but the book was probably a set text for certain schools or examinations, and supplied for that purpose at a special discount. Excluding those copies, the average annual sale over eleven years was 700 copies. The total of copies sold, at all prices, from 1898 to 1917, was 17,864.

*84.4

Title page: As for 84.3, except (a) NEW EDITION deleted; (b) date deleted; (c) changed imprint (BLACKIE AND SON LIMITED | LONDON GLASGOW AND BOMBAY).
(*Note: The* y *and final quotation marks in* "By England's Aid" *are battered*).

Contents
184 × 124 mm. (1)–384 | advertisement (i)–(ii). Frontispiece from watercolour drawing by Frank Gillett reproduced by three-colour halftone blocks; four wash-drawings by Ralph Peacock reproduced by halftone blocks, printed in black; all keyed to text pages, on coated paper, unbacked, tipped in.
  (1) Half-title p. | (2) advertisement (G.A.HENTY'S BOOKS) listing 56 titles | (frontispiece, tipped in) | (3) title p. | (4) printer's imprint (Printed in Great Britain by | Blackie & Son, Limited, Glasgow) | (5) Preface | (6) blank | (7) Contents | (8) blank | (9) list of Illustrations | (10) blank | 11–384. text | (i)–(ii) advertisement (THE NEW POPULAR HENTY) listing 60 titles.

Binding: (See Plate 174). As for 84.3, except (a) case blocked with no gilt: front-board lettering all buff, spine lettering all black; (b) title on spine now shown in four lines, and publisher's imprint changed (BLACKIE & SON LD.); (c) edges plain; (d) plain off-white endpapers.

References: Bod; PN.

Notes
1. For details of Blackie's second cheaper series, 'The New Popular Henty', and

subsequent editions of this book, see *Facing Death*, 10.7, Notes 1–3 and 6–8. This title was issued in 1922.

2. All the minor variants of *Both Sides the Border* in the series are grouped together under this 'generic' heading, *84.4.

85. AT ABOUKIR AND ACRE

85.1

AT ABOUKIR AND ACRE | A STORY OF | NAPOLEON'S INVASION OF EGYPT | BY | G.A.HENTY | Author of "The Dash for Khartoum" "By Right of Conquest" "In Greek Waters" | "St. Bartholomew's Eve" &c. | WITH EIGHT FULL-PAGE ILLUSTRATIONS BY WILLIAM RAINEY, R.I. | AND THREE PLANS | LONDON | BLACKIE & SON, LIMITED, 50 OLD BAILEY, E.C. | GLASGOW AND DUBLIN | 1899

Contents
186 × 124 mm. (i)–(x) | (11)–352 | catalogue (1)–32. Eight full-page wash-drawings by William Rainey, reproduced by halftone blocks printed in black on coated paper, unbacked, unfolioed, tipped in. Three battle-plans printed from line blocks on text pages.
    (i) Half-title p. | (ii) advertisement (MR. HENTY'S HISTORICAL TALES.) | (frontispiece, tipped in) | (iii) title p. | (iv) blank | (v)–vi. Preface | (vii) Contents | (viii) blank | (ix) list of Illustrations | (x) blank | (11)–352. text | (1)–32. catalogue.

Binding (see Plate 55)
Red cloth boards, blocked white, yellow, green, and gilt; all edges burnished olive-green; grey endpapers, lined off-white.
    Front board: At Aboukir | and Acre (gilt outline lettering) in gilt frame, cut into by gilt circle containing star within crescent moon (gilt out of green solid) over illustration of arab figures with weapons, one on a camel (white and yellow). At foot: A . STORY . OF | NAPOLEON'S | INVASION OF | EGYPT ..... | BY . G . A . HENTY (all white). **Spine:** AT | ABOUKIR | AND | ACRE (gilt open lettering) above head and shoulders of Napoleon in gilt frame with N in wreath at top (white, yellow, green, and gilt). At foot: G.A.HENTY (white). **Back board:** plain.

References: BL; Bod; PN | *Farmer*, p.5; *Dartt*, p.7.

Notes
1. The book was published on 28 July 1898 at five shillings. By the end of February 1899 Blackie had sold 8140 copies, but between then and the end of August 1915 they sold only 2907 more. The average annual sale over the seventeen-year period, boosted by initial pre-publication orders, was 650 copies, but for sixteen of those years, from 1900, it was only 182 copies. There was no sudden drop in sales in that period, the annual figure falling fairly steadily from about 260 to 100. Then the book was re-issued in the cheaper edition (see 85.3).
2. As usual at this period, the earliest issues contain catalogues with no mention of books of the current year (i.e. with title pages dated 1899), but which include Henty's novels published the previous year, with extracts from press notices.

3. Once again *Dartt* is confused by treating Blackie and Scribner editions simultaneously. Blackie editions did not have dark blue endpapers, and there are other errors of detail in the entry.

*85.2

Reprints of the five-shilling edition were in the style of 85.1, with no date on the title page. Changes were made when necessary in the title-page imprint and addresses: the Indian office was opened in 1901 although Bombay did not appear regularly in the Blackie imprint until 1906; and Dublin was omitted after 1910.

The slightly-varying issues among the reprints of the book in its first-edition format are all grouped together under this 'generic' heading, *85.2.

85.3

At Aboukir and Acre | A Story of Napoleon's Invasion of Egypt | BY | G.A.HENTY | Author of "The Dash for Khartoum" "By Right of Conquest" | "In Greek Waters" "St. Bartholomew's Eve" &c. | ILLUSTRATED BY WILLIAM RAINEY, R.I. | NEW EDITION | BLACKIE AND SON LIMITED | LONDON GLASGOW AND BOMBAY

Contents

185 × 125 mm. (1)–352 | no catalogue. Six full-page wash-drawings by William Rainey, reproduced by halftone blocks printed in black on coated paper, unbacked, unfolioed, tipped in. Three battle-plans as in 85.1.

(1) Half-title p. | (2) advertisement (NEW AND POPULAR EDITION OF | G.A.HENTY'S WORKS) listing 41 titles | (frontispiece, tipped in) | (3) title p. | (4) blank | 5. Preface | vi. [roman numerals in error] Preface, continued | 7. Contents | (8) blank | 9. list of Illustrations | (10) blank | 11–352. text, with printer's imprint on p.352 (PRINTED IN GREAT BRITAIN | At the Villafield Press, Glasgow, Scotland).

Binding (see Note 1)

Pink cloth boards, blocked black, blue, buff, and gilt; all edges stained olive-green; grey endpapers, lined off-white.

Front board: AT ABOUKIR | AND ACRE (buff) | A STORY OF NAPOLEON'S INVASION | OF EGYPT | G.A.HENTY (black) above illustration, framed by black line, of Egyptian soldier with rifle standing near the Sphinx (black, blue, buff). **Spine:** AT | ABOUKIR | AND ACRE | G.A.HENTY (all gilt) above illustration, framed by black line, of young soldier standing (black, blue, buff). At foot: BLACKIE & SON LTD (black). **Back board:** plain.

References: BL; Bod.

Notes

1. Re-issued late 1915 in the 'New and Popular Edition'. For details see *Facing Death*, 10.6, Notes 2–3; for examples of the series binding style, Plates 172–173.

2. The cheap edition of this book was long coming, and by the time it was issued the first war had started and Blackie was driven to economy measures. There was no gilt blocked on the front board, even of the first issue, although at this stage it was used on the spine. It is likely that all issues but the first had no gilt at all.

3. From the end of 1911 Blackie had dropped the dating of title pages for all books in the 'New and Popular Edition', first issues and later ones alike. Catalogues were omitted from some books, no doubt to save paper as well as expense.

4. Blackie's records end in 1917: the only sales figures known for this edition were 1178 copies and 165 copies in 1916 and 1917 respectively.

*85.4

At Aboukir and Acre I A Story of Napoleon's Invasion I of Egypt I BY I G.A.HENTY I Author of "The Dash for Khartoum" "By Right of Conquest" I "In Greek Waters" "St. Bartholomew's Eve" &c. I Illustrated I BLACKIE & SON LIMITED I LONDON AND GLASGOW

Contents

184 x 124 mm. (1)–352 I advertisement (i)–(ii). Frontispiece from watercolour drawing by Frank Gillett, reproduced by three-colour halftone blocks; four full-page wash-drawings by William Rainey reproduced by halftone blocks printed in black; all on coated paper, unbacked, keyed to text pages, tipped in. Three battle-plans printed from line blocks on text pages.

(1) Half-title p. I (2) Blackie addresses I (frontispiece, tipped in) I (3) title p. I (4) printer's imprint (Printed in Great Britain by I Blackie & Son, Limited, Glasgow) I 5. Preface I vi. [roman numerals in error] Preface, continued I 7. Contents I (8) blank I (9) list of Illustrations I (10) blank I 11–352. text I (i)–(ii) advertisement, tipped in (THE NEW POPULAR HENTY) listing 64 titles.

Binding: As for 85.3, except (a) dark-green cloth boards, blocked black, blue, and buff, with no gilt: title on front board blocked buff, all other lettering black; (b) publisher's imprint on spine changed (Blackie & Son . Ltd); (c) edges plain; (d) plain off-white endpapers.

References: BL; Bod; IM.

Notes

1. For details of Blackie's second cheaper series, 'The New Popular Henty', and subsequent editions of this book, see *Facing Death*. 10.7, Notes 1–3 and 6–8. This title was issued in 1925.

2. All the minor variants of *At Aboukir and Acre* in the series are grouped together under this 'generic' heading, *85.4.

86. CUTHBERT HARTINGTON

86.1

Cuthbert Hartington I A TALE OF TWO SIEGES OF PARIS I BY I G.A.HENTY I Author of I 'In the Days of the Mutiny,' 'The Curse of Carne's Hold,' I 'Dorothy's Double,' Etc., Etc. I WITH SIX ILLUSTRATIONS I LONDON I S.W.PARTRIDGE & CO. I 8 and 9 PATERNOSTER ROW

Contents

190 x 139 mm. (i)–(iv) I (1)–292 I catalogue (1)–24. Six full-page wash-drawings by Hal Hurst and Simon Harmon Vedder (see Note 2), reproduced by halftone

blocks printed in black on coated paper, unbacked, unfolioed but keyed to text, tipped in.

(i) Half-title p. | (ii) blank | (frontispiece, tipped in) | (iii) title p. | (iv) advertisement (BOOKS FOR THE BOYS) | (1)–292. text, with printer's imprint on p.292 (Colston & Coy, Limited, Printers, Edinburgh) | (1)–24. catalogue (see Note 4).

Binding (see Plate 12)
Red cloth boards, blocked black, blue, yellow, red, white, and gilt; all edges gilt; yellow surface-paper endpapers. See Note 4.

Front board: Cuthbert | Hartington (gilt, with black shadow) within scrolls (gilt, with red and blue) | A . TALE . OF | TWO . SIEGES . OF | PARIS (black), all above illustration of soldier taking his hat off to nurse (black, blue, yellow, red, white). At lower right corner: BY | G.A.Henty (black). **Spine:** Black and gilt rules at head, above: Cuthbert | Hartington (black over irregular decorative gilt panel, and G.A.HENTY (black) between black rules. Beneath this, illustration of soldier with sword (black, yellow, red). At foot: S.W.PARTRIDGE & CO. (gilt) between black and gilt rules. **Back board:** plain.

References: BL; Bod; PN | *Farmer*, p.23; *Dartt*, p.45, *Companion*, p.11.

Notes
1. This book was originally published in the UK in 1895 by F.V. White & Co., under the title *A Woman of the Commune*, (65.1). It was re-issued as *Cuthbert Hartington* in 1899, as described above. In 1916 it was again re-issued by Partridge under a third title, *Two Sieges*, (112.1).
2. The six illustrations are not attributed, but five by Hal Hurst appeared in *A Woman of the Commune*, of which two are initialled by V & C, a process engraver. Hurst's sixth in that book was also adapted for blocking on its front board, but is here replaced by a drawing by Simon Harmon Vedder. That in turn is adapted for the front board of *Cuthbert Hartington*, and later also for *Two Sieges*, 112.1.
3. The catalogue includes nothing by Henty. The advertisement on p.(iv) lists 12 titles, including two collections of short stories, *In Battle and Breeze*, and *Through Fire and Storm*, (see §2, 159.1 and 189.1 respectively).
4. Variant issues of 86.1 may be found with 32-page catalogues; printed endpapers; alternative colours blocked on the binding case; and slightly different forms of lettering for the publisher's imprint on the spine.
5. The titles following Henty's name on the title page include *In the Days of the Mutiny*, the title under which *Rujub, the Juggler* was sold in the United States and Canada. It is included here, however, because the story first appeared in England under that title as a newspaper serial, and would be known thus to some readers.

86.2
CUTHBERT HARTINGTON | A TALE OF TWO SIEGES OF PARIS | BY | G.A.HENTY | Author of | 'In the Days of the Mutiny,' 'The Curse of Carne's Hold,' | 'Dorothy's Double,' Etc., Etc. | WITH SIX ILLUSTRATIONS | LONDON | S.W.PARTRIDGE & CO. | 8 & 9 PATERNOSTER ROW

Contents

204 × 139 mm. (i)–(iv) | (1)–292 | no catalogue. Illustrations as in 86.1, but now printed in sepia on satin-finish coated paper.

(i) Half-title p. | (ii) blank | (frontispiece, tipped in) | (iii) title p. | (iv) blank | (1)–292. text, with printer's imprint at foot of p.292 (Roberts & Jackson, Printers, 4 Victoria Street, Grimsby.)

Binding (see Plate 12)

Red, vertically-grained cloth boards, blocked black, red, and gilt; all edges gilt; cream-laid endpapers.

Front board: CUTHBERT | HARTINGTON (red, cased black) in the upper panel of two in an over-all design of leaves, stems, and rules (black and red). In lower panel: G.A.Henty (black). **Spine:** CUTHBERT | HARTINGTON | GEO.A.HENTY (all cloth-colour out of solid-gilt rectangle, enclosed by design similar to that on front board, but with gilt blocking added to the black and red in the area below title panel. At foot, in small black rectangle: S.W.PARTRIDGE & CO. (gilt). **Back board:** plain.

Reference: PN.

Notes

1. My copy is inscribed and dated July 1908. It contains a small leaflet issued by the publisher, advertising the one-penny monthly *The British Workman*: 'Annual Volume for 1908 Now Ready. (Containing the Monthly Parts for 1907)'.

2. This is a handsome binding case, and it seems that Partridge was out to produce a 'de luxe' edition without spending more than was necessary. Unfortunately the effect is to some extent spoiled by the poor quality of the text paper. Machine-gilding of edges of leaves was still a poor substitute for hand-gilding, and in this case it is seen to least advantage on the edges of inflexible wood-bodied paper.

3. The use of sepia ink on this satin-finish art paper is a great success, appearing at first glance almost like photogravure.

4. A copy inscribed December, 1908, has the publisher's imprint blocked on the spine in gilt sans-serif (instead of serifed) lettering. Other details remain the same.

5. Probably this is the edition referred to but not described by *Farmer* (p.24) and mentioned by *Dartt* (p.45, Note). Both these copies are stated to be in blue cloth.

6. Henty's name is given on the spine of the binding case as 'GEO.A.HENTY': I have not found it so given anywhere else in his books.

87. THE LOST HEIR

87.1

THE LOST HEIR | BY | G.A.HENTY | AUTHOR OF | "THE CURSE OF CARNE'S HOLD" | "THE QUEEN'S CUP" | ETC. | ILLUSTRATED BY ERNEST PRATER | LONDON | JAMES BOWDEN | 10 HENRIETTA STREET | COVENT GARDEN, W.C. | 1899

Contents

190 × 125 mm. (1)–(408) | catalogue (1)–(8) unfolioed. Four full-page wash-

drawings by Ernest Prater, reproduced by halftone blocks printed in black on coated paper, unbacked, keyed to text pages, tipped in.

(1) Blank | (2) advertisement (NOVELS BY POPULAR AUTHORS.) | (3) half-title p. | (4) blank | (frontispiece, tipped in) | (5) title p. | (6) blank | (7)–8. Contents | (9)–407. text | (408) printer's imprint (PLYMOUTH | WILLIAM BRENDON AND SON | PRINTERS) | (1)–(8) catalogue (unfolioed).

Binding (see Plate 14)
Olive-green cloth boards, bevelled, blocked black, blue, orange, white, and gilt; edges plain; plain off-white endpapers.

Front board: THE LOST HEIR (gilt, cased black) above illustration, framed by black line, of man advancing with knife on tiger mauling another man, etc. (black, blue, orange, white). At foot: G.A.HENTY (gilt). **Spine:** THE | LOST | HEIR (gilt, cased black) above trophy of framed tiger's head and crossed rifles (black, blue, orange, white). G.A.HENTY (gilt). At foot: JAMES BOWDEN (gilt). **Back board:** plain.

References: BL; Bod; PN | *Farmer*, p.48; *Dartt*, p.93.

Notes
1. The publisher, James Bowden, had been Managing Director of Ward Lock and Bowden Limited for several years before his retirement in 1897 (see Appendix II, Part 6 for notes on both publishing firms).
2. This is an example of book production that worried Henty because it seemed to present an adult novel as a book for boys, and might therefore infringe the terms of his contract with Blackie (see Appendix VI). Some publishers of his adult novels undoubtedly appeared to be trying to lure buyers of boys' books, simply by the use of his name coupled with an 'adventure-story' illustration on the binding case.

87.2
THE LOST HEIR | BY | G.A.HENTY | AUTHOR OF | "THE CURSE OF CARNE'S HOLD" | "THE QUEEN'S CUP" | ETC. | ILLUSTRATED BY ERNEST PRATER | SECOND IMPRESSION | LONDON | T.FISHER UNWIN | ADELPHI TERRACE | 1906

Contents
185 × 120 mm. (1)–(408) | catalogue (1)–(8) unfolioed. Illustrations as in 87.1.

(1) Half-title p. | (2) advertisement (UNIFORM WITH THIS VOLUME) | (frontispiece, tipped in) | (3) title p. | (4) (All rights reserved.) | (5) Contents | (6) in error folioed 8. Contents, continued | (7) List of Illustrations | (8) blank | (9)–407. text | (408) printer's imprint (LONDON: | PRINTED BY A.BONNER, | 1 & 2 TOOK S COURT, E.C.) (*Note: apostrophe in* TOOK'S *is missing.*) | (1)–(8) catalogue (unfolioed).

Binding (see Plate 14)
Greenish-blue cloth boards, blocked yellow-green, pale blue-grey, gilt; top edge gilt; cream laid endpapers.

Front board: THE | LOST HEIR | (small leaf ornament) | G.A.HENTY (all gilt) in clear panel within over-all design of vine-leaves and tendrils (yellow-green) and pattern of rules (pale blue-grey). **Spine:** THE | LOST | HEIR | (small leaf ornament)

I G.A.HENTY (all gilt) in panel within over-all design as on front board (yellow-green and pale blue-grey). At foot: T.FISHER UNWIN (gilt). **Back board:** plain.

References: CH I *Dartt*, p.93, *Companion*, p.21.

Notes
1. The entry in *Dartt* is inaccurate, but corrected in the *Companion*.
2. I have found no records of this publisher, but notes about his business, which was ultimately taken over by Ernest Benn Limited, are in Appendix II, Part 6.
3. The advertisement on p.(2) lists five titles 'uniform with this volume', at 3s.6d. each. None are by Henty.

87.3
Title page, Contents: As for 87.2.

Binding (see Plate 14)
Blue cloth boards, blocked black; edges plain; plain off-white wove endpapers.
    Front board: THE I LOST HEIR I (inverted spade ornament) I G.A.HENTY (black). Black rule near edges of board. **Spine:** THE I LOST I HEIR I (short rule) I G.A.HENTY (all black) at head. At foot: T.FISHER UNWIN (black). **Back board:** plain.

Reference: PN.

Notes
1. The sheets are from Unwin's original impression, now in a cheaper binding case.
2. The bound-in catalogue advertises the first twelve titles in 'The First Novel Library', an enterprising venture of this publisher (see Appendix II, Part 6).

87.4
THE LOST HEIR I BY I G.A.HENTY I AUTHOR OF I "THE CURSE OF CARNE'S HOLD," "THE QUEEN'S CUP," I "DOROTHY'S DOUBLE," ETC. I LONDON: JOHN MILNE I 29 HENRIETTA STREET I COVENT GARDEN I 1908

Contents
218 x 146 mm. (1)–160 (see Note 2). No illustrations.
    (1)–160. text, set in two columns with rule between; with advertisements on pages (2) and (4); on unfolioed text leaves between pp.152–153; pp.154–155; pp.156–157; pp.158–159; and with printer's imprint at foot of p.160 (CLARKE, ALEXANDER AND CO., LTD., LONDON AND NORWICH.)

Cover (see Plate 15)
Off-white paper, printed bright-pink, royal-blue, and black; square-back, cut flush; edges plain.
(1) Front cover is divided diagonally from top left to bottom right corners by change of background-colour: upper right area is royal-blue, lower left is bright-pink. The Lost I Heir I G.A. I Henty (white out of royal-blue). The London Series (white out of bright-pink) in white frame. At bottom right: Price Sixpence (white out of bright-pink). All lettering is in a hand-drawn script.

(2) Advertisement for Automobiles De Luxe, Ltd. (black).
(3) Advertisement for Dr. J.Collis Browne's Chlorodyne (black).
(4) Advertisement for Vinolia Powder and Cream (black).
(Spine) THE LOST HEIR. G.A.HENTY. 6^D (running from head to foot).

References: Bod; NS.

Notes
1. I have been unable to find any records or information relating to this publisher, and only two copies of this paperback edition.
2. General advertisements are spread through the text, as detailed under Contents above. Publisher's advertisements appear on the page facing p.158 (NEW | Six Shilling | Novels | (list of titles and authors); and facing p.159 (The London Series | Demy 8vo. Paper Covers, 6d. | (list of five titles including this one).

88. ON THE SPANISH MAIN

88.1
CHAMBERS'S 'CONTINUOUS' READERS (underlined) | ON THE SPANISH MAIN | BY | G.A.HENTY | (publisher's device) | W.& R.CHAMBERS, LIMITED | LONDON AND EDINBURGH

Contents
175 x 122 mm. (i)–(iv) | (1)–82 | no catalogue. Frontispiece and one other full-page wash-drawing by unknown artist, reproduced by halftone blocks printed on coated text paper, unbacked, counted in pagination.
(i) Blank | (ii) frontispiece | (iii) title p. | (iv) advertisement (CHAMBERS'S 'CONTINUOUS' READERS) listing 8 titles including this one | (1)–80. text and illustration | (81)–82. Notes and Explanations, printed in two columns.

Binding (see Plate 127)
Red limp cloth, printed black; square-back, cut flush; edges plain; plain off-white endpapers.
Front: as title page; price: 6d. **Spine:** plain. **Back:** advertisement.

References: BL; Bod; BB | *Dartt*, p.101, Note.

Notes
1. For other appearances of this story see §4.
2. *Dartt*, unfortunately, is confused and inaccurate. The prelims, text, and notes, make a total of 86 pages, a strangely uneven working.
3. Chambers's 'Continuous' Readers included two other Henty titles (see Appendix V).

88.2
Title page: As for 88.1, but the full-point after 'G' in 'G A.HENTY' is missing.

Contents: 175 × 120 mm. Otherwise as for 88.1.

Cover (see Plate 127)
Red paper, printed black; square-back, cut flush; edges plain; no endpapers.
  (1) as title page, with price: 4d. (2), (3), and (4) advertisements.
(Spine) blank.

References: BB | *Farmer*, p.52; *Dartt*, p.101.

Notes
1. A re-issue of 88.1, in cheaper form.
2. It is not surprising that most copies of this fragile booklet that have survived in paper covers are those sent to teachers 'With the Publisher's Compliments'. They were sales-promotion items, and probably never entered a classroom.

89. DO YOUR DUTY

89.1
Do Your Duty | BY | G.A.HENTY | Author of | "Tales of Daring and Danger" "Sturdy and Strong" "Facing Death" | "Held Fast for England" "The Dash for Khartoum" &c. | WITH COLOURED FRONTISPIECE | AND SEVEN FULL-PAGE ILLUSTRATIONS | NEW EDITION | BLACKIE AND SON LIMITED | LONDON GLASGOW AND DUBLIN

Contents
178 × 120 mm. (1)–112 | catalogue 9–16 and 1–8. Frontispiece from watercolour drawing by H.M. Brock, reproduced by four-colour halftone blocks on coated paper, unbacked, tipped in. Seven full-page pen-drawings by R.Lillie printed from line blocks on text pages, unbacked, unfolioed but counted in pagination.
  (1) Half-title p. | (2) blank | (frontispiece, tipped in) | 93) title p. | (4) blank | (5) list of Illustrations | (6) blank | (7)–112. text | 9–16. first part of catalogue | 1–8. second part of catalogue.

Binding (see Plate 118)
Blue cloth boards, blocked black, brown, buff, and gilt; edges plain; plain off-white endpapers.
  Front board: DO . YOUR | . DUTY . | BY . G . A . HENTY (black) above illustration, framed by black line, of boy reading book and girl with large hat on her lap (black, brown, buff). **Spine:** . DO . | YOUR | DUTY | BY . G . A . | HENTY (gilt) above illustration, framed by black line, of boy, girl, cricket bat and ball, papers (black, brown, buff). **Back board:** plain.

References: BL; Bod; PN | *Farmer*, p.25; *Dartt*, p.48, *Companion*, p.13.

Notes
1. For other appearances of this story see Appendix V. It was first printed in book form in the collection of short stories, *Yarns on the Beach*, 1886 (25.1). That appearance may account for the words NEW EDITION on the present title page, its first 'solo' appearance. Also, perhaps, for the lack of a date on the title page,

Blackie's usual indication of a first issue. Publication day was 18 August 1900.

2. Dartt reports (*Companion*, p.13) copies with title-page dated 1900 in two famous collections, but both the sixth (late) Marquess of Bath and the Revd Basil Brown have assured me emphatically that they never had such copies. Those in the Copyright Libraries are also undated.

3. The numbering of the pages of the publisher's catalogue has caused confusion, not least to earlier Henty bibliographers. Dartt (*Companion*, p.13) says 'an unusual feature of the catalogue is pages number 9–16 and 25–32, indicating the practice of binding in 8-page signatures. And what happens when a printer errs.'. I have a copy of *Do Your Duty* with a similar catalogue, and another with pp.9–16 followed by 1–8 (described above). I also have a copy of *A Soldier's Daughter*, which does not differ from other copies I have seen of the first edition in having only sixteen pages of advertisements, numbered 17–32 – not thirty-two pages, as reported by Dartt, who possibly made the mistake of looking only at the final page-number when compiling his notes (see *A Soldier's Daughter*, 111.1, Note 4).

4. These are not necessarily errors by either printer or binder. It was common practice for publishers, and especially Blackie, to have their catalogues printed in sheets containing 32 or 64 pages, with an imposition scheme resulting in a number of 8-page sections. The whole catalogue was carefully designed so that the opening page of each 8-page (or 16-page) section had a strong heading: these might appear on pages 1, 9, 17, 25, etc. Each section listed books in specific categories, e.g. those for boys, those for girls, those in named series, etc. All this provided flexibility in that any individual section by itself, or any combination of sections, could be chosen for inclusion in any title, to suit the expected readership of that title, and the first page would always look like the 'beginning' even when the page-number was not '1'.

89.2

Title page: As for 89.1, but with NEW EDITION omitted.

Contents: As for 89.1, except (a) pages 5 and 7 are folioed; (b) the illustration pages are folioed.

Binding: As for 89.1.

Reference: PN.

Notes

1. It might be supposed that this issue, without NEW EDITION on the title page, preceded the one listed as 89.1. However, a great number of copies have been examined, and the presentation inscriptions show the order given here is correct. A comparable, though not exactly similar, situation exists with *John Hawke's Fortune*: see title-page details of 93.4, 93.5, and 93.6.

2. See 89.1, Notes 3 and 4.

3. For what it may be worth I mention here what appears to be a 'pirate' issue of 89.2: I have seen only one copy, in a lot of books at auction, and am unable to give any explanation of its origin. The textual content is identical with that of 89.2, but the quality of paper and printing is such that it could not possibly have come from Blackie, even as a proof. It is reminiscent of the very worst of US or Indian pirated editions. The frontispiece, on the other hand, is as good as those in normal Blackie copies. Such contrast suggests that the plate was taken from Blackie stock. But if other copies of this strange issue exist, with such frontispieces, the latter must surely have been somehow pilfered from Blackie's bindery.

The book is bound in blue cloth, blocked dark-blue and green. The front board shows an illustration of a boy and a girl on horseback, riding diagonally towards the right, in a background of trees and sky (the drawing in blue, with green sky). The picture is in a blue and green decorative frame with ornamental corners, part of which forms a lower panel in the same style, framing: DO YOUR DUTY (blue). The spine has a strange simple decoration of three birds above an elongated plant with a thin stem, in a pot, this design filling the whole spine: there is no lettering. The back board is plain. The binding design seems to have been blocked on the cloth boards, so it is likely that other copies exist. All the work, and especially the reproduction of the text, is of extremely poor quality. It is hard to understand how such a version of this book came into existence.

89.3
Blackie's I Story Book Readers I Fourth Series I (Suitable for Children of 10 to 11) I (small leaf ornament) I Do Your Duty I Adapted from Mr.G.A.Henty's Story I (small leaf ornament) I (another small leaf ornament) I London I Blackie & Son, Limited, 50 Old Bailey I Glasgow and Bombay

Contents
165 x 110 mm. (1)–80. Frontispiece by H.M. Brock, and seven pen-drawings by R.Lillie, reproduced by line blocks printed on text pages, unbacked, unfolioed but counted in pagination.
(1) Advertisement (BLACKIE'S STORY BOOK READERS) I (2) frontispiece I (3) title p. I (4) blank I 5–80. text.

Cover (see Plate 123)
Red limp cloth, printed black; lined with plain yellow paper; saddle-stitched; cut flush; edges plain.
Front: BLACKIE'S . STORY . BOOK I READERS I (printer's ornament) I DO . YOUR . DUTY I G.A.HENTY I (publisher's device) I FOURTH . SERIES . (all black) within a border of four rules with decorative corners. **Back:** plain.

References: BB; SW I *Dartt*, pp.49, 129, *Companion*, p.28.

Notes
1. As stated on the title page, the text in this edition is 'adapted' or condensed.
2. This Story Book Reader (see Appendix V) reached the Copyright Libraries in 1905.
3. The frontispiece is from the black plate of the colour-set in 89.1.
4. *Dartt* and his *Companion* are both confused. Evidence is insufficient to give details of dates, prices, and later reprints. But Stuart Wilson reports a copy of 89.3 in grey paper covers in the style described for 89.4 below, so probably 89.3 and 89.4 were each issued in both binding styles.

89.4

Title page: As for 89.3, except (a) changed imprint (BLACKIE & SON LIMITED | LONDON AND GLASGOW); (b) all the typematter is framed by rules.

Contents

165 × 110 mm. As for 89.3, except as detailed below:
(1) Half-title p. | (2) frontispiece | (3) title p. | (4) publisher's addresses; panel with list of Blackie's Story Book Readers; printer's imprint (Printed in Great Britain by Blackie & Son, Ltd, Glasgow) | 5–80. text.

Cover

Grey paper, printed black; saddle-stitched, cut flush; edges plain; no endpapers.

(1) BLACKIE'S . STORY . BOOK | READERS | (printer's ornament) | DO . YOUR . DUTY | G.A.HENTY | (publisher's device) | FOURTH . SERIES . (black) all framed by four black rules with decorative corners.
(2) blank
(3) blank
(4) advertisement (BLACKIE'S SUPPLEMENTARY READERS).

References: BB | *Dartt*, p.49, *Companion*, p.28.

Note: See 89.3, Notes 1 to 4. This is almost certainly a later issue of 89.3; note that the title 'Mr.' has been dropped before Henty's name on the title page.

89.5

Do Your Duty | BY | G.A.HENTY | Author of | "Tales of Daring and Danger" "Sturdy and Strong" "Facing Death" | "Held Fast for England" "The Dash for Khartoum" &c. | WITH COLOURED FRONTISPIECE | AND SEVEN FULL-PAGE ILLUSTRATIONS | BLACKIE AND SON LIMITED | LONDON GLASGOW DUBLIN BOMBAY

Contents: 175 × 114 mm. Otherwise as for 89.1, but catalogue folioed 25–32.

Binding (see Plate 118)

Blue cloth boards, blocked black, bistre, white, and gilt; edges plain; plain off-white endpapers.
Front board: DO YOUR | DUTY (white) in panel, framed by black rules, across illustration, also framed by black rules, of boy carrying book, and girl, with dog, running past tree (black, bistre, white). **Spine:** . DO . | YOUR | DUTY (gilt) in upper panel; in lower panel: illustration of boy, girl, dog, and book (black, bistre, white); panels divided and framed by black rules. At foot: BLACKIE & SON | LIMITED (black). **Back board:** plain.

Reference: PN.

Notes

1. The earliest inscription reported in a copy of this issue is 1910.
2. Issues later than 1910 have Dublin removed from the title-page imprint. Such a copy, with an inscription dated 1914, has the usual 8-page section of publisher's catalogue folioed 9–16 (see 89.1, Notes 3–4).
3. The text paper used for this impression is a bulky featherweight, making the book

half as thick again as 89.1 or 89.2, although considerably lighter in weight.

4. For the sake of economy the frontispiece is printed from the set of blocks used for 89.1 and 89.2 but with the black plate omitted. The most obvious result, to the layman's eye, is that the caption has to be printed in blue ink instead of black.

5. The cap D in 'Duty' on the title page has been damaged: a fault that was not corrected when 89.6, below, was printed.

6. This binding design was also used for *Bears and Dacoits and Other Stories*, 69.3.

89.6

Title page: As for 89.5, but changed addresses (LONDON GLASGOW AND BOMBAY).

Contents: 175 × 119 mm. As for 89.5, but no catalogue.

Binding (see Plate 119)

Grey cloth boards, blocked very dark green or black; illustration printed on paper, laid down; edges plain; plain off-white endpapers.

 Front board: DO YOUR | DUTY (cloth-colour out of black solid rectangle, above laid-down, run-on copy of frontispiece, reproduced by three-colour halftone blocks on coated paper. All framed by black rule. **Spine:** DO | YOUR | DUTY | G.A.HENTY (black), within ruled panel, above illustration of boy in mediaeval dress, within a second ruled panel (all black). At foot, in a third small ruled panel: BLACKIE | & SON LTD. (black). **Back board:** plain.

Reference: PN.

Notes

1. Similar full-colour illustrations printed on paper and laid down on front boards, were introduced by Blackie from 1914 onwards for other titles, including *Bears and Dacoits* and *John Hawke's Fortune*, probably as an economy during wartime.

2. The cap D in 'Duty' on the title page is damaged; see 89.5, Note 5.

89.7

Title page, Contents: As for 89.6.

Binding (see Note 1)

Grey cloth boards, blocked black; illustration printed on paper, laid down; edges plain; plain off-white endpapers.

 Front board: DO YOUR | DUTY (cloth-colour out of solid-black rectangle) above laid-down illustration, reproduced by three-colour halftone blocks on coated paper, of boy and girl playing with ball, and jumping dog, all framed by black rules. At the top, one hand of the girl, and the ball, project beyond the edge of the rectangular shape, and the plate is cut out irregularly, so that the two small projecting areas of the illustration overlap the lettering above. **Spine:** as for 89.6. **Back board:** plain.

Reference: *Dartt*, p.50.

Notes

1. See 89.6, Note 1. This binding design was also used for *Bears and Dacoits*, 69.4, Plate 122. Both titles are found in varying cloth-colours.

2. Some issues are found with a variation in the blocking of the spine on the binding case. Instead of the illustration of the boy, there is a panel containing a floral art-nouveau design.

89.8

Do Your Duty | BY | G.A. HENTY | (publisher's device) | BLACKIE AND SON LIMITED | LONDON GLASGOW AND BOMBAY

Contents
165 × 116 mm. (1)–80 | no catalogue. Frontispiece by H.M.Brock, reproduced by line block printed in black on coated paper, unbacked, tipped in; and seven pen-drawings by R.Lillie, reproduced by line blocks printed on text pages, backed by text, folioed except for the illustration on p.19.
(1) Half-title p. | (2) blank | (frontispiece, tipped in) | (3) title p. | (4) blank | 5–80. text and illustrations.

Binding (see Plate 118)
Yellow-brown cloth boards, blocked black and white; edges plain; plain off-white endpapers.
Front board: DO YOUR DUTY | G.A.Henty (black) above illustration of boy and girl with dog in snow scene (black, white), framed by black line. **Spine:** DO | YOUR | DUTY | Henty (black) in plain panel cutting across illustration of girl in white dress and shoes (black, white), both parts of illustration framed by black lines. **Back board:** plain.

References: PN | *Dartt*, p.50.

Notes
1. The text in this edition, as in 89.3 and 89.4, is abridged. The featherweight paper is less bulky than in 89.5 and 89.6. These two factors result in a thinner book than even 89.1 or 89.2.
2. *Dartt*, p.50, notes that 89.8 has 'cover and format similar to copies of *Cast Ashore* and *Charlie Marryat*'. That is misleading: *Cast Ashore*, 115.3, *Charlie Marryat*, 116.3, see Plate 133, and *The Young Captain*, 121.3, were issued, in an unnamed series, in uniform bindings, and in various cloth-colours of which one was the yellow-brown used here for 89.8. But that is as far as it goes: the board-size is bigger, the illustration is smaller, and it is of *different* children in a *different* snow scene.
3. *Dartt's* date for this impression, firmly given as (1920) but unsupported by evidence, appears to be correct, judging from inscriptions in copies examined.
4. Later issues were bound in buff, grained paper (imitating cloth). One such copy examined is inscribed with the date September 1921.

89.9

Title page: As for 89.8.

Contents
165 × 116 mm. (1)–80 | no catalogue. Frontispiece from watercolour drawing by H.M.Brock, reproduced by three-colour halftone blocks on coated paper, unbacked, tipped in. Seven full-page pen-drawings by R.Lillie reproduced by line blocks printed on text pages, backed by text, folioed except for the illustration on p.19.

(Frontispiece, tipped in) | (1) title p. | (2) blank | (3) advertisement (ISSUED UNIFORM | WITH THIS BOOK) listing 12 titles including this, the only one by Henty | (4) blank | 5–80. text and illustrations.

Binding (see Plate 118)
Grey, grained-paper boards (imitating cloth), blocked dark-blue and white; edges plain; plain off-white endpapers.
    Front board: DO | YOUR | DUTY (dark-blue) in frame of dark-blue and white lines within over-all pattern of leaves and cones or berries, also framed in dark-blue and white lines. **Spine:** DO | YOUR | DUTY | Henty (dark-blue) above two small sections of pattern repeated from front board. **Back board:** plain.

References: TC; BB; PN | *Dartt*, p.50.

Notes
1. Four issues of this edition have been identified. The earliest one is described above. The second issue has a list of 14 titles on p.(3), and at the foot of p.80 is the printer's imprint: (PRINTED AND BOUND IN GREAT BRITAIN | By Blackie & Son, Limited, Glasgow). Copies are inscribed with dates, 1922 or 1923.
2. The third issue varies from the second only in a line added on p.(2) in small italics (Printed and bound in Great Britain). Inscribed copies are dated 1923.
3. The fourth issue has variations in the advertisement on p.(3): (a) there is a third line added to the heading (1s. Series); (b) the advertisement lists 16 titles instead of 14; (c) beneath a rule at the foot there is an added line (BLACKIE AND SON LIMITED). In this issue the printer's imprint has been removed from p.80.
4. These issues are in paper boards of a variety of colours, including blue, brown, grey, buff, and green. Inscriptions in copies examined are dated from 1922 to 1927.
5. The return of the colour frontispiece, replaced in 89.8 by a line version of the same picture, which had been specially drawn by H.M.Brock for the Story Book Reader, 89.3, perhaps indicates better times following the end of the war.
6. *Dartt*, pp.48–50, is confused by this title, of which the many issues are certainly difficult to disentangle. He mentions at least three binding designs with 'vine', 'vine and flower', or 'vine and leaf' motifs, giving widely varying dates. They probably all originate from descriptions of 89.9 by his many well-meaning correspondents, on whom he often had to rely.

90. WON BY THE SWORD

90.1
WON BY THE SWORD | A TALE OF | THE THIRTY YEARS' WAR | BY | G.A.HENTY | Author of "The Lion of the North" "At Agincourt" | "Under Wellington's Command" &c. | (8-em rule) | WITH TWELVE ILLUSTRATIONS BY CHARLES M.SHELDON | AND FOUR PLANS | (8-em rule) | LONDON | BLACKIE & SON, LIMITED, 50 OLD BAILEY, E.C. | GLASGOW AND DUBLIN | 1900

Contents
185 x 130 mm. (i)–(x) | (11)–(384) | catalogue (1)–32. Twelve full-page wash-

drawings by Charles M. Sheldon, reproduced by halftone blocks printed in black on coated paper, unbacked, unfolioed, tipped in. Four battle-plans printed from line blocks on text pages.

(i) Half-title p. | (ii) advertisement (MR. HENTY'S HISTORICAL TALES.) listing 47 titles | (frontispiece, tipped in) | (iii) title p. | (iv) blank | (v)–vi. Preface | (vii) Contents | (viii) blank | (ix) list of Illustrations | (x) blank | (11)–383. text | (384) blank | (1)–32. catalogue.

Binding (see Plate 101)
Dark green-blue cloth boards, bevelled, blocked black, white, red, buff, and gilt; all edges burnished olive-green; grey endpapers, lined off-white.

Front board: Won . by . the . Sword (gilt) above illustration of French soldier with drawn sword (black, white, red, buff, and gilt). At right: A . Story . | of . the . | Thirty . | Years' . | War ... (gilt). At foot: By | G.A.Henty (black). **Spine:** Won | . by . the . | Sword (gilt) above illustration of head and shoulders of French soldier (black, red, white, red, buff). At foot: G.A.Henty (gilt). **Back board:** plain.

References: BL; Bod; PN | *Farmer*, p.84; *Dartt*, p.165.

Notes
1. The book was published on 1 June 1899 at six shillings. By the end of February 1900 Blackie had sold 9075 copies, and by the end of August 1917 they had sold 2877 more. That represents an average annual sale of 664 copies, not a very substantial figure by Henty's standards. A cheaper edition was not issued until after the first war. The total number of copies sold at six shillings was 11,952.
2. As usual at this period, the earliest issues contain catalogues that do not mention the books for the current year (with title pages dated 1900).

*90.2
Reprints of the first edition were in the style of 90.1, with the date removed from the title page. Changes were made when necessary to the title-page imprint and addresses: the Indian office was opened in 1901 although Bombay did not appear regularly in the Blackie imprint until 1906; and after 1910 Dublin was omitted.
The slightly-varying issues of the reprints of the book in its first-edition format are all grouped together under this 'generic' heading, *90.2.

*90.3
WON BY THE SWORD | A Tale of the Thirty Years' War | BY | G.A.HENTY | Author of "The Lion of the North" "At Agincourt" | "Under Wellington's Command" &c. | Illustrated | BLACKIE AND SON LIMITED | LONDON GLASGOW AND BOMBAY

Contents
184 × 123 mm. (1)–(384) | advertisement (1)–(2). Frontispiece from watercolour drawing by John de Walton, reproduced by three-colour halftone blocks; four full-page wash-drawings by Charles Sheldon, reproduced by halftone blocks printed in black; all on coated paper, unbacked, keyed to text pages, tipped in. Four battle-plans printed from line blocks on text pages.

(1) Half-title p. | (2) advertisement (G.A.HENTY'S BOOKS) listing 56 titles |

(frontispiece, tipped in) | (3) title p. | (4) printer's imprint (Printed in Great Britain by | Blackie & Son, Limited, Glasgow) | (5) Preface | vi. [roman numerals in error] Preface, continued | (7) Contents | (8) blank | (9) list of Illustrations | (10) blank | (11)–383. text | (384) blank | (1)–(2) advertisement (THE NEW POPULAR HENTY) listing 60 titles.

Binding (see Note 1)
Yellow-green cloth boards, blocked black, red, and warm-buff; edges plain; plain off-white endpapers.
   Front board: WON BY THE SWORD | G.A.HENTY (black) above illustration of two young armed men (black, red, warm-buff), with signature at lower left corner: J Hassall (black). **Spine:** WON | BY THE | SWORD | G.A.HENTY (black) above illustration of young man in armour, with sword (black, red, warm-buff). At foot: BLACKIE & SON LTD (black). **Back board:** plain.

Reference: PN.

Notes
1. Re-issued in the 1920s in 'The New Popular Henty', a series with a name very close to that of one begun in 1903 ('The New and Popular Edition'), in which this title never appeared (see 90.1, Note 1, above). Details of the second series, and later editions, are given under *Facing Death*, 10.7, Notes 1–3 and 6–8. Examples of 'The New Popular Henty' binding style are at Plates 174–175.
2. The single leaf of advertisements, tipped on to the end of the last gathering, was as usual printed on a heavier featherweight than that used for the text.
3. All the minor variants of *Won by the Sword* in the series are grouped together under the 'generic' heading, *90.3.

91. A ROVING COMMISSION

91.1
A ROVING COMMISSION | OR THROUGH THE | BLACK INSURRECTION OF HAYTI | BY | G.A.HENTY | Author of "With Frederick the Great" "The Dash for Khartoum" | "Both Sides the Border" &c. | (20mm. rule) | WITH TWELVE ILLUSTRATIONS BY WILLIAM RAINEY, R.I. | (20mm. rule) | LONDON | BLACKIE & SON, LIMITED, 50 OLD BAILEY, E.C. | GLASGOW AND DUBLIN | 1900

Contents
185 x 130 mm. (i)–(x) | (11)–(384) | catalogue (1)–32. Twelve full-page wash-drawings by William Rainey, reproduced by halftone blocks printed in black on coated paper, unbacked, unfolioed, tipped in.
   (i) Half-title p. | (ii) advertisement (MR. HENTY'S HISTORICAL TALES.) listing 47 titles | (frontispiece, tipped in) | (iii) title p. | (iv) blank | (v)–vi. Preface | (vii) Contents | (viii) blank | (ix) list of Illustrations | (x) blank | (11)–383. text | (384) blank | (1)–32. catalogue.

Binding (see Plate 80)
Red cloth boards, bevelled, blocked black, dark-grey, light-grey, brown, pink, and gilt; all edges burnished olive-green; grey endpapers, lined off-white.

Front board: Illustration of sailors on board ship (black, dark-grey, light-grey, brown, pink) framed by black line. At right: A ROVING I COMMISSION I OR I THROUGH THE I BLACK I INSURRECTION I OF HAYTI. I BY I G.A.HENTY. (all gilt). **Spine:** A I ROVING I COMMISSION (gilt) above illustration, framed by black line, of young sailor on board, rolling up his sleeve (black, brown, dark-grey, light-grey, pink). At foot: BY I G.A.HENTY (gilt). **Back board:** plain.

References: BL; Bod; PN I *Farmer*, p.59; *Dartt*, p.114.

Notes

1. *A Roving Commission* was published on 11 July 1899 at six shillings. By the end of August 1900 Blackie had sold 7694 copies, and during the following eighteen years they sold a further 2077. This was certainly not one of Henty's best-selling titles: it averaged sales of only 543 copies each year over those eighteen years, and over the last seventeen of those years the average was a mere 122 copies.

2. It is clear from Blackie's sales figures that by this time the regular print order for first editions of Henty's novels had grown to 10,000 copies. And yet this book had sold a total of only 9771 copies between publication date and the time Blackie's records cease, on 31 August 1917. There was no reprint of this book in its first-edition format: therefore all copies in this format had dated title pages. Following the initial impression of 10,000 copies *A Roving Commission* was not reprinted until after the end of the first war (see *91.2).

3. It is, perhaps, ironic as well as interesting that this book, which in terms of the number of copies sold was, with the sole exception of *Out with Garibaldi*, the least successful of Henty's novels published by Blackie, should have been the first choice of the historian, A.J.P. Taylor. In *The Times Literary Supplement*, 6 December 1974, 'twenty-five eminent contemporaries' were asked 'to nominate the three or four books that made the deepest impression on them in childhood'. After *Pilgrim's Progress* Taylor named 'All the works of Henty. *A Roving Commission* was the best of them, very frightening and full of colour prejudice'.

4. As usual at this period, the earliest issues contain catalogues that do not mention the books for the current year (with title pages dated 1900). Henty's earlier books, up to and including those for the previous year, are listed, with quotations from press notices.

5. Five of the twelve halftone illustrations are marked by the process engraver with the product name 'Swantype': see 76.1, Note 4.

*91.2

A Roving Commission I Or, Through the Black Insurrection of Hayti I BY I G.A.HENTY I Author of "The Dash for Khartoum" "Both Sides the Border" I "The Treasure of the Incas" &c. I Illustrated I BLACKIE AND SON LIMITED I LONDON GLASGOW AND BOMBAY

Contents

184 x 122 mm. (1)–(384) I no catalogue. Frontispiece from watercolour drawing by unknown artist, reproduced by three-colour halftone blocks; four full-page wash-drawings by William Rainey reproduced by halftone blocks printed in black; all on coated paper, unbacked, keyed to text pages, tipped in.

(1) Half-title p. I (2) advertisement (G.A.HENTY'S BOOKS) listing 56 titles I

(frontispiece, tipped in) | (3) title p. | (4) printer's imprint (Printed in Great Britain by | Blackie & Son, Limited, Glasgow) | (5) Preface | vi. [roman numerals in error] Preface, continued | 7. Contents | (8) blank | (9) list of Illustrations | (10) blank | (11)–383. text | (384) blank.

Binding

The design is based on that of 91.1, but all the brasses have been remade, smaller, and the style of lettering changed. Red cloth boards, blocked black, blue and buff; edges plain; plain off-white endpapers.

Front board: Illustration of sailors on board ship (black, blue, buff) framed by black line. At right: A ROVING | COMMISS- | ION | or | Through the | Black | Insurrection | of Hayti | G.A.HENTY (black). **Spine:** A ROVING | COMMISS- | ION | G.A.HENTY (black) above illustration, framed by black line, of young sailor on board, rolling up his sleeves (black, blue, buff). At foot: BLACKIE & SON LTD (black). **Back board:** plain.

References: BL; PN.

Note: For details of Blackie's second cheaper series, 'The New Popular Henty', and subsequent editions of the book, see *Facing Death*, 10.7, Notes 1–3 and 6–8.

92. NO SURRENDER!

92.1

NO SURRENDER! | A TALE OF | THE RISING IN LA VENDÉE | BY | G.A.HENTY | Author of "In the Reign of Terror" "Through Russian Snows" | "The Bravest of the Brave" &c. | (18mm. rule) | WITH EIGHT ILLUSTRATIONS BY STANLEY L.WOOD | (18mm. rule) | LONDON | BLACKIE & SON, LIMITED, 50 OLD BAILEY, E.C. | GLASGOW AND DUBLIN | 1900

Contents

186 × 123 mm. (i)–(x) | (11)–352 | catalogue (1)–32. Eight full-page wash-drawings by Stanley L.Wood, reproduced by halftone blocks printed in black on coated paper, unbacked, unfolioed, tipped in.

(i) Half-title p. | (ii) advertisement (MR. HENTY'S HISTORICAL TALES.) listing 47 titles | (frontispiece, tipped in) | (iii) title p. | (iv) blank | (v)–vi. Preface | (vii) Contents | (viii) blank | (ix) list of Illustrations | (x) blank | (11)–352. text | (1)–32. catalogue.

Binding (see Plate 77)

Red cloth boards, blocked black, blue, white, and gilt; all edges burnished olive-green; grey endpapers, lined off-white.

Front board: NO SURRENDER! | A TALE | OF THE RISING | IN | LA VENDÉE (all gilt) above and at right of illustration of soldier with bayonet fixed on large rifle (black, blue, white). At foot: G.A.HENTY (black). **Spine:** NO | SURRENDER! | A TALE OF | THE RISING IN | LA VENDÉE (gilt) above illustration of soldier with pistol and sword (black, blue, white). At foot: G.A.HENTY (gilt). **Back board:** plain.

References: BL; Bod; PN | *Farmer*, p.51; *Dartt*, p.99, *Companion*, p.22.

Notes
1. The book was published on 24 August 1899 at five shillings. By the end of February 1900 Blackie had sold 7809 copies, but during the following seventeen years, up to the end of August 1917, when their records cease, they sold only 3800 more. The average annual sale over the eighteen years, boosted by pre-publication orders, was 645 copies, but for the last seventeen of those years it was only 224 copies. The total number of copies sold up to 1917 at five-shillings was 11,609, and the book was not re-issued in a cheaper edition until after the first war.
2. Blackie's figures show a steadily decreasing sale over those eighteen years, apart from a very small boost in 1914, and especially in 1915, which may be accounted for by the appeal of the book's title to those giving presents to boys at the outbreak of hostilities. It may be deduced from the detailed sales record that the book was not reprinted in its first-edition format, and that the original print-run was in the region of 12,000 copies.
3. As usual at this period, the earliest issues contain catalogues that do not mention the books for the current year (with title pages dated 1900). Henty's earlier books, up to and including those published the previous year, are listed, with quotations from press reviews.

*92.2

No Surrender! | A Tale of the Rising in La Vendée | BY | G.A.HENTY | Author of "In the Reign of Terror" | "Through Russian Snows" | "The Bravest of the Brave" &c. | Illustrated | BLACKIE & SON LIMITED | LONDON AND GLASGOW

Contents
184 × 125 mm. (i)–(x) | 11–352 | advertisement (i)–(ii). Frontispiece from watercolour drawing reproduced by three-colour halftone blocks; four wash-drawings reproduced by halftone blocks printed in black; all by Stanley L.Wood; all on coated paper, unbacked, keyed to text pages, tipped in.
    (i) Half-title p. | (ii) Blackie addresses | (frontispiece, tipped in) | (iii) title p. | (iv) printer's imprint (Printed in Great Britain by | Blackie & Son, Limited, Glasgow) | v–vi. Preface | vii. Contents | (viii) blank | ix. list of Illustrations | (x) blank | 11–352. text, with printer's imprint at foot of p.352 (PRINTED IN GREAT BRITAIN | At the Villafield Press, Glasgow, Scotland) | (i)–(ii) advertisement, tipped in, (THE NEW POPULAR HENTY) listing 60 titles.

Binding
The design is the same as for 92.1, but some of the brasses were re-cut, and alterations to the lettering include the omission of the exclamation mark in the title on the spine. Red cloth boards, blocked black, blue, and white; edges plain; plain off-white endpapers.
    Front board: NO SURRENDER! | A TALE | OF THE RISING | IN | LA VENDÉE (black) above and at right of illustration of soldier with bayonet fixed on large rifle (black, blue, white). At foot: G.A.HENTY (black). **Spine:** NO | SURRENDER | A TALE OF | THE RISING IN | LA VENDÉE | G.A.HENTY (black) above illustration of soldier with pistol and sword (black, blue, white). At foot: BLACKIE (black). **Back board:** plain.

Reference: IM.

Notes

1. During the 1920s Blackie re-issued Henty's novels in a series called 'The New Popular Henty', a name very close to that of the series begun in 1903 ('The New and Popular Edition') in which this book did not appear. For details of the second cheaper series, 'The New Popular Henty', and subsequent editions of the book, see *Facing Death*, 10.7, Notes 1–3 and 6–8.

2. All the minor variants of *No Surrender!* in the series are grouped together under this 'generic' heading, *92.2.

93. JOHN HAWKE'S FORTUNE

93.1

JOHN HAWKE'S FORTUNE I A STORY OF I MONMOUTH'S REBELLION I BY I G.A.HENTY I AUTHOR OF I "FACING DEATH," "WITH BULLER IN NATAL," I AND OF OVER SEVENTY OTHER BOOKS FOR BOYS. I With Six Illustrations I LONDON: CHAPMAN & HALL, LIMITED I 11, HENRIETTA STREET, W.C. I (short rule) I 1901.
(Note: With Six Illustrations *is in gothic type).*

Contents

171 x 119 mm. (1)–(64) I no catalogue. Six full-page watercolour drawings by Lance Thackeray, reproduced by three-colour vignetted halftone blocks, unbacked, unfolioed, tipped in.

(1) Title p. I (2) Contents I (3)–63. text I (64) advertisement (THE YOUNG PEOPLE'S LIBRARY. I ILLUSTRATED.); printer's imprint at foot (EDMUND EVANS, ENGRAVER AND PRINTER, THE RACQUET COURT PRESS, SWAN STREET, LONDON, S.E.).

Cover (see Plate 105)

White paper printed in full colour; wrapped round 64 pages, saddle-stitched, two wires; cut flush; plain edges; no endpapers.

(1) Elaborate decorative and pictorial design printed in full colour. Background of stippled olive-green, with white scroll weaving between three full-colour illustrations. THE YOUNG PEOPLE'S LIBRARY (yellow at tops of letters, tinged to orange at base of letters) on scroll. Overprinted at top of scroll: John I Hawke's I Fortune I (star) I Vol. I VII. (black). Overprinted at foot of scroll, between two small ornaments: BY I G.A.HENTY. (black). Overprinted at top of green background: PRICE – – THREEPENCE NET. (black). Overprinted at foot: CHAPMAN AND HALL, LTD., 11, Henrietta Street, London, W.C. (black).

(2) blank.

(3) Advertisement (Chapman & Hall Ltd., Educational and General Publishers) (black).

(4) Advertisement (THE YOUNG PEOPLE'S LIBRARY.) (black) in decorative panel, background olive-green stipple).

References: BL; BB | *Farmer*, p.46; *Dartt*, p.88.

Notes
1. Little more than a pamphlet: very scarce and attractive. Printed by one of the finest colour-printers and engravers of his time, Edmund Evans.
2. I have not been able to find publisher's records relating to this publication.

93.2
Title page, Contents: As for 93.1.

Cover (see Plate 106)
Grey limp cloth, lined off-white paper, printed red; saddle-stitched; cut flush; edges plain; no endpapers.
   Printed in red on p.1 of cover only: The Young | People's | Library (within ruled panel, of which each of the four sides are curved like a flattened S). JOHN HAWKE'S FORTUNE | G.A.HENTY | CHAPMAN & HALL, LTD. | 11, HENRIETTA STREET | LONDON, W.C.

Reference: IM.

Note: Ivan McClymont's copy is the only one known to me of this issue of the first edition. It is likely that 93.1 and 93.2 were published simultaneously.

93.3
Title page: As for 93.1.

Contents
171 x 119 mm. (1)–64 | (1)–(64) | no catalogue. Illustrations as in 93.1.
   (1)–64. text and illustrations of *Pulabad; or, the Bravery of a Boy* by G. Manville Fenn, a story originally published separately, as No.4 in 'The Young People's Library', and now bound up with: (1)–(64). Henty's *John Hawke's Fortune*, of which details are as for 93.1.

Cover
Red limp cloth, printed blue; cut flush; plain off-white endpapers.
(1) The Young | People's | Library (blue) within ruled panel, of which each of the four sides are curved like a flattened S. Beneath this: PULABAD | GEO.MANVILLE FENN | JOHN HAWKE'S FORTUNE | G.A.HENTY | CHAPMAN & HALL, LTD. | 11, HENRIETTA STREET | LONDON, W.C. | PRICE 9d. (all blue).
(2), (3), and (4) all blank.

Reference: *Dartt*, p.89.

Notes
1. I have not been able to examine this issue of the first edition, bound up with Manville Fenn's story, *Pulabad*. I have relied entirely on *Dartt*, who reports the only recorded copy, in the Lilly Library of Indiana University.
2. Chapman & Hall were probably disposing of unsold sheets of both titles by offering them together in new packaging. But it was now necessary to charge 9d. for the two booklets bound in cloth, which had previously been sold at 3d. each.

93.4

John Hawke's Fortune | A Story of Monmouth's Rebellion | BY | G.A.HENTY | Author of "With Buller in Natal" "With Clive in India" | "By England's Aid" &c. | NEW EDITION | ILLUSTRATED | BLACKIE AND SON LIMITED | LONDON GLASGOW DUBLIN BOMBAY

Contents

165 × 118 mm. (1)–(80) | catalogue 1–12. Frontispiece from watercolour drawing by Lance Thackeray, reproduced by three-colour vignetted halftone blocks, unbacked, tipped in.

(1) Half-title | (2) blank | (frontispiece, tipped in) | (3) title p. | (4) blank | 5–79. text | (80) blank | 1–12. catalogue.

Binding (see Plate 109)

Grey cloth boards, blocked black, green, and red; edges plain; plain off-white endpapers.

Front board: JOHN | HAWKE'S | FORTUNE | BY | G.A.HENTY (black) at right of illustration, framed in broken black line, of boy leaning against tree with girl sitting reading at his feet (black, green, red). **Spine:** ornamental panels at head and foot (black and green); between them, running from foot to head: JOHN HAWKE'S FORTUNE G.A.HENTY (black). **Back board:** plain.

References: BL; Bod; PN | *Dartt*, p.89.

Notes

1. Not recorded in surviving Blackie records. Published on 14 September 1906.
2. As in *The Young Colonists*, bought from Routledge, so here, on acquiring the book from Chapman & Hall, Blackie printed the line 'NEW EDITION' on the title page.
3. Unusually, Blackie's catalogue is of 12 pages, printed on a less bulky featherweight paper than the text. Catalogues of 12 pages continued for subsequent issues, although the text itself is in 16-page gatherings.

93.5

Title page, Contents: As for 93.4, with updated catalogue.

Binding (see Plate 107)

Blue cloth boards, blocked black, yellow, and gilt; edges plain; plain off-white endpapers.

Front board: JOHN HAWKE'S | FORTUNE (yellow), and with the author's name on two lines ranged at head and foot with the second line of the title: G.A. | HENTY (yellow), all above illustration of boy and girl on sofa, both reading books (black and yellow), the whole framed by a black line near edges of board. **Spine:** Small drawing of boy, standing, with book (black and yellow) above: JOHN | HAWKE'S | FORTUNE (gilt). Beneath this, small drawings of: rope with two anchors; ball; girl standing with book (black and yellow). **Back board:** plain.

Reference: PN.

Notes

1. The editorial content is unchanged from that of 93.4, but the reduced bulk of the featherweight text paper is sufficient to confirm this is a new impression. The

catalogue is on a bulkier featherweight than any used for this title so far.
2. The content of the catalogue dates this issue somewhere between 1906 and 1911. It includes this title in 'Blackie's Ninepenny Series'.

93.6

John Hawke's Fortune I A Story of Monmouth's Rebellion I BY I G.A.HENTY I Author of "With Buller in Natal" "With Clive in India" I "By England's Aid" &c. I ILLUSTRATED I BLACKIE AND SON LIMITED I LONDON GLASGOW AND BOMBAY

Contents: As for 93.5, apart from revised title page; with catalogue as in 93.5.

Binding (see Plate 109)
Green cloth boards, blocked black, buff, white, and gilt; edges plain; plain off-white endpapers.
    Front board: JOHN HAWKE'S I FORTUNE (white) with the author's name on two lines ranged at head and foot with the second line of the title: G.A. I HENTY (white), in decorative panel (black, buff, white) above illustration, framed by black line, of boy pulling a dog-cart containing a girl with dolls and a dog (black, buff, white). **Spine:** John I Hawke's I Fortune I (row of three dots) I by G.A. I Henty (all gilt) above illustration of cat on a wall above a dog (black, buff, white). At foot: Blackie & Son I . Limited . (black). **Back board:** plain.

Reference: PN.

Notes
1. Dublin is omitted from the title-page imprint: that dates this issue after 1910. My copy has a school-prize label dated 1911–1912.
2. The words 'NEW EDITION' have been dropped from the title page (see 93.4, Note 2). This follows the practice adopted with *The Young Colonists*, 17.7, and also with *Do Your Duty*, 89.2.
3. Both text and catalogue are on the very bulky featherweight used for the catalogue in 93.5.
4. The front-board brasses for the title and author's name were used for 93.5.

93.7

Title page: As for 93.6.

Contents: 163 × 114 mm. As for 93.6.

Binding (see Plate 108)
Red cloth boards, blocked black; printed illustration laid down; edges plain; plain off-white endpapers.
    Front board: JOHN HAWKE'S I FORTUNE (black) above laid-down illustration, printed from three-colour halftone blocks on coated paper, of boy and girl feeding doves, with black dividing rule, and black rules framing the whole design. **Spine:** JOHN I HAWKE'S I FORTUNE I G.A. I HENTY I (5-panelled repeated pattern of 3 tulips) I BLACKIE & SON LTD (all black). **Back board:** plain.

Reference: TC.

Note: Terry Corrigan's copy is inscribed with the date 1914. Similar full-colour illustrations, printed on paper and laid down on front boards, were introduced by Blackie from 1914 onwards for other titles, including *Bears and Dacoits* and *Do Your Duty*, probably as an economy in wartime.

93.8
Title page, Contents: As for 93.7.

Binding: As for 93.7, except (a) dark-blue cloth boards; (b) the laid-down colour plate is an illustration of two oriental children, with a white child wearing a sun-bonnet. One of the oriental children is holding a parasol.

Reference: CT.

Note: See 93.7, Note. This is a simple variant of 93.7, the text probably from the same impression. I have seen copies dated 1916 and 1919.

93.9
JOHN HAWKE'S | FORTUNE | A Story of Monmouth's Rebellion | BY | G.A.HENTY | Author of "The Cat of Bubastes," | "By Sheer Pluck," &c. | Illustrated by T.W.Holmes | BLACKIE AND SON LIMITED | LONDON GLASGOW AND BOMBAY

Contents
179 x 137 mm. (1)–96 | no catalogue. Frontispiece from watercolour drawing by T.W. Holmes, reproduced by three-colour halftone blocks printed on coated paper, unbacked, tipped in. Three full-page and five half-page pen-drawings by T.W. Holmes, reproduced by line blocks printed on text pages.

(Frontispiece, tipped in) | (1) title p. | (2) printer's imprint (Printed in Great Britain by | Blackie & Son, Limited, Glasgow) | (3) Contents | (4) list of Illustrations | 5–96. text, set in large, bold type (see Note 1).

Binding (see Plate 109)
White paper boards, printed by colour-lithography; edges plain; plain off-white endpapers.

Front board: JOHN HAWKE'S | FORTUNE (ivory, cased black) superimposed at head of full-colour illustration of crowd waving their hats to passing horsemen. At foot: G.A.Henty (black). At lower right corner, artist's signature: T.W.HOLMES (brown). **Spine:** JOHN | HAWKE'S | FORTUNE | G.A.Henty (ivory out of brown panel) at head of continuation of full-colour picture from front board. At foot: BLACKIE (black). **Back board:** all-over ivory tint with small central panel reversed out (white), forming three small rectangles with lettering in each: BLACKIE | AND SON | LIMITED.

References: BL; Bod; PN | *Farmer*, p.46; *Dartt*, p.90.

Note: A considerably abridged edition, set in a very large, bold typeface, apparently directed at a younger audience than usual for Henty. The typeface is 18 point Gloucester Bold, Monotype 103. Received by the Copyright Libraries in 1925.

93.10

John Hawke's Fortune I AND I A Pipe of Mystery I BY I G.A.HENTY I BLACKIE & SON LIMITED I LONDON AND GLASGOW

Contents

184 x 124 mm. (1)–(80) I no catalogue. Frontispiece from watercolour drawing by T.W. Holmes, reproduced in black-and-white by halftone block, unbacked, tipped in.

   (1)–(2) leaf pasted down to form endpaper I (3) half-title p. I (4) Blackie addresses I (frontispiece, tipped in) I (5) title p. I (6) printer's imprint (Printed in Great Britain by Blackie & Son, Ltd., Glasgow) I (7) Contents I (8) blank I 9–48. text of 'John Hawke's Fortune' I (49) half-title p. I (50) blank I 51–75. text of 'A Pipe of Mystery' I (76) blank I 77. advertisement (TO THE READER) listing Henty titles published by Blackie I (78) blank I (79)–(80) leaf pasted down to form endpaper.

Binding (see Plate 109)

White paper boards, printed by colour-lithography; edges plain; plain off-white endpapers.

   Front board: JOHN HAWKE'S I FORTUNE (black); G.A. I HENTY (orange on yellow panel) between thick orange rules, across upper part of full-colour illustration. Artist's signature: T.W.HOLMES (brown) at lower right corner. **Spine:** JOHN I HAWKE'S I FORTUNE (all black); G.A.HENTY (orange on yellow panel) between thick orange rules. Panel and full-colour illustration continue from front board, but with approximately 5mm. white gap running down joint. **Back board:** Over-all blue panel with white margins. Yellow band across upper part, with: THE . PINNACLE . LIBRARY. (blue). Within yellow shield, at lower left corner: BLACKIE I & SON I LIMITED I (triangular mark) (all blue).

References: BB I *Farmer*, p.47; *Dartt*, p.90, Note.

Notes

1. As in 93.9, an abridged version of 'John Hawke's Fortune'.

2. For other appearances of 'A Pipe of Mystery' see §4.

3. The black-and-white frontispiece is a reproduction of the watercolour drawing by T.W. Holmes for 93.9. The full-length figure at the left has been painted out, but his shadow remains. The black-and-white illustrations in 93.9 are omitted.

4. The leaves forming pages (1)–(2) and (79)–(80) are pasted down as endpapers. The first leaf is included in the pagination, but p.(1) is not visible to the reader.

94. QUEEN VICTORIA

94.1

Queen Victoria I Scenes from her Life and Reign I BY I G.A.HENTY I BLACKIE & SON LIMITED I LONDON GLASGOW AND DUBLIN I 1901

Contents

176 x 120 mm. (i)–viii I (9)–260 I no catalogue. Frontispiece photograph of Queen Victoria, reproduced by halftone block printed in black on coated paper, unbacked,

tipped in. Numerous engravings reproduced by line blocks, and photographs reproduced by halftone blocks, all printed on text pages.

(i) Half-title p. | (ii) blank | (frontispiece, tipped in) | (iii) title p. | (iv) blank | (v) Preface | (vi) Note (see Note 2) | (vii)–viii. Contents | (9)–260. text.

Binding (see Plate 143)
Purple cloth boards, blocked white and gilt; edges plain; plain off-white endpapers.

Front board: QUEEN VICTORIA | (row of five ornaments) | SCENES FROM HER LIFE AND REIGN (white) above device made from parts of royal coat of arms (gilt). Beneath this: BY G.A.HENTY (white) between two white ornaments. **Spine:** QUEEN | VICTORIA (gilt) above group of six ornaments arranged in a triangle (gilt). Broad and narrow rules, with an ornament, (white) at head and foot. **Back board:** plain.

References: BL; Bod; PN | *Farmer*, p.57; *Dartt*, p.109.

Notes
1. This book grew out of *The Sovereign Reader*, 26.1, first published in (1887). Henty revised that book three times, finally completing it on the death of Queen Victoria. Blackie then re-issued it under this new title, for general reading or as a reward book. It did not include the earlier Notes, designed to help schoolchildren with the meanings of difficult words.
2. The only reference to the original title is a Note in small type on p.(vi), as follows: 'The earlier editions of this book have been known and appreciated by a wide circle under the title of *The Sovereign Reader*. The present edition completes the story of the great reign'.
3. The book was still made available for school use (see 94.2), with Henty's final additions and alterations included, plus the original Notes.
4. The halftone block for the frontispiece is marked by the process engraver with the product name 'Swantype': see 76.1, Note 4.

94.2 [26.5]
Title page: As for 94.1.

Contents, Binding: For a full description see *The Sovereign Reader*, 26.5, Plate 142.

Reference: PN.

Notes
1. This version was probably issued simultaneously with 94.1, and consisted of sheets from the same impression, trimmed to give slightly narrower margins. It was bound up with the 12 pages of Notes that had appeared in earlier editions of *The Sovereign Reader* (see 94.1, Note 1).
2. The binding case is nearer in design to that for *The Sovereign Reader* than that for 94.1, and the edition is in fact neither one book nor the other. I have entered it under both titles, and consequently given it two code numbers, 94.2 and 26.5, in the hope that that will not increase the confusion begun by its publisher!

94.3
Title page: As for 94.1.

Contents: 174 × 117 mm. Otherwise as for 94.1.

Binding (see Plate 144)
Lavender art-boards (paperback) drawn on, printed black and red; cut flush; edges plain; plain off-white endpapers.
Front cover: At head: PRICE ONE SHILLING (black). Three panels formed by a series of rules (red); top panel: QUEEN VICTORIA (black); central panel, photographic portrait of Queen Victoria (black halftone); bottom panel: SCENES FROM HER LIFE AND REIGN I BY I G.A.HENTY (black). **Spine:** plain. **Back cover:** Advertisement for The Victorian Era Series, published by Blackie & Son Limited (black).

References: BB I *Dartt*, p.110, Note (2).

Note: This paperback issue consists of sheets of the first printing, folded and sewn, with drawn-on cover, cut flush to a slightly smaller size than the hardback 94.11. It was probably offered for sale in this form on railway-station bookstalls.

94.4
Queen Victoria I Scenes from her Life and Reign I BY I G.A.HENTY I BLACKIE & SON LIMITED I LONDON GLASGOW DUBLIN BOMBAY

Contents, Binding: As for 94.1.

Reference: PN.

Notes
1. The reprint of 94.1 follows Blackie custom in having an undated title page.
2. There are other small changes in the preliminary pages: (a) following the opening of Blackie's Indian office in 1901, Bombay is added to the addresses in the title-page imprint; (b) the date (January 24, 1901.) has been removed from the end of Henty's Preface on p.(v); (c) folios have been inserted on pages vii and 9.
3. No records have survived. My copy contains a prize label dated 31 January 1907.

95. THE SOLE SURVIVORS

95.1
CHAMBERS'S 'CONTINUOUS' READERS I (three rules with ornament) I The I Sole Survivors I BY I G.A.HENTY I (publisher's device) I W.& R.CHAMBERS, Limited I LONDON AND EDINBURGH I (2-em rule) I Price 6d.
(*Note: the above is front cover used as title page*).

Contents
174 × 119 mm. (1)–96 I no catalogue. Three full-page wash-drawings by W.Boucher, reproduced by halftone blocks printed in black on text pages. Engraved headpiece printed from line block on p.(3).
(1) Blank I (2) frontispiece I (3)–91. text I (92)–96. Notes and Explanations.

Cover (see Note 3)
Red limp cloth, printed black; square back, cut flush; edges plain; plain off-white endpapers.
    Front: used as title p. (see above). **Spine:** plain. **Back:** plain.

Reference: BB.

Notes
1. For other appearances of the story see §4.
2. Two other Henty titles were included in the list of Chambers's 'Continuous' Readers: *On the Spanish Main*, 88.1, and *At Duty's Call*, 103.1. The series started publication in 1899.
3. Apart from the printed price, the cover design is as for the cheaper issue, 95.2, Plate 128.

95.2
CHAMBERS'S 'CONTINUOUS' READERS | (three rules with ornament) | The | Sole Survivors | BY | G.A.HENTY | (publisher's device) | W.& R.CHAMBERS, Limited | LONDON AND EDINBURGH | (2-em rule) | Price 4d.
(Note: above is front cover used as title page).

Contents: As for 95.1.

Cover (see Plate 128)
Red paper, printed black; square back, cut flush; edges plain; no endpapers.
    (1) used as title p. (see above).
    (2), (3), and (4) advertisements.
    (Spine) blank.

References: BL; Bod; PN | *Farmer*, p.63; *Dartt*, p.121.

Notes
1. The Copyright Libraries received the book in 1901.
2. The advertisement on cover page (4) lists seven titles in the series of 'Chambers's "Continuous" Readers'. These include this book (96 pages. Paper cover, 4d.; cloth, 6d.) and *On the Spanish Main* (88 pages. Paper cover, 4d.; cloth, 6d.). The latter book in fact makes 82 pages.

96. IN THE IRISH BRIGADE

96.1
IN THE IRISH BRIGADE | A TALE OF | WAR IN FLANDERS AND SPAIN | BY | G.A.HENTY | Author of "Won by the Sword" "For Name and Fame" | "The Young Colonists" &c. | (8-em rule) | WITH TWELVE ILLUSTRATIONS BY CHARLES M.SHELDON | (8-em rule) | LONDON | BLACKIE & SON, LIMITED, 50 OLD BAILEY, E.C | GLASGOW AND DUBLIN | 1901
(Note: the full-point after E.C *is missing).*

Contents

185 × 131 mm. (i)–(x) | (11)–384 | catalogue 1–32. Twelve full-page wash-drawings by Charles M. Sheldon, reproduced by halftone blocks printed in black on coated paper, unbacked, unfolioed, tipped in. Battle-plan from line block printed on text p.223.

(i) Half-title p. | (ii) advertisement (MR. HENTY'S HISTORICAL TALES.) listing 50 titles | (frontispiece, tipped in) | (iii) title p. | (iv) blank | (v)–vi. Preface | (vii) Contents | (viii) blank | (ix) list of Illustrations | (x) blank | (11)–384. text | 1–32. catalogue.

Binding (see Plate 73)

Green cloth boards, bevelled, blocked black, red, white, buff, and gilt; all edges burnished olive-green; grey endpapers, lined off-white.

Front board: IN THE IRISH | BRIGADE (gilt) above illustration of Irish Jacobite officer holding sword (black, red, white, buff, and gilt). At right: fleur-de-lys (gilt); at foot: BY | G.A.HENTY (black). **Spine:** IN THE | IRISH | BRIGADE (gilt) above illustration of head and shoulders of the same officer (black, red, white, buff, and gilt). At foot: BY | G.A.HENTY (black). **Back board:** plain.

References: BL; Bod; PN | *Farmer*, p.42; *Dartt*, p.84.

Notes

1. The book was published on 23 May 1900 at six shillings. By the end of February 1891 Blackie had sold 7655 copies, and by the end of August 1914 they had sold 2317 more, making a total of 9972 over the fourteen years, at an annual average of 712 copies. The last 12 copies at six shillings were sold in 1915, but Blackie had only those copies left in the autumn of 1914, out of their initial print order, and were ready to consider re-issuing the book in their cheaper series, see 96.2.

2. From the sales figures it seems likely that the standard first print order for Henty's boys' novels had from the early 1890s been set at 10,000 copies, following a number of very successful books. That optimism was generally justified by results. But some books did not sell as well as others, and some did not sell enough even to warrant a reprint in their first-edition format. This book was one of them. When copies of the first impression were running out, Blackie must have had strong doubts about re-issuing it in the cheaper 'New and Popular Edition'. But in the end they did so (see 96.2), probably printing only a small number of copies.

3. As usual with Blackie novels at this period, the earliest issues contain catalogues with no mention of the books for the current year. They give details, with extracts from press reviews, of Henty's books up to and including the previous year (those with title pages dated 1900) but nothing later.

96.2

In the Irish Brigade | A Tale of War in Flanders and Spain | BY | G.A.HENTY | Author of "The Bravest of the Brave" "A Knight of the White Cross" | "At the Point of the Bayonet" "The Tiger of Mysore" &c. | ILLUSTRATED BY CHARLES M.SHELDON | NEW EDITION | BLACKIE AND SON LIMITED | LONDON GLASGOW AND BOMBAY

Contents
183 × 125 mm. (i)–(x) | (11)–384 | no catalogue. Eight full-page wash-drawings by Charles M. Sheldon, reproduced by line blocks printed in black on coated paper, unbacked, unfolioed, tipped in. Battle plan as in 96.1.

(i) Half-title p. | (ii) advertisement (NEW AND POPULAR EDITION OF | G.A.HENTY'S WORKS) listing 39 titles | (frontispiece, tipped in) | (iii) title p. | (iv) blank | (v)–vi. Preface | (vii) Contents | (viii) blank | (ix list of Illustrations | (x) blank | (11)–384. text.

Binding (see Plate 173)
Blue cloth boards, blocked black, red, buff, and gilt; all edges stained olive-green; grey endpapers, lined off-white.

Front board: IN THE IRISH | BRIGADE | BY G.A.HENTY (all gilt) above illustration, framed by black line, of mounted Jacobite soldier with drawn sword (black, red, buff) with signature at lower left corner: J Hassall (black). **Spine:** IN THE | IRISH | BRIGADE | G.A.HENTY (all gilt) above illustration of young Jacobite soldier with hat in hand (black, red, buff). At foot: BLACKIE & SON LTD (black). **Back board:** plain.

Reference: PN.

Notes
1. Re-issued at the end of 1914 in the 'New and Popular Edition', but copies of this title in the cheaper format were not received by the Copyright Libraries. For details of the series see *Facing Death*, 10.6, Notes 2–3.
2. Sales figures barely exist, because all Blackie's records cease at the end of 1917. But they had sold 1317 copies by the end of the first year, at 31 August 1915, and in 1916 and 1917 they sold 300 copies and 188 copies respectively.
3. The book never had a great success by Henty's standards (see 96.1, Note 2), and there must have been some doubt about a further reprint when the first printing of 96.2 was sold out. However it was re-issued after the first war (see *96.3).

*96.3
In the Irish Brigade | A Tale of War in Flanders and Spain | BY | G.A.HENTY | Author of "The Bravest of the Brave" "A Knight of the White Cross" | "At the Point of the Bayonet" &c. | Illustrated | BLACKIE AND SON LIMITED | LONDON GLASGOW AND BOMBAY

Contents
185 × 122 mm. (1)–384 | no catalogue. Frontispiece from watercolour drawing by Frank Gillett, R.I., reproduced by three-colour halftone blocks; four full-page wash-drawings by Charles Sheldon reproduced by halftone blocks printed in black; all on coated paper, unbacked, keyed to text pages, tipped in.

(1) Half-title p. | (2) advertisement (G.A.HENTY'S BOOKS) listing 56 titles | (frontispiece, tipped in) | (3) title p. | (4) printer's imprint (Printed in Great Britain by | Blackie & Son, Limited, Glasgow) | (5) Preface | vi. [roman numerals in error] Preface, continued | (7) Contents | (8) blank | (9) list of Illustrations | (10) blank | (11)–384. text.

Binding: As for 96.2, except (a) dark-green cloth boards, blocked black, red, and buff, with no gilt: lettering on front board all buff, on spine all black; (b) edges plain; (c) plain off-white endpapers.

References: Bod; PN.

Notes
1. For details of Blackie's second cheaper series, 'The New Popular Henty', and subsequent editions of this book, see *Facing Death*, 10.7, Notes 1–3 and 6–8. This title was issued in (1925).
2. All the minor variants of *In the Irish Brigade* in the series are grouped together under this 'generic' heading, *96.3.

97. WITH BULLER IN NATAL

97.1
WITH BULLER IN NATAL I OR, A BORN LEADER I BY I G.A.HENTY I Author of "In the Irish Brigade" "Beric the Briton" "With Cochrane the Dauntless" I "The Dash for Khartoum" &c. I (7-em rule) I WITH TEN ILLUSTRATIONS BY W.RAINEY R.I. I (7-em rule) I LONDON I BLACKIE & SON, LIMITED, 50 OLD BAILEY, E.C. I GLASGOW AND DUBLIN I 1901
(Note: batter after Dauntless, *resulting in smudged quotation marks; the comma after* RAINEY *is missing).*

Contents
186 x 130 mm. (1)–384 I catalogue 1–32. Ten full-page wash-drawings by William Rainey, reproduced by halftone blocks; one full-page map reproduced by line block; all printed in black on coated paper, unbacked, unfolioed, tipped in.
(1) Half-title p. I (2) advertisement (MR. HENTY'S HISTORICAL TALES.) listing 50 titles I (frontispiece, tipped in) I (3) title p. I (4) blank I (5) Preface I (6) blank I (7) Contents I (8) blank I (9) list of Illustrations I (10) blank I (11)–384. text I 1–32. catalogue.

Binding (see Plates 89, 90, 91)
Dark-blue cloth boards, bevelled, blocked dark-brown, light-brown, pink, grey, white, and gilt; all edges burnished olive-green; grey endpapers, lined off-white.
Front board: With Buller I in I Natal (gilt) above illustration of soldier leaning on low rock to fire rifle (dark-brown, light-brown, pink, grey, white). At foot: G.A.Henty (gilt). **Spine:** With I Buller I in I Natal (gilt) above illustration of soldier with rifle (dark-brown, light-brown, pink, white). At foot: G.A.Henty (gilt). **Back board:** plain.

References: BL; Bod; PN I *Farmer*, p.78; *Dartt*, p.157.

Notes
1. *Dartt* declares at the start of his entry that he had a copy of the Scribner edition: it is clear he had not the Blackie edition. His description of the binding case which, as may be seen in the notes that follow, is an important feature in the various issues of this title, is a hotch-potch, with some details taken from the Scribner edition, some from 97.1, and some from 97.4. The most important points to note, so as not to be

misled by his entry, are: (a) none of the Blackie issues had the publisher's name blocked gilt on the spine; (b) on the front board of all issues except 97.4 there is no blocking in green. Other errors relate to colours of blocking, and of endpapers.

2. All issues of this book, including those blocked with variant brasses, were bound in the same dark-blue cloth.

3. The book was published on 13 July 1900 at six shillings. Pre-publication orders, and sales in the year following publication, were high: by the end of February 1901 Blackie had sold 17,342 copies. Thus the book sold more copies in its first year than most of his novels in their entire span of existence at their original published price. Henty declared he took only 24 days to write it (see Appendix I).

4. From evidence accumulated it is clear the book was reprinted twice before the end of 1900, within five months of publication. The reprints are shown as 97.2 and 97.3. It is very likely that the impression used for 97.2 was ordered before the book was put on sale.

5. Sales continued strongly. In the eight years from March 1901 to August 1909, Blackie sold 6552 more copies, and over the final eight years before Blackie's records cease, in August 1917, a further 1914. The grand total, from first publication to the end of Blackie's records, a period of seventeen years, was 25,808 copies, more than Henty had sold of any other book by that date.

6. As usual with Blackie novels of this period, the earliest issues contain catalogues that do not mention the books for the current year (with title pages dated 1901). These catalogues show Henty's books up to and including those for the previous year (dated 1900) but nothing later.

7. Owing to the high rate of sale, copies of *With Buller in Natal* containing the early catalogue are not scarce: they are still found in copies of 97.2, and even in the first issues of 97.3.

97.2

WITH BULLER IN NATAL | OR, A BORN LEADER | BY | G.A.HENTY | Author of "In the Irish Brigade" "Beric the Briton" "With Cochrane the Dauntless' | "The Dash for Khartoum" &c. | (8-em rule) | WITH TEN ILLUSTRATIONS BY W.RAINEY, R.I., AND A MAP | (8-em rule) | LONDON | BLACKIE & SON, LIMITED, 50 OLD BAILEY, E.C. | GLASGOW AND DUBLIN | 1901
(Note: batter after Dauntless *results in loss of one quotation mark).*

Contents: As for 97.1, but see Note 2.

Binding (see Plates 90, 92)
The description in words given for 97.1 almost exactly fits the binding design of 97.2. However, there are considerable differences between the two binding cases, as may be seen by comparing the enlarged details of the illustrations on front boards (Plates 91, 92) and spines (Plate 90).

For 97.2 the brasses have been completely re-cut, and are extremely crude in comparison with those for 97.1. Apart from lack of quality, the later brasses show differences in distribution and use of colour, not easily seen from the black-and-white illustrations.

The main variations are as follows. (a) On the front board the rifle-sling is shown in pink on 97.1 but in light-brown on 97.2. (b) On the front board of 97.1 there is a highlight along the upper part of the soldier's right leg, stretching from the waist to the boot, which is blocked in pink. This is entirely omitted in 97.2. (c) In the same illustration, on 97.1 there is a haversack-strap over the soldier's right shoulder, which runs down to the butt of the rifle and appears again below the butt. This is blocked in pink. In 97.2 this strap is blocked in light-brown, and it runs from the man's shoulder to the butt of the rifle but does not re-appear below the butt. (d) On the spine, the illustration for 97.1 shows the haversack-strap (over the soldier's right shoulder), and the haversack itself, in pink. On 97.2 the strap and haversack are shown in light-brown.

Reference: PN.

Notes

1. There is little to distinguish the content of this issue from 97.1 other than the preliminary pages. The text and the catalogue are unchanged, the latter showing that the reprint was ordered soon after, or even during, the printing of 97.1.

2. It is the revisions to the prelims which make it quite clear that they have been reprinted, and from that fact, taken in conjunction with the sales figures, it must be clear that the sheets of text in this altered binding are not from the same impression as 97.1. The changes made in 97.2, distinguishing it from 97.1, are: (a) on the title page the illustration credit line has had the missing comma after RAINEY inserted, and the reference to the map added after his name; (b) the rules above and below this line are now 8 ems long instead of 7 ems; (b) on p.(ix) the list of Illustrations has a rule added at the foot and, below it, an entry for the map, facing p.48. The battered quotation mark on the title page, after 'Dauntless', has not been replaced.

97.3

Title page: As for 97.2, but with the date removed.

Contents, Binding: As for 97.2.

Reference: PN.

Notes

1. A second reprint was issued in the same style as 97.2, but with the date removed from the title page. No other changes took place and, surprisingly, the earliest issues of this impression contained the very same catalogue that had appeared in 97.1 and 97.2 (see 97.1, Note 6).

2. My copy has an inscription dated Christmas 1900. That, together with the very early publisher's catalogue, makes it almost certain that this impression was being sold in December 1900.

3. There are no available records, but all the evidence points to Blackie having printed three impressions before the end of 1900. Considering the annual sales figures, my guess is that the first was for the standard 10,000 copies (97.11); the second for 5000 copies (97.2); and the third probably for another 5000 copies (97.3). 97.3 would have been on sale until some time in 1903, when sales passed the 20,000 mark and then a further reprint became necessary (see 97.4). Later issues of that impression would of course have contained later catalogues.

4. For this record-breaking book it seems that Blackie paid special regard to their arrangements for the dating of title pages. For earlier books it had apparently been decided that all reprints issued before the end of the calendar year in which the book was first published would have the title pages dated, with the same date as the first impression. That rule was followed with 97.2, but not, apparently, with 97.3. The explanation is probably that 97.3 was ordered so near the end of the year that Blackie was not confident it would reach the shops before 1901.

97.4

Title page: As for 97.3.

Contents: As for 97.3, but 53 titles listed on p.(2).

Binding (see Plate 89)
Dark-blue cloth boards, bevelled, blocked black, brown, green, and gilt; all edges burnished olive-green; grey endpapers, lined off-white.
    Front board: With Buller | in | Natal (gilt) above illustration of soldier leaning on low grass-covered rock to fire rifle (black, brown, green). At foot: G.A.Henty (gilt). **Spine:** With | Buller | in | Natal (gilt) above illustration of soldier with rifle at port position (black, brown, green). At foot: G.A.Henty (gilt). **Back board:** plain.

References: PN | Newbolt, *A.B.M.R.*, June 1977, p.258.

Notes
1. The catalogue does not mention books with title pages dated 1903, but includes books issued in 1901 with title pages dated 1902. My copy is inscribed 30 June 1903. These fact fit my suggestions about dates of print-runs made in 97.3, Note 3.
2. There is no obvious reason for changing the binding design for this book. Probably the original brasses were lost or damaged, and the crude replacements used for 97.2 and 97.3 were made in a hurry. Not only in a hurry, but perhaps also by a brass cutter who was not Blackie's regular supplier.
3. From every point of view the design of the original brasses was in any case unsatisfactory: they gave a very unexciting result, and had to be blocked in six separate colours. The combination of weak design and high cost, coupled with the poor quality of the replacement brasses, probably made Blackie decide to start all over again. The brasses used for 97.4 do produce a slightly stronger result, but their good points are really just that they use only four colours instead of six, and at the same time do not depart far enough from the original design to deceive booksellers and readers into believing they are looking at a different book. All versions of the design were bland and disappointing for Henty's best-selling book.
4. *With Buller in Natal* was never re-issued in either of the cheaper series up to the end of the 1920s.

98. OUT WITH GARIBALDI

98.1

OUT WITH GARIBALDI | A STORY OF | THE LIBERATION OF ITALY | BY | G.A.HENTY | Author of "The Lion of St. Mark" "No Surrender!" "St. George for England" | "Under Wellington's Command" &c. | (18mm. rule) | WITH EIGHT ILLUSTRATIONS BY W.RAINEY, R.I. | (18mm. rule) | LONDON | BLACKIE & SON, LIMITED, 50 OLD BAILEY, E.C | GLASGOW AND DUBLIN | 1901
(Note: the full-point is missing after E.C; the capital C is a wrong font).

Contents

184 x 124 mm. (i)–(x) | (11)–352 | catalogue 1–32. Eight full-page wash-drawings by W.Rainey, reproduced by halftone blocks printed in black on coated paper, unbacked, unfolioed, tipped in. One map and one battle-plan printed from line blocks on text pages.

(i) Half-title p. | (ii) advertisement (MR. HENTY'S HISTORICAL TALES.) listing 50 titles | (frontispiece, tipped in) | (iii) title p. | (iv) blank | (v) Preface | (vi) blank | (vii) Contents | (viii) blank | (ix) list of Illustrations | (x) blank | (11)–352. text | 1–32. catalogue.

Binding (see Plate 79)

Blue cloth boards, blocked black, orange, olive-green, buff, and gilt; all edges burnished olive-green; grey endpapers, lined off-white.

Front board: OUT WITH | GARIBALDI | A STORY | OF THE | LIBERATION | OF ITALY (gilt) above and at right of illustration of man cleaning rifle (black, orange, olive-green, buff). At foot: BY | G.A.HENTY (black). **Spine:** OUT | WITH | GARIBALDI (gilt) above illustration, framed by black line, of Garibaldi (black, orange, buff).At foot: G.A.HENTY (black). **Back board:**, plain.

References: BL; Bod; PN | *Farmer*, p.55; *Dartt*, p.105.

Notes

1. The book was published on 15 August 1900 at five shillings. By the end of February 1901 Blackie had sold 6524 copies, of which the majority were, as usual, accounted for by booksellers' pre-publication orders. Such orders were of course placed only on the strength of Henty's reputation and not on any assessment of the novel itself. At the end of August 1917, when Blackie's figures come to an end, they record the sale of only 2389 more copies: that figure represents an average annual sale, over sixteen years, of only 149 books. In the seventeen years since publication the total sales of the book amounted to 8916 copies, out of a probable first printing of about 10,000. There must have been many copies left unsold in 1917: the sales in the two previous years had dwindled to a mere 83 copies and 85 copies respectively. There are no records to show whether the first edition ever sold out; certainly the book was by Henty's standards a disaster.

2. It is remarkable that both this title and its immediate predesessor, *With Buller in Natal*, should fail to appear in either of Blackie's cheaper series. The first because it sold too well for a price reduction to be considered, the second because demand was not sufficient to sell the first impression.

3. The publisher's address on the title page is printed with a wrong-font capital C at the end of the second line. The type used for the book is a 'modern face', but this final C is in Baskerville, an 'old face' in which the capital C has two serifs. The difference may be clearly seen by comparison with the correctly-set capital C in BLACKIE at the beginning of the same line.

4. As usual with Blackie novels at this period, the earliest issues contain catalogues with no mention of the books for the current season (with title pages dated 1901). They give details, with quotations from press reviews, of Henty's books up to and including the previous year.

99. AT THE POINT OF THE BAYONET

99.1

AT THE | POINT OF THE BAYONET | A TALE OF THE MAHRATTA WAR | BY | G.A.HENTY | Author of "With Buller in Natal" "For Name and Fame" "In the Irish Brigade" | "No Surrender!" &c. | (8-em rule) | WITH TWELVE ILLUSTRATIONS BY WAL PAGET | (8-em rule) | LONDON | BLACKIE & SON, LIMITED, 50 OLD BAILEY, E.C. | GLASGOW AND DUBLIN | 1902

Contents

185 x 130 mm. (i)–(x) | (11)–384 | catalogue 1–32. Twelve full-page wash-drawings by Wal Paget, reproduced by halftone blocks printed in black on coated paper, unbacked, unfolioed, tipped in. One old wood-engraving (see Note 3), and two battle-plans, reproduced by line blocks and printed on text pages.

(i) Half-title p. | (ii) advertisement (MR. HENTY'S HISTORICAL TALES.) listing 50 titles | (frontispiece, tipped in) | (iii) title p. | (iv) blank | (v)–vi. Preface | (vii) Contents | (viii) blank | (ix) list of Illustrations | (x) blank | (11)–384. text | 1–32. catalogue.

Binding (see Plate 56)

Green cloth boards, bevelled, blocked black, red, white, and gilt; all edges burnished olive-green; grey endpapers, lined off-white.

Front board: At the Point of | the Bayonet (gilt) above illustration of British soldier running with rifle, bayonet fixed (black, red, white). At right: A Tale of the | Mahratta War (black). At foot: by | G.A.Henty. (white). **Spine:** At the | Point of | the | Bayonet (gilt) above illustration, half-framed with black line, of turbaned Indian with shield (black, red, white, and gilt). At foot: G.A.Henty. (white). **Back board:** plain.

References: BL; Bod; PN | *Farmer*, p.7; *Dartt*, p.9, *Companion*, p.2.

Notes

1. The book was published on 6 April 1901 at six shillings. By the end of February 1902 Blackie had sold 7905 copies, and eleven years later, by the end of August 1913 they had sold 2209 more. That gives an average annual sale, over the twelve years, of 843 copies. From what I believe to have been one single print order of 10,000 copies, there were then sixteen copies left. They were all sold in 1913, the year in which the book was re-issued in the cheaper edition (see 99.2).

2. The total number of copies sold at six shillings was 10,130, but more would have been actually printed, allowing for author's copies, review copies and so on: printers always aim at producing a few copies over the round figure ordered.

3. An old wood-engraving of the Rajah's Palace, Bhurtpoor, is printed on p.345, no doubt from an electro. The plate has been trimmed to fit the width of the type area.

4. As usual with Blackie novels at this period, the earliest issues contain catalogues with no mention of the books for the current year (with title pages dated 1902). They give details, with extracts from press reviews, of Henty's books up to and including the previous year.

99.2

At the | Point of the Bayonet | A Tale of the Mahratta War | BY | G.A.HENTY | Author of "With Buller in Natal" "For Name and Fame" "In the Irish Brigade" | "No Surrender!" &c. | ILLUSTRATED BY WAL PAGET | NEW EDITION | BLACKIE AND SON LIMITED | LONDON GLASGOW AND BOMBAY

Contents

185 × 126 mm. (1)–384 | catalogue 1–16. Eight full-page wash-drawings by Wal Paget, reproduced by halftone blocks printed in sepia on coated paper, unbacked, unfolioed, tipped in. Line illustrations as in 99.1.

(1) Half-title p. | (2) advertisement (NEW AND POPULAR EDITION OF | G.A.HENTY'S WORKS) listing 39 titles | (frontispiece, tipped in) | (3) title p. | (4) blank | 5. Preface | vi. [roman numerals in error] Preface, continued | 7. Contents | (8) blank | 9. list of Illustrations | (10) blank | 11–384. text, with printer's imprint at foot of p.384 (PRINTED IN GREAT BRITAIN | At the Villafield Press, Glasgow, Scotland) | 1–16. catalogue.

Binding (see Note 1)

Green cloth boards, blocked black, blue, buff, and gilt; edges plain; grey endpapers, lined off-white.

Front board: AT THE POINT | OF THE BAYONET | BY G.A.HENTY (all gilt) above illustration, framed by black line, of turbaned figure looking through archway at soldier (black, blue, buff); with signature at foot: J Hassall (black). **Spine:** AT THE POINT | OF THE | BAYONET | G.A.HENTY (all gilt) above illustration, framed by black line, of soldier with rifle (black, blue, buff). At foot: BLACKIE & SON LTD (black). **Back board:** plain.

References: BL; Bod.

Notes

1. Re-issued, late 1913, in the 'New and Popular Edition'. For details see *Facing Death*, 10.6, Notes 2–3; for examples of the series binding style, Plates 172–173.
2. In this edition Blackie sold 1850 copies by the end of August 1914, and they had sold 1044 more by the same date in 1917. At that point their records cease, but they were averaging sales of 724 copies a year over those four years, and the book would certainly have continued to sell for some time longer. The grand total of copies sold, from 1901 to 1917, at both prices, is 13,024.
3. From 1913 Blackie printed all issues of the 'New and Popular Edition' without dates on the title pages, first issues and reprints alike: the first issue in this edition of *At the Point of the Bayonet* was therefore undated.
4. This title has the edges of the leaves plain. First issues of books in the 'New and Popular Edition' normally had edges stained olive-green, but since 1912 Blackie had begun to introduce economies. They became more obvious during the war years.

*99.3

At the | Point of the Bayonet | A Tale of the Mahratta War | BY | G.A.HENTY | Author of "At Agincourt" "Facing Death" | "Maori and Settler" "The Treasure of the Incas" &c. | Illustrated | BLACKIE AND SON LIMITED | LONDON GLASGOW AND BOMBAY

Contents
185 × 123 mm. (1)–384 | advertisement (1)–(2). Frontispiece from watercolour drawing by unknown artist, reproduced by three-colour halftone blocks; four full-page wash-drawings by Wal Paget reproduced by halftone blocks printed in black; all on coated paper, unbacked, keyed to text, tipped in. Line illustrations as in 99.1.

(1) Half-title p. | (2) advertisement (G.A.HENTY'S BOOKS) listing 56 titles | (frontispiece, tipped in) | (3) title p. | (4) printer's imprint (Printed in Great Britain by | Blackie & Son, Limited, Glasgow) | 5. Preface | vi. [roman numerals in error] Preface, continued | 7. Contents | (8) blank | (9) list of Illustrations | (10) blank | 11–384. text | (1)–(2) advertisement (THE NEW POPULAR HENTY) listing 60 titles.

Binding: As for 99.2, except (a) red cloth boards, blocked black, blue, and buff, with no gilt: lettering on front board all buff, on spine all black; (b) spine lettering re-arranged (AT THE | POINT OF | THE | BAYONET | G.A.HENTY); (c) plain off-white endpapers.

Reference: PN.

Notes
1. For details of Blackie's second cheaper series, 'The New Popular Henty', and subsequent editions of the book, see *Facing Death*, 10.7, Notes 1–3 and 6–8.
2. The single leaf of advertisements, tipped on to the end of the last gathering, was as usual printed on a heavier featherweight than that used for the text.
3. All the minor variants of *At the Point of the Bayonet* in the series are grouped together under this 'generic' heading, *99.3.

100. TO HERAT AND CABUL

100.1
TO HERAT AND CABUL | A STORY OF | THE FIRST AFGHAN WAR | BY | G.A.HENTY | Author of "With Buller in Natal" "At the Point of the Bayonet" | "The Bravest of the Brave" "Won by the Sword" &c. | (6-em rule) | WITH EIGHT ILLUSTRATIONS BY CHARLES M.SHELDON | AND A MAP | (6-em rule) | LONDON | BLACKIE & SON, LIMITED, 50 OLD BAILEY, E.C. | GLASGOW AND DUBLIN | 1902

Contents
185 × 123 mm. (i)–(x) | (11)–352 | catalogue 1–32. Eight full-page wash drawings by Charles M. Sheldon, reproduced by halftone blocks printed in black on coated paper, unbacked, unfolioed, tipped in. Map printed from line block on coated paper as a double-spread, unbacked, guarded in between pages 50 and 51.

(i) Half-title p. | (ii) advertisement (MR. HENTY'S HISTORICAL TALES.) listing 53 titles | (frontispiece, tipped in) | (iii) title p. | (iv) blank | (v)–vi. Preface | (vii) Contents | (viii) blank | (ix) list of Illustrations | (x) blank | (11)–352. text | 1–32. catalogue.

Binding (see Plate 85)
Blue cloth boards, blocked black, white, red, grey, and gilt; all edges burnished olive-green; grey endpapers, lined off-white.

Front board: TO HERAT | AND CABUL (gilt) above illustration of Afghan warrior with long gun (black, white, red, grey). At right: A STORY OF THE | FIRST AFGHAN WAR (gilt) | BY | G.A.HENTY (white). **Spine:** TO | HERAT | AND | CABUL (gilt) above illustration of head and shoulders of Afghan tribesman (black, white, red, grey, and gilt). At foot: BY | G.A.HENTY (gilt). **Back board:** plain.

References: BL; Bod; PN | *Farmer*, p.71; *Dartt*, p.139.

Notes

1. The book was published on 28 June 1901 at five shillings. By the end of August 1902 Blackie had sold 7033 copies, a figure that included the booksellers' pre-publication orders. Fifteen years later, in 1917, when their records come to an end, they had sold only 2123 more, at a yearly average of a mere 142 copies. In the sixteen years the total sales were 9152 copies, at a yearly average of 572. By Henty's standards these are poor figures. The book was not reprinted until after the first war, in the second cheaper series (see *100.2).

2. It is clear from the sales figures for this and other titles that during the last five years of his life Henty's reputation remained high in the minds of booksellers, and that caused them to go on placing large pre-publication orders with Blackie. But from the decreasing sales of all but a few of his books it is equally clear that in spite of some encouraging press-notices his popularity was waning. It cannot, nevertheless, be concluded that Henty's skills were failing. His most successful book of all, *With Buller in Natal*, had been published only the previous year, and in this year, 1901, he was still to publish *With Roberts to Pretoria* and *With Kitchener in the Soudan*. Those three, with a dozen of his other most popular novels, half of them written as far back as the 1880s, were each still selling over 250 copies a year at the time of the first war.

*100.2

To Herat and Cabul | A Story of the First Afghan War | BY | G.A.HENTY | Author of "At the Point of the Bayonet" "The Bravest of the Brave" | "Won by the Sword" &c. | Illustrated | BLACKIE AND SON LIMITED | LONDON GLASGOW AND BOMBAY

Contents

185 × 123 mm. (1)–352 | no catalogue. Frontispiece from watercolour drawing by Frank Gillett, reproduced by three-colour halftone blocks; four full-page wash-drawings by Charles M. Sheldon reproduced by halftone blocks printed in black; all on coated paper, unbacked, tipped in.

(1) Half-title p. | (2) advertisement (G.A.HENTY'S BOOKS) listing 56 titles | (frontispiece, tipped in) | (3) title p. | (4) printer's imprint (Printed in Great Britain by | Blackie & Son, Limited, Glasgow) | (5) Preface | vi. [roman numerals in error] Preface, continued | (7) Contents | (8) blank | (9) list of Illustrations | (10) blank | 11–352. text.

Binding (see Note 1)

Blue cloth boards, blocked black, red, light-brown, and white; edges plain; plain off-white endpapers.

Front board: TO HERAT | AND CABUL | A STORY OF THE | FIRST

AFGHAN WAR (all black) | BY | G.A.HENTY (white) above and at right of illustration of Afghan warrior with long gun (black, red, light-brown, white). **Spine:** TO | HERAT | AND | CABUL (black) above illustration of head and shoulders of Afghan tribesman (black, red, light-brown, white). Beneath this: BY | G.A.HENTY (black). At foot: BLACKIE & SON LTD (black). **Back board:** plain.

References: BL; Bod; AK.

Notes

1. Re-issued 1925 in 'The New Popular Henty' series, a name very close to that of Blackie's first cheaper series begun in 1903, 'The New and Popular Edition', in which this title never appeared (see 100.1, Note 1). For details of the second series, and later editions, see *Facing Death*, 10.7, Notes 1–3 and 6–8. Examples of the series binding style are at Plates 174–175.

2. All the minor variants of *To Herat and Cabul* in the series are grouped together under this 'generic' heading, *100.2.

101. WITH ROBERTS TO PRETORIA

101.1

WITH ROBERTS TO PRETORIA | A TALE OF | THE SOUTH AFRICAN WAR | BY | G.A.HENTY | Author of "With Buller in Natal" "In the Irish Brigade" "For Name and Fame" | "With Cochrane the Dauntless" &c. | (17mm. rule) | WITH TWELVE ILLUSTRATIONS BY WILLIAM RAINEY, R.I. | AND A MAP | (17mm. rule) | LONDON | BLACKIE & SON, LIMITED, 50 OLD BAILEY, E.C. | GLASGOW AND DUBLIN | 1902

Contents

187 x 131 mm. (1)–384 | catalogue 1–32. Twelve full-page wash-drawings by William Rainey, reproduced by halftone blocks; one map reproduced by line block; all printed in black on coated paper, unbacked, unfolioed, tipped in.

(1) Half-title p. | (2) blank | (frontispiece, tipped in) | (3) title p. | (4) blank | 5. Preface | vi. [roman numerals in error] Preface, continued | 7. Contents | (8) blank | 9. list of Illustrations | (10) blank | 11–384. text | 1–32. catalogue.

Binding (see Plate 95)

Red cloth boards, bevelled, blocked black, white, brown, and gilt; all edges burnished olive-green; grey endpapers, lined off-white.

Front board: WITH ROBERTS TO | PRETORIA | G: A: HENTY: (all white) above and at right of illustration of officer in topi with drawn sword, against background half-framed by black line (black, white, brown, and gilt) and with artist's initials, J.A.D. (black) at left, in black rectangle (see Note 4). **Spine:** : WITH : | ROBERTS | : : TO : : | PRETORIA (gilt) above illustration of head and shoulders of soldier with topi and with bayonet fixed (black, white, brown, and gilt). At foot: : G : A : HENTY : (gilt). **Back board:** plain.

References: BL; Bod; PN | *Farmer*, p.82; *Dartt*, p.162, *Companion*, p.34.

Notes

1. The book was published on 15 August 1901 at six shillings. A year later, at the end of August 1902 Blackie had sold 15,433 copies: this figure, for the first year's sales, was the second highest among Henty's novels, being beaten only by *With Buller in Natal* (17,342 copies). Sales over the next seven years were 5532 copies, giving an annual average of 2620 for the eight-year period. In the following eight years, to the end of August 1917 when records cease, 2766 more copies were sold. The grand total of sales from 1901 to 1917, at six shillings, was 23,731 copies (*With Buller in Natal*, published a year earlier, sold 25,808 by the same date).

2. The book remained in its first-edition format throughout the period covered by Blackie's archive, and was not re-issued in the cheaper series. It was one of the Henty titles that were reprinted before publication, and it is possible that two reprints were put in hand before the end of 1901. Only one can be positively so identified, the title page still carrying the date (see 101.2).

3. As usual with Blackie novels at this period, the earliest issues contain catalogues with no mention of the books for the current season (with title pages dated 1902). These catalogues show Henty's books up to and including those for the previous year (dated 1901) but nothing later. In the case of this book, copies with the early catalogue are not scarce, owing to the large numbers sold in the first year: the same catalogues are found in copies of 101.2.

4. The signature on the front of the binding case may be that of J.A. Darbyshire (see Appendix IV, Part 2).

101.2

Title page: As for 101.1.

Contents

186 × 131 mm. (1)–384 | catalogue 1–32. Illustrations as for 101.1.

(1) Half-title p. | (2) advertisement (MR. HENTY'S HISTORICAL TALES.) listing 53 titles | (frontispiece, tipped in) | (3) title p. | (4) blank | 5. Preface | vi. [roman numerals in error] Preface, continued | 7. Contents | (8) blank | 9. list of Illustrations | (10) blank | 11–384. text | 1–32. catalogue.

Binding: As for 101.1.

References: PN | *Dartt*, p.162, *Companion*, p.34.

Notes

1. Initial sales (see 101.1, Note 1) ensured a quick reprint. By Blackie's custom, this impression made within the calendar year of first publication had the date repeated on the title page.

2. The addition of the publisher's advertisement on p.(2), previously blank, is the only change from 101.1. It is conceivable there was more than one reprint with dated title page, either with or without the addition on p.(2): thus making a possible total of three pre-publication impressions, as were made of *With Buller in Natal*. Unfortunately Blackie's surviving records show only sales figures, not print orders.

*101.3

With I Roberts to Pretoria I A Tale of the South African War I BY I G.A.HENTY I Author of "With Buller in Natal" "In the Irish Brigade" "For Name and Fame" I "With Cochrane the Dauntless" &c. I (17mm. rule) I WITH TWELVE ILLUSTRATIONS BY WILLIAM RAINEY, R.I. I AND A MAP I (17mm. rule) I BLACKIE AND SON LIMITED I LONDON GLASGOW AND BOMBAY

Contents

182 x 130 mm. (1)–384 I no catalogue. Illustrations as for 101.1.

(1) Half-title p. I (2) advertisement (HENTY'S TALES OF BRITISH HISTORY.) listing 38 titles I (frontispiece, tipped in) I (3) title p. I (4) blank I 5. Preface I vi. [roman numerals in error] Preface, continued I (7) Contents I (8) blank I (9) list of Illustrations I (10) blank I 11–384. text, with printer's imprint at foot of p.384 (PRINTED IN GREAT BRITAIN I At the Villafield Press, Glasgow, Scotland).

Binding: As for 101.1.

Reference: CH.

Notes

1. Later reprints were in the style of 101.2, but with no date on the title page. After 1910 Dublin was omitted from the imprint, and for very late issues the title page was completely reset in the typographical style of books in the 'New and Popular Edition', in which this title never appeared.

2. The example given here is one of the late issues, with the reset title page, and with the advertisement on p.(2) now limited to books dealing with British history. Blackie's imprint as printer now appears on the final page.

3. A number of issues appeared in the first-edition format: the undated reprints are all grouped together under this 'generic' heading, *101.3.

4. The book was not re-issued in either of the two cheaper series, demand remaining strong enough for Blackie to maintain the original six-shilling price.

102. IN THE HANDS OF THE CAVE-DWELLERS

102.1

In the I Hands of the Cave-Dwellers I BY I G.A.HENTY I Author of "With Roberts to Pretoria" "Won by the Sword" I "To Herat and Cabul" &c. I ILLUSTRATED BY WAT. MILLER I BLACKIE AND SON LIMITED I LONDON GLASGOW AND DUBLIN

Contents

180 x 123 mm. (1)–174 (see Note 5) I catalogue 1–32. Two full-page wash-drawings by Wat. Miller, reproduced by halftone blocks printed in black on coated paper, unbacked, unfolioed, tipped in.

(1) Half-title p. I (2) advertisement (HISTORICAL TALES BY G.A.HENTY) listing 28 titles (see Note 4) I (frontispiece, tipped in) I (3) title p. I (4) blank I 5. Contents I (6) blank I 7–174. text I 1–32. catalogue.

Binding (see Plate 117)
Blue cloth boards, blocked black, orange, grey, and gilt; edges plain; grey endpapers, lined white.
    Front board: IN THE HANDS ǀ OF THE ǀ CAVE ǀ DWELLERS (gilt) above illustration, partly framed by black lines, of Indian against background of landscape with wigwams (black, orange, grey). At lower right corner: BY ǀ G.A.HENTY (orange). **Spine:** IN THE ǀ HANDS ǀ OF THE ǀ CAVE ǀ DWELLERS (gilt) above illustration of white man with rifle (black, orange, grey). At foot: BY ǀ G.A.HENTY (orange). **Back board:** plain.

References: BL; Bod; PN ǀ *Farmer*, p.40; *Dartt*, p.82. *Companion*, p.19.

Notes
1. The story was first published in the *Boy's Own Paper*, in eight instalments, from 12 May to 7 July, 1900.
2. This first Blackie edition was published on 18 July 1902. It is Henty's only story to be published by Blackie without a dated title page for the first edition. *Do Your Duty* had no title-page date when first published, but the story had previously appeared in book form, in the dated first edition of *Yarns on the Beach*, 1886 (25.1). *Dartt* (p.82) and his *Companion* (p.19) refer to a copy in the British Library dated 1903, but it was a figment of his imagination.
3. First publication in book form was by Harper & Brothers, New York, in 1900. It was the only Henty title published in the United States before publication in the United Kingdom. Possibly that is the reason for the undated Blackie title page.
4. There are two versions of the prelims in this first UK edition, and I think it probable that they were both printed simultaneously on the same machine. Both versions have lists of 28 titles on p.(2), but the list in each is completely different from that in the other. Between them they list 56 books by Henty.
    Although bound in 16-page sections the book was printed in sheets of 32 pages. Five of them made 160 pages, and for this book there would have been an odd half-sheet (of 16 pages) left over. It would be normal practice in such a situation to make a set of duplicate stereotype plates, and to print the 16 pages two-up, so as to make another full sheet for printing on the same machine, instead of having to put the half-sheet on a smaller machine (see Appendix III, Part 1). If the preliminary pages were printed two-up, then an opportunity arose to have two versions of the publisher's advertisement on p.(2), and in this way to include the whole of Henty's now very long list of novels.
5. A strange technical 'fault' in the make-up of this book, uncharacteristic of Blackie, seems to have been deliberately made. The final text signature consists of 14 pages instead of the expected 16. The signature marks show that the section was planned normally as sixteen pages (half of one of the 32-page sheets referred to in Note 4), but the final leaf (which would have formed pp.(175)–(176)) was removed. That meant that what would have been the conjugate leaf (pp.161–162) had to be tipped on at the start of the gathering. Normal practice would have been simply to leave two blank pages at the end of the text. All copies examined are the same: perhaps Blackie had printed something on the final leaf which had to be withdrawn.
6. *Dartt*, p.83, reports 'A later Blackie'. A careful examination of this entry shows it to be a description of a reprint of 102.1, with lettering in brown instead of gilt. Dartt relied on information sent by enthusiasts in Britain or perhaps, in this case, in

Canada. The words used by two correspondents to describe the same pictorial blocking were different enough to make him think he was listing two separate editions. The result has caused problems for Dartt's readers, but would probably not have happened had he had a copy of the book.

*102.2

Later issues of 101.1 followed, with lettering on the front board, and later on the spine as well, blocked in pigment instead of gilt. The usual small changes appeared in reprints, mainly to the publisher's imprint, and the addition of Blackie's imprint as printers. Their Indian office was opened in 1901 although Bombay did not appear regularly in the imprint until 1906; Dublin was omitted after 1910.

The book was reprinted on featherweight papers, some bulkier than others: consequently the spine brasses often appeared too narrow.

As it is undated, collectors have difficulty in identifying the first issues (i.e. 102.1). These are the basic distinguishing features: (a) the title (but not the author's name) on both spine and front board are in gilt; (b) the spine brasses fit neatly, without margins at the sides of the lettering (spine width is 30mm.); (c) the advertisement on p.(2), headed 'HISTORICAL TALES BY G.A.HENTY' lists 28 titles; (d) the last line on the title page reads: LONDON GLASGOW AND DUBLIN.

All others are later issues or reprints, and they are here grouped together under this 'generic' heading, *102.2.

102.3

In the Hands of the | Cave-Dwellers | BY | G.A.HENTY | Author of "The Cat of Bubastes" "Won by the Sword" | "To Herat and Cabul" &c. | (publisher's device) | BLACKIE & SON LIMITED | LONDON AND GLASGOW

Contents
183 x 128 mm. (1)–(176) | no catalogue. Frontispiece from watercolour drawing by unknown artist, reproduced by three-colour halftone blocks printed on coated paper, unbacked, tipped in.

(1) Half-title p. | (2) Blackie's addresses | (frontispiece, tipped in) | (3) title p. | (4) printer's imprint (Printed in Great Britain by | Blackie & Son, Limited, Glasgow) | (5) Contents | (6) blank | 7–174. text | (175)–(176) blank.

Binding (see Note 5)
Possibly designed by Charles Rennie Mackintosh. Buff grained-paper boards (imitating cloth), blocked blue; edges plain; plain off-white endpapers.

Front board: IN THE HANDS | OF THE CAVE- | DWELLERS (blue) in rectangular panel within over-all geometric pattern of (?) abstract swallows (blue). **Spine:** IN THE | HANDS OF | THE CAVE- | DWELLERS (blue) in panel cutting across pattern as on front board (blue). In small rectangle at foot: BLACKIE | & SON . LTD (blue). **Back board:** plain.

References: NS; PN.

Notes
1. Part of a 1s.6d. series issued in the 1920s, 'Blackie's Library for Boys and Girls', not to be confused with 'The Boys' and Girls' Bookshelf' (see Appendix V).

2. *Dartt*, p.83, Note (1), should be ignored, as there was no such thing as a 'Library of Boys and Girls and English Authors'. He was confusing two separate series, as might be inferred from such an extraordinary name, and does not appear to have come across the editions in 'Blackie's Library for Boys and Girls'.

3. The text is printed from the type set for the first impression, or stereos taken from it. Only pages (1)–(4) have been reset.

4. The frontispiece illustration is used also for the dust-wrapper. On the back is a list of 50 books in the 'Library for Boys and Girls', including four Henty titles.

5. It has been suggested that this binding for the series was designed by Charles Rennie Mackintosh: see *Tales from Henty*, 57.6, Note 5, and Plate 111.

103. AT DUTY'S CALL

103.1

CHAMBERS'S 'CONTINUOUS' READERS (double underlining) | At Duty's Call | BY | G.A.HENTY | (publisher's device) | W.& R.CHAMBERS, LIMITED | LONDON AND EDINBURGH

Contents

174 x 119 mm. (1)–32 | no catalogue. No illustrations.

(1) title p. | (2) advertisement (CHAMBERS'S 'CONTINUOUS' READERS) listing 10 titles (see Note 4) | (3)–30. text | (31)–32. Notes and Explanations, with printer's imprint at foot of p.32 (Edinburgh: Printed by W.& R.Chambers, Limited.).

Cover (see Note 1)

(1) CHAMBERS'S 'CONTINUOUS' READERS | (three rules with vine-ornaments) | At Duty's Call | BY | G.A.HENTY | (publisher's device) | (at left) W.& R.CHAMBERS, | LIMITED, LONDON | AND EDINBURGH | (at right) Paper, 2d. | Can also be had in | Cloth, price 3d.

(2), (3), and (4) advertisements

(Spine) blank.

References: BL; Bod.

Notes

1. The copies in the Copyright Libraries, received in 1902, are in paper covers; I have not found a copy in limp cloth as advertised on p.1 of the cover. The main part of the cover design follows that of *The Sole Survivors*, 95.2, Plate 128.

2. 'At Duty's Call' was published in *Brains and Bravery*, Chambers, 1903 (§2, 134.1). It was previously issued as a pamphlet for presentation to members of The Boys' Brigade at Christmas, 1890, under the title 'Duty'. In 1903, soon after Henty's death, and in his memory, The Boys' Brigade serialised the story, with the same title, in *The Brigadier* (see §3 and §4).

3. *Dartt*, (p.9), describing the British Library copy, incorrectly included Paris in the imprint on p.1 of the cover. The imprint is partly obscured by a paper label giving the shelfmark, and Dartt guessed at the hidden word. It is in fact LIMITED, as might be deduced from the title-page imprint, PARIS being a wild flight of fancy!

4. Two other Henty titles are in the list of Chambers's 'Continuous' Readers on p.(2): *On the Spanish Main* (88.1) and *The Sole Survivors* (95.1). The series started publication in 1899, and included Readers at 2d., 3d. and 4d. in paper covers (in cloth at 3d., 5d. and 6d. respectively. The two titles mentioned here were in the highest price range.

104. WITH KITCHENER IN THE SOUDAN

104.1

WITH | KITCHENER IN THE SOUDAN | A STORY OF | ATBARA AND OMDURMAN | BY | G.A.HENTY | Author of "With Roberts to Pretoria" "The Lion of St. Mark" "The Bravest of the Brave" | "With Wolfe in Canada" &c. | (7-em rule) | WITH TEN ILLUSTRATIONS BY WILLIAM RAINEY, R.I. | AND THREE MAPS | (7-em rule) | LONDON | BLACKIE & SON, LIMITED, 50 OLD BAILEY, E.C. | GLASGOW AND DUBLIN | 1903

Contents

185 × 130 mm. (1)–384 | catalogue 1–32. Ten full-page wash-drawings by William Rainey, reproduced by halftone blocks; one map and two battle plans reproduced by line blocks; all printed in black on coated paper, unbacked, unfolioed, tipped in.

(1) Half-title p. | (2) advertisement (HISTORICAL STORIES BY G.A.HENTY) listing 28 titles | (frontispiece, tipped in) | (3) title p. | (4) blank | 5. Preface | vi. [roman numerals in error] Preface, continued | 7. Contents | (8) blank | 9. list of Illustrations | (10) blank | 11–384. text | 1–32. catalogue.

Binding (see Plate 93)

Red cloth boards, bevelled, blocked black, buff, and gilt; all edges burnished olive-green; grey endpapers, lined off-white.

Front board: WITH | KITCHENER | IN THE | SOUDAN | BY G.A.HENTY (all gilt) above and at left of illustration of Egyptian standard-bearer (black, buff, and gilt), all framed by black line, and with monogram of artist at lower right corner: JH (black) (see Note 2). **Spine:** WITH | KITCHENER | IN THE | SOUDAN | BY | G.A.HENTY (all gilt) above illustration of British officer in topi (black, buff). **Back board:** plain.

References: BL; Bod; PN | *Farmer*, p.80; *Dartt*, p.160, *Companion*, p.34.

Notes

1. The book was published on 17 May 1902 at six shillings. By the end of August 1903 Blackie had sold 12,664 copies, and thirteen years later, by the same date in 1916, 4934 more. In that year the book was re-issued in the 'New and Popular Edition' (see 104.2). Blackie's records cease at the end of August 1917, but show that the last 82 copies of the six-shilling edition were sold in that year.

2. John Hassall's initials are on the front board: he designed most bindings for the 'New and Popular Edition', which first appeared in the year this book was published.

3. *Farmer*, p.81, reports two issues of the book with differing catalogues. Some had the 1902 catalogues (advertising books up to and including 1901), the normal and expected catalogue for first issues of books dated 1903. Others had catalogues for the previous year. This was because *With Kitchener in the Soudan* was printed very early in the year, perhaps February or March, in time for publication in mid-May. The new year's catalogues would not by then have been printed.

4. *Dartt* follows *Farmer*, word for word, reporting 'two Blackie issues'. They both seem unaware that most of Henty's books had numerous issues, not just two, each containing the catalogue current at the time of binding (see Appendix III, Parts 1 and 2). The rest of his entry confuses Blackie and Scribner editions.

5. I have a copy with a catalogue advertising *By Conduct and Courage*, with press reviews, at the head of the list of Henty's books. This catalogue would have been printed in 1905, which means that at that date Blackie were still selling copies of *With Kitchener in the Soudan* from the first impression, or at least a reprint issued before the end of 1902. By the end of August 1905 they had sold 13,927 copies, so the number printed with dated title pages must have been close to 15,000.

6. During the course of printing, the second full-point in 'R.I.', following William Rainey's name on the title page, fell out of the forme. It seems to have happened early in the print-run as most copies examined show this fault.

104.2

With Kitchener in I the Soudan I A Story of Atbara and Omdurman I BY I G.A.HENTY I Author of "With Roberts to Pretoria" "St. George for England" I "With Wolfe in Canada" &c. I ILLUSTRATED BY WILLIAM RAINEY, R.I. I AND THREE MAPS I BLACKIE AND SON LIMITED I LONDON GLASGOW AND BOMBAY

Contents
185 × 125 mm. (1)–384 I no catalogue. Six full-page wash drawings by William Rainey reproduced by halftone blocks; one map and two battle-plans reproduced by line blocks; all printed in black on coated paper, unbacked, unfolioed, tipped in.

(1) Half-title p. I (2) advertisement (NEW AND POPULAR EDITION OF I G.A.HENTY'S WORKS) listing 45 titles I (frontispiece, tipped in) I (3) title p. I (4) blank I 5. Preface I vi. [roman numerals in error] Preface, continued I (7) Contents I (8) blank I (9) list of Illustrations I (10) blank I 11–384. text; printer's imprint on p.384 (PRINTED IN GREAT BRITAIN I At the Villafield Press, Glasgow, Scotland).

Binding (see Note 3)
Red cloth boards, blocked black, buff, and gilt; edges plain; grey endpapers, lined off-white.
   Front board: WITH I KITCHENER I IN THE I SOUDAN I BY G.A.HENTY (all black) above and at left of illustration of Egyptian standard-bearer (black, buff) all framed by black line, and with monogram of artist at lower right corner: JH (black). **Spine:** WITH I KITCHENER I IN THE I SOUDAN I BY I G.A.HENTY (all gilt) above illustration of British officer in topi (black, buff). **Back board:** plain.

Reference: PN.

Notes
1. The book was issued in 1916 in the 'New and Popular Edition'. For details of the series see *Facing Death*, 10.6, Notes 2–3.
2. Blackie's records end in August 1917, and show that 2229 copies of 104.2 were sold in the year to that date. This title and *St. George for England* were the last titles

in the 'New and Popular Edition' recorded by Blackie, but *Bonnie Prince Charlie* and *In the Reign of Terror* were in fact added to it the following year.

3. John Hassall designed binding cases for most of the books in this series, which began in 1903. First publication of *With Kitchener in the Soudan* was as late as 1902, however, and Hassall had designed the first binding. So his original design was retained for this edition and also for the second cheap edition (see 104.3).

4. First issues in this series customarily had dated title pages. But from 1913 no title pages were dated: it is often not easy to distinguish first issues. Likely clues are dated inscriptions, and for some titles the use of gilt (see Note 5).

5. The use of gold was restricted in wartime. First it went from front boards, later from spines as well. By 1916 no gold was used on front boards, and for this book the golden setting sun, in the front-board illustration for 104.1, has disappeared, and lettering is now in black. Later issues lost the gold blocking on the spine also.

*104.3
Title page: As for 104.2.

Contents

186 × 125 mm. (1)–384 ∣ no catalogue. Frontispiece from watercolour drawing reproduced by three-colour halftone blocks; four full-page wash-drawings reproduced by halftone blocks printed in black; all illustrations by William Rainey; one map and two battle-plans reproduced by line blocks; all printed on coated paper, unbacked, unfolioed, tipped in.

(1) Half-title p. ∣ (2) advertisement (G.A.HENTY'S BOOKS Uniform with this Edition) listing 18 titles ∣ (frontispiece, tipped in) ∣ (3) title p. ∣ (4) blank ∣ 5. Preface ∣ vi. [roman numerals in error] Preface, continued ∣ (7) Contents ∣ (8) blank ∣ (9) list of Illustrations ∣ (10) blank ∣ 11–384. text; printer's imprint on p.384 (PRINTED AND BOUND IN GREAT BRITAIN ∣ By Blackie & Son, Limited, Glasgow).

Binding: As for 104.2, except (a) no gilt used for blocking: all lettering black; (b) brasses for spine lettering re-cut smaller and re-arranged (At head: WITH ∣ KITCHENER ∣ IN THE ∣ SOUDAN ∣ G.A.HENTY; at foot: BLACKIE & SON LD.); (c) plain off-white endpapers.

Reference: PN.

Notes

1. For details of Blackie's second cheaper series, 'The New Popular Henty', and subsequent editions of the book, see *Facing Death*, 10.7, Notes 1–3 and 6–8.

2. All the minor variants of *With Kitchener in the Soudan* in the series are grouped together under the 'generic' heading, *104.3.

105. THE TREASURE OF THE INCAS

105.1

THE ∣ TREASURE OF THE INCAS ∣ A TALE OF ∣ ADVENTURE IN PERU ∣ BY ∣ G.A.HENTY ∣ Author of "With Buller in Natal" "At the Point of the Bayonet" ∣ "By England's Aid" "With Cochrane the Dauntless" &c. ∣ (18mm. rule) ∣ WITH

EIGHT ILLUSTRATIONS BY WAL PAGET | AND A MAP | (18mm. rule) | LONDON | BLACKIE & SON, LIMITED, 50 OLD BAILEY, E.C. | GLASGOW AND DUBLIN | 1903

Contents

186 × 123 mm. (1)–352 | catalogue 1–32. Eight full-page wash drawings by Wal Paget, reproduced by halftone blocks; one map reproduced by line block; all printed in black on coated paper, unbacked, unfolioed, tipped in.

(1) Half-title p. | (2) advertisement (HISTORICAL STORIES BY G.A.HENTY) listing 28 titles | (frontispiece, tipped in) | (3) title p. | (4) blank | 5. Preface | (6) blank | 7. Contents | (8) blank | 9. list of Illustrations | (10) blank | 11–352. text | 1–32. catalogue.

Binding (see Plate 84)

Green cloth boards, blocked black, white, brown, and gilt; all edges burnished olive-green; grey endpapers, lined off-white.

Front board: THE TREASURE | OF THE INCAS (gilt) above illustration of warrior with spear and shield (black, white, brown). At foot: BY G.A.HENTY (white). All framed by white line. **Spine:** THE | TREASURE | OF THE | INCAS (gilt) above illustration of head of Peruvian girl (black, white, brown, and gilt). At foot: G.A.HENTY (gilt). All framed by broken white line. **Back board:** plain.

References: BL; Bod; PN | *Farmer*, p.72; *Dartt*, p.140, *Companion*, p.31.

Notes

1. This was Henty's last five-shilling novel, published on 23 June 1902. By the end of August 1903 Blackie had sold 7477 copies. At the end of August 1917 when their records cease, they had sold 3830 more, at an annual average over the fourteen years of 274 copies. The figures showed a distinct improvement on many of Henty's recent books: at the end of fifteen years 11,307 copies had been sold at five shillings.
2. The binding is probably designed by John Hassall, but is not signed.
3. As usual with Blackie novels of this period, the earliest issues contain catalogues which do not list the books for the current season (with title pages dated 1903). They give details, with quotations from press reviews, of books up to and including those for the previous year (dated 1902).

*105.2

The book was reprinted in the style of 105.1, with the date removed from the title page. Changes were made when necessary to Blackie's imprint and addresses: the Indian office had been opened in 1901, but Bombay did not appear regularly in the imprint until 1906; after 1910 Dublin was omitted.

The general design of the books dated 1902, and of Henty's last three novels, including *The Treasure of the Incas*, changed gradually to a style close to that of the 'New and Popular Edition'.

Although the book was never issued in that series, nor reduced in price until 1922 (see 105.3), later issues in the first-edition format were printed on bulkier featherweight paper, which gave them an even closer resemblance to the 3s.6d. books.

The variants among the reprints in the first, five-shilling format are all grouped together under this 'generic' heading, *105.2.

*105.3

The | Treasure of the Incas | A Story of Adventure in Peru | BY | G.A.HENTY | Author of "Redskin and Cowboy" "By Sheer Pluck" | "Facing Death" &c. | ILLUSTRATED | BLACKIE AND SON LIMITED | LONDON GLASGOW AND BOMBAY

Contents

183 x 124 mm. (1)–352 | no catalogue. Frontispiece from watercolour drawing by Frank Gillett, R.I., reproduced by three-colour halftone blocks; four full-page wash-drawings by Wal Paget reproduced by halftone blocks printed in black; map of Peru, from line block printed in black; all on coated paper, unbacked, keyed to text pages, tipped in.

 · (1) Half-title p. | (2) advertisement (G.A.HENTY'S BOOKS) listing 56 titles | (frontispiece, tipped in) | (3) title p. | (4) printer's imprint (Printed in Great Britain by | Blackie & Son, Limited, Glasgow) | (5) Preface to the Original Edition | (6) blank | (7) Contents | (8) blank | (9) list of Illustrations | (10) blank | 11–352. text.

Binding: As for 105.1, except (a) no gold used for blocking: all lettering white; (b) spine lettering narrower, with G.A.HENTY above illustration: all framed within unbroken white line; (c) gilt in illustration is now replaced by white pigment below the level of the girl's eyes: above that omitted.

References: Bod; PN.

Notes

1. In 1922 the book was re-issued in 'The New Popular Henty' series, a name very close to that of the series begun in 1903 ('The New and Popular Edition') in which this title never appeared (but see Notes under *105.2).

2. All the minor variants of *The Treasure of the Incas* in the series are grouped together under this 'generic' heading, *105.3.

106. WITH THE BRITISH LEGION

106.1

WITH THE BRITISH LEGION | A STORY OF THE CARLIST WARS | BY | G.A.HENTY | Author of "With Roberts to Pretoria" "Held Fast for England" | "Under Drake's Flag" &c. | (27mm. rule) | WITH TEN FULL-PAGE ILLUSTRATIONS BY WAL. PAGET | (29mm. rule) | LONDON | BLACKIE & SON, LIMITED, 50 OLD BAILEY, E.C. | GLASGOW AND DUBLIN | 1903 *(Note: the rules above and below the artist's credit line are of unequal length).*

Contents

185 x 130 mm. (1)–384 | catalogue 1–32. The full-page wash drawings by Wal. Paget, reproduced by halftone blocks printed in black on coated paper, unbacked, unfolioed, tipped in.

 (1) Half-title p. | (2) advertisement (HISTORICAL TALES BY G.A.HENTY)

listing 28 titles | (frontispiece, tipped in) | (3) title p. | (4) blank | 5. Pre-face | (6) blank | 7. Contents | (8) blank | 9. list of Illustrations | (10) blank | 11–384. text | 1–32. catalogue.

Binding (see Plate 96)
Blue cloth boards, bevelled, blocked black, white, red, brown, and gilt; all edges burnished olive-green; grey endpapers, lined off-white.
Front board: WITH THE | BRITISH | LEGION | A STORY | OF THE . | CARLIST | WARS . . (all gilt) above and at right of illustration of officer carrying a child (black, white, red, brown). At lower right corner: G.A.HENTY (white).
Spine: WITH THE | BRITISH | LEGION | (row of three dots) | G.A.HENTY (all gilt) above illustration of officer cleaning a sword (black, white, red, brown). **Back board:** plain.

References: BL; Bod; PN | *Farmer*, p.83; *Dartt*, p.163, *Companion*, p.35.

Notes
1. The book was published on 2 August 1902 at six shillings. By the end of August the following year Blackie had sold 7656 copies, and over the following fourteen years they sold 1439 more. That made a total of 9095 copies, a low one by Henty's standards, up to the time Blackie's records cease, in 1917. The average annual sale over the fifteen years was 606 copies. The book was not reprinted in its first-edition format, nor was it re-issued in a cheaper series until the 1920s.
2. The binding is probably designed by John Hassall, but is not signed.

*106.2
With | The British Legion | A Story of the Carlist Wars | BY | G.A.HENTY | Author of "With Roberts to Pretoria" "Held Fast for England" | "Under Drake's Flag" &c. | Illustrated | BLACKIE & SON LIMITED | LONDON AND GLASGOW

Contents
185 × 124 mm. (1)–384 | advertisement (1)–(2). Frontispiece from watercolour drawing by unknown artist, reproduced by three-colour halftone blocks; four full-page wash-drawings by Wal Paget reproduced by halftone blocks printed in black; all on coated paper, unbacked, keyed to text pages, tipped in.
(1) Half-title p. | (2) Blackie addresses | (frontispiece, tipped in) | (3) title p. | (4) printer's imprint (Printed in Great Britain by Blackie & Son, Ltd, Glasgow) | (5) Preface | (6) blank | 7. Contents | (8) blank | (9) list of Illustrations | (10) blank | 11–384. text | (1)–(2) advertisement (THE NEW POPULAR HENTY) listing 64 titles.

Binding: As for 106.1, except (a) red cloth boards, blocked black, light-brown, and white, without gilt: lettering on front board all white, on spine all black; (b) all spine brasses re-cut smaller, and lettering re-arranged, with line of three dots under title omitted, and imprint (BLACKIE) added at foot; (c) edges plain; (d) plain off-white endpapers.

Reference: PN.

Notes
1. During the 1920s Blackie re-issued some of the novels in a second cheap series, 'The New Popular Henty'. For details see *Facing Death*, 10.7, Notes 1–3 and 6–8.

2. The single leaf of advertisements, tipped on to the end of the last gathering, was as usual printed on a heavier featherweight than the paper used for the text.
3. All the minor variants of *With the British Legion* in the series are grouped together under this 'generic' heading, *106.2.

107. THROUGH THREE CAMPAIGNS

107.1

THROUGH THREE CAMPAIGNS | A STORY OF | CHITRAL, TIRAH, AND ASHANTEE | BY | G.A.HENTY | Author of "With Buller in Natal" "The Bravest of the Brave" | "With Kitchener in the Soudan" &c. | (21mm. rule) | ILLUSTRATED BY WAL PAGET | (21mm. rule) | LONDON | BLACKIE & SON, LIMITED, 50 OLD BAILEY, E.C. | GLASGOW AND DUBLIN | 1904

Contents
186 × 130 mm. (1)–(384) | catalogue 1–32. Eight full-page wash-drawings by Wal Paget, reproduced by halftone blocks; three campaign-maps reproduced by line blocks; all printed in black on coated paper, unbacked, unfolioed, tipped in.
    (1) Half-title p. | (2) advertisement (MR. HENTY'S HISTORICAL TALES.) listing 53 titles | (frontispiece, tipped in) | (3) title p. | (4) blank | 5. Preface | vi. [roman numerals in error] Preface, continued | 7. Contents | (8) blank | 9. list of Illustrations (see Notes 2–3) | (10) blank | 11–383. text | (384) blank | 1–32. catalogue.

Binding (see Plate 83)
Red cloth boards, bevelled, blocked black, dark-brown, light-brown, and gilt; all edges burnished olive-green; grey endpapers, lined off-white.
    Front board: THROUGH THREE | CAMPAIGNS | G.A.HENTY (gilt) above illustration of fur-clad man with rifle, in snowy mountain landscape (black, dark-brown,, light-brown). **Spine:** THROUGH | THREE | CAMPAIGNS | G.A.HENTY (gilt) above illustration of man shown on front board (black, dark-brown, light-brown). **Back board:** plain.

References: BL; Bod; PN | *Farmer*, p.70; *Dartt*, p.138, *Companion*, p.31.

Notes
1. The book was published on 6 May 1903 at six shillings. By the end of February 1904 Blackie had sold 9013 copies, and during the next eight years, up to the end of 1912, a further 1536. The book was then reissued in the 'New and Popular Edition' (see 107.2). The last five copies at six-shillings were sold in 1913.
2. One minor variation between issues of this edition has required investigation: but from evidence available there can be no possible doubt that it stems from there having been two separate impressions. The first printing was probably of 5000 copies (with 'overs'). Blackie were no doubt becoming cautious about their initial print-runs. By an oversight, the three campaign maps were omitted from the list of Illustrations on p.9. They were added at the first opportunity.
3. A second printing of about 5000 copies was ordered in 1903, possibly even before publication: in accordance with Blackie custom the title page was dated 1904. The variation (see Note 2) came about as entries for the three maps were added to p.9.

4. Thus both dated impressions are distinguishable only by the variation of p.9. The same catalogue is bound in both issues. It omits books for the current year, with title pages dated 1904, but gives details of those dated 1903, with quotations from press reviews. Later issues of the second printing contain later catalogues.

5. The binding case was designed by John Hassall, who had already started work on books in 'The New and Popular Edition', launched in 1903.

6. Some copies have the imprint, BLACKIE & SON LTD, blocked in gilt on the spine.

107.2

Through Three Campaigns | A Story of Chitral, Tirah, and Ashanti | BY | G.A.HENTY | Author of "With Buller in Natal" "The Bravest of the Brave" | "With Kitchener in the Soudan" &c. | ILLUSTRATED BY WAL PAGET | NEW EDITION | BLACKIE AND SON LIMITED | LONDON GLASGOW AND BOMBAY

Contents

186 × 125 mm. (1)–(384) | no catalogue. Eight wash-drawings by Wal Paget reproduced by halftone blocks; three maps reproduced by line blocks; all printed in black on coated paper, unbacked, tipped in.

(1) Half-title p. | (2) advertisement (NEW AND POPULAR EDITION OF | G.A.HENTY'S WORKS) listing 39 titles | (frontispiece, tipped in) | (3) title p. | (4) blank | 5. Preface | vi. [roman numerals in error] Preface, continued | (7) Contents | (8) blank | (9) list of Illustrations | (10) blank | 11–383. text, printer's imprint at foot of p.383 (PRINTED IN GREAT BRITAIN | At the Villafield Press, Glasgow, Scotland) | (384) blank.

Binding: As for 107.1, except (a) addition of imprint on spine (BLACKIE & SON LTD) blocked black; (b) edges plain.

Reference: BB.

Notes

1. In 1912 *Through Three Campaigns* was re-issued in the 'New and Popular Edition'. For details of the series see *Facing Death*, 10.6, Notes 2–3.

2. In this edition Blackie sold 1773 copies by the end of August 1913, and a further 1005 copies in the following four years to the end of 1917, when their records cease. That represents an average annual sale over the five years of 556 copies. The total number sold from 1903 to 1917, both at 6s. and 3s.6d., was 13,332.

3. It had been Blackie's custom to date title pages of first impressions (only) in the series. But after 1912 they discontinued the custom, so this title is one of the first in the series of which no dated copies will be found.

*107.3

Through Three Campaigns | A Story of Chitral, Tirah, and Ashanti | BY | G.A.HENTY | Author of "Under Drake's Flag" "In Freedom's Cause" | "With Kitchener in the Soudan" &c. | Illustrated by Wal Paget | BLACKIE & SON LIMITED | LONDON AND GLASGOW

Contents

185 × 123 mm. (1)–(384) | catalogue (1)–(2). Frontispiece from watercolour drawing reproduced by three-colour halftone blocks; four full-page wash-drawings reproduced by halftone blocks printed in black; all by Wal Paget; all on coated paper, unbacked, tipped in.

(1) Half-title p. | (2) Blackie addresses (in London, Glasgow, Bombay and Toronto) | (frontispiece, tipped in) | (3) title p. | (4) printer's imprint (PRINTED IN GREAT BRITAIN BY ROBERT MACLEHOSE AND CO. LTD.) | 5. Preface | vi. [roman numerals in error] Preface, continued | (7) Contents | (8) blank | (9) list of Illustrations | (10) blank | 11–383. text | (384) blank | (1)–(2) catalogue (THE NEW POPULAR HENTY) listing 62 titles.

Binding: As for 107.1, except (a) blocking in black, brown, and buff, with no gilt: lettering on front board all buff, on spine all black; (b) addition of imprint at foot of spine (BLACKIE); (c) edges plain; (d) plain off-white endpapers.

Reference: AK.

Notes

1. For details of Blackie's second cheaper series, 'The New Popular Henty', and subsequent editions of this book, see *Facing Death*, 10.6, Notes 1–3 and 6–8.

2. This impression was by Robert MacLehose & Co. Limited, of Anniesland, Glasgow, a famous and very fine firm of Scottish bookprinters known as the Glasgow University Press: sadly it no longer exists. It is one of only three impressions I have seen of Henty's books outworked by Blackie. (See *A Knight of the White Cross*, *72.5, and *With Frederick the Great*, *82.4, both printed by yet another Glasgow firm).

3. The binding design (see 107.1, Note 5) is that used for the first edition.

4. The imprint on the spine of the binding case is here simply 'BLACKIE', instead of the usual 'BLACKIE & SON LTD' of this period.

5. All minor variants of *Through Three Campaigns* in the series are grouped together under this 'generic' heading, *107.3.

108. WITH THE ALLIES TO PEKIN

108.1

WITH THE ALLIES TO PEKIN | A TALE OF | THE RELIEF OF THE LEGATIONS | BY | G.A.HENTY | Author of "With Roberts to Pretoria" "Redskin and Cowboy" | "With the British Legion" &c. | (18mm. rule) | ILLUSTRATED BY WAL PAGET | (18mm. rule) | LONDON | BLACKIE & SON, LIMITED, 50 OLD BAILEY, E.C. | GLASGOW AND DUBLIN | 1904

Contents

185 × 131 mm. (1)–384 | catalogue 1–32. Eight full-page wash-drawings by Wal Paget, reproduced by halftone blocks; map reproduced by line block; all printed in black on coated paper, unbacked, unfolioed, tipped in.

(1) Half-title p. | (2) advertisement (MR. HENTY'S HISTORICAL TALES.) listing 53 titles | (frontispiece, tipped in) | (3) title p. | (4) blank | 5. Preface | vi.

[roman numerals in error] Preface, continued | (7) Contents | (8) blank | (9) list of Illustrations | (10) blank | 11–384. text | 1–32. catalogue.

Binding (see Plate 95)
Green cloth boards, bevelled, blocked black, orange, yellow-brown, and gilt; all edges burnished olive-green; grey endpapers, lined off-white.
    Front board: WITH THE ALLIES | TO PEKIN | A STORY | OF THE RELIEF | OF THE | LEGATIONS (all gilt) above and at right of illustration of Chinese man with pistol (black, orange, yellow-brown). At foot: BY G.A.HENTY (black). **Spine:** WITH THE | ALLIES | TO | PEKIN | BY | G.A.HENTY (all gilt) above illustration of Chinese man with rifle (black, orange, yellow-brown). **Back board:** plain.

References: BL; Bod; PN | *Farmer*, p.82; *Dartt*, p.162.

Notes
1. The book was published on 29 May 1903 at six shillings. By the end of August 1904 Blackie had sold 8446 copies; the book remained on sale at the published price for a further thirteen years, until the end of August 1917, when Blackie's records cease. In that time they sold 2335 more copies, making a total sale of 10,781, at an average of 770 copies a year of the fourteen-year period.
2. 599 copies were sold in 1905, but Blackie's figures show a low and declining record from 1906 onwards, the average annual sale over twelve years being only 145 copies. It is reasonable to assume the book was not reprinted in its first-edition format. Nor was it re-issued in the cheaper 'New and Popular Edition'.
3. On 31 January 1903 Blackie wrote to Scribners of New York, Henty's authorised publisher of Blackie titles in the USA, to let them know of manuscripts in their hands at Henty's death. This was one of them, but at that time the title had not been finally decided, Blackie being 'not altogether satisfied' with the one then given to it: *Cutting the Dragon's Tail: Relief of Foreign Legations at Pekin*. By 25 April proofs were being sent to Scribners under the title finally chosen by Blackie. Perhaps Andrew Chatto would have again remarked that Henty had a better feel for a title than his publisher (see 56.1, Note 6).

*108.2
WITH THE ALLIES | TO PEKIN | A Tale of the Relief of the Legations | BY | G.A.HENTY | Author of "With Roberts to Pretoria" "Redskin and Cowboy" | "With the British Legion" &c. | Illustrated | BLACKIE & SON LIMITED | LONDON AND GLASGOW

Contents
183 x 125 mm. (1)–384 | advertisement (i)–(ii). Frontispiece from watercolour drawing by Frank Gillett, reproduced by three-colour halftone blocks; four full-page wash-drawings by Wal Paget, reproduced by halftone blocks printed in black; all on coated paper, unbacked, keyed to text pages, tipped in. Map, reproduced by line block, printed in black on page (10) of text.
    (1) Half-title p. | (2) Blackie addresses | (frontispiece, tipped in) | (3) title p. | (4) printer's imprint (Printed in Great Britain by | Blackie & Son, Limited, Glasgow) | 5. Preface | vi. [roman numerals in error] Preface, continued | (7) Contents | (8) blank | (9) list of Illustrations | (10) map | 11–384. text, with printer's imprint at foot

of p.384 (PRINTED IN GREAT BRITAIN | At the Villafield Press, Glasgow, Scotland) | (i)–(ii) advertisement, tipped in, (THE NEW POPULAR HENTY) listing 60 titles.

Binding: As for 108.1, except (a) no gold used for blocking: all lettering black; (b) spine brasses re-cut, narrower, and re-arranged with addition of imprint at foot (BLACKIE); (c) edges plain; (d) plain off-white endpapers.

Reference: IM.

Notes
1. For details of Blackie's second cheaper series, 'The New Popular Henty', and subsequent editions of this book, see *Facing Death*, 10.7, Notes 1–3 and 6–8.
2. All the minor variants of *With the Allies to Pekin* in the series are grouped together under this 'generic' heading, *108.2.

109. BY CONDUCT AND COURAGE

109.1

BY CONDUCT AND COURAGE | A STORY OF THE DAYS OF NELSON | BY | G.A.HENTY | Author of "With Roberts to Pretoria" "With Buller in Natal" | "With Kitchener in the Soudan" &c. | (5-em rule) | ILLUSTRATED BY WILLIAM RAINEY, R.I. | (5-em rule) | BLACKIE AND SON LIMITED | LONDON GLASGOW DUBLIN BOMBAY | 1905

Contents
185 × 131 mm. (1)–384 | catalogue 1–32. Eight full-page wash-drawings by William Rainey, reproduced by halftone blocks printed in sepia on coated paper, unbacked, unfolioed, tipped in.
(1) Half-title p. | (2) advertisement (MR. HENTY'S HISTORICAL TALES.) listing 53 titles | (frontispiece, tipped in) | (3) title p. | (4) blank | 5. Publishers' Note | (6) blank | 7. Contents | (8) blank | 9. list of Illustrations | (10) blank | 11–384. text | 1–32. catalogue.

Binding (see Plate 58)
Red cloth boards, bevelled, blocked black, orange, buff, and gilt; all edges burnished olive-green; grey endpapers, lined off-white.
Front board: BY CONDUCT | & COURAGE | G.A.HENTY. (gilt) above illustration of young British officer with sword and pistol fighting two armed sailors (black, orange, buff, and gilt). **Spine:** BY | CONDUCT | AND | COURAGE | G.A.HENTY. (gilt) above illustration of young naval officer in shirtsleeves, with sword (black, orange, buff). At foot: BLACKIE & SON LTD (gilt). **Back board:** plain.

References: BL; Bod; PN | *Farmer*, p.15; *Dartt*, p.27, *Companion*, pp.6, 39.

Notes
1. The Publishers' Note, on p.5, reads: 'Mr. George A. Henty, who died in November, 1902, had completed three new stories, *With the Allies to Pekin, Through*

Three Campaigns, and *By Conduct and Courage*. Of these, *Through Three Campaigns* and *With the Allies to Pekin* were published in the autumn of 1903; the present story is therefore the last of Mr. Henty's great series of historical stories for boys. The proofs have been revised by Mr. G.A. Henty's son, Captain C.G. Henty.'

2. The book was published on 15 July 1904 at six shillings. By the end of August 1905 Blackie had sold 10,340 copies, and during the following twelve years they sold 2750 more, making a total of 13,090 copies. At the end of August 1917, Blackie's records cease. The book was not re-issued until 1922, in the second of Blackie's cheaper editions (see 109.2).

3. *Dartt*, p.28, and *Companion*, p.6, report a copy with a variant subtitle, 'A Story of Nelson's Days', but this was one of his confusions with Scribner editions.

4. *Dartt* also theorises about the determination of 'issues' by cloth-colour, and by the presence in some catalogues of a full-page portrait of Henty. These variations cannot be used to determine the chronological order of different issues (see Appendix III, Part 2), although it is possible that the portraits were inserted in only one issue, or perhaps a limited number of issues.

5. The book is found in two cloth-colours only, red and green. *Dartt Companion* claims that green is the 'more common' colour, but I cannot confirm that. Several sources consulted have come to the conclusion I have reached by observation, that copies in red cloth are more frequently found than those in green. But this seems to be a fruitless argument. More interesting, perhaps, is the choice of those two colours to the exclusion of others. The two illustrations on the binding case seem to cry out for the use of blue, which would be appropriate to the uniforms shown on the front board and the spine. The use of red, in particular, appears unsuitable in that it gives a military rather than a naval flavour.

6. This is only the second time that Blackie illustrated the first edition of a Henty novel with halftone illustrations in sepia ink. The first halftones so printed, sixteen years earlier, were in *The Cat of Bubastes*: see 38.1, Note 3.

*109.2

By | Conduct and Courage | A Story of the Days of Nelson | BY | G.A.HENTY | Author of "With Roberts to Pretoria" "With Buller in Natal" | "With Kitchener in the Soudan" &c. | ILLUSTRATED BY WILLIAM RAINEY, R.I. | BLACKIE AND SON LIMITED | LONDON GLASGOW AND BOMBAY

Contents

185 x 125 mm. (1)–384 | no catalogue. Frontispiece from watercolour drawing reproduced by three-colour halftone blocks; four full-page wash-drawings reproduced by halftone blocks printed in black; all illustrations by William Rainey; all on coated paper, unbacked, keyed to text pages, tipped in.

(1) Half-title p. | (2) advertisement (G.A.HENTY'S BOOKS) listing 56 titles | (frontispiece, tipped in) | (3) title p. | (4) printer's imprint (Printed in Great Britain by | Blackie & Son, Limited, Glasgow) | (5) Publisher's Note | (6) blank | (7) Contents | (8) blank | (9) list of Illustrations | (10) blank | 11–384. text.

Binding: As for 109.1, except (a) light-green cloth boards, blocked black, orange, and buff, with no gilt: gilt on front-board replaced by orange, on spine by black; (b) spine lettering re-cut narrower; (c) edges plain; (d) plain off-white endpapers,

References: Bod; PN.

Notes

1. For details of Blackie's second cheaper series, 'The New Popular Henty', and subsequent editions of this title, see *Facing Death*, 10.7, Notes 1–3 and 6–8.
By Conduct and Courage was issued in the series in 1922.

2. All the minor variants of this title within the series are grouped together under this 'generic' heading, *109.2.

110. GALLANT DEEDS

110.1

CHAMBERS'S SUPPLEMENTARY READERS (with double underline) | GALLANT | DEEDS | BEING | STORIES | TOLD | BY | G.A.HENTY | (the following six lines are at the right of printer's floral ornament) WITH | ILLUSTRATIONS | BY | ARTHUR RACKHAM, A.R.W.S. | AND | W.BOUCHER | W.& R.CHAMBERS, LIMITED | LONDON & EDINBURGH | 1905

Contents

176 x 117 mm. (1)–168 | no catalogue. Two full-page watercolour-drawings, one each by Arthur Rackham and W. Boucher, reproduced by three-colour halftone blocks printed on text pages, folioed, and backed up.

(1) Blank | (2) frontispiece | (3) title p. | (4) advertisement (CHAMBERS'S SUPPLEMENTARY READERS.) | (5) Preface | (6) Contents | (7)–78. text of 'The Golden Cañon' | 79–132. text of 'On an Indian Trail' | 133–148. text of 'In the Hands of Sicilian Brigands' | 149-157. text of 'Down a Crevasse' | 158–168. text of 'The Old Pit Shaft'; printer's imprint on p.168 (Edinburgh: Printed by W.& R.Chambers, Limited.).

Binding

Mottled, grey-blue cloth boards, blocked black and dark-blue; edges plain; plain off-white endpapers.
Front board: Chambers's | Supplementary | Readers ..... (all black) framed in panel with decoration at left of second and third lines. Gallant | Deeds | 1 shilling (black) above second panel, joined to first by decorative rules at left. In second panel: By G.A.Henty (black). **Spine:** (reading from tail to head): Chambers's | Supplementary Readers. (two vertical rules) GALLANT DEEDS. 1s. (all black). **Back board:** plain.

References: BL | *Farmer*, p.36; *Dartt*, p.63, *Companion*, p.15.

Notes

1. This is the only Henty work in Chambers's Supplementary Readers, a series not to be confused with Chambers's 'Continuous' Readers, in which three of his stories appeared in condensed form (see Appendix V).

2. This scarce publication is sought after by collectors of Arthur Rackham's work as well as by collectors of G.A. Henty.

110.2

CHAMBERS'S SUPPLEMENTARY READERS (with double underline) |
GALLANT | DEEDS | BEING | STORIES | TOLD | BY | G.A.HENTY | (the
following six lines are at the right of printer's floral ornament) WITH |
ILLUSTRATIONS | BY | ARTHUR RACKHAM, A.R.W.S. | AND | W.BOUCHER
| LONDON: 38 Soho Square, W. | W.& R.CHAMBERS, LIMITED |
EDINBURGH: 339 High Street | 1909

Contents: As for 110.1.

Binding (see Plate 129)
Red cloth boards, printed in red to imitate straight-grained morocco, with grain-lines
vertical, blocked black; edges plain; plain off-white endpapers.
  Front board: Chambers's | Supplementary | Readers ..... (all black) framed in
panel with decoration at left of second and third lines. Gallant | Deeds | 8d. (black)
above second panel, joined to the first by decorative rules at left. In second panel:
By G.A.Henty (black). **Spine:** (reading from foot to head) Chambers's |
Supplementary Readers. (two vertical rules) GALLANT DEEDS. 8d. (all black).
Back board: plain.

References: BB | *Dartt*, p.63.

110.3

Title page: As for 110.2, but with no date.

Contents: As for 110.1, but at foot of p.(4) some copies have line added (Reprinted
1910).

Binding: As for 110.2, except (a) blue-grey cloth boards, printed to imitate straight-
grained morocco, with grain-lines horizontal, blocked black; (b) price on both front
board and spine shown as 1/- (not 1s.).

Reference: BB; TC.

110.4

Title page, Contents: As for 110.3.

Binding
Red limp cloth, square back, cut flush, printed black; edges plain; plain off-white
endpapers.
  Blocking details as for 110.2.

Reference: BB.

111. A SOLDIER'S DAUGHTER

111.1

A Soldier's Daughter | AND OTHER STORIES | BY | G.A.HENTY | Author of
"With Buller in Natal" "The Lion of St. Mark" | "The Young Carthaginian" "In
Freedom's Cause" &c. | ILLUSTRATED BY FRANCES EWAN | BLACKIE AND
SON LIMITED | LONDON GLASGOW DUBLIN BOMBAY | 1906

Contents

181 x 123 mm. (1)–200 I catalogue 17–32. Six full-page wash-drawings by Frances Ewan, reproduced by halftone blocks printed in sepia on coated paper, unbacked, unfolioed, tipped in.

(Frontispiece, tipped in) I (1) title p. I (2) blank I 3. Contents I (4) blank I 5. list of Illustrations I (6) blank I 7–113. text of 'A Soldier's Daughter' I (114) blank I 115–170. text of 'How Count Conrad von Waldensturm took Goldstein' I 171–197. text of 'A Raid by the Blacks' I (198)–(200) blank I 17–32. catalogue.

Binding (see Plate 112)

Red cloth boards, blocked black, olive, orange, and gilt; edges plain; grey endpapers, lined white.

Front board: A SOLDIER'S I DAUGHTER I & OTHER STORIES (gilt) above illustration of Afridi warrior with sword and shield (black, olive, orange). **Spine:** A I SOLDIER'S I DAUGHTER I G.A.HENTY (all gilt) above illustration of Nita, the eponymous heroine, dressed as a boy (black, olive, orange). At foot: BLACKIE & SON LTD (gilt). **Back board:** plain.

References: BL; Bod; PN I *Farmer*, p.61; *Dartt*, p.120, *Companion*, p.26.

Notes

1. The story 'A Soldier's Daughter' was first serialised in *The Girl's Realm*, Vol.5, in three parts, from May to July 1903 (see §3, 210). The other stories did not appear elsewhere.
2. Frances Ewan drew six illustrations for the magazine. Blackie omitted two of them, but commissioned two new ones to take their place (see Appendix IV, Part 2).
3. Publication day was 24 June 1905, but the book does not appear in Blackie's surviving records, so no figures are available relating to editions or sales.
4. There are 16 pages of catalogue bound in, not 32 as reported by *Dartt*. The pages are folioed 17–32, and the explanation of this apparent error is given under *Do Your Duty*, 89.1, Notes 3–4. This section of catalogue is headed 'Story Books for Girls'.
5. Uncharacteristically of Blackie, the book is carelessly planned, with twelve 16-page gatherings followed by an 8-page gathering with three blank pages.

*111.2

Reprints were in the style of 111.1, with the date removed from the title page. After 1910 Dublin was removed from the imprint. In some issues Blackie inserted a list of books by Henty on p.2, and sometimes the catalogue was omitted.

Later issues were printed on a bulky featherweight paper, and eventually the brasses for the title-lettering were re-cut to fit the wider spine. The increased size of lettering made it necessary to omit the author's name from the spine; the design of the front board was not affected.

Before and during the first war Blackie were forced to economise by substituting pigment for gilt lettering on front boards of all books, and later on spines too. These and other small changes over the years produced a number of variant issues: all are grouped together under this 'generic' heading, *111.2.

111.3

A I Soldier's Daughter I And Other Stories I BY I G.A.HENTY I Author of "The

Lion of St. Mark" "The Young Carthaginian" | "In Freedom's Cause" "Wulf the Saxon" &c. | (publisher's device) | BLACKIE & SON LIMITED | LONDON AND GLASGOW

Contents

172 × 115 mm. (1)–200 | advertisement (i)–(ii). Frontispiece from watercolour drawing by unknown artist, reproduced by three-colour halftone blocks printed on coated paper, unbacked, tipped in.

(1) Half-title p. | (2) Blackie addresses | (frontispiece, tipped in) | (3) title p. | (4) printer's imprint (Printed in Great Britain by Blackie & Son, Ltd., Glasgow) | (5) Contents | (6) blank | 7–113. text of 'A Soldier's Daughter' | (114) blank | 115–197. text, as in 111.1 | (198) blank | (i)–(ii) advertisement, tipped in (not present in all copies, see Note 2) | (199)–(200) blank.

Binding (see Note 3)

Possibly designed by Charles Rennie Mackintosh. Light-brown grained-paper boards, blocked blue; edges plain; plain off-white endpapers.

Front board: A SOLDIER'S | DAUGHTER | G.A.HENTY in rectangular panel within over-all geometric pattern of (?) abstract swallows (blue). **Spine:** A | SOLDIER'S | DAUGHTER | HENTY (blue) in panel cutting across pattern as on front board (blue). In small rectangle at foot: BLACKIE | & SON . LTD (blue). **Back board:** plain.

Reference: BB.

Notes

1. Part of a 1s.6d. series that appeared in the 1920s: 'Blackie's Library for Boys and Girls', which should not be confused with 'The Boys' and Girls' Bookshelf' (see Appendix V). For other appearances of the stories see §4.

2. When present, the two-page list is, inconveniently for the binder, tipped on to p.(198), just before the final (blank) leaf. It names books in 'The Boys' and Girls' Bookshelf', 'The Young Folk's Library', 'Blackie's Library for Boys and Girls', and 'The Happy Home Library', in all of which Henty is represented.

3. It has been suggested that the binding was designed by Charles Rennie Mackintosh: see *Tales from Henty*, 57.6, Note 5, Plate 111, and Appendix IV, Part 2.

112. TWO SIEGES

112.1

TWO SIEGES | OR | CUTHBERT HARTINGTON'S ADVENTURES | BY | G.A.HENTY | Author of | 'In the Days of the Mutiny,' 'The Curse of Carne's Hold,' | 'Dorothy's Double,' Etc., Etc. | WITH SIX ILLUSTRATIONS | LONDON | S.W.PARTRIDGE & CO., LTD., | OLD BAILEY

Contents

181 × 122 mm. (i)–(iv) | (1)–292 | no catalogue. Six full-page wash-drawings by Hal Hurst and Simon Harmon Vedder, reproduced by halftone blocks printed in black on imitation art-paper, unbacked, unfolioed but keyed to text, tipped in. (See Note 3).

(i) Half-title p. | (ii) blank | (frontispiece, tipped in) | (iii) title p. | (iv) publisher's device | (1)–292. text, with printer's imprint at foot of p.292 (Roberts & Jackson, Printers, 4 Victoria Street, Grimsby.).

Binding (see Plate 13)
Grey-blue cloth boards, blocked black, red, white merging to buff, light-blue merging to dark-blue, and imitation gold; edges plain; plain off-white endpapers.

Front board: TWO SIEGES (red, cased black) | OR, CUTHBERT | HARTINGTON'S | ADVENTURES (black), over upper part of illustration of soldier taking his hat off to nurse (black, white merging to buff, light-blue merging to dark-blue). At foot: G.A.HENTY. (black). All framed by black line. **Spine:** TWO | SIEGES (cloth-colour out of solid imitation-gold rectangle) framed by black rule, with floral art-nouveau decoration above (black, red, light-blue), and below (black, white merging to buff, dark-blue), the merging of both sets of colours corresponding with that on front board. At centre of decoration: G.A.HENTY (black); at foot: PARTRIDGE (black). All framed by black lines. **Back board:** plain.

References: BL; Bod; PN | *Dartt*, p.143, *Companion*, p.32.

Notes
1. Originally published in 1895 by F.V. White & Co., under the title *A Woman of the Commune* (65.1). Re-issued in 1899 by S.W. Partridge & Co. as *Cuthbert Hartington* (86.1). It reached the Copyright Libraries under this third title in 1916. (Also published, in USA only, under two additional titles: *A Girl of the Commune*, and *Two Sieges of Paris*).
2. *In the Days of the Mutiny*, shown after Henty's name on the title page of all Partridge editions of this novel, was the title under which *Rujub, the Juggler* was first published as a newspaper serial (see *Rujub, the Juggler*, 56.1, Notes 3–6). That title was also used by book publishers in the United States and Canada.
3. The illustrations are not attributed, but are the same as in *Cuthbert Hartington*. The five by Hal Hurst originally appeared in *A Woman of the Commune*, and his sixth in that book was also adapted for blocking on its front board. In *Cuthbert Hartington*, and again here, it was replaced by a drawing by Simon Harmon Vedder, in turn adapted for blocking on the front boards of both Partridge titles. Two of the Hurst halftones are marked with a process engraver's initials, V & C.
4. The illustration blocked on the front board is the same as that on the front board of *Cuthbert Hartington*, 86.1, but the brasses were re-cut for this version, with slight differences of detail in the drawing. Additional brasses were also cut for the two sets of merging colours, covering larger areas than on the earlier book.
5. The imitation gold used for blocking the spine is also far from the real thing. Various such materials were made, but all deteriorated in time, most going almost black soon after use. It was not until the 1950s that a good, non-tarnishing imitation gold appeared on the market.
6. The paper used for the illustrations is an 'imitation art-paper' (see Glossary), not suitable for high-quality halftone printing.
7. The book is printed by Roberts and Jackson of Grimsby from stereos of the type set for *Cuthbert Hartington*, 86.1, by Colston & Coy, Limited, of Edinburgh. In spite of the change of title, the running headlines throughout the book, and the book-title printed at the head of Chapter I, still read 'Cuthbert Hartington'.

112.2

Title page: As for 112.1.

Contents: 186 × 125 mm. As for 112.1.

Binding (see Plate 13)
Light olive-green cloth boards, blocked black; edges plain; plain off-white endpapers.
Front board: TWO SIEGES | OR, CUTHBERT | HARTINGTON'S | ADVENTURES (black) above illustration, and, at foot: G.A.HENTY (all black), framed by black line, the whole being blocked from the brasses used for the black impression on the front board of 112.1, the title therefore being in 'open' lettering, and the illustration lacking some detail. **Spine:** TWO | SIEGES (cloth-colour out of solid-black rectangle) with floral art-nouveau decoration above and below, again blocked only from the brasses used for the black impression on the spine of 112.1. At centre: G.A.HENTY (black); at foot: PARTRIDGE (black). **Back board:** plain.

Reference: PN.

Note: A re-issue of sheets left over from 112.1, in a cheap binding: the boards are slightly lighter in weight than for 112.1, and the endpapers slightly heavier.

113. IN THE HANDS OF THE MALAYS

113.1

IN THE | HANDS OF THE MALAYS | AND OTHER STORIES | BY | G.A.HENTY | Author of "With Roberts to Pretoria" "With Kitchener in the Soudan" | "Beric the Briton" | "For Name and Fame" &c. | (5-em rule) | ILLUSTRATED BY J.JELLICOE | (5-em rule) | BLACKIE AND SON LIMITED | LONDON GLASGOW DUBLIN BOMBAY | 1905

Contents
182 × 122 mm. (1)–176 | catalogue 1–16. Four wash-drawings by J.Jellicoe, reproduced by halftone blocks printed in dark-sepia on coated paper, unbacked, unfolioed, tipped in.
(1) Half-title p. | (2) blank | (frontispiece, tipped in) | (3) title p. | (4) blank | 5. Contents | (6) blank | 7–54. text of 'In the Hands of the Malays' | 55–147. text of 'On the Track' | (148) blank | (149–176. text of 'A Frontier Girl' | 1–16. catalogue.

Binding (see Plate 117)
Green cloth boards, blocked black, brown, buff, and gilt; edges plain; grey endpapers, lined off-white.
Front board: IN THE HANDS | OF THE MALAYS | G.A.HENTY (gilt) above illustration of armed seventeenth-century man with wide-brimmed hat, standing over a grave (black, brown, buff). **Spine:** IN THE | HANDS | OF THE | MALAYS | G.A.HENTY (gilt) above illustration of young man tied to mast of ship (black, brown, buff). At foot: BLACKIE & SON. LTD (black). **Back board:** plain.

References: BL; Bod; PN | *Farmer*, p.41; *Dartt*, p.83, *Companion*, p.19.

Notes

1. Published on 9 September 1904: Blackie's surviving records tell no more.

2. The story 'A Frontier Girl' was first published in *The Girl's Realm*, 1901 (see §3, 210). The other stories were not printed elsewhere.

*113.2

The first reprints were in the style of 113.1, with the date removed from the title page. The earliest of them contain the same catalogue, with no mention of the titles for the current year (with title pages dated 1905). After 1910 Dublin no longer appeared in the imprint.

The general style changed gradually, with the loss of gilt blocking from the front board, and further typographical changes to the prelims and advertisements. All the early variants are grouped together under this 'generic' heading, *113.2. Later variants, with re-set title page, are described under *113.3, below.

*113.3

In the | Hands of the Malays | And Other Stories | BY | G.A.HENTY | Author of "With Roberts to Pretoria" "With Kitchener in the Soudan" | "Beric the Briton" "For Name and Fame" &c. | ILLUSTRATED BY J.JELLICOE | BLACKIE AND SON LIMITED | LONDON GLASGOW AND BOMBAY

Contents

179 x 120 mm. (1)–176 | no catalogue. Illustrations as in 113.1, but printed in sepia.

(1) Half-title p. | (2) advertisement (G.A.HENTY'S BOOKS) listing 45 titles | (frontispiece, tipped in) | (3) title p. | (4) blank | (5) Contents | (6) blank | 7–54. text of 'In the Hands of the Malays' | 55–147. text of 'On the Track' | (148) blank | 149–176. text of 'A Frontier Girl', with printer's imprint at foot of p.176 (PRINTED AND BOUND IN GREAT BRITAIN | By Blackie & Son, Limited, Glasgow).

Binding: As for 113.1, except (a) blue cloth boards, blocked black, brown, and buff, with no gilt: imprint on spine in black, all other lettering buff; (b) brasses for spine lettering re-cut more than once in a serifed face, to varying widths and spacing: imprint varies between BLACKIE & SON LTD. and BLACKIE & SON LD.; (c) edges plain; (d) plain off-white endpapers.

Reference: PN.

Notes

1. Reprints later than *113.2 were on bulkier featherweight, with illustrations on bulky one-sided coated paper. Soon after 1910 the title page was re-set, in the style of novels in the 'New and Popular Edition' (issued 1903–1918), with the title in upper and lower case. The copy described here is representative of a number of minor variants which appeared through the 1920s and 1930s, see Notes 2–4.

2. Changes were made, as usual, to title-page imprint and addresses, and during the 1920s the preliminary pages were completely re-set in the style of books in 'The New Popular Henty'. But that (1920s) series included only novels, with new frontispieces in colour. The use of colour for this title was to follow: see 113.5.

3. The binding case is as for *113.2, modified as detailed above.

4. Variant issues among the later reprints are all grouped together under this 'generic' heading, *113.3.

113.4

The book was advertised by Blackie in the series of 'English Authors for School Reading', but I have not found a copy. The other books in the series are *A Chapter of Adventures*, 48.6, Plate 103, *Tales from Henty*, 57.3, and *Sturdy and Strong*, 34.4, of which a copy has also eluded me. The series does not appear in Blackie's surviving records, but the title-page imprints of 48.6 and 57.3 both indicate publication after 1910.

113.5

In the | Hands of the Malays | And Other Stories | BY | G.A.HENTY | Author of "The Cat of Bubastes" "With Kitchener in the Soudan" | "Beric the Briton" "For Name and Fame" &c. | (publisher's device) | BLACKIE & SON LIMITED | LONDON AND GLASGOW

Contents
181 x 126 mm. (1)–176 | advertisement (1)–(2) (see Note 3). Frontispiece from watercolour drawing by unknown hand, reproduced by three-colour halftone blocks printed on coated paper, unbacked, tipped in.

(1) Half-title p. | (2) Blackie's addresses | (frontispiece, tipped in) | (3) title p. | (4) printer's imprint (Printed in Great Britain by | Blackie & Son, Limited, Glasgow) | (5) Contents | (6) blank | 7–54. text of 'In the Hands of the Malays' | 55–147. text of 'On the Track' | (148) blank | 149–176. text of 'A Frontier Girl' | (1)–(2) advertisement (see Note 3).

Binding (see Note 2)
Possibly designed by Charles Rennie Mackintosh. Buff grained-paper boards (imitating cloth), blocked blue; edges plain; plain off-white endpapers.

Front board: IN THE HANDS | OF THE MALAYS | G.A.HENTY (blue) in rectangular panel within over-all geometric pattern of (?) abstract swallows (blue). **Spine:** IN THE | HANDS | OF THE | MALAYS (blue) in panel cutting across pattern as on front board (blue). In small rectangle at foot: BLACKIE & SON . LTD (blue). **Back board:** plain.

Reference: PN.

Notes
1. Part of a 1s.6d. series that appeared in the 1920s: 'Blackie's Library for Boys and Girls', which should not be confused with 'The Boys' and Girls' Bookshelf' (see Appendix V). For other appearances of the short stories see §4.
2. It has been suggested that the binding was designed by Charles Rennie Mackintosh: see *Tales from Henty*, 57.6, Note 5, Plate 111, and Appendix IV, Part 2.
3. The two-page list, tipped on to p.176, is not present in all copies. It names books in 'The Boys' and Girls' Bookshelf', 'The Young Folk's Library', 'Blackie's Library for Boys and Girls', and 'The Happy Home Library', in all of which Henty is represented.

114. AMONG THE BUSHRANGERS

114.1

G.A.Henty | (3-em rule) | AMONG | THE BUSHRANGERS | FROM | A FINAL RECKONING | LONDON | BLACKIE & SON, LIMITED, 50 OLD BAILEY, E.C. | GLASGOW AND DUBLIN | 1906

Contents

175 × 118 mm. (1)–88. Three full-page drawings by W.B.Wollen, taken from *A Final Reckoning*, reduced and reproduced by line blocks printed in black on text paper, as frontispiece and on pages 35 and 66.

(1) Advertisement (BLACKIE'S STORY-BOOK READERS) | (2) frontispiece | (3) title p. | (4) blank | 5-88. text.

Cover (see Note 2)

Red cloth, printed black; lined with plain yellow paper; saddle-stitched, cut flush.

Front: BLACKIE'S . STORY-BOOK | : : READERS : : | (printer's ornament) | AMONG . THE | BUSHRANGERS | G.A.HENTY | (publisher's device) | 4d. (in small circle, all black) within quadruple-ruled frame with decorative corners. **Back:** plain.

References: *Farmer*, pp.93, 94 (addenda); *Dartt*, pp.4, 129, *Companion*, p.28.

Notes

1. One of nine 'Story-Book Readers', all excerpts from longer works by Henty. Only one was for children in Standard IV, price 3d. (see *Do Your Duty*, 89.3 and 89.4). The others were for Standards V and VI, price 4d. Titles are listed in Appendix V.
2. The binding design is as for *Cast Ashore*, 115.1: see Plate 125.
3. The entries in *Dartt* are amended in his *Companion*. He specifically states (*Companion*, p.28) that all copies he had seen were dated 1906.

114.2

G.A.Henty | (3-em rule) | AMONG | THE BUSHRANGERS | FROM | A FINAL RECKONING | BLACKIE AND SON LIMITED | LONDON GLASGOW AND BOMBAY

Contents: 167 × 110 mm. As for 114.1.

Cover (see Plate 126)

Green paper, printed black; saddle-stitched, cut flush.
(1) BLACKIE'S . STORY-BOOK | : : READERS : : | (printer's ornament) | AMONG . THE | BUSHRANGERS | G.A.HENTY | (publisher's device) (all black) within quadruple-ruled frame with decorative corners.
(2) and (3) blank.
(4) advertisement (BLACKIE'S SUPPLEMENTARY READERS).

References: BB | *Farmer*, pp.93, 94 (addenda); *Dartt*, p.129, *Companion*, p.28.

Notes

1. This issue does not have the words FIFTH SERIES on the cover, but apart from that is similar in all respects to the reprints of other titles I have seen.
2. *Farmer* and *Dartt* give the date 1915 to the FIFTH SERIES issues.

114.3

Among | The Bushrangers | From "A FINAL RECKONING" | BY G.A.HENTY | (publisher's device) BLACKIE AND SON LIMITED | LONDON GLASGOW AND BOMBAY

Contents

170 × 113 mm. (1)–88 | no catalogue. Three full-page drawings by W.B.Wollen, taken from *A Final Reckoning*, reduced and printed in black from line blocks: frontispiece on coated paper, unbacked, tipped in; the other two on text pages 35 and 66.

(1) Half-title p. | (2) advertisement (OTHER BOOKS IN | THIS SERIES) listing 18 titles including 6 by Henty | (frontispiece, tipped in) | (3) title p. | (4) blank | 5–88. text.

Binding (see Note 2)

Brown paper boards, grained to imitate cloth, blocked black, white, and green; edges plain; plain off-white endpapers.

Front board: AMONG THE | BUSHRANGERS (black) framed by green rules, across pattern of long-stemmed dianthus-type flowers (black, white, green). **Spine:** AMONG | THE | BUSH- | RAN- | GERS (black) above panel with pattern as on front board, and wide green rules above and below. At foot: BLACKIE (black). **Back board:** plain.

References: PN | *Dartt*, pp.4, 70.

Notes

1. One of six titles by Henty in the 'Happy Home Library' (see Appendix V). The first titles were published in 1922; the last, *A Highland Chief*, probably in 1923.
2. Alternative paper-colours were used for the binding cases, but blocking-pigments remained constant. The series design is as for *Charlie Marryat*, 116.4, Plate 133.
3. Late impressions in the 'Happy Home Library' have the printer's imprint added on p.(4): 'Printed in Great Britain by | Blackie & Son, Limited, Glasgow'.

114.4

AMONG | THE BUSHRANGERS | FROM | "A Final Reckoning" | BY | G.A.HENTY | BLACKIE & SON LIMITED | LONDON AND GLASGOW

Contents

183 × 122 mm. (1)–(96) | no catalogue. Frontispiece from wash-drawing by William Rainey, reproduced by halftone block printed in black on coated paper, unbacked, keyed to text p., tipped in.

(Frontispiece, tipped in) | (1) title p. | (2) Publisher's addresses; advertisement (Summit Library: Books of this Series); printer's imprint (Printed in Great Britain by Blackie & Son, Ltd., Glasgow) | (3) Contents | (4) blank | 5–95. text | (96) blank.

Binding (see Plate 136)

White paper boards, printed by litho in four process-colours (yellow, red, blue, black); edges plain; plain white endpapers.

Front board: AMONG | THE | BUSHRANGERS (black) | G.A.Henty (red) all on yellow circular panel at upper right corner of all-over full-colour illustration, signed 'Nick' (see Note 1), of mounted cowboy, with others in distance. **Spine:** AMONG | THE | BUSHRANGERS (black) | G.A.Henty (red) all on yellow circular panel at head of spine out of all-over continuation of colour illustration from front board. At foot: BLACKIE (in paler, indeterminate colour, out of illustration). **Back board:** Large solid-red panel, cut into at top by yellow strip, with: THE . SUMMIT . LIBRARY (red), and at the lower left corner by circular yellow panel, with: BLACKIE | & SON | LIMITED (red). White margins at all edges.

References: BL; PN | *Farmer*, p.5; *Dartt*, p.4.

Notes
1. Published 1929: the only other Henty title in the 'Summit Library' is *The Two Prisoners*, 120.4. Both binding designs are by (?) Nick (see Appendix IV, Part 2).
2. Re-set in a larger typeface, heavily leaded, to make more pages, and printed on a very bulky featherweight antique wove. It is nearly twice as thick as 114.3.
3. Details of the publisher's addresses, and also of the titles in the 'Summit Library', given on p.(2), show slight variations from one printing to another.

114.5
Title page: As for 114.4.

Contents: As for 114.4, except (a) featherweight paper is much less bulky; (b) on p.(2) advertisement is deleted, and list of addresses up-dated.

Binding (see Plate 136)
White paper boards, printed by litho in four process-colours (yellow, red, blue, black); edges plain; plain white endpapers.
    Front board: as for 114.4. **Spine:** AMONG THE BUSHRANGERS (red) running from foot to head, above: BLACKIE (red) from left to right at foot. At head: G.A. | HENTY (red) running from foot to head. All on solid-yellow background. **Back board:** as for 114.4.

References: PN | *Dartt Companion*, p.39.

Notes
1. The spine of the binding case had to be re-designed because of the change to a much thinner paper. I do not know how soon 114.5 followed 114.4.
2. Details of addresses, and of titles in the 'Summit Library', on p.(2), continue to vary as in 114.4. Dartt makes this point (*Companion*, p.39), but the changes are more frequent and far-reaching than he realised.

114.6
Among the Bushrangers | from | "A Final Reckoning" | by | G.A.HENTY | (row of 14 stars) | With frontispiece by | F.COCKERTON | BLACKIE & SON LIMITED | London and Glasgow

Contents
185 x 122 mm. (1)–(96) | no catalogue. Frontispiece from drawing by F.Cockerton, reproduced by line block on text paper.
    (Unfolioed leaf pasted down as endpaper) | (1) half-title p. | (2) frontispiece | (3) title p. | (4) Contents, with publisher's addresses at head of page, and printer's

imprint at foot (Printed in Great Britain by Blackie & Son, Ltd., Glasgow) | 5–92. text | (unfolioed leaf pasted down as endpaper).

Binding
White paper boards, printed by litho in four process-colours; edges plain; endpapers made from first and last leaves of text.
    Front board: AMONG THE | BUSHRANGERS (black) over sky in full-colour illustration of cowboys riding in landscape. At foot: G.A.HENTY (blue) overprinting illustration. **Spine:** lettering running from foot to head: BLACKIE (blue overprinting yellow to make green): AMONG THE BUSHRANGERS (white out of blue decorated panel on white rectangle): G.A.HENTY (blue overprinting yellow to make green). **Back board:** THE . SUMMIT . LIBRARY (blue) on white strip across head of board, out of solid-blue background. At lower left corner: BLACKIE | & SON | LIMITED (blue) in white circular panel out of solid-blue background.

Reference: BB.

Notes
1. This copy is inscribed 1963–64, but the impression may be considerably earlier.
2. The publisher's addresses on p.(4) are the same as those in 114.5, p.(2).

115. CAST ASHORE

115.1
G.A.Henty | (3-em rule) | CAST ASHORE | FROM UNDER DRAKE'S FLAG | LONDON | BLACKIE & SON, LIMITED, 50 OLD BAILEY, E.C. | GLASGOW AND DUBLIN | 1906

Contents
173 x 118 mm. (1)–96. Three full-page drawings by Gordon Browne, taken from *Under Drake's Flag*, reduced and reproduced by line blocks printed in black on text paper, as frontispiece and on pages 27 and 70.
    (1) Advertisement (BLACKIE'S STORY-BOOK READERS) | (2) frontispiece | (3) title p. | (4) blank | 5–96. text.

Cover (see Plate 125)
Red cloth, printed black; lined with plain yellow paper; saddle-stitched, cut flush.
    Front: BLACKIE'S . STORY-BOOK | : : READERS : : | (printer's ornament) | CAST . ASHORE | G.A.HENTY | (publisher's device) | 4d. (in small circle, all black) within quadruple-ruled frame with decorative corners. **Back:** plain.

References: BB | *Farmer*, pp.93, 94 (addenda); *Dartt*, pp.34, 129, *Companion*, p.8.

Notes
1. The entry in *Dartt* (p.34) is very confused, and amended in his *Companion*, p.8.
2. On p.(1) the list of titles shows a misprint *Last Ashore* for *Cast Ashore*.
3. For further details of Blackie's 'Story-Book Readers' see *Among the Bushrangers*, 114.1, Notes 1 and 2.

115.2

G.A.Henty | (3-em rule) | CAST ASHORE | FROM | UNDER DRAKE'S FLAG | BLACKIE & SON LIMITED | LONDON AND GLASGOW

Contents: 165 × 111 mm. As for 115.1, except p.(4): publisher's imprint with addresses; printer's imprint (Printed in Great Britain by Blackie & Son, Ltd., Glasgow).

Cover (see Plate 126)
Red cloth, printed black; lined with plain yellow paper; saddle-stitched, cut flush.
Front: BLACKIE'S . STORY-BOOK | : : | READERS : : | (printer's ornament) | CAST . ASHORE | G.A.HENTY | (publisher's device) FIFTH . SERIES . (all black) enclosed by quadruple-ruled frame with decorative corners. **Back:** plain.

References: BB | *Farmer*, pp.93, 94 (addenda); *Dartt*, pp.34, 129, *Companion*, p.28.

Notes
1. *Farmer* and *Dartt* give the date 1915 to the FIFTH SERIES issues.
2. The original 1906 issues seem to have been all in limp red cloth, and the reprints, or fifth series, both in limp red cloth and in paper covers. *Dartt* describes a fifth series copy in grey paper.

115.3s

Cast Ashore | From "UNDER DRAKE'S FLAG" | BY G.A.HENTY | (publisher's device) | BLACKIE AND SON LIMITED | LONDON GLASGOW AND BOMBAY

Contents
171 × 115 mm. (but see Note 4). (1)–96 | no catalogue. Three full-page drawings by Gordon Browne, taken from *Under Drake's Flag*, reduced and reproduced by line blocks printed in black; the frontispiece on smooth MF paper, unbacked, tipped in; the other two on text pages 27 and 70.
(1) Half-title p. | (2) blank | (frontispiece, tipped in) | (3) title p. | (4) blank | 5–96. text.

Binding (see Note 1)
Pink cloth boards, blocked black, white, and yellow; edges plain; plain off-white endpapers.
Front board: CAST ASHORE | G.A.HENTY (black) above illustration of boy and girl, carrying skates, in snow-scene (black, white, yellow) in narrow rectangular panel framed by black rules. **Spine:** CAST | ASHORE | (printer's ornament) | Henty (all black) above three-panelled art-nouveau design (black). At foot, above two black rules: BLACKIE | & SON LD (black). **Back board:** plain.

References: BL; PN | *Farmer*, p.19; *Dartt*, p.34.

Notes
1. One of three Henty titles published in this style in 1920. The other two are: *Charlie Marryat*, 116.3, Plate 133, and *The Young Captain*, 121.3. *Dartt* incorrectly names *Do Your Duty* (see 89.8, Note 3) in place of *The Young Captain*.
2. The series seems not to have been given a name. The contents vary from those in

the 'Happy Home Library' only in having a half-title page instead of a page listing titles in that series. But *Cast Ashore* is the only one of the three Henty titles in the present series which is not also in the 'Happy Home Library'.

3. All three titles were bound in a variety of cloth-colours, and by 1926 were issued in grained-paper boards (imitating cloth).

4. All copies of *Cast Ashore* I have seen are in this page-size. Copies of both the other titles were also issued in an alternative page-size (176 x 119 mm.). Issues in the smaller size have the letter **s** at the end of their coding.

116. CHARLIE MARRYAT

116.1

G.A.Henty | (3-em rule) | CHARLIE MARRYAT | FROM | WITH CLIVE IN INDIA | LONDON | BLACKIE & SON, LIMITED, 50 OLD BAILEY, E.C. | GLASGOW AND DUBLIN | 1906

Contents

175 x 117 mm. (1)–(96). Three full-page drawings by Gordon Browne, taken from *With Clive in India*, reduced and reproduced by line blocks printed in black on text pages, as frontispiece and on pages 17 and 43.

(1) Advertisement (BLACKIE'S STORY-BOOK READERS) listing 8 titles | (2) frontispiece | (3) title p. | (4) blank | 5–94. text | (95)–(96) blank.

Cover (see Note 1)

Red cloth, printed black; lined with plain yellow paper; saddle-stitched, cut flush.

Front: BLACKIE'S . STORY-BOOK | : : READERS : : | (printer's ornament) | CHARLIE | . MARRYAT . | G.A.HENTY | (publisher's device) | 4d. (in small circle, all black) within quadruple-ruled frame with decorative corners. **Back:** plain.

References: *Farmer*, pp.93, 94 (addenda); *Dartt*, p.129, *Companion*, p.28.

Notes

1. I have not seen the first issue of *Charlie Marryat*: my information is from various sources. The cover design is as for *Cast Ashore*, 115.1, Plate 125.

2. For further details of Blackie 'Story-Book Readers' see *Among the Bushrangers*, 114.1, Notes 1–3, and Appendix V.

116.2

G.A.Henty | (3-em rule) | CHARLIE MARRYAT | FROM | WITH CLIVE IN INDIA | BLACKIE AND SON LIMITED | LONDON AND GLASGOW

Contents: 165 x 111 mm. As for 116.1.

Cover (see Note 1)

Grey paper, printed black; saddle-stitched; cut flush.

(1) BLACKIE'S . STORY-BOOK | : : READERS : : | (printer's ornament) | CHARLIE | . MARRYAT . | G.A.HENTY | (publisher's device) | FIFTH . SERIES . (all black) within quadruple-ruled frame with decorative corners.

(2) and (3) blank.

(4) advertisement (BLACKIE'S SUPPLEMENTARY READERS).

References: *Farmer*, pp.93, 94 (addenda); *Dartt*, pp.37, 129, *Companion*, p.28.

Notes
1. I have not seen this issue of *Charlie Marryat*: my information is from various sources. The cover design is as for *Cast Ashore*, 115.2, Plate 126.
2. See also *Cast Ashore*, 115.2, Note 2.

116.3 and 116.3s
Charlie Marryat I From "WITH CLIVE IN INDIA" I BY G.A.HENTY I (publisher's device) I BLACKIE AND SON LIMITED I LONDON GLASGOW AND BOMBAY

Contents
176 x 117 mm. (but see Note 4). (1)–(96) I no catalogue. Three full-page drawings by Gordon Browne, taken from *With Clive in India*, reduced and printed in black from line blocks; frontispiece on MF paper, unbacked, tipped in; the others on text pages 17 and 43.
   (1) Half-title p. I (2) blank I (frontispiece, tipped in) I (3) title p. I (4) blank I 5–94. text I (95)–(96) blank.

Binding (see Plate 133, and Note 4)
Green cloth boards, blocked black, white and yellow; edges plain; plain off-white endpapers.
   Front board: CHARLIE I MARRYAT (black) above illustration of boy and girl, carrying skates, in snow-scene (black, white, yellow) in narrow rectangular panel framed by black line. **Spine:** CHARLIE I MARR- I YAT I Henty (all black) above three-panelled art-nouveau design (black). At foot, above two black rules: BLACKIE I & SON LD (black). **Back board:** plain.

References: BL; PN I *Dartt*, p.37.

Notes
1. One of three Henty titles published in this style in 1920. The other two are: *Cast Ashore*, 115.3, and *The Young Captain*, 121.3. *Dartt* incorrectly names *Do Your Duty* (see 89.8, Note 3) in place of *The Young Captain*.
2. The series seems not to have been given a name. The contents vary from those in the 'Happy Home Library' (see 116.4, below) only in having a half-title page instead of a page listing titles in that series.
3. All three titles were bound in a variety of cloth-colours, and by 1926 had been issued in grained-paper boards (imitating cloth).
4. This title and *The Young Captain* were issued in an alternative page-size of 171 x 115 mm.: issues in the smaller size have the letter **s** at the end of their coding. The variations are shown at Plate 133. I have found *Cast Ashore* in the smaller size only (see 115.3s, Note 4).

116.4
Charlie Marryat I From "WITH CLIVE IN INDIA" I BY G.A.HENTY I (publisher's device) I BLACKIE AND SON LIMITED I LONDON GLASGOW AND BOMBAY

Contents

170 × 114 mm. (1)–(96) | no catalogue. Three full-page drawings by Gordon Browne, taken from *With Clive in India*, reduced and reproduced by line blocks printed in black; the frontispiece on coated paper, unbacked, tipped in; the other two on text pages 17 and 43.

(Frontispiece, tipped in) | (1) title p. | (2) blank | (3) advertisement (OTHER BOOKS IN | THIS SERIES) listing 12 titles including 6 by Henty | (4) blank | 5–94. text | (95)–(96) blank.

Binding (see Plate 133)

Blue paper boards, grained to imitate cloth, blocked black, white, and green; edges plain; plain off-white endpapers.

Front board: CHARLIE | MARRYAT (black) framed by green rules, across pattern of long-stemmed dianthus-type flowers (black, white, green). **Spine:** CHARLIE | MARR- | YAT | Henty (all black) above panel with pattern as on front board, with wide green rules above and below. At foot: BLACKIE (black). **Back board:** plain.

References: PN | *Farmer*, p.91 (addenda); *Dartt*, pp.37, 70.

Note: *Farmer*, p.91, and *Dartt*, p.37, incorrectly date the impression 1906 and 1915 respectively. It was published in 1922. For details of the 'Happy Home Library' see *Among the Bushrangers*, 114.3, Notes 1–3, and Appendix V.

117. CORNET WALTER

117.1

G.A.Henty | (3-em rule) | CORNET WALTER | FROM ORANGE AND GREEN | LONDON | BLACKIE & SON, LIMITED, 50 OLD BAILEY, E.C. | GLASGOW AND DUBLIN | 1906

Contents

175 × 118 mm. (1)–(88). Two full-page drawings by Gordon Browne, taken from *Orange and Green*, reduced and reproduced by line blocks printed in black on text paper, as frontispiece and on p.53.

(1) Advertisement (BLACKIE'S STORY-BOOK READERS) listing 8 titles | (2) frontispiece | (3) title p. | (4) blank | 5–87. text | (88) blank.

Cover (see Note 1)

Red cloth, printed black; lined with plain yellow paper; saddle-stitched, cut flush.

Front: BLACKIE'S . STORY-BOOK | : : READERS : : | (printer's ornament) | CORNET | . WALTER . | G.A.HENTY | (publisher's device) | 4d. (in small circle, all black) within quadruple-ruled frame with decorative corners. **Back:** plain.

References: *Farmer*, p.94 (addenda); *Dartt*, pp.41, 129, *Companion*, p.10.

Notes

1. I have not seen this issue of *Cornet Walter*: my information is from various sources. The cover design is as for *Cast Ashore*, 115.1, Plate 125.

2. In his *Companion*, p.10, Dartt corrects errors in his earlier entries.

3. For further details of Blackie's 'Story-Book Readers' see *Among the Bushrangers*, 114.1, Notes 1–3, and Appendix V.

117.2

G.A.Henty | (3-em rule) | CORNET WALTER | FROM | ORANGE AND GREEN | BLACKIE & SON LIMITED | LONDON AND GLASGOW

Contents: 165 × 111 mm. As for 117.1, except p.(4) Blackie addresses; printer's imprint (Printed in Great Britain by Blackie & Son, Ltd., Glasgow).

Cover (see Plate 126)
Red cloth, printed black; lined with plain yellow paper; saddle-stitched, cut flush.
  Front: BLACKIE'S . STORY-BOOK | : : READERS : : | (printer's ornament) | CORNET | . WALTER . | G.A.HENTY | (publisher's device) | FIFTH . SERIES . (all black) within quadruple-ruled frame with decorative corners. **Back:** plain.

References: BB | *Farmer*, pp.93, 94 (addenda); *Dartt*, pp.41, 129, *Companion*, p.10.

Notes
1. *Farmer* and *Dartt* give the date 1915 to the FIFTH SERIES.
2. It appears that the original 1906 issues of the 'Story-Book Readers' were all in limp red cloth, but that the reprints, or fifth series, were issued both in limp red cloth and in paper covers. I have not seen a copy of this title in paper covers.

118. A HIGHLAND CHIEF

118.1

G.A.Henty | (3-em rule) | A HIGHLAND CHIEF | FROM | IN FREEDOM'S CAUSE | LONDON | BLACKIE & SON, LIMITED, 50 OLD BAILEY, E.C. | GLASGOW AND DUBLIN | 1906

Contents
175 × 115 mm. (1)–88. Two full-page drawings by Gordon Browne, taken from *In Freedom's Cause*, reduced and reproduced by line blocks, printed in black on text pages as frontispiece and on p.57.
  (1) Advertisement (BLACKIE'S | STORY-BOOK READERS) listing 8 titles | 2. frontispiece | (3) title p. | (4) blank | 5–88. text.

Cover (see Note 1)
Red cloth, printed black; lined with plain yellow paper; saddle-stitched, cut flush.
  Front: BLACKIE'S . STORY-BOOK | : : READERS : : | (printer's ornament) | A . HIGHLAND | . CHIEF . | G.A.HENTY | (publisher's device) | 4d. (in small circle, all black) within quadruple-ruled frame with decorative corners. **Back:** plain.

References: AG | *Farmer*, pp.93, 94 (addenda); *Dartt*, pp.74, 129, *Companion*, p.28.

Notes
1. This and the eight other 'Story-Book Readers' of Henty's work are listed in

Appendix V. The cover design is as for *Cast Ashore*, 115.1, Plate 125.
2. For details of the series see *Among the Bushrangers*, 114.1, Notes 1–3.

118.2

G.A.Henty | (3-em rule) | A HIGHLAND CHIEF | FROM | IN FREEDOM'S CAUSE | BLACKIE & SON LIMITED | LONDON GLASGOW AND BOMBAY

Contents: 165 × 111 mm. As for 118.1, except p.(4) Blackie addresses; printer's imprint (Printed in Great Britain by Blackie & Son, Ltd., Glasgow).

Cover (see Note 1)
Red cloth, printed black; lined with plain yellow paper; saddle-stitched, cut flush.
    Front: BLACKIE'S . STORY-BOOK | : : READERS : : | (printer's ornament) | A . HIGHLAND | . CHIEF . | G.A.HENTY | (publisher's device) | FIFTH . SERIES . (all black) within quadruple-ruled frame with decorative corners. **Back:** plain.

References: *Farmer*, pp.93, 94 (addenda); *Dartt*, pp.74, 129, *Companion*, p.28.

Notes
1. I have not seen this issue of *A Highland Chief*: my information is from various sources. The cover design is as for *Cast Ashore*, 115.2, Plate 126.
2. *Farmer* and *Dartt* give the date 1915 to the FIFTH SERIES.
3. It appears that the original 1906 issues of the 'Story-Book Readers' were all in limp red cloth, but that the reprints, or fifth series, were issued both in limp red cloth and in paper covers.

118.3

A Highland Chief | From "IN FREEDOM'S CAUSE" | BY G.A.HENTY | (publisher's device) | BLACKIE AND SON LIMITED | LONDON GLASGOW AND BOMBAY

Contents
170 × 111 mm. (1)–88 | no catalogue. Two full-page drawings by Gordon Browne, taken from *In Freedom's Cause*, reduced and reproduced by line blocks printed black; the frontispiece on coated paper, unbacked, tipped in; the other on text p. 57.
    (Frontispiece, tipped in) | (1) title p. | (2) blank | (3) advertisement (OTHER BOOKS IN THIS SERIES) listing 12 titles including 6 by Henty | (4) blank | 5-88. text.

Binding (see Note 2)
Brown paper boards, grained to imitate cloth, blocked black, white, and green; edges plain; plain off-white endpapers.
    Front board: A HIGHLAND | CHIEF (black) framed by green line, across pattern of long-stemmed dianthus-type flowers (black, white, green). **Spine:** A | HIGH- | LAND | CHIEF (black) above panel wih pattern as on front board, with wide green rules above and below. At foot: BLACKIE (black). **Back board:** plain.

References: PN | *Farmer*, pp.39, 91 (addenda); *Dartt*, pp.70, 74, *Companion*, p.17.

Notes
1. Published 1923, the last of six Henty titles in the 'Happy Home Library'. For

details of the series see *Among the Bushrangers*, 114.3, Notes 1–3, and Appendix V.
2. The binding design is as for *Charlie Marryat*, 116.4, Plate 133.

119. AN INDIAN RAID

119.1

G.A.Henty | (3-em rule) | AN INDIAN RAID | FROM | REDSKIN AND COW-BOY | LONDON | BLACKIE & SON, LIMITED, 50 OLD BAILEY, E.C. | GLASGOW AND DUBLIN | 1906

Contents

175 × 117 mm. (1)–88. Two full-page drawings by an unknown hand, re-drawn in line from the original wash-drawings by Alfred Pearse for *Redskin and Cow-boy,* reproduced by line blocks printed in black on text paper as frontispiece and on p. 40.

(1) Advertisement (BLACKIE'S STORY-BOOK READERS) listing 8 titles | (2) frontispiece | (3) title p. | (4) blank | 5–88. text.

Cover (see Plate 125)

Red cloth, printed black; lined with plain yellow paper; saddle-stitched, cut flush.

Front: BLACKIE'S . STORY-BOOK | : : READERS : : | (printer's ornament) | AN . INDIAN | . RAID . | G.A.HENTY | (publisher's device) | 4d. (in small circle, all black) within quadruple-ruled frame with decorative corners. **Back:** plain.

References: BB | *Farmer*, pp.93, 94 (addenda); *Dartt*, pp.78, 129, *Companion*, pp.18, 28.

Notes

1. One of nine 'Story-Book Readers' containing work by Henty. For details of the series see *Among the Bushrangers*, 114.1, Notes 1–3, and Appendix V.
2. In his *Companion*, p.10, Dartt corrects errors in his earlier entries.

119.2

G.A.Henty | (3-em rule) | AN INDIAN RAID | FROM | REDSKIN AND COW-BOY | BLACKIE AND SON LIMITED | LONDON GLASGOW AND BOMBAY

Contents: 164 × 109 mm. As for 119.1, except p.(4) printer's imprint (Printed in Great Britain by | Blackie & Son, Limited, Glasgow)

Cover (see Plate 126)

Green paper, printed black; saddle-stitched, cut flush.

(1) BLACKIE'S . STORY-BOOK | : : READERS : : | AN . INDIAN | . RAID . | G.A.HENTY | (publisher's device) | FIFTH . SERIES . (all black) within quadruple-ruled frame with decorative corners.
(2) and (3) blank.
(4) advertisement (BLACKIE'S SUPPLEMENTARY READERS).

References: BB | *Farmer*, pp.93, 94 (addenda); *Dartt*, pp.78 Note, 129, *Companion*, p.18.

Notes

1. *Farmer* and *Dartt* give the date 1915 to the FIFTH SERIES.

2. It appears that the original 1906 issues of the 'Story-Book Readers' were all in limp red cloth, but that the reprints, or fifth series, were issued both in limp red cloth and in paper covers.

119.3

An Indian Raid I From "REDSKIN AND COWBOY" I BY G.A.HENTY I (publisher's device) I BLACKIE AND SON LIMITED I LONDON GLASGOW AND BOMBAY

Contents

170 × 114 mm. (1)–88 I no catalogue. Illustrations as in 119.1, but the frontispiece now on coated paper, unbacked, tipped in; the other on text page 40 as before.

(Frontispiece, tipped in) I (1) title p. I (2) blank I (3) advertisement (OTHER BOOKS IN I THIS SERIES) listing 12 titles including 6 by Henty I (4) blank I 5–88. text.

Binding (see Note 2)

Brown paper boards, grained to imitate cloth, blocked black, white and green; edges plain; plain off-white endpapers.

Front board: AN INDIAN I RAID (black) framed by green line, across pattern of long-stemmed dianthus-type flowers (black, white, green). **Spine:** AN I INDIAN I RAID I Henty (black) above panel with pattern as on front board, with wide green rules above and below. At foot: BLACKIE (black). **Back board:** plain.

References: PN I *Farmer*, pp.40, 91 (addenda); *Dartt*, p.70, *Companion*, pp.17, 18.

Notes

1. One of six Henty titles in the 'Happy Home Library', first published in 1922. For details of the series see *Among the Bushrangers*, 114.3, Notes 1–3, and Appendix V.
2. The binding design is as for *Charlie Marryat*, 116.4, Plate 133.
3. *Farmer*, p.40, incorrectly dates this issue 1906.

120. THE TWO PRISONERS

120.1

G.A.Henty I (3-em rule) I THE TWO PRISONERS I FROM I A SOLDIER'S DAUGHTER I LONDON I BLACKIE & SON, LIMITED, 50 OLD BAILEY, E.C. I GLASGOW AND DUBLIN I 1906

Contents

175 × 117 mm. (1)–88. Three full-page drawings by an unknown hand, redrawn in line from the original wash-drawings by Frances Ewan for *A Soldier's Daughter*, reproduced by line blocks printed black on text paper, as frontispiece and on pages 19 and 45.

(1) Advertisement (BLACKIE'S STORY-BOOK READERS) I (2) frontispiece I (3) title p. I (4) blank I 5–88. text.

Cover (see Plate 124)

Red cloth, printed black; lined with plain yellow paper; saddle-stitched, cut flush.

Front: BLACKIE'S . STORY-BOOK | : : READERS : : | (printer's ornament) | THE . TWO | . PRISONERS . | G.A.HENTY | (publisher's device) | 4d. (in small circle, all black) within quadruple-ruled frame with decorative corners. **Back:** plain.

References: BB | *Farmer*, pp.93, 94 (addenda); *Dartt*, p.129, *Companion*, pp.28, 32.

Note: One of nine 'Story-Book Readers': for details of the series see *Among the Bushrangers*, 114.1, Notes 1–3, and Appendix V.

120.2

G.A.Henty | (3-em rule) | THE TWO PRISONERS | FROM | A SOLDIER'S DAUGHTER | BLACKIE AND SON LIMITED | LONDON GLASGOW AND BOMBAY

Contents: 164 × 109 mm. As for 120.1, except p.(4) Blackie addresses; printer's imprint (Printed in Great Britain by Blackie & Son, Ltd., Glasgow).

Cover (see Note 1)

Red cloth, printed black; lined with plain yellow paper; saddle-stitched, cut flush.

Front: BLACKIE'S . STORY-BOOK | : : READERS : : | (printer's ornament) | THE . TWO | . PRISONERS . | G.A.HENTY | (publisher's device) | FIFTH . SERIES . (all black) within quadruple-ruled frame with decorative corners. **Back:** plain.

References: *Farmer*, pp.93, 94 (addenda); *Dartt*, p.129, *Companion*, p.28.

Notes

1. I have not seen this issue of *The Two Prisoners*: my information is from various sources. The cover design is as for *Cast Ashore*, 115.2, Plate 126.

2. *Farmer* and *Dartt* give the date 1915 to the FIFTH SERIES issues.

3. It appears that the original 1906 issues of these readers were all in limp red cloth, but that the reprints, or fifth series, were issued both in limp red cloth and in paper covers.

120.3

The Two Prisoners | From "A SOLDIER'S DAUGHTER" | BY G.A.HENTY | (publisher's device) | BLACKIE AND SON LIMITED | LONDON GLASGOW AND BOMBAY

Contents

170 × 114 mm. (1)–88 | no catalogue. Illustrations as in 120.1; the frontispiece block now printed in black on coated paper, unbacked, tipped in; the others on text pp.19 and 45 as before.

(Frontispiece, tipped in) | (1) title p. | (2) blank | (3) advertisement (OTHER BOOKS IN | THIS SERIES) listing 13 titles including 5 by Henty | (4) blank | 5–88. text, with printer's imprint at foot of p.88 (PRINTED AND BOUND IN GREAT BRITAIN | By Blackie & Son, Limited, Glasgow).

Binding (see Note 2)
Green paper boards, grained to imitate cloth, blocked black, white, and green; edges plain; plain off-white endpapers.
 Front board: THE TWO | PRISONERS (black) framed by green line, across pattern of long-stemmed dianthus-type flowers (black, white, green). **Spine:** THE | TWO | PRIS- | ONERS (black) above panel with pattern as on front board, and wide green rules above and below. At foot: BLACKIE (black). **Back board:** plain.

References: PN | *Farmer*, p.91 (addenda); *Dartt*, pp.70, 142, *Companion*, p.17.

Notes
1. One of six titles in the 'Happy Home Library', first issued thus in 1922: for details of the series see *Among the Bushrangers*, 114.3, Notes 1–3, and Appendix V.
2. The binding design is as for *Charlie Marryat*, 116.4, Plate 133.
3. The Henty title missing from the list on p.(3) is *A Highland Chief*, 118.3, which was published in 1923, a year later than the other five.

120.4
The Two Prisoners | FROM | "A Soldier's Daughter" | BY | G.A.HENTY | BLACKIE & SON LIMITED | LONDON AND GLASGOW

Contents
180 × 122 mm. (1)–96 | no catalogue. Frontispiece from a wash-drawing by Frances Ewan, reproduced by halftone block, as it appeared in *A Soldier's Daughter* but now printed in black, on coated paper, unbacked, tipped in.
 (1) Half-title p. | (2) Blackie addresses | (frontispiece, tipped in) | (3) title p. | (4) advertisement (Summit Library : Books of this Series) listing 12 titles including 2 by Henty | (5) Contents | (6) blank | 7–96. text.

Binding (see Plate 136)
White paper boards, printed by litho in four process-colours (yellow, red, blue, black); edges plain; plain off-white endpapers.
 Front board: THE | TWO | PRISONERS (black) | G.A.Henty (red) all on yellow circular panel at upper right corner of all-over full-colour illustration, by (?) Nick (see Note 1), of the heroine and young officer with bandaged head. **Spine:** THE | TWO | PRISONERS (black) | G.A.HENTY (red) all on yellow circular panel at head, with all-over continuation of landscape in full-colour illustration from front board. At foot: BLACKIE (black). **Back board:** Large solid-red panel, cut into at the top by yellow strip, with: THE . SUMMIT . LIBRARY (red), and at the lower left corner by circular yellow panel, with: BLACKIE | & SON | LIMITED (red). White margins.

References: BL; PN | *Farmer*, p.74; *Dartt*, p.143.

Notes
1. Published 1929: the only other Henty title in the 'Summit Library' is *Among the Bushrangers*, 114.4. Both binding cases were illustrated by (?) Nick (see Appendix IV, Part 2). *Farmer* incorrectly dated the edition 1906.
2. Re-set in a larger typeface, heavily leaded, to make more pages, and printed on a very bulky featherweight antique wove.

3. Details of the publisher's addresses on p.(2) and also of the titles in the series, given on p.(4), vary from one impression to another.

4. This title was not reprinted on thinner paper, as was the case with *Among the Bushrangers* (see 114.4 and 114.5).

121. THE YOUNG CAPTAIN

121.1

G.A.Henty | (3-em rule) | THE YOUNG CAPTAIN | FROM | WITH CLIVE IN INDIA | LONDON | BLACKIE & SON, LIMITED, 50 OLD BAILEY, E.C. | GLASGOW AND DUBLIN | 1906

Contents

175 x 117 mm. (1)–(96). Three full-page drawings by Gordon Browne, taken from *With Clive in India*, reproduced from electros of the original line blocks, reduced in size by having the edges trimmed away, printed in black on text paper, as frontispiece and on pages 45 and 91.

(1) Advertisement (BLACKIE'S STORY-BOOK READERS) listing 8 titles | (2) frontispiece | (3) title p. | (4) blank | 5–94. text | (95)–(96) blank.

Cover (see Note 1)

Red cloth, printed black; lined with plain yellow paper; saddle-stitched, cut flush.

Front: BLACKIE'S . STORY-BOOK | : : READERS : : | (printer's ornament) | THE . YOUNG | . CAPTAIN . | G.A.HENTY | (publisher's device) | 4d. (in small circle, all black) within quadruple-ruled frame with decorative corners. **Back:** plain.

References: *Farmer*, pp.93, 94 (addenda); *Dartt*, pp.129, 167, *Companion*, p.28.

Notes

1. I have not seen this issue of *The Young Captain*: my information is from various sources. The cover design is as for *Cast Ashore*, 115.1, Plate 125.

2. For further details of the series see *Among the Bushrangers*, 114.1, Notes 1–3.

121.2

G.A.Henty | (3-em rule) | THE YOUNG CAPTAIN | FROM | WITH CLIVE IN INDIA | BLACKIE & SON LIMITED | LONDON GLASGOW AND BOMBAY

Contents: 165 x 111 mm. As for 121.1, except p.(4) Blackie addresses; printer's imprint (Printed in Great Britain by Blackie & Son, Ltd., Glasgow).

Cover (see Note 2)

Brown paper, printed black; saddle-stitched, cut flush.

(1) BLACKIE'S . STORY-BOOK | : : READERS : : | (printer's ornament) | THE . YOUNG | . CAPTAIN . | G.A.HENTY | (publisher's device) | FIFTH . SERIES . (all black) within quadruple-ruled frame with decorative corners.

(2) and (3) blank.

(4) advertisement (BLACKIE'S SUPPLEMENTARY READERS).

References: CT I *Farmer*, pp.93, 94 (addenda); *Dartt*, p.129, *Companion*, p.28.

Notes
1. *Farmer* and *Dartt* give the date 1915 to the FIFTH SERIES.
2. It appears that the original 1906 issues of the 'Story-Book Readers' were all in limp red cloth, but that the reprints, or fifth series, were issued both in limp red cloth and in paper covers. The cover design is as for *Cast Ashore*, 115.2, Plate 126.

121.3 and 121.3s
The I Young Captain I From "WITH CLIVE IN INDIA" I BY G.A.HENTY I (publisher's device) I BLACKIE AND SON LIMITED I LONDON GLASGOW AND BOMBAY

Contents
176 x 118 mm. (but see Note 1). (1)–(96) I no catalogue. Illustrations as in 121.1, but with the frontispiece block printed in black on coated paper, unbacked, tipped in; the others as before, on text pages 45 and 91.
  (1) Half-title p. I (2) blank I (frontispiece, tipped in) I (3) title p. I (4) blank I 5–94. text I (95)–(96) blank.

Binding (see Note 1)
Mustard-yellow cloth boards, blocked black, white, and yellow; edges plain; plain off-white endpapers.
  Front board: THE YOUNG I CAPTAIN (black) above illustration of boy and girl, carrying skates, in snow-scene (black, white, yellow) in narrow rectangular panel framed by black rules. **Spine:** THE I YOUNG I CAP- I TAIN (black) above three-panelled art-nouveau design (black). At foot, above two black rules: BLACKIE I & SON LD (black). **Back board:** plain.

References: BL; PN; CH I *Dartt*, p.168.

Notes
1. One of three titles issued in this style in 1920. This title and *Charlie Marryat* (see 116.3 and 116.3s, Plate 133) were issued in an alternative page-size of 171 x 115 mm.: issues in the smaller size have the letter **s** at the end of their coding. The third title is *Cast Ashore*, 115.3s. *Dartt* incorrectly names *Do Your Duty* (see 89.8, Note 3) in place of *The Young Captain*.
2. *Dartt*, p.168, describes the copy in the British Library, but mistakenly reports it to be part of the 'Happy Home Library' (see 121.4).
3. The only copy of this title I have seen in the smaller size, 121.3s, is a late issue, with an inscription dated 1926, and bound in grained paper, imitating cloth.

121.4
The I Young Captain I From "WITH CLIVE IN INDIA" I BY G.A.HENTY I (publisher's device) I BLACKIE AND SON LIMITED I LONDON GLASGOW AND BOMBAY

Contents
170 x 117 mm. (1)–(96) I no catalogue. Illustrations as in 121.3.
  (Frontispiece, tipped in) I (1) title p. I (2) blank I (3) advertisement (OTHER

BOOKS IN | THIS SERIES) listing 12 titles including 6 by Henty (see Note 2) | (4) blank | 5–94. text | (95)–(96) blank.

Binding (see Note 2)

Blue paper boards, grained to imitate cloth, blocked black. white, and green; edges plain; plain off-white endpapers.

Front board: THE YOUNG | CAPTAIN (black) framed by green line, across pattern of long-stemmed dianthus-type flowers (black, white, green). **Spine:** THE | YOUNG | CAP- | TAIN (black) above panel with pattern as on front board, and wide green rules above and below. At foot: BLACKIE (black). **Back board:** plain.

References: PN | *Farmer*, p.86; *Dartt*, p.70, *Companion*, pp.17, 36.

Notes

1. One of six Henty titles published in the 'Happy Home Library' in 1922. For details of the series see *Among the Bushrangers*, 114.3, Notes 1–3, and Appendix V.

2. The binding design is as for *Charlie Marryat*, 116.4, Plate 133.

3. I have a second copy, a late issue inscribed 1929, with a list of 22 titles on p.(3), including the six by Henty. Other variations in it are the wording of the publisher's title-page imprint (BLACKIE & SON LIMITED | LONDON AND GLASGOW), and the addition of the printer's imprint on p.(2) (Printed in Great Britain by | Blackie & Son, Limited, Glasgow). Also, on p.(3), beneath the longer list of titles, is added the publisher's imprint with the Bombay address included: no imprint at all was included here in the earlier issues. (No doubt there was an intermediate issue, listing more than 12 and less than 22 titles, for which the publisher's imprint was added to the advertisement panel while the Bombay address was still being used. In the issue inscribed 1929 the need to change it was overlooked when the title page was amended).

122. A YOUNG PATRIOT

122.1

A YOUNG PATRIOT | FROM | G.A.HENTY'S | "ORANGE AND GREEN" | A STORY READER FOR SENIOR | STANDARDS IN IRISH NATIONAL SCHOOLS | ADAPTED BY | H.P.COURTNEY | DUBLIN | BLACKIE & SON, LIMITED, 89 TALBOT STREET | BELFAST: 44 WELLINGTON PLACE | 1906 | (Printed and bound in Ireland)

Contents

166 × 112 mm. (1)–192 | no catalogue. Three full-page drawings by Gordon Browne, taken from *Orange and Green*, and now printed in black on text pages from electros of the original line blocks, reduced in size by having the edges trimmed away.

(1) Title p. | (2) blank | (3) Editor's Preface | (4) blank | 5–192. text and illustrations.

Binding (see Plate 132)

Red cloth boards, blocked black; edges plain; plain off-white endpapers.

Front board: A : YOUNG | : PATRIOT : | : G : A : HENTY : (all black) above decorative emblem. Beneath this: BLACKIE : & : SON : LTD : | 8d. (black) all within decorative framework. **Spine:** : A : YOUNG : PATRIOT : (black) running from foot to head. **Back board:** plain.

References: PN | *Dartt Companion*, p.37.

Notes

1. The copy described by Dartt (*Companion*, p.37) varies from the above, having the price blocked on the front board 10d. instead of 8d. It is also described as having no spine.

2. This is the only book by Henty to have both Dublin and Belfast in the imprint, and the only one to have an Irish imprint not coupled with Scottish and English addresses. In her history of the publishing house, *Blackie & Son, 1809–1959* (p.52), Agnes Blackie wrote: 'Blackie & Son had been operating their printing establishment in Dublin, entirely devoted to the production of the Vere Foster Copy Books, since 1878. By the end of the nineties it became apparent that (they) were beginning to decline from their high peak of popularity. In response to these signs of change and to insure the future of the Dublin factory, Blackie & Son embarked on general educational publishing in Ireland, and were for a time extremely successful. As the Sinn Fein movement grew stronger, however, business became more difficult, and in 1910 the Irish branch was made a separate Company with an all Irish board, known as The Educational Company of Ireland Ltd. In this Company Blackie & Son retained a controlling financial interest until 1919, when the connection was severed by the sale of shares to Mr. W. Lyon, who had originally been Manager of the Dublin branch'.

BOOKS AND ANNUALS
TO WHICH HENTY CONTRIBUTED

123. THE ADVENTURES OF TWO BRAVE BOYS
and Other Stories

123.1

THE ADVENTURES OF | TWO BRAVE BOYS | AND OTHER STORIES | INCLUDING | THE HEIR OF LANGBRIDGE TOWERS | BY R.M.FREEMAN. | AND | KING LION: A STORY OF STRANGE ADVENTURES | WITH | INTERESTING ZOOLOGICAL SKETCHES, AND USEFUL AND | AMUSING MISCELLANEOUS ARTICLES. | EDITED BY | G.A.HENTY. | WITH FULL-PAGE AND OTHER ENGRAVINGS. | WARD, LOCK AND CO., | LONDON, NEW YORK, AND MELBOURNE | (15-point rule) | (All rights reserved.)

Contents
210 x 136 mm. (i)–iv | B1–B512 | no catalogue. Frontispiece and eleven plates, from wash-drawings by W.S.Stacey reproduced by halftone blocks, and from wood-engravings by T. W. Wood; all in black on ivory MF paper, unbacked, unfolioed, tipped in. Many smaller engravings by various artists on text pages.
    (Frontispiece, tipped in) | (i) title p. | (ii) blank | (iii)–iv. Contents | B1–B512. text and illustrations.

Binding (see Plate 169)
Green cloth boards, blocked black, red, dark-blue merging to light-blue, warm buff, and gilt; edges plain; yellow surface-paper endpapers.
    Front board: BEETON'S . BOY'S OWN BOOKS | (ornament) Edited by G.A.HENTY (ornament) (black) within rectangular panel (red) framed by double rules with decorations at each end (black), above: The ADVENTURES of | TWO . BRAVE . BOYS | AND | Other | Stories (gilt). Beneath this, two overlapping illustrations, both partly framed by decorative rules (black and blue), of man riding through canyon (black, dark-blue merging to light-blue, warm buff), and boy with sword fighting man with club (black, warm buff). At foot: PROFUSELY ILLUSTRATED (black). **Spine:** . BEETON'S . | BOY'S OWN BOOKS (black) within rectangular panel (red) framed by double rules with decorations on all four sides (black) above: THE | ADVENTURES | of | TWO | BRAVE | BOYS (gilt). Beneath this is illustration of man and woman on horse, led by another man (black, warm buff), above: EDITED | BY (black) | G.A.HENTY (black on solid-gilt rectangle) framed by double rules, decorated (black). At foot: WARD . LOCK & Co. (gilt). **Back board:** plain.

References: PN | *Dartt*, p.1.

Notes
1. This fifth volume in the series, 'Beeton's Boy's Own Books', which re-uses material from *Beeton's Boy's Own Magazine* (§3, 197), edited by Henty, contains nothing written by Henty himself.
2. For further details of the series, and the numerous variant volumes within it, see §2, 127, Notes, and also Notes 3–4 below.
3. Reprints included amendments to the publisher's imprint; the date was given on the title page of the first printing only. The picture used as frontispiece varied.
4. I have a second copy of this title, with the imprint on the title page changed to: 'LONDON: | WARD, LOCK & BOWDEN, LIMITED, | WARWICK HOUSE, SALISBURY SQUARE, E.C. | NEW YORK AND MELBOURNE.'. (Bowden became a director of Ward Lock in 1878, see Appendix II, Part 6). The binding case varies in some details: (a) on the front board the title is blocked in red instead of gilt, and at the foot the words PROFUSELY ILLUSTRATED have been removed; (b) all reference to Beeton has been removed. The red panel at the head of the front board reads, simply: 'Edited by G.A.HENTY', and the one at the head of the spine reads: 'Illustrated.'; (c) the brasses used for 'EDITED | BY | G.A.HENTY', blocked in black and gilt on the spine, have been removed.

124. THE ART OF AUTHORSHIP

124.1
THE | ART OF AUTHORSHIP | Literary Reminiscences, | Methods of Work, and Advice to Young Beginners, | PERSONALLY CONTRIBUTED BY | LEADING AUTHORS OF THE DAY. | COMPILED AND EDITED BY | GEORGE BAINTON. | London: | JAMES CLARKE & CO., 13 & 14, FLEET STREET. | 8-pt rule) | 1890.
(Note: London *is in gothic type).*

Contents
192 x 125 mm. (i)–(xii) | (1)–(356) | catalogue (1)–8. No illustrations.
   (i)–(ii) Blank | (iii) half-title p. | (iv) blank | (v) title p. | (vi) blank | (vii)–x. Introduction | (xi) Contents | (xii) blank | (1) half-title p. to 'Good Writing – Is it a Gift or an Art?' | (2) blank | (3)–53. text | (54) blank | (55) half-title p. to 'Methods: Conscious and Unconscious.' | (57)–118. text | (119) half-title p. to 'The Influence of Reading on Literary Style.' | (120) blank | (121)–187. text | (188) blank | (189) half-title p. to 'The Strength of Simplicity.' | (190) blank | (191)–240. text | (241) half-title to 'A Protest against Obscurity.' | (242) blank | (243)–285. text | (286) blank | (287) half-title p. to 'Truthfulness to One's Self.' | (288) blank | (289)–352. text | (353)–355. Index of Contributing Authors | (356) printer's imprint (LONDON: | W.SPEAIGHT AND SONS, PRINTERS, | FETTER LANE.) | (1)–8. catalogue, dated 19/11/89.

Binding (see Plate 30)
Blue cloth boards, blocked black and gilt, edges uncut; brown surface-paper endpapers.

Front board: THE ART I OF I AUTHORSHIP (gilt) within frame of black rules; 'woven' pattern (black) at upper left corner; geometrical and floral decoration (black and gilt) below. **Spine:** THE I ART I OF I AUTHORSHIP (gilt) below 'woven' pattern and rules. Beneath this, gilt and black floral decoration as on front board. At foot: J.CLARKE & CO. (gilt) above two black rules. **Back board:** plain.

References: BL; Bod; PN I *Farmer*, p.8; *Dartt*, p.9.

Notes
1. The book is advertised on p.2 of the bound-in catalogue: 'Crown 8vo, cloth 5s.'.
2. Henty's contribution is at pp.19–21, in the section headed 'Good Writing – Is it a Gift or an Art?'.
3. *Dartt* omits the fourth line of the title page. *Farmer* reports white endpapers.

125. THE ASHANTEES

125.1
THE ASHANTEES: I THEIR COUNTRY, HISTORY, WARS, GOVERNMENT, I CUSTOMS, CLIMATE, RELIGION, AND I PRESENT POSITION; I With a Description of the Neighbouring Territories. I BY I A.C.BEATON. I With Map. I PORTRAITS OF SIR GARNET WOLSELEY, COLONEL HARLEY, I AND OTHER ILLUSTRATIONS. I LONDON: I JAMES BLACKWOOD AND CO., I LOVELL'S COURT, PATERNOSTER ROW. I [The right of translation is reserved.] *(Note:* With Map. *is in gothic type).*

Contents
161 x 101 mm. (i)–iv I (9)–140 I catalogue (1)–(32). Map of Ashanti, folded twice and tipped in to face title p.

(Map, tipped in) I (i) title p. I (ii) printer's imprint (LONDON I PRINTED BY J.OGDEN AND CO., I 172, ST. JOHN STREET, E.C.) I (iii)–iv. Contents I 9–140. text, with printer's imprint on p.140 (J.Ogden & Co., Printers, 172, St. John Street, E.C.) I (1)–31. catalogue I (32) blank.

Binding (see Plate 31)
Paper boards, printed black, yellow, and orange; edges plain; plain off-white endpapers.
Front board: PRICE ONE (space) SHILLING I THE (black) I ASHANTEES (yellow, cased and shaded black) over upper part of illustration, framed by black line, of man with wide-brimmed hat and short skirt, matchet at waist-belt, axe lying on ground, carrying bundle of logs in front of blazing forest (black, yellow, orange). At foot: LONDON: JAMES BLACKWOOD & CO., PATERNOSTER ROW (black) on plain yellow ground, framed by black lines. **Spine:** Stated by *Farmer* to show: THE ASHANTEES (black) on yellow background (see Note 2). **Back board:** advertisement printed in black on yellow ground, listing 39 titles, with heading: BLACKWOOD'S LONDON LIBRARY.

References: B-R; BB I *Farmer*, p.8; *Dartt*, p.7.

Notes

1. All copies inspected are folioed as shown above, from (i) to iv, and then from (9) to 140, and show no signs of having had leaves removed.

2. *Farmer* describes the cover, but not in detail; *Dartt* illustrated the front cover only. The spine is missing from all copies seen.

3. This book by A.C.Beaton contains no original contribution by Henty. But at pp.122–140 the author gives an extended quotation from a dispatch from 'the Special Correspondent of *The Standard*'.

126. BATTLES OF THE NINETEENTH CENTURY

126.1

VOLUME I
BATTLES | OF THE | NINETEENTH CENTURY | DESCRIBED BY | ARCHIBALD FORBES, G.A.HENTY, | MAJOR ARTHUR GRIFFITHS, | And other Well-known Writers | WITH A CHRONOLOGICAL LIST OF THE MORE IMPORTANT BATTLES OF THE CENTURY | VOL.I | WITH ABOUT 370 ILLUSTRATIONS AND 85 PLANS | CASSELL AND COMPANY, LIMITED | LONDON, PARIS & MELBOURNE | 1896 | ALL RIGHTS RESERVED

Contents
251 × 177 mm. (i)–viii | (1)–760 | no catalogue. Frontispiece from watercolour drawing by W.B.Wollen, reproduced by three-colour halftone blocks; nine full-page wash-drawings by W.B.Wollen (2), Alfred Pearse, J.Le Blant, Paul Hardy (2), W.H.Overend (2), Stanley L.Wood, and reproductions of paintings by Lady Butler and Ernest Crofts, A.R.A., all reproduced by halftone blocks in black on coated paper, unbacked, tipped in. Numerous plans, and illustrations by Gordon Browne, R.Caton Woodville, W.H.Overend and Paul Hardy, from wood-engravings, line plates and halftone blocks on text pages. Fold-out engraving, approx. 33 x 45 mm., of 'Badajos, 1812', from painting by R.Caton Woodville, R.I., printed in black line, and guarded in before p.(1).

(Frontispiece, tipped in) | (i) title p. | (ii) publisher's device | (iii)–iv. Contents | (v)–(viii) List of Illustrations | (Fold-out engraving, guarded in) | (1)–752. text | (753)–760. Appendix: Chronological List of Battles, with printer's imprint at foot of p.760 (PRINTED BY CASSELL & COMPANY, LIMITED, LA BELLE SAUVAGE, LUDGATE HILL, LONDON, E.C.).

VOLUME II
BATTLES | OF THE | NINETEENTH CENTURY | DESCRIBED BY | ARCHIBALD FORBES, G.A.HENTY, | MAJOR ARTHUR GRIFFITHS, | And other Well-known Writers | VOL.II | WITH ABOUT 320 ILLUSTRATIONS AND PLANS | CASSELL AND COMPANY, LIMITED | LONDON, PARIS AND MELBOURNE | 1897 | ALL RIGHTS RESERVED

Contents
251 × 177 mm. (i)–viii | (1)–760 | no catalogue. Frontispiece and three full-page

plates from reproductions of paintings by Thomas J. Barker, E. Boutigny and R. Caton Woodville, and of an engraving from a painting by D. Maclise, R.A., and from eight wash-drawings by Wal Paget (3), W.B. Wollen, Stanley L. Wood, Stanley Berkeley, Sidney Paget and an unknown artist, all printed from halftone blocks in black on coated paper, unbacked, tipped in. Numerous plans, and illustrations by Gordon Browne, W.H. Overend and Sidney Paget from wood-engravings, line plates and halftone blocks printed on text pages.

(Frontispiece, tipped in) | (i) title p. | (ii) publisher's device | (iii)–iv. Contents | (v)–viii. List of Illustrations | (1)–748. text | (749)–760. Index, with printer's imprint at foot of p.760 (PRINTED BY CASSELL & COMPANY, LIMITED, LA BELLE SAUVAGE, LUDGATE HILL, LONDON, E.C.)

Binding

Maroon leathercloth boards, blind-embossed, blocked gilt. Binding-cases were supplied by the publisher to individual subscribers, so details of endpapers and treatment of edges of leaves will vary from set to set.

Front board: BATTLES | OF THE | NINETEENTH | CENTURY (gilt) in upper panel in decorative blind-embossed design with repeated wreath and branch motifs; illustration of soldiers in battle (gilt) in lower, rectangular panel. **Spine:** BATTLES | OF THE | NINETEENTH | CENTURY (gilt) above wreath and branch design (gilt) in blind-embossed panel; ILLUSTRATED | (single rose-head design) (double rose-head design for Volume II) (gilt) above wreath and branch design (gilt) in blind-embossed panel. At foot: CASSELL & COMPANY LIMITED (gilt). Gilt rule at head and foot. **Back board:** wreath and branch design in square ruled panel at centre; rules near edges of board (all blind-embossed).

References: PN; SW | *Farmer*, p.9; *Dartt*, p.10; Cinamon, 'Talwin Morris, Blackie and The Glasgow Style' in *The Private Library*, Vol.10, No.1.

Notes

1. These volumes were first issued in 24 monthly parts in red paper covers, from February 1895 to January 1897, at 7d. each. The covers show the title and a battle scene on page 1, with a list of the Contents of the Part. Other pages of the cover carry general advertisements.

2. For readers wishing to bind the parts, title page and prelims for Volume I were given with Part 12, and for Volume 2 with the final part. The eleventh part is numbered in roman numerals, whereas the rest are in arabic. That was to avoid confusion with the numbering of Volume II. It was repeated when the work was re-issued in Parts ten years later (see 126.4, Note 4).

3. The work consists of a series of articles by many authors, named in the lists of Contents, although only three of them are named on the title pages. Henty's articles are identified in the lists of Contents in the two volumes, as follows. In Volume I: 'Amoaful. January 31, 1874', pp.215–223; 'Aroghee. April 10, 1868', pp.408–415. In Volume II: 'The Indian Mutiny: Lucknow. Part I. May–September, 1857', pp.27–37; 'The Turks before Alexinatz. August–October, 1876', pp.194–201; 'The First Burmese War. 1824', pp.396–404; 'The Indian Mutiny: Lucknow. Part II. September, 1857 – March, 1858', pp.620–626.

4. *Dartt* describes a set as above, but with publisher's catalogues in both volumes. He also describes a set in binder's cloth (as opposed to publisher's binding), as he does for other works, apparently unaware that these were 'one-off' bindings ordered by private customers, and that descriptions of them are of negligible interest.

5. At this date Talwin Morris was employed by Blackie as Art Manager (see Appendix II, Part 5, and Appendix IV, Part 2). Cinamon wrote: 'Morris's delight in lettering, as well as his much-simplified drawing – now much in the Glasgow Style – are clearly seen in the 150 headpieces drawn in 1895 and 1896 as a freelance commission for *Battles of the Nineteenth Century*'. Cinamon, (op.cit, p.9).

126.2

VOLUME I

BATTLES | OF THE | NINETEENTH CENTURY | DESCRIBED BY | ARCHIBALD FORBES, G.A.HENTY, | MAJOR ARTHUR GRIFFITHS, | And other Well-known Writers | VOL.I | WITH COLOURED FRONTISPIECE AND NUMEROUS OTHER | ILLUSTRATIONS AND PLANS | CASSELL AND COMPANY, LIMITED | LONDON, PARIS, NEW YORK & MELBOURNE | MCMII | ALL RIGHTS RESERVED

Contents

251 x 177 mm. (i)–viii | (1)–752. Frontispiece and illustrations as in 126.1, Volume I, except fold-out engraving is now omitted.

(Frontispiece, tipped in) | (i) title p. | (ii) publisher's device | (iii)–iv. Contents | (v)–viii. List of Illustrations | (1)–752. text | (753)–760. Appendix: Chronological List of Battles, with printer's imprint at foot of p.760 (PRINTED BY CASSELL & COMPANY, LIMITED, LA BELLE SAUVAGE, LUDGATE HILL, LONDON, E.C.).

VOLUME II

BATTLES | OF THE | NINETEENTH CENTURY | DESCRIBED BY | ARCHIBALD FORBES, G.A.HENTY, | MAJOR ARTHUR GRIFFITHS, | And other Well-known Writers | VOL.II | WITH NUMEROUS ILLUSTRATIONS AND PLANS | CASSELL AND COMPANY, LIMITED | LONDON, PARIS, NEW YORK & MELBOURNE | MCMII | ALL RIGHTS RESERVED

Contents

251 x 177 mm. (i)–viii | (1)–760. Frontispiece and illustrations as in 126.1, Volume II.

(Frontispiece, tipped in) | (i) title p. | (ii) publisher's device | (iii)–iv. Contents | (v)–viii. List of Illustrations | (full-page plate, tipped in) | (1)–748. text | (749)–760. Index, with printer's imprint at foot of p.760 (PRINTED BY CASSELL & COMPANY, LIMITED, LA BELLE SAUVAGE, LUDGATE HILL, LONDON, E.C.)

VOLUME III

BATTLES | OF THE | NINETEENTH CENTURY | VOL.III | THE BOER WAR OF 1899–1902 | THE CHINESE WAR OF 1900–1901 | THE ASHANTI WAR OF 1900 | WITH TWELVE FULL-PAGE PLATES AND NUMEROUS OTHER | ILLUSTRATIONS AND PLANS | CASSELL AND COMPANY, LIMITED | LONDON, PARIS, NEW YORK & MELBOURNE | MCMII | ALL RIGHTS RESERVED

Contents

251 × 177 mm. (i)–(xii) | (1)–(744). Frontispiece and eleven full-page wash-drawings by Allan Stewart (2), Sidney Paget, R. Caton Woodville (3), L. Thackeray, Edward Read, H.O. Seppings, and unknown artists (3), reproduced by halftone blocks in black on coated paper, unbacked, unfolioed, tipped in. Numerous plans and illustrations from line and halftone blocks on text pages.

(Frontispiece, tipped in) | (i) title p. | (ii) publisher's device | (iii)–v. Contents | (vi) blank | (vii)–x. List of Illustrations | (xi) List of Plates | (xii) blank | (1)–736. text | (737)–743. Index, with printer's imprint at foot of p.743 (PRINTED BY CASSELL & COMPANY, LA BELLE SAUVAGE, LONDON, E.C.) | (744) blank.

Binding

Maroon leathercloth boards, blind-embossed, blocked gilt. As for 126.1, binding-cases were supplied by the publisher to individual subscribers, so details of endpapers and treatment of edges of leaves will vary from set to set.

Details of cases as for 126.1, but instead of rose-heads to show volume-numbers, gilt roman numerals are now used, above the publisher's imprint on spines.

Reference: PN.

Notes

1. A re-issue of 126.1, with an additional, anonymous, third volume.

2. This three-volume edition was not issued in monthly or fortnightly parts, as were 126.1 and 126.4. Instead the publisher produced, simultaneously with 126.2, an alternative edition of the work for 'subscribers' only. It was issued in smaller volumes, two of which contained the material in each volume of 126.2. The set was published over a period, one volume at a time, and eventually included an extra, seventh, volume. It is described as 126.3 below.

3. The quality of paper is poor compared with that of 126.1: this particularly affected the quality of illustrations on text paper.

4. The word LIMITED is omitted from the printer's imprint on p.743.

126.3

BATTLES | OF THE | NINETEENTH CENTURY | DESCRIBED BY | ARCHIBALD FORBES, G.A.HENTY, | MAJOR ARTHUR GRIFFITHS, | And other Well-known Writers | VOL.I. (VOL.II., VOL.III., VOL.IV.) | SPECIAL EDITION | WITH COLOURED PLATES AND NUMEROUS OTHER ILLUSTRATIONS | CASSELL AND COMPANY, LIMITED | LONDON, PARIS, NEW YORK AND MELBOURNE | ALL RIGHTS RESERVED

Contents, Volume I

252 × 174 mm. (i)–(viii) | (1)–370. Three full-page watercolour drawings by unknown artist, reproduced by three-colour halftone blocks; three full-page wash-drawings by Alfred Pearse, W.B.Wollen, and Paul Hardy, reproduced by halftone blocks in black; all on coated paper, unbacked, keyed to text, tipped in. Many plans and illustrations from line and halftone blocks on text pages.

(Frontispiece, tipped in) | (i) title p. | (ii) publisher's device | (iii) Contents | (iv) blank | (v)–vi. List of Illustrations | (vii) List of Plates | (viii) blank | (1)–370. text.

Contents, Volume II

252 × 174 mm. (i)–(viii) | 371–760. Two full-page watercolour drawings by unknown artist, reproduced by three-colour halftone blocks; two full-page wash-drawings by Paul Hardy and Stanley L.Wood, and reproductions of paintings by Lady Butler and Ernest Crofts, A.R.A., all reproduced by halftone blocks in black; all on coated paper, unbacked, keyed to text pages, tipped in. Numerous plans and illustrations from line and halftone blocks on text pages.

(Frontispiece, tipped in) | (i) title p. | (ii) publisher's device | (iii)–iv. Contents | (v)–vi. List of Illustrations | (vii) List of Plates | (viii) blank | 371–752. text | (753)–760. Appendix: Chronological List of Battles, with printer's imprint at foot of p.760 (PRINTED BY CASSELL & COMPANY, LIMITED, LA BELLE SAUVAGE, LUDGATE HILL, LONDON, E.C.).

Contents, Volume III

252 × 174 mm. (i)–(viii) | (1)–382. Three full-page watercolour drawings by unknown artist, reproduced by three-colour halftone blocks; full-page wash-drawing by Stanley L.Wood, reproductions of a painting by Thomas J.Barker, and an engraving from a painting by D.Maclise, R.A., all printed from halftone blocks in black; all on coated paper, unbacked, keyed to text pages, tipped in. Numerous plans and illustrations from line and halftone blocks on text pages.

(Frontispiece, tipped in) | (i) title p. | (ii) publisher's device | (iii)–iv. Contents | (v)–vi. List of Illustrations | (vii) List of Plates | (viii) blank | (1)–382. text.

Contents, Volume IV

252 × 174 mm. (i)–(viii) | 383–748. Two full-page watercolour drawings by unknown artist, reproduced by three-colour halftone blocks; two full-page wash-drawings by Wal Paget and unknown artist, reproductions of a painting by E.Boutigny and an engraving from a painting by R.Caton Woodville, all printed from halftone blocks in black; all on coated paper, unbacked, keyed to text pages, tipped in. Numerous plans and illustrations from line and halftone blocks on text pages.

(Frontispiece, tipped in) | (i) title p. | (ii) publisher's device | (iii)–iv. Contents | (v)–vi. List of Illustrations | (vii) List of Plates | (viii) blank | 383–748. text.

BATTLES | OF THE | NINETEENTH CENTURY | VOL.V. | CAMPAIGNS OF THE NINETIES | BY | A.HILLIARD ATTERIDGE | SPECIAL EDITION | WITH COLOURED PLATES AND NUMEROUS OTHER ILLUSTRATIONS | CASSELL AND COMPANY, LIMITED | LONDON, PARIS, NEW YORK & MELBOURNE | ALL RIGHTS RESERVED

Contents, Volume V

252 × 174 mm. (i)–(viii) | (1)–372. Two full-page unsigned watercolour drawings, reproduced by three-colour halftone blocks; four full-page wash-drawings by Ernest Prater, R.Caton Woodville, and unknown artist (2), printed from halftone blocks in black; all on coated paper, unbacked, keyed to text pages, tipped in. Numerous plans and illustrations from line and halftone blocks on text pages.

(Frontispiece, tipped in) | (i) title p. | (ii) publisher's device | (iii)–iv. Contents | (v)–vi. List of Illustrations | (vii) List of Plates | (viii) blank | (1)–360. text | (361)–372. Index, with printer's imprint at foot of p.372 (PRINTED BY CASSELL & COMPANY, LIMITED, LA BELLE SAUVAGE, LONDON, E.C.).

BATTLES | OF THE | NINETEENTH CENTURY | VOL.VI. | THE BOER WAR
OF 1899–1900 | DOWN TO THE OCCUPATION OF PRETORIA | SPECIAL
EDITION | WITH COLOURED PLATES AND NUMEROUS OTHER
ILLUSTRATIONS | CASSELL AND COMPANY, LIMITED | LONDON, PARIS,
NEW YORK & MELBOURNE | ALL RIGHTS RESERVED

Contents, Volume VI
252 × 174 mm. (i)–(viii) | (1)–368. Three full-page watercolour drawings, one by
R. Caton Woodville and two by unknown artist, reproduced by three-colour halftone
blocks; three full-page wash-drawings by Sidney Paget, L. Thackeray and Allan
Stewart, printed from halftone blocks in black; all on coated paper, unbacked, keyed
to text pages, tipped in. Numerous plans and illustrations from line and halftone
blocks on text pages.
    (Frontispiece, tipped in) | (i) title p. | (ii) publisher's device | (iii)–iv. Contents |
(v)–vi. List of Illustrations | (vii) List of Plates | (viii) blank | (1)–364. text |
(365)–368. Chronology of the Boer War.

BATTLES | OF THE | NINETEENTH CENTURY | VOL.VII. | THE BOER WAR:
MAY–DECEMBER, 1900 | THE CHINESE WAR OF 1900–1901 | THE ASHANTI
WAR OF 1900 | SPECIAL EDITION | WITH COLOURED PLATES AND
NUMEROUS OTHER ILLUSTRATIONS | CASSELL AND COMPANY,
LIMITED | LONDON, PARIS, NEW YORK & MELBOURNE | ALL RIGHTS
RESERVED

Contents, Volume VII
252 × 174 mm. (i)–(viii) | (369)–(744). Three full-page watercolour drawings by
unknown artist, reproduced by three-colour halftone blocks; three full-page wash-
drawings, one by R. Caton Woodville, and two by unknown artists including one
from a photograph, printed from halftone blocks in black; all on coated paper,
unbacked, keyed to text pages, tipped in. Numerous plans and illustrations from line
and halftone blocks on text pages.
    (Frontispiece, tipped in) | (i) title p. | (ii) publisher's device | (iii)–iv. Contents |
(v)–vi. List of Illustrations | (vii) List of Plates | (viii) blank | (369)–523. text |
524–528. Chronology of the Boer War | (colour plate, tipped in) | (529)–652. text |
653–656. Chronology of the Chinese War | (657)–733. text | 734–736. Chronology
of the Ashanti War | (737)–743. Index, with printer's imprint at foot of p.743
(PRINTED BY CASSELLL & COMPANY, LA BELLE SAUVAGE, LONDON,
E.C.) | (744) blank.

Binding
Green cloth boards, blocked black, yellow and gilt; edges plain; plain off-white
endpapers.
    Front board: BATTLES . OF . THE | NINETEENTH . . . | (small illustration of
pistol and pouch, black and ochre) CENTURY (black), within the angle of
illustration in an inverted L, framed by black and ochre lines, of men on horseback
and on foot attacking across open country towards foreground figures of British
officer with sword raised, and soldiers with heavy gun half-sunk in mud (black and
ochre). At foot: ILLUSTRATED (ochre, cased black). **Spine:** BATTLES | OF THE
| NINETEENTH | CENTURY (gilt) in second of six panels, the others decorated

with wreaths, and, the top one with medal, the fourth with: VOL I I (II, III, IV, V, VI, VII), and the others with small illustrations of pistol and pouch (all gilt). Black and gilt rules between the panels, and at head and foot. **Back board:** Wreath at centre, framed in small rectangle of four rules, with dot at centre of each side (black).

References: PN I *Farmer*, p.9; *Dartt*, p.10, *Companion*, p.2.

Notes

1. This edition was issued to subscribers, volume by volume, and many 'sets' are in collectors' hands which purport to be complete (and indeed were so at the time of issue), consisting of four, five, six, or seven volumes. When the issue began it was intended either to complete the set in four volumes, which would have included all the material in 126.1, or, perhaps, in six volumes, to include all material in 126.1 and 126.2. But in the end it was decided to add an extra volume, containing work not published previously (see Note 3).

2. Slips of paper were tipped in, before the frontispiece, explaining that 'This Edition, being specially prepared for Subscription, is not available through the general Booksellers'. That was the wording in the first volume of the initial issue. As the series built up, the words were augmented to state the number of volumes in the set (at the time of issue) and the price. The slips in the final issue read 'This Edition, published in Seven Volumes at 6s.6d. each, net, includes the History of the Boer and China Wars, 1899–1900, and, being specially prepared for Subscription …' etc. Although the Ashanti War is not specifically mentioned, it is in fact included in the seventh volume, as it had been in 126.2, Volume III.

3. The title page of Volume V gives the author's name as A. Hilliard Atteridge, who had been one of the contributors to 126.1. The contents of that volume were not published elsewhere, and the events described fit chronologically between those in Volumes II and III of 126.2. The contents of 126.3, Volumes VI and VII, correspond to those of 126.2, Volume III, and remain anonymous.

4. Volume V was compiled, and illustrated, later than the others, and nearly all the pictures, including photographs, are consequently reproduced by halftone blocks.

5. No dates are visibly printed in this edition. There is, however, a strange series of binder's marks on the back folds of the gatherings throughout the volumes. These can only be seen by opening the books carefully but deeply at the hinges. In each volume the first binder's mark appears between the frontispiece and the title page. These first marks, in my own set, read, in volume order: 2/1900; 2/1900; 2/1900; 4/1900; 5/1900; 1/1901; 10/1900; 4/1901.

6. Binders' marks in this position are usually intended to show at a glance the correct sequence of gatherings when the books are collated ready for sewing. They are therefore printed progressively higher on the back of each successive gathering, and often also numbered in sequence. When the book is still unbound the marks will be seen running diagonally up the back (or what will, in effect, become the spine) of the book. But it is clear that the marks on these volumes, inserted by the printer, perform a double function. They act as binders' marks in the usual way, but also give the month and year of printing of each gathering.

7. In each volume of my seven-volume set the marks on individual gatherings show that the sections were printed at varying dates, not necessarily in chronological sequence.

8. Individual gatherings show one date in one set of volumes and another date in what otherwise appears to be a duplicate set. It is therefore clear that some, if not all, gatherings were reprinted when necessary.

9. I have an extra copy of Volume I, which was originally sold as a single-volume 'set'. The legible marks (not all can be deciphered) read: 9/99 (the first, title-page gathering), 1/99 (two gatherings), 3/99 (2 gatherings, 6/99 (six gatherings) 8/99 (one gathering) 7/99 (two gatherings). From them it is clear that this copy of Volume I was printed some months earlier than the copy of the set described above.

10. It appears that the work was started in September 1899, and that the volumes were printed and/or reprinted at least into the middle of 1901. They must, therefore, have been available to subscribers at the same time as 126.2 was on general sale, with the advantage to subscribers of an extra volume.

126.4
VOLUME I
BATTLES | OF THE | NINETEENTH CENTURY | DESCRIBED BY | ARCHIBALD FORBES, G.A.HENTY, | MAJOR ARTHUR GRIFFITHS, | And other Well-known Writers | VOL.I. | WITH A CHRONOLOGICAL LIST OF THE MORE IMPORTANT BATTLES OF THE CENTURY | WITH A SERIES OF FULL-PAGE PLATES AND NUMEROUS | ILLUSTRATIONS AND PLANS | CASSELL AND COMPANY, LIMITED | LONDON, PARIS, NEW YORK & MELBOURNE. MCMVI | ALL RIGHTS RESERVED

Contents
263 x 190 mm. (i)–viii | (1)–752. Frontispiece by W.B.Wollen and seven other full-page watercolour drawings by an unknown artist, reproduced by three-colour halftone blocks; two full-page wash-drawings by W.H.Overend, Paul Hardy, and reproductions of paintings by Lady Butler and Ernest Crofts, A.R.A., printed from halftone blocks in black; all on coated paper, unbacked, tipped in. Numerous plans and illustrations from line and halftone blocks on text pages.

(Frontispiece, tipped in) | (i) title p. | (ii) publisher's device | (iii)–iv. Contents | (v)–viii. List of Illustrations | (1)–752. text | (753)–760. Appendix: Chronological List of Battles, with printer's imprint at foot of p.760 (PRINTED BY CASSELL & COMPANY, LIMITED, LA BELLE SAUVAGE, LUDGATE HILL, LONDON, E.C.).

VOLUME II
BATTLES | OF THE | NINETEENTH CENTURY | DESCRIBED BY | ARCHIBALD FORBES, G.A. HENTY, | MAJOR ARTHUR GRIFFITHS, | And other Well-known Writers | VOL.II. | WITH A SERIES OF FULL-PAGE PLATES AND NUMEROUS | ILLUSTRATIONS AND PLANS | CASSELL AND COMPANY, LIMITED | LONDON, PARIS, NEW YORK & MELBOURNE. MCMVI | ALL RIGHTS RESERVED

Contents
263 x 190 mm. (i)–viii | (1)–760. Frontispiece and three watercolour drawings by unknown artist, reproduced by three-colour halftone blocks; three full-page wash-drawings by Stanley L.Wood, Stanley Berkeley, and an unknown artist, reproductions of paintings by E.Boutigny, Thomas J.Barker, and R.Caton

Woodville, and of an engraving from a painting by D. Maclise, R.A., printed from halftone blocks in black; all on coated paper, unbacked, unfolioed, tipped in. Many plans and illustrations from line and halftone blocks on text pages.

(Frontispiece, tipped in) | (i) title p. | (ii) publisher's device | (iii)–iv. Contents | (v)–viii. List of Illustrations | (1)–748. text | (749)–760. Index, with printer's imprint at foot of p.760 (PRINTED BY CASSELL & COMPANY, LIMITED, LA BELLE SAUVAGE, LUDGATE HILL, LONDON, E.C.).

Binding
My copy is in binder's cloth, but it is likely that, as for 126.1 and 126.2, binding cases would have been made available by the publisher to individual subscribers.

Reference: PN.

Notes
1. A straightforward re-issue of the text in 126.1, with new plates added, including a number in colour. The contents of 126.2, Volume III, published four years earlier, are not reprinted. Nor are the contents of 126.3, Volumes V to VII.
2. The contents of these volumes were first issued in 24 fortnightly parts in red paper covers, from 25 February 1905 to 10 January 1906, at 6d. each. The covers show the title and a battle scene on page 1, with a list of Contents of the Part. Other pages of the cover carry general advertisements.
3. The title page and prelims for both volumes were included at the end of Part 24, together with the Index and the Chronological List of Battles. As a result of this arrangement some copies of the bound volumes are found with the Chronological List bound in error at the end of Volume II instead of Volume I.
4. The eleventh part is numbered in roman numerals, not arabic. See 126.1, Note 1.
5. A set of the sheets forming the original Volume II (only) was issued with a cancel title page, and a new title, *The World's Battles, 1800 to 1900*, as a presentation volume, by C. Combridge, Publisher of Prize Literature, of Birmingham (see §2, 192).

127. BEETON'S BOY'S OWN BOOKS

GENERAL NOTES

1. These books contain material published by Ward Lock in their reprints of *Beeton's Boy's Own Magazine*, (§3, 197). They are listed here in §2 under their own titles, although only three contain original material by Henty.
2. The first six titles in the series were:
    (1) *Stories of Sea and Land*, §2, 187
    (2) *Stories of History*, §2, 185
    (3) *Stories of Peril and Adventure*, §2, 186
    (4) *Stories of Brave Boys and Gallant Heroes*, §2, 184
    (5) *The Adventures of Two Brave Boys, and Other Stories*, §2, 123
    (6) *Stirring Adventures Afloat and Ashore*, §2, 179
They all consist of material used in the magazine during the two years of Henty's Editorship: consequently the publisher gives his name as Editor of the books also, both on title pages and binding cases.

3. Through no fault of Henty's, the magazine was clearly not a big success. But Ward Lock seem to have done better with the material in book form, for subsequently three more volumes were added to the series. These later volumes contain more material purchased by Ward Lock from Beeton, some of it previously published in his own Magazine, but mainly in a series of books, known as 'Beeton's Boy's Own Library'. None of it was from magazine issues edited by Henty: therefore the later books should not bear his name. Their titles are:

(7) *Stories of Adventure and Heroism*

(8) *Fact, Fiction, History and Adventure*

(9) *Brave Tales of Daring Deeds and Adventure at Home and Abroad.*

4. John Cargill Thompson, by his own admission in his *The Boys' Dumas*, enjoyed speculating in a vague and optimistic way about Henty's possible authorship or editorship of work published anonymously. In his early days Henty's work in *Tinsleys' Magazine, All the Year Round,* and the *Cornhill Magazine* was unsigned, for anonymity was then the norm for contributors to those journals. But it is very unlikely that, once his name was known, he would have wished to work in other fields without recognition, or that his publishers would have allowed him to do so. That should be borne in mind when considering Cargill Thompson's remarks (*The Boys' Dumas*, pp.11–14) in connection with this series of books, and particularly the first of the three later volumes, *Stories of Adventure and Heroism.*

5. The latter book has aroused particular interest because it is sometimes found with Henty's name, as Editor, on the binding case but not on the title page. Cargill Thompson rightly draws attention to a number of variants of this title. In all he lists seven, but of those the last three differ from each other only in cloth-colour and choice of frontispiece. Variations of cloth-colour are discussed in Appendix III. For most British publishers in the last half of the nineteenth century a book for children that appeared in only one cloth-colour was something of a scarcity. And to vary, from one impression to another, the picture used as frontispiece in a book with many illustrations, was a frequent habit. I suggest, therefore, that those three variants should be considered as a single entity. So, taking it with Cargill Thompson's four other variants, I consequently deal with five issues that differ distinctly. He lists them as follows:

(1) Edited by Henty, contains *Silas Horner's Adventures*; *Wild Sports of the World*; and *Jewel Mysteries I have Known.*

(2) Edited by Henty, contains *Robinson Crusoe*; *Silas Horner's Adventures*; and *Brave British Soldiers and the Victoria Cross.*

(3) Edited by Henty, contains *Silas Horner's Adventures*; *Wild Sports of the World*; and *Robinson Crusoe.*

(4) Edited by Henty, contains *Silas Horner's Adventures*; *Wild Sports of the World*; and *Lady Turpin.*

(5) No credited Editor, contains *Robinson Crusoe*; *Silas Horner's Adventures*; and *Brave British Soldiers and the Victoria Cross.* (Found in various cloth-colours).

6. Each of the volumes contains three separate books. The first impressions of those books, before the volumes were made up, had been printed independently, often on differing papers. Each book has its own pagination, so page 1, for example, occurs three times in the volume. The title page, and a varying number of preliminary pages, were removed from each book: the surviving page-numbers show in each case how much is missing. For each book a new half-title page was printed on a single leaf and pasted in at the appropriate place, and a title page for the volume was added, specifying the component parts.

7. All this was common practice at the time, especially among publishers of children's books, such as Groombridge, and the S.P.C.K. Here, Ward Lock was binding in one volume the sheets of three books previously published separately, giving the combined volume a new title, and hoping thus to dispose of material they found hard to sell in its earlier form.

It was inevitable that, at some point, the available sheets of one or another of the three component parts would run out. Sheets of an alternative, fourth, title were then introduced to fill the gap, and at once a variant volume was created, requiring, of course, an amended title page, even if not a new binding design.

It may be noted in passing that one of the books, mentioned under *Beeton's Boy's Own Magazine* (see §3, 197), was an old Beeton title called *Our Soldiers and the Victoria Cross*. When re-used in *Stories of Adventure and Heroism*, it was given a new title, *Brave British Soldiers and the Victoria Cross*. That appears on the new title page, and on the binding case as well. But the running headlines on left-hand pages are still the original title, because, for the first issues, original sheets were used, and any later impressions would still have been printed from stereos of the original setting.

8. That system of using up old material is, I have no doubt, the explanation of all the variations of content described by Cargill Thompson. But a much more important variation in this particular title, *Stories of Adventure and Heroism*, is the wording on binding cases (see Note 5 above). Some have the words 'Edited by G.A.HENTY' on the front board, and some do not. Before considering this it will help to note how the binding-design for the later volumes (containing material not in the magazine-issues edited by Henty) was adapted to 'match' the binding of the first six books.

9. The original six volumes had an immediately-recognisable red panel at the head of the front board, and a red panel and a gilt panel on the spine, with the words 'BEETON'S BOY'S OWN BOOKS' and 'Edited by G.A.HENTY'. The three later volumes, when first issued, had a similar panel on the front board, and retained only one of the two spine panels. For these books no reference was made to Henty, but they were clearly labelled, in both places, 'BEETON'S BOY'S OWN BOOKS'. And, to retain the balance of the original, the word 'ILLUSTRATED' replaced Henty's name on the spine.

10. Later, Ward Lock abandoned reference to Beeton on *all* the books in the series. The six original volumes were labelled simply 'Edited by G.A.Henty' on the front board, and 'Illustrated' replaced the Beeton credit on the spine. At this point there was a small problem about the three later volumes. If the familiar design was to continue, how was the red (Henty) panel on the front board to be filled?

11. It was also at this point that a strange issue of *Stories of Adventure and Heroism*, the seventh title in the series, and the first non-Henty title, appeared with Henty's name as Editor blocked on the front board. We shall never know the true reason for this: whether the error was the binder's, or the publisher's. I very much doubt that it was, as has been suggested, a 'deliberate mistake' by Ward Lock to help sales. The blocking piece used for Henty's name is clearly the standard brass that had been cut and used for the first six volumes in their second state, i.e. those without any reference to Beeton's name. I incline to the kindest and most likely explanation: that

Henty's name appeared because the publisher forgot to give new instructions to the binder, and he simply followed the old standing orders.

12. Ward Lock had based this series of books on the famous names of Beeton and Henty. Beeton had suffered, not through any failure in his publishing business, the loss of his fortune shortly after the tragic early death of his wife Isabella, the author of *Household Management.* He was forced to sell, and joined the firm of Ward Lock when they acquired his business. Things did not turn out well for Beeton and, after a strange series of events, culminating in litigation, he and Ward Lock parted company. Beeton died in 1877, but even in the last years of his life had continued, once more as an independent publisher, to be a thorn in the side of Ward Lock.

Henty had never been very enthusiastic about Ward Lock's handling of the Beeton material, see *Beeton's Boy's Own Magazine,* §3, 197. While he was content for his name to be associated with the first six volumes in the series, he made it clear that thereafter the contract was terminated. For future volumes in the series, therefore, Beeton's name had lost its magic for the public and become repugnant to Ward Lock: Henty's was no longer available. That was the publisher's problem, rather than details of the design of the books, and it was a problem in need of attention.

13. The dual solution found by Ward Lock appears to be one that Cargill Thompson came very close to spotting, without realising it. It was, first, to continue the six Henty volumes in their existing format, but otherwise to abandon the series altogether. And, second, to go on using all the old material that was not included in the six Henty volumes, but in a totally new binding style that the public would not associate with the earlier presentation. Thus it was, I believe, that *Stories of Adventure and Heroism* was re-born as *Forest, Field and Flood.*

The binding of the new book is smart, with good-quality ribbed cloth on bevelled boards, blocked in gilt on front board and spine, and with all edges gilt. The contents are embellished with colour plates, but otherwise the same. Here are the old favourites that were listed by Cargill Thompson: *Wild Sports of the World*; *Brave British Soldiers and the Victoria Cross*; and *Robinson Crusoe*. And there is nothing to suggest to new readers that either Henty, or Beeton, had anything to do with it.

14. In fairness to Cargill Thompson it must be said that he was probably misled by Dartt (*Companion*, p.3A) who gives incorrect information about the Ward Lock imprint and addresses. *Forest, Field and Flood* did not appear as early as he thought, being published a year or two after the last issues of *Stories of Adventure and Heroism.*

128. BEVIS by Richard Jefferies

GENERAL NOTES

1. *Bevis* was originally published by Sampson Low in three volumes in 1882, only five years before the death of the author, Richard Jefferies. Its inclusion here is explained by the publisher's repeated advertisements, between 1891 and 1897, of a single-volume edition, 'Edited by G.A.Henty'. Apart from these otherwise uninformative announcements there is nothing to link Henty with *Bevis*, and his name does not appear in any editions of the book. It is therefore of interest to inquire into Sampson Low's reasons for believing such editorial work to be desirable, and into Henty's involvement in changing Jefferies' text.

2. Those who have enjoyed *Bevis* in their youth, as one of the great stories of boyhood, and later read the book aloud to sons, and perhaps to grandsons, will know that there are a few passages that often tended to get skipped, and that can set young ones yawning. They include some very detailed descriptions of natural landscapes, which seem to go on just a bit too long, and to hold up the plot; matters such as Bevis's Zodiac, or even the Ballad of King Estmere, can do the same thing. Edward Thomas wrote in his biography of Jefferies: 'As a boy's book – I speak under correction from boys – it has no fault, except, perhaps, that the exactness and abundance of detail is disproportionate in a work that has, alas! to end. It is too dramatic for an epic, and its movement is confused, not to speak of its being shamefully interrupted by the description of an anemone-leaf'.

John Cargill Thompson quotes Sir Walter Besant (novelist and writer, 1836–1901, whose work included *The Eulogy of Richard Jefferies*, 1888), writing to the son of a friend, another author, 'This is the best boy's book in the world, but it's a bit too long, and if I were you I should skip'. Sampson Low decided, after Jefferies' death, to produce an abridged version. Later, *Farmer*, without evidence of his actual involvement, thought it was 'at least doubtful if Henty would feel qualified to edit the work of the great naturalist'. But Henty had been, if only briefly, Sampson Low's foremost writer for boys. I believe that Marston's business relationship with Henty developed into a friendship that later provided a special reason for asking him to undertake the work (see Appendix II, Part 3). And of course Farmer didn't know, as both Henty and Marston did, that no more was intended than abridgement.

3. Cargill Thompson, in *The Boys' Dumas*, pp.87–100, shows that Henty's editorial work consisted only of cutting. No words were added, apart from a minimum required to cover the joins. After reading Cargill Thompson's detailed analysis, Jefferies' bibliographers, Miller and Matthews, wrote: 'Henty consistently removed passages of make-believe, fantasy and poetic description on the one hand, and Jefferies' realistic observation of children's cruelty on the other, frustrating his intention "to create a mood and show a true picture of childhood rather than simply tell a story".' But they continue: 'It might be added, however, in Henty's defence, that he took an obscure three-decker by a writer whose reputation lay in other directions, and launched it as a classic of boys' fiction, a reputation which, in complete and shorter versions, it has enjoyed ever since. Jefferies would probably not have objected' (*Richard Jefferies, a bibliographical study*, p.280).

4. Whether anyone doing the job today would cut the same passages is very doubtful. Henty's aim seems to have been to bring the book 'down to earth' for the readership of the 'dear Lads' whom he believed he understood through his magazine editing. He cut sections he thought 'unsuitable', and allowed to stand passages that modern feminist readers would think objectionable. But it was not the nature of the cuts that caused indignation later, it was the fact that no attempt was made to let the reader know that the abridged edition was not the complete work.

5. E.V. Lucas, another Jefferies enthusiast, wrote the Introduction to a later edition, published by Duckworth in 1904. In it, he wrote: '[*Bevis*] was published in 1882 in three volumes, thus obeying a convention to which we now look back with

426 · *G. A. Henty: A Bibliographical Study*

astonishment and effectively preventing its true reader – the boy – from approaching it. A few years later it was reissued in a more reasonable form, in one volume, with pictures; but the book had ceased to be as Jefferies wrote it, abridgment having been made without the reader's knowledge – that unpardonable fault'.

6. The book was issued at least four times in its abridged form, advertised in Sampson Low's catalogues as 'Edited by G.A.Henty', but in none of the impressions does Henty's name appear. How did this come about? The clues all lie, I think, in the foregoing notes. Some years ago I wrote (*A.B.M.R.*, November 1977): 'Henty added nothing of his own to Jefferies' text, and it is quite possible that in spite of the advertising he asked that his name should not be given on the title page. He may well have felt reluctant to be closely associated with the surgery he had been hired to perform'. It is also possible that Sampson Low, being denied by Henty the use of his name, decided not to mention the words 'edited' or 'abridged' on the title page at all, thus arriving at the situation very rightly deplored by E.V.Lucas.

7. The known impressions of Henty's abridged version of *Bevis* are described below. I would like to thank the bibliographers of Richard Jefferies for their help with the descriptions of these books, generously given in considerable detail, some time before the publication of their work.

128.1

BEVIS. | THE STORY OF A BOY. | BY | RICHARD JEFFERIES, | AUTHOR OF "THE GAMEKEEPER AT HOME," "WILD LIFE IN A | SOUTHERN COUNTY," "THE AMATEUR POACHER," GREENE | FERNE FARM," "HODGE AND HIS MASTERS," "ROUND | ABOUT A GREAT ESTATE," "WOOD MAGIC." | "But natures of the noblest frame | These toyles and dangers please; | And they take comfort in the same, | As much as you in ease." | Ulysses and the Syren. | London: | SAMPSON LOW, MARSTON, SEARLE, AND RIVINGTON, | ST. DUNSTAN'S HOUSE, FETTER LANE, FLEET STREET. | 1891. | [All rights reserved.]

(*Note: the quotation marks before GREENE in the titles following the author's name are lacking;* London: *is in gothic type*).

Contents

180 x 121 mm. (i)–(vi) | (1)–362 | catalogue (1)–32. Eight full-page drawings by A.V.Poncy reproduced by line blocks printed on calendered MF paper, unbacked, keyed to text pages, tipped in.

(i) Half-title p. | (ii) blank | (frontispiece, tipped in) | (iii) title p. | (iv) printer's imprint (LONDON: | ALLEN, SCOTT & CO., 30, BOUVERIE STREET, E.C.) | (v) List of Illustrations | (vi) blank | (1)–362. text | (final plate, tipped in) | (1)–32. catalogue, dated October 1889.

Binding

Dark-red cloth boards, bevelled, blocked black, green, buff, and gilt; all edges gilt; brown flowered endpapers.

Front board: BEVIS (gilt, with elaborate black and green casing, black hatching and decoration) | . THE . STORY . OF . (black) | A | BOY (gilt, cased and decorated green and gilt), above illustration of Bevis leading group of boys, all with sticks (black, green, buff). At foot: BY | RICHARD | JEFFERIES (gilt). **Spine:** BEVIS (gilt, with black and green casing and decoration) | THE | STORY of | A BOY (gilt)

above illustration of boy punting raft in river (black, green, buff). At foot: BY |
RICHARD | JEFFERIES (gilt, with decoration) | S. LOW . MARSTON & Co (gilt).
Back board: plain.

References: *Farmer*, p.15; *Dartt*, p.18, *Companion*, p.3; Miller and Matthews,
Richard Jefferies: A bibliographical study, p.277 (B15.2); Edward Thomas, *Richard
Jefferies, his Life and Work*, passim; Cargill Thompson, *The Boys' Dumas*, pp.17,
87–100; Newbolt, *A.B.M.R.*, November 1977, p.443.

Notes
1. The first issue of the book abridged by Henty. It is fairly lavishly made, for a
publisher who was not renowned for fine production of fiction or books for children.
Bevis was advertised from 1891 in 'Low's Standard Books for Boys', at the fixed
prices for books in that series: 'With numerous Illustrations, 2s.6d.; gilt edges, 3s.6d.
each'. Henty's own books from Sampson Low became familiar in those formats.
2. This book, however, was also advertised at 5s., and that is the issue described
above. Even after Henty's work the book is considerably longer than others in the
Sampson Low series, and it was, after all, the first single-volume edition of a work
that had been on sale as a three-decker. Illustrations had been added, and, as often
for first single-volume editions, the binding was more lavish than for issues that
were to follow. It included not only gilt edges, but bevelled (and therefore heavier)
boards, with blocking in gold and three pigment-workings. The papers used for both
text and illustrations are of higher quality than that of Sampson Low's usual MFs.
These refinements were perhaps necessary to justify the higher price.
3. The imposition and make-up of the book show a lack of careful planning and
organisation noticeable in other books from this publisher. The text is imposed to
make up as 16-page signatures, starting at p.(1). There are eleven of these, ending at
p.352. Then follows sig.AA, which makes ten pages (353–362): this consists of a
half-sheet (8 pages) with a single leaf tipped on. No doubt these pages were all
printed with the prelims, which consist of one folded leaf (4 pages) with a single leaf
tipped on, making six pages. For machining, the book therefore consists of an even
working of 356 pages (twelve 16-page gatherings), but from the binder's point of
view it is cumbersome and uneconomic, with much hand-work involved. The
illustrations make a complete, one-sided, sheet, on heavier paper, to be cut up for
insertion as single leaves. (The final plate is keyed to page 363 of the text, which
does not exist, and the caption is misprinted, 'Francis' for 'Frances').
4. A later issue of this impression has bound-in catalogues dated October 1890. I am
told by the bibliographers of Richard Jefferies that while the first issue was thread-
sewn, some later issues of this edition were wire-stitched (see 128.2, Note 5, below,
and Appendix III, Part 2).
5. The fee paid to Henty, and the terms of his contract with Sampson Low, are not
known. There is a record in Sampson Low's Agreement Book No.2, at folio
161–162, that the Agreement with G.A.Henty for *Bevis* was sent to Duckworth on
13 July 1904.
6. Both *Farmer* and *Dartt* knew of the possible existence of an edition of *Bevis*
edited by Henty, but their researches produced no results.

128.2

BEVIS | THE STORY OF A BOY | BY | RICHARD JEFFERIES | AUTHOR OF "THE GAMEKEEPER AT HOME," "WILD LIFE IN A | SOUTHERN COUNTY," "THE AMATEUR POACHER," "GREENE | FERNE FARM," "HODGE AND HIS MASTERS," "ROUND | ABOUT A GREAT ESTATE," "WOOD MAGIC." | "But natures of the noblest frame | These toyles and dangers please; | And they take comfort in the same, | As much as you in ease." | Ulysses and the Syren. | NEW AND CHEAPER EDITION | LONDON | SAMPSON LOW, MARSTON & COMPANY | Limited | St. Dunstan's House | FETTER LANE, FLEET STREET, E.C.

(*Note:* St. Dunstan's House *is in gothic type*).

Contents

182 × 121 mm. (i)–(vi) | (1)–362 | catalogue (1)–(32). Illustrations as in 128.1.

(1) Half-title p. | (2) blank | (frontispiece, tipped in) | (3) title p. | (4) blank | (5) List of Illustrations | (6) blank | (1)–362. text | (final plate, tipped in) | (1)–(32) catalogue, dated 1892.

Binding: (See Plate 135). As for 128.1, except (a) blue cloth boards, not bevelled; (b) edges plain; (c) yellow surface-paper endpapers; (d) on both front board and spine: BY | RICHARD | JEFFERIES is buff, not gilt.

References: PN | Miller and Matthews, *Richard Jefferies: A bibliographical study*, p.281 (B15.3).

Notes

1. Miller and Matthews report that this is 'a re-issue of the 1891 sheets with a cancel title page and at a reduced price … probably issued soon after and sold concurrently with the 1891 dated 5s. copies'.

2. Copies of 128.2 are also found without the bound-in publisher's catalogue. The 1892 catalogue advertises '*Bevis*, new edit. 5s.', but does not include it in the list of 'Low's Standard Books for Boys', where Henty's own books appear, and with which it had been repeatedly advertised from as early as the 1891 issue of *The Cornet of Horse* (verso of title page: 'Uniform with this Volume: With numerous Illustrations, 2s.6d.; gilt edges, 3s.6d.').

3. There is no title-page date, and no printer's imprint (previously on the verso of the title page). These omissions have little significance when compared with those from many other Sampson Low reprints. Henty's own books went through numerous issues, and some have dated title pages and some do not: the usage appears to have been quite arbitrary. When printing a cancel page for 128.2 it probably seemed not worth the expense of printing the verso.

4. The words 'NEW AND CHEAPER EDITION' probably refer to the difference in price between the 5s. edition and the 'Standard' edition (at 2s.6d. or 3s.6d. with or without gilt edges). The words do not appear again in the 1893 impression (128.3), but I do not think much significance should be attached to that. Parallel examples of the use of such words in one impression of a book and their immediate banishment from subsequent printings may be found in other works listed in this bibliography, regardless of the actual selling prices involved. The words return to the title page of 128.4, a year or two later.

5. An unpleasant feature of this otherwise good-looking issue is the use of wire-stitching instead of thread-sewing. In my copy the wire stitches have, as usual, gone rusty, but by some stroke of fortune the book is sound and the damage is scarcely apparent. It must have been kept in a dry atmosphere, but the preservation may be partly due to the good-quality text-paper which shows none of the usual signs of disintegration following the oxidation of the metal: certainly the quality of this paper was not maintained for the 1893 impression.

6. Note the 'modernisation' of the typography of the cancel title page, evident in the dropping of the punctuation at the ends of display lines (i.e. after BEVIS and BOY and JEFFERIES).

128.3

BEVIS I THE STORY OF A BOY I BY I RICHARD JEFFERIES I AUTHOR OF "THE GAMEKEEPER AT HOME," "WILD LIFE IN A I SOUTHERN COUNTY," "THE AMATEUR POACHER," "GREENE I FERNE FARM," "HODGE AND HIS MASTERS," "ROUND I ABOUT A GREAT ESTATE," "WOOD MAGIC." I "But natures of the noblest frame I These toyles and dangers please; I And they take comfort in the same, I As much as you in ease." I Ulysses and the Syren. I LONDON I SAMPSON LOW, MARSTON & COMPANY, I LIMITED I St. Dunstan's House I FETTER LANE, FLEET STREET, E.C. I 1893
(*Note: The full point after MAGIC in the titles following the author's name is battered and barely visible; St. Dunstan's House is in gothic type*).

Contents
182 x 121 mm. (i)–(vi) I (1)–362 I catalogue (1)–(32). Illustrations as in 128.1. Single leaf printed in black on cheap MF paper, one side only, giving list of publications 'Uniform with this Volume', unfolioed, tipped in immediately after title page.

(i) Half-title p. I (ii) blank I (frontispiece, tipped in) I (iii) title p. I (iv) printer's imprint (LONDON: PRINTED BY WOODFALL AND KINDER, 70 TO 76, LONG ACRE, W.C.) I (single-leaf advertisement, tipped in) I (v) List of Illustrations I (vi) blank I (1)–362. text I (final plate, tipped in) I (1)–(32) catalogue, dated 1894 (see Note 1).

Binding: As for 128.2, except (a) brown cloth boards; (b) plain off-white endpapers.

References: TC I Miller and Matthews, *Richard Jefferies: A bibliographical study*, p.282 (B15.4)

Notes
1. The first issues of this impression have bound-in catalogues dated 1893. Some copies have no advertisement leaf tipped in following the title page.

2. The printer has been changed. Miller and Matthews report that the prelims and the following text pages have been entirely reset: pp.69, 154, 155, 159, 161, 164, 165, 168, 169, 172, 173, 176, 281, 287, 297, and 331; they add: 'The page resetting involves no textual changes or variation in the number of lines per page, except p.164, where the same matter makes 33 instead of 32 lines'.

3. Miller and Matthews report that this issue was listed in the *Publishers' Circular* of 15 October 1892 as published that week, and advertised as 'edited by G.A. Henty'.

128.4

Title page: As for 128.2, but the word LIMITED in the imprint is now in capitals.

Contents: 181 x 120 mm. As for 128.3.

Binding: As for 128.3, but olive-green cloth boards, and other colours known.

Reference: Miller and Matthews, *Richard Jefferies: A bibliographical study*, p.284 (B15.5)

Notes
1. Reprinted from the plates used for 128.3, which have been allowed to become very worn, as usual with cheaper Sampson Low publications. The prelims are reset.
2. Miller and Matthews report: 'The Beinecke copy at Yale has a presentation date of 22 March 1897. This is probably the final year in which Henty's abridged *Bevis* was in print, as the last known advertisement for it is in a copy of *Winning his Spurs* dated 1897'. Since their work was published I have found and notified them of a later advertisement, in a catalogue forming an integral part of a paperback, double-column edition of *Jack Archer*, with title page dated 1898 (see 14.4, Note 4).
3. For a so-far unexplained reason Sampson Low disposed of their rights in the book to Duckworth in 1904. See 128.1, Note 5.

129–130. BLACKIE'S CENTURY READERS

129.1

THE | CENTURY READERS. | READER III. (within box rules) | (publisher's device) | LONDON: | BLACKIE & SON, 49 & 50 OLD BAILEY, E.C. | GLASGOW, EDINBURGH, AND DUBLIN. | 1888.

Contents
163 x 108 mm. (1)–192 | no catalogue. Numerous small (anonymous) line engravings printed in black on text pages.
    (1) Title p. | (2) blank | (3) Preface | (4) Contents | (5)–192. text and illustrations.

Binding (see Plate 130)
Red cloth boards, blocked black; edges plain; pale olive-green endpapers, printed in black with publisher's advertisements for educational works on pages 2 and 3 of both upper and lower ends, the former folioed (1) and (2), the latter (3) and (4).
    Front board: (decorative rule) THE (decorative rule) | CENTURY | READERS. | No. III (three rules) 1s. | BLACKIE & SON, PUBLISHERS. (all black) within panel framed by rules in over-all pattern of leaves and berries (black). **Spine:** THIRD . READER (black) running from foot to head, in panel framed by rules between two panels of over-all pattern of leaves and berries (all black). **Back board:** plain.

Reference: TC.

Notes
1. 'The Boatman's Story', better known as 'Surly Joe' (see §4), is printed in six parts

at pages 142–160. The author's name is not given. Each Part is accompanied by glossary, notes, dictation exercise, and grammar exercise. There are three small line engravings, unsigned and unascribed.

2. Announcements on p.(2) of the upper endpapers include details of 'A NEW SERIES OF READERS. | THE CENTURY READERS.', specifying eight volumes (two Primers, one Infant Reader, and Readers I–V). The (varying) prices of the volumes, and the (varying) number of pages in each volume, are given, except for Reader V. It seems probable, therefore, that it was issued later than the other books in the series. No copy of Reader V (see 130.1) has been reported with a dated title page.

130.1

THE | CENTURY READERS. | READER V. (within box rules) | (publisher's device) | BLACKIE & SON, 49 & 50 OLD BAILEY, E.C. | GLASGOW, EDINBURGH, AND DUBLIN.

Contents

171 × 115 mm. (1)–256 | no catalogue. Frontispiece, full-page and smaller line engravings, by unknown artists, printed in black on text pages.

(1) Blank | (2) frontispiece | (3) title p. | (4) Preface | (5) Contents | (6) blank | 7–256. text and illustrations.

Binding: (See Plate 130). As for 129.1, except lettering (a) on front board (CENTURY | READERS | No. V (three rules) 1s.6d. | BLACKIE & SON, LIMITED.) (b) on spine (FIFTH . READER).

Reference: Cargill Thompson, *The Boys' Dumas*, p.6.

Notes

1. At pages 139–208 appears 'The "Golden Hind": A Story of the Time of Drake', in seventeen chapters, or lessons, each with notes, vocabularies, dictation and grammar exercises. Authorship is given in a footnote on p.139: 'Adapted from *Under Drake's Flag*, by G.A. Henty'. Ten unsigned wood engravings include two that appear to be re-worked versions of Gordon Browne's illustrations in *Under Drake's Flag*.

2. The page size is slightly larger than that of Reader III (see 129.1).

3. Cargill Thompson, being unaware of 129.1, with title page dated 1888, dates this book 'c.1890', and notes that the advertisements in the endpapers include an announcement of *The Sovereign Reader* 'which helps to set the date of this book as after 1887'. In view of the advertisements in Reader III, however, it is likely that this book was first published in the same year, 1888. The first issue was probably dated on the title page, but no such copy has come to light.

130.2

THE | CENTURY READERS. | READER V. (within box rules) | BLACKIE AND SON LIMITED | 50 OLD BAILEY LONDON | GLASGOW AND BOMBAY

Contents: As for 130.1.

Binding: As for 130.1, but plain off-white endpapers.

Reference: PN.

Notes
1. This late issue, of about 1904, has no advertisements on the endpapers.
2. The title page omits the publisher's device, and has a later version of the imprint and address. The contents are otherwise unaltered from those of 130.1.

131–131A. BLACKIE'S ENGLISH-STUDY READERS

131.1
BLACKIE'S I ENGLISH-STUDY I READERS I Fourth Reader I (publisher's device) I BLACKIE . & SON . LIMITED I London . & . Glasgow

Contents
189 × 128 mm. (1)–240 I no catalogue. Eight full-page colour reproductions of paintings in British Art Galleries, by three-colour halftone blocks; a line drawing and seven wash-drawings printed from full-page line and halftone blocks in black; all on paper coated one side only, the colour plates unbacked and unfolioed, the others backed by text and folioed, all counted in the pagination. All plates arranged in pairs to wrap-round, or be inserted in, 16-page text gatherings. Many drawings printed from line blocks on text pages.
   (1) Blank I (2) frontispiece I (3) title p. I (4) publisher's addresses; printer's imprint (Printed in Great Britain by Blackie & Son, Ltd., Glasgow) I (5) Prefatory Note I (6) blank I 7–8. Contents I 9–240. text and illustrations.

Binding (see Plate 134)
Grey cloth boards, blocked dark-blue and green; edges plain; plain off-white endpapers.
   Front board: BLACKIE'S I ENGLISH= I . STUDY . I READERS (green) in plain rectangular panel out of pattern of repeated flower heads (dark-blue). In smaller panel, beneath this: BOOK I . IV . (green). At foot: BLACKIE . & . SON . LIMITED (green). All framed by green rules. **Spine:** ENGLISH-STUDY READERS IV (green) running from foot to head. **Back board:** plain.

Reference: PN.

Notes
1. 'Effie to the Rescue' appears in two Parts, at pages 161 to 170. Each Part is followed by a short series of questions. There are two line-drawings by Radcliffe Wilson. Henty is acknowledged in the list of Contents, on p.8. At the end of the text, on p.169, his name appears in small italics.
2. Published about 1927. The story consists of very brief extracts from 'A Raid by the Blacks', published by Blackie in *A Soldier's Daughter*, 1906 (§1, 111).

131A.1
BLACKIE'S I ENGLISH-STUDY I READERS I Fifth Reader I (publisher's device) I BLACKIE . & SON . LIMITED I London . & . Glasgow

Contents
189 × 128 mm. (1)–256 | no catalogue. Eight full-page colour reproductions of paintings in British Art Galleries, by three-colour halftone blocks; a line drawing, five wash-drawings, an oil painting, and an aerial photograph, printed from full-page halftone blocks in black, all on paper coated one side only, the colour plates unbacked and unfolioed, the others backed by text and folioed, all counted in the pagination. Plates arranged in pairs to wrap-round, or be inserted in, 16-page text gatherings. Many drawings printed from line blocks on text pages.

(1) Blank | (2) frontispiece | (3) title p. | (4) publisher's addresses; Book Production War Economy device with three-line statement; printer's imprint (Printed in Great Britain by Blackie & Son, Ltd., Glasgow) | (5) Prefatory Note | (6) Acknowledgments | 7–8. Contents | 9–256. text and illustrations.

Binding: As for 131.1 but with volume number changed on front board and spine.

Reference: AK.

Notes
1. That Henty is represented in this volume of the *English-Study Readers* came to my notice when this bibliography was already at the press. It was consequently not possible to include it in the consecutive numerical coding, and it has therefore been coded 131A.
2. The *English-Study Readers* were probably published in the 1920s, but, unlike the copy of 131.1 described above, the copy of 131A.1 described here contains the War Economy device on p.(4), and is a later reprint.
3. 'Rescued!' appears in two parts, at pp.9–18, each part followed by a short series of questions. Henty's contribution is given in the list of Contents on p.7. On p.18 is the credit line: *'From "Facing Death", by G.A.Henty.'*
4. Two line drawings are by Gordon Browne, the first, on p.11, is signed with his initials, the other, on p.15, is from the black plate of a two-colour drawing used to illustrate the first edition of *Facing Death*, 10.1.

132. BLACKIE'S MODEL READERS

132.1
BLACKIE'S | MODEL . READERS | BOOK . IV . | (decoration) | LONDON | BLACKIE & SON . LTD 50 OLD . BAILEY | . GLASGOW & DUBLIN .
(Note: all lettering is hand-drawn within decorative framework).

Contents
175 × 120 mm. (1)–240 | no catalogue. Eight full-page plates from a photograph, and watercolour drawings by H.M.Brock, Warwick Goble, and S.T.Dadd, reproduced by three-colour halftone blocks, all except the frontispiece backed with black-and-white illustrations from photographs, wash-drawings and line-drawings, printed from halftone and line blocks; all on coated paper, unfolioed but counted in pagination. All the plates arranged in pairs to wrap-around 16-page gatherings of text paper. Many full-page and smaller drawings printed from line blocks on text pages.

(1) Blank | (2) frontispiece | (3) title p. | (4) small decorative drawing | (5)–(6) Contents | 7–240. text and illustrations.

Binding (see Plate 131)
Dark-green cloth boards, blocked light-green; edges plain; plain off-white endpapers.
    Front board: BLACKIE'S | . MODEL . | READERS | . BOOK . IV . (light green) in light-green decorative art-nouveau design of leaves, etc. At foot: BLACKIE . | . AND . SON | LIMITED (cloth-colour out of solid light-green area) with, at right: 1/4 (light-green). **Spine:** BLACKIE'S . MODEL . READERS . IV (light-green) framed by light-green rule. **Back board:** plain.

References: OD | Cargill Thompson, *The Boys' Dumas*, p.6.

Notes
1. This series of Readers was probably published between 1905 and 1910.
2. 'The Christians to the Lions!' appears in two Parts at pages 156–165. There are no notes or questions. Both Parts are extracted from *Beric the Briton* (see §1), and this is briefly acknowledged at the end of the text on p.165.
3. Facing p.159 is a wash-drawing by W. Parkinson, used, in a larger size, as frontispiece to *Beric the Briton*, 59.1. On p.165 is a line-drawing by H.M. Brock.

132.2
Title page, Contents: 170 x 115 mm. As for 132.1.

Cover
Buff limp cloth, printed black; square back, cut flush; plain endpapers.
    Front: Design and lettering as for 132.1, except that the lines forming framework to panel are thinner, and price (1/4) is omitted at right of publisher's name (all black). **Spine:** as for 132.1, but ruled frame omitted (black). **Back:** plain.

Reference: BB.

Note: A cheaper format probably issued simultaneously with the hardback edition.

132.3
Title page: As for 132.1, but BOMBAY substituted for DUBLIN in imprint.

Contents, Binding: As for 132.1.

Reference: PN.

Notes
1. A post-1910 reprint: Dublin was then removed from the Blackie imprint on a re-organisation of the Irish branch (see *A Young Patriot*, §1, 122, Note 2).
2. The title page was hand-drawn and reproduced as a single line block, so an alteration to the address line was not easy. It was necessary to re-draw part of the artwork, copying the style used by the original lettering-artist, and to make a new line block. It has been well done, but the newly-inserted word, BOMBAY, is noticeably lighter in weight than the rest of the lettering.

133. THE BOYS' STORY BOOK

133.1

The | Boys' Story Book | Edited by Herbert Strang | (illustration of sailing ship at sea) | London: | Henry Frowde and Hodder & Stoughton
(*Note: The page is printed in red and black, red being used for the initial letters in the title, in* London, *and in the illustration*).

Contents

225 x 175 mm. (i)–(iv) | (1)–(144) | catalogue (i)–(iv) (see Note 2). Six full-page watercolours by various artists, reproduced by three-colour halftone blocks, printed on coated paper, unbacked, tipped in, not keyed to text. Many line drawings printed by line blocks on text pages.

(i) (Pasted down to front board as endpaper) | (ii) full-page illustrated bookplate with panel for owner's name (black and red) | (frontispiece, tipped in) | (iii) title page | (iv) editor's note, and printer's imprint (Richard Clay & Sons, Limited, London and Bungay.) | (1)–(144) text and illustrations | (i)–(iv) catalogue.

Binding (see Note 3)

Quarter-bound blue-green cloth, blocked black; paper boards printed dark-green and light-green, with colour plate laid down; edges plain; upper endpapers formed by leaf of text paper pasted down to board; lower endpapers plain ivory cartridge.

Front board: Edited by Herbert Strang | The Boys' Story Book (white out of dark-green and light-green textile-texture pattern, shaded dark-green) above decorative panel enclosing laid-down colour plate. **Spine:** The Boys' Story Book (black) on blue-green cloth, running from foot to head. **Back board:** over-all textile-texture pattern (dark-green and light-green).

Reference: SW.

Notes

1. The book consists of reprints of sections originally used in *The Red Book for Boys*, 174.1, as does also *Brave and True*, 135.1. The colour plates were in 174.1.
2. A 4-page, single-fold, sheet of text paper, forms the upper endpapers, on which are printed the title page and other matter described above; then follow nine 16-page gatherings, with signature marks: G, H, I, K, L, M, A, B, C; and finally a 4-page catalogue, also printed on text paper.
3. The blocks used for printing the paper on both boards are, apart from the lettering, similar to those used for *Brave and True*, 135.1, Plate 147.
4. The first 27 pages of signature A, starting on the 97th unfolioed page of the text proper, contain Henty's story 'Trapped. A Tale of the Mexican War' (see §4), extracted from *Out on the Pampas* (§1, 4.1), here edited by Herbert Strang.

134. BRAINS & BRAVERY

134.1

Brains & Bravery | BEING STORIES TOLD BY | (with double flower-head decoration at left of seven lines of names) G.A.HENTY | GUY BOOTHBY |

L.T.MEADE | J.ARTHUR BARRY | KATHARINE TYNAN | H.A.BRYDEN | and Others | EIGHT ILLUSTRATIONS BY | ARTHUR RACKHAM, A.R.W.S. | (single flower-head decoration) | LONDON | 1903 W.& R.CHAMBERS, LIMITED | EDINBURGH

Contents

184 x 130 mm. (i)–(viii) | (1)–(400) | no catalogue. Eight full-page wash-drawings by Arthur Rackham, reproduced by halftone blocks printed in black on coated paper, unbacked, keyed to text, tipped in.

(i) Half-title p. | (ii) blank | (frontispiece, tipped in) | (iii) title p. | (iv) printer's imprint (Edinburgh: | Printed by W.& R.Chambers, Limited.) | (v) Contents | (vi) advertisement (BOOKS BY G.MANVILLE FENN.) listing 15 titles | (vii) List of Illustrations | (viii) advertisement (UNIFORM WITH THIS VOLUME) listing this and 5 other titles | (1)–398. text | (399) advertisement (UNIFORM WITH THIS VOLUME) listing 5 other titles only | (400) printer's imprint, as on p.(iv).

Binding (see Plate 151)

Green cloth boards, bevelled, blocked black, grey, ochre, and gilt; edges plain; dark-brown endpapers, lined off-white.

Front board: BRAINS & BRAVERY (cloth-colour out of solid-gilt irregular panel above illustration of man on foot with pistol holding up horseman (black, grey, ochre). At foot: STORIES TOLD BY | G.A.HENTY | GUY BOOTHBY | KATHARINE TYNAN | L.T.MEADE | H.A.BRYDEN | J.ARTHUR BARRY etc. (cloth-colour out of solid-gilt irregular panel. **Spine:** BRAINS | & | BRAVERY (cloth colour out of solid-gilt irregular panel) above illustration of Chinaman with flying pigtail, holding knife (black, grey, ochre). At foot: STORIES TOLD BY | (then follows list of names in two columns, each of four lines) G.A.HENTY | GUY BOOTHBY | KATHARINE | TYNAN | L.T.MEADE | H.A.BRYDEN | J.ARTHUR | BARRY | ETC. | W.& R.CHAMBERS (all cloth-colour out of solid-gilt irregular panel). **Back board:** plain.

References: BL; Bod; PN | *Farmer*, p.14; *Dartt*, p.26.

Notes

1. There are four Henty stories (see §4): 'On an Indian Trail', pp.(1)–54; 'Gallant Deeds', pp.55–82; 'Working Up', pp.83–105; and 'Down a Crevasse', pp.106–114.
2. Title pages in later impressions were undated.
3. The other five titles, 'uniform with this book', listed on pp.(viii) and 399, all contain work by Henty: *Grit and Go*, 157; *Venture and Valour*, 190; *Peril and Prowess*, 170; *Dash and Daring*, 140; and *Courage and Conflict*, 139.
4. 'Down a Crevasse' has been carefully edited since it appeared in the 1901 Summer Number of the *Boy's Own Paper*, and on the whole the prose is much improved. There is, however, a strange error of punctuation in the last line of p.109. *For:* 'We had walked steadily and even. With the greatest efforts . . .', *read:* 'We had walked steadily, and even with the greatest efforts ...'.

135. BRAVE AND TRUE

135.1

Brave and True | Edited by Herbert Strang | (illustration of boy with tent, waving to sailing ship at sea) | London: | Henry Frowde and Hodder & Stoughton
(Note: the title is printed in black with red decorative initials; the illustration is in black and red. The title page is p.3 of the upper endpapers).

Contents

226 × 175 mm. Unfolioed book consisting of 4 pages printed black and red, plus six sections each of 16 pages, signatures A to F inclusive, printed black. Four full-page plates from watercolour drawings by P.A. Staynes, W.H.C. Groome, Arch Webb, and one unknown artist, reproduced by three-colour halftone blocks printed on coated paper, unbacked, unfolioed, tipped in. Eighteen black-and-white illustrations from line drawings by various artists, printed in black on text pages. No catalogue.

(i) Blank | (ii) full-page illustrated bookplate with panel for owner's name (black and red) | (frontispiece, tipped in) | (iii) title p. | (iv) editor's note, including 'Some of the pieces in this collection appeared first in my Annual'. At foot, beneath rule, printer's imprint (Richard Clay & Sons, Limited, London and Bungay.) | (1)–(96) text and illustrations.

Binding (see Plate 147)

Quarter-bound blue cloth, blocked black; paper boards printed turquoise and black, with colour-plate laid down; edges plain; upper endpapers formed by leaf of text paper, pasted down to board; lower endpapers plain off-white antique-wove.

Front board: Edited by Herbert Strang | Brave and True (white out of turquoise and black textile-texture pattern, shaded black) above decorative panel enclosing laid-down colour-plate. **Spine:** Brave and True (black) on blue cloth, running from foot to head. **Back board:** over-all textile-texture pattern (turquoise and black).

Reference: PN.

Notes

1. The book consists of sections used in *The Red Book for Boys*, 174, as also does *The Boys' Story Book*, 133. The colour plates were also in the earlier books.
2. Pages (1)–(27) contain the text and line-illustrations of Henty's 'Trapped. A Tale of the Mexican War', extracted from *Out on the Pampas* (§1, 4), here edited by Herbert Strang. The four illustrations, and one of the colour plates which forms the frontispiece and also illustrates this story, are by P.A. Staynes.
3. *The Red Book for Boys*, 174, and *The Green Book for Boys*, 156, and the various shorter volumes that emanated from them, were produced during the period of the 'Joint Venture' and later by the O.U.P. (see Appendix II, Part 2). All were on very bulky featherweight paper, with bindings not made to last.

136. BRITISH BATTLES ON LAND AND SEA

GENERAL NOTE

These volumes do not, strictly, warrant an entry in this book, as they contain no original contributions from Henty. They do, however, contain in Volume III extensive quotations from his war reports to the *Standard*, and for that reason I have thought them worthy of inclusion. As will be seen from the Notes below, the work was issued numerous times in varying forms. I do not give details of issues and editions: the quotations from Henty are common to all, in the pages indicated in Note 4 below. The edition described appears to give the most comprehensive coverage and illustration of the subject matter. I give it no specific code number.

BRITISH BATTLES | ON LAND AND SEA. | BY | JAMES GRANT, | Author of "The Romance of War," &c. | WITH NUMEROUS ILLUSTRATIONS. | (31mm. rule) | SPECIAL EDITION. | (31mm. rule) | VOLUME I. (VOLUME II., VOLUME III., VOLUME IV.) | CASSELL & COMPANY, LIMITED: | LONDON, PARIS & MELBOURNE.

Contents, Volume I
257 × 180 mm. (i)–viii | (1)–576 | no catalogue. Twenty full-page plates from engravings and photographs, printed on heavier paper in line or by photogravure in colours including black, grey, blue, and green, all unbacked, unfolioed and tipped in. Over 200 illustrations, including some full-page, from line engravings by numerous artists, printed on text pages.
(i) Blank | (ii) frontispiece | (iii) title p., printed in black and red | (iv) publisher's device | (v) Contents | vi. Contents, continued, and List of Full-page Plates | (vii)–viii. List of Illustrations | (full-page plate, tipped in) | (1)–576. text.

Volume II
257 × 180 mm. (i)–viii | (1)–576 | no catalogue. Twenty full-page plates in same style as in Volume I, but all printed in black. Over 200 illustrations from line engravings, as in Volume I, printed on text pages.
Details as for Volume I.

Volume III
257 × 180 mm. (i)–viii | (1)–(580) | no catalogue. Twenty full-page plates in same style as in Volume I, but printed in black or blue. Over 200 illustrations from line engravings, as in earlier volumes, printed on text pages.
(i) Blank | (ii) frontispiece | (iii) title p., printed in black and red | (iv) publisher's device | (v) Contents | vi. Contents, continued, and List of Full-page Plates | (vii)–viii. List of Illustrations | (full-page plate, tipped in) | (1)–374. text | 375–554. Chronological Résumé of British Battles on Land and Sea, 1066–1875 | (555)–579. Index, with printer's imprint at foot of p.579 (PRINTED BY CASSELL & COMPANY, LIMITED, LA BELLE SAUVAGE, LONDON, E.C.) | (580) blank.

Volume IV
257 × 180 mm. (i)–(xii) | (1)–624 | no catalogue. Twenty full-page plates in same style as in Volume I, but printed in black or blue. Over 220 illustrations and plans from line engravings, as in earlier volumes, printed on text pages.

(i) Blank | (ii) frontispiece | (iii) title p., printed in black and red | (iv) publisher's device | (v)–viii. Contents | (ix)–xi. List of Illustrations | (xii) List of Full-page Plates | (full-page plate, tipped in) | (1)–616. text | (617)–624. Index, with printer's imprint at foot of p.624, as on p.579 of Volume III.

Binding
Bright-blue, pebble-grained cloth boards, bevelled, blocked black, blind, and gilt. Binding cases were supplied by the publisher to individual subscribers (see Note 2).
Front board: BRITISH | BATTLES (gilt, with black and gilt decorative initials) | ON | LAND & SEA (black) in upper panel of complicated design of rules, crown, trident, weapons, etc. (black) and two illustrations in lower panels (black and gilt) showing land battle and sea battle. **Spine:** BRITISH | BATTLES | ON | Land & Sea (cloth-colour out of solid gilt decorative panel) over upper part of illustration (black) of soldier and sailor above: JAMES | GRANT (black). Black and gilt rules above and below, with further black and gilt rules at foot, below: CASSELL & COMPANY | LIMITED (black), the first of the two lines forming the upper arc of a circle. **Back board:** three rules near edges of bevel; ornamental design at centre of board (all blind).

References: BL; PN | *Dartt Companion*, p.5.

Notes
1. As pointed out by *Dartt*, there were numerous issues of this work, which was almost certainly published in parts in the same manner as *Battles of the Nineteenth Century* (§2, 126). It was designed as a three-volume set, dated 1873 to 1875, and then appeared in various four-volume editions over the following two decades. The set described above is undated, and later than any in the British Library: it has the words 'SPECIAL EDITION' on the title page, which is printed in two colours; it has all edges gilt; and it has twenty full-page plates in each volume, making it the most complete set I have been able to find.
2. The binding cases were offered to subscribers for private binding; the gilt edges of this set have, therefore, no significance, as each subscriber would have made his own arrangements. All binding cases are identical, with space left for the subscriber's binder to insert the appropriate volume numbers, so their style will also vary. This system implies that the work was not issued 'ready-bound'.
3. I have a second set of four volumes not in the British Library, dated between 1891 and 1894. The title pages, printed in black only, are as follows: BRITISH BATTLES | ON LAND AND SEA | BY | JAMES GRANT | Author of "Old and New Edinburgh," "The Romance of War," &c. | WITH NUMEROUS ILLUSTRATIONS. | * (**, ***, ****) | CASSELL & COMPANY, LIMITED: | LONDON, PARIS & MELBOURNE. | 1891. (1892., (n.d.), 1894.) | [ALL RIGHTS RESERVED.]
This set omits the twenty full-page plates per volume (although the regular full-page illustrations are printed on text pages), and has decorative engravings replacing the lists of plates described in the above entry. It is bound in the same publisher's binding cases as before.
4. The textual content of the various issues appears to be the same. Volume I opens with this paragraph: 'In these pages we propose to detail the exploits and glories by which our empire has become so vast that the sun never sets upon it, and by which we have maintained for ages long past the unquestionable supremacy of the sea'.

The history then begins with the Battle of Hastings, 1066, and the volume ends with the Battle of Dettingen, 1743. Volume II continues, from Fontenoy, 1745, to Bhurtpore, 1825–26; Volume III covers less than fifty years, from Navarino, 1827, to the end of the Ashantee War, 1874, and also contains a Chronological Résumé of land and sea battles from 1066 to 1875. Finally, Volume IV takes the history from the Expedition to Perak, 1875–76, to the end of the war in the Soudan, 1885.

5. Volume III contains numerous quotations from Henty's dispatches as Special Correspondent to the *Standard* during the Abyssinian campaign, and the Ashantee campaign: these will be found between pages 279 and 370. There are also quotations from the reports of military correspondents to other journals, including the *Scotsman*, the *Daily News*, and the *Telegraph*, and it appears that the compiler worked directly from copies of the main contemporary newspapers.

137. BY LAND AND SEA

137.1

. BY . LAND . | . AND . SEA . | Edited by Herbert Strang | (illustration of rifleman and drummer in action, in double decorative frame, all red and black) | London: | Henry Frowde and Hodder & Stoughton
(Note: The title is in red lettering, cased black; the imprint is in black over a red panel).

Contents
223 × 174 mm. Unfolioed book of nine 16-page sections, printed in black; plus 4 pages tipped on, to form upper-endpaper paste-down and title page, printed in red and black. Frontispiece from watercolour by unknown artist reproduced by three-colour halftone blocks on coated paper, unbacked, tipped in.

(i) Pasted down inside front board | (ii) panel for owner's name, with illustration, printed red and black | (frontispiece, tipped in) | (iii) title p., printed red and black | (iv) publisher's advertisement (UNIFORM WITH THIS VOLUME) listing 7 titles for boys, 6 titles for girls, and 4 titles for children. Below this: 'Some of the pieces in this collection appeared | first in my Annual. | H.S.' At foot, printer's imprint (Richard Clay & Sons, Limited, London and Bungay.) | (1)–(96) text.

Binding (see Plate 147)
Quarter blue cloth, printed paper boards; edges plain; upper endpaper formed from first text leaf, plain off-white lower endpapers.

Front board: By Land and Sea | Edited by Herbert Strang (reversed white out of blue decorated panel forming part of trompe l'oeil three-dimensional design of carved frame with leaves and flowers (blue). Tipped in central panel is illustration of hand-fighting on board ship, printed in three-colour halftone on coated paper. **Spine:** By Land and Sea (black) on blue cloth, running from foot to head. **Back board:** Decorative trompe-l'oeil design of carved frame with flowers and fleurs-de-lys at centre (blue).

Reference: BB.

Notes

1. The book is a selection of unfolioed sections from *The Green Book for Boys*, §2, 156. (For another series of extracts from that title see *Stirring Tales*, §2, 180).

2. Henty's 'Through the Enemy Lines', a condensed version of a part of his *The Young Franc-Tireurs* (§1, 5.1), is here edited by Herbert Strang, with five line-illustrations by T.C. Dugdale (see Appendix IV, Part 2).

138. CAMPS AND QUARTERS

138.1

CAMPS | AND | QUARTERS | An Annual | BY | ARCHIBALD FORBES | GEORGE HENTY | AND | CHARLES WILLIAMS. | WARD LOCK AND CO. | LONDON, NEW YORK, AND MELBOURNE. | 1889
(Note: An Annual *is in gothic type)*.

Contents

216 x 139 mm. (i)–(x) | (1)–(116) plus unfolioed pages, and general advertisements through text pages.

(i) (Leaf pasted down to inside cover as endpaper) | (ii)–(iv) advertisements | (v) half-title p. | (vi) advertisements | (vii) title p. | (viii) advertisement for Priestley's Dress Fabrics | (ix) Contents | (x) advertisements | (1)–5. Introduction | (6) Jellypod; alias The Muleteer. | 18. short editorial note | (4 unfolioed pages, tipped in) | (19)–23. A Relict and a Relic. | 24. short editorial note | (25)–28. A Passing Face. | 29. editorial note | (30)–41. Faithful to the Death. | 42. editorial note | (2 unfolioed pages, tipped in: advertisements) | (43)–45. Zeal in the Ranks. | 46. editorial note | (47)–54. The Divine Figure from the North. | 55. editorial note | (56)–71. Archmet's Treason. | 72. short editorial note | (73)–81. Turning the Tables. | 82. editorial note | (83)–100. The Building of the Yacht. | 101. editorial note | (102)–111. Out with the Red-Shirts. | 112. editorial note | (113)–(115) advertisements | (116) (leaf pasted down to inside cover as endpaper).

Cover (see Plate 158)

White coated-paper drawn on to first and last leaves of text, which form endpapers, square back.

Front: 1/- | CAMPS | AND | QUARTERS (printed diagonally, running up, across top left corner) | A SPRING | ANNUAL. | BY | ARCHIBALD FORBES, | GEORGE HENTY, | AND | CHARLES WILLIAMS. | WARD, LOCK AND CO., | LONDON, NEW YORK, AND MELBOURNE. | 1889. (all red) with border of two rules (red). **Spine:** plain. **Back:** Advertisement for Andersons' Regulation Waterproof Army Cloak, with printer's imprint at foot (GILBERT & RIVINGTON, LD., PRINTERS, ST. JOHN'S HOUSE, CLERKENWELL RD., E.C.).

References: Bod | *Farmer*, p.17; *Dartt*, p.31, *Companion*, p.7.

Notes

1. *Dartt* reports that one of Henty's own copies of this 'Annual', now in the Lilly Library of Indiana University, indicates that he wrote the Introduction, 'A Passing Face', 'Faithful to the Death', 'Turning the Tables', and 'Out with the Red-Shirts'.

Perhaps he also wrote the editorial notes between the stories, which act as a thread of continuity through the publication.

2. *Farmer* had to rely on a description of a copy not in original covers.

3. The publication is described on title page and cover as an Annual, but no subsequent issues are recorded.

139. COURAGE AND CONFLICT

139.1

Courage and Conflict I A I SERIES I OF STORIES I BY G.A.HENTY I F.T.BULLEN, G.M.FENN I Captain C.NORTH, HAROLD BINDLOSS I ANDREW BALFOUR, AND FRED WHISHAW I WITH EIGHT ILLUSTRATIONS I BY I W.BOUCHER I W.& R.CHAMBERS, LIMITED I LONDON AND EDINBURGH I 1901

Contents
185 x 131 mm. (i)–(viii) I (1)–416 I no catalogue. Eight full-page wash-drawings by W. Boucher, printed from halftone blocks in black on coated paper, unbacked, keyed to text pages, tipped in.

(i) Half-title p. I (ii) blank I (frontispiece, tipped in) I (iii) title p. I (iv) printer's imprint (Edinburgh: I Printed by W.& R.Chambers, Limited.) I (v) Contents I (vi) blank I (vii) List of Illustrations I (viii) advertisement (UNIFORM WITH THIS VOLUME.) listing this and 3 other titles I (1)–416. text, with printer's imprint at foot of p.416, as on p.(iv).

Binding (see Plate 151)
Red cloth boards, bevelled, blocked black, white, yellow, blue, brown, and gilt; edges plain; grey endpapers, lined off-white.

Front board: COURAGE and I CONFLICT (gilt, cased black) superimposed over illustration of Elizabethan soldiers lighting a beacon (black, white, yellow, brown). At lower left corner: STORIES Told By I G.A.HENTY I G.M.FENN I F.T.BULLEN I FRED. I WHISHAW I Etc. (black). All framed by black line. **Spine:** Courage I and I Conflict (decorative lettering using only one large capital C for the two main words of the title: cloth-colour out of solid-gilt irregular panel) above decorative trophy of crowned lion on a larger crown with rose and thistle (black, white, blue, brown). At foot: W.& R.CHAMBERS (cloth-colour out of solid-gilt irregular panel). **Back board:** plain.

References: BL; PN I *Farmer*, p.24; *Dartt*, p.43, *Companion*, p.10.

Notes
1. 'The Sole Survivors' (see §4) appears at pp.(1)–95.
2. The 'uniform' titles, listed on p.(viii), contain Henty's work: *Venture and Valour*, §2, 190; *Peril and Prowess*, §2, 170; and *Dash and Daring*, §2, 140.
3. Later impressions were printed with undated title pages, but within a short time the discovery of a serious error led to more extensive changes, see 139.2 below.

139.2

Courage and Conflict | A | SERIES | OF STORIES | BY G.A.HENTY | F.T.BULLEN, W.W.FENN | Captain C.NORTH, HAROLD BINDLOSS | ANDREW BALFOUR, AND FRED WHISHAW | WITH EIGHT ILLUSTRATIONS | BY | W.BOUCHER | LONDON: 38 Soho Square, W. | W.& R.CHAMBERS, LIMITED | EDINBURGH: 339 High Street.

Contents: As for 139.1, but (a) see Note 1; (b) on p.(viii) advertisement now lists this and 7 other titles.

Binding (see Plate 155)
Red cloth boards, bevelled, blocked black, green, and gilt; edges plain; grey endpapers, lined off-white.
   Front board: COURAGE and | CONFLICT (cloth-colour, cased black, out of solid-gilt decorative panel framed by black line) above illustration of night-scene of man tied to tree with Indians around fire in clearing beyond (black, green, gilt). At lower right corner: (ornament) Told by (ornament) | G.A.HENTY (two ornaments) | F.T.BULLEN (two ornaments) | FRED WHISHAW | HAROLD BINDLOSS | W.W.FENN (two ornaments) | ANDREW BALFOUR (all cloth-colour out of solid-gilt irregular panel framed by black line). **Spine:** Courage | and | Conflict (cloth-colour out of solid-gilt irregular panel framed by black line) above illustration of man seated under trees, with gun (black, green, gilt). At foot: W. & R. CHAMBERS (cloth-colour out of solid-gilt irregular panel framed by black line). **Back board:** plain.

References: RH | *Dartt*, p.44, Note (2), *Companion*, p.10.

Notes
1. On the title page, on pages (v) and 96, and on the front board of the binding case, the name of W.W. Fenn is now correctly given in place of G.M. Fenn in 139.1.
2. When it came to putting right this publisher's blunder, the corrections to the standing type would have been a simple matter, especially as only three pages in the book were affected. But to replace the brasses for blocking the binding case would, in this instance, have been costly. On the front board of 139.1 the names of the authors are part of a blocking piece cut for the whole of the black working, and closely knit into the drawing of the illustration itself. That made it virtually impossible to cut away part of the brass and insert a new section. To alter the existing design would have involved re-cutting the entire black plate, an expensive operation because of the size and detail, and the need for precise register.
3. Chambers looked for an easier and cheaper way out, and decided to abandon the original design altogether. Instead, they adapted brasses already cut for another book, *Peril and Prowess*, 170.1. It was necessary only to cut three simple reversed-out plates to substitute for those making the gilt panels on the front board and spine of that book, and one simple plate for the black casing of the title-lettering on the front board. Apart from the leaves of the illustration cutting into the lower left corner of the title-panel on the front board, no close-register work was involved. There was a further, continuing, economy, in that the new brasses were blocked in only three workings, whereas the old set involved twice that number.

140. DASH AND DARING

140.1

Dash and Daring | BEING | STORIES | TOLD BY | (list of names at right of floral ornament:) G.A.HENTY | GEO. MANVILLE FENN | DAVID KER | HEADON HILL | W.H.G.KINGSTON | REGINALD HORSLEY | HAROLD BINDLOSS | AND MANY OTHERS | WITH EIGHT ILLUSTRATIONS | BY | W.H.C.GROOME | LONDON | W.& R.CHAMBERS, LIMITED | 1898

Contents

185 × 131 mm. (i)–(viii) | (1)–414 | advertisement (415)–(416). Eight full-page wash-drawings by W.H.C. Groome, printed from halftone blocks in black on coated paper, unbacked, keyed to text pages, tipped in. Small line-engravings as headpieces and tailpieces.

(i) Half-title p. | (ii) blank | (frontispiece, tipped in) | (iii) title p. | (iv) printer's imprint (Edinburgh: | Printed by W.& Chambers, Limited.) | (v) Contents | (vi) blank | (vii) List of Illustrations | (viii) blank | (1)–414. text, with printer's imprint at foot of p.414 (Edinburgh: | Printed by W.& R.Chambers, Limited) | (415)–(416) advertisement (BOOKS FOR BOYS.).

Binding (see Plate 152)

Blue cloth boards, bevelled, blocked black and gilt; edges plain; grey endpapers, lined off-white.

Front board: Dash | & Daring (gilt, shaded black) above decorative trophy of flags, rifles & bayonets, swords, with small illustrations of drum, and sailing ships in battle (black and gilt); with lettering at right: STORIES | TOLD BY | G.A.HENTY | G.MANVILLE FENN | DAVID KER | W.H.G.KINGSTON | REGINALD HORSLEY | AND MANY OTHERS (all black). **Spine:** Dash & | Daring (gilt, shaded black) | STORIES | TOLD BY /. G.A.HENTY . | G.MANVILLE FENN | . DAVID KER . | W.H.G.KINGSTON | REGINALD HORSLEY | AND MANY OTHERS (all gilt) above trophy of Royal Standard and Union Flag (gilt) | W & R.Chambers (all gilt) (*n.b. no full point after W*). **Back board:** publisher's floral device as central medallion (black).

References: BL; PN | *Farmer*, p.24; *Dartt*, p.45, *Companion*, p.12.

Notes

1. 'On the Spanish Main', is at pp.(1)–80, and 'Joe Polwreath, the Hunchback', at pp.81–116, for both of which see §4.

2. Later impressions were printed with undated title pages.

3. The publisher's lists, pp.(415)–(416), form the last leaf of the final gathering.

141. A DOZEN ALL TOLD

141.1

A . DOZEN . ALL . TOLD | BEING A SET OF TWELVE STORIES BY (row of 4 ornaments) | (the following 12 names are set out in two columns, with varying numbers of printer's ornaments after each name so as to 'justify' each line:)

W.E.NORRIS | MRS. ALEXANDER | FLORENCE MARRYATT | GEORGE R.SIMS | JOHN STRANGE WINTER | ADELINE SERGEANT | F.W.ROBINSON | MONA CAIRD | HELEN MATHERS | G.A.HENTY | WILLIAM WESTALL | FREDERICK BOYLE | WITH TWELVE ILLUSTRATIONS BY (row of 7 ornaments) | (the following 12 names are set out in two columns with ornaments in same style as those above:) W.PARKINSON | FRANK BRANGWYN | WALTER S.STACEY | J.FINNEMORE | L.LESLIE BROOK | PAUL HARDY | ALFRED PEARSE | JOHN H.BACON | HAL HURST | W.H.MARGETSON | HERBERT J.DRAPER | W.HATHERELL, R.I. | LONDON, 1894. (row of 5 ornaments) BLACKIE AND SON, | LIMITED, FORTY-NINE OLD BAILEY, E.C. | GLASGOW, EDINBURGH, AND DUBLIN. (2 ornaments)

Contents

185 × 124 mm. (1)–(352) | no catalogue. Twelve full-page wash-drawings printed from halftone blocks in black on coated paper, unbacked, unfolioed, tipped in.

(1) Half-title p. | (2) blank | (frontispiece, tipped in) | (3) title p. | (4) blank | (5) Contents | (6) blank | (7) list of Illustrations | (8) blank | (9) half-title p. to first story | (10) blank | (11)–34. 'The Duffer' by W.E. Norris | (35) half-title p. to second story | (36) blank | (37)–64. 'To Paris, for Pleasure' by Mrs. Alexander | (65) half-title p. to third story | (66) blank | (67)–86. 'Jenny's Girl' by F.W. Robinson | (87) half-title p. to fourth story | (88) blank | (89)–149. 'For Money or for Love' by Mona Caird | (150) blank | (151) half-title p. to fifth story | (152) blank | (153)–168. 'Hunks' by John Strange Winter | (169) half-title p. to sixth story | (170) blank | (171)–190. 'Where is Mrs. Smith' by George R. Sims | (191) half-title p. to seventh story | (192) blank | (193)–219. 'Where the Chain Galls' by Florence Marryatt | (220) blank | (221) half-title p. to eighth story | (222) blank | (223)–240. 'A Shark's Fin' by G.A.Henty | (241) half-title p. to ninth story | (242) blank | (243)–271. 'Two Brothers' by Helen Mathers | (272) blank | (273) half-title p. to tenth story | (274) blank | (275)–288. 'Love and War' by William Westall | (289) half-title p. to eleventh story | (290) blank | (291)–318. 'A Fatal Choice' by Adeline Sergeant | (319) half-title p. to twelfth story | (320) blank | (321)–351. 'The Bordone Girl' by Frederick Boyle | (352) blank.

Binding (see Plate 146)

Dark grey-blue cloth boards, blocked black, green, ochre, blind, and gilt; edges plain; dark-blue surface-paper endpapers.

Front board: A . DOZEN, | ALL . TOLD (gilt, cased black) with row of three authors' names (gilt), each enclosed in floral design (black, green, ochre, and gilt) above, and three similar rows of authors' names, etc., below. The whole enclosed in wavy lines near edges of board (black and ochre). **Spine:** A . Dozen, | All . Told (gilt) placed similarly to title on front board, with one pair of decorative floral designs above, and three pairs below (black, green, ochre, gilt). The designs on the spine are smaller than those on the front board, have additional gilding, and the authors' names are omitted. At foot: . Blackie . and | . Son . Lim: (gilt). A pair of wavy lines (ochre and gilt) at head and foot. **Back board:** three rules (thin, thick, thin) at edges of board (blind).

References: PN | *Farmer*, p.26; *Dartt*, p.50.

Notes

1. Henty's 'A Shark's Fin' is probably his only adult fiction published by Blackie. It is illustrated by Frank Brangwyn.

2. *Farmer*, overstating the case, says 'This first edition is a very rare book', but he adds, correctly, 'There is no copy in the British Library'.

142. EMPIRE ANNUAL FOR BOYS

142.1

EMPIRE | ANNUAL | for | BOYS | (small diamond ornament) | Edited by A.R.BUCKLAND, M.A. | With Contributions by | (list of writers follows in two columns with vertical rule between) J.W.BACHE | PAUL BLAKE | WILLIAM CANTON | HAROLD DORNING | FRANK ELIAS | CLUCAS JOUGHIN | DAVID KER | E.C.KENYON | WALKER KING | ANGUS R.MACBEE | J.A.OWEN | GORDON STABLES | G.A.WADE | H.A.WOOLLEY | AND OTHER AUTHORS. | (35mm. double rule) | With Coloured Plates and | Sixteen Black and White | Illustrations. | 4 BOUVERIE ST. | LONDON E.C
(Note: The above is printed in red and blue, and apart from the publisher's address, is within a wreath-like oval border with decorations, set from standard printer's 'flowers', in yellow, green and red. There are seven small stars grouped within a shield at the head of the page (see Note 3)).

Contents

211 × 140 mm. (1)–(384) | no catalogue. Frontispiece, from watercolour drawing, together with title page as 4-page insert, printed in three-colour process inks on single-sided coated paper, unbacked. Six other full-page watercolour drawings reproduced by three-colour halftone blocks; sixteen full-page plates from wash-drawings and photographs, printed in black from halftone blocks; all on coated paper, unbacked, unfolioed, tipped in.

(1) Half-title p. | (2) publisher's advertisement (THE EMPIRE ANNUAL FOR GIRLS) | (frontispiece and title page, tipped in) | 3–6. Contents | 7. list of Illustrations | 8. Index to Authors | 9–(384) text, with printer's imprint at foot of p.(384) (UNWIN BROTHERS, LIMITED THE GRESHAM PRESS, WOKING AND LONDON).

Binding

Brown cloth boards, blocked black, dark-brown, yellowish-buff, blue, white, green, grey, and gilt; edges plain; plain off-white endpapers.
Front board: THE | EMPIRE ANNUAL | FOR | BOYS (yellowish-buff, cased black) superimposed on upper part of illustration, framed by black line, of soldiers on horseback attacking troops in military vehicle (black, dark-brown, yellowish buff, blue, white, green, and grey). **Spine:** THE | EMPIRE | ANNUAL | FOR | BOYS (gilt) above illustration of Scout riding bicycle down lane, waving his hat (black, dark-brown, yellowish buff, blue, white, green, and grey). At foot: publisher's monogram, R.T.S (black). **Back board:** plain.

References: PN | *Dartt*, p.177.

Notes
1. The publisher's name is on the spine of the binding case, but not on the title page. R.T.S., the Religious Tract Society, was a very large commercial publishing house (see Appendix II, Part 6).
2. Henty's 'Life of a Special Correspondent' appears at pp.284–290, without illustration. It is a shortened version of the serialised article in the *Boy's Own Paper*, Volume XVIII, see §3, 201.
3. The volume cannot be dated from internal sources. But the contents make it seem not earlier than 1917. Another issue of the same Annual, which contains an article on 'Four Famous Authors for Boys', including Henty, has the date, 1911, on the title page, in the position here occupied by the group of seven stars. If that 1911 Annual were the first in a series, later 'dated' by stars, this issue would be six years later, thus giving it the date 1917.

143. FIFTY-TWO FURTHER STORIES FOR BOYS

143.1
FIFTY-TWO | FURTHER | STORIES FOR BOYS | BY | GEORGE A.HENTY, GEORGE MANVILLE FENN | OLIVER WENDELL HOLMES, ASCOTT R.HOPE, ROBERT | OVERTON, DAVID KER, ROSA MULHOLLAND, | AND OTHER WRITERS. | EDITED BY | ALFRED H.MILES. | WITH ILLUSTRATIONS. | LONDON: | HUTCHINSON & CO. | 25, PATERNOSTER SQUARE.

Contents
195 × 132 mm. (i)–x | 11–460 | no catalogue. Seven full-page wood-engravings (artists and engravers unknown) printed in black on text pages.

(i) Blank | (ii) frontispiece | (iii) title p. | (iv) printer's imprint (PRINTED BY | HAZELL, WATSON, AND VINEY, LD. | LONDON AND AYLESBURY.) | (v)–vi. Preface | (vii) Table of Authors | (viii) blank | (ix)–x. Index | 11–460. text and illustrations.

Binding (see Plate 148)
Red cloth boards, bevelled, blocked black, white, and gilt; all edges gilt; blue-black surface-paper endpapers.
Front board: 52 (black, cased gilt, and again cased black) FURTHER (gilt, cased black) | STORIES FOR | BOYS (gilt, cased black), all above illustration of polar bears on boat in ice-landscape (black, white, gilt). At foot: ALFRED H.MILES (gilt). **Spine:** FIFTY-TWO | FURTHER (gilt) above solid-black rectangle with gilt and black rules above and below, and: STORIES | FOR | BOYS (reversed out gilt). Beneath this: ALFRED H.MILES (gilt) above illustration of man with balaclava, and holding gun (black, white, gilt), and: HUTCHINSON & Co. (gilt) below black rule. Black and gilt rules at head and foot. **Back board:** plain.

References: PN | *Farmer*, p.32; *Dartt*, p.57, *Companion*, p.14.

Notes
1. 'The Burman's Treasure' (see §4) is at pp.11–23. It does not appear elsewhere.
2. The Editor's Preface is dated 1 October 1891.

3. Reprints have the title-page reference to illustrations replaced by, e.g., SEVENTH THOUSAND.

144. FIFTY-TWO HOLIDAY STORIES FOR BOYS

144.1

FIFTY-TWO | HOLIDAY STORIES | FOR BOYS | BY | G.A.HENTY, GEO. MANVILLE FENN, COULSO– | KERNEHAN, C.A.STEPHENS, WILLIAM DRYSDALE, ALICE | F.JACKSON, CAPTAIN ALEXANDER, LIEUT. CLARKE | AND OTHER WRITERS. | EDITED BY | ALFRED H.MILES | ILLUSTRATED | LONDON | HUTCHINSON & CO. | 34, PATERNOSTER ROW.

Contents
195 x 130 mm. (1)–456 | catalogue (457)–(450). Five full-page wood engravings (artists and engravers unknown, but one signed 'EWM') on text pages.
(1) Blank | (2) frontispiece | (3) title p. | (4) printer's imprint (PRINTED AT NIMEGUEN (HOLLAND) | BY H.C.A.THIEME OF NIMEGUEN (HOLLAND) | AND | 36, ESSEX STREET, STRAND, LONDON, W.C.) | (5)–6. Preface | (7) Table of Authors | (8) blank | (9)–10. Index | 11–456. text and illustrations | (457)–(460) catalogue.

Binding (see Plate 148)
Grey cloth boards, bevelled, blocked black, white, buff, and gilt; all edges gilt; blue-black surface-paper endpapers.
Front board: 52 | HOLIDAY | STORIES | FOR BOYS (gilt, cased black) above illustration of diver at bottom of sea with squid (black, white, buff). At foot: ALFRED.H.MILES (gilt). **Spine:** FIFTY-TWO | HOLIDAY (gilt) above solid-black rectangle with black and gilt rules above and below, and: STORIES | FOR | BOYS (gilt reversed out). Beneath this: ALFRED.H.MILES (gilt) and illustration of diver standing at bottom of sea holding rope (buff and gilt). Below black and buff rules: HUTCHINSON & Co. (gilt). Black, buff, and gilt rules at head and foot. **Back board:** plain.

References: PN | *Farmer*, p.32; *Dartt*, p.57, *Companion*, p.14.

Notes
1. 'A Death Warning' (see §4) is at pp.11–23. It does not appear elsewhere.
2. The Editor's Preface is dated 1 September 1898.
3. Title pages in reprints have ILLUSTRATED replaced by, e.g., FIFTH THOUSAND.
4. The catalogue includes 26 books in the 'Fifty-Two Series'.

145. FIFTY-TWO OTHER STORIES FOR BOYS

145.1

FIFTY-TWO | OTHER | STORIES FOR BOYS. | BY | GEORGE A.HENTY | GEORGE MANVILLE FENN, R.E. | FRANCILLON, ASCOTT HOPE, GORDON

STABLES, | M.D., R.N., ROBERT OVERTON, DAVID KER, | AND OTHER WRITERS. | EDITED BY | ALFRED H.MILES | WITH ILLUSTRATIONS. | LONDON: HUTCHINSON & CO., | 25, PATERNOSTER SQUARE

Contents
194 × 130 mm. (1)–450 | no catalogue. Six full-page wood-engravings (artists and engravers unknown, though one signed 'GLS') printed in black on text pages.

(1) Blank | (2) frontispiece | (3) title p. | (4) printer's imprint (PRINTED BY | HAZELL, WATSON, AND VINEY, LIMITED, | LONDON AND AYLESBURY.) | (5)–6. Preface | (7) Table of Authors | (8) blank | (9)–10. Index | 11–450. text and illustrations, with printer's imprint on p.450 (Printed by Hazell, Watson, & Viney, Ld., London and Aylesbury.).

Binding (see Plate 148)
Green cloth boards, bevelled, blocked black, blue, and gilt; all edges gilt; dark olive-green surface-paper endpapers.

Front board: 52 OTHER | STORIES FOR BOYS (gilt, shadowed black) above illustration of boy with roped basket clinging to weathercock at top of church steeple, with birds, and landscape far below (black, blue, gilt). At lower left corner, diagonally: ALFRED | H.MILES (gilt). Black rules at head and foot. **Spine:** FIFTY-TWO | OTHER (gilt) above solid-blue rectangle with black and gilt rules above and below, and: STORIES | FOR | BOYS (reversed out, gilt). Beneath this: ALFRED H.MILES (gilt); illustration of seaman standing, with telescope under his arm (black, blue, gilt), and: HUTCHINSON & Co. (gilt). Black, blue and gilt rules at head and foot. **Back board:** plain.

References: PN | *Farmer*, p.32; *Dartt*, p.57, *Companion*, p.14.

Notes
1. 'An Indian's Gratitude' (see §4) is at pp.289–300, with an anonymous illustration on p.288, keyed in error to p.229. The story does not appear elsewhere.
2. The Editor's Preface is dated 1 August 1892.
3. Reprints have the title-page reference to illustrations replaced by, e.g., SEVENTH THOUSAND.

146. FIFTY-TWO STIRRING STORIES FOR BOYS

146.1
FIFTY-TWO | STIRRING STORIES | FOR BOYS. | BY | G.A.HENTY, G.MANVILLE FENN, FRANK H.CONVERSE, | DAVID KER, J.L.HARBOUR, MANLEY H.PIKE, | COULSON KERNAHAN, H.HERVEY, | ALICE F.JACKSON, | AND OTHER WRITERS. | EDITED BY | ALFRED H.MILES | ILLUSTRATED. | LONDON: | HUTCHINSON & CO., | 34, PATERNOSTER ROW

Contents
195 × 130 mm. (1)–458 | catalogue (459)–(460). Three full-page wash-drawings, including one by Stanley L.Wood, reproduced by halftone blocks, all with hand-engraving done after the blocks were etched; one pen-drawing reproduced by line

block, with hand-engraving after etching; one wood-engraving, signed P.Grenier; all printed in black on coated paper, unbacked, keyed to text pages, tipped in.

(1)–(2) Blank | (frontispiece, tipped in) | (3) title p. | (4) printer's imprint (PRINTED BY | HAZELL, WATSON, AND VINEY, LD., | LONDON AND AYLESBURY.) | 5–6. Preface | (7) Table of Authors | (8) blank | 9–10. Index | 11–458. text | (459)–(460) catalogue.

Binding (see Plate 148)
Green, diagonally-ribbed cloth boards, bevelled, blocked black, brown, white, and gilt; all edges gilt; blue-black surface-paper endpapers.

Front board: 52 STIRRING | STORIES FOR | BOYS (gilt, cased black) above illustration of two horsemen, one carrying barefoot girl across saddle (black, brown, white). At foot: ALFRED.H.MILES (gilt). **Spine:** FIFTY-TWO | STIRRING (gilt) above solid-gilt rectangle with gilt and black rules above and below, and: STORIES | FOR | BOYS (reversed out, and brown). Beneath this: ALFRED.H.MILES (gilt) and illustration of cavalier drawing sword (black and gilt). At foot: HUTCHINSON & Co. (gilt) below black and brown rules. Black, brown, and gilt rules at head and foot. **Back board:** plain.

References: PN | *Farmer*, p.32; *Dartt*, p.57, *Companion*, p.14.

Notes
1. 'A Brave Châtelaine' (see §4) is at pp.225–238. It was not printed elsewhere.
2. The Editor's Preface is dated 1 October 1900.
3. Title pages in reprints have ILLUSTRATED replaced by, e.g., FIFTH THOUSAND.
4. The catalogue lists 32 titles in 'The Fifty-Two Library'.

147. FIFTY-TWO STORIES FOR BOYHOOD AND YOUTH

147.1
FIFTY-TWO STORIES | FOR | BOYHOOD AND YOUTH. | BY | GEORGE A.HENTY, GEORGE MANVILLE FENN, ASCOTT HOPE, | GORDON STABLES, M.D., R.N., ROBERT OVERTON, A. | EUBULE-EVANS, ROSA MULHOLLAND, DAVID KER, | AND OTHER WRITERS. | EDITED BY | ALFRED H.MILES. | ILLUSTRATED. | LONDON: HUTCHINSON & CO., | 34, PATERNOSTER ROW.

Contents
194 × 131 mm. (1)–454 | catalogue (455)–(456). Five full-page wood-engravings (one signed, J.Nash, otherwise by unknown artists and engravers) on text pages.

(1) Blank | (2) frontispiece | (3) title p. | (4) printer's imprint (PRINTED BY | HAZELL, WATSON, AND VINEY, LD., | LONDON AND AYLESBURY.) | (5)–6. Preface | (7) Table of Authors | (8) blank | (9)–10. Index | 11–454. text and illustrations, with printer's imprint on p.454 (Printed by Hazell, Watson, & Viney, Ld., London and Aylesbury.) | (455)–(456) catalogue.

Binding (see Plate 148)
Blue cloth boards, bevelled, blocked black, brown, white, and gilt; all edges gilt; dark-blue surface-paper endpapers.

Front board: 52 STORIES | FOR | BOYHOOD | AND YOUTH (gilt, cased black) above illustration of soldier holding rifle facing jaguar advancing across tree-trunk bridge over ravine (black, brown, white). At foot: ALFRED H.MILES (gilt). **Spine:** FIFTY-TWO | STORIES (gilt) above solid-brown rectangle, with gilt and black rules above and below, and: FOR | BOYHOOD | AND | YOUTH (reversed out, and gilt). Beneath this: ALFRED H.MILES (gilt) and illustration of young soldier with gun, with rocks underfoot (black, brown, gilt). At foot, below black and brown rules: HUTCHINSON & Co. (gilt). Black, brown and gilt rules at head and foot. **Back board:** plain.

References: PN | *Farmer*, p.32; *Dartt*, p.57, *Companion*, p.14.

Notes
1. 'Hunted by an Elephant' (see §4) is at pp.97–106, with an anonymous wood-engraving on p.96. See 154.1, Note 3.
2. The Editor's Preface is dated September 1893.
3. Title pages in reprints have ILLUSTRATED replaced by, e.g., FIFTH THOUSAND.
4. The catalogue is on the last leaf of the final text gathering listing 14 titles. The books are advertised as 'Large Crown 8vo, 456 pages, cloth, bevelled boards, richly gilt, gilt edges. Well illustrated. Price Five Shillings Each'.

148. FIFTY-TWO STORIES OF BOY-LIFE AT HOME AND ABROAD

148.1
FIFTY-TWO | STORIES OF BOY-LIFE | At Home and Abroad. | BY | G.A.HENTY, G.MANVILLE FENN, ASCOTT R.HOPE, | W.CLARK RUSSELL, HALL BYRNE, EUBULE-EVANS, | DAVID KER, LIEUT.-COL. MACPHERSON, | AND OTHER WRITERS. | EDITED BY | ALFRED H.MILES. | ILLUSTRATED. | LONDON: | HUTCHINSON & CO., | 34, PATERNOSTER ROW.
(*Note:* At Home and Abroad. *is in gothic type*).

Contents
194 x 130 mm. (1)–450 | catalogue (451)–(452). Five full-page wood-engravings by unknown artists and engravers, printed in black on text pages.
(1) Blank | (2) frontispiece | (3) title p. | (4) printer's imprint (PRINTED BY | HAZELL, WATSON, AND VINEY, LD., | LONDON AND AYLESBURY.) | (5)–6. Preface | (7) Table of Authors | (8) blank | (9)–10. Index | 11–450. text and illustrations | (451)–(452) catalogue.

Binding (see Plate 148)
Blue cloth boards, bevelled, blocked black, red, yellow, and gilt; all edges gilt; blue-black surface-paper endpapers.
Front board: 52 | STORIES OF | BOY-LIFE (gilt, cased black) | AT HOME AND ABROAD (gilt) above illustration of man lying across railway line while another waves torch to stop oncoming train (black, red, yellow). At foot: ALFRED

H.MILES (gilt). **Spine:** FIFTY-TWO I STORIES (gilt) above solid-red rectangle with black and gilt rules above and below, and: OF I BOY-LIFE I AT HOME I AND ABROAD (reversed out, and gilt). Beneath this: ALFRED H.MILES (gilt) and illustration of railwayman holding up red lamp (black, red, gilt). At foot, below black and red rules: HUTCHINSON & CO (gilt). Red, black and gilt rules at head and foot. **Back board:** plain.

References: BL; PN I *Farmer*, p.32; *Dartt*, p.57, *Companion*, p.14.

Notes
1. 'The Man-Eater of the Terai' (see §4) is at pp.348–360, with an anonymous wood-engraving frontispiece to the book. The story does not appear elsewhere.
2. The Editor's Preface is dated September 1894.
3. Title pages in reprints have ILLUSTRATED replaced by, e.g., FIFTH THOUSAND.
4. The catalogue is on the last leaf of the final text gathering.

149. FIFTY-TWO STORIES OF COURAGE AND ENDEAVOUR FOR BOYS

149.1

FIFTY-TWO STORIES I OF I COURAGE AND ENDEAVOUR I FOR BOYS. I BY I GEORGE A.HENTY, HANS OLAFSON, EDWARD W.THOMPSON, I H.HERVEY, J.L.HARBOUR, GRACE SCHUYLER, I L.J.BATES, STINSON JARVIS, LELAND RANKIN, I MANLEY H.PIKE, W.MURRAY GRAYDON, I COL. G.W.SYMONDS, I AND OTHER WRITERS. I EDITED BY I ALFRED H.MILES. I ILLUSTRATED. I LONDON: I HUTCHINSON & CO., I 34, PATERNOSTER ROW.

Contents
195 × 130 mm. (1)–462 I catalogue (463)–(464). Two full-page wood-engravings; four full-page wash-drawings printed from halftone blocks, one hand-engraved after etching, another deep-etched and similarly hand-engraved. The last is signed, H. Burgess; other artists and engravers unknown. All printed in black on coated paper, tipped in, and all except the frontispiece are backed, as half-title pages to sections of the book.

(1)–(2) Blank I (frontispiece, tipped in) I (3) title p. I (4) printer's imprint (PRINTED BY I HAZELL, WATSON, AND VINEY, LD. I LONDON AND AYLESBURY) I 5–6. Preface I (7) Table of Authors I (8) blank I 9–10. Index I 11–462. text, with printer's imprint on p.462 (Printed by Hazell, Watson, & Viney, Ld., London and Aylesbury.) I (463)–(464) catalogue.

Binding (see Plate 148)
Red, diagonally-grained cloth boards, bevelled, blocked black, dark-grey, light-grey, and gilt; all edges gilt; blue-black surface-paper endpapers.
Front board: 52 STORIES OF I COURAGE & ENDEAVOUR I FOR BOYS (gilt, cased black) above illustration of three horsemen galloping across bridge, one firing at figures in distance (black, dark-grey, light-grey). At foot:

ALFRED.H.MILES (gilt). **Spine:** FIFTY-TWO | STORIES OF (gilt) above solid-gilt rectangle with black and gilt rules above and below, and: COURAGE & . | . ENDEAVOUR | FOR BOYS (reversed out, and dark-grey). Beneath this: ALFRED.H.MILES (gilt) and illustration of officer with sword and fur-collared coat (dark-grey and gilt). At foot, and below dark-grey and black rules: HUTCHINSON & Co. (gilt). Dark-grey, black and gilt rules at head and foot. **Back board:** plain.

References: BL; PN | *Farmer*, p.32; *Dartt*, p.57, *Companion*, p.14.

Notes
1. 'At Talavera' (see §4) is at pp.353–360. It is not printed elsewhere.
2. The Editor's Preface is dated 1 October 1901.
3. Title pages in reprints have ILLUSTRATED replaced by, e.g., FIFTH THOUSAND.

150. FIFTY-TWO STORIES OF DUTY AND DARING FOR BOYS

150.1
FIFTY-TWO STORIES | OF | DUTY AND DARING | FOR BOYS. | BY | G.A.HENTY, G.MANVILLE FENN, GRACE STEBBING, | ALICE F.JACKSON, DAVID KER, W.J.HENDERSON, | WILLIAM DRYSDALE, EDWARD W.THOMPSON, | AND OTHER WRITERS. | EDITED BY | ALFRED H.MILES. | ILLUSTRATED. | LONDON: | HUTCHINSON & CO., | 34, PATERNOSTER ROW.

Contents
193 x 128 mm. (1)–452 | catalogue (453)–(456). Five full-page wood-engravings (one after W.H. Overend, one signed R. & E. Taylor, other artists and engravers unknown) printed in black on text pages.
  (1) Blank | (2) frontispiece | (3) title p. | (4) printer's imprint (PRINTED BY | HAZELL, WATSON, AND VINEY, LD., | LONDON AND AYLESBURY.) | 5–6. Preface | (7) Table of Authors | (8) blank | 9–10. Index | 11–452. text and illustrations, with printer's imprint on p.452 (Printed by Hazell, Watson, & Viney, Ld., London and Aylesbury) | (453)–(456) catalogue.

Binding (see Plate 148)
Green, diagonally ribbed, cloth boards, blocked black, white, blue, and gilt; all edges gilt; black surface-paper endpapers.
  Front board: 52 STORIES | of DUTY & DARING | FOR BOYS (gilt, cased black) above illustration of hand-to-hand fighting on ship (black, white, blue). At foot: ALFRED.H.MILES (gilt). **Spine:** FIFTY-TWO | STORIES OF (gilt) above solid-blue rectangle with black and gilt rules above and below, and: DUTY & DARING . FOR BOYS (reversed out, and gilt). Beneath this: ALFRED H.MILES (gilt) and illustration of figure in turban with knife tucked in waistband (black and gilt). At foot: HUTCHINSON & Co. (gilt) between black rules. Black, blue, and gilt rules at head and foot. **Back board:** plain.

References: BL; PN | *Farmer*, p.32; *Dartt*, p.57, *Companion*, p.14.

Notes
1. 'The Son of a Cavalier' (see §4) is at pp.231–243. It does not appear elsewhere.
2. The Editor's Preface is dated 1 September 1897.
3. Title pages in reprints have ILLUSTRATED replaced by, e.g., FIFTH THOUSAND.
4. The catalogue lists 44 titles in the 'Fifty-Two Series', at five shillings each.

151. FIFTY-TWO STORIES OF HEROISM IN LIFE AND ACTION FOR BOYS

151.1
FIFTY-TWO | STORIES OF HEROISM | IN LIFE AND ACTION FOR BOYS | BY | G.A.HENTY; GEORGE MANVILLE FENN; ROBERT | OVERTON; DAVID KER; SYDNEY DAYRE; C.A. | STEPHENS; CAPTAIN KING; CAPTAIN LEACH; | J.L.HARBOUR; WILLIAM DRYSDALE; | AND OTHER WRITERS | EDITED BY | ALFRED H.MILES | ILLUSTRATED | LONDON | HUTCHINSON & CO. | PATERNOSTER ROW, E.C.

Contents
194 x 129 mm. (i)–(viii) | (9)–452 | catalogue (453)–(456). Two full-page wood engravings (signed by Harold Copping and Stanley Berkeley); two full-page wash-drawings printed from halftone blocks (one signed Lancelot Speed; the other unsigned, and hand-engraved after etching); one full-page pen-drawing, unsigned, printed from line block; all in black on coated paper, unbacked, keyed to text pages, tipped in.

(Frontispiece, tipped in) | (i) title p. | (ii) blank | iii–iv. Preface | (v) Table of Authors | (vi) blank | vii–viii. Contents | (9)–452. text, with printer's imprint on p.452 (Printed by Cowan & Co., Limited, Perth.) | (453)–(456) catalogue, including a description of the 'Fifty-Two Series' with a list of 75 contributing authors, headed by G.A.Henty, and a list of 29 titles.

Binding (see Plate 148)
Red cloth boards, bevelled, blocked black, orange, white, buff-pink, and gilt; all edges gilt; black surface-paper endpapers.
Front board: 52 STORIES OF | HEROISM | IN . LIFE . AND . ACTION | FOR BOYS (gilt) above and overlapping illustration of two men hauling alligator on end of rope, with third man astride it (black, white, buff-pink). At foot: ALFRED.H.MILES (gilt). **Spine:** FIFTY-TWO | STORIES OF (gilt) above solid-orange rectangular panel with black and gilt rules above and below, and: HEROISM | FOR BOYS (reversed out, and gilt). Beneath this: ALFRED H.MILES (gilt) and illustration of turbaned figure (black and gilt). At foot: HUTCHINSON & Co. (gilt) below black and gilt rules. Black, orange and gilt rules at head and foot. **Back board:** plain.

References: BL; PN | *Farmer*, p.32; *Dartt*, p.57, *Companion*, p.14.

Notes
1. 'A Traitor in Camp' (see §4) is at pp.139–153, with an unsigned wash-drawing to face p.139. The story does not appear elsewhere.
2. The Editor's Preface is dated 1 October 1899.
3. Title pages in reprints have ILLUSTRATED replaced by, e.g., FIFTH THOUSAND.

152. FIFTY-TWO STORIES OF LIFE AND ADVENTURE FOR BOYS

152.1
FIFTY-TWO STORIES | OF | LIFE AND ADVENTURE | FOR BOYS. | BY | G.A.HENTY, G.MANVILLE FENN, HENRY FRITH, ALBERT E. | HOOPER, KIRK MUNROE, ELIOT McCORMICK, DAVID KER | AND OTHER WRITERS. | EDITED BY | ALFRED H.MILES. | ILLUSTRATED. | LONDON: | HUTCHINSON & CO., | 34, PATERNOSTER ROW.

Contents
195 × 132 mm. (1)–450 | catalogue (451)–(452). Five full-page wood-engravings (one signed Gordon Browne, at p.170, other artists and engravers unknown) on text pages.
(1) Blank | (2) frontispiece | (3) title p. | (4) printer's imprint (PRINTED BY | HAZELL, WATSON, AND VINEY, LD., | LONDON AND AYLESBURY.) | (5)–6. Preface | (7) Table of Authors | (8) blank | 9–10. Index | 11–450. text and illustrations | (451)–(452) catalogue of 'The Fifty-Two Library', listing 16 titles.

Binding (see Plate 148)
Light-blue cloth boards, bevelled, blocked black, white, red merging to grey, back to red, then to green, and gilt; all edges gilt; blue-black surface-paper endpapers.
Front board: 52 | STORIES OF | LIFE & ADVENTURE | FOR BOYS (all gilt, cased red) above illustration of man with gun on horseback in setting sun (black, white, red merging to grey, back to red, then to green). At foot: ALFRED H.MILES (gilt). **Spine:** FIFTY-TWO | STORIES OF (gilt) above solid-red panel with black and gilt rules above and below, and: LIFE & ADVENTURE | FOR BOYS (reversed-out and gilt). Beneath this: ALFRED H.MILES (gilt) and illustration of cavalryman with rifle on horseback (black and gilt). At foot: HUTCHINSON & Co (gilt) between black and green rules. Black, gilt and red rules at head; black and gilt rules at foot. **Back board:** plain.

References: PN | *Farmer*, p.32; *Dartt*, p.57, *Companion*, p.14.

Notes
1. 'An Escape from Massacre. A Big Boy's Story of the Mutiny', at pp.200–213, not printed elsewhere, is illustrated by an unsigned wood-engraving as frontispiece.
2. The Editor's preface is dated September 1895.
3. Title pages in reprints have ILLUSTRATED replaced by, e.g., FIFTH THOUSAND.

153. FIFTY-TWO STORIES OF PLUCK AND PERIL FOR BOYS

153.1
FIFTY-TWO STORIES | OF | PLUCK AND PERIL | FOR BOYS. | BY | G.A.HENTY, G.MANVILLE FENN, ROBERT LEIGHTON, | LIEUT.-COL. MACPHERSON, ROBERT OVERTON, | CAPTAIN H.PATTERSON, C.G.D.ROBERTS | LUCY HARDY, ALICE F.JACKSON, | AND OTHER WRITERS. | EDITED BY | ALFRED H.MILES. | ILLUSTRATED. | LONDON: | HUTCHINSON & CO., | 34, PATERNOSTER ROW.

Contents
191 x 130 mm. (1)–454 | catalogue (455)–(456). Five full-page wood-engravings, by unknown artists and engravers, printed in black on text pages.
(1) Blank | (2) frontispiece | (3) title p. | (4) printer's imprint (PRINTED BY | HAZELL, WATSON, AND VINEY, LD., | LONDON AND AYLESBURY.) | (5) Preface | vi. [roman numerals in error] Preface, continued | (7) Table of Authors | (8) blank | 9–10. Index | 11–454. text and illustrations | (455)–(456) catalogue of 'The Fifty-Two Library', listing 41 titles.

Binding (see Plate 148)
Green, diagonally-grained cloth boards, bevelled, blocked black, brown, yellow, blue, and gilt; all edges gilt; black surface-paper endpapers.
Front board: 52 STORIES | OF PLUCK | & PERIL | FOR BOYS (gilt, cased black) above illustration of bearded man fighting hound over body of girl (black, yellow, blue). At foot: ALFRED | H.MILES (gilt). **Spine:** FIFTY-TWO | STORIES OF (gilt) above solid-brown panel, between rules (black, gilt). Below: ALFRED H.MILES (gilt); illustration of bearded man (black, gilt). At foot: HUTCHINSON & Co. (gilt) between black and brown rules. Black, brown and gilt rules, head and foot. **Back board:** plain.

References: BL; PN | *Farmer*, p.32; *Dartt*, p.57, *Companion*, p.14.

Notes
1. 'An Indian Surround' (see §4) is at pp.257–269. It does not appear elsewhere.
2. The Editor's Preface is dated September 1896.
3. Title pages in reprints have ILLUSTRATED replaced by, e.g., FIFTH THOUSAND.
4. The publisher's catalogue lists 41 titles in 'The Fifty-Two Library'.

154. FIFTY-TWO STORIES OF THE BRAVE AND TRUE FOR BOYS

154.1
FIFTY-TWO STORIES OF | THE BRAVE AND TRUE | FOR BOYS. | BY | G.A.HENTY, THEODORE ROOSEVELT, H.HERVEY, | G.MANVILLE FENN, DAVID KER, ALBERT KINROSS, | CLUCAS JOUGHIN, JAAKOV

PRELOOKER, | ALICE F.JACKSON, N.HOLDERNESS, | LIEUT. H.P.WHITMARSH, R.N., | AND OTHER WRITERS. | EDITED BY | ALFRED H.MILES. | ILLUSTRATED. | LONDON: | HUTCHINSON & CO., | PATERNOSTER ROW.

Contents
195 × 130 mm. (1)–462 | catalogue (463)–(464). Four full-page wood-engravings by unknown artists and engravers; two full-page wash-drawings by unknown artists printed from halftone blocks; all black on coated paper; all except frontispiece backed on rectos as half-title pages to Sections, keyed to text pages, tipped in.

(1)–(2) Blank | (frontispiece, tipped in) | (3) title p. | (4) printer's imprint (PRINTED BY | HAZELL, WATSON, AND VINEY, LD., | LONDON AND AYLESBURY.) | (5)–6. Preface | (7) Table of Authors | (8) blank | 9–10. Index | 11–462. text, with printer's imprint of p.462 (Printed by Hazell, Watson, & Viney, Ld., London and Aylesbury.) | (463)–(464) catalogue of 'The Fifty-Two Library', listing 38 titles.

Binding (see Plate 148)
Red cloth boards with light diagonal-grain, bevelled, blocked black, buff, dark-blue merging to grey, and gilt; all edges gilt; dark-blue surface-paper endpapers.
Front board: 52 STORIES OF THE | BRAVE & TRUE | FOR | BOYS (gilt, cased black) above illustration of officer carrying girl on horseback, looking back at fallen horseman (black, buff, dark-blue merging to grey). At foot: ALFRED.H.MILES (gilt). **Spine:** FIFTY-TWO | STORIES OF THE (gilt) above solid-gilt rectangular panel between rules (black, gilt), and: BRAVE . | AND . TRUE | FOR BOYS (reversed out, dark-blue). Beneath this: ALFRED.H.MILES (gilt); illustration of dismounted officer with drawn sword (grey and gilt). At foot: HUTCHINSON & Co. (gilt) below black and grey rules. Black and gilt rules at head; black, grey and gilt rules at foot. **Back board:** plain.

References: PN | *Farmer*, p.32; *Dartt*, p.57, *Companion*, p.14.

Notes
1. 'A Sioux Raid. A North American Story' (see §4) is at pp.353–365, with an anonymous wood-engraving facing p.353. The story does not appear elsewhere.
2. Title pages in reprints have ILLUSTRATED replaced by, e.g., FIFTH THOUSAND.
3. The Editor's Preface is dated 1 October 1902, the year Henty died. He had written twelve short stories for the 'Fifty-Two Library', one each year from 1891. Only one was later reprinted (see *Fifty-Two Stories for Boyhood and Youth*, 147.1, Note 1).

155. THE GOLDEN STORY BOOK

155.1
The | Golden Story Book | by | G.Manville Fenn, D.H.Parry, | G.A.Henty, Sheila Brayne, | L.L.Weedon, etc. | (line illustration) | ERNEST . NISTER . LONDON. (space) No. 3800. (space) E.P.DUTTON & Co. NEW YORK | IP.

Contents
259 x 210 mm. (1)–108. Numerous black and white illustrations in line and tone by various artists, all printed in black on text pages.

(1) Illustrated half-title p. | (2) blank | (3) title p. | (4)–108. text and illustrations, with imprint on p.108 (Printed in Bavaria.).

Binding (see Plate 171)
Quarter-bound grey cloth, varnished off-white paper boards, front board printed in full colour; edges browned (from poor-quality paper); plain off-white endpapers.

Front board: The | Golden Story Book (all basically yellow and brown, cased dark-brown) the last three words in a scroll-panel with holly leaves and berries in green and red. Full colour illustration of young children on frozen pond, with, at left: trade mark, imprint, etc., in small type at foot: (device, containing the words: ALTIORA PETO (dark-brown) above: EN | TRADE MARK). I.P. | ERNEST . NISTER . LONDON (all dark-brown). At centre: solid rectangular strip; floral decoration, obscuring earlier printing: below it: No. 3800 (dark-brown). At right: E.P.DUTTON & Co. NEW YORK. (dark-brown). **Spine:** plain grey cloth. **Back board:** plain varnished paper.

References: BL; PN | *Farmer*, p.35; *Dartt*, p.67, *Companion*, p.16.

Notes
1. Published in 1913. *Dartt* (p.68) reports a copy, probably a Dutton US edition, with '3 pp. of catalogue, including inside rear advertisement for Nister's Holiday Annual, 25th year'. The 25th year of *Nister's Holiday Annual* was 1913.
2. 'How a Drummer Boy Saved a Regiment' (see §4), at pp.(49)–61, is illustrated by F.A. Stewart. The story appeared in other Nister publications (see 160.1 and 164.1).

156. THE GREEN BOOK FOR BOYS

156.1
THE | GREEN BOOK | FOR BOYS | Edited by Herbert Strang | (illustration of young man firing cannon) | London: | Henry Frowde and Hodder & Stoughton
(Note: The title, printed in green, cased black, and the editor's name, black, are in a panel with the illustration, black and green, the whole being within another illustrated panel, black and green, containing the publisher's imprint).

Contents
221 x 176 mm. Unfolioed book: 4 pages printed black and green, plus eighteen sections of 16 pages each, signatures A to I and K to S, printed black. Twelve full-page plates from watercolour drawings by various artists, printed from three-colour halftone blocks on coated paper, unbacked, tipped in. Many drawings by various artists, printed from line blocks on text pages. No catalogue.

(i) Blank | (ii) full-page 'bookplate' (black and green) | (frontispiece, tipped in) | (iii) title p. | (iv) Contents | (5)–(292) text and illustrations.

Binding (see Plate 147)
Quarter-bound green cloth with printed paper boards. Cloth yellow-green, blocked darker blue-green. Paper white, printed green (halftone), with full-colour plate laid down in panel on front board. Edges plain; plain off-white endpapers.

Front board: THE | Green Book for Boys | Edited by Herbert Strang (all greenish-white out of green background) in oval-ended panel above larger one, with decorative border, containing laid-down colour plate. **Spine:** The | GREEN | BOOK | for | BOYS | Edited by | Herbert | Strang (all cloth-colour out of dark-green panel with ornamental framework), above decorative illustration of steamship (dark-green) and: HENRY FROWDE | & HODDER & | STOUGHTON | (row of three dots) (all dark-green). Dark-green rules at head and foot. **Back board:** Wash-drawing representing decorative panel in bas-relief with fleurs-de-lys and floral motifs, all printed in green halftone.

References: PN | *Farmer*, p.92 (addenda); *Dartt*, p.68.

Notes
1. Henty's 27-page 'Through the Enemy Lines. A Story of the Franco-German War', is extracted from *The Young Franc-Tireurs*, (§1, 5). It starts at sig.N, with five line-drawings by T. Dugdale on text pages and one anonymous colour-plate, tipped in.
2. See Appendix II, Part 2, for this publisher's acquisition from Griffith & Farran of their rights in Henty's work, including *The Young Franc-Tireurs*.
3. For notes on the pseudonym, 'Herbert Strang', also see Appendix II, Part 2.
4. The book was first published in 1910, together with *The Red Book for Boys* (§2, 174). Produced not to last, on bulky featherweight paper, with cheap binding.
5. *Not* an Annual, as described by *Dartt*. The Editor's note on the Contents page refers to *Herbert Strang's Annual* for boys, in which some stories first appeared.
6. See also *By Land and Sea* (§2, 137), and *Stirring Tales* (§2, 180), both of which consist of signatures extracted and reprinted from this book.

156.2
THE | GREEN BOOK | FOR BOYS | Edited by Herbert Strang | (illustration of young man firing a cannon) | HUMPHREY . MILFORD | OXFORD . UNIVERSITY . PRESS . LONDON
(*Note: the only variation from 156.1 is the publisher's imprint*).

Contents: 223 x 178 mm. As for 156.1, except (a) p.(i): Publisher's advertisement for nine books each, edited by Herbert Strang and Mrs Herbert Strang. (b) p.(iv): Contents page has printer's imprint added at foot (Reprinted 1917 in Great Britain by | Richard Clay & Sons, Limited, | London and Bungay.). (See Notes 2–3 below.)

Binding: As for 156,1, but the cloth colour is a bluer green, blocked in black, and the publisher's imprint at the foot of the spine now reads: MILFORD (black) without the row of three dots below it.

References: PN | *Dartt*, p.68.

Notes
1. For explanation of the change of publisher, see Appendix II, Part 2.
2. This edition was reprinted by Richard Clay & Sons Limited in 1926, and by The Garden City Press Ltd, Letchworth, in 1928. The page size of the latter impression, varies from the earlier ones, being 232 x 175 mm. The printer's imprint on p.(292) reads 'Printed 1928 in Great Britain at the Garden City Press Ltd, | Letchworth.', but

on p.(iv) the earlier imprint has not been deleted, and still reads 'Reprinted 1926 in Great Britain by R. Clay & Sons, Ltd., Bungay, Suffolk.'.

3. In these later issues there are only six tipped-in colour plates, and the title page is printed in black only. The book is also bound in full mid-green linen-textured cloth, blocked black; edges plain; plain off-white endpapers. Front board: THE GREEN BOOK I FOR BOYS (black) above illustration of two men seated, smoking pipes, beside camp fire, one wearing stetson and spurs; heads of two horses (black). Spine: THE I GREEN I BOOK I FOR I BOYS (black) above illustration of eight oxen pulling covered wagon driven by man with long whip; another man walking alongside (black). At foot, between two rules: OXFORD (all black). Back board: plain.

157. GRIT AND GO

157.1

GRIT and GO I STORIES TOLD BY I (with double flower-head decoration at left of list of names) G.A.HENTY I GUY BOOTHBY I D.CHRISTIE MURRAY I H.A.BRYDEN I D.L.JOHNSTONE I HAROLD BINDLOSS I F.R.O'NEILL I S.ANNESLEY I EIGHT ILLUSTRATIONS BY I W.RAINEY I (single flower-head decoration) I LONDON I 1902 W.& R.CHAMBERS, LIMITED I EDINBURGH

Contents
186 x 129 mm. (i)–(viii) I (1)–400 I no catalogue. Eight full-page wash-drawings by W.Rainey, printed from halftone blocks in black on coated paper, unbacked, keyed to text pages, tipped in.

(i) Half-title p. I (ii) blank I (frontispiece, tipped in) I (iii) title p. I (iv) printer's imprint (Edinburgh: I Printed by W.& R.Chambers, Limited.) I (v) Contents I (vi) advertisement (BOOKS BY G.MANVILLE FENN.) listing 14 titles I (vii) List of Illustrations I (viii) advertisement (UNIFORM WITH THIS VOLUME.) listing this and 4 other titles I (1)–400. text, with printer's imprint at foot of p.400, as on p.(iv).

Binding (see Plate 152)
Blue cloth boards, bevelled, blocked black, grey-blue, ochre, and gilt; edges plain; dark-blue surface-paper endpapers.

Front board: GRIT and GO (gilt, cased black) above, and overlapping, illustration of man with gun hunting lion (black, grey-blue, ochre). At lower right corner, on ochre panel framed black: STORIES TOLD BY I G.A.HENTY (two leaf ornaments) I GUY BOOTHBY (leaf ornament) I D.CHRISTIE MURRAY I H.A.BRYDEN (two leaf ornaments) I D.L.JOHNSTONE (leaf ornament) I H.BINDLOSS (two leaf ornaments) I (leaf ornament) ETC. (leaf ornament) (all black). **Spine:** GRIT I AND I GO (gilt, cased black) overlapping top of illustration of figure as on front board, walking, full-face (black, grey-blue, ochre) with thick rule (ochre) at top and upper parts of sides of spine. Beneath this: STORIES TOLD BY I G.A.HENTY (two leaf ornaments) I GUY BOOTHBY (leaf ornament) I D.CHRISTIE MURRAY I H.A.BRYDEN (two leaf ornaments) I D.L.JOHNSTONE (leaf ornament) I H.BINDLOSS (two leaf ornaments) I (leaf ornament) ETC. (leaf ornament) (all black) above: W.& R.CHAMBERS (gilt). **Back board:** plain.

References: PN | *Farmer*, p.35; *Dartt*, p.69, *Companion*, p.17.

Notes

1. 'Burton & Son; or, Found on the Shore' (see §4) is at pp.(1)–75.
2. The uniform volumes, listed on p.(viii), contain Henty's work: *Venture and Valour*, §2, 190; *Peril and Prowess*, §2, 170; *Dash and Daring*, §2, 140; and *Courage and Conflict*, §2, 139.
3. Reprints were issued with undated title pages. *Dartt*, p.69, reports 'Also reprinted with title page date': this is a misprint ('with' for 'without').
4. Reprints show variation in the publisher's imprint and advertisements; simplifications of the binding design; and, later, the use of featherweight paper.

158. HAZARD AND HEROISM

158.1

Hazard and Heroism | Being Stories Told by | G.A.HENTY | LOUIS TRACY | HAROLD BINDLOSS | EDWIN LESTER ARNOLD | Lt.-Col. A.F.MOCKLER-FERRYMAN | &c., &c. | WITH EIGHT ILLUSTRATIONS | BY | W.H.C.GROOME, R.B.A. | LONDON | 1904 W.& R.CHAMBERS, LIMITED | EDINBURGH

Contents

184 × 131 mm. (i)–(viii) | (1)–404 | catalogue (1)–(32). Eight full-page wash-drawings by W.H.C. Groome, printed from halftone blocks in black on coated paper, unbacked, keyed to text pages, tipped in.

(i) Half-title p. | (ii) blank | (frontispiece, tipped in) | (iii) title p. | (iv) printer's imprint (Edinburgh: | Printed by W.& R.Chambers, Limited.) | (v) Contents | (vi) advertisement (BOOKS BY G.MANVILLE FENN.) listing 16 titles | (vii) List of Illustrations | (viii) advertisement (UNIFORM WITH THIS VOLUME.) listing this and 6 other titles | (1)–403. text | (404) printer's imprint, as on p.(iv) | (1)–(32) catalogue.

Binding (see Plate 153)

Green cloth boards, bevelled, blocked black, red, white, and gilt: edges plain; dark brown endpapers, lined off-white.

Front board: HAZARD (red, cased black) | AND (black) HEROISM (red, cased black) (all out of solid gilt in black and gilt scrolls) | STORIES TOLD BY (white, cased black) above and overlapping illustration of man in armour, on horseback, being attacked by foot-soldiers with bows and arrows (black, white, red, gilt). At left of upper part of illustration: G.A.HENTY | E.L.ARNOLD | LT.Col. A.F.MOCKLER | FERRYMAN | HAROLD BINDLOSS | LOUIS TRACY | &c &c (all black). The whole framed by gilt line. **Spine:** HAZARD (red, cased black) | AND (black) | HEROISM (red, cased black) all out of solid-gilt rectangle framed by black line, above: STORIES TOLD BY (black). Beneath this: G.A.HENTY | E.L.ARNOLD | Lt.COL. A.F.MOCKLER | FERRYMAN | HAROLD BINDLOSS | LOUIS TRACY | &c &c (all black) within decorative gilt and black frame. Below, is illustration of British soldier with sword, being attacked by man wearing turban (black, red, white), the top and both sides enclosed by thick gilt line. At foot: W.& R.CHAMBERS (gilt). **Back board:** plain.

References: BL; PN | *Farmer*, p.38; *Dartt*, p.70.

Notes

1. Henty's 'The Wreck on the Goodwins', is at pp.(1)–19; 'The Thug's Revenge', pp.20–36; 'A Fishwife's Dream', pp.37–52; 'The Old Pit Shaft', pp.53–66; and 'On the Cliff', pp.67–85. For all of these see §4.
2. Later issues have yellow pigment substituted for gilt in the blocking of the front board and spine. Also, sometimes, the publisher's catalogue is omitted.
3. Reprints were issued with no date on the title page.
4. Six uniform titles listed on p.(viii), contain Henty's work: *Brains & Bravery*, §2, 134; *Grit and Go*, §2, 157; *Venture and Valour*, §2, 190; *Peril and Prowess*, §2, 170; *Dash and Daring*, §2, 140; and *Courage and Conflict*, §2, 139.

159. IN BATTLE AND BREEZE

159.1

IN | BATTLE AND BREEZE | Sea Stories | BY | G.A.HENTY, GEO. MANVILLE FENN, AND | W.CLARK RUSSELL | FRONTISPIECE BY LANCELOT SPEED. | LONDON | S.W.PARTRIDGE & CO. | 8 & 9 PATERNOSTER ROW, E.C.
(Note: Sea Stories *is in gothic type).*

Contents
189 × 129 mm. (1)–320 | catalogue (1)–16. Frontispiece from wash-drawing by Lancelot Speed, printed from halftone block on text paper.
  (1) Blank | (2) frontispiece | (3) title p. | (4) blank | (5) Contents | (6) blank | (7)–320. text, with printer's imprint on p.320 (NEILL AND COMPANY, PRINTERS, EDINBURGH.) | (1)–16. catalogue.

Binding (see Plate 149)
Blue cloth boards, blocked black, grey merging to white, and gilt; top edge gilt; grey flowered endpapers.
  Front board: In Battle | and Breeze (gilt, shaded black) over part of illustration of sailing ships in sea battle (black, grey merging to white). **Spine:** Black rule at head. In | Battle | and | Breeze (cloth-colour out of solid gilt rectangle; pairs of black rules above and below) above: G.A.HENTY | G.M.FENN | W.CLARK RUSSELL (black); illustration of cannon on board ship (black, grey merging to white). At foot: S.W.PARTRIDGE & CO. (gilt) between two black rules. **Back board:** plain.

References: BL; Bod; PN | *Farmer*, p.40; *Dartt*, p.77, *Companion*, p.18.

Notes

1. The Copyright Libraries received the book in 1896.
2. 'In the Grip of the Press Gang' (see §4) is at pp.(1)–84.
3. An issue exists with the publisher's device blocked blind on the back board.
4. The frontispiece halftone bears the monogram of a distinguished Viennese firm of process engravers, Angerer & Göschl.

159.2

IN | BATTLE AND BREEZE | Sea Stories | BY | G.A.HENTY, GEO. MANVILLE

FENN, AND | E.HARCOURT BURRAGE | NEW EDITION | LONDON |
S.W.PARTRIDGE & CO. | 8 & 9 PATERNOSTER ROW, E.C.
(*Note:* Sea Stories *is in gothic type*).

Contents
186 × 124 mm. (1)–320 | catalogue (1)–20. Frontispiece from wash-drawing by
Lancelot Speed, printed in black from halftone block on coated paper, unbacked,
tipped in.
   (1)–(2) Blank | (frontispiece, tipped in) | (3) title p. | (4) blank | (5) Contents | (6)
blank | (7)–320. text, with printer's imprint on p.320 (NEILL AND COMPANY
LTD., PRINTERS, EDINBURGH.) | (1)–20. catalogue.

Binding: (See Plate 149). As for 159.1, except (a) smaller board area; (b)
E.HARCOURT BURRAGE instead of W.CLARK RUSSELL on spine; (c) edges
plain; (d) yellow surface-paper endpapers.

References: PN | *Dartt*, p.77, *Companion*, p.18.

Notes
1. In this edition 'The Voyage of the "Benbow"', by E. Harcourt Burrage, replaces
the story by W. Clark Russell. The reason for the change is not known. E.H. Burrage
also wrote under pseudonyms, including 'Philander Jackson'. Percy Muir remarks:
'This worthy usually added the initials "H.U.A." after his name, which he once
admitted stood for nothing but "Hard Up Author" (*English Children's Books*, p.111).
2. The frontispiece, printed from the block used for the first edition, is now on coated
paper, giving a far better impression. Consequently the first text leaf is now totally
blank, and the frontispiece tipped in immediately following it.
3. For this impression an antique laid text paper is printed the 'wrong way' of the
grain, making it hard to fold and to use. The 'chain lines' (see 'Laid paper' in
Glossary) are consequently the wrong way for an 8vo book, i.e. left to right instead
of head to foot). It replaces the wove used for 159.1, and has a smaller page-size.
4. The catalogue (p.2) announces, as a new title, a book issued in series with this
one: *Through Fire and Storm* (§2, 189). Copies were received by the Libraries in
1898: it is likely, therefore, that 159.2 was also issued close to that date.

159.3

Title page: As for 159.2, but NEW IMPRESSION instead of NEW EDITION.

Contents: 183 × 122 mm. As for 159.2, but catalogue (1)–32 instead of (1)–20.

Binding (see Plate 149)
Red cloth boards, blocked black, blue-grey, buff, and gilt; edges plain; plain off-
white laid endpapers.
   Front board: IN BATTLE | AND BREEZE (gilt) within rules and panelling
(buff) which also enclose, below, illustration of two sailors scrubbing the deck of a
ship, one of whom is being threatened by a Chinese man with a knife (black, blue-
grey, buff). **Spine:** IN | BATTLE | AND | BREEZE (cloth-colour out of solid-gilt
rectangle, framed black). Above and below: art-nouveau floral pattern (black, blue-
grey, buff). At foot: PARTRIDGE & Co (gilt) between black and buff rules. **Back
board:** plain.

Reference: PN | *Dartt*, p.77, Note 2; *Companion*, p.18.

Notes

1. An antique laid is again used: this time the right way of the grain, with chain lines running properly for an 8vo book, i.e. from head to foot (see 159.2, Note 3).

2. Copies seen have 1906 inscriptions. A copy in red cloth with a 1908 inscription has a loosely inserted leaflet: '*British Workman* Annual Volume for 1908, Now Ready'.

3. The spine of the binding case follows a standard design for this publisher, and is a slightly simplified version of that used for *Two Sieges*, §1, 112.

4. Henty's contribution remains as in 159.1 and 159.2.

160. IN STORYLAND

160.1

IN | STORYLAND | A Volume of Original Pictures, | Stories, and Verses. | Written by | G.A.Henty, L.T.Meade, | G.Manville Fenn, | Evelyn Everett-Green, | Paul Creswick, | F.E.Weatherly, | Maggie Brown | Sheila E.Braine, Etc. Etc. | And Illustrated by | Ada Dennis, E.Stuart Hardy, | E.Lance, Hilda Robinson, | and others. | Edited and Arranged by | Alfred J.Fuller. | (at left) London: | Ernest Nister | (at right) New York: | E.P.Dutton & Co. | (centred at foot) 1505.
(Note: The title page is hand-drawn, with scrolls and floral panelling in line).

Contents

236 × 192 mm. (1)–144 | no catalogue. Twelve full-page watercolour drawings by various artists, reproduced by colour-lithography on coated paper, unbacked, tipped in. Numerous black-and-white illustrations reproduced in line or halftone on the calendered text-paper.

(1) Half-title p. | (2) 8-line verse | (frontispiece, tipped in) | (3) title p. | (4)–5. Contents | (6)–(144) text and illustrations, with imprint on p.144 (Printed in Bavaria).

Binding (see Plate 171, and Notes 2–3)

Quarter-bound grey cloth, printed paper boards; edges plain; off-white endpapers with line illustrations printed in grey.

Front board: (all lettering included in over-all, full-colour lithographed illustration): IN STORYLAND (initial letters red in small red panels, remainder blue) at head of illustration of two young girls dressed up in flowing garments, playing panpipes, with pigeons in the foreground and a fountain behind. In very small lettering at foot: (left) Ernest . Nister . London. | (centre) 1505 | (right) E.P. Dutton & Co. New York. (all grey). **Spine:** plain grey cloth. **Back board:** Plain off-white paper, varnished.

References: BL; PN | *Farmer*, p.44; *Dartt*, p.80, *Companion*, p.19.

Notes

1. The Copyright Libraries received the book in 1900.

2. Later issues had a different binding design, and the reference number 3536 on title page and front board, in place of the number 1505. The front board shows two children behind a screen, and a piano (see *Dartt Companion*, p.19). The contents are otherwise unchanged, although the vignette tailpiece on p.5 is printed upside down. Copies of the later issues have been found with inscriptions dated 1912 and 1916.

3. *Dartt*, p.80, briefly describes, and illustrates following his p.94, yet another issue with a front-board illustration of a small boy riding a tricycle in the form of a rocking horse. See 161.1, Note 2, final sentence.

4. 'How a Drummer Boy Saved a Regiment' (see §4), is at pp.(7)–14. The vignette heading, with title-lettering, and vignette tailpiece, are from wash-drawings signed with the initials A.W. Three illustrations are from line drawings by F.A. Stewart. The story appeared in other Nister publications (see 155.1 and 164.1).

161. IN THE CHIMNEY CORNER

161.1

In the | Chimney Corner | A Volume of Original Pictures, | Stories, and Verses. | Written by | G.A.Henty, | L.T.Meade, | G.Manville Fenn, | Evelyn Everett-Green, | F.E.Weatherly, | Frances E.Crompton, | Etc. Etc. | And Illustrated by | Ada Dennis, | E.Stuart Hardy, | Hilda Robinson, | and others. | (vignette illustration at right of the above lists of authors and artists) | Edited and Arranged by | Alfred J.Fuller. | (at left) London: | Ernest Nister | (at right) New York: | E.P.Dutton & Co. | (centred at foot) No. 463.

Contents
236 x 191 mm. (1)–144 | no catalogue. Twelve full-page watercolour drawings by various artists, reproduced by colour-lithography on coated paper, unbacked, tipped in. Numerous black-and-white illustrations, full-page and smaller, reproduced in line and halftone on the calendered text-paper, the full-page illustrations being unbacked, unfolioed, and not counted in the pagination.

(1) Illustrated half-title p. | (2) 8-line verse | (colour-frontispiece, tipped in) | (3) title p. | (4)–5. Contents | (6)–144. text and illustrations, with imprint on p.144 (Printed in Bavaria).

Binding (see Plate 171, and Note 2)
Quarter-bound blue cloth, printed paper boards; edges plain; off-white endpapers with line illustrations printed in grey.
Front board: (all lettering included in full-colour illustration covering entire board area): In the | Chimney Corner (mainly red, shaded dark-brown and yellow) above illustration of small girl sitting on floor in front of bench, reading book, with doll, kittens, etc. At right: by | G.A.Henty, | L.T.Meade, | G.Manville | Fenn, | etc., etc. (dark-brown). At foot: (at left) ERNEST . NISTER . LONDON | (at centre) 463 | (at right) E.P. DUTTON & CO. NEW YORK. (all brown). **Spine** plain blue cloth. **Back board:** Plain, pale-blue paper, varnished.

References: PN | *Farmer*, p.40; *Dartt*, p.80.

Notes
1. *Farmer* lists the book but reports he never saw a copy: he gives publication date as 1899. Not in British Library.

2. *Dartt* confirms the date, probably using *Farmer* as his source. His copy has the reference number 463 (as above), but has a different binding design, illustrated following his p.94. It shows two girls on a sofa, reading a book, with a younger child; dolls, toys, etc. He also reports a third binding-design, illustrating a girl and a dog, with a cat looking over her shoulder. That version is reported with inscriptions dated 1902 and 1910. Ernest Nister regularly reprinted material many times in different publications.

3. 'Little Miss Valentia' (see §4), is at pp. (7)–16. The vignette heading, with the title, is from an unsigned wash-drawing; five small line-illustrations are by E. Stuart Hardy. Nister published the story elsewhere (see 163.1 and 169.1).

162–164. NISTER'S HOLIDAY ANNUAL

162.1

Nister's | Holiday Annual | for | 1902 | With Stories by | G.A.Henty, | G.Manville Fenn, | L.T.Meade, D.H.Parry, | Evelyn Everett-Green, | and other | well-known Authors. | Edited and Arranged | by | Alfred J.Fuller. | (this all arranged above and at right and left of illustration, in black line, of children on a seesaw; at foot: (left) London: | ERNEST NISTER | (centre) New York: E.P.DUTTON & CO. | (right) Printed in Bavaria. | 746a.

Contents
251 × 205 mm. (1)–(128) | no catalogue. Frontispiece and five other full-page watercolour drawings reproduced by colour-lithography, unbacked, tipped in. Numerous other full-page, and smaller, illustrations printed by lithography in line or tone in single colours, including brown, green, blue or black, on text pages.

(1) Illustrated half-title p. | (2) alternative design for illustrated half-title p. | (colour-frontispiece, tipped in) | (3) title p. | (4) small line-illustration | (5)–6. Contents | (7) small line-illustration | (8)–(128) text and illustrations.

Binding (see Plate 170, and Note 1)
Chestnut-brown cloth boards, bevelled, blocked and printed by silk-screen in black, white, red, blue, green, yellow, and gilt; all edges gilt; off-white endpapers printed with line illustrations in grey.

Front board: Nister's (gilt, shaded black) | Holiday Annual (initials red, shaded black, cased gilt; remainder green, shaded black, cased gilt) | 1902 (gilt, shaded black) above illustration of three children in rowing-boat with bearded man, towing toy boats (black, white, red, blue. green, yellow). **Spine:** NISTER'S | HOLIDAY | ANNUAL | 1902 (gilt) above floral decoration in line (black). **Back board:** plain.

References: PN | *Dartt*, p.97, *Companion*, p.21.

Notes
1. *Nister's Holiday Annuals* were produced in two alternative styles: (a) in cloth elegant, gilt edges, at 5s.; (b) in pictorial paper boards, cloth back, at 3s.6d. The copy described above is in style (a); the two that follow are in style (b).
2. 'In Troubled Times', at pp.(49)–63, has eight drawings by E.S.Hardy: one vignette incorporates the title. Nister published the story elsewhere, see 171.1 and 181.1).

163.1

NISTER'S | HOLIDAY | ANNUAL | (2 leaf ornaments) FOR 1905. (2 leaf ornaments) | WITH | STORIES . BY G . A . HENTY | G . MANVILLE . FENN (3 leaf ornaments) | (2 leaf ornaments) REV . THEO . WOOD . F.E.S; | D.H. PARRY . G.E. FARROW | L.T. MEADE . SHEILA BRAINE | AND . OTHER . WELL-KNOWN | AUTHORS | Edited by ALFRED . C . PLAYNE | LONDON: ERNEST . NISTER . | NEW YORK: E.P. DUTTON & Co. | (at foot) 1140
(Note: the whole page is wreathed with pictorial decorations in line).

Contents
251 × 200 mm. (1)–(132) | no catalogue. Five full-page watercolour drawings reproduced by colour-lithography, unbacked, tipped in. Numerous other illustrations, some in black-and-white, and some in two colours, all backed, printed on text pages, in line or tone, by photo-lithography.
(1) Illustrated half-title p. | (2) small line-drawing | (colour-frontispiece, tipped in) | (3) title p. | (4) small line-drawing | (5)–6–7. Contents | (8)–(132) text and illustrations: imprint on p.(132) (Printed in Bavaria).

Binding (see Plate 170, and Note 2)
Quarter-bound blue cloth, printed paper boards; edges plain; endpapers printed mottled blue.
Front board: (all lettering included in over-all, full-colour lithographed illustration): Nister's (red, cased dark-brown) | Holiday Annual (initials red and white, remainder grey and white, all shaded dark-brown) at head of illustration of three children, and dog, with snowman; at foot: ERNEST . NISTER . LONDON . | E.P.DUTTON & Co. NEW YORK . | Printed in Bavaria | 1140 **Spine:** plain blue cloth. **Back board:** plain, very-pale blue paper, varnished.

References: PN | *Dartt*, p.98.

Notes
1. 'Little Mistress Valentia', at pp.(77)–83, appeared also at 161.1 and 169.1.
2. See 162.1, Note 1.

164.1

Twenty-first Year | of Publication | Nister's | Holiday Annual | Edited by Alfred C.Playne. | With Stories by | W.H.D.Rouse, Litt.D. E.Nesbit | G.A.Henty. Sheila Braine. | D.H.Parry. L.L.Weedon. | C.Bingham. G.R.Glasgow. etc. | Illustrated by | Rosa C.Petherick. E.Lance. | Arch. Webb. Sybil Tawse. | E.Stuart.Hardy. Lizzie Lawson. | Ernest . Nister . London. EN. No. 2047. E.P.Dutton & Co. New York.
(Note: the page is divided into panels and decorated with black line-drawings of holly and mistletoe).

Contents
250 × 200 mm. (1)–132 | no catalogue. Six full-page watercolour drawings reproduced by colour-lithography, unbacked, tipped in. Numerous black-and-white illustrations, some full-page, in line or tone, printed on text pages, all by photo-lithography, all backed.
(1) Illustrated half-title p. | (2) decorative line-vignette | (frontispiece, tipped in) | (3) title p. | (4) decorative halftone-vignette | (5)–7. Contents | (8)–132. text and illustrations, with imprint on p.132 (Printed in Bavaria).

Binding (see Plate 170, and Note 2)
Quarter-bound grey cloth, printed paper boards; edges plain; off-white endpapers printed with line-illustrations in grey.

Front board: (all lettering included in over-all, full-page illustration in colour-lithography): Nister's (light-blue and dark-blue, cased black) | Holiday Annual (initials mainly red, cased dark-brown; remainder light-blue and dark-blue, cased black) above illustration of two boys and a girl in a donkey-cart, with basket of groceries. At foot: (left) ERNEST . NISTER . LONDON . | (centre) E.N. 2047 | (right) E.P.DUTTON & Co. NEW YORK. **Spine:** plain grey cloth. **Back board:** very-pale greenish-blue paper, varnished.

References: PN | *Dartt*, p.98, *Companion*, p.21.

Notes
1. 'How a Drummer Boy Saved a Regiment' is at pp. (111)–121. A vignette-heading including title-lettering, and tailpiece, both from wash-drawings, are signed 'A.W.'; three line-illustrations are by F.A. Stewart. Nister published the story elsewhere (see 155.1 and 160.1).
2. See 162.1, Note 1.

165. NOW FOR A STORY!

165.1
Now for a Story! | A COLLECTION OF SHORT ORIGINAL | STORIES FOR CHILDREN. | BY | (list of authors follows, in two columns with vertical rule between, the final name centred beneath the rule) FANNY BARRY. | FRANCES CLARE. | MRS. E.M.FIELD. | G.A.HENTY. | MARY HOLDSWORTH. | ANDREW HOME. | ASCOTT R.HOPE. | KATHARINE S.MACQUOID. |` L.T.MEADE. | MRS. MOLESWORTH. | CONSTANCE M.PREVOST. | EMMA WOOD. | MABEL E.WOTTON . | London: | SKEFFINGTON AND SON, PICCADILLY, W. | PUBLISHERS TO H.R.H. THE PRINCE OF WALES. | (8-point rule) | 1893.
(Note: London: *is in gothic type).*

Contents
172 x 128 mm. One unfolioed leaf, plus (i)–vi | (1)–248. Frontispiece and two full-page plates from drawings in line by Palmer Cox; one full-page wash-drawing by Fanny Barry; all printed in black on MF wove paper, unbacked, unfolioed, tipped in.

(Two unfolioed blank pages) | (i) half-title p. | (ii) blank | (frontispiece, tipped in) | (iii) title p. | (iv) blank | (v)–vi. Contents | (1)–241. text | (242)–(244) blank.

Binding (see Plate 165)
Blue paper boards, imitation-pigskin grained, printed black, green, pink, and white; edges plain; brown flowered endpapers.

Front board: NOW FOR A | STORY ! (black and green) at right of decoration of three storks flying, with manuscripts in their bills, towards flowers at left; landscape with trees and buildings beneath heavy black line at foot (black, green, pink, white). **Spine:** NOW | FOR A | STORY ! (pink, outlined black) above continuation of decorations from front board (black, green, pink. white). Beneath this: BY | FANNY BARRY. | MRS. E.M.FIELD. | G.A.HENTY. | ANDREW HOME. | ASCOTT R.HOPE. | MRS. MACQUOID. | L.T.MEADE. | MRS. MOLESWORTH. | C.M.PREVOST. | MABEL E.WOTTON. (black). Landscape at foot beneath heavy black line, continued from front board. **Back board:** plain.

References: PN | *Dartt*, p.99.

Notes
1. 'The Wreckers of Pendarven' (see §4) is at pp.(47)–63.
2. In 1979 Richard Gilbertson, a bookdealer, of Angel Hill Publications, Launceston, Cornwall, reproduced by photo-lithography (with the original folio numbers) the pages of 165.1 that contain Henty's story, to make a 20-page booklet. It was wire-stitched (with consequential rust-marking later) within a 4-page blue card cover carrying a black line-reproduction of the design on the front board of the book (showing the title NOW FOR A STORY!). The edition was limited to 200 copies.

166. OUR ANNUAL

166.1
OUR ANNUAL | A BOOK FOR BOYS AND GIRLS | STORIES BY G.A.HENTY, CAPTAIN MAYNE REID, | H.B.MARRIOTT WATSON, HUME NISBET, | HUGH ST.LEGER, AND OTHERS | With Eight Coloured Plates | and many Black and White Illustrations | GRIFFITH FARRAN BROWNE & CO. LIMITED | 35 BOW STREET, COVENT GARDEN | LONDON

Contents
248 x 188 mm. 256 unfolioed pages of text; no catalogue. Eight full-page watercolour drawings reproduced by three-colour halftone blocks printed on imitation art paper, unbacked, unfolioed, tipped in. Numerous black-and-white illustrations in line and tone printed in black on text pages.
    (Frontispiece, tipped in) | (1) title p. | (2) blank | (3)–(256) text and illustrations.

Binding
Green cloth boards, blocked black, pale-yellow, light-blue merging to dark-blue, and gilt; top edge gilt, others plain; plain off-white endpapers. (See Note 3).
    Front board: OUR ANNUAL (gilt, cased black) in rectangular panel framed by black lines, above illustration, in a second rectangle framed by black lines, of boys and girls playing hockey (black, pale-yellow, light-blue merging to dark-blue). Beneath this, in a third rectangle framed by black lines: STORIES BY G.A.HENTY, | CAPT. MAYNE REID, HUME NISBET, | HUGH ST.LEGER, & OTHERS (black). The whole framed by heavy pale-yellow lines. **Spine:** OUR | ANNUAL (gilt) | A BOOK | FOR BOYS | & GIRLS (black) above trophy of tennis rackets, hockey sticks and croquet mallets tied with ribbon (black, pale-yellow, blue). At foot: GRIFFITH, FARRAN | BROWNE & Co. (black). Thick and thin black rules at head and foot. **Back board:** plain.

References: PN | *Farmer*, p.91 (addenda); *Dartt*, p.102, *Companion*, p.41.

Notes

1. 'A Coaching Adventure' (see §4) is at pp.(3)–(9), with two unsigned illustrations in line, engraved by W.H.

2. A cheaply produced book, on poor-quality paper. The lack of folio-numbers possibly indicates an intention to use some of the sixteen 16-page gatherings in other publications. All but the last three are complete in themselves, in the sense that a story starts on the first page and a story finishes on the last page.

3. Also issued in a cheaper binding, see 166.2 below.

4. Although called an 'Annual', no further editions were issued after this one, which was received by the Copyright Libraries in 1883.

166.2

Title page, Contents: As for 166.1.

Binding

Quarter-bound red cloth, blocked black; printed paper boards; edges plain; plain off-white endpapers.

Front board: OUR ANNUAL (black) set in arc on yellow curved panel, framed by dark-green line, and forming part of larger frame, with leaf-decoration (dark-green and yellow). Within it is watercolour drawing, reproduced by four-colour halftone blocks, of gun on carriage, being fired, with cavalry officers and men in full uniform. In small yellow panel at foot of frame: GRIFFITH FARRAN BROWNE & Co Ltd. LONDON. (dark green). **Spine:** OUR ANNUAL (black) A BOOK FOR I BOYS AND GIRLS (black), all running from head to foot. **Back board:** Publisher's type-set advertisement (GRIFFITH FARRAN BROWNE & CO.'S I PICTURE=BOOKS.), with line illustration (black).

References: PN I *Dartt Companion*, p.41.

Notes

1. The advertisement on the back of the case announces this book, as 'Crown 4to. Picture Boards, price 3s.6d.; or cloth elegant, gilt top, price 5s.'.

2. See 166.1, Notes 1, 2, and 4.

167. OUR SAILORS

GENERAL NOTE

Our Sailors by William H.G. Kingston was edited, after the author's death, by G.A. Henty. In view of the great amount of inaccurate information that has been published elsewhere about the extent of Henty's involvement as editor, I think it proper to treat the title as fully as possible, even to the extent of starting with the book under its original title, *Blue Jackets*, although it will ultimately be seen that Henty's participation was slighter than has perhaps been believed.

167.A

BLUE JACKETS: I OR, I CHIPS OF THE OLD BLOCK. I A NARRATIVE OF I The Gallant Exploits of British Seamen, I AND OF I THE PRINCIPAL EVENTS

IN THE NAVAL SERVICE, | DURING THE REIGN OF | HER MOST GRACIOUS MAJESTY | QUEEN VICTORIA. | BY | W.H.G.KINGSTON, ESQ. | AUTHOR OF | "PETER THE WHALER," "MARK SEAWORTH," "MANCO, THE PERUVIAN CHIEF," ETC. | (device of anchor with cable) | LONDON: GRANT AND GRIFFITH, | (SUCCESSORS TO NEWBERY AND HARRIS,) | CORNER OF ST. PAUL'S CHURCHYARD. | 1854.
(*Note:* The Gallant Exploits of British Seamen, *is in gothic type*).

Contents

201 × 121 mm. (i)–xiv | (1)–434 | no catalogue. (See Note 1).
    (i) Title p. | (ii) printer's imprint (LONDON: PRINTED BY W.CLOWES AND SONS, STAMFORD STREET.) | (iii)–viii. Preface | (ix)–xiv. Contents | (1)–434. text, with printer's imprint on p.434, exactly as on p.(ii).

Binding (see Plate 159)

Blue ('X Quality') grained cloth boards, blocked blind and gilt; edges rough-trimmed (heads uncut); yellow surface-paper endpapers. Blank leaf tipped on to face title page, see Note 1, below).
    Front board: decorative rules and border at edges; four-petalled star-shaped flower at centre (all blind), the blocking smoothing out the graining of the cloth. **Spine:** BLUE | JACKETS; | OR, | CHIPS | OF THE | OLD BLOCK. | (5mm. rule) | KINGSTON. (all gilt) above centre, and within very decorative gilt panel showing trident ornamented with leaves and berries and topped by crown partly made of parts of ships. Beneath title-lettering the shaft of the trident has lettered scrolls: ADEN. 1839 | SYRIA. 1840 | CHINA. 1840 | NIGER. 1841 | BURMAH. 1851 | POLAR SEAS | &c. (cloth-colour out of gilt). **Back board:** as front board.

Reference: PN.

Notes

1. The final leaf of the prelims, folioed xiii–xiv, is tipped on at the end of the 12-page gathering. A blank leaf, of slightly thinner paper, is tipped on at the beginning of the gathering, to face the title page: it is not part of the endpapers. The final leaf of text, signed 2F, is also a singleton, and evidently printed with the seven leaves of prelims, to form a 16-page working. Page (iii) is signed a2.
2. This is a much more substantial work than the first edition of *Our Sailors*: that followed nine years later and was edited to less than two thirds of the original length.

167.1

OUR SAILORS: | OR, | ANECDOTES OF THE ENGAGEMENTS | AND GALLANT DEEDS OF THE | BRITISH NAVY | During the Reign of | HER MAJESTY QUEEN VICTORIA. | BY | WILLIAM H.G.KINGSTON, | AUTHOR OF "PETER THE WHALER," "MARK SEAWORTH," | "TRUE BLUE," ETC. | LONDON: | GRIFFITH AND FARRAN, | (SUCCESSORS TO NEWBERY AND HARRIS), | CORNER OF ST. PAUL'S CHURCH YARD. | MDCCCLXIII.
(*Note:* During the Reign of *is in gothic type*).

Contents

172 × 108 mm. One unfolioed leaf plus (i)–xii | (1)–282 (plus one unfolioed leaf of

advertisements | catalogue (1)–32. Frontispiece of an engraving by Swain 'from a painting by L.W. Desanges, in the Victoria Cross Gallery', printed in black on MF paper, keyed to p.107, unbacked, tipped in.

(Unfolioed page) advertisement for *Our Soldiers* ('uniform with this volume') | (unfolioed page) blank | (frontispiece, tipped in) | (i) title p. | (ii) blank | (iii)–vi. Preface, with signature mark a2 on p.(iii) | (vii)–xii. Contents, with signature mark a2 repeated on p.(vii) | (1)–282. text, with printer's imprint at foot of p.282 (BILLING, PRINTER AND STEREOTYPER, GUILDFORD, SURREY.) | (unfolioed leaf) advertisement for two titles by W.H.Adams | (1)–32. catalogue.

Binding (see Plate 159)
Designed by Robert Dudley (see Note 5). Blue ('X Quality') grained cloth boards, blocked blind and gilt; edges rough-trimmed, heads uncut (or gilt edges, see Note 4); yellow surface-paper endpapers.

Front board: OUR . SAILORS (cloth-colour out of gilt) on scroll, forming part of a decoration, under a crown, that includes representation of a Victoria Cross: FOR VALOUR (cloth-colour out of gilt), the inscription on the Cross; beneath this: R.D (gilt), the designer's initials. All this enclosed in a frame of rules and floral ornaments (blind). **Spine:** OUR | SAILORS | OR | ANECDOTES | OF THE | BRITISH | . NAVY . (cloth-colour out of gilt) on shield, forming part of gilt decoration: READY STEADY (cloth-colour out of gilt) on scroll, above: RD (gilt), the designer's initials. At foot: LONDON | GRIFFITH & FARRAN (gilt), with three gilt rules at extreme head and foot. **Back board:** frame of rules and floral ornaments (blind) as on front board.

References: BL; CH.

Notes
1. The prelims are in a strange muddle and, judging from the repetition of the signature mark, a2, were re-arranged at least once during the production of the book. The first gathering consists of eight pages, with the frontispiece tipped in to face the title page (see fig.1). Of these eight pages the first two are unfolioed and not counted in the pagination, the rest forming pp.(i)–vi. The signature mark, a2, makes its first appearance on p.(iii).
2. The second gathering consists of a straightforward 16-page section, but with the clumsy addition of both a single leaf and a pair of conjugate leaves, tipped on at the same place (see fig.2). The single leaf is folioed xi and xii; the pair of conjugate leaves forms folios (vii)–x. The signature mark, a2, makes its second appearance on p.(vii)!
3. The catalogue bound in at the end of the book forms a complete 32-page section (see fig.4). Preceding this, the final section of the text ends with an unfolioed leaf of advertisements. This makes a total of 12 pages (see fig.3), which may have been printed as two workings, of eight pages and four pages respectively, or possibly a full sheet of 16 pages may have been made up with the odd four pages tipped-in to the prelims, i.e. pages (vii)–x. Even if this degree of tidying up took place there would still have been an odd 8-page working and an odd 2-page working to be dealt with. Altogether this is an example of appallingly bad planning and, as will be seen below, may have been the cause of a rift between publisher and printer (see 167.2, Note 2).

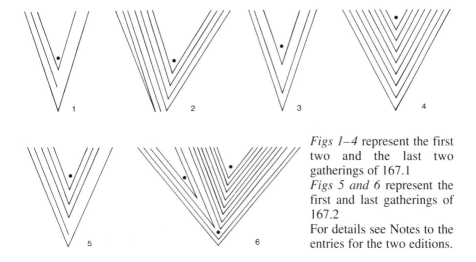

Figs 1–4 represent the first two and the last two gatherings of 167.1

Figs 5 and 6 represent the first and last gatherings of 167.2

For details see Notes to the entries for the two editions.

4. *Our Sailors* first appeared in 1862, as did Kingston's companion volume *Our Soldiers* (also edited in later years by Henty, see §2, 168), both books having title-page dates of 1863. The price of each was 3s., with rough-trimmed edges, or 3s.6d. with all edges gilt.

5. The binding design, and that of the corresponding edition of *Our Soldiers*, 168.1, are ascribed to Robert Dudley by Douglas Ball (see Appendix IV, Part 2), in his *Victorian Publishers' Bindings*, p.148.

167.2

OUR SAILORS: | OR, | ANECDOTES OF THE ENGAGEMENTS AND | GALLANT DEEDS OF | THE BRITISH NAVY | During the Reign of | HER MAJESTY QUEEN VICTORIA. | BY | WILLIAM H.G. KINGSTON, | AUTHOR OF "PETER THE WHALER," "MARK SEAWORTH," | "TRUE BLUE," "OUR SOLDIERS," ETC. | SECOND EDITION. | LONDON: | GRIFFITH AND FARRAN, | SUCCESSORS TO NEWBERY AND HARRIS, | CORNER OF ST. PAUL'S CHURCHYARD. | MDCCCLXV.

(*Note:* During the Reign of, *is in gothic type*).

Contents

171 × 108 mm. (i)–(xvi) | (1)–282 (plus one unfolioed leaf of advertisements) | catalogue (1)–36 (plus two unfolioed blank leaves). Frontispiece as in 167.1.

(i)–(ii) see Note 1 | (frontispiece, tipped in) | (iii) title p. | (iv) printer's imprint (MURRAY AND GIBB, PRINTERS, EDINBURGH.) | (v)–viii. Preface | (ix)–xv. Contents | (xvi) blank | (1)–282. text, with printer's imprint at foot of p.282, as on p.(iv) | (unfolioed leaf: advertisements) | (1)–36. catalogue, dated MDCCCLXV, with printer's imprint on p.36 (Savill and Edwards, Printers, Chandos Street, Covent Garden.) | (37)–(40) blank.

Binding: As for 167.1, except that the grain of the blue cloth has a 'random pebble' finish instead of the uneven 'broken line' (three dots between dashes).

Reference: PN.

Notes

1. I have been able to find only one copy, which lacks the first leaf. It was probably similar to the first, unfolioed, leaf in 167.1.

2. This edition is completely re-set, by a new printer, in a typeface different from that used for the first edition. It may be that the reason for a change of printer was the previous confusion, which may well have been costly, although such an outcome would have been sad in view of Billing's reputation (see 167.1, Notes 1 to 3 above). His imprint (on p.282 of 167.1) confirms him as 'printer and stereotyper', but that he was not apparently even asked to provide the publisher with stereotype plates from his typesetting, for the use of the new printer, seems also to confirm a current lack of normal friendly relationships.

3. The prelims now make an even working of 16 pages, with the frontispiece tipped in after the first leaf, to face the title page (see fig.5). The final 16-page text-gathering, sig.S, starts on p.273, with pp.(283) and (284) containing publisher's advertisements, and the final four pages blank. To avoid those four pages coming between the publisher's advertisements and the bound-in 36-page catalogue (which was produced as a complete entity by another printer), the latter is inserted in an unusual position – following the twelfth page of the section. That involved double sewing through the outer eight pages of the gathering (see fig.6). A similar arrangement occurs in *The Cornet of Horse*, see §1, 8.1, Note 8.

4. Additional text has been added by the author at the end of the book, under the heading 'Acts of Heroism Performed of late by Naval Men'. It appears on pp.280–282, and can be fitted in because the more condensed typeface used by Murray and Gibb in this edition allows for the original text to finish on p.279.

5. This edition was reprinted at least twice: the British Library records that 8000 copies had been printed by 1877.

167.3

OUR SAILORS | ANECDOTES OF THE ENGAGEMENTS & GALLANT | DEEDS OF THE BRITISH NAVY | DURING THE REIGN OF | HER MAJESTY QUEEN VICTORIA | BY | WILLIAM H.G.KINGSTON | AUTHOR OF 'OUR SOLDIERS' 'PETER THE WHALER MARK SEAWORTH' | 'TRUE BLUE' ETC. | (publisher's device) | GRIFFITH AND FARRAN | SUCCESSORS TO NEWBERY AND HARRIS | CORNER OF ST. PAUL'S CHURCHYARD, LONDON | E.P.DUTTON AND CO., NEW YORK.

(*Note: In the titles following the author's name, quotation marks are missing after* WHALER *and before* MARK; *that after* SEAWORTH *is battered. In the publisher's imprint the* W *in* NEWBERY *is battered*).

Contents

181 x 121 mm. (i)–(xvi) | (1)–(336) | catalogue (1)–(32). Frontispiece as in earlier editions, but without caption, printed in black on text page, unbacked, unfolioed.

(i) Blank | (ii) frontispiece | (iii) title p. | (iv) advertisement for *Our Soldiers* ('uniform with this volume', 'ninth thousand') | (v)–viii. Preface | (ix)–xv. Contents | (xvi) blank | (1)–332. text | (333)–(336) advertisements | (1)–(32) catalogue, dated

10.82, and including *Our Sailors* as the last title in the list of books in 'The Boys' Own Favourite Library'.

Binding (see Note 1)
Dark-blue, diagonally grained cloth boards, blocked black, light-blue, blind, and gilt; edges plain; grey flowered endpapers.
   Front board: Our Sailors | W.H.G.Kingston (black out of stippled-gilt panel) over illustration, in ornamental frame, of boy sitting in branches of a tree, reading a book, with superimposed lettering: THE BOYS' OWN | FAVOURITE | LIBRARY (all black and light-blue). **Spine:** OUR | SAILORS (black out of gilt panels), partly overlapping and partly overlapped by continuation of illustration of tree-branches from front board. Beneath this: W.H.G. | KINGSTON (gilt); GRIFFITH & FARRAN (cloth-colour out of black rectangle). **Back board:** three rules across head and foot of board; publisher's device at centre (all blind).

References: PN | Cargill Thompson: *The Boys' Dumas*, p.16.

Notes
1. The first appearance of *Our Sailors* in the earliest binding design for 'The Boys' Own Favourite Library'. For details of the series, begun in 1881, see *Out on the Pampas*, §1, 4.3, Notes 3–5, and Plate 33.
2. Cargill Thompson reports that this (1882) edition is 'identical in contents to those bearing Henty's name on the title page but gives no evidence of his participation', and from this comes to the conclusion that 'Here then is another boys' book [i.e. in addition to *Bevis*, by Richard Jefferies, §2, 128] edited by Henty but without any indication of his involvement'. Unfortunately, both Cargill Thompson's report and his conclusion are inaccurate, as is his description of the title page of the 1882 edition. The first issue of the book to bear Henty's name on the title page, 167.4, does in fact contain an additional chapter. But it is inserted before the end of Kingston's text, so that the final chapters of 167.3 and 167.4 are identical, and although Henty's contribution added 16 pages to the book, its position caused Cargill Thompson to overlook it.
3. Kingston died in 1880, and had added chapters and corrected the text in certain places since the second edition (167.2) of 1865.
4. The unfolioed pages (333)–(336), which carry publisher's advertisements, are the last two leaves of the final gathering of the text.

167.4
OUR SAILORS | ANECDOTES OF THE ENGAGEMENTS & GALLANT DEEDS | OF THE BRITISH NAVY DURING THE REIGN | OF HER MAJESTY QUEEN VICTORIA | BY | W.H.G.KINGSTON | AUTHOR OF 'OUR SOLDIERS,' 'PETER THE WHALER,' ETC. | A NEW EDITION, REVISED AND BROUGHT DOWN TO THE PRESENT TIME | BY | G.A.HENTY | (publisher's device) | GRIFFITH, FARRAN, OKEDEN & WELSH | SUCCESSORS TO NEWBERY AND HARRIS | WEST CORNER OF ST. PAUL'S CHURCHYARD, LONDON | E.P.DUTTON AND CO., NEW YORK | 1885

Contents
186 x 124 mm. (i)–(xvi) | (1)–348 | catalogues (1)–4, and (1)–(32). Frontispiece as in 167.3.

(i) Blank | (ii) frontispiece | (iii) title p. | (iv) advertisement for *Our Soldiers* ('uniform with this volume', 'ninth thousand') | (v)–viii. Preface | (ix)–xv. Contents | (xvi) blank | (1)–348. text | (1)–4. catalogue of books by the late W.H.G. Kingston | (1)–(32) catalogue of BOOKS FOR THE YOUNG (Catalogue A), dated 11.84.

Binding (see Notes 1 and 3)
Cobalt-blue, diagonally grained cloth, blocked black, pink, silver, and gilt; edges plain; yellow-green flowered endpapers.
   Front board: OUR | SAILORS (black, and cloth-colour out of solid-gilt rectangular panel) superimposed over a confused multiple illustration, including palm trees, sunset, gun on carriage, anchor, sailing ship in moonlight, etc. (black, pink, and silver), with: By | W.H.G. | KINGSTON (black) beneath title, and: ILLUSTRATED (black over pink shading) at foot. **Spine:** OUR | SAILORS (black and cloth-colour out of solid-gilt rectangle with pink and black rules above and below. By W.H.G | KINGSTON (cloth-colour out of smaller solid-gilt rectangle) with similar rules above and below. At foot: GRIFFITH, FARRAN & Co. (cloth-colour out of even-smaller solid-gilt rectangle) with similar rules above and below. Illustration of weapons and satchel, as a trophy, above cricket and tennis equipment, etc. (black and pink) between top and bottom rectangles and running behind the central one. **Back board:** publisher's monogram in roughly-rectangular panel in design of palm tree (all black) at centre.

References: PN | Cargill Thompson: *The Boys' Dumas*, p.16.

Notes
1. This 1885 edition is in the second of the binding designs used by Griffith & Farran for 'The Boys' Own Favourite Library' (see 167.3, Note 1, and Plate 33).
2. It is the first issue of *Our Sailors* to be edited by Henty, perhaps the reason for the dated title page. There were several reprints, issued in various bindings, with Henty's name on the title page, but he never made further additions to the text. Henty's sole contribution to Kingston's work is that now appearing for the first time in 167.4. It is a chapter on 'The Egyptian Campaign', which adds 16 pages to the extent of the book and is inserted at pp.316–331. This material could not possibly have appeared in 167.3 (1882), as suggested by Cargill Thompson, as it describes events which took place from 1882 to 1884. He probably overlooked the new chapter because of its position (see 167.3, Note 2).
3. This edition was reprinted and appeared later in the third of the four binding styles used for 'The Boys' Own Favourite Library' (examples at Plate 33), from about 1886. That issue is the only one recorded by *Farmer*, p.54, and has been confirmed to me by Stuart Wilson, whose copy is dated January 1895 by printer's code on p.348.
4. The catalogue immediately following the text, on pages folioed (1)–4, in fact occupies the last two leaves of the final text gathering, which would otherwise be folioed (349)–352.

167.5

OUR SAILORS | ANECDOTES OF THE ENGAGEMENTS | AND GALLANT DEEDS OF THE | BRITISH NAVY DURING THE REIGN | OF HER MAJESTY QUEEN VICTORIA | BY | WILLIAM H.G.KINGSTON | AUTHOR OF 'OUR

SOLDIERS' 'THE THREE MIDSHIPMEN' I 'PETER THE WHALER' ETC. ETC. I A NEW EDITION, REVISED I BY I G.A.HENTY I GRIFFITH FARRAN BROWNE & CO. LIMITED I 35 BOW STREET, COVENT GARDEN I LONDON

Contents

184 x 121 mm. (i)–(xiv) I (1)–348 I no catalogue. Four full-page wash-drawings by Charles J. de Lacy, reproduced by halftone blocks printed in black on text pages, unbacked, unfolioed and except for frontispiece not counted in pagination.

(i) Half-title p. I (ii) blank I (iii) blank I (iv) frontispiece I (v) title p. I (vi) [The Rights of Translation and of Reproduction are Reserved] I vii–xiii. Contents I (xiv) blank I (1)–348. text, with printer's imprint at foot of p.348 (PRINTED BY MORRISON AND GIBB LIMITED, EDINBURGH), and with printer's code showing that the impression of 2000 copies was made in October 1898.

Binding (see Plate 160)

Light-blue cloth boards, blocked black, dark-blue, red, white, green, and gilt; edges plain; plain off-white endpapers.

Front board: OUR I SAILORS (gilt) above and at right of illustration of sailing ship firing salvo, and close-up of sailor hoisting the Union flag (black, dark-blue, red, white, green). At lower right corner: W.H.G. I KINGSTON (black). **Spine:** OUR I SAILORS I W.H.G.KINGSTON (gilt) below decoration of ropes (black and red) and above illustration of sailing ship in calm water (black, white, green). At foot: GRIFFITH FARRAN I . BROWNE & Co. . (green) above rope (black and white). **Back board:** plain.

References: PN I *Dartt*, p.103, *Companion*, p.41.

Notes

1. The prelims have been re-set, but the textual content of this impression remains unchanged from that of 167.4. *Dartt* describes it as though it were the first to be edited by Henty, in spite of his Note 2, 'the book was brought up to date by Henty in 1882'. This latter error, in the Note, is understandable since the date 1882 was given erroneously in place of 1885 in a new editor's Preface which appears in later issues (see 167.6, Note 2).

2. In his *Companion*, p.41, Dartt amends his original dating of the book (1898) to (1893). That may have been taken from *Farmer*, who does little more than mention the book but dates it (1893). Any copy issued in 1893 would have been a late issue of 167.4 (as, briefly, described by *Farmer*), not an issue of 167.5 (see 167.4, Note 2), and been in one of the binding designs for 'The Boy's Own Favourite Library'.

3. *Dartt*, p.103, Note (1) states that this edition 'contains Henty's "Gallant Deeds", a section so titled on pp.210–227', and confirms this, on his p.64, under the heading 'Gallant Deeds'. He is mistaken. The section he refers to originally appeared in the first edition of *Our Sailors*, 167.1, and was written by Kingston. Dartt was possibly confused by Henty's *Gallant Deeds* (§1, 110), a Chambers's Supplementary Reader, 1905, containing a number of short stories.

4. For this edition the publisher introduced four wash-drawings, unfortunately reproduced by halftone blocks of much too fine a screen for the paper used.

167.6

OUR SAILORS | GALLANT DEEDS OF THE | BRITISH NAVY DURING THE | REIGN OF QUEEN VICTORIA | BY | WILLIAM H.G.KINGSTON | A NEW EDITION, REVISED | AND | BROUGHT DOWN TO THE END OF 1900 | ILLUSTRATED | GRIFFITH FARRAN BROWNE & CO. LIMITED | 35 BOW STREET, COVENT GARDEN | LONDON

Contents

187 × 127 mm. (1)–334 | no catalogue. Five full-page wash drawings, of which four are by Charles de Lacy and one by an unknown artist, printed from halftone blocks on text pages, unbacked, except for frontispiece, folioed on rectos.

(1) Blank | (2) frontispiece | (3) title p. | (4) blank | 5. Editor's Preface | (6) blank | 7. Contents | 8. Contents, continued, and List of Illustrations | 9–334. text, with printer's imprint at foot of p.334 (PRINTED BY MORRISON AND GIBB LIMITED, EDINBURGH) | (335)–(336) blank.

Binding (see Plate 160)

Brown cloth boards, blocked black, dark-blue, grey, yellow, green, and gilt; edges plain; plain off-white endpapers.

Front board: OUR | SAILORS (gilt) above illustration of sailor firing gun on carriage with soldier half-kneeling on guard in foreground (black, dark-blue, grey, yellow, green). At lower right corner: W.H.G. | KINGSTON (black). **Spine:** OUR | SAILORS | W.H.G.KINGSTON (gilt) above trophy of weapons, ship's wheel, cannon balls, etc. (black, dark-blue, yellow). At foot: GRIFFITH FARRAN | . BROWNE & Co. . (black). **Back board:** plain.

References: BL; PN.

Notes

1. Heavily revised by a new un-named editor, with additions and alterations (mainly to statistics relating to the size of forces and casualties) to Henty's Egyptian Campaign chapter. The whole text is re-set, and presented in a more modern manner.

2. Henty's name has now gone from the title page, but the following is an extract from the new Editor's Preface: 'After going through several editions it [*Our Sailors*] was, after the death of the author, revised and brought up to 1882 by Mr. G.A. Henty. It has now been further revised and brought down to the end of 1900'. The date 1882 is an error. The entries for 167.3, 167.4 and 167.5, show that Henty brought the work up to 1884, and the first edition containing his contribution appeared, probably in that year, with the date 1885 on the title page.

3. New chapters cover later campaigns, and there is an extra illustration, by an unnamed artist. The paper is quite unsuitable for the fine-screen halftone blocks.

4. The new Preface begins: 'The first edition of *Our Sailors* was published, under the title, *Anecdotes of Sailors*, in 1862'. This is of course incorrect: we have followed the book's history from its beginnings in 1854, as Kingston's *Blue Jackets*. The word 'Anecdotes' featured in the subtitle for many years, and that may have confused the new Editor. My own searches have revealed no trace of publication, or periodical serialisation, of Kingston's work under the heading 'Anecdotes of Sailors'. It never appeared in his own *Kingston's Magazine for Boys*, which was published from 1859 to 1863 – the years immediately preceding, and including, the date of the first edition of *Our Sailors*.

5. It is worth remarking that the publisher's expenditure on this edition (no fewer than six colour workings, including gold, in the blocking of the binding case, the complete revision and consequent re-setting of the text, and the introduction of a new picture) is hardly justified by the finished product. I have commented on the illustrations (Note 3 above); and the picture on the binding case is surely too small and insignificant to justify so many colours. Such extravagance would never have been countenanced by, for instance, the more imaginative firm of Blackie.

6. This edition reached the Libraries in 1902: it was probably published in 1901.

167.7

OUR SAILORS | GALLANT DEEDS OF THE | BRITISH NAVY DURING THE | REIGN OF QUEEN VICTORIA | BY | WILLIAM H.G.KINGSTON | A NEW EDITION, REVISED | GRIFFITH FARRAN BROWNE & CO. LIMITED | 35 BOW STREET, COVENT GARDEN | LONDON

Contents

191 x 128 mm. (1)–328) | no catalogue. Frontispiece from a wash-drawing by Charles de Lacy, reproduced by halftone block printed in greenish-blue on coated paper, unbacked, keyed to text page, tipped in.

(1) Half-title p. | (2) blank | (frontispiece, tipped in) | (3) title p. | (4) blank | 5. Editor's Preface | (6) blank | 7–8. Contents | 9–326. text, with printer's imprint at foot of p.326 (PRINTED BY MORRISON AND GIBB LIMITED, EDINBURGH) | (327)–(328) blank.

Binding (see Plate 161)

Bluish-grey cloth boards, blocked green, red, and gilt; edges plain; ivory laid endpapers.

Front board: OUR | SAILORS (gilt) within floral wreath with ribbons (green and red), the whole surrounded and enclosed by art-nouveau line-panelling (green). **Spine:** OUR | SAILORS | KINGSTON (gilt) in space between wreath and panelling similar to that on front board (green and red). At foot: GRIFFITH FARRAN | BROWNE & Co. (red). **Back board:** plain.

Reference: PN.

Notes

1. The binding case is from a 'binder's blank'.

2. The contents appear to be as in 167.6 except for the removal of the halftone plates from text pages, and the consequent re-imposition of the text to make 328 pages. After the last extravagant production (see 167.6, Note 5), economies here, in addition to the cheaper binding, are not surprising. The text paper is lighter: the frontispiece the only surviving illustration – at last on a worthy coated stock.

3. The Preface is unaltered, with previous errors (see 167.6, Notes 2 and 4).

4. My copy contains a school-prize label inscribed February 1908.

167.8

OUR SAILORS | GALLANT DEEDS OF THE | BRITISH NAVY DURING THE | REIGN OF QUEEN VICTORIA | BY | WILLIAM H.G.KINGSTON | A NEW

EDITION, REVISED | GRIFFITH FARRAN BROWNE & CO. LIMITED | 35 BOW STREET, COVENT GARDEN | LONDON

Contents: 184 × 122 mm. As for 167.7.

Binding (see Plate 161)
Red cloth boards, blocked black, orange, cream, and gilt; edges plain; plain off-white endpapers.
    Front board: OUR | SAILORS (black and orange) in decorated rectangular panel (black) above illustration of boy holding on to rigging of ship, looking towards distant sailing ship against setting sun (black, orange, cream). **Spine:** OUR | SAILORS (gilt) | KINGSTON (orange) in decorated rectangular panel (black), above illustration of standing figure (black and cream). At foot: GRIFFITH FARRAN | BROWNE, & CO. (black). **Back board:** plain.

Reference: CH.

Notes
1. A more cheaply produced reprint of 167.7, on bulkier featherweight antique wove with a smaller page size.
2. Again the binding case appears to be blocked from a binder's blank, although the design does not allow as much flexibility as some others. But many similar examples are found on children's books: publishers were not concerned that pictures should relate to the content of all books for which they were used.

167.9

OUR SAILORS | BY | W.H.G.KINGSTON | (vignetted illustration printed in three-colour halftone) | LONDON | HENRY FROWDE | HODDER AND STOUGHTON | 1910
(Note: The A in AND (publisher's imprint) is a wrong font, and appears bolder than the rest of the line).

Contents
185 × 120 mm. (1)–(328) | catalogue 1–16. Four-page insert of single-sided coated paper tipped in between pages (4) and 5, printed in three-colour process inks on pages 2 and 3, and black on page 3 only, unbacked: on p.2, watercolour drawing (signed ARCH WEBB) as frontispiece, reproduced by three-colour halftone blocks; on p.3, title page with all lettering in black (plus red for initial O in title), and small illustration at centre reproduced by vignetted three-colour halftone blocks.
    (1)–(2) Blank | (3) half-title p. | (4) blank | (4-page insert, as described above, forming frontispiece and title p.) | 5. Editor's Preface | (6) blank | 7–8. Contents | 9–326. text | (327) printer's imprint (RICHARD CLAY & SONS, LIMITED, | BRUNSWICK STREET, STAMFORD STREET, S.E., | AND BUNGAY, SUFFOLK.) | (328) blank | 1–16. catalogue.

Binding (see Note 4)
Red cloth boards, blocked black, white, blue, brown, buff-pink, and gilt; edges plain; plain off-white endpapers.
    Front board: OUR SAILORS (black, and cloth-colour reversed out of solid-gilt rectangle) framed by black line, over illustration of Scout standing in front of Union

Flag (black, white, blue, brown, and buff-pink). **Spine:** OUR | SAILORS | KINGSTON (cloth-colour out of solid-gilt rectangle) framed by two black lines, above illustration of two schoolboys standing, talking (black, white, blue, brown, buff-pink). At foot, above black rule: HENRY FROWDE | HODDER & STOUGHTON (black). **Back board:** plain.

References: BL; PN.

Notes

1. The text remains unchanged from 167.7 and 167.8. The new printer worked from stereos of the setting used by Morrison and Gibb.

2. The prelims are re-imposed: the original half-title page is now blank; the original title page becomes the half-title page; and a 4-page insert, providing a new frontispiece and title page, is tipped in immediately before p.5.

3. A short account of the purchase of the stock and goodwill of Griffith & Farran by Hodder and Stoughton, the formation of the 'Joint Venture' of that firm with the Oxford University Press, and their publication of the children's books originally published by Griffith & Farran, is at Appendix II, Part 2.

4. This binding design was also used for *Our Soldiers*, 168.10, Plate 162.

5. My attention has been drawn by Alex Pyne and by Ivan McClymont to another title, properly outside the scope of this bibliography: *Fifty Famous Sea Stories*, published in 1961 by the Burke Publishing Company Limited. The Editor of the book, writing as 'Mainsail', includes at pp.106–111, 'The Destruction of Lagos', ascribing it to G.A.Henty. That passage occurs in the earliest editions of *Our Sailors*, and it should be credited to Kingston.

168. OUR SOLDIERS

GENERAL NOTE

Our Soldiers by William H.G. Kingston was edited, after the author's death, by G.A.Henty, as also was *Our Sailors*, §2, 167. This book may, like the other, have had its origins in a work with a different title. According to a Publisher's Note in a late edition (1905) of *Our Soldiers* (see 168.7, Note 2), it was originally published by Kingston in 1862 as *Anecdotes of Soldiers*.

But a similar Editor's Note in a late edition of *Our Sailors*, stating that that book had originally been published as *Anecdotes of Sailors*, is certainly erroneous (see 167.6, Note 4). Neither *Anecdotes of Sailors* nor *Anecdotes of Soldiers* appears in catalogues of the Copyright Libraries, and I have been unable to trace the existence of such titles elsewhere. Nor have I been able to find any other title to which *Our Soldiers* might owe its origins. I begin here with the first edition of the book under its recognised title, corresponding in date and format with the first edition of its companion volume, *Our Sailors*, 167.1.

168.1

OUR SOLDIERS: | OR, | ANECDOTES OF THE CAMPAIGNS | AND GALLANT DEEDS OF THE | BRITISH ARMY | During the Reign of | HER

MAJESTY QUEEN VICTORIA. I BY I WILLIAM H.G.KINGSTON, I AUTHOR OF "PETER THE WHALER," "MARK SEAWORTH," I "TRUE BLUE," ETC. I LONDON: I GRIFFITH AND FARRAN, I (SUCCESSORS TO NEWBERY AND HARRIS), I CORNER OF ST. PAUL'S CHURCH YARD. I MDCCCLXIII.
(*Note:* During the Reign of *is in gothic type*).

Contents
172 × 105 mm. (i)–(x) I (1)–284 I catalogue (1)–36. Frontispiece from an engraved portrait of Lt. Farquharson, 42nd Highlanders, after a painting by L.W. Desanges in the Victoria Cross Gallery, reproduced by line block, printed in black on MF paper, unbacked, tipped in.

(i) Advertisement for *Our Sailors* ('uniform with this volume') I (ii) blank I (frontispiece, tipped in) I (iii) title p. I (iv) blank I (v)–vi. Preface I (vii)–ix. Contents I (x) blank I (1)–284. text, with printer's imprint at foot of p.284 (BILLING, PRINTER AND STEREOTYPER, GUILDFORD, SURREY.) I (1)–36. catalogue, dated MDCCCLXIII.

Binding (see Plate 163)
Designed by Robert Dudley (see Note 3). Red ('X Quality') grained cloth boards, blocked blind and gilt; edges rough-trimmed, heads uncut (see Note 3); yellow surface-paper endpapers.

Front board: OUR . SOLDIERS (cloth-colour out of gilt) on scroll, forming part of a decoration, under a crown, that includes representation of a Victoria Cross: FOR VALOUR (cloth colour out of gilt), the inscription on the Cross; beneath this: R.D (gilt), the designer's initials. All this enclosed in a frame of rules and floral ornaments (blind). **Spine:** OUR I SOLDIERS I OR I ANECDOTES I OF THE I BRITISH I . ARMY . (cloth colour out of gilt) on panel forming part of gilt decoration with battlements, leaves, and scroll with: VALOUR MERCY (cloth-colour out of gilt). At foot: LONDON I GRIFFITH & FARRAN (gilt), with three gilt rules at head and foot. **Back board:** frame of rules and floral ornaments (blind) as on front board.

References: BL; Bod.

Notes
1. The imposition and make-up of this book is almost as much of a muddle as that of the companion volume, *Our Sailors*, 167.1, with which it was published in 1862 (title-page date 1863). The prelims, consisting of ten pages, are made up of two conjugate leaves, forming pp.(i)–(iv), with the frontispiece tipped in between them so as to face p.(iii), and a singleton (pp.(v)–vi) tipped on to p.(iv), plus another pair of conjugate leaves (pp.(vii) to (x)) tipped on to the singleton. This is appalling planning: there seems to be no possible reason why this gathering could not have consisted of an 8-page section with the singleton tipped on to it, or, better still, an 8-page section with a pair of conjugate leaves wrapped round it to make a secure 12-page gathering (even if it would then not have been possible to avoid starting the book with a blank leaf).

2. The text itself is also badly planned, being four pages short of an even working and therefore having an odd 4-page section as well as a half sheet. All this would have been costly both to fit on machine, and to bind. It is possible that one of the pairs of conjugate leaves in the prelims was printed with the text, to make up the even working of 288 pages, but even this arrangement would have been clumsy, and would not have reduced the cost of binding so many odd bits and pieces.

3. The price of the book, and of its companion volume, *Our Sailors*, was 3s., with rough-trimmed edges, or 3s.6d., all edges gilt. The bindings were designed in 1862 for both titles by Robert Dudley: see *Our Sailors*, 167.1, Note 5, and Plate 159.

168.2

OUR SOLDIERS | ANECDOTES OF THE CAMPAIGNS AND GALLANT | DEEDS OF THE BRITISH ARMY | DURING THE REIGN OF | HER MAJESTY QUEEN VICTORIA | BY | WILLIAM H.G.KINGSTON | AUTHOR OF 'OUR SAILORS' 'PETER THE WHALER' 'MARK SEAWORTH' | 'TRUE BLUE' ETC. | EIGHTH THOUSAND. | (publisher's device) | GRIFFITH AND FARRAN | SUCCESSORS TO NEWBERY AND HARRIS | CORNER OF ST. PAUL'S CHURCHYARD, LONDON

Contents
164 x 102 mm. (i)–(viii) | (1)–(320) | catalogue (1)–32. Frontispiece as in 168.1, but with re-set caption (LIEUT. FARQUHARSON, 42ND HIGHLANDERS, BEFORE LUCKNOW. From a painting by L.W. Desanges.) and keyed to p.261.

(Frontispiece, tipped in) | (i) title p. | (ii) advertisement for *Our Sailors*, 'uniform with this volume … eighth thousand … price 3s. cloth, 3s.6d. gilt edges', and, at foot: The Rights of Translation and Reproduction are reserved. | (iii)–iv. Preface, and Preface to Fourth Edition, the latter dated August 1877 | (v)–vii. Contents | (viii) blank | (1)–319. text | (320) printer's imprint (MURRAY AND GIBB, EDINBURGH, PRINTERS TO HER MAJESTY'S STATIONERY OFFICE.) | (1)–32. catalogue.

Binding: As for 168.1 (in spite of smaller board-size), except (a) Indian-red smooth linen boards, blocked black, blind, and gilt; (b) all edges trimmed; (c) brown surface-paper endpapers; (d) blocking on front board previously blind is now black. All other blocking as before.

Reference: BL.

Notes
1. This seems to have been Kingston's final edition: it includes chapters on the Indian Mutiny; the Second Chinese War; the New Zealand War; the Abyssinian Expedition; and the Ashantee War including a section on the March to Coomassie.
2. The catalogue is dated by printer's code, June 1877, and the British Library copy (the only one known to me) was received on 10 October 1877.

168.3

OUR SOLDIERS | ANECDOTES OF THE CAMPAIGNS AND GALLANT | DEEDS OF THE BRITISH ARMY | DURING THE REIGN OF | HER MAJESTY QUEEN VICTORIA | BY THE LATE | WILLIAM H.G.KINGSTON | AUTHOR OF 'OUR SAILORS' 'PETER THE WHALER' 'MARK SEAWORTH' | 'TRUE BLUE' ETC. | EDITED AND BROUGHT DOWN TO DATE BY | G.A.HENTY | AUTHOR OF 'THE YOUNG BUGLERS' 'CORNET OF HORSE' ETC. |

(publisher's device) | GRIFFITH AND FARRAN | SUCCESSORS TO NEWBERY AND HARRIS | WEST CORNER OF ST. PAUL'S CHURCHYARD, LONDON | E.P.DUTTON & CO., NEW YORK

Contents

181 × 121 mm. (i)–viii | (1)–(376) | catalogue (1)–(32). Frontispiece as in 168.1, but without caption, only the keyword (Frontispiece.) remaining.

(Frontispiece, tipped in) | (i) title p. | (ii) advertisement for *Our Sailors* ('uniform with this volume'), and 'The Rights of Translation and of Reproduction are reserved.' | iii. Preface | iv. Preface, continued, and Preface to Fourth Edition, with date, August 1877 | v. publisher's Note (see Note 2) | vi–viii. Contents | (1)–375. text, with printer's imprint at foot of p.375 (Morrison & Gibb, Edinburgh, | Printers to Her Majesty's Stationery Office.) | (376) blank | (1)–(32) catalogue, dated June 1882 or November 1882.

Binding (see Note 1)

Red, diagonally grained cloth boards, blocked black, light-blue, blind, and gilt; edges plain; grey-green flowered endpapers.

Front board: Our Soldiers | W.H.G.Kingston. (black out of stippled-gilt panel) over illustration, in ornamental frame, of boy sitting in branches of tree, reading a book, with superimposed lettering: THE BOYS' OWN | FAVOURITE | LIBRARY (all black and light-blue). **Spine:** OUR | SOLDIERS (black out of gilt panels) partly overlapping and partly overlapped by continuation of illustration of tree-branches from front board. Beneath this: W.H.G. | KINGSTON (gilt); GRIFFITH & FARRAN (cloth-colour out of black rectangle). **Back board:** three rules across head and foot of board; publisher's device at centre (all blind).

References: BB; PN.

Notes

1. The first issue of *Our Soldiers* in 'The Boys' Own Favourite Library', begun by Griffith and Farran in 1881. For details of the series see *Out on the Pampas*, §1, 4.3, Notes 3–5; for examples of binding styles, of which this is the first, see Plate 33.
2. This is also the first issue to be edited and enlarged by Henty. The publisher's Note on p.v reads as follows: 'In preparing the present edition of this book for the press, the publishers felt that they could not do better than ask Mr.G.A.Henty, whose experiences not only among '*Our* Soldiers' but with other armies in the field are so well known, to make the additions necessary to bring the record down to the present time. This he has done; and by his description of the Afghan, Zulu, and Transvaal wars, he has made this history so far complete'.

168.4

Title page: As for 168.3.

Contents

186 × 124 mm. (i)–viii | (1)–384 | catalogue (1)–(32). Frontispiece as in 168.3.

(Frontispiece, tipped in) | (i) title p. | (ii) advertisement for *Our Sailors* ('uniform with this volume'), and 'The Rights of Translation and of Reproduction are reserved.' | iii. Preface | iv. Preface, continued, and Preface to Fourth Edition, with date, August 1877 | v. publisher's Note (see Note 2) | vi–viii. Contents | (1)–384.

text, with printer's imprint at foot of p.384 (MORRISON AND GIBB, EDINBURGH, I PRINTERS TO HER MAJESTY'S STATIONERY OFFICE.), and printer's code (see Note 1) I (1)–(32) catalogue, dated February 1884.

Binding: As for 168.3, but the red cloth is smooth and ungrained.

Reference: PN.

Notes

1. The printer's code on p.384 indicates an impression of 2000 copies, November 1833. The bound-in catalogue is dated February 1884.

2. The text is nine pages longer than in 168.3: Henty had worked on the text a second time. That is confirmed by the publisher's Note on p.v, where the wording of the last sentence has been altered to include the Egyptian war. There is now no blank page at the end of the text, and an added final 8-page gathering.

3. Sheets from this impression, dated November 1883, are also found in the second binding style of 'The Boys' Own Favourite Library', coded below as 168.5. That, in turn, was also used for one or more later reprints, as will be seen.

168.5

OUR SOLDIERS I ANECDOTES OF THE CAMPAIGNS AND GALLANT I DEEDS OF THE BRITISH ARMY I DURING THE REIGN OF I HER MAJESTY QUEEN VICTORIA I BY THE LATE I WILLIAM H.G.KINGSTON I AUTHOR OF 'OUR SAILORS' 'PETER THE WHALER' 'MARK SEAWORTH' I 'TRUE BLUE' ETC. I EDITED AND BROUGHT DOWN TO DATE BY I G.A.HENTY I AUTHOR OF 'THE YOUNG BUGLERS' 'CORNET OF HORSE' ETC. I (publisher's device) I GRIFFITH, FARRAN, OKEDEN & WELSH, I SUCCESSORS TO NEWBERY AND HARRIS, I WEST CORNER OF ST. PAUL'S CHURCHYARD, LONDON. I E.P.DUTTON & CO., NEW YORK.

Contents

185 × 122 mm. (i)–viii I (1)–384 I catalogue (1)–16. Frontispiece as in 168.3.

(Frontispiece, tipped in) I (i) title p. I (ii) advertisement for *Our Sailors* ('uniform with this volume'), and 'The rights of translation and of reproduction are reserved.' I iii. Preface I iv. Preface, continued, and Preface to Fourth Edition, with date, August 1877 I v. publisher's Note I vi–viii. Contents I (1)–384. text, with printer's imprint at foot of p.384 (MORRISON AND GIBB, EDINBURGH, I PRINTERS TO HER MAJESTY'S STATIONERY OFFICE.), and printer's code (see Note 2) I (1)–16. catalogue, dated August 1886.

Binding (see Note 1)

Red, diagonally grained cloth boards, blocked black, light-green, silver, and gilt; edges plain; yellow-green flowered endpapers.

Front board: OUR I SOLDIERS (black, and cloth-colour out of solid-gilt rectangular panel) superimposed over a confused multiple illustration, including palm trees, sunset, gun on carriage, anchor, sailing ship in moonlight, etc. (black, light-green, silver), with: By I W.H.G. I KINGSTON (black) beneath title, and: ILLUSTRATED (black over light-green shading) at foot. **Spine:** OUR I SOLDIERS (black and cloth-colour out of solid-gilt rectangle) with light-green and black rules above and below. By W.H.G. I KINGSTON (cloth-colour out of smaller solid-gilt rectangle) with similar rules above and below. At foot: GRIFFITH, FARRAN & Co. (cloth-colour out of even smaller solid-gilt rectangle) again with similar rules above and below. Illustration of weapons and satchel, as a trophy, above tennis and cricket equipment, etc. (black and light-green) between top and bottom rectangles, and running behind the central one. **Back board:** publisher's monogram in roughly-rectangular panel in design of palm tree (all black) at centre.

References: PN | *Farmer*, p.54; *Dartt*, p.103.

Notes

1. The second binding design used for 'The Boys' Own Favourite Library' (see 168.3, Note 1). As explained in notes on the series (see *Out on the Pampas*, §1, 4.3, Notes 3–5), Griffith & Farran changed the style from time to time, using four designs altogether. One result of this policy was not only that most of the the books appeared in several different binding designs over the years, but also that sheets from one impression of a given book were sometimes bound in two different styles. In this case, sheets from the November 1883 impression of *Our Soldiers* are found in both the first and second binding designs (see 168.4, Note 3, and Plate 33).

2. As also explained in the same Notes, Griffith & Farran altered the form of their imprint several times, following changes of management. This impression of *Our Soldiers* is shown by the printer's code on p.384 to be of only 1000 copies, dated October 1886, and the title-page imprint has changed since the 1883 impression.

3. No further alterations or additions appear to have been made by Henty, and the publisher's Note on p.v remains as in 168.4.

4. This is the only edition mentioned by *Farmer* and *Dartt*. In a Note at the end of his entry (p.104), *Dartt* makes the strange and erroneous comment, 'This apparently contains nothing by Henty'!

168.6

Title page: As for 168.5, except changed imprint (LONDON | GRIFFITH FARRAN OKEDEN & WELSH | SUCCESSORS TO NEWBERY AND HARRIS | AND SYDNEY).

Contents: 184 x 123 mm. As for 168.5, except (a) no catalogue; (b) p.(ii) advertisement reset; at foot, wording and punctuation of line changed ([The Rights of Translation and Reproduction are Reserved.]).

Binding (see Note 1)
Red, diagonally grained boards, bevelled, blocked black, light-brown, and gilt; all edges gilt; yellow-green flowered endpapers.
   Front board: OUR SOLDIERS (black, and cloth-colour out of solid-gilt rectangular panel) with rules (black and light-brown) above and below, superimposed across a trophy (black, light-brown, and gilt) of rifles, oars, and an anchor. Beneath this: By | W.H.G.KINGSTON (black) above crossed swords (black and light-brown). **Spine:** Six bands across width of spine (light-brown, with black above and below); between the second and third bands: OUR | SOLDIERS (black, and cloth-colour out of solid-gilt panel). Between fourth and fifth bands: KINGSTON (black, and cloth-colour out of smaller solid-gilt panel). Above sixth band: GRIFFITH, FARRAN & Co. (gilt). **Back board:** plain.

Reference: PN.

Notes
1. The third binding style used by Griffith & Farran for 'The Boys' Own Favourite Library' (see Plate 33). The textual content is unchanged from that of 168.5.
2. The printer's code on p.384 indicates an impression of 1000 copies, April 1889.

168.7

Title page: As for 168.5, except changed imprint (LONDON: | GRIFFITH FARRAN & CO., | NEWBERY HOUSE, 39 CHARING CROSS ROAD.).

Contents: 181 × 121 mm. As for 168.6, except (a) Keyword (Frontispiece.) now deleted on frontispiece (see 168.3 under 'Contents'); (b) text now ends in a 12-page gathering, imposed to include four final pages of publisher's lists; (c) no printer's imprint, nor printer's code.

Binding (see Note 1)
Blue, vertically ribbed cloth boards, bevelled, blocked black, red, white, and gilt; all edges gilt; black surface-paper endpapers.
　　Front board: Elaborate decorative framework at edges, illustrating military and naval equipment, etc. (black and, at foot, red) and sailing ship against setting sun (gilt) at top left corner. At right, in scrolls (outlined black): BoYS' [*sic*] OWN | FAVOURITE | LIBRARY. (red). At centre: OUR | SOLDIERS (gilt) | BY (black) | W.H.G.KINGSTON (gilt). **Spine:** OUR | SOLDIERS (gilt) above trophy of flags, anchor, rifles, etc. (black, white, red). Beneath: BY (black) | W.H.G. | KINGSTON (gilt). Emblem of bugle and palm leaves (red) above: GRIFFITH FARRAN | BROWNE & CO. (black). **Back board:** plain.

Reference: BB.

Notes:
1. The fourth, and last, binding style used for 'The Boys' Own Favourite Library' (see Plate 33).
2. The textual content is unchanged from that of 168.6. The publisher's imprint in the advertisement on p.(ii) is still given as 'Griffith Farran Okeden and Welsh.'.

168.8

OUR SOLDIERS | GALLANT DEEDS OF THE | BRITISH ARMY DURING THE | REIGN OF QUEEN VICTORIA | BY | WILLIAM H.G.KINGSTON | A NEW EDITION, REVISED | AND BROUGHT DOWN TO THE END OF 1898 | ILLUSTRATED. | GRIFFITH FARRAN BROWNE & CO. LIMITED | 35 BOW STREET, COVENT GARDEN | LONDON

Contents
188 × 126 mm. (1)–352 | no catalogue. Four engraved portraits from photographs of generals, three reproduced by line blocks, one by halftone block, printed in black on text pages, folioed, but unbacked.
　　(1) Blank | (2) frontispiece | (3) title p. | (4) [The Rights of Translation and of Reproduction are Reserved] | 5. Editor's Preface | 6. Titles of British Regiments | 7. Contents | 8. List of Illustrations | 9–352. text, with printer's imprint at foot of p.352 (PRINTED BY MORRISON AND GIBB LIMITED, EDINBURGH).

Binding (see Plate 162)

Grey-green cloth boards, blocked black, red, and gilt; edges plain; plain off-white endpapers.

Front board: OUR | SOLDIERS (gilt) above illustration of battle scene with British soldiers under attack (black and red). At foot: W.H.G.KINGSTON (black). **Spine:** OUR | SOLDIERS (gilt) | W.H.G. | KINGSTON (black) above illustration of African tribesman with spear and shield (black). At foot: GRIFFITH FARRAN | . BROWNE & Co . (black). **Back board:** plain.

References: BL; CH.

Notes

1. The Editor of this edition, published in 1899, was William Moxon: his name did not appear on the title page until four years later when he again brought it up to date (see 168.9). Here he continues the narrative up to the fall of Khartoum.

2. The Editor's Preface on p.5 gives erroneous information about the origin of the book, similar to that in the corresponding edition of *Our Sailors*, 167.6, about the origins of that book: 'The first edition of *Our Soldiers* was published under the title of *Anecdotes of Soldiers*, in 1862 . . .'. This is discussed in the General Notes at the beginning of this entry for 168. *Our Soldiers.*

168.9

OUR SOLDIERS | GALLANT DEEDS OF THE | BRITISH ARMY | BY | WILLIAM H.G.KINGSTON | A NEW EDITION | REVISED AND BROUGHT DOWN TO THE END OF THE | BOER WAR, 1902 | BY | WILLIAM MOXON | AUTHOR OF | "STORIES FROM SOUTH AFRICAN HISTORY" | GRIFFITH FARRAN BROWNE & CO. LIMITED | 35 BOW STREET, COVENT GARDEN | LONDON

Contents

188 x 128 mm. (1)–(376) | no catalogue. Illustrations as in 168.8.

(1) Blank | (2) frontispiece | (3) title p. | (4) [The Rights of Translation and of Reproduction are Reserved] | 5. Publisher's Note | 6. Titles of British Regiments | 7. Contents | 8. List of Illustrations | 9–374. text, with printer's imprint at foot of p.374 (PRINTED BY MORRISON AND GIBB LIMITED, EDINBURGH) | (375)–(376) blank.

Binding (see Plate 162)

Brown cloth boards, blocked black, dark-blue, grey merging to yellow, green, and gilt; edges plain; plain off-white endpapers.

Front board: OUR | SOLDIERS (gilt) above illustration of sailor firing gun on carriage with half-kneeling soldier on guard in foreground (black, dark-blue, grey merging to yellow, green). At lower right corner: W.H.G. | KINGSTON (black). **Spine:** OUR | SOLDIERS | W.H.G.KINGSTON (gilt) above trophy of weapons, ship's wheel, cannon balls, etc. (dark-blue, yellow). At foot: GRIFFITH FARRAN | . BROWNE & Co. . (black). **Back board:** plain.

References: BL; PN.

Notes
1. The Publisher's Note on p.5 includes the following: 'The present edition simply adds a brief narrative of the principal events of the Boer Wars of 1881 and 1900–1902. In the space allowed it was impossible to mention acts of individual heroism and courage for which this last war has been so remarkable; and it was found necessary to omit the accounts of the Persian, Chinese, and New Zealand Wars contained in the former editions. No reference is made to the recent events in China, as an account of these will be found in the current edition of *Our Sailors*.'.
2. This binding design was also used for *Our Sailors*, 167.6.
3. The Publisher's Note on p.5 repeats the errors mentioned in 168.8, Note 2.

168.10
OUR SOLDIERS | BY | W.H.G.KINGSTON | (vignetted illustration printed in three-colour halftone) | LONDON | HENRY FROWDE | HODDER AND STOUGHTON | 1910

Contents
184 x 122 mm. 5–(372) | catalogue (1)–16. Four-page insert of single-sided coated paper tipped in before first leaf of first text gathering, unfolioed, but counted in pagination as folios (1)–(4), printed in three-colour process inks on pages 2 and 3, and black on page 3 only. On p.2, watercolour drawing, unsigned, as frontispiece, reproduced by three-colour halftone blocks; on p.3, title page with all lettering in black (plus red for initial O in title), and small illustration at centre reproduced by vignetted three-colour halftone blocks.

(1) Blank | (2) frontispiece | (3) title p. | (4) blank | 5. Publisher's Note | 6. Titles of British Regiments | 7. Contents | (8) blank | 9–368. text, with printer's imprint at foot of p.368 (R.CLAY AND SONS, LTD., BREAD ST. HILL, E.C., AND BUNGAY, SUFFOLK.) | (369)–(372) advertisements | (1)–16. catalogue.

Binding (see Plate 162)
Red cloth boards, blocked black, white, blue, brown, buff-pink, and gilt; edges plain; plain off-white endpapers.
   Front board: OUR SOLDIERS (black and cloth-colour reversed out of solid-gilt rectangle) framed by black line, over illustration of Scout standing in front of Union Flag (black, white, blue, brown, and buff-pink). **Spine:** OUR | SOLDIERS | KINGSTON (cloth-colour reversed out of solid-gilt rectangle) framed by two black lines, above illustration of two schoolboys standing, talking (black, white, blue, brown, buff-pink). At foot, above black rule: HENRY FROWDE | HODDER & STOUGHTON (black). **Back board:** plain.

References: BL; Bod; PN.

Notes
1. The text is unchanged from 168.9. The new publisher has used a different printer, but the text is printed from stereos of the setting used by Morrison and Gibb.
2. The book is re-imposed, the first page on text paper being folioed 5, the four unfolioed and pasted-in pages on coated paper being counted in the pagination as pages (1)–(4). This arrangement is quite different from that in *Our Sailors* (167.9),

which was issued simultaneously with the same binding design. In *Our Soldiers* the four pages on coated paper are not included in the pagination; the text finishes four pages short of the even working, and the last two leaves of the final gathering are used for publisher's advertisements.

3. For details of the purchase of the stock and goodwill of Griffith & Farran by Hodder & Stoughton, the formation of the 'Joint Venture' by that firm with the Oxford University Press, and their publication of the children's books originally published by Griffith & Farran, see Appendix II, Part 2.

4. The advertisement on p.(369) names this book and five others including *Our Sailors* in the 'New Two-Shilling Series of Reward Books', uniform with this volume.

5. A later reprint of this edition, with title page still dated 1910, but with the printer's imprint on p.368 reset (Richard Clay and Sons, Limited, London and Bungay.), has a total of eight books in the series listed on p.(369). This copy has the publisher's imprint on the spine of the binding case in lettering 4mm. high: on the earlier issue it is between 2mm. and 3mm. high.

169. PASTIME TALES

169.1

PASTIME TALES | by | G.Manville Fenn, | E.Everett Green, | D.H.Parry, L.T.Meade, | etc. | (large vignette illustration of boy and girl on hobby-horses) | (at left) ERNEST . NISTER . LONDON | IP. | (at centre) No.3801 | (at right) E.P.DUTTON & Co. NEW YORK.

Contents

261 × 211 mm. (1)–108 | no catalogue (but publisher's advertisements on lower endpapers). Numerous full-page and smaller illustrations by various artists, reproduced in line and halftone on text pages.

(1) Illustrated half-title p. | (2) blank | (3) title p. | (4) illustration from wash-drawing | (5)–108. text and illustrations, with imprint at foot of p.108 (Printed in Bavaria.)

Binding (see Plate 171)

Quarter-bound pink cloth, varnished white paper boards, the upper board printed in full colour; edges plain; upper endpapers plain white, lower endpapers printed in black with publisher's advertisements on pp.1–3.

Front board: Pastime Tales (brown with grey shadow; initials red, outlined black) on white panel above illustration, framed by brown line, of woman reading from book to four children, with decoration of reeds in grey margin (all in full colour). At foot: (Nister Trade Mark) | ERNEST . NISTER . LONDON . (space) Printed in Bavaria. (space) E.P.DUTTON & Co. NEW YORK. | (centred under above line) No. 3801. (all brown). **Spine:** plain pink cloth. **Back board:** plain varnished paper.

Reference: PN.

Notes
1. 'Little Mistress Valentia' (see §4) is at pp.(16)–31, illustrated by E. Stuart Hardy.
It appeared in other Nister publications (see 161.1 and 163.1).
2. Among the collections of short stories, etc., containing work by Henty, this
compilation most unusually does not give his name on the title page.
3. The advertisements printed on the lower endpapers include an announcement of
Nister's Holiday Annual in its 'twenty-fifth year of publication'. This was the
Annual for 1913, published in the autumn of 1912, and the advertisement thus
provides a date for *Pastime Tales*.

170. PERIL AND PROWESS

170.1
Peril and Prowess I BEING I STORIES TOLD BY I G.A.HENTY I G.M.FENN I
A.CONAN DOYLE I W.W.JACOBS I D.L.JOHNSTONE I D.KER I ANDREW
BALFOUR I C.R.LOW I &c., &c. I WITH EIGHT ILLUSTRATIONS I BY I
W.BOUCHER I W.& R.CHAMBERS, LIMITED I LONDON AND EDINBURGH
I 1899

Contents
184 x 131 mm. (i)–(viii) I (1)–(424) I no catalogue. Eight full-page wash-drawings
by W. Boucher, reproduced by halftone blocks printed in black on coated paper,
unbacked, keyed to text pages, tipped in. Small black line engravings used as head
and tail pieces.
(i) Half-title p. I (ii) blank I (frontispiece, tipped in) I (iii) title p. I (iv) printer's
imprint (Edinburgh: I Printed by W.& R.Chambers, Limited.) I (v) Contents I (vi)
blank I (vii) List of Illustrations I (viii) blank I (1)–423. text, with printer's imprint
at foot of p.423 as on p.(iv) I (424) blank.

Binding (see Plate 153)
Red cloth boards, bevelled, blocked black, green, and gilt; edges plain; brown
surface-paper endpapers.
Front board: PERIL & I PROWESS (red, cased black, out of solid-gilt
decorative panel framed by black line) above illustration of night-scene of man tied
to tree with Indians around fire in clearing beyond (black, green, gilt). At lower right
corner: (ornament) TOLD By (ornament) I G.A.HENTY (ornament) I G.M.FENN
(two ornaments) I A.CONAN DOYLE I W.W.JACOBS (ornament) I
D.LAWSON.JOHNSTONE I D.KER : ETC. ETC. ETC. (all cloth-colour out of
solid-gilt irregular panel framed by black line). **Spine:** PERIL I and I PROWESS
(cloth-colour out of solid-gilt irregular panel framed by black line) above illustration
of man seated under trees, with gun (black, green, gilt). At foot: W.&
R.CHAMBERS (cloth-colour out of solid-gilt irregular panel framed by black line).
Back board: plain.

References: PN I *Farmer*, p.55; *Dartt*, p.106, *Companion*, p.22, 41

Notes

1. 'The Ranche in the Valley' is at pp.(1)–63, and 'The Golden Cañon' is at pp.64–133. For both of these see §4.

2. Later impressions were printed with undated title pages.

3. *Dartt*, p.106, is misleading about the front board of the binding case, describing it as 'same design as *Grit & Go*'. The design was used for the US edition of *Grit and Go* (E.P. Dutton & Co., New York), but not for the UK edition (§2, 157).

171. PICTURE BOOK TREASURES

171.1

Picture Book Treasures | (line drawing of girl with hoop and posy of flowers talking to boy with smaller child on his shoulder) | ERNEST . NISTER . LONDON. (space) E.N. No. 2002. (space) E.P.DUTTON & Co. NEW YORK.

Contents

244 × 198 mm. Unfolioed book consisting of: one 8-page signature and five 16-page signatures, of text and numerous line illustrations printed in black on bulky featherweight paper. One full-colour plate, varnished, is laid down on p.(2) as frontispiece. (Publisher's catalogue on lower endpapers).

(1) Illustrated half-title p. | (2) frontispiece | (3) title p. | (4) small line-illustration | (5)–(88). text and illustrations, with imprint at foot of p.(88) (Printed in Bavaria).

Binding

Quarter-bound grey cloth, printed paper boards; edges plain; upper endpapers plain off-white, lower endpapers printed on pp.(i)–(iii) with publisher's catalogue.

Front board: (lettering included in over-all, full-colour, varnished lithograph): Picture Book Treasures (mainly blue, maroon, brown) on green background, with leaves and flowers at left (green and pink), above full-colour illustration of woman and two children having a picnic in a boat tied up at river bank. At foot: . ERNEST . NISTER . LONDON. (space) EN. 2002. (space) E.P.DUTTON & Co. NEW YORK. (brown). **Spine:** plain grey cloth. **Back board:** plain ivory varnished paper. colour).

Reference: AP.

Notes

1. 'In Troubled Times' is at pp.(30)–(52), with one full-page and seven smaller illustrations in line by E.S.Hardy (see §4).

2. As customary with Nister, the story appeared in other publications, using the same illustrations. In *Nister's Holiday Annual*, 1902 (§2, 162), the type was set in two columns: here, and in 181.1, it is in a larger size in a single column.

3. The catalogue on the lower endpapers includes an advertisement for *Nister's Holiday Annual* in its 'twentieth year of publication'. That was 1908, which corresponds with a dated inscription in the copy described.

172. PLEASE TELL ME ANOTHER TALE

172.1

Please Tell Me | Another Tale. | A COLLECTION OF SHORT ORIGINAL STORIES | FOR CHILDREN. | BY | (list of authors follows, in two columns with vertical rule between, the final name centred beneath the rule) G.A.HENTY. | FANNY BARRY. | THERESA I.DENT. | MRS. MOLESWORTH. | MRS. A.M.GOODHART. | MARY HOLDSWORTH. | AGNES GIBERNE. | London: | SKEFFINGTON & SON, 163, PICCADILLY, W. | (8-point rule) | 1890.
(Note: London: *is in gothic type).*

Contents
173 x 129 mm. One unfolioed leaf, plus (i)–vi | (1)–220 | no catalogue. Frontispiece and two full-page plates from pen drawings by Palmer Cox, printed in black on MF paper from line blocks, unbacked, unfolioed, tipped in. Decorative dropped initials, and occasional engraved head and tail pieces.

(Unfolioed) blank | (unfolioed) blank | (i) half-title p. | (ii) blank | (frontispiece, tipped in) | (iii) title p. | (iv) blank | (v)–vi. Contents | (1)–220. text.

Binding (see Plate 165)
Blue cloth boards, blocked silver; edges plain; grey flowered endpapers.
Front board: PLEASE TELL ME (silver) above decoration of spray of a climbing plant with flowers, leaves and tendrils (silver); ANOTHER TALE (silver). **Spine:** PLEASE | TELL ME | ANOTHER | TALE (silver) above continuation of decoration from front board (silver). At foot: SKEFFINGTONS (silver). **Back board:** plain.

References: PN; RC | *Farmer*, p.56; *Dartt*, p.108, *Companion*, p.23.

Notes
1. 'Faithful' is at pp.(115)–150, unillustrated (see §4).
2. This is one of a series of collections of short stories produced by Skeffington & Son. Only one other contains work by Henty: *Now for a Story*, (§2, 165).
3. The make-up of the book is clumsy and uneconomical. The prelims make eight pages, although the first two are not folioed. There follow thirteen gatherings of 16 pages each, and the last two gatherings are of eight pages and four pages respectively. The final four pages are tipped on to the 8-page section, instead of being wrapped around it to give a 12-page gathering: that would have made the binding stronger, as the sewing would have gone through the hinges of all the pairs of conjugate leaves. It is possible the prelims were printed with the odd 8-page section of text, thus leaving only the 4-page section as an oddment for machining. But that would not have cut out extra expense in the bindery.
4. Roger Childs tells me the book was reprinted in 1890. The only change is the addition of the line 'SECOND EDITION.' above the title-page imprint.

173. PLUCK

173.1

PLUCK | Stories of Life and Adventure | in Many Lands | WITH ILLUSTRATIONS BY | A.B.WHITE | JOHN F. SHAW (1928) & CO. LTD. | 3 PILGRIM STREET, LONDON

Contents

176 x 130 mm. Unfolioed volume of 96 pages on bulky featherweight antique. First and last leaves of text paper are pasted down as endpapers. Colour frontispiece from (?)watercolour drawing, printed in four-colour lithography, tipped in. Numerous line drawings, full-page and half-page, throughout text.

(1)–(2) pasted down as endpaper | (3)–(4) blank, as free endpaper | (frontispiece, tipped in) | (5) title p. | (6) printer's imprint (Printed and made in Great Britain by | BISHOP & SONS LTD. | EDINBURGH AND LONDON) | (7)–(92) text and illustrations | (93)–(94) blank, as free endpaper | (95)–(96) pasted down as endpaper.

Binding

Paper boards, printed by four-colour lithography; edges plain; endpapers formed by text pages (see Contents above).

Front board: PLUCK (red, cased black) above illustration of elephant pursuing man and woman in tropical kit, on horseback, with rifles (full-colour). **Spine:** Pluck (red, cased black) above illustration, continued from front board, showing Arabic horseman in pursuit of elephant (full-colour). **Back board:** continuation of illustration, showing another mounted Arab with rifle, at full-gallop (full-colour).

Reference: BB.

Notes

1. 'Hunted by an Elephant' (see §4) is at (unfolioed) pp.(5)–(22), with 3 full-page and 4 half-page illustrations in line by A.B. White, and also illustrated in colour across the full width of the binding case. The story had appeared earlier in *Fifty-two Stories for Boyhood and Youth*, (1893), see §2, 147.
2. The book is cheaply produced on a bulky featherweight, and the omission of folio numbers suggests that parts of the book may have been used in other publications. But no other volume containing Henty's work is known from this publisher.

174. THE RED BOOK FOR BOYS

174.1

The | Red Book for Boys | Edited by Herbert Strang | (illustration of young sailor on sailing ship firing cannon) London: | Henry Frowde and Hodder & Stoughton *(Note: The title is printed in black with decorative red capital letters; the illustration is in black and red).*

Contents

221 x 174 mm. Unfolioed book consisting of: 4 pages printed red and black, plus eighteen sections each of 16 pages, signatures A to I and K to S, printed black.

Twelve full-page plates from watercolour drawings by various artists, reproduced by three-colour halftone blocks printed on coated paper, unbacked, tipped in. Many black-and-white illustrations from line drawings by various artists, printed in black on text pages. No catalogue.

(i) Blank | (ii) full-page illustrated bookplate (black and red) | (frontispiece, tipped in) | (iii) title p. | (iv) Contents | (5)–(292) text and illustrations.

Binding (see Plate 147)
Quarter-bound red cloth, blocked black; white paper boards printed red (halftone), with full-colour plate laid down in panel on front board. Edges plain; plain off-white endpapers.

Front board: Edited by Herbert Strang | The Red Book for Boys (white out of red halftone background, shaded solid red) above panel with decorative border containing laid-down colour plate (which also appears as the fourth plate in the book). **Spine:** The | RED | BOOK | (shield ornament) for (shield ornament) | BOYS | Edited by | Herbert | Strang (cloth colour out of solid black rectangle) above illustration of sailing ship (black). At foot: HENRY FROWDE | & HODDER & | STOUGHTON (black). **Back board:** all-over muslin-textured halftone tint (red).

References: PN | *Farmer*, p.58; *Dartt*, p.112, *Companion*, p.24.

Notes
1. 'Trapped. A Tale of the Mexican War', extracted from *Out on the Pampas* (§1, 4), starts at sig.A and runs for 27 pages, with four line-drawings on text pages, and one full-colour plate, tipped in, all by P.A. Staynes.
2. For notes on this publisher's acquisition of the rights in work published by Griffith & Farran, including *Out on the Pampas*, see Appendix II, Part 2.
3. Herbert Strang was the pseudonym of two men, George Herbert Ely and C.J. L'Estrange, who wrote and edited a great quantity of children's books. Those for girls were issued under the pseudonym, 'Mrs. Herbert Strang'.
4. The book was first published in 1910, together with *The Green Book for Boys* (§2, 156). It is cheaply produced, and printed on bulky featherweight paper. The binding is poor, and copies are seldom found in good condition.
5. *Dartt* incorrectly calls this an Annual. On the Contents page the Editor refers to *Herbert Strang's Annual* for boys, in which some of the stories first appeared.
6. See *The Boys' Story Book* (§2, 133), and *Brave and True* (§2, 135), both of which consist of certain signatures reprinted from this book, including Henty's story.

174.2
Title page: As for 174.1.

Contents: As for 174.1, except (a) p.(iv) has no list of Contents, and the short paragraph of acknowledgements is reset and centred on the page, with printer's imprint at foot (Richard Clay & Sons, Limited, London and Bungay.); (b) the colour plate illustrating Henty's story is transposed to face its opening page; (c) a publisher's catalogue of 4 pages, printed on same paper as the text, is tipped on the end of the final text gathering.

Binding

Quarter-bound red cloth, bright-red cloth boards, blocked gilt; edges plain; plain off-white endpapers.

Front board: Illustration of sailing ship (gilt) at lower right corner. **Spine:** THE RED | BOOK | FOR BOYS | EDITED BY | HERBERT . STRANG (gilt) above illustration of naval officer, with sword drawn, on board ship (gilt). At foot: HENRY FROWDE | HODDER & STOUGHTON (gilt). **Back board:** plain.

Reference: CH.

Note: This binding style was probably issued simultaneously with, or very shortly after, 174.1. It was used again with the imprint of the Oxford University Press after the Joint Venture came to an end, about 1917.

174.3

Title page: As for 174.1, but printed in black only.

Contents: As for 174.1, but the illustrated bookplate previously on p.(ii) now transferred to upper endpapers.

Binding

Quarter-bound red cloth, blocked black; white paper boards printed light-vermilion; edges plain; plain white paper endpapers..

Front board: THE | RED . BOOK | FOR . BOYS | EDITED . BY . HERBERT STRANG (white, reversed out of vermilion in panel with elaborate decorative framework (reversed out, white), enclosing laid-down oval section of colour plate (that appears complete on front board of 174.1). **Spine:** The | RED | BOOK | FOR | BOYS | EDITED . BY | HERBERT | STRANG (cloth-colour out of solid black) forming part of illustration of aeroplane flying over river with church and buildings behind, seen through trees (all black). At foot: OXFORD (black). **Back board:** heraldic trophy of royal arms on shield, with halberd, etc. (white) reversed out of vermilion.

Reference: CH.

Notes

1. This issue consists of sheets printed for the Joint Venture that were later bound up with the O.U.P. imprint on the binding case (see 174.2, Note).

2. In 1926 the book was again reprinted by Richard Clay & Sons, this time with the title-page imprint: HUMPHREY . MILFORD | OXFORD . UNIVERSITY . PRESS . LONDON. The book was quarter-bound in red cloth; paper boards printed with illustrations on both boards by Wyndham Payne (black, yellow-green, and red). Spine: THE | RED . BOOK | FOR | (ornament) BOYS (ornament) | (ornament) | Edited by | HERBERT STRANG | (illustration) | OXFORD (all black). As in late issues of *The Green Book for Boys* (see 156.2, Note 3) there were only six colour plates.

175. THE SAVAGE CLUB PAPERS

175.1

THE SAVAGE | CLUB PAPERS | EDITED BY | J.E.MUDDOCK | ART EDITOR | HERBERT JOHNSON | London, 1897 | HUTCHINSON & CO. | 34, PATERNOSTER ROW
(Note: London, 1897 *is in gothic type).*

Contents

198 x 147 mm. (i)–xvi | 1–376 | no catalogue. Forty-eight full-page and smaller illustrations from pen-, pencil-, and wash-drawings by various artists, reproduced by line blocks and halftone blocks printed on text pages (calendered paper), the full-page pictures unbacked, unfolioed but included in the pagination.

(i) Blank | (ii) frontispiece | (iii) title p. | (iv) printer's imprint (PRINTED BY | HAZELL, WATSON, AND VINEY, LD., | LONDON AND AYLESBURY.) | v–vii Preface | (viii) blank | ix. List of Contributors | x. List of Artists | xi–xiv. Contents | xv–xvi. List of Illustrations | (1)–376. text and illustrations, with printer's imprint on p.376 (Printed by Hazell, Watson, and Viney, Ld., London and Aylesbury.)

Binding (see Plate 164)

White cloth boards, printed pale yellow-grey, black, and light Indian-red; edges plain; grey flowered endpapers.

Front board: All lettering and decorations on irregular rectangle giving effect of paper (Indian red) with torn edges on pale yellow-grey background: SAVAGe CLUb [*sic*] (black and pale yellow-grey) above trophy of actors' masks, writers' and artists' materials, musical pipes, etc., and banner inscribed: 1897 (black and pale yellow-grey); PApers (black and pale yellow-grey). Note: almost the entire area of cloth is printed pale yellow-grey, leaving the white cloth to show only as highlights in the trophy and to outline the initial letters. **Spine:** Savage | Club. | Papers (all black) in panel of black rules, above second panel with Indian red background, and trophy of writers' and artists' material, etc., with inscription: 1897 (black and pale yellow-grey). At foot, in panel of black rules: HUTCHINSON & Co. (black). **Back board:** Panel of Indian red on background of pale yellow-grey, with trophy and decorations in panel (black and pale yellow-grey).

References: PN; BB | *Farmer*, p.60; *Dartt*, p.117.

Notes

1. 'Only a Hunchback', pp.203–221, has two line drawings by H.Petherick (see §4).
2. The Preface mentions the two earlier collections of work by members of the Savage Club, published in 1868 and 1869. Henty was a prominent member of the Club.
3. A later issue of this impression (or a reprint is remotely possible) in red cloth boards, was simply blocked thus: Front board: Savage Club | Papers | 1897 (gilt). Spine: Savage | Club | Papers | 1897 (gilt) at head; at foot: HUTCHINSON & CO. (gilt). Back board: plain. All contents, including the endpapers, remain unchanged.
4. Illustrations from halftone blocks are signed by the three following process engravers: Sedgwick, P.N., and Bursill & Ladyman.

176. SEASIDE MAIDENS

176.1

SEASIDE MAIDENS. | BY G.A.HENTY. | Being the Summer Number | OF | TINSLEYS' MAGAZINE. | TEN PAGES OF ILLUSTRATIONS | BY HARRY FURNISS. | (6-em decorative rule) | CONTENTS. (Here follows tabulated list of Contents, for details see under 'Contents' below) | (8-em rule) | LONDON: | TINSLEY BROTHERS, 8 CATHERINE STREET, STRAND. | 1880.
(Note: Being the Summer Number *is in gothic type).*

Contents

224 x 142 mm. Advertisements (1)–12 | title p. backed with advertisements (15)–16 (see Note 2) | (1)–98 | (1)–(4) Chapman & Hall catalogue (The Select Library of Fiction), printed in violet ink, not in all copies (see Note 4). Ten full-page pen-drawings by Harry Furniss (one for each story), printed from line blocks in black on MF paper, unbacked, unfolioed, tipped in.

(1)–12. 'Seaside Maidens' Advertiser. | AUGUST 1880. (*the first line in gothic type*) over numerous general advertisements, and several for Tinsley Brothers' publications, the *Union Jack*, etc. | (15) title page with list of Contents | 16. general advertisements | (full-page illustration, tipped in) | (1)–11. text of 'Surly Joe' | (12)–22. text of 'The Smuggler's Cutter' | 22–30. text of 'The Wreck on the Goodwins' | (31)–39. text of 'The Queen's Cup' | (40)–49. text of 'The Rivals' | (50)–56. text of 'A Fish-Wife's Dream' | (57)–66. text of 'A Narrow Escape' | 66–79. text of 'A Piece of Orange-Peel' | 79–89. text of 'Working Up' | (90)–98. text of 'On the Cliff', with printer's imprint at foot of p.98 (LONDON | ROBSON AND SONS, PRINTERS, PANCRAS ROAD, N.W.) | (1)–(4) Chapman & Hall catalogue, only present in certain, probably late, copies.

Cover (see Plate 157)

Light-buff paper, printed black and blue.

(1) PRICE ONE SHILLING. | SEASIDE | MAIDENS (all black); BY | G.A. HENTY | 1880 | SUMMER NUMBER (all black and blue); OF TINSLEYS' MAGAZINE (blue) | WITH TEN PAGES OF ILLUSTRATIONS BY HARRY FURNISS (black). All but the first and last lines are hand-drawn lettering and form part of the illustration by Harry Furniss, printed in black and blue, of many young ladies in a pleasure-boat.

(2) various small advertisements, printed in black.

(3) advertisements for Goodall's Household Specialities, and Kaberry's Liver Pills, printed in black.

(4) advertisement for Cadbury's Cocoa Essence, printed in black and blue.

Spine: SEASIDE MAIDENS: ONE SHILLING (black) running from foot to head.

References: HE; JJ; SW | *Sadleir*, I, 1191; Edmund Downey, *Twenty Years Ago*, p.115.

Notes

1. In 1880, following the success of earlier Christmas Numbers, Edmund Downey suggested to William Tinsley a Summer Number of *Tinsleys' Magazine*. This, the first such issue, is unusual for any publication of its kind in containing the work of only one author: as a 'special' annual issue it is included here in §2 rather than in §1 or §3. The title was to have been *On the Beach*, but was changed by the publisher in spite, according to Edmund Downey, of Henty's protests. Stuart Wilson has kindly shown me, from his collection, the briefest of letters from Henty, dated as late as 26 June: 'My dear Tinsley, I am still without proofs of "On the Beach". What is your printer up to? Yours very truly, G.A. Henty'. The date shows that the change of title cannot have taken place long before publication (see also Note 5).

2. Signature *a* (advertisements and title page) does appear regularly to have made 14 pages, consisting of (1)–12 and (15)–16, probably as a late adjustment from a planned 16 pages – which would account for the folio 16 (by then in error) on the verso of the title page. That the publication was issued thus is made virtually certain by the title page having set-off on to page 12, thus showing that those pages did face each other before the ink was properly dry. Sadleir confirms that his copy is the same as the others (*XIX Century Fiction*, I, 1191).

3. As will be seen from the description above, the text proper makes 98 pages, the final leaf (pp.97–98) carrying the signature mark *h* and consisting of a singleton tipped on to the end of the last full 16-page gathering. Thus the book, with the leaf 'missing' in signature *a*, was probably machined as an even working of 112 pages, signatures *a* and *h* forming one sheet of sixteen pages. The binder would have been instructed to cut off the odd leaf (sig. *h*), and to secure with paste both it and the other consequent singleton in their proper places.

4. I have seen two copies in private collections, with front cover (only) and sig. *a* present. They have the title page on page 15 (unfolioed) and advertisements for 'Liebig Company's Extract of Meat' and for 'Zoedone' on page 16 (which is folioed). Neither contain pages folioed 13 and 14. Kate and Tom Jackson, of Ilkley, Yorkshire, published a fine facsimile in a limited edition of 200 copies in 1986. This was made from a similar copy, that had been privately bound for protection. All include the full set of general advertisements (omitted from 176.2 and 176.3) as well as the 4-page Chapman & Hall catalogue tipped on to p.98. It is probable that these were late copies (see 176.2, Note 4): the Chapman & Hall catalogue does not appear in Michael Sadleir's or Harland Eastman's copies.

5. Commenting on Edmund Downey's report (*Twenty Years Ago*, p.115) that the new title was forced on the unwilling author by Tinsley, Michael Sadleir adds: 'Presumably he also chose the wrapper-drawing, which is of the C.H. Ross-Stage-Whispers school and unsuited both to Henty and his work.' (*XIX Century Fiction*, I, 1191).

176.2

Title page: Not present: see Notes 2 and 3.

Contents

224 × 142 mm. (1)–(2) Front cover (only) of 176.1 (see Note 3) | (1)–98 | Chapman & Hall catalogue (The Select Library of Fiction) (1)–(4), printed in violet ink (see Note 4), tipped on to p.98. Illustrations as in 176.1.

(1)–(2) Front cover and verso of 176.1, as described under entry for that issue, see Note 3 | (unfolioed frontispiece to 'Surly Joe', tipped in) | (1) Headings (SEASIDE MAIDENS. | By G.A.HENTY. | Being the Summer Number of 'Tinsleys' Magazine.' (*this line in gothic type*). All printed above opening of first story, 'Surly

Joe'. | 2–98. text, with nine more unfolioed, unbacked, illustrations tipped in to face openings of stories. Printer's imprint at foot of p.98 (LONDON | ROBSON AND SONS, PRINTERS, PANCRAS ROAD, N.W.). | (1)–(4) Chapman & Hall catalogue (The Select Library of Fiction), see Note 4.

Binding

Brown, green or orange stipple-grained cloth boards, blocked black, gilt, and blind; edges plain; plain off-white endpapers.

Front board: SEASIDE MAIDENS. (gilt) diagonally. Rules forming frame at edges of board (black). **Spine:** plain. **Back board:** Rules as on front board (blind).

References: SH | *Farmer*, p.65; *Dartt*, p.119; *Sadleir*, I, 1191; but see Note 5.

Notes

1. The existence of copies in cloth boards is mentioned in Editor's announcements in the *Union Jack*, Vol.II, No.43, 21 October 1880, p.48, and Vol.II, No.75, 2 June 1881, p.560. Henty appeared somewhat desperate to increase the circulation of his magazine and offered various prizes to helpful readers. Among other incentives he adds 'To any lad who shall obtain twelve new subscribers [to the *Union Jack*] I will send a copy of my "Seaside Maidens," bound in cloth'. Whether many lads managed to achieve this prize remains undisclosed, but copies were available for the purpose.
2. These copies were produced as books rather than as magazine-issues, without the general advertisements, which in 176.1 appeared preceding the text and on pages (3)–(4) of cover, and were considered inappropriate. Thus the first gathering was omitted, and the book started at page (1) of text, signature mark *b*. The title page had been printed in signature *a*, with advertisements for invalid foods on the verso, and was therefore not included. That seems to have resulted from bad planning, but Tinsley probably felt the headings on p.(1) would suffice: they mention *Tinsleys' Magazine* but not the publisher's address. Both *Farmer* and *Dartt* note that all copies examined by them lacked title pages, *Dartt* remarking 'There apparently was none'.
3. In all known copies of this issue the illustrated front cover of 176.1 was included, in spite of advertisements on its p.(2). The spine and pages (3)–(4) of cover were cut away, and pages (1)–(2) tipped on at the front of the book.
4. The four-page Chapman & Hall catalogue, printed in violet ink and supplied by the advertiser, followed the text in all known copies of this issue: being tipped in it did not affect the make-up. Unlike general advertisements (see Note 2), it was acceptable for inclusion in this cloth-bound 'book', although it is unlikely that Tinsley would have agreed to insert it in his novels, unless by some reciprocal agreement with the rival firm. Chapman & Hall probably contracted for a fixed number of copies to be inserted in monthly issues of *Tinsleys' Magazine*. The consignment reached the bindery in time to catch some late issues of 176.1 (see 176.1, Note 4).
5. Unfortunately the paucity of information given by *Farmer*, *Dartt*, and *Sadleir*, makes it impossible to know whether they saw copies of 176.2 or 176.3.

176.3

Title page: Not present: see 176.2, Note 2.

Contents

212 × 137 mm. (1)–98. Illustrations as in 176.1.

(Unfolioed frontispiece to 'Surly Joe', tipped in) | (1) Headings (SEASIDE MAIDENS. | By G.A.HENTY. | Being the Summer Number of 'Tinsleys' Magazine.' (*this line in gothic type*). All printed above opening of first story, 'Surly Joe'. | 2–98. text, with nine more unfolioed, unbacked, illustrations tipped in to face openings of stories. Printer's imprint at foot of p.98 (LONDON | ROBSON AND SONS, PRINTERS, PANCRAS ROAD, N.W.).

Binding: As for 176.2, but smaller boards, and seen in red cloth.

References: HE | *Farmer*, p.65; *Dartt*, p.119; *Sadleir*, I, 1191; see 176.2, Note 5.

Notes

1. Further cloth-bound copies were produced by modifying and re-binding existing copies of 176.1. The covers were completely removed, as were pp.(1)–12, headed 'Seaside Maidens' Advertiser. The Chapman & Hall catalogue does not appear in any known copy.

2. In removing the 'Seaside Maidens' Advertiser the binding thread had to be cut, and the sheets re-sewn. In rebinding, the gatherings were heavily trimmed by guillotine, thus severely reducing the page size in at least one copy. The margins would thus have been almost lost from the front cover, which would in any case have suffered in being removed from the original Summer Number, to which it was firmly glued. The cover was therefore omitted.

3. I cannot be certain whether the issues numbered 176.2 and 176.3 were actually produced in the given sequence. But it seems to me more likely that Tinsley would first have had copies made up from unused sheets lying in the binder's warehouse, and only later have embarked on the more messy, and more costly, processes outlined in Notes 1 and 2 above.

177. S.P.C.K. LIBRARY OF FICTION

177.1

S.P.C.K. LIBRARY OF FICTION | [Third Series] | SIX COMPLETE STORIES | BY THE FOLLOWING AUTHORS – | GRANT ALLEN G.A.HENTY | GEORGE MANVILLE FENN | MRS. NEWMAN AND JESSIE M.E.SAXBY | (publisher's device) | LONDON: | NORTHUMBERLAND AVENUE, CHARING CROSS, W.C.: | 43, QUEEN VICTORIA STREET, E.C.; 97, WESTBOURNE GROVE, W. | BRIGHTON: 135, NORTH STREET.
(Note: S.P.C.K. is in the form of a logotype; Third Series is in gothic type; there is a printed mark made by a raised space after the em-dash following AUTHORS).

Contents

213 × 138 mm. The upper free endpaper is used as a text leaf and contains the title page and list of Contents (see 'Binding' below). The book consists of six booklets

from the 'S.P.C.K. Penny Library of Fiction', bound together; consequently the pagination starts at (1) for each of the six, as follows: (1)–32. title p. and text of 'Constable A1' by Jessie M.E. Saxby I (1)–32. title p., text and illustrations of 'The Plague Ship' by G.A. Henty I (1)–32. title p. and text of 'Staunch: A Story of Steel' by George Manville Fenn I (1)–31. title p. and text of 'A Living Apparition' by Grant Allen I (32) publisher's advertisement (The Penny Library of Fiction) I (1)–32. title p. and text of 'Brought to Light' by Mrs. Newman I (1)-32. title p. and text of 'The Mutiny of the *Helen Gray*' by George Manville Fenn I (1)–(4) advertisements for Brooke's Soap, printed in black on pages (1) and (4); in red on pages (2) and (3).

Binding (see Plate 138)
Paper boards, cut flush, printed in full colour by photo-lithography; edges plain. Upper free endpaper printed in black on plain off-white paper: title p. on recto; list of Contents on verso. Lower endpapers plain.
    Front board: SIX COMPLETE STORIES. (white out of red background) I 6d. 6d. (white out of red background, at outer corners) all above representations, drawn in line, of the cover illustrations of the six booklets, with floral decorations around them, all on red background. Between the upper three and lower three titles: (S.P.C.K. logotype) LIBRARY OF FICTION (white, out of red, outlined with irregular black lines). At foot: Vol.3 (black); RIDDLE & OVERMAN, LONDON, S.E. (black). **Spine:** 6d (black in oval, white out of red, outlined black) I (publisher's device) (black and blue) I . LIBRARY (black and white) OF (black) FICTION . (black and white) I (publisher's device) (black and blue) I 6d (black in oval, white out of red, outlined black). All running from foot to head. **Back board:** advertisement for Fry's Cocoa in full colour with typematter in black.

Reference: NS; BB.

Notes
1. The sheets of Henty's story are exactly as described for *The Plague Ship* (see §1, 41), and are either left-over sheets from the first printing or a straight reprint. The copy at Edinburgh is catalogued (1896).
2. *The Ranche in the Valley* (§1, 52), may have been bound up in another volume of this series, *S.P.C.K. Library of Fiction*, but, if so, it has not come to light.

178. STEADY & STRONG

178.1
Steady & Strong I STORIES TOLD BY I G.A.Henty I G.Manville Fenn I John Oxenham I Louis Becke I &c. I WITH EIGHT ILLUSTRATIONS BY I W.H.C.Groome I LONDON: 47 Paternoster Row, E.C. I 1905 W.& R.CHAMBERS, Limited I EDINBURGH: 339 High Street

Contents
184 × 131 mm. (i)–(viii) I (1)–404 I catalogue (1)–32. Eight full-page wash-drawings by W.H.C. Groome, reproduced by halftone blocks printed on coated paper, unbacked, keyed to text pages, tipped in.
    (i) Half-title p. I (ii) blank I (frontispiece, tipped in) I (iii) title p. I (iv) printer's

imprint (Edinburgh: Printed by W.& R.Chambers, Limited.) | (v) Contents | (vi) blank | (vii) List of Illustrations | (viii) advertisement (UNIFORM WITH THIS VOLUME.) listing eight titles including this one | (1)–404. text, with printer's imprint at foot of p.404 as on p.(iv) | (1)–32. catalogue.

Binding (see Plate 154)
Red cloth boards, bevelled, blocked black, blue, orange, buff, and gilt; edges plain; brown endpapers, lined off-white.
   Front board: STEADY | AND STRONG (orange cased black) out of solid-gilt panels in scrollwork (black, blue, gilt) | STORIES | TOLD BY (black) above rectangular solid-gilt panel with black rules above and below, overblocked: G.A.HENTY. G.MANVILLE FENN. | JOHN OXENHAM. LOUIS BECKE. | R.E.FRANCILLON. WILLIAM ATKINSON. | &c. &c. (all black). Beneath this is illustration, partly enclosed by black line, of dog jumping at man holding knife, who is falling on stony ground near trees (black, blue, buff). **Spine:** STEADY | AND | STRONG (orange, cased black) out of solid-gilt panel in scroll (black, orange, gilt) | STORIES | TOLD BY (black) above rectangular solid-gilt panel with black rules above and below, overblocked: G.A.HENTY | G.MANVILLE FENN | JOHN OXENHAM | LOUIS BECKE | R.E.FRANCILLON | WILLIAM ATKINSON | &c &c (all black). Beneath this is illustration, partly framed by black and buff lines, of man firing at a figure in a window (black, blue, buff). At foot: W.& R.CHAMBERS (gilt). **Back board:** plain.

References: BL; PN | *Farmer*, p.64; *Dartt*, p.123.

Notes
1. 'In the Hands of Sicilian Brigands' is at pp.(1)–18; 'The Smuggler's Cutter' at pp.19–43; 'Gerald Mayfield's Reward' at pp.44–67; 'A Narrow Escape' at pp.68–87. For all of them see §4.
2. Later impressions were printed with undated title pages.
3. Spines of pictorial cloth bindings are often likely to fade. Red is always vulnerable, as here, but frequently the cloth is not the only victim of the sun: on some copies the orange pigment has retained its colour on the front board but faded almost to yellow on the spine. Less noticeably, perhaps, while the buff blocking is almost pink on the front board, on the spine it may have turned to a yellowish-grey.

179. STIRRING ADVENTURES AFLOAT AND ASHORE

179.1
STIRRING ADVENTURES | AFLOAT AND ASHORE; | INCLUDING | ANTONY WAYMOUTH; | OR, THE GENTLEMEN ADVENTURERS: | BY W.H.G.KINGSTON. | NED BURTON'S ADVENTURE | BY ARTHUR LEE KNIGHT. | FRANK ALLREDDY'S FORTUNE | BY FRANKLIN FOX. | AND NUMEROUS INTERESTING ARTICLES | ON MISCELLANEOUS SUBJECTS. | EDITED BY | G.A.HENTY. | WITH FULL-PAGE AND OTHER ENGRAVINGS | WARD, LOCK, BOWDEN AND CO., | LONDON, NEW YORK, MELBOURNE, AND SYDNEY. | (21-point rule) | [All rights reserved.]

Contents

212 x 137 mm. (i)–(iv) | C1–C512 | no catalogue. Eight full-page illustrations from line-drawings, and wash-drawings by W.S. Stacey, reproduced by line blocks and halftone blocks, printed on MF paper, unbacked, tipped in. Numerous smaller drawings and engravings reproduced by line blocks and printed on text pages.

(Frontispiece, tipped in) | (i) title p. | (ii) blank | (iii)–iv. Contents | C1–C512. text and illustrations.

Binding (see Plate 169)

Brown cloth boards, blocked black, red, blue merging to yellowish-buff, and gilt; edges plain; poor-quality yellow surface-paper endpapers.

Front board: BEETON'S . BOY'S OWN BOOKS | (ornament) Edited by G.A.HENTY (ornament) (all black) within rectangular panel (red) framed by double rules with decorations at each end (black) above: STIRRING ADVENTURES | AFLOAT and | ASHORE (gilt). Beneath this, two overlapping illustrations, both partly framed by decorative black rules, of man riding through canyon (black, blue merging to yellowish-buff), and native warrior being shot by white sailor (black, yellowish-buff). At foot: PROFUSELY ILLUSTRATED (black). **Spine:** . BEETON'S . | BOY'S OWN BOOKS (black) within rectangular panel (red) framed by double rules with decorations on all four sides (black) above: STIRRING | ADVENTURES | AFLOAT (underlined) | AND | ASHORE (underlined) (all gilt). Beneath this is illustration of two castaways with barrel, one waving, one holding head in hands (black, yellowish-buff), above: EDITED | BY (black) | G.A. HENTY (black on solid-gilt rectangle) framed by double rules, decorated (black). At foot: WARD, LOCK & BOWDEN LTD. (gilt). **Back board:** plain.

References: PN | *Farmer*, p.63; *Dartt*, p.124, *Companion*, p.27.

Notes

1. The sixth volume in the series of 'Beeton's Boy's Own Books' (§2, 127) consisting of material published in *Beeton's Boy's Own Magazine*, §3, 197, under Henty's editorship.

2. This is one of only three books in the series that contain work written by Henty. Under the heading 'The Editor's Table' he wrote for the magazine a series of essays, ten of which re-appear in this volume. There is one more, the first to have appeared, in another Volume, *Stories of Peril and Adventure* (§2, 186). The articles deal with a wide range of subjects including Behaviour, and Life, but not much reminiscence. Directed very much at Henty's 'Dear Lads', they perhaps tell us more about himself than anything else. Their subjects were summarised by *Dartt* (p.124) as follows: 'Grumbling', at pp.75–76; 'How to Spend Holidays at Home', at pp.124–125; 'Tale-bearing', at pp.156–157; 'The Disadvantages of being a Clerk', at pp.203–204; 'What to Read', at pp.252–253; 'Summertime' at pp.284–285; 'Strikes', at pp.332–333; 'Don't be Selfish during Holidays', at pp.379–380; 'Disadvantages of being an African Explorer', at pp.412–413; and 'Keep your Minds Open', at pp.459–460.

3. The final article in this series, 'The Editor's Table', was in Henty's last issue of the magazine. The list of Contents shows it as on p.507 of this book, but in fact it was replaced by the first of a number of 'Puzzle Pages'. It had been Henty's personal farewell to his readership, and so had no place in the book: 'I find the conduct of the

Magazine demands more time than with my other work, I can devote to it. I have resigned my Editorial chair and the next volume ... will be edited by other hands'. Henty's private view of the situation was more succinctly expressed in a letter to a friend (see *Beeton's Boy's Own Magazine*, §3, 197).

4. *Dartt* carelessly misquotes *Farmer*, who, he says 'stated that this volume did not have the characteristic red panel at top of cover', asserting that his own copy did have it. What *Farmer* in fact wrote was, 'It does not contain the words Beeton's Boy's Own Books, as do the earlier volumes in this series'. The publisher changed the wording on the red panels for later issues of the books in the series, cutting out references to Beeton: see *Beeton's Boy's Own Books*, §2, 127, Note 9, et seq.

180. STIRRING TALES

180.1

STIRRING TALES | Edited by Herbert Strang | (illustration of kilted Scottish soldier with shield and drawn sword in battle scene) | London: | Henry Frowde and Hodder & Stoughton
(Note: The title, printed in green, cased black, and the second line, black, are in a panel with the illustration, black and green, the whole being within another illustrated panel, black and green, containing the publisher's imprint).

Contents
222 × 172 mm. Unfolioed book, consisting of 4 pages printed black and green, plus six sections each of 16 pages, signatures N to S inclusive, printed black. Four full-page plates from watercolour drawings by various artists, reproduced by three-colour halftone blocks printed on coated paper, unbacked, tipped in. Twenty-three black-and-white illustrations from line drawings by various artists, printed in black on text pages. No catalogue.

(i) Blank | (ii) full-page illustrated bookplate with panel for owner's name (black and green) | (frontispiece, tipped in) | (iii) title p. | (iv) 'Some of the pieces in this collection appeared | first in my Annual. | H.S.' At foot, below rule, printer's imprint (Richard Clay & Sons, Limited, London and Bungay.). | (1)–(96) text.

Binding
Quarter-bound red cloth, blocked black; paper boards printed red and light-brown, with colour-plate laid down; edges plain; upper endpapers formed by first leaf of text paper, pasted down to board; lower endpapers plain off-white wove.
 Front board: Stirring Tales (white, stippled light-brown) | Edited by Herbert Strang (light-brown) all out of red panel framed by white line within red decorative framework, containing laid-down colour plate (which also appears as the second colour-plate in the book). **Spine:** Stirring Tales (black) on red cloth, running from foot to head. **Back board:** Wash-drawing representing decorative panel in bas-relief with fleurs-de-lys and floral motifs, all printed in red and light-brown halftone.

References: Bod | *Dartt*, p.125.

Notes
1. The book consists of unfolioed gatherings originally forming part of *The Green*

Book for Boys (§2, 156) which were later re-issued as part of a shorter book, *By Land and Sea* (§2, 137). Both are at Plate 147. The colour plates also appeared in the earlier books: only one of them in this title is legibly signed, by Arch Webb. *Stirring Tales* was received by the Bodleian Library in 1912.

2. Pages (1)–(27) contain the text and line-illustrations of Henty's 'Through the Enemy Lines', a condensed extract from *The Young Franc-Tireurs* (§1, 5), edited by Herbert Strang. The five illustrations are by T.C. Dugdale (see Appendix IV, Part 2).

181. STORIES FOR MERRY HEARTS

181.1
STORIES I FOR I MERRY I HEARTS (at right of illustration of boy and girl in wicker armchair, fairy with wand standing behind; kitten with ball of wool on floor) I ERNEST . NISTER . LONDON . (space) . E.P.DUTTON & CO. NEW YORK . I 10. (at left) No.4205 (at centre).

Contents
246 × 199 mm. (1)–(88) I no catalogue. Frontispiece illustration of two small girls in garden, in sun-hat and sun-bonnet, the younger washing puppy in bucket, the other with rake and watering-can, unsigned, printed in 4-colour lithography and tipped on to text page printed with black rule surround. Numerous black-and-white illustrations by various artists in line and tone throughout text.

(1) Illustrated half-title p. I (2) frontispiece I (3) title p. I (4) vignette line-drawing I (5)–(88) text and illustrations, imprint on p.88 (Printed in Bavaria).

Binding
Quarter-bound maroon paper, paper boards, upper board only printed in full colour; edges plain; plain off-white endpapers.

Front board: Printed full colour, white margins all edges; "Merry Hearts" Series (black) at top right corner of dark red background area I STORIES (reversed white out of dark red, cased and shaded maroon, the initial letter larger and decorated with green tracery; similar green tracery as rectangular decoration at end of line I FOR MERRY HEARTS (reversed out white, cased and shaded maroon). All above illustration, framed black and orange, of little girl kneeling on chair overlooking kitten and spilled milk-jug on table. In red margin, at lower left corner, publisher's trade mark, above: 10. (all black). Below picture: ERNEST . NISTER: LONDON . (space) No. 4205 (space) E.P.DUTTON & Co. NEW YORK. (all black). **Spine:** plain. **Back board:** Plain unprinted, pinkish-buff, matt paper.

References: BG I *Dartt*, p.178

Notes
1. A collection of stories and verses. Henty's 'In Troubled Times' (see §4) is at pp.18–39, with eight pen-drawings by E.S.Hardy; it appears also in 162.1 and 171.1.
2. The scarcest of the Nister publications that include Henty's work. No copies were deposited with the Copyright Libraries: the only copy I have been able to find in this country is in the Renier Collection at Bethnal Green Museum of Childhood. The Curator, Tessa Chester, kindly allowed me to examine it before the Collection was available to the public.

182. STORIES JOLLY: STORIES NEW: STORIES STRANGE & STORIES TRUE

182.1

Stories Jolly: Stories New: | Stories Strange & Stories True. | A SERIES OF NEW AND ORIGINAL TALES | FOR BOYS AND GIRLS | FROM SIX TO FOURTEEN YEARS OLD. | BY | (list of authors follows in two columns with vertical rule between, the final name centred beneath the rule) H.C.ADAMS. | R.M.BALLANTYNE. | S.BARING-GOULD. | FANNY BARRY. | FRANCES CLARE. | ALICE CORKRAN. | G.MANVILLE FENN. | AGNES GIBERNE. | MRS. A.M.GOODHART. | G.A.HENTY. | KATHARINE S.MACQUOID. | MRS. MOLESWORTH. | HELEN WILMOT-BUXTON. | EMMA WOOD. | CHARLOTTE M.YONGE. | London: | SKEFFINGTON & SON, 163, PICCADILLY, W. | (8-point rule) | 1889.
(*Note: The title, and* London:, *are in gothic type*).

Contents
187 x 140 mm. (i)–viii | (1)–(268) | no catalogue. Frontispiece and four full-page plates from wood-engravings and pen-drawings, the frontispiece signed by Palmer Cox, all reproduced by line blocks printed in black on MF paper, unbacked, unfolioed, tipped in. Two smaller illustrations reproduced by line blocks on text pages. Numerous small engraved head and tail pieces from standard electros.

   (i) Half-title p. | (ii) blank | (frontispiece, tipped in) | (iii) title p. | (iv) blank | (v) Preface | (vi) blank | (vii)–viii. Contents | (1)–265. text | (266)–(268) advertisement (Gift Books for Children) listing seven titles.

Binding (see Plate 150)
Light-blue cloth boards, bevelled, blocked black, green, yellow, and gilt; all edges stained yellow; grey flowered endpapers.
   Front board: STORIES JOLLY, | STORIES NEW, | STORIES STRANGE | & STORIES TRUE. (all black) framed by black line at centre of illustration of bunch of primroses and grass (black, green, yellow). **Spine:** STORIES JOLLY | STORIES NEW | STORIES STRANGE | AND | STORIES TRUE (gilt); H.C.ADAMS | R.M.BALLANTYNE | ALICE CORKRAN | G.M.FENN | AGNES GIBERNE | BARING-GOULD | G.A.HENTY | MRS. MACQUOID | MRS. MOLESWORTH | C.M.YONGE | ETC. | SKEFFINGTONS (all black). **Back board:** landscape vignette at centre (black).

References: PN | *Farmer*, p.64; *Dartt*, p.125.

Notes
1. 'True to her Charge' appears at pp.(45)–57, unillustrated (see §4).
2. *Dartt's* report, p.126, that the Preface precedes the title page, refers only to a binding fault in one copy.

183. STORIES OF ADVENTURE AND HEROISM

183.1

STORIES | OF | ADVENTURE AND HEROISM. | COMPRISING: | ROBINSON CRUSOE, | BY DANIEL DEFOE: | SILAS HORNER'S ADVENTURES, | BY JAMES GREENWOOD; | AND | BRAVE BRITISH SOLDIERS | AND THE | VICTORIA CROSS. | (6-em rule) | With full-page Plates and about 120 Engravings in the Text. | (6-em rule) | WARD, LOCK AND CO., | LONDON, NEW YORK, AND MELBOURNE.
(Note: The line detailing the illustrations is in gothic type).

Contents

208 × 136 mm. (i)–(ii) | (i)–(ii) | (xii)–(xxxii) | (1)–384 | (i)–(ii) | (1)–346 | (i)–(ii) | (1)–(384) | no catalogue. Six full-page plates from wood-engravings by various artists, printed in black on ivory MF paper, unbacked, unfolioed, tipped in. Numerous smaller engravings printed on text pages.

(i) Half-title p. | (ii) blank | (frontispiece, illustrating 'Crusoe and his Goat', tipped in) | (i) half-title to 'The Adventures of Robinson Crusoe' | (ii) blank | (xiii)–xxxi. Memoir of Daniel Defoe | (xxxii) blank | (1)–384. text and illustrations of 'The Adventures of Robinson Crusoe' | (i) half-title to 'Silas Horner's Adventures' | (ii) blank | (1)–346. text and illustrations of 'Silas Horner's Adventures' | (i) half-title to 'Brave British Soldiers and the Victoria Cross' | (ii) blank | (frontispiece, tipped in) | (1)–383. text and illustrations of 'Brave British Soldiers and the Victoria Cross' | (384) blank.

Binding

Brown cloth boards, blocked black, red, blue merging to warm buff, and gilt; edges plain; yellow surface-paper endpapers.
Front board: BEETON'S . BOY'S OWN BOOKS (black) within rectangular panel (red) framed by double rules with decorations at each end (black), above: STORIES of | ADVENTURE | AND | HEROISM (gilt). Beneath this is illustration, partly framed by decorative rules (black and blue) of man riding through canyon (black, blue merging to warm buff) overlapped by panel, partly framed by black decorative rules, with: Containing | ROBINSON CRUSOE. | By Daniel Defoe. | (ornamental rule) | SILAS HORNER'S ADVENTURES. | By James Greenwood. | (ornamental rule) | AND | BRAVE BRITISH SOLDIERS | AND THE VICTORIA CROSS. | (ornamental rule) | COMPRISING 1100 PAGES AND 120 ILLUSTRATIONS. (all black). **Spine:** . BEETON'S . | BOY'S OWN BOOKS (black) within rectangular panel (red) framed by double rules with decorations on all four sides (black), above: STORIES of | ADVENTURE | AND | Heroism (gilt). Beneath this is illustration of boy lookout at top of mast, waving (black, warm buff), above: ILLUSTRATED (cloth-colour out of solid-gilt rectangle) framed by double rules, decorated (black). At foot: WARD . LOCK & CO (gilt). **Back board:** plain.

References: PN | Cargill Thompson, *The Boys' Dumas*, p.11.

Notes

1. This, the seventh volume in the series of 'Beeton's Boy's Own Books', contains material from three books originally published by S.O.Beeton many years earlier, in which the rights were acquired by Ward Lock. The first six volumes in the series consisted of material, also acquired from Beeton, that had been published by Ward Lock in *Beeton's Boy's Own Magazine* (§3, 197), edited by Henty. This volume, however, contains nothing by Henty, nor was any part of it edited by him.

2. Nevertheless, a later issue was published with the words 'Edited by G.A.HENTY' erroneously blocked on the front board (see 183.2 below). As might be expected, that has led to many misunderstandings. While the relevant volumes are listed and described here, I have made an attempt under the heading 'Beeton's Boy's Own Books' (§2, 127) to explain, with particular reference to Cargill Thompson's comments (*The Boys' Dumas*, p.11), what I think probably happened.

3. The strange make-up of this volume, with its apparently eccentric page-numbering, is also explained in the Notes under 'Beeton's Boy's Own Books'. The running headlines, on recto pages of the second and third books in this volume, differ from the titles now given to the books on their half-title pages, and on the title page of the volume. That shows that their original titles, when published by S.O. Beeton, were *Silas the Conjurer*, and *Our Soldiers and the Victoria Cross* respectively.

4. This entry describes the first issue of the book, before the publisher decided to drop all reference to the name of Beeton.

183.2

STORIES OF | ADVENTURE AND HEROISM. | COMPRISING | ROBINSON CRUSOE, | BY DANIEL DEFOE. | SILAS HORNER'S ADVENTURES, | BY JAMES GREENWOOD. | AND | WILD SPORTS OF THE WORLD. | With Full-page Plates and about 120 Engravings in the Text. | LONDON: | WARD, LOCK & CO., LIMITED, | WARWICK HOUSE, SALISBURY SQUARE, E.C., | NEW YORK AND MELBOURNE.
(Note: the line detailing the illustrations is in gothic type).

Contents

200 x 131 mm. (i)–(ii) | (i)–(xxxii) | (1)–384 | (i)–(ii) | (v)–viii | (1)–346 | (iii)–xxii | 1–426 | no catalogue. Frontispiece from line drawing by unknown artist printed in black on coated paper, unbacked, tipped in. Numerous smaller engravings printed on text pages.

(i) Half-title p. | (ii) blank | (frontispiece, illustrating 'A Religious Conversation', tipped in) | (i) title p. | (ii) blank | (iii) half-title to 'The Adventures of Robinson Crusoe' | (iv) blank | (v)–x. Contents of 'Robinson Crusoe' | (xi) Index to Woodcuts | (xii) blank | (xiii)–xxxi. Memoir of Daniel Defoe | (xxxii) blank | (1)–384. text and illustrations of 'The Adventures of Robinson Crusoe' | (i) half-title to 'Silas Horner's Adventures | (ii) blank | (v)–viii. Contents | (1)–346. text and illustrations of 'Silas Horner's Adventures' | (i) half-title to 'Wild Sports of the World' | (ii) blank | (v)–viii. Preface | (ix)–xvii. Analysis of Contents | (xviii) List of Portraits | (xix)–xxii. List of Wood-Cuts | 1–426. text and illustrations of 'Wild Sports of the World'.

Binding

Blue cloth boards, blocked black, red, darker red, blue merging to white, warm buff, and gilt; edges plain; yellow surface-paper endpapers.

Front board: (ornament) Edited by G.A.HENTY (ornament) (black) within rectangular panel (red) framed by double rules with decorations at each end (black), above: STORIES of | ADVENTURE | AND | HEROISM (darker red). Beneath this is illustration, partly framed by decorative rules (black and blue) of man riding through canyon (black, blue merging to white, warm buff) overlapped by panel, partly framed by black decorative rules, with: Containing | ROBINSON CRUSOE, | By Daniel Defoe. | (ornamental rule) | SILAS HORNER'S ADVENTURES, | By James Greenwood. | (ornamental rule) | WILD SPORTS OF THE WORLD. | (ornamental rule) | WITH ILLUSTRATIONS. (all black). **Spine:** Illustrated. (black) within rectangular panel (red), framed by double rules with decorations at each end (black), above: STORIES of | ADVENTURE | AND | Heroism (gilt). Beneath this is illustration of boy lookout at top of mast, waving (black, warm buff). At foot: WARD . LOCK . & . Co (gilt). **Back board:** plain.

References: PN | *Dartt*, p.126, *Companion*, p.27; Cargill Thompson, *The Boys' Dumas*, p.11.

Notes

1. The entries for 183.1 and 183.2 show that Ward Lock produced the series in a very muddled and confusing way. In the two issues there are many small discrepancies between treatments of the contents that are common to both. In 183.1 there are two full-page plates to illustrate 'Robinson Crusoe'; in 183.2 there are none. The frontispiece in 183.2 appears to have no relevance to this volume at all. Of the original prelims for 'Robinson Crusoe', pp.(v)–(xxxii) are in 183.2, but only pp.(xiii)–(xxxii) in 183.1. Similarly there are in 183.2 four pages of the original prelims from 'Silas Horner', but none in 183.1.

2. This issue is the one that has caused most confusion, having Henty's name, as Editor, blocked on the front board. For an explanation see the Notes under 'Beeton's Boy's Own Books' (§2, 127). To complete the history of this seventh volume in the series, it is necessary to give an entry for the book in its final form, as described in those Notes, with its new title, *Forest, Field and Flood*: see 183.3 below.

183.3

FOREST, FIELD AND FLOOD | BEING | Stories of Adventures | IN | SPORT, TRAVEL AND WAR. | (1cm. rule) | Illustrated. | (1cm. rule) | LONDON: | WARD, LOCK & BOWDEN, LIMITED, | WARWICK HOUSE, SALISBURY SQUARE, E.C. | NEW YORK AND MELBOURNE.
(Note: Illustrated. *is in gothic type).*

Contents

205 × 135 mm. (i)–(ii) | (i)–xxii | 1–426 | (i)–(ii) | (vii)–viii | (1)–(384) | (i)–(ii) | (v)–(xxxii) | (1)–384 | no catalogue. Six full-page plates printed by colour-lithography on off-white cartridge paper; six full-page wood engravings printed in black on ivory MF paper; all unbacked, unfolioed, tipped in. Numerous smaller engravings printed in black on text pages.

(Frontispiece, tipped in) | (i) title p. | (ii) blank | (i) Contents | (ii) blank | (iii) half-title to 'Wild Sports of the World' | (iv) small vignette engraving of hare | (v)–viii. Preface | (ix)–xvii. Analysis of Contents | (xviii) List of Portraits | (xix)–xxii. List of Wood-Cuts | 1–426. text and illustrations of 'Wild Sports of the World' | (i) half-title to 'Brave British Soldiers and the Victoria Cross' | (ii) blank |

(frontispiece, tipped in) | (vii)–viii. Contents | (1)–383. text and illustrations of 'Brave British Soldiers and the Victoria Cross' | (384) blank | (i) half-title to 'Robinson Crusoe' | (ii) blank | (v)–x. Contents | (xi)–(xii) Index to Woodcuts | (xiii)-xxxi. Memoir of Daniel Defoe | (xxxii) blank | (1)–384. text and illustrations of 'Robinson Crusoe', with printer's imprint at foot of p.384 (Butler & Tanner, The Selwood Printing Works, Frome, and London.).

Binding
Dark-blue, vertically-grained boards, bevelled, blocked gilt; all edges gilt; plain off-white endpapers.
    Front board: small vignette illustration of man on horseback about to lasso a bull (gilt). **Spine:** FOREST | FIELD | AND | FLOOD | (ornamental cross) (all gilt) above illustration, framed by rules, of sailing ship at sea (gilt). **Back board:** plain.

References: PN | Cargill Thompson, *The Boys' Dumas*, p.12.

Notes
1. This is the final presentation of material that was first issued by Ward Lock under the title *Stories of Adventure and Heroism*. For an explanation of the inclusion here of a book in which Henty had no part, see the Notes under 'Beeton's Boy's Own Books', §2, 127.
2. Four of the lithographed colour plates appear in *Wild Sports of the World*, and the other two illustrate *The Adventures of Robinson Crusoe*. As they had not appeared in earlier issues it seems probable they were commissioned for this edition.
3. The printer's imprint on the final page of 'Robinson Crusoe' shows that this part of the volume was reprinted. No imprint appears on the page in earlier issues.

184. STORIES OF BRAVE BOYS AND GALLANT HEROES

184.1
STORIES OF BRAVE BOYS | AND GALLANT HEROES | INCLUDING | NEVER SAY DIE | BY CECIL MARRYAT NORRIS. | RUNNYMEDE AND LINCOLN FAIR | BY JOHN G.EDGAR. | DICKY BEAUMONT'S PERILS AND ADVENTURES | BY ARTHUR LEE KNIGHT. | AND | STORIES OF GLORIOUS ACHIEVEMENTS | IN ENGLAND'S ARMY AND NAVY. | ETC., ETC. | EDITED BY | G.A.HENTY. | WITH FULL-PAGE AND OTHER ENGRAVINGS. | WARD, LOCK AND CO., | LONDON, NEW YORK, AND MELBOURNE. | (15-point rule) | (All rights reserved.)

Contents
210 x 138 mm. (i)–iv | A1–A512 | no catalogue. Frontispiece and twenty full-page plates from line-drawings and wash-drawings by various artists, reproduced by line blocks and halftone blocks, printed in black on ivory MF paper, unbacked, unfolioed, tipped in. Smaller illustrations printed by line blocks on text pages.
    (Frontispiece, tipped in) | (i) title p. | (ii) blank | (iii)–iv. Contents | A1–A512. text and illustrations.

Binding (see Plate 169)
Light-brown cloth boards, blocked black, red, blue merging to pinkish-buff, and gilt; edges plain; yellow surface-paper endpapers.

Front board: BEETON'S . BOY'S OWN BOOKS | (ornament) Edited by G.A.HENTY (ornament) (all black) within rectangular panel (red) framed by double rules with decorations at each end (black) above: STORIES of | BRAVE . LADS | AND | Gallant | Heroes (gilt). Beneath this, two overlapping illustrations, both partly framed by decorative black rules, of man riding through canyon (black, blue merging to pinkish-buff), and boy with stave fighting Indian with knife on small boat, another Indian in water (black, pinkish-buff). At foot: PROFUSELY ILLUSTRATED (black). **Spine:** . BEETON'S . | BOY'S OWN BOOKS (black) within rectangular panel (red) framed by double rules with decorations on all four sides (black) above: STORIES of | BRAVE LADS | AND | Gallant | Heroes (gilt). Beneath this is illustration of two boys climbing crags at edge of sea (black, pinkish-buff), above: EDITED | BY (black) | G.A.HENTY (black on solid-gilt rectangle) framed by double rules, decorated (black). At foot: WARD . LOCK & CO. (gilt). **Back board:** plain.

References: PN | *Dartt*, p.127.

Notes

1. This, the fourth volume in the series of 'Beeton's Boy's Own Books' (§2, 127), re-using material from *Beeton's Boy's Own Magazine* (§3, 197), edited by Henty, contains nothing written by Henty himself.

2. The title of the book is incorrectly given on both the front board and the spine of the binding case, the word 'Lads' being substituted for 'Boys'.

3. The publisher's imprint was amended in reprints; the date was shown on the title page in the first printing only. The picture used as frontispiece varied.

185. STORIES OF HISTORY

185.1

STORIES OF HISTORY | CONTAINING | CRESSY AND POICTIERS | BY JOHN G.EDGAR. | THE SEIGE AND RELIEF OF GIBRALTAR; | OUR SOLDIERS AND THE VICTORIA CROSS, &c. | WITH | STUDIES OF THE ANIMAL AND PLANT WORLD | BY THE REV. J.G.WOOD. | AND OTHER INTERESTING ARTICLES. | EDITED BY | G.A.HENTY. | WITH FULL-PAGE AND OTHER ENGRAVINGS. | WARD, LOCK, BOWDEN, & CO., | LONDON, NEW YORK, AND MELBOURNE. | 1891 | (All rights reserved.)
(Note: The word SIEGE, in the fifth line, is spelt incorrectly).

Contents

214 × 139 mm. (i)–iv | B1–B512 | no catalogue. Frontispiece and nine full-page plates from wash-drawings by W.S.Stacey and wood-engravings, reproduced by halftone blocks and line blocks printed in black on ivory MF paper, unbacked, unfolioed, tipped in. Numerous smaller illustrations printed from line blocks on text pages.

(Frontispiece, tipped in) | (i) title p. | (ii) advertisement (UNIFORM WITH THIS VOLUME.) listing two other books in the series | (iii)–iv. Contents | B1–B512. text and illustrations.

Binding (see Plate 168)

Yellow-green cloth boards, blocked black, red, blue merging to pinkish-buff, and gilt; edges plain; poor quality yellow surface-paper endpapers.

Front board: BEETON'S . BOY'S OWN BOOKS | (ornament) Edited by G.A.HENTY (ornament) (all black) within rectangular panel (red) framed by double rules with decorations at each end (black) above: STORIES | of HISTORY (gilt). Beneath this, two overlapping illustrations, both partly framed by decorative black rules, of man riding through canyon (black, blue merging to pinkish-buff), and two men in armour fighting, one with broken sword (black, pinkish-buff). At foot: PROFUSELY ILLUSTRATED (black). **Spine:** . BEETON'S . | BOY'S OWN BOOKS (black) within rectangular panel (red) framed by double rules with decorations on all four sides (black) above: STORIES | of | HISTORY (gilt). Beneath this is illustration of courtier kneeling and adjusting dress of Elizabethan lady (black, pinkish-buff), above: EDITED | BY (black) G.A.HENTY (black on solid-gilt rectangle) framed by double rules, decorated (black). At foot: WARD . LOCK & BOWDEN LTD (gilt). **Back board:** plain.

References: PN | *Dartt*, p.127, *Companion*, p.27.

Notes

1. This, the second volume of 'Beeton's Boy's Own Books' (§2, 127), re-using material from *Beeton's Boy's Own Magazine* (§3, 197) edited by Henty, contains 'White-Faced Dick' (see §4) at pp.B20–B27, with an anonymous wood-engraving.

2. The spelling mistake on the title page was repeated in subsequent reprints.

3. Reprints included up-dating of the publisher's imprint, omission of the title-page date, and addition of later titles on p.(ii). The frontispiece picture varied.

186. STORIES OF PERIL AND ADVENTURE

186.1

STORIES OF | PERIL AND ADVENTURE | CONTAINING | THE BLACK MAN'S GHOST | BY JOHN C.HUTCHESON. | THE ADVENTURES OF REUBEN DAVIDGER | BY JAMES GREENWOOD. | AND | NUMEROUS INTERESTING AND USEFUL ARTICLES: | HISTORICAL AND BIOGRAPHICAL, SCIENTIFIC AND | MISCELLANEOUS. | EDITED BY | G.A.HENTY. | WITH FULL-PAGE AND OTHER ILLUSTRATIONS. | WARD, LOCK, BOWDEN, & CO., | LONDON, NEW YORK, AND MELBOURNE. | 1891 | (All rights reserved.)

Contents

208 × 135 mm. (i)–iv | C1–C512 | no catalogue. Seven full-page wash-drawings by W.S.Stacey, reproduced by halftone blocks; wood engravings and pen-drawings reproduced by line blocks; printed on MF paper, unbacked, unfolioed, tipped in.

(Frontispiece, tipped in) | (i) title p. | (ii) advertisement (UNIFORM WITH THIS VOLUME.) listing two titles in the series | (iii)–iv. Contents | C1–C512. text and illustrations.

Binding (see Plate 168)
Yellow-ochre cloth boards, blocked black, red, blue merging to brown, and gilt; edges plain; yellow surface-paper endpapers.

Front board: BEETON'S . BOY'S OWN BOOKS | (ornament) Edited by G.A.HENTY (ornament) (all black) within rectangular panel (red) framed by double rules with decorations at each end (black), above: STORIES of PERIL | AND ADVENTURE (gilt). Beneath this, two overlapping illustrations, both partly framed by decorative black rules, of man riding through canyon (black, blue merging to brown), and man wrestling with bear, and about to strike it with dagger (black, brown). At foot: PROFUSELY ILLUSTRATED (black). **Spine:** . BEETON'S . | BOY'S OWN BOOKS (black) within rectangular panel (red) framed by double rules with decorations on all four sides (black), above: STORIES | of | PERIL | AND | ADVENTURE (gilt). Beneath this is illustration of man shooting snake (black, brown), above: EDITED | BY (black) | G.A.HENTY (black on solid-gilt rectangle) framed by double rules, decorated (black). At foot: WARD . LOCK & CO (gilt). **Back board:** plain.

References: PN | *Dartt*, p.128, *Companion*, p.27.

Notes
1. This is the third volume in the series of 'Beeton's Boy's Own Books' (§2, 127), re-using material from *Beeton's Boy's Own Magazine* (§3, 197), edited by Henty.
2. As a result of the special system of pagination in the magazine, explained at §3, 197, Henty's Editorials ended up in odd places in the books. This volume contains the Editorial that appeared in the first issue of the magazine, at page C47.

187. STORIES OF SEA AND LAND

187.1
STORIES OF SEA AND LAND | INCLUDING | THE MIDS OF THE RATTLESNAKE | BY ARTHUR LEE KNIGHT. | THE YOUNG NORSEMAN | BY WILLIAM BRIGHTY RANDS. | WITH | VARIOUS NARRATIVES OF HEROIC DEEDS & ACHIEVEMENTS, | AND INTERESTING TALES AND ARTICLES ON | MISCELLANEOUS SUBJECTS. | EDITED BY | G.A.HENTY. | WITH FULL-PAGE AND OTHER ENGRAVINGS. | WARD, LOCK AND CO., | LONDON, NEW YORK, AND MELBOURNE. | (15-point rule) | (All rights reserved.)

Contents
209 x 137 mm. (i)–iv | A1–A512 | catalogue (1)–(4). Frontispiece and twelve full-page plates from wash-drawings by W.S. Stacey and wood-engravings, reproduced by halftone blocks and line plates, printed in black on ivory MF paper, unbacked, unfolioed, tipped in. Numerous smaller illustrations from line blocks on text pages.

(Frontispiece, tipped in) | (i) title p. | (ii) advertisement (UNIFORM WITH THIS VOLUME.) listing two other titles in the series | (iii)–iv. Contents | (full-page plate, tipped in) | A1–A512. text | (1)–(4) catalogue, dated November 1889.

Binding (see Plate 168)
Red cloth boards, blocked black, red, blue merging to pinkish-buff, and gilt; edges
plain; yellow surface-paper endpapers.
Front board: BEETON'S . BOY'S OWN BOOKS | (ornament) Edited by
G.A.HENTY (ornament) (all black) within rectangular panel (red) framed by double
rules with decorations at each end (black) above: STORIES of | SEA AND LAND
(gilt). Beneath this, two overlapping illustrations, both partly framed by decorative
black rules, of man riding through canyon (black, blue merging to pinkish-buff), and
boy with books, reading on rocky seashore, with sailing boat in setting sun behind
(black, pinkish-buff). At foot: PROFUSELY ILLUSTRATED (black). **Spine:** .
BEETON'S . | BOY'S OWN BOOKS (black) within rectangular panel (red) framed
by double rules with decorations on all four sides (black) above: STORIES | of |
SEA | AND | LAND (gilt). Beneath this is illustration of boy look-out at top of mast,
waving (black, pinkish-buff), above: EDITED | BY (black) | G.A.HENTY (black on
solid-gilt rectangle) framed by double rules, decorated (black). At foot: WARD .
LOCK & CO (gilt). **Back board:** plain.

References: PN | *Dartt*, p.129, *Companion*, p.27.

Notes
1. This, the first volume in the series of 'Beeton's Boy's Own Books' (§2. 127), re-
using material from *Beeton's Boy's Own Magazine* (§3, 197) edited by Henty,
contains nothing written by Henty himself.
2. Reprints included up-dating of the publisher's imprint, and of the list of titles on
p.(ii). The date was shown on the title page of the first printing only.
3. It is clear from my copy of the book that it was made up from disbound copies of
the magazine. An impression of the magazine front cover, showing matter printed on
both sides of the paper, has 'photographed' through very distinctly to the recto of the
plate following p.iv.
4. I have a second copy of this title, with the imprint on the title page updated to
'WARD, LOCK & BOWDEN, LIMITED, | LONDON, NEW YORK, AND
MELBOURNE.'. The binding case varies in some details: (a) the title on the front
board is blocked in red instead of gilt; (b) all reference to Beeton has been removed;
the red panel at the head of the front board now reads simply: 'Edited by
G.A.Henty'; the red panel at the head of the spine reads: 'Illustrated.'; and the
brasses used for 'EDITED | BY | G.A.HENTY', blocked in black and gilt on the
spine, have been removed. For an explanation of all those changes, see 'Beeton's
Boy's Own Books', §2, 127, Note 9 et seq.; (c) the blue pigment used for blocking
the front board merges to white, the buff being a totally separate working; (d) the
publisher's imprint at the foot of the spine is blocked from a brass of a slightly
different design: 'WARD . LOCK . & . Co'. This copy has an inscription dated
Easter 1900.

188. STUDY AND STIMULANTS

188.1

STUDY AND STIMULANTS; | OR, | THE USE OF INTOXICANTS AND NARCOTICS | IN RELATION TO INTELLECTUAL LIFE, | AS ILLUSTRATED BY PERSONAL COMMUNICATION ON THE SUBJECT, | FROM MEN OF LETTERS AND OF SCIENCE. | EDITED BY | A.ARTHUR READE. | (14mm. rule) | MANCHESTER: | ABEL HEYWOOD AND SON, 56 AND 58, OLDHAM STREET. | LONDON: | SIMPKIN, MARSHALL AND CO. | 1883. | (8mm. rule) | [The right of translation is reserved.]

Contents

185 x 124 mm. (1)–(4) | (i)–(viii) | (9)–(208) | catalogue (1)–20. No illustrations.

(1) Half-title p. | (2) blank | (3) title p. | (4) blank | (i)–iii. Introduction | (iv) blank | (v)–vii. Contents | (viii) blank | (1)–201. text | (202) blank | (203)–206. Index | (207) printer's imprint (PRINTERS, | ABEL HEYWOOD AND SON, | MANCHESTER.) | (208) blank | (1)–20. catalogue.

Binding (see Plate 29)

Brown cloth boards, with fine diagonal ribbing, blocked blind and gilt; edges plain; off-white endpapers, printed with small overall grey pattern.

Front board: Three plain rules across top of board (blind). At centre: device in diamond frame with corners broached, consisting of heads of wheat, bunches of grapes and vine leaves. Three plain rules and one decorative rule across lower part of board. (all black). **Spine:** Two black rules and one gilt rule at head. STUDY | AND | STIMULANTS | (8mm. rule) | A.A.READE. | (trophy wih decorative leaves) | A.HEYWOOD | & SON. (all gilt). Three plain rules (gilt) and one decorative rule (black) at foot. **Back board:** Rules as at head and foot of front board, but all blind.

References: BB | *Farmer*, p.93 (addenda); *Dartt*, p.130, *Companion*, p.28.

Notes

1. The first four pages, containing the half-title and title pages, consist of a single folded leaf, unfolioed, tipped on to the front of the first gathering.

2. The catalogue is made up and sewn as a single gathering of 20 pages.

3. Henty's contribution is at pp.67–68: he found smoking helpful, and advantageous alike to health, temper and intellect, and thought it was in no way deleterious.

189. THROUGH FIRE AND STORM

189.1

THROUGH FIRE | AND STORM | Stories of Adventure and Peril | BY | G.A.HENTY, GEO. MANVILLE FENN, AND | JOHN A.HIGGINSON | LONDON | S.W.PARTRIDGE & CO. | 8 & 9 PATERNOSTER ROW | 1898

Contents

188 x 130 mm. (1)–320 | catalogue (1)–20. Frontispiece from wash-drawing by

Lancelot Speed, reproduced by halftone block printed in black on coated paper, unbacked, tipped in.

(1) Half-title p. | (2) blank | (frontispiece, tipped in) | (3) title p. | (4) blank | (5) Contents | (6) blank | 7–320. text, with printer's imprint on p.320 (Printed by BALLANTYNE, HANSON & Co. | Edinburgh & London) | (1)–20. catalogue.

Binding (see Plate 150)
Red cloth boards, blocked black, green, red merging to yellow, blue and gilt; top edge gilt; grey flowered endpapers.
Front board: Through (gilt, shadowed black) | FIRE | & STORM (gilt, shadowed black, with red inside lower parts of letters), all above and overlapping upper part of illustration of boys and girl with flaming torches, being fired on from house behind (black, green, red merging to yellow, blue). **Spine:** Through | FIRE & | STORM (cloth-colour out of solid-gilt rectangle) framed by black lines and with black rule above and below. G.A.HENTY | G.M.FENN | J.A.HIGGINSON (black) above illustration of boy holding short knife, and waving (black, blue). At foot: PARTRIDGE & Co, (gilt) between two black rules. **Back board:** plain.

References: BL; Bod; PN /*Farmer*, p.69; *Dartt*, p.136, *Companion*, p.30.

Notes
1. 'A Desperate Gang' is at pp.7–98 (see §4).
2. The frontispiece halftone is signed by the process engraver 'Harker'(?).
3. Later issues of 189.1 show one or more of the following variations in binding:

(a) No yellow used for illustration on front board. The three torches, originally shown in yellow, with the uppermost merging from red (used in the lettering above) to yellow, now blocked in a single working with red and blue, the two colours merging at the centre into grey. The blue also merges into the green at the foot: so an economy was made by blocking all pigments except black in a single working.

(b) Grey flowered endpapers replaced by yellow surface-paper endpapers, of the same poor quality as in later editions of the companion volume from Partridge, *In Battle and Breeze*, §2, 159.

(c) 24 pages of publisher's catalogue instead of 20 pages.
4. Later impressions of the book were printed with no date on the title page, and bound with all edges of the leaves plain.

190. VENTURE AND VALOUR

190.1
Venture and Valour | STORIES | TOLD | BY | (list of authors in two columns) G.A.HENTY | A.CONAN DOYLE | W.W.JACOBS | TOM GALLON | GORDON STABLES | &c. | G.MANVILLE FENN | JAMES PAYN | F.T.BULLEN | D.L.JOHNSTONE | DAVID KER | &c. | WITH EIGHT PAGE ILLUSTRATIONS BY | W.BOUCHER | W.& R.CHAMBERS, LIMITED | LONDON AND EDINBURGH | 1900

Contents
185 x 131 mm. (i)–(viii) | (1)–(408) | catalogue (1)–32. Eight full-page wash-

drawings by W. Boucher, reproduced by halftone blocks printed in black on coated paper, unbacked, keyed to text pages, tipped in.

(i) Half-title p. I (ii) blank I (frontispiece, tipped in) I (iii) title p. I (iv) printer's imprint (Edinburgh: I Printed by W.& R.Chambers, Limited.) I (v) Contents I (vi) blank I (vii) List of illustrations I (viii) blank I (1)–404. text, with printer's imprint on p.404, as on p.(iv) I (405) advertisement (BOOKS FOR BOYS.) I (406)–(408) three full-page illustrations from other books published by Chambers I (1)–32. catalogue.

Binding (see Plate 154)
Light-brown cloth boards, bevelled, blocked dark-brown, white, yellow, blue, and gilt; edges plain; grey endpapers, lined off-white.
   Front board: VENTURE I AND VALOUR. (gilt, cased dark-brown) over upper part of illustration of knight at doorway of castle with lady, holding his lance, etc. (dark-brown, white, yellow, blue, and gilt). At lower part of left side: BEING I STORIES (yellow, cased dark-brown) I TOLD BY I G.A.HENTY I A.CONAN DOYLE I G.M.FENN I W.W.JACOBS I TOM . GALLON I D.LAWSON-JOHNSTONE I GORDON STABLES I D.KER I &c. &c. (all dark-brown). **Spine:** VENTURE I AND I VALOUR (gilt) over dark-brown shield, outlined gilt, and above decoration of sword and crown (dark-brown, white, yellow). At foot, in irregular-shaped yellow panel, outlined dark-brown, W & R I CHAMBERS (dark-brown). **Back board:** plain.

References: Bod; PN I *Farmer*, p.76; *Dartt*, p.175, *Companion*, p.33.

Notes
1. 'Torpedo-Boat 240. A Tale of the Naval Manoeuvres' is at pp. (1)–40, with one full-page illustration (see §4).
2. Later impressions of the book were printed with no date on the title page.
3. The cloth and pigments chosen for the first issues of the book seem very drab by the standards of this publisher and others of the time. I have a second copy, of a later impression, bound in red cloth in place of the dull light-brown, and with black substituted for the dark-brown blocking; this copy also has gilt edges to the tops of the leaves: all this makes a great deal of difference to the general appearance of the book. The only variations in content are: (a) endpapers dark-brown, lined off-white (instead of grey); (b) undated title page; (c) publisher's advertisement is transposed from p.(405) to p.(408), with the three full-page illustrations now preceding it; (d) the catalogue has 48 pages.

191. WITH HUNTER, TRAPPER AND SCOUT

191.1
WITH HUNTER, TRAPPER I AND SCOUT IN CAMP I AND FIELD (printer's ornament) I PERSONAL STORIES TOLD BY LT.-GEN. SIR R.S.BADEN-POWELL, I F.C.SELOUS, C.M.Z.S., SIR ERNEST SHACKLETON, COL. I CODY, ADMIRAL ROBERT PEARY, SIR E.ARNOLD, ARCHI- I BALD FORBES, SIR H.M.STANLEY, GORDON CUMMING, I AND OTHERS I EDITED BY I ALFRED H.MILES I AUTHOR OF A BOOK OF HEROES I THE

FIFTY-TWO SERIES | AND NUMEROUS OTHER WORKS | (1cm. rule) | WITH ILLUSTRATIONS | (1cm. rule) | LONDON: HOLDEN & HARDINGHAM, | 12, YORK BUILDINGS, ADELPHI, W.C.

Contents
190 × 136 mm. Two unfolioed leaves, plus i–viii | 9–(384) | no catalogue. Frontispiece from watercolour drawing reproduced by three-colour halftone blocks, and four full-page wash-drawings reproduced by halftone blocks printed in black, all apparently by the same hand, but unsigned and unascribed; all on coated paper, unbacked, unfolioed, tipped in.
(Unfolioed) Half-title p. | (unfolioed) blank | (frontispiece, tipped in) | (unfolioed) title p. | (unfolioed) blank | i–iii. Preface (see Note 4) | (iv) blank | v. list of Illustrations | (vi) blank | vii–viii. Contents | 9–(382) text | (383) advertisement (HOLDEN & HARDINGHAM'S GIFT BOOKS), see Note 3 | (384) printer's imprint (Printed by Ebenr. Baylis & Son, Trinity Works, Worcester.).

Binding (see Plate 156)
Grey cloth boards, blocked black, brown, buff, grey-blue merging to white, and gilt; all edges stained green; plain off-white endpapers.
Front board: WITH | HUNTER . TRAPPER | AND SCOUT | COL. W.F.CODY | LT.-GEN. BADEN-POWELL | RR.-ADMIRAL PEARY | SIR GILBERT PARKER | F.C.SELOUS | SIR ERNEST SHACKLETON | FRANK T.BULLEN | SIR EDWIN ARNOLD | G.A.HENTY | SIR H.M.STANLEY | ARCHIBALD FORBES | & Others (all gilt) above and at left of illustration of man climbing up a cliff-face to escape from a rhinocerous (black, brown, buff, grey-blue merging to white). **Spine:** WITH | HUNTER | TRAPPER | AND | SCOUT | (8mm. rule) (all gilt), above: COL. W.F.CODY | LT-GEN. BADEN-POWELL | RR.-ADMIRAL PEARY | SIR GILBERT PARKER | F.C.SELOUS | SIR ERNEST SHACKLETON | FRANK T.BULLEN | SIR EDWIN ARNOLD | G.A.HENTY | SIR H.M.STANLEY | ARCHIBALD FORBES | & Others | A.H.MILES | (8mm. rule) (all black) | HOLDEN & | HARDINGHAM (gilt). **Back board:** plain.

References: PN | *Dartt Companion*, p.34.

Notes
1. 'Seth Harpur's Story', at pp.98–126, is an edited version of 'Seth Harper's Story', serialised in the *Union Jack* in three weekly instalments starting on 27 May 1880. That was itself an edited extract from *Out on the Pampas*, p.85 et seq. (see §1, 4). I do not know why the spelling of Harper was changed.
2. The list of Illustrations on p.v. includes an entry for the picture on the binding case, there referred to as 'Cover', with a key-reference to the relevant text page. I have never seen such a thing done in any other book.
3. The publisher's advertisement on p.(383) lists three titles, of which the first is 'A Fine Edition of | G.A.HENTY'S POPULAR STORY | Out on the Pampas | In cloth gilt, with coloured frontispiece, | 2/6d.' See *Out on the Pampas*, §1, 4.16.
4. *Farmer* describes the second issue (191.2) and incorrectly dates the book 1903. The Preface in this first issue, and in 191.2, is dated October 1913. In his *Companion* Dartt makes it clear that he saw a copy of 191.1, but did not realise its significance (see 191.2, Note). Books from this publisher appear not to have reached the Copyright Libraries.

5. The first four pages of the book are unfolioed although they form part of the first 16-page gathering, the pagination starting only on the third leaf. This eccentricity occurs also in the same publisher's *Out on the Pampas*, see §1, 4.16. It was possibly intended that in some later and cheaper issue the two leaves might be used to form endpapers, the first being pasted down on the front board.

191.2

Title page, Contents: As for 191.1.

Binding
Blue cloth boards, blocked black; edges plain; plain off-white endpapers.
    Front board: WITH I HUNTER . TRAPPER I AND SCOUT I COL. W.F.CODY I LT-GEN BADEN-POWELL I RR.-ADMIRAL PEARY I SIR GILBERT PARKER I F.C.SELOUS I SIR ERNEST SHACKLETON I & Others (black), above and at left of illustration of man scaling cliff to escape rhinoceros (black). **Spine:** WITH I HUNTER I TRAPPER I AND I SCOUT I (8mm. rule) I COL. W.F.CODY I LT-GEN BADEN-POWELL I RR.-ADMIRAL PEARY I SIR GILBERT PARKER I F.C.SELOUS I SIR ERNEST SHACKLETON I & Others I HOLDEN & I HARDINGHAM I LTD.

References: BB I *Farmer*, p.81; *Dartt*, p.160, *Companion*, p,34.

Notes
1. *Farmer* and *Dartt* both report only this second issue, without Henty's name blocked on the binding case, although the latter had seen a copy of 191.1 in the Marquess of Bath's collection (*Companion*, p.34). This version consists of sheets of the first impression, or possibly of a reprint, in a cheaper binding. A saving was made by not blocking all the colours of the original illustration, and by using black instead of gilt for the lettering, but it is hard to see any economy achieved by remaking the lettering brasses and leaving out a few names.
2. The list of Holden & Hardingham was taken over by the Oxford University Press in the early 1920s (see §1, 4.17, Notes).

192. THE WORLD'S BATTLES, 1800 TO 1900

192.1

THE I WORLD'S BATTLES I 1800 TO 1900 I DESCRIBED BY I ARCHIBALD FORBES, G.A.HENTY I MAJOR ARTHUR GRIFFITHS I AND OTHER WELL-KNOWN WRITERS I WITH A SERIES OF FULL-PAGE PLATES AND NUMEROUS I ILLUSTRATIONS AND PLANS I BIRMINGHAM I C.COMBRIDGE I PUBLISHER OF PRIZE LITERATURE I 4 & 5 NEW STREET

Contents
262 × 190 mm. (i)–viii I (1)–748 I no catalogue. Three full-page watercolour drawings by various artists reproduced by three-colour halftone blocks; eight full-page black-and-white plates from wash-drawings, engravings, and photographs of paintings, reproduced by halftone blocks printed in black; all on coated paper, unbacked, unfolioed, tipped in. Numerous plans and illustrations from line and halftone blocks printed on text pages.

(Frontispiece, tipped in) I (i) title p. I (ii) blank I (iii)–iv. Contents I (v)–viii. List of Illustrations I (1)–748. text and illustrations.

Binding
Red leathercloth boards, blocked black; edges plain; plain off-white endpapers.
Front board: THE I WORLD'S I BATTLES I 1800 TO 1900 (black) at top left; illustration of galloping horsemen fighting with swords (black) at bottom right. All framed by double rules (black) near edges of board. **Spine:** THE I WORLD'S I BATTLES I 1800 TO 1900 (black) above illustration of soldier holding hand of wounded comrade, and firing pistol with other hand (black), At foot: COMBRIDGE I BIRMINGHAM (black). Double black rules at extreme head and foot. **Back board:** plain.

Reference: PN.

Notes
1. The title page is a cancel, in a reprint of the second volume of *Battles of the Nineteenth Century* (see §2, 126.4, Note 5). My copy is inscribed April 1914.
2. Combridge of Birmingham, as indicated on the title page, bound books for presentation purposes. Another firm doing much the same thing at that time was James Askew & Son of Preston (see §1, 7.9, Notes 2–3).
3. Combridge used only the second volume of 126.4. The Index is included in the list of Contents, but omitted from the book. It was, of course, a combined Index to both volumes, and would have shown recipients that their award was not a complete work.

193. YULE LOGS

193.1
Longman's Christmas Annual for 1898 I YULE LOGS I Edited by I G.A.Henty I With Sixty-one Illustrations I (vignette halftone illustration) I Longmans, Green and Co. I 39 Paternoster Row, London I New York and Bombay I 1898 I All rights reserved
(*Note: The first line is underlined*).

Contents
191 x 141 mm. (i)–(xii) I (1)–(432) I no catalogue. Sixty-one wash-drawings by various artists, reproduced by halftone blocks printed in black on text pages. Of these twenty-six are full-page illustrations, unbacked, unfolioed but counted in the pagination.
(i) Half-title p. I (ii)–(iii) blank I (iv) frontispiece I (v) title p. I (vi) printer's imprint (Printed by BALLANTYNE, HANSON & Co. I At the Ballantyne Press) I vii–viii. Contents I ix–xi. List of Illustrations I (xii) blank I (1)–430. text and illustrations, with printer's imprint at foot of p.430 (Printed by BALLANTYNE, HANSON & Co. I Edinburgh & London) I (431)–(432) blank.

Binding (see Plate 166)
Red cloth boards, bevelled, blocked white and gilt; all edges gilt; black endpapers, lined off-white.

Front board: YULE-LOGS (white, cased cloth-colour) out of gilt part of illustration, of smoke and sparks rising from fire in grate (white and gilt). At left, and overlapping illustration: BEING . LONGMANS' | XMAS . ANNUAL . FOR . | 1898 . EDITED . BY ... | G.A.HENTY .... (white). **Spine:** YULE | LOGS | G.A.HENTY (white, cased cloth-colour) out of solid-gilt areas of illustration of smoke rising and curling from series of five logs (gilt). At foot: LONGMANS . & | CO . LONDON. (white). **Back board:** plain.

References: BL; Bod; PN | *Farmer*, p.89; *Dartt*, p.174, *Companion*, p.38.

Notes

1. 'On a Mexican Ranche' is at pp.383–430, illustrated with three full-page and three smaller wash-drawings by Harington Bird (see §4).

2. The book is well printed on a calendered paper of very good quality, which does justice to the halftone blocks. Nine well-known illustrators of the day were chosen, including Gordon Browne, who illustrated two of the stories.

3. On the spine of the binding case the words 'EDITED BY' do not appear above Henty's name. They were added for all subsequent issues of the book. *Dartt* misses this point, reporting the omission 'only on Colonial copy' (see Note 4). (Dartt's copy was almost certainly 193.2 or 193.3, confusing his description of the title page). In his *Companion*, p.38, he re-writes the entry, but I find it more confusing than ever, as he attempts to deal with four or five issues simultaneously. Here he reports 'Probably reprinted bearing 1898 date without bevelled edges and with only tops of leaves gilt', but gives no evidence for this 'probable' issue. I have found no trace of it.

4. *Farmer* and *Dartt* both report a Colonial Edition, issued by Longmans in conjunction with Copp, Clark Co., Limited, Toronto. It is said to have an underlined line at the head of the title page: 'Longman's Colonial Library Christmas Volume 1898', and, at the foot, in place of 'All rights reserved', the line: 'This Edition is intended for circulation only in India | and in the British Colonies'. The imprint reported is: 'Toronto | The Copp, Clark Co., Limited | London: Longmans, Green, & Co. | 1898', and the binding, apparently, green cloth in the same design as 193.1, blocked in grey and red, and with plain off-white endpapers.

5. The Henty Society has a copy of Henty's letter to Robert Leighton, 30 September (1897): 'Longmans are going to bring out a volume of stories for boys next year, and have asked me to arrange with good men for the tales. Will you write one for me to run to about 10,000 words? Remuneration 2¹/₂ guineas 1000. Either in the style of your Orkney stories or of that Yarmouth one. I should like it by the end of December. If this book is successful a volume will probably be brought out each year'.

193.2

YULE | LOGS | Edited by | G.A.Henty | With Sixty-one Illustrations | (vignette halftone illustration) | REISSUE | Longmans, Green, and Co. | 39 Paternoster Row, London | New York and Bombay | 1901 | All rights reserved

Contents: As for 193.1, but with a single unfolioed leaf inserted between pp.(iv) and (v): it has the new title page (as above) on the recto, and a bibliographical note on the verso (see Note 3).

Binding: (See Plate 166). As for 193.1, but the following is deleted from the brass for blocking the front board in white: (BEING . LONGMANS' I XMAS . ANNUAL . FOR . I 1898 .). The remainder of the white blocking remains in its original position.

References: PN I *Dartt*, p.175; *Companion*, p.38.

Notes
1. The early issues of 193.2 have two title pages, the new one, for this 1901 re-issue being tipped in to appear before the original one, dated 1898.
2. Later issues had the preliminary pages reprinted, with the 1901 title page replacing the original, but no other changes to content or binding.
3. The Bibliographical Note on the verso of the 1901 title page reads: 'First Printed, September 1898   Cheaper Reissue, July 1901'.
4. The confusing entry in *Dartt Companion*, p.38, deals with many editions simultaneously, omitting any description of this one. But in his penultimate line he quotes the Bibliographical Note on p.(vi) of 193.3, in which 193.2 is mentioned.

193.3
YULE LOGS I Edited by I G.A.Henty I With Sixty-one Illustrations I (vignette halftone illustration) I New Impression I Longmans, Green, and Co. I 39 Paternoster Row, London I New York and Bombay I 1903 I All rights reserved

Contents
191 x 139 mm. (i)–(xii) I (1)–(432) I no catalogue. Illustrations as in 193.1.
  (i) Half-title p. I (ii)–(iii) blank I (iv) frontispiece I (v) title p. I (vi) Bibliographical Note I vii–viii. Contents I ix–xi. List of Illustrations I (xii) blank I (1)–430. text and illustrations, with printer's imprint at foot of p.430 (Printed by BALLANTYNE, HANSON & Co. I Edinburgh & London) I (431)–(432) blank.

Binding: As for 193.2, but with plain off-white endpapers.

References: PN I *Dartt Companion*, p.38.

Notes
1. Here, as in the later issues of 193.2 (see 193.2, Note 2), the prelims are reprinted with the revised title page and verso forming an integral part.
2. The Bibliographical Note on p.(vi) reads: 'First Printed, September 1898 I Cheaper Reissue, July 1901 I Reprinted, October 1903'.

193.4
YULE LOGS I Edited by I G.A.Henty I With Sixty-one Illustrations I (vignette halftone illustration) I New Impression I Longmans, Green, and Co. I 39 Paternoster Row, London I New York, Bombay, and Calcutta I 1914 I All rights reserved

Contents
192 x 140 mm. (i)–(xii) I (1)–(432) I no catalogue. Illustrations as in 193.1.
  (i) Half-title p. I (ii) advertisement (EDITED BY G.A.HENTY) listing this book and *Yule-Tide Yarns* I (iii) blank I (iv) frontispiece I (v) title p. I (vi) Bibliographical Note I vii–viii. Contents I ix–xi. List of Illustrations I (xii) blank I (1)–430. text and illustrations, with printer's imprint at foot of p.430 (Printed by BALLANTYNE, HANSON & Co. I at Paul's Work, Edinburgh) I (431)–(432) blank.

Binding (see Plate 166)

Red cloth boards, blocked black and grey; edges plain; plain off-white endpapers.

Front board: YULE-LOGS (black, cased cloth-colour) out of grey part of illustration, of smoke, etc., rising from fire in grate (black and grey). At left, and overlapping illustration: EDITED . BY ... | G.A.HENTY .... (black). **Spine:** YULE | LOGS | EDITED BY | G.A. HENTY (black, cased cloth-colour) out of solid-grey areas of illustration of smoke rising and series of five logs (all grey). At foot: LONGMANS . & | CO . LONDON. (black). **Back board:** plain.

References: PN | *Dartt Companion*, p.38.

Notes

1. Compared with previous issues this one is very cheaply produced, but although the paper is of poorer quality it still gives good results from the halftone blocks.

2. *Dartt Companion* gives this issue a bare mention in the final line of p.38.

3. The Bibliographical Note on p.(vi) is as in 193.3, with a final line added: 'Reprinted, January 1914'.

4. The advertisement on p.(ii) lists this book and *Yule-Tide Yarns*, the latter with ten stories and 45 illustrations: both are 'Crown 8vo, gilt edges, 3s. net'. This issue, however, has plain edges.

194. YULE-TIDE YARNS

194.1

Yule-Tide Yarns | Edited by | G.A.Henty | With Forty-five Illustrations | (vignette halftone illustration) | Longmans, Green, and Co. | 39 Paternoster Row, London | New York and Bombay | 1899 | All rights reserved

Contents

193 x 140 mm. (i)–(xii) | (1)–(372) | no catalogue. Forty-six wash-drawings by various artists, reproduced by halftone blocks printed in black on text pages. Of these, twenty-one are full-page plates, unbacked, unfolioed but counted in the pagination.

(i) Half-title p. | (ii)–(iii) blank | (iv) frontispiece | (v) title p. | (vi) blank | vii–viii. Contents | ix–xi. List of Illustrations | (xii) blank | (1)–370. text and illustrations, with printer's imprint at foot of p.370 (Printed by BALLANTYNE, HANSON & Co. | Edinburgh & London) | (371)–(372) blank.

Binding (see Plate 167)

Light-brown cloth boards, bevelled, blocked dark-brown, white, and gilt; all edges gilt; black endpapers, lined off-white.

Front board: YULE TIDE | YARNS (gilt) above decoration of shield, helmet, and crossed halberds (dark-brown, white, gilt), with two sailing ships (gilt) beneath it. At foot: EDITED BY G.A.HENTY (gilt). **Spine:** YULE : | : . TIDE | YARNS | EDITED BY | G.A.HENTY (all gilt), above decoration, between two gilt rules, of mailed fist holding lance (dark-brown, gilt). At foot: LONGMANS & | Co LONDON (gilt). **Back board:** plain.

References: BL; Bod; PN I *Farmer*, p.89; *Dartt*, p.175, *Companion*, p.39.

Notes
1. 'Chateau and Ship' is at pp.(1)–53, illustrated with three full-page and four smaller drawings by Gordon Browne (see §4).
2. *Farmer* confuses the binding of this first edition with that of the Colonial Edition (see 194.2).
3. Gerald Duin of California has pointed out that, in spite of the wording on the title page, the book contains forty-six illustrations. As with *Yule Logs* (see above), the vignette on the title page is not included in the stated totals.
4. There is a hyphen in 'Yule-Tide' on the title page, but not on the binding case.

194.2
Longmans' Colonial Library I Yule-Tide Yarns I Edited by I G.A.Henty I With Forty-five Illustrations I (vignette halftone illustration) I Longmans, Green, & Co. I 39 Paternoster Row, London I And Bombay I 1899 I This Edition is intended for circulation only in India and the I British Colonies

Contents: 193 x 142 mm. As for 194.1.

Binding: (See Plate 167). As for 194.1, except (a) grey cloth boards, blocked dark-brown, white, and dark-blue (with all previously gilt blocking now in dark-blue); (b) edges plain; (c) plain off-white endpapers.

References: PN I *Farmer*, p.89; *Dartt*, p.175, *Companion*, p.39.

Notes
1. An issue produced more cheaply than 194.1, with no changes in content apart from the wording on the title page.
2. The Colonial Edition appears to have been issued simultaneously with 194.1: both my copies are inscribed as Christmas gifts, 1899.

194.3
Yule-Tide Yarns I Edited by I G.A. Henty I With Forty-five Illustrations I (vignette halftone illustration) I REISSUE I Longmans, Green, and Co. I 39 Paternoster Row, London I New York and Bombay I 1901 I All rights reserved

Contents: 193 x 139 mm. As for 194.1, but with a single unfolioed leaf inserted between pp.(iv) and (v): it has the new title page (as above) on the recto, and a bibliographical note on the verso (see Note 2).

Binding: As for 194.1.

References: SW I *Dartt*, p.175.

Notes
1. As with *Yule Logs*, 193.2, the first reissue had two title pages, the new one being tipped in to appear before the original one for 1899. The preliminary pages for that book were eventually reprinted, with the new title page displacing the earlier one: I have not found a similar reprint of 194.3.
2. The Bibliographical Note on the verso of the 1901 title page reads: 'First Printed, September 1899 Cheaper Reissue, July 1901'.
3. *Dartt* erroneously reports that the 1901 reissue 'lacks half-title'.

194.4

Yule-Tide Yarns | Edited by | G.A.Henty | With Forty-five Illustrations | vignette halftone illustration | NEW IMPRESSION | Longmans, Green, and Co. | 39 Paternoster Row, London | New York, Bombay, and Calcutta | 1910 | All rights reserved

Contents: 193 × 139 mm. As for 194.1, but with a single unfolioed leaf inserted between pp.(iv) and (v): it has the new title page (as above) on the recto, and a bibliographical note on the verso (see Note 1).

Binding: As for 194.1, except (a) light-brown boards, blocked dark-brown, cream, and gilt, see Note 2; (b) top edge gilt, other edges plain; (c) plain off-white endpapers.

References: CH | *Dartt*, p.175.

Notes

1. The title page is now an integral part of the prelims. The Bibliographical Note on p.(vi) is similar to that in 194.3, with a third line added: 'Reprinted, September 1910'. The heading does not align with the three lines beneath it.

2. Economies have been made in the binding. The boards are of a slightly lighter weight, and are not bevelled. The use of gold in the blocking is now confined to the helmet on the front board and the lettering of title and editor (only) on the spine. Only the top edges of leaves are gilded.

§3

PERIODICALS AND NEWSPAPERS
TO WHICH HENTY CONTRIBUTED

195. ALL THE YEAR ROUND

A Weekly Journal, price 2d., conducted by Charles Dickens, with which is incorporated *Household Words*. Published at 26 Wellington Street, and by Chapman and Hall, 193 Piccadilly, London.

Volume XX: includes issues from No.477, Saturday 13 June 1868, to No.501, Saturday 28 November 1868. In the Index to the bound volume are the following two entries, each in their correct alphabetical position:

Baggage under Difficulties   233, 254
Sixty-Eight in Abyssinia   233, 254

    The fact that the two articles are linked in this way in the Index has led to a supposition that they are by the same author, although this is not explicitly stated, and all articles in this periodical are anonymous, as was customary with many periodicals of that date. 'Baggage under Difficulties', in issue No.486, 15 August 1868, runs from page 233 to page 235, and the other piece from page 254 to page 261, in the following issue, No.487, 22 August.

    The second article, 'Sixty-Eight in Abyssinia', was attributed to Henty by Dartt (*Companion*, p.26), on the strength of a claim of verification by Dr C.F. Willey of Connecticut. He makes no mention of the article 'Baggage under Difficulties'.

    Since the death of Dr Willey the Henty Society has acquired, among a collection of papers, a document he wrote to a friend. It tells how he 'found in the Beinecke Library of Yale University a letter by GAH's friend, George Augustus Sala, to GAH himself ... dated at "Putney: Wednesday, July Fifteenth". I assign the date 1868 to it because the 15th does fall on a Wednesday in 1868 ...

    'Sala tells Henty that his (Sala's) letter to Dickens had been lying around the *All the Year Round* office for some days, but that Dickens had written this morning from Gadshill to Sala telling him (Sala) that GAH's Abyssinian article was "all right" and that he (Sala) was enclosing Dickens's note to that effect with his letter to GAH'.

    Dr Willey concluded that the article in question was 'Sixty-Eight in Abyssinia', and that is what he told Dartt. Indeed, it is clear that Willey was not even aware of the first article. The only link between the two is in the Index to Volume XX, and Dr Willey probably had access only to individual issues, or to a set bound, as sets often were, without the Index. Searching through the pages, his eye would no doubt have been caught by the word Abyssinia in the title.

    Periodicals at that date received dispatches and letters from many correspondents and also from military officers involved in the Abyssinian Expedition. Information from several sources was often intermingled in the published reports: this is particularly evident in the pages of the *Illustrated London News* (§3, 214). I am sure the two articles in *All the Year Round* were linked in the index because they both concerned the Abyssinian campaign, and not for any reason of shared authorship.

According to Willey's account, Sala and Dickens referred to only one 'Abyssinian article'. What I believe to be the origins of 'Baggage under Difficulties' are traced under *The Cornhill Magazine* (§3, 206). Years later it was re-told by Henty as one of the 'Editor's Yarns' in the *Union Jack*, (§3, 225), Volume III, No.105, 29 December 1881, with the title 'Among the Gallas'. Although in places virtually word for word the same, it demonstrates Henty's own adaptation for his younger readers of a story originally written for adults. Also, perhaps, a mellowing of style in the thirteen years that had passed between the two versions.

'Sixty-Eight in Abyssinia', on the other hand, is a long, not very exciting, account of its experiences, told in the first person by a mule. In style, and use of language, it is quite unlike anything else by Henty. There are no grounds for attributing it to him, and I do not believe he wrote it.

196. ANSWERS

A weekly periodical, founded by Lord Northcliffe. Started publication 2 June 1888.

18 December, 1902: Henty's 'Writing Books for Boys', published posthumously.

197. BEETON'S BOY'S OWN MAGAZINE

An Illustrated Journal of Fact, Fiction, History and Adventure, edited by G.A. Henty, published by Ward, Lock and Co., London, 1889–1890, price 6d. monthly.

Between 1855 and 1874 S.O. Beeton edited and published a magazine with this title, and in the 1870s he also published, in book form, titles which had been serialised in the magazine (such as *Our Soldiers and the Victoria Cross*, and *Don Quixote*, etc.). A number of these were issued in a series called 'Beeton's Boy's Own Library'.

In the 1880s Ward & Lock (see Appendix II, Part 6) took over the publishing business of S.O.Beeton. They thus acquired rights in a quantity of juvenile material, much of which was out of print but seemed to them worthy of re-issue. A decision was taken to use some of the old material in a magazine, which Henty was invited to edit, although with considerable limitation on his responsibilities. He wrote in his first Editorial, in 1889:

'... while ready to listen to suggestions, I would point out that except as to the new matter, I have no responsibility, and that, with the exception of the addition of this matter, the magazine is already mapped out, and no changes are possible. *Beeton's Boy's Own Magazine* was so great a favourite with the boys of the last generation that I have no fear whatever that you will find it less interesting than your fathers did; and I can only say that I will do my best to make the new part equal to the old. Many of the very best of the writers of boys' stories have promised me their aid; and although I know that boys are rather hard to please, I think that they will be satisfied with the wonderful sixpennyworth that Messrs. Ward, Lock and Co. are going to give them'.

It was clearly, with or without hindsight, a very doubtful publishing venture by Ward Lock. They were to produce a magazine 'on the cheap', using little else than material of no great quality that had already been published once, often twice, in the previous twenty years. It is doubtful whether any fees or royalties would have been payable. Henty's remarks about 'the wonderful sixpennyworth' are not very convincing when compared with the value offered in the same year by the *Boy's Own Paper* (§3, 201). The latter gave 16 quarto pages (twice the size of Beeton's) of all new (and better quality) material, plus fine colour-plates, for one penny a week. Ward Lock gave 128 octavo pages (equal to 64 quarto pages) and no colour plates for sixpence a month.

Terry Corrigan has kindly shown me a letter in his collection, written by Henty from 6 Ravenna Road, Putney, on 3 December (?1890), and addressed almost certainly to William Henry Davenport Adams (1828–1891), an Editor and journalist, and a fellow-writer for boys. This throws some light on his true feelings about the new venture: 'My dear Mr Adams', he wrote, 'Ward & Lock's boys' magazine expired at the end of its first year of life. I told them from the first that the idea of a reprint was a mistake, and as they never made the slightest effort to push it, of course it fell through'.

Why, then, did Henty undertake the Editorship of this magazine for which all was mapped out in advance, and in which no changes were possible, and for which he had so little responsibility? As Cargill Thompson wrote (*The Boys' Dumas*, p.12), 'this is out of character. Henty was not a man who would simply allow his name to be used to endorse a product'. The truth, I think, was that Henty enjoyed the letters he received from his young readership: he had a need to be in touch with youth, and he very much missed the pleasure he had had from that contact when he was Editor of the *Union Jack*. In his first Editorial, quoted above, he describes the variety of his correspondence, and adds, 'Now, I own I like all this frank outspokenness and candid expression of opinion. It brings me closer to my readers, and is absolutely refreshing in an age when people do not often speak out their minds. It is, therefore, with pleasure that I once more assume the duties of Editor of a Boy's Magazine, and I shall be happy to hear from my readers at all times'.

I wonder how far Ward Lock's approach to Henty was due to a single-minded desire to recover some of the cost of the Beeton take-over by squeezing the last drops out of the material; and how keen they were to get Henty on their list. Henty himself, by now firmly attached to Blackie as his book-publisher, clearly found it impossible to refuse the offer, in spite of the misgivings he later admitted to. The acquisition of the juvenile material must have been considered a trifle by Ward Lock, whose main interest in Beeton lay no doubt in the widely known reference books, and above all in Mrs Beeton's celebrated *Household Management*.

The publishers realised, before publication began, that annual volumes containing all the monthly parts were out of the question, and that even half-yearly volumes would contain 768 pages and be very cumbersome. So a plan was made to bind the monthly parts in three volumes, each of 512 pages, every year. This was explained in Henty's first Editorial, following the paragraph quoted above. The plan ensured that by an ingenious system of numbering the pages, with letters, A, B, and

C, preceding the figures in each case, the sections could later be bound into volumes in which all the parts of any serialised story, and those of any other serialised items appearing in special sections, would be brought together and given complete in one or other of the volumes. As a consequence of these unusual arrangements the Editorial itself, which was in the first Number of the magazine, did not appear in the bound-up copies until Volume III.

The strange pagination system was doubtless devised by the publisher's production department. But it is likely that Henty himself would have been as concerned as the publisher that all items should be found complete within one volume when the material was re-issued in book form. So he would have agreed that an explanation of the system was most conveniently given in the editorial column.

It was common practice for magazine publishers to produce decorative binding cases, for the use of local binders asked to make up sets of issues. In this case there would have been three binding cases on sale together at the end of each year. But there seems to have been little demand for them and they are now extremely scarce: Dartt had an incomplete set (*Dartt*, p.15), but they were not used for the copies to be found in the Copyright Libraries.

Apart from the lack of demand for the publisher's binding cases, it seems that there was unexpectedly little demand, over the two years of its existence, for the magazine itself. Indeed that is a far more likely reason for its demise, than the one announced by Henty, in Vol.VI, p.503, that the conduct of the magazine demanded more time than he could give to it.

Further evidence is provided actually within copies of the first six 'Beeton's Boy's Own Books' (§2, 127). They were made not only of remaining flat sheets, taken from the printer's warehouse, but also of sections of bound, but unsold, copies of the magazines, from which the original paper covers had been removed. The first and last pages of the magazines, often bound before the printing ink had fully dried, showed 'set-off' of advertising matter from the paper covers. These traces of advertising matter, and even of the outer covers, are also found in the books.

Twelve Editorials by Henty were published under the heading 'Editor's Table', and they were, with one exception, reprinted in the subsequent books, *Stories of Peril and Adventure* (§2, 186), and *Stirring Adventures Afloat and Ashore* (§2, 179). Apart from those articles, only one of his short stories appeared in the magazine, 'White-Faced Dick' (see §4), illustrated with an anonymous wood-engraving, in *Stories of History* (§2, 185).

198. THE BOHEMIAN

An Unconventional Magazine, published by The Bohemian Publishing Co., 6 Dorset Street, Fleet Street, London, E.C., and by John Heywood, 2 Amen Corner, E.C.

Issue No.28, September 1895, contains 'An Anxious Time' (see §4).

199. BOYS

An Illustrated Weekly magazine, published by The UK Band of Hope Union, Old

Bailey, London, E.C., 17 September 1892. Taken over six months later by Sampson Low, Marston & Co., St Dunstan's House, London, E.C., with the original Editor, Edward Step. In September 1894 the magazine was absorbed into the *Boy's Own Paper* (§3, 201).

Volume I: 'The Golden Cañon' (see §4) is serialised in eight instalments starting in the first issue, p.6; it has four illustrations by Stanley L. Wood. A long biographical note by R. McCall Barbour appears on p.155, under the heading 'Boys' Favourite Authors. George Alfred Henty'. There are further editorial references to Henty and his work on pages 254 and 270.

Volume II: 'A Desperate Gang' (see §4) is serialised in ten instalments starting in number 79, 17 March 1894, p.438; it has six illustrations by Arthur J. Wall and others (two by Wall, and one each by four other artists).

200. THE BOYS' BRIGADE GAZETTE

(Also known as *The B.B.*): see YOUNG ENGLAND (§3, 228).

201. THE BOY'S OWN PAPER

Illustrated magazine, 'with which are incorporated *Boys* (see §3, 199) and *Every Boy's Magazine* (§3, 209)', published by the Religious Tract Society, 56 Paternoster Row, London, E.C., at one penny per week. First published 18 January 1879. (See Appendix II, Part 6).

Volume XVIII: Henty's autobiographical 'Life of a Special Correspondent' is serialised in three instalments, appearing in alternate issues, starting in No.908, Saturday 6 June 1896, p.570. It has an illustration by F.W. Burton to the final instalment, and anonymous decorative illustrations to the first two.

In No.910, Saturday 20 June 1896, p.607, is a brief laudatory announcement of the publication of the first volume of *Battles of the Nineteenth Century* (§2, 126).

Volume XIX: 'The Fetish Hole' (see §4) is serialised in nine instalments, starting in No.925, Saturday 3 October 1896, p.1. Alfred Pearse illustrated every instalment but the last, which has a picture by F.W. Burton.

Volume XX: 'Among Malay Pirates' (see §4) is serialised in eleven instalments, starting in No.977, Saturday 2 October 1897, p.1. It has eight illustrations by G.E. Robertson and others. The story was published in collections of Henty's stories by numerous 'pirate' book-publishers in the U.S., but never appeared elsewhere in this country.

Volume XXI: 'Burton & Son' (see §4) is serialised in seven instalments, starting in No.1035, Saturday 12 November 1898, p.97. Every instalment is illustrated by G.E. Robertson.

Volume XXII: 'In the Hands of the Cave Dwellers' (§1, 102) is serialised in eight instalments, starting in No.1113, Saturday 12 May 1900, p.505. Every instalment is illustrated by Alfred Pearse.

Summer Number for 1901: 'Down a Crevasse' (see §4) appears on pages 4-6. There is a decorative heading, signed by Whymper, and the illustration facing it, although unsigned, is almost certainly also by him.

The special Summer and Christmas Numbers of this magazine were not bound up in the Annual volumes, and are consequently scarce. This number consisted of 64 pages, bound in wrappers printed in red and black, and including two full-colour plates, one full-page, the other a double-page fold-out.

202. THE BRIGADIER

A monthly Magazine published from January 1902 by The Boys' Brigade, Head Quarters Office, 68 Bath Street, Glasgow, for its members, price one penny. Edited by Herbert Reid; believed to have ceased publication in 1904. (See also *The Boys' Brigade Gazette*, §3, 200).

Volume II: 'Duty' (see §4) is serialised in three instalments, starting in Issue 14, February 1903.

The story was first published by The Boys' Brigade as a 24-page 8vo leaflet for Christmas 1890. It has one illustration, engraved on wood by Hildibrand, a French engraver, but the artist is unknown. Copies were probably given to all members by their Company Commanders. Each included a presentation leaf with spaces for the recipient, his rank, and Captain's signature under the inscription 'With Sincere Wishes for I A MERRY CHRISTMAS I AND I A HAPPY NEW YEAR I From the OFFICERS of the (blank) Company, I THE BOYS' BRIGADE. There is also a motto for 1891, with two biblical quotations. A copy without its original cover is bound up with Henty's own copies of *Tales from Henty*, 1893 (§1, 57), and *The Sovereign Reader*, n.d. (§1, 26) now in the Wandsworth Collection of Early Children's Books. Its appearance in *The Brigadier* was a tribute to Henty following his death late in 1902.

In 1902 the story was published for schools as one of Chambers's Continuous Readers, without illustration and under the title *At Duty's Call*, price 2d. in paper cover, or 3d. in cloth. (see §1, 103.1).

203. THE CAPTAIN

A monthly Magazine for Boys and 'Old Boys', published by George Newnes Limited, Southampton Street, London.

Volume V: 'The Old Pit Shaft' (see §4) appears in the issue for August 1901, pp.435–439. There are four illustrations by Rex Osborne.

204. CHAMBERS'S JOURNAL

A weekly magazine printed and published by W.&R. Chambers Limited, 47 Paternoster Row, London and Edinburgh.

Sixth Series, Volume II: 'Torpedo-Boat 240' (see §4) is serialised in four instalments, starting in No.92, 2 September 1899, p.625. There are no illustrations.

205. CHUMS

An Illustrated Paper for Boys, first published by Cassell and Company Limited, 12 September 1892, from La Belle Sauvage, Ludgate Hill, London, E.C., price one penny per week.

Volume I: 'Jack Dillon of Dunnamore' (see §4) is serialised in six instalments, starting in No.42, 28 June 1893, p.660. There are five illustrations, signed with initials but not credited to the artist.

Simon Nowell-Smith wrote in 1958 of the teething troubles of *Chums:* 'An appearance forbidding to the boys for whom it was intended, and a layout ill-adapted to illustration, hampered its start; but Max Pemberton fought successfully for a format resembling that of the old *Boy's Own Paper*'. (*The House of Cassell*, p.184).

206. THE CORNHILL MAGAZINE

A monthly magazine first published in 1860 by Smith, Elder & Co., 65 Cornhill, London, E.C.

Volume XVII: Henty's unsigned article 'Camp Life in Abyssinia' appears in No.102, June 1868, pp.696–706, without illustration.

This dispatch is headed 'Antalo, March 10 (1868)'. A copy is bound up with Henty's own copy of *Seaside Maidens*, now in the Lilly Library of Indiana University. With it is a copy (taken from the *Cornhill* files) of a letter, from 23 St. Ann's Villas, Royal Crescent, Notting Hill Gate, dated 8 June 1868 and addressed to Smith, Elder. *Dartt* (p.42) inaccurately reports that the letter offered this contribution and asked if they required others. The details are more interesting than that: 'Sir, I arrived from Abyssinia yesterday, and find that you have inserted my article "Camp Life in Abyssinia" in your number of this month. I have another article, in continuation of the narrative up to the taking of Magdala, which is nearly completed. Will you kindly write me a line to let me know if you would take it for next month's Cornhill. Yours faithfully, G.A. Henty, late Special Correspondent "Standard" Abyssinia'.

A printed slip from the magazine is attached to the letter, marked in ink 'Answered June 13/68'. There is also a pencil inscription: 'Interest of subject will have passed'. Henty's offer was presumably not accepted, but it seems that the second piece, 'nearly completed' was then sent to Charles Dickens, possibly at the suggestion of George Augustus Sala, a Savage Club friend. Dickens seems to have been in no great hurry, but the matter was chased up by Sala, who wrote to Henty on 15 July. A résumé of the letter is given under *All the Year Round* (§3, 195), together with details of the publication of the article.

As he did with the article in *All the Year Round*, Henty re-wrote 'Camp Life in Abyssinia' years later, for publication in the *Union Jack*, this time under the heading 'An Editor's Yarns: IV. Camp Life', 25 August 1881.

The editorial account books for the *Cornhill* are held by The National Library of Scotland: MS.23189 shows that Henty received a fee of £12.12s. for this article.

207. DARK BLUE

A shilling monthly magazine published by British and Colonial Publishing Company Limited, 81a Fleet Street, London, E.C., edited by the writer, John C. Freund. Founded 1871, but closed 1873, in spite of notable literary and artistic contents (see Gleeson White, *English Illustration, 'The Sixties': 1855–1870*, pp.80–81).

Volume III: 'A Pipe of Opium' (see §4) appears in No.13, March 1872, pp.27–42.

208. THE EVENING STANDARD

Started as an evening paper called *The Standard*, 21 May 1827 to 29 June 1857, when it became a morning paper, with an evening edition. The evening paper was re-started on 11 June 1860 as a separate publication, *The Evening Standard*. Edited, 1874–1900, by W.H. Mudford. During Henty's time the two papers shared resources, including the services of their Special Correspondent. (See also *The Standard*, §3. 222).

At the end of his Preface to *Those Other Animals*, (1891), Henty wrote: 'some of these essays were first presented to the world in the columns of the *Evening Standard* (see §1, 51.1, Note 2).

209. EVERY BOY'S MAGAZINE

Monthly illustrated magazine published by George Routledge & Sons, Broadway, Ludgate Hill, London, E.C., edited by Edmund Routledge, F.R.G.S. It was later taken over by the *Boy's Own Paper*, §3, 201.

Volume for 1886: 'For Name and Fame' (see §1) is serialised in twelve instalments, starting in No.XXXVII, p.38. There are no illustrations, in spite of the announcement on the Contents page of the annual volume.

210. THE GIRL'S REALM

A monthly illustrated magazine published by S.H. Bousfield and Co., Limited, Norfolk House, Norfolk Street, Strand, London, W.C., edited by S.H. Leeder.

Volume 3: 'A Frontier Girl' (see §4) appears in No.25, November 1900, pp.169–176, with four illustrations by Victor Venner.

Volume 5: 'A Soldier's Daughter' (see §1, 111) is serialised in three instalments, starting in No.55, May 1903, p.553. There are six illustrations by Frances Ewan, in addition to an illustrative heading common to each instalment.

211. GRIP

A Weekly Journal for British Boys, published and edited by Major Arthur Griffiths from November 1883, for only three months. Cover designed by Harry Furniss.

Volume I: 'The Spy of Belfort' (see §4) appears in No.1, 15 November 1883, pp.10–12. It is illustrated with one wood-engraving.

212. THE HOME MESSENGER

A monthly magazine published by Horace Marshall & Son, Temple House, Temple Avenue, London, E.C., edited by Frederick A. Atkins.

Volume XII: Henty's 'True Heroism; a Talk with the Boys' appears in the issue for February 1903, pp.54 and 56. This was the last magazine article written by G.A. Henty, and appears with his portrait.

213. THE HOUR GLASS

An illustrated monthly magazine, published by A.G. Dawson, 14 Ivy Lane, Paternoster Row, London, E.C.

Volume II: 'Till Death, and After' (see §4) appears in issue No.11, November 1887, pp.34–42. There are no illustrations.

214. THE ILLUSTRATED LONDON NEWS

A weekly illustrated magazine, printed and published by George C. Leighton, 198 Strand, London, W.C., price, with a Supplement, fivepence.

Volume LII: In issue 1474, 21 March 1868, pp.288–290, is an article, 'The Abyssinian Expedition', in which various correspondents are mentioned, and Henty is introduced to readers. It is explained that the Commander-in-Chief, Sir Robert

Napier, was to meet ambassadors from the Court of the King of Tigre, Prince Kassai. 'Their arrival is the subject of one of our Illustrations. It is from a sketch by Mr. G. A. Henty, the special correspondent of one of the London daily newspapers, who gives the following description of the scene…'. Then follows a dispatch from Henty, and 'The Engraving on our front page is from Mr. Henty's sketch'. A description is given of the groups of figures, and individuals, in the illustration, on p.269, captioned 'Arrival at Adigerat of an Ambassador from Kassai, King of Tigre'.

Volume LII: In issue 1475, 28 March 1868, pp.312–314, another article, 'The Abyssinian Expedition', includes dispatches from correspondents and military officers, of which one is from G. A. Henty. The article is accompanied by engravings based on drawings from the correspondents, of which one, on p.309, is referred to thus: 'The sketch of the camp at Ad Abaga was drawn by Mr. G. A. Henty, who was there on Feb.21, at which date he writes to us'.

The illustration is captioned 'Camp of General Sir R. Napier at Ad-Abaga'. The article continues with a brief note, in a couple of sentences, about the meeting between Napier and Prince Kassa [whose name was here and subsequently spelt thus] 'which took place, on the 25th [February], in the plain of Mai Deha, five miles from Ad Abaga. The interview, of which we may give some illustrations, was quite satisfactory to both parties'. Illustrations appeared a fortnight later (see below).

Volume LII: In issue 1477, 11 April 1868, pp.343–344, there is a further article, 'The Abyssinian Expedition', referring to 'the interview, near Ad-Abaga, on Feb. 25, between the commander-in-chief of the British army and the reigning Prince Kassa of Tigré'. It is illustrated with several engravings, based on sketches attributed to specified military officers, and 'the two sketches of the subject last mentioned [i.e. the interview] are from the pencil of Mr. G. A. Henty'. The drawings appear on page 341 (captioned 'Sir Robert Napier entertained by the Prince of Tigre') and page 361 (captioned 'Meeting of the Prince of Tigre with Sir Robert Napier').

The first picture, on the front page of the issue, is an interior scene showing food and drink being served, and includes nearly thirty members of the entourages. The second, of a valley with tents on high mountains beyond, shows Napier leaving his tent, guarded by a long line of infantry. Napier rides out on his elephant, accompanied by following cavalry, towards the Prince, who is on horseback, and accompanied by several large groups of warriors, both mounted and on foot.

A description of the mountainous Abyssinian landscape is given by another correspondent. Then follows a long account of the interview, within quotation marks. It is not specifically attributed, but contains a reference to one of Henty's illustrations, and in the context of the editorial comment in both articles is clearly Henty's work.

The four drawings by Henty were engraved on wood and are all half-pages, measuring about 17 x 24 centimetres. The engravers of the first two pictures are not indicated, but the others are signed with initials, 'A.H.' and 'C.R.' respectively. I cannot be certain about their identity, but suggest the names of two engravers on the staff of the *Illustrated London News* at the time. Alfred Hunt joined the magazine in 1860, and was known for drawings including crowds of figures. Charles Robinson joined the staff in about 1861 and did regular work for twenty years until his death in 1881. Notes on both are given in Appendix IV, Part 2.

In his biography, *George Alfred Henty* (pp.26–27), Fenn wrote 'Not only the pen, but the pencil had become familiar to his fingers, and possibly to fill up dull moments, he began to make sketches of such objects as took his attention; and the idea striking him that such subjects might prove attractive to one of the editors of an illustrated paper at home, he from time to time tried his hand at some little scene or some quaint-looking character which had caught his eye. These supplemented his long letters to a relative ... The sketches were duly taken by their recipient to the different London illustrated papers, but whether from not being up to the editorial artistic mark, or from the fact that each paper was fully represented, no success attended their presentation'. Fenn goes on to say that the letters themselves were accepted by the *Morning Advertiser* (§3, 217), which dates the unsuccessful attempt to sell pictures considerably earlier than the ones described above, which were unknown to Fenn. I have found no other examples of Henty's work being illustrated by his own drawings.

Volume LXIV: In issue 1795, 17 January 1874, Melton Prior is introduced as 'our Special Artist' for the Ashanti War. He 'was to start, on the 20th [December], in company with the *Standard* correspondent [G.A. Henty], for the advanced guard of the expedition on the banks of the Prah. General Sir Garnet Wolsley had allowed him all the facilities and needful accomodation he could reasonably desire'. Two weeks later, in issue 1797, the article headed 'The Ashantee War' notes that the Camp at Addah, near the mouth of the Volta, seventy miles east of Cape Coast Castle, 'is described by Mr Henty, correspondent of the *Standard*, in a letter of Dec.20, from which some particulars may be cited'. What follows is not within quotation marks, so Henty's exact writing is not reproduced. In the following issue, 1798, 7 February 1874, Melton Prior reports his arrival at Dunquah on 26 December, where 'next morning Mr Henty, of the *Standard*, and Mr Stanley, of the *New York Herald*, arrived with their enormous train of servants'. He also reports that two days later 'Mr Henty left with his retinue'.

In issue 1801, 28 February 1874, p.194, the article on the Ashantee War is headed 'Capture of Coomassie'. Once again there is no contribution by Henty. However, following the official accounts of the end of the campaign, there is a report based on letters from Melton Prior, the war-artist and correspondent (see Appendix IV, Part 2). It includes the following: 'Our Artist, while sojourning at Prah-su, found convenient accomodation in a hut, shared with him by Mr. Henry Stanley, of the *New York Herald*, and Mr. Henty, of the *Standard*. He has acknowledged their friendly aid in more than one letter, and his sketch of "the newspaper correspondents' quarters" will serve as a token of remembrance'. The drawing, reproduced by a fine engraving, appears on the front page of the issue, and shows a self-portrait of Prior standing with the other two, Henty in a characteristic pose, pipe in hand. At a discreetly aloof distance, sitting in a wicker chair, is the correspondent of *The Times*, reading a book. (See page 635.)

Volume LXVII: In issue 1892, 13 November 1875, Special Supplement 'Visit of the Prince of Wales to India', p.490, is printed a 'description of the Prince's arrival at Bombay ... sent by the *Standard* special correspondent, which was somewhat fuller than the others'. Henty wrote some 2500 words, headed 'Bombay, Monday Evening' [8 November]: it appears to be the full dispatch he sent to the *Standard*. It was customary for the *Illustrated London News* to quote *in extenso* from the dispatches sent to the London dailies, and many were drawn upon in this way during the months of the royal visit.

Henty's drawing of the 'Meeting of the Prince of Tigre with Sir Robert Napier', from *Illustrated London News*, 11 April 1868. (Probably engraved by Charles Robinson).

Henty's drawing of 'Sir Robert Napier entertained by the Prince of Tigre', from *Illustrated London News*, 11 April 1868. (Probably engraved by Alfred Hunt).

Volume LXVII: In issue 1895, 4 December 1875, Special Supplement 'Visit of the Prince of Wales to India', p.562, is an even longer piece by Henty, of about 2600 words, introduced thus: 'The following description of the prince's reception [in Bombay], on Monday the 8th ult., is taken from the *Standard* correspondent's letter of that date:'.

Volume LXVIII: In issue 1902, 8 January 1876, p.34, in an article 'The Prince of Wales in India.', is Henty's account of the Perehara, described as 'the central point of the Prince's visit to Kandy'. It took place at the beginning of December: the paragraphs quoted from the *Standard* correspondent amount to about 1350 words.

Volume LXVIII: In issue 1903, 15 January 1876, p.54, an article, 'The Royal Visit to India' includes: 'The arrival of the Prince at Kandy was an important incident of the Royal progress in Ceylon. It is thus described by the *Standard* correspondent:'. Henty's piece is of about 550 words. Another paragraph on the same page of this article includes a further 150 words by Henty: 'Some Veddas which were at Kandy during the Prince's visit are thus described by the *Standard* correspondent:'.

Volume LXVIII: In issue 1904, 22 January 1876, p.90, is a description by Henty, as the *Standard* correspondent, of a the setting for a successful ball, given in the Prince's honour, at the Madras Club in December. It amounts to about 400 words.

Volume LXVIII: In issue 1911, 11 March 1876, p.262, are short extracts from Henty's account of the Royal Procession at Agra, which took place on 25 January.

Volume LXVIII: In issue 1912, 18 March 1876, p.282, under the heading 'Our Sketches from India' are references to the Prince's visit to Jeypore: 'The city is described as very different from any other Indian or Asiatic town. We borrow the following from the *Standard* correspondent:'. Henty wrote well over 1000 words to set the scene in considerable detail.

215. LONGMAN'S SCHOOL MAGAZINE

A monthly illustrated paper for school and home reading, published by Longmans, Green, and Co., from February 1892 to March 1903.

Volume IX: 'Chateau and Ship' (see §4) appears in No.100, May 1900, following its appearance the previous year in *Yule-Tide Yarns* (§2, 194).

216. THE LUDGATE ILLUSTRATED MAGAZINE

A monthly magazine first published in 1891 from 53 Fleet Street, London, E.C.

Volume VI: 'A Close Shave' (see §4) appears in the issue for April 1894, pp.612–617. There are six illustrations by J. Barnard Davis.

217. THE MORNING ADVERTISER

Organ of the Licensed Victuallers. A London morning daily paper, first published 8 February 1794.

In 1855 (see B. McCall Barbour in *Boys*, Vol.I, No.10, 19 November 1892, p.155; and Gabriel S.Woods, entry for G.A.Henty in *Dictionary of National Biography*), some letters Henty had written home from the Crimea, while in the Commissariat Department of the army, were shown by his father to the Editor of the *Morning Advertiser*. He is stated by William Allan to have been J.C.Robinson (see *The Cornhill Magazine*, No.1082, Winter 1974/75), but recorded in the *Cambridge Bibliography of English Literature* as James Grant. The letters were apparently accepted for publication, and followed by further dispatches.

This newspaper covered the Crimean War very thoroughly, publishing long and regular dispatches from their own Special Correspondent. From early May, 1855, they also published a few occasional dispatches from 'A Military Correspondent'. Some of them deal with supply, provisions, hospitals, etc., and the arrival of Miss Nightingale at Scutari, and they are all probably Henty's work.

218. THE PRESTON GUARDIAN

A weekly newspaper, price one penny.

May to September, 1895: Henty's 'A Woman of the Commune' (see §1) is serialised from issue 4106, Saturday 4 May, for 25 episodes, ending in issue 4130, Saturday 19 October 1895. The serialisation was announced in issue 4105, a week before the first instalment. The paper was not owned by Tillotsons, but the serialisation was arranged by the Tillotson Newspaper Syndicate, of Bolton, with whom Henty was under contract (see *A Woman of the Commune*, §1, 65.1, Note 1).

219. ST. NICHOLAS

An illustrated monthly magazine, published by The Century Co., New York; Macmillan and Co., London.

Volume XXVI: 'The Sole Survivors' (see §4) is serialised in six instalments, starting in No.1, November 1898, pp.20–27. Eleven illustrations are credited to G.Varian in the list of Contents of the annual volume, but only seven are by him. Of the others one is unsigned, two bear an unidentified monogram, and the last, the only one in line, is by Reginald B.Birch (illustrator of *Little Lord Fauntleroy*).

220. SCOTTISH NIGHTS

A weekly magazine of sixteen pages, price one penny. Also issued in monthly parts, price 4d., with pink paper covers, printed in black on page 1 with list of contents below the banner. Edited by Charles Maclaren, and published by MacLaren and Sons, 128 Renfield Street, Glasgow.

Volumes XIII and XIV: 'The Curse of Carne's Hold. A Tale of Adventure.' (§1, 40) was announced three times, in the issues for 16, 23, and 30 March 1889, as 'Will Shortly Appear: A New and Brilliant Story of Love and War, Romance and Adventure, by G.A. Henty, Author of "The Lion of the North," "With Clive in India,"etc., etc." The serialisation began on p.210 of the issue for 6 April 1889, each instalment consisting of one chapter. The first six parts (only) started with a 'synopsis of previous chapters'. Chapter XIII is in the final issue of Volume XIII, 29 June 1889. Chapter XIV is in the first issue of Volume XIV, dated Saturday 6 July 1889, and the story ends with Chapter XX in the issue for 17 August 1889.

Volume XX: 'Saved by a Woman' (see §4) appears in the issue for 29 April 1893.

221. SEASIDE MAIDENS

See TINSLEYS' MAGAZINE (224, below), and §2, 176.

222. THE STANDARD

Appeared with this name as a London evening paper from 21 May 1827 to 29 June 1857, when it became a morning daily. Ceased publication 16 March 1916. An evening edition was published from June 1860 as the *Evening Standard*, which still continues.

Henty was first appointed a Special Correspondent in 1865, and continued from time to time in that capacity until 1876. It was for the *Standard* that most, though not all, of his journalistic work was done. He gives (in *Who's Who, 1898*) details of his periods as War Correspondent and as Special Correspondent as follows: 'was through Austro-Italian, Franco-German, and Turco-Servian wars; Abyssinian and Ashanti Expeditions; with Garibaldi in the Tyrol, etc.' His dispatches as Special Correspondent are too numerous to be detailed here. They were shared by this newspaper with its associated *Evening Standard*, §3, 208.

The Editor from 1857–1872 was Thomas Hamber, who was later Editor of the *Morning Advertiser* (§3, 217). Subsequent Editors in Henty's time were: from 1872, James Johnstone, Jnr, the proprietor's son, in tandem for less than a year with Sir John Gorst (see below), who then took over alone until 1874; and, from 1874 to 1900, W.H.Mudford.

I am indebted for historical information to David Gunby of Canterbury University, New Zealand, and to Dr Dennis Griffiths, official historian of the *Standard* and the *Evening Standard* (q.v.), whose work, *Plant Here The Standard*, is to be published shortly. He first kindly confirmed my suspicion that the Editor, Sir John (Eldon) Gorst (M.A., LL.D., F.R.S., Q.C., M.P. for Cambridge 1866–1868) was in fact the author, J.E. Gorst, who had published in 1864 *The Maori King*. That book, described by M.P.K. Sorrenson in the *Dictionary of New Zealand Biography*, Vol.I, p.155, as 'one of the classics of New Zealand literature', is one for which Henty was later taken to task for plagiarising in his *Maori and Settler* (1891), §1, 49, (see Appendix I, Notes 15–16). In a substantial entry in the *Dictionary of National Biography* Myra Curtis describes Gorst's distinguished career, but both she, and Sorrenson in the *D.N.Z.B.*, omit any reference to the *Standard* newspapers. Gorst himself showed the same reticence in his entry for *Who's Who, 1898.*

223. THE TEMPLE MAGAZINE

An illustrated monthly magazine for Home and Sunday Reading, published by Horace Marshall & Son, Temple House, Temple Avenue, London, E.C., edited by John Foster Fraser.

Volume IV: 'Plucky and Cool' (see §4), published five years earlier in the *Western Weekly News* (227, below), is in the issue for February 1900, pp.371–377, with two illustrations by Sydney Cowell (see Appendix IV, Part 2).

224. TINSLEYS' MAGAZINE

A monthly magazine with illustrations, founded by William Tinsley shortly after the death of his younger brother, Edward, in 1868, and published at one shilling by Tinsley Brothers, 8 Catherine Street, Strand, London, W.C.

For four years it was edited by Edmund Yates, and thereafter by William Tinsley or his assistant William Croft (see Appendix II, Part 2), until Edmund Downey was appointed Editor in 1879. About 1881, Tinsley sold the magazine, retaining a controlling interest. In the end this, too, was sold, Tinsley expressed horror at subsequent activities. Tinsley Brothers had ceased business by 1884.

Volume IV: 'Coming Together' (see §4) appears in the issue for March 1869, pp.182–192, anonymously, and without illustration.

Volume V: 'The King of Clubs' (see §4) appears in the issue for September 1869, pp.235–240, anonymously, and without illustration.

Volume V: 'A Simple Story' (see §4) appears in the issue for November 1869, pp.472–480, anonymously, and without illustration.

Volume XVIII: Henty's 'Sir Sala Jung and the Berars' appears in the issue for June 1876, pp.617–626. This (signed) report resulted from Henty's tour in India.

Summer Number, 1880: Seaside Maidens (§2, 176).

The three short stories that appeared in Volumes IV and V were reported by *Dartt* (p.120, Note 1, under *Seaside Maidens*, and elsewhere under the names of each story), as leaves from magazines, 'origin unknown', bound up with other items in one of Henty's own volumes of his work, now in the Lilly Library of Indiana University.

At my request, William Cagle, Librarian of the Lilly Library, kindly sent me xerox copies of the leaves, and by studying the typography I was able to identify their source. It turned out less difficult than anticipated: all three were from issues of the same magazine. The stories follow the publication by Tinsley Brothers of Henty's first two books, *A Search for a Secret*, 1867, (§1, 1) and *The March to Magdala*, 1868 (§1, 2). 'A Simple Story' may well have been written for his own young children, and is very much in the style of such stories published at that date. In *The Art of Authorship* (§2, 124) Henty wrote: 'I used always to have my children with me for an hour after dinner, and to tell them stories' (see Appendix II, Part 1).

225. THE UNION JACK

A weekly Magazine of Healthy, Stirring Tales of Adventure by Land and Sea for Boys, price one penny, published by Griffith and Farran, West Corner of St Paul's Churchyard, London, E.C., edited by W.H.G. Kingston up to issue No.18, 29 April 1880, and thereafter by G.A. Henty. The magazine failed, and from Volume 2, No.60, 17 February 1881, Henty commissioned Cecil Brooks & Co., a small publishing business at 12 Catherine Street, Strand, London, W.C., to issue it at his expense. In No.79, 7 June 1881, Henty announced he had managed to get the magazine taken over by Sampson Low, Marston, Searle and Rivington, and that Cecil Brooks & Co. would continue to publish it for them. The new imprint, in the back fold of the next issue, confirms that, but the name of Cecil Brooks is omitted in No.83, 28 July 1881. From No.84 the imprint changes to 'Published for Sampson Low & Co. by Mr E.R. Curtice, 12 and 14 Strand': Curtice is listed in the Post Office Directory for 1882 as a wholesale newspaper agent, of 12–14 Catherine Street, Strand, and this correct address (in the same building as Cecil Brooks & Co.) is given in No.85. By October 1881 the name of Sampson Low appears alone as publisher.

Griffith & Farran, and later Sampson Low, sold annual binding cases, in decorative cloth of various colours and designs, so that readers could have their sets of weekly issues bound privately. Printed title pages and lists of Contents were also issued for that purpose. Both publishers also offered for sale ready-bound annual volumes as they were completed. In spite of poor circulation figures for the periodical there was clearly some demand for bound volumes: and Sampson Low even went to the expense of reprinting title pages for Volume I with their own imprint replacing that of Griffith & Farran.

Volume I: 'Times of Peril' is serialised, starting in issue No.1, 1 January 1880, p.9, for six instalments. Serialisation was resumed in issue No.21, 20 May 1880, p.329, under the revised title 'In Times of Peril' for a further twenty instalments. For further details of this arrangement see *In Times of Peril*, §1, 9.1, Note 1; and for details of the illustrations in the *Union Jack* and in the book, 9.1, Notes 4–11.

In his Editorial in No.21, Henty remarked that many of his readers would 'see that I have acceded to their request, and have continued the publication of *In Times of Peril*. I fear that here and there the story will be found almost too historical for a magazine appearing weekly. However, if occasionally they get a number in which the story seems a little dull, they will get so much adventure at other times that they will, I hope, be pleased with it in the long run'. It is not impossible that the original

Editor, W.H.G. Kingston, had criticised the story and brought the serialisation to an end. Henty brought it back when he was in charge as Editor.

Volume I: Between the two periods of serialisation described above, another Henty story was printed in its place. 'Facing Death' began in No.16, 15 April 1880, at p.244, and ran for five instalments, finishing in No.20, 13 May 1880. There are four unacknowledged wood-engravings, two of which are probably by John Jellicoe.

Facing Death was published in book form by Blackie two years later (§1, 10). New illustrations were commissioned from Gordon Browne, and the story is much longer than in this serialised version. Dennis Butts wrote, in the *Henty Society Bulletin*, Volume VII, No.56, Summer 1991: 'What Henty does in the serial version of "Facing Death" is to concentrate on those parts of the story which he considers dramatic and exciting, the great strike, the threatened violence, and the explosion. The serial omits the references to Nelly Hardy, the heroine, and minimises all Jack's hard work to improve himself. Everything happens very quickly, with little sense of time passing, and Jack's ultimate success thus seems to come very easily'.

If Kingston did criticise 'In Times of Peril' as 'dull' and 'too historical for a magazine', Henty may have wanted to show he really could write an exciting story, even if it meant fairly hefty cuts in his original manuscript of *Facing Death*.

Volume I: 'Seth Harper's Story' is in three instalments, starting in No.22, 27 May 1880, at p.341. There are three illustrations by John Jellicoe, engraved on wood by W.J. Welch; also three small decorative headpieces which have been trimmed to fit, and probably came from printer's or publisher's stock. The story consists of edited extracts from *Out on the Pampas* (§1, 4): starting at p.85 in 4.1.

Volume II: 'The Cornet of Horse', in twenty-six instalments, starts in No.41, 7 October 1880, at p.5, illustrated by H. Petherick and others. For notes on the title, and its illustration, see *The Cornet of Horse*, §1. 8.

Volume II: 'A Pipe of Mystery' (see §4) appears in No.52, 23 December 1880, pp.177–182, with one illustration by John Jellicoe.

Volume II: 'An Indian Cattle Raid' is in two instalments, starting in No.64, 17 March 1881, at p.369, with three illustrations. The story is extracted from *Out on the Pampas* (§1, 4), published ten years previously, as is one of the illustrations by J.B. Zwecker. The other two are by John Jellicoe.

Volume II: 'The Young Franc-Tireurs' (§1, 5) is in twenty-two instalments, starting in No.67, 7 April 1881, at p.417. There are twenty-eight illustrations by various artists. They include six of the eight engravings of R.T. Landells's drawings used by Griffith & Farran in the book, 5.1, dated 1872, and eighteen of the twenty by Janet-Lange in a French edition of the book dated 1873. There are also two illustrations by A.S.Lumley, and two by unknown artists (one probably from printer's or publisher's stock). The arrangement of the text and illustrations in the magazine is appallingly haphazard, many pictures being placed within the text of other stories, with no cross-reference. Henty had announced this serial over six months earlier in Volume I of the *Union Jack*: on 23 September 1880 (p.624) he wrote that the book had 'been for some time out of print'.

Volume II: 'Bears and Dacoits' (see §4) is in two parts, starting in issue No.78, 23 June 1881, p.604, with one illustration by a French artist (? P. Benett) probably from publisher's stock. A number of such illustrations were used in the *Union Jack*, possibly from a stock collection acquired in Sampson Low's dealings with French publishers (see Appendix II, Part 3).

Volume II: The first five true stories of Henty's adventures appear in various issues of this Volume, under the heading 'An Editor's Yarns'. The Introduction to the series appears in No.71, 5 May 1881, at p.495: this and the stories that follow represent virtually all Henty's autobiographical writing:

1. 'How I was nearly Hung' is in two parts, in No.74, 26 May 1881, p.542, and No.75, 2 June 1881, p.558.

2. 'A Trip in a Steam Launch', in three parts, is in No.77, 16 June 1881, No.81, p.591, 14 July 1881, p.655, and No.83. 28 July 1881, p.686.

3. 'Too Close to be Pleasant' appears in No.85, 11 August 1881, p.719.

4. 'Camp Life', in two parts, is in No.87, 25 August 1881, p.750, and No.89, 8 September 1881, p.781. This is a re-written version of the dispatch that was originally published anonymously in the *Cornhill Magazine*, June 1868, under the title 'Camp Life in Abyssinia' (see 206, above).

5. This fifth article under the heading 'An Editor's Yarns' is untitled, but relates to his assignment as a Special Correspondent in the Franco-German War. It appears in No.91, 22 September 1881, p.815.

Volume III: 'The Wreck on the Goodwins' (see §4) is in No.103, 15 December 1881, at p.173, with one illustration, probably taken from stock. In a footnote to the heading Henty acknowledges Tinsley Brothers and *Seaside Maidens* (§2, 221).

Volume III: 'The Queen's Cup. A Yachting Incident' (see §4), in No.106, 5 January 1882, p.220, is not illustrated. Not to be confused with *The Queen's Cup*, (§1, 78).

Volume III: 'A Fishwife's Dream' (see §4) is in No.107, 12 January 1882, p.236, without illustration.

Volume III: 'Surly Joe' (see §4) is in No.113, 23 February 1882, p.333, without illustration.

Volume III: 'Winning his Spurs' is in twenty-six instalments, starting in No.119, 6 April 1882, at p.425. Seventy-five of the eighty-one illustrations are by Horace Petherick, and were subsequently used in the book, *Winning his Spurs*, Sampson Low, 1882 (§1, 11). The others are wood-engravings, probably from publisher's stock.

Volume III: 'Presence of Mind in a Collier Boy', in No.127, 1 June 1882, at p.560, is an account of an incident in a coal mine, coupled with an appeal for money for the boy in question. I agree with the attribution to Henty (*Dartt*, p.152).

Volume III: A further six true stories by Henty of his adventures appear under the heading 'An Editor's Yarns' as follows:

6. 'Among the Gold and Silver Mines', in four instalments, starts in No.93, 6 October 1881, at p.16.

7. 'Out with Garibaldi' is in No.101, 7 December 1881, p.142. Not to be confused with Henty's novel with the same title (§1, 98).

8. 'Among the Gallas' is in No.105, 29 December 1881, at p.207. This is a re-written version of Henty's dispatch published anonymously in *All the Year Round* (195, above), Volume XX, 1868.

9. 'Out to the Crimea', in two parts, is in No.108, 19 January 1882, p.255, and No.110, 2 February 1882, p.287.

10. 'The Hospital at Scutari' is in No.112, 16 February 1882, p.319.

Volume III: 'Working Up' (see §4), in two parts, is in No.138, 17 August 1882, p.734, and No.139, 24 August 1882, p.750. Part I has a small vignette wood-engraving of a dog, artist unknown.

Volume III: 'The Smuggler's Cutter' (see §4) is in No.142, 14 September 1882, p.795, without illustration.

Christmas Number, 1882: *Old England's Flag:* Henty's 'Do Your Duty' (see §1) appears at pages 1–13, with four pen-drawings by John Jellicoe. This is the only Special Number issued during the four years of publication of the *Union Jack*, and it was bound up in the Annual Volume for the final year of issue, being printed on paper of the larger size used for all issues from 3 October 1882. The paper was also smoother and whiter than that used previously, but the improvement was not maintained and the quality deteriorated from the issue of 3 April 1883.

New Series, Volume I: 'Jack Archer' is in twenty-five instalments, starting in No.27, 3 April 1883, at p.426. There were five battle-plans, and seventeen illustrations of which eleven are wood-engravings after John Jellicoe. One pen-drawing is possibly also his. There is also a wood-engraving after Gordon Browne. Three engravings in a different style and by unknown hands include a seascape and two battle-scenes in landscapes. All were used in the book, *Jack Archer*, Sampson Low, 1883 (§1, 14). A battle-scene, also anonymous, was not re-used in the book.

From the first issue of the fourth year (New Series, Vol.1, No.1) Bernard Heldmann worked with Henty as joint Editor, and his name appeared in the banner. The magazine was produced in a larger page size, and generally more lavishly. There must, however, have been some serious disagreement: at the end of No.36, 5 June 1883, a curt NOTICE appears: 'Mr Heldmann has ceased to be connected in any way with the *Union Jack*'. No explanation was ever given, and Heldmann's name disappeared from the banner of that and subsequent issues.

Another, slightly longer, statement appeared on the final page of No.52, 25 September 1883, in the form of a letter from the Editor, announcing that the *Union Jack* had ceased publication.

226. THE UNITED SERVICE GAZETTE

A weekly periodical dealing with Military and Naval Service matters. Subtitled 'Auxiliary, Reserve, and Colonial Forces Chronicle'. Published for the Proprietor at 4 and 6 Catherine Street, Strand, W.C., price 6d. First issue, 9 February 1833.

There is no indication, in copies examined, of the identity of either the proprietor or the editor. Unsigned leading articles are written with expert or specialist knowledge of either military or naval matters, not all of which is likely to have been available to a single writer. In the months before the summer of 1885 the periodical showed considerable political opposition to the current management of the army and selection of senior officers.

In a letter to General Lord Wolsley dated 15 August 1885, in the Wolsley Autograph Collection held by Hove Public Library, Henty wrote: 'Permit me to add my congratulations to the many which you must have received upon your safe return home [from Khartoum], and the honours which you have won. I am now Editor of the above paper, and in todays issue have ventured to express my appreciation of your work. I wrote to Sir A[rchibald] Alison when I assumed the reins here, and said that so long as I remained here, there would be no renewal of the very hostile tone to the War Office which had previously marked the paper. I need not repeat that to you, but my view of the matter is that a Service paper has scarcely the same freedom of criticism that other newspapers possess, as it is contrary to all discipline for a journal read by men of all ranks in the service persistently to attack the doings and decisions of the heads of that service. Criticism is one thing, persistent hostility another'.

In another letter, the following December, he told Wolsley he had retired from the editorship three months previously 'owing to a change in the proprietorship'. From the letters, and from a perusal of a number of issues of 1884 and 1885, it appears that Henty's tenure of office was brief. But he clearly made strong efforts to change the policy of the paper, and in the issues of both 15 and 29 August 1885 published strong leaders supporting Wolsley, many years of whose life were spent campaigning for army reform.

Henty's leading article in the latter issue begins 'Viscount Wolsley wields the pen as ably as he wields the sword', referring to his final despatch from Cairo to the Secretary of State for War, published in full in the same issue. The article ends, with reference to the failure of the expedition to relieve Gordon: 'When the history of the campaign is written in cool, unimpassioned language, apart from politics and divested of party bias, the deeds of Lord Wolsley and his gallant band will stand out brightly in the annals of military history, and no discredit will attach to him or them for having been "two days too late!".'

That the readership of the paper was by no means confined to commissioned ranks is borne out by the contents of its sometimes lively correspondence columns.

227. THE WESTERN WEEKLY NEWS

A weekly newspaper published in Plymouth, Devon.

1893: 'Dorothy's Double. The Story of a Great Deception' is serialised from Saturday, 16 September, to Saturday 30 December 1893. The first instalment, consisting of the Prologue and Chapter I, has two illustrations in line, signed 'Hare'. The artist is probably St. George Hare, R.I. (see Appendix IV, Part 2).

Christmas Number, 1893: 'A Prevision of Evil' (see §4) is published at pp.18–19.

Summer Number, 1894: 'An Anxious Time' (see §4) is published on page 24.

1895: 'Plucky and Cool' (see §4) is in the issue for 7 December, at page 2.

228. YOUNG ENGLAND

An Illustrated Magazine for Recreation and Instruction, published by the Young England Office, 55 and 56 Old Bailey, London, E.C.; Book Saloon, 57 and 59 Ludgate Hill, London, E.C. Price threepence monthly.

From 1 January 1895 for several years, sheets of the magazine were bought by The Boys' Brigade and bound in their own covers for sale to their members, still at threepence monthly, as *The Boys' Brigade Gazette*, (or *The B.B.*, as it was also given on the cover). Volume II of this venture contained the material published as Volume XVII of *Young England* (see below).

Volume X: 'Joe Polwreath, the Hunchback' (see §4) is in three instalments, starting in No.2, February 1889, at p.1. There are two illustrations.

Volume XIII: 'In the Grip of the Press Gang' (see §4), in five instalments, starting in No.1, January 1892, p.1, has a full-page plate in black and brown, presented with an issue of the magazine, and later used as frontispiece to the bound Annual Volume.

Volume XVII: 'On the Spanish Main' (see §4) is in five instalments, starting in No.1, January 1896, p.1. There are four illustrations by Ayton Symington.

SHORT STORIES BY HENTY

Among Malay Pirates	§3, 201	*The Boy's Own Paper*, Volume XX, 1897, serial.
An Anxious Time	§3, 227	*The Western Weekly News*, Summer Number, 1894.
	§3, 198	*The Bohemian*, September 1895.
At Duty's Call*	§1, 103	*At Duty's Call*, Chambers's Continuous Reader (1902).
	§2, 134	*Brains and Bravery*, Chambers, 1903.
At Talavera	§2, 149	*52 Stories of Courage and Endeavour*, Hutchinson (1901).
Bears and Dacoits	§3, 225	*The Union Jack*, Volume II, June 1881.
	§1, 42	*Tales of Daring and Danger*, Blackie 1890.
	§1, 69	*Bears and Dacoits*, Blackie (1896).
	§1, 69	*Bears and Dacoits and Other Stories*, Blackie, (1901).
The Boatman's Story†	§2, 129	*Blackie's Century Readers*, Reader III, 1888.
A Brave Châtelaine	§2, 146	*52 Stirring Stories for Boys*, Hutchinson, (1900).
A Brush with the Chinese	§1, 42	*Tales of Daring and Danger*, Blackie, 1890.
	§1, 57	*Tales from Henty*, Blackie 1893.
	§1, 69	*Bears and Dacoits and Other Stories*, Blackie (1901).
	§1, 71	*White-Faced Dick And Two Other Stories*, Blackie, n.d.
	§1, 71	*White-Faced Dick & Another Story*, Blackie, n.d.
The Burman's Treasure	§2, 143	*52 Further Stories for Boys*, Hutchinson, (1891).
Burton and Son	§3, 201	*The Boy's Own Paper*, Volume XXI, 1898, serial.
	§2, 157	*Grit and Go*, Chambers, 1902.
Chateau and Ship	§2, 194	*Yule-Tide Yarns*, Longmans, Green, 1899.
	§3, 215	*Longman's School Magazine*, Volume IX, May 1900.
A Close Shave	§3, 216	*The Ludgate Illustrated Magazine*, Volume VI, April 1894.
A Coaching Adventure	§2, 166	*Our Annual*, Griffith Farran Browne & Co., (1883).
Coming Together	§3, 224	*Tinsleys' Magazine*, Volume IV, March 1869.
A Death Warning	§2, 144	*52 Holiday Stories for Boys*, Hutchinson, (1899).
A Desperate Gang	§3, 199	*Boys*, Volume II, 1894, serial.
	§2, 189	*Through Fire and Storm*, Partridge, 1898.

*First published as 'Duty' (q.v.).   †Also entitled 'Surly Joe' (q.v.).

Do Your Duty	§3, 225	*The Union Jack*, Christmas Number, 1882.
	§1, 25	*Yarns on the Beach*, Blackie, 1886.
	§1, 89	*Do Your Duty*, Blackie (1900).
	§1, 89	*Do Your Duty*, Blackie's Story-Book Reader (1905).
Down a Crevasse	§3, 201	*The Boy's Own Paper*, Summer Number 1901.
	§2, 134	*Brains and Bravery*, Chambers, 1903.
	§1, 110	*Gallant Deeds*, Chambers's Supplementary Reader, 1905.
Duty*	§3, 202	*The Brigadier*, as a pamphlet for presentation to members of The Boys' Brigade, Christmas 1890, and later as a serial in the periodical, Volume II, 1903 (see also §1, 103.1).
Escape from Massacre	§2, 152	*52 Stories of Life and Adventure for Boys*, Hutchinson (1895).
Faithful	§2, 172	*Please Tell me Another Tale*, Skeffington, 1890.
Faithful to the Death	§2, 138	*Camps and Quarters*, Ward Lock, 1889.
The Fetish Hole	§3, 201	*The Boy's Own Paper*, Volume XIX, 1896, serial.
A Fish-Wife's Dream	§3, 224	*Tinsleys' Magazine*, Summer Number, 1880
	§2, 176	('Seaside Maidens').
	§3, 225	*The Union Jack*, Volume III, January 1882.
	§1, 25	*Yarns on the Beach*, Blackie, 1886.
	§2, 158	*Hazard and Heroism*, Chambers, 1904.
A Frontier Girl	§3, 210	*The Girl's Realm*, Volume 3, November 1900.
	§1, 113	*In the Hands of the Malays*, Blackie, 1905.
Gerald Mayfield's Reward	§2, 178	*Steady and Strong*, Chambers, 1905.
The Golden Cañon	§3, 199	*Boys*, Volume I, 1892, serial.
	§2, 170	*Peril and Prowess*, Chambers, 1899.
	§1, 110	*Gallant Deeds*, Chambers's Supplementary Reader, 1905.
How a Drummer Boy Saved the Regiment	§2, 164	*Nister's Holiday Annual*, 1909
	§2, 155	*The Golden Story Book*, Nister (1913).
	§2, 160	*In Storyland*, Nister, n.d.
How Count Conrad von Waldensturm took Goldstein	§1, 111	*A Soldier's Daughter*, Blackie, 1906.
Hunted by an Elephant	§2, 147	*52 Stories for Boyhood and Youth*, Hutchinson (1893).
	§2, 173	*Pluck*, Shaw, n.d. (post 1928).
In the Grip of the Press Gang	§3, 228	*Young England*, Volume XIII, 1892, serial.
	§2, 159	*In Battle and Breeze*, Partridge, 1896.
In the Hands of Sicilian Brigands	§2, 178	*Steady and Strong*, Chambers, 1905.
	§1, 110	*Gallant Deeds*, Chambers's Supplementary Reader, 1905.

*Also published as 'At Duty's Call' (q.v.).

In the Hands of the Malays	§1, 113	*In the Hands of the Malays*, Blackie, 1905.
In Troubled Times	§2, 162	*Nister's Holiday Annual*, 1902.
	§2, 181	*Stories for Merry Hearts*, Nister, n.d.
	§2, 171	*Picture Book Treasures*, Nister, n.d.
An Indian Surround	§2, 153	*52 Stories of Pluck and Peril*, Hutchinson (1896).
An Indian's Gratitude	§2, 145	*52 Other Stories for Boys*, Hutchinson (1892).
Jack Dillon of Dunnamore	§3, 205	*Chums*, Volume I, 1893, serial.
Joe Polwreath, the Hunchback	§3, 228	*Young England*, Volume X, 1889, serial.
	§2, 140	*Dash and Daring*, Chambers, 1898.
John Hawke's Fortune*	§1, 93	*John Hawke's Fortune*, Chapman & Hall, 1901; Blackie, 1906.
The King of Clubs	§3, 224	*Tinsleys' Magazine*, Volume V, September 1869.
Little Mistress Valentia	§2, 161	*In the Chimney Corner*, Nister (1899).
	§2, 163	*Nister's Holiday Annual*, 1905.
	§2, 169	*Pastime Tales*, Nister (1913).
The Man-Eater of the Terai	§2, 148	*52 Stories of Boy Life at Home and Abroad*, Hutchinson (1894).
A Notable Christmas Dinner		*The Sunny South*, Atlanta, Ga., Vol.XXXIX, No.44, w/ending 21 December 1901: no record of publication in United Kingdom.
A Narrow Escape	§3, 224	*Tinsleys' Magazine*, Summer Number 1880
	§2, 176	('Seaside Maidens').
	§2, 178	*Steady and Strong*, Chambers, 1905.
The Old Pit Shaft	§3, 203	*The Captain*, Volume V, August 1901.
	§2, 158	*Hazard and Heroism*, Chambers, 1904.
	§1, 110	*Gallant Deeds*, Chambers's Supplementary Reader, 1905.
On a Mexican Ranche	§2, 193	*Yule Logs*, Longmans, Green, 1898.
On an Indian Trail	§2, 134	*Brains and Bravery*, Chambers, 1903.
	§1, 110	*Gallant Deeds*, Chambers's Supplementary Reader, 1905.
On the Cliff	§3, 224	*Tinsleys' Magazine*, Summer Number 1880
	§2, 176	('Seaside Maidens').
	§2, 158	*Hazard and Heroism*, Chambers, 1904.
On the Spanish Main	§3, 228	*Young England*, Volume XVII, 1893, serial.
	§3, 200	*The Boys' Brigade Gazette* (*The B.B.*), Volume II, 1893, serial.
	§2, 140	*Dash and Daring*, Chambers, 1898.
	§1, 88	*On the Spanish Main*, Chambers's Continuous Reader, 1899.

*See this title at §1, 93. Some editions were reduced in length.

*Not to be confused with the book of the same name.
[†]'A Pipe of Mystery' and 'A Pipe of Opium' are two versions of the same story.

The Son of a Cavalier	§2, 150	*52 Stories of Duty and Daring for Boys*, Hutchinson (1897).
The Spy of Belfort	§3, 211	*Grip*, Volume I, November 1883.
Surly Joe[†]	§3, 224	*Tinsleys' Magazine*, Summer Number 1880
	§2, 176	('Seaside Maidens').
	§3, 225	*The Union Jack*, Volume III, February 1882.
	§1, 25	*Yarns on the Beach*, Blackie, 1886.
	§1, 70	*Surly Joe*, Blackie (1896).
The Thug's Revenge	§2, 158	*Hazard and Heroism*, Chambers, 1904.
Till Death, and After	§3, 213	*The Hour Glass*, Volume II, November 1887.
Torpedo Boat 240	§3, 204	*Chambers's Journal*, Volume II, 1899, serial.
	§2, 190	*Venture and Valour*, Chambers, 1900.
A Traitor in Camp	§2, 151	*52 Stories of Heroism in Life and Action*, Hutchinson (1898).
True to Her Charge	§2, 182	*Stories Jolly, Stories New, Stories Strange and Stories True*, Skeffington, 1889.
Turning the Tables	§2, 138	*Camps and Quarters*, Ward Lock, 1889.
White-Faced Dick	§3, 197	*Beeton's Boy's Own Magazine*, 1889.
	§2, 185	*Stories of History* (Beeton's Boys' Own Books), Ward Lock, 1890.
	§1, 42	*Tales of Daring and Danger*, Blackie, 1890.
	§1, 69	*Bears and Dacoits & Other Stories*, Blackie, (1901).
	§1, 71	*White-Faced Dick*, Blackie (1896).
	§1, 71	*White-Faced Dick And Two Other Stories*, Blackie, n.d.
	§1, 71	*White-Faced Dick And Another Story*, Blackie, n.d.
Working Up	§3, 224	*Tinsleys' Magazine*, Summer Number 1880
	§2, 176	('Seaside Maidens').
	§3, 225	*The Union Jack*, Volume III, 1882, serial.
	§1, 110	*Gallant Deeds*, Chambers's Supplementary Reader, 1905.
The Wreck on the Goodwins	§3, 224	*Tinsleys' Magazine*, Summer Number 1880,
	§2, 176	('Seaside Maidens').
	§3, 225	*The Union Jack*, Volume III, December 1881.
	§2, 158	*Hazard and Heroism*, Chambers, 1904.
The Wreckers of Pendarven	§2, 165	*Now for a Story!*, Skeffington, 1893.
	§2, 165	*The Wreckers of Pendarven*, Angel Hill Publications, 1979.

†Also published as 'The Boatman's Story' (q.v.).

APPENDIX I

THE HENTY FORMULA FOR BOYS

'It is no harsh criticism', wrote F.J. Harvey Darton, 'to say that if you have read only two or three of the seventy-odd books [Henty] wrote for boys you know the rest, even if you like the one first encountered better than those you met later when you could recognise the formula'. He wrote of George Manville Fenn insisting on 'Henty's avowed enthusiam for "manliness"', and that the artists who illustrated his books, including Gordon Browne, 'usually drew a stock figure of a manly young Briton of seventeen or so who could never be mistaken for anything more flexible or temperamental'.[1]

Henty's formula, once established, was there for others to copy. Henty 'had many followers, and books as good as his, on much the same lines, though with all the adornments of later science and discovery to vary the incidents, appear in great numbers to this day'. Perhaps Darton is being a little harsh: Henty was writing post-Walter Scott, but was nevertheless the originator of a form of literature that was not simply an 'adventure-story'. It was an episode of history, told as accurately as Henty could manage, into which an adventure-story was woven. No one was writing similar books. Darton admits that 'Henty's own career – Westminster, Caius, the Army, special correspondent for *The Standard* – ensured not only that it could be manufactured readily but that the goods were of thoroughly sound quality'.[2]

The essayist Bernard Darwin wrote an anonymous fourth leader in *The Times* inspired by a just-published report on 'the taste in literature of the boy readers of Shoreditch between fourteen and eighteen'. That report had shown Henty was, in 1950, 'a great deal more popular than would be commonly thought': there was still a 'regular consistent demand for him'. Darwin recalled his own preparatory-school days at the end of the 1880s when Henty's novels were first appearing: 'There was the practical certainty, as Christmas drew near, of at least one brand-new Henty with a liberal splash of gilding on the cover. It more than compensated for the irritation of being annually and condescendingly addressed in the preface as "My dear lads". To some there may return a very particular vision. It is tea-time in the dining hall of a private school. The sound of the chumping of bread and butter is gradually dying away. Then there is heard from the dais a voice proclaiming "Those who have finished may read". Instantly, as if by a conjuring trick, some fifty or sixty Hentys are produced from nowhere and slapped down upon the table'.[3] For the boys for whom the formula was devised it worked, and it was still working, apparently, in 1950. According to members of The Henty Society there are those for whom it still works, more than ninety years after Henty's death.

In the latter part of his life journalists, keen to tap the fountainhead of the flourishing formula, were granted interviews. Resulting articles about Henty's books, and particularly his method of writing, are very repetitious. Perhaps the most readable was by Raymond Blathwayt, a skilled and well-known interviewer. What he wrote was later confirmed and enlarged upon by Henty himself in a little-known article written just before his death and published posthumously.[4]

'When I have once fixed, not on the story but on the epoch', Henty wrote, ' I send up to a London library and procure ten books on the subject. I glance through these. Perhaps only two of them will suit my purpose, so I send the others back and get another batch, until I have got everything I want. I get these books about ten days before I start writing. Then I have on my shelves at least a dozen atlases, some of them being amongst the earliest printed. These are very useful to me for stories of the Middle Ages, as I get the roads and coast lines that then existed, and in which many places have changed materially during the last three hundred years. I have, of course, a number of encyclopaedias from which I glean a lot of information about the character of the country, its population, products, and so on. Thus equipped I am able to start off on the story without having to pause to look up information. I lie on my sofa and smoke with two or three books open before me, the sofa being shared by three or four of my five dogs'.[4]

He had told Blathwayt he began work without any previous idea whatever of what the story was going to be. 'It gradually builds itself up from its surroundings. I dictate every word – in that way I think you obtain larger, finer sentences'. And he continued, in his own account, 'I work from half-past nine in the morning until one, and from half-past seven in the evening until ten. That is my regular programme for six months in the year; the other six I devote to yachting. I consider a fair day's work to be 6,500 words. The shortest time in which I ever wrote a book was when I did *With Buller in Natal*. I had not intended to write a story of the war, as I thought it would be too up-to-date. I had already finished my three books [for that year]; they were set up in type and ready to be printed. My publishers, however, urged me to write a war book. "How long can you give me?", I asked. "A month", they replied. I did it in twenty-four days counting in the Sundays, though I never work on Sundays. The book ran to 140,000 words, so that it is quite easy to calculate the daily average rate at which it was written'.[4]

Much earlier, in 1879, Edmund Downey had been appointed Editor of *Tinsleys' Magazine*: Henty asked 'if I knew any young fellow of intelligence who would act as his amanuensis. He did not want a shorthand writer; he wanted a smart long-hand man. I happened to know the ideal youth, and Henty engaged him. He worked with him for about two years, taking down stories for boys at Henty's dictation. My young friend told me that Henty used to walk up and down his study, smoking the eternal clay pipe, and reeling off stories as fast as he (the amanuensis) could write. Sometimes the author would say: "I'll leave you to yourself for the day. Boil down the official report of the battle of So-and-So – or this passage out of So-and-So's book." The work after a time seemed to the amanuensis to be so mechanical and so easy, that he assured me he could go on for at least a year writing automatically "Henty tales". I asked him to try how far the mechanism would go. He discovered that a chapter or two exhausted the powers of the machine minus Henty'.[5]

That the amanuensis was left alone to make such digests is revealing. No doubt Henty would have read, and perhaps corrected, each précis made for him, but it may be thought his interest lay more in the adventure story than in the historical narrative. Those two component parts of each story were clearly separated in his mind: that is confirmed by his remarks about readers of the *Union Jack* in 1880 on resuming the interrupted serialisation of *In Times of Peril*: 'I fear that here and there the story will be found almost too historical. However, if occasionally the story seems a little dull, they will get so much adventure at other times that they will, I hope, be pleased with it in the long run'.[6]

It is perhaps surprising that Henty should admit to his young readers that the history in his own books seemed dull. But less so when we know he left it to his amanuensis to 'boil down' books from the London Library. That he worked in this way, not attempting to re-write and instil new vigour into the historical sequences, leads one to suppose that he himself found some of the history not very gripping.

Although a reporter in *Chums* wrote that Henty 'informed me he carefully reads up the history of the period',[7] both Blathwayt's and Henty's own accounts disclaim very close advance study. And he apparently made no preliminary sketch of his plot nor any plan for the shape of his book before he started dictating. He just plunged straight in and let the story look after itself.

Many writers of fiction claim that once a story is started the characters take over and control the development of the plot. In Henty's case the main plots are pre-ordained by events of history, and the sub-plots can hardly be said to be controlled by the cardboard characters he repeatedly invented. A.J.P. Taylor wrote: 'Henty's books are not novels in the accepted sense at all. They are tales of adventure such as have been told from the beginning of time. Developed characters would get in the way of the narrative. All the reader wanted was a slightly idealised version of himself – moral integrity combined with physical prowess, quick in mind and body, and success guaranteed after the occasional setback'.[8]

Henty's history has not pleased everyone. But criticisms that have been made, apart from matters of detail, are sometimes those of his sources. Historians writing many years later may be expected frequently to have a changed view of history. In 1955, Godfrey Davies mounted a general attack on Henty's historical reliability, but limited his study to only four of his books, dealing with the Peninsular War and Waterloo.[9] His strongly worded criticism is in reality of Sir William Napier's 'political prejudices', but is aimed at Henty for having 'swallowed' those prejudices in relying on Napier's *History of the War in the Peninsular*. As to details, Davies agrees, 'Small mistakes matter little in novels written for boys, but the distortion of the whole course of the war is serious'. He also believes, however, that no one who relied solely on those source books could have arrived at an intelligible account of events.

Davies starts by noting 'the contrast between Napier's vivid style, and Henty's very pedestrian prose', but ends that 'Henty is at his best when describing incidents any time within half a century or so'. Bryher was one of many for whom Henty first stirred a lifelong interest in history. Among them, A.J.P.Taylor declared Henty 'a conscientious amateur historian', and if his work 'may seem dull to a later generation brought up on instant history, it was a great deal livelier than most of the textbooks then current'. Certainly, Henty was not gifted with great creative imagination. By nature he was a reporter, and it is widely held that the best of his writing was his journalism. He 'displayed in his novels the virtues of a newspaper correspondent – direct, clear and with no literary frills. Henty never aspired to be a "writer". He was merely doing an artisan's job. That won him 25 million readers. Probably it also deprived him of immortality. A journeyman, by definition, has no long staying power'.[10] Indeed, his adult novels and those written for boys came out of very much the same mould, some of the former being later issued as boys' books, changed only by the addition of illustration.

The essential bones of the plots in many of the boys' novels have more than a little in common: the hero is about fifteen when the story starts and owing to some family misfortune is thrown on his own resources. He finds a young friend who acts as a foil throughout the book, perhaps one saves the other's life; they somehow get involved in the main action, meet the chief historical figure, are captured and escape, perhaps more than once, meet and perhaps rescue a young girl who will clearly become the hero's wife in the final chapter. During the course of the narrative the hero meets as many historical figures as possible, both friends and enemies; eventually a reward, prize money, or a legacy come his way, and he returns home and settles down. There are endless variations, but the general pattern, as Darton implied, is constant. The habit of driving himself to produce three or four novels every year for over twenty years seems rather to have produced the success of the plodder than of the gifted storyteller. But plodder seems hardly the right word for a man who claims to have had an average output of 6,500 words a day.[11]

Henty has described some of his restrictions. 'It is a necessity of books for boys that the time of the action shall not extend over four, or, at most, five years, as the boys want their heroes to be boys; and, as they cannot well begin any exploits till they get to the age of sixteen, and as boys would cease to feel any vivid interest in them after they were one-and-twenty, the story has practically to finish at that age. The great difficulty is to introduce boys into military stories. In sea stories they are midshipmen, and the matter is easy. In land battles they must either be drummers, fifers, or trumpeters. In stories of the Middle Ages one has the assistance of pages, and I have frequently regretted that they have gone out of fashion, as they would be of great assistance to me.

'Of course, the hero must be British. That boys would have this so is evident from the fact that the sale of *The Cat of Bubastes*, *The Destruction of Jerusalem*, and *The Young Carthaginian*, in none of which could I possibly place a British boy, has been smaller than that of any books I have written; and they are the three stories that I rather expected would do especially well'.[12]

The rapidity of his work should perhaps have left Henty time for more serious digestion and more elegant paraphrasing of the borrowed history books. But his great concern for speed seems to have driven out the desire for such refinement. That the stories varied in quality was to be expected, from the rate at which the stock fictional figures were churned out, without development of character, and also according to the reliability of the history 'cribs' and the way they were transcribed. Manville Fenn, whose superficial biography of Henty shows he was not a close friend, writes that J.P. Griffith, 'a very rapid scribe, became the amanuensis and writer to whom he dictated every one of the books'.[13] Downey's young friend, mentioned above, had started in 1879, and Griffith worked for Henty from 1881 until his death, no doubt giving Henty's his first experience of shorthand. Griffith would have been as capable of editing his dictation as of boiling down history books.

In the *Chums* interview in 1893 Henty is reported to have said 'It all comes out of my head, but he does the actual writing. I never see any of my work until it comes to me from the printer's in the shape of proof sheets'.[14] If Griffith found occasion to improve the dictated word – and we know from Henty's surviving letters and inscriptions that his own grammar was far from flawless – the opportunity would have been there: by the time the proofs arrived from the printer Griffith could bank on a small amount of judicious editing not being noticed by the author.

Of Henty's publishers Blackie & Son were probably the best equipped to sub-edit manuscripts and 'prepare copy for the printer'. In earlier days publishers' readers met with wary disapproval, some having their very existence concealed. But Henty would have been well accustomed to having his work as a newspaper correspondent heavily 'subbed', and is even said to have briefly worked as a Reader himself.[15] Probably he not only accepted but actually expected a certain amount of 'cleaning up and polishing' to be done for him by Blackie's editorial staff.

Henty has been accused of plagiarism. Sometimes he does at least acknowledge his sources, as in the Prefaces to *With Clive in India* and *True to the Old Flag*. But more often he does not name the historians whose books he has drawn on. David Gunby, in New Zealand, has studied one example and suggests that 'Henty surpasses himself in *Maori and Settler* by the crudity of his method' of incorporating 'great slabs of historical background. . . Although it is not unnatural that, on arrival in Wellington, the Renshaws should want to know something about New Zealand, there is nothing natural about the "conversation", between Wilfrid and an obliging Mr Jackson which takes up the bulk of Chapter Nine. Mr Jackson releases a veritable flood of information, which, despite the inverted commas surrounding each paragraph, reads like nothing so much as a transcription from some history book. In fact some three-quarters of it is taken more or less verbatim (and unacknowledged) from J.E. Gorst's *The Maori King* (1864)'.[16] That is, of course, precisely the method reported by Edmund Downey from the account of his young friend who became Henty's amanuensis. Used in this way historical detail becomes dull, conversation wooden and narrative lacking in vitality.

As well as plagiarism Henty is accused of imperialism and racialism. What are we to think of his attitudes to such things? They have something in common. Plagiarism originally meant the kidnapping of slaves, then the appropriation of someone else's thoughts and ideas, and writings. Imperialism and racialism involve the domination or maltreatment of human beings, and of their ideas and ways of life. Humanity is unbelievably slow in coming to grips with such things. When Henty was a boy slavery had not yet been abolished. Even slaves in British colonies were declared free as late as 1833, and the world was only beginning to contemplate the impossible problem of righting the injustices the slave trade had caused. Imperialism, which cannot exist without racialism, was in Britain in the full flush of development.

'Above all', wrote the Revd Hugh Pruen, 'Henty is the great Imperialist. His writing days coincided with the high-water mark of Jingoism, with the premierships of Disraeli, Salisbury and Rosebery, and with the Jubilees, when the English were conscious for a brief period of a manifest destiny to which Kipling was to give matchless expression in his "Recessional" '.[17] Enlarging on this theme J.S. Bratton writes 'Henty's imperialism suffers from no sudden doubts about the legitimacy of violence; his conviction of English superiority is visited with no qualms about the failure of most Englishmen to live up to their Christian profession, and his racial generalisations make a simple dichotomy between "us" and "them", untroubled by any Christian conviction that all men are equal'.[18]

Guy Arnold made a serious study of Henty's work, but was rather carried away, I think, in one of his conclusions. He wrote: 'His books were still to be found on school shelves fifty years after his death and at least some of the racial arrogance which, unhappily, has been so marked a characteristic of British behaviour in what is now termed "The Third World" can be attributed to his influence'.[19] Those coming upon his books for the first time may certainly be unpleasantly surprised by the vehemence of Henty's convictions in, for instance, the final paragraph of *A Roving Commission*: 'the majority of the blacks [in Hayti under Toussaint L'Ouverture] are as savage, ignorant and superstitious as their forefathers in Africa. Fetish worship and human sacrifices are carried on in secret, and the fairest island in the western seas lies sunk in the lowest degradation – a proof of the utter incapacity of the negro race to evolve, or even maintain, civilization, without the example and the curb of a white population among them'. Arnold's reaction to that was: 'Henty must take a full share of responsibility for propagating the kind of views which have done such damage to British relations with African or Asian people during the present century'.[20]

Readers with a sense of history will relate men to the period in which they lived, and not judge them by the standards of later times. They will see flaws in Arnold's extreme view. Henty and his contemporaries had been brought up to think it as natural as breathing that they should foster the growth and prosperity of the British Empire. 'Of course Henty was an imperialist.', wrote C.P. Snow, 'So were most middle-class Englishmen of his kind, including many intellectuals, Fabians thrown in. It was a natural response to the national security, and it shows a lack of historical sense to expect anything different, or to regard it with a tinge of implied blame'.[21]

Other reviewers of Arnold's book joined in the chorus of protest: 'He would have been [an imperialist ogre] if he had been a voice crying in the wilderness; he wasn't, rather he was expressing the received opinion of his age. The public school virtues he expressed were the norm',[22] and 'So far from imposing his views on the younger generation, Henty's keen sensitivity to the market prompted him to shape his work to the exact tastes of the time'.[23]

Vanessa Furse Jackson has recently published a comprehensive study of another English writer, born exactly thirty years later than Henty and having little in common with him except that both have lately been called jingoists. Of the English public schools in the 1870s and 1880s she writes 'It was a golden age of great unity and great brotherhood . . . It was an age that could assume that the form its values took was widely shared and also that it was shared because the chivalric ideal that gave the values their expression was essentially a Christian and a just system of belief'. The ethos was shaken by the Boer War, and by 1914 many 'had become unable to see any ends at all in the means still rigorously promoted by the public school system'. But when Henty began writing books for boys, 'the ends – service to Empire, to country, to one's fellow man, and chivalric conduct in all things – were eminently clear, and the brotherhood inculcated by the system fostered a good that was rarely questioned. We are a questioning generation, and we would no longer agree that the sharing of certain beliefs in itself confirms the validity of those beliefs, but we must realise that to late-Victorians of a certain age and background, it did. To such people, unity promoted strength, and strength gave England her greatness, in which there was still, at that time, much national pride'.[24]

Critics sometimes fall into the age-old trap of taking the expressed views of characters in novels to be those of the author. It seems to me from careful reading of *With Lee in Virginia* that Bratton is incorrect in her assertion that Henty 'enunciates with approval the argument for slavery as a kindness to feckless black races'.[25] Henty clearly believed slavery was wrong, and was entirely aware of its miserable and cruel consequences.

He believed, certainly, that Imperialism would educate, care for and discipline the 'lesser breeds without the law', making them healthier and happier under the glorious rule of the British Queen and Empress. He could never have conceived that it might be seen as another form of slavery. As for Plagiarism, well, by comparison, what was that? In any case, everyone did it, and surely thoughts and ideas, even when written down, could hardly be regarded as belonging to only one person?[26] We see it differently now, and copyright laws have more force. But we still have racialism, and sexism, and terrorism, and ethnic cleansing, and weapons of mass destruction. It may be that we are hardly in a position to stand in judgement now over the nineteenth-century attitude to plagiarism.

' "It's a funny thing," said Mr Henty, "but I generally find that boys prefer those of my books which deal with modern times to those that embrace ancient history" '.[27] That remark from the interview reported in *Chums* shows Henty knew that when he was writing from his own experience, or of matters that had taken place in his own lifetime, as in his journalism, his touch was more sure. Certainly, *With Buller in Natal* and *With Roberts to Pretoria* are the two books that sold the most copies. But he always maintained that his favourite among his own books was

Facing Death, A Tale of the Coal Mines, with a quite different sort of plot,[28] in which no accounts of battles had to be boiled down and for which no history books had to be read.

Letter to William H. Davenport Adams: *6, Ravenna Road, Putney, Decr. 3 [1890?]*
My dear Mr. Adams – I am tied to Blackie for boy's books, and to Tillotson for novels, so that practically I am not open to engagements of any kind. Ward & Locks boys magazine expired at the end of its first year of life. I told them from the first that the idea of a reprint was a mistake, and as they never made the slightest effort to push it, of course it fell through. – Yours truly G.A.Henty.

For explanatory notes see *Those Other Animals*, §1, 51.1, Note 2; and *Beeton's Boy's Own Magazine*, §3, 197.   (Terry Corrigan collection).

HENTY'S PUBLISHERS AND THE BOOK TRADE IN HENTY'S TIME

1. TINSLEY BROTHERS, AND THE MUDIE LEVIATHAN

At the beginning of the 1850s William and Edward Tinsley, sons of a Hertfordshire gamekeeper and brought up on a farm as working boys, came to London to find their fortunes. Edward, the younger by about four years, was the brighter and probably the more gifted. He arrived some months ahead of his brother, and at first worked at the engineering workshops of the South-Western Railway at Nine Elms. While there he met the youngest of four talented brothers, Lionel Brough, who had just been appointed Assistant Publisher of the *Daily Telegraph*, one of several jobs he held with the press near the start of his successful theatrical career as a comedian.

The two young men were of the same age and a close friendship between them developed. While Brough had the imagination to devise the original scheme for selling newspapers on the streets of London, and was organising a staff of 240 boys to do this for his employers, Edward began writing articles and reviews and left his engineering job. He developed a serious leaning towards the world of publishing, and soon found employment in the office of a periodical, *Diogenes*. Almost certainly he would have been helped in his ambitions by his friend's three brothers, all of whom were writers, the second-eldest and most successful being Robert Brough, eight years his senior.

During Edward Tinsley's various ventures in publishing offices William was dealing in secondhand books and in review-copies sent to newspapers: he had no publishing experience at all. But in 1854 the brothers began to set up in business together, being interested in producing books for the circulating libraries. At first, possibly because of Edward's existing commitments, they traded under William's name. But in 1858 the firm of Tinsley Brothers was started, and that name continued in spite of Edward's early death in 1866. Much was to happen before that, however, and the new publishing house prospered almost immediately, largely because of business contacts made through their new London friends, and of more than a fair share of good luck.

The formation of Tinsley Brothers happened to coincide with a national growth of flourishing activity in literature and entertainment. In his history of Chapman & Hall, Arthur Waugh writes of the opportunities made throughout the country for book-wholesalers by the 'spread of education, the increase in railway traffic, the desire of the country parsonage and the cathedral close to keep pace with the newest intellectual interests'.[1] The great interest in books, especially in novels, resulted in a huge increase in the number of titles printed. While the practice of issuing monthly parts declined, there was another increase, this time in prices, as it became customary to publish popular novels in three volumes. These were generally priced at 31s.6d., which put them out of the regular reach of most private buyers, and it was not long before the growing and fashionable book trade was dominated by the 'circulating' or 'subscription' library.

Public Lending Libraries, as we now know them, barely existed until the time of the first world war: in spite of the Public Libraries Act, passed in 1850, only 48 'free' libraries existed in Britain in 1870 and about 350 more by the turn of the century. Libraries with members paying an annual fee had existed in the eighteenth century, but it was from small beginnings in 1842 that Charles Mudie, a stationer-bookseller in Southampton Row, was to lead a major revolution in the book trade. He rapidly built up a leviathan of a business, and although smaller libraries struggled to compete during the decades in which the three-decker novel flourished, few of them could survive for long and a number were swallowed up by Mudie's. W.H. Smith & Son, after an attempt to join forces, were rejected by Mudie and built up their own nation-wide library system. It was based on their railway-station bookstalls, for which one of their contracts stipulated that books should be available on loan as well as on sale. They became Mudie's only serious rival.

Mudie fixed an annual rate of one guinea a year, which entitled a subscriber to borrow one volume at a time, and a higher rate of two guineas for which subscribers might take four volumes at a time. Smith's annual rates were identical. Other arrangements for larger quantities were available for clubs and institutions, and Smith's had special terms for Country Bookstalls. The rates were carefully planned to fit with the vogue for three-volume novels, and the 'library-publishing' system was established on a scale never known before. There was a clear incentive for private members to subscribe at the higher rate, for in advertising the basic one guinea a year fee in 1879 Smith clearly stipulated 'Novels in more than One Volume are not available for this class of Subscription'. A similar restriction was placed on three-deckers at Smith's special subscription rate of £1.11s.6d. for borrowing two volumes at a time.

The libraries demanded of publishers that novels should be produced as three-deckers, thus keeping retail prices too high for virtually all buyers, and so increasing the library membership, especially at the higher rate. Publishers were by no means all in agreement about their attitude to the system. Some saw it as a death-knell for booksellers, and a strait-jacket for novelists. Others saw it as doubly to their advantage. For them the selling-price of novels was inevitably raised, and the editions required by libraries rose to sizes never previously contemplated. Each of those changes could only mean higher profits.

While this situation lasted Charles Mudie found himself in an outrageously strong position, being more or less able to dictate what should be published. Without an order from him a novel could be condemned to oblivion. Publishers therefore took care to assess his likely opinion, and indeed to obtain his actual opinion, before fixing print orders for new works. Mudie was not a dishonest man, but he was running a big business. It was more important to him that he could decide, and supply, 'what the public wants', which came to mean what he believed was suitable for all members of all families to read, than that he should necessarily support the finest literature.

He was, like Smith, a devout Nonconformist, and they came to wield a form of moral censorship over what subscribers might read, and consequently over what publishers could sell. Furthermore he made problems for publishers by driving hard bargains: these took much of the gilt off the gingerbread of larger editions and increased sales. As will be seen in Part 4 of this Appendix, other terms and conditions were to be imposed, which, after half a century of Mudie's domination of the writing, publication, and reading of fiction, resulted in the end of the three-volume novel, in a total reversal of the initial library policies.

But meanwhile the three-decker was the order of the day. Mudie virtually controlled the market the Tinsley brothers found themselves in when they set up their London office, close to the Strand. They had little knowledge or experience of the book business, but were clearly quick to learn, and came to early success in their dealings with Mudie, so that within a year or two 'none entered into sharper competition with Chapman & Hall than the Tinsley Brothers, who soon got round them a showy list, including Wilkie Collins, William Black, Walter Besant, Mrs. Henry Wood, and Miss Braddon'.[2] Both firms 'had cash at their disposal' according to Waugh, and it may be wondered how that came about.

It was in some degree due to the activities of the Brough family. Michael Sadleir wrote of Mary Elizabeth Braddon and her novel, *Lady Audley's Secret*: 'it attracted the attention of Lionel Brough, then acting as literary adviser to the speculative publishing firm of Tinsley Brothers. Late in 1862 it appeared as a three-volume novel and had a success both immediate and irresistible. From 1862 to the present day [1927] it has not ceased to sell. In various forms nearly a million copies must have gone into circulation … the book which made her publisher's fortune (out of the proceeds William Tinsley built himself a villa at Barnes and called it Audley Lodge) also made her own, and she became before long a wealthy woman'.[3]

There were many other successes, if not quite on so grand a scale. Their authors, though not all profitable to Tinsleys, included Harrison Ainsworth, Rhoda Broughton, George Manville Fenn, G.A. Henty, Richard Jefferies, Thomas Hardy, Thomas Hood, Jean Ingelow, George MacDonald, Florence Marryat, George Meredith, Mrs Molesworth, Mrs Oliphant, Ouida, Mayne Reid, George Augustus Sala, and Anthony Trollope.

Both brothers contributed to the fortunes of their business, but accounts of their activities indicate that at first Edward was the stronger force in the partnership. As we have seen, Tinsley Brothers and Chapman & Hall 'were keen rivals, and kept close on the trail of other people's successes, while in no way lacking the judgement to make successes of their own'.[4] Suddenly the rivalry was brought to a head by

Edward, and soon afterwards there followed an unexpected tragedy. 'About 1865 this competition became so acute that Edward Tinsley had the happy idea of ending it by the simple method of purchasing the rival firm outright. So he offered Frederic Chapman £50,000 for his business, stock, copyrights and premises, and was disappointed at finding his proposal turned down without discussion. A year later Edward Tinsley, who was an excitable creature, died in an apoplectic fit'.[5]

Edmund Downey, who for five years worked for William Tinsley as editor and office manager, recorded that 'Edward Tinsley had decided, in 1866, to leave the firm of Tinsley Brothers and to join Virtue and Co. His reasons for arriving at the decision were that he saw Catherine Street was incapable of supporting, in its then style, his own house and the house of his brother. The brothers had differences of opinion, too, on questions as to the commercial values of certain authors. And Edward Tinsley believed that his chance of increased success in the future lay in the line of publishing books appealing directly to the million, rather than the publishing of books intended mainly for the Circulating Libraries. Edward died suddenly at Catherine Street. In his hand was the pen and in front of him were the deeds which were to sever him from Tinsley Brothers and to make him a member of the firm of Virtue and Co.'.[6]

After that tragic day William Tinsley must have found life much more of a struggle, and he was to go through disastrous periods financially. Michael Sadleir, writing of Mary Elizabeth Braddon, who died in 1915, had referred to Tinsley Brothers as a 'speculative publishing firm'. Although it might be said that all publishing was essentially speculative, it is interesting, in view of Tinsleys' offer for Chapman & Hall, that Sadleir should later have taken that remark further: 'Tinsley's firm, in comparison with Chapman & Hall or Smith, Elder, was a speculative affair which did not command the real confidence of the trade'.[7] George Moore spent much time attacking the three-volume novel and the library system, and years later wrote of Tinsley: 'This worthy man conducted his business as he dressed himself, sloppily; a dear kind soul, quite witless and quite h-less. From long habit he would make a feeble attempt to drive a bargain, but he was duped generally'.[8] Nevertheless, William Tinsley began with a natural talent in the business of working with Mudie's, and managed to keep a fair general list as well as his novels.

Troubles were brewing, however. Tinsley's management of his business was never a matter of clockwork, and there were repeated moments of serious difficulty. The nature of novel publishing was changing, and no doubt Tinsley's comparatively short experience combined with his financial insecurity exaggerated for him what was a general worry.

In 1882 an anonymous article appeared in *Tinsleys' Magazine* entitled 'Is the Novel Moribund?'. It was probably written jointly by Tinsley and Downey, and dwells on the disquiet of authors, publishers, booksellers, and readers. Perhaps in jumping rather disjointedly from one aspect to another it succeeds in conveying the problems of the protagonists, and the general confusion of mind at the time: 'Now from every quarter, sacred to literature and its professors, one can hear wails for the downfall of the novel'.[9]

As we shall see, some believed that the three-decker still had some years in which to flourish. It certainly had some years of life, but in spite of his wishful thinking I believe Tinsley really understood it was dying. Only Andrew Chatto was perhaps financially secure enough to go on deluding himself to the bitter end. The troubles grew: 'Fiction was being affected by its very popularity: in the last twenty-five years . . . the number of novels published seemed to be increasing faster than the increase in novel readers. Between 1880 and 1881 there had been a 17 per cent increase in the number of novels published. The other factor hurting the traditional three-volume novel was the introduction of the American idea of serialised novels in newspapers'.[10] Henty himself entered into agreements with Tillotsons of Bolton for the serialisation in newspapers of his later novels, the first of them being published in book form by Spencer Blackett in 1889 (see Part 6 of this Appendix).

Tinsley's biographer in the *Dictionary of National Biography* seems to have relied largely on his own two-volume *Random Recollections of an Old Publisher*, clearly the work of an old man, and published two years before his death. The biographer is, however, in some matters less reliable than Tinsley's own memory, quite incorrectly attributing to Tinsley Brothers the publication of *The New Quarterly Review* (1854–59) and believing that the firm 'lost money in supporting "The Library Company" founded to rival Messrs. Mudie's'.[11]

Both these errors derive from careless misreading of Tinsley's book. The formation of 'The Library Company, Limited' was a disastrous and clearly suicidal venture and, far from supporting it, Tinsley claimed to have been among the first to sound alarms, trying to warn those associated with it, and regretting that he 'never could get them to see, until it was too late, that their venture spelt ruin from the first hour they began business'.[12] The Library Company had set up in Tinsleys' early years a business 'which endeavoured to undermine Mudie's with a half-guinea subscription', and as forecast by Tinsley it crashed within a short time, having 'created a boom in fiction which, from the publishers' point of view, was too good to last'.[13] During its short life it also proved to be the last nail in the coffin of other smaller, but much older, lending libraries, one at least dating from the middle of the eighteenth century.

Authors, readers, critics, publishers and booksellers continued for decades to blow hot and cold about the state of novel-publishing, and the strangle-hold that Mudie's exerted over all of them. New predictions were constantly being made by well-known figures in all branches of the book trade that the three-volume novel, and Mudie's with it, were due, one or both, to come to a sudden end at any moment. But the three-decker, and Mudie's system, survived well into the 1890s in spite of all the assaults made on them.

At Mudie's door were laid the necessity for inherently absurd prices for fiction; the enforcement of change in the nature of novel-writing; and the condemnation of works by reputable authors by his arbitrary 'censorship'. He was accused of interfering in the businesses of publishers by his monopolistic control of their financial affairs; even of meddling in their arrangements with their authors; and of ruining the bookselling trade.

There were at all stages of this vituperative debate those who spoke out for Mudie,[14] although the protagonists changed sides, whether authors. publishers or readers, as all parties blamed each other for the state of affairs they found themselves in. The arguments continued, and articles and letters appeared frequently in literary journals and the national press. The final stages of the battle in the book trade, when Henty's own last three-deckers were published, are briefly described in Part 4 of this Appendix.

The two adjectives in the title of Tinsley's book of memoirs are undoubtedly well chosen. It wanders about in time and place, with few dates given, and has no index. It nevertheless includes some vivid and fascinating pictures of social history, and of an eventful life in his own worlds of literature and the theatre. Tinsley's casual and romantic view of publishing, and his obsession with, and participation in, the current forms of Bohemianism, conflicted with his business sense, and in the end damaged it fatally. He was a great admirer of Mudie, and believed strongly in the virtues of the three-decker novel. It had certainly done well for him, but his feelings, although expressed from time to time in public with serious attempts at rationality, were really founded less on any original reasoning than on a heartfelt wish for prestige to be universally bestowed on it. The three-decker was an institution in which he had almost devout faith.[15]

He says nothing of his private life, beyond a brief acknowledgement to his daughter in the Preface, but there is no reason to suppose he did not have the support of his family. He says little, either, of his business failures which, according to the brief accounts that exist, took place on at least two or three occasions. Certainly he was able to rely with confidence on the support and friendship, both private and in business, given and received between most of the numerous literary and theatrical members of the Savage Club. It may have been Tinsley who introduced Henty to the Club in 1874.

The anecdotes recalled by Tinsley himself, and by Edmund Downey, about the Tinsley way of business at Catherine Street, are too numerous to digest. They do, however, show clearly that his methods would have been regarded by most of his rivals as little short of a shambles. Tinsley preferred no written agreements with his authors, many of whom enjoyed his 'open house' hospitality, dropping in without invitation at all times of day.

George Moore wrote after Tinsley's death: 'There was a long counter, and the way to be published by Mr. Tinsley was to straddle on the counter and play with a black cat . . . instead of troubling Messrs. Macmillan and Messrs. Longman with polite requests to look at my MSS., I straddled, played with the cat, joked with the Irishman [Downey], drank with Mr. Tinsley, and in the natural order of things my stories went into the magazine and were paid for. Strange were the ways of this office; Shakespeare might have sent in prose and poetry, but he would have gone into the waste-paper basket had he not straddled'.[16]

But even if a few of his authors deserted him, and if on occasion he had an unwisely sharp eye to his own financial advantage, Tinsley looked after them as friends, and especially at lunchtime and in the evening when it might be convenient to take the half-dozen steps to the side door of the old Gaiety restaurant. There was, however, no suggestion of over-indulgence, simply of a great need for company and conversation. Moore tells how he and a group of friends used to sit 'in the semi-circular nooks under the cathedral windows, and at six, Tinsley, the publisher from Catherine Street, would come in, room being made for him instantly. He used to carry a bag containing fish for the family and a manuscript novel; and until seven whisky was drunk'.[17] Tinsley liked to be trusted and felt a corresponding need to trust others. As might be expected, this approach to life sometimes let him down.

Tinsley was bored by accounts and employed a valued and devoted accountant, William Croft, who 'carried with him an air of "safety". You felt that nothing could go wrong, financially, when Croft was at your elbow'.[18] And yet Tinsley seems often to have made offers for rights without serious consideration or consultation with anyone. He made many mistakes, and was lucky on rare occasions when these turned a financial balance in his favour. Once he found he had been cheated by a novelist, Edmund Yates, some of whose books had been written entirely or in part by another writer, and who, as we shall see, had for a time been Editor of *Tinsleys' Magazine*.

The story unfolds briefly in Tinsley's own words: 'It seems fairly clear', he writes, 'that I as publisher ought to have known who were the authors of books I published, and had Mr. Yates been an unknown author, I should of course have seen the manuscript of at least the first book before I published it. But before he came to me he had made a name as a writer of fiction, and I did not trouble to see or read his MS., so he, or rather Mrs. [Cashel] Hoey, sent their matter direct to the printers ... I was very vexed when I found out the deception, but as I had published four or five novels before I did so, it was too late to make much bother about the matter. To the uninitiated in literary matters it doubtless seems strange that publishers should not see the wares they purchase. But in my time as a publisher well-known authors seldom submitted their works for approval, and I suppose do not now. Agreements were made about the length and size of the works to be written, and very often the authors sent their copy direct to their favourite printers'.[19] It does indeed seem strange, and not only to the uninitiated, that Tinsley should be so inattentive to his firm's reputation, to the choice of printers, and to all the risks incurred, including libel.

In 1868, soon after the death of his brother, William had started *Tinsleys' Magazine* (see §3, 224). For four years the Editor was the controversial Edmund Yates, who had some success in this job as in many others in his life, but who seemed unable to live without stirring up trouble, most notably perhaps between Dickens and Thackeray. Tinsley claims he lost over three thousand pounds on the first twelve numbers, but 'I am bound to admit', he adds, 'that during the few months [actually four years!] Yates edited *Tinsleys' Magazine* he worked fairly well to make it a success ... After Mr. Yates left my magazine I practically conducted it myself, with the aid of William Croft, an excellent printer's reader'.[20]

Seven years later Edmund Downey took over the Editorship: '*Tinsley's Magazine* was started under the editorship of Edmund Yates, who was also part-proprietor', he wrote. 'When Yates and Tinsley separated the Magazine might easily have been saved. But the opportunity was not seized. William Tinsley became suddenly timorous ... he commenced the cutting-down process ... he lopped off the illustrations, and, by degrees, he cut the standard price for contributions to such a low figure that it was well-nigh impossible to keep any life in the Magazine. The circulation, after Edmund Yates's departure, dropped slowly, steadily, and with it the income derived from advertisements ... Towards the latter part of the 'Seventies, the Magazine was edited "anyhow". When I was put in charge of it, *Tinsleys*' was at its lowest ebb'.[21] Catherine Street, at that time, 'was an asylum for lame ducks, literary and theatrical, especially theatrical'; Tinsley would even encourage them and 'on his return from a Gaiety bar prowl' produce a manuscript from his pocket and instruct Downey to 'find a corner for the rubbish ... give the poor devil something for it – he's on his uppers'.[22]

William Croft, Tinsley's chief accountant, and highly valued but only part-time right-hand man for many years, had 'edited *Tinsleys' Magazine* – that is to say, he had looked after its interests generally, whenever he could spare the time. His duties outside the office of Tinsley Brothers were multifarious. He compiled and edited at one time no less than thirteen almanacs. He had a connection with a printing house, and for a time he managed a publishing and bookselling business'.[23]

It may be seen that at certain periods the conduct of this periodical was even more haphazard than the management of Tinsleys' book-publishing business. In spite of his own personal modesty it does emerge from Downey's story that as the new Editor he did a great deal to improve matters: 'During the five years I spent at Catherine Street, the loss on *Tinsleys' Magazine* did not exceed at any period twenty-five pounds a month, and this was re-couped by profits on his Christmas and Summer Annuals. Moreover, as he frequently said to me, "What cheaper advertisement can I have for twenty-five pounds a month? It advertises my name and publications and it keeps my authors together"'.[24]

In the early 1880s Tinsley's grip on the business slipped away. The exact date of the final failure is not explicitly recorded: various writers mention 'failures' at dates from 1870 onwards, and there were clearly several times of crisis, but it is likely that William finally gave up at a point which Downey, uncharacteristically as a historian but perhaps characteristically as a friend, almost glosses over: 'My connection with William Tinsley terminated abruptly in September 1884'.[25] It is hard to believe that either of the two would have abandoned the other, or that Downey would not have explained the parting to the readers of his book had he either resigned or been sacked in anger. It is also significant that ten years later Tinsley wrote a long letter to Downey, 'He had just completed his Recollections and he was anxious I should publish the book for him'.[25]

During the period of Henty's association with Tinsley Brothers 'he was for a time one of the most regular of the callers at Catherine Street. He usually arrived (direct from the office of the *Standard*) about eleven o'clock, smoking his short, well-coloured, clay pipe'.[26] William Tinsley tells at length the story of a projected new magazine, *England in the Nineteenth Century*, that was to be published by Tinsley

Brothers for Willing & Co., the well-known advertising firm, and was planned for a date he unfortunately does not specify. The appointed Editor was George Augustus Sala, the first issue was written, designed, illustrated with engravings, and, according to Tinsley, printed, including an article by Henty on 'Seven Dials'.

'But', Tinsley writes, 'the most substantial matter for that or any other periodical was not to hand – namely, a good sheet of advertisements ... So no doubt Mr. Willing saw that the venture did not look promising; and, without the least hesitation, he ordered the finishing of the preparations . . . there and then to be stopped, and all accounts to be paid up at once'.[27] No trace has been found of any proofs or other remains of the project, nor of the article by Henty.

Tinsley Brothers published Henty's first two novels as three-deckers; they also published his *The March to Magdala* and *The March to Coomassie*, and three short stories and an article in *Tinsleys' Magazine* . After his death it was written of Henty's volumes of collected war correspondence that 'they were not so popular with the reading public as those of Sir William Russell and Archibald Forbes'.[28] *The March to Coomassie* was certainly reprinted, although I wonder whether some accident possibly overtook most of the first printing. It would be of great interest to know how the novels fared with Mudie, and how many copies were printed. But, sadly, no publishing records or accounts have been found.

A belief has grown up that Henty's adult fiction was never successful. This is very far from the truth: although not a runaway best-seller, one of the novels from Chatto & Windus was a substantial success. The novels published by Tinsleys did not achieve similar popularity, and in those early days newspaper-serialisation had not begun in this country. But at worst it was possible for novels by new authors to be issued in quite small editions as three-deckers and to be, in effect, automatically subsidised by the library-publishing system. Even if they made no profit for author or publisher they could, with the help of a modest order from Mudie, still leave all concerned without loss, a situation impossible with single-volume first-editions.

Things may have been better than that. Neither the lack of Tinsleys' sales records, nor the current scarcity of copies of *All but Lost* and *A Search for a Secret*, are grounds for presuming the failure of those books. Most three-decker novels of the period are scarce today: their life was as library books, and it was largely old favourites that found their way, second-hand from Mudie's, on to private shelves. By that time they had lost the smartness of new books, and they were bulky compared with their single-volume neighbours. When space had to be saved, or when wartime appeals were made for paper-salvage, they were always likely candidates for oblivion. And it must not be forgotten that *A Search for a Secret* was found worthy of being re-issued in a single volume some twenty-five years after the demise of its original publisher.

2. GRIFFITH & FARRAN, THE JOINT VENTURE, AND THE O.U.P.

Henty married in 1858 and soon had four young children. It was for them that he started storytelling, beginning no doubt with short tales when they were very small, and moving on to longer narratives. 'I used always to have my children with me for an hour after dinner, and to tell them stories', he wrote years later, 'These stories were continuous, and often lasted for weeks. One day it struck me, If my young ones like my stories, why should not others? I, therefore, each day wrote a chapter and read it to them, instead of telling it; and when the story was of proper length sent it to a publisher who at once accepted it'.[29]

Henty's first publisher, William Tinsley, had published three of his short stories in *Tinsleys' Magazine* in 1869; one of them was written for children, but was not the usual fare for Tinsley's readers, and no doubt Henty agreed with Tinsley that if he was going to write that kind of material regularly he should find a second, specialist, publisher. By that time Henty already had the completed manuscript of his first full-length novel for children, written in 1868, and he probably sent it to Griffith & Farran in the following year.

He would have found a very different atmosphere from that at Catherine Street when he went to see the children's publishers at 2 Ludgate Hill. Griffith & Farran had eventually become the owners of a business that had been started in Reading, Berkshire, in 1740, by John Newbery, and passed down, not in a direct line but through various members of his family, until it was taken over by John Harris and his son at the beginning of the nineteenth century. By that time it had become established, even if under a variety of imprints, as a publisher of books for young people, and when the younger Harris retired in 1843 the tradition was maintained by the new owners, E.C. Grant, and his partner William Darling Griffith (1805–1877).

Little is known of Grant, but he left the business after a few years and Griffith took a new partner, Robert Farran, in 1856. The emphasis was still on children's and educational books, but with a growing general list including religious works, and also three-volume and two-volume novels. The 1860s and 1870s seem to have been the most prosperous period for this publishing house.

It was probably Farran who dealt with Henty and signed the contracts for his books. *Out on the Pampas* was published in 1870, with title page dated 1871: no doubt the book Henty said he had written for his own children. Their names are given to the four main characters. *The Young Franc-Tireurs* followed a year later, based on his experiences in the Franco-Prussian War.

The first two books were published too early to reach the increased market and readership that followed the Education Acts of the 1870s. In the levels of society most affected by the changes it would have taken at least ten years for the wider spread of reading skills to benefit boys of an age to appreciate Henty. To the earlier, more privileged readership, *Out on the Pampas* and *The Young Franc-Tireurs* must each have sold a total of 3000 copies in their first and second impressions, which was by no means a poor sales record, especially for an unknown author.

Late in 1879 Henty had been invited to attend a meeting at the house of W.H.G. Kingston, at which R.M. Ballantyne was also present, to discuss the founding by Griffith & Farran of a new magazine for boys, to be called the *Union Jack*. It was published on 1 January 1880, with Kingston as Editor. But within six months Kingston was overtaken by an illness from which he did not recover, and Henty was asked to become Editor in his place.

In 1880 and 1881 Henty's third and fourth boys' books were published by Griffith & Farran: some eight years after the appearance of the second. In 1881 Farran also started the 'Boys' Own Favourite Library', which soon included several of Henty's books. Farran was in sole charge of the publishing business, as W.D. Griffith had died in 1877. That situation lasted for seven years before two new partners joined the firm and the imprint was changed to Griffith, Farran, Okeden and Welsh[30] (sometimes shortened to Griffith, Farran & Co.). During that time Henty's books were never out of print, all running through a number of small editions. They were selling satisfactorily, but Henty was still learning his trade, and some years were to pass before he produced a best-seller for any of his publishers. He had also taken over two books, *Our Sailors* and *Our Soldiers*, published by Griffith and Farran for W.H.G.Kingston, editing them and bringing them up to date: those, too, were kept in print.

Commentators have tended to underrate the early books for boys, believing they did not succeed until after his work had been popularised by Blackie in the 1880s. Eric Quayle does not mention Blackie in this connection, but reports that 'despite its historical accuracy, drawn from the author's first-hand knowledge of events, *The Young Franc-Tireurs* was no more successful than *Out on the Pampas*. Both sold moderately well, but neither appeared as a second edition until well after Henty had established himself as a popular editor of boys' magazines that carried his stories into thousands of homes throughout the land'.[31]

I think Quayle is using the word 'edition' in the Griffith & Farran sense, meaning an impression, rather than in the true bibliographical sense. In fact *The Young Franc-Tireurs* was reprinted in the year of first publication (with the words 'Second Edition' on the title page). Quayle is right in thinking that sales increased considerably in the years after 1881, but not, I think, because Henty had established himself as a popular editor of boys' magazines. Henty never did establish himself as a popular editor, and never succeeded in raising the circulation of the *Union Jack* to a point where it was not making a loss.

Griffith & Farran suffered from a number of organisational problems during the 1880s and 1890s. The *Union Jack* was not a great success, to the distress of Henty, who had set his heart on being the Editor of a boys' magazine. He repeatedly stated that ambition throughout his life, but a study of the magazines he edited shows that he was never very good at the job. I think his pleasure was mainly from correspondence with his readers and from feeling he was in touch with youth, rather than from the day-to-day work of a managing editor.[32]

Perhaps he also hoped to provide for a new generation of boys something that he had consciously lacked in his own youth. More than once he remarked to journalists that his childhood had been spent in bed. That was probably an exaggeration, but he did have a very inactive existence at home as result of ill-health, and no doubt felt frequently bored by the children's literature of the 1840s. He must have read Walter Scott, but no one else wrote historical adventure stories approaching those he was to provide for his 'dear lads', and his habit of writing may have been subconsciously altruistic, as well as a newly discovered source of income.

When Farran decided to close the magazine Henty tried desperately to find another publisher for it. To keep the ship afloat he was driven to persuade Cecil Brooks & Co., a small publisher in Catherine Street, close to the Tinsley Brothers' offices, to distribute it temporarily for him, financing the venture himself. Later, it was taken over by Sampson Low (see Part 3 of this Appendix). When that happened they also took over the publication of Henty's books for boys, although one more, *Friends, though Divided*, was published in 1883 by Griffith and Farran. In 1888 Farran was forced by illness to retire. The premises at 2 Ludgate Hill, at the corner of St Paul's Churchyard, which included a retail bookshop, were closed, and book publishing was carried on from 39 Charing Cross Road in a building named Newbery House, after the founder of the firm.

Management problems continued to beset the business. Although Sampson Low were now publishing the *Union Jack*, to Henty's great relief, as well as his new books, the five original Griffith & Farran publications continued under the old imprint. Early in 1897 more organisational changes took place. By then H.G.P. Okeden and Charles Welsh, both still in their forties, had disappeared from the imprint, and the business was taken over by a new entrepreneur called Browne. There are almost no surviving records: all papers were destroyed in the bombing of London in the second war, and consequently I am unable even to give Mr Browne's full name.

According to F.J. Harvey Darton, 'From this time on the publishing interest fades, and the last fugitive years of the firm appear to be increasingly devoted to selling stock rather than to implementing new enterprises'.[33] That statement is in a sense true, but Browne was certainly responsible for the issue of new editions of works in the list he had acquired, even if he did not commission new ones. Some of the books by Henty, as he re-issued them, are produced more smartly than many of the drab issues that had gone before.

By 1906 the business had gone a long way downhill, and was in that year put on the market. Darton gives further changes of address, covering the period from 1908 to 1911, but these are puzzling, as it was in 1906 that the stock and goodwill of Griffith & Farran was bought outright for £5000 by the London general publisher, Hodder & Stoughton.

The subsequent history of Henty's books involved in that sale is complicated only by further transfers of ownership. Those that continued to be published, apart from the two Kingston titles which he had edited (see above), were *Out on the Pampas*, *The Young Franc-Tireurs, The Young Buglers, In Times of Peril* and *Friends, though Divided*. A sixth title, *The Curse of Carne's Hold*, was in the Griffith & Farran list in 1892 as a popular work for adults, before being included in their 'Boys' Own

Favourite Library'. It had originally been issued as an adult novel by the London publishers, Spencer Blackett & Hallam in 1889 (see Part 6 of this Appendix). The book was apparently not included in the Griffith & Farran sale to Hodders and was not re-issued: it is probable that they had not acquired the full rights from Spencer Blackett & Hallam, when that business came to an end, about 1890.

In the year they acquired the Griffith & Farran business Hodder & Stoughton were in a position very similar to that of Blackie & Son of Glasgow twenty-five years earlier. At those different dates both firms of publishers wished to add a new line to their existing lists in the shape of books for schools. John Attenborough, the firm's historian, writes that for Ernest Hodder-Williams, filled with this enthusiasm, 'the only problem was shortage of capital, or so it seemed to the young partner who knew from his grandfather's reservations that the capital sums required for text-book publishing had always presented too great a financial risk'.[34] Both Hodders and Blackie found in the end, although in different ways, that they were to reach their goals by publishing a combination of educational and 'reward' books for children.

Ernest Hodder-Williams had become friendly with Humphrey Milford, who was second-in-command to Henry Frowde at the Oxford University Press. The two publishing houses were virtually next-door neighbours, and Hodder-Williams found that 'Milford's appetite was whetted by the thought of entering the lucrative juvenile market with what were euphemistically called "prize books". Literature for the amusement and entertainment of children had undoubtedly been neglected in Oxford, where it was difficult to reconcile it with the purposes of a University Press. But "recreative" literature could be educational as well. Moreover as educational publishing in Oxford was uncoordinated ... Milford could claim to be making good a flaw in the general structure'.[35]

Both he and Hodder-Williams were fired by contemplating the possibilities, and each was equally keen to make a start. 'So in 1906, the Joint Venture, known as Henry Frowde, Hodder & Stoughton, was born on an equal partnership basis... It looked like a sensible move by the Oxford University Press to enter the popular children's book market without compromising its academic reputation' and to Hodders 'the alliance was no less attractive ... the agreement signed on 18 December 1906 specifically covered educational as well as children's books'.[36]

The contract was signed for five years. 'Two editors, Herbert Ely and Charles James L'Estrange, were appointed to run the Joint Venture. Under the terms of the contract, their services were to be exclusively devoted to the Press . . . Apart from finding authors and preparing books for press, they were themselves to write an annual volume'.[36] Perhaps without exactly realising it the publishers had instituted another joint venture: this was the beginning of the vast output of annuals and other children's literature issued for many years under the shared pseudonyms of Herbert Strang, who wrote for boys, and of Mrs Herbert Strang, for girls.

The new undertaking started with material already to hand, in the form of the stock and copyrights from Griffith & Farran. As far as Henty's books were concerned, the five titles, and the two old Kingston titles he had edited, were kept securely in print, reissued with new illustrations, and sold simultaneously in editions at two different prices. The Joint Venture ran smoothly and with success. Indeed the two participants were so pleased with the arrangement that it was extended, with different editors, into medical publishing.

The only brake on development, later on, was a shortage of materials, including paper, caused by the first war, when all the partners could muster was patience. 'During these waiting years, the "Joint Venture" agreements with the Oxford University Press were revived and revised. As to the Joint Medical Publications, the partnership was renewed for a further seven years from 1 April 1916... But on the same date, all interest and stock in the elementary school texts and juveniles edited by Herbert Ely and C.J. L'Estrange were bought by the Oxford University Press. This marks the beginning of the famous Oxford Children's List'.[37]

Subsequently the Henty interest was looked after exactly as before, most of the Joint Venture editions being reprinted with the new imprint, and others re-issued with fresh trimmings. The first issues of Henty's novels for boys by the Joint Venture in 1910 and 1911 had certainly been finer examples of book production than any in which those titles had previously been published, and good standards of presentation were maintained by the Oxford University Press up to the end of the second war.

3. SAMPSON LOW; THE *UNION JACK*; A BOOK FOR GEORGE ROUTLEDGE

In 1819, when he was twenty-one, Sampson Low set up in business as a bookseller and stationer at 42 Lamb's Conduit Street in London. His father, also called Sampson, had been a printer and publisher, but died when the boy was only three years old. Before 1819 the young Sampson had spent a short time working for Lionel Booth, proprietor of one of the early circulating libraries, and a few years with Longman & Co., the distinguished English house that had already been publishing books for a hundred years.

It was not until 1848 that Sampson Low started in general book-publishing, in Red Lion Court, Fleet Street, with his 26-year old invalid son, also called Sampson after his father and his grandfather. He took an assistant, Edward Marston, who in 1856 became a partner.

Later, Marston was described by the journalist Raymond Blathwayt as 'not only one of the best-known publishers of the day, but ... also a keenly literary and cultured travelled man of the world'. Blathwayt tells of 'the estimation in which he was held in the highest literary circles in New York and Boston', and believed 'few men have a keener instinct for the right thing in the way of books than he has; he is one of the best judges of ... biography in London, though his speciality has generally been the production of books of travel and exploration'.[38]

An author whose name appears elsewhere in this bibliography, W. Clark Russell,[39] wrote his 'Recollections of Edward Marston', and told of their first meeting. 'One afternoon I received a letter from Sampson Low stating that they were willing to publish the novel [*The Wreck of the Grosvenor*] and offering me twenty-

177. *Edward Marston*

176. *William Tinsley*

179. *Andrew Chatto*

178. *Alexander Blackie*

five pounds for it'. Russell called and was received by Marston: 'I was struck by his good looks, his soft, dark, intelligent eyes, his agreeable manner, and a pleasant reserve which as I afterwards came to know, easily thawed when you gained his acquaintance or friendship... After commenting on my book in a very kindly manner he said, "Twenty-five pounds is not much to offer for a three-volume novel... But," he said with an arch look, "we can do without it" '.[40]

Russell and Marston became great friends in and out of the office. Russell's memoir illustrates the amount a still-unknown author might expect for the rights in a three-volume novel. In 1870, Thomas Hardy had had to pay William Tinsley £75 to publish his first novel, *Desperate Remedies*.[41] But a year later, for his second, *Under the Greenwood Tree*, Tinsley matched Marston's outright payment to Russell of £25. We do not know what financial arrangement the same publisher had made with Henty, only a year or two earlier, for his first three-deckers, *A Search for a Secret* and *All but Lost*.

In 1871 Sampson Low's invalid son died, and his place in the partnership was taken by his younger brother, William. Four years later, in 1875, Sampson Low retired after more than twenty-five profitable years of general publishing. He had built up a substantial list, and Marston now took charge of the business. He it was who signed contracts with Henty for his boys' books, following the firm's take-over of the *Union Jack*, originally published by Griffith & Farran. By 31 May 1881, when the first of them was drawn up, for *The Cornet of Horse*, Marston had taken more partners, and the agreement is 'between Edward Marston, William Henry Low, Samuel Warren Searle, and William John Rivington trading as "Sampson Low, Marston, Searle and Rivington," of No. 188 Fleet Street, London, English, American and Colonial Booksellers and Publishers ... and G.A. Henty Esq. 23 St. Anne's Villas, Notting Hill' (see Appendix VI).

William Low, whose name appears in the contract for *The Cornet of Horse*, died ten years after his brother, in 1881. When Henty's later books, *Winning his Spurs*, 1882, and *Jack Archer*, 1883, were published from 188 Fleet Street, Edward Marston was the owner of the business.

It is noticeable that many illustrations in the *Union Jack* under the Sampson Low régime are by French artists. Also that many of them, even those by English artists, were reproduced by French wood-engravers, and, later, by French photo-engravers. The latter came to acquire a great reputation, and Blackie's first illustrator of Henty, Gordon Browne, used both Lefman, and Guillaume Frères (see Appendix IV, Part 2). But at this date it was mainly wood-engravings that Sampson Low was buying from France.

It was understandable that this should come about as they were the publishers of many books by Jules Verne, and afterwards by other French authors. Edward Marston had made the first agreement with M. Hetzel, of Paris, for the publication of *Twenty Thousand Leagues under the Sea*, in 1871. But the links with France were older than that. Sampson Low had already published in 1852 a work in English and French by Peter Burke, *Law of International Copyright between England and France*. In 1865 the firm had acquired the English rights in Victor Hugo's *The*

Toilers of the Sea, and in connection with this and other works Marston had made visits to Paris. He took care to keep up his French connections, and ultimately played an important personal part in events which irrevocably endeared him to the French publishing profession.

In 1870 a Fund was formed for the collection and distribution of food to the inhabitants of the besieged city of Paris in the Franco-Prussian War. It was organised jointly by Sampson Low and Joseph Whitaker (of *Almanac* fame), and a committee of eighteen members of the publishing profession was formed: Marston was appointed Hon. Secretary. M. René Fouret, partner in the leading French publishing house, Hachette, acted as liaison. The scheme had successful results, and in later recognition Marston was awarded a gold medal and a diploma conferring on him a life membership of the Cercle de la Librairie. 'That medal', Marston wrote, 'which I regard as a treasure, has been to me an *open sesame* whenever I have visited Paris since that time'.[42]

In 1873 a French edition of *The Young Franc-Tireurs* had been published in Paris by Librairie Hachette. It was illustrated by a series of excellent engravings by the French artist, Janet-Lange, and they were used in the serialisation of the story in the *Union Jack* in 1881, in preference to most of the English illustrations that had appeared ten years earlier in the first edition of the book.

Things did not go well, however, with the finances of the *Union Jack*. In September 1883 Henty had to announce to his young readers its final closure by Sampson Low, for him an occasion of the greatest sadness. It was a serious blow, and his anger and frustration seem to have brought about, at least for a time, a sudden end to his association with Marston.

Henty had signed a contract with Sampson Low on 24 October 1883 for the outright sale of the copyright in a boys' book, *The Young Colonists*. That was a month after he had announced the end of the magazine. But perhaps an inner rage grew over the next few weeks. Five months later, having progressed well with the book, Sampson Low re-sold the copyright, plus illustrations, plates, and some printed sheets to George Routledge & Sons. Details of the sale and the various contracts concerned have all survived, and are given in Appendix VI and in §1, 17.

The Young Colonists was published the following year, and Routledge used all the material they had bought. By the time it was re-issued in 1892 the Routledge partnership had become a Limited Company: the first American edition was printed from plates supplied from London, and published by George Routledge & Sons Limited, from their later New York address at 9 Lafayette Place. Both American and U.K. editions were printed and bound in New York, an unusual arrangement in British book-publishing (for further details see §1, 17).

By this time Henty was beginning negotiations with Blackie & Son, of Glasgow, and these were to lead eventually to an agreement giving them rights in all his future boys' books (see Appendix VI). In 1897 Blackie bought from Routledge the rights in *The Young Colonists*, together with some of the sheets printed in America. Their use of those sheets, when they came to re-issue the book, resulted in the imprints of two different publishers appearing in separate parts of a single volume.

Meanwhile Henty had come to an agreement with Routledge that they should serialise his next story, *For Name and Fame*, in their monthly *Every Boy's Magazine*, and it was announced to start in the first issue of the new volume on 1 October 1884. The story ran throughout that year, the final instalment appearing in the December issue. But Routledge never published the story in book form: Blackie enforced their contract for the book rights, and it was issued the following May in their 5s. series.

Whether or not Henty had made up his mind at the end of 1883 to have no more to do with Sampson Low must remain a matter for conjecture. But in view of what happened to his beloved *Union Jack*, after all his hard work and earlier personal expense to keep it alive, and bearing in mind his known temperament, it seems more than likely that he made it clear to Marston that he was in no mood to continue with him in producing *The Young Colonists*. Sampson Low had, of course, bought the copyright, and would have been justified in going ahead without troubling to send proofs to the author. But Marston was a man who could not bear uncomfortable relationships, and not relishing the prospect of unpleasantness, he decided to get shot of the book.

It seems, however, that after an interval he wanted to repair the friendship. An opportunity to do so came eight years later. In 1891 he needed an editor to abridge a book for boys by Richard Jefferies, published in three volumes by Sampson Low in 1882. It had been well received, but found only a limited market and was criticised for being too long. The book, *Bevis*, is indeed a classic of boys' literature, but had not yet been recognised as such. Marston asked Henty if he would abridge it for him. The story of the editing of *Bevis*, as far as it is known, is given at §2, 128. But it is possible that the story, from Henty's point of view, goes a little further.

It was in the same year, 1891, that Sampson Low published the adult novel, *A Hidden Foe*. Although Henty was contracted to Blackie for children's books he was not yet similarly bound to Tillotsons for adult novels (see Part 4 of this Appendix). By sending the book to Marston he seems to have shown he wanted to register his gratitude for the gesture over *Bevis*, and to bury the hatchet as far as Sampson Low was concerned. The contract was dated 21 January 1891 (see Appendix VI).

A Hidden Foe was published in two volumes, a format not much liked by the circulating libraries. No records survive to show how many copies were printed or sold. It was later issued in a single volume, with illustrations, but only after an interval of ten years. It then appeared to fall between the two stools of adult and boys' literature, as later editions of many of Henty's 'adult' novels tended to do.[43]

In the year following publication of *A Hidden Foe*, Sampson Low bought the rights in a magazine, *Boys* (§3, 199), that had been started only six months earlier by The UK Band of Hope Union. The Editor was Edward Step, who had had experience of magazine work with Alexander Strachan & Co., including George MacDonald's *Good Words for the Young*, and later with S.W. Partridge & Co. (see Part 6 of this Appendix). The first issue of *Boys* contained a glowing biographical note by B. McCall Barbour, describing Henty as 'The Prince of Storytellers'.[44] In the same issue Henty's story 'The Golden Cañon' began an eight-part serialisation, and the following year 'A Desperate Gang' appeared in ten instalments. It all seems to have been arranged as a warm welcome back for Henty to the house of Sampson Low, even possibly with a thought by Marston towards replacing, in Barbour's words, the 'now defunct *Union Jack*'. Whether that had crossed Marston's mind can only be guessed at, but Edward Step remained Editor, and in any case the magazine was absorbed into the *Boy's Own Paper* after only two years existence.

In his book of memoirs, published two years after Henty's death, Marston writes some extremely friendly and affectionate paragraphs about him. He also mentions in passing that Henty once told him 'he had for some years been a great sufferer from gouty diabetes'.[45] Perhaps Henty confessed to this while making some sort of apology for his anger over the closing down of the *Union Jack* in 1883. In any case it may explain other difficulties in relationships in the later years of his life.

After Marston's death the name of Sampson Low continued to be well known, and business, although on the wane, continued up to the second war. In the 1920s and 1930s Henty's books were published from Southwark Street, London, S.E., while the old St Dunstan's House was reported destroyed in the bombing of London in 1940. The later impressions fall outside the period covered by this bibliography, but the imprint was then taken under the wing of Macdonald & Co., an imprint itself acquired by the Somerset printers, Purnell & Sons, who were still using worn plates from the original settings of Henty's books. Purnells and Macdonald in turn became part of the British Printing Corporation, ultimately to fall to the notorious Robert Maxwell. The Macdonald imprint is now owned by Little, Brown & Co., part of the Time-Life Group. I have not seen Sampson Low editions of Henty issued after the second war.

4. CHATTO & WINDUS; TILLOTSONS; THE END OF THREE-DECKERS

The firm of Chatto & Windus had its origins in a business begun in 1855 by John Camden Hotten. Now a notable name in bookselling circles, and a publisher whose books are collected, Hotten had built up a varied list when he died in 1873 at the early age of 41. He had been a publisher for only eighteen years: in that time he was responsible for introducing many important American authors to English readers, and he made a courageous decision to publish Swinburne when he was under strong attack by critics and the public.

Hotten had taken on a fifteen-year old assistant, Andrew Chatto, who later bought the business, for £25,000, from his widow. Chatto was 'joined in not very active partnership by W.E. Windus, who wrote narrative and lyric verses', but 'as a man of business, remains shadowy'. In 1876 he took another partner, Percy Spalding, and 'these two men, between them could have claimed credit for establishing the firm not merely on a respectable but an assured basis'.[46] Their list included Sir Walter Besant, Wilkie Collins, Justin McCarthy, George MacDonald, Thomas Hardy, Ouida, Charles Reade, R.L. Stevenson and Anthony Trollope. In order to acquire such a list, with strong competition from publishing houses already greater in age and experience, it was necessary, at the very least, to have a keen business sense.

During the 1880s Chatto & Windus were determined to make themselves the leading publishers of novels in London, and set out to increase their list very substantially, not only by encouraging new authors but by enticing established writers away from rival firms. We have seen earlier in this Appendix that the Tinsley Brothers had been recognised by Chapman & Hall as their chief rivals in the field, but the Tinsley empire had crumbled and lost its position, certainly by 1880. Michael Sadleir describes the situation in 1883:

'Chatto & Windus were at this date the hustlers of the trade. Over the crumbling supremacy of Chapman and Hall they were climbing to prominence, buying copyright after copyright from their failing rivals, securing fresh names for their list by paying big prices and much ostentatious advertisement. The periodical uprush into notoriety of some energetically ambitious publisher is a continuing feature of the trade's history. There is always someone "buying a fiction list", over-paying and over-advertising, forcing his way into established prominence so that, once arrived, he can settle down to sober economics. But I know of no more strongly marked happening of this kind than the rapid emergence during the late 'seventies and early eighties of the firm of Chatto & Windus. Hardly a well-known novelist (apart from those happily settled with such classical firms as Longmans, Smith Elder or Macmillan) but transferred from his previous publishers to the new and glittering Piccadilly list'.[47]

In 1892 Henty had entered into a contract with Tillotson and Son of Bolton, newspaper publishers, and general printers, who had set up a Newspaper Literature Syndicate 'For Supplying the Newspaper Press with Special Articles and the Works of Popular Novelists'. As far as Henty was concerned, Tillotsons had the exclusive serial rights in any adult fiction he wrote, and could dispose of the rights to newspapers, including their own, on a world-wide basis.[48]

Tillotsons were one of the most important organisations to whom it had occurred that novels in weekly instalments could increase sales of newspapers, and also provide an income for themselves from the sale of second rights. Naturally book publishers would offer less for a story that had already appeared in print, but the author would have received an outright payment from Tillotson, usually equal to what he would have expected from a book publisher under the old system. It had been pointed out in the 1882 article in *Tinsleys' Magazine*, already mentioned in this Appendix, that in the days before the practice of newspaper serialisation the rights in a three-decker had been worth 'about twice as much as they will fetch today'.[49]

The evidence now available is confused about whether anyone other than Tillotson actually benefited from the sale of the second rights to book publishers. At the start of his scheme, according to Frank Singleton, W.F. Tillotson, 'in effect said "Here is a sum down for you" – it would range from £10 to £1,000 according to the popularity of the author – "give me for that the right of publishing your next work in newspapers. Your rights of publication in book form are untouched. Make what arrangement you please about that" '.[50] The surviving Tillotson archive shows that many novelists, including such names as Wilkie Collins, R.D. Blackmore, Hall

Caine, Marie Corelli, Conan Doyle, were evidently happy with whatever terms their contracts with Tillotson did allow them. Tillotson assured them, Singleton tells us, that they would gain hosts of new readers, and that as their fame so increased they would be in a position to make better terms for each successive book, not only with Tillotsons, but with the book publishers.

Details of Henty's contract have not survived, but there is a letter from him in the records of the Tillotson Fiction Department which begins: 'In my agreement with you it was stipulated that you should have the offer of any book upon the same terms that anyone else was ready to give me', and reveals an offer for a story of £150 from an American publisher. The letter ends: 'Before writing to accept the offer, I feel bound by my agreement to acquaint you with it'.[51]

Should Tillotson have offered a matching sum he would have had to recover his money, and make his profit, by first selling the serial rights to a newspaper, and then selling rights for publication in book form. Tillotson's historian, Singleton, described the agreement whereby authors were to make their own arrangements with book publishers. But either Singleton misunderstood the form of contract used by Tillotson or there must have been two different types of contract in use. As far as Henty was concerned, at any rate, the author had no part in deals with Chatto & Windus.

In 1893 Chatto & Windus bought from Tillotson the first of four adult novels by Henty. Each would be added to their list after serialisation. At this date it had been proclaimed and denied for decades that the decline in the fortunes of the three-decker novel had really begun. But the number of titles published in that year showed only a small fall from earlier years – and indeed the air had been full of rumours and wild opinions for as long as many people could remember. Chatto went ahead with the three-decker edition of *Rujub, the Juggler* (see §1, 56.1, Notes 1–9), to sell at the still universally standard price of £1.11s.6d.

However, the great days really were over. The libraries were buying too many novels of an ephemeral nature, and Mudie's declared that less than ten per cent of those they bought were making a profit. Their own second-hand market was failing because there was insufficient demand for the number of books they could offer. And things were made worse by the publication of cheap editions before the three-deckers had had time to run their course through the libraries. The situation was no longer economically acceptable: on 27 June 1894 Smith's and Mudie's issued simultaneous circulars, announcing that they would no longer pay more than 4s. per volume, still subject to their usual discount, and free copies (25 as 24). That meant they were reducing their payment for three-decker novels by about 15%, and there were still even further demands. Thus, the libraries themselves deliberately brought about the collapse of the system.

The situation remained very confused in the minds of publishers, many of them bewildered and uncertain what policy to follow, and some of them anxious not to see the end of the three-volume novel. Two days after the Libraries issued their circular, Andrew Chatto wrote to them both to say he would support their proposals in principle, with only very minor reservations (see *Dorothy's Double*, §1, 61.1, Note

3). In November of that same year, 1894, in which the number of titles published was actually to rise again, Chatto, as a member of a symposium including Edward Marston and John Murray, expressed himself firmly, if romantically, a believer in the three-decker. 'I have a most hearty appreciation of the three-volume novel.' he declared, 'Take the great works of fiction in the past; it seems to me unquestionable that they have benefited by being published in the more luxurious form . . . My view is that the luxurious form . . . is an absolute necessity'.[52]

But the joint circular from Smith's and Mudie's was the decisive stroke in the collapse of the library publishing system, and it 'finally decided the trade to shake itself free. The tyrants had overreached themselves by demanding that no cheap reprint of a novel should be published within twelve months of its first acceptance by themselves. The London Booksellers' Society protested against this injustice and urged that the six-shilling new novel, with which many publishers were already leavening their thirty-one-and-sixpenny list, should become universal. The Society of Authors likewise condemned the three-decker, principally because of the time-lag before cheap publication – an interval in which the libraries used to sell off the three-deckers second-hand, at no profit to the authors'.[53]

In February 1895 the *Publishers' Circular* maintained it was generally recognised that the three-volume novel was doomed, but still some publishers were refusing to abandon it. Compared with 184 in the previous year, only 52 three-deckers were published in 1895. One of them, *Sons of Fire*, was the forty-seventh to be written by Mary Elizabeth Braddon, who had had such outstanding success with Tinsleys' publication of *Lady Audley's Secret* thirty-two years earlier. Mudie immediately banned the book. The authoress and her latest publisher, Simpkin Marshall, made a defiant stand, but the power of the libraries, even in this reversal of their original policy, was not shaken.

In September 1896 Henty wrote to Chatto to inquire about the merits of publishing his latest novel, *The Queen's Cup*, in a single volume. On 11 September Chatto replied: 'We are much obliged to you for the favour of your kind suggestion respecting the bringing out of your novel *The Queen's Cup* in one or two volumes. We had carefully considered the expediency of bringing it out in the first instance in one volume, but we have found that only in a few exceptional circumstances do the circulating libraries take a larger number in this form than in 2 or 3 volumes – indeed for issues in 2 volumes the demand seems rather less than for those in 3. We are hoping that this story which seems to us to in first place address the readers of library novels, may attract more attention in the three volume form than it would if issued in the first case in a cheap edition, which we propose to bring out later at 3s.6d.'.[54]

It is almost unbelievable, now, that Andrew Chatto, and his partner, Percy Spalding, who wrote the letter (widely-split infinitive and all!), could have taken such a view at that date. In 1896 only 25 three-decker novels were published in the UK, but Chatto's romantic regard for the physical nature of such books seems to have obscured his vision. He made himself appear, almost certainly to Henty, wilfully blind to the inevitability of their impending disappearance.

On 28 November 1896 Chatto wrote again to Henty to say 'we are not publishing *The Queen's Cup* until January – perhaps in the second week of the month',[55] and it duly appeared on 12 January 1897. In that year the total number of three-deckers published fell to a mere four, so the book which was Henty's final three-volume novel was also one of the very last ever published in Britain. Indeed its comparative lack of success may be due more to politics of publishing than to any literary failing: it just came out at the wrong time, or in the wrong format.

On 13 December 1897 Chatto & Windus wrote to Henty to tell him they had bought *Colonel Thorndyke's Secret* through Tillotsons. Two days later, on 15 December, they wrote again to thank him for returning the first batch of proofs, and added 'We are intending to publish the story as a 1-volume novel (the library 3-volume form being now unfortunately quite obsolete) and shall have the pleasure of sending you half-a-dozen author's copies when ready'.[56] So at long last Chatto had taken the inevitable decision. As Simon Nowell-Smith confirms, 'Chatto & Windus, one of the best-reputed library-novel publishers, announced that because the two- or three-decker at half-a-guinea a volume "no longer meets the requirements of the time" they would henceforward issue all their novels at five shillings'.[57]

Here, perhaps, we should consider the matter of publishers' print orders for first editions of three-decker novels. Fifteen years earlier the public demand for novels had not been quite so great, although Mudie was already twenty years into his domination of the book trade and more or less at the peak of his career. But he insisted that books in his Library should be *immediately* available to readers, and that meant buying in quantities to match subscribers' demands. 'In 1876 Trollope estimated that a publisher spent about £200 for a first edition of 600 copies of a three-volume novel. Such an edition could make just over £400, leaving the publisher just over £200 to pay an author and for his own profit'.[58]

Today authors rightly expect to receive fixed percentage royalties for their work. The situation was different in Victorian times. Many authors preferred to be given an outright payment for a novel, or at least payment for the first printing, believing that a publisher would work harder to sell a book that was not someone else's property. The logic in this view, provided the payment is reasonably assessed, and especially if accompanied by an arrangement for additional payment or royalties should the book run into further editions, is understandable if not unassailable. M.E. Braddon had received a whole series of payments from Tinsleys for her runaway success, *Lady Audley's Secret*.

But it might not be easy for the publisher. If he had to fork out a lump sum he was likely to need quick returns. In days when the economics of printing bear little relationship to those of today, he might have been both unwilling and unable to print a large first edition, involving a substantial down-payment. But on the other hand he would not even have needed to do so in order to make a profit. A short-run three-decker novel, at its ridiculously high standard price, could succeed with even a moderate order from the Libraries.

At the same date that Trollope made his financial calculations, however, a leading publisher, George Bentley, was quoting figures to one of his authors, based on an edition of 2000 copies. John Carter had suggested that Mudie was accustomed to take '1500 of any Bentley novel, sight unseen',[59] and Griest comments that even if this were not so '1500 copies would seem to be a reasonable estimate of his order for a work from an established writer'.[60]

Details of print orders for all editions of Henty's work published by Chatto & Windus are given in the Notes under each title in §1. The initial orders for the three-volume editions of *Rujub, the Juggler* and *Dorothy's Double* were for 500 copies and 400 copies respectively. Those quantities are very respectable for an author who, in the adult fiction market, could be regarded more as a beginner than an 'established writer'.

By 1893 he was of course a household name as a writer for boys, and no doubt his books for them were being read by many adults. Certainly, also, his adult novels were being read by the young. It is clear that their publishers generally found that by putting them in appropriate formats they could sell the majority of them in a juvenile market. That fact did not escape Henty's notice, and it gave him some concern in view of the terms of his contract with Blackie.[43] But *Rujub, the Juggler* had far more success than any other book Henty wrote for adults. Chatto printed a total of 11,000 copies, of which 9000 had come off the press within three years of first publication. Many novelists would have been jealous of such figures.[61]

5. BLACKIE, AND THE HENTY 'MONOPOLY'; THE GLASGOW STYLE

The origin of the firm was the offer of a partnership in 1809 to John Blackie, aged 27, by William Sommerville and Archibald Fullarton who were already in business as publishers, canvassers and deliverers. One of their earliest books, published under the imprint 'W.Sommerville, A.Fullarton & John Blackie & Co., Booksellers, Glasgow, 1811', was *Travels in Italy*. It was written by Dr John Moore, the father of Sir John Moore of Corunna, about whom Henty was to write a novel for John Blackie's grandson when the firm was known as Blackie & Son some eighty-five years later.

Moore's book was printed by Edward Khull, who became a partner in 1819, 'and the firm split itself into two sections, linked by partnership but each section operating as a distinct entity under its own name, in Glasgow and Edinburgh respectively. Thus came into being "Khull, Blackie & Co." as publishers and printers in Glasgow, and "Fullarton, Sommerville & Co." as booksellers only, in Edinburgh'.[62]

Two years later Sommerville resigned, leaving A. Fullarton & Co. in Edinburgh. In 1826 Khull resigned to continue alone as a printer, and the Glasgow firm became Blackie, Fullarton & Co., in which Blackie's eldest son, John Blackie Junior, became a partner. In 1831 the partnership was dissolved and finally the name of the firm, independent of Fullarton in Edinburgh, became Blackie & Son, Glasgow.

Meanwhile John Blackie Senior had entered into negotiations to buy a printing works at Villafield that had previously been owned by A. & J.M. Duncan, but was now closed down. Duncans had succeeded Robert and Andrew Foulis as printers to the University: their fine printing at the Foulis Press had been famed throughout Europe. Blackie's negotiations were complicated, and he was also involved in the take-over of an active printer and stereotyper whose business management had let him down. Both deals were successfully completed, and by 1837 John Blackie was in need of a manager for an operative printing works at Villafield.[63]

Walter Graham Blackie, his second son, was given the job although still only 21, eleven years younger than his brother John. He was a great success. Before long he became a partner in the printing business, then named W.G. Blackie & Co. Five years later the founder's third son, Robert, then aged 22, joined both his elder brothers as partners in Blackie & Son, Publishers. Gradually the three brothers took over the management from their father, who must have been fully aware of the brightness of their prospects. Although they were the only survivors of a family of eight, 'each of the three possessed such different and yet complementary abilities that together they formed a perfect business team'.[64]

John Blackie Junior, by far the eldest of the brothers, combined a great love of literature with sound business ability. He was a deeply religious man and responsible for many religious publications. Agnes Blackie notes that there was a reduction in that part of Blackie's list in the 1870s, mainly because John had been elected Lord Provost of Glasgow in 1863. That office took most of his time and was extremely exhausting, perhaps at last fatally.

The second brother, Walter, was physically strong, but had had smallpox when young. He had been sent to live in the country and from there to a small private school, which resulted in a place at the University of Glasgow. An extremely able student, practical and physically active, he was a classical scholar, and had a great talent for languages and music. Later, as Dr W.G. Blackie, he became a public figure in politics, Church politics, and University reform, and was a delegate at discussions in New York on the subject of international copyright.

The youngest, Robert, was a gifted amateur painter, and studied in Paris for a time under Ingres. Later, Dr W.G. Blackie's younger son, Walter, wrote: 'My father and his brother Robert were in many respects the opposites of each other: the one, impetuous and full of drive, the other (Robert) calm and deliberate in all things; the one rather lacking in aesthetic perception and the other devoted chiefly to art in all its aspects'.[65] As a partner in Blackie & Son, it was natural that illustrations should become Robert's special care.

Of all the family members who built up this solid and remarkable business, one was to play an important part in the life of G.A. Henty. John Alexander Blackie was the elder of Dr W.G. Blackie's two sons, born in 1850, nearly twenty years Henty's junior, and he became a partner in 1876. 'The Education Acts of 1870 (England and Wales) and 1872 (Scotland) had just made elementary education compulsory for all children, and created an unprecedented demand for school books. Many publishing firms were preparing to supply the new demand'.[66] Dr Blackie was keen that his firm should make a start as soon as possible, but there were difficulties following the deaths of his eldest brother, John Junior, in 1873, and of his father, the senior partner, at the age of 91 in 1874. 'The real starting point in educational publishing' for

Blackie & Son 'however, was the acquisition in 1878 of the rights in *Vere Foster Writing and Drawing Copy Books*. Vere Foster was one of the great philanthropists of the Victorian era'.[67] His story, and how Blackie came to publish his books, is remarkable and interesting. It is told at length by Agnes Blackie, but need not concern us here.

(John) Alexander Blackie took a leading part in the negotiations that culminated in the purchase of the Vere Foster copyrights, and soon found himself helping his father to plan Blackie's *Comprehensive Readers*, which 'were the first of a stream of school books of every sort – grammars, arithmetics, geographies. . . Indeed, once their plans were matured, Blackie & Son may be said, in 1879, to have entered the educational field at the gallop'.[68]

The production of school text books quickly became a major part of the Blackie publishing business. As soon as Dr Blackie had got a grip on the new programme he asked his younger son, Walter W. Blackie, to return to the fold and help him with them. Walter had gone to Canada in 1880, but he agreed to give up his plans to settle there and farm, and went straight to New York where he trained for a time with the American publishing house of Appleton.[69] He finally entered the London branch of Blackie at 50 Old Bailey in 1884.

Meanwhile Alexander was thinking ahead and had already started to assemble a new list of authors. 'Victorian schools – and Sunday Schools – were great prize-givers, so that the Education Act, by increasing schools and scholars, automatically multiplied the demand for "reward" books. From educational publishing to "rewards" was a natural line of progression which it took only three years for Blackie & Son to follow'.[70]

The first Blackie catalogue of publications for the young, issued in 1882, lists over sixty books for children at prices from 7s.6d. to 6d., including their first two Henty novels for boys, as well as ten pages of readers, 'school classics', dictionaries and other educational works. Alexander Blackie had certainly moved fast, and managed to persuade many leading writers for children to join his list. In this he was helped for some years by Thomas Archer, one of their leading educational writers, who had introduced G.A. Henty. Of the others in the original list many are not so well-known today, but all were then household names, and included G.Manville Fenn, Ascot R. Hope, Rosa Mulholland; Mrs Elizabeth Lysaght, Mrs Emma Pitman, Alice Corkran, and Annie S. Swan. As the editor of a new department the young partner had made an excellent start.

The list grew under his management to include many more famous names, but it was not just at building a list that he was to shine. Surviving letters and other documents show that Alexander Blackie was very skilful in dealings with his authors, and in managing copyrights and contracts. Above all, his imagination and innovation, coupled with outstanding technical and aesthetic skills, made him an outstanding organiser in both editorial and production matters.

A triumphant achievement of Blackie & Son in Alexander's time was the prosperous management of a large, diversified business. Even within a small printing factory it was often hard to arrange that both the compositors and the pressmen were kept fully occupied all the time. There would, for instance, always be jobs requiring only minimal typesetting, of which very large quantities had to be printed. This resulted in a need for compensating jobs, involving a great deal of typesetting but of which only a few copies had to be printed. Striking a balance in a print factory was sometimes managed with as much luck as planning.

Printer-binders gave themselves similar difficulties ten times over. They had to manage under one umbrella what were elsewhere regarded as two separate business enterprises. In the normal course of events the output from the printing works would rarely balance the capacity of all departments in the bindery. A solution might be to take some print work, or some binding work, from outside, to relieve the problem. But it wasn't always easy to get just the right outwork at the moment it was needed. When there was a shortage of work in the machine-room, the jobs on offer were often more likely to fit the machines that were already busy than those that were idle. And the everlasting balancing act performed by printers was no less tortuous than that carried on in a bindery.

Blackie were printer-binders on a big scale, and they had all these problems to face. But, unusually in Henty's time, they were publishers as well. It might be thought that that should have made things easier, but it is doubtful whether it did. There would have been moments when the publishing directors blessed their founder for his foresight in providing them with their factories. There would equally have been times when they did not.

Publishing is a permanently speculative business, and not just for the likes of Tinsley Brothers, as described by Michael Sadleir.[71] Disaster is likely to result if manuscripts are accepted on impulse, without sound, well-considered reasons. Imagine the temptations for a publisher with the financial responsibility for a printing works in the back of his mind. A need for more work in the composing room could be met, he might ponder, if he were to accept a certain manuscript about which no considered verdict had yet been reached. Another book could be put into production ahead of plan: it could no doubt fill a shortage of work in the machine room, but only if it were printed in a larger page-size than would normally have been chosen.

Alexander Blackie was a good business man, and a very serious-minded one. He was unlikely to have taken decisions for the wrong reasons. Just the reverse. He made constant and imaginative plans to keep production moving, and to keep the balance between departments in the factories. He devised, perhaps for the first time in a book-manufacturing concern, a system of mass-production; but it was to be one that did not turn out rows of uniform volumes. In fact, many of the volumes he produced were uniform in construction, but designed in such a way that few readers would notice the fact. Henty's books played a big part in the development of the plans, but the uniformity was planned for works of many authors.

Of course it did not happen all at once. But by 1883 Blackie's plans for reward books had taken shape, and it was clear that they could all be limited to a few alternative sizes and formats. These were planned to include books in a wide range of prices, with some uniformity within each range. For example, the novels by

Henty, George MacDonald, Manville Fenn, Harry Collingwood, Ascott R. Hope, and many others, could all be printed in the same page-size, and therefore on the same printing machines. They could also be printed on the same paper, which could therefore be ordered in bulk, at less cost. And, perhaps the master stroke, they could all be cast off and planned to make the same number of pages.

In fact, the novels were all standard crown octavos, planned to be printed on paper of the same thickness, or bulk. It was decided to produce them in two price ranges, at 5s. each and at 6s. each. Those at 5s. were designed to make 352 pages of text, and those at 6s. to make 384 pages, printed on 11 and 12 sheets of double-crown paper respectively.[72] The smaller books were generally given eight full-page plates, and the larger had twelve. The more expensive were bound in cases with bevelled edges to the boards, whereas the others were plain. Eventually all Henty's novels were given the famous 'olivine' edges.[73]

Those standardisations of page-size and bulk resulted in numerous novels of identical proportions, in the two different price-ranges. That meant that binding cases for all the books could be made in advance, and each would fit any of the books in their respective price-range. It was another example of Alexander Blackie's skill in planning. Regardless of what was going on elsewhere in the factory, the case-making department was virtually immune from problems of 'balance'. They could go on churning out blank cases in the two standard sizes, and a variety of cloth-colours, and all would be used for one book or another in due course.

The common practice of binding books for young people in differing cloth-colours (see Appendix III) made the scheme even more practical. When a binding order was received, with a decision as to the cloth to be used for the particular batch of copies, the blocking department simply collected the relevant number of blank cases and blocked them with the appropriate brasses, using pigments agreed for the particular colour of cloth selected.

These mass-production methods, used for a large output of books by a number of authors, made for great economy. After some experiments, described under the early Blackie titles in §1, all materials were eventually standardised, making bulk purchases possible. Factory procedures were also standardised, resulting in simpler and smoother production. Savings thus made enabled Blackie to lavish more on high-quality materials and design than any of his rivals could afford.[74] It was largely the varied designs for binding cases that disguised the uniformity of the make-up of so many books.

Alexander Blackie was not entirely responsible for illustration. When Henty became a Blackie author, Robert was sixty years old, and his influence was certainly still felt. But Agnes Blackie records that in 1892, only a few years before Robert's death, Talwin Morris was appointed head of the Art Department, and that this had 'tangible effect, not only on the design of book covers, but on the appearance of the office'.[75] It will be seen later that that was only one of the understatements in her book. A result of the appointment was that Blackie found themselves involved, as patrons, in an art-nouveau movement that became more famous in Europe than throughout Britain. It seems to have begun with the April 1893 issue of *The Studio*, and was known as 'The Glasgow Style': to that I shall return.

Meanwhile Alexander Blackie held the reins, and continued to do so for many years, apparently in all three departments: editorial, production and sales. Letters have survived showing his direction in all these main spheres of publishing. In 1906, four years after Henty's death, Alexander had succeeded his father as Chairman. He and his brother Walter still took responsibility for publications, 'the one looking after the "rewards" department of which he himself had been the creator, the other attending to the educational side, to assist with which he had been enticed back from Canada. Some general publishing was also undertaken, in which both brothers participated'.[76] Henty's books were still being produced in great quantities, by this time in a 'New and Popular Edition'. Later editions were to follow.

Alexander Blackie was a great publisher, and a man of imagination and vision. He saw things on a grand scale, as is clear from his creation of a solid and successful list of children's books, of a quality unmatched in his time. He was also one of the most skilful organisers of all the details involved in the management of printing, binding, and publishing. James Shand, a great printer, designer, and publisher of later times, and another Scot, told me of a derogatory comment he had heard made, that a certain printer was over-concerned with detail. 'But Printing', he had replied indignantly, is *all* detail'.[77]

Blackie understood that, and no aspect of Henty's books that came to his attention seems to have been too insignificant for serious consideration. The two men probably did not meet frequently, and certainly there was some geographical distance between them. But it is clear from surviving correspondence that Henty had developed friendships not only with Alexander but with his father and brother as well. The little that is known about Alexander suggests that few things concerned him apart from his business, and that he was probably a man without an overabundant sense of humour. His skills, however, were enormous, and have never been adequately recognised. Agnes Blackie was not given to overstating matters, as noted above, but to those who can understand and appreciate his achievements, even her summing up seems surprisingly lukewarm:

'By those who worked with him John Alexander Blackie is still remembered as a very able publisher. Besides energy and business capacity he had, in the matter of publishing, an undoubted flair, especially with regard to children's books. In every detail of book production, printing, binding, illustration, his standard was high, and equally so for old and young. In his private life this feeling for the visual was shown by his skill as an amateur photographer. But the business was always his main interest, to the extent that nothing bored him so much as a holiday from it'.[78]

At the end of 1918 John Alexander Blackie died. He was only sixty-eight, but had received a shattering blow two years earlier in the death on active service of his only son. He was succeeded as Chairman by his younger brother Walter W. Blackie. It was in Walter's time that the leading figure in The Glasgow Style, came in close contact with Blackie & Son. Charles Rennie Mackintosh, senior member of a group known as 'The Four', who were the core of the movement, was three years younger than Talwin Morris, but they were contemporaries in every sense.

Mackintosh's best-known work was the internationally celebrated Glasgow School of Art, built in two stages, a decade apart. Between the two stages he was introduced by Morris to Walter Blackie who was planning to build himself a new home. Robert J.Gibbs, writing in the *Newsletter* of the Charles Rennie Mackintosh Society,[79] reports Walter somewhat in awe of the celebrated designer, but even more surprised by his youth when they met. Mackintosh's work on The Hill House, Helensburgh, delighted him, and a lasting friendship followed between architect and client.

The graphic idiom of the Glasgow Style was already well known by Walter, through the work of Morris, his assistant Archie Campbell, and other designers commissioned by Morris. Gerald Cinamon wrote that the whole movement was, 'as its name implies, peculiar to what was then Britain's Second City ... its roots as diverse as Japanese interior design, the Aesthetic Movement, Celtic imagery, Art Nouveau, and the Arts and crafts Movement. Its young creators were students of or connected with the Glasgow School of Art ... In Britain its influence was purely local, yet it influenced designers and architects on the Continent, particularly in Vienna'.[80]

It might have been expected that Talwin Morris would ask Mackintosh to design bindings for Blackie, but Morris died a young man in 1911, and in the fifteen years of their friendship he had never done so. Quite possibly Morris admired Mackintosh's architectural work more than his graphic design. Gibbs writes 'Morris's work is notably spook-free, finer and cleaner than the Glaswegians', avoiding eccentricity and rough edges, in short, infinitely more suited to mass-production'.[81] In truth, I believe Mackintosh's book design was some way from the elegance and finesse of Morris's mature work.

However, after the first war, and some ten years after Morris's death, Walter Blackie was of a mind to produce a new cheap edition of Henty's novels, in uniform bindings. He wrote to Mackintosh to ask if he would undertake the design. The scope offered was not great: 'an ordinary colour, such as is procurable in ordinary cloths, is the thing', and 'I fear we cannot afford gilt these times: so, for the new Henty Library we shall require to use ordinary black ink'. As to the style, Mackintosh's brief was: 'The design can hardly be intimately connected with the substance of any one of Henty's books seeing the same design has to do for the lot' and Walter explained he was after an abstract expression of Henty's work, and the 'cover should be manly and full of courage not too much "expressed in fancy" '.[82]

Walter Blackie seems to have been over-parsimonious in his instructions for Henty's new edition. The restrictions on his designer were tight, and I think the idea of totally uniform abstract designs for the novels was ill-conceived. Alexander had invented mechanical mass-production for his children's books, but in such a way that no one noticed it. Walter seems to have lacked the imagination of his brother. But Mackintosh, who badly needed work in the 1920s, produced a bold, simple and striking design. His 'rough' is illustrated in Gibbs's article, and by chance confirms that this particular design was for the novels, as it includes lettering representing parts of two of their titles in the single drawing: 'THE DRAGON' [AND THE

RAVEN] and [UNDER] 'WELLINGTON'S COMMAND'.

Ultimately Walter Blackie changed his mind. The project was abandoned, and 'The New Popular Henty' volumes emerged, as described in §1, with bindings very close to those for the earlier cheap series, although with the stipulated 'no gilt'. But Mackintosh's design was not lost: Blackie used it for a slighter series called 'The Boys' and Girls' Bookshelf'. That included books by other authors and only one by Henty (see *Yarns on the Beach*, §1, 25.5, Plate 115).

Mackintosh designed other books for Blackie, but none specifically for Henty. A cheap series, given, as often by Blackie, a name easily confused with that of another, was 'Blackie's Library for Boys and Girls', and Gibbs believes the binding may have been Mackintosh's work. The series includes Henty titles (see Appendix V), and the books designed by both men are given references in the notes under their names in Appendix IV, Part 2.

Morris also designed a sans-serif letterform, used with variations for many of his bindings. It was combined with endlessly changing versions of a limited series of motifs: whiplash lines, rectangles, dots, stylised flowers, often within frames in pseudo-architectural style. Cinamon wrote of him: 'His timely tenure at Blackie, the influence upon him by the artistic work of The Four, and his encouragement as patron of their work, was immensely significant. In his position at Blackie he was hugely influential in spreading and popularising the Glasgow Style throughout the world. That Morris produced so many wonderful designs, and had the opportunity and encouragement to do so, we must thank the publishing house of Blackie & Son'.[83]

Looking back, finally, to the early days of Henty's association with Blackie & Son, it can be imagined that he and Alexander must have discussed his words in the Preface to *The Cornet of Horse* (Sampson Low, 1881): 'It is my intention to follow up the series, and I hope in time to give you histories of all the great wars in which the English people have been engaged since the Norman conquest'. Within less than a decade they were to find that in Blackie's hands the projected series increased in popularity and success virtually to the point of becoming an national institution.

On 14 May 1887 they had signed an agreement by which Blackie was bound to accept from Henty three books for young people each year, and Henty was to write such books exclusively for Blackie. This was to be binding for five years, but in fact a new contract was signed between them in September 1891, improving the terms for Henty and altering the specified maximum and minimum lengths of the books.[84]

From that time all Henty's books specifically 'written for young people' were published by Blackie, who in 1895 even acquired from Routledge the rights in *The Young Colonists*. Only novels for the young were included in the contracts, although Blackie also produced some of his volumes of collected short stories. A later letter in the Blackie archive, dated 28 September 1896, expresses Henty's pleasure and gratitude when the royalty rates were increased further, but no details of that arrangement survive.[85] Altogether Blackie published nearly eighty of Henty's books, excluding late volumes of excerpts from the earlier novels, and some of them were in print for nearly a hundred years.

6. HENTY'S OTHER PUBLISHERS, AND TWO UNPUBLISHED NOVELS

A number of publishers each issued just one or two works either written by Henty, or including contributions by him. George Routledge & Sons come into this category, and their work is mentioned in Part 3 of this Appendix. The others are listed here in roughly chronological order of publishing Henty.

Spencer Blackett produced two books by Henty, both intended for adults. In *Gabriel Allen, M.P.* the title-page imprint was: '(Successor to J. & R. Maxwell), Milton House, 35, St Bride Street, Ludgate Circus, E.C.'. The book is not dated, but believed by Farmer to have been published in 1888: certainly it was after Henty contracted with Blackie for children's books (see Appendix VI), and before his arrangement with Tillotsons for novels (Part 4 of this Appendix). J. & R. Maxwell was a publishing house owned by John Maxwell, husband of M.E. Braddon (see Part 1 of this Appendix).

The following year, 1889, Blackett published *The Curse of Carne's Hold* as a two-decker: here the imprint was changed to 'Spencer Blackett & Hallam, 35, St. Bride Street, Ludgate Circus, E.C.'. Peter Allen tells me the new imprint lasted only a few months, and that in 1890, when the business failed, copyrights and stock were acquired by Griffith & Farran. Certainly by 1893 they were issuing the book as a single-volume novel and as a yellow-back, and also added it to their 'Boys' Own Favourite Library'. But in 1906, when Hodder & Stoughton bought the stock and goodwill of Griffith & Farran, *The Curse of Carne's Hold* seems not to have been included among their copyrights, for it was never published again.

Spencer Blackett was a son of the original partner in Hurst & Blackett, publishers, who had taken over the business of Henry Colburn on his death in 1855. Years later, in 1905, Hurst & Blackett published Edmund Downey's anecdotal account of his years with Tinsley Brothers, *Twenty Years Ago* (see Part 1 of this Appendix). It is possible that Downey introduced Henty to Blackett, who had built a strong list by 1890, including four of Rider Haggard's early novels, others by Conan Doyle, Mrs Oliphant, Ouida, L.T. Meade, Mayne Reid, and many more.

The Society for the Propagation of Christian Knowledge published two short stories by Henty in their 'Penny Library of Fiction': *The Plague Ship* in 1889 and *The Ranche in the Valley* in 1892. The S.P.C.K. had been founded in 1698 for the distribution of prayer books, and only entered the field of fiction in 1814, extremely cautiously. That caution remained an overwhelming factor in the progress of the Society as publishers for children, and it is perhaps surprising that Henty's work, if it was to be suitable for such an organisation, did not find its way to another, younger and, in that field, more progressive house:

The Religious Tract Society. Both the S.P.C.K. and the R.T.S. had found it necessary, after the Education Acts of the 1870s, to brighten up their publications for children, and to give their fiction more direct appeal. Previously the Sunday Schools had been important to many parents, as they taught children to read. Now that responsibility fell to Board schools. Gradually the ability of children, and parents, to read and write came to be taken more for granted. 'The result of wider spreading literacy', wrote J.S.Bratton, 'was to increase the demand for children's books, and also to change their nature. Schools and other prize and present buyers could no longer hope to attract their readers simply by the promise of learning the skill, nor to control them by offering them anything they wished them to believe embodied in fiction: the fiction had to have an obvious and immediate appeal, if only in the form of a glittering binding'.[86]

The R.T.S. was the quicker to react to the situation, early in the 1870s changing the style of its books at all prices from 6d. upwards. In 1879 they started the *Boy's Own Paper*, and that soon developed qualities of both content and design with which the *Union Jack* could never compete, in spite of Henty's repeated denials to his young readers. After the demise of the *Union Jack* several stories by Henty, and his serialised 'Life of a Special Correspondent', appeared in the *Boy's Own Paper*.

Henry & Co., of 6 Bouverie Street, E.C., published Henty's *Those Other Animals* in 1891 in 'The Whitefriars Library of Wit and Humour'. The General Editor, William Henry Davenport Adams, who devised that series, wrote several books advertised in Henry's catalogue under his own name. He also wrote many books under various pseudonyms, and there may be other works of his in the list. He died in 1891. A second edition was published in 1897, this time in 'The Random Series', when Henry & Co. had become a Limited Company and moved to 93 St Martin's Lane, London, W.C. I have been unable to find records of this publisher, who also issued the 'Victoria Library for Gentlewomen', announced 'to supply good and wholesome Fiction, also Descriptive Sketches, and Essays on Moral and Social Questions connected with Women's Welfare ... Hygiene, Manners, Dress, the Toilette, the Boudoir, Music, and the Cuisine... Her Majesty the Queen has been graciously pleased to sanction the use of the title "The Victoria Library," and to order two copies of each volume for the Royal Library'. The authors included many titled ladies.

Ward, Lock and Co. and **Cassell & Company** are grouped together here as their activities for a time overlapped. In 1889, the year *The Curse of Carne's Hold* was published, Ward & Lock asked Henty to take on the Editorship of a re-issued version of *Beeton's Boy's Own Magazine* which had been published by its original owner twenty years earlier. It was, as Henty foresaw from the start, a doubtful project, and an account of the venture is given at §3, 197. Its main interest, now, is a series of twelve Editorials by Henty under the heading 'Editor's Table'.

Ward and Lock had entered into partnership as young men in 1854, mainly through the agency of a first cousin of George Lock, called Thomas Dixon Galpin. Only two years earlier Galpin had set up as a printer in partnership with George William Petter. Ebenezer Ward had worked for a publisher, a customer of Petter and Galpin, and he had confided to Galpin that he wanted to leave his employer and to set up his own business. George Lock, who was 22 and some twelve years younger than Ward, also asked the advice of his cousin, Galpin, about a possible career in London. Galpin introduced the two young men, and was instrumental in getting his uncle, George Lock's father, to put up £1000 capital.

A year later, in 1855, another, quite unconnected, young business reached a moment of crisis. John Cassell, born in a Manchester inn, had become a dedicated and courageous teetotaller. He had little or no education and, although apprenticed as a carpenter, was unskilled in any trade. He left home at 19, and travelled with friends made while addressing an often antagonistic public about temperance, managing to make a little money by rough carpentry. He married in 1841 at the age of 24, and a long struggle for survival ensued. From such unpromising beginnings he became, by way of a small but growing business selling coffee and tea as an acceptable alternative to alcohol, a successful publisher of temperance and radical periodicals, and, by 1850, educational paperback books. His business grew and was successful. His name became well-known, largely because it was included in the titles of nearly all his publications, as it had been on all the packets of his tea and coffee. But his finances were not well secured, and the crash came in 1855 when his backer foreclosed.

A young and enterprising firm of printers who had worked for him, Petter & Galpin, bought his business, and with it his debt. They arranged for the publication of much of Cassell's work to continue, and of course acquired more printing work for themselves in the process. It was not until three years later that John Cassell was admitted to the new partnership. 'It is a fair assumption that before the first appearance of the new imprint, "Cassell, Petter & Galpin", the debt ... had been sufficiently discharged. Cassell became senior partner by virtue of his most remunerative asset, his name: his financial interest in the publishing business was small, and in the printing business, which was separately conducted under the name Petter & Galpin, he had no interest at all'.[87]

Petter & Galpin had been giving cousinly financial assistance to Ward & Lock, and now they found themselves part of a rival publishing business. 'It is at least a possibility that, but for the opportunity offered by John Cassell's failure, the eventual amalgamation would not have been between Petter's and Cassell's but between Petter's and Ward & Lock'.[88] There were problems, and some bad feeling, arising from the conflict of interests. Ward & Lock books were even for a time advertised in Cassell publications.

But in the end common sense and family unity prevailed. La Belle Sauvage, the delapidated building in which John Cassell had his business before his failure, was restored, and the publishing firm was back on the rails. 'Petter devoted a meticulous attention to editorial affairs that was wholly foreign to John Cassell's nature, while Galpin ... had the commercial ability, shrewdness and ruthlessness for lack of which Cassell had failed'.[89] It was, nevertheless, a triumvirate of eccentrics, and although the business managed well enough it can hardly be said to have run entirely smoothly.

In 1865 John Cassell died of cancer. Only a week before his death he had been asked to join a full partnership, to include the printing activities of the business. At this time the firm was publishing about twelve part-issues each month: by 1888 the number had risen to forty. In the intervening period they had published Stevenson's *Treasure Island*, first in their children's magazine *Young Folks* and later in their growing book list. By then the list included many other important writers: Rider Haggard, Stanley Weyman, Quiller-Couch and, in the non-fiction field, Henry Morley. In 1888 Petter died, having retired from active work five years earlier, when the firm was incorporated as Cassell & Company Limited. The publishing organisation was at a high point of prosperity after a dozen years of expansion.

At about this time Ward, Lock, were also on the crest of a wave. In 1865 Charles T. Tyler joined as a partner: he brought new capital to the business, and remained for eight years as financial adviser. Little more is known about Tyler, although he was involved in the negotiations with Samuel Beeton, which resulted in the take-over of Beeton's publishing business following the failure of the Overend Gurney Bank in 1866 (see *Beeton's Boy's Own Magazine*, §3, 197). No doubt he also played an important part in the acquisition by Ward Lock & Tyler in 1870 of the important publishing house of Edward Moxon, whose authors included Robert Southey, Barry Cornwall, Monkton Milnes, and Disraeli.

In 1878 the business moved into larger premises: by then its name had reverted to Ward & Lock, and the following year they appointed two new partners. One was John Lock, younger brother of George; the other was James Bowden. Bowden had been employed by Sam Beeton and moved to Ward Lock with him, following the disasters that destroyed Beeton's business. He worked impressively with George Lock as an editorial manager, and in 1891 the firm's name became Ward Lock and Bowden. It was probably Bowden who dealt with Henty in 1889 over the Editorship of the re-issued *Beeton's Boy's Own Magazine*, though it is by no means certain that the project was his idea.

It was a good time for both Ward Lock and Cassell. From that peak, however, Cassell's business faltered, and its fortunes went steadily downhill. 'Two principal factors account for the decline: the preoccupation of the men at the head of the business with outside interests, and the workings of the Elementary Education Act which recoiled like a boomerang upon the firm that had most diligently sought to promote it and profit by it'.[90] This was the Act which had affected all publishers of books for children, making fundamental changes in both the editorial and production policies of such as the S.P.C.K. and the R.T.S., and bringing Blackie for the first time into a field they were soon to lead.

But Cassell managed to miss the boat, as they did with three-volume fiction for the circulating libraries. Their Chairman, General Manager, and Secretary were, all three, primarily politicians. They added to the book list in politics, biography and education but did little about the popular magazines and part-issues, such publications as were the money-spinning successes of their rivals, Newnes, Harmsworth and Pearson. It was only the arrival of a 'new broom', in the person of Newman Flower, that once again put the firm on the rails, rather as had happened after John Cassell's failure fifty years earlier.

It was during the period of decline, in 1892, that Henty's work first appeared in a Cassell publication. A story, 'Jack Dillon of Dunnamore', was printed in six instalments in *Chums*, a newly started and badly designed magazine (see §3, 205). Four years later some of his serious journalism appeared in *Battles of the Nineteenth Century*. One of Cassell's successful part-issues, it was issued and re-issued several times (see §2, 126).

The affairs of Ward Lock, Bowden and Company continued, without excitement and without disaster, and in 1893 James Bowden was appointed Managing Director of Ward Lock & Bowden Limited. The Chairman of the new Company was George Ernest Lock, son of George Lock and known in the business as Mr Ernest. There does seem to have been a negative quality, of restraint without adventure, in Ernest Lock's approach to publishing, which Bowden may have found constricting. Four years later he retired, and set up his own firm:

James Bowden of 10 Henrietta Street, Covent Garden, W.C., published in 1899 Henty's *The Lost Heir*, a novel for adults that was designed and produced very much in the style of Henty's boys' books. This tendency has been commented on in Part 3 of this Appendix, and it was in 1899 that Henty's concern about it became clear through the comments of a journalist who had interviewed him for *The Gem*.[43] A page of advertising, and the catalogue bound in Henty's book, show that at that date Bowden had already established a long list of novels, at least one of whose authors, Joseph Hocking, he had earlier recruited to the list of his former employers. How long James Bowden remained in business is uncertain, but in 1906 *The Lost Heir* was re-issued by

T. Fisher Unwin of Adelphi Terrace, London, W.C. From this publisher the book appeared in plain and simple bindings, without the pictorial boards of Bowden's edition. It was otherwise unchanged, and kept its illustrations; indeed, Unwin added a list of Illustrations, but even so it would probably have appeased Henty had he lived to see it.

Unwin had been born into the book world, and had a job with Hodder & Stoughton before buying a small publishing company, Marshall, Japp & Co, and starting on his own in 1883. He started publishing just as the days of three-volume novels had come to an end. 'Circulating libraries were no longer the deciding factor. The bookshops and bookstalls were feeling the influence and supplying the needs of a better-educated public, and Fisher Unwin was among the first publishers to tickle its literary palate with unaccustomed fare'.[91]

'His idea was good; he wanted to improve the opportunities of struggling authors, and made it known that he would pay £30 for the copyright of any first novel of which his [advisory] readers approved. Fisher Unwin made substantial losses on five out of every six of these titles, but did find a very few real winners'.[92] He was the first to publish Somerset Maugham and Conrad, and had a strong list in other fields than fiction. In the end 'Fisher Unwin was a victim of the error of using his publishing facilities to popularise his own political prejudices, an error which brought him to grief'.[93] Between the wars the business was taken over by Ernest Benn Limited, an offshoot of Benn Brothers.

In 1908 another publisher, **John Milne** of 29 Henrietta Street, Covent Garden, produced a paperback edition of Henty's *The Lost Heir* in 'The London Series' at 6d. The text was set in two columns and interspersed with general advertisements. Of this publisher no records, nor, indeed, any traces, have come to light.

F.V. White & Co., of 14 Bedford Street, Strand, London, W.C., published Henty's *A Woman of the Commune* in 1895, snatching it from Tillotsons, as it were, from under the nose of Chatto & Windus (see §1, 65, Notes 1–4). Peter Allen tells me that this publisher started up in 1881 by buying out Samuel Tinsley & Co. (no connection with the firm of Tinsley Brothers, but in the business of publishing novels). In 1871 Samuel Tinsley had carried on a campaign against the library system, announcing single-volume novels at 4s. each, while still taking care to cover himself by issuing the standard three-deckers.

White eventually had a very long list, including the great output of Henrietta Eliza Vaughan Stannard, novelist and occasional writer for children, whose pseudonym, or, as her own entry in *Who's Who* gives it, *nom de guerre*, was John Strange Winter. Her father had been an army officer before taking holy orders, and Ruskin said she was 'the author to whom we owe the most finished and faithful rendering ever yet given of the character of the British soldier'. Henty must have heard this famous remark, but seems not to have met her, or, if he did, remained silent, just as does, inexplicably, the *Cambridge Bibliography of English Literature*. G. Manville Fenn, and Weedon Grossmith appeared in White's list, but most of their writers were women. They advertised monthly magazines, including *London Society*, and *Belgravia*, the latter edited by M.E. Braddon until 1893.

A Woman of the Commune was first issued, with a sub-title 'A Tale of Two Sieges of Paris', in a simple binding, and could hardly have been mistaken for a boys' book. A year later it was issued in pictorial boards with bevelled edges and gilt lettering, and with a set of six illustrations. The illustrations were by Hal Hurst, grandson of Daniel, the original partner in Hurst & Blackett. This book, as well as *The Lost Heir* (see above), was almost certainly one of the titles referred to by Henty's interviewer from *The Gem*.[43] Thereafter the book passed to another publisher:

S.W. Partridge & Co. of 8 & 9 Paternoster Row, London, E.C., who re-issued it as *Cuthbert Hartington*, with the same sub-title as before, in a new binding design but still dressed up as a boys' book. In 1916 they again re-issued the book, this time under the title *Two Sieges*, with a sub-title 'Cuthbert Hartington's Adventures'. The general design was the same as for the previous version, but the quality of paper and binding are clearly affected by wartime restrictions. Partridge was a substantial publisher of books for the young, and for years specialised in moral texts campaigning against intemperance and cruelty to animals. With others mentioned earlier they both took advantage of and benefited from the Education Acts of the 1870s, and some of their publications were similar to those from the R.T.S. They also published a number of periodicals, including *The British Workman, The Friendly Visitor, The Infants' Magazine*, and *The Band of Hope Review*. From 1883 all were edited by Edward Step, who also wrote books under their imprints. He left in 1891 to become Editor of *Boys* (§3, 199), a magazine to which Henty contributed. The business was taken over in 1930 by A.& C.Black Limited.

Chapman & Hall published Henty's *John Hawke's Fortune* in 1901 as a most attractive booklet, illustrated and decorated in colour, and engraved and printed by Edmund Evans. It was Volume VII in 'The Young People's Library', and there is no evidence to show how it came to be offered to them – or perhaps commissioned by them. After it had been re-issued in a series of cheap bindings, it passed to Blackie & Son.

Chapman & Hall, founded in 1830, publisher of Dickens, and for a time of Trollope, was one of the most distinguished houses in London, and at one time regarded Tinsley Brothers as their main rival in the three-decker novel market (see Part 1 of this Appendix). For many years their reader, or literary adviser, was George Meredith. He was appointed in 1860 and was still working for them in 1894. In 1866 he was sent for a few months to Italy by the *Morning Post* as Special Correspondent, where he met Henty. William Allan gives an account of a three-round boxing match between the two of them, arranged as a private display, at the personal request of Garibaldi.[94]

Two unpublished novels. Soon after the boxing match, probably in 1867, Henty submitted the manuscript of his first adult novel to Chapman & Hall. B.W. Matz, a lifelong member of their staff, recorded many details of Meredith's work. 'During the 'sixties,' he remembered 'G.A. Henty, whose story *Frank Tressilor* was returned with instructions to "encourage the author to send any future work" '.[95] No novel of that name is heard of again, but Henty is reported by B. McCall Barbour as having spoken of it: 'Very bad, no doubt, and [it] was, of course, never published, but the plot was certainly a good one'.[96]

Towards the end of his life Henty wrote a book for boys that was never published. In March 1904 John Alexander Blackie wrote to Scribners in New York: 'Another Ms. by Mr. Henty has turned up, but we are not quite sure yet whether we shall publish it. It is an Irish story and in it there is a little feeling of partizanship which we should endeavour to eliminate, but we have at present the book before an adviser in Ireland to say whether it would be found satisfactory to Irish readers. We hope to come to a decision regarding it within the next ten days, when we shall write you'. Six days later Blackie wrote again to say 'we find that the book to which we referred is of so partizan a character that it would not be in the interest of either the author or publisher to issue it. The book therefore will not be published'.[97]

APPENDIX III

BOOK PRODUCTION METHODS

1. PRINTING

Turning a manuscript into a book is a complicated process, and the notes that follow are an attempt to explain briefly the various stages in such work on Henty's books. I deal first with the printing of the text, and then with the binding of the whole printed book. The preparation and printing of illustrations are briefly covered in Appendix IV.

A printer's responsibilities on receiving a manuscript from a publisher have always varied. Some publishers took a great interest in the appearance of their books, and always gave detailed instructions. Others, with less concern for typography and aesthetics, preferred, perhaps perilously, to leave all technical matters to the printer, avoiding as much decision-making as possible. But there were in Henty's day, and for many years later, certain universal conventions. They related to such matters as appropriate page-sizes for novels, the style for setting paragraphs, relative proportions of margins, the arrangement of preliminary pages, and so on, which were observed, in general principle, by all concerned.

The conventions were understood by recognised book printers, specialists in their field, but not necessarily by 'general' or 'jobbing' printers. Many of the latter had excellent qualities, and might be used by publishers to print catalogues or other things, but not books. In all Henty's books, other than those from Blackie, the printers' imprints that appear on text pages are not the ones that are printed at the ends of the bound-in catalogues.[1] Blackie were unique among Henty's publishers in being themselves printers, and found it more economical not to farm out the production of their own catalogues.

The publisher, then, chose his book printer. The printer's first job, for any book, was to work out the length of the manuscript, and the number of pages the volume would make. Calculations would be based on the exact page-size, and any other specifications, stipulated by the publisher. The object was to arrive at a style of typesetting that would be aesthetically pleasing, and also make the book fill a convenient and economical number of pages.

The text had to be printed on large sheets of paper in one or other of several standard sizes. For Henty's novels paper was usually bought in Quad Crown, which measured 30 x 40 inches. That would make 64 pages: 32 on each side. For editions of 2000 copies the paper would probably be printed as a full sheet, but for editions of only 1000 copies it was generally economical to cut the paper in half before printing.[2]

Eventually the printed work would be cut into Crown sheets measuring 15 × 20 inches, and folded to make 16-page sections or 'signatures'.[3] It was normal practice for the printer to insert a single letter in the foot-margin of the first page of each section, the letters continuing alphabetically[4] from one section to the next. These helped the binder to ensure the sections appeared in the right order. Sometimes consecutive figures were used instead of letters. Whether letters or figures, the characters were known as 'signatures', and that word became an alternative name for the section itself, commonly referred to as 'sig.A' or 'sig.2'.

With Quad Crown paper it was possible to print a sheet with pages numbered consecutively from, say, 1 to 64. That would be cut and folded to make four 16-page sections. It was also customary, as an alternative, to impose the type for what was known as 'half-sheet work'. That meant that 32 pages were printed on one side of the paper, which was then turned end to end, as well as being turned over, before the same forme, i.e. the same set of 32 pages, was printed again on the other side. The usual printers' term for this method was 'work-and-turn'. The resulting sheet was cut into four 16-page sections, of which two pairs were identical. By the first method 1000 sheets of paper would produce 1000 copies of each of four different sections; by the second method the same amount of paper would produce 2000 copies of each of two different sections.

If a book made an odd number of 16-page sections, one of them would probably be printed on a smaller machine, on a sheet of Double Crown paper (measuring 20 × 30 inches). Here the half-sheet, or work-and-turn, method would be used, so that 1000 sheets of paper would produce 2000 identical 16-page gatherings. A point to be borne in mind by bibliographers and serious-minded collectors is that the half-sheet printing method produced slightly-varying sets of gatherings, and the word 'identical', used in the last sentence, is not strictly accurate.

In that example the first sheet to come off the printing machine could be backed up by the 1001st impression, and the 1000th impression could be on the back of the 2000th. Thus, any damage to the type, such as sorts dropping out of the forme half-way through the run, might be apparent on pages backed up with both early and late impressions. If the two sides of the paper used for the text showed a variation in texture, as always happens with laid paper, it would be clear to the most inexperienced eye that some copies of the section existed with the first page on the rougher side of the sheet, and some had the first page on the smoother side.

To have a blank page, or even two, at the end of a book, would not matter much. But to have an odd page of text left over, at the end of the last 16-page section, could be a small disaster. It might involve printing a single leaf on a small press, and pasting it into the book by hand, for every copy of every edition printed from that typesetting of the text. Other ways existed of dealing with the situation, but any of them could prove extremely costly. It was therefore important to plan books to make 'even workings', to ensure the contents would fit neatly into a regular number of whole sheets of paper.[5] For that a 'cast off' was necessary.

A cast-off is a minutely detailed calculation of the number of characters, rather than words, in the book. From it will be determined the size of typeface (and, indeed, the typeface itself, for they all differ), length of line, spacing between lines, and the number of lines per page, that will produce exactly the right number of pages. Every chapter, every paragraph, every line of dialogue, every diagram or illustration in the text, every detail, in fact, has to be treated as a separate item. Even a small error of calculation, involving a single paragraph, could result in a chapter carrying over on to an extra page. The responsibility for accuracy was a heavy one.

The estimating clerk working on a series of books might be asked to devise several alternative styles of typesetting for a given page size. The calculations for one book, in such a series as Henty's novels, gave no more than an indication of the format required for the next. The lengths of his manuscripts differed considerably. But with variations of typographical style, skilfully managed, each title could end up making exactly the same number of pages. When a satisfactory format for a book had been worked out,[6] and approved by the publisher, the manuscript went to the printer's Reader.

The abilities of Readers, or the 'Gentlemen Correctors of the Press', varied considerably from one printing house to another, and could gain or lose business for their employers. The best of them, accustomed to dealing with the work of important authors, were men of great skill and education, some with university degrees. Every manuscript had to pass through their hands, to be 'prepared for the press'.

That preparation involved the most careful scrutiny, checking of spelling and punctuation, ensuring consistency of detail in narrative and description, querying or correction of historical fact and of statistics, checking for risks of libel, and more besides. Many authors owe much to a Reader's erudition, thoroughness, and genuine interest in each book assigned to his care. Most are never aware quite how much is done on their behalf, and many are astonished by the details of poor construction or grammar drawn to their attention.

Brooke Crutchley tells of an author who remarked 'You wouldn't think it possible for any human being to notice that you have spelt ill-will with a hyphen on page 860, when you spelt it without a hyphen on page 239. And Dr Joseph Needham was delighted to have it pointed out that he had called the Chinese language virile in one place and only a few pages later referred to it as pregnant'.[7]

At about the time wood-engravings were giving way to the photo-engraving of line blocks and halftone blocks (see Appendix IV), typesetting by hand was also in gradual decline. For Henty's early publishers, however, mechanical typesetting was still in the future. 'Various machines for composing type had been in use for years but the book trade was not affected until the Linotype and Monotype machines were perfected between 1890 and 1900. (Books were still being commonly set by hand even after 1918)'.[8] So it was to hand-compositors that most of Henty's manuscripts were entrusted after readers' queries had been sorted out.

Later, books were set by Linotype, and eventually by Monotype. To the layman the results of mechanical composition are not noticeably different from those of hand composition, although to the experienced eye setting by Linotype is the most easily recognised. The important changes brought about by mechanisation were of economics, and the availability of more and more new typefaces.

When the type for a book had been set, it was assembled in galleys, or long trays, convenient for storing in special racks. Galleys varied in size, but might hold a long stretch of undivided type for as many as three or four pages of text. Proofs were taken from the type while in this state, and galley proofs were sent to the reader. He marked any mistakes made by the typesetter, who made corrections and pulled further sets of proofs. One set became the 'Marked Set', carefully inscribed by the reader to show the author and the publisher any outstanding queries or suggested corrections.

Henty was reported in an interview to have said that, following dictation to his amanuensis, 'I never see any of my work until it comes to me from the printer's in the shape of proof sheets'.[9] It is likely that he saw most of his books only in galley-proof, and not again when the type had been made up into pages. There is a photograph of him on his yacht, captioned (perhaps more imaginatively than accurately), 'G.A. Henty reading the proofs of his last book'.[10] Whether or not you think he looks old enough for it to be his last book, the over-retouched picture certainly shows him reading what appear to be short galley-proofs, in this case the galley holding no more than about two pages.

The Marked Set of proofs found its way back to the printer via the publisher, and the type was made up into pages. Page proofs would have been pulled, and carefully checked by the reader, though for works of fiction probably not sent to the author. Even the publisher did not always ask for them, often regarding them as an unnecessary expense. But there were many conscientious editors or production managers who did, unable to brush aside their worries that the printer might at the last minute confound their latest progeny.[11]

Page proofs were basically the same as galley proofs, but divided up to show exactly what would appear on each page. At this stage the page-numbers, or 'folios' were added, the signature marks mentioned earlier, and also the running headlines, if any, on each page. Once this had been done, any further corrections to the type, especially if they involved over-running matter from one page to another, would be much more expensive.

Even on the galley proofs corrections could be troublesome, as any alterations affecting the length of a chapter would throw out the calculations made in the original cast-off. That was still true, of course, of corrections on page proofs, but having to move type from page to page was time-consuming and costly as well. So an author would be asked to keep all corrections to a minimum, and if a deletion had to be made he would be urged to insert within the same paragraph, or at least within the same page, an extra word, phrase or sentence, of equal length, to compensate.

It is probable that Henty, like most authors, found such requests an irritation, and on occasions would throw out the well-laid plans by making substantial additions or deletions. Something went wrong with the planned even workings in both *Captain Bayley's Heir* and *When London Burned*, but we shall never know whether the books suffered from miscalculations by the planners, or whether Henty himself upset the apple-cart at the proof stage.[12]

The final refinement was 'book-proofs', which were proofed after imposition, on paper of the size to be used for the book, folded, sewn and trimmed. They were in fact rough copies of the book as it would ultimately appear, and were valuable to publishers for use, in later terminology, as sales-promotion material – for coaxing pre-publication orders from booksellers.

Proofs of the preliminary pages, or prelims, of his books might not have been of much interest to Henty, except for the author's Preface. The title page, lists of Contents and Illustrations, and so on, would have been compiled, and corrected, by the publisher. And it seems likely that, at least at first, Henty did not concern himself with proofs of the captions to illustrations, judging by a persistent misprint of the name of one of the four main characters in *Out on the Pampas*, who were all called after his own children.[13] Some of Henty's books have illustrations printed on text pages. Notes on the various types of blocks from which the pictures were printed are in Appendix IV. But in the main the pictures were printed separately, and were added to the text pages in the bindery, as will be described in Part 2, below.

The printing of both text and illustrations was carried out only after very careful make-ready of each forme. The process was started when the forme was laid on the press, and the object was to reduce the pressure in areas where the type, or blocks, printed too heavily and to increase it where the impression was light. This was done by removing or adding small pieces of very thin paper on the platen of the press. The effect of this treatment had to be inspected from time to time by taking impressions before further work was done. The time spent on make-ready was often long, but for good bookwork never wasted. It varied according to the condition of the type or plates being printed, and sheets of an often-reprinted book could take several hours. There were no acceptable short cuts.[14]

2. BINDING

When making a decision to print a first edition of, say, 2000 copies, Henty's publishers would be fully aware that the cost of printing an additional 1000 copies at the same operation was not likely to be more than a few pounds. Certainly it would be very little indeed compared with the cost of the first 1000. The cost of the first edition of a book included everything from the cast-off and the typesetting onwards, including proof reading, make-ready, and the printer's general administration. But the cost of adding an extra 1000 copies to the print order involved only a short period of machine time and the value of the additional paper.

There was therefore a temptation for publishers to take a gamble with certain books by printing rather more than good judgement suggested. On the other hand the cost of binding all those extra books would be formidable, especially if they could not be sold. Sensible publishers resisted temptation. But in any case it became normal procedure to put a quantity of the printed 'flat sheets' into storage, and to send to the bindery only sufficient to meet existing sales orders and such as might be expected in the very near future.[15]

In comparatively recent times there have been radical changes in the economics, and therefore the methods, of book production. Today it is customary to print and bind complete editions or impressions as one series of consecutive operations. But the earlier method made life in one way easier for publishers, who did not at any stage have to commit themselves to the full cost of an edition of bound books before they knew whether they could sell it. And if they couldn't sell it they would be left only with flat unbound sheets, which had cost comparatively little to produce, rather than quantities of bulky, and expensive, fully-bound books.

It was not a foolproof system for publishers: they clearly had to sell a substantial part of an edition in order to recover their outlay. But it is important to understand how it worked, because it helps to provide the answer to a question frequently asked about Henty's books. Can separate issues of an edition be dated, or given a chronological order, or even identified, according to variations in the colours of binding cloth used? It has been a puzzle for many collectors, and has resulted in some believing they should make a point of acquiring copies of each title in every different cloth-colour they can find. The reasons why I have always discouraged such a plan will, I hope, become clear in the course of this essay.[16]

But it is necessary to take in proper order the various stages through which each batch of books passed when it was sent, in the form of flat sheets, to the bindery. The first batch of a new book was likely to be a large one, calculated to fulfil all the pre-publication orders from booksellers, and such further orders as might be expected when the book was in the shops and reviews were published. Subsequent batches were likely to be smaller, perhaps of only a hundred copies, often of fifty or even less. The relative values of labour and materials have been completely transformed over a hundred years, and are now the opposite of what they were. It was then, and until recently, desirable, if not necessary, for publishers to bind books only in small quantities as they were needed.

The first operation, on the arrival of a batch of printed sheets for a book, was that of folding. For Henty's early books this was done by a hand-operated machine. Automatic folding machines were not in use until his much later reprints were bound. The folded signatures were collated, or gathered, in correct sequence, and the correct catalogue, or section of catalogue, drawn from stock and added at the end.[17] Then the books were sewn. For this process too, new machines have been developed over the years, but for nearly all Henty's books it would have been done by a hand-operated sewing machine with linen thread.

There were very few exceptions: one of them was *The Young Buglers*, of which the first edition was wire-stitched with a stapling machine. This process was perhaps suitable for catalogues or other ephemeral material, but it was a deplorable one for books. It also seems an odd choice for this particular title, which was the most expensive of all Henty's novels for boys. The wire stitches usually rusted fairly quickly, and the eventual action of the rust was to cause the break up of the binding. That has caused books bound in such a way, including first issues of *The Young Buglers*, to become comparatively scarce, simply because they have not survived the effects of oxidation.

After the books were sewn, the plates, which had been printed separately, had to be individually inserted at their correct positions throughout the text. This was a hand operation, and still would be, were it not that modern books tend for the sake of economy to have illustrations printed together as complete sections, which can be collated and sewn with the text sections, by machine. For one of Henty's books with eight tipped-in plates there would be a long bench set up in the bindery at which eight girls would sit, side by side. Others would be positioned to feed in the books to the first girl and to stack the completed work at the far end.

Each girl would have in front of her a pile of illustrations, the first having all the frontispieces, the second the copies of plate 1, and so on. All these plates had been cut from the printed sheet, but trimmed only to give the correct margin in the back (or inside edge) of the leaf. One sewn but unbound book would be handed to the first girl. She pasted in the frontispiece and passed the book on, immediately receiving a second copy. The second girl opened the book at the right place for her plate, pasted it in and again passed the book on, and so the process continued. By the time the first book reached the girl at the final 'station' the first girl was pasting in her eighth frontispiece. At the far end the books would be stacked again, now having all the plates tipped in at their proper places.

The number of girls would vary according to the number of plates to be tipped in. Some of Henty's books had folded maps inserted also, and generally the folding would have been done before the tipping in stage. The method of pasting and inserting was well planned, and experienced girls could achieve high speeds of operation. As they were usually paid according to the number of books completed, it was incumbent on each one not to delay the others. The paste used was reasonably quick-drying, but not so quick as to prevent each girl from pasting the edges of about a dozen plates simultaneously by overlapping them in a staggered stack.

When the plates were all inserted, the endpapers were pasted on. Then the books went to the guillotine operator to be trimmed. If they were to be given gilt or stained edges, they were then securely clamped in a press with the edges exposed. Staining was a comparatively simple matter of spraying, or possibly brushing: a process of particular significance in Blackie's presentation of Henty.[18] Gilding was a much more skilled and costly operation (except for the machine-gilding on cheaper books, which was rather crude). Both processes involved some burnishing. Then began the heavier work of rounding and backing, forming shoulders on the books, adding headbands if required (hardly ever on Henty's books) and lining the spines.

Meanwhile a quite separate operation was going on in the case-making department. Some early preparations for the cases had been made as soon as the exact content of the book was known: those began with a white-paper dummy. The dummy, as the name implies, was a book made from the correct number of pages of text paper, with leaves to represent the tipped in illustrations, endpapers, etc., all unprinted, but assembled from the actual materials to be used. It showed the thickness of the volume, and the exact size of the binding case required. A designer was therefore able to start work on the lettering and decoration of the case before the book was printed, knowing already the precise width of the spine, and other dimensions.

The binding case itself was made of two pieces of strawboard, with edges bevelled where appropriate, and a strip of 'hollow-paper' to go between them and form the stiffening of the spine. These had all been accurately cut to size, and were correctly positioned in a hand-operated machine, glued and covered with a piece of cloth, also cut to the right size. The corners of the cloth were cut, so that when it was turned over the edges of the boards neat corners were formed. All this was done by the machine, which pressed the surface smooth and delivered a stack of completed cases ready for use when dried.

Collectors of children's books, and indeed of other books, published in the latter decades of the nineteenth century, will be aware that many of them, including first and later editions, were made available by most publishers in several differently coloured binding cloths. Some such books were put in the shops in more than one colour simultaneously, but that was by no means a universal practice.

Eric Quayle writes of R.M. Ballantyne's experience with his early publishers, Nelson, and tells how 'when his name was well-known, they allowed Ballantyne to choose his own cloth colours. His letters reveal ... that he usually selected three or four bright and contrasting colours, and these bolts of cloth the binders used as they came to hand, taking down a fresh and perhaps different colour as earlier bolts were used up'.[19]

This account is given as if in Ballantyne's own words, but not within quotation marks, and it is clear that at some point the sentence changes authorship to Quayle himself. Dartt paraphrased Quayle, managing even to put words into his mouth, 'it is the theory of Eric Quayle, that while some issues of first editions may be determined by cover color, it is also possible that bolts of cloth were stacked indiscriminately in the bindery. When a workman had exhausted his supply of one bolt of cloth, he might simply take a bolt of another color as the spirit (and his esthetic sensibilities) moved him'.[20]

Unfortunately these commentators have between them managed to conjure up a totally romantic vision of an imaginary bindery. No binding firms that were capable of producing books for either Ballantyne's or Henty's publishers could have been as primitive as they imply. Bookbinding was by then a mainly mechanised business, the various processes involved were departmentalised, and there were certainly too many books passing through the works to allow such haphazard goings-on as they suggest. The methods used by Blackie have been briefly described in Appendix II, Part 6: that firm was organised on a bigger scale than some others, but the processes involved were the same for the production of all but the later twentieth-century reprints of Henty's novels for boys.

In a commercial bindery such as Henty's publishers would have employed, fifty-yard rolls of cloth would be stored together on shelves, certainly not 'stacked indiscriminately' as suggested by Dartt. The man in charge of them would cut off a length, measured for the job in hand, and that would later be cut into pieces, each of the right size for making one case for a book. The length cut from a roll would be recorded, for charging to the job-sheet for the book, and to keep control of stocks.

It is, nevertheless, of interest to know from Ballantyne's own letters that he was asked to choose his own colours. There is no record of such choice being offered to Henty. And Quayle continues, on much firmer ground, to make an important point that should be of interest, and some comfort, to collectors of Henty's work.

Cargill Thompson had insisted 'It is not sufficient to have one example of the first edition of any title: one must have all the variants. Obvious differences to look for are of cover colour and endpapers'.[21] But Quayle rightly affirms that 'priority of issue cannot be claimed for a volume on the grounds that it is bound in a particular colour of cloth, providing that the format and internal make-up of the book equates with other copies of the same edition. This observation applies to much of the juvenile fiction issued in the latter half of the nineteenth century, and includes the work of Ballantyne, W.H.G. Kingston, G.A. Henty, and a host of similar writers in the same field'.[22] In fact Quayle does not go quite far enough. At that period most children's publishers were doing the same thing for a very wide variety of books: even publishers of books for adults followed the trend.

Once the publishers' custom of using alternative cloth-colours for a single edition is understood, the significance to a collector of any particular colour dwindles, especially as it is quite impossible to know which colour happened to be used first. In addition, the printed sheets of any given signature of an impression would have been stacked as they came from the machine, those printed first lying at the bottom of the pile. Thus the first sheets to have been impressed would be the last to reach the binder, and could not have appeared in the earliest binding cases to be made.

It is possible that the first binding order for a new book, which as already seen was likely to be a big one, was carried out in more than one cloth-colour. I have found no relevant records to show this, one way or the other, although the regular appearance of copies of *By Conduct and Courage* in both red and green cloth do confirm the possibility. Clearly, variations became easier and more likely between smaller batches that were bound later on. Changes in cloth-colour often demanded changes in the colours used for blocking the designs on the cases, and for Henty's books that could be a serious consideration. Blackie, in particular, often used many colours, with gold, and for some titles a completely new colour scheme was necessary when the ground colour changed.

When the blocking press had to be set up afresh for a particular batch it would be no more costly to use a new range of pigments than to stay with the original colours. Such considerations applied also to his books from some other publishers. 'Have you ever noticed how much more expensively boys' books are got up than are ordinary novels? Better paper, binding, illustrations', was Henty's own comment.[23] But the inclusion of paper in his remark makes it fairly certain he was thinking of Blackie rather than his earlier publishers.

When the design was approved it would be sent away to a brass-cutter, with an order to make the blocking-pieces for impressing the gold and pigments on the case. The brasses were engraved by hand by a skilled craftsman, who produced a separate set of pieces for each colour. The small brass pieces were mounted, and fitted in the blocking press, those for each working (i.e. each colour) having to register accurately with the others, as in colour printing. The assembly and mounting of the brasses was often done on sheets of cardboard with animal glue, a process that to a layman looked primitive in the extreme, but that produced reliable results and remained unchanged for many decades.

The blocking presses in use were of several kinds, and bore little resemblance to those in use now. They were mostly very similar to platen printing presses operated by a treadle – indeed I use one of those for the purpose today. The machines were heated for gold-blocking, or for the pigment foils that early in the twentieth century followed the use of coloured printing inks.

The application of gold leaf is not at all easy, and is a skill that has to be carefully learnt and practised. The leaf is beaten to a thickness of only one 250,000th of an inch, and is consequently extremely light and flimsy, very difficult to control, and to lay over the area to be blocked. Its movement has to be skilfully managed by the use of special instruments and gentle puffs of the operator's breath, so it may be seen that such work cannot be done with speed. At first, for commercial binding, 'a number of girls allocated to the blocking press operator sized the covers and laid the leaf on, for the blocker to make the impression, and then pass the covers on to a second group of girls who did the cleaning off'.[24] The last process was to remove surplus gold, and that was done with a soft putty-like substance forming a 'gold rubber', which removed the tiny fragments and collected them within itself. The rubber was eventually returned to the manufacturer who recovered the valuable metal for future use.

Later, gold leaf was supported on ribbons of waxed tissue, and then of glassine paper, that could be fed into hand-operated blocking machines in rolls of any required width. A shellac coating had been applied to the gold surface, and that eliminated the necessity, on the surface to be blocked, for glair, or any other form of mordant that would have been used for the normal application of gold leaf.[25]

Before the use of foil, the blocking of pigments was done with printing ink, and the ink duct of the machine made it possible to get unusual effects. By loading the duct with two or more colours of ink, close to each other, but so that the colours mixed together only at the points where they met, the blocked effect was of colours merging gradually from one to another. During the course of a run the mixing would tend to spread over a larger area, but the runs were generally short, for small batches of books, so this did not present a problem. For long runs it might have been necessary to wash up the machine half-way through and start again.

The later, and cleaner, pigment foils were easier to use than ink, requiring no drying time and no washing-up of the machine. But they did not have the same flexibility, and could not produce the merging effects seen on the earlier children's books. From soon after the turn of the century the R.T.S. and other publishers occasionally used silk-screen printing with coloured inks to decorate and illustrate cases, often in combination with gold blocking.

The books were at last ready to be assembled, by being inserted into the blocked cases, or 'cased in'. For the earlier books this was a hand operation, as may be seen from marks made by the hand-brush used to apply the glue for the endpapers. The books were then put in lying presses, under light pressure for a day or two. That helped them to retain their shape and smart appearance, and, however impatient the publisher was to lay his hands on them, it was an important part of the process.

Small differences in the binding processes of individual books do occur, and cannot all be covered fully here. For Henty's books such matters of detail are mentioned in the Notes under individual titles in the main Sections of this book.

Finally, I would like to mention a practice of more than one publisher I worked with, and which I believe to have been an old custom of others. It grew out of an idea adopted by bookbinders who were trying to ingratiate themselves with their customers. Their gesture of goodwill then became a 'service' that was expected of binders by some publishers, but in our context seems almost to have been planned to cause confusion for future book collectors and bibliographers.

When the case for a book had been designed, and the brass blocking-pieces made, the design and brasses were sent to the binder with instructions to make a specimen blocked case. This had to be formally approved by the publisher before he gave the first binding order. Binders developed a habit of making more than one specimen case: they followed the designer's layout and instructions for the first, and then blocked a number of similar cases using various cloth-colours and pigments. These followed the fancy of the blocking-press operator, and possibly also of the binder's salesman. Over a period the publisher consequently accumulated a stack of blocked cases in colour-schemes which he had not approved and had no intention of using.

From the early years of the reign of King Charles II, and by statutes of various later dates, it has been necessary by law for a free copy of every book to be sent to certain Libraries. By the Act of 1911 the copyright laws require that publishers shall send copies to six places: to the British Library, and on request to the Bodleian Library, the Cambridge University Library, the National Libraries of Scotland and Wales, and to the Library of Trinity College, Dublin.[26] This costly imposition made publishers give thought to ways of lightening the burden. One such idea, which I have observed in operation, has almost certainly been followed by a number of publishers.

Six binding cases for a new book, blocked in various discarded colour-schemes, and which had cost the publisher nothing, would be taken from his cupboard and returned to the binder. The resulting copies of the book were dispatched forthwith to the Copyright Libraries.

I recently heard that in some cases the practice had been developed further, by even economising with the contents of books. Whenever a publisher had asked for imposed page proofs, or book-proofs, the opportunity existed. Peter Allen, of Messrs Robert Temple, with whom I discussed many years ago these habits of publishers, has written to me about the British Library copy of Vizetelly's first English edition of *The Bohemians of the Latin Quarter* by Henri Murger. 'It is certainly a proof the thrifty publisher decided not to waste:', he writes, 'not only does it have a different title page, dated a year earlier than the published book, and a different publisher's address, but it lacks the plates (or any mention of them), is twenty pages shorter than the published book, *and has proof-reader's marks!'* .

Years later, such a volume, perhaps not so obviously phoney as the Murger, may come to be representative of a scarce title. Bibliographers have habitually tended to prefer working from a deposit copy in one of the Copyright Libraries, believing themselves to be giving a precise and guaranteed description of the details of a true first edition. In this way a unique issue comes to be described, with a variant title page, or with binding in cloth and colours not seen elsewhere. Although I have not examined every volume in the Henty collections in all the Copyright Libraries, I do not recall seeing any that are affected by this form of publisher's economy. But the possibility remains: certainly there are 'rogue' copies of books by other authors on their shelves, waiting to be discovered.

APPENDIX IV

ILLUSTRATION AND DESIGN

1. ILLUSTRATION TECHNIQUES AND PROCESSES OF REPRODUCTION

The period covered by the publication of Henty's books, and their reprints, happens to coincide with the development of almost all illustration techniques, and the processes of reproduction, associated with letterpress printing. The very earliest printed illustrations were in line, and impressed from wood blocks. They were cut on the side of a piece of wood, or plank, and for the sake of clarity are generally referred to as wood-cuts. They were followed after some years by wood-engravings,[1] which were incised into the cross-section, or grain-end, of a piece of hard wood, usually box-wood. They allowed much greater detail and richness in illustration. The first pictures in Henty's books were wood-engravings.

Unlike children's books, adult novels in Henty's time were mostly published in three volumes (see Appendix II), and not usually illustrated, although pictures were frequently added when they were re-issued as single volumes. Henty's *Out on the Pampas*, for children, was his first book to be illustrated, with four engravings from drawings by Johann Zwecker. Two of them show the engraver's signature as well as the artist's, for it was common practice for an illustrator to draw his picture on wood and send it to a professional wood engraver.[2] Sometimes such an engraver would work from a drawing on paper, even a wash-drawing, and provide his own wood.

Some of Henty's early stories for boys were first published in magazines. They were illustrated with wood engravings, often printed from the original wood blocks, which were made to the same height as the metal type, so that pictures and text could be printed together. Blocks could often be used again when stories were published in book form. But it was not always possible, as the pictures in magazines were sometimes too large to fit on to the page of a book.

If it was likely that a picture might be used again later, perhaps even to illustrate some totally different story or article, a stereotype or an electrotype would usually be made, as a form of insurance against possible damage to the original. When that was done the metal plate could sometimes be trimmed to a smaller size, so that it would fit the page of a book: there are examples of such treatment among the illustrations in *In Times of Peril* (see §1, 9.1).

Clean and sharp impressions from wood engravings depended on the skill and care of the machine-minder. Poor Thomas Bewick, the best-known of English engravers, suffered greatly over the reproduction of his work, and judging from much of the printing in Henty's day things had not greatly improved. Bewick wrote that his first difficulty was 'in getting the cuts I had executed printed so as to look anything like my drawings on the blocks of wood, and corresponding to the labour I had bestowed upon the cutting of the designs'.[3] His problems continued through the several editions of his work that were printed in his lifetime, in spite of repeated protests.

Bewick knew what he wanted from his printers, but his failure to achieve it stemmed partly from his ignorance of printing techniques. He stressed his need to pare the wood at appropriate places; 'to lower down the surface on all the parts I wished to appear pale, so as to give the appearance of the required distance',[4] 'and the same thing holds good with every figure where different shades of colour is required'.[5] That method of achieving 'tones', or grey areas, did not work and indeed, as any letterpress printer would know, could never work.

For the line blocks and halftone blocks that were to follow, letterpress machine-minders had the same aim as Bewick – to get the very best out of the engraved surfaces. By then machines, and particularly inking techniques, were easier to control, and impressions were much refined by 'make-ready'.[6] Robert Hunter Middleton, between 1940 and 1970, made a collection of many of Bewick's original wood blocks. With careful make-ready, rather more elaborate but very similar in method to those of his own time with photo-engraved blocks, he obtained the most wonderful results, far beyond anything achieved by Bewick's own printers,[7] or even, indeed, that could have been dreamed of by Bewick himself.

Fine letterpress printing, of both illustrations and type, has also always depended on the proper application of good printing ink, and on the use of suitable paper to receive the impression. Poor paper was often the cause of indifferent reproduction; in the nineteenth century this became a particular problem in the printing of halftone blocks, and one that is especially evident in some of Henty's books. John Schönberg and Frank Feller were among the artists whose work suffered most in this way (see their entries below).

Publishers and printers both came to make collections of 'second-hand' wood-engravings. Sometimes they grew into veritable libraries of illustration, and often proved great money-savers when new publications were planned. There were, of course, strange results, some ridiculous, and some enchanting. The publishers, Bell & Daldy, had in the 1870s acquired a lot of German engravings, largely of subjects suitable for children, and Mrs Ewing was invited to write verses to accompany them in print, with some charming results.[8] Even Blackie illustrated Henty with electros of engravings originally made for another purpose: there are two in *Held Fast for England* (see §1, 55.1) and one, obviously trimmed at both sides to fit the page-margins, in *At the Point of the Bayonet* (see §1, 99.1). Later, engravings made for *Under Drake's Flag* were used by Blackie in a book by another author.

Towards the end of his life Bewick made a prediction: 'seeing the practical use printers were making of woodcuts, the utility and importance of them began to be unfolded to my view; and . . . I am confirmed in the opinions I have entertained, that the use of woodcuts will know no end'.[9] They continued in Henty's books well after the advent of photo-engraving, and have been a beautiful form of illustration and decoration ever since.

The development of commercial photo-engraving revolutionised the illustration of newspapers, magazines and books, first with line blocks and later with halftones. The potentialities of both were fully exploited by Henty's illustrators. Artists commissioned to make wood-engravings had traditionally supplied blocks from which the actual impressions on paper were made, or at least from which electros for printing would be made. Publishers had had to specify the precise size of each illustration. When photo-engraving was used it was possible for an artist's drawing to be enlarged or reduced in the course of blockmaking. It seems, however, that old customs died hard, and publishers still expected artists to provide them with the actual blocks made by photo-engravers.

Later, publishers preferred to order blocks themselves, from their own chosen photo-engraver. Illustrators were asked to supply drawings, not blocks. But for the first seven books published by Blackie it is clear that Gordon Browne was still responsible for choosing his blockmakers, and other illustrators did the same for some considerable time. This system allowed them to pick blockmakers willing to help them with experimental work. A popular and early approach to photo-engraving was to treat the metal blocks as a first stage only in producing a printing surface, and to complete the process with a hand-graver. Indeed, some illustrations reproduced by halftone blocks were given special effects by such treatment. Parts of a drawing could be deliberately omitted from the original supplied to the photo-engraver, and added by hand-engraving on the metal plate. Examples may be seen in illustrations by William Parkinson (see his entry, in Part 2, below).

But the first successor to wood-engraving in Henty's books was the line-block. Bewick had puzzled over the technique of Dürer, and then mastered, and discarded, the achievement of fine cross-hatching by superimposing impressions from two blocks to make a single picture.[10] He would no doubt have discarded also the very idea of a photographically produced line-block, but it was nevertheless capable of reproducing any effect, including cross-hatching, that could be made by pen on paper.

And quite a different use of two line blocks to make one picture offered possibilities not considered by Bewick. Whether the original idea came from Blackie or from Browne we do not know, but it was decided from the start that Henty's books should be illustrated in two colours. A line block of a simple black-and-white drawing was printed consecutively with a second plate, adding the effect of a wash, or tint, in sepia. The method was soon copied by Blackie's other illustrators, but it was first developed, and explored, by Gordon Browne, as briefly described in his entry below. The two-colour line plates were a great success, but Blackie's pleasure was to be tempered when the cost they involved became fully apparent. The expense lay not so much in the price of blockmaking, more in the time and care necessary to print them.

Make-ready, as we have seen in Appendix III, was always a vitally important stage in letterpress printing, and perhaps especially for illustration. To get an even, clear impression, parts of the block would need to be printed more, or less, heavily than others. The same skill was necessary that Bewick had wanted for his wood-engravings. The make-ready of illustrations was a laborious job, and the method was very similar to that described in Appendix III, Part 1. But for blocks the thin pieces of paper could be applied for more general effect to the under side of the block ('underlaying'). For more detailed refinements, they were still applied, as before, to the platen of the press, that is, behind the paper to be printed ('overlaying').

For two-colour printing this work all had to be done for both formes, taking twice as long. And of course the make-ready stage in the machine-room was reached only after the formes had been imposed in the composing room. There, first, the black plates were locked up in a chase, imposed with correct margins for each page. Then the blocks for the second colour were locked up in another chase, identically matching the first, so that when the two impressions were made, one after the other, they would be precisely and accurately in register. It was a difficult and time-consuming process, and could be very frustrating. After precise positioning had been achieved with two or three blocks it was only too easy to upset them in the course of imposing the next two or three.

Furthermore the whole tedious process had to be gone through all over again when a reprint was required. The time involved in imposing illustrations in register was sometimes reduced by printing them on small machines. Then only four, or perhaps only two, pairs of blocks, in smaller chases, would have had to be worked together. But such an arrangement tended to be a matter of swings and roundabouts. Saving time in the composing room would result in more formes to print, which inevitably took longer in the machine room.

Blackie soon decided the two-colour process was too expensive. An easy saving was to omit the second colour altogether and reprint the pictures in black only. For many later impressions of the early Blackie editions that was done. But for some existing illustrations such treatment would have produced an unsatisfactory artistic result. For them it was decided to remake the blocks, and to include on one plate the second-colour image and the black line-drawing, thus printing everything together in black. That presented no technical problem for the blockmaker, as the two existing originals could be photographed together on to a single plate.

Unfortunately there were other difficulties. A mechanical tint would appear much darker in tone when printed in black than it would when printed with sepia ink. It must sometimes have seemed to Blackie that it would in the end be more economical in time and worry to forget the whole thing and go back to printing the pictures in the original two colours. But in 1886 Gordon Browne made illustrations for *With Wolfe in Canada* to reproduce in black only. Indeed, the whole idea of a second colour was dropped, and Browne turned his attention to other techniques such as scraper-board, or scratch-board, also described in his entry below.

After a few years Blackie began using halftone blocks, and Henty's books show them going through the teething troubles associated with that process. Here the need for careful make-ready was greater than for line work. When the new blocks first came into use that was especially true, as they were still lacking the life and vitality achieved later. Other difficulties are described in the notes below on John Schönberg and J.R. Weguelin, whose wash-drawings were the first of Henty's illustrations to be reproduced by halftone. A common cause of trouble was the over-ambitious choice of a screen too fine for the paper on which blocks were printed.

The screen consisted of two sheets of glass, firmly fixed together, after each had been ruled by diamond-point with a series of very fine, equidistant lines. The lines on one sheet were at right angles to those on the other when the two were fastened together. The screen was set in front of the film negative, inside the camera that was used to photograph the original artwork. The image passing through the lens, and eventually reaching the negative, was thus broken up into very small areas of light, varying in intensity, and strongest where the original was lightest in tone. The negative was printed down on to a sheet of copper. When that was etched, the resulting plate was covered with small raised dots of varying size, the surfaces of which would print on paper the impression familiar to us as a halftone.

At first, the most successful commercial engraver was George Meisenbach of Munich, who patented his method in London in 1882.[11] He began with a screen of parallel straight lines, which had to be rotated to a different angle during the course of photographic exposure. But he later changed to the cross-line screen described above. He made halftone blocks from the wash-drawings by Stanley Wood for the first single-volume edition of *Rujub, the Juggler* (see §1, 56.2, Note 3).

The fineness of a screen was measured by the number of ruled lines to the linear inch. The term 'half-tone' had been devised by the Bullock brothers in 1865,11 but there is of course no actual 'tone' in the printed result. The ink is black and the paper is white, and the effect of tone is in the mind's eye only, mixing the black and white to produce a kind of optical illusion. Coarse screens (down to 50 screen) were used for newspaper work, printed on cheap paper; fine screens needed an 'art paper', i.e. one coated with china-clay, with a really smooth surface.

Blackie began by using a screen that was too fine for their paper, which, even if the best they could buy, was not of sufficiently high quality. Similar errors were made by other publishers, and one of the greatest sufferers among Henty's illustrators was Frank Feller, whose much later drawings for Griffith & Farran were utterly ruined by being printed in fine screen on an uncoated text paper.

Afterwards a kind of snobbishness about screens developed: some publishers felt there was something 'infra dig' about anything below 150 or even 200 screen for their books. And they naïvely believed that the finer the screen the more justice would be done to the detail of an original. In fact that was rarely if ever true, as other factors were involved in producing the most satisfying image for the human eye. It may seem paradoxical, but often a coarser halftone screen gave a result that appeared clearer to the naked eye than the same subject reproduced with a very fine screen. Very fine screens will sometimes prevent the eye from immediately accepting the optical illusion: the surface of the paper is too densely covered, and obscures a clear vision of the mixing of the black dots with the white paper.

My experience in book production was that no screen finer than 133 consistently gave pictures of the highest quality, and that widely-shared view was based on work by many of the best halftone printers in the British Isles, using the highest quality coated paper. For Henty, even Blackie at their most successful period were using too fine a screen, and their 200 screen blocks were still tending to get clogged with bits of dust and dirty ink in 1904. Their results were, certainly, good. But a less fine screen would have made them considerably better.

In 1901 Chapman and Hall published a small booklet, *John Hawke's Fortune*, with coloured illustrations by Lance Thackeray. The watercolour drawings were reproduced by three-colour halftones, printed by Edmund Evans. A book by Henty had not previously had coloured illustrations, although there were some for stories in 'collections' published by Nister, mentioned below. The earlier colour-printing processes of Baxter, Fawcett, and especially Kronheim, were popular for children's books but had never been used for illustrations of Henty. Then, in the 1920s, Blackie issued 'The New Popular Henty' series, each with a frontispiece from a watercolour-drawing printed by three-colour halftone blocks.

The principles of halftone printing in colour were, even more than for black-and-white, based on optical illusion. Three negatives were made, one after another, using filters to separate the colours of the original into the primaries used for printing: yellow, red, and blue. The plates then made were printed, in that order, each impression carefully superimposed on the last. It was necessary for the screen to be set at a different angle for each negative, so that the printed dots of each colour did not fall exactly on top of each other, but appeared juxtaposed in a regular pattern. As before, the mind's eye does the work, mixing the colours in proportion to the density of each at any point. The result is an impression of all – well, nearly all – the colours of the spectrum.

Finer quality resulted from four plates instead of three. The fourth plate was printed in black, and was used to give only a light impression, intended just to sharpen up the picture and to add a sense of more detail and intensity. Many publishers did not use four colours, being content with what blockmakers could achieve with three, and indeed it is frequently hard to believe that a three-colour reproduction has no black ink in it. But the best work was done with four colours, and can usually be distinguished at a glance, because the caption beneath the picture would be printed in black ink. Where the caption is in blue, as in nearly all Henty's colour-illustrations, it is pretty certain that only three colours have been used.

In all colour-printing, because of the different physical natures of original and reproduction, and, frequently, the great reduction necessary from one to the other, total accuracy of colour is impossible. For instance, details such as bright blue eyes may be an important feature of a painted portrait. But they are frequently too small, in reproduction, to be visible at all as separate entities. While accuracy was important to artist, blockmaker and publisher, fine colour-precision for illustrations of fiction was rarely of vital concern, at least to the publisher. And the reader was in any case unable to compare the reproduction with the original.

So far we have considered only letterpress printing. There were several other processes in Henty's day, but only one was used for his books. The publishers, Ernest Nister, used lithography almost exclusively, and their books were printed mainly in Bavaria. Three of Henty's short stories were each issued by them in a number of collections, with black-and-white drawings reproduced both in line and halftone.

For lithography the printing surface is not raised, as in letterpress printing, but the system is based on the principle that oil and water do not mix, even on a level printing surface. Originally the printing surface was a stone, giving the process its name, and stone surfaces are still used by artists. But commercially a larger and more flexible surface was required, and the stone was replaced by a zinc or aluminium plate that could print a number of pages on a large sheet of paper.

The early stages of reproduction are much the same as for letterpress. Then the plate is sensitised with bichromated albumen, which becomes hardened when exposed to light: on to this the negative images from the camera are photographically printed. The plate is rolled with an oily ink, and then washed with water. The water removes the unexposed, and therefore unhardened, parts of the albumen: what remains is the printing image. The plate is thereafter damped with water and rolled with the oily ink for each impression.

The process was later developed much further, and a new term, 'offset-lithography', came into being at about the turn of the century. There the basic principle was the same, but in the course of machining the image was transferred from the plate to a rubber roller, known as a 'blanket'. That became the printing surface, and in turn transferred the image to the paper. The resilience of the new, and comparatively soft, printing surface made it possible for fine detail, including halftone work, to be printed on paper that had a rough texture – rough, at least, when compared with the previously essential coated paper.

Apart from the books published by Nister, and some later endpapers printed for the 'Joint Venture' and the Oxford University Press, little of Henty's work was reproduced by lithography. The process was of course used for printing in colour, and colour printing by offset-lithography was used in the 1920s for several paper-covered binding cases, including those in the 'Summit Library' (see Appendix V), those of *In Times of Peril*, and *John Hawke's Fortune* (see §1, 9.12, 93.9, respectively), and for the frontispiece and binding case of *Pluck* (see §2, 173.1).

Offset-lithography turned out to be the most revolutionary development in the entire history of printing. In this country it has finally resulted in the total abandonment of commercial operations by letterpress, the process that was for five hundred years the basis of printed communication.

2. NOTES ON ARTISTS AND DESIGNERS

BERKELEY, STANLEY, *d.* 1909
Painter and illustrator, working regularly for many of the leading London magazines in the 1880s and 1890s. He produced wood-engravings for Cassells, of action scenes often with many figures, and a wash-drawing as one of six illustrations by various artists for Henty's story 'A Desperate Gang' in *Boys* magazine. Exhibited: R.A., R.B.A.
See (§2): 126.1. (§3): 199.

BIRCH, REGINALD B.
I know little of this artist except that he illustrated books by Frances Hodgson Burnett, the best-known being *Little Lord Fauntleroy*. He made one pen-drawing for the serialisation in *St. Nicholas* of Henty's 'The Sole Survivors', which has nine illustrations by other artists, all in tone.
See (§3): 219.

BIRD, JOHN ALEXANDER H., *b.* 1846
Recorded by Houfe as a painter of animals, and illustrator specialising in horse subjects.[12] He contributed to a short-lived shilling magazine, *Dark Blue*, (§3, 207). It is possible that he was the illustrator of Henty's story 'A Mexican Ranche' for Longmans, signing his wash-drawings 'Harington Bird' or 'H. Bird'. Exhibited: R.A., R.I., and Canadian Academy.
See (§2): 193.1.

BOUCHER, WILLIAM H., A.R.W.S., *d.* 1906
Successful and popular illustrator of magazines and books in the last half of the nineteenth century. Made the original drawings for R.L.Stevenson's *Treasure Island* on its first appearance as 'The Sea Cook' in the magazine *Young Folks*, 1881–1882. He painted a watercolour for the schoolbook, *Gallant Deeds*, reproduced in colour. His other illustrations for Henty were wash-drawings reproduced by halftone blocks, some of which were heightened by hand-work with a graver. Exhibited: R.A., R.B.A.
See (§1): 95.1; 110.1. (§2): 139.1; 170.1; 190.1.

BRANGWYN, Sir FRANK, R.A., 1867–1956
Born in Bruges, the son of a Welsh architect, was extremely versatile as a painter, etcher, lithographer and designer. He worked for a time with William Morris, and then travelled extensively in the East, in Africa and in Spain. He did much illustration work, both in colour and black-and-white. His picture for Henty is a wash-drawing reproduced by a halftone block which has been worked over by hand with a graver. Exhibited: R.A., R.E., R.W.A.
See (§2): 141.1.

BROCK, HENRY MATTHEW, R.I., 1875–1960
Of four brothers working in the same field, he and C.E.Brock, who was five years

his senior, are the best known. They grew up and worked in Cambridge, where Henry attended the School of Art and then joined his brother's studio. Their work was very similar and would be hard to tell apart were it not almost always signed. He used pen-drawing for Cassell, with mechanical tint combined with 'spattering'. His illustrations for Blackie were watercolours reproduced in colour. Exhibited: R.A., 1901–1906.

See (§1): 69.2; 89.1. (§2): 126.1; 132.1.

BROWN, MAYNARD

Probably the illustrator listed by Houfe as 'M. Brown' who specialised in landscapes for the *Illustrated London News* about 1888, and who practised in Edinburgh.[13] His illustrations for Henty were fine pen-drawings, printed in black only. Exhibited: R.S.A., 1889.

See (§1): 43.1.

BROWNE, GORDON, R.I., 1858–1932

Born at Banstead, Surrey, and studied art at Heatherley's. He was more prolific than his famous father, Hablôt K. Browne ('Phiz'), and Joseph Pennell wrote that 'he seems to have the facility of Doré'. Many, including Sketchley, have written of his skill in capturing movement, and of 'the picturesque and unhesitating invention that has shaped his style'.[14] Nicolas Hawkes has pointed out that he seemed 'to have a *penchant* for figures falling through space',[15] and he certainly managed them very successfully a number of times in drawings for Henty. His first Henty illustration was in the *Union Jack* with the first instalment of *Jack Archer* on 3 April 1883. It was reproduced as a wood engraving, and later appeared in the book, printed from an electrotype slightly trimmed to fit the page size. No engraver's signature appears, and it is possible he engraved his own illustration. The only other wood engravings I have seen from Gordon Browne also appear in the *Union Jack*, to illustrate a story by Bernard Heldmann, serialised from 3 October 1882 to July 1883. There are eight illustrations only, some of them so poor in quality as to cast doubt on their origins, but the last, in issue No.18 dated 30 January 1883, is one of those undoubtedly by Browne and once again shows a man falling through space.

He illustrated fourteen of Henty's novels for Blackie, including the first seven they published. It is possible that he devised the method of using a second colour for which Blackie was praised by a reviewer in *The Academy* following the appearance of the first two titles.[16] It was, in any case, for some years an essential part of his technique, soon used by other illustrators of Henty and he was still experimenting with it even after Blackie had started using halftone blocks.

Browne's two-colour-line technique went on developing and changing during those first eight years he worked for Blackie. For the first book by Henty, *Facing Death*, he made pen-drawings to be reproduced by line blocks in black, and originals for the second-colour 'wash', to be printed in sepia. Such second-colour originals were made in one of two ways. The first was to paint, in pale-blue watercolour, over the black pen-drawing (made with waterproof drawing-ink) the area that was eventually to be printed in sepia. The pale blue did not interfere with the reproduction of the black drawing, and could itself be 'separated' photographically by the blockmaker to produce another plate. By this method there was no problem in making sure that the two plates, when printed together in two colours, would exactly 'register'.

A second method was similar but involved the use of a transparent paper 'overlay', held carefully in place over the pen-drawing by adhesive tape, while the artist made his wash-drawing on it. The blockmaker was thus presented with two originals, which would be laid side by side and photographed simultaneously. This cut out the need for photographic separation and ensured eventual 'register'.

To save time for artists, blockmakers and engravers, an American firm started in 1879 to produce sheets of a variety of designs printed on transparent paper. They consisted, for example, of straight lines, or wavy lines, drawn in many varying degrees of thickness and closeness. They could be cut out, and then into shapes, with a sharp blade, both before and after being laid down on drawings or on overlays, to produce the effect of shading. The designs became available in ever increasing variety, and included all kinds of stipples and other patterns. They were well known in this country as Ben Day Tints, after the name of their inventor.[17] Later, when others entered the field, they were generally called 'mechanical tints'.

Gordon Browne had started using Ben Day tints in a small way for the *Facing Death* illustrations, although at this stage most of his second-colour originals were made by hand with a brush. For the second Henty title, *Under Drake's Flag*, he continued experimenting and used more tints. The blocks for this book are signed by one of the earliest French process-engravers, M. Lefman, a pioneer and leader in the field, used by Horace Petherick for line work a little earlier.[18] For *With Clive in India* Browne used stipple tints, and the second-colour work became still more adventurous and complicated for *By Sheer Pluck*.

Next, Browne used another French firm of process-engravers, particularly well-known for their success with halftone blocks.[19] Their name, Guillaume Frères, may be seen inscribed on the blocks for two of the titles with 1885 dates. Although the blocks in *St. George for England* carry no engraver's name, they follow the same style, carrying even further the Guillaume expertise with stipple tints. Perhaps by then Gordon Browne felt he had taken the experiments in tint-laying as far as they could usefully go. Halftone blocks were starting to make their mark, and that may have damped enthusiasm for his two-colour-line techniques. The latter were, in any case, expensive to print (see Part 1 of this Appendix). Whatever the reason, he abandoned them for his next three books for Henty.

It was not yet, however, that Browne turned to wash-drawings. *With Wolfe in Canada* was illustrated by black line blocks with no second colour. As in the previous book, Browne used solid black areas boldly, a practice not popular with letterpress machine-minders because it involved heavier inking, which caused difficulties in getting clean results from more delicate parts of the drawings, and even from the typematter. This book also introduced a new technique. Browne used a form of scraperboard[20] for some of the *With Wolfe in Canada* drawings, and again, even more liberally for those in *Orange and Green*.

Sometimes artists used a graving tool on the metal plate to make incisions that would print white out of darker areas. That was done on both line and halftone blocks. Possibly Browne used the technique, but that he also used scraperboard, or something very similar, is shown without doubt in *Orange and Green* by pen lines in black which are drawn over the top of, and at an angle to, the incisions.

In the same year, *Bonnie Prince Charlie* was illustrated without the use of mechanical tints, but the line drawings themselves included more shading and cross-hatching than Browne normally used, and the work was very finely controlled. It seems to follow a manner of drawing used by several other artists at that period (and mentioned elsewhere in these notes), by which pen-drawings take on a superficial appearance of fine wood engravings. Here we see clearly the cross-hatching effects, discussed at length by Bewick (see Part 1 of this Appendix), obtained in print by later artists so much more easily than he could do.

For *The Lion of St. Mark* Browne went back to the use of both brush-strokes and mechanical tints for second-colour plates, with results rather like those in his earlier work. But here he combined those techniques with the use of scraperboard, and appears to have devised a way of using scraperboards for both the black plate and the second-colour plate. The last book illustrated in two-colour line is *With Lee in Virginia*, and for that Browne used some new designs of mechanical tints, and again mixed mechanical effects with those made by a brush. His versatility in this field was possibly in danger of becoming more important to him than the production of good drawings.

Gordon Browne's illustrations for Cassell are straightforward pen-drawings. The last Henty title he illustrated for Blackie was *Held Fast for England* (1892), and for the first time he used black-and-white watercolour wash-drawings. It seems that he had avoided the use of the halftone process until he was satisfied with the results it could by then produce. That technique was also used for the set of pictures in *Yule-Tide Yarns*, published by Longman.
See (§1): 10.1; 13.1; 14.1; 15.1; 16.1; 18.1; 19.1; 20.1; 22.1; 27.1; 31.1; 32.1; 34.5; 36.1; 45.1. (§2): 126.1; 194.1. (§3): 225.

BURTON, Sir FREDERICK WILLIAM, R.H.A., R.W.S., F.S.A., 1816–1900
A painter, born in County Clare, who studied in Dublin. He later studied for seven years in Munich. He had an extremely successful career as a miniature painter and watercolourist, and became Director of the National Gallery in 1874. He was knighted on his retirement, twenty years later. Shortly after that he made two wash-drawings for Henty's work in the *Boy's Own Paper*. The first illustrates part of his 'Life of a Special Correspondent', and is reproduced by a halftone block, with much handwork done with a graver. The second is for the final instalment of 'The Fetish Hole', the previous eight parts having been illustrated by Alfred Pearse (q.v.), and is engraved on wood by P. Naumann. Exhibited: R.A., R.H.A.
See (§3): 201.

CHRISTIE, J.A.
I have no information about this artist. He may have been related to James Elder Christie who worked in London and Glasgow in the 1880s and 1890s. The two Henty illustrations are pen-drawings printed in black only.
See (§1): 42.1.

COLE, A.P.
I have no information about this artist, who made six watercolour drawings for the 'Joint Venture' in 1910.
See (§1): 12.7.

COWELL, G.H.SYDNEY, *fl*. 1884–1907
Painter, sculptor, and illustrator. Worked in London for many of the well-known magazines. He made two wash-drawings to illustrate Henty's 'Plucky and Cool': they are reproduced by halftone blocks, one of which is lightly, the other heavily, worked over by hand with a graver. Exhibited: R.A., R.B.A, R.O.I.
See (§3): 223.

DADD, FRANK, R.I., 1851–1929
Born in London and studied at South Kensington and the R.A. Schools. Houfe says 'his style is very photographic with heavy application of bodycolour and clever uses of grey wash, but it is technically excellent and very accurate in detail'.[21] He made wash-drawings for Cassell. Exhibited: R.A., R.I., R.O.I..
See (§2): 126.3.

DARBYSHIRE, J.A., *fl*. 1886–1900
An illustrator, specialising in figure work. He lived near Manchester, and exhibited there in the 1890s. May perhaps have drawn the illustrations for the binding case of *With Roberts to Pretoria*, of which the one on the front board is signed 'J.A.D.'.See (§1): 101.1.

DAVIS, JOSEPH BARNARD, *b*. 1861
Painter of landscapes and portraits. Born at Bowness, Windermere, and worked in London, 1890–1911, for many of the well-known magazines. Later he worked at Gerrards Cross. He made four wash-drawings and two pen-drawings for Henty's story, 'A Close Shave', reproduced by deep-etched halftone blocks, and line blocks, one of which has a mechanical tint laid down. Exhibited: R.A., R.B.A., R.C.A., R.I., R.O.I., R.S.A.
See (§3): 216.

DRAPER, HERBERT JAMES, 1864–1920
Born in London; studied and worked in London, Paris and Rome. One of his paintings was bought by the Chantrey Bequest, 1898. His twelve wash-drawings for Henty were reproduced by halftone blocks. Exhibited: R.A., R.B.A., R.H.A.
See (§1): 63.1.

DUDLEY, ROBERT, *fl.* 1858–1893

Landscape painter, illustrator, designer of binders' brasses. Worked in London, for journals including the *Illustrated London News* and *Beeton's Boy's Own Magazine*. His many bindings included some (signed) for Griffith & Farran. Exhibited: R.A., R.I.

See (§2): 167.1; 168.1.

DUGDALE, THOMAS CANTRELL, R.A., R.O.I., 1880–1952

Born at Blackburn; studied and worked in Manchester, London and Paris. Made illustrations in woodcut style, and with pen. His work for the 'Joint Venture', published in 1910 and 1911, was in watercolour, reproduced in colour, and he also made some pen-drawings for them. Later he abandoned illustration for oil painting, and exhibited frequently in northern provincial cities, in Paris, and at R.A., R.H.A., R.O.I., R.S.A.

See (§1): 5.12; 9.8. (§2): 137.1; 156.1; 180.1.

DURAND, GODEFROY, *b.* 1832

An illustrator born in Düsseldorf but of French extraction. He settled in London after the Franco-Prussian War, and exhibited pictures of the siege of Paris at the R.B.A. in 1873. Worked on the staff of the *Graphic* for over twenty years, illustrating military and horse subjects and foreign views. Of the illustrations for *The Young Colonists*, a mixed bag of pictures commissioned by Sampson Low (see §1, 17.1), only one is his. It is a very finely detailed wood-engraving, and at this date of publication (1885) it is possibly printed from a line block made of an impression of the original, the image having been reduced in reproduction. However, much of another engraving, made for Cassell at about the same time, is equally fine in detail (see 126.1, Vol.I, p.627). Exhibited: R.A., R.B.A.

See (§1): 17.1. (§2): 126.1.

EVANS, EDMUND, 1826–1905

Aged 14 he was apprenticed to Ebenezer Landells, a pupil of Bewick; worked on his own from 1847 and soon became known for his colour printing and engraving. The Dalziell Brothers were his rivals, but in colour printing never matched him in quantity and quality. His work was in constant demand from publishers of fine books and of children's literature alike. For Blackie he made black-and-white wood engravings for seven of ten drawings by Solomon J.Solomon in *For the Temple*.

See (§1): 35.1; 93.1.

EWAN, FRANCES, *fl.* 1897–1929

A figure painter, she worked in London and St Ives, Cornwall. She made seven wash-drawings and an illustrated heading for Bousfield's serialisation of 'A Soldier's Daughter'. All are signed and dated 1903. For the book Blackie used four of the same drawings, and commissioned her to do two more. They painted out the date on three of the original illustrations, leaving it (hardly legible) on the frontispiece. One of the new drawings is dated 1905. All the drawings were reproduced by halftone blocks, those in the book having to be reduced considerably

more than those in the magazine.
Exhibited R.A., S.W.A.
See (§1): 111.1. (§3): 210.

EYLES, D.C.

Made illustrations for Baden-Powell's *The Scout* magazine and for Sampson Low publications. He made one wash-drawing for Henty's *White-Faced Dick*.
See (§1): 71.2.

FARMER, E.S.

I have no information about this artist, who made a watercolour drawing for Sampson Low in the 1920s, reproduced by three-colour halftones.
See (§1): 11.5.

FELLER, FRANK, 1848–1908

Born in Switzerland and studied in Geneva, Munich, Paris and London. He was a painter, and illustrated books and magazines. He worked in London in the 1880s and 1890s, and remained there for the rest of his life. His wash-drawings for Henty were poorly reproduced by halftone blocks made with too fine a screen for the paper they were printed on. He also made pen-drawings for Cassell.
See (§1): 4.7; 5.10; 9.6. (§2): 126.1.

FINNEMORE, JOSEPH, R.I., R.B.A., 1860–1939

Painter and illustrator, born in Birmingham where he studied at the Art School. Also studied in Antwerp, and went on a tour of European and Asiatic countries From 1884 worked in London on books and magazines. His twelve wash-drawings for Blackie were reproduced by halftone blocks. He also produced pen-drawings for Cassell, of action scenes with much figure work: some were produced as wood-engravings and some made into line blocks. One of the former (126.1, Vol.I, p.524), usually seen to better advantage in later impressions (e.g. 126.3, Vol.II, p.524), was engraved by R. Taylor (q.v.), whose work here appears to emulate the drawings of falling figures often made by Gordon Browne (q.v.).
See (§1): 68.1. (§2): 126.1.

FOWLER, ROBERT

I have no information about this artist, who made four line-drawings for Blackie, signed and dated 1887. Fowler followed the Gordon Browne technique with mechanical tints on second-colour plates printed in sepia.
See (§1): 34.1.

FURNISS, HARRY, 1854–1925

Born at Wexford in Ireland of an English father. A fellow-member with Henty of the Savage Club, for which he designed numerous menus, etc.[22] Contributed to *Punch*, worked for the *Illustrated London News*, by which he was sent to the Chicago World Fair as Special Artist. He also travelled to Canada and Australia. He was one of the best-known and most able black-and-white artists of his time, often working extremely quickly, and he established a great reputation for his parliamentary and comic sketches and caricatures. He illustrated a number of his own books of reminiscences about personalities of the day. His Henty illustrations, like most of his work, were bold pen-drawings. A second colour was used in the cover illustration for the Summer Number of *Tinsleys' Magazine*. Exhibited: R.A., R.H.A., F.A.S. See (§2): 176.1.

GILLETT, (EDWARD) FRANK, 1874–1927
Born in Suffolk, educated at Gresham's, he spent six years as a Lloyds' clerk and ten years on the staff of the *Daily Graphic*. From 1908 he worked for *Black & White* and the *Sporting & Dramatic News*, as an illustrator of sporting and equestrian subjects. He provided black-and-white wash-drawings and a large number of watercolours for Blackie's cheaper editions, all signed with his initials. Earlier he made some wash-drawings for Cassell, reproduced rather poorly on text paper. Exhibited: R.A., R.I. See (§1): 20.4; 21.4; 28.4; 30.5; 33.3; 35.4; 37.4; 38.4; 43.4; 58.4; 59.3; 60.4; 62.4; 63.4; 64.4; 67.3; 68.3; 72.4; 74.4; 75.4; 77.4; 84.4; 85.4; 96.3; 100.2; 105.3; 108.2; (§2): 126.3.

GOUGH, ARTHUR J., *fl.* 1897–1914
Worked in London as a landscape painter; and as an illustrator, mainly in black and white. His illustrations drawn in 1909 for the 'Joint Venture' were watercolours reproduced in colour. Exhibited: R.A., R.I. See (§1): 4.10.

GRETHE, CARLOS
I have no information about this artist, who made a wash-drawing as one of six illustrations of Henty's story 'A Desperate Gang' in *Boys* magazine. See (§3): 199.

GROOME, WILLIAM HENRY CHARLES, R.B.A., *fl.* 1881–1914
A landscape painter and illustrator who worked in London. The three Chambers books are each illustrated by eight wash-drawings reproduced by halftone blocks, of which some have been worked over by hand with a graving tool. He made other wash-drawings and line drawings for Cassell. Exhibited: R.A., R.B.A., R.I., R.O.I. See (§2): 126.1; 135.1; 140.1; 158.1; 174.1; 178.1.

HARDY, EVELYN STUART
I have no information about this artist who illustrated two of Henty's short stories,'In Troubled Times' and 'Little Mistress Valentia', with pen-drawings for Nister. As in most of their books the pictures were printed by lithography in Bavaria. Hardy also made many pen-drawings of action scenes for Cassell. See (§2): 126.1; 161.1; 162.1; 163.1; 169.1; 171.1; 181.1.

HARDY, PAUL, *fl.* 1886–1899
Worked in Kent; Houfe calls him prolific, competent, but unexciting, at his best in costume romances and adolescent series.[23] He made wash-drawings for Blackie and for Cassell, reproduced by halftone blocks; also numerous pen-drawings for Cassell. He probably also drew the frontispieces for *Surly Joe* and *White-Faced Dick*, both

of which are reproduced by line blocks initialled P.H. Exhibited: R.A.
See (§1): 62.1. (§2): 126.1.

HARE, ST GEORGE, R.I., 1857–1933

Illustrator, portrait and genre painter. Born in Limerick; studied with N.A. Brophy, and at the South Kensington Schools in 1875. He was almost certainly the artist who made two small line illustrations (signed 'Hare') for the first part of a newspaper serialisation, arranged by Tillotsons, of *Dorothy's Double*.
See (§3): 227.

HASSALL, JOHN, R.I., R.M.S., 1868–1948

Watercolourist, poster designer and illustrator. Educated in Devon and at Heidelberg. Gave up farming in Manitoba to study art in Antwerp and Paris. Apart from his bold poster designs he did some sensitive watercolour illustrations. He started designing Blackie's binding cases for Henty's books early in the twentieth century, when the last few novels for boys were being first published. Father of the twentieth-century wood-engraver and illustrator, Joan Hassall, and of the writer Christopher Hassall.

In 1903 Blackie started their 'New and Popular Edition' of Henty's novels: these were issued in new binding designs, most of which were Hassall's work. Many of the cases are signed by John Hassall, and many others, in the same characteristic style, are not. It seems likely that the latter were also by him, and not by some unknown person copying his style, if only because Blackie would hardly have had the gall to use such blatant imitations of a very individual artist and craftsman. Exhibited: R.A., R.I., R.M.S., R.S.W.
See: (§1): The majority of Henty's novels in the 'New and Popular Edition', 1903–1918, and also those in the 'New Popular Henty' series issued in the 1920s.

HENDERSON, JOSEPH, R.S.W., 1832–1908

I have no information about the artist who made a number of drawings for one of Henty's stories in the *Union Jack*. Nahum shows that the JH monogram with which he signed his drawings is exactly similar to that used by the Joseph Henderson named here,[24] but I have no positive identification. Electrotypes from the wood-engravings for the story, 'In Times of Peril', were later cut down to fit the page-size of the book, published by Griffith & Farran in 1881 (see §1, 9.1, Notes 4–8).
See (§1): 9.1. (§3): 225.

HINDLEY, GODFREY C., R.O.I., *fl.* 1880–1910

A figure painter who specialised in illustrating books for boys. He made eight wash-drawings for the only book of Henty's that he illustrated. He also painted flowers.
See (§1): 67.1.

HOLLOWAY, W. HERBERT

Little is known of this artist, except that Houfe reports that he illustrated *Fairy Tales from South Africa*.[25] He signed the drawing, captioned 'Sudan', that was used by the 'Joint Venture' for the endpapers of books in 'The Boys' Pocket Library'.
See (§1): 4.12; 7.11.

HOLMES, T.W., *b.* 1872

Born in Newcastle-on-Tyne, and studied at Leeds School of Art. From 1894 he worked for over thirty years in London for several publishing houses and contributed to numerous periodicals including *Chums* and the *Union Jack*. For Blackie he made watercolour drawings, reproduced by litho, for both the frontispiece and binding case for a late edition of *John Hawke's Fortune*.
See (§): 93.9.

HUNT, ALFRED, *fl.* 1860–1884

Studied at the R.A. Schools, and practised as a painter in Yorkshire. In about 1860 he joined the staff of the *Illustrated London News*. Houfe says he contributed drawings that 'present crowds of figures, usually rather wooden but interesting for their period details'.[26] It is likely that he was the engraver of one of Henty's own drawings sent to the I.L.N. from the Expedition to Abyssinia, showing Sir Robert Napier with the Prince of Tigre, 1868.
See (§3): 214.

HURST, HAL, R.B.A., R.O.I., 1865–*c*.1938

Widely talented as a painter, illustrator and miniaturist. Born in England, he was a grandson of Daniel Hurst, original partner in Hurst & Blackett, publishers. Worked with success in Ireland, drawing the eviction scenes; when 23 he went to U.S.A. and worked for several newspapers. Later studied in Paris, before returning to London, where he contributed to most of the periodicals. Is said by Houfe to have been strongly influenced by Dana Gibson.[27] All his Henty illustrations were wash-drawings. Exhibited: R.A., R.B.A., R.H.A., R.I., R.M.S., R.W.S.
See (§1): 64.1; 65.2.

JANET-LANGE, ANGE LOUIS, 1816–1872

This excellent Parisian artist studied in the ateliers of Colin, Ingres, and Vernet. Michael Bryan says he painted sacred subjects in his youth and later worked for twenty years on the paper *L'Illustration*.[28] He illustrated the French edition of *The Young Franc-Tireurs* published by Librairie Hachette in Paris, 1873. The engravings were mostly by C. Laplante, with some by Hildibrand or J. Gauchard. Henty obtained electros from the wood blocks and used them in his serialisation of the story in the *Union Jack* eight years later, in preference to the illustrations by Landells (q.v.).
See (§3): 225.

JELLICOE, JOHN, *fl.* 1865–1905

Was a painter, but mainly illustrated novels and magazine-stories of domestic life. He was one of several artists used to illustrate 'Jack Archer' in the *Union Jack*, and he also illustrated 'Seth Harper's Story', 'A Pipe of Mystery' and 'An Indian Cattle Raid' in the same magazine. The last is an extract from Henty's book *Out on the Pampas*, and also includes one of the original Zwecker illustrations from the book. The serialised 'Jack Archer' is illustrated by eleven wood-engravings, and there is one pen-drawing which may also be his. Certainly all Jellicoe's other illustrations in

the *Union Jack* are pen-drawings. His two pictures for Blackie, published in 1904 (title-page date 1905), are wash-drawings. Exhibited: R.B.A.
See (§1): 14.1; 113.1. (§3): 225.

KERR, CHARLES HENRY MALCOLM, R.B.A., 1858–1907

A portraitist and landscape painter, he lived and worked in London. He made pen-drawings for the first illustrated edition of *The Curse of Carne's Hold*. Exhibited: R.A., R.B.A., R.H.A., R.I., R.O.I.
See (§1): 40.2.

LANDELLS, ROBERT THOMAS, 1833–1877

Educated in France, studied painting and drawing in London, specialising in military subjects. His father was Ebenezer Landells (1808-1860), the originator of *Punch*, who was apprenticed to Thomas Bewick, and who in turn had Edmund Evans, the Dalziel brothers, and many other leading engravers as his pupils. Robert was 'an artist of considerable ability in black and white work; acted for many years as Art War Correspondent to the *Illustrated London News* [from 1855 to 1871], and in that capacity went through a great part of the Franco Prussian Campaign'.[29] He was awarded the Prussian Iron Cross for his drawing and for ambulance work, and the Bavarian cross for valour. He was no doubt an obvious choice to illustrate Henty's *The Young Franc-Tireurs*, soon after they both returned home. The wood-engravings from his drawings were by Swain, and nine years after the book was published Henty used some of them again for his magazine serialisation. Exhibited: R.B.A.
See (§1): 5.1. (§2): 225.

LEIGH, CONRAD H.

I have no information about this artist who made four watercolour drawings for the 'Joint Venture', reproduced in colour and published 1910.
See (§1): 5.10.

LEIGHTON, EDMUND BLAIR, R.O.I., 1853–1922

Born and educated in London, son of the artist, Charles Blair Leighton, studied at the R.A. Schools. He made impressive wood-engravings for Cassell, showing Nelson at the Battle of Copenhagen, and Napoleon entering Moscow. Nahum illustrates his usual signature, of neat block capital letters.[30] Exhibited: R.A., R.B.A., R.O.I.
See (§2): 126.1.

LILLIE, R.

I have no information about this artist, whose work for Henty seems to be limited to seven black-and-white line-drawings.
See (§1): 89.1.

LUMLEY, ARTHUR, 1837–1912

A painter and illustrator, born in Dublin, he emigrated later to the United States, where he worked in New York. A contributor to the *Illustrated London News* between 1875 and 1881. He made two pen drawings for the serialised version of *The*

Young Franc-Tireurs to illustrate an incident not covered by the pictures in either the English or French editions of the book. Exhibited: R.A.
See (§3): 225.

MACKINTOSH, CHARLES RENNIE, F.R.I.B.A., 1868–1928

Architect, designer and painter; a leading figure in the art-nouveau movement, known as 'The Glasgow Style' which became celebrated in Europe. Born and studied art in Glasgow; in 1902 he became a partner in a Glasgow firm of architects. Met with considerable success in Vienna, Venice, Munich, Dresden, Budapest and Moscow, as well as in his own city. In 1896 he won an architectural competition to design and furnish the Glasgow School of Art. A rare poster for the Glasgow Institute of the Arts, which he had designed the previous year, was sold at Christies in February 1993 for £68,200, beating the earlier record price for a British poster by over £60,000. His friend and associate Talwin Morris introduced him to Walter W. Blackie for whom he designed The Hill House, Helensburgh. In 1913 he gave up architecture and moved to London to concentrate on painting. After Morris's death, in the 1920s when he was in need of work, Blackie commissioned him to work on bindings. He produced an abstract design intended for a new uniform edition of Henty's novels. The result was striking, but used instead for a series that included *Yarns on the Beach*. A design for another series that included Henty titles may also be his. See Appendix II, Part 5, and Robert J. Gibbs, 'Mackintosh's Book Designs' in *Newsletter of the Charles Rennie Mackintosh Society*, No.12, 1976.
See (§1): 25.5; 34.6; 57.6; 102.3; 113.5.

MARGETSON, WILLIAM HENRY, R.I., 1861–1940

Painted, mainly landscapes, in oils and watercolour. Born and lived in London, where he studied at the R.A. Schools. A popular and successful illustrator, his work for Henty consisted of wash-drawings, reproduced by halftone blocks, those for *A March on London* and *With Cochrane the Dauntless* being made by the Swan Engraving Company. The drawing facing page 314 of the first edition of *Beric the Briton*, of which the title page ascribes twelve illustrations to W. Parkinson, is in fact drawn and signed by Margetson. Exhibited: R.A., R.B.A., R.I., R.O.I.
See (§1): 59.1; 74.1; 75.1; 81.1.

MILLER, WAT

I have no information about this artist, whose only work for Henty seems to be two wash-drawings reproduced by halftone blocks.
See (§1): 102.1.

MORRIS, TALWIN, 1865–1911

Born in Winchester, orphaned, articled to an architect uncle at the age of 15, he became assistant art-editor of the new weekly paper *Black and White* in 1891. Appointed Manager of Blackie's Art Department in May 1893, according to Gerald Cinamon, although Agnes Blackie gives the date as 1892.[31] He was an important figure in the art-nouveau movement known as 'The Glasgow Style' (see Appendix II, Part 5), and a friend and associate of Charles Rennie Mackintosh (q.v.). He completely changed the style of book design for Blackie, his own work on cloth binding-cases having a distinctive elegance, and finesse not matched by his imitators. He often incorporated in his designs a symbol, as a form of signature, consisting of three irregularly spaced small circles, or dots. Cinamon wrote: 'The ingenuity of the publisher's marketing methods was endless as the same titles kept reappearing in constantly changing bindings. Up-to-date cover designs for old and new titles were required in abundance, and it was Morris's job to provide them'.[32] He designed a great many himself, and commissioned many others. Designers of binding cases for Henty's books in Morris's time, whose names are given in this Appendix, include Hassall and Peacock.

He also worked for other publishers, including Cassell, for whom he designed 150 very distinctive headpieces in *Battles of the Nineteenth Century*. He died lamentably young.
See (§1): 15.5; 29.3; 42.3; 48.6; 48.7; 53.3; 57.1; 57.3; 68.3. (§2): 126.1.

NASH, JOSEPH, R.I., *c*.1835–1922
Was a landscape and seascape painter, and did illustrations for several magazines. His father, also called Joseph, was an architectural draughtsman and illustrator who worked for Pugin. Nash illustrated only one book for Henty, sharing the work with J.N. Schönberg (q.v.). Each of them drew five illustrations on wood, the two sets being cut by different engravers. Exhibited: R.A., R.H.A., R.I., R.O.I.
See (§1): 53.1.

NICK
I have no information about the Blackie artist who signed himself thus on a wash-drawing, dated 1927, reproduced by halftone, and on two watercolours, reproduced by litho, on binding cases in the 'Summit Library'.
See (§1): 25.5; 114.4; 120.4.

OVEREND, WILLIAM HEYSMAN, R.O.I., 1851–1898
A marine painter, born in Yorkshire, and educated at Charterhouse. He worked extensively for the *Illustrated London News* as an illustrator and as an engraver, and for numerous other magazines. He illustrated many books and did a prodigious amount of work in his comparatively short life. His earlier illustrations for Blackie were wood engravings, and for two later titles wash-dawings reproduced by halftone blocks. Both styles were also used in the volumes from Cassell. Exhibited: R.A., R.O.I.
See (§1): 44.1; 48.1; 73.1; 77.1. (§2): 126.1.

PAGET, HENRY MARRIOTT, R.B.A., 1856–1936
The eldest of three London brothers who all worked as painters and illustrators (see Sidney and Walter Paget, below). He attended the R.A. Schools, and made several foreign tours, to Italy, Greece, Crete, and Canada. Was Special Artist for the *Sphere* covering the Balkan War..

Paget's early work for Cassell was reproduced as wood-engraving. His first Henty illustrations for Blackie are pen-drawings, superficially appearing rather like wood-engravings, with fine detail and cross-hatching. Lines are sometimes broken, resulting in a 'dotted' effect, as may be achieved with scraper-board: in Paget's work it is more likely that it was done with a graving tool on the zinc line-block. These illustrations follow the precedent set by Gordon Browne, being printed with mechanical tints on second-colour plates, to give the effect of a wash. His later pictures, in *Captain Bayley's Heir*, were wash-drawings. They were made in the early years of halftone blocks, and although Paget sent his originals to the well-known firm of photo-engravers in Vienna, Angerer & Göschl, whose monogram appears in the plates, the results were rather flat and restricted in their tonal range. Exhibited: R.A., R.B.A., R.O.I.

See (§1): 24.1; 28.1; 37.1. (§2): 126.1.

PAGET, SIDNEY E., 1860–1908

Brother of H.M. and Walter Paget, qq.v. Studied art at the British Museum, and at Heatherley's and the R.A. Schools. Was the first illustrator of the Sherlock Holmes stories for Conan Doyle in the *Strand Magazine*. Worked on the staff of the *Illustrated London News* and the *Sphere*. Marguerite Jago made wood-engravings of his work for Cassell, and it was also reproduced by halftone. Exhibited: R.A., R.B.A., R.I.

See (§2): 126.1.

PAGET, WALTER STANLEY ('WAL'), 1863–1935

The youngest of three brothers (see H.M., and Sidney Paget, above). Sketchley calls him 'an excellent illustrator of *Robinson Crusoe* and of many boys' books and books of adventure'.[33] Those included many of Henty's later titles, and he made wash-drawings and watercolours for a number of first editions and cheaper reprints. His earliest work for Henty was dated 1893, so most of it was considerably later than that of his brother Henry (see above). Some halftones for Blackie were 'Swantypes' from the Swan Engraving Company. His work for Cassell included wood-engravings, pen-drawings, and halftone blocks from André & Sleigh. Exhibited: R.A., R.B.A., R.O.I.

See (§1): 58.1; 76.1; 76.4; 80.1; 82.1; 83.1; 83.4; 99.1; 105.1; 106.1; 107.1; 107.3; 108.1; (§2): 126.1.

PARKINSON, WILLIAM, *fl.* 1883–1895

Illustrator and cartoonist, worked for a number of London magazines and publishers. The wash-drawings made for Henty are reproduced by halftone blocks that were deep-etched on the artist's instructions, so as to produce highlights and areas of unprinted white paper. The pictures in *Beric the Briton* facing pages 72 and 148 have been worked on by hand with a graving tool, and that is almost certainly the artist's own work, rather than any fancy intrusion of the process-engraver, in both cases forming an integral part of the detail of the ground-foliage. The illustration facing page 314 is for some reason drawn and signed by W.H. Margetson, in spite of the title-page credit for twelve illustrations to Parkinson. Exhibited: R.A.

See (§1): 59.1.

PEACOCK, RALPH, 1868–1946

Portraitist and landscape painter; illustrator and designer. Studied at the Lambeth School of Art, the St John's Wood School, and the R.A. Schools where he won the gold medal and the Creswick prize. He taught at St John's Wood School for many years. His first work for Henty was a set of twelve wash-drawings for *Wulf the Saxon*, 1895. They were reproduced by halftone blocks, one of which, facing p. 12, has a blemish between the two main figures, not very successfully repaired by the engraver.

Talwin Morris (q.v.), head of Blackie's art department and himself an important designer in the art-nouveau style, commissioned in 1894 or 1895 a replacement binding case for *Under Drake's Flag*, possibly as an experiment (see §1, 13.3, Notes 1 and 2). It was certainly successful, and Peacock's design supplanted the original. He undertook further work on a number of binding cases for Henty's novels between then and 1898, and for most of them the colour of the binding cloth was not changed for subsequent binding orders. Peacock's distinctive style is easily recognisable, and the designs for three of the books are signed with his initials. In addition to that work he made wash-drawings reproduced by halftone blocks for two more Henty titles, and, some years after Talwin Morris's death, a watercolour reproduced in colour for a late edition of *Wulf the Saxon*. Exhibited: R.A., R.B.A., R.O.I.

See (§1, binding designs): 13.3; 72.1; 73.1; 76.1; 77.1; 80.1; 81.1; 84.1. (§1, illustrations): 66.1; 66.3; 72.1; 84.1.

PEARSE, ALFRED, *c.* 1854–1933

A London painter, and prolific black-and-white illustrator, whose wood-engravings in various magazines maintained a consistent and individual style, showing that he either cut his own wood blocks or employed a very distinctive engraver. His technique was particularly striking when used for large pictures on quarto magazine pages: although much of it is fine work it must be said that his illustration of Henty's 'The Fetish Hole' and 'In the Hands of the Cave Dwellers' did not give full scope to his powers. Later, his rather less effective wash-drawings, made for Blackie, were reproduced by halftone blocks, a number with deep-etching and hand-engraving. His work for Cassell included pen-drawings, wood-engravings, and halftone blocks from André & Sleigh. He also made watercolour drawings, reproduced in colour in late Blackie editions. Exhibited: R.A., R.B.A.

See (§1): 42.6; 47.1; 47.4; 49.1; 49.4; 54.1; 54.3. (§2): 126.1. (§3): 201.

PETHERICK, HORACE WILLIAM, 1839–1919

A painter and illustrator, working south of London. He specialised in children's stories and costume subjects. Henty thought very highly of his work,[34] and many of the illustrations he did for him are finely drawn with a pen to look superficially rather like wood engravings. Perhaps the most remarkable are the set of seventy-five small drawings, some no more than vignettes, often in more open style, that he did for 'Winning his Spurs', serialised in the *Union Jack*, and later re-used by Sampson Low in the book. At least a third of them were made into line blocks by M. Lefman, the French pioneering photo-engraver, who was used later by Gordon Browne, but after the middle of June 1882 Petherick seems to have sent his work elsewhere.

Exhibited: R.A., R.B.A.
See (§1): 8.1; 11.1. (§2): 175.1. (§3): 225.

PRATER, ERNEST, *fl.* 1897–1914
A black-and-white artist and illustrator, he worked for many of the leading periodicals of the day including those for boys. Sent as Special Artist by *Black and White* to cover the Sino-Japanese War of 1894. His work for Cassell was reproduced by wood-engraving, and a few years later by halftone blocks. When James Bowden set up as an independent publisher, after retiring from Ward Lock, he commissioned Prater to make four wash-drawings to illustrate *The Lost Heir*, a novel intended for adults. They were reproduced by halftone blocks: the four-colour blocking-pieces for the front board were probably engraved by the brass-cutter with no more than the frontispiece illustration as a guide.
See (§1): 87.1. (§2): 126.1; 126.3.

PRIOR, MELTON, 1845–1910
Special artist and illustrator, studied under his father, W.H. Prior, in Camden Town. From 1873 he worked regularly for the *Illustrated London News*, and was their Special Artist at many campaigns. He did not illustrate Henty's work, but during the march to Coomassie he published in the *I.L.N.*, 28 February 1874, a drawing of a camp scene, showing himself with G.A. Henty and H.M. Stanley.
See (§3): 214.

PROCTOR, J. JAMES
A black-and-white artist and illustrator of whom very little is known: he contributed to *Illustrated Bits*. His two pictures for Blackie, 1886, are pen-drawings, reproduced by line blocks printed in the old Gordon Browne style with mechanical tints on second-colour plates to give the effect of wash.
See (§1): 25.1.

PROCTOR, JOHN, *fl.* 1866–1898
Houfe records him as 'one of the best political cartoonists of the end of the Victorian period, characterised by invention and strong drawing of animals'.[35] He was the *Illustrated London News* Special Artist in St Petersburg in 1874, and worked for other London periodicals. His eight drawings for Henty, mainly of military subjects set in the Peninsular War period, were engraved on wood with great technical skill by 'W.H.' for Griffith & Farran, 1879.
See (§1): 7.1.

RACKHAM, ARTHUR, R.W.S., 1867–1939
Illustrator and watercolourist, born and educated in London. Studied art at the Lambeth School, and became one of the best-known and most-collected of English book-illustrators. His drawings have been in fashionable demand in recent decades. Some of his finest work is in colour, but he did black-and-white illustrations of remarkable quality and in great profusion. His illustrations of Henty consist of a watercolour reproduced in colour, and wash-drawings reproduced by halftone

THE ILLUSTRATED LONDON NEWS.

REGISTERED AT THE GENERAL POST-OFFICE FOR TRANSMISSION ABROAD.

No. 1801.—VOL. LXIV.   SATURDAY, FEBRUARY 28, 1874.   WITH EXTRA SUPPLEMENT   SIXPENCE. BY POST, 6½D.

Drawing by Melton Prior, Special Artist to the *Illustrated London News* during the Ashantee War, published 28 February 1874. The three figures in the foreground are H.M. Stanley, Correspondent of the *New York Herald*, a self-portrait of Melton Prior, and G.A. Henty, Correspondent of the London *Standard*. The figure seated behind is the Correspondent of *The Times* of London.

blocks. Exhibited: R.A., R.B.A., R.I., R.O.I., R.S.A., R.S.W., R.W.S.
See (§1): 110.1. (§2): 134.1.

RAILTON, HERBERT, 1857–1910

Born at Pleasington, Lancashire, and educated in Belgium and at Ampleforth. Sketchley wrote 'No architectural drawings are more popular than his, and no style is better known or more generally "adopted" … An architect's training and knowledge of structure underlies the picturesque delapidation prevalent in his version of Anglo-gothic architecture'.[36] His work was in demand for many magazines and guidebooks, and he illustrated numerous books. His drawings for Cassell are very fine pen-sketches of buildings in Delhi and elsewhere, reproduced by line blocks, and his style greatly influenced Holland Tringham (q.v.).
See (§2): 126.1.

RAINEY, WILLIAM, R.B.A., R.I., R.O.I., 1852–1936

An important artist and illustrator. Born in London, studied art at South Kensington and then attended the R.A. Schools. He had a long and successful career as a book illustrator, which continued right up to the end of his life, and some of his best work was also done for magazines. He worked on seven of Henty's first editions for Blackie, and also made wash-drawings and watercolour drawings for later editions. Those wash-drawings, and others for Chambers, were reproduced by halftone blocks, and the watercolours by three-colour sets. Exhibited: R.A., R.B.A., R.I., R.O.I.
See (§1): 28.3; 29.5; 53.4; 85.1; 91.1; 97.1; 98.1; 101.1; 104.1; 104.3; 109.1; 109.2; 114.4; (§2): 157.1.

ROBERTSON, GEORGE EDWARD, *b.* 1864

Portrait painter, and illustrator. Studied at St Martin's School of Art, and worked in London, especially for the *Graphic* and the *Boy's Own Paper*. He made wash-drawings for Henty's 'Among Malay Pirates' and 'Burton & Son', which are reproduced by halftone blocks that have been worked over with a hand-graver. The engraver's name, P. Naumann, appears on several blocks in the first set which, generally, are not as striking as the later illustrations with comparatively little hand-work. Exhibited: R.A., R.B.A., R.O.I.
See (§3): 201.

ROBERTSON, VICTOR

I have no information about this artist, whose wash-drawing for Henty's 'In the Grip of the Press-Gang' was the only illustration of the serial in *Young England*. It was reproduced as a two-colour plate by litho in brown and black, presented free with an issue of the magazine and bound up as the frontispiece to the annual volume.
See (§3): 228.

ROBINSON, CHARLES, *d.* 1881

Son of a London bookbinder and wood-engraver, apprenticed to a lithographic firm. He studied at Finsbury School of Art, and won a silver medal in the National

Competition. In about 1862 he joined the staff of the *Illustrated London News*, where, according to Houfe, 'he contributed regular and rather wooden work until his death'.[37] He had three well-known nephews: Charles, T.H., and W. Heath Robinson. It is possible that he was the engraver of one of Henty's own drawings, sent from the Expedition to Abyssinia in 1868, that appeared in the magazine.
See (§3): 214.

SCHÖNBERG, JOHANN NEPOMUK (JOHN), *b*. 1844

Born in Austria, son of the lithographer Adolf Schönberg, he studied in Vienna. Worked for illustrated periodicals in France, and then for the *Illustrated London News* for twenty-two years, following his appointment as their Special Artist in Roumania in 1877. His earliest illustrations were pen-drawings for *The Lion of the North*, finely drawn to appear superficially rather like engravings, in the manner of a number of illustrators of his time, and reproduced by line blocks. Only Gordon Browne and C.J. Staniland had preceded Schönberg in illustrating Henty for Blackie, and for his first book he followed what had become an accepted style, with mechanical tints laid on the second-colour plates. Even more than for Staniland's drawings, however, the second-colour tints for Schönberg seem superfluous.

The pictures in his second book, *In the Reign of Terror*, are black-and-white wash-drawings, reproduced by the first halftone blocks to appear in a book by Henty. The drawings have great quality, and it is a pity the new halftone process was not yet developed to do them justice. The results are flat, and lack the vitality of Schönberg's earlier illustrations. The screen here is unnecessarily fine, too fine, indeed, for the rather indifferent art-paper, and certainly for machine-minders still inexperienced in the process. The ink clogged the fine detail of the blocks, and the situation was made worse by dust settling on the plates during machining.

Perhaps it was a result of disappointment with those reproductions that Schönberg did not illustrate another Henty for four years. When he did, the work was shared with another illustrator, Joseph Nash (see above), and for *The Dash for Khartoum* they each produced a set of five drawings, engraved on wood. Of the two I prefer Schönberg's stronger and more vigorous work, which appears as the frontispiece and on pages 123, 163, 184 and 342. His work included only one other wood-engraving for Henty, and that had appeared seven years earlier, in a mixed bag of illustrations originally assembled by Sampson Low for *The Young Colonists* (see §1, 17.1).

Some seven years after his last book for Blackie, in 1899, Schönberg went back to wash-drawings for a new edition of *The Young Buglers* from Griffith & Farran. Once again he was to be disappointed. The eight halftone blocks made by the Art Repro Company (?) are no doubt of better quality than those used earlier by Blackie, but the publisher had them printed on paper totally unsuitable for their fine screen, and the results do no kind of justice to the artist. It is sad that Schönberg, who was a fine illustrator, was so badly let down by Henty's publishers.
See (§1): 7.6; 17.1; 23.1; 33.1; 53.1.

SHELDON, CHARLES M., *fl.*1891–1907
A figure artist and illustrator, apparently born in the U.S.A. He took up an assignment as Special Artist in the Sudan, 1897–1898, for *Black and White*. His wash-drawings to illustrate Henty were reproduced by halftone blocks.
See (§1): 19.3; 90.1; 96.1; 100.1.

SOLOMON, SOLOMON JOSEPH, R.A., R.B.A., 1860–1927
Born in London, attended the R.A. Schools, then studied in Munich and Paris. He travelled and worked in Italy, Spain and Morocco. Became Vice-President of the Maccabeans Society and President of the R.B.A. in 1918. He was the initiator of camouflage for the British army in the first war. His illustrations for Henty were made as wash-drawings in 1887, and beautifully engraved on wood by Edmund Evans (q.v.) and R. Taylor (q.v.) for the first edition of *For the Temple*. Those pictures show the use of wood-engraving at its finest in Henty's books. In the same year Blackie were experimenting with their first use of halftone blocks to illustrate Henty's *In the Reign of Terror* (see John Schönberg, above).

The first halftones were not a huge success, but a beginning had to be made, and the value of the process became apparent later when experience had been gained. Indeed, in 1903, when Blackie re-issued *For the Temple* in a cheaper edition (title-page date 1904), Solomon's original wash-drawings were dug out of storage, and reproduced again, this time by halftone blocks. By then, some sixteen years later, process-engraving had developed, and the work of the wood-engravers in 1887 could be seen side-by-side with the well photographed reproductions of the originals they had had to work from. The comparison is well worth making today, by those who have both editions. Exhibited: R.A., R.B.A., R.H.A., R.I.
Set (§1): 35.1; 35.3.

SPEED, LANCELOT, 1860–1931
Shipping and coastal painter, and illustrator in black and white. Born in London, educated at Rugby and at Clare College, Cambridge. Latterly worked and lived at Southend-on-Sea. The frontispiece for Partridge is from a wash-drawing, reproduced by a halftone block with some deep-etching and hand-engraving.
See (§2): 159.1.

SPENCE, PERCY F.S., 1868–1933
Painter and illustrator born at Sydney, N.S.W., he moved from Australia to London in 1895. For the rest of his life he contributed to magazines in London, with occasional book work. He had known Robert Louis Stevenson in the South Seas, and drew portraits of him. He made six wash-drawings, reproduced by halftone blocks, for Sampson Low's first single-volume edition of *A Hidden Foe*.
See (§1): 46.2.

STACEY, WALTER S., R.B.A., R.O.I., 1846–1929
Mainly a landscape painter and illustrator. Born in London, he studied at the R.A. Schools, worked in London until 1902, and later in the West Country. Most of his illustrations were for boys' and adventure books: those for Henty being black-and-

white wash-drawings, and a watercolour reproduced in colour.

It is interesting to compare the illustrations in the first edition of *By Right of Conquest* with those in the later cheap edition. The original blocks have been discarded and replaced by new ones from the Swan Engraving Company: there are differences in details of certain areas of wash, representing clouds, shadows, folds in garments, etc. The improvements may have been brought about by reworking parts of the original drawings, but more probably, in spite of the apparent scale of the changes, result from better quality of reproduction. The same blockmaking company was still producing excellent work in the 1950s.

For the original versions, which are harder in tone and texture, the earlier blockmakers probably did a certain amount of 'titivation' to the blocks themselves. 'Improvement' by supposedly judicious hand-work was often done in the early years of halftone blockmaking, and on occasion the blockmaker's re-touching artist got carried away and did more than was required or expected of him. The original version of the frontispiece shows clear signs of blockmaker's discreet 'cleaning-up work' at the lower right corner. That was no doubt necessary, and an acceptable improvement. But the variations between the two versions of the illustrations captioned 'The Pile of a Hundred Thousand Skulls' and 'The Messenger Returns at a Gallop ...' are particularly noticeable: the first in the sky at the upper right corner, and the second in the shadows on the ground. It is likely that the second, 'Swantype', versions are more accurate reproductions of the drawings, and that the earlier versions show unnecessary intrusion by the blockmaker. Exhibited: R.A., R.B.A., R.I., R.O.I.
See (§1): 50.1; 50.4; 60.1. (§2): 123.1.

STANILAND, CHARLES JOSEPH, R.I., R.O.I., 1838–1916
Born at Kingston-upon-Hull, studied at Birmingham, Heatherley's, South Kensington, and the R.A. Schools. When Van Gogh was in England he was a great admirer of Staniland. He turned out a great volume of work, and Houfe says his strength was in marine illustrations where the ships and tackle were seen at close quarters and the working seaman was observed in large scale. Unfortunately the books he was asked to illustrate for Henty do not give full scope for those particular talents. That is a pity, for Houfe continues 'his many contributions to the *Illustrated London News* and the *Graphic* were a mainstay of those periodicals in the 1870s and 1880s, readers had practically to wipe the brine from their faces as they turned the pages'.[38]

Both the books for Henty are illustrated with line blocks from fine pen-drawings drawn in a manner referred to elsewhere in these notes: it was popular with several artists of the period, and results in pictures bearing a superficial resemblance to wood-engravings. *The Dragon and the Raven* was the first from Blackie not to have been illustrated by Gordon Browne, and followed his use of mechanical stipple-tints on second-colour plates. The tints seem hardly necessary for Staniland's drawings, and for *The Young Carthaginian* they were abandoned. Exhibited: R.A., R.I.
See (§1): 21.1; 30.1.

STAYNES, PERCY ANGELO, R.I., R.O.I., *b.* 1875

Painter, designer and illustrator, studied at the Manchester School of Art, at the Royal College, and later in Paris. His work for Henty consists of three small pen-drawings reproduced by line blocks, and, more impressively, a watercolour reproduced on a quarto page by a three-colour set. They all illustrate the story, 'Trapped'. Exhibited: R.I., R.O.I.

See (§2): 135.1; 174.1.

STEWART, ALLAN, 1865–1951

Military and historical painter and illustrator. Born and educated in Edinburgh, studied at the R.S.A. Schools. Worked for the *Illustrated London News* from about 1895: he was their Special Artist in South Africa, and accompanied King Edward VII on his Mediterranean tours. He made wash-drawings for Cassell, reproduced by halftone blocks. Exhibited: R.A., R.S.A., R.S.W.

See (§2): 126.2.

STEWART, F.A.

I have no information about this artist: he made six wash-drawings for one of Blackie's cheaper editions in 1907, and illustrated for Nister 'How a Drummer Boy Saved a Regiment', with three pen-drawings dated 1899.

See (§1): 44.3. (§2): 155.1; 160.1; 164.1.

SYMINGTON, J. AYTON, *fl.* 1890–1908

Worked for a number of the London magazines, and illustrated books, mainly of adventure stories. He drew three pictures for the serialisation of Henty's 'On the Spanish Main', one of which is also signed by the engraver, C. Hentschell.

See (§3): 228.

TAYLOR, R., *fl.* 1887–1896

A very fine engraver on wood about whom I have been able to find nothing in spite of diligent searches. For Blackie he engraved the last three illustrations in the first edition of *For the Temple*, the first seven being engraved by the great Edmund Evans. The quality of Taylor's work is very high, in my opinion exceeding that of Evans for this book. For Cassell, Taylor also engraved an illustration by Joseph Finnemore (q.v.).

See (§1): 35.1. (§2): 126.1.

THACKERAY, LANCE, R.B.A., *d.* 1916

Painter, illustrator and writer, his first recorded illustrations are dated 1894. He lived in London and specialised in sporting and humorous illustration. He travelled in the Middle East, and had three one-man shows at leading galleries in London between 1908 and 1913. His work for Henty consists of a single full-page watercolour drawing in 1905, reproduced by vignetted three-colour halftones. Exhibited: R.A., R.B.A., R.I.

See (§1): 93.4. (§2): 126.2.

TRINGHAM, HOLLAND, R.B.A., *d.*1909
Painter and architectural illustrator, following very much in the style of the influential Herbert Railton (q.v.). Sketchley refers to him and Hedley Fitton as 'unmistakable in their Railtonism'.[39] His numerous fine pen-drawings for Cassell depict landscapes in European war areas. Exhibited: R.A., R.B.A.
See (§2): 126.1.

VARIAN, G.
I know nothing of this artist who made seven wash-drawings for the serialisation of Henty's 'The Sole Survivors'. They are reproduced by halftone blocks, which have been fairly heavily worked over by hand with a graver.
See (§3): 219.

VEDDER, SIMON HARMON, *b.* 1866
American painter, sculptor and illustrator, born and studied in New York. Later he studied in Paris and by 1896 had settled in London, contributing to a number of magazines. *Cuthbert Hartington* and *Two Sieges* are two titles for the same book, with the same illustrations, only one being by Vedder and the others by Hal Hurst. The original version of the book was *A Woman of the Commune*, in which the Vedder picture did not appear. Vedder's drawings for Henty, including six used in Blackie's first issue of *The Young Colonists*, were wash-drawings reproduced by halftone blocks, the latter by the Swan Engraving Company. Exhibited: R.A., R.O.I.
See (§1): 17.7; 86.1; 112.1.

VENNER, VICTOR, *fl.* 1901–1924
Houfe notes him as a humorous illustrator, contributing to *Punch* in 1904.[40] His illustrations of Henty's story, 'A Frontier Girl' are wash-drawings of figures in action, reproduced by halftone blocks.
See (§3): 210.

WALL, ARTHUR J., *fl.* 1889–1897
Illustrator who worked at Stratford-upon-Avon. Houfe says he specialised in animals and birds; also that he probably visited Australia when working for the *Illustrated London News*.[41] That may be why he was chosen to illustrate Henty's story 'A Desperate Gang', subtitled 'A Story of the Australian Bush'. His name is given as the main illustrator, but he drew only two of six pictures used for the serial.
See (§3): 199.

WALTON, JOHN DE, R.W.A., *b.* 1874
Originally employed in an architect's office, but by the age of nineteen he was working at illustration for a living, and contributed to numerous magazines, specialising in adventure and military subjects. He lived for many years in Cornwall, and was commissioned to paint a miniature portrait of King George for Queen Mary's Dolls' House. He made watercolour drawings, reproduced in colour as frontispieces for seven of Blackie's cheaper editions of Henty.
See (§1): 15.8; 19.4; 24.4; 27.3; 73.4; 81.4; 90.3.

WEBB, ARCH

I have no information about this artist who made two watercolour drawings for Blackie in the 1920s, reproduced in colour, and others for the 'Joint Venture'.
See (§1): 13.5; 22.4. (§2): 135.1; 137.1; 156.1; 174.1; 180.1.

WEGUELIN, JOHN REINHARD, R.W.S., R.O.I., 1849–1927

Painter and illustrator, born in Sussex, the son of a clergyman, and educated at Cardinal Newman's Oratory School, Edgbaston. He became a Lloyd's underwriter, and then went to the Slade School. He was a Victorian classicist and painted in the style of Alma-Tadema. Sketchley says 'few decorative artists habitually use "wash" rather than line. Among these, however, is Mr Weguelin . . . his drawings have movement and atmosphere'.[42] The wash-drawings he made for Blackie were among the first to be reproduced by the comparatively new process of halftone blocks.

There was a school of opinion, some would call a prejudice, that persisted in some degree throughout the life of the halftone process, that sepia ink would give a more satisfactory result than black. For some printers it seemed to be true, although most found, with experience, that black ink gave a stronger and more robust impression. The halftone process was patented in 1882, and it was at once used to reproduce photographs. As ordinary photographic prints had for some time been common and popular in sepia tones, it was natural that printers should copy the trend. Thus, while the halftone blocks in *In the Reign of Terror* and *Captain Bayley's Heir* were printed with black ink, Blackie tried sepia for Weguelin's illustrations in *The Cat of Bubastes*. It was the only Henty first edition for which Blackie used it.

A close examination with a magnifying glass shows that Blackie found the new blocks as difficult to print as anyone else. And the difficulties had not diminished in the year since they printed the illustrations for *In the Reign of Terror* by John Schönberg (q.v.). Blackie printed halftones very well later, as may be seen in much of Henty's work, even if they always tended to use screens that were a bit too fine (see Part 1 of this Appendix). Of course the quality of art-paper, and of blocks themselves, improved in the same period, as did the skill of machine minders, as they gradually acquired more experience in the process. Exhibited: R.A., R.B.A., R.H.A., R.O.I., R.W.S.
See (§1): 38.1.

WEIR, HARRISON WILLIAM, 1824–1906

A painter and illustrator who specialised almost exclusively in animals and birds. Born in Sussex, and educated at Camberwell, he learned colour printing when apprenticed to George Baxter. 'A gifted and brilliant conversationalist, brimful of anecdote . . . a man of many parts, poet, painter, draughtsman, and naturalist'.[43] He drew for the *Illustrated London News* for over fifty years. The Henty illustrations are in the well-known Harrison Weir style of pen-drawing, reproduced by fine line blocks. Exhibited: R.A., R.B.A.
See (§1): 51.1.

WHITE, A.B.

I have no information about this artist who illustrated the re-issued short story 'Hunted by an Elephant' for John F. Shaw in the late 1920s. There are seven drawings printed from line blocks; the frontispiece, reproduced by four-colour lithography, illustrates Henty's story and is also used for the cover illustration. It is not easy to tell exactly what illustration-technique was used to produce the original. See (§2): 173.1.

WHYMPER, EDWARD J., 1840–1911

The great mountaineer and artist, who illustrated his own famous work, *Scrambles Among the Alps*, and many other books and magazines, was part of a family wood-engraving business. He engraved a decorative headpiece for Henty's story, 'Down a Crevasse', in the *Boy's Own Paper*, and although it is unsigned the illustration on the facing page it almost certainly his too. The style is consistent with his work, and he would of course have been the obvious choice for the subject. See (§3): 201.

WILSON, RADCLIFFE

I have no information about this artist who made two pen-drawings for 'Effie to the Rescue', extracts from Henty's 'A Raid by the Blacks' (in *A Soldier's Daughter*) that appeared in *Blackie's English Study Readers*, *IV*, c.1927. See (§2): 131.

WOLLEN, WILLIAM BARNES, R.I., R.O.I., 1857–1936

A military painter and illustrator, born at Leipzig, and educated in London, he studied at the Slade. He originally intended to join the army, but became a professional painter, and was sent by the *Graphic* as Special Artist to South Africa in 1900. His illustrations for Henty's books are fine pen-drawings reproduced by line blocks, with mechanical tints on second-colour plates in the old Gordon Browne manner. The drawings are in a style common to a number of artists included in these notes, who, soon after the end of the period of the wood-engraving as the common form of illustration, used fine pen-strokes to produce a superficially rather similar effect. For Cassell he made wash-drawings and watercolour drawings reproduced in colour. Exhibited: R.A., R.H.A., R.I., R.O.I., R.S.A. See (§1): 29.1; 114.1. (§2): 126.1; 126.3.

WOOD, STANLEY L., 1866–1928

A military painter and illustrator, he worked in London for numerous magazines, and illustrated many boys' adventure stories. Much of his work was done for Chatto & Windus. Doyle says Wood had a tough adventurous life and spent many of his early years camping, riding and working in the cattle districts of Southern Texas and Southern California, virtually living the life of a cowboy.[44] His illustrations for Cassell and for Chatto & Windus are all from wash-drawings in his characteristic vigorous style, those for the first-named publisher being reproduced by wood-engravings and the later ones by halftone blocks. For Blackie his wash-drawings were reproduced by halftones, and he made one watercolour drawing for the cheap

edition of *No Surrender!* published in the 1920s. In 1892 he had made four wash-drawings to illustrate Henty's story 'The Golden Cañon' in *Boys:* they were reproduced by deep-etched halftone blocks. Exhibited: R.A., R.O.I.
See (§1): 56.2; 79.2; 92.1; 92.2; (§2): 126.1. (§3): 199.

WOODVILLE, RICHARD CATON, R.I., R.O.I., 1856–1927

Born in London, brought up in St Petersburg, he studied art in Düsseldorf. Then he lived in Paris and finally settled in London in 1875. He specialised in painting and illustrating battle scenes, and was sent by the *Illustrated London News* as Special Artist to the Turkish War of 1878. He turned more and more to painting, and gave up black-and-white work in 1897. Doyle says Queen Victoria admired his work and hung several of his paintings at Windsor and Balmoral.[45] Of the collection of pictures in *The Young Colonists* only one wood engraving bears his signature. The work is very fine, and not very well printed: it is possibly reproduced by line block from an impression of the original wood, with the image reduced in the blockmaking process. The reproductions of his paintings for Cassell are by wood-engraving and also by halftone heavily worked on by hand. In 1901 he also made watercolour drawings for them. Exhibited: R.A., R.H.A., R.I., R.O.I.
See (§1): 17.1. (§2): 126.1; 126.3.

ZWECKER, JOHANN BAPTIST, 1814–1876

Natural history painter, illustrator and etcher, born at Frankfurt. 'He was a highly-educated artist of the Düsseldorf School. He painted in oil and water colour; his work always showed good drawing and design, but was generally heavy in effect'.[46] He spent the last 26 years of his life in London, and worked for numerous magazines. Many of the books he illustrated dealt with natural history subjects. Of his four wood-engravings to illustrate Henty's first book for children, two are signed by the engraver, Pearson. Exhibited: R.A., R.B.A.
See (§1): 4.1. (§3): 225.

APPENDIX V

NAMES OF PUBLISHERS' SERIES
IN WHICH HENTY'S BOOKS APPEARED

GRIFFITH & FARRAN
The Boy's Own Favourite Library
Out on the Pampas
The Young Franc-Tireurs
In Times of Peril
The Curse of Carne's Hold
The Kingston Series of 6s. Books
The Young Buglers
The Crown Library for Boys
The Young Buglers
Friends, though Divided
Tales of Travel and Adventure
In Times of Peril
Friends, though Divided
Tales of Adventure
The Young Buglers
Friends, though Divided

SAMPSON LOW
Low's Standard Books for Boys
The Cornet of Horse
Winning his Spurs
Jack Archer
Sampson Low's New Series (1920s)
2s.6d. each
The Cornet of Horse
Winning his Spurs
Jack Archer
A Hidden Foe

S.P.C.K.
Penny Library of Fiction (later as
SHELDON PRESS)
The Plague Ship
The Ranche in the Valley

GEORGE BELL
Bell's Indian & Colonial Library
A Woman of the Commune

BLACKIE
New series of Children's Books (1896)
Twopence each
White-Faced Dick
Threepence each
Surly Joe
Bears and Dacoits
Graduated Stories (1902)
One Shilling each
Do Your Duty
Bears and Dacoits
New Graduated Series (1907)
One Shilling each
Bears and Dacoits
Excelsior Series (1907)
All at 1s.6d.
Tales of Daring and Danger
Yarns on the Beach
Crown Library (?1910)
A Chapter of Adventures
Tales from Henty
Ninepenny Series (c.1906–1911)
John Hawke's Fortune
English Authors for School Reading
A Chapter of Adventures
Tales from Henty
Sturdy and Strong
In the Hands of the Malays
The Boys' and Girls' Bookshelf
(c. 1927)
Yarns on the Beach

Library for Boys and Girls (c. 1928)
   A Soldier's Daughter
   Sturdy and Strong
   In the Hands of the Malays
   In the Hands of the Cave Dwellers
   Tales from Henty
The Sceptre Library (Boys)
   Sturdy and Strong
Library of Famous Books (1929)
   A Chapter of Adventures
   Tales from Henty
The Young Folk's Library
   Do Your Duty
The Happy Home Library
   Among the Bushrangers
   Charlie Marryat
   A Highland Chief
   An Indian Raid
   The Two Prisoners
   The Young Captain
The Talisman Library (1920–1922)
   Beric the Briton
   The Dragon and the Raven
   Redskin and Cowboy
   Under Drake's Flag
   With Clive in India
   With Wolfe in Canada
The Pinnacle Library
   White-Faced Dick
The Summit Library
   Among the Bushrangers
   The Two Prisoners
Blackie's Story-Book Readers
   Among the Bushrangers
   Cast Ashore
   Charlie Marryat
   Cornet Walter
   A Highland Chief
   An Indian Raid
   The Two Prisoners
   The Young Captain
   Do Your Duty
Blackie's Continuous Readers
   A Chapter of Adventures
Blackie's Colonial Library
   With Clive in India
   A Final Reckoning
   When London Burned

   The Dash for Khartoum
The New and Popular Edition
6s. novels, now at 3s.6d.
   Under Drake's Flag
   With Clive in India
   In Freedom's Cause
   True to the Old Flag
   The Lion of the North
   Through the Fray
   The Young Carthaginian
   For the Temple
   The Lion of St. Mark
   Captain Bayley's Heir
   By Pike and Dyke
   By England's Aid
   By Right of Conquest
   In Greek Waters
   St. Bartholomew's Eve
   Through the Sikh War
   A Knight of the White Cross
   The Tiger of Mysore
   With Cochrane the Dauntless
   At Agincourt
   With Moore at Corunna
   With Frederick the Great
   Under Wellington's Command
   Both Sides the Border
   In the Irish Brigade
   At the Point of the Bayonet
   With Kitchener in the Soudan
   Through Three Campaigns
5s. novels, now at 3s.6d.
   Facing Death
   St. George for England
   The Dragon and the Raven
   The Bravest of the Brave
   A Final Reckoning
   Orange and Green
   In the Reign of Terror
   The Cat of Bubastes
   One of the 28th
   Maori and Settler
   Condemned as a Nihilist
   A Jacobite Exile
   Through Russian Snows
   On the Irrawaddy
   A March on London
   At Aboukir and Acre

The New Popular Henty
6s. novels, now at 3s.6d.
  Under Drake's Flag
  With Clive in India
  In Freedom's Cause
  True to the Old Flag
  The Lion of the North
  Through the Fray
  The Young Carthaginian
  Bonnie Prince Charlie
  For the Temple
  The Lion of St. Mark
  Captain Bayley's Heir
  By Pike and Dyke
  With Lee in Virginia
  By England's Aid
  By Right of Conquest
  The Dash for Khartoum
  Redskin and Cowboy
  Beric the Briton
  In Greek Waters
  St. Bartholomew's Eve
  Through the Sikh War
  Wulf the Saxon
  When London Burned
  A Knight of the White Cross
  The Tiger of Mysore
  With Cochrane the Dauntless
  At Agincourt
  With Moore at Corunna
  With Frederick the Great
  Under Wellington's Command
  Both Sides the Border
  Won by the Sword
  A Roving Commission
  In the Irish Brigade
  At the Point of the Bayonet
  With Kitchener in the Soudan
  With the British Legion
  Through Three Campaigns
  With the Allies to Pekin
  By Conduct and Courage
5s. novels, now at 3s.6d.
  Facing Death
  By Sheer Pluck
  St. George for England
  The Dragon and the Raven
  For Name and Fame

  With Wolfe in Canada
  The Bravest of the Brave
  A Final Reckoning
  Orange and Green
  In the Reign of Terror
  The Cat of Bubastes
  One of the 28th
  Maori and Settler
  Held Fast for England
  Condemned as a Nihilist
  A Jacobite Exile
  In the Heart of the Rockies
  Through Russian Snows
  On the Irrawaddy
  A March on London
  At Aboukir and Acre
  No Surrender!
  The Treasure of the Incas

CHAMBERS
  Chambers's Continuous Readers
    On the Spanish Main
    The Sole Survivors
    At Duty's Call

CHATTO & WINDUS
  The Piccadilly Novels
    Rujub, the Juggler
    Dorothy's Double
    The Queen's Cup

HENRY
  The Whitefriars Library
    Those Other Animals
  The Random Series
    Those Other Animals

THE 'JOINT VENTURE',
HENRY FROWDE / HODDER &
STOUGHTON
(later OXFORD UNIVERSITY PRESS)
  The Boy's New Library
    The Young Franc-Tireurs
    In Times of Peril
    Friends, though Divided
  The Boys' New 7d. Net Library
  later renamed:
  The Boy's Pocket Library
    Out on the Pampas
    The Young Buglers

APPENDIX VI

CONTRACTS & AGREEMENTS
WITH PUBLISHERS

GENERAL NOTES

Only a few of Henty's contracts are still in existence, many having disappeared with other records of the publishers with whom they were made. Those include Tinsley Brothers and other firms whose businesses did not last for more than a few years. Many publishers' records, including those of Griffith & Farran, were lost during the bombing of London in the second war. The earliest contracts I have been able to find are some made with Sampson Low. But their records are sadly incomplete.

Owners of documents surviving have kindly given me permission to reproduce them, and they are set out below in chronological order. I have included a few notes made in publishers' contract books about Henty's work, and have added some notes of my own where it seemed some explanations might be helpful.

1. SAMPSON LOW AND ROUTLEDGE

(A) HENTY / SAMPSON LOW – The Cornet of Horse

Agreement Book 2.   Folio 85–86.

SPECIAL AGREEMENT

Title of Book: THE CORNET OF HORSE, a Tale of Marlborough's War.

MEMORANDUM of AGREEMENT entered into the Thirtyfirst day of May 1881 BETWEEN Edward Marston, William Henry Low, Samuel Warren Searle, and William John Rivington, trading as "Sampson Low, Marston, Searle and Rivington," of No.188 Fleet Street, London, English, American and Colonial Booksellers and Publishers, hereinafter called "the Publishers," for themselves and their assigns, successors for the time being in their business and firm of the one part, and G.A. Henty Esq. 23 St. Anne's Villas, Notting Hill, hereinafter called "the Author," of the other part.

The Publishers agree to print and publish for the Author the Work entitled "THE CORNET OF HORSE &c" of which he is the Author, and he on his part agrees to cede and assign to them the sole and exclusive right to publish and vend the Work, and all rights to translate or reprint the same during the legal term of copyright, upon the following terms, namely:–

1.   The Author guarantees that the Work is original, and in no way whatever an infringement of any copyright belonging to any other person, and that it contains nothing of a scandalous or libellous character, and the Author, and his executors and administrators, shall and will hold harmless the Publishers from all manner of claims and proceedings which may be made and taken against them on the ground that the Work is such an infringement or contains anything scandalous or libellous.

2.   Sampson Low, Marston, Searle and Rivington are to act as Publishers and sole Wholesale Vendors for Great Britain and Ireland, the British Dominions, the Continent of Europe, and the United States of America.

3.   The Publishers are to pay the Author a royalty of one tenth of the selling price[1] on all copies sold in the regular course of trade up to five thousand copies, and a royalty of fifteen per cent on all copies sold beyond that number, it being understood and agreed that if an Edition is sold in the American market at a specially low price the profit derived from said sale to be equally divided between Author and Publishers. Any copies sold off by auction or otherwise not to be subject to the payment of any royalty.

4.   The plates or moulds already made from text in "UNION JACK" become the property of the Publishers, who will complete the production of the Work.[2]

The Author agrees to pay all Cost of Corrections and Alterations in the proof sheets beyond ten shillings for every sixteen pages of print.

Accounts shall be made up and rendered half-yearly, in July and January, and the balance due to the Author shall be payable on application at the end of six months after such rendering of the account.

This Agreement and all its provisions are to be considered as entered into by the Author with the Publishers and their assigns, successors for the time being in their business and firm.

As witness the hands of the parties:–

(signed)

Witness:
(signed)   R.B. Marston.   Sampson Low, Marston, Searle & Rivington.

Witness:
(signed)   Wm. Judd.   G.A.Henty.

(B) HENTY / SAMPSON LOW – The Young Colonists

Agreement Book 2.   Folio 225–226.

AGREEMENT FOR PURCHASE OF COPYRIGHT.

MEMORANDUM. WHEREAS I have this day sold to Sampson Low, Marston, Searle and Rivington, of No.188 Fleet Street, London, at the price or sum of Seventy

Five Pounds all my Copyright and interest, present and future, vested and contingent or otherwise, of and in "THE YOUNG COLONIST"[3] a tale of the Zulu & Boer Wars, composed by me. AND WHEREAS the said sum of Seventy Five Pounds hath been paid to me by the said Sampson Low, Marston, Searle and Rivington, and for which I have given them a receipt duly stamped. Now in consideration of the premises and such payment to me, I hereby for myself, my executors and administrators, promise and engage to and with the said Sampson Low, Marston, Searle, and Rivington, their executors, administrators, and assigns, at their request and cost, to execute a proper Assignment of my aforesaid Copyright and Interest to the said Sampson Low, Marston, Searle and Rivington, their executors, administrators, or assigns, or as they shall direct; and also myself to pay all cost of corrections and alterations in the proof sheets beyond ten shillings for every sixteen pages of print.

Witness my hand this 24th day of October, in the year of our Lord, One thousand eight hundred and eighty three.

(signed) G.A.Henty.

FORM OF RECEIPT TO BE GIVEN.
Received of Messrs. Sampson Low, Marston, Searle and Rivington, the sum of Seventy five pounds for the absolute sale of all my Copyright and Interest, present and future, vested and contingent or otherwise, of and in "THE YOUNG COLONIST" composed by me.

(C) SAMPSON LOW / ROUTLEDGE – The Young Colonists

Agreement Book 2.   Folio 259–260.

AGREEMENT FOR PURCHASE OF COPYRIGHT.

MEMORANDUM. WHEREAS we Sampson Low, Marston, Searle and Rivington, of No.188 Fleet Street, London have this day sold to Messrs. George Routledge & Sons[4] of Broadway, London at the price or sum of two hundred and fifty pounds all our Copyright and interest, present and future, vested and contingent or otherwise, of and in the book, Illustrations, and stereotype plates of the Young Colonists composed by G.A.Henty. AND WHEREAS the said sum of two hundred and fifty pounds hath been this day paid to us by the said George Routledge & Sons and for which we have given them a receipt duly stamped. Now in consideration of the premises and such payment to us we hereby for ourselves and our successors promise and engage to and with the said George Routledge and Sons and their successors, at their request and cost, to execute a proper Assignment of our aforesaid Copyright and Interest to the said George Routledge and Sons or their successors, or as they shall direct. Witness our hand the 27th day of March, in the year of our Lord, One thousand eight hundred and eighty four.

(signed) Sampson Low, Marston, Searle & Rivington.

FORM OF RECEIPT TO BE GIVEN.

Received of Messrs. George Routledge & Sons an acceptance for the sum of two hundred and fifty pounds for the absolute sale of all our Copyright and Interest present and future, vested and contingent or otherwise, of and in THE YOUNG COLONISTS with the Illustrations, Electros & stereotype plates, composed by G.A.Henty.

(signed) Sampson Low & Co.

(D) HENTY / SAMPSON LOW – A Hidden Foe

Agreement Book 3.   Folio 135–136.

SPECIAL AGREEMENT.

Title of Book: THE HIDDEN FOE.[5]

MEMORANDUM of AGREEMENT entered into the Twentyfirst day of January 1891 BETWEEN Edward Marston as Agent for and on behalf of Sampson Low, Marston, Searle and Rivington, Limited, of St. Dunstan's House, Fetter Lane, Fleet Street, London, English, American, and Colonial Booksellers and Publishers, hereinafter called "the Publishers," which term when requisite is to include their successors and assigns, of the one part, and G.A. Henty, Ravenna Road, Putney, hereinafter called "the Author," which term when requisite is to include his executors, administrators or assigns, of the other part.

1.   The Publishers agree to manufacture and publish at their own risk and expense the Work entitled "THE HIDDEN FOE" of which the said G.A. Henty is the Author.

2.   The Author guarantees that the work is original, and in no way whatever an infringement of any copyright belonging to any other person, and that it contains nothing of a libellous or scandalous character, and the Author shall and will hold harmless the Publishers from all manner of claims and proceedings which may be made and taken against them on the ground that the Work is such an infringement or contains anything scandalous or libellous, and the Publishers shall be entitled to retain and reimburse themselves out of the Author's share all costs and expenses incurred by the Publishers in protecting the copyright of the Work, or incurred otherwise with reference to, or in consequence of, its publication.

3.   The Author agrees that the Publishers have the exclusive right during the legal term of copyright to publish the Work in any part of the world, and will not during such term employ any other publisher or publishers for the purpose, and

hereby empowers the Publishers to arrange for any translation or reprint of it in such manner as, and wheresoever, they shall from time to time think fit.

    4.   The Publishers agree to pay to the said Author the sum of sixty pounds (£60) on account of the two or three volume edition: a royalty of ten per cent on the published price of the six shilling edition; and a royalty of ten per cent on the net proceeds of popular editions: no royalty to be paid on copies which it may be necessary to sell off as a remainder or otherwise.

    7.[6]   Accounts shall be made up and rendered half-yearly, in August and February, and the proceeds to which the Author is entitled shall be payable on application at the end of six months after such rendering of the account.

    8.   The Author agrees to pay personally all cost of corrections and alterations in the proof sheets beyond ten shillings for every sixteen pages of print. As witness the hands of the parties:–

(signed) G.A. Henty.

Witness

(signed) P. Griffiths.   21 January 1891.

(E) HENTY / SAMPSON LOW – Bevis

Agreement Book 2.   Folio 161–162.

Bevis.[7]

Received 13/7/04. and sent to Duckworth's. H.M.

(F) HENTY / SAMPSON LOW – A Hidden Foe

Agreement Book 3.   Folio 135–136.

Henty "Hidden Treasure[8]"

taken out 9/8/04. H.W.

(G) HENTY'S EXECUTOR / SAMPSON LOW – (3 titles)

Agreement Book 8.   Folio 35–36.

G.A. Henty deceased.

John Shearman Esq.[9] of 4 Serjeant's Inn, Fleet Street, E.C.4 surviving[10] Executor of the above named deceased in consideration of the sum of £60 (Sixty pounds) the receipt of which he hereby acknowledges assigns to Messrs. Sampson Low Marston

& Co. Ltd. of Overy House 100 Southwark Street, London S.E.1 all the copyright and translation, serial, dramatic, cinematograph rights and any other irght [*sic*] or rights that is the Author's in and about the works entitled:–

"Cornet of Horse"[11]
"Winning his Spurs"
"Hidden Foe"

Dated this 17th day of February One thousand nine hundred and twenty three.

(signed)   John Shearman.

Witness to the signature of
John Shearman Esq.[12]

(signed)   F.M.Roberts,
4 Serjeant's Inn, London, E.C.4.
Solicitor's Clerk.

And it is certified that the transaction hereby effected does not form part of a larger transaction or a series of transactions in receipt of which the amount or value or the aggregate amount or value of the consideration of the property transferred exceeds Five Hundred Pounds.

(signed)   John Shearman.

Agreement Book 8.   Folio 35–36.

No.94.   15th February 1923.

G.A. Henty deceased.

Received of Messrs. Sampson Low, Marston & Co. Ltd. the sum of Sixty pounds for the remaining rights in "Cornet of Horse," "Winning his Spurs" and "Hidden Fox".[13]
£60.

(signed)   J.Shearman.
Executor of the above-named
deceased.

2. BLACKIE & SON

(A) HENTY / BLACKIE & SON

Literary Letter-Book No.2.   Page 892.

Agreement between Blackie & Son and Geo. A. Henty for writing juvenile books – Expires April 1892.

George A.Henty Esq
102 Upper Richmond Road
Putney, London, S.W.

Dear Sir

In order that the agreement between us may be properly recorded we now enumerate the various points which have been agreed to between us:–

1st.   That for a period of five years from this date, that is to say until April 1892, Mr. George A. Henty undertakes to write books designed for young people for Messrs. Blackie & Son only, and in consideration of this Messrs. Blackie & Son agree to accept from Mr. Henty each year three (3) Books written for young people:– Each Book to contain from 90 to 120,000 words, and Messrs. Blackie shall pay Mr. Henty for each of these books the sum of £100 (Hundred pounds sterling). Mr. Henty undertakes to supply the complete manuscript copy for these Books not later than the 30th of April in each year.

2nd.   That by mutual agreement arrangements may be made to issue these stories through Newspapers or other Periodicals, but not more than two (2) of these stories shall be so issued in one year, and no story shall be started in any Periodical except on the distinct understanding that it may be published complete in book form in the following October whether completed in the Periodical or not. And no story shall be started in any periodical between the months of July and January.

3rd.   Whatever sum is paid for the copyright of such stories by the proprietors of the periodicals in which they are to be published shall be equally divided between Messrs. Blackie & Son and Mr. Henty provided always that should more than £100 (hundred pounds stg) be received for any one story so issued: Messrs. Blackie shall not be entitled to more than £50 (Fifty pounds stg) for their share.

4th.   That before any arrangement is made with a Periodical or Newspaper by Messrs. Blackie & Son for the publication of one of these stories in a Newspaper or Periodical, Mr. Henty's consent to that arrangement must be obtained in writing, and similarly before Mr. Henty makes any such arrangement Messrs. Blackie & Son's consent must be obtained in writing.

5th.   All arrangements made to be finally carried out by Messrs. Blackie & Son, that is to say Messrs. Blackie & Son to make the necessary business arrangements and to receive the payments from the Periodicals or Newspapers.

6th.   It shall be a condition in any arrangement made with a Newspaper or Periodical that proper acknowledgement is made that the story is published by arrangement with Messrs. Blackie & Son (This is necessary to make the condition in Clause 1 of any good, that is to say that Mr. Henty writes these stories of a juvenile class for Messrs. Blackie & Son only).

7th.   That in the event of International Copyright coming into force between this country and America during the subsistence of this agreement Messrs. Blackie & Son undertake to pay Mr. Henty one half of what sums they may receive for copyright in the U.S.A.

We trust that this mode of recording the agreement is satisfactory.

We are, Dear Sir,
Yours truly   (signed) Blackie & Son.

(B) HENTY / BLACKIE & SON

Memorandum.   See Letter, 5th March 1889. (Private Letter Book No.____).

Arrangement made whereby Mr Henty gets Royalty of 2d. per copy on all of 6/– series sold to America (United States) and 1 1/2d. per copy on all 5/– books sold there.

(C) HENTY / BLACKIE & SON

Memorandum of Agreement

entered into this Fifth day of September Eighteen hundred and ninety one between Messrs. Blackie and Son, Limited, Glasgow (hereinafter called the said firm) and Mr. G.A.Henty, 6 Ravenna Road, Putney, London, (hereinafter called the said author).

Whereby it is agreed as follows:-

I.   That this agreement cancels all previous agreements.
II.   That this agreement shall subsist for seven years and from year to year thereafter.
III.   That the said author undertakes to write books designed for young people for the said firm only.
IV.   That in consideration of this the said firm agrees to accept from the said author each year three books written for young people, each book to contain from

100,000 (one hundred thousand) to 140,000 (one hundred and forty thousand) words.

V. That copyright at home and abroad of the said books shall belong to the said firm.

VI. That the said firm shall pay to the said author (1) the sum of £150:–:– (One hundred and fifty pounds sterling) for each of the three books referred to in Clause IV, and (2) after the sale of 5000 (five thousand) copies of each of the said books a Royalty (during the duration of the copyright) of 3½d (three and a half pence) per copy if the book is published at a retail price of 6/– (six shillings) and 3d (threepence) per copy if the book is published at a retail price of 5/– (five shillings).

VII. That the said firm shall pay to the said author (during the duration of copyright) (1) on the sales made on and after 31st August 1891, a Royalty of 3½d (three and a half pence) per copy of the following books which are published at a retail price of 6/– (six shillings) namely:

> Under Drake's Flag
> With Clive in India
> In Freedom's Cause
> True to the Old Flag
> The Lion of St Mark
> With Wolfe in Canada
> Bonnie Prince Charlie
> The Lion of the North

and a Royalty of 3d (threepence) per copy on the sales made on and after 31 August 1891 of the following books published at a retail price of 5/– (five shillings) namely:

> Facing Death
> By Sheer Pluck
> St George for England
> The Dragon and Raven [*sic*]
> For Name and Fame
> The Bravest of the Brave
> A Final Reckoning
> In the Reign of Terror
> One of the 28th

and (2) they shall pay a Royalty of 3½d (three and a half pence) per copy on the following books published at a retail price of 6/– (six shillings) after 5000 (five thousand) copies of each book have been sold:

> Through the Fray
> The Young Carthaginian
> For the Temple

> Captain Bayley's Heir
> With Lee in Virginia
> By Pike and Dyke
> By England's Aid
> By Right of Conquest
> A Dash for Khartoum [*sic*]
> Redskin and Cowboy

and a Royalty of 3d (threepence) per copy after a sale of 5000 (five thousand) has been made of each of the following books published at a retail price of 5/– (five shillings), namely:

> Orange and Green
> The Cat of Bubastes
> Maori and Settler
> Held Fast for England

VIII. That by mutual agreement arrangements may be made, if it can be done without interfering with American copyright, to issue these stories through newspapers or other periodicals, but not more than two shall be so issued in any one year, and no story shall be started in any periodical except on the distinct understanding that it may be published complete in book form in the following October,[14] whether completed in the periodical or not.

IX. Whatever sum is received for issuing such stories in such a way shall be equally divided between the said author and the said firm.

X. That it shall be in the power of the said author to make such arrangements as he thinks fit for the Right of Translation into Foreign Languages of any of his books published by the said firm and such sums as may be obtained for these rights shall be divided equally between the said author and the said firm.

XI. That the said firm agree to pay the said author one half of any Royalty that is obtained from the sales of such books as are copyrighted in the United States of America.

XII. That on sales of the 6/– (six shilling) books or 5/– (five shilling) books as are exported in quires or in bound copies to the United States of America by the said firm, the said author is to receive on 6/– (six shilling) books the sum of 2d (twopence) per copy, and on 5/– (five shilling) books the sum of 1½d (one and a halfpence) per copy, so long as the present price is obtained from the American publisher.

XIII. That the Royalty Statements be made up to the 31st August in each year and submitted to the said author within one month thereafter when the Royalty shall be paid.

XIV. That the Royalty Statements on American Sales be made up at such dates as shall be agreed upon with the American publisher, and the Royalty to be paid when payment has been made by the American publisher.

XV. That the Royalties referred to in Clauses VI, VII, and XII shall only be paid so long as the books are sold at the retail prices of 6/– (six shillings) and 5/– (five shillings) respectively, and in the event of a reduction in the retail price of any book a proportionate reduction in the rate of Royalty shall be made.

XVI. That the publishers shall have the right of deciding when a book should be issued at a lower price. As witness the hands of the said Parties hereto.

> (signed)   G.A. Henty
>
> Witness to the signature of G.A. Henty
> (signed)   J.P. Griffith
> 4 Lawn Terrace, Wandsworth.
>
> For Blackie & Son, Limited
>
> (signed)   J. Alexander Blackie Director.
>
> (signed)   W. Gladstone Witness
> 17 Stanhope Street, Glasgow.

(D) NOTE

A letter in the Blackie archives, from Henty to Alexander Blackie, acknowledges with gratitude a 'considerable increase' in Henty's royalty terms in September 1896. Details are not known but the letter is quoted at Appendix II, Part 5, Note 81.

APPENDIX VII

BLACKIE'S RECORDED PUBLICATION DATES AND SALES FIGURES

1. BLACKIE'S RECORDED PUBLICATION DATES

Title	Publication date	Title-page date
Facing Death	**31 May 1882**	**1882, 1883**
Under Drake's Flag	31 August 1882	1883
With Clive in India	**24 September 1883**	**1884**
By Sheer Pluck	28 September 1883	1884
In Freedom's Cause	**16 July 1884**	**1885**
True to the Old Flag	2 August 1884	1885
St. George for England	**27 August 1884**	**1885**
The Dragon and the Raven	2 May 1885	1886
For Name and Fame	**2 May 1885**	**1886**
The Lion of the North	19 August 1885	1886
Through the Fray	**5 September 1885**	**1886**
Yarns on the Beach	15 September 1885	1886
With Wolfe in Canada	**18 May 1886**	**1887**
The Bravest of the Brave	1 June 1886	1887
A Final Reckoning	**8 June 1886**	**1887**
The Young Carthaginian	8 June 1886	1887
Bonnie Prince Charlie	**6 June 1887**	**1888**
Orange and Green	2 July 1887	1888
In the Reign of Terror	**8 July 1887**	**1888**
Sturdy and Strong	27 July 1887	1888
For the Temple	**19 August 1887**	**1888**
The Sovereign Reader	26 August 1887	–
The Lion of St. Mark	**29 February 1888**	**1889**
Captain Bayley's Heir	15 August 1888	1889
The Cat of Bubastes	**3 September 1888**	**1889**
Tales of Daring and Danger	20 July 1889	1890
By Pike and Dyke	**7 August 1889**	**1890**
One of the 28th	8 August 1889	1890
With Lee in Virginia	**8 August 1889**	**1890**
By England's Aid	14 June 1890	1891
A Chapter of Adventures	**14 June 1890**	**1891**
Maori and Settler	15 July 1890	1891
By Right of Conquest	**3 October 1890**	**1891**

Title	Publication date	Title-page date
The Dash for Khartoum	14 July 1891	1892
Redskin and Cow-boy	**14 July 1891**	**1892**
Held Fast for England	1 August 1891	1892
Condemned as a Nihilist	**21 June 1892**	**1893**
Beric the Briton	22 June 1892	1893
In Greek Waters	**29 June 1892**	**1893**
A Jacobite Exile	13 June 1893	1894
St. Bartholomew's Eve	**13 June 1893**	**1894**
Through the Sikh War	13 June 1893	1894
Wulf the Saxon	**8 May 1894**	**1895**
In the Heart of the Rockies	19 July 1894	1895
When London Burned	**4 August 1894**	**1895**
A Knight of the White Cross	13 June 1895	1896
Through Russian Snows	**14 August 1895**	**1896**
The Tiger of Mysore	12 September 1895	1896
With Cochrane the Dauntless	**9 June 1896**	**1897**
At Agincourt	27 June 1896	1897
The Young Colonists	**4 August 1896**	**1897**
On the Irrawaddy	13 August 1896	1897
With Moore at Corunna	**22 May 1897**	**1898**
A March on London	15 June 1897	1898
With Frederick the Great	**26 August 1897**	**1898**
Under Wellington's Command	2 June 1898	1899
Both Sides the Border	**28 June 1898**	**1899**
At Aboukir and Acre	28 July 1898	1899
Won by the Sword	**1 June 1899**	**1900**
A Roving Commission	11 July 1899	1900
No Surrender!	**24 August 1899**	**1900**
In the Irish Brigade	23 May 1900	1901
With Buller in Natal	**13 July 1900**	**1901**
Out with Garibaldi	15 August 1900	1901
Do Your Duty	**18 August 1900**	**–**
At the Point of the Bayonet	6 April 1901	1902
Bears and Dacoits & other Stories	**28 May 1901**	**–**
To Herat and Cabul	28 June 1901	1902
With Roberts to Pretoria	**15 August 1901**	**1902**
Wih Kitchener in the Soudan	17 May 1902	1903
The Treasure of the Incas	**23 June 1902**	**1903**
In the Hands of the Cave Dwellers	18 July 1902	–
With the British Legion	**2 August 1902**	**1903**
Through Three Campaigns	6 May 1903	1904
With the Allies to Pekin	**29 May 1903**	**1904**
By Conduct and Courage	15 July 1904	1905
In the Hands of the Malays	**9 September 1904**	**1905**
A Soldier's Daughter	24 June 1905	1906
John Hawke's Fortune	**14 September 1906**	**–**

Notes

1. These publication dates were kindly supplied by Blackie & Son, from their records.

2. Blackie's practice of printing on first-edition title pages the date of the year following that of actual publication was one followed by many publishers. Blackie kept to this policy even when a book was published as early in the year as February, see *The Lion of St. Mark*, above. There has been confusion in the minds of many booksellers and writers who have not understood the practice, and have consequently believed that some American editions of Henty preceded the first Blackie issues. In fact the only Henty title to be published in the United States before the appearance of its British first edition is *In the Hands of the Cave Dwellers*: it was issued in 1900 by Harper & Brothers, New York, and in 1903 by Blackie & Son. See Introduction, p.xiv, and especially Appendix VI, Note 14.

3. The lack of publication dates on some title pages is explained in each case in the appropriate entry in §1, as is the recording of two dates for *Facing Death*.

2. SUMMARISED ANALYSIS OF BLACKIE SALES OF HENTY'S NOVELS

FROM PUBLICATION DATES TO 31 AUGUST 1917 (when records cease)

SIX-SHILLING NOVELS *(see explanatory notes at end of five-shilling novels below)*

Title	Yr 1 sales	Yrs @6s.	Av @6s.	do.ex yr 1	Total @ 6s.	Yrs @ 3s.6d.	3s.6d. sales	Total sales
Under Drake's Flag	**2,094**	**27**	**720**	**667**	**19,577**	**9**	**10,216**	**29,793**
With Clive in India	2,773	23	964	882	22,427	12	15,811	38,238
In Freedom's Cause	**2,698**	**21**	**524**	**415**	**11,006**	**13**	**12,771**	**23,777**
True to the Old Flag	2,528	28	494	419	13,859	6	3,633	17,492
The Lion of the North	**2,770**	**20**	**550**	**433**	**11,019**	**13**	**8,787**	**19,806**
Through the Fray	2,631	17	458	322	7,942	16	11,174	19,116
With Wolfe in Canada	**2,719**	**31**	**570**	**498**	**17,662**			**17,662**
The Young Carthaginian	2,561	19	475	359	9,159	13	6,732	15,891
Bonnie Prince Charlie	**3,298**	**30**	**559**	**464**	**16,759**	*		**16,759**
For the Temple	2,694	16	538	394	8,762	15	9,574	18,336
The Lion of St. Mark	**3,831**	**14**	**773**	**538**	**11,094**	**16**	**14,987**	**26,081**
Captain Bayley's Heir	3,214	16	541	363	8,815	4	8,615	17,430
By Pike and Dyke	**3,952**	**15**	**607**	**368**	**9,194**	**14**	**11,866**	**21,060**
With Lee in Virginia	4,057	29	402	271	11,652			11,652
By England's Aid	**4,270**	**11**	**876**	**537**	**9,757**	**15**	**10,295**	**20,052**
By Right of Conquest	3,780	19	521	340	9,966	8	4,404	14,370
The Dash for Khartoum	**6,465**	**27**	**868**	**653**	**23,432**			**23,432**

*Bonnie Prince Charlie was issued in the 3s.6d. 'New and Popular Edition' after the end of August, 1917: no sales figures for it at that price are available.

Title	Yr 1 sales	Yrs @6s.	Av @6s.	do.ex yr 1	Total @ 6s.	Yrs @ 3s.6d.	3s.6d. sales	Total sales
Redskin and Cow-boy	5,880	26	941	744	24,470			24,470
Beric the Briton	**7,260**	**25**	**805**	**536**	**20,122**			**20,122**
In Greek Waters	5,950	18	570	254	10,260	8	2,904	13,164
St. Bartholomew's Eve	**7,345**	**25**	**584**	**302**	**14,701**	7	**4,148**	**18,849**
Through the Sikh War	6,725	18	722	369	13,101	6	3,606	16,707
Wulf the Saxon	**8,090**	**23**	**737**	**403**	**16,962**			**16,962**
When London Burned	9,075	23	786	409	18,071			18,071
A Knight of the White Cross	**9,200**	**18**	**805**	**312**	**14,498**	4	**2,208**	**16,706**
The Tiger of Mysore	9,400	18	906	407	16,333	4	2,691	19,024
With Cochrane the Dauntless	**9,180**	**12**	**1,044**	**305**	**12,536**	9	**5,356**	**17,892**
At Agincourt	9,440	16	900	330	14,399	5	3,794	18,193
With Moore at Corunna	**9,150**	**11**	**1,121**	**318**	**12,395**	9	**6,535**	**18,930**
With Frederick the Great	8,990	11	1,034	239	11,403	9	5,558	16,961
Under Wellington's Command	**10,566**	**8**	**1,780**	**524**	**14,275**	11	**12,262**	**26,537**
Both Sides the Border	8,227	8	1,268	274	18,167	11	*8,805	26,972
Won by the Sword	**9,075**	**18**	**664**	**169**	**11,952**			**11,952**
A Roving Commission	7,694	18	543	122	9,771			9,771
In the Irish Brigade	**7,655**	**14**	**712**	**178**	**9,984**	3	**1,805**	**11,789**
With Buller in Natal	17,342	17	1,518	529	25,808			25,808
At the Point of the Bayonet	**7,905**	**12**	**843**	**201**	**10,130**	4	**2,894**	**13,024**
With Roberts to Pretoria	15,433	17	1,396	519	23,731			23,731
With Kitchener in the Soudan	**12,664**	**14**	**1,257**	**380**	**17,680**	1	**2,229**	**19,909**
With the British Legion	7,656	15	606	103	9,095			9,095
Through Three Campaigns	**9,013**	**9**	**1,172**	**192**	**10,554**	5	**2,778**	**13,332**
With the Allies to Pekin	8,446	14	770	180	10,781			10,781
By Conduct and Courage	**10,340**	**13**	**1,007**	**229**	**13,090**			**13,090**

*This figure includes 1108 copies which were sold to the London County Council as a 2s.6d. book. It is noted in Blackie's sales records without comment: possibly the book was a set subject for certain schools or examinations, and supplied for that purpose at a special discount (see *Both Sides the Border*, §1, 84.3, Note 2).

FIVE-SHILLING NOVELS

Title	Yr 1 sales	Yrs @5s.	Av @5s.	do.ex yr 1	Total @ 5s.	Yrs @ 3s.6d.	3s.6d. sales	Total sales
Facing Death	**2,162**	**25**	**802**	**745**	**20,045**	10	**8,564**	**28,609**
By Sheer Pluck	2,177	34	712	667	24,199			24,199
St. George for England	**2,650**	**32**	**644**	**579**	**20,629**	1	**1,498**	**22,127**
The Dragon and the Raven	2,628	22	509	408	11,282	10	6,414	17,696
For Name and Fame	**2,798**	**32**	**556**	**484**	**17,801**			**17,801**

Title	Yr 1 sales	Yrs @5s.	Av @5s.	do.ex yr 1	Total @ 5s.	Yrs @ 3s.6d.	3s.6d. sales	Total sales
The Bravest of the Brave	2,392	28	477	406	13,354	3	2,012	15,366
A Final Reckoning	**2,445**	**23**	**553**	**467**	**12,722**	**8**	**4,939**	**17,661**
Orange and Green	2,417	22	409	313	9,076	8	3,642	12,718
In the Reign of Terror	**2,690**	**30**	**575**	**502**	**17,246**	*		**17,246**
The Cat of Bubastes	3,529	19	552	387	10,580	10	4,738	15,318
One of the 28th	**4,581**	**18**	**947**	**733**	**17,310**	**10**	**8,429**	**25,739**
Maori and Settler	3,910	20	586	411	11,786	7	3,942	15,728
Held Fast for England	**5,880**	**26**	**775**	**570**	**20,137**			**20,137**
Condemned as a Nihilist	6,370	14	987	573	14,136	11	8,013	22,149
A Jacobite Exile	**5,590**	**15**	**633**	**279**	**9,576**	**9**	**2,061**	**11,637**
In the Heart of the Rockies	7,375	23	765	465	17,604			17,604
Through Russian Snows	**10,090**	**20**	**1,018**	**540**	**20,357**	**2**	**2,262**	**22,619**
On the Irrawaddy	8,415	15	769	223	11,607	6	3,006	14,613
A March on London	**8,870**	**14**	**888**	**274**	**12,556**	**6**	**3,117**	**15,673**
At Aboukir and Acre	8,140	17	650	182	11,047	2	1,343	12,390
No Surrender!	**7,809**	**18**	**645**	**224**	**11,609**			**11,609**
Out with Garibaldi	6,524	17	524	149	8,916			8,916
To Herat and Cabul	**7,033**	**16**	**572**	**142**	**9,152**			**9,152**
The Treasure of the Incas	7,477	15	754	274	11,307			11,307

In the Reign of Terror was issued in the 3s.6d. 'New and Popular Edition' after the end of August, 1917: no sales figures for it at that price are available.

Notes

1. All the figures shown above are taken from the archive of Blackie & Son.

2. An explanation of the eight columns shown in these tables follows:

(i)   *Yr 1 sales:* indicates the number of copies sold in the first year of publication and includes pre-publication orders from booksellers. At that stage the books had not been reviewed, and pre-publication orders were based on salesmen's recommendations or on Henty's established reputation. Thus they are sometimes unexpectedly large for books that later sold comparatively slowly.

(ii)   *Yrs @6s. or Yrs @5s.:* Shows the number of years during which the book was sold in its original first-edition format. In no case are figures available beyond the end of August 1917, when Blackie's records cease.

(iii)   *Av @6s. or Av @5s.:* Shows the annual average number of copies sold during the period indicated in the second column.

(iv)   *do. ex yr 1:* Indicates the average annual sales during the same period but omitting the first year of publication (and therefore also omitting the booksellers' pre-publication orders).

(v)   *Total @ 6s. or Total @ 5s.:* Shows the total number of copies sold at the original publication price during the years given in column (ii).

(vi)   *Yrs @ 3s.6d.:* Indicates the number of years, up to the end of August 1917, during which the titles were sold in the 'New and Popular Edition' at 3s.6d. In most cases, they continued to sell for a few years after 1917, but 23 titles were never issued in this edition at all.

(vii)   *3s.6d. sales:* Total sales in the 3s.6d. edition up to 31 August 1917.

(viii)   *Total sales:* Combined total sales in both editions up to 31 August 1917.

3. Some additional details are given in Notes under the title of each book in §1.

NOTES TO THE APPENDICES

NOTES TO APPENDIX I

1. F.J. Harvey Darton, *Children's Books in England*, pp.310–311.
2. ditto, p.311 (written in 1932). In America, seventeen years later, Louis Coffin wrote: 'Henty's faults and limitations are not inconsiderable', but, after enumerating those he detected, added, 'Nevertheless, his purpose to do justice to all sides is always apparent and generally successful, and there is not one of his tales that does not leave a boy, or a man with something of the boy left in him, better off for having read it'. *Bulletin of Bibliography*, Vol.19, No.9, 1949, p.243.
3. Bernard Darwin (anonymously), in *Fourth Leaders from The Times*, 1950, p.62.
4. Henty's own account, 'Writing Books for Boys', was in *Answers*, 18 December 1902. Raymond Blathwayt's 'How Boys' Books are Written' was one of numerous reported interviews, in *Great Thoughts from Master Minds*, in No.979, 4 October 1902, pp.8–9. The periodical was widely read by the clergy, and in the 1890s had a circulation of some 50,000. Blathwayt, ordained in the Church, and one of the most experienced interviewers of his time, received among other letters of appreciation one from J.A. Froude, the historian, congratulating him on an interview with an old friend, the eminent biologist Sir Richard Owen: 'You have hit him off to the life, and I could almost imagine I was sitting in the room and talking to him'. Quoted by Christopher Silvester, *The Penguin Book of Interviews*, p.4.
5. Edmund Downey, *Twenty Years Ago*, pp.116–117.
6. G.A. Henty, Editor of the *Union Jack*, Vol.I, No.21, 20 May 1880, p.336. In a blurb for *Under Drake's Flag* some three years later, Blackie wrote: 'The historical portion of the story is absolutely to be relied upon, but this, although very useful to lads, will perhaps be less attractive than the great variety of exciting adventure through which the young adventurers pass in the course of their voyages'.
7. Anon., 'Boys' Writers of Today' in *Chums*, Vol.II, No.60, 1 November 1893, p.159.
8. A.J.P. Taylor, 'Prince of Storytellers' (review of Guy Arnold's *Held Fast for England*, see Note 19 below) in the *Observer*, 13 April 1980.
9. Godfrey Davies, 'G.A. Henty and History' in *The Huntington Library Quarterly*, Vol.XVIII, No.2, February 1955.
10. A.J.P. Taylor, 'Prince of Storytellers' in the *Observer*, 13 April 1980.
11. It is doubtful whether Henty's amanuenses worked in longhand, as implied by Downey, especially in view of the number of words he claimed to dictate in a day. An interviewer reported Henty, in *The Gem*, issue for 16 December 1899, p.209, as saying: ' I tell

my stories – dictate them to my Secretary. He takes them in shorthand, transcribes them, and reads them to me. Thus I criticise them, and correct them if necessary'.

12. G.A. Henty, 'Writing Books for Boys', published posthumously in *Answers*, 18 December 1902. '*The Destruction of Jerusalem*' was a slip for *For the Temple*.

13. G. Manville Fenn, *George Alfred Henty, The Story of an Active Life*, 1907, p.328. On 4 August 1928 a notice was printed in *The Clique*, a booksellers' trade paper, from which the following is extracted: 'AN APPEAL. Many of our London readers may know Mr. J. Pettit Griffith who has for many years carried on a bookselling business at Brixton ... Mr. Griffith, we are sorry to say, has had nothing but illnesses and financial losses for several years past, and we know personally that his is a very deserving case.' Then is quoted part of the *D.N.B.* entry for his father, W.P. Griffith, F.S.A., R.I.B.A., which ends 'Griffith died a poor man at Highbury, 11 September 1884'. The appeal continues: 'his eldest son, John Pettit Griffith, who has been admitted as an A.R.I.B.A., in 1881 had already been obliged to abandon his profession for a quicker way of making a living. In 1881 he joined the late George Henty as his secretary, and continued to serve him for twenty years until his death; among other work making notes for the historical details of many of his long series of stories ...'. At the end of the appeal is a list of subscribers to date. It includes Walter Blackie, E.W. Marston, and the Rt.Hon. David Lloyd George.

14. Anon., 'Boys' Writers of Today' in *Chums*, Vol.II, No.60, 1 November 1893, p.159. Pete Martin's papers collected for a projected Life of Henty, now in the Lilly Library at Indiana University, include an account of a meeting in 1951 between Miss Betty Worlidge (working

for Martin) and the widowed Mrs Griffith. She had married Griffith as his second wife about 1893, and mentioned, during a long and chatty interview, that she remembered the sound of his typewriter in Lavender Gardens during her courting days. So Henty's books were being sent to Blackie as typescripts rather than as manuscripts by then. Henty's only reference to a typewriter (the word in those days meant the typist more often than the machine) was in the *Answers* article (Note 4 above).

15. An anonymous obituarist in *The Athenaeum*, No.3917, 22 November 1902, p.683, reported that after the Crimean campaign 'he acted for a time as a corrector of the press', before joining the staff of the *Standard*.

16. David Gunby, 'Maori and Settler' in *The Henty Society Bulletin*, No.6, December 1978, pp.3–6. David Gunby teaches English Literature at the University of Canterbury, New Zealand. His article first appeared in the first issue of a New Zealand literary quarterly, *Islands*, Spring, 1972. J.E. Gorst, author of *The Maori King* was born at Preston 1835, and became a Fellow of his Cambridge college at the age of 22. Went to New Zealand on the death of his father, and met his future wife, daughter of a Christchurch cleric; they married in 1890. Gorst was soon involved in New Zealand affairs. Appointed in 1862 Civil Commissioner for the Waikato district; later he founded and edited a newspaper. Back in England he had a highly successful career at the bar and in politics. In 1885 he became Solicitor General, and was knighted. For a time in the 1870s he was Editor of the *Standard* and *Evening Standard*: so Henty's plagiarism in 1890 was of the work of one of his own former Editors (see §3, 222).

17. The Revd Hugh Pruen, 'A Great Imperialist' in *The Henty Society*

Bulletin, No.5, September 1978, pp.8–10.

18. J.S. Bratton, *The Impact of Victorian Children's Fiction*, pp.197–198.

19. Guy Arnold, *Held Fast for England*, p.80.

20. ditto, p.79.

21. C.P. Snow, 'True Grit' (review of Guy Arnold's *Held Fast for England*, see Note 19 above) in the *Financial Times*, 26 April 1980.

22. David Holloway, 'Teaching the Young Idea' (review of Guy Arnold's *Held Fast for England*, see Note 19 above) in the *Daily Telegraph*, 10 April 1980.

23. Eric Stokes, 'From Mexico to Mysore' (review of Guy Arnold's *Held Fast for England*, see Note 19 above) in *The Times Literary Supplement*, 11 April 1980.

24. Vanessa Furse Jackson, *The Poetry of Henry Newbolt*, pp.33–34.

25. J.S. Bratton, *The Impact of Victorian Children's Fiction*, p.198.

26. Plagiarism had been the bane of many writers for a long time. Among them was the illustrious cookery writer, Eliza Acton, whose *Modern Cookery for Private Families* was published in 1845. 'Although plagiarism was practically the rule, it greatly incensed Miss Acton, and she was already complaining bitterly in the 1855 edition, which was almost certainly the one Isabella [Beeton] used: "At the risk of appearing extremely egotistical, I have appended ... *Author's Original Receipt* to many of the contents ... in consequence of the unscrupulous manner in which large portions of my volume have been appropriated". She died in 1859 but she must have turned in her grave when *Household Management* appeared: Isabella had used her book for about a third of her soup recipes, a quarter of her fish dishes, over a score of her sauces, and many other preparations besides, and acknowledged the origin of only two'. Sarah Freeman, *Isabella and Sam*, p.149.

27. Anon., 'Boys' Writers of Today' in *Chums*, Vol.II, No.60, 1 November 1893, p.159.

28. When advertising their first book by Henty, Blackie wrote: '*Facing Death* is a book with a purpose. It is intended to show that a lad who makes up his mind firmly and resolutely that he will rise in life, and is prepared to face toil and ridicule and hardship to carry out his determination, is sure to succeed. The hero ... is a typical British boy, dogged, earnest, generous, and though "shamefaced" to a degree, is ready to face death in the discharge of his duty. His is a character for imitation by boys in every station'.

NOTES TO APPENDIX II

1. Arthur Waugh, *A Hundred Years of Publishing*, p.99.

2. ditto, p.107

3. Michael Sadleir, 'Maxwell, Mary Elizabeth (M.E. Braddon)' in *Dictionary of National Biography*, 1927. Although M.E. Braddon had written some slight works previously this was her first three-volume novel. Brough drew Tinsley's attention to it when it was being serialised, a venture that was attempted twice but never succeeded owing to the failures of two periodicals. The sums offered by Tinsley are hinted at in his *Random Recollections*, but not explicitly divulged, although he admits 'the first agreed price for it was two hundred and fifty pounds' (Vol.II, p.343) and 'after that we gave her five hundred pounds and other handsome presents' (Vol.I, p.57). That may be contrasted with the sums offered for first novels by Tinsley and Sampson Low to other authors including Thomas Hardy (see Part 3. Sampson Low, below). Frank Mumby adds that *Lady Audley's Secret* ran through eight three-volume editions

during its first three months. See Mumby, *Publishing and Bookselling*, p.263.

4. Arthur Waugh, *A Hundred Years of Publishing*, p.107.

5. ditto, p.179.

6. Edmund Downey, *Twenty Years Ago*, p.7. Downey must have heard his version of the story from Edward's brother, William, some years later. In fact there is no evidence now that Edward intended to desert his brother. The firm of J.S.Virtue & Company, printers and publishers, had expanded and formed another publishing firm, Virtue Brothers & Company. They had invested in expensive new machinery, and also lent money to other publishing concerns among their printing customers, largely in order to keep their own business alive. Suddenly, in 1866, the elder brother, George, died at the age of 39, and James, left alone in charge, both managerially and financially, realised he had taken on more than he could cope with. He became desperate to dispose of the publishing business, and made plans to sell it to Edward Tinsley. It seems that when Edward died, two months after George Virtue, he had not informed William, although it is possible Edward had intended that the two businesses should be run together. See Srebrnik, *Alexander Strahan, Victorian Publisher*, pp.88–89.

7. Michael Sadleir, *Trollope, A Bibliography*, p.254.

8. George Moore, *Confessions of a Young Man*, p.171.

9. Anon., 'Is the Novel Moribund?' in *Tinsleys' Magazine*, Vol.XXX, April 1882, p.389.

10. Richard Mullen, *Anthony Trollope*, p.597. The article in *Tinsleys' Magazine* (see Note 9) makes the point more forcibly: 'Perhaps the most serious block to the career of the three-volume novel is the latter-day custom, imported from the other side of the Atlantic, of running serial stories in the newspapers... Before the introduction of this newspaper system, the three-volume rights of a good novel were worth about twice as much as they will fetch today' (p.393).

11. H.R.Tedder, 'Tinsley, William' in *Dictionary of National Biography*, 1909.

12. William Tinsley, *Random Recollections of an Old Publisher*, Vol.I, p.66.

13. Frank Mumby, *Publishing and Bookselling*, p.262.

14. Among them was Edward Marston who inherited from the Low family the firm of Sampson Low, and who became one of Henty's publishers (see Part 3 of this Appendix). He wrote: 'Charles Edward Mudie, the "Colossus" under whose huge legs authors and publishers alike were supposed "to walk and peep about", sometimes, to find for themselves "dishonourable graves", and sometimes great good fortunes, was, in point of fact, *not* a Colossus. On the contrary he was one of the gentlest, meekest, most kindly of human beings... He was an earnest thinker, and he drew a group of thinking men around him by his magnetic influence... I have had many a battle with him when I have taken a new book and he had to subscribe the number he would take; for that number was really a guide for others to follow. He was by no means arbitrary, as one who should say "so many will I take, no more and no less". On the contrary, he was rather fond of arguing the point; and if I have sometimes gone away with a smaller number than I asked him to take, frequently he has taken more than he at first intended'. *After Work*, pp.189–190.

15. Edmund Downey wrote, after Tinsley's death: 'Throughout almost the whole of his publishing career he devoted himself mainly to "the Library business", and, though, during the Sixties and the Seventies he published numerous successful books of travel and biography, the back-bone of "Tinsley Brothers" was the three-volume novel. The three-volume novel was killed early in the Nineties, so that in any event the house of Tinsley would hardly have survived the shock. The head of it would then have been too old to learn a new trade'. *Twenty Years Ago*, p.6.

16. George Moore, *Confessions of a Young Man*, p.171.
17. ditto, p.135.
18. Edmund Downey, *Twenty Years Ago*, p.243.
19. William Tinsley, *Random Recollections of an Old Publisher*, Vol.I, pp.138–139. In Mrs Cashel Hoey's entry in the *Dictionary of National Biography* Elizabeth Lee writes, 'Mrs. Hoey wrote in all eleven novels, dealing for the most part with fashionable society. [Titles then listed]. Mrs. Hoey was also largely responsible for ... five novels which were published under the name of Edmund Yates: of the last work Mrs. Hoey was sole author, and the secret of her authorship was divulged'. Mrs Lee refers to Tinsley's account of the episode, and says nothing to deny the conspiracy to deceive him.
20. ditto, Vol.I, pp.324–325.
21. Edmund Downey, *Twenty Years Ago*, p.247.
22. ditto, pp.215–216.
23. ditto, p.244.
24. ditto, pp.246–247.
25. ditto, p.45.
26. ditto, pp.114–117.
27. William Tinsley, *Random Recollections of an Old Publisher*, Vol.I, pp.96–104.
28. Anon., obituary notice in *The Athenaeum*, No.3917, 22 November 1902, p.684.
29. George Bainton (ed.), *The Art of Authorship*, pp.20–21.
30. A year later, in 1885, Charles Welsh published under the firm's new imprint *A Bookseller of the Last Century*, his biography of the founder of the original business, John Newbery (1713–1767). He also wrote Newbery's entry in the *Dictionary of National Biography*.
31. Eric Quayle, *The Collector's Book of Boys' Stories*, p.104.
32. The correspondence columns also help to give an impression of the qualities of Henty as Editor. His constant exhortations and promises of rewards to readers (e.g. 'I hope that now we are older friends you will ... support the Magazine and aid me in what I can assure you is an arduous and up-hill task. To any lad who shall obtain twelve new subscribers, I will send a copy of my *Seaside Maidens* bound in cloth, and to any who may get three new subscribers I will send my photograph'. Vol.II, No.43, p.48); and his readiness to point out in print a lack of intelligence in some of his readers, reveal an anxious man, often in a negative, pedagogic attitude to his public. Young readers certainly criticised the paper, and it must be said for Henty that he was not afraid to publish those criticisms. But his replies tended to admit weaknesses and to ask, in a mood of self-pity, that readers should understand his own problems and put up with sub-standard results. (e.g. 'Many of my correspondents do not like Jules Verne's story ... I can only say that I bought – at a very high price – the right of publishing this story ... and I was obliged to take what I could get. It has been pointed out to me ... that the details are not always correct, and this I admit. Jules Verne writes too much to be always accurate in detail'. Vol.II, No.53, p.208). He also defended the 'dullness' of his own story, 'In Times of Peril', in an apologetic way (Vol.I, No.21, p.336). Henty had set out in his first issue (Vol.I, No.19, p.289) what he believed to be the qualities of the editor of a boys' magazine, and expressed his obviously genuine pleasure at being 'a boy who

has got his wish' in becoming such an editor. Dartt, commenting on Henty's later editorship of the *Beeton's Boy's Own Magazine*, lists his articles published under the heading 'The Editor's Tables', and remarks 'after reading them the reader may readily see why Henty was not a success as an editor for boys' publications'. (*Dartt*, p.125).

33. F.J.Harvey Darton, *Children's Books in England*, 1982 edition, p.333.

34. John Attenborough, *A Living Memory*, p.51.

35. Peter Sutcliffe, *The Oxford University Press*, p.147.

36. John Attenborough, *A Living Memory*, pp.51-52.

37. ditto, p.82. In a letter to me dated 6 October 1991 John Attenborough wrote: 'I think it is clear that Henry Frowde was not allowed by the Delegates to issue children's books under the O.U.P. imprint; but that the change came when Milford succeeded him'.

38. Blathwayt, *Great Thoughts from Master Minds*, No.982, 15 November 1902, p.57.

39. See *In Battle and Breeze*, §2, 159.1.

40. Quoted in Edward Marston, *After Work*, pp.143–144. There is some confusion about Russell's early novels. According to Gabriel S.Woods's entry for him in the *Dictionary of National Biography* this was his second novel, published in 1877, which 'established his reputation as a graphic writer of sea stories'. His first, *John Holdsworth, Chief Mate*, was published by Tinsley Brothers in 1874 or 1875 (see Tinsley, *Recollections*, Vol.I, p.301), Woods giving the later date and reporting that it at once attracted attention. However, the *Cambridge Bibliography* in a long catalogue of his writings lists a number of earlier three-volume novels published under a pseudonym, 'Sydney Mostyn'.

41. Charles Morgan, *The House of Macmillan*, p.94, records that of five hundred copies printed three hundred and seventy were sold, and that the author lost a third of his outlay. More details of Hardy's dealings with Tinsley are given in Edmund Downey, *Twenty Years Ago*, pp.19–21.

42. Edward Marston, *After Work*, p.187.

43. It has frequently been remarked that Henty's style of writing for adults was not greatly different from that in his boys' books. A number of the novels originally published for adults were later illustrated and dressed up to look much like his books for younger readers. Some examples are: *The Curse of Carne's Hold; A Hidden Foe; Rujub, the Juggler; A Woman of the Commune*; and *Colonel Thorndyke's Secret*. This tendency among several of his publishers worried Henty, mainly because of his contract with Blackie (see Appendix VI). In 1892 he got Tillotsons to stress to Chatto & Windus that the title of a book should be chosen that did not suggest it was written for boys. And five years later he wrote to Chatto specifically about *Colonel Thorndyke's Secret*, extracting a promise in their letter to him of 21 December 1897: 'It shall be described on the title as a "novel" in accordance with your instructions' – a promise that in the event was overlooked. Two years later the matter seems to have built up in his mind: a journalist reporting an interview with Henty about his books, remarks 'How popular his writings are every one is aware, and if one desired proof of this it would be found in the fact that lately some publishers are endeavouring to bring out his novels as Boys' Books; a form of deceit which cannot be too highly reprobated'. (*The Gem*, issue dated 16 December 1899, p.209). The fact remains, of course, that of some of those books more copies were sold in their later form than as adult publications.

44. B. McCall Barbour, 'Boys' Favourite Authors: George Alfred Henty' in *Boys*, Vol.I, No.10, p.155.

45. Edward Marston, *After Work*, p.262. Several of Henty's contemporaries have written of his fiery outbursts of irritation and of embarrassments caused by them. Sir Henry Lucy described him as 'at once the warmest-hearted, shortest-tempered man in the world'. *Sixty Years in the Wilderness*, p.89.

46. Oliver Warner, *Chatto & Windus*, p.12.

47. Michael Sadleir, *Trollope: A Bibliography*, p.315.

48. In November 1871 Tillotson & Son Limited founded the *Bolton Journal*, and shortly afterwards started the 'Newspaper Literature Syndicate'. W.F. Tillotson, son of the founder of the firm, and himself the founder of its newspaper business, 'thought of the value of stories as a help to circulation, especially of the weekly journals, and to help him to meet the cost of them enlisted the support of a number of other newspapers. Ultimately, by a development of this idea, the firm became established as agents for the supply of fiction to newspapers generally' (Frank Singleton, *Tillotsons, 1850–1950*, p.41). It was a profitable venture and offered opportunities to new authors. But it is clear from Chatto & Windus correspondence with Henty and other authors, that Tillotson eventually went further than that, and acted as an active authors' agent. The Newspaper Literature Syndicate was sold by Tillotsons just before the second war.

49. Anon., 'Is the Novel Moribund?', in *Tinsleys' Magazine*, Vol.XXX, April, 1892, p.393.

50. Frank Singleton, *Tillotsons, 1850–1950*, p.42.

51. Letter from G.A. Henty to Tillotson & Son, in Archive of *Bolton Evening News*, Tillotson Fiction Department Records, ZBEN/4/1/104, headed '6 Ravenna Road, Putney. Jany 11 [no year given]'. The letter also contains the following: 'Of course you do not want another book of mine at present, but as a formal matter I think it right to tell you that I have had an offer from Mr. S.G. McPhere of the Associated Literary Press of New York of £150 for a story of 50,000 words, and half profits on the sale in book form in England and the States'. I cannot identify the story: no year is given with the date, 11 January, and there is no published story by Henty of 50,000 words. It was possibly written soon after Tillotsons had published *Colonel Thorndyke's Secret*, which would make it unlikely they would 'want another at present'. If so, the nearest to the description seems to be *In the Hands of the Cave-Dwellers*, published in New York in book form by Harpers in 1900, possibly following newspaper serialisation by the Associated Literary Press. I have not been able to get any confirmation of this possibility, which must in any case be a doubtful starter, as *In the Hands of the Cave-Dwellers* is a story of about 30,000 words. It was serialised in London, in 1900, in the *Boy's Own Paper*.

52. Andrew Chatto, November 1894, quoted in Guinevere L. Griest, *Mudie's Circulating Library*, p.199. Chatto's letters to Smith's and Mudie's, both dated 29 June 1894, virtually agreeing their new terms, are in the Chatto & Windus Archive, MS 2444/28, at folios 880 and 881. He had decided to publish three-volume novels at 15s., but determined to stick out for the full 4s. per volume from the Libraries, without the 'customary' discount, but still counting 25 sets as 24. The 'customary' discount had varied from one publisher to another, according to what they had been able to negotiate with Smith's and Mudie's, and was liable to vary also according to the size of their orders for particular books. Chatto's terms were to be fixed, for three-volume novels at 15s., at a discount of 23.2%.

53. Simon Nowell-Smith, *The House of Cassell*, p.188.

54. Letter from Chatto & Windus to G.A. Henty, 11 September 1896, in the Collection of Publishers' Archives in Reading University Library.

55. ditto, 28 November 1896.

56. ditto, 15 December 1897.

57. Simon Nowell-Smith, *The House of Cassell*, p.188.

58. Richard Mullen, *Anthony Trollope*, p.165.

59. John D. Carter & Michael Sadleir, *Victorian Fiction*, p.7.

60. Guinevere L. Griest, *Mudie's Circulating Library*, p.60.

61. It is sad that the myth about Henty's failure as a novelist should have reached such proportions. Eric Quayle wrote, 'Throughout his career he was never able to make the slightest impact on an adult readership, and one has only to wade through the introductory chapters of any of his novels of serious intent to understand instantly why this was so', and continues with two hundred words on this theme (*The Collector's Book of Boys' Stories*, p.101). Guy Arnold, in his *Held Fast for England*, p.87(n), comes to a different conclusion: 'I have read two of his adult novels, *Rujub the Juggler* and *Gabriel Allen, M.P.* and both have a period charm which I found surprising; Henty's adult novels have, I suspect, been generally underrated'.

62. Agnes A.C. Blackie, *Blackie & Son, 1809–1959*, p.9. Further information about the early history of the business may be found in W.W. Blackie's memoir of his father, *John Blackie, Senior*, whom he describes as 'the sort of man who always succeeded in doing whatever he had to do', and as having admitted 'I was very little at school after I was six years old'.

63. A hundred years later, in 1936, the buildings were sold to another famous Scottish publishing house, to whose premises they were connected by a tunnel. Walter W. Blackie (1860–1953), the younger brother of J. Alexander Blackie, wrote to William Collins: 'This is just to express my sense of satisfaction that the vacated premises of our old works should have passed into the hands of William Collins and Company and not to any outsider. The premises were originally those of Andrew and J.M. Duncan, Printers to the University, and were purchased by my grandfather in 1829. Moreover your great-grandfather and my father were, in those early days, closely associated in many philanthropic and other objects . . . Then my father and your grandfather, Sir William, were friends through life. So altogether I feel that you are the ideal custodians of the ancient printing premises'. (Quoted in David Keir, *The House of Collins*, p.262.) Within another quarter of a century Henty's books for boys were being printed, albeit abridged, by the modern presses of William Collins, the new owners of Blackie's Villafield buildings (see Preface to this book).

64. Agnes A.C. Blackie, *Blackie & Son, 1809–1959*, p.19.

65. ditto, p.21.

66. ditto, p.32.

67. ditto, p.33.

68. ditto, p.38.

69. D. Appleton & Company of New York published in 1898 the first U.S. edition of Henty's *The Queen's Cup*, an adult novel first published in England the previous year by Chatto & Windus.

70. Agnes A.C. Blackie, *Blackie & Son, 1809–1959*, p.38.

71. See Appendix II, Part 1.

72. The Blackie series consisted of 24 novels at 5s. each, and 43 at 6s. each. The fixed formats for the two price ranges came into use gradually but were fully operational by 1885. Most, but not all, were twice re-issued later in cheaper editions (see Appendix V). There were many other titles in smaller formats.

73. The earliest novels had plain edges, but in 1884 Blackie stained the edges of *In Freedom's Cause* (title-page date 1885) a rather yellowish olive-green. That was continued for later novels, the colour becoming nearer to a true olive-green, and eventually it was used for all novels, including the later issues of those published before *In Freedom's Cause*. Eric Quayle mistakenly reports that Blackie started the practice in 1883 with *With Clive in India*: 'It was on this volume that the experiment of coating the outer edges of the leaves of the book with an opaque and shiny varnish was first tried'. (*The Collector's Book of Boys' Stories*, p.105). But nothing resembling varnish could possibly have been used, as it would have caused the leaves to stick together. In fact the effect was achieved with a light water-based stain, brushed or sprayed on the edges of the leaves while the books were very tightly pressed, and then burnished. The burnishing was an important part of the process, and achieved a smooth, glossy effect on the edges of Blackie's high-quality paper. For their later, cheaper, editions, printed on increasingly rough-surfaced antiques, the burnishing grew progressively less effective. The word 'olivine', used by Blackie in advertising their books, was adopted from the name of a mineral, or chrysolite, usually of an olive-green colour.

74. Blackie's books nevertheless set the standard for imitators. 'The format of [Henty's] full-length books remained constant from 1883 until well into the Edwardian era, and the style proved so attractive to young purchasers that almost every publishing house

specializing in books for teenagers copied Blackie's original design'. Eric Quayle, *The Collector's Book of Boys' Stories*, pp.106–107.

75. Agnes A.C. Blackie, *Blackie & Son, 1809–1959*, p.43

76. ditto, pp.46–47.

77. Another incident related to me by James Shand makes the same point. It will be understood at least by the older generation of compositors and typographers. Walking one early morning through the composing room of his Shenval Press in Hertford, he overheard with delight the reply to a newly recruited comp. who had asked, 'What's the boss here like to work for?'. 'He's ok', said the old hand, 'as long as you don't forget to letterspace your small caps'.

78. Agnes A.C. Blackie, *Blackie & Son, 1809–1959*, p.47.

79. Robert J. Gibbs, *Newsletter*, Charles Rennie Mackintosh Society, Summer 1976, p.(5).

80. Gerald Cinamon, 'Talwin Morris, Blackie and The Glasgow Style' in *The Private Library*, Vol.10, No.1, p.5. This long and well-illustrated article gives much detail of the work of Talwin Morris, for Blackie and for other publishers.

81. Robert J. Gibbs, *Newsletter*, Charles Rennie Mackintosh Society, Summer 1976, p.(5).

82. Letters from Walter W. Blackie to Charles Rennie Mackintosh, December 1921, in Glasgow University Art Collections.

83. Gerald Cinamon, 'Talwin Morris, Blackie and The Glasgow Style', p.46.

84. Eric Quayle's *The Collector's Book of Boys' Stories*, in many ways an admirable and valuable book, contains (at pp.104–105) a strange and totally fictitious account of Henty's business relationships with his publishers, and the reasons he moved from one to another.

(These matters are dealt with under each publishing house in the various Parts of Appendix II). But in particular he gives details of a supposed agreement in 1882 between Henty and Blackie: 'Terms were agreed on the basis of a ten per cent royalty on all sales up to five thousand copies, increasing thereafter to a maximum of fifteen per cent. A substantial advance was made to the author, and a business friendship cemented that continued without interruption for the rest of his life'. In view of the deservedly wide readership of Quayle's book it seems right to point out here that Quayle's account is very far from reality. Henty's first agreement with Blackie, in 1887, gave him down payments only, of £100 on each book. In 1891 the down payments were increased to £150 per book, and Henty was to receive a royalty of about five per cent on each title only *after* the first 5000 copies had been sold. Details of the contracts are given in Appendix VI, and from them it may be seen that Henty had arranged very special terms with Sampson Low for *The Cornet of Horse*, which relate fairly closely to those ascribed incorrectly by Quayle to the first Blackie contract. The terms for this one book were special owing to the strange circumstances in which Henty had already begun work on producing the book himself, before it was taken over by Sampson Low (see *The Cornet of Horse*, §1, 8.1, Notes 3–5). Such terms were not repeated for other titles later.

85. Letter from G.A. Henty, 33 Lavender Gardens, Clapham Common, 28 September 1896, to John Alexander Blackie: 'I cannot be otherwise than greatly pleased at the progress made in the sales of my books, and at the amount of the cheque you have sent me. It is indeed most satisfactory, and I know that a very large part of the success is due to the manner in which the books have been got up, and the energy with which they have been pushed by your firm.
'I am very much obliged for the considerable increase in the royalties that you will pay on this years books, and hope that the outlay you have made in getting the books copyrighted in Canada will produce satisfactory results.
'With kind regards to your Father, Brother and yourself, I remain, Yours very sincerely, G.A. Henty'.

86. J.S. Bratton, *The Impact of Victorian Children's Fiction*, p.191.

87. Simon Nowell-Smith, *The House of Cassell*, p.57.

88. ditto, p.72.

89. ditto, p.75.

90. ditto, p.157.

91. Frank Mumby, *Publishing and Bookselling*, p.274.

92. Ernest Benn, *Happier Days*, p.159. Chief among Fisher Unwin's Readers was Edward Garnett, who also worked for Duckworth, and later with Jonathan Cape.

93. ditto, p.160.

94. William Allan, 'G.A. Henty' in *The Cornhill*, No.1082, Winter 1974/75, p.76

95. B.W. Matz, 'George Meredith as Publisher's Reader' in *The Fortnightly Review*, Vol.LXXXVI, 2 August 1909, p.286. Norrie incorrectly records that Meredith 'accepted G.A.Henty's offerings'. (Ian Norrie: *Mumby's Publishing and Bookselling in the Twentieth Century*, p.44).

96. B. McCall Barbour, 'Boys' Favourite Authors: George Alfred Henty' in *Boys*, Vol.I, No.10, p.155.

97. Extracts from two letters from Blackie & Son, Glasgow, to Charles Scribner's Sons, New York, dated 2 March 1904 and 8 March 1904 respectively.

NOTES TO APPENDIX III

1. 'To the uninitiated, any printer is a

potential book printer, but this is no more the case than that any tailor is competent to make a lady's costume. Either a printer is a book printer or he is not a book printer; the commercial printer who has occasionally printed a book (probably a local directory or a glorified catalogue) is a person to be avoided, if you want a presentable article.' Sir Stanley Unwin, *The Truth about Publishing*, p.109. It has always been true, nevertheless, that publishers have relied very heavily on their jobbing printers, chosen for their efficiency in carrying out numerous vital tasks, mainly concerned in one way or another with publicity. To the reader or collector of books their most obvious function was the printing of the publisher's catalogue, bound in as the last part of a volume. Catalogues were designed to be used in most titles the publisher produced, and therefore had to be printed in large quantities so as to be available when needed in each bindery he used. Very rarely a binder would find he had insufficient copies to complete an order for a specific book. At such times he would tend to continue binding the books, simply omitting the catalogues. There have, however, been even more rare occasions when a binder has drawn on old stock of outdated catalogues, and that has caused a few problems to bibliographers or collectors who have relied on a date printed in a catalogue as a means of identifying an issue of a book. The operative word here, I think, is 'few'. I have not been aware of a single example of a misleading catalogue in all the thousands of copies of Henty's books that I have examined over many years.

2. That this applied to Henty's novels for boys is directly confirmed in two ways. First, entries in Routledge's 'Publication Books' show that the text of the first edition of *The Young Colonists* was printed in 1884 on 20 reams of Quad Crown to produce 2000 copies, and that the reprint of 1000 copies in 1885 was printed on 20 reams of Double Crown to produce 1000 copies. Second, John Tannahill, the then Chairman of Blackie & Son, Limited, wrote to me, on 2 February 1977, 'In the days to which you refer we had our own factory where most of our machines were of a size which printed 32 pages on each side of a sheet.'

3. When folded, the paper area would measure $7\frac{1}{2}$ x 5 inches. As will be explained in Part 2 of this Appendix, the books were trimmed by guillotine in the course of binding, and that resulted in a page-size of $7\frac{1}{4}$ x $4\frac{7}{8}$ inches. The later use of double-quad-crown paper, measuring 40 x 60 inches, did not necessarily change the make-up of the book in the usual 16-page sections. The final size, after guillotining, was referred to by publishers and others, including most printers and booksellers, as the 'trimmed size', while binders called it the 'cut size' (see Glossary).

4. It was common practice from early days of printing to use for this purpose only 23 letters of the alphabet, omitting I or J; and U or V; and W. If there were a twenty-fourth sheet it would be 'signed' Aa, followed by Bb, etc. Leaves within a sheet were sometimes signed on their rectos, e.g., A2, A3. Customs in the use of signature marks varied from one printer to another, but the principle was constant and the results usually easy to interpret.

5. It would generally have been acceptable, though not often for perfectionists such as Blackie & Son, for a book with 16-page sections to contain a section making only eight pages. It was technically not difficult to print the same eight pages twice on one half-sheet, which would be cut again in half in the bindery. Each resulting piece was then

folded twice and sewn into the book as though it were a normal section. Other devices (wrap-rounds or inserts) were used in emergencies for four odd pages, but to have arrived at such a necessity, and it did happen not infrequently, was in the best circles considered a costly planning error, much to be frowned on.

6. For many years the larger publishers have employed typographers or designers to plan books in great detail. Some of those dealing only in fiction, or in books needing little typographical expertise, left such matters to their printers. Book printers generally employ a typographer, or at least a capable compositor who will undertake such work. Apart from Blackie, who were printers as well as publishers, it is doubtful whether the early publishers of Henty's books had qualms about leaving typographical matters to their printers.

7. Brooke Crutchley, Cambridge University Printer, 1946–1974, *To be a printer*, pp.55–56. The first customer mentioned was Monsignor Ronald Knox, speaking at a lunch to celebrate the publication of his version of the Bible in 1955.

8. Ruari McLean, *Victorian Book Design*, p.161. Details of the development of mechanical composition and of a number of type-casting and composing machines are given in the *Catalogue: Printing and the Mind of Man*, pp.85–88.

9. Interview with Henty in *Chums*, Vol.II, No.60, 1 November 1893, p.159.

10. G.M. Fenn, *George Alfred Henty*, illustration facing p.272.

11. I have described publishers' habits relating to galley proofs (or 'slip proofs') and page proofs as I understand them to have been, seen and known them before the second war, and experienced them, working with a dozen leading London publishers, and with many leading book printers throughout the country, over the past fifty years. I must, however, allow here what I find a surprisingly

controversial word from Sir Stanley Unwin, who was for long the acknowledged authority on *The Truth about Publishing*, and wrote in the 1946 (revised) edition of that book: 'It is usual nowadays in England for the first proofs to be sent out in page form... The advantages of "going straight into page" are many, and the disadvantages in most cases negligible. There will always be a few instances in which galley proofs are essential, but they will remain the exception'. Sir Stanley Unwin, *The Truth about Publishing*, p.118.

12. The texts of both these books were planned to be printed on twelve sheets of double-crown paper, and each should therefore have made 384 pages. *Captain Bayley's Heir* was printed with 386 pages, and *When London Burned* with 388. The over-running is referred to in the Notes to each title in §1.

13. The error is in the caption to the fourth plate, facing p.242 in 4.1, which reads: 'Hulbert's Escape from the Indians'. Henty's younger son, and the character in the book, were named Hubert. The misprint continued through all impressions of the book in which the original illustrations appeared.

14. 'Bear in mind, in bringing up the forme, that a perfectly even impression is the great desideratum, therefore do not be tempted to bring up the light parts by giving extra pressure to the whole'. Joseph Gould, *The Letter-Press Printer*, p.121. Brooke Crutchley tells of the perfectionist qualities of his predecessor at the Cambridge University Press, Walter Lewis: 'His speciality was presswork – the critical process of transferring the ink from the forme of type to the paper sheet. He insisted on passing the first sheet of every book, judging the nice relation of ink and impression, running his fingers over the back to satisfy himself that there was enough "tommy", spotting unfailingly a

piece of poor register or bad alignment. Nothing but the best would do; many a time the stolid press-room overseer, Harry Franklin, would leave the room cussing beneath his breath because the forme had to be made ready all over again, the ink changed or an adjustment made to the "furniture" '. Brooke Crutchley, *To be a printer*, pp.35–36.

15. 'Although the larger the number bound at once the cheaper the price of the binding, it is often unwise to bind up the whole of an edition at the outset. The cost of printing five hundred copies more than are needed is little more than the value of the additional paper, whereas the cost of binding in excess of one's requirements would be a substantial sum. Most publishers, therefore, restrict their binding orders to their immediate needs'. Sir Stanley Unwin, *The Truth about Publishing*, p.151.

16. This is not to say that variations in colour are never of interest. In Henty's early books from Blackie there are variations of cloth texture as well as of colour. The grained cloth used, for example, for the first few bindings of *Under Drake's Flag* was later changed for one of smoother texture; this happened with other titles, and the change marks a definite stage in the development of Blackie's experience and policy. There are a number of titles from the same publisher which seem always to have been bound in the same cloth: these include *With Buller in Natal*, and *With Cochrane the Dauntless*. I have, however, been told of one copy of each of these titles found in alternative shades of blue: they must have interest if only for their scarcity value.

17. Notes about the pre-printing of catalogues to provide adequate stocks for binders, are in the first Part of this Appendix III (see Note 1). Further explanation of the make-up of some publishers' catalogues, allowing certain selected parts to be used in particular books, without excisions being apparent to the ordinary reader, are given at *Do Your Duty*, §1, 89.1, Notes 3–4.

18. For notes on Blackie's famous 'olivine' edges, see Appendix II, Part 5, Note 73.

19. Eric Quayle, *The Collector's Book of Boys' Stories*, p.49. It should be mentioned here that Quayle refers to Ballantyne's 'letters, quoted in *Ballantyne the Brave*, 1967' on this subject. This is Quayle's own biography of Ballantyne, but in spite of more than one search I have not found in it any letter about cloth-colour.

20. Dartt, *Companion*, p.49.

21. John Cargill Thompson, *The Boy's Dumas*, p.5. Cargill Thompson mentions alternative endpapers as collectable variations. As with binding cloth, Blackie used surface-paper of different colours in different batches of books from the same edition. (For later books they used plain grey paper with an off-white lining). Certainly the changes in colour of surface paper may represent varying 'states' of an edition, but they seem to me to have little significance for any non-fanatical Henty-collector. On the other hand I have a first-edition copy of *A March on London*, 1898, with plain off-white endpapers. They are without doubt the original endpapers, and carry a school-prize label dated December 1897. They are the only such plain ends I have ever come across in a first edition of a Henty novel, and for that reason have some interest. The reason, probably a temporary lack of the normal grey paper owing to a failure of delivery, is as unimportant as this variant. It is simply a collector's curio.

22. Eric Quayle, *The Collector's Book of Boys' Stories*, p.47.

23. Quoted by Raymond Blathwayt, in *Great Thoughts from Master Minds*, p.9. William Davenport Adams, the son of

Henty's journalist friend,
W.H. Davenport Adams, who edited
Those Other Animals (§1, 51), wrote in
1888: 'As for gift-books, whether for
boy or girl, adult or juvenile, they have
their destination marked upon them in all
the colours of the rainbow. Some
complain of this, and call it vulgar. No
doubt it often is so. But a gift book is
produced for a definite purpose, and the
public would be surprised, and probably
annoyed, if it were not as gorgeous in
gold and colours as it was expected to
be. Gold and colours are what are
wanted, and the publishers do well to
supply them'. Wm. Davenport Adams,
By-Ways in Book-Land, pp.169–170.

24. From a letter from Barry Sitch to Peter
Newbolt, 16 March 1993. I am greatly
indebted to my friend Barry Sitch,
Technical Director of George M. Whiley
Limited, for his generously given help
and advice with many details of early
blocking processes, and of the
development of foils using gold and
pigments. These are still to be published
in his own forthcoming books.

25. A director of one of the leading
bookbinding firms in England wrote in
1959: 'all blocking is done by ribbon-
gold, which is a cellophane ribbon
coated with gold dust and adhesive.
Thus glaire-washing, the cutting and
laying on of gold and the removal of
surplus are all abolished. In their place a
two-hundred-foot long ribbon of
cellophane carries the gold and adhesive
to the heated block, stops an instant
while the impression is made, and then
moves on, carrying with it all unwanted
residue'. Lionel Darley, *Bookbinding
Then and Now*, p.75.

26. 'Is it right that the cost of these [books]
should fall on the shoulders of those who
live by providing them, authors as well
as publishers, rather than upon the
community at large? Successive
governments have held that it was, and

have declined to amend this piece of
copyright legislation, even though it
involved presenting books free to the
national library of Eire, a foreign
country'. Ian Parsons, 'Copyright and
Society', in *Essays in the history of
publishing*, p.47.

NOTES TO APPENDIX IV

1. This distinction in terminology between
wood-cuts and wood-engravings is
convenient and now generally accepted,
but is of comparatively recent and not
universal usage. As will be seen below,
Thomas Bewick, known by some as the
father of wood-engraving, commonly
referred to his work as wood-cuts. The
word 'cut', has been used ever since in
printers' colloquial terminology to refer
to all blocks for letterpress printing,
whether made to print from a wooden or
a metal surface.

2. 'In 1872 there were 128 firms of wood-
engravers listed in the *Post Office
Directory* at work in London… The
majority [of engravings were] not signed
at all, as was general throughout the
century. Much excellent work was done
anonymously'. Geoffrey Wakeman,
Victorian Book Illustration, pp.71–72.

3. Thomas Bewick, *Memoir*, p.205.

4. ditto, p.205.

5. ditto, p.208.

6. See Appendix III, Part 1, final
paragraph. Repeated make-ready,
especially of blocks, wore out printing
surfaces more effectively than actual
printing, even when runs were very long.

7. Gordon Williams, in *RHM: Robert
Hunter Middleton*, p.58, writes of
Middleton's first published portfolio of
impressions from the wood blocks: 'For
the first time Middleton had made it
possible to see Bewick's engravings as
Bewick had intended they be seen, but
as he had never found a printer able to
print them'.

8. Mrs Ewing's verses appeared first in various issues of *Aunt Judy's Magazine*, published by Bell & Daldy, and were later collected and published by the S.P.C.K. in the Collected Edition of her works, as Volume 9, *Verses for Children and Songs for Music*.

9. Thomas Bewick, *Memoir*, pp.204–205.

10. ditto, p.207: after describing at length his experimental work, and his success in 'rumbling' Dürer, he declares 'I have long been of opinion that the cross-hatching of woodcuts, for book work, is a waste of time; as every desired effect can be much easier obtained by plain parallel lines'.

11. George Meisenbach 'deserved credit for making a commercial success of what had hitherto been a more or less visionary idea. Not until Meisenbach demonstrated the possibilities of the half-tone did photo engravers take up the process in earnest'. Ellic Howe, 'From Bewick to the Halftone' in *Typography*, No.3, p.22. Howe also claims that 'In the year 1865 the brothers Bullock took out a patent which embraced the use of a ruled screen' (op.cit., p.21), but in fact the patent taken out by E.& J. Bullock of Leamington in that year, No.2954, was to produce a series of dots by a different method, and was developed for use in lithography, not letterpress printing (see Geoffrey Wakeman, *Victorian Book Illustration*, p.95 for the Bullock Brothers, and p.139 for George Meisenbach).

12. Simon Houfe, *The Dictionary of British Book Illustrators and Caricaturists, 1800–1914*, p.235.

13. ditto, p.247.

14. Joseph Pennell, *Pen Drawing and Pen Draughtsmen*, p.282, and R.E.D. Sketchley, *English Book Illustration of To-day*, p.96

15. Nicolas Hawkes, 'A Note on Gordon Browne', in *Henty Society Bulletin*, Vol.2, No.10, p.7.

16. A review of Henty in *The Academy* was frequently quoted by Blackie in their bound-in catalogues. No reference to date is given. It may be found, for instance, on the first page of the catalogue in the earliest issues of *The Dragon and the Raven*, 21.1: 'It is due to Messrs. Blackie to say that no firm of publishers turns out this class of literature with more finish. We refer not only to the novel tinting of the illustrations ...'. Another review in the same journal, again quoted by Blackie without date, and this time of *With Clive in India*, also praises Gordon Browne: 'Among writers of stories of adventure for boys Mr. Henty stands in the very first rank, and Mr. Gordon Browne occupies a similar place with his pencil'.

17. I have had in my possession since 1947 a large folded sheet of 'patterns' of tints of all kinds, supplied by a leading London process-engraver, to be used when ordering blocks from them. It is headed 'Ben Day Shading Mediums. For art work on stone, metal and card board. Invented by Benjamin Day. Used by the leading Lithographers and Photo Engravers of the World. Ben Day, Inc., 119 Kent Place, Summit, New Jersey'. This was of course a later selection of tints than that available to Gordon Browne, but probably not very different. On the front of the folder are printed the words 'Ben Day Screens have been the Standard of Quality since 1879'.

18. Gordon Browne, and Horace Petherick too, had blocks made by Lefman, a pioneer in the making of line blocks, see Wakeman, *Victorian Book Illustration*, p.131.

19. Browne also used Guillaume Frères, in Paris, who pioneered a halftone process and gained a fine reputation outside their own country, see Bland, *A History of Book Illustration*, pp.298 and 307.

20. The process is described briefly by Geoffrey Wakeman, *Victorian Book*

Illustration, p.150. The principle is that the artist draws in black ink on a card surface that has been coated with a thin layer of china clay. Lines or stipples may be 'scratched' into the ink marks he has made, or small parts of a drawing may be scraped away with a sharp tool, producing effects similar to those of an engraved image.

21. Simon Houfe, *The Dictionary of British Book Illustrators*, p.278.

22. See Aaron Watson, *The Savage Club*, pp.170, 187, etc., and illustrated examples.

23. Simon Houfe, *The Dictionary of British Book Illustrators*, p.333.

24. Peter Nahum, *Victorian Painters' Monograms*, p.116.

25. Simon Houfe, *The Dictionary of British Book Illustrators*, p.342.

26. ditto, p.349.

27. ditto, p.350.

28. Michael Bryan, *Dictionary of Painters and Engravers*, Vol.I, p.707.

29. George & Edward Dalziel, *The Brothers Dalziel*, p.12. He also, for the *I.L.N.*, 'depicted' the Crimean and Danish wars, and, 'in his later years reproduced in oil and watercolours many of the scenes he had witnessed', see Bryan, *Dictionary of Painters and Engravers*, Vol.II, p.10.

30. Peter Nahum, *Victorian Painters' Monograms*, p.52.

31. Agnes A.C. Blackie, *Blackie & Son*, p.43.

32. Gerald Cinamon, 'Talwin Morris, Blackie and The Glasgow Style' in *The Private Library*, Vol.10, No.1, p.7.

33. R.E.D. Sketchley, *English Book Illustration of To-day*, p.92.

34. In the *Union Jack*, Vol.II, No.57, 27 January 1881, on p.272, Henty wrote an editorial reply to a letter received from one of his readers: 'I am sorry that you think the illustrations in the *Boys' Own* are "more life-like and much better" than those of *The Union Jack*. It is a matter of opinion. I can only assure you that in the opinion of artists and other good judges, there is not the slightest comparison between the two, Mr. Petherick's work especially being by far the finest artistic work ever put into a magazine of the kind, and quite equal to anything in the *Illustrated* or *Graphic*. If you ask the opinion of any person of educated artistic taste, he will tell you the same thing'.

35. Simon Houfe, *The Dictionary of British Book Illustrators*, p.421.

36. R.E.D. Sketchley, *English Book Illustration of To-day*, p.45.

37. Simon Houfe, *The Dictionary of British Book Illustrators*, p.435.

38. ditto, p.463.

39. R.E.D. Sketchley, *English Book Illustration of To-day*, p.46.

40. Simon Houfe, *The Dictionary of British Book Illustrators*, p.485.

41. ditto, p.489.

42. R.E.D. Sketchley, *English Book Illustration of To-day*, p.29.

43. George & Edward Dalziel, *The Brothers Dalziel*, p.182.

44. Brian Doyle, *Who's Who of Boys' Writers and Illustrators*, p.99.

45. ditto, p.99.

46. G.& E. Dalziel, *The Brothers Dalziel*, p.270.

NOTES TO APPENDIX VI

1. The copy in the Sampson Low Contract Book has the two words 'selling price' underlined, and a note in the margin, which appears to be in Henty's handwriting: 'not published price'.

2. An explanation of the reference to the plates made from the typesetting in the *Union Jack* is given in *The Cornet of Horse*, §1, 8.1, Notes. The unusual nature of the negotiations with Sampson Low, whereby they were to take on the publication of a book which was already in production under Henty's control, no doubt accounts for the use of the words

'SPECIAL AGREEMENT' at the head of this document. It probably also accounts for the agreement to pay royalties for this book instead of the more usual outright payment to an author at that period.

3. The title of the book seems to have been changed by the time the rights were sold to Routledge (see below).

4. No relevant contract books of this publisher have survived. There are, however, entries in an account book confirming, although with slightly varied terms, the sale to them by Sampson Low of the rights and materials specified. Details are given in §1, under the book title (17.1).

5. The title of this book was changed after the contract was signed.

6. Paragraphs 7 and 8 appear to be so numbered in error. They follow straight on after paragraph 4, on the same sheet of paper, and without any break.

7. There is a handwritten mark against the title, 'Bevis', and in the margin 'G.A. Henty'. Duckworth published Richard Jefferies's book in 1904, edited by E.V. Lucas. Details of Henty's edition are given in §2, 128.

8. This appears to be a carelessly typed entry, intended to refer to Henty's *A Hidden Foe*. The Agreement Book folios are the same as those for the contract shown above. No explanation is given for the words 'taken out': the contract is in fact present in the Book to this day.

9. The name has been altered by hand in ink. The letter 'J' is typed, with the rest of the first name, 'ohn', inscribed by hand; 'Esq.' has been deleted in ink.

10. The word 'surviving' has been written in ink above the line, with a caret mark to show its insertion as indicated.

11. Against the first title in the list is written by a later hand 'See Bk 2 for original ag.'.

12. The first name has been completed, and 'Esq.' deleted, as before (see Note 9 above).

13. The word 'Fox' has been corrected by hand in ink to 'Foe'.

14. This stipulation was no doubt a precaution simply to make sure that Blackie would be able to publish any such book in time for the Christmas market of the year in which Henty had delivered the manuscript. It seems likely that this clause in the agreement had come to the attention of David A. Randall, sometime director of The Lilly Library, Indiana University, who had previously worked for Scribner in New York, and may have been the cause of a misunderstanding. According to Dartt (*Companion*, p.46) Randall published in *The New Colophon*, January 1948, his belief that Henty's books were regularly published in the UK by Blackie in October of their respective years. He therefore mistakenly claimed that in a number of cases the American Scribner editions pre-dated those from Blackie in the UK. Blackie's actual publishing dates are given at Appendix VII, Part 1.

GLOSSARY OF TECHNICAL TERMS

Antique paper: A printing paper with a rough surface, found in varying qualities. It is generally lighter in weight than cartridge paper, being made with more air in the pulp; from early in the twentieth century it has sometimes been made in a very bulky and lightweight form, known as 'featherweight'.

Art paper: A wove paper coated with china clay to give a smooth surface suitable for the printing of halftone blocks. See also 'Imitation art-paper'.

Author's corrections: Those corrections made on proofs by an author that are not related to any errors or 'literals' made by the compositor, and which represent departures from the 'copy' supplied to the printer.

Back: The back of a book, or the back edge of a leaf in a book, is that next to the sewing, i.e. the opposite side to the fore-edge.

Backing-up: Printing the second side of a sheet that has already been printed on one side, so that the impressions on each side exactly 'line up': this process is also known as 'perfecting'.

Bastard title: Another name for 'half title'.

Batter: Type accidentally damaged in a forme.

Ben Day tints: 'Mechanical tints', or designs that could be laid down on line blocks to give areas of tone, pattern, or shading (see Appendix IV, Part I).

Binder's blank: A binding case blocked with a design, simple or elaborate, with spaces or panels to allow the insertion by the binder of appropriate lettering for any title, author, and publisher. Such designs were in common use for publishers' cheap series, or as a stand-by when the proper binding cases for a book were for some reason not ready or available.

Blind blocking: A blank impression made on the case of a book by the binder's brass blocks, without gold or pigment.

Block: A general name for line blocks, halftones, stereos, electros, etc., and not normally used for binders' brass blocks which are referred to as 'brasses'.

Bolts: 1. The folded edges of a printed sheet, at the head, tail, and fore-edge, before trimming. 2. Compact rolls of (binding) cloth, usually of 40 or 50 yards.

Brasses: The binder's brass blocks, engraved by hand and deeply cut, by which the lettering and design is impressed on the binding case, either 'blind', or with gold leaf, foil, or ink.

Cancel: One or more leaves inserted in a book to replace a leaf or leaves removed, usually the result of an error by printer or publisher. A single-leaf cancel is normally tipped on to the stub of the removed leaf that it is to replace.

Caption: The title or line of type beneath (or above, or beside) an illustration, sometimes called a 'legend'.

Case: The outer covering of a book in cloth or paper boards. It consists of two pieces of board with a strip of stiffening for the spine, all covered with cloth, or, sometimes more cheaply with paper. The process of 'casing' a book is totally different from that of 'binding': in the latter the binding, usually of leather, is built around the book, whereas in the former the case is made entirely separately and the book is glued into it. The act of inserting the book in its case is often called 'casing-in'. The term 'binding', however, is also loosely used, in such terms as 'cloth-bound'.

Cast off: The careful measurement of a manuscript to determine the exact number of pages it would make when set in type of a certain size and kind. See Appendix III, Part 1.

Chase: The cast-iron frame, sometimes later made of steel, in which type, blocks and furniture were locked, ready for printing.

Coated paper: See 'Art paper'.

Collate: In the binder's sense a book is collated when all its component parts, gatherings, or sections, with inserted illustrations, are collected togther in correct order, ready for sewing. In the bookseller's sense he has collated a book when he has checked it, page by page, and satisfied himself that all the component parts are present and correct. In the bibliographer's sense it is a standard shorthand description of the physical composition of a book: this form of shorthand is not used in this bibliography, which nevertheless gives the relevant information in a manner to which most Henty collectors are accustomed.

Collotype: A high-quality printing process suitable for short runs only, whereby the image is printed from a gelatine surface. Wash-drawings and photographs are reproduced without a halftone screen, and when looked at through a glass appear scarcely different from the originals.

Colophon: A note, usually at the end of a book, but sometimes included in the prelims, giving information such as title, author, printer, place of printing, date. The note is sometimes accompanied by the printer's or publisher's device, and the device has been frequently referred to, incorrectly, as the colophon.

Conjugate leaves: Two leaves of a book which consist of a single, folded, piece of paper.

Copy: Any matter supplied to a printer to be set in type.

Cut edges: Binders' term for the finally guillotined, and so smooth, edges of the leaves of a book. Publishers and booksellers have generally used the term 'trimmed edges' to mean the same thing.

Cuts: An old word, probably deriving from woodcuts, used to mean illustrations printed with the text, as opposed to 'plates', which were printed separately.

Device: A trade mark or proprietory symbol, usually that of a publishing firm. (See also 'Colophon', for the misuse of that word).

Distribute: To break up type and return each sort to its correct box in the case when it was no longer required for printing. The common verb used by compositors was 'to dis.'.

Edition: Strictly, an edition means all copies of a book printed at any time or times from a single setting of type without substantial alterations, whether from the original type, from stereos or electros made from the type, or by any photographic or other reproduction process. The proper bibliographical meaning of the word has been confused, mainly in the nineteenth and twentieth centuries, by publishers' usages. See also 'impression', 'issue', 'reprint', and 'state'.

Egyptian typeface: (Usually written with no capital letter). A face that has square or rectangular serifs, generally used in display. (See §1, 8.3, and 8.4, bindings).

Electrotype: A printing plate made by the deposition of copper by electrolysis on to a mould of wax or lead taken from an engraving or from type, and backed with a lead alloy. Sometimes used to make duplicate blocking pieces from binder's brasses. The word is frequently abbreviated to 'electro'.

Em: The square of any size of type, not necessarily the width of the body of the cap

M. Without other specification an em is taken to mean a 12 point em, almost exactly one sixth of an inch, which was used as the standard unit of measure for the depth and width of a page.

En: Half the width of an em in any size of type, hardly ever the width of the cap N.

Endpapers: Leaves at the beginning and end of a book, usually with a single fold, tipped on to the first and last pages of the book, and with their outer leaves pasted to the boards of the binding case. They may be plain, coloured, or printed.

'Extra Quality': A manufacturer's name given to a specific cloth made for bookbinding. The Winterbottom Book Cloth Company was for decades the leading supplier to the trade, and this material was made in an enormous range of colours, all available either plain, or embossed in any of about fifty alternative patterns. See also 'X Quality'.

Featherweight: See 'Antique paper'.

Flong: A sheet of prepared papier-mâché used for making moulds for stereotyping.

Foil: A wide roll, once of thin paper, now more usually of transparent plastic, carrying a coating of pigment, or gold (either imitation or real). It is usually cut into narrower pieces, each forming a long ribbon of a width suitable for blocking a particular design on a binding case. In the process of blocking, the foil is separated from its paper or plastic carrier, which is discarded

Folio: 1. A sheet of paper folded once, to form two leaves or four pages. 2. A book of folio size. 3. The page number on a page of a book.

Font: another form of the word 'Fount'.

Foot: The lowest edge of a book or page, as opposed to the 'head'.

Fore-edge, or foredge: The edge of a book opposite the spine.

Forme: The type, blocks and furniture, locked up in a chase, ready for putting to machine.

Fount: A complete set of all characters of type, letters, figures and punctuation marks,

etc. in a particular size. The quantities of each 'sort' normally varied according to a standard assessment of the general requirements when setting the English language.

French joints: Originated from a mediaeval edict compelling French binders to use vellum reinforcements in back linings. That made wider joints necessary. Many modern continental binders have for decades made spines of cloth-bindings narrower than was traditional in Britain, and with deeply impressed grooves at the joints. Those who favour the method claim it is not just a search for cosmetic improvement, but actually a functional necessity. They claim that mechanical binding processes, that give French joints and simultaneously press each book for five seconds, will successfully eliminate warping of boards. To prevent such warping has always been an essential stage in binding: it was previously necessary to keep books in a press for a minimum of twelve hours.

Furniture: Strips of wood or metal placed around and between pages of type and blocks when imposed in a chase.

Galley: A tray, once of wood, later of metal, in which type was put when it had been set, and in which it was first made up into pages. It could be stored thus in special racks, and proofed while in galley. Galleys varied in size, and held enough type to make anything from two to four pages.

Gathering: 1. A group of leaves, folded to the size of the book, possibly a simple section, possibly two sections or parts of sections with illustrations inserted or wrapped round, ready for assembling with other gatherings for the binder. 2. The act of so assembling the component parts of the book.

Glair: A traditional form of size, or mordant, used with gold leaf. It is made from egg-white and diluted in differing ways according to the preference of the binder.

Guarded in: A plate or illustration is said

to be guarded in when it is inserted in position in the book with the back edge of the leaf folded and wrapped round the adjacent leaves; thus the thread passes through it when the book is sewn. Sometimes the same effect may be achieved by binding-in a prepared stub, to which the illustration is later tipped on.

Gutter: A frequently misused word. It was a printer's imposition term, and applied to the space comprising the fore-edges of pages, plus the area of trim, where these foredges fell internally in the forme. The spaces were the widest vertical gaps between the areas of printing surfaces in the forme. It does *not* mean the space between the printed area of a page and the fold of the leaf in the back of the book.

Half-sheet working: A system of imposing and printing often referred to as 'work-and-turn' (see below). See also Appendix III, Part 1.

Halftone block: A printing plate usually made of copper, photographically produced with a 'screen' to break up the original image, ultimately etched into the copper and resulting in a relief printing surface of small dots, varying in size according to the density of the original. See Appendix IV, Part 1.

Head: The top of a book or page, as opposed to the 'foot'.

Headband: A decorative band, usually of silk or cotton, plain or coloured, in cloth-bound books generally glued to the backs of the folded leaves under the lining, before the book is cased in.

Hinge: This word, and the word 'joint', are still carelessly used. The hinges are strictly the internal junctions of the book with the binding, and the joints the external junctions of the boards with the spine. Thus, if a secondhand bookseller describes a book as having 'hinges cracking' he is properly referring to the endpapers, whereas a 'split joint' would be a far more serious matter.

Hollow paper: The stiffening paper inside the spine of a cloth binding case.

Imitation art-paper: Devised by papermakers as a cheap substitute for coated art paper, supposedly suitable for fine-screen halftone blocks. It had china clay mixed with the pulp during manufacture, and was not coated at all. For halftone printing it was better than paper with no clay at all, but did not produce high-class work.

Imposition: 1. The arrangement of pages within a forme, in order that they shall appear in correct positions when printed and folded. 2. The act of laying down the pages in this way.

Impression: 1. A number of copies of a book printed at one time. There may be a number of impressions of one edition. (see also 'edition', 'issue', 'reprint' and 'state'). 2. The quality of a piece of printing, often used with adjectives such as fine, clear, sharp, heavy, blurred.

Imprint: 1. The publisher's name (and address), usually with the date, on the title page, sometimes on the verso of the title page. The publisher's imprint, usually consisting of his name only, also appears on the spine of a binding case. 2. The printer's imprint gives his name and address, and now usually the country of origin of the printed book. See also 'printer's code'.

Insert: One or more pairs of conjugate leaves inserted at the centre, or elsewhere within, a section, so that they are sewn with it in binding. The term can also refer to a single leaf inserted and pasted into the book. See also 'wrap round'.

Integral: A leaf is said to be integral when it forms part of a printed section. Any leaves 'tipped in' or any 'cancels' are not integral.

Issue: When alterations, corrections, additions or excisions have been made, after publication, to copies of a book forming part of one edition, such copies are said to belong to separate issues of that edition. Such alterations sometimes occur within editions of Henty's books, the prime example being the first impression of the first edition of *Facing Death* (see §1, 10.1, 10.2, 10.3, 10.4).

By proper bibliographical definition the reprints of Blackie's novels by Henty, usually having the date removed from the title page, are nevertheless later issues of the first editions, no substantial changes having been made to the typesetting. Blackie's own incorrect use of the word 'edition' (on the title page of *Facing Death*, 10.3) is typical of its use by publishers at that date and ever since, and it is hardly surprising that booksellers and collectors will not usually consider, as a Blackie first edition, anything that does not have the right date on the title page.

The determination, by both booksellers and collectors, of issues of the first editions of Henty's books has been traditionally according to the publishers' bound-in catalogues. This has applied particularly to those published by Blackie, although they never dated their catalogues, beyond possibly a headline announcing the new books for a particular season or year. The earliest issues of a new Blackie title were listed in the catalogue without quotations from press reviews, since these had not yet appeared. But, as soon as they had, suitable quotations were included in the next printing of the catalogue, and were bound in subsequent issues of the book. Later issues are recognised by the inclusion in the catalogue of books published in subsequent years.

Alterations to binding styles during the course of binding an edition also occur: the first impression of the first edition of *Friends, though Divided* (see §1, 12.1, 12.2, 12.3) is found in three slightly, but very clearly, different styles. These do not relate to the colour of the cloth and pigments used for blocking it, but to the bevelling of boards and the wording of the publisher's imprint, and all three can be shown to follow in chronological sequence.

Alternative colours of cloth and pigments on binding cases may be regarded as comprising varying states or issues. But for children's books of this period such variations were common to almost all editions, and I have declined within this book to consider them as other than minor variants (see Appendix III, Part 2).

See also 'edition', 'impression', 'reprint', and 'state'.

Joint: See 'hinge', above.

Laid down: Pasted down, or mounted.

Laid paper: Paper made, originally, in a frame on a mesh of close parallel wires, with other wires crossing them at right angles, set considerably further apart. The marks of the wires are visible as watermarks when the paper is held up to the light and are known as laid lines and chain lines respectively.

Leading: The insertion of thin strips of lead, or a lead alloy, known as 'leads', between lines of type, to space them out.

Leaf: A piece of paper comprising two pages, the 'recto' being the upper, or right-hand page, the 'verso' being the reverse side, or left-hand page.

Letterspacing: Spacing between the letters of a word. In display lines, for example on a title page, this may be quite obvious. In words set in small capitals it is not obvious to the layman, but has been usually thought essential by designers and typographers to give a pleasing effect to the eye.

Line block: A printing plate, usually of zinc, produced photographically, and etched to produce a relief printing surface representing a line original.

Lined paper: A sheet of paper that has another laminated to it by some form of adhesion. Later Henty titles from Blackie had endpapers made from thin grey paper that was lined with white paper.

Linson: The registered trade name of a paper material, now supplied by the Watson Grange Company, and 'made from highest grade fibres with the essential bookbinding qualities of toughness, durability, flexibility and scuff-resistance'. Obtainable in several grades, and grained in a variety of 'fabric' and other textures, it has to a great extent replaced cloth for inexpensive hardback books. Similar materials, perhaps originally rather less durable, have been used since about 1920.

Literals: Errors made by the printer in setting type.

Locking up: Tightening up a forme with quoins when everything within it was otherwise ready for machine.

Lower board: Another term for the back board of a book.

Make-ready: The detailed preparation on a press for the printing of a forme. It included overlaying and underlaying, and often took a considerable time, but was essential for good presswork (see Appendix III, Part 1).

Make-up: The taking of type from galleys by the compositor, and its arrangement in pages: the insertion of folios and running headlines, and any blocks required.

Measure: The width to which type was set, measured in 12-point ems.

Mechanical tints: See 'Ben Day tints', above.

MF: Machine Finished, a term describing the surface given to paper when it is manufactured. The surface of MF paper was smooth, but it varied in degree. See also 'SC'.

Octavo: 1. The size of a sheet of paper when folded in half three times so that it makes eight leaves or sixteen pages. 2. A book of octavo size.

Overlaying: Adding thin pieces of paper to the platen of a press during make-ready (see Appendix III, Part 1, and Appendix IV, Part 1).

Overrunning: Carrying words backward or forward in making corrections, particularly from page to page.

Perfecting: See 'Backing-up'.

Pie: Type that has been accidentally mixed up, and so 'pied'.

Prelims: An abbreviation for 'preliminary pages'. These are all the pages of a book before the first page of text proper, including half-title page, title page, Contents, List of Illustrations, Preface, etc.

Printer's code: In some, but by no means all, of Henty's books the printer inserted, in addition to his imprint, a short line consisting of groups of letters and figures. They give a varying amount of information as to the number of copies of that particular impression, the date, and sometimes an office reference. A simple example is '2M/8/98/K', which might signify that the book was one of an impression of 2000 copies, the date was August 1898, and the office reference was to file K.

Pull: Another term for a proof.

Quarto: 1. The size of a sheet of paper when folded in half twice so that it makes four leaves or eight pages. 2. A book of quarto size.

Quoin: A metal adjustable wedge used for tightening up and locking the contents of a forme to hold it secure when ready for machine.

Recto: The right-hand page of a book, by definition with an odd page number.

Register: 1. The exact adjustment of pages back-to-back on a sheet of paper, so that in folding all margins will be correct. 2. In colour-printing the exact positioning of the plate for each colour in relation to the others.

Reprint: Any impression of a book following the first, for which no substantial alteration has been made to the typematter. The first reprint of a book is the same as its second impression.

Running headline: Abbreviated to 'running head'. The headline, often repeating, at the head of a page. In correct typographical practice the running head on left-hand pages (versos) should always be the book title. That on recto pages may be the chapter heading, or it may vary on each page to give a summary of the content of the page. The virtue of the constant verso headline is that it has great value to librarians in identifying a leaf that has been found detached from a book.

Run on: 1. A sentence starting in the same

line as the previous one, or not beginning a new paragraph. 2. Chapters which do not start on a fresh page, are said to 'run on'.

Saddle-stitched: Any gathering of leaves when sewn through the folds of the pages is said to be saddle stitched. The word comes from the metal 'saddle' on which gatherings were laid, opened at the centre fold, to allow the needle and thread (or, sometimes, a wire-stapling machine) to pass through and make the stitches.

Sans serifs: A typeface characterised by the absence of serifs: often abbreviated to 'sans', and in earliest forms known as 'grotesques' or 'grots'.

SC: 'Super-Calendered'. A printing paper that has been pressed, usually several times, between metal rollers, to give it a highly polished surface.

Section: A synonym for 'gathering'.

Serif: A short cross-stroke at the top or bottom of the main strokes of a letter or figure.

Signature: The letter, or sometimes numeral, printed at the foot of the first page of each gathering, as a guide to the binder in collating them correctly. For a fuller description see Appendix III, Part 1.

Silk-screen printing: A development of the centuries-old stencil. It was taken up by commercial printers at the turn of the century and was sometimes, but not often, used for the decoration of cloth binding cases. Many effects can be obtained, by line and by tone, with any number of colours.

Sort: The name for a single piece of metal type.

State: When alterations, corrections, additions or excisions have been made, during the process of manufacture, and therefore before publication, to copies of a book forming part of one edition, such copies are said to belong to separate states of that edition. See 'issue', above.

Stereotype: A metal plate cast from a papier-mâché mould forming a replica of type or a block. Frequently abbreviated to 'stereo'.

Surface-paper: Paper which has been sprayed with pigment on one side only. Such paper was used for endpapers, especially by Blackie for Henty's earlier books.

Tint blocks: Blocks used for printing plain background colours, often in light shades with black line blocks. Sometimes they were made with a broken, or patterned, or halftone texture, by the use of laid-down mechanical tints. See also 'Ben Day tints'.

Tipped in: An illustration, map, or other single leaf, is said to be tipped in to the book when it is pasted along its back edge to a page of the book.

Trimmed edges: Publishers' and booksellers' term for the final state of the guillotined, and so smooth, edges of the leaves of a book. Binders have generally used the term 'edges cut' to mean the same thing, which has been known to cause confusion.

Underlaying: Adding thin pieces of paper beneath blocks, i.e. between them and the bed of the printing machine, during make-ready (see Appendix IV, Part 1).

Upper board: Another name for the front board of a book.

Verso: The left-hand page of a book, by definition with an even page number.

Work and turn: A method of imposing a forme so that its content was printed on both sides of a sheet, thus producing two complete and similar copies after cutting. Also known as 'half-sheet working'.

Wove paper: Paper with an even texture, made on close-meshed wires, so that it normally has no laid lines and chain lines as in 'laid paper'. Most of Henty's books were printed on wove paper.

Wrap-round: One or more pairs of conjugate leaves wrapped round a section and thus sewn with it in binding. See also 'insert'.

'X Quality': A manufacturer's name given to a specific cloth made for bookbinding. The Winterbottom Book Cloth Company was for decades the leading supplier to the trade, and this material was made in an enormous range of colours, all available either plain, or embossed in any of about fifty alternative patterns. It was a slightly thinner, and therefore cheaper, version of their 'Extra Quality', but the two are not easy to distinguish when used on a binding case.

PUBLISHED WORKS CONSULTED

I am very grateful to writers of works in copyright, and their publishers, for permission to quote from them. In the list below they are indicated by an asterisk. I have been unable to trace a small number, whose address or ownership has changed, and much regret any consequent omissions. All quotations from the Dictionary of National Biography *(entries listed but without asterisks) are by kind permission of Oxford University Press. Thanks for permission to quote from unpublished writings are included in the* Acknowledgements *which form the following section of this book.*

Adams, Wm. Davenport: *By-Ways in Book-Land*, London, Elliot Stock, 1888.

*Allan, William: 'G.A.Henty' in *The Cornhill*, No.1082, London, John Murray, Winter 1974/75.

Anon.: 'Boys' Writers of To-day' in *Chums*, Vol.II, No.60, London, Cassell, 1 November, 1893.

Anon.: 'Brough, Lionel, 1836–1909' in *Dictionary of National Biography*, London, Smith, Elder, 1912.

Anon.: *Catalogue of the Exhibitions: Printing and the Mind of Man*, London, Bridges, and the Association of British Manufacturers of Printers' Machinery, 1963.

Anon.: 'A Favourite of Our Boys' in *The Gem*, London, 16 December 1899.

*Anon.: *Fourth Leaders from The Times*, 1950, London, The Times, 1951.

Anon.: *Fourth Leaders from The Times*, 1953, London, The Times, 1954.

Anon.: 'George Alfred Henty', in *The Times Literary Supplement*, London, 28 November 1952.

Anon.: 'An Illustrious Illustrator' (Gordon Browne), in *Chums*, Vol.II, No.84, London, Cassell, 18 April, 1894.

Anon.: 'Mr. George Alfred Henty' in *The Athenaeum*, No.3917, London, 22 November 1902.

Anon.: Sale Catalogue, *Illustrated Books, Children's Books, Conjuring & Circus, Related Drawings* (includes Cargill Thompson collection), London, Sotheby's, June 1991.

*Arnold, Guy: *Held Fast for England*, London, Hamish Hamilton, 1980.

*Attenborough, John: *A Living Memory: Hodder & Stoughton, Publishers, 1868–1975*, London, Hodder & Stoughton, 1975.

Ball, Douglas: *Victorian Publishers' Bindings*, London, The Library Association, 1985.

Barr, James: 'A Great Writer of Christmas Books' in *The Golden Penny*, London, Parker & Thomas, Christmas Number, 1898.

Bateson, F.W. (ed.): *The Cambridge Bibliography of English Literature*, Cambridge

University Press, 1940.

*Benn, Ernest: *Happier Days: Recollections and Reflections*, London, Ernest Benn Ltd (now A. & C. Black Ltd), 1949.

Bewick, Thomas: *Memoir of Thomas Bewick, written by himself, 1822–1828*, London, Bodley Head, 1924.

*Blackie, Agnes A.C.: *Blackie & Son, 1809–1959*, London & Glasgow, Blackie & Son, 1959.

Blackie, Walter W.: *John Blackie, Senior (1782–1874)*, Privately Printed, London & Glasgow, Blackie & Son, 1933.

Blackie, Walter W.: *Walter Graham Blackie (1816–1906)*, Privately printed, London & Glasgow, Blackie & Son, 1936.

Bland, David: *A History of Book Illustration*, London, Faber & Faber, 1958.

Blathwayt, Raymond: 'A Talk with Mr. Edward Marston' in *Great Thoughts from Master Minds*, No.982, London, Smith, 15 November 1902.

Blathwayt, Raymond: 'How Boys' Books are Written: A Talk with Mr. G.A. Henty' in *Great Thoughts from Master Minds*, No.979, London, Smith, 4 October 1902.

Boase, G.C.: 'Hotten, John Camden, 1832–1873' in *Dictionary of National Biography*, London, Smith, Elder, 1908.

Boase, G.C.: 'Low, Sampson, 1797–1886' in *Dictionary of National Biography*, London, Smith, Elder, 1909.

Boase, G.C.: 'Mudie, Charles Edward, 1818–1890' in *Dictionary of National Biography*, London, Smith, Elder, 1909.

Boase, G.C.: 'Routledge, George, 1812–1888' in *Dictionary of National Biography*, London, Smith, Elder, 1909.

*Bratton, J.S.: *The Impact of Victorian Children's Fiction*, London, Croom Helm, 1984.

Briggs, Asa (ed.): *Essays in the history of publishing*, London, Longman, 1974.

Bryan, Michael: *Dictionary of Painters and Engravers*, London, George Bell & Sons, revised editions: Volume I, 1886; Volume II, 1889.

Butts, Dennis: 'Writing to a Formula: G.A. Henty, Historical Novelist or Reporter?' in *Henty Society Bulletin*, No.11, Cheltenham, March 1980.

Butts, Dennis: 'Henty's Serials and Novels' in *Henty Society Bulletin*, Vol.VII, No.56, Royston, Summer 1991.

Cargill Thompson, John: *The Boys' Dumas: G.A. Henty: Aspects of Victorian Publishing*, Cheadle, Carcanet Press, 1975.

Carter, John: *ABC for Book Collectors*, London, Hart-Davis, fifth edition, 1972.

*Carter, John, with Michael Sadleir: *Victorian Fiction*, London, Cambridge University Press for The National Book League, 1947.

*Cinamon, Gerald: 'Talwin Morris, Blackie and The Glasgow Style' in *The Private Library*, Third Series, Vol.10, No.1, Pinner, The Private Libraries Association, Spring 1987.

*Coffin, L.: 'George Alfred Henty: a Bibliographical Study of Henty and his Writings for Boys' in *Bulletin of Bibliography*, Vol.19, No.9, 1949.

Cooper, A.B.: 'John Hassall: his Posters and his Pictures' in *The Captain*, London, George Newnes, July 1901.

*Crutchley, Brooke: *To be a printer*, London, The Bodley Head, 1980.

Curtis, Myra: 'Gorst, Sir John Eldon (1835–1916)', in *Dictionary of National Biography*, London, Oxford University Press, 1927.

Curwen, Harold: *Processes of Graphic Reproduction in Printing*, London, Faber & Faber, fourth edition revised by Charles Mayo, 1966.

Cust, Lionel: 'Landells, Robert Thomas (1833–1877)' after entry for Ebenezer Landells in *Dictionary of National Biography*, London, Smith, Elder, 1909.

Dalziel, George & Edward: *The Brothers Dalziel. A Record of Work, 1840–1890*, London, Batsford, (1901) re-issued, 1978.

Darley, Lionel: *Bookbinding Then and Now*, London, Faber and Faber, 1959.

Darton, F.J. Harvey: *Children's Books in England*, Cambridge University Press, 1932, and 1982.

*Dartt, Captain Robert L.: *G.A. Henty, A Bibliography*, Altrincham, John Sherratt, 1971. [**Dartt**]

*Dartt, Captain R.L.: *A Companion to 'G.A. Henty: A Bibliography'*, Dartt, Cedar Grove, N.J., second issue, 1972. [**Companion**].

Davies, Godfrey: 'G.A.Henty and History' in *The Huntington Library Quarterly*, Vol.XVIII, No.2, San Marino, California, February 1955.

Dickens, Charles (ed.): *Dickens's Dictionary of London*, London, Charles Dickens, 1879.

Dodgson, Campbell: 'Dalziel, Edward (1817–1905)', and 'Dalziel, George (1815–1902)' in *Dictionary of National Biography*, London, Smith, Elder, 1912.

Downey, Edmund: *Twenty Years Ago: A Book of Anecdote illustrating Literary Life in London*, London, Hurst and Blackett, 1905.

Doyle, Brian: *Who's Who of Boys' Writers and Illustrators*, London, Brian Doyle, 1964.

Doyle, Brian: *Who's Who of Children's Literature*, London, Hugh Evelyn, 1968.

Egoff, Sheila A.: *Children's Periodicals of the Nineteenth Century, A Survey & Bibliography*, London, The Library Association, 1951.

Farmer, B.J., *see* Kennedy, R.S.

Fenn, G. Manville: *George Alfred Henty: The Story of an Active Life*, London, Blackie, 1907.

*Freeman, Sarah: *Isabella and Sam: The Story of Mrs Beeton*, New York, Coward, McCann and Geoghegan, 1978.

Gaskell, Philip: *A New Introduction to Bibliography*, Clarendon Press, Oxford, 1974.

Gettmann, Royal A.: *A Victorian Publisher: A Study of the Bentley Papers*, Cambridge University Press, 1960.

*Gibbs, Robert J.: 'Mackintosh's book designs' in *Newsletter of the Charles Rennie Mackintosh Society*, No.12, Glasgow, Summer 1976.

Gould, Joseph: *The Letter-Press Printer: A Complete Guide to the Art of Printing*, London, Marlborough & Co., sixth edition, (?1894).

*Griest, Guinevere L.: *Mudie's Circulating Library and the Victorian Novel*, Newton Abbot, David & Charles, 1970.

*Gunby, David: 'Maori and Settler' in *Henty Society Bulletin*, Vol.I, No.6, Cheltenham, December 1978.

Hannabuss, C.S.: *Works by George Alfred Henty included in the Wandsworth Collection of Early Children's Books*, London, Wandsworth Public Library, n.d. [**Hannabuss**]

Hardie, Martin: 'Evans, Edmund (1826–1905)' in *Dictionary of National Biography*, London, Smith, Elder, 1912.

*Hawkes, Nicolas: 'A Note on Gordon Browne' in *Henty Society Bulletin*, Vol.II, No.10, Cheltenham, December 1979,

*Holloway, David: 'Teaching the Young Idea' in the *Daily Telegraph*, London, 10 April 1980.

Houfe, Simon: 'The Dalziel Brothers', Introduction to Catalogue, *The Dalziel Family, Engravers and Illustrators*, London, Sotheby's Belgravia, 1978.

*Houfe, Simon: *The Dictionary of British Book Illustrators and Caricaturists*, Woodbridge, Suffolk, Antique Collectors' Club, 1978.

*Howe, Ellic: 'From Bewick to the Halftone: a Survey of Illustration Processes during the Nineteenth Century' in *Typography*, No.3, 1937.

Hunter, H.L., and Cecil Whiley: *Leaves of Gold*, London, George M.Whiley Ltd, 1951.

*Jackson, Vanessa Furse: *The Poetry of Henry Newbolt: Patriotism Is Not Enough*, ELT Press, University of North Carolina, Greensboro, 1994.

James, A.R.: 'Edward Step (1855–1931). A short biography', *Antiquarian Book Monthly*', Vol.XX, No.3, March 1993.

Johnson, A.E.: *John Hassall, R.I.*, London, A. & C. Black, 1907.

*Keir, David: *The House of Collins*, London, Collins (now HarperCollins), 1952

Kennedy, R.S., and B.J. Farmer: *Bibliography of G.A. Henty and Hentyana*, London, n.d. [*Farmer*].

King, Arline T.: 'Soap, Victorian Style' in *Ex Libris*, Journal of the USF Library Associates, University of South Florida, Summer/Fall, 1979.

King, Arthur, and A.F. Stuart: *The House of Warne*, London, Frederick Warne, 1965.

Knight, George: 'When I was a Boy. I. An Afternoon Talk with G.A. Henty' in *The Captain*, London, George Newnes, April 1899.

Lee, Elizabeth: 'Hoey, Mrs. Frances Sarah, (Mrs. Cashel Hoey), 1830–1908' in *Dictionary of National Biography*, London, Smith, Elder, 1912.

Liveing, Edward: *Adventure in Publishing: The House of Ward Lock*, London, Ward Lock, 1954.

Lucy, Sir Henry W.: *Sixty Years in the Wilderness*, London, Smith, Elder, fourth impression, 1911.

Mackenzie, Compton: *My Life and Times: Octave One, 1883–1891*, London, Chatto & Windus, 1963.

McKerrow, Ronald B.: *An Introduction to Bibliography*, Oxford, Clarendon Press, 1928.

McLean, Ruari: *Modern Book Design*, Fair Lawn, N.J., Essential Books (O.U.P.), 1959.

*McLean, Ruari: *Victorian book design & colour printing*, London, Faber & Faber, 1963.

Marston, Edward: *After Work: Fragments from the Workshop of an Old Publisher*, London, Heinemann, 1904.

Matz, B.W.: 'George Meredith as Publisher's Reader' in *The Fortnightly Review*, Vol.LXXXVI, London, Chapman & Hall, 2 August 1909.

Maurice, Frederick B.: 'Wolsley, Garnet Joseph, first Viscount Wolsley, 1833–1913' in *Dictionary of National Biography*, London, Oxford University Press, 1927.

Miller, George, and Hugoe Matthews: *Richard Jefferies: A bibliographical study*, Aldershot, Scolar Press, 1993.

Moore, George: *Confessions of a Young Man*, London, Heinemann, reprinted, 1952.

Morgan, Charles: *The House of Macmillan* (1843–1943), London, Macmillan, reprinted, 1944.

Muir, Percy: *English Children's Books*, London, Batsford, 1954.

*Mullen, Richard: *Anthony Trollope: A Victorian in his World*, London, Duckworth, 1990.

Mumby, F.A.: *The House of Routledge, 1834–1934*, London, Routledge, 1934.

*Mumby, Frank: *Publishing and Bookselling*, London, Jonathan Cape, fourth edition, 1956.

Nahum, Peter: *Victorian Painters' Monograms*, Slough, Foulsham, 1977.

Newbolt, Peter: 'G.A. Henty: some notes on the Blackie first editions' in *Antiquarian Book Monthly Review*, Vol.IV, No.3, Issue 35, Oxford, March 1977.

Newbolt, Peter: Letter to the Editor (*With Buller in Natal* illustrated), *Antiquarian Book Monthly Review*, Vol.IV, No.6, Issue 38, Oxford, June 1977.

Newbolt, Peter: 'G.A. Henty: the earlier books for boys, 1871–1885' in *Antiquarian Book Monthly Review*, Vol.IV, No.11, Issue 43, Oxford, November 1977.

Newbolt, Peter: 'The Nature of Henty's Novels' in *Henty Society Bulletin*, Vol.VIII, No.58, Winter 1992.

Norrie, Ian: *Mumby's Publishing and Bookselling in the Twentieth Century*, London, Bell & Hyman, 1982.

*Nowell-Smith, Simon: *The House of Cassell, 1848–1948*, London, Cassell, 1948.

Pachon, Stanley A.: 'George Alfred Henty' in *Dime Novel Round-Up*, Vol.16, No.195, Fisherville, Massachusetts, December 1948.

Pachon, Stanley A.: 'The Works of George Alfred Henty' in *Dime Novel Round-Up*, Vol.17, No.196, Fisherville, Massachusetts, January 1949.

*Parsons, Ian: 'Copyright and Society' in *Essays in the history of publishing*, London, Longman, 1974.

Pennell, Joseph: *Pen Drawing and Pen Draughtsmen*, London, Macmillan, second edition, 1894.

*Pruen, The Rev. Hugh: 'A Great Imperialist' in *Henty Society Bulletin*, No.5, Cheltenham, September 1978.

Quayle, Eric: *Ballantyne the Brave*, London, Rupert Hart-Davis, 1967.

*Quayle, Eric: *The Collector's Book of Boys' Stories*, London, Studio Vista, 1973.

Quayle, Eric: *The Collector's Book of Children's Books*, London, Studio Vista, 1971.

Quayle, Eric: 'Imperialism for Boys' in *Antiquarian Book Monthly Review*, Vol.VII, No.9, Issue 77, Oxford, September 1980.

Quayle, Eric: 'Rise and Fall of Henty's Empire', letter in *The Times Literary Supplement*, London, 7 November 1968.

Sadleir, Michael: *Excursions in Victorian Bibliography*, Folkestone & London, Dawsons, re-issued, 1974.

Sadleir, Michael: 'Maxwell, Mary Elizabeth, 1837–1915 (M.E. Braddon)' in *Dictionary of National Biography*, London, Humphrey Milford, O.U.P., 1927.

*Sadleir, Michael: *XIX Century Fiction, A Bibliographical Record*, 2 volumes, Cambridge, Massachusetts, Martino, 1951 edition, re-issued 1992. [*Sadleir*].

*Sadleir, Michael: *Trollope, A Bibliography*, London, Constable, 1928.

St. John, Judith (ed.): *The Osborne Collection of Early Children's Books, A Catalogue*, Volume I (1566–1910), Toronto Public Library, revised edition 1975. Volume II (1476–1910), Toronto Public Library, 1975.

Seccombe, Thomas: 'Adams, William Henry Davenport, 1828–1891' in *Dictionary of National Biography*, London, Smith, Elder, 1909.

Seccombe, Thomas: 'Yates, Edmund, 1831–1904' in *Dictionary of National Biography*, London, Smith, Elder, 1909.

Shand, P. Morton: 'Mackintosh, Charles Rennie' in *Dictionary of National Biography*, London, Oxford University Press, 1937.

Shane, T.N.: *Passed for Press, A Centenary History*, London, Association of Correctors of the Press, 1954.

*Silvester, Christopher (ed.): *The Penguin Book of Interviews*, London, Penguin Books, 1994.

*Singleton, Frank: *Tillotsons, 1850–1950: Centenary of a Family Business*, Bolton & London, 1950.

Sketchley, R.E.D.: *English Book Illustration of To-day*, London, Kegan Paul, Trench, Trübner & Co., 1903.

Sladen, Douglas (ed.): *Who's Who*, 1898, London, A. & C. Black, 1898.

Smith, W.J., E.L. Turner, & C.D. Hallam: *Photo-Engraving in Relief*, London, Pitman, third edition, 1951.

*Snow, C.P.: 'True Grit' in the *Financial Times*, London, 26 April 1980.

Sorrenson, M.P.K.: 'Gorst, John Eldon, 1835–1916' in *Dictionary of New Zealand Biography* (ed. W.H. Oliver), Vol.I, 1769–1869, Wellington, Allen & Unwin, 1990.

Springhall, John: 'Rise and Fall of Henty's Empire', in *The Times Literary Supplement*, London, 3 October 1968.

Srebrnik, Patricia Thomas: *Alexander Strahan, Victorian Publisher*, Ann Arbor, University of Michigan Press, 1986.

Steavenson, David: 'Invasion of Afghanistan', letter in *The Times*, London, 28 January 1980.

*Stokes, Eric: 'From Mexico to Mysore' in *The Times Literary Supplement*, London, 11 April 1980.

*Sutcliffe, Peter: *The Oxford University Press, An Informal History*, Oxford, Clarendon Press, 1978.

*Taylor, A.J.P.: 'I remember, I remember' in *The Times Literary Supplement*, London, 6 December 1974.

*Taylor, A.J.P.: 'Prince of Storytellers' in the *Observer*, London, 13 April 1980.

Tedder, Henry Richard: 'Tinsley, William, 1831–1902' in *Dictionary of National Biography*, London, Smith, Elder, 1912.

Thomas, Edward: *Richard Jefferies: His Life and Work*, London, Hutchinson, 1909.

Tinsley, William: *Random Recollections of an Old Publisher*, 2 volumes, London, Walpole Press, 1900, re-issued 1905.

Trease, Geoffrey: 'G.A. Henty: 50 Years After' in *The Junior Bookshelf*, No.XVI, October 1952.

Trollope, Anthony: *An Autobiography*, 2 volumes, Edinburgh & London, Blackwood, second edition, 1883.

*Unwin, Sir Stanley: *The Truth about Publishing*, London, Allen & Unwin (now an imprint of HarperCollins), fourth edition, 1946.

*Wakeman, Geoffrey: *Victorian Book Illustration, The Technical Revolution*, Newton Abbot, David & Charles, 1973.

*Warner, Oliver: *Chatto & Windus, A Brief Account of the Firm's Origin, History and Development*, London, Chatto & Windus, 1973.

Watson, Aaron: *The Savage Club*, London, T.Fisher Unwin, 1907.

*Waugh, Arthur: *A Hundred Years of Publishing, Being the Story of Chapman & Hall, Ltd.*, London, Chapman & Hall, 1930.

*Williams, Gordon: 'The Bewick Blocks' in *RHM: Robert Hunter Middleton, The Man and his Letters*, Chicago, The Caxton Club, 1985.

Winter, Arthur F.: *Stereotyping and Electrotyping*; London, Pitman, 1948.

Woods, Gabriel S.: 'Henty, George Alfred, 1832–1902' in *Dictionary of National Biography*, London, Smith, Elder, 1912.

Woods, Gabriel S.: 'Russell, William Clark, 1844–1911' in *Dictionary of National Biography*, London, Smith, Elder, 1912.

ACKNOWLEDGEMENTS

The compilation of this work owes much to the encouragement of the Revd Basil Brown, fellow founder-member of the Henty Society. Over the years I sometimes faltered, but his warmly rousing voice and firm arm of support seemed always behind me. Publication has been made possible by the Henty Society, whose generous financial backing proved essential for a book of such magnitude with an inevitably limited readership. Without that support the undertaking would certainly have foundered.

I owe grateful thanks to a large number of individual members and ex-members of the Henty Society, many of whom have become friends, for information about books or letters in their collections, for lending or allowing me to photograph unusual items, and for other help. I cannot mention them all, but in particular thank the sixth (late) Marquess of Bath, for many years Patron of the Henty Society, for checking and reporting on items in his collection; Roy Henty, founder, first Hon. Secretary, and now Vice-President of the Henty Society, with whom I have enjoyed years of talk and correspondence; Ann King, present Hon. Secretary of the Society, valued friend and supporter who has constantly and tirelessly gone out of her way to give help and encouragement; Dennis Butts, who succeeded me as Editor of the Henty Society Bulletin; Christopher Holtom, bookseller and fellow bibliographer, who has over the years covered quires of paper with information and lent me many items to examine; Bill Lofts, founder-member and sometime Committee member of the Henty Society, Terry Corrigan, sometime Hon. Secretary of the Henty Society, Ivan McClymont, and Stuart Wilson, four most prolific and unstinting givers of information and help; Guy Arnold, writer on Henty and many other matters, for good talk and for leading me to some of the records that Blackie had declared lost; Norman Shaw, specialist bookseller and firm support in the early days of this work; and many others including Brian Burgess; Roger Childs; David Drummond; Ian Entwistle; Anthony Gadd; Nicolas Hawkes; Mildred Hoad; Kate & Tom Jackson; the late John Laframboise; Caroline Michel; Clive Orbell-Durrant; Kathleen Packard, Henty's granddaughter; the Revd Hugh Pruen; Alex Pyne; the late David Sandler; the Revd David Shacklock; the late Cyril Smith; Ian Thompson; from the U.S.A.: Dick Dilworth of Richmond, Virginia; Gerald H. Duin, of Greenbrae, California; Harland Eastman of Springvale, Maine; the late Kenneth Wiggins Porter, sometime Professor Emeritus of History, Oregon University, with whom I corresponded at length from 1977 to 1981; and the late Professor Francis Willey of Mansfield Center, Connecticut.

I acknowledge valuable help from Clive Hurst, Head of Special Collections, and his Staff at the Bodleian Library Oxford, who spent much time and trouble making it easy and comfortable for me to examine their Henty Collection of UK editions, the most complete known to me; Nina Evans, Richard Price, and members of Staff both of the British Library and of the British Library Newspaper Library; Dr Hector Macdonald, John Morris, and members of Staff of the National Library of Scotland; Tessa Chester, Curator of Children's Books, the Bethnal Green Museum of Childhood; William Cagle, Lilly Librarian, Indiana University Library; Michael Bott, Archivist of the Collection of Publishers' Archives, Reading University Library, who somehow knew and had ready in advance every document I wished to consult; Gillian Furlong and Catherine Mainstone, of the Library of University College London; Peter G.Vasey, Assistant Registrar, National Register of Archives, Scotland; Michael S.Moss, Chief Archivist, and Vanora Skelley, Archives & Business Record Centre, Glasgow University; Joanna Soden, Royal Scottish Academy; Nigel A.Roche, St Bride Printing Library; Peter S.Foden, Archivist, Oxford University Press; Gill Thompson, Librarian, Royal Photographic Society; A.Owens, Town Clerk, Preston Borough Council; Kevin Campbell, Archivist, Local History & Archives Department, Bolton Public Libraries; Members of Staff, Norwich Central Library Reference Library; Mrs A.C.Bowden, Librarian, Bolton Evening News.

Special thanks are due to Jack Adrian, writer and editor, for his vital and generous encouragement; Peter Allen of Messrs Robert Temple, bibliographer and bookseller, for help over many years, and especially for his patient and learned reading of a first draft of Appendix II, from which it greatly benefited, but in which any errors are entirely my own; the late John Attenborough, writer, sometime Deputy Chairman, and Historian of Hodder & Stoughton for his interest and permission to quote from our correspondence; Dr Ingar Bratt of Lund University, Sweden; Carmen Callil, Jonathan Burnham, Directors of Chatto & Windus, and Gina Dobbs, Director of Random House UK Group, who severally allowed me to study and quote from their unpublished archives, and to copy their photograph of Andrew Chatto; Patricia Douglas, Director of the Charles Rennie Mackintosh Society, who generously sent me past Newsletters of the Society; Dr Dennis Griffiths, official historian of the *Standard* and the *Evening Standard* for information kindly given before the publication of his work; Julia Hunt, bibliographer of Ernest Nister publications; Patricia James of Little, Brown & Co., for permission to quote from Sampson Low unpublished archives; Andrew Lockett of the Oxford University Press; Professor Hugoe Matthews, FRCS, joint bibliographer of Richard Jefferies, who kindly gave me information about *Bevis* before his work was published; Barry McKay, bookseller, Appleby-in-Westmorland; R.Michael Miller, sometime Managing Director, Blackie & Son, who generously provided the portrait of Alexander Blackie, and allowed me to quote from unpublished Blackie archives; Victor Moss, bookseller, Preston; the late Percy Muir, learned friend and distinguished bibliophile; Harry Pitt, Emeritus Fellow of Worcester College, Oxford, my oldest friend and stalwart supporter, who gave me my first word-processor without which this book would never have appeared; Barry Sitch, Technical Director, George M.Whiley Limited, with whom I first worked on gold for books some forty years ago, for his constant friendship and most freely given technical advice; John Tannahill, sometime Chairman, Blackie & Son; D.E.Turner, Managing Director, James Askew & Son, Preston; Frank Weatherhead, distinguished bookseller, of Aylesbury, who introduced me to Farmer's bibliography nearly fifty years ago; and the late Simon Young, cousin and sometime Director, John Murray.

My thanks for permission to quote from copyright material is given, with full details of writers and publishers, under Published Works Consulted, the previous section of this book. Among sources of information about illustrators, of which I have used a number, none has been of such regular and reliable help as Simon Houfe. I owe him an enormous debt of gratitude for his invaluable *Dictionary of British Book Illustrators, 1800–1914*, which, as a bonus, unexpectedly led me to Henty's own published drawings.

I am grateful to the Bodleian Library, Oxford, for permission to reproduce copyright photographs of books, at Plates 1 (250 n. 263–265), 2 (250 w. 16–18), 3 (256 e. 4319–4320), 4 (256 e. 5612–5613), 15 (2533 e. 1328), 31 (R.H. 722.1 r. 12), 35 (254391 e. 250, and 2531 e. 199), 40 (25439 e. 10), 53 (254391 e. 235), 139 (256 e. 4760 (4)), 158 (256 e. 4286) and 163 (231 c. 176); to Stuart Wilson, Plate 25; and to Ivan McClymont, Plate 106; the rest of the photographs of books, though not all the books, are my own.

I acknowledge my debt to two men I was unlucky never to meet. First, to an unknown benefactor of my preparatory school, who by the gift of over twenty first editions in 1935 introduced me, aged 12 and just appointed school librarian, to Henty. And, second, to the late Captain Robert L. Dartt, previous bibliographer of Henty, with whom many years later I carried on a lively correspondence, and who kindly presented me with a copy of his *Companion* shortly before his planned visit.

Finally, and above all, for tolerating over twenty-five years of persistent intrusion by Henty and all his works into our lives and home, with loving encouragement, and very precious help, I express my never-ceasing amazement, admiration and gratitude to my dearest wife, Marcia.

Cley-next-the-Sea   Peter Newbolt
Norfolk

MAIN INDEX

Works written by Henty, and those to which he contributed, are shewn in ***bold italic***, followed by the section of this book in which each appears (§1, §2, or §3). The main entry for each work is also shewn in **bold**. Alternative and projected book-titles, where known, are similarly listed, even though some were never used.

Entries relating to Engravers, Printers, Publishers, Booksellers, etc., are so designated. References to major Designers, e.g. of binding-cases, are included, but not to Artists or Illustrators, whose names and details are given alphabetically in Appendix IV, (see page 619). Where one man worked both as Designer and Illustrator, e.g. Peacock, references in this index are only to his work in the former capacity.

Some matters of general or of technical interest are listed as subheadings under the following three (bold) main entries: **Dartt**, **Henty**, and **Production practices**.

Facing Death (§1), **58**.

Farran, Robert, 7, 572, 573, 574.

Fawcett, Benjamin, Driffield, Engraver and Printer, 617.

Fenn, George Manville, 310, 347, 443, 502, 507, 517, 536–537, 555, 598, 665, 675.

Fenn, W.W., 443.

Fifty-two Further Stories for Boys (§2), **447**.

Fifty-two Holiday Stories for Boys (§2), **448**.

Fifty-two Other Stories for Boys (§2), **448**.

Fifty-two Stirring Stories for Boys (§2), **449**.

Fifty-two Stories for Boyhood and Youth (§2), **450**.

Fifty-two Stories of Boy-Life at Home and Abroad (§2), **451**.

Fifty-two Stories of Courage and Endeavour for Boys (§2), **452**.

Fifty-two Stories of Duty and Daring for Boys (§2), **453**.

Fifty-two Stories of Heroism in Life and Action for Boys (§2), **454**.

Fifty-two Stories of Life and Adventure for Boys (§2), **455**.

Fifty-two Stories of Pluck and Peril for Boys (§2), **456**.

Fifty-two Stories of the Brave and True for Boys (§2), **456**.

Final Reckoning, A (§1), **150**.

Flower, Sir Newman, 596.

For Name and Fame (§1), **126**.

For the Temple (§1), **169**.

Forbes, Archibald, 413–417, 420, 441, 518–519, 520, 571.

Forest, Field and Flood (*Stories of Adventure & Heroism*, §2), **510**.

Foulis, Robert & Andrew (The Foulis Press), Glasgow, Printers, 585–586.

Foulsham & Co., Publishers, x.

Fouret, René, 578.

Frank Tressilor (Appendix II, Part 6), **599**.

Fraser, John Foster, 543.

Freeman, Sarah, 666.

Freund, John C., 534.

Friends, though Divided (§1), **73**.

Froude, J.A., 664.

Frowde, Henry, 12–15, 26, 29, 40, 192, 575, 669.

Frowde, Henry, and Hodder & Stoughton, Publishers ('The Joint Venture'), 12–15, 25–28, 39–41, 55–56, 78–79, 192, 435, 437, 440, 458–459, 480–481, 489, 494–496, 505, 575.

Fullarton, Archibald, 585.

Fuller, Alfred J., 465, 466.

Gabriel Allen, M.P. (§1), **183**.

Gall and Inglis, Printers, Edinburgh, 3.

Gall and Inglis, Publishers, 3.

Gallant Deeds (§1), **384**.

Galpin, Thomas Dixon, 594–595.

Garnett, Edward, 673.

Garden City Press, The, Letchworth, Printers, 459.

Gaskell, Philip, xiii.

Gauchard, J., Wood-engraver, 628.

Gibbs, Robert J., 250, 591, 592, 630, 672.

Gilbert and Rivington, London, Printers, 18, 19, 21, 22, 24–25, 32–33, 35, 38, 43–45, 67–70, 87–88, 91, 105–107, 112, 188–189, 441.

Gilbertson, Richard, Bookseller and Publisher, 469.

Girl's Realm, The (§3), **535**.

Glasgow Style, The, 196, 415, 589–592, 630.

Golden Story Book, The (§2), **457**.

Gorst, J.E. (later Sir John), 542, 559, 665.

Gould, Joseph, 675.

Grant, E.C., 572.

Grant, James, 438–439, 541.

Grant & Griffith, Publishers, 471.

Great Northern Printing Works, London N.W., 3.

Green Book for Boys, The (§2), **458**.

Griest, Guinevere L., 584, 670, 671.

Griffith & Farran, Publishers, ix, 5–14, 18, 19, 20, 21, 23–24, 25–26, 28–29, 31, 32–38, 39–41, 43–44, 46, 49, 51–54, 55, 60, 73–78, 90, 186, 187–188, 189–190, 191–192, 469–470, 471–480, 481, 482–488, 490, 544, 572–575, 577, 593, 616, 624, 627, 634, 637, 648.

Griffith, John Pettit, 559, 652, 665.